T2-DLO-295

A *Traveler at Forty*

THE DREISER EDITION

Sponsored at
the University of Connecticut
by
the Thomas J. Dodd Research Center,
the College of Liberal Arts and Sciences, and
the University Research Foundations
and by
the University of Pennsylvania Library

THEODORE DREISER

A Traveler at Forty

Edited by
Renate von Bardeleben

University of Illinois Press
Urbana and Chicago

Manufactured in the United States of America
C 5 4 3 2 1

∞ This book is printed on acid-free paper.

Library of Congress Cataloging-in-Publication Data
Dreiser, Theodore, 1871–1945.
A traveler at forty / Theodore Dreiser ; edited by
Renate Von Bardeleben.— Dreiser ed.
p. cm.
Includes bibliographical references and index.
ISBN 0-252-02913-5 (acid-free paper)
1. Europe—Description and travel. 2. Dreiser, Theodore,
1871–1945—Travel—Europe. 3. Americans—Europe—
History—20th century. I. Bardeleben, Renate von. II. Title.
D921.D75 2005
914.04'288'092—dc22 2004029306

CONTENTS

ILLUSTRATIONS

PREFACE

By 1912 Theodore Dreiser had acquired critical standing as a novelist, though he had published only three modestly successful books—*Sister Carrie* (1900), *Jennie Gerhardt* (1911), and *The Financier* (1912)—in thirteen years. The publication of *A Traveler at Forty* (1913) placed him at the threshold of a career as a prolific author in a half-dozen genres. Of the twenty-three books he would publish in the next thirty-two years, only five were novels—and two of these five were published posthumously. *A Traveler* contains seeds that would germinate in many of his later volumes of nonfiction. Based on the events of a trip to Europe at age forty, it is the first of three travel books; the first to contain the figure of "Dreiser," who would become world famous in large-scale memoirs; the first to advertise his complex relationship with his family and his German heritage; the first to present memorable character sketches of men and women from his time; and the first to articulate a considered perspective on certain of his abiding interests: art, death, religious belief, the power of desire, the allure of wealth, and the psychological effects of poverty.

After reading page proofs of *A Traveler,* H. L. Mencken congratulated Dreiser, saying that sections of the book "show the best writing you have done since Jennie Gerhardt." Nevertheless, he added that certain places suffer from "an effect of reticence": "You start up affairs that come to nothing." In response Dreiser justly complained that his publisher, the Century Company, had severely cut the original text, omitting over forty chapters and diluting many of the sequences that did make it into print. Dreiser later wrote Mencken with a request that went beyond the text of *A Traveler:* "After I am dead please take up my mss of The Financier, Titan & Travel book & restore some of the women stuff." Dreiser's emphasis on the "women stuff" doesn't tell the whole story. The Century editors also heavily excised autobiographical reminiscences, philosophical speculations, revealing portraits of prominent figures, and carefully observed renditions of lower-class urban life. In all, only 53 of Dreiser's original 103 chapters found their way into print.

The book was successful, going through six printings between 1913 and 1930. Dreiser was intent, however, on preserving the full text of *A Traveler.* On 31 May 1917 he noted in his diary that he had instructed his secretary, Estelle Kubitz, to "re-copy . . . the full penwritten copy of *A Traveler at Forty* . . . in order that it be left intact when I die." Fortunately, he took the time to supervise the transcription of his holograph manuscript, which has subsequently disappeared. It was last mentioned by Dreiser on 11 December 1922 in a memo he sent to a book buyer named W. W. Lange: "A Traveler at Forty. Original pen copy. This is much longer than, and contains a good deal of material not in the book. At present loaned to one who desires to retain it. Can be recovered. Property of the author." The Kubitz typescript of 1917 is the only known copy of the original manuscript. Its survival among the Dreiser papers at the University of Pennsylvania makes possible this edition of an important "lost" Dreiser text. No other Dreiser book—including *Sister Carrie* and *The "Genius"* (1915)—was as exhaustively edited by its publisher as *A Traveler at Forty.* The present edition, coming some ninety years after the book's debut, fulfills Dreiser's wish for the appearance of a more inclusive version of his travel book.

Editorial Procedures

A Traveler at Forty is part of an ongoing series, the Dreiser Edition. Each book is a product of cooperative efforts. The general editor appoints an editor for each project. The general editor and the textual editors select the text for each volume and establish the project within the framework of current editorial theory. They approve the relevant documents, devise the historical and textual principles for the edition, and work with volume editors in determining the copy-text. The general editor and textual editors verify all transcriptions and assist the volume editor in gathering the textual, historical, and bibliographical documents pertinent to the edition. At each state of preparation, they inspect the text and authenticate its contents.

The editorial principles formulated by W. W. Greg, Fredson Bowers, and G. Thomas Tanselle have guided the Dreiser Edition since its inception in 1981. As applied by the textual editor James L. W. West III, these principles provided useful techniques for determining copy-text and methodology for early Dreiser Edition volumes. The Dreiser Edition remains committed to many of the basic procedures used in preparing these first volumes. The editors continue to utilize pertinent documents among Dreiser's papers. Each edition takes into account the author's intentions for the work (insofar as they are knowable); each employs a system of emendation that considers all relevant prepublication and printed texts. There is no attempt to reproduce the text of a single historical document, nor is there any claim to be definitive. Although Dreiser Edition volumes often depend on unpublished manuscripts and typescripts, they do not aim to replace the published or historical texts of Dreiser's works.

The editors for the Dreiser Edition have long recognized that Dreiser's books resulted from collaborative efforts that began with his holograph manuscripts. Over time these manuscripts were subject to alterations, with varying degrees of authorial cooperation, by Dreiser's personal associates, publishers, professional editors, and typists. As the compositional history of Dreiser's works suggests, his intentions for publication were often problematic, even when he was cooperating with publishers and editors to take his works to print. In the case of *A Traveler,* Dreiser left clear indications that he was in many ways an unwilling participant in the publication process. We know, for instance, that the promoter of his travels, the publisher Grant Richards, and the editors at Century edited the manuscript more drastically than he had desired or anticipated. In the previously noted instances, Dreiser suggested that the manuscript Kubitz copied is a text he meant to preserve, thus implying that under certain circumstances he might have wanted to publish that version. Dreiser surely knew, however, that he could not submit such a text for publication without the sort of revision he expected of his work when it was at the stage of the Kubitz typescript.

In the absence of the holograph manuscript or a complete revised typescript, the editors have employed the Kubitz typescript as their copy-text. The copy-text has been edited as a public document, and thus the editors have emended unintelligible passages, misspellings, typographical errors, and lacunae in the Kubitz typescript. Emendations have been based on collations from existing documents, including the first edition, that have authorial sanction. To address problems where there are no authorities beyond the copy-text, including accidentals or obscure matters of substance, the volume editor took an active role and made decisions consistent with Dreiser's known habits of composition. The more significant emendations are recorded in the apparatus; all are recorded in a document on deposit at the University of Pennsylvania's Dreiser collection.

In selecting the Kubitz typescript as the basis for this edition of *A Traveler,* the editors recognize that this determination constitutes only one of several possible editorial choices, all of equal import. In this regard the Dreiser Edition has evolved naturally from its original formulations to take into account one of the central ideas common to the work of such diverse textual critics as Hans Zeller, Jerome J. McGann, and Donald H. Reiman. Accordingly, this edition of Dreiser's travel book is presented as one of a number of possible versions in a continuum of composition. Viewed together with the version Dreiser published in 1913 and the surviving Century Company typescripts (and hypothetically with the holograph manuscript, should it ever become available), this edition provides an opportunity to more fully examine the complex processes of composition, editing, censorship, and revision that characterize Dreiser's work from the 1890s to 1945.

* * *

A Traveler at Forty continues the Dreiser Edition's tradition of publishing texts that are not easily accessible, either to the specialist or the general reader. Such an undertaking would be unimaginable without the sponsorship of two institutions: the Library of the University of Pennsylvania and the University of Connecticut. Several individuals at the University of Connecticut deserve special mention for their initiatives and continuing support of this project: Ross D. MacKinnon, dean of the College of Liberal Arts and Sciences; Thomas P. Wilsted, director of the Thomas J. Dodd Research Center; and Janet Greger, vice provost and dean of the Graduate School. The goodwill and special training of the staff at the University of Pennsylvania's Annenberg Rare Book and Manuscript Library have been essential to the progress of the Dreiser Edition. Director Michael T. Ryan has generously devoted his own time and the resources of his staff to facilitating the work of the Dreiser Edition. Curator of Manuscripts Nancy M. Shawcross continues to contribute her expertise and special service to the project. John Pollack has consistently and untiringly assisted Dreiser Edition editors in their work. Finally, Dr. Willis Regier, the director of the University of Illinois Press, has provided imaginative guidance and commitment to the Dreiser Edition at a pivotal point in its history.

Thomas P. Riggio
General Editor
The Dreiser Edition

ACKNOWLEDGMENTS

I am indebted to the trustees of the University of Pennsylvania for permission to publish the complete text of *A Traveler at Forty* from the Theodore Dreiser Papers; to reprint photos; and to quote from Dreiser's travel diaries, his correspondence, and other material relevant for this travelogue. Throughout all the phases of production for this book, my work has profited from the assistance I have received from the staff at the Annenberg Rare Book and Manuscript Library at the University of Pennsylvania. I especially wish to thank Nancy M. Shawcross, the curator, who unfailingly and speedily answered all my queries.

For the permission to reproduce the portrait of Charles T. Yerkes, I am grateful to the National Portrait Gallery, Smithsonian Institution, Washington, D.C. For the use of a photo of the Dutch singer Julia Culp, I wish to thank the publisher Friese Pers Boekerij BV, Leeuwarden, the Netherlands.

Thomas P. Riggio not only suggested that I devote myself to this project but also guided it from beginning to end with unflagging interest and attention, making himself an ideal adviser. I am indebted as well to James L. W. West III, with whom I had the pleasure of discussing editorial principles and laying out the editorial groundwork. I owe many thanks to Lee Ann Draud, an experienced reader of Dreiser's texts and manuscripts. My gratitude also goes to Willis Regier and the staff of the University of Illinois Press and especially to Bruce Bethell for his careful scrutiny of the copy-text.

Moreover, I have received help and encouragement in various ways and from numerous people, institutions, libraries, archives, and museums, of whom I can name only a few. Madeline Gibson, assistant to Gene Rinkel, curator of the Rare Book and Special Collections Library of the University of Illinois Library, answered all my inquiries concerning the archives of Grant Richards. Jerome Loving provided me with important background material. Keith Newlin furnished answers to key questions. I was further aided by John Copping, the vicar of Cookham Dean, Berkshire; by the town of Mayen; and by German members of the Dreiser family, Dreiser's late cousins Karola and Wilhelmine and Dreiser's nephew Rolf Dreiser.

Finally, I thank my university for granting me two sabbaticals that allowed me to start and finish this project. This would not have been possible, however, without the contributions of David Sawyer, Jeff Clingenpeel, Rebecca Kelly, and Laura Russell, as well as the occasional assistance of Richard Henninge and Donald Kiraly. The crucial and final stage was supported by the truly dedicated work of Klaus H. Schmidt and Corinna Gaubatz. The enumeration of my indebtedness, though, would remain incomplete without recognition of my family, who gladly offered the technical and research expertise of their various professional fields.

A Traveler at Forty

Dreiser's itinerary, 1911–12. The solid line shows his route through Europe. He arrived in England at Fishguard and then traveled to Cookham, Marlow, Oxford, London, Manchester, Canterbury, and Dover. After crossing the Channel to Calais in France, he took a train to Paris. From there he departed for Menton, Monte Carlo, and Nice on the Riviera. Via Pisa he traveled to Rome and then turned north, visiting Perugia, Florence, and Venice on his way to Milan. In Switzerland he stopped at Lucerne and then headed for Germany. From Frankfurt he took a side trip to Mainz and Mayen. He proceeded to Berlin and then on to Amsterdam, Haarlem, The Hague, and Rotterdam in Holland. He returned to Paris via Belgium, seeing Bruges and Brussels, Antwerp, Ghent, and Waterloo, and then retraced his steps to London. After a final visit to Cookham, he boarded a ship at Dover for New York.

CHAPTER I

To begin this record right, I should say that on this date, Saturday, November 4th, 1911, I am living in an apartment at 3609 Broadway, New York, which is near the 145th Street subway station. I am living in a really beautiful apartment, small but delightful, in an apartment house known as the Riverview, which faces Broadway at 149th Street, but which runs through to some unimproved property owned by the same man who owns this house, and which therefore—our apartment particularly (being on the fifth floor)—commands a truly magnificent view of the Hudson River which parallels Broadway (or rather, which Broadway parallels) and also of Riverside Drive, one of the most beautiful park residence thoroughfares in all New York. The apartment has six pretty rooms and a bath, beautifully and conveniently arranged. There is an abundance of hot water, steam heat, gas and electricity, a gas range, elevator, telephone, uniformed hall service, a courteous superintendent and all those things which go to make the best type of apartment life in New York City—the first city in America.

I have just turned forty. I have seen a very, very great deal of life. I have been a newspaperman, editor, magazine contributor, author and, before these things, several odd kinds of clerk before I found out what I could do. This past winter I have been engaged in writing a novel—*Jennie Gerhardt*—which is just now on the market and, thank heaven, much to my astonishment, doing fairly well. This fall I have been at work on another novel entitled "The Financier," which I hope to complete by the spring of 1912. About one-third of it is done. I am not very well fixed financially at this moment, but because of the unexpected success of my second book, critically at least, I am beginning to see my way clear. A distinct, unequivocal literary reputation is worth something financially in the United States.

Eleven years ago I wrote my first novel called *Sister Carrie*, which was issued by Doubleday, Page & Company of New York and suppressed by them—heaven knows why, for the same fall they suppressed my book because of its alleged immoral tendencies, they published Zola's *Fecundity* and *An Englishwoman's Love-Letters*. I fancy now, after eleven years of wonder, that it was not so much the supposed immorality as the book's straightforward, plainspoken discussion of American life in general. We were not used then in America to calling a spade a spade, particularly in books. We had great admiration for Tolstoy and Flaubert and Balzac and de Maupassant at a distance—some of us—and it was quite an honor to have handsome sets of these men on our shelves, but mostly we had been schooled in the literature of Dickens, Thackeray, George Eliot, Charles Lamb and that refined company of English sentimental realists who told us something about life, but not everything. No doubt all of these great gentlemen knew how shabby a thing this world is—how full of lies, make-believe, seeming and false pretense it all is—but they had agreed among themselves or with the public or with sentiment generally not to talk about that too much.

Books were always to be built out of facts concerning "our better natures." We were always to be seen as we wish to be seen. There were villains, to be sure—liars, dogs, thieves, scoundrels—but they were strange creatures, hiding away in dark, unconventional places and scarcely seen save at night and peradventure; whereas we, all nice, clean, bright, honest, well-meaning people, were living in nice homes, going our way honestly and truthfully, going to church, raising our children, believing in a Father, a Son and a Holy Ghost, and never doing anything wrong at any time, save as these miserable liars, dogs, thieves, et cetera, might suddenly appear and make us. Our books largely showed us as heroes. If anything happened to our daughters, it was not their fault, but the fault of these miserable villains. Most of us were without original sin. The business of our books, our church, our laws, our jails, was to keep us so. I am quite sure that it never occurred to many of us that there was something really improving in a plain, straightforward understanding of life. Most of us believed that to understand life was not only to become evil, passively so, by reading but to be by the very act of so reading actively dangerous.

Sister Carrie came out, and to my astonishment I found myself the center of a storm of criticism and abuse as well as the head and front of a peculiar company of individuals who were determined to see to it that in the long run both I and my book—or perhaps I had better say my book only—had justice. They wrote me. They wrote Messrs. Doubleday & Page. I recall one perfectly delightful letter in which Christ and the ass that carried him into Jerusalem were referred to. I was praised to the skies by some critics. I was damned to the lowest depths of insanity by others. "A hack newspaper reporter," I recall one critic writing, "who would be highly flattered to be called the Zola of America." I have never read a line of Zola, I am sorry to report. "A cheap sensationalist who seeks to make capital out of all the silly newspaper horrors of the time—the bread line, the East Side lodging house, etc." Then there were those who stated publicly that it was "the best novel ever written in America," "the first piece of American realism worthy of the name," "a great human document," etc.

Do I believe all this? I don't know. Did I, at the time? I'm quite sure I didn't. I was the most surprised man or boy—for I was a boy in mind, just the same—that you ever saw. Something prompted me while I was writing to write sincerely. I would come to strange, hard, bitter, sad facts in my story, for after all, it was a story, and I would say, "Shall I put that down?" and something within the very center of my being would say, "You must! You must! You dare not do otherwise." At times, sitting at my little dining table in the flat I then occupied in 102nd Street near Central Park West, New York, I felt very much like Martin Luther must have felt when he stood before the Diet of Worms. "Here I stand. Otherwise I cannot do. God help me."

But perhaps instead of telling you about my book, I had better tell you something about myself, particularly if you intend to follow this record. My father was a woolen manufacturer at Terre Haute, Indiana, when I was a boy. He came to America from Germany as an immigrant in 1844 and ran a woolen mill for a while as a manager, finally owning it himself. He was an ardent Catholic, while my mother was first a Mennonite and later a convert. She was never the religious enthusiast that he was. I was born in Terre Haute, and when I was about eleven years old, the family removed from Terre Haute to Warsaw, Indiana, in the northern portion of the state, and there I went to school until I was sixteen. After that I spent one year at the State University of Indiana. Later, I went to Chicago and was a real estate clerk, collector, laundry clerk—anything you will—until I finally found that which I could do best—newspaper reporting. After that, as I have said, I was successively dramatic editor, traveling correspondent, magazine contributor, editor and finally author.

I never fancied I was exceptional in any of these things, and in one or two instances I have been discharged. More frequently, I have resigned of my own accord, moving on to what I hoped would be better things. I have been prosperous and hungry, applauded and looked upon as anything but worthwhile. Men have told me to my face that I am erratic, deficient, peculiar. Men have told me to my face that I am the most distinguished personality with whom they have ever come in contact. Do I believe all this? No. I am not sure that I do. I do not know anything. I know nothing about life—I know nothing about myself. I have suffered much, I have enjoyed many things intensely—oh, very intensely.

All my life I have been emotional, high strung, a victim of the lure of beauty in everything, and yet I have given many people the impression that I was cold, hard, indifferent, selfish and cruel. Perhaps I am both. I am ready to believe that I am. But beauty holds me first. I am subject to that and yet a novice in its subtleties. I do not know the history of Greece, save in a very general way. I do not know the history of various arts—poetry, prose, architecture, sculpture, painting—except in the same general way, not intimately. I do not know even the history of beauty in women, its significant emissaries in life, but I suspect many things. A single fact goes a long way with me. It suggests much.

I cannot say that I love humanity as much as I did when I was a boy, and now I suspect that I did not love it so much as a boy. From my youth, my eye was held and my feelings gripped by what might be called impersonal beauty—the beauty of rosy clouds in the early dawn, of birds flying, flowers blooming, of landscapes melting into hazy distances. I can recall rising at four and five o'clock of early spring mornings when I was seven, eight, nine and ten years of age, when the rest of the family—excepting my mother, who was also a lover of beauty—was asleep, and going forth to see what the day and the world were like. I can never hope to indicate to anyone what those hours were to me. I could not suggest what affinity lay between my blood and the faint delicate hues of the morning glory. In poetry books here and there I have found lines which bring back with cognizable sweetness something of what I felt. In Shelley's "Adonais," in Keats's "Ode on a Grecian Urn," in Wordsworth's "Excursion" and sonnets and odes I have found much. In Wordsworth's "Boy and the Owls" particularly, I recognize something of myself. And when he sang, "My heart leaps up when I behold a rainbow in the sky," he was saying what I have felt over and over without knowing why.

Life has been so beautiful to me. I have cried time and again thinking of its sweetness, its pathos, its grim, dramatic power. I have cried over the characters I have created, and I have cried over a half-witted boy in the street. I have felt sorry for endless people, and I have felt happy that life has provided warm, cozy shelter for so many. I know nothing of its mysteries. I accept now no creeds. I do not know what truth is, what beauty is, what love is, what hope is. I do not believe anyone absolutely, and I do not doubt anyone absolutely. I think people are both evil and well-intentioned.

I was raised in Western towns. I know nothing of Europe. I have never been farther west than the Mississippi nor farther south than North Carolina. But I have lived, met and talked with a vast number of people of degrees of ability, intelligence, station, and so forth. I am not a simple-minded man—quite the contrary.

In some respects, America is so gauche—so raw, as we phrase it. It reminds me sometimes of the traditional yokel who guffaws before a statue of the Venus of Milo. "Gee whiz, look at that." But it's a great, big, wonderful, forceful nation just the same, and it's going to come out of its hearty yokel point of view and write and read books and paint and hang pictures which will take the world by storm. I believe in America. I believe in its rawness—its brute force. I feel—I know—it has a tremendous work to do. I wish sincerely I could help do it. But it suppressed my feeble little bit of realism in 1900, and it may suppress me some more in time to come—but it won't suppress all realism. It can't. And it will love its realists after a while, as it now loves its patriots—Nathan Hale and Ulysses S. Grant, and Abraham Lincoln, and it will have the same noble basis for doing so.

Well, that's pretty much of a flight, isn't it, to be dated Nov. 4th, 1911, but I'm not through yet. For on this date a strange thing happened. Here I was writing, owing $300 on an insurance policy which was just about to fall due, owing $175.00 on a piece of land which I wanted very much to own free and clear at Grand View-on-the-Hudson—isn't that a typical American name—Grand View-on-the-Hudson? It sounds something like Squedunk-by-the-Sea. I owed $1,000 against an apple orchard—a yearly payment—and $1,500 in the shape of an old debt, and all I had against the things was something like $450.00 in the bank, and the obvious prosperity of my new book. At least it looked at this writing, from the critical fuss being made over it, as though it would sell, and so I was not utterly depressed, but I had been.

Fate plays queer tricks with us. Honestly, as I live, I never expected to have the money to go to Europe. I have always wanted to go and I have always said to myself that if I did go, it would be comfortably or not at all. I have a horror of little pinching calculations. I can't go about much and not put my hand in my pocket and pay freely and gladly. Most of us have a sense of dignity which we must maintain. If I could not do that, I would take off my nice clothes, get a job as a motorman and run a streetcar until I could. I have no horror of common work. I like it. I like common men. And I wasn't thinking of how I would ever go to Europe. But now since my second book was stirring things up, I was thinking how I would press on to the completion of my thirty-ninth chapter, take my story thus far done down to my publishers, say, "Here, I must have at least $3,000 to complete it"—and get it. I knew I should. I felt sure of it. Publishers are not letting go of artistic strikes if they can help it. They like to foster those whom they consider capable. They will take a chance—if it is a reasonable one. I thought they would in this case. Then, since the last one-third of my story was laid in London, I thought that possibly in February or March I would run over to that city, look up my data, run right back and complete my book.

While I was opening my mail on this morning, I encountered a now memorable note which was addressed to me at my apartment. It was, as I found on glancing at it, from an old publisher friend of mine in England who expressed himself as anxious to see me immediately, a gentleman whom I admire very much, but with whom, heretofore, I have never been able to do any business. He was one of those who helped suppress *Sister Carrie* in 1900, for he refused it for the English market. He did not think it would sell, and anyhow, he told me afterward that he did not think it amounted to so much. Still, I liked him. I have always liked him. I liked him because he struck me as amusingly English, decidedly literary and artistic in his point of view, a man with a wide vision, discriminating taste, rare selection. He wears a monocle in his right eye, *à la* Joseph Chamberlain, and I like him for that. I like people anyhow who take themselves with a grand air, whether they like me or not—particularly if the grand air is backed up by a real personality. In this case it is.

He had been over to see me once, three years before, had dined at my house, or rather, apartment. He had called on me at my office in the Butterick Building when I was editor-in-chief of the Butterick Publications. He had told me once frankly that he liked me, that in his judgment I was a great writer, that it was a scandal that I was not compelled to write. He even complained to Mrs. Dreiser for her part in the affair—my literary idleness—though as a matter of fact, he did not know all the facts. Sickness had interfered—a long period—and I was practically cheated by chance out of ten years of my literary life, but be that as it may—. Anyhow, after three years, here was this note from him and I scanned it curiously.

"Where are you?" it read. "I must see you at once. Write or phone me today. Don't fail. Yours, Grant Richards."

Why did he want to see me? I asked myself. Did he want to get my current book for England? It was too late. It was already out in England, I thought. Probably he just wanted to see me. I would call him up and make an appointment, and I did, but he was not in. Then I visited the hotel, being on my way downtown, left a card and a complimentary copy of my book and invited him to come to breakfast Sunday morning, which he did.

Next morning Grant Richards took breakfast with me; it was a most interesting affair. He was late—very—because he got on the wrong train on the subway and had been carried somewhere into the borough of the Bronx instead of up Broadway as he wished. He explained all this with his grand official air. He stalked in, his spats shining, his monocle glowing with the shrewd, inquisitive eye behind it, his whole manner genial, self-sufficient, almost dictatorial and always final—if you really will have it so. The man is positively the most interesting Englishman I have ever met. He takes charge so easily, rules so sufficiently, does so essentially well in all circumstances where he is interested so to do.

He said he had been in England in all this. He had thought of coming, but he had let the thought of not being able to—affairs—stand in his way. "That was really silly," he observed, "for, of course, one could come. Always notions, these. One could always come." How had I been? What was I doing? He was down at Mr. Doubleday's. He had seen a full-page picture of me in the *Bookman* and a very flattering notice of my following. I think this must have surprised him a little. I think it re-awakened his interest very keenly perhaps. "Why," I can see his very intellectual English mind saying, "this man has come to life. He's just the man I want to see. If I can arrange a book, now." Anyhow, here he was.

"I have decided what we shall do now," he observed with that managerial air which always delights me because my soul is not in the least managerial. "You shall come to England with me. I have my passage all arranged for the 22nd. I shall phone and say that Mr. Theodore Dreiser, a very distinguished American author, is coming back with me and that I want a first-class cabin suite reserved. You shall come to my house in England, you shall stay there a few days, then I shall take you to London and put you up at a very good hotel where the food is very good and the service excellent. You shall stay there until January 1st, and then we shall go to the south of France—Nice, the Riviera, Monte Carlo; from there you shall go on to Rome, to Paris, where I shall join you, and then sometime in the spring or summer, when you have all your notes, you shall return to London or New York and write your impressions, and I shall publish them!"

"Why? Why?" I ask, and "How? I haven't any money to go to London or Paris or anywhere else at present. My affairs are very much complicated. You say 'Come to London.' Quite so. But how about me—my financial difficulties?"

"Those things can always be arranged," observed my friend, adjusting his monocle and staring at the river. "A matter of that kind can always be arranged. It is not as though it could not. You are writing a new book, you say. Very well, that is very simple. You have thirty-nine chapters done. I shall go to my friend Mr. Scott tomorrow at the Century and I shall say, "Look hyah, what would you say if someone should have walked into your office thirty years ago and said, 'You can have now for a little consideration all the future works of Mr. Hardy or Mr. Meredith? What would you say?' Anyone knows what they would say. I know very well what they will say. In consideration of that, and on condition that I raise you, say, three hundred pounds for your immediate expenses and more later, you are to close up your affairs here and come with me on the 22nd to London."

He paused delightfully. The eye behind the monocle gleamed auspiciously, assuringly.

"Yes, I know," I replied. "That's all very fine. I don't know whether I can or not. I have certain obligations to my present publishers. I cannot just jump up and walk off to another. There is this apartment to consider. I cannot carry this lease very well. There are certain obligations now due to be met." I explained in a vague way what they were.

"Those can be met. So it is agreed. I raise you three hundred pounds for your immediate expenses. You sublet your apartment. Wednesday, the 22nd, we sail. Let me see. This is Sunday, the 5th. Tomorrow is Monday. Tomorrow I go to Philadelphia. Tuesday I shall see my friend Scott. Wednesday morning at 8 o'clock sharp you shall breakfast with me at the Knickerbocker.

I shall then tell you what I hyah. After that you shall do whatever the situation may require to expedite matters. Is that agreed?"

"It is agreed to this extent," I replied calmly and rather doubtfully, "you are at liberty to see what you can do. I should like to go to England. As a matter of fact, I must go, eventually, for I have to secure the local details for the last one-third of my new novel. However, I am really interested to know what can be done. I should like to know what the Century Company or any other company would say to such a proposition. I'll breakfast with you certainly at eight o'clock Wednesday morning. This is very flattering."

Then I showed him just what the reviewers and the news critics were saying of *Jennie Gerhardt*.

He went away seemingly very much interested in this idea of his. I was very doubtful. I did not understand it at all. It was all so sudden. He seemed very convinced that anything I might do would be very much worthwhile, and I did not and do not agree with him. Anyhow, he left, saying if all eventuated satisfactorily, he was to have the next book for the English market.

"If it *can* be arranged," I interpolated.

"It can be arranged," he replied emphatically. "I will attend to the financial part and arrange the affair with an American publisher. And, in case it does go through, you are to give me this manuscript you are now working on as a family heirloom."

"Delighted. I should be glad to do that anyhow. However—"

So away he went, and I walked over to the river, staring at it meditatively. Was this a dream, or was it true? Three hundred pounds—$1,500—for immediate expenses, and more afterward. How much more? I should have to have considerable more to straighten out things nicely. This apartment—what about that? Could I lease it?

Sometimes life is very generous. It walks in and says, "Here, I want you to do a certain thing," and it proceeds to arrange all your affairs for you. I felt curiously at this time as though I was on the edge of a great change. Something was going to happen. Fate had probably sent this man to get me out of this. Anyhow, here he was, and before leaving he had tucked six chapters of "The Financier" ("Fee-nance-yer," he insisted they called it in England) under his arm and was going to read them at once. He probably won't like them, I thought. Anyhow, no harm can come from letting him read them and seeing what he can do financially. So I went off to see some friends, and Mr. Grant Richards went on his way.

CHAPTER II

Things move swiftly when the time is ripe, the hour propitious. I had no faith in this proposed adventure, but working on quietly at my story, Wednesday morning came, and at eight o'clock I was in the lobby of the Knickerbocker Hotel. I shall not describe that glittering world, but who does not know it?—one of the best hotels in the very heart of the theater and hotel life of New York. Mr. Grant Richards was dressing and would be down. In ten minutes, there he was, fresh and brisk, his face rosy, that air which health has showing in his gestures and in his eyes.

"Oh, yes. Hyah we ah. Been waiting long? Now we shall breakfast, and then afterwards we shall talk. While you are putting up your coat, I shall be ordering," and off he was.

A table at any time in the Knickerbocker Hotel is an infinite delight to me. At breakfast it has a subtle charm all its own. The hotel is a little showy, but it has an air. The waiters, of course, are all French, well paid, well set up, thoroughly drilled in their troublesome art; the cuisine is borrowed from the very best restaurants of Paris and elsewhere that we know. It is blended with a subtle understanding of what an American dish is and just how it should be served. And it comes to you with all the airs of a French dish—for instance, my commonplace order of buckwheat cakes and Jones's sausage.

"Jones's sausage! Jones's sausage!" observed my perfect Englishman, monocle wisely alert. "What is Jones's sausage? Something very American, I suppose? You like them? You shall have them."

"And buckwheat cakes?"

"And buckwheat cakes."

"And coffee?"

"And coffee."

And now I shall tell you the history of Jones's sausage, which is very simple indeed. Plain American sausage made smokehouse fashion by a man who knows how in Wisconsin. To be cosmopolitan, to do as the Americans do, Mr. Grant Richards decided he would have some also, but he merely picked at them. I think he was thinking of a bit of smoked fish and an egg.

Anyhow, that over, and I began to hear a report of what had happened. He had not seen Mr. Scott first, but had decided to talk to a Mr. Doty, who was also very influential in the publishing affairs of this house, and interest him. Mr. Doty had responded most cordially. Although this was election day, a holiday, and Mr. Doty had decided to go somewhere and play golf, he was staying in town especially to read my mss., and I was to go now—I can hear Grant Richards's managerial executive voice call up my apartment and have it sent to him by special messenger. Then everything was to be put over until Friday, when if the strain of interest had not been interrupted, I was to meet the officers of the Century Company and the editor of the *Century Magazine* at lunch at the Aldine Club.

"Why?"

Well, they were interested in me. They wanted to meet me. It was time that I should. Mr. Johnson, the editor, was most keen to show his appreciation of my work. He wanted to write me beforehand, which, however, was finally deemed unnecessary. So come two more days of peaceful writing, in which Grant Richards is visiting another city, and then Friday at twelve-thirty sharp I am scheduled to meet Mr. Grant Richards in the lobby of the Hoffman House and there we are to dine, I fancy.

Not so. This is merely a short preliminary conversation. The lunch is at the Aldine Club. We are to go to the Century Company first, then to the Aldine Club. Mr. Doty is very much impressed. He has read all of "The Financier" and likes it very much—thinks it magnificent, in fact.

As usual, I am mistrustful of fate. We are to go to the Century Company, and because of certain predilections of the editor of the *Century*, I am to express a willingness to do a type of social essay article in Europe for the magazine. Some separate arrangement for papers of this kind with payment in advance is to be made. Mainly, however, the transfer of myself—books, papers. "The Financier" is the chief topic of interest on which the conversation is to hinge. Mr. Grant Richards has a grand scheme in his mind. They are to advance $1,500 now against a series of three papers for the magazine. They are to advance an additional $2,500 against the book, and they are to allow me fifteen percent in the first 10,000 and twenty percent on all over that. I listen solemnly, for I do not know what to think. My present terms are not nearly so advantageous. My present publishers have no intention of advancing me anything unless compelled to. Besides, I have obligations to them. It is ticklish business.

However, meeting people and talking things over, getting acquainted, never does any harm. I am pleased at the general idea of discussion. It makes it so much easier to talk "brass tacks" to my own publishers. We go. There is much general hand-shaking. I have the feeling that for once in my life I am being somewhat lionized. They are most gracious. While I am talking, my mind runs back to days when I was distinctly persona non grata here. No doubt I was a very raw, ridiculous youth. I fancy my intrusion with any thought relating to art must have seemed an anomaly. Anyhow, that is all gone and done for now, and here I am—come back a real live author with a peculiar sort of standing which speaks for itself, and it is temporarily worth-while talking to me.

I always have to smile when I think of the showy, glassy little hours of success in life. A man does a little something—sinks a ship, writes a piece of music, constructs a play, advocates a policy in politics, and behold, he has his little hour. For a moment the world pauses and listens. At first only a few pause and listen, then a reasonable number, then he is seized upon by certain significant figures and made a little something of—it depends upon the man—he does or does not strut and stare a little. Some do, some do not. I have noticed in a number of cases within my own experience that some have, and it has always seemed a pathetic spectacle. How little such a one must know about life! How mistakenly must he hold the gauds that life has to offer. They are such tinsel things—such flitter geld. I know of nothing so intangible, no mist so vague, no mirage so compounded of refraction and thin air as repute and applause. "Honor. Who has it? He that dies o' Wednesday." (I am quoting Master Will Shakespeare.) "Doth he feel it? No. Doth he hear it? No. 'Tis insensible, then? Yes, to the dead. But will he not live with the living? No. Why? Detraction will not suffer it. Therefore I'll none of it. Honor is a mere scutcheon, and so ends my catechism."

However, we went to lunch. There was a staggering array of wine glasses and plates. I was given an excellent position between the president of the company and the editor of the magazine. Opposite me sat my mentor, his monocle trimly set, and at the foot of the table, the secretary, Mr. Doty, and the treasurer, Mr. Ellsworth.

I wish I could amply and convincingly describe this intellectual and pleasant company. Business is business, but some businesses are not anything like others, and the publishing business is one of them. It isn't really so much a business as it is an art connoisseurship in its higher forms, and the company which these gentlemen represented was certainly one of its higher forms, certainly one of its best forms. I have always held the *Century Magazine* in the utmost reverence and respect. The hard brutalities of some forms of trade are not involved. This isn't tea or coffee they are dealing in, but figments of the brain, principally, fine lusterful thoughts which take on a sheen from both antiquity and posterity. It doesn't matter that it is the Aldine Club, New York, or Will's Coffee House of the sixteenth century. The fact is the same. The business of the publisher, on one side at least—and it seems to me on all sides—is with art. There is nothing but art involved in it at bottom, if no more than the art of disseminating information, which is a fine art. Pictures, stories, verses, essays, histories, biographies—this is the grist of their mill, and it is a fine grist. It is delightful wheat that comes forth in some instances—real bread of life, and I would be proud to be included in the sum total of its perfect product.

We sat down, and I looked at these gentlemen each and each by turn, for I had never seen but one of them before. A curious, pleasant, entertaining company. Mr. Scott, the president, reminded me of the late Joe Cannon, only he lacked, as one of the editors subsequently told me, the "never-say-die," which is the little wisp of hair which ornamented the late Speaker's otherwise polished bald head. He is also, like myself, from Indiana and bears some of the distinguishing features of that peculiar state, a naive simplicity of manner, a social democratic manner of address, a peculiar fresh-wood look which has some faint relationship to sound hickory—I can't tell you why. He is, I should say, a fine example of the Middle West American of the middle historic period—from 1844 to 1894. That period, to me, in the Middle West, has produced a certain type of man which I recognize in Mr. Scott, Mr. Cannon and others.

Mr. Johnson, the editor of the *Century Magazine*, is quite another sort of man, a pale sandy-bearded, sandy-haired type of man of, perhaps, fifty-five or sixty—I am no judge—the like of whom I have seen in the art and medical world more than once. He is phlegmatic, I should say, and dreamy, with an intense love of the beautiful. I would be safe in saying that, even if I did not instinctively know it to be true, for his poetic product of verse testifies to the same end. A fine understanding of the art, music, sculpture, and painting of the world, no doubt, with an undue reverence for genius, perhaps. Such men are apt to become lost in speculative abstrusities and to lose sight of current-day issues in the deep, sad music of universal art.

Mr. Johnson and I had a little tiff once. It was a silly thing, and it occurred years ago, when I was twenty-six or -seven. It came up at this meal because of his sedate courtesy in referring to it. I was writing stories at the time, and I wrote one, my first, I think, which I called, "Of the Shining Slave Makers," and sent it, among other places, to the *Century Magazine*. I sent it there first. Presently it came back with a courteous note, not a printed slip, saying it was not within their scope and they were obliged to reject it. Something in the note, or perhaps it was because it was the Century Company, and I was anxious to obtain recognition there, caused me to decide to write and ask what the reader's opinion had really been, for I judged from something else in the note that not the editor, but one of his readers, had read it. Back came the reader's opinion in a few days—clear and definite. He had given the story serious consideration, evidently, for he had written three or four hundred words as to what he thought. In it he said—oh, I forget what—that it was a straining of probabilities to attribute to an ant the emotions of a man; and being young and ambitious and anxious to get on, this angered me. I wrote back and criticized the reader scathingly. Isn't that exactly like the average literary beginner? No doubt this angered Mr. Johnson, but his note did not show it. It was far more courteous than mine.

It said, among other natural things, that that was the last time he would trouble to send a contributor a reader's opinion, for he saw plainly that it merely aroused additional ill-will if the mss. happened to be rejected. This gave me an excuse for feeling badly toward the *Century* for a time, and I so felt. But after a while other interests grew up and I finally forgot, or rather regretted, all that had been connected with it. It seemed silly and useless on my part, and it was, I suppose. But I was a boy.

Now, Mr. Johnson recalled this in a delicate way, and I explained to all present. It turned out that Mr. Ellsworth, the treasurer of the company—a gentleman with a hearing machine which looked somewhat like a fair-sized camera and which he placed on the table before him, hearing from it by means of a wire and black rubber receiver attached to his ear—had also read "The Financier" and was sincerely impressed. He was quite frank and forceful about this, and I liked him all the better for a story he told about his going to London for the first time and running quickly to the Poets' Corner at Westminster Abbey, only to find himself greatly disappointed as to its size and other charms, and hurrying swiftly away again. He was another American, with an easy, air-less, off-hand manner which I like so much. I often wonder why it is that I rejoice in the distingué air of a man like Whistler or Grant Richards and the simple, collapsible manner of so many really able, forceful Americans, when the two things are at poles' ends. The answer is of course that we can like a thing and its direct opposite at one and the same time. We do probably in everything, only we don't notice it.

The luncheon was really a gay affair. Being the hero of the hour, much attention was paid to me. I was listened to deferentially. I found myself becoming oratorical, pompous, rather superior, I think. I have to smile when I think I am not that. In the main I am rather shy. But supported by the faith of Grant Richards, and being told on all sides that I was at work on something very exceptional, I may be forgiven, I hope, if I swelled a little with pride. Pride! Pride! Pride! Heaven forbid. And I know so much of this dusty, shifty world.

Well, then, this meal went on and ended with compliments and droll stories, and we were out in the street again. Before leaving, Grant Richards had told me to see him at four o'clock at his hotel, and there I was. When he came, brisk from the publishers' office where he had been talking terms, he was obviously elate. The critical, examining eye behind the monocle was dancing a dance which was peculiarly gay.

"I've fixed it," he observed directly. "It's all arranged. You are to come with me to London. First, let me see if there is any mail, and then we go up to the room. You don't mind if I dress for dinner and talk at the same time? It is late."

"Not at all."

"Well, then," he replied, when we were in his chamber on the ninth floor, "this is how it is. I have it all figured out. They are to advance you $1,500 against a series of three articles which you are to do for the magazine, and which has nothing to do with the book which might flow from your experiences and which will be taken up under a separate head. They are to make you a definite, separate advance payment in connection with your book, $2,500, on the day on which the papers are presented for your signature, and $2,500 on the day the book is issued, or sooner, if necessary, the papers to be presented not later than next Friday at eleven o'clock or, say, the following Monday at the same hour. And meantime, you are to take this manuscript of yours, which a boy will bring here in a few moments, together with a form of letter which I shall dictate to your publishers, and ask them to read it and give you a decision by not later than next Friday morning at eleven o'clock. That is pretty short notice to give them to turn around in, but of course, as a matter of fact, I am anxious to make it just as difficult as possible for them, for of course I am anxious that they should reject the proposition as a whole. The Century Company will pay you fifteen percent on the first ten thousand and twenty percent on all over that. I am going to suggest that you ask Harper and Brothers to pay you $2,500 not later than eleven o'clock on Friday next; that they pay you an additional $2,500 on January 1st, 1912; that they give you a straight fifteen percent on the first ten thousand copies sold and a straight twenty percent on all copies sold over that, and that they relinquish rights so that I may publish it abroad."

His monocled eye gleamed intensely, and he smiled.

"I fancy they'll consider those terms rather stiff. Very good. The stiffer the better. That's just what I want. They won't accept, of course, and all will be clear sailing. Of course we shall have to have time to turn round in, and that's why I say next Friday."

He paused, gathering things from bags, adjusting his shoes and collars, looking intermittently at books which were being sent for examination by publishers.

I could not believe that what I had heard could possibly be true. The time was too short. The thing he thought could be done could not be done. I could not sublet my apartment, for one thing. Still I went away, wrote the form of letter as suggested, sent the manuscript and waited. I fancied a great storm would follow. There would be wailing and gnashing of teeth. Still, there were many things which made it possible—even probable. The reviews were most significant and coming in fresher and fresher every day. There were interviewers following my steps from the *Sun*, the *Evening Post*, the *Times*, the *Telegraph* and some syndicate or other. The house which had published the book was running significant advertisements, and, generally speaking, things were looking up. I was the recipient of congratulatory letters, phone messages, even telegrams. I was never quite so fussed about in all my life before.

And now my most insistent manager, self-constituted and rather fascinating, took a new tack. I must come and dine with himself and a certain Baron R. who was stopping, for the time being, in America, to see a little of New York life. We were to dine at the Ritz. I must go with him to see the Manets at the Museum and write a certain Mrs. Havemeyer for the privilege of looking at hers. I must breakfast with him on Friday, the day I was to hear finally from Harpers, and compose notes and arrange a method of procedure. We were sailing a difficult course. My life was rather full of invitations just at this time, what with people looking me up who had not for a long time, and renewing old ties, but I accepted these. New York is always interesting to me, and what he told me of Baron R., the kind of man he was, made me feel that I would be very much interested in him. To begin with, he was, he said, a close relation of the German royal family—how close I do not care to know, and I would not care to say if I did. He had been an officer in the German army, of course. He was an accomplished linguist, I understood, a man of the world and of refinement, and, from the point of view of women, a frank and outspoken sex enthusiast. I understood that he gambled a great deal, thought nothing of losing thousands of dollars in a night, drew on some German imperial agent for more money when he needed it and otherwise disported himself as freely as he chose. He was something in connection with the diplomatic service of Germany, but whatever it was, it was largely nominal. He was to be here only a little while longer, and then he was to be off to Russia.

"I should like you to see him," explained Grant Richards, with his usual insistence on important things. It is so nice to have someone who knows what the really interesting things of life are, who will insist at the same time on your observing them. "He is very much of a type—one you ought to know. He has a large estate in Prussia, and if you should hit it off, he might possibly extend you an invitation to spend Christmas or something on his estate. I could ask him to do that without any trouble. It would give you an insight into German life. Anyhow, he's very much worthwhile—different—not at all an ordinary person."

We went on Wednesday, as scheduled. I recall us swinging along together in the November dark, Grant Richards in his high hat and fur coat, and myself arrayed similarly, all save the fur on the coat, and coming through that storm of taxis and automobiles which makes the New York hotel and theater district, to the Ritz. By some mix-up, the baron had not received Richards's message. Some other baron—or his man, rather—had got it. Anyhow, he had to get him on the phone and tell him we were waiting, but he came immediately. We were scarcely through with our soup before he came quickly forward, a tall, lean, experienced gentleman of perhaps thirty-eight or forty, his face graced by a long, pointed nose, his hands thin, delicate, the nails long, pointed and highly polished. I noticed at once that his face, so smoothly massaged, had only a slightly German cast, not markedly so, and his eyes were soft and full of that shrewd reserve which notifies you at once that the possessor is full of a world of experience which he will never reveal.

The difference between a polished man of the world—a follower after pleasure and social delights generally—and a constructive working temperament such as that of the average American businessman or financier, of which we know so much, is just that which exists between a well-groomed Maltese cat and a bulldog or a Newfoundland. The one goes lightly, shrewdly, always—in calculating, delicate steps and ways. The other is strong, rawboned, direct, savage or good-natured, as the case may be. There is no close mental approximation in either case. The one does not understand how the other does—how he can do as he does—what he is thinking about. Your average American businessman would consider a man like Baron R. a wastrel and a stray. He would say at once that his life was a failure. What good does he do? What has he ever done? All our American plays are full of solid American fathers who give hard, practical advice to polished European aspirants for their daughters' hands, and try and do make men of them—according to the American standard. Your European, like Baron R., looks at the hard, solid American father, and says to himself, "What a hack! What a thick wit! That such a creature should be allowed within the sacred precincts of refinement!" Your Baron R. is refined, from the best points of view in which we use that word. His body is more delicately put up, his knowledge of life and social forms is fifty times as great as that of the other. He knows women, manners, appointments, service. He knows exactly how a butler ought to do, and a servant. He knows where the interesting social places of life are, what the connections of well-known people are, and so on and so forth, ad infinitum. Like Baron R., he speaks three or four or a half-dozen languages. His French is as good as his English; his Italian as his Russian. He knows what the niceties of dress are—just the things for the individual hour and the individual day. Your American businessman or financier knows little or nothing of these things—scarcely anything, relatively. He is too busy making money. He is too busy planning and devising things which the public needs greatly and which they will pay for gladly—railways, streetcar lines, public buildings, elevators, clocks, soaps, anything and everything. He knows that refinement may be ahead of him or his children, but he doesn't care anything much about that—not so very much. Let Johnny, his son, have it, or Mary, his daughter. As for him, he likes simple things, and the European polished gentleman thinks in a way that he is a clown and a boor and the less he has to do with him, the better. These things were perhaps truer twenty and thirty years ago, even, than they are today, but they are still notably true. I foresee a time when there will be a blend, but it is some distance off.

So Baron R. sat down, and with that delicate social reticence of his and Grant Richards's, we began a most interesting conversation. The baron began to explain how it was that he was late. There was some other baron in the background somewhere. He was not at all profuse about it, as an American would have been, but soft and cat-like. Grant Richards had explained to me that he, the baron, was suffering from an incurable affliction of the nerves which control the muscles about the eyes, so that they contracted involuntarily and made it seem as though he had gotten dust or something in them. I noticed this at once, for after a few moments both eyes, at intervals, began closing as swiftly and regularly as though I had thrown sand into them. Then they opened, and it was gone. I never saw an affliction like that before.

We talked, of course, about the Ritz a little, which is quite new, the principal dining room a beautiful oval, very delicately decorated. He said he liked it. Then he and Grant Richards exchanged a few subtleties concerning Europe—some references to Monte Carlo, Ostend, Paris and elsewhere. He was told by Grant Richards who I was, and I could see plainly that whoever I was, I was just another person in a long stream of people, who do things, or attempt to do them, and who get somewhere or who do not. His own station was fixed. We talked of America—its worst and best features. The most offensive thing to him was the impoliteness and crude incivility of the servants. He could not stand that. They were too gauche, too raw, too much like boors and sore thumbs, standing about. Grant Richards complained of the American habit of expectoration. I had thought we were largely over that, but it seems not. Anyhow he noticed it as a great offense, and I don't blame him. I object to it myself.

I think the baron's sense of the niceties was a little shocked by my desire to know what he thought of America for, after all, I was an American, and he could scarcely say exactly what he thought. I tried to indicate that although American-born, I was universal in my point of view, a detached spectator of life, but his hand moved in a curious gesture of unrest and uncertainty. His eyelids rose slightly.

"This fellow—really now—" I could hear him saying to himself, and you can imagine the rest. Grant Richards was a little anxious to get off the subject, and so we changed it to women and social things in general, and the atmosphere cleared nicely.

I wish I could indicate by what process of words exactly we came to talk about women, and to do what we did, but I cannot—my memory is not good enough. I could see, I think, by one or two remarks which he made at the opening of the conversation, that he was greatly interested in women—sex—and that there was no other interest in his life truly to compete with it. Grant Richards had indicated to me in one way and another by slight references that such was the case.

"Frankly, he is a hedonist," I think he said.

Anyhow, I knew beforehand that he was. He told of gambling somewhere the night before and losing five hundred or fifteen hundred dollars, and then he told of some place, some café, where the life was supposed to be high or gay, and the manner in which he did it showed that we were on the right track so far as he was concerned. The manner in which he spoke of losing the five hundred or the fifteen hundred dollars showed me that this sum, whatever it was, was no more than three or four dollars would be to me.

It is always hard for me to approach the subject of sex in the spirit in which I wish, for it is so hard to define it accurately—to say exactly what I mean. It is like attempting to handle or bottle some nebulous gas which is circumambient and which one cannot really hope to control. Sex means so many things to different people. To some it is the faintest reference to passional interest, hedged about by all the laws and conventions. To others it is a wild, raging, destroying flame, in which it is either death or delight, or both. Your man of the world like Baron R., Grant Richards, or myself, look upon it very much, I fancy, as he looks on any other fact or form of entertainment—a good meal, a play, a travel trip, or something of that sort. (I am talking of a passing sex interest, not love.) The three things are usually interrelated, somewhat. Sex facts do not shock me anymore. A woman's form is not the blinding thought it once was. There might be some chance condition where some most experienced man of the world would go wild over some subtle, lovely, artistic temperament in a woman. That is one chance in a great number. In the main, sex is thought of by the world at large as compounded of coarser things—attractive women whom you don't know very well, for instance.

It is also always a puzzle to me to define clearly and definitely just what it is that the average person means by his enthusiasm for a gay place. Is it the sex thought entirely? Sometimes I think not. Still, these places are usually frequented by young men and girls looking eagerly into each other's eyes. There is a wild, sensuous languor about some of them. About others there appears to be only glitter and show. Where is the dividing line? I suppose truly there is none. It always depends on the individual. Some of us go around sex in large far-off circles of work, trade, dress, food. Others come close in swift, narrowing circles and are scorched at last and die badly burned. I know many such. We talk of life sometimes as though sex were not a part of it, but after all, say what you will, travel we never so far in distant orbits, it is still the center of things—the blazing sun around which we are compelled to swing. Love makes the world go round, says the old saw. Substitute the word sex for those who are too lacking in temperament to understand love in its finer poetic reaches, and you have the whole answer. There is love without passion and passion without love, and also the two combined. For youth perhaps the last is best. But sex desire—plain sex interest without any of the refinements of love, save those which spring from the lovely outlines of a woman's body—controls millions.

And who shall say that really there is not something lovely here? I for one would insist that there is, if it were not for the quarrels, the low bartering, the bitter comment that goes so often with this commercialized form of passion. Say what one will, the misery of that cannot be got over. Love is better than that. Sex is better than that. It requires an understanding, a temperamental harmony, that something which springs up between two and which in its higher and more enduring forms we call love.

What I am trying to get at is that this conversation between us three gradually turned onto the subject of sex. The baron had heard of some place in New York where you phoned and at your request they had some given type of woman—or a group of them, five, ten, fifteen, twenty—waiting for you to choose from. Did you want a tall woman or girl with light hair, blue eyes, a fair complexion, she—some type of her—would be waiting for you, say six or seven specimens. Did you prefer a petite brunette or a large brunette, a German, a Frenchwoman, a Russian or any other nationality—apparently, according to him, you could be easily satisfied. The mistress of this house had a large clientele, obviously. She knew where there were hundreds of girls to your hand. Any one of them, for the occasion, would cost you twenty-five dollars. A half-hour or so in which you might inspect them would cost you a bottle of champagne, say five dollars. You did not need to take any if you did not like them, but in the main, you were sure to be satisfied. It was all very interesting—quite dramatic—as sex subjects are to men.

We listened to this, and then I think I asked where this was. He hadn't the number at hand, but could get it. He told of a particular sex development at the hotel where he was stopping. It appeared that there was a large tea room where at four in the afternoon tea is served. You could not go there to drink tea without a lady, but if you wished, if you looked as distingué and rakish perhaps as the baron, you would be provided with one. He told us, sincerely enough, that the manager, seeing him strolling about idly at tea time and glancing into the tea room, had suggested that if he really wanted to go in and had no companion, it could be arranged. The conversation was something like this, as I recall it:

"You would like to go in there, perhaps?"

"I would, but I have no lady friend. I understand—"

"Well, if you wish and will speak to me at any time, that can be arranged. I could send for someone in ten minutes."

The thought arose with me, did the management know of this—the directors—or was this just this manager? According to the baron, almost any actress, certainly any chorus girl, could be thus secured for the purpose of tea drinking. Isn't that curious? I can imagine the good Americans of Sedalia, Missouri, or Ottumwa, Iowa, lifting their eyes in horror, but the New York of today is a very different place from the New York of fifteen or twenty years ago.

We passed on to other things—a Miss Burke, for one thing, who was always cropping up in the conversation between myself and Grant Richards. She had swum somehow into my ken this last week as someone, an English actress, who had come over on the same boat with Grant Richards and the baron some few weeks before, and I vaguely understood that she was or might be going back on the same boat with Grant Richards and myself, if I went. In speaking of her, the baron said that she, Miss Burke, had invited him to dine, but he had not. Why? I understood or fancied from something Grant Richards had said that she was very good-looking. She had come over after a play in America called *The Easiest Way*, which Grant Richards insisted had been lifted, spiritually at least, from my book, *Sister Carrie*, he said, in order to inform her as to New York, the stage and the kind of woman she was expected to interpret. I was not really interested in her except vaguely, but I rather fancied that Grant Richards was. This Baron R. evidently interested her, but he did not think (from what he said) that the game was worth the candle. I fancied, from his manner, that he thought the pursuit would be too long-drawn-out.

From Miss Burke we passed to coffee, the show we were going to see, etc. It was now nine o'clock. At nine-five or -ten we strolled out and over to see a musical farce comedy called *The Little Millionaire*, which was only mildly amusing to me. Somehow we were agreed that we would stay together for a while, that after the play we were to visit some especially lively restaurant which the baron had heard of—a negro restaurant where the ragtime music was especially good and the service not absolutely bad. The baron complained that it was hard to find truly lively places—that there weren't so many in New York. He had heard of some. This was one.

We went to the Knickerbocker, because it was raining, and the hotel was near, thence in a taxi to the first restaurant, which was in a rather run-down street devoted to negroes (West 53rd Street, no less), thence to a place called Faust's at 59th Street and Broadway, and thence to another called the Garden at 50th Street and Seventh Avenue.

I mention these three places collectively because I wish to deal with them collectively, since they are one and the same thing from the restaurant—amusement—point of view. The city of New York at this time was new to this sort of thing, or perhaps I had better put it in another way and say that this sort of thing—*just* this sort of thing—was new to New York. Every city everywhere, at all times and in all climes, has its public places, its restaurants, its hotels, its dives, where its ebullient sex interest and enthusiasm find vent. The world is always busy blinking and denying this fact, one element of the world, but it is nonetheless true, nevertheless. I have never seen a city where it was not so. I have never read of a city where in the reading I could not see that it was so. Life, in spite of all our preaching and moralizing—our churches, laws and jails—is always bad and good. Evil and good. They go, universally, hand in hand.

Well, from one point of view (the earthly contrary point of view, and mind you I always think of good and evil as only relatively true, having no existence whatsoever beyond this vale of tears), these places, to me, are evil. That is, they are opposed in their spirit to the established forms and customs, to the ideals of the convention-observing classes. I do not say that insofar as I am concerned that they are evil to me. As a writer, a spectator, a believer in the joy of living where health and strength and judgment and caution permit, they are not evil to me. I do not see that they come to anything destructive so far as I am concerned, and there may be many like me. Conscience is a peculiar thing. It troubles some people greatly. The race idea of what is right and wrong holds many people—perhaps the vast majority, though I am by no means sure of that—in a vise-like grip. They bow to the time—conscience. They are stricken by current thought. They are afraid to think for themselves. If they ever chance to do so, they regret it for the rest of their lives. I am not one such.

I have another idea of life. It is that I, individually, should be free. I can't tell why exactly that I think I should, but I feel deeply that I should. I feel that I should stand up and look life in the eye, say what I think, do what I think I ought to do. Most people think otherwise for me and for themselves. They are constantly warning me against myself. You must do this! You must not do that! You must not go here! You must not go there! This is good, that is bad. Do this, ignore that. But you see I can't always agree with them. I have another idea of life. It isn't obviously the same thing to me that it is to other people. I like all kinds of life, good, bad and indifferent. I don't like a burglar or a murderer or an inveterate liar or a thief, and yet I know that they always have been and always will be, so far as this mortal state is concerned. I don't like low, foul-mouthed prostitutes, and yet I know that these are but the other extreme of pale, anemic nuns voicing their spiritual aspirations in prayer.

To me, life is, or should be, a happy medium. I don't want any pale, anemic nuns in mine. I don't like them. Life doesn't mean pale, spiritual aspiration to me. At the same time, I don't want any ranting, swearing, evil-minded women to cross my path and make my life a misery. I don't believe, for instance, that the spiritual-minded person can ever be thoroughly physically degraded, and if they are, they will come out more spiritual-minded than ever, stronger for their experience; and I don't believe that any low, coarse vulgarian of a woman or man, all sex and no aspiration, can ever be lifted into a highly spiritual state. Life is too short. Words and precepts are not sufficient. Life may destroy one such, it may grind him or her to pieces, but it won't change him or her. The chemistry of our being was compounded before we were born. We make life—collectively speaking; life doesn't make us. . . . I am talking of this visible social scheme which we know. Of course, in the last analysis, life always makes us. We are the expression of some great invisible life—its pale shadow.

But to come back to these restaurants. They represent in New York at this time an outlet for this sex enthusiasm which the world is always suffering from in one direction and another, principally in its unbridled, unrestrained, ungoverned, unconventionalized youth. We went to somebody's in 53rd Street, and here were a lot of negroes playing and singing ragtime songs. It was practically empty, and it did not look very promising from the point of view of sex entertainment. There was one boy, a very light mulatto, almost white, and one pretty white girl dining, or rather, drinking together—I didn't see that the girl drank anything at all—who interested me from the point of view of which I have been talking. The boy, for all his color, was very good-looking, as American boys of this type go. The girl, to me, was decidedly attractive. She was young, say eighteen or nineteen, full-bodied, rather shapely, with a soft, full, flower-like face, and she was bubbling with a wild, but ill-restrained, sex emotion. While the negroes were singing their stirring sex-rag melodies, this girl was swaying her hands and her body in her chair in time with the music and sometimes singing a part of the words. She and her Adonis exchanged those sudden, fierce glances from time to time, which lovers know, and once, not long before they left, she caught his cheeks between her two soft hands and gave him a long, eager, burning kiss. All could see.

I looked at Baron R. and Grant Richards, and they were looking. The situation was not lost on them. The young couple got up and went into an adjoining room where there was a tall pier mirror in which I could see them. They went to get their wraps, for the girl put on her cloak, I saw that. But before he put on his overcoat or hat, she twisted her arms under his about his back, and together they began to do a most sensuous dance. You have probably heard of the Hula-Hula—possibly you have seen it. Our American Turkey Trot is an invention of somewhat the same kind. It is plainly a bacchanal, an expression of sex desire. These two swayed about in the rhythm of this dance. They stood before each other clinging close, their lips glued together, and went through these sensuous almost barbaric motions. It was far more sensuous than the Merry Widow dance that stirred New York once several years before, or than that of the actress known as Anna Held.

It was plain desire, an invitation of the sex relationship, and I wondered as I looked at it why these two should choose to do this here where everyone could see them. What had become of conventional shame or fear? Evidently, it was quite dead. What were the conditions which produced these two? I asked myself. Where did they come from? Where was the girl's mother? Her father? Her mother may have been a hard-working woman, unschooled in all the subtleties of life, for all I knew. The average home of the poor has little or no restraining influence on the children. They are compelled to go out into the world, parents and children, and work; and that fine arrangement, control and advice, so often dreamed of for the home, goes to pieces. Anyhow, it doesn't always work when it is present. But here they were, and the end, unless it was already achieved, was plainly in sight. The girl would give herself to the boy. There would be three or four or five months of a wild sex relationship, and then the question of what to do would come. I should say that the youth would have no desire to assume any responsibility for the girl. There might be tears and woe, or there might not. Different people take life differently. It was plain to be seen that in a way this was what this restaurant was for, to provide an atmosphere in which these sex feelings could grow.

It was so at the restaurant called Faust's, only less so. Here a scene like the last would not have been tolerated. Perhaps it would not at the other place if there had been a crowd—I doubt it, though. At Faust's, the room was crowded with men and women—young men and young women. The place was somewhat dim, although the ceiling was thickly spangled with red, green and blue lights, hung like grapes in intertwined vines. Vaudeville performers were singing topical songs. Beer, wine, whiskey—all the current drinks—were being served and some food being eaten. The same lover-like glances were being exchanged here and there. The whole raison d'être was some place where this sense of desire could loose itself.

But Baron R. was not satisfied, he said. It wasn't lively enough. There wasn't enough of the spirit of deviltry and motion abroad. The singers and players didn't sing and play often enough. In Paris, now, at some place, the music went on all the time. At another place—he gave me the name—the women danced naked, some of them. At the Garden, at 50th Street and Seventh Avenue, they sang all the time. We should go there. So out we went into the rain again, our high hats attracting some little attention, and piled into a taxi. In a few moments we were at the Garden, a place hitherto unknown to me, and here we found a large crowd, singing and drinking, the ceiling set as in the other place with red, green, yellow and blue lights in vines. We ordered drinks, of course. Grant Richards, in passing one young lady, was greeted mockingly because of his monocle.

"Oh, jah me! Don't look at me like that!"

He smiled his enigmatic smile.

We listened to the music and the singing for an hour or so. We watched a young American girl, quite good-looking, urging us in her song to come and kiss her.

"I want to be cuddled, cuddled, cuddled," the song ran.

The baron ran his fine, thin fingers over his chin, descanting on women, Paris, Vienna, London. In Vienna, the women were quite smart. In Russia, Germany, France and abroad generally, the women had more temperament. Damn the American women, anyhow. They were mere sex machines. They didn't feel what they were doing. They were dry, dusty lures, beautiful to look upon, but without real feeling. Grant Richards stared amiably about and complained that the girls didn't like him as much as they might. I thought—well, I thought that singing and playing about these things doesn't amount to much. One woman's enthusiastic affection is worth a whole year of musical palaver about "cuddling me," etc.

I think I am a little brutal about sex, all told, anyhow. The relation is rather a delicious one, and I brook little interference and not much delay. If a woman will, she will. If she won't, she won't. I have little patience with long philandering, unless I am greatly interested. Tonight, that place the baron had been talking about—the one where you paid twenty-five dollars and took your choice—was running in my mind. I had never seen anything like that. I was interested to see it.

"What about that place where they show you seven, eight or ten women and let you take your choice? Why don't we go there? I should like to see that."

The baron was a little indifferent, I think. I don't believe he wanted to go. Now that I recall it, he said that really he was not interested tonight, but if I wished—. He looked at Grant Richards.

"It is all the same to me," replied that worthy. He expressed the idea then or after that ordinary promiscuous relationship was revolting to him. He could not go it. The sex relationship, so far as he was concerned, had to be based on something much more intimate in the way of temperamental affinity.

I make no such boast. I cannot definitely say when or when not I should find a temperament, even in a place like this, which drew me greatly. The world is strange. As a rule, promiscuity of this character is quite as revolting to me as it is to anyone. I shy at little bits—crudities and rudenesses. A word, and the thought of even friendly conversation is gone. Still, the bagnio or the house of assignation always interests me as a spectacle. I am curious about these women who inhabit these places, as I am about any other women or any other men. They are a part of this weird, majestic spectacle of life, and it fascinates me.

Well, once more in the rain, at three o'clock in the morning, without taking a taxi because it was only two or three blocks away, we came to this place. The baron had phoned. The lady had said, "Yes, yes," or "Certainly," or something like that. The women or girls would be there in fifteen minutes. We waited more than fifteen minutes before we started, but when we reached there, the ladies had not come. The baron was a little doubtful about the floor, but Grant Richards rang a bell, and presently a young, buxom, intelligent-looking negress opened the door, and the baron recognized her.

"Ah, yes," I can hear his slightly German accent—that faint echo of a German guttural—"Have they come? No? Well, we will wait."

We walked in. It was a charming apartment, quite tastefully furnished—white and red, if I recall aright. The pictures on the walls were good pen copies, engravings, of some excellent painters—Corot, perhaps, Detaille. There were no immoral or suggestive pictures of any kind—no pornographic statuary. We nosed about, as gentlemen of leisure will, looking at the room, talking of the exaggerated notions about the luxury of some places of ill repute. Presently, one girl came, a tall, lean, homely creature, homely to me at least, and my interest in the adventure sank a thousand percent. How could such a girl be called and be expected to interest or entertain observing men of the world? She was too raw, too homely, too silly. She wasn't even tastefully dressed.

This won't do at all, I said to myself.

Then came a second girl. Well, she was better. She looked a little like one of Gainsborough's paintings—light hair, blue eyes, a slender, graceful figure, but she was too shallow in her mood, her make-up, her mind. I thought of Macbeth's address to the ghost, "thou hast no introspection in those eyes." Still, we were here and something had to be done—wine at least provided. The negress introduced the two girls to us as Miss So-and-So, and

Miss So-and-So, and I think we nodded genially—I'm sure we did. Then we strolled back to the dining room, and the first girl, finding the atmosphere a little frigid—I'm sure all my interest had expired sometime since—put on a gay-sounding waltz of some kind, and started the phonograph which stood in the corner. This helped but little. Then we ordered champagne and opened that, but that did no good. I looked at these two girls and thought, what a dreary proposition outside of true affection the sex question is. You can't pump up an interest in women or sex. It must spring naturally.

I fancy I expected to see some marvelously attractive women—eight or ten at least, one of whom because of her ruddy beauty and smart manners and pretty speeches would interest me. Alas! Alas! The third one came, and then I knew that I had been led into a foolish adventure by my lively imagination. These things turn out to be what they are advertised to be. It isn't possible to find the truly attractive woman in a bagnio. True sex charm doesn't end so unfortunately, in the main. The third girl was better, a petite little Russian, very dark, very graceful, slightly anemic, but sweet in her fashion. She was far more mobile than the others—bright, spoke French and Russian, and I noticed that we all roused to a sort of interest in her.

Still, the baron did not want to stay; Grant Richards would not on principle. I could not, for there was not sufficient charm here to entice me. I think I finally told them that the occasion was unpropitious, that the mood was gone, and that we were going. Naturally, they were disappointed. It is not a pleasant thing to be routed out of your bed at three o'clock in the morning and sent on a profitless wild goose chase. However, we had bought three or four bottles of wine at five dollars the bottle. There was some gift on the baron's part, I think, to the negress. I gave the little Russian something because of a passing whim. The baron had said that the mistress of this place had said that she could get him, for a sufficient sum of money, any actress in New York. He could name his actress, and she would undertake to carry out the liaison quickly and pleasantly. I didn't believe it. On the face of it, to me, it is silly—for occasionally even actresses fall in love and are faithful. However, I heard him bargaining with the negro maid of this mistress, who was, apparently, the only one who ever appeared in these transactions. She, the negress, was to have fifty dollars for herself. What the mistress or the actress were to have I did not learn.

I went away in a dreary mood. These tenderloin brilliancies are not often anything more than silly mirages anyhow. And it was nearly four-thirty or five o'clock in the morning by now and pouring down rain. I got to bed at five-thirty, I think, and was up again at eight.

CHAPTER III

The Monday following the Saturday on which I sent the manuscript of "The Financier," together with my letter of terms, requesting an immediate decision, I expected to hear some word of protest. But none came. Tuesday I had a very pleasant phone message—not at all in keeping with the storm I expected—from one of the representatives of the firm, telling me that the manuscript had been safely received and that he was reading it. No word of objection. Wednesday came another message from another member, asking me to call. It was very pleasant. He wanted to see me.

This conversation, strangely enough, was one of the most amiable that I had ever had with any member of the firm.

"Why this sudden decision?" he asked in his genial, practical way. "We've been getting along fairly pleasantly, haven't we? Why do you want so much money? Is it going to cost you five thousand dollars to go to London to complete your story?"

"It isn't the story alone," I replied. "It's some current obligations also. I have a number of things to meet. Besides, I can get that much without any argument, just as I'm telling you. That more than anything else has helped to shape this situation."

"Well, now, let's see. There needn't be any real argument about this. You say you have to go to London. I see that you have to. You want to make your story just what it ought to be, and we as your publishers want you to. I don't think we're going to quarrel much on that. Anyhow, you're a very different man to what you were three months ago."

He turned over some papers on his desk and picked up a check.

"There you are," he said. "There's not much argument about that, is there?" He handed it to me.

It was a check for $2,500, payable to myself. You could have knocked me down with a feather.

"As for the rest of those terms," he went on, "we'll fix them up to suit your convenience. I'll have them made out and you can sign them any time before you go. When do you sail?"

"The twenty-second."

"Well, you are going quick, aren't you? Well, here's good luck."

He shook my hand, and I think it is just possible that I stared a little uncertainly. These things do not happen very often in the average life. The sky does not rain money on demand. On the instant, I saw how Grant Richards's transfer scheme had gone up in smoke. There was to be no transfer. On Friday I would meet him, and he would be expecting that I would be going down that morning to find out definitely whether I was to be released or not so that the Century Company could act. As a counter answer, I would have to present this check. I could see his face in prospect—the eye behind the monocle. Still, there was nothing else to do. Terms were terms. The terms were his own. He had made them exorbitantly high and stringent in order to defeat any desire on the part of Harper and Brothers to go on. As a matter of fact, they had, as one says in poker, "seen his bluff and called it." It was too late to change now.

I confess that entirely aside from my own interests and my own very comfortable profit in this case, I was glad to see the firm of Harper and Brothers so magnanimous, so willing to take a chance, so game to checkmate an untoward situation. I learned in a subsequent conversation—and in a still later one after that, for there were various minor details to be adjusted—that they had not even read the manuscript of "The Financier." One man was reading it—Mr. Hitchcock, a friend of mine of long standing—but he could not have reported favorably if he had wanted to, for he had not read it all. He may have reported that so far as he had gone, it was promising or satisfactory, but that was all. No. They had been suddenly confronted by what to them must have been an unfortunate situation—they looked at the condition of the sales of *Jennie Gerhardt*, took into consideration the value of the wave of critical approval, and said, "Here, it will not do to part with this man—at this stage, anyhow. We'll chance it."

And so out I walked with my check for two thousand five hundred dollars in my pocket, the assurance of another of the same size a little later on, and the terms of fifteen and twenty percent as to royalties accepted without a tremor. A strange world this is, surely, and none more than myself has ever had better cause to think so.

Friday came and with it the astonishment, the almost consternation of Grant Richards, if such a word could be used in connection with a so uniformly equable person. I met him at the appointed time—eight o'clock in the morning. Again, I gave him time to get seated, to order my order of "Mr. Jones's sausage," as he insisted on calling it, and then he said briskly,

"Well, tell me. What have you heard?"

"This," I replied, and I shoved the check under his nose.

I shall never forget the curious expression that swept over his face. It was a compound of astonishment, regret, satisfaction, humor and a half-dozen other minor and major emotions, all rolled into one. Of course, he never believed for one moment that such a thing could happen. To him, it was an utter impossibility from the start. I was not well enough known. I was not as yet a large enough seller. He had been satisfied that the Century

Company's attitude was very largely a reflection of his. Here was this check, however, and it threw him completely out of countenance. One fancies expletives and exclamations, forceful and strong, in connection with anyone in a situation of this kind, but not so with Grant Richards. He stared. He pressed his lips together. He screwed up his monocled eye.

"This is a most astonishing turn of affairs," he finally said. "It's quite amazing. It puts me in a rather awkward light with the Century Company. They must know—of course they do know—that we have not been attempting to play any game, to use them in any way. I shall have to go and see my friend Scott at once and tell him all about it. On second thought, we both had better go. I have it. I'll call up Doty. That would be better yet. I'll tell him to come down here. I'll warn him that things have taken a turn for the worse. That will be the best way. Then after we have talked it over with him, we can explain the whole thing afterwards to the rest of them. It's most unfortunate. It's positively extraordinary. I hadn't the slightest idea they'd do anything of the kind. In a way, I admire them for it very much. I admire their pluck. It gives me a better opinion of American publishers in general," and he stared smilingly before him.

"What about those articles for the Century Company?" I finally put in, after I had allowed him to have his say. "Do you think this hitch in regard to the book will make any difference in regard to those? For a number of reasons, I should like to be allowed to go on and do those. It makes some difference to me whether I am identified with the Century Company or not. I should like to do those articles whether I give them the book or whether I don't. I should like to make that separate article contract just as we agreed, taking a suitable advance against them, because once they are bound in this way, they will be more sincerely interested in the result. I am sure they will like some of the stuff that I do, and if by any chance they shouldn't, I can give them suggestions for something else."

He postponed the discussion of this until after he had phoned Mr. Doty to come down. The latter was with us in not more than forty-five minutes, and together we adjourned to Mr. Grant Richards's room. Before this, we had discussed the matter of the papers for the magazine and decided that the company could have no reasonable objection to that, that it would be foolish not to continue it. Mr. Doty, on his arrival, thought so also. He was rather gloomy, for evidently he had been counting strongly on obtaining "The Financier." Together, after a short discussion, we adjourned to the Century Company, explained the unexpected outcome and told them what we desired. I never saw a group of officers take a defeat more generously, although they were obviously dissatisfied. They congratulated their rival firm in spirit. They stated, as had Grant Richards, that they admired their courage and swiftness of action. Under the circumstances, they would be satisfied with half a loaf rather than no bread.

They would take the articles for the magazine. They would make the original payment subject to the privilege of rejecting a book of travel which should grow out of my observations. They would pay me a straight fifteen percent if amply illustrated. If not, twenty percent. We parted, shaking hands genially, wishing each other luck. A check for $1,500 was to reach me the next day. I was to come to the president's house for dinner on the following Monday evening. We hurried finally to look after our steamer passage, to settle on what things I should take. Curiously, this same night two friends of mine phoned and offered to take my apartment off my hands furnished. I am stating exact facts. Now, say there is no such thing as luck.

The four days following were days of swift action for me. It was necessary for me to arrange a number of things. I had my insurance account to settle, my land note to meet, my orchard payment to arrange for, my due bill for $1,500 to fix for January 1st. I had a bag to buy, two trunks to pack, a steamer rug to secure, a cap, shoes, handkerchiefs, some additional pajamas—in fact, a long list of odds and ends. I had some fifty-five farewells to write, certain individuals to see, a farewell dinner to attend. One pretty lady, heaven bless her, fairly ached at my going. How I ever got through, I don't know. It seems that necessity lent wings to my feet. I crowded every hour to the full. I slept but little. I was up at five-thirty or six and to bed again only at midnight or later.

Finally the sailing day dawned, after a delightful dinner with Mr. Scott, my American publisher, and I was off. My trunks had gone the previous morning at nine. Two bags and a rug I carried to the ship myself. I had agreed to meet Grant Richards in the writing room of the great liner at eight o'clock, and there I was. I shall not soon forget my ride down, my reading in a morning paper of the suicide of a friend of mine—a brilliant man—for love. He had fallen on hard times; his wife had decided to desert him; he was badly in debt and being prosecuted for some non-payment of debt. I cannot say that he was an intimate friend, but I knew him well. I had known his curious, erratic history. Here, on this morning when I was sailing for Europe, quite in the flush of a momentary literary and intellectual victory, he was lying in death. It gave me pause. It brought to my mind the Latin phrase *memento mori*. I saw again, right in the heart of this hour of brightness, how grim life really is. Fate is kind, or it is not. It puts you ahead, or it does not. If it does not, nothing can save you. I acknowledge the Furies. I believe in them. I have heard the disastrous beating of their wings.

CHAPTER IV

We are several days out at sea now, and I shall go back and tell you something about it, lest in these kaleidoscopic changes I shall forget all about it. I remember in the rush of leaving New York that I recalled on waking this Wednesday morning of having dreamed of a bug that could talk. I mention it because it struck me as curious at the time—a talking bug. Have you ever dreamed of one? When I reached the ship, it was already a perfect morning in full glow. The sun was up; a host of gulls were on the wing; an air of delicious adventure enveloped the great liner's dock at the foot of 13th Street. I noted at once, as something that I ought to remember, that the steerage and second-class passengers had a separate entrance from those of the first, and that over the entrance of the first-class there was a bright, brown-and-white-striped awning. In the pier entrance was an elevator. On the dock were many officers stationed to direct and explain. I inquired after my trunks. They were on board. I asked about mailing some letters—there was a mail clerk on the dock to receive mail and to sell you stamps if necessary. I went on deck, interfered with in no way, and sought the writing room. Shall I ever forget the delicious impression this great ship gave me!

In the first place, even at this hour, it was crowded with people—B deck, at least, the main lobby. I noted to my surprise and satisfaction that there was an elevator and that the writing room and dining room, which I casually inspected, were beautifully decorated and ornately equipped. There was an ample supply of pretty picture-postcards of the ship and of places, such as Nice, to which its transportation gave access. There was a large supply of variously colored and finely-woven, monogrammed writing paper. I hurried to my berth. I found a dainty little room done in white and cherry-stained wood, with a dresser, a fair-sized clothes press, fitted with a mirror, a washstand with which was combined a writing desk, several switch lights, a reading lamp over my pillow, decorated with a pretty yellow silk shade, and other small conveniences which I need not mention. The aisle which gave access to my room was handsomely finished in highly-polished cherry wood, the floor laid with thick, soft carpet. My trunks were in order. My room steward, an undersized Englishman, reported at once.

"Anything I can do for you, sir?"

"No."

"Do you wish to arrange now, sir, for a regular hour for your bawth?"

"No."

"Very well, sir," and off he went.

I went back to the writing room intending to write a few farewell notes but decided to take a turn about the deck to see what my ship was like. We are all so eager for new experiences in this world.

I must say that, as much as I know about life, I was seriously impressed. I can frankly say that I never saw so fine a ship. It seemed impressively beautiful to me. In the first place, it was so large. The writing room, easily a chamber 30 × 60, was a jewel of decoration. Its walls were of jade-gray woodwork, its curtains at either side of the ship (the ends of the room, looking at it lengthwise) were of a delicious old rose hue. They were heavily valanced and bordered with light rose and lavender-hued embroidery. The floor covering was of a slightly different shade of old rose. The lamps—tall bronze candlesticks—topped with pink silk shades, were sixteen in number and prettily arranged to light the writing desks. There was an oval dome of pork-fat-jade glass set in bright bronze, let into the roof or topmost deck, and a tall oval-topped mirror above a white marble mantel which graced the forward or prow wall. Here a cheerful electric fire was shining. The library cases which graced the stern or aft wall were full of handsomely bound volumes subject to your request, of course. There were already a half-dozen people writing industriously, and the room was snapping with an air of cheerful or pathetic departure.

The general drawing or lounging room, immediately to the rear of this but divided by a general lobby which gave onto the ship stairs, was another delightful chamber, to me. It was particularly pleasing because it was so large for a ship—easily 60 × 80. The windows were hung with charming old rose draperies, the floor covered with a rich carpet of a rosy hue. The forward or prow wall was occupied by a large fireplace and mantel, already glowing with an electric fire. The rear or stern wall of the room was ornamented by a triangular grand piano. In between were scattered all manner of chairs, settees, tête-à-têtes and those novelties devised in of deep armchairs which weary travelers relish so much. Nearly all of them, as I soon learned, were fixed solidly to the floor. I soon knew why. A few others were free.

The lights were numerous and ornate; the ceiling, a splendid and ornate glass dome. There were little tables here and there for cards and refreshments, and a group of alcoves suitable for parties of eight or ten where one might retire and feel reasonably separate and exclusive. Back of this again was a very large smoking room, handsomely furnished, which I never used, and beyond this again, quite to the stern of this A deck, a combined palm and observation room. Being protected on three sides and roofed in, and always safe from the winds against which the ship was speeding, it was a pleasant place to be if one desired the fresh air with the comfort of refreshments. I did not go here nor to the smoking room often during my trip, for I found to my satisfaction far more desirable places, the protected walking and chair lounging places on B deck, and the half-mile, free-for-all walking course around the outside of the splendid rooms I have been describing on A deck.

There were many other first-cabin decks, as I soon found—C, D and E, together with a magnificent dining room, reaching from the floor of D deck to the roof of C deck. I admired it especially because it was delightfully paneled in highly carved, plainly stained oak, with Elizabethan columns carved with the large spheres or balls and strap work of that period. It was commodious, artistic, and in every way beautiful. At luncheon and dinner I found that it was richly odorous of fresh-cut flowers, liberally distributed as decorations for the tables, flower beds before the dining room entrances, and a great attractive bank behind or rather forward of the Captain's table, between the two entrances. I had thought, from a slightly fishy odor that prevailed in the morning when I first walked about, that this was to be an undesirable accompaniment of our meals, but I was mistaken. The ample supply of delightful cut flowers overcame all that.

From the moment I came on board, I was delighted by the eager, restless movement of the throng. It was like the lobby of one of the great New York hotels at dinner time, so far as B deck—the main entrance deck—was concerned. There was much call on the part of a company of dragooned ship stewards to "keep moving, please," and the enthusiasm of farewells and inquiries after this person and that were delightful to hear. I stopped a while in the writing room and wrote some notes. I went to my stateroom—B-39—and found first a telegram of farewell and later several letters. Later still, several gift books, books which had been delivered at the ship, were brought to me. I went back on the dock and mailed my letters, encountered Grant Richards finally and exchanged greetings and then, perforce, soon found myself taken in tow by him, for he wanted obviously to instruct me in all the details of this new world upon which I was now entering.

At eight-thirty there was a general sounding of call to go ashore. At eight-fifty-five I had my first glimpse of Miss Burke, as discreet and charming a bit of English femininity as one would care to set eyes upon. She was an English actress in whose comfortable transit Mr. Grant Richards was apparently seriously interested. He discovered her about this time and shortly afterward a Miss Longfellow, who was introduced to him and Miss Burke via a third acquaintance of Miss Burke's, a Mr. Kahn, no less—a very direct, self-satisfied and aggressive type of Jew. I noticed him strolling about the deck some time before I saw him conversing with Miss Burke and later for a moment with Grant Richards.

So there were to be two women, I thought—both extremely good-looking, as I could see. Miss Burke was arrayed in a bright green corduroy coat, with gray rabbits for trimming and a dainty shovel hat of hard, bright felt,

I saw him conversing with Miss Burke

with feather decorations of a pleasing design. Miss Longfellow, a more Semitic and yet somehow distinctly American type, wore a long coat of deep purple cloth, trimmed with the fur of some gray animal, and lined with it also. She had on a dainty little gray cloth hat, somewhat of a turban design, pulled low over her eyes, and her hands and feet were daintily encased in handsome leather. I saw these women only for a moment at first, but they impressed me at once as rather attractive examples of the stage world—that world of pretty women, fine clothes, fine ornaments, jewels and the delights of a comfortable life generally.

It was soon nine o'clock after this—the hour of the ship's sailing—and I was interested to observe the general exodus of those who were not going. I noticed about now that I no longer had the undivided attention of Grant Richards, for he was obviously keenly interested in the welfare of his lady acquaintances. He disappeared for periods at a time, and when the ship moved out, I was without him. I went forward to the prow end of C deck, on which the writing room was located, and watched the sailors on B deck below me cleaning up the final details of loading, bolting down the hatches and the like. All the morning I had been particularly impressed with the cloud of gulls fluttering about the ship, those pretty sea-angels of art, but now the harbor, the magnificent wall of lower New York, set like a jewel in a green ring of sea water, took my eye. When should I see it again? How soon should I be back? I had undertaken this voyage in pell-mell haste. I had not figured at all on where I was going, or what I was going to do. London, yes—to gather the data for the last one-third of my novel. Rome—assuredly, because of all things, I wished to see Rome. The Riviera, say, and Monte Carlo, because the south of France has always appealed to me as something to see. Paris, Berlin—possibly; Holland—surely, and maybe a bit of Athens or Spain. I could not tell. As I stood here seeing this marvelous piece of sea architecture, so immense, so ornate, so expensive to travel in, point its prow outward to the broad Atlantic, a touch of real, early, youthful *Heimweh* came to me. It hurt me to pass Staten Island, seeing its green hills where I have known some happy hours, and Sea Gate, where I have spent many a lovely summer day looking wistfully at the sea. After that came the deep gray-blue of the ocean, and then I felt that it was of little use to longer stare at the water. It would now be much the same, mile after mile, until England should be reached. I started to go below, but Grant Richards overtook me.

"Come up here," he said.

We went to the topmost deck where were the huge white air funnels and the towering red smokestacks—four of them, each large enough to accommodate a tally-ho and its attendant horses. We looked at the water, talked of the sudden speed of all this, the anomaly of it. I am quite sure that Grant Richards, when he originally made his authoritative assertion of my coming with him, was in no way satisfied that I would. It was a somewhat light venture on his part, but here I was. And now, having "let himself in" for this, as he would have phrased it, I could see that he was intensely interested in his adventure and in me. He wanted to make me a success in London, to see that my book of travel was a success, to make me do and see the things that would be characteristic, dramatic, colorful. From one point of view, it was all very interesting and delightful. I felt for once as though my life were seriously and obviously being taken in hand by fate. I was doing something, evidently, that I was called to do. Things were being made right for me to do it. It was being made easy for me to do. So I speculated, Grant Richards by my side.

"You have a spare copy of your book?" he asked suddenly.

"Yes," I replied.

"I want you to let me have it. I have already given Miss Burke *Sister Carrie* to read."

"And who is this for?"

"Miss Burke and myself. I understand that George W. Smalley is on board. If possible, I hope to get him to read it. If we could get his enthusiastic approval, it would be worth something. He would stir up some interest in it."

I smiled at the honest and deft industry of the managerial brain. It knows so well how to fan into a flame the first faint flickers of popular approval.

"Very well," I said, but knowing the history of George W. Smalley from years of past observation and understanding, even before I saw him—just what manner of man he was—I did not imagine that he would approve of either me or my work, Mr. Grant Richards and his hearty enthusiasm for me to the contrary notwithstanding.

The social, domestic, culinary and other economies of a great ship like this interested me from the start. I may say I was intensely interested. My mind from the first was briskly asking itself, "How do they do on a great liner?" and I observed all developments with a keen eye. It impressed me no little that all the servants were English—not a single American anywhere—and that they were—shall I say polite?—well, if not that, nonaggressive. American servants—I could write a whole chapter on that, but we haven't any servants in America. We don't know how to be servants. It isn't in us, it isn't nice to be a servant, it isn't democratic, and spiritually, I don't blame us. In America, with our turn for mechanics, we shall have to invent something which will do away with the need of servants. What it is to be, I haven't the faintest idea at present.

Another thing that impressed and irritated me a little was the stolidity of the English countenance as I encountered it here on this ship. I didn't know then whether it was accidental in this case or national. There is a certain type of Englishman—the robust, rosy-cheeked, blue-eyed Saxon—whom I cordially dislike, I think, speaking temperamentally and artistically. They are too solid, too rosy, too immobile as to their faces, and altogether too assured and stare-y. I don't like them. They offend me. They thrust a silly race pride into my face which isn't necessary at all and which I always resent with a race pride of my own. It has even occurred to me at times that these temperamental race differences could be quickly adjusted by an appeal to arms, which is sillier yet. There you have the silly race pride on my part. But so goes life. It is foolish on both sides, but I mention it for what it is worth. I went to my room and began unpacking, but was not there long before I was called out by Grant Richards, to meet Miss Burke and Miss Longfellow.

"Get your cap and coat," he said in his authoritative way, "and come out on deck. Miss Burke is there. She's reading your book. She likes it. I tell her—" etc., the usual complimentary things that have been told about it.

I went out, interested to meet these two, for the actress—the talented, good-looking representative of that peculiarly feminine world of art—appeals to me very much. I have always thought, since I have been able to reason about it, and I may as well state it here, that the stage is almost the only ideal outlet for the artistic temperament of a talented and beautiful woman. Men—well, I don't care so much for the men of the stage. I acknowledge the distinction of such a temperament as that of David Garrick or Edwin Booth. They are great actors, and by the same token they are great artists—wonderful artists. But in the main, the men of the stage are frail skeletons of a much more real thing—the active, constructive man in other lines.

On the contrary, the women of the stage are somehow, by right of mere womanhood—the art of looks, form, temperament, mobility, imitativeness—peculiarly suited to this realm of show, color, and make-believe. The stage is fairyland, and they are of it. Women—the women of ambition, aspiration, artistic longings—act anyhow all the time. They lie like anything. They never show their true colors—or very rarely. If you want to know the truth, you must see through their pretty, petty artistry, back to the actual conditions behind them which are conditioning and driving them. Very few, if any, have a real grasp on what I call life. They have no understanding of and no love for philosophy. They do not care for the subtleties of chemistry and physics. Knowledge—book knowledge, the sciences—well, let the men have that. Your average woman cares most—almost entirely—for the politics and the abstrusities of her own little world. Is her life going right? Is she getting along? Is her skin smooth? Is her face still pretty? Are there any wrinkles? Are there any gray hairs in sight? What can she do to win one man? How can she make herself impressive to all men? Are her feet small? Are her hands pretty? Which are the really nice places in the world to visit? Do men like this trait in women, or that? What is the latest thing in dress?—in jewelry?—in hats?—in shoes? How can she keep herself spick and span? These are all leading questions with her, strong, deep, vital, painful. Let men have knowledge, strength, fame, force—that is their business. The real man, her man, should have some one of these things if she is really going to love him very much—I am talking about the semi-artistic woman with ambition. As for her, she clings to these practical details, and they make her life. Poor little frail things—fighting with every weapon at their command to buy and maintain the courtesy of the world. Truly, I pity women. I pity the strongest, most ambitious woman I ever saw. And, by the same token, I pity the poor helpless, hopeless drab and drudge, without an idea above a potato, who never had and never will have a look in on anything. I know—and there is not a beating feminine heart anywhere that will contradict me—that they are all struggling to buy this superior masculine strength against which they can lean, to which they can fly in the hour of terror. It is no answer to my statement, no contradiction of it, to say that the strongest men crave the sympathy of the tenderest women. These are complementary facts, and my statement is true. I am dealing with women now—not men. When I come to men I will tell you all about them!

But this stage world, in consequence, appeals to me as a fit and ideal showplace for many of the most delightful characteristics of women. She can dress there naturally, she can parade there. Her art of make-believe is just what the stage wants. If she is pretty, mobile, enthusiastic—the stage needs that. Our modern stage world gives the ideal outlet for all that is most worthwhile in the youth and art of the female sex. It matters not that it is notably immoral. You cannot predicate that of any individual case until afterward. At any rate, to me, and so far as women are concerned, it is distinguished, appropriate, brilliant, important. I am always interested in a well-recommended woman of the stage.

I came out. Miss Burke and Miss Longfellow were sitting side by side in steamer chairs arranged by the managerial skill of Grant Richards, for I found that this very able patron of mine was doing everything that should be done to make this trip comfortable without show or fuss. Many have this executive or managerial gift. Sometimes I think it is a natural trait of the English—of their superior classes, anyhow. They go about colonizing so efficiently, industriously. They make fine governors and patrons. I have always been told that English direction is thorough. Is this true, or is it not? At this writing, I do not know. Perhaps I never shall. Anyhow, this one particular example of the English upper classes is not only efficiently executive, but courteous, diplomatic, and so far as I can see not disagreeably intrusive.

Not only were all our chairs on deck here in a row, but our chairs at table had already been arranged for—four seats at the captain's table. It seems that from previous voyages on this ship Grant Richards knew the captain. He also knew the chairman of the company in England. No doubt he knew the chief steward. Anyhow, he knew the man who sold us our tickets, for he had introduced me to him on the previous Friday. He knew the headwaiter at the Ritz—he had seen him or been served by him somewhere in Europe. He knew some of the servitors of the Knickerbocker of old. Wherever he went, I found he was always finding somebody whom he knew. I like that social, executive, managerial instinct. It is a pleasant trait. It speaks well for one's social and intellectual ability. I have very little if any of it, scarcely any. I like to get in tow of such a man as Grant Richards and see him plow the seas. I like to see what he thinks is important. In this case, there happens to be a certain intellectual and spiritual compatibility. He likes some of the things that I like. He admires my point of view. Hence—so far at least—we have gotten along admirably. I speak for the present only. I would not answer for my moods or basic change of emotions at any time.

Well, here were the two actresses side by side, both charmingly arrayed, and with them, in a third chair, a short, stout, red-haired Jew whom I had seen talking to Miss Burke earlier in the morning. In the confusion of observations and introductions I had come into the impression that this gentleman, Mr. Kahn, was a friend of Miss Longfellow's, and that he had been introduced to Miss Burke and Grant Richards by her. As a matter of fact, he was an acquaintance of Miss Burke's, as was Miss Longfellow. She had met both of them abroad.

On sight, I did not like Mr. Kahn. In fact, he is a type of Jew I dislike very much—vain, self-satisfied, pompous, dictatorial in as far as a situation will permit, and so on and so forth. There are Jews, many of them, whom I admire greatly. Some of my closest friends are Jews, and those of them who chance to read these lines will know well how close. They will understand, and also that there is no petty race prejudice in me. I like and dislike Jews, quite as I like and dislike the varying examples of any other nationality.

However, here was Mr. Kahn, and he was talking to Miss Longfellow. Mr. Grant Richards was talking to Miss Burke. I was introduced with a flourish, and I could see at once that my friend had been singing my praises. I was a personage. They had better be interested in me. And so on, and so forth.

Do you recall in your own experience how nice pretty ladies are when they think they ought to be? They are always on the *qui vive* for what life may chance to produce in the way of a marvelous man. I was greeted with rosy smiles—pretty airs. Their eyes spoke preliminary expectation, curiosity. Was I as nice as I ought to be? Would Mr. Grant Richards's compliments be justified by my subsequent manifestations? I sat down, and we exchanged commonplaces. After all, words are rarely helpful on any occasion. Sometimes they seem to do us harm, sometimes good. In the main, I think it is the non-speaking forces of our personalities that do the talking. They make us liked or disliked. I felt here, to begin with, a certain temperamental propinquity and, as I found later, it was not entirely unjustified. Mr. Kahn, I could see, did not like me. He was in no way familiar with my type. I smiled, because I knew him instantly as well as though I had lived with him all my life. His intellectual processes were plain because they were not simple, and when you know that about a man, you know everything. The simpler a soul, the more difficult it is to fathom. Isn't that strange.

Miss Burke talked to me first. She was a very little woman, cute, petite, delicate. Her eyes were as soft as a dove's, with a form of appeal in them which was part real, part make-believe. Her face was so very lovely, so soft, so colorful, full of a pale delicacy and refinement. Her hands and feet were very small and pretty. She cooed in a soft English voice about my first trip, the sea, the dangers of seasickness. Her eyes looked into mine softly and I could see—well, I could see that she was very nice and that I was not at all objectionable to her, quite interesting to her for the present, and strange. When you come well introduced, paraded before, as it were, by a company of outrunners clanging cymbals and blowing trumpets, people are always inclined to be well-disposed toward you. They have no idea but that you may well be something wonderful, lovely, beautiful, anything you please. They are like the people who crowd around any new prophet crying, "Lo!" "Behold!" However, "the kingdom of heaven," as Jesus very accurately observed, "cometh not by observation."

Well, while I was talking to Miss Burke, making myself as nice and smiling as I could and wondering, as I usually do, just what concomitants were missing or present toward establishing that ideal relationship which sometimes exists between the sexes and which makes for what the young consider the highest form of earthly bliss, I secretly or otherwise (I do not recall whether it was very secret or not) observed the personality of Miss Longfellow. Here was someone who on sight, at a glance, attracted me far more significantly than ever Miss Burke could. I cannot tell you why exactly. In a way Miss Burke appeared at moments and from certain points of view—delicacy, refinement, sweetness of mood—the more attractive of the two. But Miss Longfellow, with her chic face, her dainty little chin, her narrow, lavender-lidded eyes, drew me quite as a magnet draws an iron filing. I liked her. I liked a certain snap and vigor which shot from her eyes and which, I could feel, represented our raw American force. A foreigner will not, I am afraid, understand exactly what I mean, but there is something about the American climate—its soil, rain, winds, race spirit—which produces a raw, direct incisiveness of soul in its children. They are strong, direct, elate, enthusiastic. They look you in the eye, cut you with a glance, say what they mean in ten thousand ways without really saying anything at all. They come upon you fresh like cold water, and they have the pull of a hard, bright jewel and the fragrance of a rich, red, full-blown rose. Americans are wonderful to me—American men and American women. I have seen some of the most delightful temperaments in that country. They are rarely polished or refined. They know little of the subtleties of life, its order and procedures, but oh, the glory of their spirit, the hope of them, the dreams of them, the desires and enthusiasms of them! That is what wins me. They give me the sense of being intensely, enthusiastically, humanly alive.

So I looked at Miss Longfellow, and after a time I got an answering glance back from her which said as well as anything could say, "I like you." She narrowed her little lavender-lidded eyes in a shrewd way, and I smiled. Delicious, I thought, and I looked forward to the time when she should sit by me. It came, after Grant Richards had taken Miss Burke for a walk, and Miss

Longfellow had gone to her room and come back again. I had gone to my room to get my steamer rug. Mr. Kahn had betaken himself elsewhere. Chicken broth had been served on deck. I think I had disappeared for a half-hour or so and unpacked some more of my things.

Anyhow, when she came back, she looked at me smilingly, and I said, "Sit here," indicating the chair beside me. It was a little forward, perhaps, but we were liking each other slightly, and why shouldn't I?

"But my chair is over here," she observed, uncertain whether to resent this forward direction or not.

"Oh, that doesn't make any difference, sit here anyhow. Come, do."

"I think I'd better not," she said cautiously, doubtfully settling herself in her chair. I think she was thinking this was rather swift procedure, and anyhow, Grant Richards had come back and was standing by. She was already tucking her rug about her.

"Come, be nice," I laughed, looking into her eyes. "Come over here by me."

She got up, moved by I can scarcely say what—the appeal of it all. She came and sat down beside me, and when she turned her pretty head, her eyes were dancing, and her even little teeth were showing between as sweet a pair of lips as you would want to see. The eyelids and the chin and the dainty low forehead and the cut of the little delicate nose all held me.

"There now, are you satisfied?" she asked.

"Quite," I replied.

"I hope you feel better."

"I do. Aren't you nice," I said, and I think she actually gurgled with delight.

As we say in America—this for her and for myself—though on second thought perhaps I had better eliminate myself—"this was going some."

We talked of the sea, London, my book, the ship. It turned out in this conversation that a certain newspaperman and critic—an American by the name of Karl Kitchen, working on the *New York World*—had brought her my two books two nights before and urged her to read them. He was wild in his praises, she said, and liked my second book even better than the first. She did not tell me anything about herself, save that she was on the stage in some capacity and that she knew a large number of newspapermen, critics, actors, etc. A chorus girl, I thought, and then by the same token—a lady of not absolutely rigid virtue. She *would* if she liked you very much—how much?

I think the average man, however much he may lie and pretend, takes considerable interest in this proposition. There are large orders and schools of mind, bound by certain variations of temperament and schools of thought, who either flee temptation of this kind, find no temptation in it, or, when confronted, resist it vigorously. The accepted theory of marriage and monogamy holds many people absolutely. There are those who would never sin (hold unsanctioned relations, I mean) with any woman. There are others who will always be true to one woman. There are those who are fortunate if they ever win a single woman. I am not one such. I do not know what I am. I know that I have loved and been loved by many women. I can see the religionist scoffing at this. I can still say that it is true. There is a strong chord of sympathy and understanding that exists between myself and every woman I have ever known intimately. They all like me. I can go back and talk things over. They are not angry. They like me.

This thought of whether she would or wouldn't held me all through this conversation. I am never sure what it is exactly that a woman expects under these circumstances—where she encounters a man to whom she is strongly drawn. Personally, I do not proceed so directly and incautiously on all occasions. I am not so easily interested in women. It is the exceptional always that fascinates me, not the commonplace, and I do not find the exceptional every moment. I cannot brook the average woman. She is too dull or too silly or too homely or something of that sort. Mere beauty—per se—will not attract me. I have known many exquisitely beautiful women to leave me as cold and distant as any human being can be left. From some, I turn away in instant weariness; from others, with positive dislike. There is a type—all my women have much in common—which appeals to me immensely. They all have charm of look and charm of manner, but better yet, they all have charm of soul, a certain sweetness of hope and intellect and youth coupled with real human understanding. I want hard common sense in my women, along with all their other lovely airs and graces, and I want reasonable human sympathy and good nature, or we part company quickly.

Well, here was Miss Longfellow beside me, and next to her Miss Burke, who had come back, and next to her Grant Richards, and here was I talking to Miss Longfellow very intimately and finding a hearty sympathy and response. She talked about London, how nice it would be, and about Paris, how she loved it, and then she said, "You're a vigorous fellow, aren't you? I think you're rather what I thought you would be from what Karl Kitchen said of your books."

"You like me, don't you?" I asked her, sinking my head back into my chair, but near to hers, so that I could talk softly. I could feel it as plainly as anything that she did, in her present ebullition of temperament, but I was curious to know whether she would admit so quickly.

"Oh, I don't know. Perhaps I do. I can't tell. I'm not sure yet."

"But you do, though. I know you do. I can tell by your manner. Come, now. Admit it. You like me, don't you?"

"Oh, I don't know. How can I tell so soon?"

"Look at me."

"No."

"Look at me just a moment."

"Be still. They'll hear. They're watching."

"Look at me anyhow."

She turned her head and opened her eyes in a wide, luring, coquettish look. There was something really human in them, kindly, aspiring, a desire to be loved, a desire to have real love always thrust upon her. They were yielding, too, slightly, and yet they weren't entirely.

"You like me, don't you?"

"Yes."

The eyes spoke with a real bolt of feeling.

"Much?"

"Much, I think."

"How much?"

"Oh, yards and yards. From here to the end of the deck."

She was like a gay little girl talking.

"I knew you did. I could feel it. And how did you feel?"

"The same. I could see."

"Then if you like me so much are you going to be very nice to me on the trip over?"

"How do you mean?"

"You know how I mean."

"I'm going to be as nice as I can. I can't be so very nice. There are other things that prevent me."

"Oh, come now. What are you talking about—someone else?"

"Yes."

"Are you married?"

"No."

"Are you in love?"

"Not in love exactly. I have someone who likes me very much and whom I like. I'm going over to join him. He's good to me. He gives me everything I want. It wouldn't be fair."

"Not even with me?"

"Not even with you."

"Come. I don't like that. You mustn't tell me that now. You don't mean that you'd just like me and then—"

"But it's true. I won't do that. I like you very much. I do." She turned her pretty face and opened her eyes. "But I have some conscience. I don't care anything about morals. I don't know anything about them. But if I did that I wouldn't feel right with myself. I have to live with my own mind."

"Well said. But I don't like that. I don't believe that you like me. You would if you liked me enough. You don't like me enough, that's all."

"It isn't that; I do like you, but I don't like you enough for that. I can't. I wouldn't feel right. I would if it weren't for that."

"Oh, pshaw! Hang the luck!"

She took my hand which was beside her muff and squeezed it underneath. She held it.

"That won't do," I said. "It won't help."

"I can't help it," she replied, with the first touch of resentment I had yet seen. "I can't do the other. I won't."

She let go my hand.

"Sweet, let's not quarrel. I think maybe you will, anyhow."

She smiled, but I could see that there was some sense of trouble here, and difficulty. She would and she wouldn't. It was myself—that was the answer, I thought. I hadn't turned the trick, and it made me a little angry.

We went to walk about the deck afterward, and though it began gaily enough, it ended in a quarrel.

"You're intensely sweet," I said, "with your cute little chin and your pretty nose, and your lavender-lidded eyes. Why don't you like me? Why won't you be nice?"

"Because I can't. Don't you see?"

"No, I don't see."

"Well, I don't want to. It isn't fair. It wouldn't be nice."

"For me it would."

"Yes, for you."

"Oh, I know," I replied sourly. "It's the same old story. Why do you want to be nice at all if you won't? Why should you look at me and hold my hand?"

"All right, I won't, if you say so. Why should you look at me?"

"Why should I look at you? What a silly question! Why should I look at you!"

"Oh, all men are brutes. They can go to the devil. Let's go back downstairs."

"No, let's go up on this upper deck."

It was the topmost deck, where the funnels and stacks were, and it was the most secluded of any.

"No, I won't."

"Come with me."

"No, let's go downstairs."

"You're simply angry now, or you're putting on."

"Oh, I'm not angry. I just don't want to walk."

"Come here."

"No."

I swung her round by the shoulders and threw her into my arms.

"There," I said, putting her lips to mine, "tell me what you'll do."

"Let me go. People will see. I'll never forgive you for this."

"Oh, back up. Cut out the bluff. Let it go. We'll go downstairs."

I was angry myself at what I considered her silly pretense—the old desire of a woman to coquet without paying any price whatsoever.

We came down to where the chairs were, but the others were absent. I was angry and she was defiant. She went off to her room, and I laughed. "She can go to the devil," I thought.

That was the beginning of an almost enduring quarrel.

CHAPTER V

This interesting ship life proceeded apace. I was fascinated every moment by the thought of being on this vast floating palace. I skipped my lunch, having had a late breakfast in my room, and at dinner was introduced to the dining room, Miss Longfellow sitting beside me to my left, a stranger to my right. Grant Richards was most brilliant in his leadership throughout this whole trip and affair. During the afternoon, when he was not talking with Miss Burke or Miss Longfellow (she suddenly ignored me for my anger, disbelief and other aggressive qualities or the lack of them, and went to walk with him), he was instructing me in the intricacies of ship life, was planning what we should do in Europe, was getting my repute as an author noised about as much as possible and was seeing to the welfare of all of us as much as possible. I never saw so comforting and efficient a man in all my life. He was in and out of my room every little while, or seeing where I was.

"Oh"—who can indicate exactly the sound of the English "Oh"?—"Oh, there you are. Now let me tell you something. You are to dress for dinner." I am giving sample conversation out of many, merely. "The etiquette requires it. You are to talk to the captain some, tell him how much you think of his ship and so forth, and you are not to neglect the neighbor to your right at table. Ship etiquette, I believe, demands that you talk to your neighbor—at least at the captain's table—that is the rule, I think. You are to take in Miss Longfellow, I am to take in Miss Burke." He made an agreement with me that he was to look after the general expenses and halve them up later and that he was to order the wine, knowing more about it. Miss Longfellow and I were at swords at dinner, but I teased her just the same.

"We are very angry, it appears."

"Oh, no. We have to have something to feel angry about."

"But we are a little sour, just the same, however infinitesimal the provocation."

"Oh, you go to the deuce."

"Come now, what's the use being angry? I don't care. You won't, so you won't. Let it go. You may change your mind later. Anyhow, we can talk. Do you remember so-and-so in New York?" and so we took up a haphazard conversation.

The captain appeared, and I saw a middle-sized man of rather stocky body with a longish face and those queer sea-gray eyes which so many sailors have—all, I think—and which talk so definitely of the sea. He was a man who had come up from the ranks—that queer type of efficient inefficiency—the man who knows one thing. I can always see behind a man of that kind long years of hard work, rough words, dirty work, oaths and cheap, artless living in his home life. I can see just the sort of house he would live in if he had one on shore—a thing stuffed with new, cheap furniture of the Sixth Avenue or Harrod's type and supplemented by prints of pictures which would give you a headache or make you cry. Such men treasure silly little things and are as jealous of their poor little earthly honors as it is possible for humans to be. Still, he was a nice enough man. Grant Richards told me he was good at card tricks and that we must visit him in his cabin some day. He (Grant Richards) was busy scanning the cabin list to see who was on board and getting a line on things generally.

After dinner we adjourned to the ship's drawing room, and there Miss Longfellow fell to playing cards with Grant Richards at first, afterwards with Mr. Kahn, who came up and joined us perforce.

This day had been a little stormy from several points of view which had no relationship to the condition of the sea. I think I have indicated in one or two places in the preceding pages that Grant Richards, being an Englishman of the artistic and intellectual classes with considerable tradition behind him and all the feeling of the worthwhileness of social order that goes with class training, has a high respect for the conventions. He is a little muddled at times as to what is what, for being essentially democratic in spirit and loving America—its raw force—he still clings almost pathetically, I think, to that vast established order which is England. It may be producing a dying condition of race, but still it is so nice, so fine. Now, one of the tenets of English social order is that being a man, you must be a gentleman, very courteous to the ladies, very observant of outward forms and appearances, very discreet in your approaches to the wickedness of the world, but nevertheless you may approach and much more, if you are cautious enough. Grant

Richards had no particular objection to sex attractions and sex liaisons if they are subtly and discreetly managed, but if there is the least flaunting of untoward conditions in the face of convention, he is off like a shot. "No, no," I can hear him say, "we must not do anything like this. This is terrible. We are flying in the face of order—we are not keeping up appearances."

I think that, like myself, he wanted to be very nice to both ladies, equally and observedly attentive to each, not to show any predilection for either, not to do any philandering, at least openly—to be nice, quiet, remote, etc.

Alas, alas, here was I, beginning all wrong. No sooner did I set eyes on Miss Longfellow than I must openly and flaringly begin to pay court to her. Scandalous! What would Miss Burke think? What would the surrounding passengers think? I think he suspected at first that Miss Burke might possibly come to like me, and later that he was pleased that Miss Longfellow and I had fallen out. I have no positive proof that he noticed it the first day, but he may have. And, anyhow, she may have told him.

For she was a peculiar woman. Her world consisted of sex interests, sex attractions and repulsions, or had up to this time, and she was still looking about, uncertain whether she would cling indefinitely to the lover with whom she was now cohabiting, but uncertain as to whether any other would arrive who was as much worthwhile. Frankly, she was a daughter of joy—I would use a much stronger word, only on mature deliberation, I do not think it applies. She told me at dinner or afterward, I forget which, that at fourteen she was a shop girl earning four dollars a week. At sixteen she claims to have been an under-stenographer to some person in New York, of whom I have heard. I think she lied, but let it go at that. At seventeen or sixteen she said she was an extra at the Opera in New York, and I can well believe that—playing a page, a seraph, a part of the chorus of nymphs—anything and everything required. At eighteen some man had found her and made her his mistress, and she was then allowed to go to the New York School of Dramatic Art. She told me also that she had studied English Literature at Columbia University, but, Shade of Addison, I don't believe it.

Anyhow, after that—well, after that, the deluge, no doubt. She would not trace her history for me. I got inklings—Monte Carlo, Aix-les-Bains, Paris, Ostend, the Riviera, here, there, everywhere. Though her father is only an alderman and her mother established in a nice apartment on the Upper West Side, we ride in taxi cabs, array ourselves in splendid furs, are injured in an automobile accident, imitate the manners and the speech of fine ladies and make the truly cultivated lift their eyes in horror at atrocious mispronunciations and misinterpretations. The truth is, we know—and we don't. We have had, as the Americans say, "a look-in." We have caught a glimpse of something finer and better, and we are wild to enjoy it—to have it. We haven't real manners or refinement; we haven't either true sweetness or gentleness of spirit. We are lustful, hungry, savage, wicked, and we grab and snap vigorously, using our pretty body, our shameless eyes, our sweet red lips and siren hair as lure.

God damns that subtlety of nature that builds mantraps and sets a lure in the path of the unwary. He writes in these faces of whoredom the signs of their own iniquity. You can tell. They are sweet, but they are disgusting also. There must be something equally evil in you before you can harmonize, and I use the term 'evil' relatively, for, after all, I do not believe in either good or evil save as vague and passing contraries which seem to be and are not.

Well, Grant Richards had been greatly disturbed at my sudden interest in this lady—for, all said and done, she was delightful anyhow—but, you see, I was the one who was creating the disturbance in an open, flagrant way, not he, and he has an inborn desire to lead. I can see him arriving on board entirely interested in Miss Burke, since he had never seen Miss Longfellow in his life, and, because of his previous interest in Miss Burke, paying no particular attention to her. She was gauche, aggressive, pushing. She had planned, he told me, to get in with Miss Burke, for she it was who had had her chair put next to Miss Burke's on the lounging deck, and she it was who had secured a seat at the captain's table next Miss Burke. Anyhow, she was pushing and uncertain and possibly very unsatisfactory, and then I come along and take up with her. I like her. By George! as we would say in America; this is very strange.

He looks at her himself now and suddenly begins to discover some very interesting things about her. She has that native force which he so admires in so many Americans. Although she is crude, she has ambition, beauty, youth, hope, and Grant Richards admires youth, ambition, beauty, hope. As a matter of fact, he is very enthusiastic about it wherever he finds it, and on seeing what had happened, he said, "Here, there must be something to this girl," and he begins to look into the matter for himself.

Witness now a very human and delightful comedy. I have quarreled with the lady, and she is angry with me. Seeing my sudden, peculiar interest, Grant Richards wakes up and proceeds to look into the situation closely. He begins to like her. I see him walking about the deck talking enthusiastically. His monocle, his English get-up, his *savoir faire*, his experience of life, never stood him to better advantage. He knows how to be nice, helpful, discreet, and he strolls about now; the lady being disgruntled with me, he is decidedly *persona grata*. I begin to suspect very seriously that what I wanted, he will get, and it makes me angry. I see very clearly how it has all come about. What a chump to urge things so briskly, and particularly in his presence. It amuses me, and yet it makes me angry.

And Miss Burke, well, I think Miss Burke felt the least something. I may be mistaken, but I think so. I think she thought she was going to be danced exclusively to by two men on this occasion, and lo and behold, both have gone off and begun dancing attendance on someone else. It is all very well, but, of course, it cannot be helped.

And to cap it all, at a late hour that night, Grant Richards comes and takes me to task for my obstreperous, unconventional, decidedly uncomfortable attitude. I almost die between the humor and the chagrin of the thing, but what of that! Once before, during the day, right after the first burst of interest on my part I think it was, he said to me with that quizzical, uncertain light in his eyes, "Here, here, this will never do!" (You will have to supply the delightful, superior English accent for yourself.) "I shall have to get the captain to put you in irons. Breaking up the order of the ship, scandalizing the passengers! It won't do at all." But I could see, for all that, that he meant a portion of it. It did not disturb me any at that time, for at that time I thought I had the lady sure.

Later, it was more curious and not quite so indifferent. We had been playing cards upstairs, or rather Miss Longfellow and Grant Richards had. Miss Burke, feeling a little weary, had retired early, and I, after a time, had left also. Before I left, however, Mr. Kahn had come up, and, as I have said, and perforce without so much as a by-your-leave, joined us. Later a friend of his, Kahn's, a man who was near the figure of the world that Kahn was, also came up. This latter unconventional soul, a heavy, impossible, inexperienced Jew, leaned over Miss Longfellow's shoulder and helped direct her play. Once he observed, "It's Longfellow's turn," which was scandalous, seeing that he did not know her save by name, and once she said to me because of something I said, "You're wrong, old dear," and it appears that in England that is the language of the loose, immoral, vulgar classes.

Anyhow and also, she had told several risqué and inappropriate stories on the lounging deck, at dinner and elsewhere, in the presence of Miss Burke and himself, and he was beginning to feel that it was high time this whole thing should be straightened out. I must cease my excited philanderings, which would probably eliminate me so far as Miss Longfellow was concerned. She must pull herself up; cut the crude, interfering barbarians; cease her vulgarities in conversation and play the role of the lady for the rest of the trip. Mr. Vulgar Kahn and his still more vulgar friend must be severely cut the next day, and Grant Richards must be permitted to enjoy the society of Miss Longfellow on such terms as he should dictate. I smile and laugh at the man's courage, subtlety, persistence and good nature. It showed such an efficient point of view. The whole situation needed to be corrected, not abandoned, which shows you the executive mind at its best. So down he comes to me.

Witness me in my berth solemnly reading the *Adonais* of Shelley—or was it the *Painters of France*? Enter Grant Richards.

"Asleep? Am I intruding? I thought I might be. Tired?"

I assure him I am not.

"A most cu-aw-rious situation that, upstairs. She's quite bright, that Miss Longfellow. I quite like her. A little crude in spots, but something could be made out of her if she could only be taken in hand. But these two friends of hers—they are impossible. I never saw anything quite like that procedure upstairs."

"What about?" I ask, but I am not very well informed, or perhaps I had better say observant, in these matters, and anyhow I have the loose American attitude toward the subtleties of good form.

"Do you see how they come up there? I was never so put out in my life. First Mr. Kahn comes, and then his friend drifts in without word or warning. In polite society, now, that is the worst of form. You couldn't do that, you know, in any place where experienced people meet. The trouble with her is she doesn't seem to know—she doesn't mind."

"She's quite young and raw," I put in rather more critically than otherwise. "She doesn't know anything about good society. She has brains, though, and wit. She'll come out right, I think, if she has time enough."

"Quite so. I like her. But that situation, now, where that friend of Kahn's said, 'It's Longfellow's turn,' and her saying to you, 'You're wrong, old dear.' Why, that sort of thing is impossible. It won't do at all. You can't do that sort of thing, you know. I shall have to talk to her tomorrow. I shall send her word by the steward the first thing in the morning to know what time she is going to breakfast, and then I shall give her a bit of advice in a nice way. She's clever, you know. She has a pretty face and a good mind. A great deal might be made out of her—but this sort of thing—"

"And then me," I observed what he was really coming to, what he was driving at. "I'm really the cause of this loose atmosphere, this trouble!"

"Well, as for you," he observed, finding his opening at last, "really, I shall have to speak to the captain about you. You're disrupting all the custom and procedure of the ship. Really, that sort of thing won't do at all, you know—" the eye behind the monocle was most curiously elate, quizzical, monitory.

"Joh! Joh!" I wanted to say in imitation of the English "Dear! Dear!" but I was in no mood. I had begun it, in a way—there was no doubt of that. Miss Longfellow and I had burst into a very curious flame. No doubt some passengers noticed it. Certainly they might have. He indicated that Miss Burke was aware of what was going on. From that, I took it that she was shocked. I should have to behave better in the future.

"Quite so," I agreed, "I understand. Mr. Kahn and his friend will have to be eliminated. I shall have to cease paying violent attention to Miss Longfellow" (that was quite easy now). "Miss Longfellow will have to cease telling her risqué stories and brace up generally. We are all going to behave," and I wanted to add, "and Grant Richards is going to be cock of the roost," but I didn't. I was so amused and entertained. I was curious to see how this whole thing would end. I wanted to see how he and Miss Longfellow would get along together. Mind you, I am of the opinion that Grant Richards doesn't mind a little philandering himself, particularly when all his other rivals have been laid low, but as to that, I had no final evidence at the time I wrote these lines.

CHAPTER VI

Let me take out of my notebook some of the comments I wrote on this ship life and just as I penned them at the time. We shall come back to the balance of this story later on.

Nov. 23: A dull crowd and small, I understand, for this ship. Evidently I am not seeing the finest type of ocean passenger. The dining room is not quite as glittering, perhaps, and the throng in the drawing room of an evening. Never mind. I am seeing enough.

A slightly more rolly night than was the day. I think of disaster and of being in an open boat in a cold, stormy sea. The wreck of the *Bourgogne* eight or ten years ago comes back to me. That was terrible. At eight I call for a bath; at nine I breakfast. No breakfast for Miss Burke or Miss Longfellow. Richards comes down late. Feels better, and we talk literature. I study the wood paneling of the dining room. Miss Longfellow does not appear till two. Miss Burke appears at eleven. Atmosphere thaws out, and we start anew on a friendly basis. I walk much. The speed of the sea rushing by amazes me. It is quite like a train, or Niagara. I am interested by the class differences on shipboard. They are so marked. I weary of doing nothing. After all, the edge of sailing on this splendid boat has been taken off by the glamour and show of American hotel life. I send Miss Longfellow *Jennie Gerhardt*. I try to read *The Vista of English Verse*. Impossible to get interested. Trying to read on shipboard is hard. I am too much interested in it as an adventure. Yesterday was hard, bright and clear, with no force of wind, but spray flying some because of the speed of the boat. Today it was clear in the morning and warm, with heavy, lowering clouds in the afternoon and evening. Clouds look so low over the sea or anywhere where you can command a wide stretch of space. Miss Burke was as nice as ever, a slightly affected little person—or perhaps it is just my preliminary mood concerning the English. Richards says she is the best-dressed woman on the English stage. She is nice, quite, with very bright lips—rouged probably—and a clear, possibly manufactured—but if so, very artistically—complexion. She has the "raather" and "I dyah say" of the English, but is, to a certain extent, sympathetic and good-natured.

Miss Longfellow is another type, obviously an adventuress. She is, say, twenty-nine years old; Miss Burke is nearer thirty-six or thirty-eight. Miss Longfellow has glittering, significant eyes. Her body is very shapely; her face daintily formed, with a cute, short little nose, Cupid's bow lips, a pert, aggressive little chin which she thrusts independently forward, and a wealth of black hair done low over her eyes. She looks like an Italian. Like Miss Burke, I think she rouges her lips, pencils her eyes, perhaps works hard over her complexion and pays endless attention to the outward appearance of her person. She is bright—very—with thick, unattractive hands. She also makes a great effort to appear just what people expect her to be wherever she is. That thing never works, quite. People are too wise. They lift their eyes at the slightest remark; they judge by the cut of one's coat or the fit of one's dress. The elite are not usually where pretension can make ready headway.

I note that Miss Longfellow uses too much perfume and walks with a languid, provocative air at times. She gambles when she gets a chance and expects all who train with her to provide money liberally. Night before last she spoke of having paid $390 duty on a dress! Today she told me of having earned her own living in London for a time by model work. This trip is costing her a few hundred. She also spoke of knowing the adventuress's world and ventured the thought that we are what we are by temperament and cannot help it. She spoke of having come up from nothing—having been born in Richmond. Not much admirable home life back of her, that is sure.

Shaved at four, got sick and vomited once. Tuesday I tried to read *Sands of Pleasure* in anticipation of meeting its author in London, but I can't. It's a dull book. Went out on deck and found Richards and Miss Burke side by side, the latter feeling very badly. It is nearly dark now. We saw the moon over our right shoulders through a slight rift in the lowering clouds just for a moment. I dressed afterward for dinner and ate heartily. Gloomy because Miss Longfellow won't be nice to me. A cross-eyed man sits opposite me at dinner. Later we all sat in the parlor and talked. Kahn came up and got "frozen." I think the sea is noble but unendurable. The motion sickens me. In the night I find out why all drawers and receptacles are made with spring locks: the motion throws everything on the floor.

It develops in a conversation with Richards that I am to go to Oxford,

Canterbury Cathedral, some typical English manufacturing towns two hours from London, etc. I see and feel romance in all this, for this trip is without plan, but I feel physically ill just the same. I thought I was a better sailor.

N.B. I walked much this day about the long decks—one on B, one on A. The sea of course is very much of a same-ish thing, but the endless water is still impressive to me. Thoughts in the night came: what if the boat should sink or strike an iceberg?—one was reported near us. The sound of the waves, the wash-wash, is always in one's ears. I saw a petrel, but no whale or fish of any kind. One thing impressed me: the backward rushing of the water with the speed of a train as if it were moving and we standing still. The dark green solidity of it moved me. And the strong, fresh winds—how good they were!

People on shipboard are peculiar. The class distinctions are sharp. You would never imagine from where we are that there is a second or third class. The second class occupy the rear one-fourth of the ship with separate dining, writing, lounging rooms, etc. The third class were forward with a promenade deck which brought them back past the gallery of the dining room. While I was walking there once, looking at a great circular bed of roses arranged in jars before the dining room balcony entrance, a door opened, and I caught a glimpse of the shabby third-class life. It smacked a little of Dives and Lazarus.

Also, I noticed, the first-class passengers were obviously so unconscious of any other form of life than that which they were enjoying; they were so magnetized and inspired by their own comfort that they could not give a thought to anything else. Humanity is constituted to look up, not down, forward, not back, I think. It always thinks of more luxury, not less; of better days, not worse. Now and then a dark fact will intrude, but humanity struggles hard and quickly to clap the door on it. These people in this sea-palace strutting to and fro in caps, canvas shoes, gay-patterned storm coats and the like were so sensitive, it seems to me, of their station, their class. Everyone seems to be saying defiantly to himself, "I am quite as good as you are." They walk with a self-conscious stride, an air. And the women! Women are always the makers of class. They cut aspiration in others with whipping glances. One sees how exclusively the rich and socially distinguished keep to themselves. It is actually fashionable to keep to one's suite. And we talk only of polite things and give ourselves airs. I saw several types of men on board who interested me considerably above the others—one a stout, ruddy American millionaire, striding to and fro masterfully; and past him, in another direction, a small, elegant mouse of an Englishman in a great white-and-brown-checked cap and checked storm coat with flaring skirts. This latter's profile was so keen and refined, a piece of cut ivory, quite Dante-like.

These two interested me especially, because I knew they would never understand each other. One represented the pride of force, the other the pride of caste and tradition. They walked purposely unconscious of each other here—delightful! Another type which interested me greatly was that of a bony, angular scion of great wealth, say fifty years of age, who obviously knew everything, had been everywhere and takes everything for granted. You can see by his walk that he admits of no superiority in anyone; that he rarely acknowledges equality in anyone and would fly unconventionality and mediocrity as he would the plague. "I do not know him; I shall never see him again. But I know him as well as though I had lived with him for years. He represents a class." I used to wonder in my silly youth how attractive women could endure a man of this type. I understand now. Position and the ability to boast of it repay a bright, ambitious woman for everything. To hell with them.

Nov. 24: The boat rocked more last night, and I slept but little. My books fell down, shaken off the trunk, and the trunk itself moved about. Richards came in at ten. I was going to my bath. Afterwards I came back and lay down reading a history of French painting and posting my notes of yesterday. I had chicken sandwiches, two hard-boiled eggs and a cup of coffee in my room. At three P.M. I got up and went on deck and walked. Phenomenon of gulls keeping up with ship surprised me. Our speed is said to be twenty-nine miles. Captain Turner says these birds can fly fifty miles an hour. No ship in sight. Rolling of boat very heavy toward six P.M.

At dinner I sat by the captain. Richards has completely cut me out with Miss Longfellow, leaving Miss Burke on my hands to entertain. She's charming but weak. Would not interest me. Miss Longfellow much more forceful, though less polished. We talked of London, Paris, music, collections—all the customary things. I listened to Mr. G. W. Smalley (an ex-newspaper correspondent and journalist of whom I know much) at dinner—an aged, dreary, antiquated man. In his time he has obviously been a tuft-hunter. At eleven P.M. I was weary and went to bed.

The barbershop on this boat is small, bad and ridiculously out of keeping with this ship. My shave cost me thirty-five cents. Angle of boat rocking said by barber and captain to reach as high as thirty-four degrees.

Nov. 25: When I went on deck this morning, the day was beautiful. In the first place, I was feeling fine. My squeamishness of the day before had gone, and during the night when the boat was rocking vastly, I felt as though I were being lulled to rest in some great hammock. I have always loved to swing, anyhow, either in a swing or a hammock or a rocking-chair, and now my dream of peace on board had come. I rested so well. I dreamed. I thought of the great, deep, dark sea under me, and the fish and the birds the captain told me about at dinner which roost on the water—sea gulls and tern and whale-birds and so on. He told me that whale-birds were something like house-martens. The name impresses me. It talks of the vasty deep. Whale-birds!

One thing he told me which interested me. He said that some people imagine that sea gulls and the like follow a ship all the way across the ocean. They don't. One flock may follow all day, but at night it will roost on the water, and the next day a new flock, any group which happens to be near at dawn, will take up the chase. They fly faster than the boat steams—forty-five to fifty miles an hour, he says. At night they roost and are forsaken. He says that you can be sure of this because on a moonlit night, you may see roosting flocks, not flying but paddling out of the way as the boat approaches.

But to come back to this morning. It was so fine. The sun was so dark, the sea so bright, the wind so cool but not at all cold—more like a cool wind on a warm summer day. One passenger told me at breakfast that it might be because we were near the Gulf Stream. Anyhow, I went on the bridge deck; I walked with great enthusiasm. My very youth came back, days when I was seven to ten years old and used to sit on our back fence and watch swallows and house-martens skim over a five-acre field of clover or timothy—it was alternated from season to season. Somehow the rolling sea brought back my youthful sense of space, and the gulls spoke of our Indiana buzzards. The sea was so fresh and cool. There is something about its dark bluish-green decks which makes me feel as though I should like to rock on it forever. For the first time in my life I saw what rollers were—I saw them coming. And I rejoiced in that expression: "The rocking floor of the sea." There was a rainbow shining away off to the west, and the wind would clip the tops off the nearer waves and turn them, with the sun's aid, into delicate spectrums of pink and purple, blue and gold. It was wonderful. There was a flock of gulls trailing behind us, and in the distance a ship or two.

It is wonderful to me how much personality has to do with life. There is a slim, young American girl on board this ship traveling first-class, whom in all probability I shall never know. She is tall, lean, swaggering, graceful. Her clothes hang and swing in foamy waves, a white belted wool coat coming almost to her feet in particular. Her hair is red-gold, and this morning, disheveled as it was, she had it bound round with a velvet ribbon of ox-blood hue. Her eyes are blue-gray; her nose long and keen but shapely; her lips thin, red, expressive. Her cheeks are pale, sunken, and yet pink and healthy-looking. She walks with a swing and a flare, and one can see that she thinks. Every time I meet her I say, "How beautiful," and think, "Oh youth, youth," but I shall never meet her. I really do not know that I should want to. She might like me, and she might not. I fancy not. She would not understand me, and I would not understand her. But she is as beautiful as a Reynolds or a Blake. Naked, she would make a splendid Diana in some hunting scene. As a mistress, unquestionably she would be imperious and hard to deal with. I should say her life will cross that of many a man, and yet I may be mistaken. Such imperial beauty is not for me. I am too imperious myself. But she fits in with this sanded deck, this blowing wind, this rolling sea.

Around twelve o'clock, by arrangement with the chief steward, Richards, Miss Burke and myself met in front of the purser's office on B deck and went over a portion of the ship—the third-class section forward, the second-class section aft, the sailor's hold forward (I went there alone) and the second- and third-class kitchens. Some people abhor the commonplace and the poor, and I myself have a strong distaste for filth, but I cannot say that I find the third-class on this boat so terrible. Everything is cheap and plain, like a first-class lodging house in the Bowery. The rooms are small and fitted with bunks. There is not so much air as in the first-class rooms, and they are not so light. The main objection is perhaps that the people are dressed poorly and that the odors are strong. The third-class deck appeared to be crowded with Italian men who had been to America and were going home for Christmas. They are a picturesque lot. Their new clothes are so store-y, so shelf-wrinkled and shoddy-made. Some have knit and some leather vests. Some have new shoes, some wide-brimmed, black felt hats. There is color here—a bright tie now and then. I must say, according to their standard, they seem to be well provided for. These bunks and decks are no worse than their own homes in New York, and it only costs them thirty-five dollars to go across.

Down in the extreme section of the forward angle, I found a section where the able seamen live. It is, I think, seven floors below the top deck. A bright room, at that, set with long, green, baize-covered tables. Some twenty or thirty men in blue jean jackets looked up when I came in, or rather put my head in. No one came down these two narrow flights of iron stairs with me. The chief steward warned me against going, but I persisted because I wanted to see how they lived. Here they were, British seamen, their faces brown and ruddy but seamed with those same lines which always bespeak a nation's, not an individual's, age. They looked at me as a drove of cows might survey a sheep, and I returned their glance. They probably did not like it; I don't blame them. I have always resented being made a show of. The nature of hard work, if it is hard for them, and of unintelligible thought, if their thoughts are unintelligible, has gone from me. Although I was once wild about uplifting the workingman, I am not so sure that I understand them any more. I am not so sure that individual temperaments can be uplifted by outside influences. I used to think so. I am not so sure now. Anyhow, I do not know what they long for exactly, what they want to be. I wish I did. But if I were Velázquez or a living Rembrandt, I would come here and paint these men, every mark and seam. I would get the look of their eyes and the weary look of their faces. I would paint these rough hands and their big feet. Why?—I don't know. They are beautiful to me, collectively speaking, sad, grim, majestic.

This morning we had a discussion at breakfast, two strange men and myself. One man, to my right, is an Englishman, evidently refined and with some feeling for art. The other is an American, not so refined, slightly cross-eyed but well-built and interesting. He has an ingratiating smile. Many would call him attractive. It started somehow about the uncertainty of life, principally because the dishes were slipping aimlessly about the table. I said how much I was enjoying it all this morning. Anyhow I ventured, as I almost always do when we get far enough along philosophically and metaphysically, that we do not know anything about anything—I mean anything beyond the little mechanical facts of this state which we call mortal. Curiously, both men agreed with me. They seemed to like the idea, but it was not at all new to them, of course. It was not old and threadbare to them, however, for they discussed it with avidity. It was almost as good as their breakfast. We talked of the abstrusities of philosophy and the subtleties of characters. Ethics, morals, standards went by the board. What are they? we asked. Still, we agreed that there was a static condition here to which one had to conform and that this was only good and endurable because it was not definitely fixed and because life was uncertain. We all agreed that life was lovely because we do not know anything about it, because we know not what a day may bring forth.

I saw the kitchens on the same trip that we saw the steerage. The third-class kitchen reminded me of that of a Bowery restaurant. The second-class was very much the same as that of the first-class. I could see no difference. And the second-class dining room was as nice as that you find on some first-class ships. (I have been over the *Baltic* and the *St. Louis*.)

At four today, after writing from half-past one until four on this diary, I went with Richards, Miss Burke, Miss Longfellow and George W. Smalley to take tea in the captain's room. He is rather a nice old fossil, this same captain, taken from a first-class passenger's point of view. I have no faith in these class appearances. He served tea and showed us card tricks, and there was (to me) silly talk of one thing and another—actors, former passengers, and so on. Finally we got away, and seeing the moon in the west through an open door and a flare of pale bluish-green light in the far west, I slipped away from the others and crossing to the extreme rear of the boat back of the second-class section, I stood there and watched the night fall. The moon was beautiful, clear and bright, leaving a silver track toward the boat. The stars were out, thick and beautiful. I have not seen such stars in some little time. The wind was cool and caressing, and the boat rolled in great, long rolls of, say, twenty degrees from side to side.

It occurred to me while there how silly is the importance we sometimes attach to the master of a great ship like this. In the eyes of some he might stand for all the wisdom connected with it; as a matter of fact he has very little. Captain though he is, he is no more to it than I am. He is not a true captain. He is not a real master. There is a chief engineer over whom he has no control. But more than that, there is the company president or chairman, all the subtleties of division and authorities, until really he is little more than a name or an idea. Standing upon the bridge deck later, with all the tall, pointed stars overhead and these great funnels and stacks standing up around me in the dark, I thought of the cargo hold, the different class cabins, the cooks, the sailors, the passengers, the company which built the ship, the company which owns it; the thought came to me that this vast leviathan is really a race expression, a time thought.

It comes into being through no single being or group of beings, but through the race ability and longing for expression. I am as much a reason for its existence as anyone else—my longing for travel and expression. All the knowledge—the race knowledge, as it were—of engineering, plumbing, carpentering, cabinet-working, cooking, serving, housekeeping, official management, navigation and the like is here accumulated and expressed. This is not the only great ship. There are hundreds of them. The race knows how to do all these things. It can do them over and over. No individual is responsible, no individual is important. This little silly captain just happens to be by chance called to preside. I happen to be so fortunate as to be able to ride. I might not. Others might be called in my place.

This vast vessel might almost go on without people, it is so wonderful. It represents the spirits of our sea-ancestors, the wisdom of our race work. We (the race) have done vast things, but we will do vaster—only you and I are nothing, fading, falling leaves on its immense tree. Tomorrow we will be gone, but ships will not, nor people, nor ideas. The race will be alive and the sea plowed and ships will be of stranger power. The thought is wearisome—but alas, great life is heavy. Our little brains cannot grasp it all. We know literally nothing, the race knows something. God, divine mind, knows all.

I stood tonight, after I had left the stern of the ship, up among the great stacks and funnels looking at the stars. This is a peculiar portion of the ship to me, quite its most distinguished section. From here, in a way, you can see how majestic it all is—how distinguished its height, how great its depth, how vast its bulk, how proudly it fronts the deep. For all its great length and breadth and height and depth, so impressive from this viewpoint as compared with the world of water about and the illimitable space of stars, it seems so puny—at once so much and so little. I had just come past the grand lounging rooms on A deck, where were smokers, readers, tipplers, all making the best of a luxurious, but to many nevertheless tedious, voyage. I was thinking as I stood up here that the worst phase of my life, and its best at times, is its loneliness. In loneliness, such as on this deck for instance, when I am shut out from the company of others by the subtleties of my own disposition, its moods, unrests, angers and the like, I come face to face with the vasty deep. I am up against that huge wall of the unknowable which is at once so penetrable and impenetrable.

Here, because of absence from familiar scenes, the enforced companionship of comparative strangers, the sense of uncertainty as to the future, the keen realization of the passing character of all forms and moods, the futility of life, oppressed me heavily. I often wonder just what is the nature, the chemical components, of a mood such as this, but there is never any answer. I sink and sink in spirits until an almost physical ache and pain supersedes the mental one. Joy in the beauty of life is so close to sorrow. These high stars, so keen, so haphazard-seeming, so innumerable—they put one out of countenance with the littler things. I listened to the swishing water, rhythmic in its outward wash from the prow. I gazed at the stacks and funnels, huge, shadowy, majestic. It seemed a wonderful trip and a wonderful situation to me in time and space, but withal I was intensely lonely, miserably so.

I sometimes think that all the heart needs in these hours of physical and mental misery, when the greatness, beauty and distinction of life falls like a tremendous requiem on the soul, is just that little glow of affection and understanding which springs between two and endures. It seems a minor thing to say in the face of the vast wash of circumstances, which we should face so bravely, but it is so. Just two, with that little fire of love or understanding which burns so briskly or so warmly, and the great dark is no longer so dark for us. Death does not matter—distant death—nor any current ill. Here is rest, here is sanctuary, here is peace. Blow the winds of life ever so bitterly—but pshaw! I struck my hands irritably together—life rarely comes so, and feeling the tang of absence more acutely than ever, I went below.

At seven o'clock, after dressing, I went to dinner, to sit by Miss Longfellow again. She was in a better mood for some reason and looking decidedly smart and interesting. Her hair is raven-black, as is Miss Burke's, and done tonight very low over her forehead. We talked of plays, the Shuberts, whom she knew, theatrical opportunities in London. It appeared that in spite of her present mission, which was to rejoin her favored flame, she was interested to get on the stage in London. The gentleman on my right, to whom Richards insisted I must talk, was very pleasant. I learned tonight that his name was Owen, and the gentleman opposite me was a Mr. McGee, controller of some great motor corporation, going to London for some financial reason. He had all the peculiar reserve and determination and resistance of the American financial mind. He told me on this occasion that he was going to learn to broaden his "a's" after the English fashion.

"But what will you do when you go to St. Louis?" I asked him, for he had observed that he had come from there.

"Well, I won't go there, that's all," was his laughing reply.

Mr. Owen and I talked some more of London, Canterbury Cathedral, the Wallace Collection and the National Museum, where I am to see certain things. He has a brother who has become an American citizen and resides in New York.

One of the most interesting persons to me, partly from an illustrative point of view, is this same G. W. Smalley, whom I have mentioned and whom Richards found to be aboard ship on the second day and who was again at the captain's table tonight. He has a seat next that worthy on the side of the table opposite me. As a publishing manager, Richards is, of course, intensely interested in any personality whose character makes for the selling of books. About fifteen or twenty years ago this man, who is now almost in his dotage—a lean and slippered pantaloon—was quite a flourishing personality in New York and London. He was the London correspondent of the *New York Herald,* a subtle and rather vigorous personality but considerable of a toady, as I happen to know, and one whose face was rather sternly set toward anything save position, lineage, triumphant power and things of that sort. We all know the type.

He was here this evening, lean and baggy of cheeks, his eyes aged and sunk in weary sockets, his hands thin and a little trembly at times, and his whole body rather sunk in upon itself and feeble to behold. He was dressed in excellent tweed, however, could ride on this ship, which cost him no less than two hundred dollars the passage, and seemed, if I could judge from Richards's attitude, to still possess some little influence in the literary and art world.

I must confess that age, quite aside from its just deserts or merits, always possesses a sentimental and a sympathetic interest for me. I am inclined to look upon it with a kindly eye. I feel sorry for the flickering end of life, quite as I feel sorry for its hungry, unrecognized beginnings. But this old dog had an evil, sly look in his eye, to me. I read his tuft-hunting past quite clearly in his wrinkled face, and I didn't like him. He began his conversation with the usual cynical, lofty references to life which all literary and artistic men, myself included, affect, but that did not irritate me so much as a feeling concerning his secret personality. I could feel it, and I didn't like it.

"Oh, yes," he began to the captain at this dinner or some other—it was at dinner, and we were all more or less cheerfully gathered, "a level sea, a pleasant captain," or some old saw like that. He fell into a discussion of books and literary and art personalities with Miss Burke, who happened to be sitting beside me at the time and who speaks French perfectly, I understand, and who is well up on the modern schools of realism and romance. She had read some memoirs in which he was particularly interested—the letters of Madame de Sévigné to her daughter—and he immediately mentioned several other books of memoirs, classic notations by distinguished women which she had not read. I noted this latter as an enfeebled and disagreeable trait of his, that he was so anxious to air his knowledge of the subtleties of publication at the expense of one who could not possibly know. These works were all strange to me, being French and I not reading French, but they were more so to her, whose profession was not literature but the stage and who could not possibly have surveyed the literary reaches which he would naturally encounter as a journalist and author. Still, she seemed quite aware of most of that to which he referred. His mind was full of memories which concerned Bernhardt, Coquelin, Réjane and a score of others whom I have forgotten. He was greatly concerned over the Goncourts, Sainte-Beuve, Michelet and so on, but when it came to the realistic writers, those interpreters of life whom some of us consider important—de Maupassant, Flaubert and others—he was silent. I fancy a man like George Moore would be anathema to him, and as for Tolstoy and Dostoyevski—let us draw the curtain.

Anyhow, the thing which amused me in connection with this old gentleman was his inability to differentiate clearly between values. How does he draw the line? One is good, the other bad. Why? The divine Sarah once leaned on his arm. He chortled joyfully as he related it. He could be of use to the divine Sarah. She was nice to him in a social way. I can explain it on no other basis. He looked to me, as Richards once said of someone of whom he did not approve, very much as though he might be the kind who would like to go about with bishops—the most contemptible specimens of humanity. In fact, he looked very much like a bishop.

I tripped him once, though, and would have done so many times if it had not been for his age and the fact that his defeat and discomfiture were really not worth the labor. He was talking of women, venting those silly old saws of the vintage of '75 concerning the vast subtlety of women. Who can know a woman? She is as deep as the sea, as dark as the night. She is as many different persons as there are birds, animals, fish, etc. Ovid in his poetic flights and after him poets and authors generally (Balzac was one of the worst offenders) have given vent to this silly gush concerning the vast subtlety of women—purely the joy of their creative imaginations.

It is silly. Everyone knows it is silly. In a lackadaisical way, more because

I was bored than anything else, I suggested that I did not believe it, that it was rather an exploded idea. The old gentleman was on me in a minute. I could see by the glint in his eye that he was about to make an intellectual killing for his own pleasure and that of others. His eyes narrowed. The superior, condescending glance of the intellectual came into his face.

"How do you make that out?" he asked. "Do you read them more clearly than the rest of us?"

"No, about the same as the rest of us, I fancy. I cannot see how they are invested in much more mystery than a man. Mind is mind. I happen to believe, with some psychologists and metaphysicians, that there is but one mind—at least we have no present proof of many. For my part I think that the one mind, or simply *mind,* works largely to one end in both. There are some sex differences under which the same mind labors—in a woman, her long hair, her shapely body, her pretty lips, her evoluted desire to tempt and to flee; and in a man his strong arms, his muscular body, his evoluted desire to conquer and pursue; and these two things make a seemingly greater difference between them than really exists. It is not so great as it seems. They work with different implements, that is all—I mean this same mind is."

"But how do you explain the origin of these differences?"

"Biologically. Biologically," I replied. "There was a time when there were no sexes, simply a physically self-dividing gender, a neuter gender, I believe. Biology teaches that fairly clearly."

The old gentleman's eye lost its fire.

"But this mind—this mind—how do you explain its tendency to differentiate?" I could see plainly that he was disturbed and out of his element. It was a little cruel.

"I don't," I replied. "I don't. The psychologists give us a fair indication of the drift of mind in the male and female. They see no vast difference, other things being equal. There is a time conscience which governs each sex, their attitude, their traditions. The truth is—"

"Truth, truth!" he grabbed at the word like a drowning man. "Pilate asked what is truth?"

"Quite so," I replied, honestly a little wearily. The game wasn't worth the powder. "We all ask the same thing."

He subsided, relieved, and so did I. It would have been a shame to have gone on. That subject, though, the subtlety of the female sex, did not come up at this table again, not on this trip.

Most of my woe on this boat has concerned Miss Longfellow. She is so beautiful. An impossible person from some points of view, wholly unschooled in letters, good society, polite manners and many other things—a real cocotte, and yet delightful, hard and cold one minute, the next soft and silly.

She depends absolutely on the charms of her body to get her what she wants. She first leaned strongly to me and now snubs me for Richards, pretending in a way that she does not. But I see plainly what is going on, and I think Richards suspects that I see. For this reason he is doubly nice, but it does not help any. My pride has been severely hurt in this instance. It is curious to me to watch myself as a writer playing this part of a hopeless gallant. Sometimes I wish I were above such things.

Richards is surely your polite host, a subtle manager of affairs and full of many graces. Tonight at table I found our little dinner-card labeled "Theodore Dreiser and Party," printed, and I knew nothing of it before. After dinner there was a concert, the first I had ever seen on a liner. It was an amazing spectacle from one point of view. The whole thing was cooked up out of such poor material, and yet it realized over sixty-four pounds for some widows and orphans of sailors. Richards had some slight hand in this. At least he managed to have Miss Longfellow and Miss Burke appointed to collect the money (pass the plate), and I was tolled off by Sir William White—or was it Sir Richard?—the chairman, to superintend the counting of the money. As we say in American slang, "What do you know about that?"

It was a dreary affair, from one point of view, amusing from another. I had to smile when the concert was opened by a Mr. Owen scheduled to render "Alice, Where Art Thou?" Mr. Owen turned out to be, to my astonishment, a short, stout, red-faced understeward of some description, in a shabby blue uniform slightly too short in the legs, who carried a faded old book of ballads and sang his song from that. Far be it from me to cavil at the physical condition of any person or his right or pleasure to sing here. I don't. The only point was he couldn't sing. His hair was anything but thick and of a sandy color; his eyes watery and blue; his face, stolid and unemotional, took me by surprise. Is he really going to sing? I asked myself. The English have a peculiar stolidity of countenance, some of them, quite a race trait, which amuses me to begin with and wearies me a little afterward. And then Mr. Owen's expressionless eyes raised to heaven in an occasional musical (I couldn't say emotional) appeal to know where Alice really was—it was too much. He sang fearfully. It was an effort to reach all the higher and lower registers, and in all the difficult passages—the song is simple enough, in all conscience—his voice all but quavered. I saw at once that this was merely a money-raising scheme for the sailors and that the idea was that any old thing would do.

I was not mistaken. The violinist of the ship's orchestra, a tall, shambling, ill-put-together youth with a peculiar and disturbingly large nose and a noticeably thin neck, rendered a selection on his instrument, and not badly. Then came the cellist of the orchestra, who also rendered something as old as the hills, but good. Then the Princess Maura Kadato—I always think of the fairy Abracadabra when I hear that—sang. Who is the Princess Maura Kadato? I expected from the program that I should see a charming lady, but alas, no. I was to be disappointed. A rather tall girl, or woman, dark-haired, dark-eyed, of a rather smudgy complexion and having a thin growth of hair on her upper lip, came out and sang. She was weak and uninteresting, undecisive, with eyes that wandered aimlessly—whom I can best describe as sicky. If she were not a princess, you would never know that she was alive. A hall-bedroom type of girl who may be brilliant but who is without physical force. Sicky is the word—the kind from which I instantly physically recoil. She sang three indifferent songs in a colorless voice, and I noticed that her nice clothes merely hung on her. No shape, no air, no *esprit de corps*, no nothing. Avaunt the Princess Maura Kadato.

Then came a young, short, bespectacled Englishman, who one individual on board told me was a London music-hall favorite, and another that he was an accountant's "clark," and he was good, quite. His first two songs did not appeal to me so much, being of a peculiarly English turn, but when his third song described a careful, stingy man, I saw the point. He was rather above the average character-interpreter, interesting and pleasant. Then came some other passengers—a silly, nervous young man with his handkerchief in his sleeve, whom his friends had induced "to oblige." He was one of our Western "good family" type, genial but an ass. He sang "I Love a Lassie," and some middle-class composition of his own. I am sorry, but I have no patience with this sort of thing.

Then Sir William White, K.C.B., got up and told us what the meeting was all about. We had enjoyed the pleasant features of this concert, he said. We were enjoying a pleasant passage on this vast liner, but did we ever give a thought to the men who carried us so safely: the engineer, the sailors, the stokers in the hold, the men who have hard lives and carry us so safely? They were just as important to us as the captain and the officers of the company. Some people had to do this work, and these people did. There were references to widows and orphans, St. James's definition of "true religion and undefiled before our God and Father." Part of the money, we learned, was given to American seamen's charities, part to English. A slip or leaflet put on each seat carried a picture of a seamen's orphanage in Liverpool and the history of deaths in the Irish Channel—whither we were steaming—during the last thirty-five years. It was a gloomy record, decidedly uncomfortable. While he was talking, the boat lurched, as it did when the Princess Maura Kadato (of Italy, I learn) was singing. The faint vibration of the boat, the slow rolling to and fro, the sound of creaking woodwork, albeit highly carved and ornately arranged, brought to my mind the great sea outside. "Suppose," I said to myself, "that just now while the Honorable Sir William White is addressing us so blandly, and there is applause and hear-hears and polite complimentary and approving nods of this very comfortable company—supposing a boiler blew up or we struck an iceberg or the ship for some strange reason turned turtle. Imagine the consternation here. Imagine the end of polite hear-hears. Imagine these very comfortable evening-dressed gentlemen becoming heroes or cowards in the twinkling of an eye, or a little of both. Imagine the rush for the boats and the end of ceremony, and screams and prayers."

Well, this was a rank, anarchistic imagining. It was crude and impolite and uncalled-for. Melodramatic, you will say. Quite so. Still, it actually occurred to me, as it has to thousands before me. The creak of the wood and the swish of the sea outside did it. I mistrust humanity so that I always think of these things. I cannot help looking under the surface of veneer. It is such a thin substance. It cloaks old, old elemental things, storms of lust and hunger and confused elemental things. I do not always care for "Oh's" and "Ah's" and "You don't tell me's" and polite, evoluted things. In the parlance of the Bowery, they sometimes "give me a pain." And yet I know they represent the substance of life to some and there are those who could not live without them. They would die among raw, elemental things, like an oyster stripped of its shell. And to me an oyster is just as important.

Well, Sir William White, K.C.B., finished his address, and then he asked our Miss Longfellow and our Miss Burke to pass the plates. And he asked me to go to the purser's room and superintend the counting, which I did, although I scarcely knew one piece from another. There was sixty-four pounds, eight shillings and three pence in American, English and Canadian money, which they said was there and so reported to Sir William. When he told the assembled company, there was much polite applause.

Then there was some need to wind up the meeting, and another Englishman, much more typical to me than Sir William, proposed in a flowery speech that we extend to Sir William a vote of thanks, which we did. We learned that Sir William was a very noted ship architect, the very best in England; that he had designed this triumph of the sea; that somehow England owed some of its mercantile greatness to him, which I do not doubt. He seemed a very simple man, kindly and fair-minded. Then we sang "America" and "God Save the King," both printed on the same sheet of paper, and then we broke up. Sir William thanked me privately for counting the money and our party for letting our ladies collect the cash.

"You know," he smiled in explanation afterwards, "handsome ladies always do better in these matters than men." And it's quite true. "Our" ladies would have drawn money from the most impecunious, I fancy. They were so distingué.

Well, that being over, I drank a brandy and soda with Messrs. Owen and

McGee, "roasted" American trusts, inquired after the commercial and political honor of England, which Mr. Owen believed to be unblemished, and so went to bed.

Oh, no. I started to go to bed, but it being warm and fresh, I stepped outside. There were no fellow passengers, apparently, on the promenade. All had retired. The sky was magnificent for stars—Orion, the Pleiades, the Milky Way, the Big Dipper, the Little Dipper. I saw one star, off to my right as I stood at the prow under the bridge, which, owing to the soft, velvety darkness, cast a faint silvery glow on the water, just a trace. Think of it: one lone, silvery star over the great dark sea doing this. I stood at the prow and watched the boat speed on. I threw back my head and drank in the salt wind. I looked and listened. England, France, Italy, Switzerland, Germany—these were all coming to me mile by mile. As I stood there, a bell over me struck eight times; then another farther off sounded the same number. Then a voice at the prow called "All's well," and another aloft on that little eyrie called the crow's nest, which was a part of the one lone mast of this ship, echoed it. "All's well!" The second voice was weak and quavering.

Something came up in my throat—a quick, unbidden lump of emotion. Was it an echo of old journeys and old seas when life was not safe? What about Columbus? and Raleigh? and the Norsemen? What about the Phoenicians? and the Egyptians? and the Greeks? St. Paul writes, "And we being exceedingly tossed with a tempest"—quite so, fears and pains and terrors. And now the world has come to this vast ship, 882 feet long, 88 feet beam, with huge pits of engines and furnaces and polite, veneered first-cabin decks and passengers. I love life. It is strange, dangerous, beautiful, cruel. I love forms and variations, but I mistrust them utterly. I do not know who I am, or whence I am, or why I am. Only I am here, and I would that I were happy and could live so always.

CHAPTER VII

November 26: It is 10 A.M. When I roused and looked at my watch I thought it might be eight-thirty or seven. The day was slightly gray with spray flying. The sea is really a boisterous thing, threshing and licking in hills and hollows. I was thinking of Kipling's "White Horses" for a while.

There are several things about this great ship which are unique. It is a beautiful thing, all told, its long, cherry-wood-paneled halls in the first-class section, its heavy porcelain baths, its dainty staterooms fitted with lamps, bureaus, writing desks, washstands, and closets. I like the idea of dressing for dinner and seeing everything quite stately and formal. The little be-buttoned call-boys in their tight-fitting blue suits amuse me, and the bugler who bugles for dinner. That is a most musical sound he makes, trilling in the various quarters gaily, as much as to say, "This is a very joyous event, ladies and gentlemen; we are all happy; come, come, it is a delightful feast." I saw him one day in the lobby of C deck, his legs spread far apart, the bugle to his lips, no evidence of the rolling ship in his erectness, bugling heartily. It was like something out of an old medieval court or a play, very nice and worthwhile.

At lunch, which is breakfast for me, Mr. Owen, Mr. McGee, Miss Longfellow and Miss Burke, Mr. Grant Richards, Mr. George W. Smalley, Captain Turner and one or two others. The captain, very gay and chipper, says we cannot stop at Fishguard but will go on to Liverpool, which no one believes. A little small talk about this. Miss Burke, I'm afraid, isn't going to think so very much of me anymore. She doesn't understand me now, but takes me on faith, Grant Richards being the religionist announcing the gospel according to Theodore Dreiser. Miss Longfellow, crude and savage as she is, is nearer my blood. We are at dagger-points at times because she seems to like Grant Richards better. She would like me to ask her her opinion of my book, but I won't. She also thinks at times that I am pettish and somewhat of an ass. Very, very true indeed. Still, I find ways of evening matters at odd moments. And I shall probably pay Grant Richards "out" in some way, as the English express it. He turned a pretty trick, frightening me by complaining of what people would think. I notice peoples' thoughts are not so much of a factor, now that he has the inside track. A very politic, sophisticated, managerial gentleman who knows a very great deal, but not everything.

After lunch I went with the chief engineer through the engine room. This is a pit eighty feet deep, forty feet wide and perhaps one hundred feet long, filled with machinery. What a strange world. I know absolutely nothing of machinery, not a single principle connected with it, and yet I am intensely interested. These boilers, pipes, funnels, pistons, gauges, registers and bright-faced register boards speak of a vast technique which to me is tremendously impressive.

I know scarcely anything of the history of mechanics, but still I am fascinated. I know, of course, how certain principles are traced back to Egypt and Archimedes. I know the story of Watt and the tea kettle; of Fulton and his steamboat; of Stephenson and his engine. I know what boilers and feed-pipes and escape-pipes are and how complicated machinery is automatically oiled and reciprocated, but there my knowledge ends. All that I know about the rest is that which the race knows. There are mechanical and electrical engineers. They devised the reciprocating engine for vessels and then the turbine. They have worked out the theory of electrical control and have installed vast systems with a wonderful economy as to power and space. This deep pit is like some vast, sad dream of a fevered mind. It clanks and rattles and hisses and squeaks with almost insane contrariety. There are little, narrow, steep, oil-stained stairs, very hot or very cold and very slippery, that wind here and there in strange ways, and if you are not careful there are moving rods and wheels to strike you. You pass from bridge to bridge under whirling wheels, over clanking pistons, past hot containers, past cold ones. Here are men standing—blue-jumpered assistants in oil-stained caps and gloves—thin caps and thick gloves—watching the maneuvers of this vast network of steel far from the passenger life of the vessel. Occasionally they touch something. They are down in the very heart or the bowels of this thing, away from the sound of the water, away partially from the heaviest motion of the ship, listening only to this clank, clank and whir, whir and hiss, hiss all day long. It is a metal world they live in, a hard, bright, metal world. Everything is hard, everything fixed, everything regular. If they look up they behold a huge, complicated scaffolding of steel. Noise and heat and regularity.

I shouldn't like that, I think. My soul would grow weary. It would pall. I like the softness of scenery, the haze, the uncertainty of the world outside. Life is better than rigidity and fixed motion, I hope. I trust the universe is not mechanical, but mystically fluid. Let's hope it's a vague, uncertain, but divine idea. We know it is beautiful. It must be so.

Mr. Gillingham, the chief engineer, was a peculiar little man. Like Captain Turner, it was obvious that he had come up from nothing—hard conditions; one could see that. He was a hard little man, grim, irritable, jealous of his hard world of machinery. When I came to his door after his orderly or steward or cabin boy—or whatever he might have been called who was sent for me—had brought me to him, he stared at me defiantly. He looked me over critically, also with the air of one who says "Who in the world are you?" He was a little man, short, stout, quite like a little sausage packed into his blue suit. He was a kindly soul in his way, as one could see, for hard knocks and years had probably removed some of his early pugnaciousness.

"Is this Mr. Gillingham's office?"

"N'Yuss."

"Is this Mr. Gillingham?"

"N'Yuss."

I noticed that his left canine showed quite savagely as he said this, quite like a dog snarls, but it was not intentional—merely habit.

"I believe I am to be allowed to go over the engine rooms."

"You may be. Come in and sit down."

He turned from me to another individual who had just preceded me: a silly, self-advertising ass of about fifty-five or sixty whom I shall proceed to describe. There was a lean, slippered pantaloon in a gray suit and cap who had been in some phase of the engineering business once and knew it all. Have you ever met the man who takes an intense delight in airing all his knowledge at your expense and by way of asking you? He was with us this day. He did not know me, hence I was a fool and nothing. He did know who the chief engineer was, so to him the latter was a shining luminary. I despise this sort of silly ass; cravens, failures, tuft-hunters—you can spot them at a glance. Treading on the aching fingers of those below and licking the boots of those above. "God made all sorts," as some American once said to me, "but he must have regretted his handicraft in some instances. May love them all, but he can't admire them."

Well, we went about after a time, the engineer leading the way, and it was obviously his desire to be courteous to us both. There was no overcoming the sense of superiority and of his own importance in the mind of this second visitor. I never knew a man to be quite so eager to show me, a total stranger to him, that I was a negligible quantity to him, and to get between myself and any possible understanding of what was going on. It was positively laughable. There was nothing so important about the whole adventure—just a notion in this whiskered silly-billy's mind that it was his hour to shine. I listened as keenly as I could in this threshing world, but he offered no syllable of advice or information. He kept constantly between myself and the engineer and took my occasional questions with quite an air of being unnecessarily interrupted. I was on the verge once of making some direct, succinct commentary as to the asininity of his procedure, but I let the thought go. What was the use? I was seeing enough.

My compliments to Mr. Gillingham, however. A hard, thorough, interesting little man. I liked him. I liked his "N'Yuss" and his self-contained and yet defiant attitude, I hope sincerely that he has a fine, big ship, full of machinery, to look after for years and years to come.

After my visit to the engine room, I washed my hands of oil and worked on these notes. Afterward I dressed and went to dinner. At table Miss Longfellow was beside me. A remarkable person—I say it again. Velázquez should have painted her, or Whistler. Either would have understood her directly. We made up slightly for a little while. She accepted an invitation to a Thanksgiving dinner with me in London, which I afterwards broke, and wanted me to give her my address, but I asked her what was the use. How curious this feeling is between us can best be illustrated by several little incidents. Grant Richards had fixed up a little dinner-party, which he pretended Miss Longfellow had given. The dinner-card read "Miss Malvina Longfellow and Party." Mine read "Mr. Theodore Dreiser and Party," though I had nothing to do with it. She had been flirting with Grant Richards. His manipulation of the whole thing has been wise and clever. She asked me to write my name on her card as a souvenir. I said, "No." "Oh, all right," she flared, and turned a chilly shoulder on me.

"I have no pen," I cuttingly added.

"Yes, quite so," she replied. "The ship is without them."

Silence for five minutes, while I talk to Mr. Owen. Then later the music struck up Offenbach's "Barcarole." I hummed it. She joined.

"Where do you stop in London?" she asked.

"I don't know. With Grant Richards for two days. With my friends, the C.'s, for several after that, I am sure. Then some London hotel. Which would you recommend?"

"The Savoy, of course. You will see all the celebrated people you wish to see."

"I am sick of them already."

"And then it's convenient."

"To what?"

"Oh," archly, "things in general."

I make no comment.

She: "That reminds me. I do not get to eat a Thanksgiving dinner this year."

"Why not?"

"Where I am none is given."

"I hereby invite you. No American should want for that."

"You give me your address, and I'll write you."

"My general address, yes." I gave it.

"When I get settled I want you to come and meet my friends."

"Hang your friends. I don't care about them. You don't like me. So why should I bother about your friends?"

"But I do like you."

"You don't. Quit kidding. Cut it out."

"But I do. You're a masterful man. You don't understand. I can't do what you want."

"For me, you mean."

"What do you mean?"

"For me. Now, of course, if it were, say—"

"Oh, nonsense. Don't be silly. That's the silliest remark you've made yet."

"But it's true."

"Oh, don't be silly. It's not. That's the last thing. Please give me a little credit for something. You are certainly impossible."

"Quite so. But the gentleman at the end of the table is not."

"That's not true, I tell you."

"Don't lie. I know better. Don't take me for an utter chump. You don't like me. So let it go. However, the Thanksgiving dinner holds."

More badinage and general talk.

After a while Mr. Owen and I are talking about the beauty of the English women. I suggest that a tall Du Maurieresque lady in rather lacy, dowdy clothes, her hair parted gracefully in the middle, is typical.

"But not all are tall and lean," he ventures. "Some are shorter and more roundly built."

"But the universal standard commands a certain leanness. The lean ones should be typical."

Miss Longfellow (entering the conversation): "I prefer to be lean myself."

"To achieve that universal standard of use, I suppose," I reply. "A most serviceable standard."

"I think you're the most brutal man I have ever known," she flared. "I despise you—"

"Oh, no, moderately truthful," I replied.

"You have said things to me—"

"Hush. I'll sign the dinner-card."

With a toss of the head, "As if that were important!"

"But you do want it signed."

"Oh, no, I don't."

"That isn't true."

"Quite, I assure you."

"You're simply angry."

"You take yourself seriously, don't you?"

"But you are."

"One must have something to be angry about."

"Me, for instance."

"I'm not feeling well tonight. I'm going to my room and to bed."

"Will you let me sign the card?"

"No."

"Do I dine with you in London?"

"No, I don't think so."

"Well, that is more in keeping, anyhow. But I will send you the list of books." I had recommended a course of reading.

"Yes, if it's not too much trouble. It must be at your pleasure, however."

She rose and strolled away. Her mood was really hard and bitter. I felt a little sorry. I think we shall try to do better from now on. This is being too mean.

The final winding-up of this day occurred in the grand lounging or reception room where, after dinner, we all retired to listen to the music. I stopped in the writing room to write a note, and when I came back Mr. Grant Richards and Miss Longfellow were in one alcove on a settee talking, and Mr. Kahn and Miss Burke were in another. This Hebrew gentleman reminded me in his looks and ways of a hundred prosperous, rather well-mannered Jews I have seen in my time—Mrs. Wharton's Jew in *The House of Mirth* and the American comedian Sam Bernard in something I have seen him in. He was so smug, so assured, so very well able to take care of himself. He had the air of ownership which comes with prosperity and looked at me at times with a lucid note of inquiry in his eye as much as to say, "Who the devil are you and how do you come to find yourself on this ship?" Of course I returned his look blandly, almost mockingly, I'm afraid. I don't think he quite understood how I came to be with two so charming ladies, even if Grant Richards was a publisher and I an author. I think, if he thought at all, that he had the usual commercial contempt for authors and authorship. Anyhow he was with Miss Burke, and he did not relish my approach.

I asked permission to sit down. It was granted. We talked of music, and I happened to know what was being played in several instances when he did not. Miss Burke looked charming in a very chic green silk evening dress relieved by touches of white and silver. I noted her dainty patent leather slippers and the odd, woven texture of her stockings. In these days, six inches of stocking is little enough to see—eight or ten is more common. And then those narrow skirts which bind the hips so suggestively and showily. However! We talked aimlessly until ten, when Grant Richards and Miss Longfellow joined us. Then Mr. Kahn left and, shortly after, Miss Burke, accompanied for the moment, as far as her room, by Grant Richards. He returned after a moment, and then began one of those really interesting conversations between Grant Richards and Miss Longfellow which sometimes illuminate life and make one see things clearer forever afterward.

It is going to be very hard for me to define just how this could be, for, after all, I might say at the moment that I had considerable contempt for the point of view which the conversation represented. Consider, first, the American attitude. With us (not the established rich but the hopeful, ambitious American who has nothing, comes from nothing, and hopes to be President of the United States or John D. Rockefeller), the business of life is not living, but achieving. Roughly speaking, we are willing to go hungry, dirty, to wait in the cold and fight gamely if in the end we can achieve one or more of the seven stars in the human crown of life—social, intellectual, moral, financial, physical, spiritual or material supremacy. Several of the forms of supremacy may seem the same, but they are not. Examine them closely. The average American is not born to place. He does not know what the English sense of order is. We have not that national *esprit de corps* which characterizes the English and the French perhaps, certainly the Germans.

One of those really interesting conversations between Grant Richards and Miss Longfellow

We are loose, uncouth, elate, but, in our way, wonderful. The spirit of God has once more breathed upon the waters.

Well, the gentleman who was doing the talking in this instance and the lady who was coinciding, inciting, aiding, abetting, approving and at times leading and demonstrating, represented two different and yet allied points of view. Mr. Richards is distinctly, as I have clearly pointed out, I hope, a product of the English conservative school of thought, a gentleman who wishes sincerely he was not so conservative. His house is in order. You can feel it. I have always felt it in relation to him. His standards and ideals are fixed. He knows what life ought to be, how it ought to be lived. You would never catch him associating with the rag-tag and bobtail of humanity with any keen sense of human brotherhood or emotional tenderness of feeling. They are human beings, of course. They are in the scheme of things, to be sure. But let it go at that. One cannot be considering the state of the underdog at any particular time. Government is established to do this sort of thing. Statesmen are large, distinguished servants who are supposed to look after all of us. The masses! Let them behave. Let them accept their state. Let them raise no undue row. And let us, above all things, have law and order.

That is a section of Grant Richards; not all, mind you, but a section.

Miss Longfellow I think I have described fully enough, but I shall add one passing thought. A little experience of Europe, quite considerable of its show-places, has taught her, or convinced her rather, that America did not know how to live. You will hear much of that fact, I am afraid, during the rest of these pages, but it is especially important just here. My lady, prettily gowned, prettily manicured, going to meet her lover in London or Fishguard or Liverpool, is absolutely satisfied that America does not know how to live. She herself has almost learned. She has been most comfortably provided for this time. Anyhow, she has champagne every night at dinner. Her equipment in the matter of toilet articles and leather traveling bags is all that it should be. The latter are colored to match her complexion and gowns. She is scented, polished, looked after, and all men pay her attention. She repeated to me some of the worst stories I ever heard, and she knew all I knew. She is vain, beautiful, and she thinks that America is raw, uncouth; that its citizens, of whom she is one, do not know how to live. Quite so. Now we come to the point.

It would be hard to describe this conversation. It began with some "have-you-been's?" I think, and concerned eating places and modes of entertainment in London, Paris, Monte Carlo and elsewhere. It would be useless for me to try to remember names, for I cannot. I gather by degrees, though, that in London, Paris and elsewhere there were a hundred restaurants, a hundred places to live, each finer than the other. I heard of liberty of thought and freedom of action and pride of motion, which made me understand that there is a freemasonry which concerns the art of living. There is a world in which conventions as to morals have no place; in which ethics and religion are taboo. Art is the point. The joys of this world are sex, beauty, food, clothing, art. I should say money, of course, but money is presupposed. You must have it.

"Oh, I went to that place one day, and then I was glad enough to get back to the Ritz at forty francs for my room." She was talking of her room by the day. Food of course was extra. The other hotel had been a little bit quiet or dingy.

I opened my eyes slightly, for I thought Paris was reasonable; but not so—not more than New York, I understood at this point, if you do the same things.

"And, oh, the life," said Miss Longfellow at one point. "Americans don't know how to live. They are all engaged in doing something. They are such beginners. They are only interested in money. They don't know. I see them in Paris now and then," she lifted her hand. "Here in Europe people understand life better. They know how to live. They know before they begin how much it will take to do the things that they want to do, and they start out to make that much—not a fortune, just enough to do the things that they want to do. When they get that they retire and *live*."

"And what do they do when they live?" I asked. "What do you call living?"

"Oh, having a nice country house within a short traveling distance of London or Paris, being able to dine at the best restaurants and visit the best theaters once or twice a week, to go to Paris or Monte Carlo or Scheveningen or Ostend two or three or four—as many times a year as they please, to wear good clothes and to be thoroughly comfortable."

That is not a bad standard, I said, and then I added,

"And what else do they do?"

"And what else should they do? Isn't that enough?"

"It is. Yes. From one point of view. Quite so."

And there you have the European standard according to Miss Longfellow as contrasted with the American standard which is, or has been up to this time, something decidedly different, I am sure. We have not been so eager to live. Our idea has been to work. No American that I have ever known has had this idea of laying up just so much, a moderate amount, and then retiring and living. He has had quite another thought in his mind. The American—the average American—I am sure loves power, the ability to do something, the ability to be doing it, far more earnestly than he loves mere living. He wants to be an officer or director of something, a mayor or governor, a businessman, an architect, a poet, anything you please, for the sake of being it—not for the sake of living. He loves power, authority, to be able to say go and thou goest or come and thou comest. The rest he will waive—mere comfort. You can have that. But even that, according to Miss Longfellow, was not enough for her.

She had told me before, and this conversation brought it out again, that her thoughts were of summer and winter resorts, low-necked dresses, diamonds, open balconies of restaurants commanding charming vistas, gambling tables at Monte Carlo, Aix-les-Bains, Ostend and elsewhere, to say nothing of absolutely untrammeled sex relations. English conventional women were frumps and fools. They had never learned how to live, they had never understood what the joy of freedom in sex was. Morals—they have been built up on lack of imagination and physical vigor; ethics—what the hell are ethics? tenderness—well, you have to take care of yourself; duty—there isn't any such thing. If there is, it's one's duty to get along and have money and be happy.

I thought I knew something more of European life and standards, for Grant Richards appeared to concur in some of these things. I cannot tell very readily exactly what he does think. I fancy, though, that English order, American force, French comfort and European smartness generally make up his idea of what is right and proper.

After beer and sandwiches at twelve or thereabouts, we all went to bed.

CHAPTER VIII

November 27, 1911: I am writing these notes on Tuesday, November 28, very close to a grate-fire in a pretty white sitting room in an English country house about twenty-five miles from London, and I am very chilly. My feet are very chilly, and I have spent the night in a decidedly cold room in a chilly, detached stable, or extra house, which is pretty, however, and calculated to accommodate supernumeraries in the way of guests. I have landed at Fishguard and proceeded to London and come back to Cookham, and now I am going to tell you what I think. What I think! What I think! Is this thought? Or some aimless bubbling of sensation or emotion, or both? What is thought, anyway?

While I was lying in my berth this morning—I prefer writing as though it were yesterday—I heard the room steward outside my door tell someone that he thought we reached Fishguard at one-thirty. Somehow, from the original talk about reaching London late Monday night, I fancied that we would not reach Fishguard before six or six-thirty. Why, I don't know. Of course I have or had no definite idea of English distances, and I fancied Fishguard must be two or three hours from London, not more. It turned out to be five of fast running, and all of two hours getting from the paused ship to the moving train.

However, when I heard that, I got up. I had intended to lie until noon, for they had been shoving the clock forward so regularly that I did not think I was getting a fair night's rest at any time anyhow. But now I arose, feeling that I had to shave and pack and breakfast and that I would surely not have so much time before I should have to leave. The result proved this.

I packed my trunks, thinking of this big ship and the fact that my trip was over and that never again could I cross the Atlantic for the first time. A queer world, this. We can only do any one thing significantly once. I remember when I first went to Chicago. I remember when I first went to St. Louis. I remember when I first went to New York. Other trips there were, but they are lost in vagueness. But the first time of any important thing sticks and lasts. It comes back at times and haunts you with its beauty and its sadness. You know so well you cannot do that anymore; and, like a clock, it ticks and tells you that life is moving on. I shall never come to England anymore for the first time. That is gone and done for—worse luck.

But I packed—will you believe it?—a little sadly. I am a silly person from many points of view. There is in me the spirit of a little wistful child somewhere, and it clings pitifully to the hand of its big mama, Life, and cries when it is frightened. It longs for love and sympathy, and aches—oh, pathetically;

and then there is a coarse, vulgar exterior which fronts the world defiantly and bids all and sundry to go to the devil. It sneers and barks and jeers bitterly at times, and guffaws and cackles and has a joyous time laughing at the follies of others.

I packed and then went to hunt Grant Richards, to find out how I should do. How much was I to give the deck steward; how much the bath steward; how much the room steward; how much the dining room steward; how much "boots," and so on.

"Look here!" observed that most efficient of all managerial souls that I have ever known. "I'll tell you what you do. No, I'll write it," and he drew forth an ever-ready envelope.

"Deck steward: so much," it read.

"Room steward: so much—" etc.

I went forthwith and paid them, relieving my wistful soul of a great weight. Then I came on deck and found that I had forgotten to pack my ship blanket or steamer rug, which I forthwith went and packed. Then I discovered that I had no place for my derby hat save on my head, so I went back and packed my cap. Then I thought I had lost one of my brushes, which I hadn't, though I did lose one of my stylo pencils. Finally I came on board and sang coon songs with Miss Longfellow, sitting in our steamer chairs. The low shore of Ireland had come into view with two faint hills in the distance, and these fascinated me. I thought I should have some slight emotion on seeing land again, but I didn't. It was gray and misty at first, but presently the sun came out beautifully clear, and the day was as warm as May in New York. I felt a sudden elation of spirits with the coming of the sun, and I began to think what a lovely time I was going to have in Europe.

Miss Longfellow was a little more friendly this morning than before. She is a tricky beast, coy, uncertain and hard to please. She liked me intellectually and thought I was able, but her physical and emotional predilections so far as men are concerned did not include me.

We rejoiced together singing, and then we fought. There is a directness between experienced intellects which waves aside all formalities. She had seen a lot of life; so had I. She said she thought she would like to walk a little.

"Certainly," I said.

We strolled back along the heaving deck to the end of the first-cabin section and then, under a rail, via the second-cabin deck to the stern. We were on B deck all the time, which really did not extend to the stern of the ship but near it. When we reached there, the sky was overcast again, but it was one of those changeable mornings which is now gray, now bright, now misty. Just now the heavens were black and lowering with soft, woolly, rain-charged clouds—like the wool of a smudgy sheep. The sea was a rich green in consequence—not a clear green but a dark, muddy, grass-green. It rose and sank in its endless unrest, and one or two boats appeared—a lightship anchored out all alone against the lowery waste, and a small, black, passenger steamer going somewhere.

"I wish my path in life were as white as that and as straight," observed Miss Longfellow, pointing to the white, propeller-churned wake which extended back for half a mile or so.

"Yes," I observed, "you do and you don't. You do, if it wouldn't cause you trouble in the future—impose the straight and narrow, as it were. Anyhow, it isn't."

"Oh, you don't know," she exclaimed irritably, that ugly fighting light coming into her eyes which I had seen there several times before. "You don't know what my life has been. I haven't been so bad. We all of us do the best we can. I have done the best I could, considering."

"Yes, yes," I observed bitterly and cynically, I think, "let it go at that. Anyhow, you have your good points. You're ambitious and alive, and you're seeking heaven knows what. You would be fine with your pretty face and body if you were not so sophisticated. The trouble with you is—"

"Oh, look at that cute little boat out there!" She was talking of the lightship. "I always feel sorry for a poor little thing like that, set aside from the main tide of life and left lonely, with no one to care for it."

"The trouble with you is," I went on, seizing this new remark as an additional pretext for analysis, "you're romantic, not sympathetic. You're interested in that poor little lonely boat because its state is romantic, not pathetic. It may be pathetic, but that isn't the point with you."

"Why isn't it?"

"Because it isn't."

She did not argue this. There was an element of straight, striking, intellectual honesty about her which I admired very much.

"Well," she said, "if you had had all the hard knocks I have had you wouldn't be sympathetic either. I've suffered, I have. My illusions have been killed as dead—"

"As a doornail," I added.

"It's so."

"Yes. Love is over with you. You can't love anymore. You can like to be loved, that's all. If it were the other way about—"

I paused to think how really lovely she would be with her narrow lavender eyelids, her delicate, almost *retroussé* little nose, her red cupid's bow mouth.

"Ah," she exclaimed with a gesture of almost religious adoration. "I cannot love any one person anymore, but I can love love, and I do—all the delicate things it stands for."

"Flowers," I observed, "jewels, automobiles, hotel bills, fine dresses."

"Oh, you're brutal! I hate you!"

"No, you don't."

"Yes, I do."

"No, you don't."

"Yes, I do. You're a brute. You've said the cruelest, meanest things that have ever been said to me."

"But they're so."

"I don't care. Why shouldn't I be hard? Why shouldn't I love, live and be loved? Look at my life. See what I've had."

"Even so. But you don't hate me."

"No, I don't like you."

"You like me, in a way."

"I admire your intellect."

"Quite so. And others receive the gifts of your personality."

"I can't help it. I can't be mean to the man I'm with. He's good to me. I won't. I'd be sinning against the only conscience I have."

"I think you're lying, but let it go at that. You're nice, anyhow."

"I know I'm nice."

"Let's walk back."

So back we came.

They were blowing a bugle for lunch when we came back, and down we went. Grant Richards, Owen, Mr. McGee, Miss Burke were all there, eating their farewell meal. The orchestra was playing "Auld Lang Syne," "Home, Sweet Home," "Dixie" and the "Swanee River." It even played one of those delicious American rags which I love so much—"The Oceana Roll." I felt a little lump in my throat at "Auld Lang Syne" and "Dixie," and together Miss Longfellow and I hummed "The Oceana Roll" as it was played. One of the girl passengers came about with a plate to obtain money for the members of the orchestra, and half-crowns were universally deposited. Then I started to eat my dessert, but Grant Richards, who had hurried off, came back to interfere.

"Come, come!" He is always most emphatic. "You're missing it all. We're landing."

I thought we were leaving at once. The eye behind the monocle was premonitory of some great loss to me. I hurried on deck—to thank his artistic and managerial instinct instantly I arrived there. Before me was Fishguard and the Welsh coast, and to my dying day I shall never forget it. It was beautiful.

Imagine, if you please, a land-locked harbor, as green as glass in this semi-cloudy, semi-gold-bathed afternoon, with a half-moon of granite scarp rising sheer and clear from the green waters to the low gray clouds overhead. On its top I could see fields laid out in pretty squares or oblongs, and at the bottom of what to me appeared to be the east end of the semi-circle was a bit of scrub or gray which was the village, no doubt. On the green water were several other boats—steamers, much smaller, with red stacks, black sides, white rails and funnels—bearing a family resemblance to the one we were on. There was a long pier extending out into the water from what I took to be the village, and something farther inland which looked like a low shed. On the face of one part of the rocky wall was a white sign in large letters—Oxo.

"What's that?" I asked of Grant Richards much later, as we were nearing the pier.

"It's a beef extract, I think, something like Liebig's."

It gave life a rough, workaday touch for the moment to me.

But when I came up on deck, not only was this lovely scene before me but there were, let us say, a thousand (there may have been only a hundred or two, but let us say a thousand) gulls or tern flying about. All my life I have loved flying birds. In a collection of essays somewhere, unpublished and perhaps worthless, I have written one on "The Flight of Pigeons." Ever since I have been old enough to know, a bird on the wing has haunted me with a suggestion of infinite beauty. In my boyhood days in Indiana, the sight of a buzzard or a hawk soaring in the sky has aroused in me an uncontrollable sense of joy. I have always wanted to fly. Time and again I have dreamed of flying beautifully over hills and valleys, seeing all that was stretched out below. The wide wings of the eagle, the pinions of the condor, the ordered ranks of wild geese flying geometrically, have literally thrilled me. I have thought of endless similes—snowflakes, wind-blown leaves, poised angels. Once in Newark, New Jersey, in some cheap, wooden-housed back street I saw a great flock of wheeling pigeons, soaring now high, now low, and once they came so near the shush of their happy wings filled my ears. I could have cried. I could have clapped my hands. I could have mounted as an eagle, never to descend to earth again. But they were gone over the black, shabby housetops, and I was still in my back street in Newark, New Jersey. So may the seraphim sweep at a trumpet's call. So may the messenger of majesty enthroned hurtle through the abyss of space.

This black hotel of a ship, so vast, so graceful, now rocking gently in this enameled bay, was surrounded this hour by wheeling, squeaking gulls. I always like the squeak of a gull, for it reminds me of a rusty car wheel, and somehow it accords with a lone, rocky coast. Here they were, their little feet coral red, their beaks jade gray, their bodies snowy white or sober gray, wheeling and crying, "My heart remembers how." I looked at them, and that old, intense sensation of joy came back, the wish to fly, the wish to be young, the wish to be happy, the wish to be loved. I think my lips framed verses, and I think I thought that if nature in her vast, sightless chemistry would only give me something to feed this intense emotion to the full, I should welcome eternal sleep.

Anyhow, my scene, beautiful as it was, was slipping away. There was one of the pretty steamers I had noted lying on the water some distance away drawing alongside. To get mails, first, they said. There were hurrying and shuffling people on all the first-cabin decks. Miss Burke was looking for Mr. Grant Richards. Mr. Grant Richards was looking after his luggage. I saw Sir William White coming forward to greet the captain where he stood in his great gold-braided blue overcoat on the bridge. I saw the captain come forward then and grasp his hand. There were mail chutes being lowered from our giant vessel's side, and then bags and trunks and boxes and bales were sent scuttling down. I saw dozens of uniformed men and scores of ununiformed laborers briskly handling these in the sunshine, and by turns my eyes would stray to the gulls, to the captain on his bridge, to the tall stone hills, to the green water, to everything. My fellow passengers in their last hurrying hour interested me, for I knew I should see them no more. Then the mail and trunks being off, that boat veered away; another and somewhat smaller one came alongside, and we first- and second-class passengers went aboard that, and I watched the great *Mauretania* growing less and less as we pulled away from it.

It was immense, curiously, from alongside—a vast skyscraper of a ship. At a hundred feet, it seemed not so immense but more distinguished as a ship. At a thousand feet, all its lines were exquisite and perfect, its bulk not so great but the pathos of its departing beauty wonderful. At two thousand feet, it was still beautiful and large against the granite ring of the harbor, but alas, it was moving. The captain was an almost indistinguishable spot upon his bridge. The stacks were, in their way, gorgeous, taking on beautiful proportions. I thought, as we veered in near to the pier and the *Mauretania* turned within her length or thereabouts and steamed out, I had never seen a more beautiful sight. Her convoy of gulls was still about her, angels of art. Her smokestacks flung back thin, graceful steamers. The propellers left a white trail of foam. I asked someone, "When does she get to Liverpool?"

"At two in the morning."

"And when do the balance of the passengers land?" We had practically emptied the first class.

"At seven, I fancy."

Just about then, the lighter bumped against the dock. I saw upon some nearby rails a strange kind of car. There was a new kind of freight car, smaller than ours, and a different passenger car. I walked under a long, low train shed covering four tracks, I fancy, and then I saw my first English passenger train—a semi-octagonal-looking affair (the ends of the cars certainly looked as though they had started out to be octagons), and there were little doors on the side labeled "First," "First," "First." On the side at the top of the car was a longer sign, "Cunard Ocean Special—London—Fishguard."

I knew of course that that was our train.

The intricacies of the English baggage-checking system had troubled me no little since I had started, for who is there that does not fret some about his baggage? In America we do differently, of course. If we are going anywhere there and our trunks are ready, or sure to be, we telephone for an expressman who takes our trunks, bags, etc. and gives us separate check stubs, one for each. These we present at the baggage room, always connected with the depot—or station, as the English speak of it—and these, if we have our tickets, are exchanged for railway baggage checks. We do not need to hunt our baggage out on any platform; we do not need to think about it anymore until we reach home or the house of our friends. There we call another expressman, give him our railway baggage checks, and he brings us our trunks. Needless to say, the large American express companies which call for and deliver trunks are reliable.

Not so in England, and I suppose elsewhere (at this writing) on the Continent. Here at Fishguard I saw the difference instantly. Indeed, I saw some of the difference on the Cunard dock in New York. Before I sent my trunks to the dock, I was compelled to label them D. with a large poster D.; also S.S. *Mauretania,* with another poster; also "First Cabin" with another poster, and so on. Truthfully, I never saw my property so well labeled and directed before in all my life. We are more easygoing than that in America.

Before I reached the dock at 13th Street in New York I was told that having done all this, I would have to sort my baggage out of many other pieces at a stand labeled D., there being a baggage stand for every letter in the alphabet. Not so. When I came, I presented my express stubs.

"In your cabin, sir."

And there they were.

Then there were letters to post and the business of unpacking, and after that I worried no more about my luggage until I reached Fishguard.

Here it was a different story. I now realized more clearly what these alphabetical stands were, and in the confusion I hurried to where I was told—the sign of the letter D. And behold, there were my trunks, safe and sound.

My porter, annexed by the executive Richards, was there with me, urging the inspector of customs to "look at these, please, sir." He didn't get much attention for all his urging, which was intended to impress me more, I think, than it was the inspector. Finally he came—a small, dark man in a blue suit, who said he would have the smaller trunk opened. There being no wines, cigars, etc., he closed it again quickly.

"Now we're all right, sir," exclaimed my porter, and I was shown to where seat #98 was.

The difference in baggage handling, of sorting out your own baggage, was really no greater than the difference in the number and temper of railway assistants here and elsewhere, as contrasted with our American scheme of things.

Right here I propose to interpolate my second dissertation on the servant question, and I can safely promise, I am sure, that it will not be the last. One night, not long before, dining in New York at the Ritz with Baron R. and Grant Richards, I asked them both what to them was the most offensive or objectionable thing about America. One said expectorating; the other said the impoliteness of servants. I know why all that is—I have studied it at leisure, but I shall not expatiate on it here. On the *Mauretania*, at Fishguard, in the train from Fishguard to London, at London, and here in this country house after but a few minutes, I saw what the difference was. Of course I have heard these differences discussed before ad lib. for years, but hearing is not believing. Seeing and experiencing is.

On shipboard I noticed for the first time in my life that there was an aloofness about the service rendered by the servants which was entirely different to that which we know in America. They did not look at one so brutally and critically as does the American menial. Their eyes did not seem to say, "I am your equal or better," and their motions did not indicate that they were doing anything unwillingly. In America—and I am a good American—I have always had the feeling that the American hotel or house servant or store clerk—particularly store clerk—male or female—was doing me a great favor if he did anything at all for me. As for trainmen and passenger boat assistants, I have never been able to look upon them as servants at all. Mostly they have looked on me as an interloper and as someone who should be put off the train instead of assisted in going anywhere. American conductors are czars. American brakemen and trainhands grand dukes at least. A porter is little less than a highwayman. And a hotel clerk—God forbid that we should mention him in the same breath with any of the foregoing.

However, as I was going on to say, when I went aboard the *Mauretania*, I felt this burden of serfdom to the American servant lifted. These people, strange to relate, did not seem anxious to fight with me. They were actually civil. They did not stare me out of countenance; they did not order me gruffly about. And really I am not a princely soul, looking for obsequious service—truly, I am not. I am, I fancy, a very humble-minded person when traveling or living, anxious to go briskly forward, not to be disturbed too much and allowed to live in quiet and seclusion.

The American servant is not built for that. In the main, he is not a servant at all. One must have great social or physical force to command him. At times, he needs literally to be cowed by threats of physical violence. You are paying him? Of course you are. You help do that when you pay your hotel bill or buy your ticket or make a purchase, but he does not know that. The officials of the companies for whom he works do not appear to know. If they do, I don't know how they would be able to do anything about it. You cannot make a whole people over by issuing a book of rules. Americans are free men. They don't want to be servants. They have despised the idea for years. I think the early Americans who lived in America after the Revolution, the anti-Tory element, thought after the war having won their nationality that there was to be an end of servants. I think they associated service of this kind with slavery, and they thought when England had been defeated all these other things such as menial service had been defeated also.

Alas, superiority and inferiority have not yet been done away with—quite. Slow brains and swift brains still exist. There are the strong and the weak; the passionate and the passionless; the hungry and the well-fed. There are those who still think that life is something which can be put into a mold and adjusted to a theory, but I am not one of them. I cannot view life or human nature save as an expression of contraries—in fact, I think that is what life is. I know there can be no sense of heat without cold; no fullness without emptiness; no force without resistance—no anything, in short, without its contrary. Consequently, I cannot see how there can be great men without little ones; wealth without poverty; social movement without willing social assistance. I may be all wrong. My social economy, chemistry, physics, biology, sociology may be pointless, but as yet I cannot see it. No high without a low, is my idea, and I would have that the low be intelligent, efficient, useful, well-paid, well-looked after. And I would have the high be sane, kindly, considerate, useful, of good report and good will to all men.

But, to proceed. When I got aboard the *Mauretania*, I felt this difference. Years of abuse and discomfort have made me rather antagonistic to servants. I felt no reasonable grounds for antagonism here. They were behaving properly. They weren't staring at me. I didn't catch them making audible remarks behind my back. They were not descanting unfavorably upon any of my fellow passengers. Things were actually going smoothly and nicely, and they seemed rather courteous about the whole thing. Isn't that strange!

Yes, and it was so in the dining room, in the bath, on deck, everywhere, with "yes, sirs" and "thank you, sirs" and two fingers raised to cap visors occasionally for good measure. Were they acting? Was this a fiercely suppressed class I was looking upon here? I could scarcely believe it. They looked too comfortable. I saw them associating with each other a great deal. I heard scraps of conversation. It was all peaceful and genial and individual enough. They were, apparently, leading unrestricted private lives. However, I reserved judgment until I should get to England. I am still reserving judgment. However, at Fishguard it was quite the same, and more also. I felt this difference between the English and American temperament, insofar as servants are concerned. These railway guards and porters and conductors were not our railway conductors, brakemen and porters by a long shot. Never, in a thousand years. They were different in their attitude, texture and general outlook on life. Physically I should say that American railway employees—I dread to use the word servant in connection with them, for servants assuredly they are not—are superior to the European brand. They are, on the whole, better fed, or at least better put up. They seem bigger to me, as I recall them; harder, stronger, though I may be mistaken. The English railway employee seems smaller and more refined physically, less vigorous.

But as to manners. Heaven save the mark! These people are civil. They are nice. They are willing. "Have you a porter, sir?" "Yessir! Thank you, sir! This way, sir! No trouble about that, sir. In a moment, sir! Certainly, sir! Very well, sir!" I heard these things on all sides, and they were like balm to a fevered brain. Life didn't seem so strenuous with these people about. They were actually trying to help me along. I was led, I was shown, I was explained to, I got under way without the least distress and I began actually to feel as though I were being coddled. Why, I said, these people are going to spoil me. I'm going to like them. And I had rather decided that I wouldn't like the English—why, I don't know—though I never read a great English novel that I didn't rather like all of the characters in it. Hardy's lovely country people have warmed the cockles of my heart. George Moore's English characters have made me feel they were excellent. I have followed Barrie with infinite zest in spots, and Jerome K. Jerome in *Three Men in a Boat* made me think the Englishmen the ultimate of compatibility. And here was Grant Richards, for instance. But the way the train employees bundled me into my seat and got my bags in after or before me, and said "We shall be starting now in a few minutes, sir," and called quietly and pleadingly—not yelling, mind you—"Take your seats, please" delighted me.

I didn't like the looks of the cars. I can prove in a moment by any traveler that our trains are infinitely more luxurious. I can see where there isn't heat enough, and where one lavatory for men and women on any train, let alone a first-class one, is an abomination, and so on and so forth, but still and notwithstanding, I say the English railway service is better. Why? Because it's more human; it's more considerate. You aren't driven and urged to step lively and called at in loud, harsh voices and made to feel that you are being tolerated aboard something which was never made for you at all but for the employees of the company. And now that I have that one distinct difference between England and America off my chest, I feel much better.

CHAPTER IX

Finally the train was started, and we were off. All the time we had been landing and getting our baggage together, I had been comparing the American railway with the English railway materially. Let me write here that from that point of view, the Englishman who has not been to the United States does not know what a real railway is. I looked at the tracks while we were waiting, and I saw that the rails were not hundred-pound rails like those on our big trunk-lines but lighter—perhaps sixty or seventy, if even so much. The track was not as wide, if I am not mistaken, and the little freight or goods cars were positively ridiculous—mere wheelbarrows. As for the passenger cars, when I came to examine them they reminded me of some of our fine streetcars that run from, say, Schenectady to Gloversville, or from Muncie to Marion, Indiana. They were the first-class cars, too—the English Pullmans. I looked at the woodwork, and it was flimsy and cheap. I studied the upholstery—our cushioned streetcars are just as nice.

The train started out briskly, and you could feel that it did not have that great powerful weight to it which the American train has. An American Pullman creaks significantly, just as a great ship does, when it begins to move. An American engine begins to pull slowly because it has something to pull, like a team with a heavy load. I didn't feel that I was in a train half so much as I did that I was in a string of baby carriages. They clicked along as gaily as a string of baby carriages might, and when you consider the size of England you immediately say "Why not?" They don't have to cross from the Atlantic to the Pacific, or from New York to the City of Mexico, as some Pullmans do. There are no extreme changes from heat to cold, and vice versa. Three hundred miles, I am told, is the average distance any train runs, and that is like going from New York to Rochester or from Chicago to St. Louis! So why heavy trains? They are cute enough and they carry one quite smoothly. It would be silly to have heavier ones.

But somehow I could not help thinking with pride of the long steel expresses—ten, twelve and fourteen cars long—with their tremendous baggage cars, their steel day-coaches, their heavy Pullmans and their gorgeous dining cars beginning slowly to move for Chicago, St. Louis, Palm Beach, Montreal, New Orleans, San Francisco and the City of Mexico. Those are trains! And to know that all those far-flung lines of steel were a part of that one great empire that has always insisted that it must be free was another interesting thought to me. But that did not alter the superiority of the English service. America is a real empire in itself, though England has the distinction of being a broken one.

These long lines are so like the visions of all our great men, from Washington to Roosevelt, from Jefferson and Lincoln to Grant and Walt Whitman—that all that is done must be done for all. We have had seemingly amazingly greedy men, but we have had them always by right of their vast ideas, and that is as true of old Commodore Vanderbilt and Jay Gould as it is of J. P. Morgan and John D. Rockefeller. We might well love those old sharks, for in spite of their shortcomings and evil deeds in many directions, we also know that in some respects, they have done wonderfully by us. America had to be materially united and quickly, and only greed and ambition would accomplish it; anyhow, what they did had to be done, the doctrine of all men being free and equal (which they're not) to the contrary notwithstanding.

But once more to this train. Will we ever get to London? I can hear you say: "Well, let's try again. Let's see." We started, and now just as we are going, I have to go back to Miss Longfellow and Miss Burke for a moment. I have commented on these two considerably, but they form an integral part of my early impressions. Even as we were coming away from the steamer I had a final word with Miss Longfellow, for she had a telegram in her hand, come from somewhere, and I saw she was smiling slightly.

"Aha! So he's coming, is he?" I commented.

"He's here," she replied. "He's on the dock."

"Now for a high old time," I commented, and for joy or for revenge—I couldn't tell which—she clasped her hands in a kind of ecstasy.

Women know how to manage subtle thrusts, but it didn't matter so much now. After watching her various gyrations I wasn't so interested. I didn't believe she would be exclusively anyone's for any reasonable period, and that thought irritates me—a strumpet of a woman. A true mistress is quite another matter—they have always been the great sex figures of the world from Helen on. I watched her movements as she neared the dock, and suddenly I saw her face light up. He was on it, looking down at her, a smooth, well-set-up figure of a man, distinctly English, very conservative in his dress, smiling, decidedly good-looking. He had that ruddy glow of health which the English gentry have, I fancy, that glow which results from the privileges of ample rest and exercise. You could tell by his very air that he was used to money. There were faint, whitish little wrinkles at the sides of his eyes—the wrinkles of forty—and his eyes were steady, blue, good-natured. I thought at once, "a fairly resourceful man. He prides himself much on this toy he has bought, but he doesn't love her wildly. He couldn't. He hasn't the temperament for it."

But not knowing him at all, I couldn't really insist on that. He might. I am very ready to jump at conclusions, I notice, which subsequently I am compelled to retract.

And meantime I had also been following Miss Burke, dear little Dresden china lady with her lovely complexion, her chic hats, her pretty, weak chin, her soft, gray-blue eyes and her smart, close-fitting gowns. I never saw a more dainty little lady in all my life nor one with a more pleasing accent nor one with a kindlier air, and yet one who I fancy had quite a little will of her own and could be very cross and very mean if she would. Kittens have almost as much facility at biting and scratching as cats, and yet I couldn't, and can't, think of her as doing very much of that. Secretly, I was very glad that she was well-known and that she had a maid and that she had money—some, I hope, anyhow. Most of the women I have seen with these jewels of fortune haven't been as dainty and sweet as she. She reminded me of George Moore's "Doris" in "The Lovers of Orelay," and I had a haunting sense that maybe she wasn't as well-off as she seemed and that maybe fortune wouldn't stay by her. I sincerely hope that the contrary is true. She was constantly looking about as we began to leave, asking "Now what do you suppose has become of Bullen?"—Bullen was her maid—and "I suppose all my trunks have gone safely aaf." She never said "Awff," as we say it.

From her I learned what the cause of all the trouble between England and America really is. It's the letter "A." We pronounce it as "a" in "hay" is pronounced, while they pronounce it as we pronounce "o" in "hot." It makes all the difference in the world. "Laughter" becomes "laafter," and "bath," "bawth," only more so, for they go still farther and linger lovingly on certain syllables. It actually surprised me to hear how long Miss Burke and others could linger on the vowels of certain words—one vowel, for instance, in one or two particular words in a sentence. Our "awfully nice" became "a-w-" (put a long pause in here) "-fully nice," and I liked to hear it. But to hear three- and four-year-old children saying "raather" in the same drawling way and calling a bath a "bawth" with the same long, lingering accent was too much. I didn't resent it. I felt lost.

Well, Miss Burke wasn't sure at first whether Bullen had got off the liner on to the lighter, and then when she was finally satisfied on that score by her maid placidly turning up at the last minute, she wasn't sure when we were on the train whether Bullen had been so foolish as to get on the second train instead of the first. (There were two trains leaving Fishguard for London, one a few minutes after the other.) There were some tea cakes in a tin or a box which were lost, and I thought at first by the excitement which followed this discovery that she had lost one of her ten handsome trunks. Bullen tickled me. She was so unconcerned.

"Well, it's gone," she said with an air of finality which was as disconcerting as it was consoling. "I told you to let me pack it, but you wouldn't. Maybe the next time you will." Her accent was almost like that of her mistress, not quite so refined.

I felt again, as I had before, that Bullen was a sort of guide and mentor to Miss Burke and that the latter's affairs could be left safely in her hands.

Miss Longfellow and her lover, Miss Burke and her maid, Grant Richards and I comfortably filled one little compartment, and now we were actually moving, and I began to look out at once to see what English scenery was really like. It was not at all strange to me, for in books and pictures I had seen it all my life, but here were the actual hills and valleys, the actual thatched cottages, if there are any, and the actual castles or moors or lovely country vistas, and I was seeing them.

As I think of it now, I can never be quite sufficiently grateful to Grant Richards for a certain affectionate, thoughtful, sympathetic regard for my every possible mood on this occasion. This was my first trip to this England of which, of course, he was intensely proud. He was so humanly anxious that I should not miss any of its charms or, if need be, defects. He wanted me to be able to judge it fairly and humanly and to see, as he phrased it, "the eventual result sieved through my temperament." The soul of attention; the soul of courtesy; patient, long-suffering, humane, gentle. How I have tried the patience of that man at times! An iron mood he has on occasion; a stoic one, always. Gentle, even, smiling, living a rule and a standard. Every thought of him produces a grateful smile. Yet he had his defects—plenty of them. Here he was at my elbow, all the way to London, momentarily suggesting that I do not miss the point, whatever the point might be, at the moment. He was a little proud of me in a superior way—a little desirous of showing me off, but what of it? He was helpful, really interested, and above all and at all times, warmly human.

We had been just two hours getting from the boat to the train. It was three-thirty when the train began to move, and from the lovely, misty sunshine of the morning the sky had become overcast with low, gray and almost black rain clouds. I looked at the hills and valleys—they told me we were in Wales—and curiously, as we sped along, first came Wordsworth into my mind, and then Thomas Hardy. I thought of Wordsworth first because these smooth, kempt hills, wet with rain and static with deep, gray shadows, suggested him. Some low stone cottages, not thatched but gray and black with moss perhaps, brought back—I can't tell you why—the dead Lucy and that soft, sweet, homey atmosphere which Wordsworth loved to picture. Perhaps I am thinking mostly of the poems called "The Solitary Reaper" and that other, "The Boy and the Owls," though neither of these suggest a gray, lowering landscape. Perhaps, better yet, it was the little low cottages of stone and whitewash, set down in green and brown angles of earth, hugging that dear brown mother of us all, that brought him back.

England owes so much to William Wordsworth, I think. So far as I can see, he epitomized in his verses this sweet, simple hominess that tugs at my heartstrings like some old call that I have heard before. My father was a German, my mother of Pennsylvania Dutch extraction, and yet there is a pull here in this Shakespearean-Wordsworthian-Hardyesque world which is precisely like the call of a tender mother to a child. I can't resist it. I love it. I love it so much that it even hurts me—and I am not English but radically American.

As we sped on and I saw that low, gray light that sometimes differentiates a sodden, rainy landscape, I thought of Shakespeare's "Weird Sisters" on the heath—"Saw you the weird sisters?" Macbeth came back and that distinguished call "All hail to thee, Macbeth, Thane of Glamis! Hail to thee, Macbeth, Thane of Cawdor! Thou shalt be king hereafter!" Oh, that majestic intellect! Oh, that lovely solvent of a nation's emotions and feelings! Shakespeare and England. We all bask in the glory of his golden ray.

And then Thomas Hardy. I understand that Hardy is not as well thought of as he might be in England, that somehow some large conservative class thinks that his books are immoral or vulgar or destructive. I say to you gentlemen and ladies of England that you had better make much of Thomas Hardy while he is alive and while you may. He is one of your great traditions. His works are beautiful. The spirit of all things he has done or attempted is lovely. His is a master mind, simple, noble, dignified, serene. He is as fine as any of your cathedrals to me. St. Paul's or Canterbury has no more significance to me than Thomas Hardy. I shall see St. Paul's. I wish I could see the spirit of Thomas Hardy indicated in some such definite way. And yet I do not.

Monuments do not indicate great men. Your fields and valleys do. Your rains, your sunshine, your roads, your cottages. I see a gardener outside my window in this suburban cottage, and he is Thomas Leaf to me or Joseph Poorgrass. Hardy has made him more real than this man, long before I saw his living counterpart, and so he shall remain. Tess D'Urberville is present in this housemaid who brings me my tea and my "bawth." I see England in Hardy, rural England, and nature has done you great honor to have created so fine a mind. Give honor unto Hardy while you may. You may not much longer, for he will not be here to honor, save in spirit.

At twenty or thirty miles from Fishguard we came to some open water—an arm of the sea, I understood—the Bay of Bristol, where boats were and tall, rain-gutted hills that looked like tumbledown castles. Then came more open country—moorland, I suppose—with some sheep; once a flock of black ones, and then the lovely, alternating hues of this rain-washed world. The water under these dark clouds took on a peculiar luster. It looked at times like burnished steel, at times like muddy lead. I felt my heart leap up as I thought of our own George Inness and what he would have done with these scenes and what the English Turner has done, though he preferred, as a rule, another key.

At four-thirty one of the charming English trainmen came and asked if we would have tea in the dining car (didn't yell, mind you, "Last call for tea in the dining car!"). We would. We arose and in a few moments were entering one of those dainty little basket cars, paneled—oh, quite like an English house—in black and bird's-eye maple or white-painted wood, I forget which. It was for all the world like a nice, sweet, cozy little dining room in a pretty English inn. (I haven't seen one yet—only pictures.) The chairs were of thin, black wood with padded cloth seats to match. The tables were covered with white linen and simple, pretty china and a silver tea service. It wasn't as if you were really traveling at all. I felt as though I were stopping at the house of a friend or were in the cozy corner of some well-known and friendly inn.

Tea was served. We ate toast and talked cheerfully. Miss Burke retailed some of her experiences with some of her relatives and stingy friends. Grant Richards was most anxious that I should not miss any of the significance of the landscape and insisted that I keep my nose to the window. Miss Longfellow and her charming protector, who insisted on joining us in the compartment we had reserved, refused tea as subsequently they did dinner. They were probably billing and cooing while we were dining. Anyhow, when they settled into their seats there was a considerable exchange of significant glances—making of eyes, we call it—and for a while I saw that he was holding her hand affectionately. Evidently he was glad to see her.

This whole trip—the landscape, the dining car, the cozy tea, Miss Longfellow and her lover, Miss Burke and her temporary escort, Grant Richards—finally enveloped my emotional fancy like a dream. I realized that I was experiencing a novel situation which would not soon come again. The idea of this pretty mistress coming to England to join her lover and so frankly admitting her history and her purpose rather took my mind as an intellectual treat. You really don't often get to see this sort of thing—I don't. It's Gallic in its flavor to me.

Grant Richards, being a man of the world, took it as a matter of course, his sole idea being, I fancy, that the refinement of personality and thought involved in the situation permit him to tolerate it. I always judge his emotions by that one gleaming eye behind the monocle. The other does not take my attention so much. On shipboard when we were dealing with Mr. Kahn and his somewhat vulgar friend, Mr. Richards was most disturbed. He didn't like the texture of their souls and bodies. They were sows' ears obviously to him and not silk purses. I knew from his attitude to Baron R. in New York and to others whom we had met together in the past or knew jointly that ethics and morals and things like that had nothing to do with his selection of what he considered interesting personal companionship. Were they interesting? could they tell him something new? would they amuse him? were they nice, socially, in their clothing, in their manners, in the hundred little material refinements which make up a fashionable lady or gentleman? If so, welcome. If not, hence. And talent—oh, yes, he had a keen eye for talent. And he loves the exceptional and will obviously do anything and everything within his power to foster it.

So Grant Richards did not object to Miss Longfellow in his compartment nor as a companion for his friend Miss Burke, who in her experienced way did not mind, and when he saw Mr. T., Miss Longfellow's lover, he obviously did not object to him.

"Rather a nice type," he said to me a little while after he saw him. "Good-looking chap. A little weak, I think, but otherwise quite all right. There you see, my dear fellow, a very good example of the English country gentleman. He isn't your lord or titled person at all, but he has a good family behind him and he has money. He knows how to live. Anyone can see that. I rather like him."

Mr. T. and Grant Richards struck up a rather friendly conversation, and as usual I sat off in one corner and looked on. I must be a very disconcerting person, by the way. I haven't the slightest idea how I look to others. I was once described by a wrathful writer in a New York paper as looking like a beef-packer, and I have been told that I look like a demon at times, but I cannot believe either. I don't care to talk unless I'm very much interested, and if I am not interested, I don't care whether anyone cares whether I talk or not. I can be perfectly happy all by myself, and I get an intense satisfaction from merely looking on. Most people must object to this, however, for most people want, each and every one, to do something—be bright, gay, useful. I'm not. I know I'm not. I sit, as we Americans say in our slang, "like a bump on a log," and there I remain. If people will only talk and not bother about me, I will get along fine. But if they concern themselves too much, I get nervous. And when I want to talk, I have the conviction that I can talk rapidly and forcefully, and I have held my room full of guests with ease and pleasure for an hour at a stretch, so I don't worry. But how must I look to others?

As we traveled, and having started so late, it grew nearly dark after tea. It was misting, and the distant landscapes were not so easy to descry. We came presently in the mist to a place called Carmarthen, I think, where were great black stacks and flaming forges and lights burning wistfully in the dark, and then to another similar place, Swansea, and finally to a third, Cardiff—great center of manufacture, I should judge, for there were flaming lights from forges (great, golden gleams from open furnaces) and dark blue smoke, visible even at this hour, from tall stacks overhead, and gleaming electric lights like bright, lucent diamonds.

I never see this sort of place but I think of Pittsburgh and Youngstown and the coke ovens of western Pennsylvania along the line of the Pennsylvania railroad. I shall never forget the first time I saw Pittsburgh and Youngstown and saw how coke was fired. I was on my way to New York. I had never seen any mountains before, and suddenly, after the low, flat plains of Indiana and Ohio with their pretty little wooden villages so suggestive of the new type of the New World, we rushed into Youngstown and then the mountains of western Pennsylvania (the Alleghenies). It was somewhat like this night coming from Fishguard, only it was not so rainy. The hills rose tall and green; the forge stacks of Pittsburgh flared with a red gleam, mill after mill, until I thought it was the most wonderful sight I had ever seen. And then came the coke ovens, beyond Pittsburgh mile after mile of them, down in the low valleys between the tall hills where our train was following a stream bed.

It seemed a great, sad, heroic thing then to me—plain day labor. Those common, ignorant men, working before flaming forges, stripped to the waist in some instances, fascinated my imagination. I have always marveled at the inequalities of nature—the way it will take one man and give him a low brow and a narrow mind, a narrow round of thought, and make a slave or horse of him, and another a light, nimble mind, a quick wit, an air, and make a gentleman of him. No human being can solve either the question of ability or utility. Is your gentleman useful?—yes and no, perhaps. Is your laborer useful?—yes and no, perhaps. I should say obviously yes. But see the difference in the reward of labor—physical labor. One eats his hard-earned crust in the sweat of his face; the other picks at his surfeit of courses and wonders why the this or the that doesn't taste better. I did not make my mind. I did not make my art. I cannot choose my state except by predestined instinct, and yet here I am sitting in a comfortable English home as I write, commiserating the poor workingman. I indict nature here and now, as I always do and always shall, as being aimless, pointless, unfair, unjust. I see in the whole thing no scheme but an accidental one, no justice save accidental justice. Now and then, in a way, by and large, some justice is done, but it is accidental. No individual man seems to will it. He can't. He doesn't know how. He can't think how. And there's an end of it.

But these queer, weird, hard, sad, drab manufacturing cities—what great writer has yet sung the song of them? Truly I do not recall one at the present clearly. Dickens, as I remember, gives some suggestion of what he considered the misery of the poor, and in *Les Misérables* there is a touch of grim poverty and want here and there. But this is something different again. This is creative toil on a vast scale, and it is a lean, hungry, savage animal to contemplate. I know it is because I have studied personally Fall River, Massachusetts and Paterson, New Jersey and Pittsburgh, Pennsylvania, and I know what I'm talking about. Life runs at a gaunt level in those places. It's a rough, hurtling world of fact.

The threshing machines begin at seven. They stop at six or take on a new shift. The mills run, run with a storm of sound, or they blaze with a golden glow of heat. I have seen the men before the furnaces in Pittsburgh, stripped to the waist, and I know how it is. I have seen them come out after ten minutes' turn at the work of transferring hot metal, and sit dripping, bare to the waist, for another ten minutes until they had to go back again. Three dollars a day was the pay, if I recall rightly. That may sound large in England. It isn't in America. They were Huns, Poles, Czechs, Croatians in Pittsburgh. In Fall River in the cotton mills they were Englishmen, Canadians, Italians and some others. You may think they were doing fairly well. I thought they were miserable specimens. I thought the appearance of the cities and towns proved it. I got a vast physical depression from walking about and looking at the drab houses and the cheap stores and listening to the stories of strikes and poor wages and dull minds and so on. I don't suppose it is any different in England.

I looked at the manufacturing towns as we flashed by in the night and got the same feeling of sad commiseration and unrest. The houses looked poor, and they had a deadly sameness. The streets were narrow and poorly lighted. Am I wrong? I am going to see. I am going to walk over one of these towns foot by foot. I am going to feel it for myself. I want to. Why? I don't know. I want to. I had the feeling that the poor and the ignorant and the savage were somehow great artistically—I have always had it. Millet saw it. He painted *The Man with the Hoe*. I feel it. I can't tell you why. These drab towns are wonderful to me. They sing a great diapason of misery. I feel hunger there and misery. I feel lust and murder and life sick of itself, stewing in its own juice. I feel women struck in the faces by brutal men; and sodden lives too low and weak to be roused by any storm of woe. I fancy there are hungry babies and dying mothers and indifferent bosses and noble directors somewhere, not caring, not knowing, not being able to do anything about it perhaps if they did.

I am not a humanitarian. I lay no claim to vast tenderness. I do very badly when it comes to personal action. I am selfish, self-centered, greedy, mean—but these things appeal to me just the same. I am sorry. As I write these lines there are hot tears in my eyes. Why, I don't know. Why does music move me? Why a great painting? Why a lovely landscape? Why, I don't know. But I'm crying now, and it's not the only time in my life that I have cried over these things—I confess it gladly. I've felt close to tears just at the sight of a large, drab, hungry manufacturing town. I feel sorry for ignorant humanity. I wish I knew how to raise the low brows; to put the clear light of intellect into sad, sodden eyes. I wish there weren't any blows, any hunger, any tears. I wish people didn't have to long bitterly for just the little, thin, bare necessities of this world, but I know also that life wouldn't be as vastly dramatic and marvelous without them. Perhaps I'm wrong. I've seen some real longing in my time, though. I've longed myself, and I've seen others die longing—

However, let's quit crying and go on to London.

At Cardiff an uncle of Miss Burke looked in the window, and then I heard some more about the typical Englishman of a certain class, the country gentleman, and that this was one. I understand that they like to ride and shoot a great deal, this class, and I heard Miss Burke say that whenever a man is given to that sort of thing, he doesn't know much of anything else. She seemed to think poorly of gentlemen who hunt and shoot, and I had the idea that almost all lords and ladies did it. But I am a citizen of Indiana and not used to these subtleties of a world which concerns itself with knowing how to live.

Between Carmarthen and Cardiff and some other places where this drab, hungry world seemed to stick its face in the window, I listened to much conversation about the joyous side of living in Paris, Monte Carlo, Ostend and elsewhere. I remember once I turned from the contemplation of a dark, sad, shabby world scuttling by in the night and rain to hear Miss Burke telling of some Parisian music-hall favorite by the name of Otéro rivaling another Parisian music-hall favorite by the name of Liane de Pougy at Monte Carlo. Of course it is understood that they were women of loose virtue. Of course it is understood that they had fine, white, fascinating bodies and lovely faces and that they were physically ideal. Of course it is understood that they were marvelous mistresses and that money was flowing freely from some source or other—perhaps from factory worlds like these—to let them work their idle, sweet wills. Anyhow they were gambling, racing, disporting themselves at Monte Carlo, and all at once they decided to rival each other in dress. Or perhaps it was that they didn't decide to but just began to, which is much more natural and human.

As I caught it, with my nose pressed to the carriage window and the sight of rain and mist in my eyes, Otéro would come down one night in splendid white silk, perhaps, her bare arms and perfect neck and hair flashing certain priceless jewels, and then Liane de Pougy would arrive a little later or at the same time with her body equally beautifully arrayed in some gorgeous material and her white arms and neck and hair equally resplendent. Then the next night there would be more lovely gowns of marvelous material and artistry and more jewels—every night more and more gowns and jewels, until one of these nights one of these women took all her jewels, to the extent of millions of francs, I presume, and arraying her maid gorgeously in silk or something of that sort, put all the jewels on her and sent her into the casino or the ballroom or the dining room—wherever it was—and she herself followed, in—let us hope—plain, jewel-less black silk, with her lovely flesh showing voluptuously against it. And the other lady was there, oh, much to her chagrin and despair now, of course, arrayed in all her own splendid jewels to the extent of an equally large number of millions of francs, and so the rivalry was ended. It was a very pretty story of pride and vanity, and I liked it.

Just as Miss Burke was telling how marvelous all this was and how beautiful both Otéro and Liane de Pougy looked on all and sundry occasions, one of those great blast furnaces which I have been telling you about and which seem to stretch for miles beside the track flashed past in the night, its open red furnace doors looking like rubies and the frosted windows of its lighted shops looking like opals and the fluttering street lamps and glittering arc lights looking like pearls and diamonds; and I said, behold, these are the only jewels of the poor, and from these come the others. And to a certain extent, in the last analysis and barring that unearned gift of brains which some have without asking and others have not at all, so they do.

Well, then, presently it was too dark to see again, and we dined: Miss Burke, Mr. Grant Richards and myself, (Miss Longfellow and Mr. T. refraining), and after that came back and sat in our compartment. We talked of war, or rather Mr. T. did, for he was intensely interested apparently in what a certain Sir Edward Grey, Minister of Foreign Affairs, was going to say that day in regard to the nation's foreign policy, particularly as this would reflect the nation's attitude toward Germany. I hadn't paid so very much attention to Mr. T. before, except as one might curiously examine the successful possessor of some woman worth having, but now I looked him over carefully. He seemed somewhat more interesting to me.

Much to my surprise, I learned that the feeling between England and Germany was still very high at this time (it had been so for years), quite warlike in fact, and he wished sincerely that England would fight Germany now while Germany was still not too strong from a naval point of view. He was satisfied apparently that France would help England and that she was just ready, you know, to pounce on Germany and thresh her. My friend Grant Richards seemed rather to agree with this, and Miss Burke was naturally enthusiastically pro-British, though being a woman and an artist rather aloof from it all. There was this fact stated: namely, that England had been ready to strike only a little while before at the highest point of some Moroccan difficulties. Her fleet in the North Sea was full coaled, all the traveling officers, relieved from duty for one reason and another, had been recalled, the nation was ready to rush a great army via France to the German borders, and so on.

What a world, I thought. Here are these two nations doing quite well side by side at present, divided comfortably and safely by the North Sea, and yet so eager about the future, which really concerns no individual man alive, that they cannot live in peace. Both are proud of their authority, their ability to fight. Both have decided to bestride the world as a Colossus, both feel that they do already. They are, no doubt, inordinately jealous. They probably pass each other, Englishmen and Germans, with heads up and shoulders back, thinking how joyously they would like to undertake to settle this question of which has the real right to be haughty before all the world by an appeal to arms. War! For after all, it always comes down to that. By blowing each other into kingdom come they get rid of each other. We brook no rivals, we who feel the richness of strength. "I come first," says the strong man. "Where I sit is the head," and if another dares to say or even look as if to say *no*, there is war or rumors of war, the thunder of the captains and the shouting of the men.

So Reading was passed, and then I was told we were going through or near Slough, and presently it was obvious that we were in railroad yards and the heart of some great center, for there were all sorts of cars about and other engines puffing to and fro, with no clatter of engine bells and flare of headlights as in America, however, and not long after we rolled into a long, smoky train shed and beside a bright, bustling, crowded platform, and there were guards opening our carriage-doors and we were out and really in London.

Once when I was ten years old, I remember being taken by my mother with my brother Ed and my sister Tillie from Sullivan, Indiana, where we had been temporarily staying, to Evansville, Indiana, where we were going to stay a little while longer before we moved into the northern part of the state. Sullivan, in Sullivan County, was a very little place, as you may well guess, raw, grass-grown—uncertain, as so many American towns are, as to whether they are going to go on growing or die out entirely, and Evansville was even at that time a stirring, bustling city of forty or fifty thousand people, with a bright brick depot where entered a number of lines of railroads and where was quite an intense show of life just about train time. I had never seen a real city—Terre Haute was so much smaller. When I had left Terre Haute, I was too young to realize what streetcars were, and I don't recall that there were any. But now on this night, lying back against the red-cushioned seat staring out at the curious bustle of life that attended the small stations of the small country towns which we passed coming into Evansville, I got a strange, childish sensation of the weird, kaleidoscopic nature of life. The lights and the people and the buses and the this and the that confused and frightened and entertained me, and I remember distinctly squeezing my mother's arm to be sure that I really had her with me and that she would not run off and leave me in this desperate tangle of events.

And then, after a long time, a tremendous city seemed to come into view. I was very tired and sleepy, but the lights and the engines and the long lines of houses—all frame, of course—stirred me up, and I shook myself in a form of ecstasy—of delight, of terror. It seemed the most wonderful thing in the world to me, this scene. What was I going to see? What was I going to hear? What delights might not exist here? It was marvelous. And presently the train rolled into the handsome new depot, very, very large to me then, and I got down, clinging to my mother's hand or skirt, and I looked at the hurrying people with amazed and wondering eyes, and then when I got outside, there was a long, bright, (to me) glittering street with an unbroken line of bright store windows on either side, and—wonder of wonders—a streetcar going by. I had never seen one before. It was red and yellow, as I recall, with a green band somewhere. It read on one side "Franklin Street and the Salt Wells." There were two mules pulling it, each with a little bell at its back, and under the projecting cap of the roof in front was a green glass eye with a light behind it. A green light was its particular signal.

I thought this really was the most marvelous thing I had ever seen. I thought it was some contrivance made in paradise. As far as the street was concerned, it might just as well have been hung with diamonds and rubies as lights. I could not possibly have been more pleased. It was a dream to me, a delicious, marvelous thing. I was as full of delight as a melon is of water. The world was going around in a dizzy, glittering ring, and as you see, I have not forgotten it. I could not enter any other great city and rival that sensation. Chicago gave me a repetition of it, New York another—London another, but alas I was comparing it all to Evansville, Indiana. It wasn't as keen, it wasn't as fine, it wasn't as wonderful. It was and it wasn't. Life cannot tingle me like that anymore. My blood does not boil for that heat.

It was seven or eight. For one moment when I stepped out of the car, the thought came to me with a tingle of glory, "I have come by land and sea three thousand miles." Then it was gone again. It was strange, this scene. I recognized at once the various London types caricatured in *Punch, Pick Me Up* and elsewhere. I saw a world of cabs and buses, of porters, gentlemen, policemen and citizens generally. I saw characters—strange ones—that brought back Dickens and Du Maurier and W. W. Jacobs, but I did not see anything that brought back the keen tingle of Evansville, Indiana. That was boyhood against maturity and inexperience against experience. I can never enter a great city or new world without some thrill—I hope I never shall—but not that thrill. Already the A.B.C. baggage scheme I had marveled at at Fishguard was not quite so marvelous, only here there was more of it. But I thrilled just the same. The station reminded me of that which once existed in St. Louis in 1892. It is no better, no worse. St. Louis subsequently erected a very marvelous depot, but that has since been surpassed a dozen times in New York, Chicago, Washington and elsewhere. After the new stations in New York and Washington, D.C., what shall one say of railway terminals, anyhow? The chief charm of this was that it was old to me. It reminded me of a condition no longer extant in America. It brought back my extreme boyhood and, oh, scores of delightful and pathetic memories. I could write on depots forever, on going and coming, but I won't.

I hunted out my trunks. I said farewell to Miss Longfellow and her lover; I said farewell to Miss Burke and was introduced to Miss Hemmerde, who was, I understood, Grant Richards's secretary, a most prim and capable-appearing young woman. The words "Booking Office" and the typical London policeman took my eye. I strolled about seeing the crowd disappear, my red-gold Diana among them (we had dined in the same car with her coming from Fishguard), and then we were scheduled to take a third-class train back to Cookham from this same depot. I won't tell you much how I nosed about, trying to sense London from this vague, noisy touch of it. I can't indicate how the peculiar-looking trains made me feel. Humanity is so very different in so many little unessential things, so utterly the same in all the large ones. I could see that it might be just as well or better to call a ticket office a "booking office"; or to have three classes of carriages instead of two, as with us; or to have carriages instead of cars; or trams instead of street railways; or lifts instead of elevators. What difference does it make? What difference does it make whether we say "laaf" or "laugh"? "Bawth" or "bath"?

Human nature is the same. An accent is nothing, a cut of cloth is nothing. I'm told by my mentor that I must get such-and-such things and wear them. All right, I will. But what of it? Life is the same old thing. Joy is the same here as elsewhere; sorrow the same; hope the same; despair the same.

I looked into the eyes of the porter who was carting our trunks about, and I saw the intense satisfaction with which he was executing this poor, little job. It meant another little tip for him. It may have meant a drink or a bed, or a part of those things which keep his poor little home going. Thank God that there is work for most of us to do. Thank heaven that we can have the pleasure of helping now and then. I see no stranger thing than I have seen anywhere else. These little differences entertain me. They make me smile or cry (in my mind only). I see poor old humanity up against it as much as ever, perhaps more so, and I know that neither I nor anyone else can do much to relieve it. Omar voiced it best, and the writer of Ecclesiastes, when he wrote, "There is a grievous evil I have seen under the sun."

Yes, there are many evils, and they are grievous. And there are many joys, and they are memorable beyond the heart to express. But this sorry scheme, this fitful fever, is at times well worth the living to me. It was this night when I entered London. But I would not have the heart nor the effrontery to speak for any other man.

CHAPTER X

It is quite a week later and more since I last wrote of my entrance into London, and I have some interesting things to record in connection with Bigfrith, Cookham Dean, Berkshire (which, by the way, I find is pronounced "Barksheer") and some other places. I fancy this is a very fair and pretty example of the average country place near London, and it certainly lacks none of the appointments which might be considered worthy of a comfortable home, but it is as cold as blazes to me, and I can't understand the evoluted system of procedure which has brought about any such uncomfortable state and maintains it as satisfactory. These Britons are actually warm when the temperature in the rooms is somewhere between forty-five and fifty, and they go about opening doors and windows with the idea that the rooms need additional airing. They build you small, weak coal fires in large, handsome fireplaces, and then if the four or five coals huddled together are managing to keep themselves warm by glowing, they tell you (or stroll about at least looking as though) everything is all right. I can't see it. Doors are left open, windows flung out. (The American up-and-down moving window doesn't prevail here, I am told.) We have nice little lead- or iron-set paned windows with clever opening contrivances which affect a portion of the window only, a quarter or a half in case of long, narrow windows. The whole effect is pleasing, and I like it—prefer it, I think—but it doesn't give you that sense of being almost outside which the wide-flung American sash does.

We reached this place up some winding road, inscrutable in the night, and I wondered keenly what sort of an atmosphere it would have. The English suburban or country home of the better class has always been a concrete thought to me—rather charming on the whole. A carriage brought us, with all the bags and trunks carefully looked after—in England you always keep your luggage with you—and we were met in the hall by a maid who took our coats and hats and brought us something to drink. There was a small fire glowing in the fireplace in the entrance hall, but it was so small—cheerful though it was—that I wondered why Grant Richards had taken all the trouble to cable from America to have it there. It seems it is a custom, insofar as his house is concerned, not to have it. But having heard something of English fires and English ideas of warmth, I was not greatly surprised.

"I am going to be cold," I said to myself at once. "I know it. The atmosphere is going to be cold and raw, and I am going to suffer greatly. I don't see how I shall ever write."

But I put my back to the small though cheerful-looking fire in the sitting room and decided to make the best of it. I was here, I should not get away very soon, and I might as well quit quarreling. I looked at the furniture, the solidity of the walls, the mode of decoration and arrangement, and decided that I liked it very much. It was simple, in good taste, orderly, and the pictures and objects of art were worthwhile.

"Now," said my host with his usual directness of speech, "I think it is best that you should go to bed at once and get a good night's rest. In the morning you shall have your breakfast at whatever hour you say. Your bawth will be brought you a haaf or three-quarters of an hour before you appear at table, so that you shall have ample time to shave and dress. I shall be here until eleven-fifteen to see how you are getting along, after which I shall go to the city. You shall have a table here, or wherever you like, and the maid will serve your lunch punctually at two o'clock. At haaf-paast four you shall have your tea brought to you, in case you are here. In the evening we dine at seven-thirty. I shall be down on the five-fifty-two train."

So he proceeded definitely to lay out my life for me, and I had to smile. "That stupendous order which is England," I thought, and took my matches. He accompanied me to my chamber door, or rather to the foot of the stairs. There he wished me pleasant dreams. "And remember," he cautioned me with the emphasis of one who has forgotten something of great significance, "this is most important. Whatever you do, don't forget to put out your boots for the maid to take and have blacked. Otherwise you will disrupt the whole social procedure of England."

I smiled.

"It shall be done. Out shall come my shoes. I wouldn't have the vast perfection of England disturbed for anything in the world."

And so we parted.

It is curious—this feeling of being quite alone for the first time in a strange land. I began to unpack my bags, solemnly thinking of New York, the ocean, the speed of all this, how it was going to eventuate. I was wondering whether I was going to like it, whether I was going to be able to write anything of value, and so on and so forth. There were strange poetic thoughts concerning Shakespeare and the men of significance who had peopled this ancient land. Was there any sense of their quondam presence still lingering? I went to the window and pressed my nose against it, but I could not make out anything. One or two small lights burned afar off. I undressed and got in bed, feeling anything but sleepy. I lay and watched the fire flickering on the hearth. So this was really England, and here I was at last—absolutely of no significance to anyone else in the world, but very important to me. An old, old dream come true, and it had passed so oddly, the trip, so almost unconsciously as it were. We make a great fuss, I thought, about the past and the future, but the actual moment is so often without significance, so dull or unconscious. Finally I slept after hearing roosters crow and thinking of Hamlet's father, his ghost, and the chill that invests the thought of cockcrow in that tragedy.

Morning came and with it a knock from the maid. I called, "Come in." In she came, neat, cleanly, rosy-cheeked, bringing a large tin basin—very much larger than an American tub but not so deep—a large water can full of hot water, towels and the like. She put the tub and water can down, drew a towel rack from the wall nearby and spread out the towels and started to leave. Before doing so, she turned.

"What time will you have your breakfast, sir?"

"What time is it?"

"Haaf-paast eight, sir."

"At nine-fifteen," I replied.

"Very well, sir," and off she went.

I did not hear her take the boots, but when I went to the door they were gone. In the afternoon they were back again, nice and bright. I speculated on all this as an interesting demonstration of English life. Grant Richards is not so very well-to-do, but he has all these things. It struck me as pleasing, soothing, orderly—quite the same thing I had been seeing on the train and the ship. It was all a part of that interesting national system which I had been hearing so much about.

At breakfast it was quite the same—a most orderly meal. Grant Richards was there to breakfast with me, to see that I was started right. His face was smiling. How did I like it? Was I comfortable? Had I slept well? Had I slept very well? It was bad weather, but I would raather have to expect that at this season of the year.

I can see his smiling face—a little cynical and disillusioned—get some faint revival of his own native interest in England in my surprise, curiosity and interest. The room was cold, but he did not seem to think so. No, no, no, it was very comfortable. I was simply not acclimated yet. I would get used to it.

This house was very charming, I thought, and here at breakfast I was introduced to the children. Gioia (pronounced Joya) Vivian Mary Elisina Grant Richards, the only girl and oldest child, looked to me at first a little pale and thin, quite peaked in fact, but which I afterward found was not true, merely a temperamental objection on my part to a type which afterwards seemed to me very attractive; a decidedly wise, high-spoken, intellectual and cynical little maid. Although only eleven years of age she spoke with the air, the manner and the words of a woman of twenty.

"Oh, yes, Amayreeka! Is that a nice place? Do you like it?"

I cannot convey in the least way the touch of lofty, well-bred feeling it had—quite the air and sound of a woman of twenty-five or thirty schooled in all the niceties of polite speech. What a child! I thought. She talks as though she were affected, but I can see that she is not. Quite different she seemed from what any American child could be—less vigorous, more intellectual, more spiritual, perhaps not so forceful, but probably infinitely more subtle, and so on. She looked delicate, remote, Burne-Jones-y—far removed from the more commonplace school of force we know—and I think I like our type better. I smiled at her, and she seemed friendly enough, but there was none of that running forward and greeting people, which is an average middle-class American habit. She was too well-bred. I learned afterward from a remark dropped at table by her, concerning American children, that it was considered bad form. "American children are the kind that run around hotel foyers with big bows in their hair and speak to people," was the substance of it apropos of something. I saw at once how bad American children were.

Well, then came the eldest boy, Gerard Franklin Grant Richards, who reminded me at first glance of that American caricature type, dear to the newspaper cartoonist, of Little Johnnie Bostonbeans. Here he was, "glawses," inquiring eyes, a bulging forehead, a learned air—and all at ten years of age—and somewhat undersized for his age. A clever child, sincere apparently, rather earnest, eager to know, full of the light of youthful understanding. Like his sister, his manners were quite perfect but unstudied. He smiled and replied, "Quite well, thank you," to my amused inquiries after him. I could see he was bright and thoughtful, but the unconscious, though (to me) affected, quality of the English voice amused me here again. Then came Charles Geoffrey Grant Richards and Geoffrey Herbert Grant Richards, the second youngest and youngest, who affected me in quite the same way as the others. They were nice, orderly children, but English—oh, so English.

It was while walking in the garden after breakfast that I encountered Geoffrey Herbert Grant Richards, the youngest, but in the confusion of meeting people generally I did not recognize him. He was outside the coach-house where are the rooms of the gardener and where my room is.

"And which little Richards might this be?" I asked genially, in that patronizing way we have with children.

"Geoffrey Herbert Grant Richards," he replied with a gravity of pronunciation which quite took my breath away. We are not used to this formal dignity of approach in children of so very few years in America. This lad was only five years of age, and he was talking to me in the educated voice of one of fifteen or sixteen. I stared, of course. And fancy a name like that in America, anyhow!

"You don't tell me!" I replied. "And what is your sister's name again?"

"Gioia Vivian Mary Elisina Grant Richards," he replied.

"Dear, dear, dear!" I sighed. "Now what do you know about that!"

Of course such a wild piece of American slang as that had no significance to him whatsoever. It fell on his ears without meaning.

"I don't know," he replied, interested in some fixture he was fastening to a toy bathtub.

"Isn't that a fine little bathtub you have!" I ventured, eager to continue the conversation because of its novelty.

"It's a nice little bawth," he went on, "but I wouldn't call it a tub."

I really did not know how to reply to this last, it took me so by surprise. A child of five, in little breeches scarcely larger than my two hands, making this fine distinction. We surely live and learn, I thought, and went on my way smiling.

But this house interested me from so many other points of view, being particularly English and new, that I was never weary of investigating it. I had a conversation with the gardener one morning concerning his duties and found that he had an exact schedule of procedure which covered every day in the year. First, he got hold of the boots, I believe—delivered to him by the maid—and did those, and then he got up his coal and wood and built the fires, and then he had some steps and paths to look after, and then some errands to do—I forget what. There was the riding pony to curry and saddle, the stable to clean—oh, quite a long list of things which he did over and over, day after day. He talked with such an air of responsibility, as so many English servants do, that I was led to reflect on the responsibility of English servants in general, and he dropped all his h's where they occurred, of course, and added them where they shouldn't be. He told me how much he received, how much he had received, how he managed to live on it, how shiftless and irresponsible some people were, and so on and so forth.

"They don't know 'ow to get along, sir," he informed me with that same solemn air of responsibility. "They just doesn't know 'ow to manige, sir, I tyke it—some people doesn't, sir. They gets sixteen or h'ighteen shillin's the same as me, sir, but hawfter they goes an' buys five or six g'uns" (I thought he said "guns"; he actually said "gallons") "o' beer in the week, there hain't much left for other things—is there, sir? Not that's no w'y, is it, sir, I hawsk you, sir?"

I had to smile at the rural accent—rural or servant or cockney class, I couldn't tell which at that time. He was so simple-minded—so innocent, apparently, and yet he might not have been. I couldn't tell. Everyone called him Spillett—not Mr. Spillett, as we might in America, or John or Jack or some sobriquet of some kind, but just Spillett. He was Spillett to everyone—the master, the maid, the children. The maid was Dora to everyone, and the nurse Nana. It was all so interesting to me because it was so utterly new.

And then this landscape round about; the feel of the country was so refreshing and peculiar. I knew absolutely nothing about it, and yet I could see and feel that we were in a region of comfortable suburban life. I could hear the popping of guns all day long, here and thereabouts, this being the open season for shooting—not hunting, as my host informed me, for there was no such thing as hunting hereabouts. In England people only *hunt* big game—deer, fox and the like—and when they are mounted and ride after the hounds. They shoot when they take gun in hand and prowl about after rabbits, pheasants and the like. I could see men strolling here and there together, guns under their arms, plaid caps on their heads, knee breeches, leather leggings and the like. I could see from my writing desk in the drawing room window clever-riding English girls bounding by on light-moving horses, and in my limited walks about, I saw plenty of comfortable-looking country places—suburban homes. I was told by a friend of mine that this was rather a pleasant suburban section but that I might see considerable of the same thing anywhere about London at this distance.

Dora interested me very much as a maid. She was so very quiet, so silent and so pretty. The door would open, any time during the day when I was writing, and in she would come to look after the fire, to open the windows, to draw the curtains, light the candles and serve the tea or to call me to lunch or dinner. Usually I ate my lunch and drank my four-o'clock tea alone, and I ate my evening meal, dinner, all alone once—to my surprise and astonishment, as I shall relate. It made no difference, my eating alone. The service was quite the same. The same candles were lit fully, several brackets on different parts of the table, the fire built in the dining room. There were four or five courses and wine. Dora stood behind me watching me eat in silence, and I confess I felt very queer. It was all so solemn, so stately. I felt like some old gray baron or bachelor shut away from the world and given to contemplating the follies of his youth. When I was through with nuts and wine—the final glass of port—it was the custom of the house to retire to the drawing room and drink the small cup of black coffee which was served there, and on this night, although I was quite alone, it was the same. The coffee was served just as promptly and dignifiedly as though there were eight or ten present. It interested me greatly, all of it, and pleased me more than I can say.

CHAPTER XI

After I had been at Cookham four or five days catching up on my accumulating notes, it was Grant Richards who, with a managerial eye fixed upon what to him was a probable interesting result, suggested that I visit Marlow, which was quite nearby on the Thames—a place which he said fairly represented the typical small country town of the old school.

"You will see there something which is not so generally common now in England as it was, a type of life which is changing greatly, I think, and perhaps you had better see that now before you see much else."

Always I have had a romantic notion of the state of the English town. From my youth I have seen pictures of it and read descriptions of it, and now I was to see a typical one for myself. He gave positive instructions as to how this was to be achieved. I was to say to the maid when I would be ready. Promptly at that hour one of the boys was to come and escort me to some point in the road where I could see Marlow. From there I was to be allowed to proceed alone.

"You won't want to be bothered with any company, so just send him back. You'll find it very interesting."

I was so busy working on my notes that I thought nothing of the matter, but one afternoon, I think it was a Friday, it faired up so beautifully that I decided I must go out of doors. I was sick of writing. I gave notice to Dora, the maid, at luncheon that I should want one of the boys for a guide at three o'clock, and at ten minutes of the hour Gerard entered my room with the air of a soldier.

"When shall you be ready for your walk to Marlow?" he asked in his stately tone.

"In just ten minutes now."

"And have you any objection to our walking to Marlow with you?"

"Are there two of you?"

"Yes. My brother Charles and myself."

"None whatever. Your father doesn't mind, does he?"

"No, he doesn't mind."

I dismissed him, and at three he and his brother appeared at the window. Their faces were eager with anticipation, and I went at once to get my cap and coat. We struck out along some strange road between green grass, and although it was December, you would have thought it April or May. The atmosphere was warm and tinged with the faintest, most delicate haze. A lovely green moss, very fine, like powdered salt, was visible on the trunks of the trees. Crows were in the air, and robins—an English robin is a solemn-looking bird—on the lawns. I heaved a breath of delight, for after days of rain and chill, this burst of golden light was most delicious.

On the way, as I was looking about, I was entertained by such delightful questions as, "Are there any trees like these in Ahmerrykaa? Do you have such fine weather as this in Ahmerrykaa? Are the roads as good as this in Ahmerrykaa?"

"Quite as good as this," I replied, referring to the one on which we were walking, for it was a little muddy.

The way lay down through a patch of nearly leafless trees, the ground strewn thick with leaves, and the sun breaking in a golden shower through the branches. I laughed for joy at being alive—the hour was so fine. Presently, after going down a bank so steep that it was impossible not to run if you attempted to walk fast, we came to an open field, the west border of which was protected by a line of willows skirting the banks of a flume giving into the Thames somewhere. Below the small bridge over which we passed was fastened a small punt, that quaint little boat form so common on the Thames. Beyond that was a very wide field, fully twenty acres square, with a yellow path running diagonally across it, and at the end of this path was Marlow.

I shall never forget it. We were discussing war between America and England, solely because the lads insisted on discussing it, and I was giggly over the fun I was having proving that England would not be able to do anything at all with the United States. It is scandalous to tease children in this way, but I could not resist the fun of it. The United States was so vast, I said. It was full of such smart people. While England was attempting to do something with its giant navy, we should be buying or building wonderful ships and inventing marvelous machines for destroying the enemy. It was useless to plead with me as they did that England had a great army and we none. "We can get one," I insisted, "—oh, a much vaster army than you could."

"And there's Kan-nee-dah," insisted Gerard wisely. "While you would be building your navy or drilling your army, we should be attacking you through Kan-nee-dah."

"But Canada doesn't amount to anything," I replied. "It doesn't like you anyhow. It only has six million people."

He insisted that Canada was a great source and hope, and I finally said, "Now I'll tell you what I'll do. You want England to whip the United States, don't you?"

"Yes," echoed both Gerard and Charles heartily.

"Very well, then, for peace and quiet's sake, I'll agree that it can. England can whip the United States both on sea and land. Now is that satisfactory?"

"Yes," they echoed unanimously.

"Entirely so?"

"Yes, quite so."

"Very well, then," I laughed. "It is agreed that the United States is badly beaten everywhere and always by England. Isn't Marlow lovely?" and I fixed my interested gaze on the approaching town.

In the first glimpse of Marlow, some of the most joyous memories of my childhood came back. I don't know whether you as a boy or a girl loved to look in your first reader at pictures of quaint little towns with birds flying above belfries and gabled roofs standing free in some clear, presumably golden air, but I did. Such pictures are among my earliest and dearest memories, and here, across this green field, lay a little town, the sweetness of which I shall not soon forget. The most prominent things were an arched bridge and a church with a square gray belfry set in a green, tree-grown churchyard. I could see the smooth surface of the Thames running beside it, and, as I live, a flock of birds in the sky.

"Are those rooks?" I asked of Gerard, hoping for poetry's sake that they were.

"Rooks or crows," he replied. "I don't know which. Are there rooks in Ahmerrykaa?"

"No, there are no rooks."

"Ah, that's something, then, we have that you haven't."

"Yes, that's something."

I walked briskly because I wanted to reach this pretty scene while the sun was still high, and in five minutes or so we were crossing the bridge. I was intensely interested in the low, gray stone houses, with here and there a wall in front with a gate, and the very pretty churchyard lying by the water, and the sylvan loveliness of the Thames itself. I suspected at once that the place was full of interesting historic facts which I ought to know about, but I had no way of knowing. In the middle of the bridge I stopped and looked at the water. It was as smooth as glass and tinged with the mellow light which the sun casts when it is low in the west. There were some small boats anchored at a gate which gave into some steps leading up to an inn—The Compleat Angler. On the other side, back of the church, was another inn—The Lion and Elk, or something like that, and below the bridge, more toward the west, an old man in a punt, fishing. There was a very old man, such as I have often seen pictured in *Punch* and the *Sketch*, sitting near a support of the bridge, a short, black pipe between his very wrinkled lips. He was clad in thick, heavy, greenish-brown clothes and heavy shoes and a low, flat hat such as some curate may have discarded. His eyes, which he turned up at me as I passed, were small and shrewd, set in a withered, wrinkled skin, and his hands were a collection of dried lines, like wrinkled leather.

"There," I thought, "is a type quite expressive of all England in its rural form. The illustrations of England have been teaching me that all my life."

I went into the church, and here I saw so much more of that which I have always heard.

For instance, I have always heard of the pride of local families which will cover the walls of their local churches with flattering commentaries on the virtues of their departed, and here they were. The church wasn't so very old. It was located on the site of one built in the thirteenth century, and on the wall near the door was a list of the resident vicars and their patrons, beginning with some long-since-forgotten soul. The monks and the abbots of the pre-Reformation period were indicated, and the wars of the Reformation also. This bridge which I had crossed had evidently been destroyed by Cromwell and had been rebuilt only sixty or seventy years before, but my memory is not good, and I will not guarantee these facts.

These virtues of the departed dead—they amused me greatly. People are such infernal fools, I was going to say, but I will change it and remark that humanity is never quite so ridiculous as when it is about the work of commemorating the virtuous deeds of the dear departed. We think so highly of those who have gone, after they have gone. We say such silly things. Listen to this. It is from that wall:

> Sacred to the Memory of John Downe, Esqu.
> late of this Parish who departed this life
> the 21. day of July 1805, Aged 62 Years.
> He was a Man of Exemplary Piety and fierier Integrity:
> Whose Many Virtues will ever Endear him to his Family & Friends.

No one, not even a country knight in rural England, is as good as this, but your fine memorial marble would have it so. Read it, and then the next also.

The rest of Marlow, as I explored it, was even more delicious still. We went out into the street and found some old stocks inside an iron fence, dating from some older day where they had punished people after this fashion. We came to a store which was signaled by a low, small-paned window let into a solid gray wall, where were chocolates and candies and foreign-manufactured goods with labels I had never seen before. It is a strange sensation to go away from home and leave all your own familiar patent medicines and candies and newspapers and whiskies and to journey to some place where they never saw nor heard of them. Here in Marlow, as lovely as it was, I was saying to myself, "Yes, yes, it is delicious, but how terrible it would be to live here. I couldn't. It's a dead world. We have done so much better than this."

I walked through the pretty streets, as smooth and clean as though they had been brushed, and between rows of low, gray, winding houses which curved in pretty lines, but for the life of me I could not help swinging between the joy of art which is alive and the sorrow for something that is gone and will never be anymore. Everything, everything spoke to me of an older day. These houses, all of them, were lower than they need be, thicker, colder, sadder. I could not think of gas or electricity being used here, although they were, or of bright, broad windows, open plumbing, modern streetcars, a stock of modern, up-to-date goods. I was impressed by a grave silence, which is as pathetic to me as nothing else, a profound peace.

"Oh, I'm away from things—I am out of them," I said to myself. "I must get out of this," and yet I was almost hugging myself for joy at the same time. What is this?

I remember going into one courtyard where an inn might once have been and finding in there a furniture shop, a tin shop, a storeroom of some kind and a stable, all invisible from the street. Do you recall Dickens's descriptions of busy inn scenes? You came into this one under a chamber belonging to some house which was built over this entryway. There was no one visible inside, though a man did cross the court finally with a wheel spoke in his hand. One of the houses or shops had a little circular cupola on it, quite white and pretty and surmounted by a faded weathercock.

"How lovely," I said, "how lovely!" but I was as sad as I could be.

In the stores in the main street were always small, many-paned windows, never one large sheet of glass glowing with a brilliant light. There were no lights as yet, and the rooms into which I peered and the private doors gave glimpses of things which reminded me of the poorest, most backward and desolate sections of our own country. All the time there was something haunting me, a memory of something, and I kept saying to myself, "What is it I am trying to think of? What is it that is coming back that this suggests?"

Our lives are queer webs of nothings. Our minds, so-called, are fevers and dreams. All life is a tissue of illusions, built up, evoluted, but illusions still. As I walked down this street, thinking of Dickens, thinking of Hardy, thinking of pictures in English weeklies of English people of all grades, I saw an automobile here and there, not many, and some girls on bicycles—not very good-looking. I missed at once the dash and go and hope of an American small town. Say what you will, you could not find an atmosphere like this in an American town, however small, unless it had already been practically abandoned. It would not contain a contented population of three or four thousand. Instead of saloons I saw "wine and spirit merchants" and also "Mrs. Jane Sawyer, licensed wine and spirit dealer." The butcher shops were the most American things I saw, because their ruddy goods were all displayed in front with good lights behind, and the next best things were the candy stores. Dressmakers, milliners, grocers, hardware stores, wine shops, anything and everything, were apparently concealed by solid gray walls or at best revealed by small-paned windows. In the fading afternoon I walked about hunting for schools, some fine private homes, some sense of modernness; but no, it was not there. I noticed that in two directions the town came abruptly to an end, as though it had been cut off by a knife, and smooth, open, green fields began. In the distance you could see other towns standing out like the castellated walls of earlier centuries—but here was an end, sharp, definite, final.

I saw at one place—the end of one of those streets and where the country began—an old gray man in a shabby black coat bending to adjust a yoke to his shoulders, to the ends of which were attached two buckets, filled with water. He had been into a low, gray, one-story inn called "Ye Bank of England," before which was set a bench and also a stone hitching post. For all the world he looked like some old man in Hardy wending his fading, reflective way homeward. I said to myself here, "England is old. It is evening in England, and they are tired."

I went back toward the heart of things along another street, but I found after a time that it was merely taking me to another outer corner of the town. It was gray now, and I was saying to my young companions that they must be hurrying on home, that I did not intend to go back so soon. "Say I will not be home for dinner," I told them, and they left after a time, blessed with some modern chocolate which they craved very much.

This street led me past low, one-story houses, the like of which, I insist, can rarely be duplicated in America. Do you recall the log cabin? In England it is preserved in stone, block after block of it. It originated there. As I went along, the people seemed so thick and stolid and silent to me. They were healthy enough, I thought, but they were raw, uncouth, mirthless. There was not a suggestion of gaiety anywhere, not a single burst of song. I heard no one whistling. A man came up behind me driving some cattle, and the oxen were quite on me before I heard them. But there were no loud cries. He was so ultra-serious. I met a man pushing a dilapidated baby carriage. He was a grinder of knives and mender of tinware, and this was his method of perambulating his equipment. I met another man pushing a handcart with some attenuated remnants of furniture in it.

"What is that?" I asked. "What is he?"

"Oh, he's somebody who's moving. He hasn't a van, you know."

Moving! Here was food for pathetic reflection.

I looked into low, dark doors where humble little tin- and glass-bodied lamps were beginning to flicker.

"Thank God my life is better than that," I said. And yet the pathos and the beauty of this town was gripping me firmly. It was as sweet as a lay out of Horace, as sad as Keats.

Before a butcher shop I saw a man trying to round up a small drove of sheep. The grayish-yellow of their round, woolly backs was pathetic in the twilight. They seemed to sense their impending doom, for they ran here and there, poking their queer little noses along the ground or in the air and refusing to enter the low, gray entryway which gave into a cobbled yard at the back and side of the shop, the deadly shambles. The farmer who was driving them wore a long black coat and he made no sound, or scarcely any.

"Sooey!" he called. "Ssh," as he ran here and there, this way and that.

The butcher or his assistant came out and caught one sheep, possibly the bellwether, by the leg and hauled him backward into the yard. Seeing this, the silly sheep, not recognizing the enforced leadership, followed after. Could there be a more convincing commentary on the probable manner in which life, its customs and forms, have originated?

I walked out another long street, quite dusk now, and met a man driving an ox, also evidently to market. There was a school in session at one place, a boys' school—low, ancient in its exterior equipment and silent as I passed. It was *out*, but there was no running, no halloing. The boys were going along chatting rather quietly in groups. I do not understand this. The

American temper is more ebullient. I went into one bar—Mrs. Davidge's—and found a low, dark room with a very small grate fire burning and a dark little bar where were some pewter mugs, some pink-colored glasses and a small brass lamp with a reflector. Mrs. Davidge must have served me herself, an old, slightly hunched lady in a black dress and gray gingham apron. "Can this place do enough business to support her?" I asked myself. There was no one in the shop while I was there.

The charm of Marlow to me was its extreme remoteness from the life I had been witnessing in London and elsewhere. It was so simple. I had seen a comfortable inn somewhere near the marketplace, and this I was idly seeking, entertaining myself with reflections the while. I passed at one place a gas-manufacturing plant which looked modern enough insofar as its tank was concerned but not otherwise, and then up one dark street under branches of large trees and between high brick walls, where in a low doorway, behind which a light was shining, I saw a shovel-hatted curate talking to an old woman in a shawl. All the rest was dark. At another corner I saw a thin old man, really quite reverential-looking, with a peaked, intelligent face, fine in its lines (like Calvin or Dante or John Knox) and long, thin white hair, who was pulling a vehicle—a sort of revised baby carriage—on which was, of all things, a phonograph with a big flower-like tin horn. He stopped at one corner, where some children were playing in the dark, and putting on a record, ground out a melody which I did not consider very gay or tuneful. The children danced, but not with the lightness of our American children. The people here seemed rather like this old man—sad and old and peaked, with a fine intellectuality apparent, or thick and dull and red and stodgy. Am I wrong? I can only say, I shall see. I doubt it. My old man wheeled his phonograph off into some side street quite as dark as the others and disappeared.

When I reached the marketplace, I saw a scene which something, some book or picture, had suggested to me before. Children were playing about, and laborers were going home, talking a dialect which I could not understand except in part. Solid women in shawls and flat, shapeless wrecks of hats, and tall shambling men in queer long coats and high boots—drovers they looked like—were going to and fro. Five men came into the square and stood there under the central gas lamp with its two arms each with a light. One of them left the others and began to sing in front of various doors. He sang and sang—"Annie Laurie," "Auld Lang Syne," "Sally in Our Alley," but no one gave him anything. Finally he came to me.

"Would you help us on our way?" he asked.

"Where are you going?" I inquired.

"We are wayfaring workmen," he replied simply, and I gave him some coppers—those large English "tuppences" that annoyed me so much.

He went back to the others, and they stood huddled in the square together like sheep, conferring, but finally they went off together in the dark.

At the inn adjacent, I expected to find an exceptional English scene of some kind, but I was more or less disappointed. It was homey but not so different from old New England life. The room was large with an open fireplace and a general table set with white linen and plates for a dozen guests or more. A shambling boy in clothes much too big for him came and took my order, turning up one of the big lights and stirring up the fire. I called for a paper and read it, and then I sat, wondering whether the food would be good or bad.

While I was waiting, a second traveler arrived, a sandy-haired person, who looked to me for all the world like an underpaid clerk of some kind. He had a quite small, dapper body, with shrewd, fresh, inquisitive eyes—a self-confident and yet clerkly man.

"Good evening," he said, and I gave him the time of day.

He bustled to a little writing table and sat down to write, calling for a pen, paper, his slippers and various other things.

I think at times that I am the most unsatisfactory person in the world when it comes to strangers. I have the silliest habit in the world of suspecting them on sight of being dull, pointless, of no interest whatsoever. I cannot imagine a worse point of view nor a more dreadful state of mind. In that direction lies isolation. On sight, this gentleman (I suppose the English would abuse me for that word) looked anything but satisfactory. I suspected he was Scotch and that he was cheap-minded and narrow. Something about his manner and the healthy, brisk way in which, when his slippers came, he took off his shoes and put them on, quite cheerful and homelike, soothed me.

"He isn't so bad," I thought. "He's probably a traveling salesman—the English type. I'd better be genial and human. I may learn something."

Soon the waiter returned (and I forgot to say that by the time the latter had arrived to serve me, he had arrayed himself in a dress-suit, the size of which was a pure piece of comedy in itself) and brought the stranger's toast and chops and tea. The latter drew up to the other end of the table from me with quite an air of appetite and satisfaction.

"They don't usually put us fellows in with you," he observed, and I replied that I didn't quite understand how that was. I knew now he was Scotch and a traveling man.

"We traveling men usually have a separate dining and writing room. Our place seems to be shut up here tonight, for some reason. I wouldn't have called for my slippers here if they had the other room open."

"Oh, that's quite all right," I replied, gathering some odd class distinction. "I prefer company to silence. You say you travel?"

"Yes, I'm connected with a house in London. I travel in the south of England."

Here was my chance. I should learn something of the south of England.

"Tell me," I said, "is this a typical English town from the point of view of life and business, or is it the only one of its kind? It's rather curious to me."

"It's one of the poorest I know—certainly the poorest I stop at. There's no life to speak of here at all. If you want to see a typical English town where there's more life and business, you want to see Canterbury or Maidenhead. No, no, you mustn't judge England by this. I suppose you're traveling to see things? You're not English, I see."

"No, I'm not English."

"You wouldn't be from America now?"

"Yes, I'm from America. I come from New York."

"I had a strong notion before I came to London to go to America after I left school"—and to have heard him pronounce *school* alone would have settled his identity for those who know the Scotch. "Some of my friends went there, but I decided not. I thought I'd try London instead, and I'm glad I did."

"You like it?"

"Oh, yes, from a money point I do. I make perhaps fifty percent more than I did in Scotland, but I may say, too, it costs me about fifty percent more to live." He said this with a sigh. I could see Scotch thrift sticking out all over him. An interesting little man he proved, very intelligent, very cautious, very saving. You could see early religious training and precepts and keen desire to get up in the world in his every gesture.

We fell into a most interesting conversation, to me, for knowing so little of England I was anxious to know more, despite the littleness of my companion and his clerkly manner. He wanted to know what I thought of England, and I told him, as much as I could judge by a few days' stay. He told me something of London life, its streets, sections and so on, and asked a great many questions about America. He had the ability to listen intelligently, which is a fine sign. He wanted to know particularly what traveling salesmen received and how far their money went. We talked of the difference between Englishmen and Americans as to their ideas of warmth, and he thought an Englishman loved to look at a fire. He was interested to know the difference between English and American railroads. By the time the meal had ended and we were toasting our toes before the fire, we were quite friendly.

"It's some little distance back to my place, and I think I'll be going," I said. "I don't know whether I really know how to get there, but I'll try. I understand there is no direct railroad connection between here and there. I may not be able to find my way at night."

"Well, I'll walk with you a little way if you don't mind," he said solicitously. "I have nothing else to do."

The idea of companionship soothed me. Walking alone and standing in the marketplace looking at the tramping men had given me the blues. I am subject to these depressions, and once with me they are sometimes hard to shake off. I felt particularly lonely at moments, being away from America, for the difference in standards of taste and action, the difference in modes of thought and practice, and the difference in money pieces and the sound of human voices was growing on me. When you have lived in one country all your life and found yourself comfortable in all its ways and notions and then suddenly find yourself out of it and trying to adjust yourself to things that are different in a hundred little ways, it is rather hard. England seemed sad and lonely to me, and I had no real joyous place to go. In America I have.

"That's very nice of you. I'd like to have you," and out we went, paying our bills and looking into a misty night. The moon was up but there was a fairly heavy fog on, and Marlow looked sadder than ever. Because I stated that I had not been in any of the public houses and was interested to go, he volunteered to accompany me, though I could see that this was against his principles.

"I don't drink myself," he observed, "but I will go in with you if you want to. Here's one."

We entered and found a rather dimly lighted room—gas with a mantle over it—set with small tables and chairs, and a short bar in one corner. Mrs. Davidge's bar had been short too, only her room was dingier and smaller. A middle-sized Englishman, rather stout, came out of a rear door, opening from behind the bar, and asked us what we would have. My friend asked for root beer. I noticed the inescapable open fire and the array of pink and green and blue wineglasses. Also the machinery for extracting beer and ale from kegs, a most brassy and glowing sight. Our host sold cigars, and there were boards about on the tables for some simple games.

This and a half-dozen other places we ventured into gave me the true spirit of Marlow's common life. I recalled at once the vast difference between this and the average American small-town saloon. In the latter (heaven preserve us from it!) the trade might be greater or it might not, but the room would be larger, the bar longer, the flies, dirt, odor abominable. I hope I am not traducing a worthy class, but the American saloon-keeper of small-town proclivities has always had a kind of horror for me. The implements of his trade have always been so nauseatingly gummy. Here in Marlow and elsewhere in England, whenever I had occasion to inspect them, the public houses of the small-town type were a great improvement over the American variety. They were clean and homelike and cheerful. The array of brass, the fire, the small tables for games, pleased me. It looked to be a place used more as a country club or meeting house than, as in our case, a grimy, orgiastic resort. If there were drunken men or women in any of these "pubs," this night I did not see them. My Scotch friend assured me that, ordinarily, he believed them to be fairly respectable.

Not knowing my way through the woods adjacent and having spent much time in this way, I finally decided to take a train or conveyance of some kind. But there was no train or conveyance to be had for some time to come. The trains that were there did not run my way, and no "fly" would convey me, as one bar mistress informed me, because there was a hard hill to climb and the rain which had fallen during the day had made the roads bad. I began to meditate on returning to the inn. Finally the bar-lady observed, "I can tell you exactly how to get there, if you want to walk. It's not more than an hour and it's a perfectly good road all the way."

She drew with her finger an outline of the twists of the road. "If you're not afraid of a few screech owls, there's nothing to harm you. You go to the bridge up here, cross it and take the first road to your left. When you come to a culvert about a mile out you will find three roads dividing there. One goes down the hollow to somewhere—I forget the name—one goes up the hill to Cookham—it's a bridle path—and one goes to the right. It's a smooth, even road—that's the one you want."

It was a lovely night. The moon overhead was clear and bright, and the fog gave the fields a white, eerie look. As we walked, my friend regaled me with what he said was a peculiar custom among English traveling men. At all English inns there is what is known as the traveling men's club. The man who has been present at any inn on any stated occasions for the greatest number of hours or days is *ipso facto* president of this club. The traveling man who has been there next longest, if only for ten minutes less than the first or more than the third, is vice president. Every inn serves what is known as the traveling man's dinner at twelve o'clock or thereabouts, and he who is president by virtue of the qualifications above described is entitled to sit at the head of the table and carve and serve the roast. The vice president, if there be one, sits at the foot of the table and carves and serves the fowl. When there are two or more traveling men present—enough to provide a president and a vice president for this dinner—there is a regular order of procedure to be observed.

The president arriving takes his seat first at the head of the table; the vice president then takes his place at the foot of the table. The president, when the roast beef is served, lifts the cover of his dish and says, "Mr. Vice President, we have here, I see, some roast beef." The vice president then lifts the cover of his dish and says, "Mr. President, we have here, I see, some roast goose." "Gentlemen," then says the president, bowing to the others present, "the dinner is for all," and begins serving the roast. The vice president later does his duty in turn. The next day, in all likelihood, the vice president or some other becomes president, and so it goes. My little Scotsman was most interested in telling me this, for it appealed to his fancy as it did to mine, and I could see he relished the honor of being president in his turn.

It was while he was telling this that we reached the culvert and we saw before us three paths—the middle one and the one to the right going up through the dark woods, the one to the left merely skirting the woods and keeping out in the light.

"Let's see, it's the left you want, isn't it?" he asked.

"No, it's the right," I replied.

"I think she said the left," he cautioned. "Well, anyhow, here's a signpost. You lift me up and I'll read what it says."

It wasn't visible from the ground.

I caught him about the legs and hoisted him aloft, and he peered closely at all three signs. He was a dapper, light little man.

"You're right," he said. I lowered him to the ground.

"Well, here's to you," I said. "I'm surely much obliged. It's been a pleasant evening."

"I've enjoyed it ever so much."

We shook hands and wished each other luck. He struck off along the road he had come in the fog, and I mounted musingly through the woods. It was dark and delightfully odorous, the fog in the trees, struck by the moonlight, looking like moving sheeted ghosts. I went on gaily, expecting to hear a screech owl, but not one sounded. After perhaps fifteen minutes of walking I came out into the open road and then I found that I really did not know where Cookham was after all. There was no sign.

I went from house to house in the moonlight—it was after midnight—rousing up drowsy Englishmen who courteously gave me directions and facing yowling dogs who stood in the open roadway and barked. I had to push one barking guardian out of the way with my hand. All was silent as a churchyard. Finally I came to a family of Americans who were newly locating for the winter not far from Cookham, and they put me right. I recall the comment of the woman who opened the door—"You're an American, aren't you?" and the interest she took in being sure that I would find my way. When I finally reached my door I paused in the garden to survey the fog-lined valley, from which came the distant bark of a dog. The wayfaring laborers, the careful Scotsman, the man with the yoke, the man with the sheep, Marlow itself—how odd it all seemed. After London and New York, it was another world. And yet so life sags to the innocuous at every turn, I thought. Take away trade and stark necessity, and what have you?

What, indeed!

CHAPTER XII

After a few days I went to London for the first time—I do not count the night of my arrival, for I saw nothing but the railway terminus—and I confess I was not impressed as much as I might have been. After years in New York, Chicago and other American cities, the architecture of any city from an imposing point of view would, I should think, fail to impress me. The buildings are not as high as they are in America, any American city of any size, and they are not large in their coordinated masses. I could not help thinking, as we passed from Paddington via Hyde Park, Marble Arch, Park Lane, Brook Street, Grosvenor Square, Berkeley Square, Piccadilly and other streets to Regent Street and the neighborhood of the Carlton hotel, that it was beautiful, spacious, cleanly, dignified and well-ordered, but not astonishingly imposing. Fortunately it was a bright and comfortable morning, and the air was soft. There was a faint, bluish haze over the city, or that part which we traversed, which I took to be smoke, and certainly the city smelled as though it were smoky. I had a sense of great life, but not of crowded life, if I manage to make myself clear by that. It seemed to me at first blush as if the city might be so vast that no part was important. At every turn, Grant Richards, who was my ever-present monitor, was explaining, "Now this that we are coming to," or "This that we are passing," or "That is so-and-so," and so we sped by interesting things, the city impressing itself on me in a vague way but meaning very little in the vast mass of things present. We must have passed through a long stretch of Piccadilly, for Grant Richards pointed out a line of clubs, naming them—the St. James's Club, the Savile Club, the Lyceum Club, and then St. James's Palace, where he said the king lived at times. Next door, I learned later, was a noble pile where the dowager Queen Alexandra lived, and in some other place a dark-looking building of some charm which he said was the residence of the Duke of Portland.

I was duly impressed. I was seeing things which, after all, I thought, did not depend so much upon their exterior beauty or vast presence as upon the distinction of their lineage and connections. They were beautiful in a low, dark way, and certainly they were tinged with an atmosphere of age and respectability. After all, since life is a figment of the brain, the built-up notions of things are in many cases really far more impressive than the things themselves, and this was what I felt to be true of many of these things. London is a fanfare of great names; it is a clatter of vast reputations; it is a swirl of memories and celebrated beauties and orders and distinctions. It is almost impossible anymore to disassociate the real from the fictitious or, better, the spiritual. There is something here which is not of brick and stone at all, but which is purely a matter of thought. It is disembodied poetry, noble ideas, delicious memories of great things; and these, after all, are better than brick and stone. If the latter be not bad—and who, looking at London, could say that of it?—it is wonderful. The city is low, generally not more than five stories high, but it is beautiful. And it alternates great spaces with narrow crevices in such a way as to give a splendid idea of variety. You have at once a sense of being very crowded and of being very free. It looks at times as though you had all space and no space. A fine human touch, this, and quite like life.

The thing that struck me most in so brief a survey—we were surely not more than twenty minutes in reaching our destination—was that the buildings were largely a golden yellow in color, quite as if they had been white and time had stained them. Many other buildings looked as though they had been white also but had been covered with a thick black soot which the wind and rain had whipped in spots and made white again. At first I thought, "How homely." Later I thought, "This effect is quite charming."

We are so used to the new and shiny and tall in America, particularly in our larger cities, that it is very hard at first blush to estimate a city of equal or greater rank, which is old and low, and, to a certain extent, smoky. My first thought was, "Why, this is like St. Louis in 1891," and then it reminded me again of Philadelphia and Rittenhouse Square. Grosvenor Square and some of the other squares are quite like that. It was better than Philadelphia and St. Louis combined, as I could see at a glance, for there was a different order of life holding here. There was, off-hand, more beauty, more surety, more dignity, more space. The people walking were not more leisurely, but, by and large, I should say, they were better dressed. The police had an air of dignity and intelligence such as I have never seen anywhere in America, and it was obvious at a glance. The streets were so beautifully swept and cleaned, and I saw soldiers here and there in brilliant uniforms, standing outside palaces and walking in the public ways. That alone was sufficient to differentiate London from any American city. We rarely see our soldiers. They are too few. I think what I felt most of all was that I could not feel anything very definite about so great a city, and that there was no use trying.

"Here is a famous bachelor neighborhood," Grant Richards pointed out to me, nodding. "The comfortable man-about-town finds this convenient."

I looked and saw a very respectable row of buildings—no one more than five stories, clean, orderly, attractive. It was like every other neighborhood I had seen thus far, orderly, well-paved, ornate, each building looking as though it had received the undivided care of some able architect. I think that is one thing you feel keenly about London, that somehow great individual care has been put on each separate building in the better neighborhoods, and that each is a product of some taste and skill. One can see where styles have been borrowed from Rome, Venice, Florence and elsewhere and only slightly modified to meet the local needs. But the architecture is good, reserved, conservative, even delicate in some instances.

We were soon at some bank where I was to have my American order for money cashed; and then, after a short walk in some narrow street, we were at the office of my friend Grant Richards, where I caught my first glimpse of an English publishing house. It was very different from an American house of the same kind, for it was in an old and dark building of not more than four stories, such as in America would not be allowed to stand, and set down in a narrow angle off Regent Street and lighted by small, lead-paned windows, which in America would smack strongly of Revolutionary days. In fact we have scarcely any such buildings left. Grant Richards's offices were on the second floor, up a small dingy staircase, and his private room itself was so small that it surprised me by its coziness. I could not call it dingy. It was quaint, rather, Georgian in its atmosphere, with a small open fire glowing in one corner, a great rolltop desk entirely out of keeping with the place in another, a table, a bookcase, a number of photos of celebrities framed, and the rest books. I think he apologized for, or explained the difference between, this and the average American business house, but I do not think explanations are in order. London is London. I should be sorry if it were exactly like New York, as it may yet become. The smallness and quaintness appealed to me as a fit atmosphere for good books.

I should say here that this preliminary trip to London from Cookham, so far as Grant Richards was concerned, was intended to accomplish three things: first, to give me a preliminary glimpse of London; second, to see that I was measured and examined for certain necessary articles of clothing in which I was, according to Grant Richards, woefully lacking; and third, to see that I attended the concert of a certain German singer in whom he was interested and whose singing he thought I might enjoy. It was most important that I should go, because he had to go; and since all that I did or could do was merely grist for my mill, I was delighted to accompany him.

Grant Richards, in many respects, I wish to repeat here, is one of the most delightful persons in the world. He is a sort of modern Beau Brummell with literary, artistic and gourmandizing leanings. He loves order and refinement, of course—things in their proper ways and places—as he loves life: its dress, food, appearances and the like. I suspect him at times of being somewhat of a martinet in home and office matters; but I am by no means sure that I am not doing him a grave injustice. A more even, complaisant, well-mannered and stoical soul, who manages to get his way in some fashion or other, if it takes him years to do it, I never met. He surely has the soul of a stoic, the patience of fate and, I think, the true charity of a great heart.

However, looking me over as I was in America, I fancy he said to himself, "This individual, whom I rather like, is deficient in many things. Plainly, America, in its larger aspects, knows little of the fine details of raiment and living; and this man is—well—an American. Now before he can be properly presented in London and elsewhere, he needs—well, let me see." So this morning I had to be measured for waistcoats and shirts, some ties to be made to order, some shoes to be made to order, a fur overcoat to be measured for, some socks, silk and otherwise, to be purchased, and things of that sort. My silk hat needed to be ironed, my eyeglasses to be mended. I was to look after a mackintosh and a knit vest and buy myself, under Grant Richards's direction, a sovereign purse. The latter was due to the difference between English and American money, whereof I here and now complain.

English money is peculiar to me. It is based, as I am told, on some theory of multiplying the shilling, but I have never been able to figure out how that is. Our American decimal system—one cent, five cents, ten cents, twenty-five cents and so on up to five thousand cents—seems ideal to me. But of course I am used to that. The English are used to their money. I missed my nickels, dimes, quarters and dollar bills from the start and paid my way uncertainly with my shilling, two-shilling and half-crown pieces. The idea that there should be a fifty-cent piece and a sixty-cent piece so nearly alike that you can scarcely tell them apart seems to me the height of the ridiculous—but again I am used to a different system. One night I surprised a London policeman by showing him a two-shilling piece and sixpence piece in one hand and asking "How much is that?"

"Three shillings," he answered.

"And how much is that?" I asked, showing him a sixpence piece and a half-crown in the other hand.

"Three shillings," he replied.

"Isn't that silly to have two sets of money so nearly alike which amount to the same thing?" I observed, and he smiled oddly but did not reply.

I was badly confused at first as to this relationship, and it is not clear in my mind yet. Later, however, I had a typewritten statement of what all the pieces of money I was apt to encounter were worth in American money, and this I consulted in moments of doubt.

This matter of English and American money began to trouble me the moment I reached that stage on my voyage where I began to pay for things out of my own pocket to the ship's servants. I couldn't figure out the tips to my own satisfaction, and this irritated me. I remember urging Grant Richards to make the whole matter clear to me, which he did much later. He gave me a typewritten statement as to what tips I should pay at hotels and country houses and how and when, and this I followed religiously. Here it is:

"In leaving the hotel tomorrow, give the following tips:

Maid	3/-
Valet	3/-
Gold-braid boy	1/-
Porter who looks after telephone	1/-
Outside man (doorman)	1/-

If you reckon at a hotel to give 9d. a day to the maid and the valet, with a minimum of 1/-, you will be doing handsomely. At a country house, on the supposition that they have only maids, give the two maids whom you are likely to come across 2/6 each when you come away on Monday. (I am speaking of weekends.) Longer periods should be figured at 9d. a day. If, on the other hand, it is a large establishment—butler and footman—you would have to give the butler 10/- and the footman 5/- for a weekend; for longer periods more."

While we were discussing money at different times, I was warned that I should need a coin-purse for holding gold-pieces, and after carrying a few half-sovereigns and sovereigns in my vest and trousers pockets along with my other change, I soon agreed. The half-sovereigns were so small (the same size as our $ 2.50 gold piece) that I was always losing them or dropping them, and at one of the public houses in Marlow I was sure for a time that I had lost one. Some of my pennies and sixpences dropped on the floor and with it my gold. However, later I concluded not. So this morning I agreed, on going to London, that I must surely have a coin-purse.

I cannot imagine anything more delightful than being introduced, as I was by Grant Richards, to the social character of London. He was so intelligent and so very nice about it all. "Now, first," he said, "we will get your glasses mended, and then you want a traveling bag, and then some ties and socks, and so on. Well, come along. I have an appointment with you at your tailor's at eleven o'clock, where you are to be measured for your waistcoats, and at eleven-thirty at your furrier's, where you are to be measured for your fur coat," and so on and so forth. "Well, come along. We'll be off."

I was pleased, for I had just received a package of interesting and congratulatory letters, and I was feeling very good indeed. We went out into Carlton Street through Regent Street to an optician's, where I left my distance glasses; thence to a leather goods house, where I bought a bag for six pounds; then to a hatter's, where my silk hat was ironed; then to my tailor's, where I was measured for waistcoats; thence to a shirtmaker's, where I was measured for shirts and bought ties and socks; and thence to my furrier's, where I was measured for a fur coat.

I have to smile when I think of it, for I of all people am the least given to this matter of proper dressing and self-presentation, and Grant Richards, within reasonable limits, represents the other extreme. To him, as I have said, these things are exceedingly important. The delicate manner in which he indicated and nudged me into getting the things which would be right, without openly insisting on them, was most pleasing. "In England, you know," he would hint, "it isn't quite good form to wear a heavy-striped tie with a frock coat—never a straight black. And we never tie them in that fashion—always a simple knot." My socks had to be striped for morning wear and my collars winged, else I was in very bad form indeed. I fell into the habit of asking, "What now?" and I think that system of procedure might well have continued throughout the entire trip.

London streets and shops, as I first saw them, interested me greatly. I saw at once more uniforms than one would ordinarily see in New York and more high hats and presumably—I could not tell for the overcoats—cutaway coats. The uniforms were of mailmen, porters, messenger boys and soldiers; and all being different from what I had been accustomed to, they interested me—the mailmen particularly, with a form of service helmet cut square off at the top; and the little messenger boys with their tambourine caps cocked joyously over one ear amused me. The policeman's helmet strap under his chin was new and interesting.

The first thing that took my attention in the stores was the clerks, but I may say that the stores and shops themselves, after New York, seemed small and old. New York is so new; the space given to the more important shops is so considerable. In London it struck me that the space was not much and that the woodwork and walls were dingy. One can tell by the feel of a place whether it is exceptional and profitable, and all of these were; but they were dingy. The English clerk, too, had an air of civility—I had almost said servility—which was different. They looked to me like individuals born to a condition and a point of view, and I think they are. In America any clerk may subsequently be anything he chooses (ability guaranteed), but I'm not so sure that this is true in England. Anyhow, the American clerk always looks his possibilities—his problematic future; the English clerk looks as though he were to be one indefinitely.

We were through with this (to me, novel) round by one o'clock, and Grant Richards explained that we would now go to the Carlton Grill. All my life—certainly all my literary life—I had been hearing of the Carlton, its distinction, its air; and now I said to myself, "Here I am, and I shall be able to judge it for myself." We stopped at a barber's for a few minutes to be shaved, and, to my astonishment, I saw a barbershop which in America would be considered ridiculous anywhere. It was not dirty; you could see quite plainly that it was clean, well-conditioned, and probably enjoying a profitable patronage; but for smallness, meanness, the age of the woodwork and the chairs, commend me to America of, say, 1865. It was the poorest little threadbare thing I have yet seen in that line, and it was directly adjoining the Carlton, I think. Grant Richards spoke of it as "his barber's."

"You won't see the same thing hyah that you do in America. Ouah babahshops are much less imposing. In America you make a function of shaving. Hyah we do it quickly—get it ovah with. We waste no time. In America your babahshops are palaces compared to ouahs." Quite so. An American barber's chair is worth, I should say, just fifty English chairs. Its appearance is showy, ornate, quite magnificent. The walls of a good American barbershop are marble or fine white plaster or hardwood heavily mirrored. The mirrors are large, engrossing. The bottles, towels, razor-racks, shaving mugs constitute a blazing curio case—a glittering museum. I think old English prints of 1732 and earlier show the English barbershop quite as it is today—no better, no worse. And I had fancied when looking at these prints that all such things had gone long ago.

The Carlton was another blow. I had fancied that I was going to see something on the order of the Plaza or the Ritz in New York—certainly as distinguished, let us say, as the Manhattan or the Belmont. Not so. It can only be compared, and I think fairly so, to the Lafayette or the Brevoort in New York. There was the same air of age here that there was about those two old but very excellent hotels. The woodwork was plain, quite simple (I am speaking of the grill); the coatroom was commonplace; the lavatories were certainly no better than those of the Brevoort; the carpets were red and a little worn in spots; the woodwork had obviously been repainted white from time to time. Several of the stairsteps squeaked as we went down. "The Lafayette, the Brevoort," I said to myself over and over in descending; and the cuisine and the general appearance of the dining room reminded me of the same type of room in these hotels.

As for the crowd—well, Grant Richards stated that it might be smart and it might not. Certain publishers, rich Jewish merchants, a few actors and some Americans would probably be here. This grill was affected by the foreign element. The *maître d'hôtel* was French, of course—a short, fat, black-whiskered man who amused me by his urbanity. The waiters were, I believe, German, as they are largely in London and elsewhere in England. One might almost imagine Germany intended to invade England via its waiters. The china and plate were simple and inexpensive, almost poor. A great hotel can afford to be simple. We had what we would have had at any good French restaurant, and the crowd was rather commonplace-looking to me. Several American girls came in, and they were good-looking—smart but silly. I cannot say that I was impressed at all, and my subsequent experiences confirm that impression. I am inclined to think that London hasn't one hotel of the material splendor of either the Ritz-Carlton, the Plaza or the Vanderbilt in New York. But let that go for the present.

While we were sipping our coffee, Grant Richards told me of a Mrs. Stoop, a friend of his, who was already most anxious to meet me. What he had been telling her you can guess as well as I, for he did not tell me. She was, he said, a lion-hunter. She tried to make her somewhat interesting personality felt in so large a sea as London by taking up with promising talent before it was already commonplace. She had asked him to bring me to lunch this day, but he did not think it wise. Come to think of it, he had consulted me earlier in the day in his office concerning this same lady, and I had refused to go. But I believe it was arranged over the phone then that I should lunch at her house the following day at one and be introduced to a certain Lady O., the daughter of a duke and a patron of the arts, and a certain Miss Villars, an interesting English type. Why Mrs. Stoop should be so anxious to meet me and introduce me to her friends was somewhat of a mystery to me, but I was pleased with the idea of going. I had never seen an English lady lion-hunter. I had never met the daughter of a duke, nor yet a typical English girl. There might be others present. I was also informed that Mrs. Stoop was really not English but Dutch, but she and her husband, who was also Dutch and a wealthy London banker, had resided in London so long that they were to all intents and purposes English, and besides, they were in rather interesting standing socially, being rich. It might pay for me to go. I stated that I was very glad to go.

We then arose and went to hear a certain Miss Culp, a German of about thirty years of age, sing at some important hall in London—Bechstein, I think it was—and on the way I was told something of her. It seemed that she was very promising—quite a success in Germany and elsewhere as a concert singer—and that she might be coming to America at some time or other. Grant Richards had known her in Berlin. He told me an amusing story of how he had begged her to sing at her very charming home near Berlin, where he was once staying, and that, she having complied, he fell sound asleep during the performance. He seemed to think I would like her. I tell all this because of subsequent developments. We went, and I heard a very lovely set of songs—oh, quite delightful—rendered in a warm, sympathetic, enthusiastic manner and representing the most characteristic type of German love sentiment. It is a peculiar sentiment—tender, wistful, smacking of the sun at evening and of lovely tarns on which the moon is shining. German sentiment verges on the mushy—is always close to tears—but anything more expressive of a certain phase of life I do not know.

Miss Culp sang forcefully, joyously, vigorously, and I wished sincerely that I might meet her and tell her so, but that was not to be then. After the concert Grant Richards disappeared behind the scenes, and I waited. When he came out, we agreed to separate until it was time to take the train to Cookham, for I wished to seek a stylographic pen, and he had an appointment with Miss Culp and Mrs. Stoop—I fancy to give them tea. I struck out to wander idly for an hour and find my way about, and so I secured another short impression of London which pleased me very much.

All the while in these dark streets—for it was quite dark when I came out of the concert hall—I was thinking of St. Louis, Philadelphia, Baltimore (the older portions), and all the while getting a sense of a life that was vast, complicated, rich, ornate, full of the smack of Empire and great ambassadorial functions and exchanges of great thought and taste and art with the whole world. One feels the absence of that in New York, and of course decidedly more so in any of the lesser American cities. They are important, distinguished from a trade point of view, but this quality of "knowing how to live," as Miss Longfellow had pointed out, and of having the intellectual and artistic and social authority to do so, is quite wanting. Say what you will, this life takes itself quite seriously, as though it were the last word, not beholden to any other section of the world for a standard, and that you can feel. In America we always appear to be wondering how they would do it elsewhere. Here is no questioning, not the least suggestion of it. It is all dignified, forceful, ordered, finished. You know it is right according to their standard, because this is the way they know it must be done. If you ask how do they know, the answer is tradition, age, a built-up order of procedure. There is no other answer. It is like English law. There is no written code, merely an index of precedent.

I came through Harley Street, Cavendish Square—where are the great doctors—Portland Place and somehow into Oxford Street; along that to Selfridge's store and much farther, and then back along this same street to a much busier world which was in the neighborhood of a famous restaurant. Since the London subways concerned my next novel, "The Financier," I was determined to ride in them as much as possible in order to get a sense of their order and character instead of riding in taxis, as Grant Richards suggested. I was entertained deliciously by the spectacle of the swarming life about me, for London appears to be crowded everywhere. "Is this more crowded than New York?" I asked myself, and at times I thought it was.

Nowhere could I find the type of pen I wanted, and I got the impression that the London type of stationery shop was inferior to ours. However, I can offer no surety as to that. They seemed more crowded, less ordered, less interesting-looking, but the attendance was always more courteous. The business of clerks thanking you when you finally decided that you could not be satisfied, after having put them to so much trouble, was quite too much for me. It was so un-American—so much better, need I say?

Well, I did take the subway—the tube, I should say—and hunted my way back to Paddington, where I found Grant Richards brisk and smiling.

"Were you amused?"

"Quite."

"Well, then, this afternoon was not wasted. I shall always be satisfied if you are amused. As for myself, I have been horribly bored. I don't care for music, and I abominate—I confess it to you—talking art when I must as a duty. It is quite impossible."

I smiled, and we rode sleepily back to Cookham to dine and thence to bed.

CHAPTER XIII

I recall Sunday, December 3rd, 1911, with as much interest as any date, for on that day at one-thirty I encountered my first London drawing room and some personalities that interested and amused me greatly. Grant Richards and I went into town at eleven via the Great Western, agreeing to meet at the Paddington Station at about five-forty-five and return to Cookham together. As usual we talked of literature and art. I recall now as a part of this fortunate adventure that we had been talking of a new development in French art, which Grant Richards approved in part and disapproved in part—the Post-Impressionists, I think he termed them—and there was mention also of the Cubists, a still more radical departure from conventional forms, in which, if I caught it right, the artist passes from any attempt at transcribing the visible scene and becomes wholly geometric, metaphysical and symbolic—a phase of art with which I was not sufficiently familiar at this time to judge.

I recall that when he first spoke of leaving New York, I had been presented with a book on French art by one of my friends in the Century Company, and in that I read of this latest development, but only with passing interest. I rather drew the conclusion at the time that the Post-Impressionist movement was a reaction against the superficial refinement of such work as that of Reynolds in England or Greuze and Cabanel in France, a protest in fact, and as such lacked the authority of true art. The fact that after a very short while I began to suspect that I might be mistaken is neither here nor there. The truth is that Manet, Degas and Cézanne were little more than names to me and that the works of van Gogh, Paul Gauguin, Matisse, Picasso and Epstein were entirely unknown. I think I did know the theory on which Manet worked, the value of depending upon atmosphere to harmonize primary colors, and I may have seen an example or two of his work—in an indifferent way, however. There was what appeared to me a puzzle picture by one of the present-day leaders of the new movement in one of the London weeklies a few nights after I arrived, and we had discussed that with varying opinions. I am inclined to mistrust my opinion of anything new. Things grow on me by degrees, and I change my mind so. In this instance I declared that I could not tell. We might be evoluting into a higher or different understanding of life which would require only symbols to represent the art of nature. The truth was, the picture had no immediate appeal for me, and I admitted that.

When I reached the home of Mrs. Stoop, which was in one of those lovely squares that constitute such a striking feature of the West End and other portions of London, I was ushered upstairs to the drawing room, where I found my host, a rather practical and shrewd-looking Dutchman, and his less obviously Dutch wife, discussing a peculiar picture.

"Oh, Mr. D-r-r-izer," exclaimed my hostess on sight as she came forward to greet me, a decidedly engaging woman of something over forty whose bronze hair and ruddy complexion and distinguished gown of green silk, cut after the latest mode, stamped her in my mind as of a romantic, artistic, eager disposition. "You must come and tell us at once what you thingk of the pigture ve are discussing. It is downstairs. Lady O. and Miss Villars are already there. Ve are trying to see if ve can get a better light on it. Mr. Grant Richards has told me of you. You are from America. You must tell us how you like London, after you see the Day-gah"—the proper pronunciation, I was finding, of Degas.

I think I liked this lady thoroughly at a glance and felt at home with her, for I know the type. It is the same to which Bernhardt, Réjane and Mrs. Leslie Carter belong. It is the mobile, artistic type, with not much practical judgment in great matters, but bubbling with enthusiasm, temperament, life. I quite possessed her on sight, for I felt that I could command her interest and artistic admiration if I chose.

"Certainly. Delighted. I know too little of London to talk of it. I shall be interested in your picture."

We were downstairs again by this time.

"Mr. D-r-r-izer, the Lady O."

A modern suggestion of the fair Joanne, considerably withered by time, tall, astonishingly lissome, done—as to clothes—after the best manner of the romanticists and suggesting one of Wagner's most warlike goddesses because of a winged hat, grown thin and tall. Such was the Lady O. She looked a little too made-up for comfort, a little dusty as to complexion, and that is always uncomfortable. A more fascinating type—from the point of view of stagecraft—I never saw. I never saw anyone made up better. And the languor and lofty elevation of her gestures and eyebrows defy description. She could say, "Oh, I am so weary of all this," with a slight elevation of her eyebrows a hundred times more definitely and forcefully than if it had been shouted in stentorian tones through a megaphone.

She gave me the fingers of an archly poised hand.

"It is a pleasure."

"And Miss Villars, Mr. D-r-r-izer."

"I am very pleased."

A pink, slim lily of a woman, say twenty-eight or thirty, very fragile-seeming, very Dresden china-like as to color, a dream of light and Tyrian blue with some white interwoven, very keen as to eye, the perfection of hauteur as to manner, so well-bred that her voice seemed subtly suggestive of it all—that was Miss Villars. I thought her as delicate and characteristic a piece of humanity as I have ever known, so vastly different to the types we breed in America.

To say that I was interested in this company is putting it mildly. The three women were so distinct, so individual, so characteristic, each in a different way. The Lady O. was all peace and repose—statuesque, weary, dark. Miss Villars was like a ray of sunshine, pure morning light, delicate, gay, mobile. Mrs. Stoop was of thicker texture, redder blood, more human fire. She had a vigor past the comprehension of either, if not their subtlety of intellect—which latter is often so much better.

Mr. Stoop stood in the background, a short, stocky provider—a little uncertain as to his place in this world, a little suspicious of his wife's temperament, I fancied—a typical money-grubber of, say, Threadneedle Street, in tow of a once pretty and still not unattractive woman.

"Ah, yes, Day-gah! You like Day-gah, no doubt?" interpolated Mrs. Stoop, recalling us. "A lovely pigture, don't you thingk? Such color! such depth! such sympathy of treatment! Oh!"

Mrs. Stoop's hands were up in a pretty artistic gesture of delight.

"Oh yes," continued the Lady O., taking up the rapture. "It is so human—so perfect in its harmony. The hair—it is divine! And the poor man—he lives alone now in Paris, quite dreary, not seeing anyone. Aw, the tragedy of it! The tragedy of it!" A delicately carved vanity box she carried, of some odd workmanship—blue and white enamel with points of coral in it—was lifted in one hand as expressing her great distress. I confess I was not much moved by what seemed purely conventional, albeit highly artistic, pathos, and I looked quickly at Miss Villars. Her eyes, it seemed to me, held a subtle, apprehending twinkle in them, but I could not be sure.

"And you?" It was Mrs. Stoop addressing me.

"It is impressive, I think. I don't know as much of his work as I might, I am sorry to say."

I was really very uncertain as to the value of the picture, for the method was quite new to me. Besides, I was satisfied that I was not seeing it across a sufficient space. Being impressionistic, it needed, I thought, more distance and the play of interesting atmosphere. I am not an ultimate art critic.

"Aw, he is marvelous! Wonderful! I am transported by the beauty and the depth of it all!" It was Mrs. Stoop talking, and I could not help rejoicing in the quality of her accent. Nothing is so pleasing to me in a woman of culture and refinement as that additional tang of remoteness which a foreign accent lends. If only all the lovely, cultured women of the world could speak with a foreign accent in their native tongue I would like it better. It lends a touch of piquancy not otherwise obtainable.

A delightful woman, this, I said to myself. Charming. And these other two—the Lady O., as a type, and Miss Villars, a pure, dainty, delicate Dresden china.

By this time a third gentleman had been announced, a Mr. K., a dwarf and, as I understood it, a most accomplished violinist. He was, as I understood, the friend and mentor of the Miss Culp whom I had heard sing the previous afternoon. I had understood that Mrs. Stoop had also assisted to get Miss Culp her London hearing, or at least that she had been working to make her concert a success.

Our luncheon party was complete now, and we would probably have gone immediately into the dining room except for another picture—by Picasso. Let me repeat here that before Grant Richards called my attention to Picasso's cubical uncertainty in the London Exhibition, I had never heard of him. I have explained how I felt. Here in a dark corner of the room was the nude torso of a consumptive girl, her ribs showing, her cheeks colorless and sunken, her nose a wasted point, her eyes as hungry and sharp and lustrous as a bird's. Her hair was really not hair, but strings. And her thin, bony arms and shoulders were pathetic, decidedly morbid in their quality. To add to the morgue-like aspect of the whole thing, the picture was painted in a pale bluish-green key.

I wish to state here that now, after a little lapse of time, this conception—the thought and execution of it—is growing on me. I am not sure that this work, which has rather haunted me, is not much more than a protest—the expression and realization of a great temperament. But at the moment it struck me as dreary, gruesome, decadent, and I said so. I was in no mood to say anything at all because my current temperament was repelled by it. Lady O. was expressing unbounded satisfaction, Miss Villars was looking at it quite uncertainly. Mrs. Stoop was quite near me, eagerly insistent, I thought.

"And what do you think?"

"I'm afraid I don't like it."

"Aw, don't like—my Picasso!"

I felt a shrinking sense of dissatisfaction and defeat in her. I was falling in her estimation rapidly. Really, I could feel the atmosphere change.

"It strikes me as a little gloomy—morbid."

"Gloomy! Morbid!" Mrs. Stoop fired in her quite lovely accent. "What have they to do with art?"

"Luncheon is served, Madame."

The double doors of the dining room were flung open, and we were called to pass the erect flunky, as firm in his attitude as a piece of wood.

"That is quite too bad! He doesn't like my Picasso! I can't understand that. From what Mr. Grant Richards said, I thought you would be just the one—" the remark ended by my interrupting.

"But I don't think I do—I'm not absolutely sure—but I don't think so."

She was busy for the moment arranging us, and then I found myself sitting between Mrs. Stoop and Miss Villars, with the violinist opposite me. The conversation fell to pairs for the moment, I addressing myself to Miss Villars.

"I was so glad to hear you say you didn't like it," Miss Villars applauded, her eyes sparkling, her lips moving with a delicate little smile. "You know, I abhor those things. They *are* decadent, like the rest of France and England. We are going backward instead of forward, I am quite sure. We have not the force we once had. It is all a race after pleasure and living and an interest in subjects of that kind. I am quite sure it isn't healthy, normal art. I am sure life is better and brighter than that."

"I am inclined to think so myself at times," I replied.

We talked further, and I learned to my surprise that she suspected England to be decadent as a whole, falling behind in brain, brawn and spirit, and that she thought America was much better.

"Do you know," she observed, "I really think it would be a very good thing for us if we were conquered by Germany."

I was quite astonished at this. I had found here, I fancied, someone who was really thinking for herself, and a very charming young lady in the bargain. She was quick, apprehensive, all for a heartier point of view. I am not sure now that she was not merely being nice to me, and that anyhow she is not all wrong, and that the heartier point of view is the courage which can front life unashamed, which sees the divinity of fact and of beauty in the utmost seeming tragedy. Picasso's weak flower of decay and degradation is beginning to teach me something—the marvelous perfection of the spirit which is concerned with neither perfection nor decay, but life. It haunts me.

However, I agreed with her heartily then, and we struck up a laughing friendship. I told her of my interest in London—the differences, the notable differences which occurred to me between America and England. Mrs. Stoop questioned me concerning my experiences. I was drawn into an exchange of experiences with the dwarf, who had been to America. American railroads, American health, American size—oh, many things came up. I presently fell crosswise of the Lady O., whom I found to be a profound admirer of Henry James, for I did not quite agree that the involved sentence of labyrinthine depths was absolutely necessary. She seemed to think the more difficult the nut to crack, the more significant the food. I yield to none in my understanding of James and my appreciation of what he has to say, but I insist that a less convolute process of thought would give him a more enduring place. It is somewhat like those who admire George Meredith. I am accused of using poor English, and I know no ready method of remedying it. It is no answer to say, "Use better English." Defects are temperamental, and we rise or fall by our temperaments. People who live in glass houses, etc.

This very charming luncheon was quickly over, and I think I gathered a very clear impression of the status of my host and hostess from their surroundings. There were pictures and tapestries and china and glass, to say nothing of furniture and rugs, of rare selection. The walls and room spaces were not exactly crowded, but they had a sense of fullness of important living material. Money here was reasonably plentiful. Mr. Stoop was evidently liberal in his understanding of what constitutes a satisfactory home. It was not exceptional in that it differed greatly from the prevailing standard of luxury. There was nothing that one might call strikingly different here. The rooms had rather an early Flemish look which consorted but poorly with Picasso's grim representation of life and Degas's revolutionary opposition to conventional standards. I worked this out later in my defense of my attitude in regard to Picasso when we were once more upstairs, looking at more drawings of the disciples of the Post-Impressionists and the Cubists then residing in London.

It is curious how friendships spring up. Miss Villars and I were all for each other on sight, I fancy. Her glances were most kindly, her smile most radiant, and I'm sure I reciprocated in spirit, if not in kind. We stood side by side after I ended a long dissertation on American force in the dining room, after the women had gone, Mr. K., the dwarf, and Mr. Stoop being my auditors. They seemed to approve rather cheerfully, though I knew it was courtesy more than approval.

"At last I have found someone who will stand with me," said Miss Villars.

"Indeed I will. But tell me of the Lady O.—a most remarkable type."

"It's too long," she laughed. "She is Lucrezia Borgia come to life—in appearance only. Quite your subtle poisoner."

"More like the fair Joanne, only a little *passée*."

"I like my comparison best. You will never see a better. She is a fair example of what I was saying—English decadence."

"But surely English women are better than that—not more artistic. They couldn't be. She is really a great achievement."

"No, that is the direction. English society is tending that way. I feel it."

"And the mass?"

"They are worn out. They need a transfusion of blood."

"Aren't you shrewd! We get along fine. We agree intellectually. Surely we must continue this."

"I hope so. It would be a pleasure."

Just as we were talking a fourth man made his appearance—an artist. I shall not forget him soon, for you do not often meet people who have the courage to appear at a Sunday afternoon sociable in a shabby, workaday business suit, unpolished shoes, a green neckerchief in lieu of collar and tie, and cuffless sleeves. I admired the quality—the workmanship—of the silver-set scarab which held his green silk neckerchief together, but I was a little puzzled as to whether he was very poor and his presence insisted upon or comfortably progressive and posing thus as a means of attracting attention. His face and body were quite thin, his hands delicate. There was a fine line from the forehead to the end of the nose, quite fine. The mouth, the lips were not too wide, and thin. I noted a peaked interest in things and, I thought, an exceptional subtlety—say, one who would not be quite frank at any time. His eye was not a straight staring eye—quite moving and almost apprehensive. I learned afterward that his name was Henry Lamb and that he was an artist of some force and distinction. Grant Richards had been one of those who had first taken him in hand.

I am not sure that Miss Villars had ever seen him before. She seemed quite surprised by his appearance. The Lady O. was interested and, I think, took his hand for the first time. By some oversight neither Miss Villars nor myself was introduced. Art was in the air, and Picasso up for further discussion. During our absence—the men over the coffee—Picasso and Degas had been reintroduced on this floor and a number of drawings of some German follower of Cézanne and Matisse. They were black like partitioned fields, raw reds and greens and browns placed sharply side by side and the eye left to introduce atmosphere sufficient to harmonize them all. They were not bad.

"Now, Mr. Lamb, what do you think of my Day-gah?"

The painter shrugged his shoulder as if he were cold. "I rather like them," he said. "I am not exactly a convert. They are not bad."

"And yet once I thought—"

"But I do not think I care for them so much now."

The green silk neckerchief was fascinating us all. Think of this combination: Henry Lamb, Mrs. Stoop, Miss Villars, the dwarf, the Lady O. and Mr. Stoop, uncertain and commonplace.

"This is quite the most interesting thing yet," I heard the dwarf say to Miss Villars.

She moved to my side.

"Do you think art really needs that?" she asked me. She was alluding to the green silk neckerchief.

"It does not offend me. I admire the courage. It is at least individual."

"That I could not do," volunteered the dwarf.

"It is after George Bernard Shaw. It has been done before," replied Miss Villars.

"Then it requires almost more courage," I said.

"And what about Picasso? Are you as fond of him? Do you like this?" Here Mrs. Stoop moved the sad excerpt from the morgue to the center of the room that he of the green neckerchief might gaze at it.

"I like it," he pronounced. "The note is somber, but it is excellent work"

"I like it," he pronounced. "The note is somber, but it is excellent work. Quite an achievement, I should say."

Mrs. Stoop was comforted a little. "These others do not like it—Miss Villars and Mr. K. and Mr. D-r-r-izer."

"I like it," returned Henry Lamb simply.

He left after a moment or two quite abruptly, and then the Lady O. extended her hand in an almost pathetic farewell. I wish I could describe it. Lady Macbeth in the sleepwalking scene could not have been more strange. The voice was lofty, sad, sustained.

"Good-bye. So sorry! I shall not see you soon. We are leaving for Rome Wednesday. You go to Berlin. I shall hope to see you there later. Perhaps you will see me once before I go," she was talking in a perfectly delightful strain to Mrs. Stoop.

"Good-bye!" to me. "So charmed!"

"Good-bye!" still in that same high, aloof key to Miss Villars and the dwarf. "This has been most pleasant."

It would have brought a round of hearty applause at a theater.

She went out, and I said to myself that I treasured each particular movement and word. As an artistic presentation of a mood, it was perfect. Life does not know how to produce many Lady O.'s.

We were considerably reduced now, and Mrs. Stoop turned to me as a source of interest and a point of attack. "So you don't like my Picasso?" I am sure she felt that I had made a grave mistake. Either I was much overrated intellectually, or I had some sound, deep-seated reason.

"So you don't like my Picasso?" she repeated.

"I like it as a piece of painting, not as a subject. It is in my judgment too morbid—decadent, I should say. Life is better than that—healthier, more brilliant."

"And you call yourself a realist. You write realistic books. You see how life is. As though art must concern itself with health or color or brilliancy! I don't understand that. I don't accept it. Art is something more than that—greater than that."

She was working herself up into quite a destructive mood, and I felt myself called upon to defend myself vigorously or accept a humiliating defeat here and now and retire discredited, unable to enlist her sympathy and interest any longer.

Women are so peculiar in this way—this type of woman. They need intellectual dominance by someone—crave it. No man can hope to hold their interest who cannot in a way browbeat them thoroughly. They crave it. They are happy to receive it. They slip out so gracefully via the door of their womanhood and their sex. "Oh, but you are so much more clever!" How often I have heard that!

"Art is what life is," I exclaimed easily and rather airily, "and life is not morbidity. It is better than that. I am perfectly willing to admit for argument's sake that morbidity is a part of life. What part? An infinitesimal fraction. Life is not concerned with it. Life is concerned with construction, building up a lovely illusion, not destroying itself via death and despair. I call life to witness. Look out of the window! Look at this room! Look at yourself! Look at what you desire! That? Never! If you thought it were approaching you personally, you would flee in terror. Your house does not show that you crave morbidity. I fancy only healthy people are invited. Your companionship, I'll venture to say, does not show it. Young love flees morbidity. Life is busy creating an illusion of joy, happiness, gaiety, hope. How can you say that life, or art, which is an expression of life, will sanction that? You can't. You don't. This is a temporary interest, a pose, a passing enthusiasm. These people, like Picasso, are merely protesting against the undue predominance of the other. If the thing they do has no vitality, no authority, no permanence, life itself will not sanction it. Look out of the window."

"Life, life! The artist is not concerned with what life sanctions. He is above life. He is better than life."

She was quite excited.

"Oh, no," I said laughingly, "not as good as that. He is of life. Life produces him in its struggle for healthy expression. He is better than his work. Life is better than he is because life produces him."

I went on gaily, piling words on words, but to tell you the truth I was merely befogging the issue. The questions are entirely insoluble. No one can say definitely what is art. Everyone views art through his own temperament, and agreeing temperaments make a school. Picasso may be right. No doubt he is. Anyhow, I am not an art authority. But I had defeated milady by merely talking faster, and she fell back first on my books, which she had not read, but which Grant Richards had described to her, and then on the phrase, "But you are so much more clever." When that came, I laughed wearily. I could have said, "My thumbs are up." As it was, I added one more paragraph of the same kind, pointless because, as I say, art cannot be generalized upon in this way, and then she threw herself back pettishly on her divan. "Very well, we will not talk about art any more. Put the picture away. We will talk about books, streets, engines, not art."

"Clever woman," I laughed. "But you mustn't get angry. You must answer me."

"Answer! Answer!"

She was merely waiting to be coaxed. She saw that I liked her. My smile won a smile in return, and then Miss Villars praised me.

"Oh, that was so good. I'm so glad. You said what I have been wanting to say."

"We two must meet again," I whispered.

"But we do—Tuesday. Are you not coming to the concert Tuesday evening?"

"So I am. I had forgotten that. That is most fortunate."

I had forgotten that Grant Richards's first arrangement with Mrs. Stoop was to bring me to this concert, but she had insisted on seeing me earlier in order that she might talk with me.

"I'm sorry to see you go."

"I've been charmed to meet you. I hope we meet again," she said aloud.

"Oho!" exclaimed Mrs. Stoop. "That is quite a compliment. You find each other interesting. I am glad."

Miss Villars went quickly out.

I extended my hand.

"Delightful woman. Perfectly charming."

"But you don't like my picture."

"Give me time. I may."

"Yes, time—but that is all wrong. I shall see you Tuesday, though?"

"Without fail."

"And you sit by Miss Villars."

"That is very nice."

I went out breathing the London air, wondering at this odd gathering. Personalities affect me quite like winds and storms. They are the realest, most forceful things. They are like lovely sounds, colors, odors, dreams. I walked through Cadogan Place, down some unknown street, down another, wondering how I should spend my time until five-forty-five. I came out into some pleasing harmonious triangle where was a statue of a lord named Strathnairn, and a policeman, erect, his black leather strap under his chin. London life, on this delicious wine-colored Sunday afternoon, was like a song. The sky was a pale opal, the west red, a blue, opalescent haze in the air.

"Officer, where shall I find a Catholic church?" I asked.

I was thinking of vespers. Maybe I was not too late to witness the glow of candles and hear the poetic echoes of an older world.

"Well, there's the Oratory just below here. You might like to see that. And then there's St. Somebody's—I've forgotten the name—beyond the park." He was speaking of Hyde Park.

I decided to go to the Oratory, because he explained that it was a noble building, one of the largest in London, and I hurried down this street, wondering how near it was. Londoners were out in force here, a high-hatted, cutaway-coated mass, swinging canes and talking to none-too-pretty women. I passed Harrod's for the first time and was astonished to find it so large—quite larger than anything in New York, I thought. I understood that American department stores were always much larger. By pleasant ways I came to the Oratory, passing a tube station as I did so, and I saw I was late, for the vesper throng was coming out. I hurried in anyhow, for I wanted to see it.

A great building, dim in the fading afternoon light, odorous of incense, a few candles still burning on the altar, a light here and there, and in the pulpit an aged, gray-haired priest with a face as fine as that of Schubert or Schumann addressing a handful of people seated about the noble piece of carving which was his temporary throne. A great black wooden cross bearing a silver figure of the Christ stood beside him, and some nearby light cast a pale radiance on his face.

"He is some Catholic missionary," I thought, "ordered to address this company. A revival mission is being held here. What a slim group to address."

His subject was God—the love of God, the pointlessness of life, the security of faith—and I found that a fitting end to such a fleeting panorama as today had been. How often have I said that life is meaningless to me, a tale told by an idiot, sound and fury, signifying nothing! If anything were needed to prove it, the swirling streets running black with aimless humanity were enough. Aimless humanity! I maintain that. Listen to what I saw and heard here:

First, this stately pile, a composite of vague, flattering notions of art—coming from where? Going where? Next, this dim light, these silly people, gaping, praying, wondering whether they should stay, wondering whether they should go, some leaving in the midst of his finest periods and thoughts. You could look at them and then him and see how futile it was for that mind to be addressing these sheep. His discourse was eloquent, noble, logical, metaphysical, as religious discourses go. His face was old, gray, sad, weary.

God, he said, was an idea, the word, the be-all and the end-all of this seeming existence. Beyond Him was nothing. What was life? He demonstrated it as a collection of beliefs, desires to be, a thing of hope and fame and strength and appetite. What was fame? A silly fancy concerning the thoughts of others which could mean nothing to the individual beyond self-hypnotism of thinking so. What was a hope—a figment of the mind based solely on past gratifications and rumors of good to others and pleasures attained by others, but bringing no real satisfaction, for it was without definite realization. What was strength? A seeming. For one man one thing, for another another. Useless to fight off the growth of age, weariness, disappointment, dissatisfaction. What was appetite? Built-up illusions as to pleasure which is in the thought always, never in the deed. The actual deed, the moment, was rarely pleasurable. What was wealth? Accumulated care and duty.

I watched his face as he pronounced the doom of each earthly quality and then pointed with almost mumbling lips to the one great force which never changes, which always was, always will be. "I am the vine, ye are the branches," he quoted. "If you are connected with Him in thought," he went on, "all the rest is without significance. Thought of Him is all there is, because He is all there is. The rest is errant nonsense, meaning nothing. Life, so-called life, withers, but God endures."

I looked at the silly faces beneath him, a mere handful—they were really not listening, most of them. They were praying or drawing some vague satisfaction from being in the precincts of seemingly sacred things. The Catholic church offers shadows, incense, symbolic music as signs of divinity, and the world accepts them. This old man, tottering to his grave, must have been his own best listener, for at his age I can well imagine he believed what he said. He should.

I got up after a time and went out into the street. I asked four passersby what the next great building to this was, standing up so majestically in the gloom. No one knew. It was the South Kensington Museum. I went through the fast falling night to the tube and took my way to Paddington, wondering at all I had seen. There was Grant Richards waiting. He had gone around to Mrs. Stoop's after I had left. They had been most interested. I had created a real impression. The old, pale man in the pulpit at the Oratory was in my mind.

We rode to Cookham and walked home under a starry sky to Bigfrith. The fields were soft and hazy, glamorous. "Would a bottle of champagne cheer you up?" asked Grant Richards genially. "This is very important. What wine will you have?"

"Champagne will do," I said.

We came to a lovely little church in a hollow. The windows were lighted. They were singing. I wanted to go in.

"No, no," he said. "It is against the custom of the country to interrupt in this way. I couldn't let you. You shall come some Sunday with Gioia."

I gave up this vague tendency.

Finally we were home, at dinner, through it, through sherry, champagne, port, coffee, and finally were off to bed. As usual I lay and mused one hour, two, three. I heard a screech owl cry and some roosters crow. Then I slept. But I think I said over and over a score of times, "Sound and fury, signifying nothing."

And so it is.

CHAPTER XIV

London is lost in a fog at this period for me, for it is now December 20th, and I am writing of December 4th. All that day I wrote steadily at Bigfrith, and it rained, so I have nothing to record. I wrote until nearly four P.M. and then went into London, carrying some belongings of Grant Richards, a mirror among other things, and was comfortably installed at the Capitol Hotel. Grant Richards had told me about this as being central, convenient, cheap and reliable. I found I had a good room there, and I liked it very much, barring the age of all London buildings, the lack of steam heat, the slowness of telephones and many little odds and ends that seem slow to Americans. What London lacks in speed, mechanical equipment, newness and things of that sort, it makes up in civility, thoroughness, good cooking and general attention, which is pleasant. Nothing has overcome for me at present the sense of age in things and that absence of hard, raw force, which gives significance to America.

I must pass over many little things now which at first I thought I would record, for in retrospect they are unimportant. We are always doing something, and in the vast accumulation of things done, only a few things stand out. I remember dining with Grant Richards at a typical London chophouse—Scott's, I believe, not bad—and meeting there some member of a European gambling fraternity whom Grant Richards knew and who invited us around to the Raleigh Club to have coffee. He looked like King Edward VII, quite the same type, and Grant Richards looked like your typical lord in evening clothes, fur coat, monocle and opera hat. I have no idea what I looked like. I was dressed to match. Afterwards we went to Mrs. Stoop's, and there again was a company of all sorts, pretty girls and women in evening gowns, men of considerable repute or talent in evening clothes, my artist of the green silk handkerchief, Miss Villars and, I believe, at least one painter and one musician of great repute—John Sargent and Percy Grainger.

These evenings as a rule do not interest me very much—they are the same the world over. Mrs. Stoop did, however, for this interesting company, the music provided, the excellent supper afterwards, was an expression of her, I thought. Grant Richards had been telling me that she was very nice in her sympathetic attitude toward new talent and really helpful. I fancied I discerned the unrest of an unsatisfied youth, so far as love was concerned, and as I discovered later, I was not mistaken.

To really indicate what all this meant to me and to demonstrate clearly what subsequently transpired, I must animadvert a little to what has become, for me, a very significant and interesting fact in life: namely, the people who have lost their youth. I do not think that the average person under thirty really realizes what this means or has worked it out intellectually for himself, but for myself I can only say that it has become quite clear that for one reason and another—bashfulness, fear, poverty, homeliness, disadvantage of location and so on and so forth—one person here and there, perhaps many, between fifteen and thirty or forty have never had any sense of what a really joyous youth is. So many, on the contrary, have an ideal youth. They have happy homes, considerate parents, ample companionship of an age and temperament calculated to produce pleasure, and in their early years they are fed up on those things which are considered to constitute happiness in youth; consequently, as they grow older, they do not miss them, are satisfied they have had their share and go gracefully from single responsibility to marriage, children, and the pleasure of seeing their youth repeated in those who are younger than themselves and whom perchance they love dearly. For the non-constructive, unpropagandizing mind, this is quite an ideal progress, and many follow it without the least understanding of what stress, unrest, unhappiness may lie outside for those temperaments which for one reason and another may not be able to achieve it.

I have the profoundest pity for the person who, for any cause whatsoever, has missed that natural progress (whether as intellectuals we deem it essential or not), has fallen outside the procreative scheme of things. There is a mating season for us all. There is a temperamental inclination to build a home or a nest, though in so many it is purely rudimentary. Leading to that is all the enthusiasm of youth, its flare and gaiety. We dance our way to love. We sing our way to it. We run, laugh, posture, gesture. If by any chance we lose that at the time when it is best, sweetest, most delicious, heaven help us. The sting and the ache come after. We wake to find ourselves old and youth gone, and then for some it is "God damn the world!" Life is really not so unendurable under any circumstances, but by contrast with this we imagine it so. Poor little losers of their youth. I pity them.

There is the other nature which, meeting with all the details of this situation, is cursed with the imaginative or creative temperament in the bargain. This multiplies its woes. It sees not only the actual loss which can be borne by some temperament—the average temperament—with equanimity but also the spiritual deprivation, the vast possibility of joy, which is always a thousand times greater in the artistic imagination than it could possibly have been in fact. After all, we have but one little body, and it cannot eat up the whole world, however brilliantly the imaginative temper conceives that it can. So runs the situation.

Well, in Mrs. Stoop I perceived at once an example of something of this sort. Life had obviously not given her enough. I suspected a somnolent youth in which days and years had slipped away in a dream, and suddenly she had awakened to find herself, say, thirty-five or thirty-eight. Suppose she discovered a gray hair; suppose a wrinkle appeared. The young were more successful in love than she was. Gay youth was no longer so much interested in her. She may have married without much reflection, without real understanding, and now—now—life is slipping away.

It pleases me to think of her as I saw her among her guests that night. She was so eager, so forceful, so conscious of a rather triumphant situation. Clever people were about her—very clever. She was considered, in a way, a patron of the arts, music, painting, fiction, perhaps other things. A very talented group of musicians was rendering most interesting and affecting chamber music. A lovely English folk song was given, a new, strange, weird Irish reel. She was in close touch and harmony with the new art movement—Post-Impressionism, Cézanne, Gauguin, van Gogh, Picasso. I wonder whether Epstein and Gill were not in her rooms. She was on close terms of friendship with Grainger, Sargent, Grant Richards and now myself. Her greenish-blue eyes were quite lustrous. Her plump, not unattractive form was swathed in a close-drawn gown of dark-green silk. She had the vivacity of Bernhardt and our American Leslie Carter—and, alas, the unfortunate suggestion of approaching age. I read in her face the signs of and the opposition to growing old. Grant Richards voiced it very nicely in some preliminary remark, "She's growing old, and she isn't doing it very gracefully."

Well, I watched her talking to Miss Villars, to some very pretty black-haired girl whom I did not know, to some very interesting but contemptuous and vague middle-aged woman who interested me as a temperament. I saw my artist Henry Lamb in the room and some curiously self-conscious girl of delicious but entirely artificial poses who sang the English folk song I admired so much. Finally she came and sat opposite me, and we exchanged a series of curious glances.

I must say I delight in this—to some seemingly insipid—rapprochement between two temperaments. Nothing interests me quite so much as the psychology of the human mind, and to analyze a temperament from a face and a few remarks and a few actions is a great delight. It is like some complicated picture puzzle of which you have not the whole drawing but only a suggestion of what it might be. It is a great pleasure.

Let me say here and now that I was not at all interested in the lady physically. She did not stir me the least bit. From that point of view, I was far more interested in Miss Villars, who sat close to me and was most friendly. In fact she had indicated in every way to date that she liked me very much. I had warned Grant Richards, after my row with him in regard to Miss Longfellow on the steamer, to "keep out." Because I had expressed an interest in her, he was becoming interested, and in the outcome of any contest for possession of a lady, if he were really interested, I would have small hope. "I shan't look at her," he had promised going to the house, and he was obviously keeping his word. Mrs. Stoop sat down near me, though, and our eyes strayed together at least once in every ten seconds. I was wondering what she was thinking, and she was estimating my temperament. I know this from after facts. She occasionally addressed a remark to me or to her husband beyond me, and finally she left.

"That lady is not true to her husband," I said. "She is eager for passional experiences—not so much to love as to be loved. She wants to be the force that she might have been at eighteen or twenty or twenty-five." Alas!

I was sorry for her and delighted with her, for I approve of this human fire that fights and defies age. It may be useless and foolish, but it is interesting, dramatic, at times sad—a wonderful commentary on the force that makes life what it is.

After music we went in to supper, and by the kindly manners of Grant Richards I was placed by Miss Villars. Mrs. Stoop had promised me that she would see to this—after Miss Villars openly expressed a desire to know me better, but for some reason she didn't do it. Grant Richards lauded himself afterward for having done most excellently—"didn't he deserve some praise for his conduct?" I agreed that he did. Miss Villars and I fell into a passionate discussion of London, the decadence of England, what there was to see. Finally we agreed that we would meet—we were getting along so fine—and that she would show me some important thing in London—Hampton Court or the National Gallery or some park—and we could continue this pleasant discussion. She was to call me up and make an appointment, or I was to write her, and so we left it.

It was after supper that the interesting thing happened, for having messed over the food until quite late, the guests began to leave at once. There was quite a flurry of leave-taking. I talked with first one and then another, watching Mrs. Stoop about the artistic labor of her farewells. Finally my turn came, and I complimented her on her generalship. "You are a past master—you do it excellently well."

"Why do you leave so soon?" she asked. "I expected you and Grant Richards to stay a while and talk."

"But it is very late."

"I know, but what is time? And I may not see you so much more."

"That is so. You are going to Berlin on Tuesday next. Well then, I shall not see you anymore this season."

"Oh, but I wanted you to come and lunch with me on Friday. We will be all alone. We will have a nice, quiet talk."

"But I mustn't crowd your last remaining hours here. It is getting near Christmas."

"You will not. I want you to come. I should be disappointed if you should not. I must know more of you. Wait. Where is Grant Richards?"

"He's getting ready to leave, I think."

Just then the pianist came, Mr. Percy Grainger. He had on a handsome fur coat, and his light hair, suggestive of Paderewski, seemed to be blowing lightly about his head. A fine, Byronic head with bright-blue, fascinating eyes.

"Oah! There you are!" One could scent the female philanderer in Mrs. Stoop's voice, the lady of many passional interests. "What a fine coat—so-a soft! I will not see you then till we get to Berlin. You are there soon, now. I like these soft big coats—" She was stroking the fur.

Instantly I wished mine were finished. The remembrance of that amuses me.

He said some delicate artistic thing, smiled wisely, grasped her hand lightly.

"Good-bye! Good-bye!"

Her voice quite cooed.

The lady of a thousand interests, I thought.

"Now, where is Grant Richards?" she asked, and went in search of him.

Though he was outside the door in his fur coat, he was brought back. With him was a certain Archibald Russell, whom I had never met before, a pale, delicate, soi-disant soul, who shook my hand gingerly on introduction.

"You are to stay a little while. It is not late. We are to smoke and talk." It was Mrs. Stoop talking.

Grant Richards protested it was late. Mr. Archibald Russell was for going anyhow. Because she was interested I begged them to remain. And finally she had her way.

We adjourned to the combination reception and smoking room, where were Picasso's consumptive girl and Degas's stribbly-haired lady, and there we had more discussion of art. It was useless, mere patter, but I could see more of her human enthusiasm, and so I did not mind. Several times she looked winsomely into my eyes, and I smiled.

"A great kid," I observed, laughing at her enthusiasm and make-believe.

"That is American for what?"

"A clever lady."

"Oo-ah! I like that then."

Finally we got out.

CHAPTER XV

I would not stop to record the walk home from Mrs. Stoop's except that it introduced to me a very interesting view of London life as quite a different matter entirely. We had come away first with a Mr. Eric MacLagan, a critic, writer and curator of sculpture at the South Kensington Museum, and second with a Mr. Archibald Russell, a lean, conservative gentleman of, say, thirty, a critic of art, a writer and man-about-town who was a product of Christ Church, Oxford, and a representative, I should say, of quite the conservative point of view in regard to England—i.e., that there is nothing at all the matter with England and that, barring an occasional trifle, it is not England but the outsider who is very wrong.

An evening such as this had proved to be does a number of curious things for the intellectual. It reconfirms, as it were, his faith in things artistic. It gives him an opportunity to cut his steel against that of others and to measure the deficiencies of those who pretend to a world of which, of course, he is a radiant member. It gives him a chance to say bright things, to shine, as it were, and most intellectuals spruce up quite noticeably on such occasions and show of what they are made.

I was particularly interested in the key of the conversation after we left and the tone in which it was given. The English of the intellectual and artistic worlds have an air of ultra-refinement, quite different to that with which we—or perhaps I had better say I—are familiar in America. We are less refined, less air-ish. Our men of intellectual force are apt to converse more simply, to abandon manners and delicate, airy asides and to come down to the "brass tacks" of things. Your Englishman of this grade, so far as I can make out, never abandons a certain air of insouciance, of great ease in action.

Of course there was much talk at once as to who so-and-so was and how Miss So-and-so or Mr. So-and-so was appearing. It so happened that the young lady who had sung the folk song was open to some criticism for the unsatisfactory character of her mouth—it was hard, thin and not pretty—and a certain titled lady was interesting solely for being vapid and, consequently, easy to jest with. I noted particularly Mr. Archibald Russell's manner, for he struck me at once as a man who should give an excellent account of himself intellectually. It was typically British, the "aw haw" of the broad "a" in everything. His "Hyah! Hyah! Hyah!" in answer to everything, quite as I would say "yes" and meaning the same thing, quite amused me. He was full of a delicate sarcasm, quite as delicate as his face and hands, which he evinced for personages and things in general.

"Quite a good little song, that. Hyah! Hyah! I didn't quite like her mouth—too small, I should say. Hyah! Not a bad song, that. Who was your artist friend—quite a peculiar person, that—most extrawdinary."

I was quite waiting for this. The remark was not addressed to me. He was talking to Grant Richards.

We strolled out into the night, intending to return along Hyde Park and Piccadilly to Regent Street. It was two o'clock in the morning. I had been interested by the atmosphere of the street, for London at this hour of the night was new to me. So much is lighted not by electricity but by the softer gas lamps. The buildings in this region reminded me of those to be found in Park Avenue, New York, between 34th and 42nd Streets, and there were square miles of them—four, five and six stories high, reddish-brown, conservative, in the night quite shadowy. Mr. Russell was criticizing Henry Lamb, who had been present, for wearing a shabby street suit without a waistcoat and a green linen neckerchief instead of black evening clothes and a high collar.

"He ought to be drummed out of society," he said with what I took to be asperity but which I learned afterwards was intended as a jest.

"Quite so," observed MacLagan, who, whatever his tolerance might be, was one who would never offend in this way. They agreed between them that he was probably doing it for advertising purposes only. This shocked me as indicating a spirit of ultra-conservatism which I did not like—the English spirit of ultra-conservatism, which in contradistinction to the American spirit of the same caliber must be worse because it is in England. I did not see this until a little while after. We all leave our native shore for the first time, I fancy, in a hypercritical spirit.

Opposite Hyde Park entrance we came to a wooden shelf or board of great thickness set on two posts some four feet from the ground which Richards called my attention to as being an object of interest. It was no more nor less than a resting post, dating from the fifteenth or sixteenth century or earlier, for carriers bearing burdens of one description and another and making for London town. At that time they still had several miles to go before reaching the city. Here they put down their loads and conversed, no doubt, or wiped their brows wearily. The place is now so near the heart of things that it might be called a center.

Just beyond this a little way and nearer the city, at the upper end of Piccadilly, we encountered the beginnings of that peculiar nightlife which extends from there and crosswise along Regent Street for a little way to Leicester Square. It is a peculiar world, not different in spirit perhaps from that which may be found manifesting itself about the Grand Opera House at Paris, or from 34th to 50th Streets along Broadway, or in Unter den Linden and along Friedrichstrasse in Berlin, but it has its national characteristics and is therefore interesting. The girls, it struck me at once, were so much more attractive than the general run of that class of woman I had thus far encountered—shopgirls, salesgirls, house servants, the ladies at Mrs. Stoop's reception, the women buying in the superior stores and the women one sees in carriages. I use the word attractive in a reserved way, for the charm, I fancy, must have been in most cases purely superficial. Their clothing was so much better cut and draped than that of the girls of the shops. Their hats, shoes and gloves were so superior in taste. They carried themselves with an air in most cases, and they had the advantage of blooming youth and beauty. This electric-lit thoroughfare, with its now silent buildings on either hand, was alive with them, like bats that circle after dark.

Wandering home from clubs and receptions or possibly from club to club were scores of young and middle-aged men—the typical British Johnnie—his opera hat shoved back on his forehead, his white shirt and tie contrasting sharply with his correctly-cut black clothes, his shoulders enveloped in a soft black overcoat or cape of some kind, and usually carrying a cane. In most cases he—or they, for he came in pairs or threes—paid no attention to these rosy-cheeked nymphs of the street, who saluted him with the most engaging remarks. It is against the law, as I found later, for any street woman to say anything to anybody, but the law in this case, so far as I could judge, is almost entirely ignored.

"Aren't you lonely, sweetheart? Don't you want to go with me?"

"Hello, dear! My, but you're handsome!"

"See my nice new shoes. Aren't they pretty?"

These are intended purely as opening remarks—anything to break the reserve of the possibly bashful or doubtful observer. A connoisseur of youthful beauty would certainly look twice at any of these women. Their faces in so many cases were so oval, their eyes so bright, their air so assured. The English climate does not require rouge; it brings the flush of health to almost every normal cheek. In this are not included the thousands and thousands of the underfed. It struck me as so evident that poverty, not vice, is the thing which fills this midnight pavement with what should be innocent girlhood. Men talk about the innate wickedness of these human souls, but I have never been able to discover that their meager understanding permitted as large a grasp of vice as those who stand higher in the world esteem. The circumstances from which they spring are obviously so confined. The answer is that they should work in the shops, but one could introduce ten thousand reasons why this very respectable lure might fail. To indicate one, namely—let us think of the high spirit that rebels at the commonplace and longs for a glitter which it cannot understand. At my reception, which I had just left in my comfortable evening clothes, there were women who were far more subtle but not more virtuous, as I have reason to know. Their position was unquestioned; their means and the social environment from which they had sprung gave them a certain distinction of bearing. But as for being less evil—let us put it in another way. They were far more comprehensive and artistic in their moods. Let him who is without sin cast the first stone.

At Hyde Park Corner we lost our companions, MacLagan and Archibald Russell, and Grant Richards and I returned to our hotel alone. At one corner he indicated a perfect face under a wide-brimmed hat of flaring lines, saying, "Could anything be more perfect than that?" The girl smiled at him, a radiant, luring smile. "Some of these women," he remarked condescendingly, "are really attractive."

The next day I went to a Neo-Impressionist exhibition at the Stafford Gallery, for a walk in Soho, for a ride in the city proper (the financial district), to the Cheshire Cheese for dinner, to the Shepherd's Bush Empire to hear an American vaudeville singer of great repute, and so on for days and days, making social calls and visiting museums, churches, public restaurants, the interesting hotels and theaters, until at times I was fairly weary of London and what it had to show. The most interesting impression I gained at once and the one that remained the longest is that there is not the least hope of anyone ever knowing London thoroughly. It is quite as much of an uncharted sea of conditions, classes, hopes, despairs, failure and success as ever was sailed by a medieval navigator when the world was not known to be round.

For days and days I rode on the tops of buses, intensely interested in the city as it passed in review below. I traveled from Barking and Seven Kings on the east to Twickenham, Shepherd's Bush, Warenwood Scrubbs and Kensal Rise on the west. From West Dulwich and Camberwell Green on the south, I rode to Hampstead Heath, North Finchley on the north—but I never got out of London. I remember riding seventeen miles on one bus line for a very modest price, but I was all the while in London. The only time that I ever seemed to get out of it was when I took a train for Manchester or Canterbury or for the country house at which I was stopping at Cookham Dean in Berkshire. The general impression that I got was of a city ranging from two to four stories in height, seldom more than five or six in the business heart, and stretching away in endless reaches of drab grays and yellows, which struck me at first as exceedingly depressing. The streets, so far as I could make out, were absolutely without order so far as direction or persistence was concerned. The vast majority of them run but a very little way, compared to the great lengths of streets in America, and then suddenly cease, or curve, or change their names. They are lined, in the main, with homes so tasteless and so uniform that you cease after a time to consider them individually at all. The facade of a block is the thing that you see. The twists and turns of a street are what you see, its drabness, its narrowness, its pathos—rarely, if ever, a house.

It is curious, now that I think of it, that I recall very few individual homes in all London, yet I must have walked or ridden hundreds of miles and surveyed casually thousands upon thousands of houses. I recall many charming neighborhoods, sections where drab gray masses blended into something inexpressibly sweet, and I can honestly say that in many sections London appeared to possess a home charm unrivaled—the best that one finds indicated in Dickens or Thackeray—but the exterior is always in a minor key. Gray clouds hang over the city; it rains or mists frequently; the tree-trunks, when you find them in the parks or elsewhere, have a lovely patina of bright moss. The people go about mostly—the middle class I am referring to—in clothes which struck me as anything but noticeable save for their commonplaceness. Your young man clerk was dapper enough in his tight trousers, his closely-fitting coat, his derby hat pushed well back on his head, and not infrequently carrying a stick. The women, young and old, barring a few that are encountered in the more imposing sections of the city, were shabby to a degree. Never in my life have I seen worse dressed women than I did in England.

The morning following my visit to Mrs. Stoop's I went, as I have said, to view exhibitions of Neo-Impressionist art at the Stafford Gallery, where originals by Cézanne, Gauguin and van Gogh greeted my astonished gaze. I shall never forget my intense desire to see the merit in these things, coupled with an uncertainty as to their significance when contrasted with my own personal idea of beauty. There is a type of progressive mind in art, or was at this time, which would sneer at the necessity for beauty in a picture—at least such a necessity as I at the moment might have indicated. Although there were some truly vivid landscapes, the figures of which most of the pictures were composed seemed to be so out of drawing, the colors so crude and coarse, laid on in many instances in flat masses side by side. I did not know at the moment how far even these Neo-Impressionists were removed from the real radicals of the art realm, though I was beginning to have a faint notion.

My theory of art, or to be quite correct, the theory of art which had been imposed upon me by my early training, was that pictures should not only be correct in drawing, suggestive and artistic in arrangement, harmonize in color, but also be true without suggestion of method. The subject should be one in which the innate refinement complemented the skill of the painter. Imagine, then, van Gogh's Christ—long-faced, red-haired, lantern-jawed, bony, a figure drawn from the worst horrors of a famine and hung naked with a filthy rag about his loins upon a wooden cross which looked to be made of the roughest of posts—his lips animal, his misshapen hands and feet pierced by perfectly horrible spikes, and his face askew with a sickening grimace in a kind of agony. The colors were truly raw and brutal—yellows, browns, blues—I would not venture to say now exactly what. Evidence of brush strokes was not absent, quite the contrary—significant spots where the painter had added a particular color with a single stroke. This picture was one which I knew to be seriously applauded, and I gave it among the others its proper consideration. It struck me as having a raw, crude sincerity. All the older theories of art were obviously put rudely to one side. Evidence of brush strokes was not feared; the most startling contrasts of color not evaded, but almost courted; beauty of line and form, save for accuracy of drawing, fled from as one would flee from the plague.

The crude, sad brutality of life itself, stripped of all its rosy filaments of romance and shown hard and bitter and naked as it sometimes is, was here quite plainly set forth. These pictures were much more than vital—they were more like slaps, kicks and loud shouts. I can imagine one of these painters saying to a devotee of the older school, "To hell with art as you understand it. This is also art," and by this process we arrive at that very interesting Tower of Babel—the moot question, to twist a simile, "What is art?" I, for one, give place to the Neo-Impressionist and to every other who sincerely believes in what he does; and some of these pictures I sincerely enjoyed. They provided a contrast to my understanding of art as it had been; they gave me a measure wherewith I might measure; and having seen these, and others which I saw later, art can never again be wholly the perfection of line and form which a Lawrence, a Watteau, a Van Dyck or a Rubens would have it. Both are valid—they must be.

From here I went to my furrier's to look after a handsome fur coat which was an experience for myself, and thence into Soho to get a taste of an older literary world of which De Quincey and Lamb were a part. I visited the co-operative stores, which interested me as an idea which has run to seed, and the Embankment, hunting below London Bridge for No. 5 Old Swan Lane and finding it after much difficulty. I cannot hope to indicate what a swirling delight London was; only those who understand and enjoy a tide race can understand. There are no streetcars to speak of in the vast central portion of London—the bus, the taxi and the tube substitute for the long miles of car lines in New York. Streets, courts, squares, circles whirl round in a dizzy ring. Lanes no bigger than a man's hand ooze streams of people; tall iron fences give glimpses of lovely green trees; shaded courts, green so far as the grass is concerned all winter long.

My first glimpse of the Thames and the Embankment was on this same day whirling down toward London Bridge, my neck twisting in almost a vain attempt to see everything at once—Somerset House, where taxes are paid and wills registered, the Hotels Cecil and Savoy, the Inns of Court and other important structures and places. It struck me so forcibly in looking at Somerset House that in order to be impressive, a building need not necessarily be so high as long. This thought in itself after a time struck me as curious, for why should I think of a building as being necessarily high in order to be impressive? America, was my answer. America. London was not high, merely far-flung and old and, to a certain extent, shabby. Only this and nothing more.

This day, my first free one in which I was not in a way piloted hourly, was bringing me a jumbled impression of fascinating human activities—trade, religion, law, art, government, the sea, anything you will. It was a city—8,000,000 people—and I was swimming enthusiastically in it. That night, by arrangement with Grant Richards, I was to visit the Cheshire Cheese, which I had long heard of and of which I was doubtful. I am sorry to state that my peculiar temperament will not often permit me a natural comfort in the resort of great fame. I am haunted by the idea of how tawdry and make-believe it all is, which in a way is carrying the supersensitive too far. It struck me as a dreary place at first, maintained, as so many of these things are, for the benefit of the traveling public. The Londoner, I am sure, cares little for the Cheshire Cheese. I was duly shown the chair in which Doctor Johnson sat and the corner which he and his friends occupied, but for me it had not the faintest glamour of the past. The high-backed settees in which you found yourself compelled to squeeze in order to be seated at your table may have been delightful in older days, but it was not very pleasant here—at least not on this occasion. The very low ceiling, the plain brown walls decorated with prints of former days, the sawdust-covered floor, the heavy white stoneware from which the food was served, and other points of this character made up an excellent stage setting for an old inn.

Appreciation of these things depends upon a mood, and my mood was surely not right, yet I was entertained by the spectacle of several groups of Americans in full evening dress, as I was myself, dining at the various tables about. The enthusiasm of one group, hailing evidently from Lynchburg, Virginia, was exceedingly keen. An intense sense of strangeness and variety showed in their eyes. They were Americans, they were in England, and they were doing wonderfully novel things. Hence the joy.

On this occasion I was introduced by Grant Richards to his aunt, the wife of a celebrated English novelist and naturalist, and to her son and daughter—the former a theatrical manager of some distinction, and the latter the wife of a professional man who had died some time before. It is curious how my moods betray me at times. The son, who subsequently came to have an actual fascination for me, was perhaps for the first two or three hours as unsatisfactory a person as ever I listened to. He was somewhat under the medium in height—stocky, smooth-shaven, buoyantly cheerful. He seemed to be doing his best to be more than nice to me—cheerful, inquiring, interested. I resented it greatly. It seemed to me that I was listening to the enthusiastic babblings of an eighth-rate mind; and for the sister, a pale, lymphatic woman with an eager eye, I had no more regard. It seemed to me that she was asking sly, silly questions in order to betray me into some ill-considered opinion for which she could criticize me. It made not the slightest difference to me what any of those present thought. (And I really think that such an attitude is both boorish and ungrateful, but I resented this kindly effort to entertain me nevertheless.)

As a matter of fact, I was expecting a better restaurant and more charming company, and I was disappointed. I recall Grant Richards's long-suffering efforts to be courteous and helpful. "For heaven's sake, do buck up! Come now, do be cheerful. Isn't this rather good after all? You will find Jerrard here exceedingly entertaining if you will just talk to him. My dear aunt, now, is dying to know all about you." I sat like a Hindu idol on a dusty throne, refusing to smile or be in any wise gay. Only the ale, which was served in large tankards, interested me in the least, and that because through it I thought I might manage to change my mood. I did not really want to be uncivil, but unquestionably some of us are victims of our temperaments. I know I am of mine. It is as impossible for me to lift myself out of a given state of mind at times as it would be to lift myself over a fence by means of my bootstraps. If I am brought out of it, it must be by means of outside agencies, or by concentrated effort which causes me to try various remedies and finally wears away the state. I know that Jerrard Grant Allen, the son, made as interesting a commentary on the importance of the American character, contrasted with that of the English, as I have ever heard, but it struck me at the time as silly.

We finally arose and left, making our way under a high moon along High Holborn to a tube station. I think I was shown where Doctor Johnson lived, a thundering printing office with green lights standing next door. I also saw some old, quaint inn in Holborn, now completely deserted but bearing all the earmarks of a charming period of English life. The tube interested me as a contrast to what I had known of the New York subway—for one went up and down deep shafts in elevators to get in and out of it, and the distances you walked in tunnels to find the tracks was to me astonishing. I could not imagine why a subway entrance should be put so far from the actual track where you were to take the train—sometimes quite as much as two short New York blocks, I am sure. The cars were apparently not any smaller, the seats much more comfortable, for they were nicely cushioned in the first- and second-class compartments, and the whole train was comfortably lighted. There was no straphanging, so far as I could see. I never saw any in all the time I was in London. I do not recall that there were even straps to hang to. The only fault I had to find was, being an American, that the people in the cars were not Americans. Naturally that was a great defect.

It is a curious matter, this of differences in national temperaments. I found it disturbing me later every time I changed from one country to another. I had no sooner left the United States than the English—whom I found in charge of the great international steamship on which I was traveling—irritated me by their somewhat different manner of doing things and by their method of speaking. But when I arrived in England, I was in a perfect sea of difference. It was not so much in degree; if one had been referring to it in terms of heat or cold, you could have said that it was only a little warmer or a little colder. Of the English I should say that their temperament is somewhat colder than that of the Americans. But the sight of thousands of people who speak the language that you speak in just a slightly different manner; who wear the clothes that you wear, but in a somewhat different way; who hand you a different money in a different voice; who call directions, sing songs, and make their motions in a manner somewhat varied from that to which you have been accustomed—it is really a constant source of irritation. No one knows how fixed in his notions he has become until he travels in a foreign land. Then he will find that for no reason under the sun, save that he has long been accustomed to it, his way is the best way. The Englishman says "tube" where you say "subway"; hence for the time being he is almost persona non grata. It is so with these and other minor matters.

On this particular subway ride I found myself in a heated argument with Mrs. Bicknell in regard to whether or not America was influencing England—favorably, unfavorably or not at all. As a matter of fact—and I say it quite impartially—all the facts of the argument were on my side. The subway system on which we were riding was due to the influence of an American who came to London to make a fortune. The car advertising, as one saw it displayed everywhere, had been borrowed absolutely from America. A large number of the car advertisements which our eyes studied in an effort to obtain corroboration concerned American-made products. I recall distinctly the Walk-Over Shoe, Armour's Extract of Beef, the Gillette Safety Razor, the Eastman Kodak, the Waterman Pen, the Ingersoll Dollar Watch and a half-dozen other things, all of which were shown in the particular car in which we were riding. I recalled to Mrs. Bicknell's mind that a large number of the stores which I had seen advertised American products for sale quite broadly in the windows, and the department store as best exemplified in London was an American idea. We went all through various facts—the telephones, the telegraph, the electric light, the streetcar, the complicated American plumbing system with its convenient baths, the stock ticker and other mechanical ingenuities which have been completely revolutionizing England are all American. I went back and recalled the cotton gin, which had revolutionized English manufacturing nearly a hundred years before, and wound up by referring to the flying machine, which seemed to be adding insult to injury. She herself admitted that English shoes and English ready-made clothing had been transformed for the better because of American methods, the adoption of which was compulsory. Had I already paid the visit to Manchester, which I subsequently did, I could have told her that the English cotton mills were even then being reconstructed amazingly on American principles—in fact that they were even better than the American mills because the English manufacturers had been able to avoid the errors which inexperience had caused the Americans to make. It was an interesting argument to me, because it cleared my own mind on the subject and made me realize what I really thought. All that I subsequently saw confirmed the statements I made to Mrs. Bicknell.

Another point in illustration of this came out when we reached Shepherd's Bush Empire, a vaudeville theater built and conducted on the latest American plan. Mr. Allen, who, as I have said, was taking me to see an interesting American singer who was creating a stir in English vaudeville, confided to me as we entered that this theater was of a kind which had completely changed the London vaudeville world since 1900.

"They're building them everywhere," he assured me. "It's a good thing you came when you did, or you wouldn't have a chance to see an old-style variety house at all. I'll have to take you to see the Hoxton Pantomime and the Elephant and Castle if you want to see an old-style English theater. This is the last word in vaudeville newness. You'll see a lot of typical English acts all right, and the crowd is something like it used to be, but I think even the crowd is different. I think this style of show is drawing out a different type of person."

We had to wait because some act was on which did not permit immediate entrance. When we finally entered, I saw an interesting West End audience drawn from the neighborhood of Hammersmith, Ealing and Warenwood Scrubbs. It was quite British in its flavor—different, I thought, from the same type of audience in New York in one respect, namely, that it appeared to be all of one nationality. One sees so much of Germans, Italians, Jews and Irish in New York, or at least the generations derived from them. If there ever was a type that looked like the pictures of John Bull, it has largely disappeared. In its place there are various individuals who suggest in a minor way such people as George Moore, George Grossmith, Junior, Winston Churchill, Sir Thomas Lipton and others. The average Englishman of London, it strikes me, is fairly well-set-up and reasonably healthy. There are whole neighborhoods where they appear to lack a physical constitution, but that is not London generally by any means.

I was intensely interested in this, my first London vaudeville performance, because I always feel that the average vaudeville performance is fairly indicative of the humor of the people. What will they laugh at, what will they applaud? I witnessed a series of acts which seemed to me above the average in merit. Fortunately, two of the best things were purely English, though five or six acts which were not so good were English also. The star act was an American girl singing slightly risqué songs and changing her costume each time from something very glittering to something more glittering. There was also a Japanese troupe and several American "teams," who were as bad as those who go abroad to amuse Europe usually are, though the star act, which, as I have said, I was brought to see, was the singing American girl, and she was given the best place on the program. I cannot say really that she interested me very much at all. She was beautiful, as so many of the women vaudeville performers who do turns of this kind are. The American woman, when she is built properly, is usually so attractive that all Europe stops to look at her. This one had the customary robust, shapely form, the pink and white complexion, the clear eyes and the white teeth. Her hair was plentiful and of a light corn color, and her voice was not bad. I am sure this Shepherd's Bush audience was more interested in her healthy youth than in anything else—though they did not realize it. She was so much more of a charming physical spectacle than you usually see on the British vaudeville stage. Beyond that she was not important, but she received by far the most applause and was no doubt considered the most important turn of the evening.

The act that interested me most was that of a rather slim, somewhat academic and not too good-looking girl by the name of Wish Wynne, who gave interpretations of English farmgirls such as one encounters in Thomas Hardy's novels and the English slavey as she is at times indicated on the stage. I never saw a better act in my life, and I was astonished when I had to consider that such true art was receiving the lesser consideration of the evening. My buxom American girl with her risqué songs was a clown compared to this woman. In the first place, Miss Wynne's art of impersonation was perfect. She looked exactly the character she wished to suggest, and her voice and her mood changed completely with her impersonation. I shall never forget how pathetically unsophisticated she looked as the little English farmgirl carrying a bundle of straw, her bonnet fallen back from her head over her shoulders, telling of her love for a farmhand and of his awkward proposal. I was glad to note afterwards that if this Shepherd's Bush audience did not see the significance of her art, the great English dramatic critics did, for I read lengthy appreciative notices of her work in the *Chronicle* and the *Telegraph*, and I trust that it did not stop with those papers. The woman should be celebrated far and wide as an artist of great merit.

A second English act which amused me and struck me as thoroughly characteristic was that of a man who looked for all the world like a character in one of Hogarth's pictures or Fielding's novels. He might have been one of the rural clowns whom Joseph Andrews encountered on his journey to London. He was so, one might say, grossly proportioned—very stout, very round of stomach, very fatheaded in the true sense, with undersized ears and fat lips. He wore a small pointed hat and looked as though he had been jailed many times for drunkenness and other offenses. I resented his presence greatly when he first stepped out on the stage. Could this be the type of thing that Englishmen could interest themselves in, I asked myself. Surely the slummy character of London life was here well indicated. In three minutes I was shaking with laughter, and continued so, being the most vociferous among the many who recalled him for a third and a fourth time. It was largely because his humor was accurately English for the class he represented—the sort of barrelhouse wit that one might expect in a drunken rural community. I remember Mr. Grant Allen and Mrs. Bicknell being slightly disgusted, and I could not tell from Richards's imperturbable face whether he was amused or not. I believe it is bad form to laugh in a theater. But Mr. Allen, the manager, told me that this man had a fair professional standard as a humorist, though he was not as good now as he had been formerly.

The other English acts were exceedingly sad, dull, mistaken in their humor or their pathos. You would have to see them to realize that they really represented an older form of entertainment that was dying out before the onslaught of an American invasion. It is very hard to indicate just what it is that makes the difference between the excellent work of one period and that of another, but if some second-rate music-hall artist should come out on the stage of Hammerstein's Victoria in New York and recite "Over the Hill to the Poor House," the effect could not be worse. They were out of date, musty, absolutely as old in their atmosphere as some of the old streets and houses in London which indicate a former day. I was astonished, but I could see from this what England would have still been like if it had not been for the rise and influence of the United States. This whole city and nation had been and is still being shot through with American influence, and this theater in which we were sitting and the second-rate American act which they applauded so vociferously was simply a testimony to the youth and novelty of the American world which they crave. England will unquestionably be made over radically by United States experience—probably somewhat by those emanating from its own colonies also, but much more by those coming from the States. When it has been, it will be a much more active England than it is today. Whether it will be better than America remains to be seen.

CHAPTER XVI

"London sings in my ears." I remember writing this somewhere about the fourth or fifth day of my stay. It was delicious, the sense of novelty and wonder it gave me. I am one of those who was raised on Charles Dickens and Thackeray and Lamb but I must confess I found little to corroborate the world of vague impressions I had formed. Novels are a mere expression of temperament anyhow, where they are truly appealing, and those of Dickens and Thackeray are rather less than more the exception. London was so low, I saw at once, as to its building height—so comfortably old. New York and America are all so new, so lustful of change. Here, in these streets, when you walk out of a morning or an evening, you feel a pleasing stability. London is not going to change under your very eyes. You are not going to turn your back to find, on looking again, a whole skyline effaced. The city is restful, naive, in a way tender and sweet like an old song, and I felt that. London is more fatalistic and therefore less hopeful than New York, but how interesting and wonderful it seemed to me.

The first thing that impressed me was the grayish tinge of smoke that was over everything—a faint haze—and the next that as a city, street for street and square for square, it was not so strident as New York—not nearly so harsh. The traffic was less noisy, the people more thoughtful and considerate, the so-called rush, which characterizes New York, less foolish. There is something rowdyish and ill-mannered about the street life of New York—a thing I have complained of for years. This was not true of London. It struck me as simple, sedate, thoughtful, and I could only conclude that it sprang from a less stirring atmosphere of opportunity. I fancy it is harder to get along in London. People do not change from one thing to another so much. The world there is more fixed in a pathetic routine, and people are more conscious of their so-called betters. I hope not, but I felt it to be true. But London was beautiful in its way, quaint, naive, sad.

I do not believe that it is given any writer to wholly suggest a city. The mind is like a voracious fish: it would like to eat up all the experiences and characteristics of a city or a nation, but this, fortunately, is not possible. My own mind was busy pounding at the gates of fact, but during all the while I was there, I got but a little way.

I remember being struck with the nature of St. James's Park, the great column to the Duke of Marlborough at the end of the street and the whirl of life in Trafalgar Square and Piccadilly Circus, all of which were very near. Grant Richards's office in narrow Carlton Street interested me, as did the storm of cabs which whirled by all the corners of this region. It was described to me as the center of London, and I am quite sure it was—for clubs, theaters, hotels, smart shops and the like. The heavy trading section was farther east along the banks of the Thames, and between that and Regent Street, where my little hotel was located, lay the financial section, sprawling around St. Paul's Cathedral and the Bank of England. One could get out

Piccadilly Circus

of this great central world easily enough—but it was only, apparently, to go into minor centers such as that about Victoria Station, Kensington, Paddington, Liverpool Street and the Elephant and Castle. It was all decidedly pleasing because it was new and strange and because there was a world of civility prevailing which does not exist in America.

I recall venturing one noon into one of the Lyons restaurants just above Regent Street in Piccadilly and being struck with the size and importance of it, even though it was intensely middle-class. It was a great chamber, decorated after the fashion of a palace ballroom, with immense chandeliers of prismed glass hanging from the ceiling and a balcony furnished in cream and gold where other tables were set and where a large stringed orchestra played continuously during lunch and dinner. An enormous crowd of very commonplace people were there—clerks, minor officials, clergymen, small shopkeepers—and the bill of fare was composed of many homely dishes, such as beef and kidney pudding, combined with others bearing high-sounding French names. I mention this Lyons restaurant because there were several quite like it and because it catered to an element not reached in quite the same way in America. Perhaps the Horn & Hardart Company of Philadelphia and the Kohlsaat Company in Chicago may serve some such patronage. I doubt it. I think the Lyons Company reaches a somewhat better class. Proportionately they pay more.

The thing that interested me was that I expected to find London very old in this matter of eating accommodations—why, I cannot say. Certainly I did not expect to find anything which rivaled the Harlem Casino of New York and the big middle-class restaurants of Chicago. Nevertheless, here it was; and I was told afterwards that the man who had started it made a great fortune, somewhat like that of Childs in New York, and that he was expecting to build shortly a great hotel which should be run on the same basis. In spite of the lifted eyebrows with which Richards greeted my announcement that I had been there, the food was very good; and the service, while a little slow for a place of popular patronage, was quite good. I recall being amused by the tall, thin, solemn English headwaiters in long black frock coats, leading the exceedingly bourgeois customers to their tables. The English curate with his shovel hat was here in evidence and the minor clerk. I found great pleasure in studying this world, listening to the music, and thinking of the vast ramifications of London which it represented; for every institution of this kind represents a perfect world of people.

It was one evening shortly after I had lunched with Mrs. Stoop that Grant Richards decided that I must visit two critics, one of art, the other of literature, who lived together in a kind of bachelor studio in Upper Brooke Street—very close, by the way, to that of Miss Burke, the young actress who had come over on the steamer with us and with whom we had since lunched. It was interesting to find her in her own rather smart London quarters, surrounded by maid and cook and a male figure of the usual significance in the immediate background. Not unlike many actresses and lonely women of the mentally liberated school, Miss Burke, delicate, fragile bit of Dresden china that she was, had a lover, a ruddy, handsome, slightly corpulent French count of manners the pink of perfection. He looked for all the world like the French counts introduced into American musical comedy—just the right type of collar about his neck, the perfect shoe, the close-fitting, well-tailored suit, the mustachios and hair barbered to the last touch. He was charming, too, in his easy, gracious aloofness, saying only the few things that would be of momentary interest and pressing nothing.

Miss Burke had prepared an appetizing lunch. It was not as good a lunch as we would have had at Grant Richards's or Mrs. Stoop's nor done with the air of either establishment. There were little hitches which indicated effort and strain, as when a certain wine was no more, but on the whole, it was charming. She had managed to collect a group of really interesting people—a Mr. T., for instance, whose bête noire was clergymen and who stood prepared by collected newspaper clippings and court proceedings, gathered over a period of years, to prove that all clergymen were scoundrels. He had, as he insisted, the most amazing data showing that the most perverted of all English criminals were usually sons of bishops and that the higher you rose in the scale of hieratic authority, the worse were the men in charge. The delightful part of it all was the man's profound seriousness of manner—a thin, magnetic, albeit candle-waxy type of person of about sixty-five who had the force and enthusiasm of a boy.

"Ah, yes," you would hear him exclaim every so often during lunch, "I know him well. A greater scoundrel never lived. His father is bishop of Wimbledon"—or, for variation—"his father was once rector of Christ Church, Mayfair." That amused me.

There was a thin, hard, sharp-nosed literary lady present, of the obviously and militantly virgin type, who seemed to regret, cynically and acidly, the limitations which her mental state involved. There are many such. Their quarrel is with the vice and evil of the world while they themselves are wretchedly unhappy. My advice to such would be to go over into the camp of the enemy. She was at the foot of the table, next to the count, but we fell into a discussion of the English woman's suffrage activity under his very nose, the while he talked lightly to Grant Richards. She was for more freedom for women, politically and otherwise, in order that they might accomplish certain social reforms. You know the type. She was not very successful in her chosen profession, and that made her bitter. How like a sympathetic actress,

I thought, of such loose proclivities as Miss Burke to pick a lady of this character to associate with. I have never known it to fail. And how this Miss X., literary underbrush that she was, must have envied Miss Burke her humanly feminine comfort in her liaison with the handsome count.

The thing that interested me was to see this charming little actress, obviously on the fringe of society but not of it, keeping up as smart a social form as her means would permit and still hoping after years of effort and some considerable success to be taken up and made much of. These understrappers of art are never ready or willing to believe that society, in its last reaches, is composed of dullness and heaviness of soul, great well-guarded fortunes, iron-bound forms and heavy, rigid mating instincts which respond to no schools of the unconventional or the unmoral and know neither flights of fancy nor delicacy and tenderness of emotion. Individuals like Miss Burke think, somehow, that if they achieve a great artistic success they will be admitted everywhere. Dear little Miss Burke! I am quite sure that only persistent rebuffs as she rose artistically, if that had been possible, would have made it clear that there are walls that are never scaled by art. And morality, any more than immorality or religion, has nothing to do with some other walls. Force is the thing, and the ultimate art force she did not possess. If she had, she would have been admitted to a certain interchange in certain fields. Society is composed of slightly interchanging groups, some members of which enter all, most members of which never venture beyond their immediate individual circles. And only the most catholic-minded and energetic would attempt or care to bother with the labor of keeping in touch with more than one single, agreeable circle.

But her French count—he was so very dapper. I asked Grant Richards about him, and, as usual, he was reticent. Was he rich? No, he thought not. I told him that I gathered from various things—the seeming private boudoir of the count—that there was an intimacy here. He admitted it. Miss Burke possessed some means; she was entitled to so human a diversion. The social thing was not to see anything in these matters—socially they do not exist; it isn't kind to let them.

But to return to the two critics, one of whom—a Mr. Archibald Russell—had amused me at Mrs. Stoop's reception, and the other of whom—a Mr. Filson Young—had written a novel that made a considerable stir some few years before. Grant Richards was his publisher. I merely mention this, however, because it brought about a return date or luncheon between me and Mr. Young which did prove very interesting. These two men lived in charming, though small quarters in Upper Brooke Street, not far from Grosvenor Square, on the fringe of ultra-respectability, if not of it. Mr. Russell, as I have perhaps indicated, was a very finicky man, thirty-two or thirty-three years of age, pale, slender, remote, artistic. Mr. Young was somewhat an imitation of Mr. Russell, I should have said, though he was the older man—artistic, remote, ostensibly cultured, living and doing all the refined things on principle more than anything else.

It always interests me to find the purely literary or artistic type in this world, the semi-successful, who make the cultivation of beauty a profession and monger art. Here was one—this Young. His principal book, a novel, had been fairly successful, largely—as I learned subsequently—because it was based on a personal experience. His subsequent volumes were rather dull, one of them relating to music—the "How To Listen" variety, of which there is such a plague. He was an excellent organist, a critic of some insight, an engineer originally by training, and several other things. At present he was writing for the *English Review* and living here in Upper Brooke Street, fretting to some extent, I think, about an income.

The rooms of the two men, occupying separate floors but having a common dining room between them, were charmingly decorated. Mr. Young had a built-in organ in his section, rows upon rows of built-in bookcases, excellent prints and original paintings, strong, stable furniture of the Jacobean type and the usual bits of porcelain, bronze, brass and copper which make such places attractive. His light was furnished by candles, of course, and he greeted us arrayed in dark trousers and waistcoat to match and a dark-brown velvet smoking jacket. Being very pale, smooth-shaven and his hair parted smoothly on one side, he presented a very kempt and conservative air. Mr. Russell, who appeared a few moments afterward, quite languidly, was more conservatively dressed in a dinner coat. The air of an occasion was about the place, for, as usual, Grant Richards had made much of me, and while Mr. Young had read one of my books and thought very little of it, nevertheless he was prepared to accept me on what Grant Richards insisted was my crescent reputation.

It amuses me now when I think of it, for of course neither of these gentlemen cared for me in the least beyond my momentary vogue or repute in their small world. I must have appeared somewhat boorish and supercilious, but they were exceedingly pleasant. Art was the underlying theme, of course, with my arrival, impressions, introductions, acquaintances and the like as means to this end. How did I like London? What did I think of the English? How did London contrast with New York? What were some of the things I had seen?

My head was ringing with what I had seen already. London was going around in a ring for me. Its vast reaches were ever in my mind. I was puzzled as to what I did think, as I am generally by this phantasmagoria called life. While Mr. Young served an opening glass of port and I toasted my feet before a delicious grate fire, I stated as succinctly as I could what I had seen thus far, which was not much. Already, as I have indicated in a way, I had decided that England was deficient in the vitality which America now possesses—certainly deficient in the raw, creative imagination which is producing so many new things in America, but far superior in what, for want of a better phrase, I must call social organization as it relates to social and commercial interchange generally. Something—perhaps the British climate—has developed in the English social animal a sense of responsibility. I really think that the English climate has had a great deal to do with this. It is so uniformly damp and cold and raw that it has produced a sober-minded person. When subsequently I encountered the climates of Paris, Rome and the Riviera, I realized quite clearly how impossible it would be to produce the English temperament there. One can see the dark, moody, passionate temperament of the Italians evolving to perfection under their brilliant skies. The wine-like atmosphere of Paris speaks for itself. London is what it is, and the Englishman likewise, because of the climate in which he has been reared.

I said as much without much protest, but when I ventured that the English might possibly be falling behind in the world's race and that other nations, such as the Germans and the Americans, might rapidly be displacing them, I evoked a storm of opposition. I have to smile when I think how the sedate Mr. Russell rose to this argument. It began at the dinner table and was continued in the general living room later. He sneered at the suggestion that the Germans could possibly conquer or displace England and hoped for the day when the issue might be tried out physically. Mr. Young laughed as he spoke of the long way America had to go before it could achieve any social importance even within itself. It was a thrashing whirlpool of foreign elements. He had recently been to the United States, and in one of the British quarterlies then on the stands was a long estimate by him of America's weaknesses and potentialities. He poked fun at the careless, insulting manners of the people, their love of show, their love of praise. No Englishman, having tasted the comforts of civilized life in England, could ever live happily in America. There was no such thing as a serving class. He objected to American business methods as he had encountered them, and I could see that he really disliked America. To a certain extent he disliked me for being an American and resented my literary prosperity for obtruding itself upon England. Being the hero of the hour, however, I was in a very comfortable position and could afford to take things quietly, which I did. I enjoyed these two men as exceedingly able combatants, men against whose wits I could sharpen my own.

Mr. Russell invited me to visit the famous Wallace Collection with him the next morning, and for the following Thursday I made an appointment

Hoped for the day when the issue
might be tried out physically

with Mr. Young for a lunch at the Royal Automobile Club and to visit St. Paul's and the Roman Catholic Cathedral. Grant Richards and I left them in the early hours of the morning after I had heard Mr. Young play on his pipe organ, which he assured me had notable range for its size, and its small volume was carefully calculated to sound impressive in so small a space. He played Bach with real distinction and feeling. The next morning I visited the Wallace Collection with Mr. Russell to see primarily the Watteaus and the splendid period furniture which is there displayed. It is an excellent collection, though of no vast size, and charmingly housed. I noted curiously that most of the art displayed was foreign to England, particularly the furniture and the modeled objects of art.

I mention these two men because, in a minute way, they suggested the literary and artistic atmosphere of London. They went about, as Grant Richards informed me, to one London drawing room and another. Mr. Russell was considered an excellent judge of art; Mr. Young, an important critic. Their mode of living constituted a touch of the better Grub Street of today. It was not bad.

CHAPTER XVII

From this idle promenade through the Wallace Collection the next morning with Mr. Russell, I hurried at the last moment to the residence of Mrs. Stoop to keep my luncheon appointment—a luncheon in which I was not interested for myself but which I argued was going to give me an opportunity to study a very interesting type much more intimately than I had. Her peculiar temperament and her interest in me made her an object well worthy of observation. She struck me as having so much more temperament than intellect, and yet the intellect that she had was so sophisticated and so inclined to the purely artistic. Looking at her and her house, seeing that her husband was practically valueless from this point of view, one could see that all her days she had been straining after an artistic perfection in her home, her dress, her social relations and whatever else was connected with her.

Her house, as I have said, was a sort of jewel-box, elaborate in its decorations, full of many charming things, but fortunately not stuffy. The examples of Picasso, Matisse, Degas on her walls indicated quite plainly that she was in touch with the latest movements in art; and her receptions, which included such men as Shaw, Sargent, Henry Lamb and various artistic duchesses and countesses, testified to the same fact. She was not without an interesting part in the distinguished social movements of the city. Her refusal to grow old gracefully, as Richards had put it, had interested me, because it was quite obvious that she could have been more conservative in her dress and manner without conflicting with her appearance of maturity. She arranged herself, as many society women do, with all the sharpness of outline and éclat of jewelry which one forgives in age, though the simple charms of youth are better. The resources of the rouge pot were not beyond her; but, as in the arrangement of her home and in her dress, she was much of the artist. On the few occasions that I saw her, she looked charming, gay, brilliant.

When I arrived at her house, she was not present, but I was ushered into the reception room, where books and pictures entertained me for the while. Presently she came, fresh from the shops, a harmony in brown, her hat of an outré but distinguished design, her long, heavy, yellow gloves buttoned to the elbows. She had apparently the physical vigor and the bounding enthusiasm of a girl of eighteen and greeted me with a light and airy gaiety and warmth worthy of a better cause.

"Ah, so you are here! I am so-oh glad. How have you been? How are you enjoying London? Now you must come and tell me all about it. I know that luncheon is ready. We will have a nice little tête-à-tête."

She tapped a bell and said to the servant who appeared, "You may serve the luncheon at once." She threw aside a muff and stole of brown fur and pulled two chairs together close in front of the fire. "Now I am going to have the pleasure of hearing all that you have been doing."

I am a very placid person. As I looked at her, I thought that she would be a very interesting person to describe. Her temperament would be such an interesting study. I spoke of the Wallace Collection and the Watteaus I had seen there, of the fact that the swirl of the London life was making my head go round in a ring, that the concentric streets were confusing. I mentioned the delight of a long ride to Shepherd's Bush and the pleasure of seeing Miss Wynne, whom I described. She made a note of her name, for she intended to have her perform at one of her evenings. Then we went in to lunch.

Only those with discrimination and means could afford or would have the taste to serve what followed. Hors d'oeuvres, a soup, a fish, an entrée, a hot bird, several kinds of wine, a selection of pastry were offered—though we contented ourselves with a bit of fish and the roast. "You will sit here," she said when we came in, "and I will sit here. We do not need Henry. I will send him away shortly. Now talk to me. You must be very nice. I have had a hard morning and I am tired." Her manner bespoke anything save weariness as she poured me a light wine and offered me a small roll. Her eyes had an eager, fatuous light in them, that round, ogling look with which women so easily impress the impressionable. Her red-gold hair gave a peculiar brilliancy to her complexion. She looked keen, intense, vital.

"I'll be as charming as I can, but you must tell me about yourself. I have so little to tell that you would care to know."

"Oh, now," she said with the least touch of irritation, "I don't like that. You must be simple."

"But I am—quite so. I never thought that my life was very complicated. What would you have me tell you?"

"America is such an interesting country. It produces such remarkable people. You must have had a world of experiences before you came to London." She smiled encouragingly and helped me to something else—I forget what.

"Well, let me see," I replied. "I was born in Indiana. That means nothing to you. It is a state. I was educated in the public schools of my native town. I have been a newspaperman, an editor, and have lived and worked in quite a number of American cities. I am married and am no longer living with my wife. I have no children and have written two books. Now what else can I tell you?"

She looked at me curiously. "You Americans are so fresh and new."

"Oh, no more so than the young of other nations," I replied. "But you tell me about yourself. I am much more interested in you than in anything that concerns me."

"Why should you be interested in me?" she asked coyly. "I have not done anything of any importance. My life is rather dull, I think."

"On the contrary, it is very interesting to me. You are a Dutchwoman. You are an interesting figure in London. Then you represent a certain attitude of mind"—I would not have been frank about this for anything under the circumstances—"which interests me greatly. I can't help wondering what sort of girl you must have been at eighteen."

This matter of age is a ticklish affair with a woman of Mrs. Stoop's age, but I intended to avoid that. I was thinking that there must have been, in a measure, a repressed girlhood here to permit of such bounding enthusiasm later, or that she had always been exceptionally passionate and emotional and had merely never recovered. So many women give a great demonstration of vitality because they have never been satisfied in anything and are still eager.

"Oh, my youth! My youth!" she exclaimed. "When I think of that—" she sighed. "But why do you say I represent a certain attitude of mind? Just what do you mean by that?"

I felt that she suspected a possible criticism here, but I did not intend to be trapped.

"Just your extreme youth and enthusiasm. Nothing more. You have such a vital attitude toward life. Most of us lose our interest in things so very young."

She felt satisfied. I could see it. Her inquiring eyes colored with a smile. She felt that I was taking her age at her own valuation and giving her credit for youth.

"Yes, my girlhood," she said, returning to her former topic. "I can scarcely understand what sort of a creature I was myself—so naive, so unsophisticated. I hardly knew anything about life before I was married—and then—" She lifted her eyes in dreary recollection.

"You did not love your husband?" I volunteered. It was the obvious thing to say. It was quite plain that the present occupant of this position (I did not know whether there had ever been another or not) did not share her affections or interests to an extent, if at all.

"Oh no, of course not. I was too young to understand. I was raised in such a conventional atmosphere. But how I talk to you! How do I know that you understand?"

I merely looked at her without saying anything at all. Henry came in finally to serve the roast.

"You need not do that," she said to him. "I will attend to it. I will ring if

I need you." He went silently out. She turned and looked at me with large, round—what she intended to be captivating—eyes. I had already heard that she was interested in some artist somewhere—Holland, I believe—and I suspected the general philanderer in her, as I know it to exist in myself. I do not care so much for eternal fealty in most people as I do for current merit. Her current merit was not so very attractive to me, though she was interesting enough.

"You are a curious woman," I said after a time, in which we surveyed each other in silence. I was conscious of the charming artistry of the room, the richness of the service on the table, her own exquisite toilet.

"Why curious?" she asked me, quite eagerly.

"You are so young, so childish. I would have given much to have known you when you were a nebulous girl in Holland. You must have been charming. You and I have very much in common—very much. I hope I have your enthusiasm. I wish I had your faith in life to satisfy. If I were to be in London long, I should like to know you better."

I was thinking of her extreme interest in Percy Grainger, the pianist, the night I had been here before. Her attitude toward him then was quite like hers to me at this moment. There is no leashing the philandering woman.

She put her pretty arms on the table and laid her chin meditatively in her hands. One could see that she had been a radiant beauty in her day. Her red-gold hair, her long, almond-shaped eyes and oval face gave her a decidedly Sarah Bernhardt effect.

"It's too bad that you are not," she said. "Why can't you stay? Can you not write as well in London as anywhere else? I should think London would be a charming atmosphere for you to work in."

I smiled cynically.

"What good would that do me?" I asked. "You are leaving soon. I heard you say so. Besides, I have come to see Europe."

"Oh yes, but you are not going to be seeing Europe forever. I will be back here in January. You won't be here then, no?"

I shook my head negatively.

"That is too bad. You will be coming back in the spring, though. I can see you then."

I had to smile. The desire of the philanderer to philander is incurable. I felt as satisfied as I ever felt of anything that her interest in me was not very great—more curiosity than anything, a novelty. She felt she had met her intellectual match, and that was something. I might possibly, if Grant Richards's praises were to be trusted, be going to stir the world greatly. She could not possibly tell. I was not utterly socially objectionable and quite satisfied in my way apparently. All these things were having their weight.

"No," I said rather dolefully, for I was beginning to act a part—the part I felt she wanted me to act. I was really not interested in her beyond a very temporary interest. She would have bored me greatly after a very little while. Still, she was pleasant enough for a momentary flirtation. "It would come to nothing. You are interested in very many things, but you would never be interested in me. You really do not know me. I think I understand you. You would like to do many things, but in the last analysis you would never do them."

She rose to come round to my side of the table and fill my wineglass—an obvious ruse.

"How do you know what I would do? You don't know. I would do anything I pleased where I was interested. I tell you I would do anything."

She poured my wine and looked down on me with a beaming countenance. Her face and manner betokened a very warm personal interest.

"Anything," she repeated.

This is a curious world. The situation was quite abnormal. I felt as though I were on the verge of an enforced proposal, and yet one in which I was not very much interested. Mrs. Stoop expected me to be greatly fascinated by her, which I was not. She stood beside me, but I made no move to touch her. Instead, I said rather mockingly:

"No, you say that, but you really don't mean it. I know your type. You are emotional, impetuous, dramatic."

I paused, for under this rough analysis she went about to her seat, studying me with round eyes. She sat down and put her elbows on the table once more, her face flushed.

"I don't understand you," she said.

"I understand you," I said. I got up, for she kept studying me with her wide, acquisitive gaze. She was disappointed that I did not make love to her.

"Get up," I said authoritatively and with the feeling that somehow she would be glad to obey me, which she did. She upset a cup of red wine as she did so.

"Never mind that," I added as I saw her pause to remedy the evil. "Come here."

She abandoned the cup, coming round the table toward me, looking at me all the while with that assumption of fearsome innocence which the experienced in philandering know so well how to assume. It was a curious, dumb show, quite ridiculous to me who admires so much the splendor of true affection. The stage on which it was being enacted was most picturesque.

When she reached me, I took her arms and studied her face. "Now," I said, "if you really mean it, tell me how much you like me? Will you do, as you say, anything?"

Her face clouded slightly. She had, I am sure, intended by her flirtatious attitude to start a pursuit which would make an attending devotee of me socially. This was apparently not so clear now as when she began. My manner was too direct, incisive, without tenderness or even the assumption of it.

"Oh," she said, "I hardly know what you mean. I have known you such a little while."

"I thought so," I replied smilingly.

"There is someone else. I like you very much. I—"

I saw through the silly little game so constantly played in this silly world and was glad I had been so matter-of-fact about it all. I had not given any evidence of sudden fascination—rather of doubtful curiosity. Nevertheless she was flustered, wrought up, emotionally disturbed. I looked at her quite solemnly, critically. "Just as I thought," I repeated. "Who is he?"

She shook her head. "And yet you are very much like him. That's why I am drawn to you, I think. You are so sympathetic."

The mysteries of sex attraction are beyond any words to describe. They are as fluid as water, as treacherous as the sea. Those who know most of them are the most amazed, the most puzzled. I looked at her curiously, in feigned surprise, I think, only to see her eyes brim.

"Oh," she exclaimed, "I am so unhappy at times. That is it. That explains it all." Her semi-Dutch voice had a most appealing ring.

When a woman cries, the mystery is still further complicated. I fancied I knew the person to whom the compliment of tears was paid. It did not flatter me any that being somewhat like him, I should be sought for my sympathy. As a matter of fact I saw quite clearly that I might so soothe her that she would accept me in lieu—it was quite possible, but I did not care for that. She was too old, too much of a philanderer and an actress. She was interesting to talk to, but not very. Her chief interest in life was to shine in every possible way—socially, intellectually, emotionally, and to be admired and petted. It was something to have men of exceptional merit run after her. I was one such—let us say the latest.

I pretended great sympathy. I listened to her woes. Her life was so dreary. Her husband did not really share her artistic ambitions. Her artist friend was so fine. If she could just make him successful! Then she paid me various compliments for my fineness of spirit. Having small faith in mortality in any form, this did not interest me much. She finally took me in her automobile to Regent Street, telling me, as we passed Buckingham Palace, of a ball she had attended there recently and what she had worn. We got on famously. My one feeling all the while was that I was dealing with a typical social butterfly, vain, vapid, insincere, magnetic; the kind who mean excellently well but who by their unchained desires hold vast potentiality for evil. She might readily involve anyone in a most disturbing scandal. And she was not beautiful either. She was merely not growing old gracefully.

CHAPTER XVIII

I went this same evening, after a reasonable afternoon's work, to see where I should dine. It was after six, and I had worked from a little before four until then. I was a little lonely, although it must seem foolish to the reader of these notes, for I had certainly been entertained quite enough. But the older I grow, the more lonely I become. A half-hour of my own company is quite sufficient, unless I am walking or working—then nothing matters, for I am really very much entertained by life or my comments concerning it. But Grant Richards had gone, and here I was with an evening and a day before me, and I speculated solemnly as to where I should dine. The Savoy, the Cecil, the Ritz, all came into my mind, and after that the Piccadilly and some minor places such as Lyons, where I saw the interesting noonday luncheon crowd, and so on.

As I was going out to walk about and see for myself, the porter handed me several unimportant letters, and at the door a footman handed me a package.

"Those ladies just brought you that. In the car." He was nodding to where a large purple-hued automobile was standing in the glare of the electric lights. I looked and recognized the face of Mrs. Stoop. She was smiling her luminous affected smile—the joy of the artist who is representing life in a distinguished manner.

"I thought," she said in her sweet Dutch accent, "that you would like to have it. I brought it."

I bowed and smiled. "So nice of you. I'm delighted. Really, this is charming of you."

"No." Her voice had a Bernhardt lure to it—the long, sad drawl of the voice of gold. "No—I'm glad."

She looked at me with significant eyes, and I bowed again. The folly of romance, I thought. It means so little—it means nothing. We love once or twice. After that, there is only the sad phantom of delight which can never be attained.

I went up the street, and her car sped away. In Piccadilly I stared into the bright shop windows. London's display of haberdashery and gold and silver ornaments interests me intensely. Because it was drizzling and I had no umbrella, I thought of buying one but changed my mind. They are such a nuisance. I walked on into Regent Street. I had no idea where I was going and looked at the home-surging crowds under the arc lights, wondering what sort of people they were, how they differed from Americans, how I could detect that difference. It was delightful to me to watch the clerks, men and women, the old men and the old women, the young men and the young women, the boys and girls. Youth and age offer such a never-ending and dramatic contrast—the old broken-down feeble men and women to whom life has become a deadly round of reiterated cares, and the young hopeful buoyant boys and girls who think life is so lovely. Everything is before them. Their eyes dance. They run and laugh and sing. They have strength and hope wherewith to meet the cares of the day. But age! Age!! Age!!!

Well, here I was in Regent Street, and the thought was with me as I walked in the rain, "Where shall I dine? How shall I do it? Shall I phone for Miss Villars and take her to see Wish Wynne after dinner—or what? Or shall I find some peculiarly interesting-looking girl of the streets and see what she can tell me of London? What can I learn of London through her?" I had been thinking of the London street girls ever since Grant Richards and myself had strolled home along Piccadilly from Mrs. Stoop's musical at two o'clock in the morning. They had been so attractive-looking, so much prettier, truly, than the average woman of class and distinction whom I had seen. It had raised the question why the unschooled daughters of the poor are so often so much more attractive physically—I am not talking now of either mind or temperament. In those matters they are usually woefully deficient—from a social point of view, quite impossible, I suppose, or nearly so. Now it occurred to me, however, that some of them might operate as a refuge from loneliness, though I confess—perhaps I had better say insist—that the thought of anything physical between myself and her, whoever she should be, left me quite cold.

I think I have already pointed out that I am not as enthusiastic about women as I once was—the average woman. I cannot stand them. My idea of beauty and charm in sex is too high. As a rule, the average woman knows little or nothing of life. Her proportion of physical or mental charm is meager. She has too many defects of thought and character. I follow them with interest—a very little interest—a very little way. Then my feelings revolt, and I want no more.

But tonight I was thinking of some agreeable individual of reasonable intelligence, some simple-mannered girl who would not really be too bad and who would talk with me without any wild desire to rob me. It is bad business, this of having to do with street women, and in all my life, boyhood included, I think, I have picked up just three—possibly four or five, I forget. The last one was in New York, some three years before this, and I did so on that occasion because the girl ahead of me had a rippling motion to her large, easy body. She was pretty, and I was interested to see why. I was not disappointed physically, but mentally she was impossible, and as in most such cases where intelligent men are concerned, the adventure came to nothing. She was nice, but not as nice as I thought she ought to be.

Tonight I looked about, largely because a girl—a shopgirl, I fancy—looked willingly at me, but she was not pretty enough. Then I decided to call up Miss Villars and did so, but she could not join me. She wanted to, but there was someone coming to see her. I hung up the receiver and went out into the rain, strolling through New Bond Street and looking idly at the dark stores. In Piccadilly again I saw a girl—two of them, really, but only one interested me—who looked over her shoulder at me and smiled. She was of medium size, dressed rather as the American girl dresses herself, and quite pretty. Her eyes were large and simple and her figure excellent. Her hips and bust had a peculiar sway to them which spoke of fair proportions.

"Shall I or shall I not?" I thought, and finally decided for the adventure of it that I would. I followed her up the street, for she and her companion had disappeared, and presently overtook them where they paused to look into a shop window. I signaled to her, and she came over.

"Wouldn't you like to take the two of us?" she asked with that quaint odd accent of the English or Welsh, which is not London cockney but rural. Her voice was soft, and her eyes were as blue and weak in their force as any unsophisticated girl's might well be.

"This girl isn't hard and vulgar. She's simply weak," I said to myself. "Her eyes are too soft and vague. She wouldn't know how to be really brutal. I'll talk to her." I suppose we all pride ourselves on knowing something of character in women. I thought I did.

"No," I replied rather directly to her question. "I don't want your companion. She isn't quite what I want. I prefer you. You must send her away."

"Would you mind givin' her a shillin'?" she asked simply—not graspingly as these women are inclined to ask at times.

"Not at all," I replied. "Here you are."

It was a wet night, chill and dreary, and on second thought I made it a half-crown. The second girl went away—a girl thinner and not so attractive to me—and I turned to my companion.

"Now," I said, "what shall we do? Let me see." It was nearly eight o'clock, and I was wondering where I could go with such a girl to dine—certainly not to a conspicuous public restaurant. Her clothes were not good enough. I was a little doubtful about the whole procedure anyhow, and looking at her, I wondered whether I should really care to do anything more than talk to her. Because she reminded me the least bit of the country girl interpreted by Miss Wynne, I felt a literary interest in her. Her chin and nose were not bad, her teeth clean and even. But her clothes were a mere patchwork—the cheapest kind of a feather boa, the cheapest kind of an imitation American hat, imitating its breadth and chicness. Her suit was of blue twill but old, or rather, well worn. The color of her cheeks was that wonderful apple color of the English, and her eyes—really her eyes were quite a triumph of nature—soft and simple and deeply blue and not very self-protective.

"Poor little storm-blown soul," I thought as I looked at her. "Your life isn't much. A vague, conscienceless (in the softer sense of that word) thing. You have a chilly future before you."

She looked as though she might be about nineteen, certainly not more—the foolish age for girls.

"Let's see! Have you had your dinner?" I asked.

"No, sir."

"Where is there a good restaurant—not too conspicuous—not too well-known?"

"Well, there's ——" (I forget what the name was) "and the Lyons Corner House."

"Ah yes, where is that?" I asked, thinking of the other Lyons which I had seen. It would be something in her class. "Do you go there yourself occasionally?"

"Oh yes, quite often. It's very nice, I think."

I fancied I knew the sort of place it was—cheap, frequented by middle-class people or those somewhat below that in the social scale, but fairly decent. The other Lyons place indicated as much.

"We might go there," I said. "Still, on second thought, I don't think we will just now. Where is this place you go to—the place you take your friends?"

I forgot to say that with my consent she had agreed to meet her friend again at eleven at some place which they knew of.

"It's at No. 38 Great Titchfield Street."

"Is that an apartment or a hotel?"

"It's a flat, sir—my flat. The lady lets me bring my friends there. If you like, though, we could go to a hotel. Perhaps it would be better."

I could see that she was uncertain in a vague way as to what I would think of her apartment.

"And where is the hotel? Is that nice?"

"It's pretty good, sir, not so bad."

I smiled. She was holding a small umbrella over her head.

"We'd better take a taxi and get out of this rain, anyhow."

I put up my hand and hailed one. We got in, the driver obviously realizing that this was a street liaison, but giving no sign. London taxi drivers, like London policemen, are the pink of civility. I never witnessed such a generally pleasing attitude as the police, the drivers, the trainmen and the clerks generally have in London. This girl was civil, obliging. I was contrasting her with the Broadway and the American type generally—hard, cynical little beasts, however they come to be so. The English, from prostitutes to queens, must have an innate sense of decency in the social relationship, of live and let live. I say this in all sincerity and with the utmost feeling of respect for the nation that has produced it. They ought to rule—by right of courtesy. Alas, I fear me greatly that the force and speed of the American, his disregard for civility and the waste of time involved in standing on the order of his going, will change all this.

In the taxi I did not touch her, though she moved over near me in that desire to be amorously friendly, but instead I contented myself with looking out into the streets where the rain was falling.

"Have we far to go?" I asked perfunctorily.

"Not very. Only a little way."

"How much ought the cab charge to be?"

"Not more than eight or ten pence, sir."

Then, "I am wondering whether I am going to like you," I said, thinking of the cheapness of fares in London generally. I was thinking also of whether there were ruses and traps in the shape of dangerous houses where men might be taken and robbed. I decided I would judge for myself.

"There's one of the restaurants I was thinkin' of," she observed as we passed a third- or fourth-rate place—the kind I would never enter myself, except on advice, so cheap and poor was it.

"Well, we wouldn't go there," I observed.

"Do you like girls, sir?" she asked quaintly in a very human attempt to be pleasant under the circumstances.

"No," I replied, lying cautiously. "I think not—not as a rule, certainly." I wanted to see what she would say, what effect a distant attitude would have on her.

"Why not?"

"Well, as a rule they are not nice enough. They don't know enough. They are what I call dull."

She looked at me uncertainly—a little overawed, I think. I was certainly a strange fish to swim into her net, anyhow.

"Very likely you don't like me, then?"

"I am not sure that I do. How should I know? I never saw you before in my life. I must say you have mighty nice eyes," was my rather banal reply.

"Do you think so?" She gave me a sidelong, speculative look.

"Yes. They're soft and pleasant. I can't tell about the rest of you. You may be pretty."

"But you don't like women, do you?" she asked.

"No, not very much."

"You're a woman-hater. That's what you are. I've seen such."

"Not a woman-hater. No. Simply not very much interested in them. They're not very clever as a rule. They lie and pretend, and they're not nice enough either."

"You don't like me, do you?"

"Not very much. You're a little nice. You have nice eyes."

"My eyes," she echoed, "yes. Well, it's all right. I don't mind. I don't care."

"You have a nice form?"

"They tell me so."

"Well, we'll see."

I had to smile at the seemingly cold-blooded quality of my procedure. I was not so hard-hearted by any means, but it must have sounded as though I was no more interested than I would have been in an array of fish at a market. I was curious about her intellectually—what she could teach me of London life generally and of her little world in particular. I was sorry for the moment that I couldn't take a physical interest in her, but I couldn't. I am too suspicious of disease and the temperaments of people. As a rule, these women are not nice. Besides, in spite of my fine preliminary opinions, she might try to rob or overcharge me or take me to some place where some wretched game would be worked. I had no fear of this, however, or at least not sufficient to let it interfere with an interesting adventure. Adventure is almost the only spice left in life, and there is very little of that. I had not asked her what she would charge, preferring not to. I wondered what she would attempt to build out of that.

"What nationality are you?" I asked.

"I'm Welsh," she replied.

"I didn't think you were English exactly. Your tone is softer."

The taxi stopped abruptly before the number she had given the driver, and we got out. It was a shabby-looking building with a tea or coffee room on the ground floor, and the woman who came to change me a half-sovereign ($2.50 American money), in order that I might pay the driver, was French, small and cleanly-looking. She was pleasant and brisk, and her whole attitude reassured me at once. She did not look like a person who would take part in any scheme to rob anyone, and I had good reason to think more clearly of this as we came out later.

"This way," said my street girl, "we go up here." And I followed her—up two flights of thinly-carpeted, cheaply-built stairs, into a small, dingy room.

It was clean, after the French fashion. There was a gas-jet covered by a Welsbach burner and one window hung with cheap machine-made lace. The bed was very cheap but clean and sound-looking.

"It's not so bad?" she asked with a touch of pride.

"No. Not at all."

"Will you pay for the room, please?"

The landlady had followed and was standing by.

I asked how much and found I was to be charged five shillings, which seemed cheap enough, considering.

"I wonder what she will want?" I thought, thinking of the girl. "Now we'll see whether her soft eyes belie her. If she's savage and evil, she'll attempt to overcharge me." Still I did not inquire.

She locked the door as the landlady went out and began taking off her hat and jacket. I took off my hat and overcoat and hung them up, but no more. I was really in no mood for the whole adventure. She was not bad, but there is an ideal in life I have to contend with, a certain one somewhere, whom in all probability I shall never see anymore but with whose beauty and charm, as by a yardstick, I must measure the whole race of womankind. I may not speak of her more, but it cannot be helped. Measured by that individual standard, many fail utterly—the good and the evil, the beautiful and the homely alike—for the time being.

There is something about the clothing of the street girls at times—the less efficient ones, I fancy—which possesses an indescribable pathos for me. In the bright gaslight of this room I examined her—Lilly Edwards, she told me afterwards her name was—and her clothes were pathetic. They were not exactly unclean—they really were not that—but shabby and threadbare. When she took off her jacket, for instance, I saw that her shirtwaist was cheap, worn and broken. She took off her outer skirt, and the next, a black one, was of thin material, and after that came a poor corset-cover, a worn corset, a pair of cheap cotton drawers, and under it all a cheap cotton chemise without the least touch of artistry or suggestion of worth about it.

"This poor little girl doesn't make much," I said to myself. "She isn't clever enough. Her eyes show it."

"So you think you have a pretty form," I said drearily as she undressed. The room was anything but comfortably warm to me, but I do not pretend to understand the English standard. I am sure it did not seem cold to her.

"Some think so," she replied with a touch of bravado in her eyes. With a faint breath of gaiety, "Look at that."

She drew herself up and filled out her chest. Her bosom swelled stiff, and I felt one of her breasts under her chemise.

"Yes, that's not bad. Take it off. I'll see for myself." I was pointing to her chemise.

She took it off quickly, thinking to impress me, I fancy, or hoping to, and stood beside me quite naked, save for shoes and stockings. Her breasts stood forth from her chest smartly, and her body was graceful, shapely.

"I'm going to have a child in six or seven months," she observed in a curious, off-hand way, thinking possibly that she ought to tell me for fear that I would notice that she was rather full in the abdomen. I had not noticed. It surprised me the least bit—disgusted me for a second, say—and then I thought why should I feel so. She is only a street girl. It is sordid and pitiful and mean, but why should I object? She is common property, and I know it. I shall not see her anymore.

I was quite passionless, for all her nakedness, and looked at her body critically: the shape of her legs and arms, which were not rounded enough, and the texture of her skin. Now that she was stripped, I saw that her skin was a little too dark—dusty-looking—her elbow and knee joints rough with what is called gooseflesh, I believe, and her lips and the underside of her nose chafed a little by the cold weather, I suppose.

"Are you cold?" I asked.

"No," she replied. "I'm comfortable enough."

"This room isn't chilly to you?"

"No."

"I don't understand you English. You don't seem to know what cold is. I'm cold right now."

"I'm not."

We were standing in front of the mantelpiece, below which was the empty, fireless grate and above a fair-sized mirror. She was crowding close to me, attempting by rubbing against me to arouse that desire which only intense sympathy or compatibility of temper, where beauty is, can arouse. If I had liked her much, felt sorry for her, seeing that she was not really homely, I might have. Her eyes, so curiously soft and blue, had a soft, gentle appeal. Her hair, I noticed, was brown but coarse and dusty—not well kept. These poor little wastrels know absolutely nothing of the art of living or fascination. They are the shabbiest pawns in life, mere husks of beauty and living on husks.

"Sit down, please," I said. She obeyed like a child. "So you're Welsh. What part of Wales do you come from?" I asked, ignoring the attempted lure of her body.

She told me—some outlandish name.

"What were your parents? Poor, I suppose?"

"Indeed not," she bridled with that quaint country accent. "My father was a grocer. He had three stores."

"I don't believe it," I said mockingly. "You women lie so. I don't believe you're telling me the truth."

"Why not?" Her clear eyes sought mine.

"Oh, I don't. You'd naturally attempt to make things look better than they are."

She bristled vaguely but without force. It was pathetic.

"Believe it or not," she said sullenly. "It's so. My father is a grocer."

"More likely he is a miner," I said or thought—I forget which, but anyhow I recall no reply.

"What are you going to do with your baby when it comes—give it away?"

"I am not. I'm going to keep it."

"Yes. Like hell you are. You're going to give it to some hospital or put it on some doorstep."

"I am not. I'm going to keep it. I'd like a child of my own. I don't like children, it's true, but one of your own is different."

"Aren't you afraid?"

"I'm not. I'll come out all right."

I thought of the probably wretched fate of this life coming, of its probable career! There ought to be some form of social gardening undertaken in this world, I said to myself at the moment. Humanity can be made better at the door of life, I think. Certainly it would do no harm to try. I myself need governing.

"Perhaps you will and perhaps not. You don't look so strong to me. You may not come through."

"Well, if I die, I die," she said.

I liked that. More particularly I liked the way she said it. There was something right decent about the mental feel of the girl—something better than her state.

"Tell me," I said, rubbing the flesh of her back near her hips with my hand, "how much can you make out of this business? A good living?"

"Oh, sometimes more, sometimes less. I don't walk every day, you know. I only walk when I have to. If I pick up a gentleman and if he gives me a good lot, I don't walk very soon again—not until that's gone. I—I don't like to very much."

"What do you call a good lot?" Now we were coming to the money question. I was going to see how she measured me.

"Oh, all sorts of sums. I have been given as high as six pounds."

"That isn't true," I said. "You know it isn't true. You're talking for effect. You know no man ever gave you six pounds in your life."

"It *is* true. As I'm alive, it's true. I swear by anything. It wasn't in this very room, but it was in this house, and what's more, he spent seventeen pounds on me on wine downstairs."

"What silly rot!" I said. "Seventeen pounds on wine in this house! You're lying out of the whole cloth. Why do you talk such nonsense? Your eyes are better than that."

"It's true, as I live. He was a rich American. He was from New York. All Americans have money—and he was drunk."

"Yes, all Americans may have money," I smiled sardonically, "but they don't go round spending it on such as you in that way. You're not worth it."

"Why ain't I?"

She was such a weak little creature; it was a shame to be so brutal.

"Because you're not. You're not attractive enough. You're not interesting enough. You don't know enough."

She looked at me, but no angry rage sprang to her eyes. She didn't know how to take me, how to think of me. I was puzzling her, I suppose, and she felt out of place and rather put under possibly.

"It's true just the same," she said meekly.

She was a little cold finally, and I made her sit on the bed and draw some of the clothes around her. She was puzzled, perplexed, uncertain. She told me, via questions and answers, of the police regulations which permit a woman to go with a man, if he speaks to her first, without being arrested—but not otherwise—and of the large number of women who are in the business. She told me of French, German, English and American men and their characteristics. The Americans, English and Germans she appeared to like well enough, but the French were brutes, she insisted. Just how she wouldn't explain. They wanted women to do things they shouldn't. Even a prostitute may have prejudices and standards. Piccadilly is the great walking ground, I understood, after one o'clock in the morning; Leicester Square and the regions adjacent, between seven and eleven. There is another place in the East End—I don't recall where—where the poor Jews and others walk, but they are a dreadful lot, she assured me. The men expect the girls to go for three shillings, and the girls are poor, miserable drabs. I thought at the time that if she would look down on them, what must they be!

Then, somehow, because the conversation was getting friendly, I fancy, this little Welsh girl decided perhaps that I was not as severe as I seemed. This type is always trained by experience to think constantly of how much money can be extracted from men—not the normal fee, since there is little more than a poor living in that, but extravagant sums which produce fine clothes and jewels, according to their estimate of these things. It is an old story. Other women had told her of their successes. Those who know anything of women—the street type—know how often this is tried. She told the customary story of the man who picked her up and, having escorted her to her room, offered her a pound, when two pounds or a much larger sum was expected. The result was, of course, according to her, dreadful for the man. She created a great scene, broke some pottery over his head, or beat him with some brushes. It is an old story of the bagnio, an old trick. Your timid man, hearing this and being possibly a new or infrequent adventurer in this world, becomes fearful of a scene. Many men are timid about bargaining with a woman beforehand. It smacks too much of the brutal and evil, and after all, there is a certain element of romance involved in these drabby liaisons for the average man, even if there is none—*as there is none*—for the woman. It is an old, sad, sickening, grim story to most of them, and in their eyes men are fools, dogs, idiots, but rarely anything fine or interesting. When they see the least chance to betray one of them, to browbeat and rob or overcharge him in any way and by any trick, they are ready to do it. This girl, Lilly Edwards, had been schooled by perhaps a hundred experienced advisers of the street as to how this was done. I know this is so, for afterwards she told me of how other women did it.

But to continue: "He laid a sovereign on the table, and I went for him," she said.

I smiled, not so much in derision as amusement. The story did not fit her. Obviously it was not true.

"Oh, no you didn't," I replied. "You are telling me one of the oldest stories of the trade. Bless your soul, I was caught by it once. You frightened him and he paid, or you found that he resisted and you beat him up so that he would never try to give any girl like you less than fifteen or twenty pounds! Now the truth is you are a silly little liar, and you think you are going to frighten me by telling me this into giving you two or three pounds. You can save yourself the trouble. I don't intend to do it. I wouldn't do it if you were much more attractive than you are, and to me you are not attractive at all. You haven't really a nice figure. And certainly you haven't a nice mind. Why do you spring such an old chestnut as that on me?"

"What's a chestnut?" she asked, surprised by the expression.

"Oh, it's American for a fake or stale old story. We say that of something that we've heard so often that we are tired of it—that it's a chestnut."

My little Welsh girl was all at sea at once. Her powerless but really sweet eyes showed it. I pitied her weak, sweet eyes.

"It is true," she exclaimed, trying to show a little anger and fire. "I did do it. I wouldn't let any man treat me like that!"

"You didn't do it. It's a lie, and you know it's a lie. You have been taught how to say and try this by others. Why, hang it all, you haven't the force. Your eyes won't let you get away with it. You can't do what you say you can. I wouldn't give you any such sum as that, nor anything more than I thought was right and fair. I might wreck you and the place first. But we won't talk about that. I'll give you what I please—exactly and no more. But I'm sorry you've begun this silly lying, for I like you even less now. I did like your eyes—but, pshaw! you're not worth talking about. Put on your clothes."

I never saw a more troubled little maid in all my life. She didn't know what to make of me. Her normally soft eyes were filled with a kind of wonder and, I fancy, apprehension. I had no intention of not paying her well. This was all acting, a kind of dumb show.

"I didn't say you'd give it to me," she explained warily. "I said I'd got it. I don't know what you'll give me. What did you expect to pay?"

Poor little street waif! She was going about putting on her rags of clothes, and I actually grew sorry watching her. Something hurt—the pathos of her courage and endurance in the face of such a contemptuous attitude. I had pretended not to like her body and told her so. I had made fun of her lies and flouted her tricks. She said once, with a kind of weak anger or self-justifying resentment, "I suppose maybe you're played out. I've seen men like that."

"Oh, am I?" I replied, keeping up that show. "That's all you know. Because you can't interest me, I'm impotent. You're silly. You can't turn the trick, that's all."

She was hooking her corset briskly and putting on her skirt in a gloomy, despondent way—the depression that follows defeat.

"I don't understand you. I never saw anybody like you before."

"This is a new experience for you," I said. "It will teach you something more about men."

"I don't want to know anything more about them," she returned with sudden fury. "I'm sick of them—the whole lot of them! If I could get out of this, I would. I wish I need never see another man!"

I did not doubt the sincerity of this outburst, but I affected not to believe her.

"Oh, surely not!"

"I do!" she insisted sullenly.

"You say that, but it's all talk. If you wanted to get out, you would. Why don't you get a job at something? You can work."

"I don't know any trade now, and I'm too old to learn."

"What nonsense! You're not more than nineteen, and you could do anything you pleased. You won't, though. You're like all the others. This is the easy way. You won't do it because you can lie and browbeat and lie about and smoke—"

"Oh, you—" she started, but stopped. Her weak, pretty eyes held a dumb pathos (as I am living, I testify to this). She was quite fully dressed now and ready to go. It touched me, and I took her arm. She was adjusting a final pin of some kind in her hat.

"I'm really not as bad as I seem," I said gently, trying to make up to her for the insults and cruelty. "It's a rainy, bad night. This room is gloomy. I like you a little better now, in spite of your lies and your silly talk. You can't help yourself. You're not such a bad little girl if you do hate men—you're just a little hurt. And I'm not so bad either. Really I'm not. I'm simply teasing you."

"Oh no, I don't care." Her eyes looked hurt and angry.

"Are you sure you don't? Look me in the eyes."

"Oh, I can't help it if you don't like me. You don't like me, so that's all there is to it."

"I do like you a little better now than I did before. Really I do. I like you because it is possible to hurt you. There is some hope in that. Come. Take off your coat and hat. I'll show you something."

Her eyes lighted with a peculiarly friendly gleam. There was a touch of triumph in them, of self-recovery. Then she really wasn't as bad as I thought her.

"Well, you're funny," she replied, laughing. "You really are funny." And I could see that for once, in a long time, perhaps, the faintest touch of romance had entered this sordid world for her.

CHAPTER XIX

I would not continue this romance of Lilly Edwards save for the fact that the last half of this shabby evening proved better than the first. When we came out of this commonplace rooming establishment, which was about ten or fifteen minutes later, I said, "Now we'll go and have something to eat," and, seeing that my attitude had changed so radically, she asked, "Would you get me a box of cigarettes? I haven't any change."

"Surely," I said, and we stepped into a tobacconist's shop. From there we took a taxi to Lyons Corner House, which she seemed to regard as sufficiently luxurious, and from there—but I'll tell this in detail.

At this meal I talked to her much more pleasantly about London street life. I had given her a sovereign and purchased her a double-sized box of excellent cigarettes, and now I was paying for her supper. Her whole attitude had changed. From plodding the streets in the rain and being browbeaten shamefully, she was being treated in a most gallant manner. I was most friendly and kindly, I think. She interested me a lot.

"Tell me," I said after she had given the order, picking something for herself and me, "you say you come from Wales. Tell me the name of a typical mining town which is nearer London than some of the others—some place which is really poor and hard-worked."

"Well, where I came from was pretty bad," she ventured, giving me some unpronounceable name. "The people haven't got much to live on there."

I wish you might have heard the peculiar purr of her accent.

"And how far is that?"

She gave me the hours from London and the railroad fare in shillings. I think it was about three hours at most.

"And Cardiff's pretty bad," she added. "There's lots of mines there. Very deep ones, too. The people are poor there."

"Have you ever been in a mine?"

"Yes, sir."

I smiled at her civility, for in entering and leaving the room of the house of assignation, she had helped me on and off with my overcoat—quite as a servant might.

I learned a little about Wales through her—its ill-paid life—and then we came back to London. How much did the average street girl really make? I wanted to know. She couldn't tell me, and she was quite honest about it.

"Some make more than others," she said. "I'm not very good at it," she confessed. "I can't make much. I don't know how to get money out of men."

"I know you don't," I replied with real sympathy. "You're not mean enough. Those eyes of yours are too soft. You shouldn't lie though, Lilly. You're better than that. You ought to be in some other work, worse luck."

She didn't answer, choosing to ignore my petty philosophizing concern over something of which I knew so little. For who can explain life? And why will we, who are in sin, insist on casting the first stone?

We talked of girls—the different kinds. Some were really very pretty, some were not. Some had really nice figures, she said. You could see it. Others were made up terribly and depended on their courage or their audacity to trick money out of men—dissatisfied men. There were regular places they haunted, Piccadilly being the best—the only profitable place for her kind—and there were no houses of ill repute. The police did not allow them.

"Yes, but that can't be," I said. "All the vice of London isn't concentrated in just this single spot." The restaurant we were in—a large but cheap affair—was quite a center, she said. "There must be other places," I suggested. "All the women who do this sort of thing don't come here. Where do they go?"

"There's another place along Cheapside, where the society women go."

"The society women?" I asked. "You don't mean to tell me the society women go and walk? I can't believe it." I was curious to know on what she based her statement.

"Yes, I do," she replied. "Society women. You wouldn't believe how many of them do that. They go down there in the afternoon between three and five and wait for the men with money when they are going home. I've seen them myself. I didn't believe it either, but I went down there and saw them."

"I wonder if you know a society woman when you see one?" I queried.

"Indeed I do. I see them coming out of the theaters and the opera house."

"I doubt that," I replied, restraining my amusement. "You might have, however. They don't go to either place very often, I'm afraid."

She looked at me curiously, but we talked on. It appeared that there were certain places where the girls congregated in this district—saloons or quasi-restaurants, probably like the Dewey in New York, where they could go and wait for men to speak to them. They could wait twenty minutes at a time, and then if no one spoke to them, they had to get up and leave, but after twenty minutes or so they could come back again and try their luck, which meant that they would have to buy another drink. In the meantime, there were other places, and they were always full of girls.

"You shall take me to that Cheapside place," I suggested. "I will buy you more cigarettes and a nice box of candy. Afterwards I will pay you for your time."

She thought about her traveling companion whom she had agreed to meet at eleven, and finally promised. The companion was to be left to her fate. I don't think she had a serious engagement with her.

While we dined, we talked of men and what they liked. Englishmen, she thought, liked French girls pretty well, and Americans liked English girls, but the great trick was to get yourself up like an American girl and speak her patois—imitate her slang, because she was the most popular of all. "Americans and English gentlemen"—she herself made that odd distinction—"like the American girl. I'm sometimes taken for one," she informed me, "and this hat is like the American hats."

It was. I smiled at the compliment, sordid as it may appear.

"Why do they like them?" I asked.

"Oh, the American girl is smarter. She walks quicker. She carries herself better. That's what the men tell me."

"And are you able to deceive them?"

"Yes."

"Well then," I thought, "it's those who know very little of America," for I could not see how an American could help escaping that soft rural pathos which in the English and Welsh country voice moves me so much.

"How do you do that?" I asked. "They must know. Do you know American slang?"

"Yes, sir."

"Let me hear some."

"Well, I guess I'll have to go now," she began, trying to imitate the American voice. It was a little like it. "All Americans say 'I guess,'" she informed me.

"And what else?" I asked.

"Well, 'sure.' We say 'sure' in Wales, too."

"That's interesting. And what else?"

"Oh, let me see." She seemed lost for more. "You teach me some," she said. "I know some other words, but I forget."

For half an hour I coached her in "lemon," "frost," "fake," "bluff," "four-flusher," "hot-air artist," "dope," "mutt," "dippy," "pie-eyed," and those more interesting phrases such as "Officer, he's in again," "for the love of Mike," "what do you know about that" and things of that sort. She sat there, intensely interested, while I drilled her simple memory and her lips in these odd American phrases, and I confess I took real delight in teaching her. In a way I was sorry for the abuse I had heaped upon her, and I wanted to make her more efficient. Poor little Lilly Edwards! She will end soon enough. If a few silly phrases would aid, I would drill her longer and help her in many other ways besides.

At eleven we departed for one of the places where she said these women congregated, and then I saw what the London underworld of this kind was like. I was told afterwards that it was fairly representative and even exceptional, in a criminal or immoral way. New York's vice is far more varied and subtle; it is much more brilliant, if you would have it so. There was something soggy and brutal about this. Aside from this particular characterization, this Piccadilly neighborhood, which is supposed to be the center of sex attraction for all London, is scarcely more significant, more individual, than anything you would find in Cincinnati or St. Louis, if as much so; but I am thinking of these places as they were years ago. New York has its notable houses of vice, scores of them, and hotels by the dozen, which are visiting places for the sexually inclined, but in addition to this it has areas—Broadway from 34th to 42nd Streets; Broadway from 26th to 34th; 14th Street from Irving Place to Third Avenue, and even up Fourth Avenue from 23rd to 28th. There are other really gay vice centers, such as 125th Street and Eighth Avenue, and 125th Street and Third Avenue, and all of these concern Manhattan Island only. Brooklyn, the Bronx, Jersey City and Newark have centers of vice of their own. I should say London's Piccadilly could best be compared to the vice section lying between Irving Place and Third Avenue. The women are more or less of the same caliber, ignorant and degraded, and the meeting places I saw were about as sordid as the Dewey, Sharkey's and the like.

This little girl took me to a place on a corner just below the theater known as the Empire and very close to the restaurant we were leaving—I should say two blocks. It was on the second floor and was reached by a wide stairway which gave into a room like a circle, surrounding the head of the stairs as a center. To the left, as we came up, was a bar attended by four or five pretty barmaids, and the room, quite small, was crowded with men and women. The women—or girls, rather, for I should say they all ranged somewhere between seventeen and twenty-six—were good-looking in an ordinary way, but they weren't chic like the French, nor smart and aware like the Americans of the same class. In all sincerity I should say that American women of this class were greatly superior, not so dull and serious.

The tables at which they were seated were arranged around the walls, and they were drinking solely to pay the house for allowing them to sit there. Men were coming in and going out, as were other girls. Sometimes they came in or went out alone. At other times they came in or went out in pairs. Waiters strolled to and fro, and the etiquette of the situation seemed to demand that the women should buy port wine—why, I don't know. It was vile stuff, tasting as though it were prepared of chemicals, and I refused to touch it. I was shown local detectives, lesbians, girls who worked in pairs—why, I did not understand until later—and pimps. I was assured that the maids behind the bar were available, that you could make arrangements with them to meet you "afterwards," as they speak of the London closing hour. I did not understand until now that London closes all its restaurants, saloons, hotel bars and institutions of this kind promptly at twelve-thirty, and then these women are turned out on the streets.

"You should see Piccadilly around one o'clock in the morning," my guide had said to me a little while before, and now I understood. They were all forced out into Piccadilly from everywhere.

It was rather a dismal thing to be sitting there, I must confess. The room was lively enough, but this type of life is so vacant of soul. It is precisely as though one stirred in straw and sawdust, expecting it to be vigorous with the feel of growing life and freshness, such as one finds in a stalk or tree. It is a world of dead ideals, I should say—or, better yet, a world in which ideals never had a chance to grow. The women were the veriest birds of prey—cold, weary, disillusioned, angry, dull, sad perhaps; the men were victims of carnal desire without the ability to understand how weary and disgusted the women were who sought to satisfy them. No clear understanding of life on either side; no suggestion of delicacy or romance. No subtlety of lure or parade. Rather, coarse, hard bargaining in which robbery and abuse and bitter recrimination play a sodden part. I know of nothing so ghastly, so suggestive of a totally dead spirit, so bitter a comment as a street girl's weary, speculative, commercial cry of "Hello, sweetheart!"

From this first place we went to another—not so good, Lilly told me, although in the matter of size it was large. I think she was thinking of "good" in the sense of profitable to herself or the girls. It was a block or two nearer the old city of London than the other and in a basement instead of upstairs—in quite a deep basement. It was full of tables, and some waiters and some guests were there, but it didn't have the sense of life that the other had, although I was informed that in a little while it would be livelier. Once more a table, port for Miss Edwards, beer this time for myself, and I was shown the London type of pederast or sodomite, locally known as a "poof." These individuals appeared to be the same dreary victims of congenital defects that I have always observed them to be. Here they wore long poetic hair and a look that to me was terrorizing. The sodden face of life numbs my soul at times. I wonder how the silly moralists and religionists explain this type, how they would go about reclaiming them from the error of their ways. They have no mental faculties to speak of, no understanding. They are weird, sad, terrible. You might as well speak of reforming a toad into a bluebird, or something of that sort. Who's going to do it? And here we have the tall spires of churches and the grace of Almighty God spoken about, and then you have the congenitally deformed, just as you have the idiot who could not be reformed if he would. I have to smile. A dustier, weirder, more inexplicable thing than life I cannot possibly conceive.

Well, from here we went to a third place across the street, also in a basement, which my guide told me was the worst. I fancied, as I strolled about with Lilly from place to place in the drizzling rain and dark, that people must be looking at me as a rather shameless example of degeneracy myself, for I scarcely looked a fit companion for Lilly. I was too intellectual-looking, she too foolishly and gaudily young. We went into the basement about one-half or a third as large as the other and found it packed with young men and women as in the first place. It was interesting to note that in those three instances, the more or less mature man, middle-aged, was absent. The males were boyish, the girls all under twenty-six surely. Wild oats, disease, decay and death.

It did not strike me as a much coarser atmosphere than had prevailed in the first room, but this may have been a misapprehension on my part. The men and women looked the same. Port wine and beer were being consumed. There was none of that looking eagerly into each other's eyes which you find in the better grade of public restaurant in America where the young congregate. But they talked with each other. That is what I deplore and miss in vice—the utter lack of sentiment. It is horrible.

An incident occurred here which both shocked and amused me, hardened investigator that I am, for we took seats side by side at a small oblong table, the three remaining sides of which were occupied by four unaccompanied women of this world. The one that sat next to me at my end was a blonde girl of about twenty with rich, yellow hair and a flat, peculiarly spready type of nose. She had blue eyes and a weary, sophisticated air. The other one at the other end was black, very: black hair, black eyes, a white face, white teeth, red lips—a peculiarly vital and savage-looking little thing, apparently older than the others and more experienced. The third was brown-haired and white-faced, and the fourth, the youngest and smallest of all, a pale, lymphatic brunette with small, hard, pointed features. They were having an argument concerning some fifth woman or girl who was not present and who had evidently said something about somebody else—perhaps one of those present.

"Oh, well, what's the use fighting about her?" the yellow-haired girl who was sitting nearest me kept saying. "You had to learn, didn't you? She doesn't mean all she says. She isn't old enough. Give her a chance, I say. I'm willing to live and let live."

"Give her a chance! Give her a chance!" replied one of the others. "Don't she know! She's pretty near as old as I am, and I know. I didn't have to be on the town eighteen months before I knew." It was the black-haired girl opposite me who was speaking.

"Yes, I know, but she's young just the same. She don't know any better. I know her, and I think she's a sort of a fool yet. She'll grow out of that if you give her time enough."

There was some talk of somebody who had written this girl's mother and accused her of being diseased and of having been turned out of somewhere—a pretty mess of degradation and false witness.

"Well," chirped the little girl opposite me, "I've been on the town eighteen months, and I know better. She's as old as I am."

"And I've only been on it two years," observed the one next to her, "and I know better."

"Well, I've been on it three years—ever since I was eighteen—and I saw stacks of pricks before then (ever since I was fifteen, only I did it for love then), and I know better too, but just the same I don't want to see her abused. She don't know, I tell you." It was the yellow-haired girl with the flat nose.

"Stacks of pricks!" I thought. "What vicious language! How hard these women become!" And then I fell to speculating as to just why this language should shock me, if at all. What was it that created this standard of good and evil words and ideas? My little Welsh girl, in spite of her own experience, winced at this rough language. Her eyes moved oddly when the expression came brazenly and defiantly forth. "Even she objects to this," I thought, "and she considers this place bad. So she has some standard of life, below which this is."

I smiled genially at these women, and they grew very boisterous under my approbation. They called to two young men who came in to give them a cigarette, and getting the loan of the box, each took three. Just previous to this, in some spirit of show or make-believe, my street girl had opened her packet and passed it round, but then they took only one each and with quite an air of reserve. Now it was quite different.

"I call that a dirty trick," jested the man who had handed them the case.

I was getting a little weary of my adventure now, but I went to a fourth place, upstairs this time, hearing stories by the way of girls who work in teams—one to rob, the other to sit by and allow herself to be taken to court if discovered, the real associate criminal meanwhile having disappeared with the booty and so having made it impossible for the second one to be punished. There is no punishment without proof—the goods stolen in possession of the victim arrested. She herself had been an unwitting victim of a girl who used her as a stool pigeon once, persuading a man to take them both to a room, robbing him and jumping out of the taxi, leaving her to be charged. Fortunately the man did not discover the ruse, though she was frightened to death. I wouldn't have believed this except for her peculiar conduct with me. She also told me of girls who never went with men except for the purpose of robbing and browbeating them, never to copulate if possible, and that they were the financially prosperous of this world, the ones who wore jewels and fine clothes. Again she complained in her simple way of not being able to make money, and I believed her.

She told me of falling in love with a beau of this world—a pimp, I suppose, he would be called, or a cadet—who made her give him all she earned and then gambled it away. He was a veritable lord and master to her, and she obeyed him until she hated him, and then she ran away. He had met her since and wanted her to return, but she wouldn't. She was afraid he might pursue and threaten her, but he hadn't. She gave him as much as thirty-five pounds one week and worked to a certain extent under his instructions.

It was a dreary world, all told. There wasn't enough show or glitter. Compared to the New York worlds of the same class, it was drab and second-rate, much more dispiriting. Think of this being Piccadilly above the Strand, and then think of Broadway and 42nd Street!

It is a poor world. I do not attempt to explain it. I think, viewing it all in all, that the man or woman of bridled passions is much better off. This fever of lust on the part of men is not blamable, though not profitable. They are obviously not deliberately so. In women of meager intelligence and poor skill in life, vice leads to this, alas. Circumstances have so large a part in it. I think, all in all, it is a deadly hellhole, a weariness; and yet I know that talking is not going to reform it. Life, in my judgment, does not reform. The world is old. Passions in all classes are about the same. We think this shabby world is worst because it is shabby. But is it? Isn't it merely that we are different, used to different things? I think so. The one pity is that here all this degenerates into stark crime, violence, perversion, robbery, murder—possibly, occasionally—and a wallow and ferment of cheap gauds and desires.

After buying her a large box of candy, I hailed a taxi and took my little girl home to her shabby room and left her. She was very gay. Quite a little had been made of her since we started from the bagnio of rented rooms. Her purse was now the richer by three pounds. Her opinion had been asked, her advice taken; she had been allowed to order; I had tried to make her feel that I admired her a little and that I was sorry for her a little. At her door, in the rain, I told her I might use some of this experience in a book sometime. She said, "Send me a copy of your book. Will I be in it?"

"Yes."

"Send it to me, will you?"

"If you're here."

"Oh, I'll be here. I don't move often."

Poor little Welsh waif! How long, how long, I thought, will she be "here"? And as though she would really be there for any reasonable length of time anyhow! Disease, ill health, weariness, despair—these things lurk in her dreary path—and yet she thought she would be there!

Yes, life will be there in some cosmic shape, and she and I in some vague way, such as this perhaps, on this written page. No more. Of such is the underworld of London.

CHAPTER XX

If I should attempt to dilate on all the interesting adventures that befell me, this would prove a never-ending diary. The amazing metropolitan atmosphere in which I found myself satisfied me completely for the time being. Life here was complex and so extended that for days and days that involved visits (breakfasts, luncheons, dinners, suppers) with one personage and another, political, social, artistic, I was still busy snatching glimpses of the great lake of life that spread on every hand. Insofar as I could judge on so short a notice, London seemed to me to represent a mood—a uniform, aware, conservative state of being, neither brilliant nor gay anywhere, although interesting always.

About Piccadilly Circus, Trafalgar Square, Leicester Square, Charing Cross and the Strand, I suppose the average Londoner would insist that

London is very gay, but I could not see it—certainly not as similar sections in New York are gay. It is not in the Londoner himself to be so. He is solid, hard, phlegmatic, a little dreary, like a certain type of rain-bird or Northern loon, content to make the best of a rather dreary situation. On the other hand, I would not say that the city is depressing—far from it—though there are many who have told me they found it so. You have to represent a certain attitude or state of mind to be a Londoner, or a Britisher even, a true one, and on the whole I think it is a more pleasant attitude than one finds in America, though not so brilliant. Creature comforts run high in this type of mind and, after that, a certain happy acceptance of the commonplace. Nothing less than that could possibly explain the mile on mile of drab houses, of streets all alike, of doorways all alike, of chimneys all alike. That is what you feel all over England—a drab acceptance of the commonplace—and yet, when all is said and done, it works out into something so charming in its commonplaceness that it is almost irresistible. All the while I was in London, I was never tired of looking at those dreary streets and congratulating myself that they composed so well. I do not wonder that Whistler found so much to admire at Chelsea or that Turner could paint Thames water scenes. I could, too, if I were an artist. As it was, I could see Goldsmith and Lamb and Gray and Dickens and much of Shakespeare in all that I saw here. It must be the genius of the English people to be homey and simple and yet charmingly idyllic in their very lack of imagination. It must be so.

This particular afternoon along the Thames, for instance, it was raining. I saw the river in varying moods—all the way from Blackfriars Bridge to Chelsea—and never once was it anything more than a black gray, varying at times from a pale or almost sunlit yellow to a solid leaden-black hue. It looked at times as though something remarkable were about to happen, so weirdly greenish-yellow was the sky above the water, and the tall chimneys of Lambeth over the way, appearing and disappearing in the mist, were irresistible. There is a certain kind of barge which plies up and down the Thames with a collapsible mast and sail which looks for all the world like something off the Nile. They harmonize with the smoke and the gray, lowery skies. I was never weary of looking at them in the changing light and mist and rain. Gulls skimmed over the water here very freely, all the way from Blackfriars to Battersea, and along the Embankment they sat in scores, solemnly cogitating the state of the weather, perhaps. I was delighted with the picture they made in places—greedy, wide-winged, artistic.

I had a novel experience with these same gulls one Sunday afternoon, which I may as well relate here. I had been out all morning reconnoitering strange sections of London, and arrived near Blackfriars Bridge about one o'clock. I was attracted by what seemed to me at first glance thousands of gulls, lovely clouds of them, swirling about the heads of several different men at various points along the wall. It was too beautiful to miss. It reminded me of the gulls about the *Mauretania* at Fishguard. I drew near. The first man I saw was feeding them minnows out of a small box he had purchased for a penny, throwing the tiny fish aloft in the air and letting the gulls dive for them. They ate from his hand, circled above and about his head, walked on the wall before him, their jade bills and salmon-pink feet showing delightfully. I was thrilled and hurried to the second. It was the same. I found the vendor of small minnows nearby, a man who sold them in small boxes for this purpose, and purchased a few boxes. Instantly I became the center of another swirling cloud, wheeling and squeaking in hungry anticipation. It was a great sight. Finally I threw out the last minnows, tossing them all high in the air and seeing not one escape, while I meditated on the speed of these birds which, while scarcely moving a wing, rise and fall with incredible swiftness. It is a matter of gliding up and down with them. I left, my head full of birds, the Thames forever fixed in my mind.

It seems odd to make separate comment on something so thoroughly involved with everything else in a trip of this kind as the streets of London, but they contrasted so strangely with those of other cities I have seen that I am forced to comment on them. For one thing, they are seldom straight for any distance, and they change their names as frequently and as unexpectedly as a thief. Bond Street speedily becomes Old Bond Street or New Bond Street, according to the direction in which you are going, and I never could see why the Strand should turn into Fleet Street as it went along, and then into Ludgate Hill, and then into Cannon Street. Neither could I understand why Whitechapel Road should change to Mile End Road, but that is neither here nor there.

The thing that interested me about London streets first was that there were no high buildings—nothing over four or five stories, as a rule, though here and there you actually find the eight- and nine-story building. There are some near Victoria Street in the vicinity of the Roman Catholic Cathedral of Westminster. The vast majority of these buildings are comparatively old—not new, like those in New York or Rome or Berlin or Paris or Milan. London is older in its seeming than almost any of these other cities, and yet this may be due to the fact that it is smokier than any of the others. I saw it always in gray weather or through, at best, a sunlit golden haze, when it looked more like burnished brass than anything else. Then it was lovely. The buildings in almost all cases were of a vintage which has passed in America. Back in 1840, 1850, 1860 and as late as 1870 they built such buildings in America as are being built in London today—dull, ochre-hued four-to seven-story affairs with elevators, which are really not satisfactory and have architectural details which ought to be suppressed. Outside of some of the old palaces and castles in London—St. James, Buckingham, the Tower—there are no fine buildings. The Houses of Parliament and the cathedrals are excluded, of course. Even the new Christian Science churches are dull, and they pretend to some architectural charm in America.

Nevertheless, London is delightful. You find that it bears more relationship in its quirks and turns to all the older portions of the very old cities: Paris, Rome, Florence, Venice, Frankfort and the extreme lower section of Manhattan Island. I was reminded of the twists of London by Perugia in Italy and by the odd quarters of Lucerne in Switzerland and Mayence in Germany. These things date from a time when straightness of ingress and egress was not an advantage, though commercially I am satisfied that they are of small advantage today—quite a hindrance, in fact.

Another thing that interested me about London was the fact that if you walk in any direction you chose, guide your steps ever so carefully, you still could not make your way in any given direction without a map or compass, and you were always striking odd corners or sections, little centers of life which seemed individual and exclusive to themselves. This is certainly true of Camberwell Green, Clapham Common, Belgravia, West Hampstead, Hammersmith, Stratford, Islington and a score of other places. I wandered and wandered, ad lib, always to find that I could never really walk or ride out of London before it was too late to go further. A perfect sea of life it always seemed to me, surging with a strange enthusiasm which was nevertheless homey, courteous, good-natured and, in a way, gay.

I went one morning in search of the Tower, and coming into the neighborhood of Eastcheap, witnessed that peculiar scene which concerns fish. A fish-dealer, or at least his hirelings, always look as though they had never known a bath and are covered with slime and scales, but here, in addition to these other virtues, they wore a peculiar kind of rubber hat on which tubs or pans of fish could be carried. The hats were quite flat and round and reminded me of a smashed "stovepipe," as the silk hat has been derisively called. The peasant habit of carrying bundles on the head was here demonstrated to be a common characteristic of London. On another morning I visited Pimlico and the neighborhood of Vincent Square. I was delighted with the jumble of life I found here, particularly in Strutton Ground and Churton Street. Horse Ferry Road touched me as a name, and Lupus Street was strangely suggestive of a hospital.

It was here that I encountered my first coster cart, drawn by the tiniest little donkey you ever saw, his ears standing up most nobly and his eyes suggesting the mellow philosophy of indifference. The load he hauled, spread out on a large table-like rack and arranged neatly in baskets, consisted of vegetables—potatoes, tomatoes, cabbage, lettuce and the like. A bawling merchant or peddler followed in its wake, calling out his wares. He was not arrayed in coster uniform, however, as it has been pictured in America. It was delightful to listen to the cockney accent in Strutton Ground where "'ere you are, loidy" could be constantly heard, and "foine potitoes these are, Madam, hextra nice." In Earl Street I found an old cab-yard now turned into an automobile garage, where the remnants of a church tower were visible, tucked away among the ruck of other things. I did my best to discover of what it had been a part. No one knew. The ex-cabman whom I discovered here, now dolefully washing the wheels of an automobile, informed me that he had "only been workin' 'ere a little w'ile," and the foreman could not remember. It was before his time. Just beyond this again I found the saddest little chapel, part of an abandoned machine-shop with a small handbell over the door, which was rung by means of a piece of common binding twine! Who could possibly hear it, I reflected. Inside was a wee chapel, filled with benches constructed of store-boxes and provided with an altar where some form of services were conducted. There was no one to guard the shabby belongings of the place, and I sat down and meditated at length on the curiosity of the religious ideal.

In another section of the city where I walked—Hammersmith—and still another—Seven Kings—I found conditions which I thought approximated those in the Bronx, New York or Brooklyn or Chicago. I could not see any difference between the lines of store-front apartment houses in Seven Kings and Hammersmith—and Shepherd's Bush, for that matter—and those in Flatbush, Brooklyn or the south end of Philadelphia. You saw the difference when you looked at the people, and if you entered a tavern, America was gone on the instant. The barmaid settled that and the peculiar type of idler found here. I recall being entertained by the appearance of the workingmen assembled in Seven Kings, their trousers strapped about the knees, their hats or caps pulled jauntily awry. Always the English accent was strong, and at times, here in London, it became unintelligible to me. They had a lingo of their own. In the main I could make it out, allowing for the appearance or disappearance of "h's" at the most unexpected moments. The streetcars in the outlying sections are quite the same as they are anywhere in America, and the variety of stores about as large and bright.

In the older portions, however, the twisting streets, the presence of the omnibus in great numbers, the presence of the taxi stand at the more frequented corners, the peculiar uniforms of policemen, mailmen, street-sweepers (dressed like Tyrolean mountaineers), messenger-boys, and the varied uniforms of the soldiery gave the city an individuality which caused me to realize clearly that I was far from home—a stranger in a strange land.

CHAPTER XXI

As interesting as any days that I spent in London were two in the East End. I do not know how it comes about, but the west end of nearly every city with which I have been familiar has been the respectable end and the east end poor, if not disreputable. This is true of New York, Boston, Chicago, St. Louis, Philadelphia, Baltimore and other cities, and it is certainly true of London. Some physical or spiritual fact quite above the willing of man seems to have something to do with this.

All my life I had heard of this particular section as grim, doleful, drab, a center and sea of depraved and depressed life. "Nothing like the East End of London," I have heard people say, and before I left I expected to look it over, of course. The thing that whetted my desire in the first place was a conversation I had with a certain London poet who was creating quite a stir at the time, John Masefield, who had been a bartender in the extreme East End of London, Canningtown. He told me of the curious physical condition of the people, which he described as "bluggy" or stagnant. They were, he said, like stale ditch-water, souring in their own sty. Little intelligence in the first place, according to him, seemed to be breeding less and less intelligence as time went on. Poverty, lack of wits, lack of ambition were fostering inbreeding. Such things are easy to say. No one can really tell. The thing that was more interesting to me was the proffered information concerning East End amusements—calf-eating contests, canary-singing contests, whippet races, pigeon-eating contests. Many of these contests seemed to relate to eating, but the canary-singing contest idea delighted me, one bird matched to sing against the other. He said it would be hard to indicate how simple-minded the people were in many things and yet how low and dark in their moods, physical and moral. I got an impression of this some days later, when I discovered in connection with the police courts that every little while the courtroom is cleared in order that terrible, unprintable, almost unbearable testimony may be taken. What he said to me somehow suggested the atmosphere of the Whitechapel murders, those demoniac crimes that had thrilled the world a few years before.

It so happened that just about this time, when I was thinking of going there, another crime occurred—the very latest murder in Whitechapel, though it had nothing to do with a woman. It was a drab basement affair, relating to a secret gambling room conducted by an East End Jew and his wife, who murdered a Jewish tailor for the little money he was supposed to have—not more than thirty-five dollars, all told. It sounded so East Endy and the London papers indulged in such a long discussion that I finally took the tube and went out there one afternoon.

I must confess that my first impression was one of disappointment. America is strident, and its typical "East Side" and slum conditions are strident also. There is no voiceless degradation that I have ever seen in America. The East Side of New York is unquestionably one of the noisiest spots in the world, if not the worst. Nothing could be noisier. Children swarm in the streets, peddlers' pushcarts line the way, and gutter merchants cry and jest; the wagons and trucks rattle over cobblestones or broken asphalt pavements, and women call or talk from window to window or scream blatantly in the streets. This is not only true of New York, but of Chicago and other American cities that I have seen, and springs probably from the fact that manufacturing and living go on in the same realm. I am told this is true of the East End of London, but if so, it gives no evidence of it. I was surprised to find how distinctly different are the two realms of poverty in New York and London.

On my first visit I took the subway or tube to St. Mary's Station, Whitechapel, and, getting out, investigated all that region which lies between there and the Great Eastern Railway Goods Station and Bethnal Green and Shoreditch. I also reconnoitered Bethnal Green. The impression I gained, and which was not changed by the several subsequent visits which I made, was one of vast, sad, vacuous depression.

It was a chill, gray January day. The London haze was gray and heavy, quite depressing. Almost at once I noticed that this region which I was in, instead of being strident and blatant as in America, was peculiarly still and quiet. The houses, as in all parts of London, were exceedingly low, two and three stories, with occasional four- and five-story buildings for variation, but all built out of that drab, brownish-gray brick which, when properly smoked, has such a sad and yet effective air. The streets were not narrow, as in New York's East Side—quite the contrary; but the difference in crowds, color, noise, life was astonishing. In New York the East Side streets, as I have said, are almost invariably crowded. Here they were almost empty. The low doors and areaways oozed occasional figures who were either thin or shabby or dirty or sickly, but a crowd was not visible anywhere. They seemed to me to slink along in a half-hearted way, and I, for one, experienced no sense of desperado criminality of any kind, only a low despair. The people looked too weak, too law-governed. The policeman must be an immense power in London. Vice?—yes. Poverty?—yes. I saw young boys and girls with bodies which seemed to me to be but half-made-up by nature, half-done. They were ambling, lackadaisical, weary-looking. Low? Yes, in many cases. Filthy? Yes. Savage or dangerous? Not at all. What I did notice was the large number of cheap cloth caps worn by the men and boys, and the large number of dull, gray shawls wrapped slattern-wise about the shoulders of the women. This world looked sad enough in all conscience, inexpressibly so, but because of the individual houses in many instances, the clean streets and the dark tiny shops, not unendurable—even homey in instances. I ventured to ask a stalwart London policeman—they are all stalwart in London—"Where are the very poor in the East End—the poorest there are?"

"Well," he observed, looking straight before him with that charming, soldierly air the London policemen have, his black strap under his chin, "most of these people hereabouts have little enough to live on."

I walked long distances through such streets as Old Montague, King Edward, Great Carden, Hope, Brick Lane, Salesworthy, Flower, Dean, Hare, Fuller, Church Row, Cheshire, Hereford—a long, long list, too long to give here, coming out finally at St. John's Catholic Church at Bethnal Green and taking a car line for streets still farther out. I had studied shops, doorways, areas, windows, with constant curiosity. The only variations I saw to a dead level of sameness—unbroken by trees, green places or handsome buildings of any kind—were factory chimneys and endless charitable institutions for the care of the aged or the homeless or girls and boys, and occasional churches and churchyards, gray, sad, dull. Life certainly sinks to a low level at times. The principal characteristics of this region, insofar as I could discover, were these same institutions, covering apparently every form of human weakness or deficiency but looking as if they were much drearier than the thing they were attempting to cure. One of them, I remember, was an institution for the orphans of seamen, and another a hospital for sick Spanish Jews. The lodging houses for working girls and working boys were so numerous as to be discouraging and so dreary-looking that I marveled that any boy or girl should endure to live in them. One could sense all forms of abuse and distress here. It would spring naturally out of so low a grade of intelligence. Only a Dickens, guided by the lamp of genius, could get at the inward spirit of these, and then perhaps it would not avail. Life, in its farthest reaches, sinks to a sad, ugly mess and stays there.

One of the places that I came upon in my perambulations was a public washhouse, laundry and bath, established by the London County Council, if I remember rightly, and this interested me greatly. It was near Winchester Street and looked not unlike a low, one-story factory building. Since these things are always fair indications of neighborhoods, I entered and asked permission to inspect it. I was directed to the home or apartment of a small martinet of a director or manager, quite spare and dark and cockney, who frowned on me quizzically when he opened his door—a perfect devil of a cheap superior who was for putting me down with almost a black look. I could see that it was one of the natives he was expecting to encounter.

"I would like to look over the laundry and baths," I said.

"Where do you come from?" he asked.

"America," I replied.

"Oh! Have you a card?"

I gave him one.

He examined it as though by some chance it might reveal something concerning me. Then he said if I would go round to the other side he would admit me. I went and waited a considerable time before he appeared. When he did, it was to lead me with a very uncertain air first into the room filled with homely bath-closets, where you were charged a penny more or less according to whether you had soap and towel or not and where the tubs were dreary affairs with damp-looking wooden taps or flanges, and thence into the washroom and laundry, where at this time in the afternoon—about four o'clock—perhaps a score of women of the neighborhood were either washing or ironing.

Dreary! dreary! dreary! Ghastly! In Italy, later, and southern France I saw public washing under the sky, beside a stream or near a fountain—a broken, picturesque, deliciously archaic fountain in one instance. Here, under gray skies in a gray neighborhood and in this prison-like washroom, it was one of the most doleful pictures of life the mind of man could imagine. Always when I think of the English, I want to go off into some long analysis of their character. We have so much to learn of life, it seems to me, and among the first things is the chemistry of the human body. I always marvel at the nature of the fluids which make up some people. Different climates must produce different kinds, just as they produce strange kinds of trees and animals. Here in England this damp, gray climate produces a muggy sort of soul which you only find *au naturel* when you walk among the very poor in such a neighborhood as this. Here in this washhouse I saw the low English *au naturel*, but no passing commentary such as this could do them justice. One would have to write a book in order to present the fine differences. Meekness, lowness of spirit, a vague comprehension of only the simplest things, combined with a certain meaty solidarity, gave me the creeps. Imagine living all your days a semi-conscious meat machine! Here they were, scrubbing or ironing; strings tied about their protuberant stomachs to keep their skirts up; clothes the color of lead or darker, and about as cheerful; hair gray or brownish-black, thin, unkempt; all of them pale and weary-looking—about the atmosphere one would find in an American poorhouse. They washed here because there were no washing facilities in their own homes, no stationary tubs, no hot or cold water, no suitable stoves to boil water on. It was equally true of ironing facilities, the director told me. They came from four blocks away. Some women washed here for whole vicinities—the more industrious ones. And yet few came here, at that; the more self-respecting ones stayed away. I learned this after a long conversation with my guide, whose principal commentary was that they were a worthless lot and that you had to watch them all the time.

"If you don't," he said in Cockney English, "they won't keep things clean. You can't teach 'em scarcely how to do things right. Now and then they gets their hands caught." He was referring to the washing drums and the mangles. It was a long story, but all I got out of it was that this was a dreary world, that he was sick of his position but compelled to keep it for financial reasons, that he wanted as little as possible to do with the kind of cattle which he considered these people to be and that he would prefer to give it up. There was a touch of socialism in all this—trying to do for the masses—but I argued that perhaps under more general socialistic conditions things would be better; certainly one would have to secure more considerate feelings on the part of directors and some public approval which would bring out the better elements. Perhaps under truer socialism, however, public washhouses would not be necessary at all. Anyhow, the cry from here to Bond Street and the Houses of Parliament and the stately world of the Lords seemed endless. What can society do with the sad, shadowy base on which it rests?

I came another day to another section of this world, approaching the East End via Aldgate and Commercial Road and cutting through to Bethnal Green via Stepney. I found the same conditions, clean streets, low, gray buildings, shabby people, a large museum whose chief distinction was that the floor of its central rotunda had been laid by women convicts! So little life existed in the streets, generally speaking, that I confess I was depressed. London is so far-flung. There were a great many Jews of Russian, Roumanian and Slavic extraction, nearly all bearing the marks of poverty and ignorance but looking shrewd enough at that, and a great many physically deteriorated English. The long-bearded Jew with trousers sagging about his big feet, his small derby hat pulled low over his ears, his hands folded tightly across his back, was as much in evidence here as on the East Side in New York. I looked in vain for restaurants or showplaces of any kind (saloons, moving pictures, etc.). There were scarcely any here. This whole vicinity seemed to me to be given up to the poorest kind of living—sad, drab, gray. No wonder the policeman said to me, "Most of these people hereabouts have little enough to live on." I'm sure of it. Finally, after a third visit, I consulted with another writer, a reputed authority on the East End, who gave me a list of particular neighborhoods to look at. If anything exceptional was to be detected from the appearance of the people beyond what I have noted, I could not see it. I found no poor East End costers with buttons all over their clothes, although they once existed here. I found no evidence of the overcrowded home life, because I could not get into the houses to see.

Children, it seemed to me, were not nearly as numerous as in similar areas in American cities. Even a police-court proceeding I saw in Avon Square was too dull to be interesting. I was told I might expect the most startling crimes. The two hours I spent in court developed only drunkenness and adultery. But, as my English literary guide informed me, only time and familiarity with a given neighborhood would develop anything. I believe this. All I felt was that in such a dull, sad, gray, poor-bodied world any depth of filth or crime might be reached, but who cares to know?

CHAPTER XXII

Before parting with my general impression of London I should like to return once more to the Thames, for that of all things that I saw—largely because of my own river-loving disposition and the significance rivers always have in every city where one passes—interested me most. The Thames—mainly due to the things I had read of it—first called me, but later it seized my fancy on its own account. It was at Marlow that I first saw its dull surface of brown water. There is a quality about English rural scenery which is touching in the extreme, and the Thames at Marlow was exquisite. It was so narrow, so still, so smooth, the banks on either side fringed with green curving shores. Marlow Church was at the water's edge with gravestones showing in ordered rows and several inns for the refreshment of the traveler—white, quaint-chimneyed institutions, which, because of green grass and some flying rooks and the presence of an evening sun shining like red blood in the water of the river, seemed to me unutterably lovely. I could think of nothing so delightful as dining here upon an open veranda and watching the small flat-nosed punts on the river and the evening sun. Afterwards I stood in the dark at the end of a quaint old street, exquisite in gloom, and saw a small green and red-lighted tug come drifting up out of the dark and stop stock-still for some reason. It stayed here quite strangely while I watched it, without anyone stirring on board. I finally concluded that it had anchored for the night.

Another day I saw the Thames in a driving rain. It was dreary in my hotel, and having an afternoon, I decided to follow it for a diversion. I consulted my Baedeker for directions, but finally threw it down in disgust, for of all dreary things, Baedeker in connection with a river is the dreariest. The long list of palaces, bridges, monuments, schools, fountains, etc., all minutely described in a dry-as-dust manner, hurriedly catalogued, and yet all this in connection with so fluid a thing as a river! The sipping and sucking of immemorial waters never mentioned. No suggestion of color or light or air or rain. Just a catalogue of institutions, all as dreary as dust! I did note that a Cleopatra's Needle, a companion to the one in Central Park in New York, ornamented one bank of the river and that Battersea Park and Battersea Bridge, sacred to Turner and Whistler and William Blake and Thomas Carlyle, were farther upstream, opposite Chelsea. My mind was on the wind and the rain that go with flowing water, and I paid little attention to the catalogued things. I was sorry afterward that I failed to take my Baedeker with me. Instead I took a cloth cap and raincoat and sallied forth, rejoicing in the wet wind and rain.

The Thames from Blackfriars Bridge to the Tower Bridge, along Upper and Lower Thames Street, which is on the right bank of the river going upstream, was my first experiment, though in making it, I saw little of the river. It is a street that runs parallel with it and is intersected every fifty or one hundred feet by narrow lanes which lead down to docks at the water's edge. I always think of the average city having its typical water-scene—Rome its Tiber, Venice its Lagoon, Florence its Arno, Boston its Charles, Paris its Seine, New York its North and East Rivers, Philadelphia its Delaware, Berlin its Spree, Chicago its Chicago River, and so on ad infinitum. Here was London with its Thames, a murky little stream above London Bridge compared to such vast bodies as the Hudson and the Mississippi, but utterly delightful as I saw it here. I admired it on several occasions before and after—once in a driving rain off London Bridge, where twenty thousand vehicles were passing in the hour, it was said; once after eight at night, when the boats below were faint, wind-driven lights and the crowd on the bridge black shadows. Once I walked along the upper reaches of the Thames from Blackfriars Bridge to Battersea Bridge and beyond to the giant plant of the General Electric Company—a very charming section of London—in a driving rain and partially in the dark.

But I was never more impressed than I was this day walking from Cleopatra's Needle to the Tower. I question whether the section I am thinking of—from Blackfriars Bridge to the Tower Bridge—is not from some points of view the most interesting in London, though it gives only occasional glimpses of the river. The afternoon and evening (or night, for it turned dark at four o'clock) I followed it, it was raining hard and misting, and perhaps on account of this and the dark, I was impressed with the strange quality of the life here abounding. London is so queer. It is very modern in spots. The taxicab and the telephone take away much of the illusion of age. It is too much like New York and Chicago and Philadelphia and Boston to make you generally conscious of older days except in spots, but here between

Blackfriars Bridge and the Tower, along Upper and Lower Thames Street, I found something that suited me very much. It smacked of Dickens, of Charles II, of Old England and of a great many old, forgotten, far-off things which I could not readily call to mind but which I felt. It was delicious—this narrow, winding street with its high walls, quite high because the street was so narrow, and alive with people bobbing along under umbrellas or walking stodgily in the rain. Lights were burning in all the stores and warehouses, dark recesses running back to the restless tide of the Thames, and they were full of an industrious world of commercial life. I smelled printing plants, drughouses, hide and leather houses, flour and the like, and I saw such queer names of small lanes running through to the river (which I wrote down but afterwards found on every map)—Puddle Dock, Wheatsheaf Wharf, Trig Lane, Lambeth Hill, Red Bull Wharf, Little Narrow Alley, Dyers Hall Wharf, Dock House Lane, Huggin Lane, Kennet Wharf, Anchor Lane, Southwark Bridge, Three Cranes Lane, Bell Wharf, Joiners Wharf, Friars Lane, Dowgate Dock, Cousin Lane and Allhallows Alley. I have not named them all, only some, but they struck me as delightful at the time, quite wonderful.

I knew, from bits I had read in the past—heaven knows where—and in my more immediate Baedeker, that I was in the heart of Old London. Somewhere near here was London Stone, an old Roman milestone supposed to have something to do with an old Roman Forum in London, and also the site of a house of Chaucer. St. Paul's was not so very far away, and the Bank. What could be older than London Bridge or the Tower of London, which ended this street along which I was moving in the dark? Or Billingsgate Market? The latter I did not see save in the dark—the site of it only—but I had read enough to imagine what it must be like.

It was interesting to me to think that I was in the center of so much that was old, but for the exact details, I confess, I cared little. It was far more comfortable to think that I could turn to a certain page in my guidebook and find them all carefully listed. Here the Thames to me was especially delightful. It presented such odd vistas. I watched the tumbling tide of water, whipped by gusty wind, where moderate-sized tugs and tows were going by in the mist and rain. It was quite a spectacle—delicious, artistic, far more significant than quiescence and sunlight could have made it. In spite of all this I could see that architecturally this section was startlingly different from the very oldest sections of New York about Peck Slip, though certain types of small London restaurants of the cheapest character in here interested me, and the people who worked here were so different.

In New York and Chicago and elsewhere I have been quite familiar with the underpaid and the underfed, but I have never seen anything more interesting in the way of humanity than I saw here. They were all so white,

Here the Thames to me was especially delightful

so pasty-faced, so lymphatic, I thought, and they looked to me to be so dull, yet so full of a rich color, too. I would have given anything, for instance, to have had a Frans Hals or a Rembrandt here with me to paint a crowd of apprentices or workers (boys and girls, from heaven knows where, what types of shop), gathered in a small milk and pastry store which I found, a shop where meat-pies and beef-and-kidney puddings were sold and where they bought enough to stay their appetites for the night's work. To me, although they were meaty-faced and messy-looking, they were fascinating. Somehow they seemed fair examples of what London could do at its worst, and yet I liked them. I could talk of the houses, the doorways, the quaint, winding passages, the water, the distinguished events which had occurred here, but for significance and charm they did not compare with the nebulous, intangible mass of humanity which moved before my gaze. The mouths of many of them were so weak, their noses so snub, their eyes so squint, their chins so undershot, their ears so stub, their chests so flat. Most of them had a waxy, meaty look, but for interest they were incomparable. American working crowds may be much more chipper, but not more interesting. I could not weary of looking at them.

I remember going to some barber near here afterwards and having my hair brushed by a marvelous brush which was driven by a belt system—and I did so solely because the idea was so amusingly novel. Then I went off to get a good dinner, but the neighborhood was with me like a great symphony and is so to this day.

The upper reaches of the river above Blackfriars Bridge to Chelsea and beyond, which I explored another afternoon, were more pretentious from a scenic point of view, though not so human. For the entire distance, which is something over four miles, the river here is in constant view. One follows along the Victoria Embankment from Blackfriars Bridge to Westminster Bridge, a most imposing section including such things as the Temple, Somerset House, the hotels Savoy and Cecil and the Houses of Parliament to Westminster Bridge; but beyond that, after you go around the Houses of Parliament to reach it, the character of the waterside life simplifies greatly. It takes on a kind of drab respectability. At one place I encountered my old friend Horse Ferry Road, of the day I discovered the Roman Catholic Cathedral. It crosses the river via Lambeth Bridge, and here it was that I learned that the Thames at high tide is higher than the ground on which a part of the city stands. A gate in the wall which encloses the river was being washed by this tide, and if it had been open, the water would have poured out in the street and flooded the neighborhood. I asked a policeman.

"Yes," he said, "there's much ground around here which would be under water if it weren't for that wall."

I walked on past the Tate Gallery, which I never visited, the Equitable Gas Works, the Army Clothing Depot, the Castles Ship Building Company and the Chelsea Park Gardens and Chelsea Hospital—a world of commonplace life scarcely worth the mentioning and yet interesting. I remember thinking that Pulford Street was a monument to dreariness, and that nothing could be either worse or better, according to how you looked at it, than St. George's Square, Aylesford Street, Pimlico Gardens and the like. They all looked to me as though they were occupied by people who were on the ragged edge of poverty—sad, dreary souls battling wearily with untoward conditions. Beyond Chelsea Park Gardens things improved considerably, and the houses took on the distinction of those private dwellings which originally occupied Riverside Drive in New York—but only for a little way. After that it died down into something less showy, though much more artistic and poetic, as it merged into Old Chelsea proper at Battersea Bridge.

But what interested me most was not so much the life of the inhabitants here as the shore line and the river itself. Its character varied so, without at the same time varying radically. At one place along the Embankment, for instance, between Lambeth and Chelsea, I found an old haven or junkyard for decadent ship materials—ships, prows, wheels, masts and the like, particularly those curious ornaments of now defunct ships which have breasted heaven knows what seas. It was a great yard labeled "The Castle Ship Building Company," with enormous white prow-head figures of Britannia, George III and others over the gate and prows from H.M.S. *Collingwood*, H.M.S. *Formidable*, H.M.S. *Edinburgh*, H.M.S. *Leander* and dozens of others—ships which must have been built of wood, before the day of the steel battleship, scattered profusely about. They were mostly highly conventionalized figures, after the fashion of caryatids, intended to rest under the prow proper—figures of mermaids, sea horses, old Triton with his horn, Venus, Pallas Athena, Minerva and many others out of the Greek and Roman legends. One of the most interesting was a wooden figure of an old witch with her high, peaked hat and rough broom. The name of the ship from which this was detached was not given. But I could see her riding forward in a storm, the ship plunging and tossing, her rough broom held defiantly aloft, her painted wooden eyes agleam. The thought was quite wild to me, strange, grim.

Beyond Chelsea Park Gardens came Chelsea proper, with its simple houses and tendency to fade away into cheap, unsatisfactory neighborhoods. Here, as I learned later, lived Sir Thomas More, George Eliot, Dante Gabriel Rossetti, Carlyle and Whistler, and over the river Turner and Blake. It was interesting to me to think that so many such meditative and beauty-loving minds should have chosen this spot. The houses on the right bank, going upstream—Cheyne Walk, no less—were so respectable that one felt that they must be occupied by people who in a way had achieved some form of distinction—earned it—before coming here. It was all suggestive of a deep peace and spiritual content. I followed the Thames in the rain to the giant plant of the General Electric Company, not unlike those which supply the power to drive the subway trains in New York, and thought of Sir Thomas More and Henry VIII, who had married Anne Boleyn at the Old Church near Battersea Bridge, and wondered what they would think of this modern powerhouse! What a change from Henry VIII and Sir Thomas More to vast, whirling electric dynamos and a London subway system! A little below this, coming once more into a dreary neighborhood of the cheapest sort of houses—mud-colored brick—I turned off into a street called Lots Road, drab and gray, and, being weary of rain and gloom, took a bus to my hotel. What I know of the Thames I have described. It is beautiful.

CHAPTER XXIII

During all my stay at Cookham I had been hearing more or less, an occasional remark, of a certain Sir Hugh Lane, an Irish knight and art critic, a gentleman who had some of the finest Manets in the world. He had given Dublin its only significant collection of modern pictures—in fact Ireland should be substituted for Dublin—and for this he was knighted. He was the art representative of some great museum in South Africa—at Johannesburg, I think—and he was generally looked upon as an authority in the matter of pictures.

Grant Richards had evidently been talking to him of me in a flattering way, for he (Grant Richards) came one evening to my hotel with the announcement that Sir Scorp (Sir Hugh Lane) was coming down to Cookham to spend Saturday and Sunday, that he would bring his car and that together on Sunday we three would motor to Oxford. The latter was, as I understood it, some sixty-five miles away, and Grant Richards beamed through his monocle as he explained that it would be very interesting to see. He had an uncle who was a very learned master of Greek at Oxford, whom he described as a "crusty old fish," who, if we were quite nice and pleasant, might give us lunch. Grant Richards's father, now dead, had been something rather important at Oxford, and there was still another uncle who was also something important there. In fact, Grant Richards had wished to go to Oxford himself at one time, but circumstances had prevented him, and after entering for training somewhere else, he had abandoned it all and entered the publishing field.

Friday went by, and Grant Richards remained home on Saturday to welcome his guest. We were, I found, to take a little side trip on Saturday afternoon to a place called Penn, some twenty or twenty-five miles from Cookham, whence William Penn had come originally. Saturday was rainy and gloomy, and I doubted whether we should do anything in such weather, but Grant Richards was not so easily put out. I wrote all morning in my alcove, while Grant Richards examined papers, and sometime after two o'clock Sir Hugh arrived. A Miss Hemmerde, Grant Richards's secretary and general assistant, had come down the night before, late, I fancy, and she and Grant Richards discussed his arrival at breakfast and lunch. It seems that Miss Hemmerde had been in communication with him and knew of his probable movements. Finally he arrived however, a pale, slender, dark-eyed man of forty or thereabouts, with a keen, bird-like glance, a poised, nervous, sensitive manner and that elusive subtlety of reference and speech which makes the notable intellectual wherever you find him. For the ten thousandth time in my life, where intellectuals are concerned, I noticed that peculiarity of mind which will not brook equality save under compulsion. "Where are your credentials?" such minds invariably seem to ask. "How do you come to be what you think you are? Is there a flaw in your intellectual or artistic armor? Let us see." So the duel of ideas and forms and methods of procedure begins, and you are made or unmade, in the momentary estimate of the individual, by your ability to withstand criticism. I think I liked Sir

Hugh, as intellectuals go. I am not sure I should care for him so much on additional examination. I liked his pale face, his trim, black beard, his pale hands and his poised, nervous, elusive manner.

"Oh yes. So you're new to England? I envy you your early impressions. I am reserving for the future the extreme pleasure of reading you."

These little opening civilities always amuse me. I love to act and to see other people do so. We are all on the stage and we play our parts perforce, whether we do so consciously or not.

It appeared that the chauffeur had to be provided for; Sir Hugh had to be given a hasty lunch. He seemed to fall in with the idea of a short run to Penn before dark, even if the day were gloomy, and so after feeding him quickly before the grate fire in the drawing room, we were off—Sir Hugh, Grant Richards, Miss Hemmerde, Gerard (Grant Richards's son), the chauffeur and myself. Sir Hugh seemed opposed to taking too many in his machine, and I thought he was unduly inconsiderate in expressing his fears, but that may have sprung from his long familiarity with Grant Richards. He seemed to take Grant Richards too lightly, and yet at other times I judged not. They were possibly just very good friends of long standing.

I am inclined to oppose intellectual superiority in others. I am inclined to oppose on principle any attempt to estimate me quickly or lightly, and nothing gives me quite so much satisfaction as to drop a trapdoor of intellectual subtlety under the feet of those who are so sure of their own point of view that the views of all others are insignificant. Like the bull in the herd and the cock in the roost, I have a natural opposition to rivalry, and particularly superiority, in another, and I tolerate it only to cut deep if I can or to observe it as a spectacle, which is better yet and less harmful and reprehensible.

As I say, I liked Sir Hugh in a general way, and his light, quick, delicate observations concerning art, literature, painting and life in general caught my fancy. He made no effort to strike up any quick relationship with me but remained quite aloof and talked in generalities. I could see that he took himself very seriously—as well he might, seeing that, as I understood it, he had begun life with nothing. There were remarks, familiar ones, concerning well-known painters, sculptors, architects and the social life of England generally. He seemed to know C. H. Shannon, John Lavery, William Orpen, John Sargent and other English, American, Irish and French painters intimately, and he spoke of a young architect who had come from South Africa to spend a year in England, studying architectural conditions here, and with whom he was at present going about. He told us that this young man knew much more of the wonders and perfections of English and American architecture than he (Sir Hugh) did, and that his special preferences among historic Englishmen in this field were Sir Christopher Wren and Inigo Jones. I could see at once that he himself was at present saturated with enthusiasm over the historic specimens of the work of Wren and Jones and that any other forms of architecture were to be waved aside as inadequate and subversive of good taste in this field. I had to smile, for I have seen so many enthusiasts in my time, preaching one thing and another as the last word, they being for the moment transported or self-hypnotized. There were, of course, splendid forms of architecture before Wren and Jones, and there will be others in the future. However, for the present we were to have nothing save the doctrines of architecture according to Wren and Jones.

This first afternoon's trip was pleasant enough, acquainting me as it did with the character of the country about Cookham for miles and miles. Up to this time I had been commiserated on the fact that it was winter and I was seeing England under the worst possible conditions, but I am not so sure that it was such a great disadvantage. Nature, grave or gay, is quite fascinating to me, and a rain-soaked, cloud-mantled atmosphere is quite as distinguished in its way as a glittering, sunlit world. England especially, I must say, I enjoy as I saw it then, and some of the finest prospects I hold in memory were seen in gray, cold, lowery weather. Today as we sped down some dank, slippery hillside, where the river Thames was to be seen far below twisting like the letter *S* in the rain, I thought to myself that light and color, summer light and color, would help but little. In fact there are many things which too much color and bright sunshine mar.

Anyhow, there was no complaint to make on this score today. The villages that we passed were all rain-soaked and preternaturally solemn. There were few if any people abroad. We did not pass a single automobile on the way to Penn and but a single railroad track. For all the extended English railway system, these little English villages are practically without direct railway communication. You have to drive or walk a number of miles to obtain suitable railway connection.

I think I never saw a prettier sight than those villages presented on this day. Of course, up to this time I had only seen Marlow, through which we passed again. I have no memory for names, and really names are not important in England; they are all, apparently, equally quaint and poetic. I do recall High Wycombe, Lane End and Hazlemere, but they are only three out of many equally lovely. I recall the sag-roofed, moss-patterned, vine-covered cottages of once red but now brownish-green brick, half-hidden behind high brick walls, where curiously clipped trees sometimes stood up in sentinel order and vines and bushes seemed in a conspiracy to smother the doors and windows in an excess of knitted leafage. Until you see these villages, no words can adequately suggest the subtlety of age and some old order of comfort, once prevailing but now obsolete, which these little towns and separate houses convey. You know at a glance that they are not of this modern workaday world. You know at a glance that no power under the sun can save them. They are of an older day and an older thought—the thought that goes with Goldsmith's "Traveller" and "Deserted Village" and Gray's "Elegy."

The sweetest of these little homes or cots are low one-story affairs with curiously rough-hewn slate shingles, extending eaves, small, narrow, thick-walled, many-paned windows and a general suggestion of rude, solid masonry which is delightful. Nothing so enthuses me as the peculiarity and unexpectedness of the angles in connection with them: the varieties of roofs that are apt to go with the collection of additions, which sometimes make a single home. I can imagine nothing more delicious than the haphazard arrangement of buildings in a street or around a square or a triangle of ground. These little villages appear never to be scattered but pulled and huddled together like sheep in a storm, and they suggest an age when it was well that men should so congregate. I am sorry that this world does not often permit us to go back and see an older civilization in full swing. It would be so interesting to see one of these villages as it was. The stout, stolid rustic, his wife, his daughter, his son—I should like to have seen the innkeeper of 1632, let us say, the stagecoach driver, the parson, the farrier. I should like to have seen the plowman and village lout, idle and drunken. Alas, there is no suggestion of that left. Somehow, now, you feel only the absence of the railroad, the fact that it cannot endure, that rooms are damp and dark and that bathrooms, telephones, electric lights and phonographs are somehow inappropriate, crude, new and destructive of all this quaintness. The English mailman in his uniform is visible even on a rainy day. And our speeding automobile—what a sacrilege! All the while I had the feeling that somehow the dear, delicious little streets should be covered with glass and preserved as curios, and then having done this, the world should once more go about its workaday business.

They cannot endure. I say it over and over. They cannot endure. The railroads are destroying them, the newspapers, the telephones. Every single blessed soul in this world is becoming smart. There are no boors, no churls, no strange, hairy, shaggy men. All are smart clerks at least with canes and "ready-to-wear" clothes. Vines and flowers and pent-roofs and narrow lead-paned windows—these do not belong to ready-made clothes. Fancy a smart clerk emerging from one of these low, quaint doorways, or even an up-to-date farmer! No, Hardy has gathered the last examples in his gallery of masterpieces. After him Piccadilly and the sightseer and the man who is a good businessman—for a time, anyhow.

By ways such as these we came to Penn finally, but it was darkening and we did not seek the Penn House, which was somewhere in a grove. Grant Richards leaned out and inquired of an old laboring man, sunken-eyed, leather-faced, toothless, where such-and-such a place was. His face lit up with a flickering, toothless smile.

"The first road to your left. You can't miss it," he observed in some quaint, odd accent, and we were off again, rushing at high speed over level, wet roads.

"Now if you want to see a bit of ancient England, there you have it," observed Sir Hugh. He was referring to the old man.

We were back in an hour by ways that were just as lovely as those by which we had come. I observed that the landscape was simple, quite like any other landscapes of its kind. The difference between America and England is hedges, neatly divided fields, roads that are skirted on one or both sides by a row of trees, and those dear little roofs and spires which peek over distant hillsides, where tall trees stand up and birds are in the sky. You get the feeling that all of this land is carefully gone over annually by men who are intensely interested in it, in what it will yield or do, whereas in America there are large stretches where you feel that nothing can be done as yet, that it will take time and more people to bring them into cultivation. England, the bits I have seen, give me no such impression. It is one continual succession of well-ordered fields and quaint, moss-covered, angular-roofed towns which have turned and twisted and sunk in upon themselves until they are dreams of darkness, inconvenience, beauty and pure romance.

I shall not stop to tell how marvelously the old sunken roofs have taken on lovely curves instead of the original—I fancy they were original—straight lines. It is something you never see in America, at least I never have. I never saw cottages so quaint and strange in all my life. We boast of the Colonial beauty of bits of Boston, Marlborough, New York and Philadelphia. One needs to see England, whence these came. Our ancient bits do not even suggest the sweetness of the things which, no doubt, can be witnessed by the thousands in England and, no doubt, Scotland and Ireland also.

That evening at dinner Sir Hugh appeared by some mistake in his evening clothes, we having agreed beforehand that such should not be worn. Afterwards, drinking our coffee in the drawing room, Sir Hugh and Miss Hemmerde played by turns, and the children sang those lovely little songs which relate to the flight and return of Charles II, called "Songs of the North"—"Over the Sea to Skye," "Lizzie Lindsay" and "Return Ye to Me." I think I began to like Sir Hugh better then, for I began to find him simple and human under all his airs. He played and sang with the children, expatiated more upon his beloved Wren and Jones, and finally fell into a hot argument over the schools of architecture which involved America and

England—Gothic, Byzantine, Colonial and the variations introduced by Wren and Jones.

It began, I think, by his insisting that St. Paul's in London, which is a product of the skill of Sir Christopher, as are so many of the smaller churches of London, was infinitely superior, internally and externally, to the comparatively new and still unfinished Roman Catholic Cathedral of Westminster. With that I could not agree. I have always objected to the ground plan of the Gothic cathedral anyhow, namely the cross, as being the worst possible arrangement which could be devised for an interior. It is excellent as a scheme for three or four interiors—the arms of the cross being always invisible from the nave—but as one interior, how can it compare with the straight-lying basilica, which gives you one grand forward sweep, or the solemn Greek temple with its pediment and glorifying rows of columns? Of all forms of architecture, other things being equal, I most admire the Greek, though the Gothic, exteriorly even more than interiorly, has a tremendous appeal. It is so airy and florate. I rejoice in the Roman modification of the Greek, the great vault with the interwoven colonnade and frieze. Nothing is more suggestive of art in life to me than the Gothic, and the Egyptian and Byzantine expressions of temperament are altogether lovely. I am not sure but that I treasure the American Colonial, borrowed from Adam in England, most of all, but now that I see the beauty of the work of Wren and Jones, I give them high place as noble, artistic temperaments. However, as I have shown, the artistic effect of the Byzantine Catholic Cathedral had appealed to me too much to have it thus ruthlessly swept aside as inferior to St. Paul's. I do not think so, and, interior for interior, there is no comparison. Both are great. St. Paul's appeals to me in one way, Westminster in another. The Westminster interior is larger, more somber, more musically unbroken. It is like a vast organ peal, sad and dark.

However, this divergence led to an animated discussion, and it came about that I stated pro and con about what I have said here. We could not agree. Interiorly, St. Paul's, according to Sir Hugh, was vastly superior. We diverged to America by my stating that in addition to the several vast older schools, which were entirely satisfactory to me in their way, America had evolved still another—the skyscraper, which, whatever may be said, is different.

"Was it not a patchwork of older things?" queried Sir Hugh rather contemptuously.

"Was it not an expression of a great necessity and an entirely new form, and did not that justify it as a school?"

More argument. He doubted whether America had produced anything new. I advised him to travel there and see the suggestions of a great approaching change. European standards had practically gone by the board. We were seeking new forms and finding them. Witness the American state capitols, which are individual, though they all voice one school, the new terminals at Washington and New York, the mission buildings of the California and Leland Stanford Universities and the skyscrapers. No architectural effect can be entirely new. There is always a trace of the old, but in these have we not diverged distinctly and given life something different? He was not sure.

The subject then veered to the English proletariat—the common people from whom, or because of whom, all things are made to rise, and this was based on the final conclusion that all architecture is, or should be, an expression of national temperament, and this as a fact was partly questioned and partly denied. I think it began by my asking whether the low little cottages we had been seeing this afternoon—the quaint windows, varying gables, pointless but delicious angles, and the battered, time-worn state of homes generally—was an expression of the English temperament. Mind you, I love what these things stand for. I love the simpleness of soul which somehow is conveyed by Burns and Wordsworth and Hardy, and I would have none change if life could be ordered so sweetly—if it could really stay. Alas, I know it cannot. Compared to the speed and skill which is required to manipulate the modern railway trains, the express companies, the hotels, the newspapers, which are compelled to handle an increasing speed of shift and change—all this is helpless, pathetic. It is like the modest violet blooming by the mossy stone. Life has become harder, swifter, surer, more desperate than these darling little huts indicate. They are little flowers blooming by the wayside, sad, lovely, pathetic, delicious. Oh, to save them from the harm that must eventually befall!

Sir Hugh's answer was that yes, they were an expression, but that, nevertheless, the English mass was a beast of muddy brain. It did not, could not, quite understand what was being done. Above it were superimposed intellectual classes, each smaller and more enthusiastic and aware as you reach the top. At least it has been so, he said, but now democracy, newspapers, "every-man-no-better-than-I-am" were beginning to break up this lovely solidarity of simplicity and ignorance into something that was not so nice. "People want to get on now," he declared. "They want each to be greater than the other. They must have baths and telephones and railways, and they want to undo this simplicity. The greatness of England has been due to the fact that the intellectual superior classes with higher artistic impulses and lovelier tendencies generally could direct the masses, and like sheep they would follow. Hence all the lovely qualities of England—its ordered households, its beautiful cathedrals, its charming castles and estates, its good roads, its delicate homes and order and precedences. The magnificent princes of the realm have been able to do so much for art and science because their great impulses need not be referred back to the masses—the ignorant, non-understanding masses—for sanction."

Sir Hugh sprang with ease to Lorenzo the Magnificent, to the princes of Italy, to Rome and the Caesars for illustration. He cited France and Louis. Democracy, he declared, is never going to be able to do for art what the established princes could do. Democracy is going to be the death of art.

Not so, I thought and said, for democracy can never alter the unalterable difference between high and low; rich and poor; little brain and big brain; strength and weakness. It cannot abolish difference and make a level plane. It simply permits the several planes to rise higher together. What is happening is that the human pot is boiling again. Nations are undergoing a transition period. We are in a stew which means change and reconstruction. America is going to flower next, and grandly, and perhaps after that Africa or Australia. Then, say, South America, and we come back to Europe by way of India, China, Japan and through Russia all in turn, and new great things from each again. Let's hope so. A pretty speculation, anyhow.

We could not get anywhere, however, because we could not agree. Sir Hugh did believe that the next great hope was America, which was a part of my contention. But Americans—Pah! they are a bad lot more or less, at present principally more, and rather unendurable.

Well, then, we came to one real American—a Jew by blood—Oscar Hammerstein, who had just opened his London opera house and who before coming here and attempting to revolutionize London musical procedure had done such wonders in America. I recall when he built the Olympia in New York, at Broadway and 43rd Street, which started the theatrical change which brought about the present Times Square in New York and its whirl of congested theatrical life, and before that I recall his days as manager of Koster and Bial's, or his fame at least as manager of that peculiar music hall. I saw how he revised the New York operatic situation, sweeping out the silly old stolidity of the Wagnerian clique at the Metropolitan, and I suggested to Grant Richards, for a change in the conversation, that he support Oscar Hammerstein intellectually in London, for I believed he would do great things there.

I had heard that London operatic conditions had crystallized into some staid and indifferent state solely because of the lack of competition and a new idea. I had heard that it was tradition that opera could not be given in winter in London, successfully. Englishmen could not go because, forsooth, it was the custom not to go. I am an iconoclast by disposition, and such a situation always invites my direst opposition. I wanted to see this situation changed, smashed, and I was wishing Oscar Hammerstein luck on that score. I wanted

Grant Richards, who is essentially progressive and democratic if not iconoclastic, to see the value of this operatic change and to aid it by his good word.

Sir Hugh was on me in a moment with vital criticism and I think some measure of insular solidarity. The English do not love the Americans, that is sure. They admire their traits—some of them—but they resent their commercial progress. The wretched Americans will not listen to the wise British. They will not adhere to their noble and magnificent traditions. They go and do things quite out of order from the way in which they should be done, and then they come over to England and flaunt the fact in the noble Britisher's face. This is above all things sad. It is evil, crass, reprehensible, anything you will, and the Englishman resents it. He even resents it when he is an Irish Englishman. He dislikes the Germans much, fears the outcome of a war from that quarter, but really he dislikes the Americans more. I honestly think he considers America far more dangerous than Germany. What are you going to do with that vast realm which is "the States"? It is upsetting the whole world by its nasty progressiveness, and this it should not be permitted to do. England should really lead. England should have invented all the things which the Americans have invented. England should be permitted to dictate today and to set the order of forms and procedures, but somehow it isn't doing it. And, hang it all! the Americans *are*! They are coming over here and imposing their ideas, their machinery, their shoes and their ready-made clothes on Englishmen, and now comes this nasty Oscar Hammerstein and tries to impose a new system of operagoing and opera procedure on London. It may be very good; his opera house may be splendid; he may have a fine idea, and it may be necessary, but he is a coarse, crude American, an interloper doing things which an Englishman should have done, and there you have it. Alas! Alas!

Grant Richards had been telling me from time to time that the alleged success of certain singers introduced by Hammerstein to London was all a cooked-up newspaper story fostered by subservient English newspaper paragraphers who had been suborned by Hammerstein's gold. The opera house was really a failure. He had produced no new talent. Now came Sir Hugh with much the same thought in mind, and I did my best to stir up a noble argument.

"He's fine," I said, "he's forceful. He revolutionized opera in New York. He brought *Pelléas et Mélisande* by Debussy, *Thaïs* by Massenet, *Louise* by Charpentier, *Salome* by Strauss and a dozen other things when the Metropolitan Opera House was insisting on the unending reiteration of Wagner, Verdi, Gounod, Offenbach and the ancient list of masters whom we have seen over and over and over. He brought us new talent—Tetrazzini, Cavalieri, Mary Garden—in fact, a whole company of capable singers whom we had never heard before, and he made the musical seasons when he was in charge of the Manhattan Opera House brilliant affairs. He will do so here. Why shouldn't you support him?"

Well, the answer was, he hadn't done so much. He had been here six weeks now, and he had produced one singer whose claim to fame was doubtful. What had he done, produced? There was nothing of any significance to these things. What did Massenet amount to? What Puccini? It was not as if he were really trying to do anything artistic, trying to produce remarkable, truly artistic operas and notable singers. As a matter of fact, he couldn't very well. There weren't any after Wagner—Well, after Wagner what was there?

So the argument drifted.

The fact was, these contentions were rather sound, and I was distressed to think that Hammerstein had not done anything more. Nevertheless, from all I had heard, I was convinced that there was room for improvement here. We argued further concerning singers, the value of doing things in a new way, the question whether the old English opera had been doing all that it was essential for it to do. In the face of the assertion that Hammerstein had done nothing, there was little to be said. Lacking accurate facts, I had to cease.

The next morning I was up bright and early and glad that we had had such a forceful argument. It was worthwhile, for it brought us all a little closer together. I should have stated that Miss Hemmerde left shortly before the argument began, and so we were without her company. Grant Richards, the children and I ate a hearty breakfast together while we were waiting for Sir Hugh to come down and wondering whether we should really go, it was so rainy. Grant Richards gave me a book on Oxford, saying that if I were truly interested I should look up beforehand the things that I was to see. Before a pleasant grate fire I studied this volume, but somehow my mind was disturbed by the steadily approaching fact of the trip itself, and I made small progress. Somehow during the morning the plan that Grant Richards had of getting us invited to lunch by his uncle at Oxford disappeared, and it turned out that we were to go the whole distance and back in some five or six hours, leaving only two or three hours for sightseeing. Tea, perhaps, was to be had at Oxford. Sir Hugh was to look up some paintings he was interested in in the Oxford art gallery, and I was to be allowed to ramble at liberty with Grant Richards as guide and to be shown the character of the city and colleges in general.

To my surprise, on examining the little book he gave me—*Oxford and Its Colleges* by one J. Wells—I found that the town consisted of twenty-two colleges, one cathedral, the Bodleian Library, the Ashmolean Museum and an art gallery. It was a charmingly written and illustrated little book, which I studied with interest for an hour, reading of the history of Oxford, catching glimpses of individuality in the different schools or colleges and learning how it was organized. It appeared that all the colleges were not of equal date, that while the earliest went back to the ninth and tenth centuries, one, Keble, had been founded so late as 1870 and that all trained their scholars for the general examinations, which took place in one building. A classical course was compulsory, but in addition to that you could take law, medicine, music, economics and things of that sort. It gave me a better idea of what I was to see, and I was glad that I had found the book.

The things that interested me most were the lovely pictures—pen drawings by Edmund H. New—which showed so many lovely bits: High Street and Queen's College, the porch of St. Mary the Virgin, Balliol College, Oriel College, Radcliffe Library and other, many other, exquisite nooks and corners. The pictures were small and exquisite—birds flying high above Tom Tower and the towers of Christ Church, and vines festooning St. John's College garden front. So much of American college architecture is borrowed from the standards indicated here that one could not but thrill at beholding the original, which in some respects is much better. Age, even in this little volume, was indicated very clearly, and a fine architectural sentiment, which has somehow blended all in an exquisite whole, was quite apparent.

After this, of course, I was eager to start and sorry that the rain was whipping the windows. Grant Richards was teasing Gioia with the thought that we would not go. At eleven Sir Hugh came down, and then it was agreed that the rain should make no difference. We would go anyhow.

I think I actually thrilled as we stepped into the car—not that trips of this character were new to me, but somehow the exquisite flavor and sentiment of Oxford was reaching me here. It must be beautiful, I thought, and I hoped the car would go fast so that I should have an opportunity to see much of it. We did speed swiftly past open fields where haycocks were standing drearily in the drizzling rain, and down dank aisles of bare but vine-hung trees, and through lovely villages where vines and small, oddly-placed windows and angles and green-grown, sunken roofs made me gasp for joy. I imagined how they would look in April and May with the sun shining, the birds flying, a soft wind blowing. I think I could smell the odor of the roses here in the wind and rain. We tore through them, it seemed to me, and I said once to the driver, "Is there no law against speeding in England?"

"Yes," he replied, "there is, but you can't pay any attention to that if you want to get anywhere."

There were graceful flocks of crows flying here and there. There were the same gray little moss-grown churches with quaint belfries and odd vine-covered windows. There were the same tree-protected borders of fields, some of them most stately, where the trees were tall and dark and sad in the rain.

I think an open landscape such as this, with green, wet grass or brown stubble and low, sad, heavy, gray clouds for sky and background, is as delicious as any landscape that ever was.

By and by we came to Oxford. It was surely not more than one hour and a half after we left Cookham before we began to rush through the narrow, winding streets where houses, always brick and stone and red walls to the fore with tall gates and vines above them, lined either side of the way. It was old—you could see that. Even much that would be considered new in England was old according to the American standard. The plan of the city was odd to me, because unlike the American city—praise be—there was no plan! Not an east and west street anywhere. Not a north and south one. Not a four- or five-story building anywhere apparently, and no wood, just wet, gray stone and reddish-brown brick and vines. When I saw High Street and the facade of Queen's College I leaped for joy.

There is something about lovely architecture that is like lovely painting or beautiful verse. It is sad like a sonnet by Keats or Shelley, stately like the lines of Shakespeare, suggestive of melancholy, like the "Ode on a Grecian Urn." I can think of nothing lovelier in life than this building line in High Street, Oxford, either in marble or bronze. It is so gentle, so persuasive of beautiful thought, such an invitation to reflection and tender romance. It is so obvious that men have worked lovingly over this. It is so plain that there have been great care and pains and that life has dealt tenderly with all. It has not been sacked and destroyed or revised and revivified, but just allowed to grow old softly and gracefully. I can think of nothing lovelier—the spires, the corbels and gutters, the quaint paned windows, the narrow arched doorways and gateways, the vistas, vistas, vistas which greet one at every turn, tender, graceful, delicious, soothing. Love is not better than that. The beauty of the human body has nothing to defy the beauty of a perfect building. Architecture sings. It chants alleluias of delight. It shares with all the sisterhood of art that divine afflatus which is perfection. There is nothing finer, neither in heaven nor on earth. It is as beautiful as beauty can be.

Owing to our revised plans for luncheon I had several marmalade sandwiches in my hand, laid in an open, white piece of paper, which Grant Richards had brought and passed around, the idea being that we did not have time for lunch if we wished to complete our visit and get back by dark. Sir Hugh had several meat sandwiches in another piece of paper equally flamboyant. I was eating vigorously, for the ride had made me hungry, the while my eyes searched out the jeweled wonders of the delicious prospect before me.

"This will never do," observed Sir Hugh, folding up his paper thoughtfully, "invading these sacred precincts in this ribald manner. They'll think we're a lot of American sightseers come to despoil the place."

"Such being the case," I replied, "we'll disgrace Richards for life. He has relatives here. Nothing would give me greater pleasure."

"Come, Dreiser. Give me those sandwiches." I put them away. "We can't go on like this."

It was Richards, of course.

I gave over my feast reluctantly. Then we went up the street, shoulder to shoulder, as it were, Gioia walking with first one and then another. I had thought to bring my little book on Oxford, and to my delight I could see that it was even much better than the book indicated.

"Oh, beautiful, beautiful, beautiful!" I exclaimed, and if I said it once I said it a hundred times. I had reason to say it a thousand and more.

How shall one do justice to so exquisite a thing as Oxford—twenty-two colleges and halls, churches, museums and the like, with all their lovely spires, towers, buttresses, ancient walls, ancient doors, pinnacles, gardens, courts, angles and nooks which turn and wind and confront each other and break into broad views and delicious narrow vistas with a grace and an uncertainty which delights and surprises the imagination at every turn. I can think of nothing more exquisite than these wonderful walls, so old that whatever color they were originally, they are now a fine mottled black and gray with uncertain patches of smoky hue and places where the stone has crumbled to a dead white. Time has done so much; tradition has done so much; pageantry and memory; the art of the architecture, the perfection of the labor of the builders, the beauty of the stone itself, and then nature—leaves and trees and the sky! This day of rain and lowery clouds, though Sir Hugh insisted it could stand no comparison with sunshine and spring and the pathos of a delicious twilight, was yet wonderful to me. Grays and blacks and dreary alterations of storm clouds have a remarkable value when joined with so delicate and gracious a thing as perfectly arranged stone.

We wandered through alleys and courts and across the swards of University College, Balliol College, Wadham College, Oriel College, up High Street, through Park Street, into the Chapel of Queens College, into the banquet hall of Balliol, out again to the Bodleian Library and thence by some strange turns and lovely gateways to an inn for tea. It was raining all the while, and I listened to Sir Hugh's disquisitions on the effect of the personalities, or theories, of both Inigo Jones and Christopher Wren, not only on these buildings but on the little residences in the streets. Everywhere Sir Hugh, enthusiast that he is, found something—a line of windows done in pure Tudor, a clock tower after the best fashion of Jones, a facade which was Wren pure and simple. He quarreled delightfully, as the artist always will, with the atrocity of this restoration or that failure to combine something after the best manner, but—barring the worst errors which showed quite plainly enough in such things as the Oxford art gallery and a modern church or two—it was all perfect. Time and tradition have softened, petted, made lovely even the plainest surfaces.

I learned from Richards where Walter Pater and Oscar Wilde lived, where Shelley's essay on the value of atheism was burned, and where afterwards a monument was erected to him, where some English bishops were burned for refusing to recant their religious beliefs, and where the dukes and princes of the realm were quartered in their college days. Sir Hugh descanted on the pity of the fact that some, who would have loved a world such as this in their youth, could never afford to come here, while others who were as ignorant as boors and as dull as swine were for reasons of wealth and family allowed to wallow in a world of art which they could not possibly appreciate. Here as elsewhere I learned that professors were cads and pedants, eager, greedy, jealous, narrow, academic. Here as elsewhere precedence was the great fetish of brain, and the silly riot of the average student was as common as in the meanest school. Life is the same, be art great or little, and the fame of even Oxford cannot gloss over the weakness of a humanity that will alternately be low and high, shabby and gorgeous, narrow and generous.

The last things we saw were some very old portions of Christ Church, which had been inhabited by Dominican monks, I believe, in their day, and this thrilled and delighted me quite as much as anything. I forgot all about the rain in trying to recall the type of man and the type of thought that must have passed in and out of those bolt-riven doors, but it was getting time to leave, and my companions would have none of my lagging delight. Sir Hugh had missed out on the pictures he had come to see; Richards's crusty uncle had failed to invite us up because, as I understood it, he disliked Sir Hugh. We were wet, and Sir Hugh a little tired, and it was decided that tea was essential and then we would go and hunt up our chauffeur in some square or triangle known as Carfax, whither he was to bring the car promptly at three-thirty. It was now two forty-five, and Grant Richards, with his noble passion for promptness and regularity, was determined that we should be off and home by dark or nearly so, because Sir Hugh complained that the lamps of his machine were not in the best working order.

I recall walking with them to an inn which was surely an echo of older days—a queer, rambling, ramshackle thing of brick and stone, with a coach entrance and passage of cobbles and a rear collection of old sheds, slant-roofed washhouses, upper living rooms and so on, places no doubt for porters and stablemen to sleep, and a general air of cleanly, comfortable antiquity. I wandered back through here, while the others were ordering tea, but was soon recalled by a very ordinary-looking German waiter. I was to come and drink tea and not waste time. So in I went. Grant Richards and Sir Hugh were drying their coats, and the tea was already served.

In a few moments we were sipping reflectively, wondering whether the car was at the corner, exchanging badinage concerning America and England, recounting incidents of beauty which in the general hurry of things had been neglected. Sir Hugh had a bone to pick with Richards because of his indefinite connection with this Oxford world and all its privileges. I, being an American, was subject to criticism because of our national errors, riches and lack of taste; and the talk went so far as to object to my watch-chain and the ring which I wore on my forefinger. Grant Richards's weakness for good food and fine wines came up for excoriation, and then it was time for the car to be sought. To see more of the city I went along from the inn with Grant Richards, though the rain was settling down to a heavy, dreary downpour, and there were no umbrellas. We loitered at Carfax corner awaiting the arrival of the chauffeur, who finally did appear, but only after we had huddled ourselves into an idle taxi and gone in search of him. He had some excuse about having been here over and over at odd moments, but Richards would not believe him. To me he consigned him to the nethermost parts of hell. "I hope he grills in hell," was, if I recall rightly, his exact expression.

The hour had struck, and in a fading light we started on the return trip. It was blowing rain, and as we were leaving Oxford, I lost my cap and had to walk back after it. Later I lost a knit glove, of great comfort in cold weather, but I did not mind. I was on the front seat, I could bundle my steamer rug about me for protection and hum snatches of song to myself as we sped on, and that was worth something. I take great delight in speeding and looking at any landscape when it is not too glaring, and this today was ideal. We rushed with lovely engine speed up hill and down dale, the quaint little towns flying past, tented haycocks standing out in wet fields, low, soft, wet, black clouds lying low on the horizon, and after a time a light beginning to twinkle here and there. My mind sang itself a song of old England. One dim light far off on a hillside brought back an old country scene in the West, and then I wished that I might live years and years, hale and strong to enjoy much of life. This sense of a warm, healthy body is a wonderful thing. And speed and hunger and warmth and the beauty of nature make a wonderful combination.

As we rode, my mind went back over the ancient chambers, paneled woodwork, stained glass windows and high-vaulted ceilings I had just seen. The heavy benches and somber portraits in oil sustained themselves in my mind clearly. Oxford, I said to myself, was a jewel architecturally. It was so beautiful it was sad. Another thousand years and it would be as a dream of the imagination, a figment of a poetic brain. I feel now as if its day were done; as if so much gentle beauty cannot endure. I myself had seen the invasion of the electric switchboard and the streetcar in High Street, and of course other things will come. Already the Western world is smiling at a solemnity and a beauty which are noble and lovely to look upon, but which cannot keep pace with a new order and a new need. But if that must be, I said to myself, Oxford should be built over like other things, with crystal glass so that the winds and rains may be at it in vain and only the shadows and the sunlight darken or gild its fine perfections. It should be given to the poets, the singers of fine songs, the dreamers of exquisite dreams. Let it be for love to live in and death to die in, but take away the turbulent stream of common men.

I asked Gioia if she would like to live here, young ardent soul that she is.

"No," she said, "it is too gloomy."

If she were eighteen, I thought, and it were spring and Romeo whispered to her under one of the lovely balconies, on one of the delicious swards, it would not be lonely then.

CHAPTER XXIV

Among the most interesting characters that I met in London was that same Sir Hugh Lane, with whom and Grant Richards as guides and mentors I had journeyed to Oxford. After that utterly delightful and individual weekend in which Sir Hugh had arrived at Cookham Dean with his car to undertake that trip to Oxford, I had come to look on him as a character. I importuned Grant Richards for additional information. "Who is he, exactly?" "Where does he come from?" "How does he come to be Sir Hugh?"

As usual Grant Richards, for reasons of temperament solely, was reticent. He doles out information sparingly on all occasions, bits and scraps which you can piece together as you like or not. There is something almost archaeological about his revelations, much as scraps and shards yielded by Nippur or Nineveh. You delve into him and you get much or little or nothing, unless by revealing he has some particular aim to achieve. Then it comes fast enough.

"Oh, he is a knight," he explained, "made so because of his discrimination and taste in art. He is really a great connoisseur. Years ago, when I first knew him, he was near starving—very poor. He lived in a small room and, by hook or by crook, picked up one small picture after another—pictures of merit—which he sold for higher prices. The man has taste and discrimination. I am afraid his early poverty has injured his constitution. His stomach is very bad, due to irregular eating in those days. His house at Chelsea is a great gallery. He has some pictures there—a Frans Hals and a Rembrandt among others—that are almost priceless. How he has done it is beyond me. He practically introduced Manet into England, and he gave Dublin a really fine gallery, though I don't think he gets much thanks for it, to tell you the truth. You have seen the man. Judge for yourself. He is charming. He will invite you to dinner, I am sure. Then you can see for yourself."

After that remarkably contentious ride to Oxford and our long argument the evening before, I was intensely interested in the man. He vibrated with a strange individuality. His dark eyes burned with an almost sickly luster; his pale skin was not healthy. I recalled Grant Richards's cautioning me not to argue with him vehemently, that it "broke him up nervously." I began to think of him as one might think of a fine-blooded horse or one of those early Victorian beauties of whom it was said they were "bred under glass." His companions in his large house or neighborhood appeared to be George Moore, Philip Wilson Steer, the English landscapist, and, less frequently, John Sargent. I have told how he was interested to find an Inigo Jones Castle (very dilapidated) which he might restore, fill with art objects and beautiful pictures and leave it all to England, as, perhaps, a memorial of himself. Quite a definite art personage, as you may see.

Not so much more than a week or ten days had gone after I had settled in London before I received the invitation suggested by Grant Richards, and perhaps a week later I journeyed to Chelsea in a taxi, being received in the hall of his large private house by a solemn factotum who took my hat and coat and ushered me into the general living room, where a weak English fire was burning. To the inhabitants, no doubt, the house seemed fairly comfortable. To me it seemed a crime that any man who could purchase and retain paintings by Rembrandt and Frans Hals should be so cheerlessly accommodated in the matter of heat.

The house was one of that famous row known as Cheyne Walk—houses once occupied by Whistler, Rossetti, Carlyle, George Eliot and others. This particular mansion, facing the Thames opposite Battersea Bridge—the region painted by Whistler and Turner—was an old brownstone affair, gloomy in the dark, with a solemn, non-decorative but imposing facade which somehow bespoke the taste of the occupant. The rooms, as I found, were large and hung in gallery fashion to some extent with significant canvases of the Dutch, Flemish and French schools. At a glance, as I walked in, I recognized Van Dycks, van der Neers, de Heems and a Manet. A brilliant bit of color, with a portrait as a base or excuse, hung near a door, turned out later, as I learned, to be a Mancini, a painter whose work I had never seen. It scintillated with all the force of a rich, almost feverish palette. There was a wonderfully rich Van Dyck in the general reception room, a portrait, as I learned later, of John Oxenstierna, Count of Södermöre, who was the plenipotentiary minister of Gustavus Adolphus at the Peace of Münster. The count was in a rich gold tunic with slashed sleeves, black breeches and black cloak thrown over the left shoulder—a showy person, whose white lace collar and cuffs emphasized it all. I stopped to admire it.

"Ah, there you are," called Sir Hugh, advancing. "Ha! Ha!" (the latter was a mere nervous mannerism at times, at others an aloof sarcasm). "Come to the fire. You Americans like to be warm, I believe. That is a Van Dyck—John Oxenstierna. Rather nice, I think. I bought it at a sale a few years ago. Ha! Ha! Hum!"

He had a most remote, aloof atmosphere. He seemed to be enveloped in a cloud or rather crystalline veil of translucent but impervious force.

"So you are all alone," I said, "with your pictures. A goodly company they can easily be. I went by here the other day in the rain and saw these houses, but I did not recall that you lived here."

"It's a pleasant location. I find it comfortable. This was Whistler's first house. I have altered one or two rooms to make a better space for my pictures. In other ways I have restored it. I have been putting up old carved doors which I found discarded in the cellar, and scraping the paint off some very fine hardwoods. I find it pleasant."

You could feel the man's profound respect and reverence even for artistry in materials. Life, at its best, was dignified and only made endurable by art for him. It would be a simple matter to tear such a soul as his to bits by compelling it to accept disjointed surroundings. He fairly breathed order, cleanliness and, above all, a high sanctuary feeling for color, arrangement, mood, light, atmosphere. Your true connoisseur—not collector—your lover of art for art's sake.

"I thought I would have you come a little early so we might sit about and talk. The others will be along later. I hope you haven't been saving any large appetite—Ha! Ha!—for our dinner will be a very simple affair. Hum! We will go out for it. There is a charming little one-shilling restaurant around the corner where I often take visiting celebrities. Hum! Ha! Ha! We will go there when the others come. Mr. Moore cannot be here. We will have to reserve our dinner for you and him until you come back. Richards tells me you will be here again in April."

"Good Lord!" I thought. "A one-shilling restaurant! And here I was expecting a good dinner! The idea of his eating in such a place—the stingy beast! No wonder he has priceless Rembrandts. No wonder his stomach is out of order. Well, I'm no worse off than the rest of them, whoever they are."

At the same time I said, "Very good. Produce the one-shilling restaurant in due season. I admire your selection of pictures."

"Oh, these—they are merely a few that I could not distribute elsewhere. When you get warm we must look at them. I suppose you are enjoying London?"

We drifted off at once into an analysis of certain phases of it. With true art understanding he made several suggestions, all highly selective—bits of architecture, the interior of the Roman Catholic Cathedral, a portrait or two in the Wallace Collection.

"There is a young South African architect coming here tonight—ha! ha!—with whom you should see London. I have told him about you, don't you see" (another mannerism). "He is looking up Inigo Jones and Wren. You must see some of those things with him. I should think that would interest you."

"It would," I said, pleased to have the company of a really talented architect but thinking of the one-shilling dinner.

"Before anyone else comes," he added, "we might look at the pictures," and so together we strolled about studying the principal portions of the house and the art—brilliant pictures, selected with rare judgment, which constituted in themselves a great, if limited, gallery. They could have been purchased just as they stood, I thought, by some government and retained as a fine, artistic memorial as well as a public museum of inestimable value.

I say all this with caution, for I never saw a finer Frans Hals or a better Rembrandt than graced two easels standing in an adjoining room. The Rembrandt, I think, he spoke of as the Demidoff Rembrandt, a portrait of a young woman done in pale cream and silver, sold at a famous sale in Italy. As Rembrandts go today, it might bring three or four hundred thousand dollars or more under favorable circumstances. In treatment, it was not unlike the Elizabeth Bas, once exhibited in New York but belonging permanently to the Rijksmuseum at Amsterdam. It had more of the Rembrandt feeling for artificial lighting than the other. A brilliant, human thing, disturbing in its psychology, elusive in the mystery of its paint and light, reflecting the subtlety of the great master of mood and reality—truly a great picture. I marveled that any man who had once lived on bread and water almost in order to be able to buy art should eventually, even then, have achieved it, but it was a fitting climax. I was glad he had it.

The Frans Hals was another—truly an amazing picture, one of the rarest Hals in the world. Those who admire the roistering realist of Haarlem—and is there one who does not?—would have thrilled responsively to the velvet blacks that were in this picture, silvery grays, whites mellow with a soothing yellow mellowness, and reds and yellows that never flare but blend with the glassy suggestiveness of the scales of a fish. It is a portrait of an old lady—some other Dutch Elizabeth Bas—broad-faced, flat-eyed, phlegmatic, stolid, ox-like, clean, exhibiting all the simplicity and all the naive beauty of the Dutch costume. I take off my hat to Hals of Haarlem. I know how marvelously art runs off into metaphysics, and upliftingly so in others, but this drunken Dutchman—I hope he was so—painted things as they were. Too great to be great. Too compact of reality to care about the unreal, the *un-human* and remote. Now that we adore the metaphysics of Botticelli and Rembrandt, we can still pay honor to him. How that Dutchwoman stepped out and occupied the place! She was more real than Lane or myself, by far. Of all the company gathered this evening, she was the most significant. I can see her now sitting in her chair in Lane's house in Cheyne Walk, looking at me. Those simple, honest, real, human Dutch eyes! I take off my hat to Frans Hals. In art I sit at his feet. Other gods there are—at times seemingly before him—but when the subtleties of color and light mystify and the metaphysics of temperament elude and disturb, one may return to him to witness again the perfection of the surface of things and rise up refreshed and renewed, ready to face the world as it singingly maintains itself—this tremendous illusion of reality.

Besides this perfect Hals there were so many others of such great charm—Ruysdael's *The Hill of Bentheim*, for instance; Snyders's *Concert of Birds;* one of Van der Veer's interiors, and then Van Dycks, Metsu, I believe a Manet and the previously mentioned Mancini, wherewith went an interesting story.

It appeared that Sir Hugh was an ardent admirer of the temperamental Italian, that he had followed his work with interest for years. When the Italian was in England or Ireland—I forget which—he painted the portrait of the daughter of a lady of distinction, who, having no judgment or taste in matters of this kind and knowing nothing much of this painter, soon wearied of it, because of idle, casual, pointless opinion, and thinking it a daub, sold it along with some old furniture to a curio dealer for, let us say, two or three pounds or less—very likely less. The furniture-dealer, knowing nothing of art, cast it into the limbo of the junk-pile, where along with old clocks and tables it gathered much dust and discredit. Then one day, several years later; along came Sir Hugh. He was looking for just such stray packets as this.

"How much for the picture?"

"Three pounds," said the dealer, seeking to drive a hard bargain.

"I'll give you one."

The deal was completed.

He brought it home, dusted and varnished its despised surface and hung it among his treasures. There it hung, gleaming and scintillating, when I entered, with the riches of flaming tubes, orchestrated in oil rainbows, vibrating with fairy tints and jewels of rare color.

"What a brilliant picture!" I observed.

"Oh yes. Ha! Ha! Hum!" Then came the story. "And now Mrs. Y. doesn't like me anymore. She heard of its being here, and then she heard of what others thought of it here, and now she wants me to sell it back to her. Ha! Ha! Hum! It's become a little disgraceful, selling out a thing like that. It impeaches her art judgment, of course. The idea of my being compelled to sell it to her again because it is of her daughter—ha! ha! hum!—absurd! Of course I wouldn't do it—under a very high figure. She claims now that she never sold it at all, that it was stolen. Ha! Ha! Hum! Absurd! Isn't it charming?"

We laughed over this, so human and so true, just the sort of thing that was likely to happen to this Irish-English knight with his keen feelings and discrimination. Just then the South African architect arrived—a Jew, eager in his enthusiasm for life and England and the works of Wren and Jones, and after him Philip Wilson Steer, the English landscapist, a large, placid, bovine gentleman who looked more like a stockbroker or a country gentleman than a landscapist. George Moore was not coming, and John Sargent did not appear, so we adjourned after a time to this approved one-shilling restaurant—a heavy art company gracing the cleanest, cheapest little dining room you would wish to see—very spindling with vague, tasty rations of limited quantity which were supposed to be sufficient because of the simple humanity of the place—its accidental individuality. Why do some eighteenth-rate restaurants achieve, quite by accident apparently, this marvel of individuality?

I am sure I grew swiftly in fondness for Sir Hugh on this occasion, even more than at Oxford. There was a wry, acrid flavor to the man, combined with a rich, sentient humanity which was tonic.

"Oh yes," he said to me, by way not so much of apology as of warning. "I must really caution you against Richards. You are going abroad with him. It is so easy, when you are with him, to fall into expensive habits. He pretends a gourmet's interest in things. He loves the flair of expensive places. He assumes to have a critical knowledge of the haute cuisine of France. I'm not so sure. It is a rather shabby distinction at best—ha! ha! hum! We do not live by bread alone."

"We come very near doing it in this place," I suggested.

He ignored my thrust.

"It always seems to me," he went on, "that he would do so much better by himself if he were to devote what little money he has to the real factors in art—to invest in objects rather than in his stomach. I think he is merely striking at a standard which he does not artistically realize—not even in his own mind—ha! ha! hum! It is so much better, don't you see, to live very simply like this and save your money for better things. Hum! I refuse to be led into his extravagances. When I am out with him, I let him buy what he chooses and take something very simple myself. The fact is, I cannot afford it, whatever he can. You are probably in much the same position as myself—ha! ha! hum!—so you will have to be careful, don't you see!"

What a dreadfully penurious knight, I thought, buying Rembrandts and castles and delivering homilies on simple eating and living in a place like this!

The young Jewish architect, Solomon, much more than the English landscapist, was a full-blooded personality. A press could have squeezed much of the wine of life out of him. He seemed to radiate much of the expansive freedom of the South African veld. Call him thirty-eight or forty, see him short, stout, chunky, thick-set, with a broad, full, expressive face. Very psychologic, as most Jews are, a fine reader of character, tolerant, judicious, critical, with a feeling—or a hope, rather—for always newer and better things.

By hook or by crook I managed to worm a disquisition on South African architecture out of him—whether it was different, new, likely to prove a highly individual contribution to the world's few schools of really significant architecture. "Yes, probably so," he said. "South African architecture has already borrowed something from the Kaffir's kraal from the almost necessitously white walls of that glaring, sunlit world." He described a Dutch fan window that had originally come from Holland but had been elaborated here in some strange way so as to give it South African individuality. Climate and strong light were making flat, windowless wall spaces desirable, which naturally gave the houses a touch of individuality. His hope was for something as distinctive as the Colonial architecture of America, only with the atmosphere and feeling of South Africa strongly indicated. How fine it is, I thought, that different lands do develop different phases—art aspects—so that we all may be entertained by variety and individuality.

Mr. Philip Wilson Steer, to tell you the truth, I found very dull. His chief distinction appeared to be that he was the bosom friend of John Sargent and the intimate of George Moore. "I can rarely get Moore these days," observed Lane, "because he's always 'dining with Stee-ah.'" He was mocking Moore. "I think it's because Steer coddles him and I don't."

"Depend on it, you don't," I interpolated.

"We are all living in terror of what he is about to write of us. I suppose he'll say something friendly of Steer, though it's a question, but as for myself I tremble. I try to placate him as much as possible, but I suppose it is useless—ha! ha! ha!"

"I can see you placating him, Lane," I observed, "—the whole gentle process."

Both Steer and Solomon smiled broadly.

We indulged in a critical analysis of London architecture and English food, and then after registering our names in some cheap yellow book kept here for the purpose as a memorial to our distinguished presence, we returned to Lane's house.

It was most amusing, in spite of his absence, to see how the personality of Moore loomed up in the background of this small group—Lane, Steer, Sargent and Solomon all living in this vicinity. Together they formed a little social world, bent on looking after their individual art labors and longing for a family atmosphere in this world. The old, trite "man is a social animal" never quite forsakes us. Even such individualists as Lane and Moore and Sargent come to lean heavily on companionship, I found, and it brought back to me the loneliness of such individualists as Rembrandt and Schopenhauer, to say nothing of Spencer, who suffered bitterly for the want of it. No women, insofar as I could make out, were intimately connected with this group, but they were eager for each other's company, quarreling and criticizing the while, as is the human way.

"What sort of a man is Moore, anyhow?" I asked Lane, after we had consumed our thin vegetable soup, our plain boiled fish and had drunk a little—to me wretched—ginger beer. (I had not then learned to put gin in it, and such an extravagance would never have been suggested, let alone countenanced, by Lane.) He got great spiritual satisfaction out of seeing us eat so thinly and meagerly.

"Oh, very contentious, ha! ha! A very small man. He loves to prick all our bubbles of egotism. He comes in here now and then to see me."

"A fine pair you must make—you and Moore! Ye gods—a case of steel cut steel."

"Oh, he is far more observant than I am, I assure you; he is full of a boundless contempt and reserve. We all have to walk very softly to escape analysis."

It turned out, according to Steer, that Moore claimed to be impotent, that his days of earthly pleasure were over and that, consequently, he was now free to go about criticizing and painting life in an unremitting, realistic mood.

"Ha! ha! hum! I tremble as to what he will say about me—" Lane repeated this observation several times.

A terrible intellectual conflagration ensued a little later when, before going home, I attempted a justification of Neo-Impressionism and even Cubism, without, I confess, either sufficient understanding or data. My knowledge of these art phases, as I have indicated, was very recent. It so happened that there was an exhibition of Neo-Impressionistic art then on in London—Cézanne, Gauguin, van Gogh, Matisse, Picasso and others. I believe there were several German and even one or two Norwegian examples.

"What do you think of the Neo-Impressionists, anyhow?" I asked of Lane.

He bristled irritably, like a disturbed dog.

"Oh, there is some little something to Cézanne and Gauguin. I have no quarrel with van Gogh surfaces. Picasso can paint to a certain extent. But as for the drawing, the harmony—a child could do as well. I believe they pride themselves in some instances on achieving the child's viewpoint. They neglect the high significance of temperament completely. Art isn't for barbarians, even if they manage to attract attention. They may overrun us for the time being, but they cannot establish their loud braying as art singing."

"I believe you admire Degas, however."

"Degas—yes. Truly. Ha! ha! hum! It's a far cry from Degas to Matisse and the Cubists. It is no trick to paint red eyes and green hair. They insist that they trust to atmosphere to blend raw colors for the eye. The most of them can't draw, and temperamental blending such as the eye achieves with perspective is beyond them. It's an easy way to self-advertisement." His voice had an acrid, bitter quality.

"But the other day I saw van Gogh's *Christ on the Cross*—you don't deny value to that, do you?"

"What is it," put in Steer defensively, "—a raw, bloody farmhand hung on a pole! I see no art in it. Just an attempt to be noisily offensive. Anyone can become conspicuous and wipe their feet on the draperies or expectorate on the floor. I know one art connoisseur in London who goes to one side and expectorates every time you mention Neo-Impressionism."

"I confess that the *Christ* has a grim veracity to me, and anyhow, it's tonic aside from being good painting. The portrait of Père Tanguy is certainly admirable."

"I will admit for argument's sake that there is something to the work of Cézanne, Gauguin, van Gogh and even Picasso. As a matter of fact, there is. Call it good painting if you want. It lacks superior art value—ha! ha! There is such a thing as refinement in the matter of taste and of selection and presentation. Rembrandt painted the operating table, but he didn't go out of his way to add red eyes and green hair. It is more subtle and difficult to get the flesh values and the surfaces he obtains. They are not just laid on raw and left to luck. Take the Frans Hals in the next room, or the Rembrandt —you certainly cannot contend that there is a paint and character value equal to these in the pictures you are talking about. One is art, the other travesty, in my judgment—a cheap way to notoriety."

"I hold no brief for Neo-Impressionism," I suggested, "but certainly there is something to be said for a reaction against the polished inanities and super-refined spiritualities of some painters and schools. Certainly Watteau and Fortuny paint an unreal world. It is widely removed from reality. The *Way-*

side Christ of Gauguin and the *Père Tanguy* of van Gogh are no farther removed from actuality in one direction as Botticelli's *Primavera* is in another. Why are they so reprehensible? They present—suggest—a grim reality to me. It isn't pleasant, but what of it? The sad, dirty face of life is never pleasant. Is it without art?"

"I know one of these fellows," put in Steer, whose polished canvases show no straying from accepted paths, "who suggests that there is often a better picture on his palette at the end of the day than there is on the canvas on which he has been working. Anyone can squeeze color tubes onto a palette."

"What do you think?" I asked of Solomon.

"To tell you the truth, I haven't seen enough to know. I can imagine a sharp variation from accepted stands that might be valuable."

Lane merely meditated in his fine, remote way. "In Paris it has gotten so now," he suggested, "that they draw—paint, I mean; I won't call it drawing—anything and call it rain or snow or love. They haven't even the acrid validity of such things as van Gogh and Gauguin's paintings. They aren't even moods. Who is to cherish such sickening cross-sticks and scarecrows, even if they happened to be well-painted? Life is seeking to escape from dust and inefficiency and disease. I should not care for syphilis in my parlor, however well-painted. You may like a high-colored chrome of a cancer. Art should suggest a rare metaphysical harmony, I should say."

I stuck grimly to Cézanne, Gauguin, van Gogh and Picasso for justification, introducing Degas by way of defense and re-enforcement, his hard, shabby, stribbly-haired women in morning negligee, realizing from what I had seen that here was something—a new, invigorating, tonic force—destined to blow the breath of life into older forms. I could see what this violent Neo-Impressionistic and even Cubistic art was destined to do for me with its hard, impatient protest against violet skies and delicate drapery—its tonic reaction against spindling over-refinement. I could see I was in bad company, however. Steer was merely cynically condescending. Lane was artistically irritated, Solomon was a student spectator. We talked and talked, but it came to nothing, the upshot being that I was looked upon as arguing more for argument's sake than because of any depth of conviction or art understanding. I saw once more how dangerous it is to do battle for our nebulous inclinations and faiths. Nevertheless this argument strengthened my own faith in the significance of this school as an art variation, and I decided to follow it closely. Before I left Europe I should see much more of it, particularly at Paris and Berlin. Time has only strengthened, not shaken, my belief that Neo-Impressionism heralds a return to artistic force and sanity—the force that produced the great original schools of Italy.

CHAPTER XXV

The period in which all occurred that I have narrated covered six weeks, during which time the Christmas holidays were drawing near and Grant Richards was making due preparation for the celebration of that event. As perhaps the reader is now aware, he was a stickler for the appropriate observance of those things which have national significance and national or international feeling behind them. Whatever joy he might get out of such things, much or little, I am convinced that he was much more concerned lest someone should fail of their appropriate share of happiness than anything else. I like that in Grant Richards. It touched me greatly and made me feel at times as though I should like to pat him on the head, particularly at such times as I was not enraged beyond measure and ready to tear him to bits. But to return to this matter of the Christmas holidays.

During all my youth in Indiana and elsewhere I had been fed on that delightful picture "Christmas in England," concocted first, I believe (for general consumption, anyhow), by Washington Irving—and from him rehashed for magazine and newspaper purposes and by various more or less unimportant personalities—until it had become romance ad nauseam. The boar's head carried in by the butler of Squire Bracebridge; the ancient peacock pie with the gorgeous tail feathers arranged at one end of the platter and the crested head at the other; the yule log; the mistletoe berries and the Christmas choristers singing outside of windows and doors of echoing halls—all had vaguely stood their ground and as such had rooted themselves in my mind as something connected with ancestral England. I am sure I did not anticipate anything of this kind as being connected with present-day England, or with Grant Richards's simple country residence, but, nevertheless, I was in England, and he was making Christmas preparations of one kind and another, and my mind had a perfect right to ramble a little.

So many things go to make up that very amiable feast when it is successful that I hesitate to think now of all the things that contributed to this one. There was Sir Hugh Lane (Lord Scorp, as I had now come to call him), a slim, anemic, ascetic-souled man who was coming to spend the holidays; Jerrard Grant Allen, a cousin of Grant Richards's, a jolly, roistering theatrical manager who was unquestionably, after Grant Richards, one of the most pleasing figures I met in England, a whimsical, comic, ballad-singing, character-loving soul, who was as great a favorite with children and ladies as one would want to find. He knew all sorts of ladies, apparently, of high and low degree, rich and poor, beautiful and otherwise, and apparently he was kindly disposed towards them all. I could write a splendid human-interest sketch of Jerrard Grant Allen alone. Then there was Mr. Eric MacLagan, a pale, thoughtful person, artistic and poetic to his fingertips, curator of one of the splendid divisions of the South Kensington Museum, a lover of Mr. Housman's *A Shropshire Lad,* a lover of ancient glass and silver, whose hair hung in a sweet mop over his high, pale forehead, and whose limpid, dark eyes shone with a kindly, artistic light. Then there was Grant Richards's aunt and her daughter (mother and sister, respectively, of the highly joyous Jerrard Grant Allen, and wife and daughter of a famous litterateur); also the daughter of a professor of philosophy somewhere; and then, to cap it all, the total of Grant Richards's very interesting household: housekeeper, governess, maid, cook, gardener and, last but not least, the four charming, I might almost say adorable, children.

And then there was Grant Richards, a host in himself. For weeks beforehand he kept saying on occasion as we wandered about London together, "No, we can't go there," or, "You mustn't accept that, because we have reserved the Saturday and Sunday for Christmas at my place," and so nothing was done to interfere with it. Being in his hands, I finally consulted him completely as to Christmas presents and found that I was to be limited to very small gifts, mere tokens of goodwill, I being his guest. I did manage to get him a supply of his favorite cigarettes, however, unknown to himself—the ones his clever secretary told me he much preferred—and had them sent out to the house with some favorite books for the remaining members of the household.

But the man was in such high spirits over the whole program he had laid out for me—winter and spring, the thought of Paris and the Riviera—that he was quite beside himself. More than once he said to me, beaming through his monocle, "We shall have a delightful time on the continent soon. I'm looking forward to it and to your first impressions." Every evening he wanted to take my hastily scribbled notes and read them, and after doing so he was strong for having me do them all just that way, that is, day by day, as I experienced them. I found that quite impossible, however. Once he wanted to know if I had any special preference in wines or cordials, and I knew very well why he asked. Another time he overheard me make the statement that I had always longed to get the rich, odorous Limburger cheese from Germany.

"Done!" he exclaimed. "We shall have it for Christmas."

"But, Papa," piped up Gioia maliciously, "we don't all have to have it at the same time, do we?"

"No, my dear," replied Grant Richards solemnly, with that amazing patronizing and parental air which almost always convulsed me—a sort of a gay deviltry always lurking behind it. "Only Mr. Dreiser need have it. He is German and likes it."

I assumed as German a look as I might—profound, Limburgy.

"And I believe you like Mr. Jones's sausage," he observed on another occasion, referring to an American commodity known as Jones's sausage, which he had heard me say in New York that I liked. "We shall have some of those."

"Christmas is certainly looking up," I replied. "If I come out alive, in good condition for Paris and the Riviera, I shall be grateful."

He merely beamed on me reprovingly.

Well, finally, to make a long story short, the day came, or at least the day before. We were all assembled for a joyous Christmas Eve: Eric MacLagan; Lord Scorp; Jerrard Grant Allen; the dearest aunt and the charming daughter-cousin—extremely intelligent and artistic women both; the four children; Grant Richards's very intelligent and appealing secretary, Miss Hemmerde; the daughter of the college philosopher; and myself. There was a delightful dinner spread at seven-thirty, when we all assembled to discuss the prospects of the morrow. It was on the program, as I discovered, that I should arise and accompany Grant Richards, his aunt, his cousin and the children to a nearby abbey church, a lovely affair, as I was told, on the banks of the Thames, while Jerrard Grant Allen, who positively refused to have anything to do with religion of any kind, quality or description, was to go and reconnoiter a certain house, of which more anon, and to take young Geoffrey Grant Richards (he of the bawth) for a fine and long-anticipated ride on his motorcycle. Lord Scorp and Eric MacLagan were to remain behind to discuss art, perhaps, or literature, being late risers. If there was to be any Santa Claus, which the children doubted, owing to Grant Richards's rather grave asseverations to the contrary (there having been a number of reasons why a severely righteous Santa might see fit to remain away), he was not to make his appearance until rather late in the afternoon. Meanwhile we had all adjourned to the general living room, where a heavy coal-fire blazed on the hearth (for once) and candles were lighted in profusion. The children sang "Songs of the North," accompanied by their governess. I can see their quaint faces in the candlelight now, gathered about the piano. Sir Hugh Lane, MacLagan and myself indulged in various artistic discussions and badinage; Mrs. Grant Allen, the aunt, told me the brilliant story of her husband's life—a great naturalistic philosopher and novelist; and finally after coffee, sherry, nuts and much music and songs—some comic ones by Jerrard Grant Allen—we retired for the night.

It is necessary, to prepare the reader properly for the morrow, to go back a few days or weeks, possibly, and tell of a sentimental encounter that befell me one day as I was going for a walk in that green world which encompassed Cookham Dean. It was a most delightful spectacle. Along the yellowish road before me, with its borders of green grass and green though leafless trees, there was approaching a most interesting figure of a woman, a chic, dashing bit of femininity—at once wife, mother, chatelaine (the presumption, owing to various accompanying details, was mine)—as charming a bit of womanhood and English family sweetness as I had yet seen in England. English women, by and large, let me state here, are not smart—at least not those I had so far encountered—but here was one dressed after the French fashion in trig, close-fitting blue, outlining her form perfectly, a little ermine cap of snowy whiteness set jauntily over her ear, her smooth, black hair parted demurely over her forehead, a white muff warming her hands, and white spats emphasizing the trim leather of her footgear. Her eyes were dark-brown, her cheeks rosy, her gait smart and tense. I could scarcely believe she was English, the mother of the ruddy three-year-old in white and red wool, a little girl who was sitting astride a snow-white donkey, which in turn was led by a trim maid or governess in somber brown, but it was quite plain also that English she was. There was such a wise, sober look about her, for all her smartness—a sort of taunt, buttressed by conservatism. It was such a delightful picture to encounter thus early of a clear December morning that in the fashion of the English I exclaimed, "My word! This is something like!"

What is more, as she passed she gave me a saucy look, as much as to say, "Don't you be too free with your glances, kind sir—just free enough."

I went back to the house that afternoon, determined to make inquiries. Perhaps she was a neighbor, a friend of the family.

Of all individuals who have an appropriate and commendable taste for the smart efforts of the fair sex, commend me to Grant Richards. His interest and enthusiasm neither flags nor fails. Being a widower of discretion, he knows exactly what is smart for a woman as well as a man, and all you have to do to make him prick up his ears attentively is to mention trig beauty as existing in some form, somewhere, not too distant for his adventuring.

"What's this?" I can see his eye lighting. "Beauty? A lovely woman? When? Where?"

This day, finding Spillett in the garden trimming some bushes, I said, "Spillett, do you know any family hereabouts that keeps a white donkey?"

Spillett paused and scratched his ear reflectively.

"No, sir. I cawn't say as I do, sir. I might harsk, sir, down in the village hif you're hanxious to know, sir."

"Never mind for the present, Spillett," I replied. "I may want to know. If so, I'll ask you."

I knew he would inquire anyhow.

That night at dinner, the family being all present, Grant Richards in his chair at the head of the table, the wine at his right, I said mildly, "I saw the most beautiful woman today I have yet seen in England."

Grant Richards was just in the act of elevating a glass of champagne to his lips, but he paused to fix me with an inquiring eye.

"Where?" he inquired solemnly. "Were you in the city?"

"Not at all. I rarely, if ever, see them in the city. It was very near here. A most beautiful woman. Very French. Trim figure, small feet, a gay air. She had a lovely three-year-old child with her riding on a white donkey."

"A white donkey! Trim? Very French, you say? This is most interesting! I don't recall anyone about here who keeps a white donkey. Gioia," he turned to his young daughter, "do you recall anyone hereabouts who keeps a white donkey?"

Gioia, a wizard of the future, merely smiled wisely.

"I do not, Papa."

"This is very curious, very curious indeed," continued Grant Richards, returning to me. "For the life of me, I cannot think of anyone who keeps a white donkey. Who can she be? Walking very near here? I shall have to look into this. She may be the holiday guest of some family. But the donkey and child and maid—and young, you say? Jerrard, you don't recall anyone hereabouts who owns a white donkey—anyone with a maid and a three-year-old child?"

Jerrard smiled broadly. "No, I don't," he said.

Grant Richards shook his head in mock perturbation. "It's very strange," he said. "I don't like the thought of there being any really striking women hereabouts of whom I know nothing." He drank his wine.

There was no more of that then, but I knew in all probability that the subject would come up again. Grant Richards inquired, and Spillett inquired, and, as was natural enough, the lady was located. She turned out to be the wife of a tennis, golf and aeroplane expert or champion, a man who held records for fast automobiling and the like and who was independently settled in the matter of means. Mrs. Eric Saunders was her name, as I recall. But it also turned out that Grant Richards did not know her and did not recall anyone who did.

"This is all very trying," he said when he discovered this much. "Here you are, a celebrated American author, admiring a very attractive woman whom you meet on the public highway, and here am I, a resident of the neighborhood in which she is living, and I do not even know her. If I did, it would all be very simple. I could take you over, she would be immensely flattered at the nice things you have said about her. She would be grateful to me for bringing you. Presto—we should be fast friends."

"Exactly," I replied sourly, "you and she would be fast friends. After I am

Grant Richards

gone in a few days, all would be lovely. I shall not be here to protect my interests. It is always that way. I am the cat's paw, the bait, the trap. I won't stand for it. I saw her first, and she is mine."

"My dear fellow," he exclaimed banteringly, "how you go on! I don't understand you at all. This is England. The lady is married. A little neighborly friendship."

"Yes, yes," I replied, "I know all about neighborly friendship. You get me an introduction to the lady, and I shall speak for myself."

"As for that matter," he added thoughtfully, "it would not be inappropriate, under the circumstances, for me to introduce myself on your behalf. She would be pleased, I am sure. You are a writer, you admire her. Why shouldn't she be pleased?"

"Curses!" I exclaimed. "Always in the way. Always stepping in just when I fancy I have found something for myself!"

But nothing was done until Jerrard Grant Allen arrived, a day or two before Christmas. That worthy had traveled all over England with various theatrical companies. Being the son of so eminent a literary man as his father, he had been received in all circles and apparently knew comfortable and interesting people in every walk everywhere. Grant Richards, who at times, I think, resented his artistic sufficiency, was nevertheless prone to call on him on occasion for advice. On this occasion, since Jerrard Grant Allen knew this neighborhood almost as well as his cousin, he consulted him as to his possible knowledge of our lady of the donkey.

"Mrs. Saunders? Mrs. Eric Saunders?" I can still see his interested look. "Why, it seems to me I do know someone of that name. If I am not mistaken, I know her husband's brother, Harris Saunders, up in Liverpool. He's connected with a bank up there. We've motored all over England together, pretty nearly. I'll stop in Christmas morning and see if it isn't the same family. The description you give suits the lady I know almost exactly."

I was all agog. The picture she had presented was so smart. Grant Richards was intensely interested, though perhaps disappointed too, that Jerrard Grant Allen should know her when he didn't.

"This is most fortunate," he said to me solemnly. "Now if it should turn out that he does know her, we can call there Christmas day after dinner. Or perhaps he will take you."

This last a little regretfully, I think, for Jerrard Grant Allen counted himself an equal master in the matter of the ladies and was not to be so easily set aside. So Christmas Eve it was decided that on the morrow Jerrard Grant Allen should reconnoiter the Saunders country house early and report progress, while we went to church. Fancy Grant Richards and me walking to church Christmas morning with the children!

Christmas in England! The day broke clear and bright, for Christmas day in England, and there we all were. It was not cold, and as is usual, there was little, if any, wind. I remember looking out of my window down into the valley toward Cookham and admiring the green rime upon the trees, the clustered chimneys of groups of farmers' or workingmen's cottages, the low, sagging roofs of red tile or thatch, and the small windowpanes that always somehow suggest a homey simplicity which I can scarcely resist. The English milkmaid of fiction, the simple cottages, the ordered hierarchy of powers are, willy-nilly, fixtures in my mind. I cannot get them out.

First, then, came breakfast in our best bibs and tuckers, for were we not—Grant Richards, Mrs. Grant Allen, her daughter and the children—to depart immediately afterwards to hear an English Christmas service? Imagine Grant Richards, the pride of Piccadilly, marching solemnly off at the head of his family to an old, gray abbey church. As the French say, "I smile." We all sat around and had our heavy English breakfast tea, and, to my comfort and delight, "Mr. Jones's sausages." Grant Richards had secured a string of them from somewhere.

"Think of it," commented Gioia, sardonically. "Mr. Jones's sausages for breakfast! Aren't they comic? Do you like them?"

"I most assuredly do."

"And do you eat them every day in Ah-mair-ree-kaa?" queried Gerard, the younger, with a touch of latent laughter in his voice.

"When I can afford them, yes."

"They're quite small, aren't they?" commented five-year-old Geoffrey.

"Precisely," I replied, unabashed by this fire of inquiry. "That's their charm."

Jerrard Grant Allen was already striking up a tuneful ballad to add to the joy of the occasion, and Mrs. Grant Allen was wondering whether "really" I was going to be interested in this dull old English church. Perhaps Grant Richards was making me go against my will and I would rather do something else.

The church that we visited was one of those semi-ancient affairs done in good English-Gothic, with a touch of Tudor here and there, and was located outside the village of Cookham, perhaps one, two or three miles from Grant Richards's home. I recall with simple pleasure the smug, self-righteous, Sunday-go-to-meeting air with which we all set forth, crossing homey fields via diagonal paths, passing through stiles and along streams and country roads past simple little cottages that left me breathless with delight. I wish truly that England could be put under glass and retained as a perfect specimen of unconscious poetry. The pots and pans outside kitchen doorways! The simple stoops ornamented with clambering vines! The reddish-green sagging roofs and clustered cylindrical chimney pots! When we came to the top of a hill, we could see the church in the valley below, nestling beside one bank of the Thames which wound here and there in delightful S's. A square tower, as I recall, rose quaintly out of a surrounding square of trees, grass, gravestones and box hedge.

There was much ado in this semi-ancient place as we came up, for Christmas day, of all days, naturally drew forth a tradition-loving English audience. Choirboys were scurrying here and there, some ladies of solemn demeanor, who looked as if they might be assisting at the service in some way or other, were dawdling about, and I even saw the rector in full canonicals, hastening up a gravel path toward a side door as though matters needed to be expedited considerably. The interior was dark, heavy-beamed and by no means richly ornamented with stained glass, but redolent of bygone generations at that. The walls were studded with those customary slabs and memorial carvings with which the English love to ornament their church interiors. A fair-sized and yet, for so large an edifice, meager audience was present; an evidence, it seemed to me, of the validity of the protest against state support for the established church. There was a great storm in England at this time against the further state support of an institution that was not answering the religious needs of the people, and there had been some discussion of the matter at Grant Richards's house. As was natural, the artistically inclined were in favor of anything which would sustain, unimpaired, whether they had religious value or not, all of the old cathedrals, abbeys and neighborhood churches, solely because of their poetic appearance. On the other hand, an immense class, derisively spoken of, I learned, as "chapel people," were heartily in favor of the ruder disposition of the matter. Grant Richards, in his best Piccadilly clothing, was for their maintenance.

To be frank, as charming as this semi-ancient church atmosphere was—and possibly suited to the current English neighborhood mood and thought (I could not say as to that)—it did not appeal to me as strongly on this occasion as did many a similar service in American churches of the same size. The vestments were pleasing, as high church vestments go; the choir, made up of boys and men from the surrounding countryside no doubt, was not absolutely villainous, but it could have been much better. It seemed to me, to tell the truth, that I was witnessing the last and rather threadbare evidences of an older and much more prosperous order of things. Beautiful in its way? Yes. Quaint? Yes. Naive? Yes. But smacking more of poverty and an ordered system continued past its day than anything else. I felt a little sorry for the old church and the thin minister or rector and the goodly, albeit a little provincial, citizens who clung so fatuously to an older order of things. They have their place, no doubt, and it makes that sweet, old lavender atmosphere which seems to hover over so much that one encounters in England. Nevertheless life does move on, and we must say good-bye to many a once delightful thing. Why not set these old churches aside as museums or art galleries or any other public use, as they do many of them in Italy, and let the matter go at that? It is not necessary that a service be kept up in them day by day and year by year. Services on special or state occasions would be sufficient. Let bygones be bygones, and let the people tax themselves for the things they really do want, perhaps skating rinks and moving pictures. They seemed to flourish even in these elderly and more sedate neighborhoods.

Outside in the graveyard, however, after the services were over and we were idling about a few moments, I found a number of touches of that valiant simplicity in ability which is such a splendid characteristic of the English. Although there were many graves here of the nobility and gentry, dating from as far back as the sixteenth century, there was no least indication, as far as I could see, of ostentation, but everywhere simple headstones recording names only and not virtues—sometimes, perhaps, a stately verse or a stoic line. I noticed, with a kind of English-speaking pride, the narrow new-made grave of Sir Robert Hart, the late great English financial administrator of China, who, recently deceased, had been brought overseas to this simple churchyard to lie here with other members of his family in what I assumed to be the neighborhood of his youth and nativity. It is rather fine, I think, when a nation's sons go forth over the world to render honorable service, each after his capacity, and then to come back in death to an ancient and beloved soil. The very obscurity of this little grave with its two-foot six-inch headstone and flowerless mound spoke more to me for the dignity and the ability that is in true greatness of soul than a heaven-soaring shaft might otherwise do.

On the way home, I remember, we discussed Christian Science and its relative metaphysical merits in a world where all creeds and doctrines blow, apparently, so aimlessly about. Like all sojourners in this fitful fever of existence, Mrs. Grant Allen and her daughter and her son, the cheerful Jerrard Grant Allen, were not without their troubles, so much so that being the intelligent woman that she was and quite aware of the subtleties and uncertainties of religious dogma, she was nevertheless eager to find something upon which she could lean, spiritually speaking—the strong arm, let us say, of an Almighty, no less, who would perchance heal her of her griefs and ills. I take it, as I look at life, that only the intellectually very able or the materially very rock-ribbed and dull can front the storms and disasters which beset us or the ultimate dark which only the gifted, the imaginative, see, without quakes and fears. So often I have noted this to be true, that those who stand up brave and strong in their youth turn a nervous and anguished eye upon this troubled seeming in later years. They have no longer any heart for a battle that is only rhyme and no reason, and, whether they can conceive why or not, they must have a god.

I, for one, would be the last person in the world to deny that everywhere I find boundless evidence of an intelligence far superior to my own. I, for one, am inclined to agree with the poet that "if my bark sinks, 'tis to another sea." In fact, I have always innately presumed the existence of a force or forces that, possibly ordered in some noble way, maintain a mathematical purity and order in visible things. I have always felt, in spite of all my carpings, that somehow in a large way there is a rude justice done under the sun, and that a balance for—I will not say right, but for happiness, is maintained. The world has long since gathered to itself a vast basket of names, such as Right, Truth, Justice, Mercy. My thinking has nothing to do with these. I do not believe that we can conceive what the ultimate significance of anything is; therefore, why label it? I have seen good come to the seemingly evil and evil come to the seemingly good. But if a religion will do anybody any good, for heaven's sake, let him have it. To me it is a case of individual, sometimes of race, weakness. A stronger mind would not attempt to define what may not be defined, nor to lean upon what, to an infinite mind, must be utterly insubstantial and thin air. Obviously there is a vast sea of force. Is it good? Is it evil? Give that to the philosophers to fight over, and to the fearful and timid give a religion. "A mighty fortress is our God," sang Luther. He may be; I do not know.

But to return to Mrs. Grant Allen and her daughter and Grant Richards's children and Grant Richards ambling across the sunny English landscape this Christmas morning. It was a fine thing to see the green patina of the trees and the richer green grass, growing lush and thick all winter long, and to see the roofs of little towns like Cookham—for we were walking on high ground—and the silvery windings of the Thames in the valley below, whence we had just come. I think I established the metaphysical basis of life quite ably, for myself, and urged Mrs. Grant Allen to take up Christian Science. I assailed the wisdom of maintaining the Established Church by state funds largely, I think, to irritate Grant Richards, and protested that the "chapel people" had a great deal of wisdom on their side. As we drew near Cookham Dean and Grant Richards's country place, it occurred to me that Jerrard Grant Allen had gone to discover whether he really knew our lady of the donkey, and I was all agog to find out. Grant Richards himself was perking up considerably, and it was agreed that first we would have an early afternoon feast, all the Christmas dainties of the day, and then, if Jerrard Grant Allen really knew the lady, we were to visit her and then return to Bigfrith, where, I now learned, there was to be a Santa Claus. He was to arrive via the courtesy of Jerrard Grant Allen, who was to impersonate him, and on that account, Grant Richards announced, we might have to cut any impending visit to our lady short in order not to disappoint the children, but visit her we would. Knowing Jerrard Grant Allen to be a good actor and intensely fond of children—Grant Richards's especially—I anticipated some pleasure here. But I will be honest. The great event of the day was our lady of the donkey, her white furs, and whether she was really as striking as I had imagined. I was afraid Jerrard Grant Allen would return to report that either he did not know her or that she was not as fascinating as I had imagined. In either case my anticipated pleasure would come to the ground with a crash. We entered, shall I say, with beating hearts.

Jerrard Grant Allen had returned. With Lane and Eric MacLagan he was now toasting his English legs in front of the open fire and discoursing on some vanity of the day. At sight of the children he began his customary badinage, but I would have none of it. Grant Richards fixed him with a monitory eye. "Well," he said, putting the burden of the inquiry on me, "our friend here has been quite restless during the services this morning. What did you find out?"

"Yes," chimed Mrs. Grant Allen, who had been informed as to this romantic encounter. "For goodness' sake, tell us, we are all dying to know."

"Yes, tell them," interpolated Lane sarcastically. "There will be no peace, believe me, until you do."

"To be sure, to be sure," cheerfully exclaimed Jerrard Grant Allen, straightening up from jouncing Geoffrey. "I know her well. Her sister and her husband are with her. That little baby is hers, of course. They live just over the hill here. I admire your taste. She is one of the smartest women I know. I told her that you were stopping here, and she wants you to come over and see the Christmas tree lighted. We are all invited after dinner."

"Very good," observed Grant Richards, rubbing his hands. "Now that is settled."

"Isn't she charming," observed Mrs. Grant Allen, "to be so politely disposed?"

"And," added Jerrard Grant Allen, leaning toward me and whispering, "I have something else to tell you. She is very unhappy. Her husband is somewhat of a stick. She married him, I think, for his money."

"Come now," observed Grant Richards, "we'll have no confidences. What is that you are telling him?"

"Some unwholesome thought, I'll warrant," said Lane.

But Jerrard Grant Allen did not confess. He was merely saying, he said, that two brothers had married two sisters, and that while the wives were smart as any he knew, the husbands were dull. Thereafter the dinner could not come too soon, and by two-thirty we were quite ready to depart, having consumed heaven knows how many kinds of wines and meats, English plum pudding and—especially for me—real German Limburger. It was a splendid dinner.

Shall I stop to describe it? I cannot say, outside of the interesting English company, that it was any better or any worse than many another Christmas feast in which I have participated. Imagine the English dining room, the English maid, the housekeeper in watchful attendance on the children, the maid, like a bit of Dresden china on guard over the service, Grant Richards, monocle in eye, sitting solemnly in state at the head of the board, Sir Hugh Lane, Eric MacLagan, Jerrard Grant Allen, Mrs. Grant Allen, her daughter, myself, the children, all chattering and gabbling. The high-sounding English voices, the balanced English phrases, the quaint English scene through the windows—it all comes back, a bit of sweet color. Was I happy? Very. Did I enjoy myself? Quite.

But as to this other matter. It was a splendid afternoon. On the way over Grant Richards and myself—the others refusing contemptuously to have anything to do with this sentimental affair—had the full story of our lady of the donkey and her sister and the two brothers that they married. It appeared truly enough that the men were dullards, younger sons of a good family, with money. The girls were ambitious, emotional daughters of a family perhaps not so good, certainly without much means. The woman whom I had met on the highway was the better-looking of the two and the more talented. She was dissatisfied because her interests were, to a certain extent, literary and artistic, or, perhaps better yet, smart, whereas her husband's soul was devoted to such things as flying machines, automobiles, mines, ranching and the like. Jerrard Grant Allen informed us quite smilingly that the husbands were athletic men both, a little dull and very fond of their wives. "Harris Saunders," he observed naively, "is a crack shot. He took a prize here somewhere not long ago."

We turned eventually into one of those charming lawns enclosed by a high, concealing English fence, and up a graveled automobile path to a snow-white Georgian door. We were admitted to a hall which at once bore out the testimony as to the athletic prowess of the husbands twain. There were guns, knives, golf-sticks, tennis rackets, automobile togs and swords. I think there were deer and fox heads in the bargain. By a ruddy, stocky, sporty man of perhaps thirty-eight, and all of six feet tall, who now appeared, we were invited to drink what we would—whiskey, sherry, ale—a suitable list. We declined the drink, put up our fur coats and sticks and were immediately asked into the billiard room where the Christmas tree and other festivities were holding—or about to be. Here, at last, was my lady of the donkey and the child and the maid and our lady's sister, and alas, our lady's husband, full six feet tall and vigorous—and, of all tragic things, fingering a forty-caliber sixteen-shot magazine pistol which his beloved brother of sporting proclivities had given him as a Christmas present! I eyed it as one might a special dispensation of Providence.

But our lady of the donkey? A very charming woman she proved, intelligent, smiling, very chic, quite aware of all the nice things that had been said about her, very clever in making light of it for propriety's sake, unwilling really to have anything made of it for the present, for husband's sake. But that Anglicized French air! And that romantic smile!

We talked—of what do people talk on such occasions? Jerrard Grant Allen was full of the gayest references to the fact that Grant Richards had such interesting neighbors as the Saunderses and did not know it and that they had once motored to Blackpool together. I shall not forget either how artfully Grant Richards conveyed to Mrs. Eric Saunders, our lady of the donkey, that I had been most intensely taken with her looks, while at the same time presenting himself in the best possible light. Grant Richards is always at his best on such occasions, Chesterfieldian, and with an air that says, "—a mere protégé of mine. Do not forget the managerial skill that is making this interesting encounter possible." But Mrs. Saunders, as I could see, was not utterly unmindful of the fact that I was the one who had been heralded to her as a noted writer, and that I had made the great fuss and said all the nice things about her after a single encounter on a country road, which had brought about this afternoon visit. She was gracious without being forward or provocative and ordered the Christmas tree lighted and had the young heir's most interesting toys spread out on the billiard table. I remember picking up a linen storybook, labeled Laughlin Bros., New York.

"From America," I said—quite unwisely, I think.

"Oh, yes, you Americans," she replied, eyeing me archly. "Everything comes from America these days, even our toys. But it's rather ungracious to make us admit it, don't you think?"

I picked up a train of cars and, to my astonishment, found it stamped with the name of a Connecticut firm. I hesitated to say more, for I knew that I was on dangerous ground, but after that I looked at every book or box of blocks and the like, to find that my suspicions were well-founded. England gets many of its Christmas toys from America.

Nothing came of this episode except a pleasant introduction for Grant Richards, who had all the future before him. I was leaving for Paris a week or two later. It was all in vain, as I foresaw, that I was invited to call again, or that she hoped to see something of me among her friends in London. I think I said as much to Grant Richards with many unkind remarks about the type of mind that manages to secure all merely by a process of waiting. Jerrard Grant Allen added fuel to the flames by gently remarking on occasion that she was very unhappy, poor dear, and that her temperament would probably find, some day, some satisfying outlet. Meantime Grant Richards walked bravely forward, his overcoat snugly buttoned, his cane executing an idle circle, his monocle on straight, his nose in the air. I could have made away with him for much less.

The last of this very gallant day came in the home of Grant Richards himself. As we neared the house, we were told to hurry forward and state that Jerrard Grant Allen had remained at the Saunderses for dinner, while he made a wide detour, ending up, I think, in some chamber in the coachhouse. I did not see him again until much later in the evening, but meantime the children, the relatives, the friends and the family servants were all gathered in the nursery on the second floor. There was much palaver and badinage concerning the fact that Santa Claus had really had such bad reports that he had found it much against his will to come here, early at least. There were really some excellent things that had been reported to him later, however, and he had, so someone had heard, changed his mind.

Whether there would be little or much for such a collection of ne'er-do-wells was open to question. However, if we were all very quiet for a little while, we should see. I can see Grant Richards now in his Sunday cutaway, stalking nobly about, and the four little Grant Richardses surveying rather incredulously but expectantly the maid, the nurse, the governess and their father. I was wondering what had become of my small mementos and whether my special cigarettes for Grant Richards were in safety in Santa Claus's pack. It was small stock, I fear me much, that these well-behaved little English children took in this make-believe, but presently there was a loud hammering at the nursery door, and without a "by your leave" the same was opened, and a vigorous, woolly-headed Santa Claus put his rosy face in the chamber.

"Is there anyone living here by the name of Geoffrey Grant Richards, or Gioia Grant Richards, or Gerard Grant Richards?" I shall not repeat all the names he called after in a high, falsetto voice. "I've been a long way today, and I've had a great deal to do, and I haven't had the least assistance from anybody. They're so busy having a good time themselves."

I never saw a redder nose or more shaggy eyebrowed eyes or a gayer twinkle in them, and the pack that he carried was simply enormous. It could barely be squeezed through the door, and as he made his way to the center of the room, he looked quizzically about, groaning and squeaking in his funny voice and wanting to know if the man in the monocle were really Grant Richards, and whether the fat lady in the corner were really a nurse or an interloper, and if the four children that had been reported to him as present were really there. Having satisfied himself on various counts and evoked a great deal of innocent laughter, to say nothing of awe as to his next probable comment, he finally untied the enormous bag and began to consult the labels.

"Here's a package marked Gerard Grant Richards. It's rather large. It's been very heavy to carry, all this distance. Can anybody tell me whether he's been a reasonably good child? It's very hard to go to all this trouble, if children really aren't deserving. He has a very impish look in his eye, it seems to me," he added as he came forward. "But I suppose I ought to let him have it." And so the gift was handed over. One by one the gifts came forth, commented on in this fashion, only the comments varied with the age and the personality of the recipient. There was no lack of humor or intimacy of application, for this Santa Claus knew apparently whereof he spoke.

"Is there a writer in the room by the name of Theodore Dreiser? I've heard of him faintly, and he isn't a very good writer. But I suppose he's entitled to a slight remembrance. I hope you reform, Mr. Dreiser," the Santa Claus said wisely. "It's very plain to me that a little improvement could be effected." I acknowledged the wisdom of the comment.

When my cigarettes were handed to Grant Richards, Santa tapped them sapiently. "More wretched cigarettes! I know them well! If it isn't one vice that has to be pampered, it's another. I would have brought him pâté de foie gras or wine if I didn't think this was less harmful. He's very fond of prawns too, but they're very expensive at this time of the year. A little economy wouldn't hurt him."

Dora, the maid, and Nana, the nurse, and Miss C., the governess, came in for really brilliant compliments. Sir Hugh Lane was told that an old English castle or a Rembrandt would be most suitable, but that Santa was all out at present, and that if he would just be a little more cheerful in the future, he might manage to get him one. Eric MacLagan was given books, as was very fitting, and in a trice the place was literally littered with wonders. There were immense baskets and boxes of candied fruit from Holland; toys, books and fruit from Grant Richards's mother in Rome; more toys and useful presents from ladies in London and the north of England and France and the Isle of Wight—a goodly company of mementos. It's something to be an attractive widower. I never saw children more handsomely or bountifully provided for, and a new saddle, whip and bridle for Gioia's riding pony struck me as extremely appropriate. There were other things, curious puzzles, German mechanical toys from Berlin and certain ornamental articles of dress, which, by the astonishing bursts of excitement which they provoked, seemed exceedingly welcome.

Santa now drew off his cap and whiskers to reveal himself as Jerrard Grant Allen, and we all literally got down on the floor to play with the children. You can imagine, with each particular present to examine, how much there was to do. Teatime came and went unnoticed, a state occasion in England. Supper, a meal not offered except on Christmas, was spread some time about eight o'clock. About nine-thirty an automobile took Sir Hugh Lane and Eric MacLagan away, and after that we all returned to the nursery until about ten-thirty, when even by the most liberal interpretation of holiday license it was bedtime. We soberer elders (I hope no one sets up a loud guffaw at that phrase) adjourned to the drawing room for nuts and wine, and finally, as the beloved Pepys was accustomed to remark, "So to bed." But what with the abbey church, the discourse on Christian Science, our lady of the donkey, a very full stomach and a phantasmagoria of toys spinning before my eyes, to say nothing of various abstruse speculations as to the source of all the presents, I went to bed thinking of—well, now, what do you suppose I went to bed thinking of?

CHAPTER XXVI

One of the most interesting phases of all my stay in England was this same trip to Manchester which I had been planning for some days. My head was full of London—the strangeness of its various characteristics—but I was eager to know something more of England, the England outside of London. I had always heard of the manufacturing life represented by Leeds, Sheffield, Manchester, Birmingham, Nottingham and the like. I had been told that if I went to Nottingham I would see some fifty thousand women operatives, with scarcely a man in the place, and I had thought some of witnessing this interesting spectacle. After some deliberation I changed my mind, however, and decided to visit Manchester instead, because I heard of various outlying towns—Stockport, Oldham, Rochdale, Middleton, Summit, Wigan and the like. Mr. Jerrard Grant Allen had told me that the conditions at Wigan were so bad that when a stage comedian anywhere in England was in need of a laugh, all he had to say was that his address was Eight, or any number, Sea View Terrace, Wigan, whereupon the audience would burst into loud applause. This struck me as fairly indicative of wretched conditions, and I was eager to see Wigan.

My principal object in going to Manchester at all was to see whether the laboring and living conditions were as bad as they have frequently been described by various agitators. I bought my ticket at eleven o'clock of this Sunday night, the last of the old year, with the curious feeling of being on the edge of an interesting adventure. I had in my pocket several letters of introduction—one to the wife of a wealthy machinery supplies agent at Manchester, a Mrs. Stubbs, and another to a steamship agent, a certain K. Kabura, a Jew—neither of which was I certain whether I would use. I had so little time. Mr. Jerrard Grant Allen, who gave me the letter to Mrs. Stubbs, assured me that her interest in literature and art was great, that she would be interested to show me Manchester in her car if I would let her, that she could unquestionably open various opportunities to me—mines, mills, the courtesies of the Lord Mayor, etc. I only had two days that I really cared to give to Manchester. I merely wished to see it. London interested me much more.

I took the train first-class, reading by the way that this was the last night on which second-class tickets would be sold on this line—the Midland. The second-class compartment had evidently proved unpopular, satisfying my theory that in life only extremes are appreciated, that no one cares for that lack of distinction which is indicated by the word normal. I had a copy of a new play by a new writer, John Masefield, of which I approved in spots only. I read it to while away the time.

England was so interesting to me and my total stay so short that everything I saw was most important. To a hungry man, little bread is much. I was interested in the type of solemn Englishman who was journeying from London to Manchester on this New Year's Eve. My own gyrations at this particular period were unimportant, for I was following my own whim. I might have stayed with Richards in London over the holidays. But these solemn Londoners, I thought—where were they going on New Year's Eve?

Once more I was impressed with the comfort of English railway riding. England is homey. My fur overcoat and my steamer rug were ample protection against the damp—it always seemed damp to me in England—and the separate compartment always appealed to me as so much more satisfactory than the crowded American car. There was no opportunity to take a sleeper here; the distance was too short (three and a half hours), and so I wrapped myself in my rug and thought to sleep. Thoughts of England, the country we were passing through, kept me wide awake, however, and at Crewe, three-quarters of an hour from Manchester, I was compelled to change. I recall now with what interest I surveyed the English and Scotch working classes whom I encountered on this platform, the sense of great travel activity which the depot had, the grim workaday life which it all suggested. It was not until long afterward that I learned that six hundred trains passed here daily and that some engine works nearby employed 21,000 men. I thought of the Earl of Crewe, of whom I had heard. Somehow, by intuition merely, I was reminded of Pittsburgh and Wheeling and those coarse manufacturing towns of western Pennsylvania and West Virginia. I was interested by the thought that I was now nearing the center of that vast manufacturing section of England to which, once, the whole world responded. It is still vast enough, but America and Germany have risen since then. I sensed, without having any evidence to confirm it, vast factories, warehouses, mines, coal pockets. The very atmosphere of life seemed to have changed, and where in London were thoughts of Empire and social life, great peace and pride, here were struggle and effort. I am quite sure that only the temperamentally dull need to see the actual visible face of things to know where they are.

At Stockport, a few minutes out of Manchester, I had a most interesting experience. At Crewe I had entered another first-class carriage and was quarreling with it because it was dirtier and generally more reprehensible than the one in which I had left London, when I was joined by a young Scotch-Englishman of what to me was a very interesting but unsatisfactory type. He looked much like a Scotchman of education and refinement, or at least someone who had been trained in a world where money was plentiful. His clothing was of the best, his portmanteau and golf bag were of the best leather. He had a handsomely striped steamer rug and seemed generally to be fitted out with all the comforts of existence.

It would be useless to try to explain why I took a violent dislike to him, but I did. He reminded me of a youth of my schooldays whose very existence at that time I resented very much. Not a popinjay, by any means, but an able, resourceful snob. I speculated, as I sometimes do when I take violent dislikes to anyone, of what a pleasure it would be to get into a pointless quarrel with him and give him a good beating, if I could. The gallants of the Middle Ages had the pleasure of doing this occasionally. It seemed to me that in him I saw typified all the wrongs of 500,000 overworked, underpaid wastrels of fortune—the poor, half-equipped fools at the bottom who are harnessed to this treadmill of earthly events and exploited by the strong in order that such young heirs as these may flourish. I remember looking at his jaw, which was prognathous and defiant, and at his deep-set young eyes, which lurked like dark spiders in brown-tanned holes of skin and bone. His hands were long, shapely, strong.

As we neared Stockport, I decided to speak to him to test the quality of his voice. I have considerable faith in voices of certain kinds. I asked him the time. He looked at his watch, which was fastened about his left wrist in the form of a leather bracelet, and then in a soft, pleasing, disarming, cultivated tone replied, "A quarter of three. We're late."

I subsided, meditating upon the ladylike wristwatch.

"Are there any cathedrals or abbeys near Manchester which are of any importance?" I inquired.

"Now let me see," he speculated most courteously. "I don't believe so. Not near. There is a cathedral at Chester, twenty-one miles from Crewe, and an abbey church at Leicester, but they are not near here. Manchester Cathedral does not amount to anything." He ran them over in his mind out loud. "Ely, Gloucester, Norwich, Titchfield, Lincoln, Wells, Winchester, Peterborough—No," he said, "not within any reasonable striking distance. There is little but manufacturing in this section of England."

I remember doing my best to adjust his voice to his physique. His voice belied his looks. He seemed anything but the creature I had fancied him to be. I speculated on his voice and his looks all the way to Manchester, unable to adjust the two. At the station he advised me to take a "fly" when he saw me hesitating and asking for a taxi. "There are very few here," he said.

I went off, meditating on his courtesy. I was compelled to admit that my instinct, if it amounted to anything at all, was badly baffled in this case. Yet, I consoled myself, I might be right after all. The immedicable woes of many might shine out through his gracious comfort and irritate me after all. It was not very intelligent comfort, however. The man was very pleasing.

In coming into Manchester, I had seen all the signs of the kind of city it was to prove to be. Endless "goods" cars were standing on sidings. The air was smoky, hazy, choky. Cinders seemed everywhere, plentiful. Tall coal chutes, chimneys, factory windows gleaming under the hard glitter of electric lights, showed me that we were in a dreary world of work, a rough kind of work. The charming intellectual, conventional smoothness of the south of England was gone.

"Exactly like a manufacturing city," I thought as I came out on the station platform and saw the dreary cobbled street nearby, the beggarly row of run-down "hacks" or closed carriages which ply between stations and hotels in a city of this caliber. No art, no taste, no nothing. Some few have a little money, a great deal of money—too few, however, to make public conveniences general. The rest are drudges. I rode to the Midland—the only decent hotel in England, Jerrard Grant Allen had described it to be—and went to a room which had been engaged in advance. I was too tired to quarrel, but if I had not been, there would have been no excuse. Since I had left America, I had seen nothing one-half as good, though many much more expensive. I recalled Grant Richards sniffing when Allen had described it as excellent, and I could see why. It was bourgeois. The same hotel located in America would have received praise from Grant Richards as being excellently American. Located in London or patronized by the smart crowd, it would have been all that a hotel should be. Here in Manchester—well, what could be excellent in Manchester? That was the end of it.

Let me here digress for once and thoroughly on the subject of English hotels—not inns. During my total stay of six weeks in England I encountered a number of them, mostly in London. One of them, the Cecil, in spite of its advertised American reputation, I found to be abominable—a perfect barn. Its halls were narrow and not properly lighted, its furnishings old and hardly on a par with those of the Galt House of Louisville, Kentucky. Its lighting equipment was supposed to be electric, but gas still served in spots. The ceilings of the rooms were low, a magnificent view of the Thames half destroyed by high-placed windows. The elevators were slow and stuffy. Any fourth-rate hotel in America would be better equipped, and yet it has been advertised far and wide as one of London's great hotels—solely for the benefit of unsophisticated Americans, as the English are always pleased to note. The Savoy, its neighbor, is considered by the stranger to be the smart hotel of London and so is frequented by them. It contains the only really smart restaurant in London, the one most talked of. There is much to-do over the restaurants of the Carlton and Claridge's, but the Savoy is better. However, I could not see that it was much of an improvement on the better hotels in New York—certainly not better than the Ritz or the Plaza—and Richards was constantly telling me that it was not nearly as attractive as those in Paris. It was quite expensive. Besides, the building is old and not very impressive.

The hotel that did appeal to me out of the few that I saw was Claridge's.

Not that it was smart, but solely because of its delicious atmosphere of conservatism. Here one found a richly appointed world, very still, very phlegmatic, with servants who were obviously of the best family caliber and whose manners were perfect. I remember dining there one evening and being impressed with the exceedingly homelike atmosphere of the great lobby and dining room. It was like a large private manor. The general reception room was graced by a large fireplace that blazed very cheerfully. The dining room looked as though it were reserved for the immediate private family of somebody. The various servants approached you with the air of being especially in your employ. Yet it was only comparatively recently that this hotel was remodeled so as to make it modern—to introduce electricity, elevators, a central heating system and the like. To this day, baths are not considered so essential that they are connected with every suite, and yet the best of English society stops here. It was not really nice to want things too up-to-date. The really important people were not too particular about these things. Only Americans were so brash and raw and impetuous as to want things perfect. I could quite see the logic of it. It appealed to me very much—so long as I could keep reasonably comfortable myself.

The one really modern, up-to-date hotel that I saw in London, and that did appeal to me as having much of the atmosphere of the average first-class American hotel, was the Piccadilly, in Piccadilly, and it, I soon learned, was not really successful. Its dining room, foyer, halls and landings were properly spaced, decorated, lighted and reached by a swift elevator service, but they had an air of being deserted. The public did not come here. Why, I could not understand. My friend Richards informed me that it was not *smart*. The Carlton, with its frayed carpets, worn and insufficient plumbing, creaky stairs and the like, was much better. I ate in the restaurants of both on several occasions, and I could not see that either in the matter of food, service or appointments the Carlton was better than, if as good as, the Piccadilly, but it was much more popular—much more the place to be. An air of success, great importance, pervaded the Carlton, whereas the Piccadilly was almost morbid in its gloom. It was in danger, I learned, of going into the hands of a receiver.

It is in this matter of heat, light, elevator service and the absolutely necessary bath that the London hotels are still lacking, and, if I could believe those who should know, nearly all the hotels of England. Mr. Jerrard Grant Allen, who had piloted various theatrical troupes of excellent standing to all parts of England and Scotland—Edinburgh, Glasgow, Liverpool, Birmingham and the like—told me that in but one city in England (Manchester) was there a really first-class hotel, one in which you could be truly comfortable—the one I was in now. You need scarcely expect steam heat anywhere else. I doubt whether it will ever be popular. The climate is raw and damp, but it is rarely if ever freezing cold. A moderate-sized grate-fire actually serves to take the chill off a room that is not actually cold. In the next place, the bath as it is served you—in a little tin tub with a pitcher of hot water put down beside it and a large towel spread out to receive the flying spray—is considered entirely satisfactory. The colder the room, the better. In the third place, space devoted to a bathtub in connection with your room is considered folly. If the tub is fifty or one hundred feet down a hall, it is considered near enough. The most amusing thing of all in connection with this matter of modern comfort occurred in connection with this same "one perfect hotel" at Manchester, which I am about to relate.

All during my stay in London I complained of the absence of bathrooms, cold bathrooms, misplaced electric lights or no electric lights, no elevators, smoky grate-fires, no telephones in many of the rooms, a perfectly marvelous system of letting water in and out when there was a bathtub at all—which amused me greatly. The idea of a bathtub at all is so novel to the English that they surround it with a kind of panoply of procedure so far as letting the water in or out is concerned. Both at Grant Richards's, Mr. Stubbs's, Mr. Allen's, the Hotel Capitol and the Hotel Cecil, I noticed that the water-cock was equipped with some strange contrivance for regulating the height of the water and for blending it—three cocks, where one would have been ample. Here at the Midland in Manchester, the bath was indeed in connection with the room, but the space devoted to it was almost as large as the room itself, and, having no radiator, it was cold. Then there was the same wonderful water-letting arrangement and, most amusing of all, though the hotel was entirely new, no toilet in connection with the bathroom at all. For that, a walk of fifty to two hundred feet was necessary, this arrangement being evidently considered the most sanitary. When I spoke to my valet about the curiosity of it, he replied, "I'm sure they didn't want to do that. It wasn't that they didn't think of it. They didn't want to do it."

So the management was imposing its notions of how things ought to be on the traveler. Nevertheless there were so many other compensations and comforts in this great hotel that I really thought no more about this. It was delightful to be here after all the tin tubs, misplaced lights, no phone in room and the like. Here all these little details were carefully worked out, and they made it pleasant.

CHAPTER XXVII

Since my first impressions of Manchester and the north of England were gained from the rooms and windows of this particular hotel, and it was considered to be the best hotel in England, it interested me very much. I think I never saw so large a hotel. It sprawled over a very large block in a heavy, impressive, smoky way. It had, as I quickly discovered, an excellent Turkish and Russian bath in connection with it and five separate restaurants—German, French, English, etc.—and an American bar. The hall distances in it were something enormous—blocks, it seemed to me—and the general equipment plain but effective. I admired the speedy elevator service and the several restaurant decorations, though in the main they were a little showy. The most important travel life of Manchester centered here—that was obvious. I was told that buyers and sellers came here from all parts of the world and that they mostly congregated in this particular caravansary. I myself saw at once on the first morning after my arrival some French, Germans and Armenians, but no Americans. The Englishmen who were present looked to me very much like Americans.

The hotel was located near what is known as the Central Station at St. Peter's Square in the heart of the theatrical and shopping district, and the first impression I received, looking out into the square from the windows of the breakfast room, was that I was in a city very much like St. Louis, Pittsburgh or Baltimore. The air was hazy with bluish smoke, the buildings black from soot, the streets granite-paved to withstand heavy traffic. It was New Year's Day, and the streets were comparatively empty, but this large, showy, heavily-furnished breakfast room was fairly well sprinkled with men whom I took to be cotton operatives. There was a great mill strike on at this time, and these men were gathered for conference, representatives of all the principal interests involved. I was glad to see this, for I had always wondered what type of man it was that conducted the great manufacturing interests of England—particularly this one of cotton. The struggle was over the matter of the recognition of the unions and a slight raise in the wage scale. Here they were, some of the men who were to decide whether the unions were to be recognized or not.

As I cogitated on the fact that the little I had seen of Manchester so far, including this hotel, was like St. Louis, Missouri, so I also meditated on the fact that these men were very much like a similar collection of wealthy manufacturers in the United States, no more and no less. Great industries seem to breed a certain type of mind and body. You can draw a mental picture of a certain keen, dressy, phlegmatic individual—not tall, not small, round, solid, ruddy—and have them all. These men who were in this breakfast room were so comfortably solid physically. They looked so content with themselves and the world, so firm and sure. Nearly all of them were between forty-five and sixty, cold, hard, quick-minded, alert. They all had on such nice clothes, made of the best material, and wore but little jewelry. They talked quietly among themselves where they were together, and very little. They seemed to be thinking. In most cases their voices were low, tough, guttural. They looked anything but like the typical Englishman of the south and much more—in fact, quite like—the American businessman of the same station. One could see that the average labor leader would get short shrift from them unless he had the sword of compulsion in his hand. Whatever the justice of his claim, one could hear them answering "business is business," or not answering at all. I liked their looks. It struck me at once that if England were to be kept commercially dominant, it would be this type of man, not that of the south, who would keep it so.

And now I could understand, from looking at these men, why it was that the north of England was supposed to hate the south of England, and vice versa. I had sat at a dinner table in Portland Place one evening and heard this matter of the sectional feeling discussed. Why does it exist? was the question before the guests. Well, the south of England is intellectual, academic, historic, highly socialized. It is rich in military, governmental, ambassadorial and titled life. The very scenery is more exquisite. The culture of the people, because of the more generally distributed wealth, is so much better. In the north of England the poor are very poor and contentious. The men of wealth are not historically wealthy or titled. In many cases they are hard, greedy upstarts like the irrepressible Americans. They have no real culture or refinement. They manage to buy their way in from time to time, but that does not really count. They are essentially raw and brutal trash, and that was the end of it.

Looking at these men breakfasting quietly, I could understand it exactly. Their hard, direct efficiency would but poorly adjust itself to the soft speculative intellectuality of the south. Nothing so wearies the man of affairs as intellectual abstrusities, arguments about art, literature, life, social procedure; nothing so wearies the intellectual as hard, unwearied insistence on the necessity of constructive commercial thought. Hence the drawn swords. Yet no country is anything without its commercial greatness, any more than it is without its intellectual and artistic significance. The two things go hand in hand. I enjoyed my breakfast, thinking on these things, and then struck out to see what I could see of the city alone.

I shall not attempt to describe Manchester in detail—never fear. I saw a great deal of it—portions of the Irwell and Irk, where large smoky manufacturing warehouses, iron foundries and the like were located, and sections around Albert Square, St. Peter's Square, Piccadilly Square or Place, and the like. I also took a car to Salford and another to Stockport, in order to gather as quick a picture of the Manchester neighborhood as I could, of its general facial aspect. I could not see that it was in any way superior to St. Louis or Pittsburgh as these two cities existed fifteen or twenty years ago.

All of the great cities of present-day Europe are practically of modern construction. Most of them have grown to their present great population in the last fifty years. Hence they have been built—not rebuilt—in that time. An old thing in any of these modern cities is quite as conspicuous as the same thing would be in an American city—not more so. Manchester has no distinguished cathedral, only a shabby little parish church masquerading as one. It has five railway stations, three of them very large; and four or five fair-sized hotels, but only one of any distinction. The depots, while busy, seemed to be indescribably shabby—largely, I suppose, because of the grime and dark weather—but it seemed to me also that they lacked any distinction of design. The City Hall was large, with many gingerbready convolutions of stone, and the stock exchange was impressive, particularly the great interior room, 200 × 190 with twenty red marble columns nearly seventy feet high, and its round dome of colored glass dignified with a ribbon of biblical text—"A good name is rather to be chosen than great riches, and loving favour rather than silver and gold." I wondered how often, if ever, any of the anxious traders here ever speculated on that statement. The Bible propounds such knotty propositions for the average soul to contend with.

Salford, a part of Manchester, was nothing: great cotton and machine works and warehouses. Stockport was not anything either, save long lines of low brick cottages one and two stories high and mills, mills, mills, mills! It always astounds me how life repeats itself—any idea in life such as a design for a house—over and over and over. These houses in Salford, Stockport and Manchester proper were such as you might see anywhere in Chicago, St. Louis, Cincinnati, Baltimore—in the cheap streets. I had the sense of being pursued by a deadly commonplace. It all looked as people do when they think very little, know very little, see very little, do very little. I expected to learn that the churches flourished here very greatly and that there was an enormous Sunday school somewhere about. There was—at Stockport—the largest in the world, I was told, 50,000 students attending. What resources thoughts of infinity offer in contradistinction to such a life as this!

One of the things I did notice was my first pair of clogs or wooden-soled shoes with brass toe-clips, which the poorer working classes wear here. I had read of these things in some book—the clatter of them on the hard stone pavements in the morning, when the people were going off to work, or in the evening, when they were coming home. It had sounded rather sad and dramatic to me, and I was on the *qui vive* to see a pair. As I was boarding a car somewhere to go to Stockport, I heard a peculiar clattering behind me, and turned. A man was approaching, a marked peasant type such as the Huns and Slavs whom we import, only he was an Englishman. This struck me as strange. I had not got it into my head quite yet that England had a peasant class too, an English peasant class quite on a par intellectually and physically with the Huns and Poles. It astonished me. His clothes were very shabby, his face slightly rummy. He clattered past, solemnly sucking a pipe, and I said to myself quite distinctly, "Why, that man is an Englishman! He isn't a 'foreigner' at all!"

It all came to me in a flash then—the presence of an English peasant class—and I could scarcely get over it. I had always fancied that the English were above that, that they imported peasants ("foreigners") as we do. To think that this man should be bone of my bone and blood of my blood shocked me. I rode to Stockport, thinking about it, and walked all around there, up one long street and down another, only to be convinced by house after house and street after street that if England hasn't the equivalent of Austro-Hungarian low life, it is so near it that the difference is negligible. In America we import "foreigners." Here they grow.

I saw scores of children clattering about in what were practically wooden shoes. I saw houses of the smallest, cheapest kind, but always of brick paved with stone or brick floor. Always the kitchen, dining room and living room seemed to be just one—the same. Men and women both looked in a way so dull and stodgy. I was glad to see that most of them seemed clean—very. I wondered whether religion had anything to do with this. There was a drab silence hanging over it all, the pathetic dullness of the laborer when he has nothing to do save the one thing he cannot do—think. The streets were largely empty and silent—a dreary, narrow-minded, probably religious, conventional world which accepts this blank drabness as natural, ordered, probably even necessary. To the west and the south and the east and the north are great worlds of strangeness and wonder—new lands, new people—but these people can neither see nor hear. Here they are, harnessed to cotton mills, believing no doubt that God intended it to be so, working from youth to age without ever an inkling of the fascinating ramifications of life. It appalled me.

One of the things I did see and that interested me greatly was a football match which occurred later in the afternoon and which gave me my first and only view of a tremendous football crowd in England. It began in such a curious way, my discovery of it. I was walking down a rather bleak and shabby street with a tall chimney stack at the end of it, when I saw a young man come briskly out of a gate and strike out in the direction that I was going. I looked at him as a type, with his wooden shoes. Presently, as we turned a corner, another came out and went in the direction that I was going, quite smartly. Down this long street I saw three or four more all going in the same direction, and from a side street which emptied into this were trickling a few more.

The thought that all of these people might be going in any particular direction did not strike me at first. Later, as I saw them all turning in one direction around a given corner and that they were momentarily being added to by outpourings from houses and intersecting street corners, I became greatly interested. "This is something strange," I said. "Where can they all be going?" The idea of some church, a fire, a public square which I had not seen, all occurred to me. I followed on briskly.

In five minutes the original trickling stream became a torrent. This narrow red-walled street, through which we were pouring like a foaming stream between narrow banks, was resounding with the clatter of human feet, many of them shod with wooden shoes. It was not a gay crowd in any way. There was not much talking. It surged on and on, until I confess I was possessed by a vast enthusiasm to see the end of it. I was delighted to think that I should have been privileged to witness such a spectacle. Suddenly I saw the whole stream disappearing around a distant corner, and I hurried to that. What was my surprise to find a low wooden gate giving entrance to a large football field, possibly five acres in extent, which was surrounded by unprotected wooden seats.

A vast crowd was here, principally men and boys with a sprinkling of women, and the ground between the seats and the fence protecting the playing green proper was also preempted. A workaday crowd such as you might see at Lawrence or Lowell or Fall River, Massachusetts. I noted the commonplace character of their get-up. There was scarcely a well-dressed youth in the crowd. They were talking a form of English which I could not understand. It was fair English no doubt, but with such a queer accent and spoken so fast that I could not make it out. Now and then, when someone spoke slowly and distinctly, I caught a phrase or a sentence which I could understand. It struck me as so strange that in England I should not be able to understand offhand the workaday conversation of the English. The English papers and books are quite the same as ours. Why a difference in pronunciation that makes the language non-understandable to the ear?

I journeyed back to my car line, thinking of this and so many other things. The admission to this football game, which was obviously an event of great importance (one of the star games of the year, as I read the next morning), was sixpence, or a little more than ten cents in our money. The men who were playing were fine, rollicking specimens of manhood, stocky legs and arms and big chests—just the sort of animal a lush, damp climate should produce. At the end of the street, at an inn where I stopped for some toast and tea before returning to Manchester, I finally saw the aftermath of it all—a great crowd of hearty, enthusiastic Britons, part Irish, part Scotch, indulging in brandy and soda and rejoicing in the outcome. The inn was so old-fashioned, the toast and tea so good and so inexpensive, the room in which they all were before an open coal fire so charming that I began to think that Stockport and the north of England were not so bad. Anyhow they were used to it—smoke, rain, cotton mills, wooden shoes and all. I saw much worse than Stockport in the same vicinity, a grim, dark world generally. Fish manage to survive in any depth of sea, some sort of fish. Those who live in Manchester and its vicinage are one sort.

CHAPTER XXVIII

This same evening, by invitation, I attended a New Year's dinner at the Midland, the one grand annual public feast of the city, as I was told it was, at which the best and wealthiest of Manchester's society, its gayest blades and prettiest women, were supposed to attend. This interested me very much. In so dark and smoky a world, a gay scene as a contrast to the various facets of labor, grime, poverty, depression, etc., would be worthwhile. I accepted with alacrity. Mrs. Stubbs, to whom I had brought a letter and to whom Jerrard Grant Allen had written before my arrival, had phoned me and wanted to know if she could not show me a portion of the city in her automobile—for an hour or so in the afternoon, all the time she had. I declined, for I wanted to see one or two of the outlying places at my leisure, and I had no idea where I would wind up. Would I be back by seven or eight o'clock? Yes. Had I any engagement for the evening? No. Would I do her the honor to attend a New Year's Night dinner which was going to be held in this hotel beginning at nine? Some peculiarity of the local closing law, its rigidity, made it necessary to begin at this hour in order to be through by twelve, and some other difficulty in connection with the time which could be devoted to this function by local members of society made it necessary to give it on New Year's Night instead of New Year's Eve, which was the time for which it was intended. I did not get the significance of it all until I had talked considerably at the dinner table in the evening, but I agreed to come and find Mr. Stubbs, who was to seek me at the proper hour in the lobby.

At the stipulated time I met him.

From the description furnished me by Jerrard Grant Allen of Mrs. Stubbs, I was prepared to encounter a very charming woman, but I was certainly not prepared to encounter Mr. Stubbs and at such a gala function as this. He was a very little man, short, stocky, contentious, sour-looking. I do not think I ever met a more contentious or an artistically duller person in my life. He was quite bearish and disgruntled-looking. He did not seem to have a single idea outside of the machinery business in which he told me he was engaged. He met me with a peculiarly inquisitive glance, his eyes screwed up in a semicantankerous manner.

"Mr. Dreiser?" he asked.

"The same," I replied. "This is Mr. Stubbs?"

"My wife said I would find you here," he began indifferently. "She wants me to bring you over to her table. I'm glad to meet you. We'll find her in a moment. I understand you're an American. What part of America do you come from?"

"New York," I replied. "New York and the West. I was born in the West."

"You're a writer, as I understand it. Newspaperman?"

"I have been," I replied, not troubling to explain any further.

"We had a newspaperman come here from America three or four years ago. He came to look up the working conditions here. We showed him a lot of attention, but he did not get things right. Most of us felt pretty dissatisfied."

I had to smile. This unkindly reference to newspapermen, seeing I had just admitted that I was one, was most ungallant. I thought he might have been more courtly, seeing that I was his guest for the evening. Nevertheless he was interesting as a character. He seemed to resent my coming at all. He introduced me to some bystander who exchanged a few commonplaces with me, and then he led me to his wife.

As I had quite suspected, I found one of those faint, neurotic, nebulous types of middle-class business wives—not at all unpleasing to look upon, still comparatively young, devoted to art and reform, anxious to be a *grande dame* without the necessary aplomb, savoir faire, insight, etc. to be one. Really, in life I know of nothing more wearisome or pathetic. A little bit of the climber, let us say, without any real talent for it. A hazy, rag-bag thinker, caught by all the socialistic theories in regard to the relief of the masses, but quite without the courage or ability to espouse them in any large way; believing in universal peace, the recognition of the unions, the public ownership of some utilities, but uncertain about the emancipation of women, and so on. I had to smile at the tolerant way in which her husband spoke of her and her reforms—"My wife thinks so and so"—and at the same time her own serious air of weight and importance. At the same time, I was thoroughly convinced from a general survey of the situation that in addition to this mental and temperamental difference between them, she was either unfaithful to him in a minor way or wanted to be. She probably did not have the innate courage for that. I speculated casually as to how two such people ever came to marry each other. Money must have been the reason on one side, love of feminine beauty on the other.

This room in which we were was rapidly filling up, and I was interested to see the type of people who were entering to fill it—the best of Manchester's wealth and position, or wealth anyhow. There were scores of tables set with flowers and labeled with the names of the guests who were to sit at them. There was a central table, heavily decorated, reserved to the Lord Mayor and his friends. I noticed the presence of a number of navy and army officers and a large number of Jewish men and women. The latter looked exceedingly prosperous; they usually do. I was told afterward that the tremendous shipping interests of Manchester, to say nothing of much of the machinery world, was in their hands, that the wealthiest citizens were of that persuasion. Certainly those who were here tonight, pointed out to me as leading citizens, were forceful-looking enough. The women of this race, the young ones, were, as usual, the most attractive physically of all those present. They were large, plump, blonde, rosy-cheeked, much like large lily-white orchids bursting out of their corsages, their arms and shoulders were so plump and white. They displayed all the nervous, ambitious enthusiasm so characteristic of the Jewish women. All the time I could not get the notion out of my mind that I was not in Manchester, England, but St. Louis, Missouri. The temper of the two places is about identical. There are a large number of Germans in both. Music is cultivated to about the same extent. Beer is notably consumed. The manufacturing atmosphere is quite the same, only for cotton and machinery in the case of Manchester, substitute shoes and tobacco for St. Louis. The shipping interests are not so vastly different, although Manchester has only a canal. The negligible condition of art and letters is quite the same.

I have a warm spot in my heart for the purely dull, commonplace commercial conditions, wherever I find them, providing they are strong and stirring. It is always so interesting to me to be in an atmosphere in which people are hoping to be something. It is always a little savage and coarse where the strongest are concerned and a little hopeless and depressing where the weakest are seen, but as compared with the lackadaisical, condescending, nothing-further-to-be-done insouciance of those who have achieved or are definitely placed socially (which is the condition of so many in the south of England), give me the atmosphere of intense ambition, of combined hope and despair which you find in a place like Manchester or St. Louis.

I know that in the south of England, strange as it may seem to say it, the social conditions are not so marked (they are and they aren't), that is, the struggle between the rich and the poor is not so great. More small intellectual people in the south have a little money to live on. Nevertheless the conditions are worse. In the north of England, grim as the conditions are, there is still a chance for the common individual, slight as it may be. He can get rich. In the south of England, rich or not rich, he can never be anything, anyhow. There the noble lord, the friendly peer, lives with his commonalty in charming social civility, seemingly democratic recognition of the fact that they are human beings like himself, but there is nothing to it. He cannot see any of the commonalty rising to his level. In the north, the rich may exploit the poor, the strong the weak, but the poor and weak can nevertheless become rich and strong. You can feel it. It is in the air. The very atmosphere of class struggle and contention indicates it. The ability to succeed is the test in the north; the fortune of being born properly is the test in the south. Of course the new-rich in the north long to be taken up by the peerage of the south, to be made one of them, but that is neither here nor there. The conditions of opportunity are in the north, not the south.

And as I looked at this interesting gathering as it ate and chattered this night and talked with Mr. and Mrs. Stubbs and a Mr. and Mrs. Samble, to whom I was introduced and whom they sought and brought to this table, I realized that all this was true. This was not an English but an American atmosphere in which I found myself, with some modifications as to custom, climate, political and social beliefs. The women had all the eager, strident, showiness of the American woman, though the English women, barring the Jewesses who can scarcely be considered English any more than they can be American, were not as good-looking as the American women. The Jewesses were mostly beautiful, as I have said, bursting from their corsages and white satins and silks like great, wet water lilies. They wore the now rather wide bands of commonplace but effective white, blue, pink or orange ribbon around their heads; their garments were creamy with rich lace; their necks and arms a-glitter with diamonds and jewels of other kinds. They were gay and forceful—quite sensual. Laughing mouths, dancing eyes, high-pitched conversation of much gaiety was everywhere.

One of the amusing things was that this being Sunday, no liquor of any kind was supposed to be served—the "chapel people," as the religious-minded are dubbed in England, are strong enough to prevent this—but, in spite of the blue laws without, champagne was being consumed here in large quantities. Insofar as I could see, there was no one whose conscience was troubled about it. The usual air of the sophisticated prevailed, the freemasonry of the successful. Only this exotic burst of nature in this supposedly suppressed northern religious atmosphere was interesting. The chapel people might close the saloons and restaurants on Sunday at twelve midnight; they might prevent the sale of liquor to the rabble and the hoi polloi and close all stores and theaters, giving the city an absolutely funereal gloom, but they could not, however, suppress the moods of the strong and the sensuous, nor prevent them from having what they wished as elsewhere. I asked Mrs. Stubbs as a reformer what she thought of this. Her answer was an evasion. The ignorant sometimes carried their dullness too far. Still, the rich ought to be willing to conform. "Anyhow, they can go to London and Paris," she replied innocently. "They ought not to flaunt their superiority here." Later she admitted that she for one could not stand this atmosphere indefinitely. "It gets on one's nerves a little," she added.

Quite so. The strong, being properly suppressed here, go elsewhere to sip their joys, and so vice or human enthusiasm is properly segregated. The weak and inefficient or narrow and prejudiced are left to stew in their own juice of dreariness, which they make still drearier by driving out the only opportunity for contrast which the situation affords.

I had an inkling of how this spirit of religious oppression works and what it leads to (for want of contrast) right here in this room before I left, but before seeing it I had a long interesting talk concerning things English and American. Mrs. Stubbs had been to "the States." She had traveled from New York to San Francisco. I asked her what was the one thing she noticed most as standing out markedly in contrast to her life in England.

"Your lack of privacy," she replied.

"Lack of what?" I exclaimed.

"Privacy," she insisted. "You Americans have to do everything in public. I shall never forget the long trains on your roads full of people, all sitting together in cars. It was the same way in your restaurants. You all love to eat where everyone can see you. I wonder all the young men and women don't make love in public."

"I believe they are beginning to," I replied, thinking of our American parks.

"I shall never forget my sufferings on one of your Pullman trains. I couldn't get a separate compartment and I had to undress in the car—as much as I dared. I cried."

The enormity of the Pullman system came home to me at once. It was like a flash of lightning. Being purely American raised, I had always imagined, as Americans always do, that the American Pullman system, like the

American everything else, was the best in the world. Here was someone who did not see it at all, a woman of refinement who despised it. In Euston and Waterloo and Charing Cross and other sections in London, I had seen many of the comfortable little sleeping cars, furnishing a single section to each person—a bed, washstand, small table, dressing mirror, clothes hooks and the like, and all for no more money than the American Pullman Company charges. I took umbrage at my odd, silly belief at once. An old notion had died a sudden death in my head, killed by a fact. After that, my eyes began to open to some other defects of the American railway system.

But to continue. At twelve o'clock it became necessary for all to rise, join hands and sing "God Save the King." This was because this should have been done the preceding evening. We crossed hands in the center of the table and sang loudly. It was then that Mr. Stubbs made his only interesting remark.

"When we say 'God save the King,'" he confided to me, "we mean the government." His eye was screwed up most defiantly. I had to laugh.

At twelve-thirty I had eaten my way through a somewhat dull but ample dinner, and then it was that the general exodus began. I had learned why Mrs. Stubbs favored recognition of the unions and why Mr. Stubbs did not. He was down on them, and she opposed him. Universal peace had been disposed of by me by some interesting remarks in regard to the uselessness of peace as an implement of progress. There was much criticism of the unsatisfactory Americans as being not yet quite national, and some pride displayed on her part because she was "frequently taken for an American woman." We talked of the movement to establish a republic in China, which was then being fought out. Mrs. Stubbs had met Dr. Sun Yat-sen, the prime instigator. Suddenly the lights went out, as they invariably do all over England, at twelve-thirty o'clock, as a signal that by one all the guests must have departed.

Naturally, those who were most conservative, the Lord Mayor among them, arose and departed. Others not quite so responsible lingered until one, when the lights were turned low. After that, between one and two, many tables were cleared away, leaving considerable free space, and the manager and the headwaiters, as is the custom, were going about in the gloom, urging the remaining guests to depart.

"Gentlemen—please!"

"Gentlemen, it is time to leave!"

In one corner a drunken naval officer, surrounded by his fellow roisterers, was doing his best to engage in a fight with the manager of the hotel because the latter had urged him not to sing "God Save the King" so persistently when no one else was singing and not to throw wine on the floor. The charge of the naval officer was that this attitude was unpatriotic and that the manager, who, by the way, was a German, was a "middle-class dog." There were many sneering remarks indulged in by the officer as to breeding, training and the like. It looked like a real fracas for a while. In another section of this interesting caravansary, some of the young men and women were dancing, or trying to, which was also against the rules, though the management courteously refused to dismiss the orchestra until the very last had gone. All the conservatives, men and women, had departed by this time. Only the young, attractive or fiery remained.

In the half-light which was now the only illumination furnished—a single red or green table lamp here and there—might be seen the young bloods of the city and their inamoratas flirting vigorously. Some of the prettiest of the young women were sitting in the laps of the men. Champagne was being consumed lavishly. Bodices and hair-ribbons were sadly ruffled, and there was considerable preemptory and compulsory kissing behind the large, brown granite columns which aid in supporting the building here and there. I saw one girl, a flushed, lovely creature, charming to look on physically, kick a silver champagne bucket filled with cracked ice over on the floor and laugh heartily. Several others occasionally mounted tables and chairs. A few moments later a man near me, a rather gross specimen of the city's trader but very gay and genial, picked up a long, thin length of robin's egg blue ribbon, which had been pulled from someone's lingerie, and gathering it up in his brown hands, pressed it eagerly to his nose.

"How would you like to be where that came from?" he asked cheerfully.

I smiled sociably, taking the remark in good part.

"Give me that!" called another of his own type, seizing it and trying to pull it away. "I need something like that to sleep with."

"Not on your life," replied the first in typical American English. "That goes under my pillow." He pulled it back and stuffed it in his waistcoat pocket. This went on until nearly three, when the various members of the company, after much urging on the part of the management, were bundled into automobiles and disappeared.

In spite of the gloom and the smoke of the north, I had seen that the orgiastic temperament of the race was not cured by any means by law, that it was merely suppressed. "They go to Paris or London," Mrs. Stubbs had said.

Quite so—or they conduct themselves wildly and vigorously at home behind expensive doors.

CHAPTER XXIX

After my dinner of the evening before, at which I had seen so much of what might be called the *haut monde* of this northern world, I was all the more interested to visit the outlying sections of this region which I had come to see—Rochdale, Middleton, Oldham, Bolton, Wigan, etc.—all of which were nearby and all of which had been reported to me as grim, dark, sad, pointless—a world concerned with pathetic labor only and in no way lightened by gaiety or amusements of any kind. I wanted to see for myself. I have a theory that there is a grandeur of darkness, bleakness, sadness, dullness, quite as there is of spirit and light. It requires but the eye to see. Wherein is light better than darkness and white better than black, and how would the one have its value without the other? I may as well say at the opening that I was well repaid.

In some respects, I think, I never saw so dreary a world. Yet in saying this, I do not wish to indicate that the working conditions are any worse than, if as bad as, those which prevail in various American cities such as Pittsburgh, Philadelphia, Boston, Chicago, and especially in the minor cities such as Lowell, Lawrence, Fall River, Providence, New Brunswick and cities of that level. I don't think I ever saw or could see worse conditions than I saw in Lawrence and Fall River. But be that as it may; here was a dark workaday world, quite unfavored by climate, a country in which damp and fogs prevail for fully three-fourths of the year and where a pall of smoke is always present. I remember reading a sign on one of the railway platforms leading to Bolton this second day, which stated that owing to the prevalence of fogs the company could not be held responsible for the running of trains on time. I noticed, too, that the smoke and damp were so thick everywhere that occasionally the trees on the roadside or the houses over the way would disappear in lovely, Corot-like mist. Lamps were burning in all stores and office buildings this morning I ventured out. Streetcars carried headlamps and dawned upon you out of a hazy gloom. Traffic disappeared in a thick blanket a half-block away. I was delighted that anything so black and grimy as this workaday life should have such an artistic setting of mist.

The second thing that contributed greatly to the character of this world was the smallness and the cheapness and the sameness of the houses. There is much of that everywhere in this world, but there could not possibly be more than there is here—long lines of one- and two-story houses, deeply tinged with soot, their windows quite small and set with narrow panes of glass, the chimneys all of the same size and shape and all in the same position. I noticed that, as in London, many of the houses were built of a gray or mud-colored brick which, when tinged with smoke, made them far more pleasing to look on than those built of the more expensive red. Insofar as the shops and stores were concerned, I could see no variation from what one finds in the poorer streets of London, Chicago, St. Louis, what you will.

Most of these outlying towns had populations ranging from 90,000 to 100,000, but insofar as interesting or entertaining developments of civic life were concerned, proportioned to their size, there were none. They might as well have been villages of 500 or 1,000. Houses, houses, houses, all of the same size, all the same color, all of the same interior arrangement, virtually. It is always astonishing to me to find how nature loves to repeat itself in everything. There are two billion people on this earth, all with two legs, two arms, two eyes, two ears, etc., and the only reason we don't become nauseated with the whole proposition and die is because we see so little of them—we meet really so few intimately in the course of a single life. It is equally true of ducks, green apples, any minor-sized thing. Only the relatively large is scarce—mountains, moons, seas. Every other thing is repeated ad nauseam.

Here in Middleton, Oldham, Rochdale, which I visited the first day, and in Bolton, Blackburn and Wigan, which I visited the next, I found this curious multiplication of the same thing which you could dismiss with a glance—whole streets, areas, neighborhoods, of which you could say, "All alike." In Middleton I was impressed with the constant repetition of "front rooms" or "parlors" all alike. You could look in through scores of partly open doors (this climate is damp but not cold) and see in each a chest of drawers exactly like every other chest in this place, and in the same position relative to the door. Nearly all the round tables which these front rooms contained were covered with a pink-patterned tablecloth. The small single windows, one to each house, contained a blue or yellow jardiniere set on a small table and containing geraniums. The fireplace, always to the right of the room as you looked in the window, glowed with a small coal fire. There were no other ornaments that I saw. The ceilings of the rooms were exceedingly low and the total effect was one of clean, frugal poverty, such as you see in Holland.

One of the most interesting things to me was to see this low, humble world of cottages, little huts of brick hugging the ground, dominated as to skyline by tall, imposing cotton mill buildings of red brick, oblong, seven or eight stories high, pierced with endless windows and ornamented by an immense round stack of the same color which soared high in the air over all and emitted a lovely plume of black smoke, blending artistically into the gray sky and air. As usual I was told it was threatening rain. These mills, bearing pleasing names such as Rob Roy, Tabitha, Marietta, looked down upon the humbler habitations at their base much as the famous castles of the feudal barons must have looked down upon the huts of their retainers. I was constrained to think of the workaday existence that all this suggested, the long lines of cotton-mill employees going in at seven o'clock in the morning in the dark and coming out at six at night in the dark. Many of these mills employ a day and a night shift. Their windows, when agleam in the smoke or rain, are like patins of fine gold. I saw them gleaming at the end of dull streets or across the smooth, olive-colored surface of millponds. In going home this night (home being the Midland hotel), I saw them gleaming through mist and rain. The few that I heard (the majority of them were shut down because of the strike) had a roar like that of Niagara tumbling over its rocks—a delicious, ominous thunder. I could not help thinking of the vast quantities of cotton cloth these mills must weave.

In recent years, because of American and possibly German competition—I don't know—the mill owners have abandoned the old low, two-story type of building with its narrow windows and dingy aspect of gray stones, and erected the enormous structures, the only approach to the American skyscraper I saw in England, in their stead. They are wonderful mills, far superior to the ones you will see today in Fall River, Providence and Lawrence. They are really magnificent as mill structures, clean, bright and, every one that I saw, new. If I should rely upon my merely casual impression, I should say that there were a thousand such within twenty-five miles of Manchester. When seen across a foreground of low cottages such as I have described, they have all the dignity of cathedrals—vast temples of labor. I was told by the American Consul-General at London that they are equipped with the very latest cotton-spinning machinery and are now in a position to hold their own on equal terms with, if not utterly to defy, American competition. The intricacy and efficiency of the machinery is greater than that employed in American mills.

I could not help thinking what a far cry it was from these humble cottages, some few of which in odd corners looked like the simple thatched huts sacred to Burns and "The Cotter's Saturday Night," to these lordly mills and the lordly owners behind them—the strong, able, ruthless men whom I saw eating in the breakfast room at the Midland the day before. Think of the poor little girls and boys—principally girls—clattering to work in the dark of a misty morning in their wooden shoes, and if you will believe it (I saw it at Bolton in January and a cold rain), in thin black shawls and *white straw hats* much darkened by continuous wear! I never saw a more pathetic sight in my life. The particular crowd that I saw was pouring out at high noon. I heard a great whistle yelling its information in regard to noon, and then a little mouse-hole of a door in one corner of the great structure opened, and out poured this little black stream. By comparison it looked like a small procession of ants or a trickle of black water. Small as it was, however, it soon filled the street, and then I heard the great clattering of wooden-soled clogs. Someone ought to write the song of the clogs. They came, a dreary mass in the rain, some of them carrying umbrellas, some not, *all* wearing straw hats and black shawls! Can you imagine anything drabbier than a black shawl and a dirty, wide-brimmed straw hat in a rain? Don't forget the climate—wet, smoky, gray. Don't forget the general effect of the atmosphere—dark. Don't forget the windows gleaming here and there at high noon with lights. There you have it. It touched me deeply.

I looked at the faces of these women—pale, waxy, dull, inefficient. I looked at their shapeless skirts hanging like bags about their feet. I looked at their flat chests, their graceless hands, and then I thought of the strong men who know how to use (I will not say exploit) inefficiency. What would these women do if they could not work in these mills? What would they learn, sitting at home? What would they do with much money if they had it? Give it to some cause, buy trash with it. I am not sure. One thing that I am sure of is that these great big mills, whatever charges may be brought against their owners in regard to hours, insufficiency of payment, indifference of treatment, are nevertheless better places to me than these humble little cottages with their commonplace little round of duties. What can one learn washing dishes and scrubbing floors in a cottage? I can see someone jumping up exclaiming, "What can one learn tying commonplace threads in a cotton mill, taking care of eight or nine machines, one lone woman? What has she time to learn?" This, if you ask me: the single thought of organization, if nothing more. The thought that there is such a thing as a great machine that can do the work of fifty or a hundred men. It will not do to say the average individual can learn this without working in a mill. It is not true.

What the race needs is ideas. It needs thoughts of life and injustice and justice and opportunity, or the lack of it, kicked into its senseless clay. It needs to be made to think by some rough process or other (gentleness won't do it), and this is one way. I like labor leaders. I like big, raw, crude, hungry men who are eager for gain, for self-glorification. I like to see them plotting to force such men as I saw breakfasting at the Midland to give them something—and the people beneath them. I am glad to think that the ground that has got up, that walks, that runs, that sings, that wears black shawls and straw hats in January, has sense enough at last to appoint these raw, angry fellows who scheme and struggle and fight and show their teeth and call great bitter strikes such as I saw here and such as had shut tight so many of those great solemn mills. It speaks much for the race. It speaks much for *thinking*, which is becoming more and more common. There won't be so many women with drabby skirts and flat chests and straw hats in January if this goes on.

There won't be so many strong, able men sitting at sumptuous breakfasts at the Midland saying in polite language "to hell with them." There will still be strong men and weak—we will never do away with the mountains—but the conditions may not be so severe. Anyhow, let us hope so, for it is such a nice, optimistic thought, and I like it. It cheers one in the face of all the drab streets and the drab people. I have no hope of making millionaires of everybody, nor of establishing that futile abstraction, justice; but I do cherish the idea of seeing the world growing better and more interesting for everybody. And the ills which make for thinking are the only things which will bring this about.

At Middleton I had a very interesting experience. Middleton is such a dull old hole. Its mills are majestically large and its cottages relatively minute. There is a famous old inn here, very picturesque to look upon, and Somebody of Something's comfortable manor, but they were not the point for me. In one of its old streets, in the dark doorway of an old house, I encountered an old woman, very heavy, very pale, very weary, who stood leaning against her doorpost.

"What do you burn here, gas or oil?" I asked, interested to obtain information on almost any topic and seeking a pretext for talking to her.

"Hey?" she replied, looking at me wearily but making no other move.

"What do you burn?" I asked, "What do you use for light—gas or oil?"

"Ile," she replied heavily, as though she were very tired. "You'll have to talk very loud," she mumbled. "I'm gettin' old and I'm goin' to die pretty soon."

"Oh, no," I said, "you're not old enough for that. You're going to live a long time yet."

"Hey?" she asked.

I repeated what I had said.

"No," she mumbled, and now I saw she had no teeth, "I'm gettin' old. I'm eighty-two and I'm goin' to die. I been workin' in the mills all my life."

"Have you ever been out of Middleton?" I asked.

"Hey?" she replied.

I repeated.

"Yes, to Manchester, Saturdays. Not of late, though. Not in years and years. I'm very sick, though, now. I'm goin' to die."

I could see from her looks that what she said was true. Only her exceeding weariness employed her mind. I learned that water came from a hydrant in the yard, that the kitchen floor was of earth. Then I left, turning to see if her shoes were of wood as to their soles. They were. Weariness and an earth floor were all that life had left her.

At Rochdale I saw where John Bright once lived and where the few mill-hands with twenty-eight pounds capital started the Society of Equitable Pioneers, now numbering over 13,000 members and having 390,000 pounds capital. At Oldham I saw the largest collection of mill stacks I ever saw anywhere, seemingly endless mills. On a clear day, so said the Baedeker I carried, six hundred could be seen. At Bolton I saw the City Hall, a not unattractive structure, completely surrounded by a shabby circus, the small stone-paved public square having been let for that purpose. I never saw so dreary a scene. Dauby, flaring pictures of the fat lady and the two-headed boy were strung along the sidewalks, yellow and red show and animal wagons were backed up against the walls of the City Hall. A small dining room tent was under the Mayor's window, and a horrible, stuffy cooking wagon stood to one side of the main entrance. I never saw so peculiar a scene. The whole square was crowded with tents great and small, but there was little going on, for there was a drizzling rain in progress. Can human dullness sink lower, I asked myself, feeling that the civic heart of things was being profaned. Could utmost drabbiness out-drab this? I doubt it. Why should the aldermen permit it? Yet I have no doubt this situation appealed exactly to the imagination of the working population. I can conceive that it would be about the only thing that would. It was just raw and cheap and homely enough to do it. I left with pleasure.

CHAPTER XXX

I reserve for this final chapter my impressions of Oldham. I might say much of Wigan, with its sooty-faced miners and frowsy-looking women and children in the poorer sections; or of Bolton, with its tall factories and grimy streets; but I reserve for Oldham the rest that I have to say. I consider Oldham an idyll in drab. When I came into the city in a streetcar from Rochdale, it was with my head swimming from the number of mills I had seen. I have described the kind—all new. It was misting or about to rain, and the streets were quite gloomy, lowery. I was hungry and wanted to find the best restaurant. The place has 150,000 inhabitants. At the principal corner, where two lines of cars crossed and where a policeman stood on guard, I dismounted. Here was the man who could tell me what I wished to know.

"Where shall I find the best restaurant, officer?" I asked, observing him with that care with which one "takes in" a local type.

"Well, now, let me see," he cogitated, adjusting his short truncheon to his chin and surveying the street philosophically. "About the best we have here is the Kafe Monaco—I think you'll find that'll be the best. If you will just go to the next corner there and turn up two blocks, you'll see it. It's in a basement. You can't miss it."

"The Cave Monaco," I repeated. I thought he had said "Cave."

"The Kafe Monaco," he replied with genial dignity. "Just around the corner."

Many Americans have the idea, I am sure, the vast majority of them, that the genus Rube, meaning in the language of the cognoscenti "hayseed," "farmer," "backwoodsman," "jay"—that interesting type of uninformed, inexperienced, good-natured, curious albeit intelligent individual—is common to America and has not even an approximate counterpart anywhere. They are wrong. I had the idea, like most others, that this was true, and was compelled to smile on encountering him here in Oldham in the form of a policeman. Although occupying the central position at the principal street crossing in a city of 150,000, his idea of the pronunciation of café was *kafe*, and his whole manner indicated a naive curiosity. For a policeman he had a peculiarly American backwoodsy look, for an Englishman a kind of sprawling nonchalance which was as humorous as it was inquisitive, and I had to abandon my idea that America had the only species of backwoodsman fit for humorous consumption. Like the idea of the American sleeping car I had entertained—namely, that it was the best in the world—here was another, that the naive "Rube" exists only in the United States, gone glimmering. England in the north here, where the citizens are more like American types than they are Englishmen and the cities and towns are more like American cities and towns of the same class than they are like those of the rest of England, produces the "country jake," who is more like the American product described by this term than he is like anything else in England. It was delightful.

I did not go to the "Kafe" Monaco direct, however, in spite of my hunger. Once I had time to survey this center of things, I decided that it was worth much more attention. Because of the heavy, damp, gray, smoky atmosphere, the reddish-black and blackish-gray color of the buildings, their low size, the cheap, unimportant displays of goods in windows and the general atmosphere of narrow workaday life, I decided to remain and investigate. Lunch could wait. In several places I found small eating places labeled "fish, chip and pea restaurant" and "tripe, trotters and cow-heels restaurant," which astonished me greatly, really astonished me. I had seen only one such before in my life, and that was this same morning in Middleton—a "fish, chip and pea restaurant," but I did not get the point sufficiently clear to make a note of it. The one that I encountered this afternoon had a sign in the window which stated that unquestionably its chips were the best to be procured anywhere and very nourishing. A plate of them standing close by made it perfectly plain that it was potato chips which were meant. No recommendation was given to either the fish or the peas. I pondered over this, thinking that such restaurants must be due to the poverty of the people and that prices for meat being very high, these three things were substituted. Here in Oldham, however, I saw that several of these restaurants stood in very central places where the rents should be reasonably high and the traffic brisk. It looked as though they were popular for some other reason. I asked a policeman.

"What is a 'fish, chip and pea restaurant'?" I asked.

"Well, to tell you the truth," he said, "it's a place where a man who's getting over a spree goes to eat. Those things are good for the stomach."

I pondered over this curiously, because in the first place, matters of diet interest me, and because in the second, there were four such restaurants in this immediate vicinity, to say nothing of one labeled "tripe, trotters and cow-heels," which astonished me still more.

"And what's that for?" I asked of the same officer.

"The same thing. A man who's been drinking eats those things."

I had to laugh, and yet this indicated another thing characteristic of a wet, rainy climate—namely, considerable drinking. I wondered whether Oldham men were particularly drunken, strolled on to the next corner and was slightly confirmed in this by seeing a man, a woman and a child conferring. "Come on," said the man to the woman all at once. "Let's go to the pub. A beer'll do you good." The three started off together, the child hanging by the woman's hand. I followed them with my eyes, for I could not imagine quite such a scene in America, not done just in this way. Women—a certain type—go to the back rooms of saloons well enough; children are sent with pails for beer. But just this particular combination of husband, wife and child is rare, I am sure.

And such public houses! To satisfy myself of their character, I went to three in three different neighborhoods. Like those I saw in London and elsewhere around it, they were pleasant enough in their arrangement, but gloomy. The light from the outside was meager, darkened as it was by smoke and rain. If you went on back into the general lounging room, lights were immediately turned on, for it was not bright enough to see otherwise. If you stayed in the front at the bar proper, it was still dark, and one light, a mantled gas-jet, was kept burning. I asked the second barmaid with whom I conferred about this, "You don't always have to keep a light burning here, do you?"

"Always, except two or three months in summer," she replied. "Sometimes in July and August we don't need it. As a rule we do."

"Surely it isn't always dark and smoky like this?"

"You should see it sometimes, if you call this bad," she replied contemptuously. "It's black."

"I should say it's very near that now," I commented.

"Oh no, most of the mills are not running. You should see it when it's foggy and the mills are running."

She seemed to take a sort of pride in the matter, and I sympathized with her. It is rather distinguished to live in an extreme of any kind, even if it is only that of a smoky wetness of climate. I went out, making my way to the "Kafe" Monaco, where I enjoyed such a meal as only a third-rate restaurant, which is considered first by the local inhabitants, would supply.

This matter of a city's restaurants always interests me. In manufacturing towns of any size they are the most interesting indications of local conditions that one could desire. If there is any liberality of spending in any community, it usually shows itself in some form of public amusement or entertainment, most usually in a good restaurant. You can almost always depend on this—that if there is not at least one restaurant in a city of a population of one hundred thousand which is not moderately satisfactory in the way of food and is not somewhat gay and showy in its atmosphere, the general life of the city will be found to be unutterably workaday and drab. I found this to be true in my examination of so many American cities—Fall River, Lawrence, Lowell, Providence, Paterson and New Brunswick—and I am prone to believe it is true of other places. Not a single restaurant worthy of the name did any of them contain. And the life!

Here in Oldham I was prepared for a similar revelation, and I was not disappointed. The "Kafe" Monaco was in a basement, entered by an outside stairway which was lined with marble in a showy way, but this did not reassure me. A post somewhere, a supporting pillar, was completely covered with polished brass, a solecism characteristic of modern saloon life for some reason. The tables I saw at once were nicely equipped with good linen—perhaps due to the manufacturing of this article which goes on here—but for the rest I could not say much in praise. The dishes were notably commonplace—porcelain and cutlery, cheap. The food was not good at all, rather bad in a pretentious way, and it did not help any that a large and closely-printed bill of fare was furnished. When I called for the filet of flounder which was so briskly announced, I found that they did not have it, and the French pancakes listed among the sweets were a myth. I had hoped to discover my old friend and standby, steak-and-kidney pudding, but alas, this bill of fare was above anything so lowly. Chops and steaks were the distinguishing feature of this restaurant, and so I contented myself with a poorly-broiled chop and tea, swearing internally at the cheap make-believe which will offer the shadow of superiority without the substance. Oldham must have a "Kafe" Monaco with a long list of interesting dishes, but no real restaurant. It is always so.

I journeyed from here into the streets once more, interested by the fact that Baedeker had said that from one point somewhere, *on a clear day*, whenever that might be, six hundred stacks might be seen. Six hundred stacks is some stacks, I would have you know. If one could see them together, they would be worth looking at. In this fog it was no good looking for them. Instead, I contented myself with studying the architecture of the streets and noting how in so many cases the end of a street, or the sheer dismal length of an unbroken row of houses, all alike, was honored, made picturesque, made grand, even, by the presence of these gloomy monuments of labor.

There is an architecture of manufacture, almost invariably as dreary and shabby as its setting, which to me in its solemnity, strangeness of outline, pathos and dignity, quite rivals, if it does not surpass, the more heralded forms of the world—its cathedrals, parthenons, Moorish temples and the like. I have seen it often in America and elsewhere, where a group of factory buildings, unplanned as to arrangement and undignified as to substance, would yet take on exquisite harmony of line and order after which a much more pretentious institution might well have been modeled. At Stockport, near Manchester, for instance, on the Mersey, which is here little more than a rivulet but picturesque and lovely, I saw grouped a half-dozen immense mills with towering chimneys which, for architectural composition, from the vantage point of the stream, could not have been surpassed. They had much of the dignity of vast temples, and I thought of them in that light, housing a world of underpaid life which was nevertheless rich in color and enthusiasm. Sometimes I fancy the modern world has produced nothing more significant, architecturally speaking, than the vast manufactory. Here in Oldham again they were gathered in notable clusters, towering over the business heart and the various residence sections, so that the whole scene might well be said to have been dominated by it. Involuntarily there rose in me a strange feeling of narrowness and repression. For the time being, I took on the hunger, the poverty, that general attitude of mind in which little is much. I think that is what we all do—more or less—under such circumstances, only some resent it and hurry away. To me, the point of view of the man at the bottom is always fascinating and well worth considering.

I wandered the streets, looking in the store windows and seeing what was sold. I must say it was not inspiring. The clothing, for instance, such of it as was displayed, was not smart—anything but—and the material calculated to gratify or entertain the artistic side of the population was practically nothing. I did see a piano store where phonographs were principally sold, and a leather goods emporium, though the material offered was trashy. In one store window, though, I found a pair of gold and a pair of silver slippers offered for sale—for what feet in Oldham? They were not of good gold or silver cloth, and the price was negligible, but this sudden burst of romance in a dark workaday world took my fancy. I wondered what mill girl, if any, would wear them, and what illusion of high life they would give her. They seemed so out of place here. Better the clogs, it seemed to me, which I heard clattering about me, or the "tripe, trotters and cow-heels" of the drunkard, than this. And yet, why not? Do they really not harmonize well together?

It was at four o'clock, after several hours of wandering about the dull, rain-sodden streets, that I returned to the main thoroughfare, the market-place, in order to see what it was the 150,000 found to entertain themselves with. I looked for theaters and found two, one of them a large motion-picture affair. If there were any restaurants other than the "Kafe" Monaco, I did not find them. Drug stores, boot-and-shoe places, groceries, hardware, small dry-goods—so it went, an endless ruck of little businesses. For entertainment I suppose those who are not religiously-minded do as they do in Fall River and elsewhere: walk up and down past the bright shop windows or sit in the public houses (unquestionably far more cheerful by night than by day) and drink.

But the thing that interested me most of all happened in connection with this same motion-picture theater—the Grand Palace, I think it was called. I had been speculating on this same matter of entertainment when, of a sudden, walking in a certain direction, my ears were greeted by a most euphonious, and I can even say mellifluous, clatter—so interwoven were the particular sounds which I recognized at once as coming from the feet of a multitude shod with wooden-soled clogs. Where were they coming from? I saw no crowd. Suddenly, up a side street, coming toward me down a slope, I detected them, a vast throng. The immense motion-picture theater had closed for the afternoon, and its entire audience, perhaps 2,000 in all, was descending toward this main street. In connection with this crowd, as with the other at Bolton, I noted the phenomenon of the black or white straw hat, the black or brown shawl, the shapeless skirts and wooden-soled clogs of the women; the dull, commonplace suit and wooden clogs of the men. Where were they going now? Home, of course. These must be a portion of the strikers. They looked to me like typical mill workers out on a holiday, and their faces mostly had a waxy pallor. I liked this sound of their shoes, though, as they came along—this song of the clogs. It was like a grand clatter of small drums. They might have been dancing or waltzing on a wooden floor. The thing had a swing and a rhythm of its own. "What if a marching army were shod with wooden shoes?" I thought, and then, "What if a mob with guns and swords came clattering so?"

A crowd like this is like a flood of water pouring downhill. They came into the dark main street, and it was quite brisk for a time with their presence. Then they melted away into the totality of the stream, as rivers do into the sea, and things were as they had been before.

The thing that struck me about Oldham, as it has about nearly every other place of the same kind that I have ever been in, is that if the moving pictures or cheap theaters of one form and another furnish some slight entertainment in this workaday world, the vast majority who live here must fall back on other things—their work, their church, their family duties or their vices—for diversion. I am satisfied, for one thing, that under such conditions sex plays a far more vital part in cities of this description than almost anywhere else. For although the streets be dull and the duties of life commonplace, sex and the mysteries of temperament weave their spells quite as effectively here as elsewhere, if not more so. In fact, denied the more varied outlets of a more interesting world, humanity falls back almost exclusively on sex, and I felt this this afternoon in this main street.

Women and men, or rather boys and girls (for most of the women and men grown had a drudgy, disillusioned, wearied look), went by each other glancing and smiling. They were alert to be entertained by each other, and while I saw little that I would call beauty in the women, or charm and smartness in the men—on the contrary—nevertheless I could understand how New York and Paris standards might not necessarily prevail here. Clothes may not fit, fashion may find no suggestion of its dictates, but after all, underneath, the lure of temperament and of beauty is the same. And so these same murky streets may burn with a rich passional life of their own. I left Oldham finally in the dark and in a driving rain, but not without a sense of the sturdy vigor of the place, keen if drab. Through the rain and the mist I saw great mills gleaming in the dark, lovely phantasms of labor, and I realized that here, no less than in the most perfect haunts of pleasure, the palaces of light and color, this wonderful warp of life is being spun. Its diaphanous weft is a little darker here, but what of it? This is the dark that contrasts so well with light elsewhere, and there always is the dark.

"And must be?" I can hear some eager reformer exclaiming critically.

Let him who has discovered paradise lead the way.

CHAPTER XXXI

One evening I went with a friend of mine to visit the Houses of Parliament, that noble pile of buildings on the banks of the Thames. For days I had been skirting about them, interested in other things. The clock-tower, with its great round clock-face—twenty-three feet in diameter, someone told me—had been staring me in the face over a stretch of park space and intervening buildings on such evenings as Parliament was in session, and I frequently debated with myself whether I should trouble to go or not, even if someone invited me. I grow so weary of standard, completed things at times! However, I did go. It came about through the Hon. T. P. O'Connor, M.P., an old admirer of *Sister Carrie*, who, hearing that I was in London, invited me. He had just finished reading *Jennie Gerhardt* the night I met him, and I shall never forget the kindly glow of his face as, on meeting me in the dining room of the House of Commons, he exclaimed:

"Ah, the biographer of that poor girl! And how charming she was, too! Ah me! Ah me!"

I can hear the soft brogue in his voice yet and see the gay romance of his Irish eye. Are not the Irish all inborn cavaliers, anyhow?

I had been out in various poor sections of the city all day, speculating on that shabby mass that have nothing, know nothing, dream nothing; or do they? It was most depressing, as dark fell, to return through long, humble streets alive with a home-hurrying mass of people—clouds of people not knowing whence they came or why. And now I was to return and go to dine where the laws are made for all England.

I was escorted by another friend, a Mr. M., since dead, who was, when I reached the hotel, quite disturbed lest we be late. I like the man who takes society and social forms seriously, though I would not be that man for all the world. M. was one such. He was, if you please, a stickler for law and order. The Houses of Parliament and the repute of the Hon. T. P. O'Connor meant much to him. I can see O'Connor's friendly, comprehensive eye understanding it all—understanding in his deep, literary way why it should be so.

As I hurried through Westminster Hall, the great general entrance, once itself the ancient Parliament of England, the scene of the deposition of Edward II, of the condemnation of Charles I, of the trial of Warren Hastings and the poling of the exhumed head of Cromwell, I was thinking, thinking, thinking. What is a place like this, anyhow, but a fanfare of names? If you know history, the long, strange tangle of steps or actions by which life ambles crabwise from nothing to nothing, you know that it is little more than this. The present places are the thing, the present forms, salaries, benefices and that dream of the mind which makes it all into something. As I walked through into Central Hall, where we had to wait until Mr. O'Connor was found, I studied the high, groined arches, the Gothic walls, the graven figures of the general anteroom. It was all rich, gilded, dark, lovely. And about me was a room full of men all titillating with a sense of their own importance—commoners, lords possibly, callboys, ushers, and here and there persons crying of "Division! Division!" while a bell somewhere clanged raucously.

"There's a vote on," observed Mr. M. "Perhaps they won't find him right away. Never mind; he'll come."

He did come finally, with, after his first greetings, a "Well, now we'll eat, drink, and be merry," and then we went in.

At table, being an old member of Parliament, he explained many things swiftly and interestingly, how the buildings were arranged, the number of members, the procedure and the like. He was, he told me, a member from Liverpool, which, by the way, returns some Irish members, which struck me as rather strange for an English city.

"Not at all, not at all. The English like the Irish—at times," he added softly.

"I have just been out in your East End," I said, "trying to find out how tragic London is, and I think my mood has made me a little color-blind. It's rather a dreary world, I should say, and I often wonder whether lawmaking ever helps these people."

He smiled that genial, equivocal, sophisticated smile of the Irish that always bespeaks the bland acceptance of things as they are, and tries to make the best of a bad mess.

"Yes, it's bad"—and nothing could possibly suggest the aroma of a brogue that went with this—"but it's no worse than some of your American cities—Lawrence, Lowell, Fall River." (Trust the Irish to hand you an intellectual "You're another!") "Conditions in Pittsburgh are as bad as anywhere, I think; but it's true the East End is pretty bad. You want to remember that it's typical London winter weather we're having, and London smoke makes those gray buildings look rather forlorn, it's true. But there's some comfort there, as there is everywhere. My old Irish father was one for thinking that we all have our rewards here or hereafter. Perhaps theirs is to be hereafter." And he rolled his eyes humorously and sanctimoniously heavenward.

An able man this, full, as I knew, from reading his weekly and his books, of a deep, kindly understanding of life, but one who, despite his knowledge of the tragedies of existence, refused to be cast down.

He was going up the Nile shortly in a houseboat with a party of wealthy friends, and he told me that Lloyd George, the champion of the poor, was just making off for a winter outing on the Riviera, but that I might, if I would come some morning, have breakfast with him. He was sure that the great commoner would be glad to see me. He wanted me to call at his rooms, his London official offices, as it were, at 5 Morpeth Mansions, and have a pleasant talk with him, which latterly I did.

While he was in the midst of it, the call of "Division!" sounded once more through the halls, and he ran to take his place with his fellow parliamentarians on some question of presumably vital importance. I can see him bustling away in his long frock coat, his napkin in his hand, ready to be counted yea or nay, as the case might be.

Afterwards when he had outlined for me a tour in Ireland which I must sometime take, he took us up into the members' gallery of the Commons in order to see how wonderful it was, and we sat as solemn as owls, contemplating the rather interesting scene below. I cannot say that I was seriously impressed. The Hall of Commons, I thought, was small and stuffy, not so large as the House of Representatives at Washington, by any means.

In delicious Irish whispers he explained a little concerning the arrangement of the place. The seat of the speaker was at the north end of the chamber on a straight line with the sacred woolsack of the House of Lords in another part of the building, however important that may be. If I would look under the rather shadowy canopy at the north end of this extremely square chamber, I would see him, "smothering under an immense white wig," he explained. In front of the canopy was a table, the speaker's table, with presumably the speaker's official mace lying upon it. To the right of the speaker were the recognized seats of the government party, the ministers occupying the front bench. And then he pointed out to me Mr. Lloyd George, Mr. Bonar Law (Unionist member and leader of the opposition), and Mr. Winston Churchill, all men creating a great stir at the time. They were whispering and smiling in genial concert, while opposite them, on the left hand of the speaker, where the opposition was gathered, some droning M.P. from the North, I understood, a noble lord, was delivering one of those typically intellectual commentaries in which the British are fond of indulging. I could not see him from where I sat, but I could see him just the same. I knew that he was standing very straight, in the most suitable clothes for the occasion, his linen immaculate, one hand poised gracefully, ready to emphasize some rather obscure point, while he stated in the best English why this and this must be done. Every now and then, at a suitable point in his argument, some friendly and equally intelligent member would give voice to a soothing "Hyah! hyah!" or "Rathah!" Of the four hundred and seventy-six provided seats, I fancy, something like over four hundred were vacant, their occupants being out in the dining rooms, or off in those adjoining chambers where parliamentarians confer during hours that are not pressing, and where they are sought at the call for a division. I do not presume, however, that they were all in any so safe or sane places. I mock-reproachfully asked Mr. O'Connor why he was not in his seat, and he said in good Irish:

"Me boy, there are thricks in every thrade. I'll be there whin me vote is wanted."

We came away finally through long, floriated passages and towering rooms, where I paused to admire the intricate woodwork, the splendid gilding and the tier upon tier of carven kings and queens in their respective niches. There was for me a flavor of great romance over it all. I could not help thinking that, pointless as it all might be, such joys and glories as we have are thus compounded. Out of the dull blatherings of half-articulate members, the maunderings of dreamers and schemers, come such laws and such policies as best express the moods of the time—of the British or any other empire. I have no great faith in laws. To me, they are ill-fitting garments at best, traps and mental catchpoles for the unwary only. But I thought, as I came out into the swirling city again, "It is a strange world. These clock-towers and halls will sometime fall into decay. The dome of our own Capitol will be rent and broken, and through its ragged interstices will fall the pallor of the moon." But life does not depend upon parliaments or men.

Another afternoon we went to the new Roman Catholic Cathedral in Westminster to hear a fourteenth-century chant which was given every afternoon between two and three by a company of monks who were attached to this church. It was interesting to come out of the swirling streets of London into this dark church, not much larger than Westminster Abbey, and hear this solemn chanting going on. My friend explained to me the peculiarities of the music involved, the endings on a rising inflection, the quaint breaking in of sets of voices at different points carrying the chant a little way and then dropping it. He explained why one of the monks came to the center of the choir at regular intervals and apparently sang alone. This was to give the key of the new division of the music, common at a time when organs were not common. I was more interested in the shadowy expanse of the dome, which is as yet of plain brick, and the tall brick walls, innocent of any marble. In the foggy London atmosphere a church of this size takes on great gloom, and the sound of these voices rolling about in it was very impressive. Religion seems of so little avail these days, however, that I wondered why money should be invested in any such structure or liturgy. There were scarcely a half-dozen people present, if so many, and yet this vast edifice echoes every day at this hour with these voices—a company of twenty or thirty fat monks who might seemingly be employed in something better. Of religion—the spirit as opposed to the form—one might well guess that there was little.

From this cathedral we took a taxi, and bustling down Victoria Street past the Houses of Parliament and into the Strand, we came eventually to St. Paul's. Although it was only four o'clock when we reached there, this huge structure was growing dusky, and the tombs of Wellington and Marlborough were already dim. The organist here was a friend, and because of this we were permitted to sit in the choir stalls with the choristers, a company of boys who entered after a time headed by deacons and sub-deacons and possibly a canon. A solitary circle of electric bulbs flamed gloomily overhead. By the light of this we were able to make out the liturgy covering this service, the psalms and prayers which swept sonorously through the building. As in the Roman Catholic Cathedral we had just left, I was impressed with the futility of the procedure. There are some eight million people in London—but there were only twenty-five or thirty here, and I was told that this service was never much more popular. On occasions the church is full enough, full to overflowing, but not at this time of day. The best I could say for it was that it had a lovely, artistic significance which ought to be encouraged; and no doubt the whole procedure is so viewed by those in authority. As a spectacle seen from the Thames or other sections of the city, the dome of St. Paul's is impressive enough, and as an example of English architecture it is sufficiently dignified, though in my judgment not to be compared with either Canterbury or Salisbury. But the interesting company of noble dead, the fact that the public now looks upon it as a national mausoleum and that it is a monument to the genius of Christopher Wren makes it worthwhile. As I look back upon all the other cathedrals I saw, I think that its chief charm was that it was individual and different. In actual beauty, the pure Gothic or Byzantine or Greek examples surpass it greatly.

It was not so long after this that I journeyed down to Canterbury on my way to Paris. All the time I could give to London had virtually been exhausted, and I was now going to catch a glimpse of Paris and the Riviera. In preparation for this, various things had been purchased—a summer straw hat and outing hat and shoes, a light summer suit, a canvas traveling bag to carry the ever-necessary rug, galoshes, umbrellas and so forth. In order to dispense with one of my trunks, I had been compelled to purchase a leather bag of good size which could endure rough usage and would hold a great deal. As I finally found myself equipped, I was carrying five pieces of baggage in addition to a steamer rug and my fur coat, which was as good as a bag itself. My plan was to leave London two days ahead of Grant Richards, visit Canterbury and Dover, and meet with him there to travel to Paris together. He had a number of acquaintances in Paris to whom he was going to introduce me, leaving me in their charge until such time as he could join me, some three weeks later, for the trip to the Riviera. From the Riviera I was to go on to Rome, and he was to return to England.

Among other things I paid a farewell visit to Sir Scorp in his lovely mansion in Cheyne Walk, where I found him surrounded by what one might really call the grandeur of his pictures. I have said before how his house contained distinguished examples of Rembrandt, Frans Hals, Van Dyck, Paul Potter, Velázquez, Mancini and others, and as I contemplated him on this occasion, he looked not unlike one of the lymphatic cavaliers of one of Van Dyck's canvases. A pale gentleman, this—very remote in his spirit, very far removed from the common run of life, concerned only with the ultimately artistic and wishing to be free of everything save the leisure to attend to this. He was not going to leave London, he thought, at this time, except possibly for a short visit to Paris. He was greatly concerned with the problem of finding his dilapidated "castle" which he could restore, live in, and eventually sell, I suppose. It must be a perfect example of Tudor architecture—that he invariably repeated. I gained the impression that he might fill it with interesting examples of some given school or artist and leave it as a public monument.

He repeated his thought that I ought to go about the work of getting up a local exhibit of representative American art and have it brought to London. He commended me to the joys of certain cities and scenes—Pisa, San Miniato outside Florence, the Villa Doria at Rome. I had to smile at the man's profound artistic assurance, for he spoke exactly as a grandee recounting the glories of his kingdom. I admired the paleness of his forehead and his hands and cast one longing look at his inestimable Frans Hals. To think that any man in these days should have purchased for little a picture that can in all likelihood be sold for $500,000. It was like walking into Aladdin's cave.

The morning I left it was gray as usual. I had brought in all my necessary belongings from Cookham Dean and installed them in my room at the hotel, packed and ready. The executive mind of Grant Richards was on the *qui vive* to see that nothing was forgotten. A certain type of tie must be purchased for use on the Riviera—he had overlooked that. He did not think that my outing hat was quite light enough in color, so we went back to change it. I had lost my umbrella in the excitement, and that had to be replaced. But finally, rushing to and fro in a taxi, loaded like a van with belongings, Grant Richards breathing stertorously after each venture into a shop, we finally arrived at the Victoria Station. Never having been on the Continent before, I did not realize until we got there the wisdom of Grant Richards's insistence that I pack as much of my belongings as possible in bags and as little as possible in trunks. Traveling first-class, as most of those who have much luggage do, it is cheaper. One can take as many as five or six parcels or bags with one and stow them on racks and under the seats, which saves a heavy charge for excess baggage. In some countries, such as Italy, nothing is carried free save your hand-luggage, which you take in your compartment with you. In addition the rates are high. I think I paid as much as thirty shillings for the little baggage I had, over and above that which I took in my compartment with me. To a person with a frugal temperament such as mine, that is positively disconcerting. I saw my reserve outing money dwindling rapidly away into the maws of voracious railway magnates. It was my first taste of what I came subsequently to look upon as greedy Europe.

Like a true traveler of little experience, I was as eager to see as much as possible, and so as the train rushed southeast, I did my best to see the pleasant country through which we were speeding, the region indicated on the maps as North Downs. I never saw any portion of English country anywhere that I did not marvel at the charming simplicity of it and understand and appreciate the Englishman's pride in it. It has all the quality of a pastoral poem, the charm of Arcady—fields of sheep, rows of quaint chimney pots and odd houses tucked away among the trees, exquisite moldy and sagging roofs, doorways and windows which look as though loving care had been spent on them. Although this was January, all the leafless trees were covered with a fine thin mold as green as spring leaves themselves, which gave the landscape a charming look. At Rochester the ruins of an ancient castle came into view and a cathedral which I was not to see. At Faversham I had to change from the Dover express to a local in order to be able to stop at Canterbury. By noon I was there and was looking for the Fleur de Lys, which had been recommended to me as the best hotel there. "At least," observed Grant Richards quite solemnly to me as we parted, "I think you can drink the wine." I smiled, for my taste in that respect was not as cultivated as his.

Of all the places I visited in England, not excluding Oxford, I believe that Canterbury pleased me most. The day may have had something to do with it. It was warm and gray, threatening rain at times, but at times also the sun came out and gave the old English town a glow which was not unrelated to spring and paradise. You will have to have a fondness for things English to like it. Small, quaint two-story houses with unexpected twists to their roofs and oriel and bay windows which had been fastened on in the most unexpected places and in the strangest fashion. The colors, too, in some instances, are charmingly high for England—reds and yellows and blues; but in the main, a smoky red brick tone prevails. The River Stour, which in America would be known as Stour's Creek, runs through the city in two branches, and you find it in odd places—walled in closely by the buildings, hung over by little balconies and doorsteps—the like of which I did not see again until I reached Venice. There were rooks in the sky, as I noticed when I came out of the railway station; and winding streets and a general air of peace and quiet—but I could not descry the cathedral anywhere. I made my way up High Street—which is English for "Main"—and finally found my recommended inn, small and dark, but in the hands of Frenchmen and consequently well furnished in the matter of food. I came out after a time and followed this same street to its end, passing the famous gate where the pilgrims used to sink on their knees and in that position pray their way to the cathedral. As usual my Baedeker gave me a world of information, but I could not stomach it and preferred to look at the old stones of which the gate was composed, wondering that it had endured so long. The little that I knew of St. Augustine and King Ethelbert and Chaucer and Thomas à Becket and Laud came back to me. I could not have called it sacred ground, but it was colored at least with the romance of history, and I have great respect for what people once believed, whether it was sensible or not.

If I should write a hundred volumes of European travel I am satisfied I should never be weary of singing the charms of English rural and village life. Canterbury is a city of twenty-eight thousand, with gasworks and railroads and an electric power plant and moving pictures and a skating rink—but though it has all these and much more of the same kind, it nevertheless retains that indefinable something which is pure poetry, if not art, and which makes England exquisite. As I look at it now, having seen much more of other parts of Europe, the quality which produces this indefinable beauty in England is not so much embodied in the individual as in the race. If you look at architectural developments in other countries, you have the feeling at times as if certain individuals had greatly influenced the appearance of a city or a country. This is true of Paris and Berlin, Florence and Milan. Someone seems to have worked out a scheme at some time or other. In England I could never detect an individual or public scheme of any kind. It all seemed to have grown up like an unheralded bed of flowers somewhere. Again, I am satisfied that it is the English temperament which, at its best, provides this indefinable lure which exists in all these places. I noticed it in the towns around Manchester where, in spite of rain and smoke, the same poetic hominess prevails.

Here in Canterbury, where the architecture dates in its variations through all of eight centuries, you still feel the dominance of the English temperament which has produced it. Today, in the newest sections of London—Hammersmith and Seven Kings, West Dulwich and North Finchley—you still feel it at work, occasionally or instinctively constructing this atmosphere which is common to Oxford and Canterbury. It is compounded of a sense of responsibility and cleanliness and religious feeling and strong national and family ties. You really feel in England the distinction of the fireside and the family heirloom and the fact that a person must always keep a nice face on things, however bad they may be. The same spirit erects bird-boxes on poles in the yard and lays charming white stone doorsteps and plants vines to clamber over walls and windows. It is a charming and poetic spirit, however dull it may seem by comparison with the brilliant iniquities of other realms. Here along this little river Stour, which I traced out in different places, the lawns of the houses came down to the water in some instances; the bridges over it were built with the greatest care; and although houses lined it on either side for several miles of its ramblings, it was nevertheless a clean stream. I noticed in different places, where the walls were quite free of any other marks, a poster giving the picture and the history of a murderer who was wanted by the police in Nottingham, and it came to me, in looking at it, that he would have a hard time anywhere in England concealing his identity. The natives' horror of disorder and scandal would cause him to be yielded up on the moment.

In my wanderings, which were purely casual and haphazard, I finally came upon the cathedral, which loomed up suddenly through a curving street under a leaden sky. It was for all the world like a lovely song, rendered with great pathos. Over a Gothic gate of exquisite workmanship and endless labor, it soared—two lovely black stone towers rising shapely and ornate into the gray air. I looked up to some lattices which gave into what might have been the belfry and saw birds perched just as they should have been. The walls, originally gray, had been turned by time and weather into a soft, spongy black which somehow fitted in exquisitely with the haze of the landscape. I had a curious sensation of darker and lighter shades of gray, lurking pools of darkness here and there, and brightness in spots that became almost silver.

The cathedral grounds were charmingly enclosed in vine-covered walls that were nevertheless worked out in harmonious details of stone. An ancient walk of some kind, overhung with broken arches that had fallen into decay, led away into a green court which, by a devious process of other courts and covered arches, gave into the cloister proper. I saw an old deacon, or canon, of the church, walking here in stately meditation; and a typical English yeoman, his trousers fastened about the knee by the useless but immemorial straps, came by wheeling a few bricks in a barrow. There were endless courts, it seemed to me, surrounded by two-story buildings, all quaint in design and housing heaven knows what subsidiary factors of the archiepiscopal life. They seemed very simple habitations to me. Children played here on the walks and grass, gardeners worked at vines and fences, and occasional workmen appeared—men whom I supposed were connected with the architectural repairs which were being made to the facade. As I stood in the courtyard of the archbishop's house, which was in front and to the left of the cathedral as you faced it, a large blue-gray touring car suddenly appeared, and a distinguished ecclesiastic in a shovel hat stepped out. I had the wish and the fancy that I was looking at the archbishop himself—a sound, stern, intellectual-looking person—but I did not ask. He gave me a sharp, inquiring look, and I withdrew beyond these sacred precincts and into the cathedral itself, where a tinny-voiced bell was beginning to ring for afternoon service.

I am sure I shall never forget the interior of Canterbury. It was the first really old great cathedral that I had seen—for I had not prized very highly either St. Paul's or St. Alban's. I had never quite realized how significant these structures must have been in an age when they were by far the most important buildings of the time. No king's palace could ever have had the distinction of Canterbury, and the cry from the common peasant to the archiepiscopal see must have been immense. Here really ruled the primate of all England, and here Becket was murdered.

Of all known architectural forms, I am satisfied that the Gothic appeals to me most. It seems to me to correspond absolutely to the finest impulses in nature itself—that is, to produce the floriated form. The aisles of the trees are no more distinguished artistically than those of a great cathedral, and the overhanging branches through which the light falls have not much more charm for me than some of these perfect Gothic ceilings sustained by their many branching arms of stone. Much had happened apparently to the magnificent stained-glass windows which must have filled the tall-pointed openings at different periods, but many of them have been replaced by plain frosted glass. Those that remained were of such richness of color and such delightful variety of workmanship that, seen at the end of long stretches of aisles and ambulatories, they were like splotches of blood or deep indigo, throwing a strange light on the surrounding stone. A great tablet near the entranceway gave the names of all the archbishops since the beginning, and along the aisles between the columns were the customary sarcophagi of the famous dead. Only a specialist in history or architecture could be entertained by the minute perfections of this vast interior.

I was never wearied of looking at the details of the stonework, the richness of the wood carving in the choir stalls, the full perfection of the ironwork, the carvings on the tombs and the decorations of the walls generally. After the services, which were not unlike those of St. Paul's, I got in tow of a guide—the first of the European brand, of which I was to see so much later—who was one of three or four evidently licensed for the purpose.

It is said today that Americans are more like the Germans than like the English, but from the types I encountered in England I think the variety of American temperaments spring naturally from the mother country. Four more typical New England village specimens I never saw than these cathedral ushers or guides. They would do credit to the current-day stories of Mrs. Wilkins Freeman. The quizzical New England expression, the sharp-pointed chin, the short growth of whiskers sticking straight out—even the nasal twang was present in one of them. They were sitting on the steps leading up to the choir, and gossiped like a lot of old women. I heard them clattering about what George Somebody was going to do and whether Mrs. So-and-So was getting round again. If they had referred to old Sy Perkins up Merrimac way I would not have been in the least astonished; and they were sharp after the money which their perquisite involves as any New Englander could possibly have been. They were all clad in cap and gown, and when the tallest of the three spied me he got up. "Your turn, Henry," said a guide almost enviously, one might have said; and Henry came around and unlocked the great iron gates which give into the choir. Then began, for my special benefit, as magnificent an oration on history as I have heard in many a day. It was horribly dry and parrot-like, however, in its expression, and I could take no particular interest in it, for watching his whiskers go up and down on his chin. There was something strangely automatic and humorous about the movement of his jaw, and he bit off his sentences at the end quite in the New England fashion. If he had only said "anythin'," "nothin'," and "somethin'," the similarity would have been complete.

We were joined, after we had gone a little way, by a party of old maids from Pennsylvania who were lurking in one of the transepts, and I had the horror of seeing my guide go back to the iron entranceway to the choir and begin all over. Not a sentence was twisted, not a pause misplaced. "Good heavens," I thought, "he does that every day in the year, perhaps a dozen times a day." He was like a phonograph with but one record, which is repeated endlessly. Nevertheless the history of the archbishops, the Black Prince, the Huguenot refugees, the carving of the woodwork and the disappearance of the windows was all interesting. He really rose to great heights of expression when, after having made the rounds of the cathedral, we came out into the cloister, the corridors of which were all black and crumbling with age, and he indicated the spot and described the manner in which Becket had been stabbed and had fallen. I don't know when a bit of history has moved me so much.

It was the day, the gentle quality of it, its very spring-like texture that caused it all. The grass in this black court was as green as new lettuce; the pendants and facets of the arches were crumbling into black sand—and spoke seemingly of a thousand years. High overhead the towers and the pinnacles, soaring as gracefully as winged living things, looked down. There is something airy and spiritual about Canterbury—delicate, diaphanous, web-like. It has no more sense of the heaviness of St. Paul's than an egret has of a toad. It seems to beat with an airy rhythm of its own; its pinnacles and spandrels have wings; its trefoils and facets are true flowers; and it sings, sings, sings, in the storied air like a wonderful song. It seemed to me to swim in an amethystine glamour of its own, and as I looked at the black-gowned figure of my guide and thought of the ancient archbishop crossing this selfsame grass, I felt as though life might truly reach perfection at times, that one such moment was here and now. Nothing—no scene, no song, no book, no picture—has ever held more of that ultimate perfection than this cloistered green with its onlooking towers and pinnacles. Tears truly came to my eyes, and I laughed at the same time in pure happiness over the pathos and the beauty of life. No words may describe Canterbury, however. Its charm should be sung, and only so.

When I came outside the gate into the little square or triangle which faces it, I found a lovely statue of the lyric muse—a semi-nude dancing girl erected to the memory of Christopher Marlowe. It surprised me a little to find it here, facing Canterbury, in what may be called the sacred precincts of religious art; but it is suitably placed and brought me back in mind to the related kingdom of poetry. All the little houses about have heavy, overhanging eaves and diamond-shaped, lead-paned windows. The walls are thick and whitewashed, ranging in colors from cream to brown. They seem so unsuited to modern life, and yet they were full of all the things that make it: picture-postcards, American shoes, advertised candy such as chocolate, the latest books and magazines. It was charming to find them here crowded against the ancient walls of Canterbury and fronting the lyric muse.

I sought a tearoom nearby and had tea, looking joyously out against the wall where some vines clambered, and then wandered back to the depot to get my mackintosh and umbrella—for it was beginning to rain. For two hours more I walked up and down in the rain and dark, looking into occasional windows when the blinds had not been drawn, stopping in taprooms or public houses where rosy barmaids waited on me with courteous smiles, examining the shops of High Street which were not much better than those of a fourth-rate American town, finding St. Martin's church, the monastery of St. Augustine, the town police station and other objects of interest. I could see plainly from the shop windows, however, that all that was old was of little interest to modern Canterburians, for they were full of the latest inventions of all kinds—stationery, books, pictures, leather goods, hats, canes, shoes, the whole roster of social equipment—and the boys and girls went laughing by in delicious unconsciousness of anything that related to the past. If you had mentioned Thomas à Becket, they would have looked at you in surprise, and as for Laud or St. Augustine or King Ethelbert—you had far better have asked them about the latest football score. But charming they were, nevertheless, fit descendants and continuances of that English spirit which makes for simple beauty. The land that has produced Marlow and Salisbury and Canterbury and Oxford can never ultimately be spoken of as artistically deficient.

CHAPTER XXXII

One of the things which dawned upon me in moving about England, and particularly as I was leaving it, was the reason for the inestimable charm of Dickens. I do not know that anywhere in London or England I encountered any types which forcefully manifested the characters he described. It is probable that they were all exaggerated—somewhat. But of the charm of Dickens's settings there can be no doubt. He appeared at a time when the old order was giving away, and the new—the new as we have known it in the last sixty years—was manifesting itself very sharply. Railroads were just coming in and coaches being dispensed with; the modern hotel was not yet even thought of, but it was impending.

Dickens, born and raised in Landport, was among the first to perceive the wonder of the change and to contrast it graphically with what had been and still was. In such places as St. Alban's, Marlow, Canterbury, Oxford and others I could see what the old life must have been like when the stagecoach ruled and made the principal highways lively with traffic. Here in Canterbury and elsewhere there were inns sacred to the characters of Dickens, and you could see how charming that world must have appeared to a man who felt that it was passing. He saw it in its heyday, just before its decay, and he recorded it as it could not have been recorded before and can never be again. He saw also the charm of simple English life—the native love of cleanly pots and pans and ordered dooryards; and that, fortunately, has not changed. You can see it. I cannot think of anyone doing England as Dickens did it until there is something new to be done—the old spirit manifested in a new way. From Shakespeare to Dickens the cry is long; from Dickens to his successors it may be longer still.

I was amused on leaving Canterbury to think that on the morrow at this same time I should catch my first glimpse of Paris. The clerk at the station who kept my bags for me noted that I came from New York and told me he had a brother in Wisconsin and that he liked it very much out there. I said, "I suppose you will be coming to America yourself one of these days?"

"Oh, yes," he said, "the big chances are out there. I'll either go to Canada or Wisconsin."

"Well, there are plenty of states to choose from," I said.

"A lot of people have gone from this place," he replied.

It rained hard all the way to Dover; but when I reached there, it had ceased, and I even went so far as to leave my umbrella in the train. The line terminates in some gloomy, unprepossessing shed, and in the center of a welter of docks, warehouses and shipping facilities I had time just to get the feeling that I was in the center of an exceedingly jumbled seafaring world when I discovered the absence of my lately purchased umbrella. Now for another demonstration of English honesty: I said to the porter who was carrying my belongings, "I have forgotten my umbrella."

"Don't let that worry you," he replied in the calmest and most assuring of English tones. "They always look through the trains. You'll find it in the parcel room."

Sure enough, when I returned, there it was behind the clerk's desk, and it was handed to me promptly. If I had not had everything which I had lost, barring one stick, promptly returned to me since I had been in England, I would not have thought so much of this; but it confirmed my impression that I was among a people who are temperamentally honest. I believe now that, generally speaking, the English are absolutely honest—certainly in all the minor affairs of life. In the major ones it is possibly very different. But who is to account for the twisting of major affairs anywhere?

My guide led me to the Lord Warden Hotel, where I ate a hearty meal and arranged myself comfortably in a good room for the night. It pleased me, on throwing open my windows, to see that this hotel fronted a bay or the sea and that I was in the realm of great ships and sea traffic instead of the noisy heart of a city. Because of a slight haze, not strong enough to shut out the lights entirely, foghorns and fog bells were going, and I could hear the smash of waves on the shore. I decided that after dinner I would reconnoiter Dover and see what I could see.

I think I gained as interesting an impression as any of England in these last few hours just before sailing for Calais. By some good fortune there was a review of warships in this harbor at the time; and the principal streets of Dover were crowded with marines in red jackets and white belts and the comic little tambourine caps cocked jauntily over one ear. Many of them carried the little stick which they use as a substitute for a cane, not more than twenty inches long, and walked with a jaunty stride. I soon found that the worst sections of the town lay between the Lord Warden, which is the principal hotel, and High Street, perhaps a mile and a half or two miles away. Its worst thoroughfare was a street called Snargate, and here all the underlings of the vessels were congregated. Such a swarm of red jackets I never saw in my life. They were walking up and down in pairs, trios, quartets and even quintets, talking briskly and flirting with the girls. I fancy that those representatives of the underworld of women who prey on this type of youth were here in force. They were certainly not very attractive to look upon, but it is just possible that the best representatives were not in the streets at all. Many a house with shuttered windows looked suggestive to me, but I kept religiously on my way, anxious to see as much of the exterior face of the city as I could.

Much to my astonishment in this Snargate Street I found a south-of-England replica of the "fish, chip and pea" institution of the Manchester district. I concluded from this that it must be an all-English institution, and wherever there was much drunkenness there would be these restaurants. In such a port as Dover, where sailors freely congregate, it would be apt to be common; and so it proved.

Farther up High Street, in its uttermost reaches in fact, I saw a sign which read, "Thomas Davidge: Bone-setter and Tooth-surgeon"—whatever that may be. Its only rival was another I had seen in Bolton which ran, "Temperance Bar and Herbal Stores." The two should have been side by side.

For amusement, after I had watched the soldiers' efficiency, I went to the center of greatest excitement—a triangular space near the juncture of High and Snargate Streets—and entered a motion-picture theater which was the principal attraction. As in Manchester, the principal feature was the coronation of the king and queen at Simla in India. I was interested to see that in this collection of motion pictures, as in those of Manchester, London and elsewhere, a number of American scenes were given, principally of the West and Southwest. Looking over my experiences of Europe as a whole, I should say that the life of our western and southwestern regions and historical pictures relating to our Civil War are very popular throughout Europe generally. I saw Western and Civil War pictures in Paris, Rome, Milan, Frankfort, Berlin and Amsterdam. The motion-picture programs here were about as good as they were anywhere and seemed to create about as much excitement. The prices were rather high, all told, compared to the same class of entertainment in America—being sixpence and a shilling. I have seen many a good picture show for a nickel in the United States. When this was over, I returned to the hotel through Snargate Street, still crowded with marines; and because of the fog bells and foghorns in the harbor, I dreamed that I was in a shipwreck. The moon had come out before I went to bed, and I could see long piers reaching out into the water and a world of masts and lights. The sound of great waves pounding a beach still came from somewhere.

The next morning I was up early and sought the famous castle on the hill, but could not gain admission and could not see it for the fog. I returned to the beach, and by that time the fog had lifted and I could not only see the castle on the hill but the wonderful harbor besides. I saw only two coast scenes all the time I was in Europe—the one at Fishguard when I arrived and the one at Dover when I left and returned. Fishguard was more romantic in its general contour, but Dover was far more impressive. The great cliffs were truly chalk-like in their color and rose like great battlements, English Gibraltars, on either hand. I never saw a finer beach or a finer surf or a more pleasing sea walk and residence district. A long line of handsome residences faced this imposing seawall and splendid surf. The waves were rolling in great foamy masses, thundering on the shore, and the water beyond was a milky blue. The sky was blue and the high cliffs white. It seemed to me a delightful place to spend a summer, if it were not too warm. This section of Dover had a very distinguished air.

At ten-thirty this morning the last train from London making the boat for Calais was to arrive and with it Grant Richards and all his paraphernalia bound for Paris. I spent the last half-hour in a Dover barbershop and in purchasing some picture-postcards. So far as I could make out, the customary barber pole was absent in Dover, and the upstairs room in which I was shaved was more like a conservatory for flowers than a place of business. In spite of the absence of all the glittering contraptions which make up the American "tonsorial parlor," I much preferred this simple little English room with its immovable chair and excellent razor. The polite "if you pleases" and "thank yous" of the barber made up for the absence of the twenty-one perfumes and powders which usually accompany the same operation in America. He did not try to make me talk and, as far as I could make out, was really an intelligent, home-loving citizen.

It seems to me that I have sung the praises of Grant Richards as a directing manager quite sufficiently for one book, but I shall have to begin anew. He arrived as usual very brisk, a porter carrying four or five pieces of luggage, his fur coat over his arm, his monocle gleaming as though it had been freshly polished, a cane and an umbrella in hand and inquiring crisply whether I had secured the particular position on deck which he had requested me to hold. If it were raining, according to a slip of paper on which he had written instructions days before I ever left London, I was to enter the cabin of the vessel which crossed the Channel, preempt a section of seat along the sidewall by putting all my luggage there, and bribe a porter to place two chairs in a comfortable windless position on deck to which we could repair in case it should clear up on the way over. All of this I faithfully did. The chairs had the best possible position behind the deckhouse, and one of my pieces of luggage was left there as a guarantee that they belonged to me.

It looked like rain when the train arrived, and we went below for a sandwich and a cup of coffee; but before the boat left, it faired up somewhat, and we sat on deck studying the harbor and the interesting company which was to cross with us. A company of twenty English schoolgirls in the charge of several severe-looking chaperones were crossing to Paris, either for a holiday or, as Grant Richards suggested, to renew their studies in a Paris school. A duller lot of maidens it would be hard to conceive of, and yet some of them were not at all bad-looking. Conservatism and proper conduct were written all over them. Their clothing was severely plain and their manners most circumspect. None of that vivacity which characterizes the average American girl would have been tolerated under the circumstances. There was no undue giggling and little, if any, jesting. They interested me, because I instantly imagined twenty American girls of the same age in their place. They would have manifested twenty times the interest and enthusiasm which these did, only in England that would have been the height of bad manners. As it was, these English maidens sat in a quaint row all the way over, and disappeared quite conservatively into the train at Calais.

This English steamer crossing the Channel to France was a disappointment to me in one way. I had heard for some time past that the old uncomfortable Channel boats had been dispensed with and new, commodious steamers put in their place. As a matter of fact, these boats were not nearly as large as those that run from New York to Coney Island, nor as commodious, though much cleaner and brighter. If it had rained, as Grant Richards anticipated, the cabin below would have been intolerably overcrowded and stuffy. As it was, all the passengers were on the upper deck, sitting on camp chairs and preparing stoically to be sick. It was impossible to conceive that a distance so short, not more than twenty-three or -four miles, should be so disagreeable as Grant Richards said it was at times. The boat did not pitch to any extent on this trip over—on my return, some three months later, I had a different experience. But now the wind blew fiercely, and it was cold. The Channel was as gray as a rabbit and offensively bleak. I did not imagine the sea could be so dull-looking, and France, when it appeared in the distance, struck me as equally bleak in appearance—a land crowded with dull peasants who would not know a lovely landscape if they saw it.

As we drew near Calais, it was no better—a shoreline beset with gas tanks and iron foundries. It was not until we actually reached the dock that I saw a line of sparkling French *facteurs* looking down on the boat from the platform above. Presto! England was gone. Gone all the solemnity and the politeness of the porters who had brought our luggage aboard, gone the quiet civility of ship officers and trainmen, gone the solid dough-like quiescence of the whole English race. It seemed to me on the instant as if the sky had changed and instead of the gray, misty pathos of English life—albeit sweet and romantic—had come the lively slapdash of another world. These men who looked down on us with their snappy, bird-like eyes were no more like the English than a sparrow is like a great auk. They were black-haired, black-eyed, lean, brown, active. They had on blue aprons and blue jackets and a kind of military cap, the crown of which sagged in and to one side in accordion pleats. There was a touch of scarlet somewhere, either in their caps or their jackets, I forget which; and somewhere nearby I saw a French soldier—his scarlet woolen trousers and lead-blue coat contrasting poorly, so far as *éclat* goes, with the splendid trimness of the British. Nevertheless he did not look inefficient but raw and forceful, like one imagines the soldiers of Napoleon should be. The vividness of the coloring made up for much, and I said at once that I would not give one France for fifty million Englands. I felt, although I did not speak the language, as though I had returned to America.

It is curious how one feels about France, or at least how I feel about it. For all of six weeks I had been rejoicing in the charms and the virtues of the English. London is a great city—splendid—the intellectual capital of the world. Manchester and the north represent as forceful a manufacturing realm as the world holds—there is no doubt of that. The quaintness and sweetness of English country life is not to be surpassed for charm and beauty. But France has fifty times the spirit and enthusiasm of England. After London and the English country it seems strangely young and vital. As you step off the boat to the dock, coming from England, you could imagine the French doing anything—writing great poetry, fighting great battles, producing great things in art, literature and commerce. As you look at these bustling, cheerful people, you can hardly imagine anything being wrong with France. It is often spoken of as decadent, but I said to myself, "Good Lord, let us get some of this decadence and take it home with us. It is such a cheerful thing to have around." I would commend it to the English particularly.

On the way over Grant Richards had been giving me additional instructions. I was to stay on board when the boat arrived and signal a *facteur* who would then come and get my luggage. I was to say to him, "*Dix colis*," whereupon he would gather up the ten bundles and lead the way to the dock. I was to be sure and get his number, for all French *facteurs* were scoundrels and likely to rob you. I did exactly as I was told, while Grant Richards went forward to secure a section, first-class, and to see that we had places in the dining car for the first service. Then he returned and found me on the dock, doing my best to keep track of the various pieces of luggage, while the *facteur* did his best to attract the attention of a customs inspector who would order such bags as he fixed upon to be opened and pass on their contents. As I understood it, only whiskey, cigars and cigarettes were contraband, and as we had none of these, I felt perfectly safe.

It was certainly interesting to see the difference between the arrival of this boat at Calais and the similar boat which took us off the *Mauretania* at Fishguard. There, although the crowd which had arrived was equally large, all was peaceful and rather still. The porters went about their work in such a matter-of-fact manner. All was in apple-pie order. There was no shouting to speak of. Here all was hubbub and confusion, apparently, although it was little more than French enthusiasm. You would have fancied that the French guards and *facteurs* were doing their best to liberate their pent-up feelings. They bustled restlessly to and fro; they grimaced; they reassured you frequently by look and sign that all would be well, must be so. Inside of five minutes—during which time I examined the French newsstand and saw how marvelously English conservatism had disappeared in this distance of twenty miles—the luggage had been passed on, and we were ready to enter the train.

Grant Richards had purchased a number of papers—*Figaro*, *Gil Blas* and others—in order to indicate the difference between the national lives of the two countries which I was now to contrast. I never saw a man so eager to see what effect a new country would have on another. He wanted me to see the difference between the English and the French papers at once; and although I was thoroughly familiar with it already, I carefully examined these latest productions of the French presses. The same delicious nudities that have been flourishing in the French papers for years were there—the same subtle Gallic penchant for the absurd and the ridiculous. I marveled anew at the sprightliness of these figures, which never cross the Atlantic into American papers. We do not know how to draw them because we are not accustomed to them in our lives. As a matter of fact the American weeklies and magazines adhere rigorously to the English standards. We have varied some in presentation but have not broadened the least in treatment. As a matter of fact I believe that the American weekly and monthly are even more conservative than the British paper of the same standard. We think we are different, but we are not. We have not even anything in common with the Germans, from whom we are supposed to have drawn so much of our national personality.

However, the train started after a few moments, and soon we were speeding through that low, flat country which lies between Calais and Paris. It was a five hours' run direct, but we were going to stop off at Amiens to see the great cathedral. I was struck at once by the difference between the English and the French landscape. Here the trees were far fewer, and what there were of them were not tinged with that rich green mold which is characteristic of every tree in England. The towns, too, as they flashed past—for this was an express—were radically different in their appearance. I noted the superabundance of conical red roofs swimming in a silvery light and hard white walls that you could see for miles. No trees intervened to break the view, and now and then a silvery thread of a river appeared. We passed a church with white walls and blue windowsills, to say nothing of its red roof, and small hamlets, the houses of which were crowded together in what appeared to be an almost smothering embrace. There were factories, too, American fashion, but they also in many instances had white walls and red roofs. Imagine an American factory which could be described in this manner!

This train we were on was different from the English trains, for the track was standard gauge, American fashion, and the cars as large as American cars. I took a good look at the engine before we got on, and it struck me as a homely mechanism, not having the artistic lines which characterize the great flyers that pull the American trains. The smokestack was low and stubby, the sandbar dumpy, and there was no bell and no headlight. One thing I did like were the drivers. Inside the cars the corridor and section system had been followed as in England; and those who have ever ridden in these will not rejoice in the American trains anymore. It seems strange now to me that the barbaric system which prevails here should ever have been imposed on us. I can no longer take pleasure in the stuffy, sickening Pullman.

Grant Richards slept until we neared Amiens, while I studied what I ought to know about Paris and European cathedrals generally. Amiens, when we reached there, proved to be one of the most interesting of French towns. Once outside its railway station—which was not unlike that of any other anywhere, size for size—I was charmed with its very medieval air. National architecture, I find, is compounded of a repetition of a very few peculiar and simple lines. The English Tudor, which is the best that England has to show, is really a combination of the round tower, the castellated wall, the narrow window and the French door. A town embellished with any of these structures takes on the national air at once. In France I found that the conical-roofed tower, the high-peaked roof, the solid gray or white wall, and the thick red tile, fluted or flat, combined to produce what may be looked upon as the national touch. The houses here varied considerably from the English standard by being in many cases very narrow and quite high for their width—four and five stories. They are crowded together, too, in a seemingly defensive way, and seem to lack light and air. The solid white or gray shutters, the thick-fluted rain pipe and the severe, simple thickness of the walls produced an atmosphere which I came to look upon after a time as supremely Gallic, lingering on from a time when France was a very different country than what it is today.

Amiens was all of this. It would have seemed hard and cold and bare and dry except for these little quirks of roofs and the lightness of the spirit of the people. Wherever you saw a Frenchman, he was walking with a brisker air, a jerkier motion, than is customary with the Englishman. We wandered through high-walled, cobble-paved streets until suddenly we came to the cathedral, soaring upward out of a welter of the dreary and commonplace. I had thought Canterbury was wonderful—but now I knew that I had never seen anything in my life before so imposing as Amiens. Pure Gothic, like Canterbury, it was so much larger. A perfect maze of pinnacles, towers, arches, buttresses and flying buttresses; carven saint piled on carven saint, and gargoyles leering from every cranny. I could scarcely believe that the faith of man had ever reared so lovely a thing. What a power religion must have been in those days! To what perfection the art of architecture had attained! Villon's most poetic mood is no finer than these walls. The loving care that has been exercised in designing, shaping and placing these stones is enough to stagger the brain. I did not wonder when I saw it that Ruskin and Morris had attained to a sort of frenzy over the Gothic. It is a thing for sighs and tears.

Both Grant Richards and I walked around it in reverent silence, and I knew that he was rejoicing to know that I was feeling what I ought to feel. I felt as though a great song ought to be written about this, that artists ought to paint it, poets sing of it, travelers rave over it. It was a thing well worth coming miles and miles to see. I should say it would be nothing to cross many seas and many continents to see so fine a thing as Amiens. There are not many structures in the world like it. I saw many cathedrals afterward—Rouen, Notre-Dame, Milan, Florence, Pisa, Rome, Cologne, Antwerp, Brussels—but no one of the others really approached it in quality. Rouen is almost as good, the Duomo at Florence is astonishing, Milan is a dream of pinnacles, but Amiens was something of all of these and more. It is simply astounding.

We went inside after a time because it was threatening dusk, and the light was failing, and we had to make our train for Paris. I shall never forget the vast space within those wondrous doors—the world of purple and gold and orange and blue in the windows, the blaze of a hundred and more candles upon the great altar, the shrines with their votive offerings of flaming tapers, the fat, waddling mothers in bunchy skirts, the heavy priests with shovel hats and pig-like faces, the order of attendant sisters in blue collars and flaring linen headgear, the worshipful figures scattered here and there upon the hard stone floor on their knees. The vast space was full of a delicious incense; faint shadows were already pooling themselves in the arches above to blend into a great darkness. Up rose the columns, giant redwoods of stone supporting the far-off roof. All the glory of pointed windows, all the richness of foliated decorations, all the worshipfulness of graven saints set in shrines whose details seemed the tendrils of spring—whatever the flower, the fruit, the leaf, the branch could contribute in the way of artistic suggestion had here been seized upon. Only the highest order of inspiration could have conceived or planned or executed this delicious dream in stone.

Why, a common building would be honored by any one of ten thousand fragments which might be removed from this great pile. A single pinnacle would make a sufficient monument for any man. One of its adorable trefoils would make a window for a small church. It is a veritable pantheon of saints and a Mecca of shrines. I looked vaguely at the description of it in my Baedeker but gave it up. What more could printed type tell me than what I could see and feel? A guide, for a franc or two, took us high up into the organ loft and out upon a narrow balustrade leading about the roof. Below, all France was spread out; the city of Amiens, its contour, was defined accurately. You could see some little stream, the Somme, coming into the city and leaving it. Wonderful figures of saints and devils were on every hand. We were shown a high tower in which a treaty between France and Spain had been signed. I looked down into the great well of the nave inside and saw the candles gleaming like gold and the people moving like small bugs across the floor. It was a delicious confirmation of the majesty of man, the power of his ideals, the richness and extent of his imagination, the sheer ability of his hands. I would not give up my fleeting impression of Amiens for anything that I know.

CHAPTER XXXIII

As we came away from the cathedral in the dusk, we walked along some branch or canal of the Somme, and I saw for the first time the peculiar kind of boat or punt used on French streams—a long affair, stub-pointed at either end. It was black and had somewhat the effect of a gondola. A Frenchman in baggy corduroy trousers and a soft wool cap pulled over one ear was poling it along. It contained hay piled in a rude mass. It was warm here, in spite of the fact that it was the middle of January, and there was a feeling of spring in the air. Grant Richards informed me that the worst of winter in Paris appeared between January fifteenth and the middle of March, that the spring did not really show itself until the first of April or a little later.

"You will be coming back by then," he said, "and you will see it in all its glory. I will come over, and we will go to Fontainebleau and ride." That sounded very promising to me.

I could not believe that these dull cobblestone streets through which we were passing were part of a city of over ninety thousand and that there was much manufacturing here. There were so few people in sight. It had a gray, shut-up appearance—none of the flare and spirit of the towns of the American Middle West. It occurred to me at once that although I might like to travel here, I would never like to live here. Then we reached the railway station again.

There is something about the French nation which, in spite of its dreary-looking cities, gives them an air of metropolitan up-to-date-ness. I don't know where outside of America you would find the snap and intensity of emotion, ambition and romance which you find everywhere in French streets. This station, when we returned to it, was alive with a crowd of bustling, hurrying people—buying books and papers at newsstands, looking after their luggage in the baggage room and chattering to the ticket-sellers through their windows. Some train was just in out of Paris, and they were hurrying to catch that, and as I made my first French purchase—twenty centimes' worth of postcards of Amiens—our train rolled in. It was from the north, such a long train as you frequently see in America, with cars labeled Milan, Trieste, Marseilles, Florence and Rome. I could hardly believe it and asked Grant Richards, as he bustled about seeing that the luggage was put in the proper carriage, where it came from. He thought that some of these cars started from St. Petersburg and others from Denmark and Holland. They had a long run ahead of them yet—over thirty hours to Rome, and Paris was just one point in their journey. The run from Amiens to Paris requires several hours.

We crowded into one car—stuffy with baggage, its windows damp with human breath, various nationalities occupying the sections—and disposed of our grips, portmanteaus, rugs and so on as best we could. I slipped the bustling old *facteur* a franc—not so much because he deserved it, but because he had such a gay and rakish air. His apron swung around his legs like a skirt, and his accordion-pleated cap was lolling gaily over one ear. He waved me a smiling farewell and said something in French which I wished I could understand. Then I realized for the first time what a pity it is not to understand the language of the country in which you are traveling.

As the train sped through the dark to Paris, I fell to speculating on the wonders I was to see. Grant Richards, with the patience of a father and the interest of a mother, was explaining to me that now we would meet two cocottes whom he had specially engaged in order to make my entrance into Paris properly gay and interesting. We were to dine at the Café de Paris and then visit the Folies-Bergère and afterward have supper at the Abbaye de

Thélème, and after that, if the ladies were in a proper mood, we could take them further or deliver them at their own door and return to our hotel. He was not sure that I would be interested in sightseeing until morning because of the long day of travel. He hoped I would like the ladies, but he could not guarantee that. One of them, he said, was exceedingly charming, an ideal type of the cocotte. The other, her sister, was a somewhat different type—he had seen her once. I might like her better. The pathetic drawback to this whole proposition was that neither of them spoke English and I spoke no French, so that I would have to sit and admire them or talk by signs. That did not enthuse me very much, and I wished that Miss Longfellow had come to Paris, as she had once thought she would, or Miss Villars. I think if I had persuaded her a little more she would have, and we could have done the city together. However, I looked forward to having a good time anyhow, and in this mood we reached Paris.

I should say here that of all people I know, Grant Richards is as capable of creating an atmosphere as any—perhaps more so. I think sometimes that he has more of that ability than I have. The man lives so heartily in his moods; he sets the stage for his actions long beforehand and then walks on like a good actor and plays his part thoroughly. All the way over—from the very first day we met in New York, I think—he was either consciously or unconsciously building up for me the glamour of smart and artistic life in Europe. Now these things are absolutely according to your capacity to understand and appreciate them; they are, if you please, a figment of the brain, a fume of the mind. If you love art, if you love history, if the romance of sex and beauty enthralls you, Europe in places offers tremendous possibilities. To reach these ethereal paradises of charm, you must skip and blink and dispense with many things. All the long lines of commonplaces through which you travel must be as nothing. You buy and prepare and travel and polish, and finally you reach the center of this thing which is so wonderful; and then when you get there, it is a figment of your own mind. Paris and the Riviera are great realities—there are houses and crowds of people and great institutions and the remembrance and flavor of great deeds; but the thing that you get out of all this for yourself is born of the attitude or mood which you take with you.

Toward gambling, show, romance, a delicious scene, Grant Richards carries a special mood. Life is only significant because of these things. His great struggle is to avoid the dingy and the dull, and to escape, if possible, the penalties of encroaching age. I think he looks back on the glitter of his youth with a pathetic eye, and I know he looks forward into the dark with stoic solemnity. Just one more hour of beauty, is his private cry, one more day of delight. Let the future take care of itself. He realizes, too, with the keenness of a realist, that if youth is not most vivid in yourself, it can sometimes be achieved through the moods of others. I know he found in me a zest and a curiosity and a wonder which he was keen to satisfy. Now he would see this thing over as he had seen it years before. He would observe me thrilling and marveling, and so he would be able to thrill and marvel himself once more. He clung to me with delicious enthusiasm, and every now and then would say, "Come now, what are you thinking? I want to know. I am enjoying this as much as you are."

He had a delicious vivacity which acted on me like wine. It was a case of action and reaction, and we mounted in our moods until we were positively brilliant, gay, sarcastic, witty. I would not attempt to suggest all the badgering and humorous nagging that went on from hour to hour, but it was a case of dissecting life and character, scalpel in hand. I did not hesitate to strike at his inmost convictions, to reveal himself to himself in spite of himself—and he returned the compliment with interest. I never had a better time in my life.

As we neared Paris, he had built this city up so thoroughly in my mood that I am satisfied that I could not have seen it with a realistic eye if I had tried. It was something—I cannot tell you what—Napoleon, the Louvre, the art quarters, Montmartre, the gay restaurants, the boulevards, Balzac, Hugo, the Seine and the soldiery—a score and a hundred things too numerous to mention and all greatly exaggerated. I hoped to see something which was perfect in its artistic appearance, exteriorly speaking. I expected, after reading George Moore and E. V. Lucas, a wine-like atmosphere, a throbbing world of gay life, women of exceptional charm of face and dress, the bizarre, the unique, the emotional, the spirited. At Amiens I had seen enough women entering the trains to realize that the dreary commonplace of the English woman was gone. Instead, the young married women that we saw were positively dashing compared to what England could show—shapely, piquant, sensitive, their eyes showing a bird-like awareness of what this world has to offer. I fancied that Paris would be like that, only more so; and as I look back on it now, I can honestly say that I was not greatly disappointed. It was not all that I thought it would be, but it was near enough. It is a gay, brilliant, beautiful city, with the spirit of New York and more than the distinction of London. It is like a brilliant, fragile child—not made for contests and brutal battles, but gay beyond reproach.

I shall not stop to expatiate on the history of Paris here—others must do that. When the train rolled into the Gare du Nord, it must have been about eight o'clock. Grant Richards, as usual, was on the *qui vive* for precedence and advantage. He had industriously piled all the bags out close to the door and was hanging out of a window doing his best to signal a *facteur*.

I was to stay in the car and hand all the packages down rapidly, while he ran to secure a taxi and an inspector and in other ways to clear away the impediments to our progress. With great executive enthusiasm he told me that we must be at the Hôtel Normandy by eight-fifteen or -twenty and that by nine o'clock we must be ready to sit down in the Café de Paris to an excellent dinner which he had ordered by telegraph. He was to go and fetch the mesdames—in a taxi, and then this charming evening would begin.

I recall my wonder in entering Paris—the lack of any long-extended suburbs, the sudden flash of electric lights and electric cars. Mostly we seemed to be entering through a tunnel or gully, and then we were there. The noisy *facteurs* in their caps and blue aprons were all around the cars. They ran and chattered and gesticulated—so unlike the porters in Paddington and Waterloo and Victoria and Euston. The one we finally secured, a husky little enthusiast, did his best to gather all our packages in one grand mass and shoulder them, stringing them on a single strap. The result of it was that the strap broke right over a small pool of water, and among other things the canvas bag containing my blanket and magnificent shoes fell into the water. "Oh, my God!" exclaimed Richards, "My hatbox! Look at that! Of course this damned ass would have to try to break his neck in order to get all the money. I knew the strap would break."

The excited *facteur* was fairly dancing in anguish, doing his best to get the packages together and make another brilliant attempt. Between us we relieved him of about half of them, and from around his waist he unwrapped another large strap and strung the remainder on that. Then we hurried agonizedly on, for nothing would do but that we must hurry. A taxi was secured and all our luggage piled on it. It looked half-suffocated under bundles as it swung out into the street, and we were off at a mad clip through crowded, electric-lit streets. I pressed my nose to the window and took in as much as I could, while Grant Richards, between calculations as to how much time this would take and that would take and whether my trunk had arrived safely, expatiated laconically on French characteristics.

"You smell this air?—It is all over Paris."

"The taxis always go like this." (We were going like mad.)

"There is an excellent type—look at her."

"Now you see the chairs out in front—they are this way all over Paris."

I was looking at the interesting restaurant life which never really seems to be interrupted anywhere in Paris. You can always find a dozen chairs somewhere, if not fifty or a hundred, out on the sidewalk under the open sky or a glass roof—little stone-topped tables beside them, the crowd surging to and fro in front. Here you can sit and have your coffee, your liqueur, your sandwich. Everybody seems to do it—it is as common as walking in the streets.

We whirled through street after street, partaking of this atmosphere, and finally swung up in front of a rather plain hotel which I learned this same night was close to the Avenue de l'Opéra on the corner of the Rue de L'Echelle and the Rue St-Honoré. Our luggage was quickly distributed, and I was shown into my room by a maid who could not speak English. Downstairs the clerk, the elevator man and the hall porters understood well enough, for they were accustomed to dealing with English travelers. As a matter of fact it was supposed to be an English hotel. I unlocked my belongings and rapidly changed my clothes, while Grant Richards, breathing mightily, fully arrayed, soon appeared, saying that I should await him at the door below where he would arrive with our guests. I did so, and in fifteen minutes he returned, the taxi fairly whirling up out of a steady stream that was spinning by. I think my head was dizzy with the whirl of impressions which I was garnering, but I did my best to keep a sane view of things and to get my impressions as sharp and clear as I could.

I am quite satisfied of one thing in this world, and that is that the most common intelligences are very frequently confused or hypnotized or overpersuaded by certain situations and that the weaker ones are never free of the wildest forms of illusion. We talk about the sanity of life—I question whether it exists. Mostly it is a succession of confusing, disturbing impressions which are only rarely valid. This night I know I was moving in a sort of maze, and when I stepped into the taxi and saw the two girls whom Grant Richards had produced, I easily succumbed to what was obviously their great beauty.

The artist Greuze has painted the type that I saw before me over and over and over—soft, buxom, ruddy womanhood. I think the two may have been twenty-four and twenty-six, respectively. The elder was smaller than the younger—although both were of good size—and not so ruddy, but they were both perfectly plump, round-faced, dimpled and with a wealth of brownish-black hair, even, white teeth, smooth, plump arms and necks and shoulders. Their chins were adorably round, their lips red, their eyes laughing and gay. They began laughing and chattering the moment I entered, extending their soft, white hands and saying things in French which I could not understand. Grant Richards was smiling, beaming through his monocle in an amused, superior way. I noticed that the elder girl was arrayed in pearl-colored silk with a black mantilla spangled with silver, and the younger had a dress of peach-blow hue with a white lace mantilla that was also spangled. Their slippers were of white satin, and they breathed of a faint perfume. We were obviously in beautiful, if not moral, company.

I shall never forget the grand air with which Grant Richards led this noble company into the Café de Paris. Both he and I were in fine feather so far as our own clothing was concerned—fur overcoats, silk opera hats, white gloves, all the requirements of the occasion. The ladies radiated a charm and a flavor which immediately attracted attention. This café was aglow with lights and alive with people. It is not large in size—quite small in fact—and triangular in shape. The charm of it comes not so much from the luxury of the fittings, which are luxurious enough, but from their exceeding good taste and the fame of the cuisine. One does not see a bill of fare here that indicates prices. You order what you like and are charged what is suitable. Champagne is not an essential wine, as it is in some restaurants—you may drink what you like. There is a delicious sparkle and spirit to the place which can only spring from a high sense of individuality. Paris is supposed to provide nothing better than the Café de Paris insofar as food is concerned. It is as good a place to go for dinner as the city provides. We disposed ourselves at the table reserved for us and enjoyed a delicious meal—a soup, a fish, a roast, several kinds of wine and a sweet.

It amuses me now when I think of how the managerial ability of Grant Richards had been working through all this. As the program had been arranged in his mind, I was to take the elder of the two ladies as my partner, and he had reserved the younger for himself. As a matter of fact there was really small choice between the two, and I was really interested in both until after a few parleys; and when I had exchanged a few laughing signs with the younger, he informed me that she was really closely tied up with someone else and was not available. This I really did not believe, but it did not make any particular difference. I turned my attention to the elder, who was quite as vivacious, if not quite as forceful, as her younger sister. I never knew what it meant before to sit in a company of this kind—welcome as a friend, looked to for gaiety as a companion and admirer, and yet not able to say a word in the language of the occasion. There were certain words which could be quickly acquired on an occasion of this kind, such as "beautiful," "charming," "very delightful," and so on—for which Grant Richards gave me the French equivalent—and then I could make complimentary remarks which he would translate for me, and the ladies would say things in reply which would come to me by the same source. It went gaily enough, for the conversation would not have been of a high order if I had been able to speak French. Grant Richards objected to being used constantly as an interpreter, and when he became stubborn and chattered gaily without stopping to explain, I was compelled to fall back on the resources of looks and smiles and gestures. It interested me to see how quick these women were to adapt themselves to the difficulties of the situation. They were constantly laughing and chatting between themselves, looking at me and saying obviously flattering things and then laughing at my discomfiture in not being able to understand.

The elder explained what certain objects were by lifting them up and insisting on the French name. Grant Richards was constantly telling me of the compliments they made and how sad they thought it was that I could not speak French.

We departed finally for the Folies-Bergère, where the newest sensation of Paris, Mistinguett, was playing. She proved to be a brilliant hoyden to look upon, a gay, slim, yellow-haired tomboy who seemed to fascinate the large audience by her boyish manners and her wayward air. There was a brilliant chorus in spangled silks and satins and finally a beautiful maiden without any clothing at all who was cloaked by the soldiery of the stage before she had half crossed it. The vaudeville acts were about as good as they are anywhere. I did not think the performance was any better than one might see in one or two places in New York, but of course the humor was much broader. Now and then one of their remarkable *bons mots* was translated for me by Grant Richards, just to give me an inkling of the character of the place. Back of the seats was a great lobby or promenade where a fragment of the demimonde of Paris was congregated—beautiful creatures, in many instances, and as gay as you please. I was particularly struck with the smartness of their costumes and the cheerful character of their faces. The companion type in London and New York is somewhat colder-looking. Their eyes snapped with Gallic intelligence, and they walked as though the whole world held their point of view and no other.

From here at midnight we left for the Abbaye de Thélème, and here I encountered the best that Paris has to show in the way of that gaiety and color and beauty and smartness for which it is famous. One really ought to say a great deal about the Abbaye de Thélème, because it is the last word, the quintessence, of midnight excitement and international savoir faire. The Russian and the Brazilian, the Frenchman, the American, the Englishman, the German and the Italian—all meet here on common ground. I saw much of restaurant life in Paris while I was there, but nothing better than this. Like the Café de Paris, it was small, very small, when compared to restaurants of similar repute in New York and London. I fancy it was not more than sixty feet square—only it was not square, but pentagonal, almost circular. The tables, to begin with, went around the walls, with seats which have the wall for their back; and then, as the guests pour in, the interior space is filled up with tables which are brought in for the purpose; and, later in the morning, when the guests begin to leave, these tables are taken out again and the space devoted to dancing and entertainers.

As in the Café de Paris, I noticed that it was not as much the quality of the furnishings as the spirit of the place which was important. This latter was compounded of various elements—success being the first one, perfection of service a second, absolute distinction of cooking, and lastly, the subtlety and magnetism of sex, which is capitalized and used in Paris as it is nowhere else in the world. I never actually realized until I stepped into this restaurant what it is that draws a certain monied element to Paris. The tomb of Napoleon and the Panthéon and the Louvre are not the significant attractions of that important city. Those things have their value, and they constitute a historical and artistic element that is distinguished, romantic, forceful, but over and above that there is something else—and sex is it. I did not learn until later what I am going to say now, but it might as well be said here, for it illustrates the point exactly.

The same management that controls this restaurant controls a large, gaudy, immoral dance hall in the same vicinity and a hotel next door whose gorgeously furnished rooms are let but for one purpose. The dance hall, the hotel and the restaurant are run as a joint commercial enterprise, and they supplement each other to perfection. A little experience and inquiry in Paris quickly taught me that the owners and managers of the more successful restaurants encourage and help to sustain a certain type of woman whose presence is desirable. She must be young, beautiful, or attractive, and, above all things, possessed of a temperament. A woman can rise in the café and restaurant world of Paris quite as she can on the stage, and she can easily graduate from the Abbaye de Thélème and Maxim's to the stage; and on the other hand the stage contributes freely to the atmosphere of Maxim's, the Abbaye de Thélème and others. A large number of the figures seen here and at the Folies-Bergère and other places of the same type are interchangeable. They are in the restaurants when they are not on the stage, and they are on the stage when they are not in the restaurants. They rise or fall by a world of strange devices, and you can hear positively brilliant or ghastly stories illustrating either conclusion. Paris—this aspect of it—is a perfect maelstrom of sex, and it is sustained by the wealth, the curiosity, the hedonism and the lechery of the world.

The Abbaye de Thélème on this occasion presented a brilliant scene. The carpet, as I recall it, was a rich velvet-green, the walls a lavender-white. From the ceiling six magnificently prismed electroliers were suspended, three glowing with a clear peach-blow hue and three with a brilliant white. Outside a small railing near the door, several negro singers, a mandolin and a guitar player, several stage dancers and others were congregated. A perfect storm of people was pouring through the doors, all with their tables previously arranged for. Out in the lobby, where a January wind was blowing, you could hear a wild uproar of slamming taxi doors and the calls of doormen and chauffeurs getting their vehicles in and out of the way.

The company generally, as on all such occasions, was on the *qui vive* to see who else was present and what the general spirit of the occasion was to be. Instantly I detected a number of Americans, three amazingly beautiful English women such as I never saw in England and their escorts, a few Spaniards or South Americans and, after that, a variety of individuals whom I took to be largely French, although it was impossible to tell. The English women interested me, because during all my stay in Europe, I never saw three other women quite so beautiful, and because during all my stay in England, I scarcely saw a good-looking English woman. Grant Richards suggested that they were of that high realm of fashion which rarely remains in England during the winter season—when I was there—and that if I came again in May and June I would see plenty of them. Their lovely hair was straw-colored and their cheeks pink and cream. Their arms and shoulders were delightfully bare, and they carried themselves with amazing hauteur. By one o'clock, when the majority of the guests had arrived, this room fairly shimmered with white silks and satins, white arms and shoulders, roses in black hair, and blue and lavender ribbons fastened about coiffures of lighter complexion. There were jewels in plenty—opals and amethysts and turquoises and rubies—and there was a perfect artillery of champagne corks. Every table was attended by its silver bucket of ice, and the mandolins and guitars in their crowded angle were strumming mightily.

As we seated ourselves, I speculated interestedly as to what drew all these people from all parts of the world to see this, to be here together. Grant Richards was most eager to come here first and to see that I saw this without delay. I do not know where you could go and see more of really amazing feminine beauty for a hundred francs. I do not know where for the same money you could buy the same atmosphere of lightness and gaiety and enthusiasm. This place was fairly vibrating with a wild desire to live. I fancy the majority of those who were here for the first time—particularly of the young—would tell you that they would rather be here than any place they had ever been in their life. The place had a peculiar glitter of beauty which was compounded by the managers with great skill. The waiters were all deft, swift, suave, good-looking; the dancers who stepped out on the floor after a few moments were of an orchid-like Spanish type—ruddy, brown, full-bodied, black-haired, black-eyed. They had on dresses that were as close-fitting as the scales of a fish and that glittered with the same radiance. They waved and rattled and clashed castanets and tambourines and danced wildly and sinuously to and fro among the tables. Some of them sang, or voices accompanied them from the raised platform devoted to music.

After a while, red, blue, pink and green balloons were introduced, anchored to the champagne bottles and allowed to float gaily in the air. Paper parcels of small paste balls of all colors, as light as feathers, were distributed for the guests to throw at one another. In ten minutes a pandemonium of sex enthusiasm raged. Young girls were up on their feet, their hands full of these colored weapons, pelting the male strangers of their selection. You would see tall Englishmen and Americans exchanging a perfect volley of these colored spheres with girls of various nationalities—laughing, chattering, calling, screaming. The cocotte in all her dazzling radiance was here—exquisitely dressed, her white arms shimmering, perfectly willing to strike up an understanding with the admirer who was pelting her. After a time, when the audience had worn itself through fever and frenzy to satisfaction or weariness, or both, a few of the tables were cleared away, and the dancing began. Occasional guests joined. There were charming dances in costume from Russia, from Scotland, from Hungary and from Spain. I myself joined with a Spanish dancer for a waltz and had the wonder of seeing an American girl rise from her table and dance with more skill and grace than the employed talent. A wine-enthused Englishman took the floor—a handsome youth of twenty-six or -eight—and remained there, gaily prancing about from table to table, dancing alone or with whomsoever would welcome him. What looked like a dangerous argument started at one time, because some high-mettled Brazilian considered himself insulted. A cordon of waiters and the managers soon adjusted that.

It was between three and four in the morning when we finally left, and I was very tired. Between the amount of champagne I had consumed and the glitter of the evening, I was a little dizzy. Owing to the fact that I could not speak French and because, from observation, I had confirmed myself in the feeling that Grant Richards had arranged our companionship with the mesdames for his convenience, reserving the younger of the two for himself, I had about made up my mind that I cared for neither of them. I think the champagne had something to do with this, as did the fact, to which this restaurant testified, that there were many such women in Paris, all equally beautiful. At the Folies-Bergère, sitting back of my companion, I had reached a sort of understanding with her, but later, in the Abbaye de Thélème, I did not think so well of it and rather ignored her. When we were in the taxi, it was decided that we would meet again for dinner; and since it was practically daylight, I was glad when we had seen them to their apartment and returned to the hotel. In one way this seemed a fitting introduction to Paris; and yet from another point of view it had not ended quite right. I should have gone with the lady; it was the customary thing; it was the way the majority of such dinner parties end—in Paris.

CHAPTER XXXIV

I shall never forget my first morning in Paris—I woke up after about two hours' sleep or less, prepared to put in a hard day at sightseeing, because Grant Richards had a program which must be adhered to and because he could only be with me until Monday, when he had to return. It was a bright day, fortunately, a little hazy and chill, but agreeable. I looked out of the window of my very comfortable room on the fifth floor, which gave out on a balcony overhanging the Rue St-Honoré, and watched the crowd of French people below coming to shop or to work. It would be hard to say what makes the difference between a crowd of Englishmen and a crowd of Frenchmen, but there is a difference. It struck me that these French men and women walked faster and that their every movement was more spirited than either that of the English or the Americans. They looked more like Americans, though, than like the English, and they were much more cheerful than either, chatting and talking as they came. Rue St-Honoré, being identified with Balzac, interested me, and the Rue de l'Echelle, having had something to do with the Swiss Guards, interested me also. I could not help wondering what parts these streets had played in the French Revolution, if any, and just where the dead had fallen.

I was so interested to see whether I could make the French maid understand that I wanted coffee and rolls without talking French that I gave up my speculations and returned, meanwhile taking my bath. American travelers wanting coffee and rolls for breakfast are an old story to French maids, and no sooner did I say *café* and make the sign of drinking from a cup than she said, "*Oh, oui, oui, oui—oh, oui, oui, oui!*" and disappeared. Presently the coffee was brought me and rolls and butter and hot milk, and I ate my breakfast as I dressed. About nine o'clock Grant Richards arrived with his program. I was to walk in the Tuileries—which was close at hand—while he got a shave. We were to go for a walk in the Rue de Rivoli as far as a certain bootmaker's, who was to make me a pair of shoes for the Riviera. Then we were to visit a haberdasher's or two and after that go straight about the work of sightseeing—visiting the old bookstalls on the Seine, the churches of St. Étienne-du-Mont, Notre-Dame, Sainte-Chapelle, stopping at Foyot's for lunch; and thereafter regulating our conduct by the wishes of several guests who were to appear—Anne Estelle Rice and J. D. Fergusson, two Neo-Impressionist artists, and a certain Mme. Wanita de Villiers, who spoke English and would not mind showing me around Paris if I cared for her company.

We started off quite briskly about this, and my first adventure in Paris led me straight to the gardens of the Tuileries, lying west of the Louvre. If anyone wanted a proper introduction to Paris, I should recommend this above all others. It is a strip of ground lying between the Rue St-Honoré and the Seine and stretching for several miles in the direction of the Bois, into which it gives. Such a noble piece of gardening as this is the best testimony France has to offer as to its taste, discrimination and sense of the magnificent. I should say, on mature thought, that we shall never have anything like it in America. We have not the same lightness of fancy. And besides, the Tuileries represent a classic period.

I recall walking in here and being struck at once with the magnificent proportions of it all, the breadth and stately lengths of its walks, the utter wonder and charm of its statuary—snow-white marble nudes standing out on the green grass and marking the circles, squares and paths of its entire length. No such charm and beauty could be attained in America, because we would not permit the public use of the nude in this fashion. Only the fancy of a monarch could create a realm such as this; and the Tuileries and the Place du Carrousel and the Place de la Concorde and the whole stretch of lovely tree-lined walks and drives that give into the Bois de Boulogne and lead to the Arc de Triomphe speak loudly of a noble fancy untrammeled by the dictates of an inartistic public opinion.

I was astonished to find how much of its heart Paris has devoted to public usage in this manner. It corresponds, in theory at least, to the space devoted to Central Park in New York—but this is so much more beautiful, or at least it is so much more in accord with the spirit of Paris. These splendid walks, devoted solely to the idling pedestrian and set with a hundred sculptural fancies in marble, show the gay, pleasure-loving character of the life which created them. The grand monarchs of France knew what beauty was, and they had the courage and the taste to fulfill their desires. Look as you will, either from the Place de la Concorde to the Louvre, or from the Louvre to the Place de la Concorde, and you have a spectacle of beauty such as no other city affords. To crown it all, you can look from the Place de la Concorde across the Seine to the Esplanade des Invalides and see the Napoleonic supplement to what had gone before; with the space lying between the Trocadéro and the École Militaire, containing the Eiffel Tower, which soars like a bit of lacework a thousand feet in the air and commands the whole, and the connecting Cours la Reine—all this constitutes a public park or space of almost perfect qualities. If the Seine is not a majestic river, at least it is a gay and dashing one—quick-tempered, rapid-flowing, artistically walled, crossed by a score of handsome bridges and ornamented in every notable way. I got an inkling of it all in the fifteen minutes that I walked here in the morning sun, waiting for Grant Richards to get his shave.

From here we went to a Paris florist's where Madame pinned bright boutonnieres on our coats, and thence to the bootmaker's where Madame assisted her husband in the conduct of his business. Everywhere I went in Paris I was struck by this charming unity of husband and wife and son and daughter. We talk much about the economic independence of women in America. It seems to me that the French have solved it in the only way that it can be solved. Madame helps her husband in his business, and they make a success of it together. Monsieur Galoyer took the measurements for my shoes, but Madame entered them in a book; and to me, the shop was fifty times as charming for her presence. She was pleasingly dressed, and the shop looked as though it had experienced the tasteful touches of a woman's hand. It was clean and bright and smart and smacked of good housekeeping; and this was equally true of bookstalls, haberdashers, art stores, coffee rooms and places of public sale generally. Wherever Madame was, and she looked nice, there was a nice store; and Monsieur looked as fat and contented as could reasonably be expected under the circumstances.

As far as I could make out, Grant Richards had fixed in his own mind on the few historic things—outside of the gay life which he loves so much—which were important to see. One of these was the church of St. Étienne-du-Mont, and although I was for lingering by the way and sidetracking into other institutions, he would not have it. I could see all those when he was gone.

I shall never forget this first morning impression of Paris, although all my impressions of it were delightful and enthusing, from the poorest quarter of the Charenton district to the perfections of the Bois and the region about the Arc de Triomphe. It chanced that this morning was bright, and I saw the Seine glimmering over the stones of its shallow banks and racing madly. It was so interesting to me how much the French had made of so little in the way of a river. It is not very wide—about one-half as wide as the Thames at Blackfriars Bridge, and no whit wider than the Harlem River which makes Manhattan an island or the Chicago River east of the juncture of its two branches. It is about as wide as the Schuylkill in Philadelphia or the Charles in Boston or the Tiber at Rome or the Spree in Berlin. It is interesting how rivers do vary in their character. Here the Seine was as bright as new buttons—its banks properly lined with gray but not dull-looking walls, the two streets which parallel it on either side alive with traffic, every few blocks a handsome bridge, every block a row of very habitable, if not imposing, apartment houses, at various points views of Notre-Dame, the Tuileries, the Cours la Reine, of the Trocadéro and the Eiffel Tower.

I followed the Seine from city wall to city wall one day, from Charenton to Issy, and found every inch of it delightful, heavenly. I was never tired of looking at the wine barges near Charenton, the little bathing pavilions and passenger boats in the vicinity of the Louvre, the brick barges, hay barges,

How much the French had made of so little in the way of a river

coal barges and heaven knows what else, plying between the city's heart and points downstream past Issy. It gave me the impression of being one of the brightest, cleanest rivers in the world—a river on a holiday. Its water is not blue, but it has some such effect at times. It looks as though one might drink it, which is more than you can say for the Thames or the Tiber or the Arno or the Spree; and as for spirit, I can only say that it gave me an intense sense of lightness and freedom from care.

I was always happy, gay, poetic in my mood when I walked along its banks, wherever I happened to be. It seemed to me to be compounded of all the joys and all the beauties that one could wish in a river. Once at Issy at what is known as the "green hour," which is five o'clock—when the sun was going down and a perfume wafted from a vast manufactory of perfume and men were poling boats of hay, and laborers were trudging home in their great wide-bottomed corduroy trousers, blue shirts and inimitable French caps—I felt as though the world had nothing to offer Paris which it did not already have—even the joy of simple labor amid great beauty. I could have settled in a small house in Issy and been a laborer in a perfume factory, carrying my dinner pail with me every morning, with a right goodwill—or so I thought at the time. As I write this, the mood comes back, and I feel as though I would rather live in Paris in any one of a hundred obscure realms I discovered than be the occupant of more pretentious quarters in any other city in the world. Paris sings constantly with a light, gay voice and a thrilling sense of life which I did not find anywhere else in my travels.

This morning, on our way to St. Étienne-du-Mont and the cathedral, we examined the bookstalls along the Seine and tried to recall offhand the interesting comments that have been made on them by great authors and travelers. My poor wit brought back only the references of Balzac, but Grant Richards was livelier with thoughts from Rousseau to George Moore. They have a magnificent literary history; but it is only because they are on the banks of the Seine in the center of this whirling pageant of life that they are so delightful.

One has to be in an idle mood and love out-of-doors to enjoy the bookstalls, for they consist of a dusty row of four-legged boxes with lids coming quite to your chest in height and reminding one of those high-legged counting tables at which clerks sit on tall stools and write. These boxes are old and paintless and weather-beaten, and at night the very dusty-looking keepers, who from early morning until dark have had their shabby-backed wares spread out where dust and sunlight and wind and rain can attack them, pack them in the body of the box on which they are lying and close the lid. You can always see an idler or two here—perhaps many idlers—between the Quai d'Orsay and the Quai Voltaire, and I studied some of them purely because of curiosity aroused by previous comment. They seemed to be interested enough, for this is a dreary business spot, no doubt, to the native Parisian and those who come here come to buy. It reminded me curiously of the thrill of life that once existed about the old Madison Street Bridge in Chicago when that was the chief artery to the West Side, and also of the old bookstalls that used to exist on Fourth Avenue between Astor Place and 14th Street, New York. New York and Chicago, I beg to state, have much in common with Paris in their intense love of life, their gay sense and suggestion of ability to live and to live gladly. And that is what I felt on the banks of the Seine on this, my first morning in Paris.

We made our way through the Rue Mazarin and Rue de l'Ancienne-Comédie into that region which surrounds the École de Médecine and the Luxembourg. In his enthusiastic way Grant Richards tried to indicate to me that I was in the most historic section of the left bank of the Seine, where were St. Étienne-du-Mont, the Panthéon, the Sorbonne, the Luxembourg, the École des Beaux-Arts and the Latin Quarter. In this same Rue Mazarin we came upon a society of secessionists in art—and, of all things, secessionists from the Neo-Impressionists—which surprised me greatly. "In God's name, what can that be?" I asked Grant Richards. "What do they paint?"

A command of his best American slang, on which he prides himself, came to Grant Richards's rescue. "Search me—as you Americans say," he replied. "I did not know that anyone had seceded, but you can always predict that in Paris. I must go and see what they have to show." That was the last I heard of these secessionists, however, while I was in Paris.

This region, for a first adventure in Paris, proved as delightful as any. We came for a little way into the Boulevard St-Michel, and there I saw my first artists in velvet suits, long hair and broad-brimmed hats; but I was told that they were poseurs—the kind of artist that is so by profession, not by accomplishment. They were poetic-looking youths—the two that I saw swinging along together—with pale, thin faces and slim hands. I was informed that the type had almost entirely disappeared and that the art student of today prefers to be distinctly inconspicuous. From what I saw of them later, I can confirm this; for the schools which I visited revealed a type of boy and girl who, while being romantic enough in all conscience, were nevertheless inconspicuously dressed and very simple and offhand in their manner. I visited this region later with artists who had made a name for themselves in the radical world, and with students who were hoping to make a name for themselves—sitting in their cafés, examining their studios and sensing the atmosphere of their streets and public amusements. There is an art atmosphere, strong and clear, compounded of romance, emotion, desire, love of beauty and determination of purpose, which is thrilling to feel. There may be as many as thirty or forty thousand art students in Paris—possibly more—and they live a life which has been written of and sung of until it is stale; but it is still there in all its richness and color, and it will glow no doubt long after we are dead, as it has this long while before we came.

My impression of this region, as I saw it this morning, was as good as any I secured later. It was merely confirmed by a subsequent visit. The houses are old—not so old that they have any flavor of the antique, but older than the newer portions of Paris. The streets are narrower than they are in some of the other sections, except where they are cut through by the magnificent boulevards which have come since the Empire. The "Boule Miche" and the "Boule St-Germain" are, of course, lined with shops, but they have that delicious Parisian characteristic which is nowhere else in the world—the wide sidewalk and the café with its many chairs. The streets, although looking a little murky as compared with the rest of Paris, were nevertheless throbbing with that life which is purely Parisian.

Paris, as far as I can make out, is as young in its mood as any city in the world. It is as wildly enthusiastic as a child. I noticed here this morning the strange characteristic of old, battered-looking individuals singing to themselves, which I never noticed anywhere else in this world. Age sits lightly on the Parisian, I am sure; and youth is a wild fantasy, an exciting realm of romantic dreams. There may run through it all a practical conservatism which works out to the financial salvation of millions; but it is nevertheless delicious in its erotic enthusiasm. The Parisian—from the keeper of a market stall to the prince of the money world, or of art—wants to live gaily, briskly, laughingly, and he will not let the necessity of earning his living deny him.

I felt it in the churches, the depots, the restaurants, the streets—a wild, keen desire for life, with the blood and the body to back it up. It must be in the soil and the air, for Paris sings. It is like poison in the veins, and I felt myself growing positively giddy with enthusiasm. I believe that for the first six months Paris would be a disease from which one would suffer greatly and recover slowly. After that you would settle down to live the life you found there in contentment and with delight, but you would not be in so much danger of wrecking your very mortal body and your uncertainly immortal soul.

The church of St. Étienne-du-Mont is really quite central to a number of important features of the left bank of the Seine—the Sorbonne, the Panthéon, the Luxembourg, the École de Médecine, the Musée de Cluny, the Jardin des Plantes and the Halle aux Vins. The church is as fine as possible, a type of the kind of architecture which is no type and ought to have a new name—"modern" is as good as any. It has a creamish-gray effect, exceedingly ornate, with all the artificery of a jewel-box. The striped black-and-white layers of the columns that support the Greek pediment which surmounts the door suggest the Orient. So does the mosque-like cupola of the tower, but the remainder of the church suggests anything you please—a jumble of all the variations that have occurred in the last five hundred years. It is not Gothic, not Greek, not Byzantine, and yet it is very charming to look upon—an accidental artistic creation compounded of many things.

It is not a notably large church and yet not very small, amazingly ornate on the interior, plastered with rich marbles, and containing the tomb of Sainte Geneviève, who seems to have routed out Saint Denis, the patron saint of Paris. I learned a little of the almost humorous history of the latter saint from Grant Richards as we walked and later from guidebooks which were in my possession. The Panthéon, which is so very nearby and which contains the tombs of Voltaire and Zola and Hugo, was built as a church to house the miracle-working remains of this particular lady. Revolutions, Communes and changes of government turned the Panthéon back and forth from church to Panthéon until finally the saint's body was destroyed and the tomb removed to this church. I was not very much interested, save that the tomb was interesting to look at, being covered with a hundred candles, all lighted, and having a score of supplicants kneeling before it. There was also a funeral ceremony in progress in the church at the time, with the casket standing in the central aisle and the nave full of a great company of mourners. In addition there were vendors of picture-postcards and a guide or two, all doing business uninterrupted. I could not help admiring the design of the interior, though it would be hard to describe it. As rich and slender columns as I ever saw supported a high, many-angled, many-windowed roof. The magnificent arch or bridge of pierced stone revealing exquisite and almost endless workmanship divides the nave from the choir. Back of the central altar are other shrines and many rich windows—obviously a church fostered by wealth. Personally I would not exchange a single Greek temple or a Gothic chapter house for a score of it.

The one thing that interested me in this neighborhood, as we hurried through and away from it to the Ile-de-la-Cité and Notre-Dame, was that it has always been a center for students of the Sorbonne and art strugglers of the Latin Quarter. I was told that there were thousands upon thousands of students from various countries at the Sorbonne—among them eight thousand from Russia alone. How they live my informant did not seem to know, except that, in the main, they lived very badly. Baths, clean linen and three meals a day, according to him, were not at all common, and in the majority of instances they starve their way through, going back to their native countries to take up the practice of law, medicine, politics and other professions. After Oxford and the American universities this region and the Sorbonne itself were anything but attractive. It is too hard and bare, somewhat like a university located on the East Side in New York would be. Yet for those who rejoice in Parisian atmospheres and an ancient and quaint vicinity, it would be attractive enough.

My first impression of Notre-Dame was spoiled for me by my having first seen Canterbury and Amiens. Notre-Dame is Gothic—magnificent Gothic after its kind—but exceedingly heavy and not too ornate. It has a splendid position on its little island in the Seine, and seen from day to day, as a local pedestrian would see it, it would take on great magnificence and charm. But after Amiens and Canterbury it was not light enough for me, not airy enough, not graceful enough. It was really not sufficiently a flight of fancy. Somehow it was deliciously suggestive of all the history that is connected with it, from Saint Denis down, but it is nevertheless heavy and dark and somber. Any great pile like this is necessarily impressive, both on the interior and the exterior, and it has amazing buttresses, sturdy towers, solid round columns of granite that are impressive, but not airy as Gothic should be. I read all the history connected with it this day and evening, but it was more precious to me for the references in Balzac and Hugo. Balzac really estimated it best at its true worth in connection with the life of the city; and the touches you will find in the *Great Man from the Provinces* and the *Wild Ass's Skin* cast over it the glamour of genius which can nevermore be taken away.

From Notre-Dame we passed by the Hôtel-Dieu and the Pont St. Michel to the Palais de Justice and Sainte-Chapelle. I thought at first that all the policemen about were soldiers, and that this was some sort of barracks where a daily drill occurred. I was not yet used to the red-lined capes, short swords and soldierly caps of the Paris police. So many of the public buildings of Paris, like the Hôtel-Dieu, the Hôtel de Ville, the Palais de Justice, the Louvre and other institutions which have come down from an older day, are reminiscent of the worst in American architecture—the old city hall and court house of Chicago and the deadly commonplace city hall of Philadelphia. In some respects they are not even as imposing. As a rule they are very large, very gray or brown, very stuffy and without that lightness or distinctness of treatment which characterizes other great buildings in Paris and elsewhere.

In looking at these things, one often wonders why the architects of public buildings have not borrowed more heavily from the old ducal palaces of Italy or the splendid Tudor achievements of England. We have done much better with our Capitol at Washington and with many of our state capitols and city halls. In these older institutions so famed in literature and, to a certain extent, in historic art, the architects did not realize the value of simplicity. There is nowhere that the eye can follow a smooth line or clear space. It is endless convolutions and flutings and gingerbread excrescences, until the eye cannot rest. Here and there, in such buildings as the Musée Galliera, the Musée de Cluny, the Musée Carnavalet, the Petit Palais, the church of the Madeleine, the Palais Royal and others, one realizes what the genius of French architecture has accomplished. To deny that these other institutions are imposing and impressive because of their mere bulk would be folly. They rank with such institutions as Somerset House in London, the new city hall in Brussels and the Metropolitan Museum of Art in New York. If these have artistic value, then all these great institutions in Paris have that. To me, their only distinction is their tremendous size.

But in the courtyard of the Palais de Justice, alive with policemen and French barristers in their robes and black caps, is the Sainte-Chapelle—to me, it was one of the most charming exteriors and interiors I saw in Paris. It is so exquisite, this chapel which was once the scene of the private prayers of a king, but it is now merely an open showplace into which anyone can walk during the hours when it is exhibited. This day that I saw it, the sun was pouring through its tall, narrow, prismatic windows, and the interior was transfused with light broken into ten thousand shades and colors and melted into one. Although it is only a little chapel, it is such a brilliant illustration of what can be done with the Gothic, whether the building is large or small. The Greek temple, the Italian basilica, the Byzantine mosque, the Gothic chapels and cathedrals seem to me to be the only true church forms anyhow, and Sainte-Chapelle shows what can be done with a little Gothic. In one of the walls of the chapel there is a small latticework behind which, it is said, Louis XI sat to hear his mass. This brought back a suggestion of that interesting French life which is so vivid in history, but I confess it is hard for me to appreciate the suggestions of the old in such a whirling modern metropolis as Paris is today. Now and then it came back—beautiful touches; and, as if these things were stained-glass windows through which the light of the past were streaming, all Paris is transfigured by it. But to take the individual thing and have the past come back is hard.

By this time the semi-circle of significant institutions, seen in the light of an entirely new social atmosphere, had set my brain in a whirl. My head was going around in a ring, and there were still so many things to see. There was a luncheon at Foyot's, a little restaurant near the Luxembourg and the Musée de Cluny, where the wise in the matter of food love to dine and where, as usual, Grant Richards was at his best. He had, as I have said, invited two Neo-Impressionists—one an American girl hailing from Philadelphia and one a Scotch artist from Edinburgh, I believe—both greatly interested in the radical movement in art and working together in some way which I did not quite understand at first. I sometimes think that Grant Richards is one of the most secretive men I ever knew, for in many simple matters in regard to the people we were to meet, he would leave me entirely in the dark. I would get some vague impression of something, and then the whole matter would come to light of its own accord. In this instance, the relations of Mr. Fergusson and Miss Rice did not come to light until some little time after, but when it did, it was all as clear as day and frankly admitted on both sides. I was prepared to meet two interesting people, for I never knew my mentor to produce uninteresting ones, but I was not very much impressed at first. It was interesting to sit in Foyot's, however, and contrast the clean but commonplace little rooms with restaurants of similar reputation in America.

Foyot's, as the initiated will attest, is a delightful place to lunch or dine, for the cooking is perfection itself. The French, while discarding show in many instances entirely and leaving their restaurant chambers to look as though they had been put together with an effort, nevertheless attain a distinction of atmosphere which is astonishing. For the life of me, I could not tell why this little restaurant seemed so smart and bright, for there was nothing either smart or bright about it when you examined it in detail; and so I was compelled to attribute my impression to the probably all-pervading temperament of the owner. Always, in these cases, there is a man, or a woman, quite remarkable for his point of view, and although I did not see him, I fancied the owner, whatever his name, must be such a man. Otherwise you could not take plain white tables and brown leather wall seats and rooms with ceilings not more than ten feet from the floor and make them into anything so pleasing and enthusing and soothing. A lunch which had been ordered by telephone was now served, and at the beginning of its gastronomic wonders Mr. Fergusson and Miss Rice arrived.

I shall not soon forget the interesting temperaments of these two, for even more than great institutions, individuals who come reasonably close to you make up the atmosphere of the city, and these two did. Mr. Fergusson was a solid, sandy, steady-eyed Scotchman who looked as though, had he not been an artist, he might have been a kilted soldier, swinging along with the enviable Scotch stride. Miss Rice was a delightfully Parisianized American, without the slightest affectation, however, so far as I could make out—of either speech or manner. She was pleasingly good-looking, with black hair, a healthy, rounded face and figure and a cheerful, good-natured air. There was no sense of either that aggressiveness or superiority which so often characterizes the female artist.

We launched at once upon a discussion of Paris, London and New York and upon the delights of Paris and the progress of the Neo-Impressionist cult. I could see plainly that these two did not care to force their conviction with that art development on my attention, but I was interested to know of it. There was something so solid and self-reliant about Mr. Fergusson that although I did not care for him to begin with, before the meal was over I had taken a fancy to him. He had the least suggestion of a Scotch burr in his voice which might have said, "awau" instead of "away" and "doon" instead of "down," but it resulted in nothing so broad as that. They immediately gave me a list of restaurants that I must see in the Latin Quarter and asked me to come with them to the Café d'Harcourt and to Bullier's to dance and to some of the brasseries to see what they were like.

Between two and three, Mr. Fergusson left because of an errand, and Grant Richards and I accompanied Miss Rice to the Gardens of the Luxembourg to her studio in the Rue Denfert-Rochereau. I shall not soon forget my impression of this delightful public garden which, not unlike the Tuileries on the other side of the Seine, was set with charming statues, embellished by a magnificent fountain, and alive with French nursemaids and their charges, idling Parisians in cutaways and derbies, and a smart world of pedestrians generally. The wonder of Paris, as I was discovering, was that, walk where you will, it was hard to escape the sense of breadth, space, art, history, romance and a lovely sense of lightness and enthusiasm for life.

CHAPTER XXXV

Since the two studios occupied by Miss Rice and Mr. Fergusson formed an interesting part of the art atmosphere I witnessed in Paris, I shall describe them in detail. Miss Rice's, in the Rue Denfert-Rochereau, had a pleasing sense of light and space, an exceedingly high ceiling and tall windows which opened out on one side (to the northeast) in the Rue Denfert-Rochereau and to the southeast into the court on which it was placed. In calling here I had my first taste of the Paris concierge, the janitress who has charge of all entrées and exits and to whom all those not having keys must apply. In many cases, as I learned, not even keys are given to the outer gate or door. One must ring and be admitted. This gives this person a complete espionage over the affairs of all the tenants, mail, groceries, guests, purchases, messages—anything and everything. If you have a charming concierge, well and good; if not, not. In the studio of Mr. Fergusson in the Boulevard Raspail, it was the same, only here his studio overlooked a lovely garden—a heavenly place set with trees and flowers and reminiscent of an older day in the shape of bits of broken stonework lying about, which suggested the architecture of a bygone period. His windows, reaching from floor to ceiling and supplemented by exterior balconies, were overhung by trees. In both were scores of canvases done in the Neo-Impressionistic style, which made a profound impression on me.

It is one thing to see Neo-Impressionism hung upon the walls of a gallery in London or disputed over in a West End residence. It is quite another to come upon it fresh from the easel in the studio of the artist or still in process of production, defended by every thought and principle of which the artist is capable. In Miss Rice's studio were a series of decorative canvases, intended for the walls of a great department store in America, which were done in raw reds, yellows, blues and greens of the Neo-Impressionist cult—flowers which stood out with the coarse distinctness of hollyhocks and sunflowers; architectural outlines which were as sharp as those of rough buildings; and men and women whose details of dress and feature were characterized by colors which the uncultivated eye would pronounce unnatural. Looking at life, however, one wonders whether the average picture reflects the actual force of things, whether we have risen mentally to the place where we can transfer our very sharp impression of physical objects to canvas and not feel them to be exaggerations. We pay so little attention to what we see as a rule—chair, book, table, lamppost—anything you please; but if we see it at all, for even so brief a time, we see it clearly. Yet transfer a book or a chair to canvas, literally as it looks when it strikes the eye, and it is apt to appear hard, forced, exaggerated. So seemed most of the things in Miss Rice's pictures.

It was the same in the studio of Mr. Fergusson, to which we journeyed after some three-quarters of an hour. To me, of the two painters, Mr. Fergusson seemed the more forceful. Grant Richards confided to me that he thought Miss Rice had been greatly influenced by him. But in spite of this close relationship, I decided later that she had managed to retain her artistic individuality and integrity. She worked in a softer mood, with more of what might be called an emotional attitude towards life. His canvases were unquestionably brilliant realism after their kind and were highly appreciated in certain directions. When we visited there, he was already gathering them up for an exhibition in London; and it was because of admiration enthusiastically expressed that he gave Grant Richards one of his charcoal sketches, a drawing of a café type which netted him considerable praise later. It was in the Scotchman's best Neo-Impressionist vein—a daring, undecipherable, emotional Gaelic type.

Grant Richards was in the heyday of his Parisian glory and appropriately cheerful. We took a taxi through singing streets lighted by a spring-like evening sun and came finally to the Restaurant Prunier, where it was necessary for him to reserve a table and order dinner in advance; and thence to the Théâtre des Capucines in the Rue des Capucines, where tickets for a farce had to be secured; and thence to Gerny's Bar near the Avenue de l'Opéra, where we were to meet the previously mentioned Mme. de Villiers, who was, out of the goodness of her heart and for other considerations, to help entertain me while I was in the city. Although I do not take the feminine type which Mme. de Villiers represents very seriously, I shall never forget this remarkable woman, who by her beauty, simplicity, utter frankness and moody immorality would shock the average woman into a deadly fear of life and make a horror of what seems a gaudy pleasure world to some. Yet I think it was more a matter of Mme. de Villiers's attitude than the things which she did which made them so terrible. But that is a long story.

We came to her out of the whirl of the "green hour," when the Paris boulevards in this vicinity were fairly swarming with people—the gayest swarming world I have ever seen. We have enormous crowds in New York, but they seem to be going somewhere very much more definitely than the Paris crowd. In New York there is an eager, strident, almost objectionable effort to get home or to the theater or to the restaurant which one can easily resent—it is so inconsiderate and indifferent. In London you do not feel that there are any crowds that are going either to the theaters or the restaurants, and if they are, they are not very cheerful about it; they are enduring life. In Bishopsgate and Canon Street and the Strand and Piccadilly I marked storms of people who were going everywhere at this same hour, but they had none of the lightness of the Parisian world. I think it is all explained by the fact that the Parisians feel keenly that they are living now and that they wish to enjoy themselves as they go. The American and the Englishman—the Englishman much more than the American—have decided that they are going to live in the future. Only the American is a little angry about his decision and the Englishman a little meek or patient. They both feel that life is intensely grim. But the Parisian, while he may feel or believe it, decides wilfully to cast it off. He lives by the way, out of books, restaurants, theaters, boulevards and the spectacle of life generally. They trot briskly, and they come out where they can see each other into the great wide-sidewalked boulevards and the thousands upon thousands of cafés and make themselves comfortable and talkative and gay on the streets.

It is so obvious that everybody is having a good time—not merely trying to have it—that they are enjoying the wine-like air, the cordials and *apéritifs* of the brasseries, the net-like movements of the cabs, the dancing lights of the roadways and the flare of the shops. It may be chill or drizzling in Paris, but you scarcely feel it. Rain can scarcely drive the people off the streets. Literally it does not. There are crowds whether it rains or not, and they are not despondent. This particular hour in which we made our way from Prunier's to the Théâtre des Capucines, and from the Théâtre des Capucines to Gerny's Bar, was essentially thrilling, and I was interested to see what Mme. de Villiers was like.

A charmingly proportioned girl of twenty-two or -three with really a flower-like face of much beauty—But first let me describe Gerny's Bar. It was only by intuition, and by asking many questions, that at times I was able to extract the significance of certain atmospheres from Grant Richards as quickly as I wished. He was always reticent or a little cryptic in his allusions. In this instance I gathered rapidly, however, that Gerny's Bar was a very

The thousands upon thousands of cafés

extraordinary little restaurant presided over by one Mme. Gerny, a woman of a most pleasant and practical type. She could not have been much over forty—buxom, good-looking, self-reliant, efficient. She moved about the two rooms which constituted her restaurant, insofar as the average diner was concerned, with the air of a hostess of considerable significance. Her dresses, as I noticed, were always sober but in excellent taste. About this time of day the two rooms were a little dark, the electric lights being reserved for the more crowded hours, yet there were always a few people here. This evening when we entered I noticed a half-dozen men and three or four young women lounging here in a preliminary way, consuming *apéritifs* and chatting socially.

I made out by degrees that Mme. Gerny was a patroness of sorts, that she had a following of a kind in the Parisian scheme of things, that certain men and certain women came here for reasons of good fellowship; and that she would take a certain type of struggling maiden, if she were good-looking and ambitious and smart, under her wing. The girl would have to know how to dress well, to be able to carry herself with an air—and when money was being spent very freely by an admirer, it might as well be spent at Gerny's Bar on occasion as anywhere else. There seemed to be, it was quite obvious, an *entente cordiale* between Mme. Gerny and all the young women who came in here. They seemed so much at home that it was quite like a family party. Everybody appeared to be genial, cheerful, and to know everybody else. To enter here was to feel as though you had lived in Paris for years.

While we were sitting at a table sipping a brandy and soda, Mme. de Villiers entered, a brisk, genial, sympathetic French personage whose voice on the instant gave me a delightful impression of her. It was, as I have repeatedly said, the loveliest voice I ever heard. It was so soft and cooing and musical. It had a combined atmosphere of gaiety and sadness, touched with a suggestion of color—what, it would be impossible to say. Her eyes were of a light blue and her hair brown and her manner sinuous and insinuating. She seemed to have the spirit of a delightfully friendly collie dog or child and all the spirit and alertness that goes with them.

"Oh yes, there you are, you Grant Richards!" and after I had been introduced, "You know, he is the worst, he never tells me when he is coming. I never know beforehand. I just get a note, and then here he is." She laughed, and putting aside her muff and stole, shook herself into a comfortable position in a corner and accepted a brandy and soda. She was so interested for the moment, exchanging whys and wherefores with Grant Richards that I had a chance to observe her carefully and to decide whether I liked her at all or not. In a moment she turned to me and wanted to know whether I knew either of two American authors whom she knew—men of considerable repute. Knowing them both very well, it surprised me to think that she knew them. She seemed, from the way she spoke, to have been on the friendliest terms with both of them, and anyone by looking at her could have understood why they should have taken such an interest in her.

"Now, you know, that Mistaire N., he is very nice. I was very fond of him. And Mr. R., he is clever, don't you think?"

I admitted at once that they were both very able men and that I was glad that she knew them. She informed me that she had known Mr. R. and Mr. N. in London and that she had there perfected her English, which was very good indeed. I was amused to think what Grant Richards's relationship to her must have been, for she chided him gaily, but in a way wistfully, for negligence. To avoid teasing on that score, he explained in full who I was and how long I would be in Paris and that he had written her from America because he wanted her to show me some attention during my stay in Paris.

If Mme. de Villiers had been of a somewhat more calculating type, I fancy that with her intense charm of face and manner and her intellect and voice, she would have been very successful. I gained the impression that she had been on the stage in some small capacity, but she had been too diffident—not really brazen enough—for the grim world in which the French actress rises. Callousness extending far into the realms of brutality is the be-all and the end-all for the talented in that realm. I soon gained the impression that Mme. de Villiers was a charming blend of emotion, desire and refinement which had strayed into the wrong field. She would have done better in literature or music or art, and she seemed fitted by her moods and her understanding to be a light in any one of them, or all.

I shall never forget how she looked at me, quite in the spirit of a gay, uncertain child, and how quickly we reached the feeling that we would get along very well together. "Why, yes," she said quite easily in her soft voice, "I will go about with you, although I would not know what is best to see. But I shall be here, and if you want to come for me, we can see things together." Suddenly she reached over and took my hand and squeezed it genially. We had more drinks to seal the rather festive occasion, and then Mme. de Villiers went away. It was high time then to dress for dinner at Prunier's, and so we returned to the hotel.

It was a peculiar and an amusing evening which followed, for, as it turned out, the two cocottes whom we had taken to the Abbaye de Thélème the evening before were again invited to dinner—why, I did not know. By contrast with Mme. de Villiers and Miss Rice, they were not very interesting, but Grant Richards seemed to think that some connection which he had intended should be made had not been made and that tonight would adjust matters. I was really in no mood to see them anymore, for I had been caught by the desire to see Paris this night alone with Grant Richards; but no, that would not do. One must always have feminine companionship in Paris, according to him. And so we journeyed to Prunier's to await their coming. As it turned out, fortunately, they did not arrive. Some disagreement or misunderstanding between them and their host which was never straightened out caused them to fail to keep their appointment, though we saw them later on the Riviera. We ate a companionable meal, watching the Parisian and his ladylove or his wife arrive in droves and dine with that gusto and enthusiasm which is so characteristic of the French. Like Foyot's it was decidedly unpretentious, surprisingly so to retain the patronage which it had. I was again satisfied that the temperament of the owner and the perfection of the cuisine must be responsible.

To make up for the defection of our invited guests, it was necessary to send for someone to complete the evening, and so Mme. de Villiers was thought of—Mme. de Villiers and any friend who would occupy the seats intended for the mesdames—at the Théâtre des Capucines. A taxi driver was dispatched bearing a note and soon returned with the reply that Mme. de Villiers would join us later at the theater, and so we finished our meal in comfort.

I would not say more of this evening except that it gave me another glimpse of this unquestionably remarkable woman, who was especially charming in a pale bluish-gray dress and gray furs. She wore a gray fur cap, which gave her face a roguish look, and a gray muff and stole. She helped entertain us through what, to me, was a somewhat dull performance of a farce in a tongue that I did not understand. I was entertained by the effective character work of the actors, but nothing compensates, as I found everywhere, for my ignorance of French. In Germany, where I understood the language sufficiently well to talk it slowly, certain plays or scenes were ruined for me by the fast talking of the actors.

By now it was that I was gaining the impression that Paris was not unlike New York—very much like it, in fact, so much so that barring the quantity of force involved and the intention of the people to succeed greatly, there is no real difference. The spirit and atmosphere of the two cities, where the notable difference comes in, is in a certain superior buoyancy which the French have and a certain ultra-daring and give-and-take which we lack. New York buildings are superior to Parisian buildings in size and solidity—some of them—but they do not give one the impression of artistic plan which characterizes many French structures. All of Paris is laid out on a wider and lighter and airier plan, and it seems in all its phases to suit the temperament of the French people. New York is larger, fiercer, grosser, but with the same spirit. I think New York bears the same relation to Paris that Rome did to Athens. The Greeks were gay and meticulously effective; Rome was gay also, but its lines of power were flung to the farthest reaches of the known world. That is really the difference between Paris and New York.

When we came out of this theater at half after eleven, Mme. de Villiers was anxious to return to her apartment, and Grant Richards was anxious to give me a taste of all the significant café life of Paris before he should leave the next night for London. "If you know where they are and see whether you like them, you can tell whether you want to see any more of them after I'm gone—which I hope you won't," said Grant Richards loftily, leading the way through a swirling crowd that was for all the world like a rushing tide of the sea.

Certain sections of Paris at this time of night reminded me of the vicinity of the Metropolitan Opera House at the closing hour, when a thousand carriages are doing their best to make the doors, and the neighboring streets are a helter-skelter of vehicles and pedestrians endeavoring to escape with their lives. There are no traffic laws in Paris, so far as I could make out; it is silly to quote the old joke about being arrested if you are run over by a Parisian cab, but truly I imagine there is something in it. They certainly have the right-of-way, and they go like mad. I read of the Parisian authorities having imported a London policeman to teach the Paris police the art of traffic regulation, but if so, their instruction has been wasted. This night in which we put Mme. de Villiers in a taxi and sent her spinning away reminded me of a bedlam of vehicles and people.

A Paris guide, one of the tribe that conducts the pornographic-minded stranger through scenes that are supposedly evil and through immorality that I know from observation to be utterly vain, approached us somewhere in the Boulevard des Capucines with the suggestion that he be allowed to conduct us through a realm of filthy sights, some of which he catalogued. I would give a list of them if I thought that any human organization would ever print them, or that any individual would ever care to read them—which I don't. I have indicated before that Grant Richards is essentially clean-minded, for all his flirtations with romantic mistresses. He is really and solely interested in the art of the demimondaine and the spectacle which their showy and, to a certain extent, pornographic lives present. No one in this world ever saw more clearly through the shallow make-believe of this realm than he does.

Like all really thinking persons, his mind is confused by the spectacle in contradictions which life presents, and not being willing to accept any theory as to how it should be lived, he contents himself with admiring the art and the tragedy and the pathos of it. I fancy I am in much the same position intellectually. This world of women in the Abbaye de Thélème, Gerny's Bar, the Théâtre des Capucines interested him as examples of the struggle for existence and the artistic pretense which it sometimes compels.

To him, the vast majority of these women in Paris were artistic—whatever one might say for their morals, their honesty, their brutality and the other qualities which they possess or lack; and whatever they were, life made them so—conditions over which their temperaments, understandings and wills had little or no control. He is an amazingly tolerant man, one of the most tolerant I have ever known, and kindly in his manner and intention.

Nevertheless he has an innate horror of the purely physical when it descends to inartistic brutality. There is much of that in Paris, and these guides advertise it, but it is filth especially arranged for the stranger. I fancy the average Parisian knows nothing about it, and if he does, he has a profound contempt for it. So has the well-intentioned stranger, but there is always an audience of pornographic-minded yokels who are willing to pay a fair price to see what Paris has to offer. So when this guide approached us with the proposition to show us a selected line of vice, Grant Richards took him genially in hand.

"Stop a moment, now," he said, with his high hat on the back of his head, his fur coat expansively open and his monocled eye fixing the intruder with an inquiring eye. "Tell me one thing—have you a mother?"

I paused in delight, for in this swirling Paris where vice of sorts was usually rampant, this was too much. The small Jew who was the industrious salesman for this particular type of ware paused in astonishment also and cocked his eye curiously on this stranger who was obviously preparing to josh him in a novel way.

They are used to all sorts of setbacks, these particular guides, for they encounter all sorts of people, severely moral and the reverse; and I fancy on occasion they would be soundly trounced if it were not for the police who stand in with them and receive a modicum for their protection. They certainly learn to understand something of the type of man who will listen to their propositions; for I have never seen them more than ignored and I have frequently seen them talked to in an offhand way, though I was pleased to note that their customers were few. This particular little Jew had a quizzical, screwed-up expression on his face and did not care to answer the question at first, but resumed his announcement of his various delights and the price it would all cost.

"Wait, wait, wait!" insisted Grant Richards. "Answer my question. Have you a mother?"

"What has that got to do with it?" asked the guide. "Of course I have a mother."

"Where is she?" demanded Grant Richards authoritatively.

"She's at home," replied the guide, with an air of mingled astonishment, irritation and a desire not to lose a customer.

"Does she know that you are out here on the streets of Paris doing what you are doing tonight?" Grant Richards asked with a very noble air.

"Ho!" replied the man. "You're kiddin' me."

"Answer me," persisted Grant Richards, still fixing him solemnly through his monocle. "Does she?"

"Why no, of course she doesn't," replied the Jew sheepishly.

"Would you want her to know?"—this in sepulchral or at least cathedral-like tones.

"No, I don't think so."

"Have you a sister?"

"Yes."

"Would you want her to know?"

"I don't know," replied the guide defiantly. "She might know anyhow."

"Tell me truly—if she did not know, would you want her to know?"

The poor vendor looked as if he had got into some silly, inexplicable mess from which he would be glad to free himself, but he did not seem to have sense enough to walk briskly away and leave us. Perhaps he did not care to admit defeat so easily.

"No, I suppose not," replied the interrogated vainly.

"There you have it!" exclaimed Richards triumphantly. "You have a mother—you would not want her to know. You have a sister—you would not want her to know. And yet you solicit me here on the street to see things which I do not want to see or know. Think of your poor gray-headed mother," he exclaimed grandiloquently and with a mock air of shame and sorrow. "Once, no doubt, you prayed at her knee, an innocent boy yourself."

The man looked at him much as if to say, "For God's sake, what have I got into—what am I up against?"

"No doubt if she saw you here tonight, selling your manhood for a small sum of money, pandering to the lowest and most vicious elements in life, she would weep bitter tears. And your sister—Don't you think now you had better give up this evil life? Don't you think you had better accept any sort of position and earn an honest living rather than do what you are doing?"

"Well, I don't know," said the man. "This living is as good as any other living. I've worked hard to get my knowledge."

"Good God, do you call this knowledge?" inquired Grant Richards solemnly.

"Yes, I do," replied the man. "I've worked hard to get it."

"My poor friend," said Grant Richards, "I pity you. From the bottom of my heart, I pity you. You are degrading your life and ruining your soul. Come now, tomorrow is Sunday. The church bells will be ringing. Go to church. Reform your life. Make a new start—do. You will never regret it. Your old mother will be so glad—and your sister."

"Oh, say," said the man, walking off. "You don't want a guide. You want a church." And he did not even look back.

"It is the only way I have of getting rid of them," commented Grant Richards. "They always stop when I begin to talk to them about their mother. They can't stand the thought of their mother."

"Very true," I said. "Cut it out now, and come on. You have preached enough. Let us see the worst that Paris has to show," and off we went, arm in arm, to the nearest restaurant, which was the Bar Fysher, and after that to Gerny's Bar, Palmyre's Bar, to the Grelot, the Rabelais, the Abbaye de Thélème, the Rat Mort, the Pigalle, the Monico, les Hannetons, the Royale, la Jeunie, the Capital, the Café Américain, and finally Maxim's when the dark was fading into a silvery dawn.

I shall never forget the strange impression which all this world of restaurant life gave me. Obviously, when we arrived at Fysher's at twelve o'clock, the fun was just getting under way. Some of these places, like this Bar Fysher, were no larger than a fair-sized room in an apartment, but crowded with a gay and festive throng—Americans, South Americans, English and others. One of the tricks in Paris to make a restaurant successful is to keep it small, so that it has an air of overflow and activity. Here at Fysher's Bar, after allowing room for the red-jacketed orchestra, the piano and the waiters, there was scarcely space for the forty or fifty guests who were present. But what guests! All of them in evening clothes, the gentlemen in high hats and expensive shirtfronts, the ladies in the costume of the ballroom and the polite restaurant. All of them were comparatively young—the women particularly—all of them bursting with health and having plenty of money in their pockets, or appearing to. They would not be welcome long in this dizzy café world if they did not, for champagne was twenty francs the bottle, and champagne was all they served. It was necessary here, as at all the restaurants, to contribute to the support of the musicians; and if a strange young woman should sit at your table for a moment and share either the wine or the fruit which would be quickly offered, you would have to pay for that. Peaches were three francs each and grapes five francs the bunch. It was plain that all these things were offered in order that the house might thrive and prosper. It was so at each and all of those that I have mentioned.

As we walked or taxied from place to place—they were all in the vicinity of the Place Pigalle and the Boulevard de Clichy—I was astounded by the whirling enthusiasm of this night life which surrounded these restaurants. Taxis were as thick as flies and far more noisy. The air was redolent of gasoline, with an occasional suggestion of perfume from one source or other. Nearly all the women one saw either entering or coming out of the restaurants and taxis were in daring, or at least pronounced, costumes. You were not in a world of tall or imposing buildings—quite the contrary. The neigh-

Crowded with a gay and festive throng

borhood seemed to me rather run-down and even shabby. But it was full of whirling champagne-drinkers who were interested in but two things: the flare and glow of these restaurants, which were always brightly lighted and packed with people—and women.

In the last analysis, women—the young women of easy virtue—were the glittering attraction, and truly one might say they were glittering. Under the flare of brilliant glass-prismed electroliers, in costumes which were most frequently of white satin or silk or of cloth sewn with sequins or beads of glistening hue, their backs, bosoms and arms bare, their dresses displaying the outlines of their figures like a tight skin, they were, in a great many instances, ravishing figures to behold. Fine feathers make fine birds, and nowhere more so than in Paris. But there were many birds here who would have been fine in much less showy feathers. In many instances they craved and secured a demure simplicity which was even more convincing than the flaring costumes of the demimonde. It was strange to see American innocence—the products of Petoskey, Michigan, and Hannibal, Missouri—cheek by jowl with the most daring and the most vicious women which the great metropolis could produce. I did not know until sometime later how hard some of these women were, how schooled in vice, how weary of everything save this atmosphere of festivity and the privilege of wearing beautiful clothes. It was a scorching lesson, and it displayed vice as an upper and a nether millstone between which youth and beauty are ground or pressed quickly to a worthless mass. I would defy anybody to live in this atmosphere as long as five years and not exhibit strongly the telltale marks of decay.

Mostly, those who come here come for a night or two, or a month or two, or once in a year or so, and then disappear again back into the comparatively dull world from which they emanated—which is fortunate. If they were here for a little while, this deceptive world of delight would lose all its glamour, but a very few days and you see through the dreary mechanism by which it is produced: the browbeating of shabby waiters by greedy managers; the extortionate charges and tricks by which money is lured from the pockets of the unwary; the wretched hallrooms and garrets from which some of these butterflies emerge to wing here in seeming delight and then disappear. When the natural glow of youth has gone come powder and paint for the face, belladonna for the eyes, rouge for the lips, palms and the nails, and perfumes and ornaments and the glister of good clothing; but underneath it all one reads the weariness of the eye, the sickening distaste for bargaining hour by hour and day by day, the cold mechanism of what was once natural, instinctive coquetry. You feel constantly that so many of these demimondaines would sell their souls for one last hour of delight and then gladly take poison, as so many of them do, to end it all.

Consumption, cocaine and opium maintain their persistent toll, and in a little while the doormen, waiters, managers and guests who now smile and show gleaming teeth in approval will promptly lock their doors or turn away in loathing or disgust. This is a furnace of desire—this Montmartre district—and it burns furiously with a hard, white-hot flame until there is nothing left save black cinders and white ashes. Those who can endure its consuming heat are welcome to its wonders until emotion and feeling and beauty are no more.

CHAPTER XXXVI

The time that I spent in Paris was from the twelfth to the twenty-sixth of January, during which I am quite satisfied that I visited every important section within the walls, to say nothing of most of the principal museums and public institutions. The part that interested me most from the point of view of age and strangeness was the Marais, that section of narrow streets and high buildings which lies between the Rue St-Antoine on the south, the Rue de Turenne on the east, the Rue du Temple on the west and disappears in the north toward the Rue de Bretagne. The Rue des Francs-Bourgeois is its central highway east and west. I found it by accident. I did not know that there was such a thing as the Marais or that it had a name, but after having seen all the wide boulevards and magnificent circles, I knew that any such narrow welter of streets as these represent an older order. That night, after having spent a good portion of the day here, I looked it up and found that this was true. London has narrow streets, and Rome and Florence. The old Roman Forum district I found to have been built on streets so narrow that they would not make respectable alleys today. But however narrow the streets of the world's earliest civilization were—and obviously they were very narrow, for defensive purposes—they were never any narrower than the streets of the Marais.

There were actually thoroughfares which I could span from wall to wall by stretching out my two arms, and you see the great hooks set in the walls on which chains were strung to impede the progress of an invading enemy. You could also see the narrow windows high up in these solid walls from which defenders could lean and pour boiling water and hot lead. The entryways of the old palaces which are to be found at frequent intervals dating back to the fourteenth and fifteenth centuries were not made for show but for defense. You could see where great wrought iron doors were set in solid walls and gave into narrow passages which were easily defended. It was so plain that a palace set in a narrow street of this kind and approached only through a narrow and easily-defended gate was a much safer affair than a palace set in a wide thoroughfare and easily surrounded by a clamoring horde. I am satisfied that not more than a thousand men could be packed in one of these narrow passages between two intersecting streets, and if they were, they would not have room to turn around, let alone fight. The grand duke or prince who was defending his noble domain could have his inner courtyard filled with defenders and all who crawled through his narrow entryway would be clouted or cut to death.

There is one tablet over the passage at No. 38 Rue des Francs-Bourgeois which reads: "In this passage, while leaving the Hôtel Barbette, Duke Louis of Orleans, brother of King Charles VI, was assassinated by Jean the Fearless, Duke of Bourgogne, on the night of the 23rd or 24th of November, 1407." I could not read this, but I found another who was contemplating it with as much curiosity as I subsequently evinced and who explained to me its significance. We had some slight discussion as to the character of this neighborhood, enough to confirm my suspicions, and then we parted. It seemed such a fitting inscription for this district.

All these streets reek of a grim, defensive life which was no doubt imposing and glorious in its day, but that is now all over. There is a scheme for cutting wide streets all through this region, and when I was there, the wreckers were already at work, tearing wide gaps through stout walls that had not seen the light of day for centuries. One hundred and fifty million dollars have been set aside by some public authority in France for the promotion of this work, and it looked to me as though, given a few more years, there would be no more Marais; but it was delightful to wander into these old courtyards, look at interior entranceways that were designed with the greatest artistic taste, and really realize that this was the center of a distinguished life that was gone forever. I found stone quarries, soap companies, chemical companies, all sorts and conditions of small industries flourishing in different parts of these one-time palaces. Now and then you would find a great stone urn or a bit of carving that had fallen from some cornice or balustrade lying broken and moldy on the ground below.

The narrow streets were alive with a clattering mass of French laborers and small tradesmen and the type of citizen that would live in such a run-down region. At the noon hour the French factory girls in shawls and dark-colored skirts could be seen walking up and down arm in arm all through this region. It is a region that gives one the last taste of old France, and it occurred to me at the time that steps ought to be taken to preserve some phases of it intact. But the property owner must have his profit, and if he cannot rent or sell it in its old form, he must perforce tear it down and build something new. In England they have an ultra-conservative care for these old things and much is preserved—perhaps too much. In Paris the tendency seems to be to alter radically, but there may be forces at work caring for these things, of which I naturally would not know. Certainly the old museums of Paris—the Cluny and the Carnavalet—are splendid examples of saving an old phase of life to modern usage.

I wonder if I can ever indicate briefly the charm and delight I found in the museums of Paris—the smaller ones, not the Louvre. That vast structure with its miles and miles of pictures, although I attacked it voraciously at different times, signally defeated me. I first had the idea of attacking it room by room and not missing anything. After a brain-aching morning, during which I nearly suffered a mental art-stroke and could not find my way out because I did not know what the word *sortie* meant, I escaped, only to meditate how I would really achieve this purpose which I had in mind. I returned courageously in the afternoon with another thought. This time I would see certain collections—that of Chauchard, for one—and then special groups and schools. I was deterred in this honest adventure by finding, purely accidentally, the Winged Victory of Samothrace, the Venus of Milo, a collection of old Roman bas-reliefs showing sacerdotal processions, religious choruses and the like, which were amazingly beautiful to me.

By chance I stumbled on a badly organized chamber where were a number of Watteaus, Fragonards, Bouchers, Lancrets, Paters, which held my attention for the rest of the time I had to spare. Nevertheless I made a third attempt and this time succeeded in viewing much of what the museum had to show of Rubens, Botticelli, Rembrandt, Velázquez, Meissonier, Corot, Daubigny, Millet and that lovely company of minor Dutch painters whose simple studies of ordinary life seemed to me at times to be the best of all. At the time I saw these, I really looked forward to the day when I should be in Holland and should see them in plenty—not knowing that a large portion of them had been scattered far and wide. This was as fine a collection as any I saw in Berlin, but it seemed strangest of all to me to encounter them in Rome and Florence and Venice, where they do not in the least belong. To see van Ostade and Metsu and de Hooch in the Uffizi was too much. They were lost in a perfect storm of religious art.

But if the marvels of the Louvre gave me a brain-ache—the miles and miles of wonders which no human brain could reasonably contrast or compare—the romance and simplicity of the Carnavalet and Cluny restored my soul. I sat one whole morning in the sunlight which fills the courtyard of the Carnavalet on a cool mossy bench, looking at an ancient carved well-top; fragments of gargoyles from old churches long since disappeared; fragments of pulpits, windows; an armorial capital from the mortuary chapel of the Requiers family out of the ancient church of the White Mantle; a mounted horseman from the gate of the Hôtel de Ville; two delicious terracotta lions from the garden of a house in the Rue Raspede; a lovely Gothic niche for some saint.

This lovely old building, which is only two stories high and of a somber brown stone which has a charm far exceeding any newer brighter hue, was at one time the house of Madame de Sévigné and is now the official museum of the city of Paris. In it are those quaint and varied collections which relate to old Paris and the French Revolution—the Bastille, the campaigns of Napoleon, the life of old Paris and things of that sort. It is so very soothing because its contents are so varied and in a way so human and unexpected. You walk from a lovely collection of old fans to the room which Louis XVI occupied in the Bastille, from costumes which the French ladies wore in the sixteenth century to the pikes and staves and flags which did service at the storming of the Bastille. There are letters and orders from Napoleon, memorials of Gambetta, a valuable collection of porcelains bequeathed by M. de Yiesville, little trinkets that belonged to Mme. de Sévigné and a Chinese room which shows the exquisite taste of someone. You would hardly believe that a public museum could be so personal, so intimate, so like a charming private home to which you had been admitted by courtesy. You feel all the while as if you were in the house of a celebrated friend, and out in the lovely central courtyard the pigeons that occupy a number of cots in the walls are walking in and out on the parapets and fluttering to and fro among the carved stone memories of delicious France.

I think, on the whole, Carnavalet is so lovely that I would put it above everything save the Musée de Cluny, which is on the other side of the river in the Latin Quarter and is just as sweet and old and delicious as the perfect refinement of France could make it. I wish I could define for myself, let alone for the reader, what it is that makes the charm of these two museums. Balzac suggests them in the refined social life which he indicates as once centering around the Boulevard St-Germain, and our own George W. Cable suggests it as having been reflected in the New Orleans life of which he writes in the *Grandissimes* and *Old Creole Days*. There is a touch of it in the home built by that ardent admirer of France, Thomas Jefferson, and wherever you encounter the perfections of the simpler pieces of the Louis furniture there, you have a touch of the spirit that made these museums. Without, the Cluny is a poetic blend of the Gothic and the Renaissance. It is as simple in its outlines as a Tudor palace, but much more ornate in its decorations. Like Carnavalet, it is a demure brown structure standing in the heart of that beloved Latin Quarter where stand the Sorbonne, the Panthéon, the Luxembourg, St. Étienne-du-Mont, St. Sulpice and St. Germain-des-Prés.

The first Monday I was in Paris I tried to go there but not knowing the rule of Paris—not open Mondays—I was unkindly carried there by the thieving cabby, who knew well enough that it was closed. That is the way of the Parisian cabby. And then he made a great to-do about "*très triste*" and "*Mon Dieu!*"—he was very sorry—all in French. I walked away sorrowfully to inspect other things, and came another Monday, making the same mistake a second time. I was so eager to see this institution that I came the next day at ten o'clock in the morning and was promptly told that I was an hour early. At eleven I was admitted, free of charge.

I fairly devoured those wonderful rooms with their low, dark ceilings and deep windows. I shall never forget the spell the novelty and variety of this delicious collection cast upon me. Imagine the wonderful charm and delight of carefully, artistically selected collections of jewels, ironwork, fireplaces, Spanish leather, lace, gold work, pottery, tapestries, lace. Somehow it is not as if you were in an ordinary museum but, as in the Carnavalet, in a private mansion of a great and subtle collector.

I can never tire of thinking of the wonder and beauty of things that I saw—not too much and not too little. Listen: the state bed of the time of Francis I; a pastoral staff in boxwood and ivory; a crosier from the abbey of St. Martin at Pontoise (thirteenth century); a collection of toys found in the Seine; a collection of shoes of different periods, illustrating the richness and fancy of different days; candlesticks and lanterns of the fourteenth century; the nine gold crowns of the Visigoth King Recceswinth, A.D. 649; a Merovingian scabbard ornamented in gold, with a bronze guard; smelling bottles of the sixteenth and eighteenth centuries; two interesting girdles of chastity; a collection of mirror boxes; the fine bronze serpents from a fountain in the Château Villette in the seventeenth century; the golden hinge ornaments from Notre-Dame; the spurs of Francis I, adorned with salamanders; the gold rose of Basle, presented by Pope Clement V to the Prince Bishop of Basle—a lovely object. What would you? I could go on and on.

Outside in the garden, the only entrance to which is through the court of the "hôtel," or museum, are medieval sculptures and architectural remains so soft, so convolute, so gray that they are like music. I reserve to the last the Thermes or ruins of the baths—sixty-five-and-a-half by thirty-seven-and-a-half, and fifty-nine feet in height—once belonging to the ancient palace of the emperors (not of France but of Rome) which were here. I never knew it until I got here that Paris, such as it was, or the present site of Paris at least, was once the summer home of some of the Roman emperors. In this hall or baths there is a fragmentary Roman altar dedicated to Jupiter that bears an inscription to the effect that as far back as the time of Tiberius (A.D. 37) there existed a corporation of Parisian watermen. This adds for me the last touch of delicacy and aroma which the Cluny does not need but has, connecting in this vague romantic way old Paris with old Rome. What more could a museum want or be?

About the fifth day I was in Paris, there arrived from London a gentleman by the name of Hale, a Boston publisher whom I had met in London and who had amused me greatly by his comments on the differences he found existing between America and England. He had amused me vastly by the vivid account he gave of a newly rich drug manufacturer, a Jew, who had come over on the same boat with him and whom he constantly referred to as the author of the Cold Cream. Hale was a little less than medium in height, quite dark, and preternaturally grave in his speech and manner. He reminded me almost always of a judge delivering an opinion, and the first time I saw him he strolled into my room in answer to my call pursuant to his knock and looked me over almost before he greeted me. He said he was Mr. Hale of whom Grant Richards had spoken and wanted to know whether I was interested in London. I recall that at the time I was terribly resentful toward all Americans—may God forgive me!—for I had just discovered after a little taste of England that America was entirely without civility, breeding, manners, training, anything you please. I did not want to see any more Americans because the thought of them annoyed me—but here all at once Hale was stuffed down my throat, and I decided to make short work of it and get rid of him as soon as possible. Instead of that, to my astonishment, and in spite of all his characteristics, which were offensively American, I took a fancy to him.

He had the drawl and the poise and the nonchalance of the Middle West, and although apparently he had none of the qualities for which he was so enthusiastic in his praise of the English, he nevertheless charmed me by the accuracy of his estimate of them and the ease and good nature with which he disposed of them and pretension in anyone. This manufacturer with whom he had crossed, evidently on the best of terms, had, as an evidence of his regard and affection for the passengers on the ship, been handing out samples of cold cream and had been constantly referring to his friends in the manufacturing world as "one of our largest iron dealers" or "one of our largest furniture manufacturers." Hale amused me by explaining that in turn he had referred to some of his friends as "one of our largest poets" and "one of our largest artists." But he was enthusiastic over the civility of England, and that interested me.

"Say," he said when he came in. (He turned out to be a Harvard graduate and was born in Boston. The atmosphere of the Middle West that was about him was due to his experiences there and his admiration for it.) "I don't get it at first, do you? It's sort of hard to realize, the way they carry on here."

"You mean the atmosphere of civility and politeness?" I replied. "It is a little strange after New York."

"Yes," he said, taking the chair I offered him and arranging his feet before the fender, "it's hard to understand. Why, a man actually apologized over here at the Victoria Station for dropping my trunk! I never saw anything like it. They ask you where you want to go and whether they can do anything for you, and then they really do it. It beats me. I never saw anything like that in Boston."

"You never saw anything like that anywhere in the United States," I replied, "if my observation is worth anything. They really have time to be nice over here, and it doesn't seem to interfere with business either."

We fell into a lively discussion concerning this, the result of which was that we agreed to breakfast together the next morning, and so this very interesting friendship began. Afterward I heard but little save the interesting civility of the English until I left for France; and then came a letter saying that he was coming over for a few days and wanted to know if he could not see me there. I was quite pleased because although I had the friendship of Mme. de Villiers and that of Miss Rice and Mr. Fergusson, who were doing their best to entertain me, I had no male companion who was as idle as myself. I wrote him to come on at once.

On the fifth morning at eight o'clock he knocked at my door, having newly arrived and wearing that same undisturbed air which had pleased me so much in London.

"These Frenchmen are a brisk lot," he observed, and then wanted to know what the odor was which pervades Paris everywhere. We discussed that and his trip over and then went out to breakfast.

It was exceedingly interesting to me to get a second American point of view on this European life, for I was inclined to look upon my own as possibly eccentric. Hale had never been to Europe either. He had one American friend, an author who lived at Versailles, and a second, an art student who lived in the Latin Quarter. Both of these he was anxious to notify at once by telegraph, and he was very keen to see all that he could of Paris in three days. This struck me as a worthwhile adventure, and we began to plan at once what the different things should be. He wanted to see the Tuileries, the Louvre, the Luxembourg, the Panthéon, Napoleon's tomb, Notre-Dame, the Latin Quarter, the Moulin Rouge, Montmartre, some of the most exciting restaurants, and then, as he naively added, "any other little thing that I can." I said, "Certainly, Hale. Us for the Moulin Rouge and the Tuileries. We'll do the Louvre in about nine long steps, and we'll just brush by the Luxembourg and the Latin Quarter. My five days have taught me a lot about Paris, and you are going to have the full benefit of it. We'll run right out now and see the Tuileries, if you don't mind, and then we'll hurry to the Louvre. I've only been there three times myself trying to see it, but a fourth time won't matter. I may have missed something."

We were having our coffee and rolls at a little table outside a restaurant near the Comédie-Française, and he was doing his best to recall the French which he had studied in America, repeating odd phrases to himself like a parrot. "Now let me see," he observed. "I believe I can pay for this in French," and he began to calculate what it would come to, meanwhile eyeing the hovering waiter with some misgivings.

"Dooks franks does it—dooks franks for each of us," I explained. "Every breakfast I have ever had here has cost me dooks franks."

He laughed and calculated, and sure enough, with the tips it came to about four francs, which he paid with some remark about the weather.

"You know," he said, "what astonishes me about this country is that when I talk French to these people they seem to understand me. It's very strange—Look at the Knights of Pythias!"

He was referring to two French messengers in cocked hats and blue uniforms who were crossing on the other side of the street.

"Knights of Pythias your grandmother!" I replied. "Those are French messengers. You see them here and there all over Paris."

"Well, well," he replied in mock stupidity. "They look very much like the parades of those fellows we have in America."

We went back to the hotel to await the arrival of his artist friend, Mr. Hart, who was to join us, and when that individual, who looked more like a Western cowboy than an artist, arrived, we made our way to the Tuileries, out the Champs-Élysées to the Arc de Triomphe, out the Boulevard Kléber to the Trocadéro, the Champs-de-Mars to Napoleon's tomb and from there to the Luxembourg. For three days I wandered thus with Hale, and I can honestly say that I was never more entertained in my life. When we came to the Arc de Triomphe, he observed in his dry way, "Well now, that is something like," and had a long argument with his friend as to whether he should be permitted to go to the top of it, which project I approved greatly but which Mr. Hart objected to. Nevertheless, Hale went. The Trocadéro pleased him greatly. "Say, that's like an American World's Fair, ain't it?" he remarked—which it is. A single upward look at the Eiffel Tower thrusting its thousand feet of red iron into the gray morning air extracted a delicious, "What do you know about that!" from him, and looking down into the circular crypt of the dome of the Invalides upon the reddish-brown porphyry sarcophagus of Napoleon, he observed, "There certainly, as the author of the Cold Cream would say, lies our largest general." I was certainly impressed with the richness of the tomb, although it could have been much simpler. The only perfect tombs of that kind are the tombs of the Medici in Florence, and they do not depend upon the room in which they stand.

From here we went directly to the Luxembourg, and I shall never forget the manner in which Hale picked out the interesting pictures of which he had seen reproductions or had studied at college. It was constantly, "George! that's fine, isn't it? I had a copy of that when I was at college." "Well, if here isn't the—! One of our best men did that." He was referring to an American picture hung there. Or "Well, well! That's been one of my favorite pictures all my life." I could not interest him very much in the Neo-Impressionists, of which there were one or two very conservative examples in the museum. His friend Hart's face was set hard against them, for one thing, and he quoted someone as having said that it was unquestionably a way to paint, but the worst way. It is useless to discuss art anyhow, and we took our delight in wandering through room after room of brilliant pictures—the last word of modernism before the arrival of the Neo-Impressionists. I could not help wondering how many of these thousands of delicious genre pictures would be saved for posterity. They are so far removed from religious art and have so little of that purely decorative value which saves so many things. They can only be retained for their individual charm as pictures, and yet as a record of their day they are perhaps as valuable as those the Dutch did in Holland. It is a question—but the Luxembourg is splendid.

It was to Foyot's to lunch in order to air my knowledge of French restaurants, and then St. Étienne-du-Mont and the Panthéon, Sorbonne and the gardens of the Tuileries; but because we were a little slow in lunching, we missed the wonders of Notre-Dame and Sainte-Chapelle this day. Hale's artistic friend was interested to show him a bit of the Latin Quarter proper, and as this was the only day he could devote to him, we decided to go there. I shall never forget the old house in which Hart lived, where there was a Merovingian tower known as the tower of Clovis still in existence and where John Calvin had once had a workroom and written many of the religious feuilletons which so greatly stirred his day. Hale's comment on the ancient tower, that "it made Plymouth Rock look like thirty cents," suited my mood exactly, and his "to think that anybody would leave their happy steam-heated flat for a joint like this" described the interior exactly. We went out in search of true bohemianism in the shape of student restaurants, ateliers and the student chambers generally. We found the restaurants—full only of those dull girls and boys who come because they have no better place to go and who take these rather comfortable public places with their tables as matter-of-factly as you would your dining room or kitchen. They can get pen, ink and paper here from the waiter and can sit and sketch idly by the hour where it is warm and fairly bright for the price of a beer or two. They can meet their latest affinity, and when they do—the right one—they do not come so often anymore. This student who was with us told me that when a girl found a man she usually disappeared for a long time to keep house for him, sometimes forever, and when their youth and illusion are gone, all disappear.

We went to several ateliers—now in the early dark—and to avoid attracting attention and disturbing the class, we bought conventional drawing books and pencils and pretended to sketch. The arrival or departure of strangers under such circumstances is nothing. They are coming and going all the time, and we did not even attract a glance. In one atelier, before a great class, a little French girl with bushy black hair and a flower-like body was posing in the nude. The room resounded to the scratching of pencils, and many a charming outline was drawn. It was the one thing that Hale was most anxious to see. He was satisfied now that his day was a great success, and I saw nothing in Paris that seemed more suitably Parisian. The old neighborhood in which this atelier was located was characteristically French, with central doorways that gave into courts and no light showing in any windows. So often a French street presents this peculiar spectacle at night—long lines of buildings with shutters closed tight, a blank wall, yet unquestionably teeming with life within.

I wish I had space to tell all the things I saw with Hale and the manner in which I saw them. We visited the Moulin Rouge, after a dinner at the Café de Paris, and inspected that tinsel world where vice is paraded as a staple and simple nudity would be great virtue. I was glad to see that, as in the case of myself, the tawdriness and stupidity of all this irritated Hale. Vice does become so mechanical after a time. The various artifices of dress, motion, salute, seduction are of the tawdriest and dreary beyond words. These women—particularly about the Moulin Rouge, it seemed to me—seemed more than many others to be in revolt against the dreariness of the business of exciting lust. For all the spirit which their salutes or their dances contained, they might as well have been day laborers with their buckets going wearily to work. The large promenade back of the stalls where the women walked as at the Empire in London, and the small chambers belowstairs where special performances of vice were to be given between the acts, were so cheap and wearisome that they could not have obtained place on Coney Island.

"Well, that'll be about all for that," said Hale, as we walked out, and I agreed with him. "If that's the best Paris can do, take me back to Coney Island."

I took him to the Abbaye de Thélème, which was now opening, and where at least he could see an artistic scene, and where high-priced vice hides all its weariness behind charming toilettes and an educated demeanor.

CHAPTER XXXVII

From the Place Pigalle as a center we visited all that was to be seen in that vicinity. From the Abbaye de Thélème, which is the center of excitement of this character in the Place Pigalle and where we witnessed quite the same scene as had occurred the night before, we crossed the street to the Rat Mort, which is on another corner, and saw a scene which, if not as artistically brilliant, was as gaudy as a slightly less refined type of frequenter could make it.

This matter of differences in patronage was noticeable at once. The Bar Fysher seemed crowded with those who were thoroughly versed in the ways of Paris and provided with ample means. They seemed to be individuals who were opposed to moving about much and preferred to sit and be entertained. Gerny's Bar, which we found glowing with a comfortable little light of its own, was apparently composed of those who knew each other fairly well and preferred their mutual society to that of strangers. Palmyre's Bar, the Grelot and the Rabelais struck me as decidedly vicious—a type of young woman gathered here which may be described as tired of the glittering world of the Abbaye de Thélème and Maxim's and a little down on her luck. Les Hannetons was frequented by perverts of the male sex, and we were asked at the door whether we were looking for young men or young women.

Over the way we entered the hotel run in connection with the Abbaye de Thélème—that gorgeous collection of boudoirs which is always at your service—and farther down the street we sought out the apartment of a young girl whom Grant Richards announced was the type beloved of the art student—the type so proud of her art connections that she will not associate with members of any other world—"a true Montmartreuse," an appellation which she used to describe herself originally. Repeated ringings at a darksome doorway caused it eventually to spring open, and by the aid of matches we made our way to the third floor, where persistent knocking finally produced an inquiry. When Grant Richards explained concerning himself, there was a staccato, "*Oh, oui, oui, oui,*" and the door opened.

A charming young lady of not more than twenty-one, clad only in her nightdress, scurried away to light another light in an inner room, and then we were made welcome. I noticed at once a dangerous-looking revolver which had been flung carelessly on the bed and a yellow-backed book which she had been reading before she went to sleep. A stuffy room it was, dingy, with all sorts of knick-knacks scattered about on tables, the mantel, the dresser, and it breathed as though every breath of air had been shut out. She was slender and lymphatic and very excitable and evidently pleased to see her friend of recent years. Not understanding French, I could only judge what it was all about, but obviously there were many exchanges of humor and persiflage, and I could see that he was asking her to take me under her wing for the time being.

As he told me afterwards, she explained that she was, for the present at least, the friend of a student and that she did not care to be entertained otherwise. It was plain to me that a controlling attraction towards Grant Richards himself existed and that this was another of his numerous conquests. The fact that she had been and still was keenly interested in him did not, owing to his desire to further my Parisian adventures, deter him from attempting to make me an unworthy successor in the young lady's good graces. She was interesting enough, but I was not greatly stirred, for this was a crowded sea in which many fish were swimming, and it seemed to me that I was fairly well provided for as it was. So much for friendship—

The lady was too sleepy to come to supper, and speculating on what else we should see, we made our way to the Café Américain and Maxim's. After the Abbaye de Thélème I should place Maxim's as the most desperately showy of all Parisian resorts and the one as well calculated as any other to illustrate the mechanical insobriety of this world. The majority of these restaurants have red-jacketed orchestras, but Maxim's was the only place where I saw the leader leave his rostrum and play on his violin before individual tables. It is a nightly trick, and yet there is a certain thrill to it, for the gentleman, a Slavic type with burning eyes and black hair, fixed his gaze in each instance on some particular woman and played to her as though he were a lover under her balcony. It interested me to see how the orchestra, wearied as they must have been by years and years of nightly playing in some such resort as this, still followed him closely with their eyes, gathering the significance of his leadership from his movements. It is something when musicians, in a world as commonplace as this must have been to them, should care enough for the art of music to wish to make the playing of it perfect, even in so tawdry a world as this. It was good music—snatches from the operas of Wagner, Puccini and others and ragtime songs from America. As usual the walls were lined with a brilliant company and the intermediate space packed with tables at which the same brilliant company accustomed to the Abbaye de Thélème was visible.

Here it was that I learned that fruit was especially brought to any table where one of the young women connected with the place chose to seat herself for a moment. It cannot be said that these girls who lend so much grace and color to these restaurants have as a rule any definite working connection with any particular establishment, but they have an understanding with many. Their presence is tolerated only because they are attractive and modish and as long as they consent to make friends with the lone gentlemen present and eat the fruit and drink the wine offered; thereafter a sizable bill is presented, which is the restaurant's pay for its courtesy. The lady's pay comes from the gentlemen directly, if ever. There are those not above asking for a louis as a gratuity if they are hard pressed, and now and then there are men who freely give it if they have been entertained or amused in the least way.

It was after Maxim's and the Café Américain that I first saw the Parisian dawn. We came along the Port de la Conférence and the Quai des Tuileries through that wonderful architectural world which concerns the Place des Invalides, the Garden of the Tuileries, the Eiffel Tower, the Louvre and the Seine. We walked for a time under the arcade that spans the sidewalk of the Rue de Rivoli. The sky was being slowly and faintly illuminated with a weak electric blue; the trees and monuments and buildings stood out faintly in a strange light. It was deliciously artistic, this atmosphere, quite unreal and theatric, like the light you sometimes see produced on the stage or in grand opera. Paris, even at this hour, was only reasonably still. In the distance you could hear the spinning of taxis and the footfall of pedestrians—strangers in opera hats and cape coats were idling homeward, not at all weary apparently and quite gay. We both agreed that in this deliciously illuminated world it was a pity to go to bed, but since Grant Richards had an appointment at nine-thirty and wished to change his clothes, and I felt out of place strolling around in a high hat and fur overcoat, I decided to return also. I had an ambition to see some of the Paris boulevards of a Sunday morning, and since we were to meet at the Café Marguery for lunch and entertain Mme. de Villiers anew, it was also deemed necessary to get a little sleep, and so we returned to the Hôtel Normandy for about four hours. By that time I was up and away, seeing what the city had to offer in sights, and I enjoyed this first Parisian Sunday morning immensely.

Paris of a Sunday is quite unlike any city in which I have ever been. The effect of life and charm of movement produced here on almost every street is due to the fact, I think, that there are no suburbs in the sense of those that exist about London, Chicago, New York and elsewhere. Manhattan Island, on the West Side from 59th to 157th of a Sunday morning, presents more of the atmosphere of Paris than any other place I have ever been. The interesting sections of most cities are drained early Saturday afternoon by the suburbs and do not resume that quickened life which they present on a weekday until Monday comes again. Then these streets have the crowds but not the atmosphere which Paris has on Sunday. There, all is strolling ease and a rather refined atmosphere of good-natured prosperity and comfort.

Paris is a walled city. It seems silly to give this as a piece of information, but I do not believe that the average person really understands it. All of Paris is literally confined within a wall twenty-one miles in circumference which in turn is strengthened by bastions and a moat, and the moat is filled with water. When you step outside this wall at any one of the fifty or more gates, the character of the city changes instantly. In the vast majority of cases there is no city; you step out to view green fields and roads leading to no visible place. At these gates officers who represent the inland customs are stationed—men carrying long, thin rods of steel, somewhat like a rapier, who jab them quite inconsiderately into loads of straw, hay, bags, baskets, coal and the like. It amused me to see them punching thus indiscriminately into merchandise of all kinds, and I thought at first that it had something to do with spies, but I learned later that it concerned only cigars, tobacco and whiskey. These are national monopolies, and Paris is the great center where they are consumed. If you can get tobacco and spirits into Paris without paying the high fees demanded, you are in the way of making an exceptional profit, so this is not infrequently attempted. The old lady who was arrested because she was so fat is an old story—her fatness being due to cigarettes exteriorly applied.

But to return to Paris on Sunday. This wall which encloses the city encloses the vast bulk of the population. The Paris subway, which turns in circles and cross sections, does not go outside the walls. Neither do many of the Paris electric lines or bus lines, which run from one important point in the city to another. All these streets within these walls, narrow and wide, are lined with buildings from six to eight stories high and crowded with people, of course. You can have the curious experience of stepping inside the gates at any one of a score of places in this wall, and from seeing open fields on the outside, you can contemplate a new eight-story elevator apartment building with all the conveniences which these modern structures contain. Outside the walls, green fields; within, the marble-lined lobby of an imposing building with highly-polished electroliers and uniformed hall service. Such is Paris.

Naturally such a confined world as this, containing several million people as it does, presents lively industrious throngs on weekdays and a pleasing idling mass on Sunday. London, which covers perhaps five times as much territory as Paris and is, in the main, only two and three stories high, sinks away into respectable silence and the occasional Sabbath-minded pedestrian. New York, except on Manhattan Island, loses much of its appearance of crowded enthusiasm. Paris retains it all—in Sunday clothes, frock coats, smart waistcoats, patent leather shoes, a world of dogs leashed to smart leather straps, and ladies looking their airiest and best. I will say that Paris on Sunday has a most respectable and conservative atmosphere—smart, reserved. You could really believe that once you get all the night-prowling element confined to their hotels, which are not so numerous, the rest of Paris is what it should be—home-loving, church-going, family-visiting. The streets are so wide and clean, the views and vistas so delightful. One should really see Paris on a bright, sunny Sunday morning such as this was to understand how thoroughly charming it can be.

All the cabs and taxis were prowling briskly about or hurrying swiftly on distant errands. The streetcars and buses were crowded. You have but to walk a little way in any direction until you come to some view of importance—the Place de la Concorde, the Madeleine, the Avenue de l'Opéra, the Arc de Triomphe, the Tour St. Jacques or some other monument in any one of the grand circles in which so many of the streets of Paris terminate. It was really delightful to see and feel this Sunday air, to see how thoroughly these particular people take their ease. In London I suffered from an atmosphere of severe depression on Sunday, due entirely to the gray, empty streets, the vistas of silent houses, the sense of reserve and repression. Here it was as if all Paris had determined to come out of doors to enjoy the sunlight, the crowds, the cafés, and to take their ease generally. I know of no other city which gives one this sense of ease and companionship in solitude.

At twelve o'clock I joined Grant Richards and Mme. de Villiers at Marguery's and enjoyed the sole which bears that restaurant's name. We discussed this matter of Sunday appearance of Paris, and Grant Richards was recognized by a waiter who had once worked at Martin's in New York—

which pleased him greatly. After an hour here we strolled up one of the streets which lead up the high hill on which is located Sacré-Coeur, and coming to the Moulin de la Galette, one of the famous dance halls of Paris, we entered. I was told that since this was in the heart of the Montmartre district, the new center for painters and students, we would see plenty of the type of maiden known as the Montmartreuse—the young girl whose youth and beauty are dedicated to the comfort of the struggling student.

Insofar as charm and interest were concerned, I could not see that this was superior to many of the great dance halls that are to be found in New York and elsewhere. The floor was not as large as several to be found in Coney Island, Atlantic City and other resorts of that kind. The crowd was not any larger, if as large, although this building (quite new) was much more charmingly designed than many that are built and used for dancing. It was constructed of light iron and pine, all decoratively treated, with the visible ironwork supporting the balconies and the dull, green-painted roof having the effect of decorative loopings.

The large floor and the tables on raised platforms or balconies above it were filled with young men and women who were supposed to be, according to Grant Richards, young art students and their affinities. I expected to see much of the long hair, the corduroy suit and the flowing tie, but they were conspicuously absent. I do not think I saw a single example of the old art student type. The young girls were peculiarly Parisian in their appearance, if you will accept *Figaro* as a guide to what is Parisian in this matter. Their eyebrows were, in the main, properly carboned, their lips and cheeks rouged, and the outlines of their bodies sharply emphasized by tight-fitting dresses and high-colored ribbons used to pull in their skirts about their hips and to decorate their neckbands and sleeves.

The surprising thing to me was their extreme youth—from sixteen to twenty—and the wealth of a certain form of experience which, according to Mme. de Villiers, went with them at this age. Most of them, according to her and Grant Richards, were already disillusioned, bitterly weary of life, selling their virtue for a moderate price or taking up with students for little or nothing—largely to maintain themselves in the atmosphere in which they found themselves. Virtue and beauty are truly cheap in this realm; and the worst of it, according to Mme. de Villiers, is that they have not the talent to make anything of themselves mentally or artistically. They will never come to anything in the cafés or on the stage or elsewhere, and, being dissatisfied with the commonplace and humdrum of house-wifely existence after a brief and disillusioning taste of this café and studio realm, they are no longer suited to any usable social purpose. They become—a certain percentage of them—girls of the streets, and you will see their wonderful flower-like faces in the cafés of the Boulevard des Capucines and the Boulevard des Halles and that sharp world that exists around the Place de l'Opéra. They are wonderful, good-natured, possibly prosperous, possibly not; but that, without the talent that makes the actress or the singer, is where they end.

At the Moulin de la Galette Grant Richards, Mme. de Villiers and myself parted company. He had his bags to pack—since he was leaving on a nine o'clock train for London—several calls to make, and wished to see Mme. de Villiers to her rooms. As we had entered, I had seen farther up this same hill the imposing outlines of Sacré-Coeur towering above Paris like a white mosque. It seemed to me that this was a church that I had heard of for years, although I found when I was there that it was still not completed. Those high board fences which contractors love to place about uncompleted buildings were still in place, and you went up a boarded stairs, in one place, to reach it. Nevertheless the best general view I had of Paris I obtained from the hilltop on which this stands, although subsequently I also looked down on Paris from a tower of Notre-Dame and from the top of the Arc de Triomphe.

Sacré-Coeur is considered by all the architectural wiseacres as another bastard example of nothing—a botch of Byzantine, Romanesque, Moorish and whatever the modern examples of architecture can be called. It is nevertheless an interesting building in its way—certainly as attractive as St. Étienne-du-Mont, St. Augustin, La Trinité, St. Germain-des-Prés and others which I saw, which are interesting, if not pure, examples of any given school. The most interesting thing about this church to me was that the fathers who had designed it had chosen this perfectly amazing site. From the clock tower which I visited later on a clear day, all of Paris can be seen—the Seine, the Tuileries, Notre-Dame, the Trocadéro and many institutions which I, not being familiar with Paris, could not name. The interesting thing to me was to see how modern apartment houses of the type which prevails on the Upper West Side in New York were climbing up the hill toward this church on all sides. Large studio apartment houses, if you please, where the studios range from three to nine thousand francs in rent. No ordinary student and his Montmartreuse will ever occupy these. They are intended for iron manufacturers in Pittsburgh who like to live in art studios in Paris and are convinced that the Montmartre district provides the ideal art atmosphere in which to abide. Thus these shabby little creatures I saw dancing in the Moulin de la Galette and their student friends do accomplish one thing—a high real estate value for landowners. The atmosphere which they create, while disapproved of morally, is obviously valued financially, and why should the rich not be made to pay if they want to live where people are free and bad?

The interior of Sacré-Coeur is really imposing. The great windows are already completely filled with rich stained glass, and the altars, choir stalls, chapels, columns and arches are of valuable marbles. I found an altar to St. Joseph, before which, as before many others, was placed a large brass candelabra and boxes of candles which you could buy for a franc and place and light them as a votive offering. All of these in the chapels back of the main altar were ablaze with light. One day some time later, having a wish which I wanted to come true and being up here for a morning walk, I lighted a candle and placed it on an outer and more remote candelabra. A black-cassocked priest strolling up and down, seeing me putting it there, said in English which I could see was very carefully calculated, so poor was it, "Wouldn't you like to put your candle a little nearer the altar?"

"Yes, thank you," I said, "I will," and I did so, putting it very near St. Joseph's feet. I wondered what this black-cassocked priest thought of superstition in general and of me in particular, for I was so amused at my own venture that I could hardly keep from smiling. Nevertheless I stood at a distance and admired my handiwork and wished that St. Joseph would be so kind as to make my wish come true—which he did, for several days later I got what I wanted. What it was I will not tell.

Wandering down from here in a gray haze which soon became dark, I followed that line of boulevards that leads to the Place de l'Étoile, marveling at the Sunday evening crowds which filled the streets, and finally was compelled to take a taxi in order to be able to reach my friend Grant Richards in time to see him off. As usual I found him wildly stuffing things into boxes, breathing stertorously and calling maids and hall boys to his assistance to get them to the lobby. We arrived just in time for the night train for London, and the last thing I saw him doing was hanging out of his carriage window purchasing a sanitary pillow and warning me with his monocle eye fixed on me in great solemnity against going about Paris at night alone. "Don't do anything startling till I get back," was his chief plea. "If you are going to do anything desperate, let me be with you," and the most enigmatic of smiles flitted over his face.

The train was gone, amid a great clattering of "*avant*," and I once more turned into the streets of Paris—quite alone now, not speaking any French, but quite sure that I could find out all I wanted to know without much assistance from anyone—which I did.

CHAPTER XXXVIII

The next day, in company with my new friend, I visited Versailles. We rose early, for we had to make an eight o'clock train, and we had only retired some three or four hours before. That is the way you go on in Paris, according to Grant Richards, and I think it is true. The amount of sleep I had there was negligible, but the electric quality of the Parisian atmosphere makes up for it. I often thought of the strangeness of people living in Oldham and Bolton when they could live in Paris. Even London is a dreary horror after Paris.

We had to run to find a taxi, none responding to the call of the hotel, it being Sunday morning and taxis being few and far between. We heard their rumble in the distance, but they would not respond to our frantic signals, and we had the pain of running blocks down the Rue de Rivoli and across the Pont Royal before we found a muddy four-wheeler which would take us to the Gare des Invalides, from which the train started. All the way along I was trying to recall what I knew about Versailles, having forgotten my Baedeker and Hale having only fragmentary information. He kept telling me that his friend Mr. Dawson was an authority on Versailles, that he spoke perfect French, wrote books there and would tell us all about it. "He's some potatoes when it comes to Versailles," he said, "and he knows the ropes." So we settled in the wretched boxcar which does service on the average French road for suburban traffic and waited to see what we should see. We had run the last block after leaving the cab in order to get this train, and Hale's meager French had been compelled to do yeoman's service in order to find out whether we were in the right depot and the right train.

Deliver any human being from any such suburban service as this. You could take any half-dozen American freight cars anywhere and, by a little tinkering, convert them into as good an accommodation. Although even at this hour quite a number of people were going out of Paris into the country, there was nothing save these greenish-black cabooses to carry them. I could not discover any first- or second-class cars at all. Army officers, citizens, laborers, women, all collected in these smoky, tobaccoy, bony, hard, wooden-seated cars which seemed to be without springs and which clattered over the rails and out through endless high-walled cuts and smoky towns to Versailles. Because of these same tunnels and cuts, we were almost there before we saw any of the country, and I longed for the picturesque scenes which most American cities present as you enter or leave them by train.

When we reached Versailles, it was chill, a little foggy, and with the plain, gray, cream-colored and lead-colored fronts of the French houses standing out hard and bare. Only the fog and the trees saved them from being most unsatisfactory. I have this to say about most of the houses that I saw in France outside of Paris: they have a chill, blank, conservative look; they are all crowded together—three, four, five stories high; they are narrow as to their fronts, built of drab stone; their shutters, usually green and of solid wood, are closed distressingly tight. If there is any life it always concerns some inner court, and when you reach that, you feel as though you have gotten back into a reasonably human world. Deliver me from a French street in a country town or small city.

Mr. Dawson, who met us at the depot, was as lofty a person intellectually and artistically as I have known in years. Nice, but lofty. He was very youthful—not more than twenty-eight or thirty—tall, well-built physically, with a fine face and head and hands, but a very ladylike manner. He had a rather ladylike voice which was saturated with hauteur, and with him was a little dog to whom he talked in the most affectionate terms. "Dodo is very nervous," he observed. "She doesn't like country trains and this morning damp, do you, Dodo? She doesn't like this cold damp ground under her feet. Well, how are you?"

He took the arrival of Hale, whom he had not seen for several years, as the simplest matter of course and talked as though they had parted the day before. I recall now that he had a wristwatch and that he walked in a mincing way. Nevertheless I liked him after I had recovered from the original shock he gave me and felt satisfied that I should like to know him better. Hale was so unkind as to tell him that I was an American author, which made it necessary for him, he being a fellow author, to put me in my place. He did much to suppress or at least ignore me, but I went joyously along, for I was interested in his general appearance and what he might say or do.

He began at once, much to my satisfaction and delight, a very interesting account of Versailles—the general conditions prevailing, pointing out where some playwright of great note had a splendid collection of something. He showed us where the French Assembly—both houses, both the Senate and the Deputies—met in one body to elect a president. He had represented the American Associated Press in Paris some time before and had later beaten that organization by thirty-five minutes on the election of Fallières, which was consummated here by figuring out which way the crowd would run when the successful vote was cast and getting out by another door. He reminded me of another lady-killer I had known years before—a certain Edward Garfield Wriothesley Russell—who was never out of my mind as long as we were with him. Before entering the grounds of Versailles, we looked into the old courtyard of his house, an old courtyard which had been there all of a hundred and fifty years, and it was charming with vines, flowers, a stone bench and a small, broken fountain. He left an order for lunch for three, I think, and then we struck out into the grounds of Versailles, the wonderful aisles of trees and woodland pathways still clothed in a faint mist.

One could easily believe in looking at the palace and the grounds that they cost one hundred million dollars to prepare and six hundred thousand yearly to maintain. I was told, and it was obvious in looking at the statues and grounds, that the one hundred thousand at present devoted to its care barely kept it in order. The wonderful chariot of Apollo half-buried in water was, in addition, partly hidden by mist, which gave it a semi-spectral aspect, and the long lines of white urns and marble statues which lead from there to the palace itself disappeared in a vague gray. Not a soul outside of ourselves was anywhere to be seen. We followed these various alleys of clipped trees from round point to round point where splendid aisles radiated, all vacant and silent. There was no wind stirring, and the trees were absolutely still. We came to the Petit Trianon, closed tight and in the charge of a lonely caretaker, which we looked into through some of the windows. The small, white pavilion of music embowered in trees, the charming temple of love, the mill and cottage of Marie Antoinette and the long lanes through which the cavaliers and ladies of the court were wont to canter were all visited. The knowledge of Mr. Dawson was almost disturbing—he had the history of it at his fingertips.

It was pathetic to see the action of the chill winters on the delicate features of the nude statues, fingers, ears and toes being frequently broken off by the frost and not always promptly replaced. "It is hard for the director to do it," explained Mr. Dawson, "with the money he has at his command. He does his best, but a severe winter is expensive." A day at Versailles in summer would be delightful, but it ought to be nearer Paris. It is an expensive public park to maintain at so great a distance from the city.

The only sensation I can get from walking through a structure so vast as the palace of Versailles proper is one of great weariness because of its size and preciosity. The extent of the facade facing the park is 2222 feet, which after a fashion approximates a half mile, and counting in the central court which sets back of the face line proper, it is probably a half mile in length. Preciosity is the word to describe it all—vast rococo walls, amazing rows of mirrors, floriated windows, capitals, red and gold and prismed glass and, seemingly, miles upon miles of pictures. They are dull pictures after a fashion—historical scenes of the career of Napoleon, the lines of the Louis and so forth. There is nothing to say about these pictures except that possibly they have some slight photographic value. My wonder was that any human being could ever get it in his brain to paint on so large a canvas as most of these frames contained. Literally hundreds of figures of men, horses, guns, explosions, generals in conference—an astounding array. Perhaps they are of value. My one desire was to escape. I had one chortle of delight when, encountering a secret stair leading out of the chambers of Marie Antoinette, the irrepressible Hale remarked, "Well, I suppose Louis XVI took many a sneak down here."

"Oh yes, oh yes," I replied, "that will help a little," and I laughed my way past the state coach and out into the Avenue de Paris and all the way to the chambers of Mr. Dawson—for it was the one thing I had really saved out of Versailles. The rest was mere gilt and glass and fulsome ornamentation and great space—which kings must have but no ordinary human being could endure. It just occurs to me now what a terrific job it would be to sweep it all with a broom.

Our journey back to Paris was a sort of terror to me, for after leaving the boxcar we were to examine the Napoleon collection in the Musée des Invalides and then visit the Louvre in order to allow Hale a flying inspection of that institution. I have, as I write, an agonizing sense of Napoleon's hat, coat, pistols, handwriting and masses of other material belonging to him, and then of the agonizing miles of pictures in the Louvre which Hale insisted on inspecting in masses, accompanied by a German guide who spoke English and who agreed to point out the very exceptional things to him for five francs. "Europe from crag to crag," I called this, and it seemed to me that we fairly leaped from room to room. Vast masses of pictures went by in pyrotechnic blurs, and I think I saw all of Rubens as a red splotch and all of Titian as a blue one. I am sure the Meissoniers had a general dark effect, and Watteau and his pupils looked somewhat green. In one of the chambers of sculpture, two great porphyry basins explained the mystery of the Oracles and their revelations to me at last, for by putting your head in one basin at one end of the hall, you could hear the whisper of another person who might have his head in the basin at the other end. So if two such basins were employed—one in the antechamber of a temple and one in a curtained recess far from the view of the inquirer—mystic answers might readily be supplied. How well the word "priestcraft" symbolizes the subtlety of these ancient representatives and advocates of religious emotion, and how useful art and literature and physics and chemistry have been for their very sinister purposes. "To Gerny's Bar for dinner," read my notes, for having acquired a real brain-ache, I refused to go a step further, courtesy or no. And with the Louvre ended this day's investigation of classic Paris.

It was a relief to sit in the comfortable home-like atmosphere of Mme. Gerny's restaurant and watch her making herself gracious to her attendant damsels and their escorts and to listen to the red-coated minstrels and hear Hale talk uncertain French to an adjacent maiden who was not at all unfriendly. We returned as usual at a late hour, satisfied that Paris was like New York—only better organized, more artistic, more subtle, a perfect expression of the Latin temperament.

The remainder of the days I spent in Paris were seven, and during that time it seems to me that I saw an absolutely astonishing collection of notable things—things more distinguished than London has to show. For instance, I never saw a graveyard as strange as that of Père-Lachaise, with its narrow streets or paths packed with small temples or tombs, each one labeled "Family So-and-So." It was so crowded with these little houses of the dead that it induced a vast depression, a morbidness of soul such as I have not experienced in years.

I hunted out the tombs of Rachel and Abélard and Héloïse, of Daudet, de Musset, Corot, Daubigny, Chopin, Balzac and Hugo. It was astonishing to me to see how well the memory of so many of these celebrities were kept in mind. On Chopin's grave were at least a dozen bouquets of flowers of recent dates, cast here by admirers. Wreaths were exceedingly common—a kind of dull, gray mortuary wreath that is manufactured in Paris, and single roses and bunches of violets. I believe there is great family feeling in Paris and great emotional and sentimental reverence for art and literature and music. Corot's and Daubigny's graves were especially favored, and the sad avenues were literally strewn with fresh flowers. I think I got here this day an intense sense of what it means to be alive, to come home of an evening to a cottage or an apartment, to be able to eat a meal and sit before a fire and converse with friends. Actually, when I came away from this vast collection of memories—mere names—the human force that was selling shoes in stores, running streetcars, calling newspapers, lighting lamps and hurrying to and fro in great masses seemed strange and delicious and wonderful. Outside of this clanging, clattering illusion of existence, with people hurrying about their loves and their sorrows, their ambitions and enthusiasms, was nothing but an abstraction, a name on a stone, a memory of something that was once a part of this. I felt that if I could not immediately come into contact with friends and relations, I should die of despair, and yet as I got back into the swirling life of the city, the pathos of annihilation gradually disappeared, and the morbid spell of Père-Lachaise disappeared. No other cemetery ever did that for me—and I should not want to put myself in a position where another one could.

Another thing that interested me for an hour was the Bal Bullier, a huge and popular dance hall in the Avenue de l'Observatoire, where I went with Mr. Fergusson and Miss Rice and a party of their friends to see young Paris dance. Since I was told that one never sees children of the better, or even middle-class, families in a place of this kind, I could scarcely tell what element it was I was observing. Obviously it was not the same as that to be seen at the Moulin de la Galette. The girls were not of the same accentuated type, and the men seemed nearer clerks than artists, although there were many young artists present. I know of no place in New York as convenient to the mass of the people which is as large and imposing. Like the Moulin de la Galette it was well and pleasingly built of good wood and steel and painted within a light green and seal brown. It was well, even brilliantly lighted, and the floor was crowded with possibly a thousand dancers. A heavy admission fee of four francs was charged, and something extra for the care of hats and robes. There was an elevated platform extending all around the room containing chairs and tables where refreshments were served, and where a great crowd of spectators were sitting.

It was here that I noticed that the French dancing was not at all like that in vogue when I left New York. There was no particular swiftness nor speed of motion nor progress in any given direction. A couple would not go once around the floor in a given dance. It was more a matter of graceful physical motions of the hips and the feet and confined to a very narrow circle of space. A great deal of graceful walking and fancy kicking was done, but in a reserved way. I could not see that it was anywhere near as suggestive as the dance known as the "Turkey Trot," and I am satisfied that the suggestive motions permitted in East Side New York dance halls would not have been tolerated on the floor. There was no noise, only a gay chatter, and the sense of immoral relationship so characteristic of the Moulin de la Galette was absent. It was a healthy place, the Bullier, interesting and bright, and if there were more of that in Paris, it would be wanting in its lure for the international traveler of a certain type of mind.

This brings me to the interesting relationship that existed between Mr. Fergusson and Miss Rice, who maintained their separate studios in different sections of this region and yet who, nevertheless, were mistress and man and who were the center of a very interesting circle of talented friends. Among those who visited their studios, I met authors and artists of considerable ability and a number of journalists and magazine writers of international connections. Miss Rice was a personality all by herself—a good painter, a student of character, a good housekeeper and an intense lover of life. Her philosophy was of the broadest and kindest. She was a hard and enthusiastic worker. Mr. Fergusson was equally forceful, his studio a delightful place to see and his friends numerous and of considerable influence. I had to smile at the artistic scorn with which he told me that it was a poor type of artist who could not obtain a woman of means to support him in Paris—if he were that kind of an artist. He never told me that he and Miss Rice were definitely associated in an affectionate way, but it was so obvious from the frank social relationship that existed between them. "Sandy" was always invited to dinner when there was anything of importance at Miss Rice's studio, and at other times it was quite plain that he took his meals there unless they were lunching or dining out. While he was taking his bath, I saw her arrive at his studio with the ingredients of a dinner in a basket and prepare to serve it.

As a rule they adjourned after their day's work to some café or theater of varieties where they found amusement in each other's company. I went with them to the Café d'Harcourt and several student restaurants which had once been frequented by Baudelaire and Oscar Wilde. She was tremendously clever at sketching and, with her notebook before her, would pencil type after type of those notably characteristic faces of the restaurants. Once in the Café Olympia in the Boulevard des Capucines between one and three in the morning, she held an informal levee, sketching the wonderful types of which the room was full, and having them gather around her in swarms in order to be sketched.

It was not unlike a scene in musical comedy, and I know of no place else in the world where it could occur. Nowhere in the world, to begin with, could you find a room so thoroughly crowded with women who were of the lowest strata socially and yet who were so amazingly beautiful. There were types so artistically perfect as to feature, so graceful in their motions, and so tastefully dressed that you would marvel to be told that they were not fresh from the stage, but rather from the street. They were as experienced and blasé as long service in the streets could make them, as weary, as *désillusioné* and as gay as only French women could be. They exercised a splendid savoir faire, I thought, smiling cheerfully, gathering about like happy children, striking attitudes which they thought would be effective in a sketch, and going to bring others whom they thought would look better in a picture of this kind. It seemed to me as though they felt that they had the reputation of Paris for spirit and smartness and gaiety to sustain, and they did their parts with the air and the enthusiasm of trained actresses. This basement café was literally packed with beauty—costumes which would win a burst of applause if a curtain went up on them and dancing as graceful as I have seen anywhere. When we left at three, the place was still full, and Miss Rice's notebook was the richer for twenty sketches.

CHAPTER XXXIX

About the twenty-second of January I received word that on Friday the twenty-sixth Grant Richards would arrive from London prepared to journey with me to the Riviera; with my permission he would bring Sir Hugh Lane, who wished to go with us, and the latter might continue with me to Rome. The charming knight was not feeling very well; a season on the Riviera would do him good, and our company, in Grant Richards's high-flown language, would cheer him up. I, for one, was pleased at the thought of more company and looked forward to their arrival with interest.

Meanwhile, since their coming meant the end of all my observations of Paris, I bestirred myself to see as much more as I could before I left.

Since the arrival of Grant Richards ended once and for all my relationship with Mme. de Villiers, I should like to tell the story of that very remarkable woman. My memory of her ends in a peculiar and colorful way. During my stay in Paris I had been going to see her from time to time, inviting her out to lunch and dinner and occasionally strolling with her in some interesting neighborhood which I had not yet visited. Although so comparatively young, she had lived a remarkable and dramatic life. If one believed her—and I had no reason to judge that she was not absolutely sincere and truthful—she was the illegitimate daughter of a French army officer whose interesting and well-to-do family in Paris would, of course, have nothing to do with her. By the same woman who had given birth to her, there was a full brother who was doing well somewhere in Paris but who would have nothing to do with her, because he was anxious to get along in the world and was not willing to brook a possible investigation of his family connections. Yet she was obviously very fond of him and showed me a picture of this very pleasing-looking young man, whom she inordinately praised.

Her mother, it appears, had died when she was comparatively young, and her father had placed her and her brother in the charge of a small family some distance from Paris, where they were looked after with considerable care until she was fifteen years of age. At that time, obviously because he was anxious to dispose of her in some unobtrusive way, he endeavored to persuade her to enter upon a novitiate in a certain convent, which she refused to do. "I was too fond of life," she said in those amazingly beautiful tones which sprang from her throat, "to be a nun. Pah! I did not want to be a nun! I wanted to see the world and to meet people, and I would not listen to that at all!"

Her father, it appears, had persuaded the local priest, a young man of considerable education and charm, to work upon her sympathies and persuade her to accept his plan. This he attempted to do, but rather disastrously for himself, for he fell in love with Wanita and came within an ace of sacrificing her to his own passion.

"I was very passionate," she told me of herself. "I did not know anything about life. I thought he was a nice young man, and I liked him." It ended in some way in a dramatic scene between him and her in which he kissed her bosom and told her on recovering his self-possession that she would either become a saint or a devil, and he believed she would become a saint. Then he withdrew emotionally and spiritually from the contest and left her to her own devices.

Now, whether it was that there was some young lady in this village whom she knew and with whom she came to Paris, or whether she ran away of her own accord and made dangerous connections, or whether her brother brought her there, I do not recall; but anyhow, she came to Paris and, with some money which her father had given her, managed to live for a while and to connect herself with the chorus world of the French stage. The young lady who appeared as her companion at this time was an adventurous, dramatic spirit who earned her living now and then as a clerk, obtained some money from her relatives and was courted and entertained by young men of means because she was good-looking and temperamentally attractive. Mme. de Villiers told me that at this time she had no idea of doing anything wrong socially. Her father, seeing the course she was determined to take, contributed some money to her support. She early found herself handicapped, from the social point of view, because she could give no intelligent account of her family connections, and she had no birth certificate—most important in France. With her friend, however, she visited in different places—London, the Riviera, Vincennes, Marseilles—and through her met other women. In London Mme. de Villiers met a young doctor who took a great interest in her because of her personal charm and intellectuality, and who endeavored to guide her so that she might marry and socially place herself. He kept telling her that she ought to accept some modest position of some kind and marry as well as she could. "But pshaw!" she said in her soft Bernhardt tones, "that did not interest me. I wanted to live and have a good time as long as I was young, and I thought he was talking just to hear himself talk."

Her gay girlfriend, whom she described to me only vaguely as being rather subtle and designing but attractive, was secretly having relations with men which she knew nothing of. She invited Mme. de Villiers into company which was destructive, from a moral point of view. "And I did not understand then," she said, "just what it all meant." Mme. de Villiers was ill several times and was treated by her doctor friend, which cemented their friendship. Among other things, her girlfriend borrowed money from her and finally departed in a terrified state of mind that she was enceinte and that she knew no way of escaping the consequences of her condition.

"I was frightened," said Mme. de Villiers. "I did not know what to do, and I went to consult with my doctor friend, who, because he liked me, told me to bring her to him. He got her out of that—and during all this she told me of the good times she had been having and laughed because she had escaped so easily."

"My doctor friend," she told me, "was very much disturbed over the company I was keeping. He wanted me to leave London and go back to the town where I had been raised, but I would not. When he saw that I continued to run with my friend and go about as before, his attitude changed, and he began to make love to me himself. I think I was to blame, though, for I hung around him a great deal and ran to him with every problem I had. He liked me very much, and I liked him; and finally, because I was curious about the whole relationship, I went with him. We were friends in that way for nearly a year, and then because I discovered him with another woman, I left him. I did not love him—I never had—but I was disgusted, and so I just left."

The remainder of Mme. de Villiers's story I gathered piecemeal. Through her reckless girlfriend and through the doctor, who, if I am not mistaken, was married, she met a number of men and women who were well-to-do. Among them was a young Englishman, a clubman and a man of means, who took a great fancy to her and persuaded her to become his mistress. Mme. de Villiers was unquestionably in love with him. He established her in an apartment in London, and together they traveled some on the Continent—particularly to such places as Scheveningen, Ostend, Biarritz, Aix-les-Bains and the Riviera. While she was with him, so far as I could judge, she was perfectly faithful, and it is within the possibilities that she might have remained so—although I doubt it. The time came when his family wished him to marry, and he finally announced the fact of his impending marriage, leaving her in the apartment and supplying her with some money but refusing to see her. It was at this time that the most unfortunate portion of her career began.

Living in this apartment and connecting herself with her old friends, she met, among others, women of means with whom she began to practice lesbianism and to extend her favors to any attractive man, not so much for money as for the pleasure of companionship. Among others whom she met in this way was a certain American poet and novelist, who, because of his sybaritic and emotional temperament, became wildly infatuated with her and, with her permission, assumed full charge of her ménage. There was then established here a rather gay literary and bohemian atmosphere which lasted for some little while until another American short story writer and novelist—a warm friend of the poet's—appeared on the scene and began visiting with them. The temporary Mrs. Poet, on her part, became badly smitten with the newcomer and, without her master's consent, persuaded the novelist to take her to dinner and attempted to seduce him into a physical relationship with her. This, because of his friendship for the poet, he refused to do—which disappointed her greatly. In a way, according to her, it disgusted her with the poet himself, and when he discovered that she was going out to dinner with his friend without his knowledge, he became greatly enraged, reproached her bitterly and turned on his friend with the charge that he had seduced his mistress—which was not true. Exit the novelist, and after that, exit the poet. Mme. de Villiers deserted him because she no longer cared for him. "Oh, he was crazy," she said. "I could not endure him. And he was so passionate he was silly."

"How was he silly, Mme. de Villiers?" I asked curiously.

"Oh, when he would see me at times," she replied, "he would speak a lot of stuff out of his poems and dance in a foolish way. I could not stand him. He made me tired, as you say."

One could have forgiven a poet becoming foolish over Mme. de Villiers, for she was very charming indeed.

After the poet and the novelist, her life, so far as I could understand it, went off into a haze of disappointment and dissatisfaction. Being no longer happy in London, she decided to return to Paris and see if she could make anything out of her life there. Her father, having endeavored to persuade her to undertake something serious or marry, deserted her entirely. I think she had the stage in view on her return to Paris, or at least the semi-successful life of the cocotte—that type of woman whom I have indicated as frequenting the cafés, making brilliant catches now and then and being rewarded with ample funds. Her disposition, as I could have told her with my slight knowledge of Paris, was not fitted to the role which she was attempting to essay.

A charming woman, physically and mentally, with exquisite taste in dress and manners, she was far from being sufficiently calculating, sufficiently shrewd, to practice those arts which the cocotte must practice to succeed. To blackmail, for instance, would have been as foreign to Mme. de Villiers's nature as to fly. She had neither the taste nor the desire to connect herself with a group of women such as one occasionally discovers in the world who work together, introducing friends and planning campaigns. Her personal predilections and sympathies were always dominant, and this would naturally inhibit her from allying herself with that hard, indifferent type of individual who has means. She would not do or, rather, submit to the perversions which those sufficiently powerful to make a place for her on the stage would demand. She told me of perfectly revolting suggestions made to her by men of means who would have fostered her career if she had submitted, but turned their backs quite coldly when she refused.

"Oh, you don't know! You don't know!" she exclaimed once in an ecstasy of moral despair, staring at the floor—and when I finally extracted the truth, I myself was severely shocked. Her tendency was to seek those with whom she could live in a sort of childish good nature and sympathy, and to waste her days in a gay career of badinage and sympathetic humor. Paris, however—the stage and the restaurant world—is a terrific battleground, and without the ability to fight, and fight hard, one is doomed unless possessed of that open sesame, a striking voice or the ability to act in a distinguished way. Of these I am quite sure Mme. de Villiers possessed neither. She was merely a lovely flower of great tenderness, capable of suffering intensely and certain to be made to do so unless she was found by some genius of wealth or willing to accept a very simple existence in an inconspicuous world.

I came across her at a time, as I learned, when she was in the doldrums, and while she had plenty of good clothes and a pleasant place to live, she was seeing quite clearly the truth of the things that I have indicated, and it was weighing terribly on her spirits. A certain Mistinguett, with whom she had been intimate, was just at this time blazoned on all the billboards of Paris as the reigning success at the Folies-Bergère—a tall, lissome, tow-headed girl whom Mme. de Villiers had taught a little English and whose "Jiv me akeess" (Give me a kiss) was nightly producing rounds of applause from the jaded frequenters of the Folies. Mme. de Villiers had to witness this spectacle of glittering success on the part of one so close to her, as juxtaposed to her own apparent failure. She was dreadfully morbid, and at times her voice was as unendurable as music of great pathos. "Then," she said to me one night as we came out of the Folies, stopping in front of the posters of Mistinguett, a dashing composition in yellows, reds and blues which showed the reigning music hall favorite in a rakish cap and an absolutely glittering smile, "she was no better off than I was last year. I taught her to speak English."

"I know, Wanita," I said, "but your turn will come, maybe."

"Oh, no," she replied, "I know," and it was almost impossible to console her. It was with some thought of discussing her condition that I looked forward to Grant Richards's arrival, for it seemed that some suggestion might be made or some letters given which might improve her condition—but of that more anon.

CHAPTER XL

The arrival of Grant Richards created a great change of atmosphere, for although my days had been full of sightseeing and interchange of courtesies of one kind and another, there was not that homey quality about it all which his personality supplies. Grant Richards is somewhat like a furnace or an immense radiating blazing fireplace, for he is so full of a youthful zest to live and so keen after the shows and customs of the world that to be near him is to enjoy the privilege of great company. I have never wondered why he is so popular with women, or that his friends in different walks of life constitute so great a company. He seems to have known thousands of all sorts, and to be at home under all conditions. That persistent, unchanging atmosphere of "all is well with me," to maintain which is as much a duty as a tradition with him, makes for exceedingly pleasant companionship.

I did not see him when he first arrived, for I was off bidding farewell to a certain journalist to whom I had been introduced, and to Mme. de Villiers, whom I was not sure whether I would see anymore. Grant Richards had come from London not only with Sir Hugh Lane, who was bringing all his belongings for an extended stay on the Riviera, but a certain Sir Arthur Calvin, curator of the collection in the South Kensington Museum, whom I had met at Grant Richards's house, and also the scientific representative of a famous American millionaire, a Mr. Flexner, who was traveling over Europe making a study of prostitution with a view to throwing some light on that world-old problem and who was coming to Paris to see what he could discover there. As a matter of fact he considered Paris a pivotal point in his European investigations. A large sum of money had been set aside by his millionaire patron for use in gathering data. There was also a fifth person, who had joined at the last hour, the representative of a famous American publishing house who was coming to Paris to see a certain American diplomat about a book.

All but one of this goodly company descended upon the Hôtel Normandy late on Friday afternoon, and when I returned to the hotel I was notified that they were variously distributed about the place. Sir Hugh Lane had retired to his bed for a little rest before venturing out in the evening. The curator and the scientist were unpacking their several belongings, and Grant Richards had already gone off to see friends. A party of the whole was at once organized to dine at the Café de Paris and to see the café life, of which I was by now exceedingly weary. I really groaned within my soul when I learned that in the cause of the scientist and for the sake of Sir Hugh Lane, who had never seen the deepest Parisian underworld, a new expedition was to be undertaken. I thought at first it was to include or confine itself to that world which I had never seen, but of which the street guides were always palavering—those unmentionable sights to which Grant Richards invariably applied the "mother" cure. It turned out, as I half suspected it would, that Grant Richards would really have nothing to do with it. He was perfectly willing to lead the way into that showy world of immoral relations which he considered to have some artistic value as a spectacle, but he would not lend himself to purely sodden spectacles of vice, and I applauded him for it. Strangely enough, the Irish knight, chill religionist and fastidious aesthete, concerned only with the perfections of art, was anxious to see the worst that Paris had to show. The scientist, a small, canny Hebrew, was smartly interested—quite spruce—but talked solemnly of the profundity and dignity of his undertaking, and how serious his intention was to get at the causes of prostitution. The curator, a tall, wax-like lover of the exceptional in art, had a distant, indifferent air—good-natured and cheerful, but only mildly interested. The young publishers' representative could not come. His wife, coming over on the train from London to Paris, had heard that some such expedition was under way and put her foot down. Grant Richards informed me, looking at me solemnly through his monocle, that he thought that tears had been involved. He was quite sorry, for he was quite sure that the young publisher was very eager to come. Like a good-natured showman he was concerned lest any should miss his interesting wares.

Before this grand pilgrimage to the temples of vice and excitement Grant Richards and I spent a remarkable evening, revisiting most of the restaurants we had visited the second night we were in Paris—partly, as I was led to believe later, in order to permit him to run across Miss Longfellow, who was in Paris at the time, and partly to see if he could not by any chance locate a certain Mlle. Freyl, who, he had informed me when we first came to Paris, had been one of the most distinguished restaurant and Folies stage figures. Four or five years before she had held at the Folies-Bergère much the same position now recently attained by Mistinguett—in other words, she was the sensation of that stormy world of art and romance of which these restaurants are a part. She had had a wonderful mezzo-soprano voice of great color and richness and a spirit for dancing that was Greek in its quality. He told me that her every motion was artistic, that there was no thing so simple or plain which, if she chose to wear it, was not instantly transmuted into the dashing and the wonderful. "Why, if she were to tie a rag around her hair, it would smack of the revolution, and if she wore torn shoes of necessity, you would fancy she was doing it for effect. Nothing that she could put on would be unbecoming. I hope we find her." He was most anxious that I should get at least a glimpse of this exceptional Parisian type—the real spirit of this fast world, the poison flower, the hooded cobra, the ruddy rose of hell. He expected some day, he said, that we would run across her here in Palmyre's Bar, for he fancied she was down on her luck; and it was here that we actually did get wind of her. Already he feared that lesbianism, syphilis, morphine and a general tendency to strain her physical and mental powers in order to be happy had had their deadly effect and that we would find her faded and uninteresting. Nevertheless he was anxious that I should see her for what she had been.

Our evening's path lay through Gerny's Bar, the Café de la Paix, Fysher's Bar and Palmyre's Bar, on to the Abbaye de Thélème, the Café Américain, Maxim's and so forth. At Fysher's Bar, quite accidentally apparently, we encountered Miss Longfellow, whom I had not seen since we left Fishguard and who was here in Paris doing her best to outvie the women of these gay restaurants in the matter of her dresses, her hats and her beauty. I must say she presented a ravishing spectacle—quite as wonderful as any of the other women who were to be seen here—but she lacked, as I was to note, the natural vivacity of the French. We Americans, in spite of our high spirits and our healthy enthusiasm for life, are nevertheless a blend of the English, the German and some of the sedater nations of the north; and we are inclined to a physical and mental passivity which is not common to the Latins. Miss Longfellow did not have the spiritual vibration which accompanies the French women. As far as spirit was concerned, she seemed superior to most of the foreign types present, but the French women are naturally gayer, their eyes brighter, their motions lighter.

She resumed at once her posey account of her adventures since I had seen her—where she had been living, what places she had visited, and what a good time she was having. I could not help marveling at the disposition which set above everything else in the world the privilege of moving in this peculiar realm which fascinated her so much. Socially she was an outcast, but she did not trouble about this. As she told me on the *Mauretania*, all she hoped for was to become a woman of Machiavellian finesse and to have some money. If she had money and attained to real social wisdom, conventional society could go to the devil; for the adventuress, according to her, was welcome anywhere. She did not expect to retain her beauty entirely, but she did expect to have some money, and meanwhile to live brilliantly, as she deemed that she was now doing.

Her love of champagne was quite as marked as ever and her comments on the various women of her class as hard and accurate and brilliant. I noticed that, quite like myself, Grant Richards was occasionally shocked by her brutal comments on women, their lacks and their weaknesses. I remember her saying of one woman, with an easy sweep of her hand, "Like a willow, don't you think?"—and of another, "She glows like a ruby." It was true—fine character delineation.

My principal irritation this evening was that I was convinced that Grant Richards had been in touch with her for some time and had brought about this encounter for his own amusement and to see what I would say. I treated him and the lady so very badly that at Maxim's, an hour later, she decided to go home, so we took her to her hotel and then resumed our investigations alone.

Our next adventure was in Palmyre's Bar, where we went to make inquiry of Freyl, and there learned that she was really extant, had been seen at several places and was probably at the Rat Mort. We went there, but she was not present. We went in and out of one famous café and another, peering among the hosts of giddy diners—the dancers dancing, the music strumming as though it had never been done before, and finally we returned to the Rat Mort—this time to be rewarded; Freyl was present.

"Oh yes, there she is," Grant Richards exclaimed with considerable excitement, and I looked to a distant table to see the figure he indicated—that of a young girl seemingly not more than twenty-four or -five, a white silk neckerchief tied about her brown hair, her body clothed in a rather nondescript costume for a world so showy as this. Most of the dresses of the women were of white silk and satin cut low in the neck and with bare arms. Freyl had on a skirt of light-brown wool, a white shirtwaist open in the front and the collar turned down, showing her pretty neck. Her skirt was short, and I noticed that she had pleasing ankles and pretty feet, and her sleeves were short, showing a solid forearm. Before she noticed Grant Richards, she took a shapely-bodied girl in black silk for a partner and danced with others in the open space between the tables which circled the walls. I took a good look at her because of Grant Richards's description, because of the fact that she had been married twice and because the physical and mental ruin of a dozen girls was, falsely or not, laid at her door. Her face did not suggest the depravity which her career would indicate, although it was by no means ruddy; but she seemed to scorn rouge. Her eyes—eyes are always significant in a forceful personage—were large and vague and brown, set beneath a wide, full forehead—very wonderful eyes. She looked a little, in her idle security and profound nonchalance, like a figure out of the Revolution or the Commune. She would have looked splendid in a riot marching up a Parisian street, her white band about her brown hair, carrying a knife, a gun or a flag. She would have had the courage, too, for it was so plain that life had lost much of its charm and she nearly all of her care. She came over when her dance was done, having seen Grant Richards, and extended an indifferent hand. He told me, after their light conversation in French, that he had chided her to the effect

I looked to a distant table to see
the figure he indicated

that her career was ruining her once lovely voice. "I shall find it again at the next corner," she said, and walked smartly away.

He was all agog over this simple event, and I could see that the woman was wonderful to him. In all her simple clothes and ways she was far more important to him than all the fine women in all their showy garments, surging about us. "Someone should write a novel about a woman like that," he explained urgently. "She ought to be painted. It is amazing the sufficiency of soul that goes with that type. There aren't many like her. She could be the sensation again of Paris if she wanted to—would try. But she won't. See what she said of her voice just now." He shook his head. I smiled approvingly, for obviously the appearance of the woman—her full, rich eyes—bore him out.

She was obviously a figure of distinction in this restaurant world, for many knew her and kept track of her. I was told that for the last two or three years she had scorned all men, her affection being for women only, and that some young girl who was with her then was her mistress. I watched her from time to time talking with the guests of one table and another, and the chemical content which made her exceptional was as obvious as though she were a bottle and bore a label. To this day she stands out in my mind in her simple dress and indifferent manner as perhaps the one forceful, significant figure that I saw in all the cafés. The only one who compared with her in quality was Mistinguett, the glittering, vital figure of the Folies—a woman of Freyl's own temperament and vices and quite as forceful, only Mistinguett was still not weary of life and effort.

It was in this café, the Rat Mort, that we had one of those peculiar encounters which stamp Paris for me as being something different from anything I have ever known. Beside us, at an adjoining table, sat two young women of perhaps twenty-four or twenty-five, beautifully gowned, who were drinking champagne and amusing themselves by contemplating the scene.

"Great God!" said Grant Richards to the one nearest us, in French, "how you have fallen off since last year!" (I am transcribing this from his exact translation later.)

"Why, how ungallant!" replied the lady. "I think I am about the same. You think you know me, don't you? You mistake me for someone else."

"Aren't you ——— ———?" he asked. "I am certainly not mistaken. I think I know that chin and that ear." (All acting and pretense on Grant Richards's part.)

"You are mistaken, just the same. I am quite sure that I am as nice as I ever was."

Then followed one of those smart conversations in which the effort was to establish the exact place of this last encounter, the reason why he thought she had fallen off in looks, a general give and take of persiflage, with smart teasing on his part and coquetting on hers. We had some wine together. The girl beside her was a little dull—no particular friend of hers—and went her way alone after it was all over. This particular lady tried to establish the fact that she was no roving cocotte of this world, but a mistress with an establishment, and we wound up being invited to her chambers in the Avenue Malakoff, to which we journeyed in a taxi. It was after three in the morning. Having arrived there, we were shown into a decidedly attractive apartment in one of those very modern French apartment houses which have all modern conveniences and are furnished after the best manner of the style known as rococo. Her several rooms, some five in number, with a snowy bath, were furnished in excellent taste—rich hangings, charming pictures, expensive tables, chairs, bureaus and the like and closets full of gowns which probably fitted the lady exquisitely. She was the happy possessor of a dog and a maid and made much over the former, insisting on the old saw that if we did not love the dog we might not love her. The master of this house was away for the present—hence she was amusing herself these idle evenings visiting the restaurants of the Place Pigalle. She offered us wine and urged us to make ourselves comfortable. Our proposed trip to the Riviera aroused memories of her own connected with that world and with other European watering places. She finally assured Grant Richards that if with the first of his winnings at Monte Carlo he did not rush out and telegraph her some flowers, he would have no luck. We learned that her first name was Angèle, and then we came away.

My last adventure in this world, barring a few days the following spring, occurred the same evening of this day, which was now breaking, when Grant Richards as master of ceremonies led the Irish knight, the curator, the scientist and myself over this now exceedingly familiar ground. It began, heaven knows why, with a dinner at Palmyre's Bar—the dullest of all Parisian places for such a purpose—and before we were through we had lost Sir Hugh Lane and were within an ace of losing Mr. Calvin. It all sprang from Grant Richards's opposition to presenting the worst side of Paris, and with his choosing this particular occasion to write parting letters to his friends in Paris. I also had been so foolish as to suggest in the company's presence that we send a note to Mme. de Villiers asking her to join us. My object was to introduce her to the scientist, who, since he was seeking to obtain some philosophic and scientific light on the question of prostitution in Paris, seemed to me to stand in need of the intellectual service which Mme. de Villiers could render him. Her point of view on this score was at once philosophic and unique. She had had a world of experience and, I thought, could point out ways and means of approaching this subject intelligently. Mr. Flexner had struck me as being not of the order mentally or temperamentally which gains anything save a superficial and exterior and more or less academic view of this subject. Mme. de Villiers, because of her astonishing intellectual frankness, would take him close to the heart of the subject. Through her and those whom she knew he could learn of the congenital and conditional prostitutes. I sent off my letter, and Mr. Flexner seemed very pleased with the idea. But the Irish knight suddenly announced that he was exceedingly bored, that we were embarking on an exceedingly dreary evening, that he was not feeling exceedingly well and that he was going home.

"Wretched old middle-class restaurant," he observed sarcastically. "The same dreary atmosphere that you can see anywhere in London. I thought we were going to really visit something interesting."

Grant Richards did not apologize, but endeavored to reassure him. Something interesting would develop later. He would have none of it, however, and took his overcoat and left. Thereafter the four of us adjourned to another place, a repetition in part of the promenade atmosphere of the Moulin Rouge. This giddy world of showy dancers, staged solely for the benefit of the stranger, was dull to all of us, and we tried more of the restaurants—without effect. Finally Mr. Calvin departed without having seen anything to interest him, and now the three of us made our way to the Abbaye de Thélème in order to await the coming of Mme. de Villiers.

Being Saturday night, it was exceedingly crowded and gay here—quite the scene that I have described before. She arrived at one o'clock, looking as charming as I have ever seen her, and I explained to her in full what the object of the invitation was. If she could be of service to Mr. Flexner he would probably reward her with an amount which we had suggested would be about right, and with which he seemed to concur. Although a little moody at first, she could not withstand the infectious gaiety of the place, which was rapidly becoming riotous, and the last picture I had of her, after having decided to leave her in the company of Mr. Flexner and return to the hotel, was of her and some young American who had been attracted by her beauty exchanging a fusillade of those small colored wafer-balls which are given all the guests to throw. She had on a little fur cap of some silver-gray skin from which was suspended over her forehead a row of silver pendants which vibrated and trembled as she tossed her head to and fro. Readily susceptible to the charms of a scene of this kind, the joy of it had gone to her head; her eyes were sparkling, her lips parted, and she had the color and the pretty enthusiasm of a child. So wild did she become, as I stood contemplating her from the door, that she finally leaned over the table of her antagonist and beat his solid brown hands with her little white ones. The air was full of floating balloons and flying colored balls and the glittering light of the pink and white chandeliers. We waved Mr. Flexner a genial farewell as he sat gazing at her in uncertain speculation, and we made our way back to the hotel. Between three and four I packed my trunks, and at nine the next morning we were at the Gare de Lyon, ready for our journey to the Riviera, and mine to Rome.

CHAPTER XLI

All my life before going abroad I had been filled with a curiosity as to the character of the Riviera and Monte Carlo. I had never quite understood that Nice, Cannes, Mentone, and Monte Carlo were all in the same vicinity—a stone's throw apart, as it were, and that this world is as distinct from the spirit of the north of France as the south of England is from the north of England. As Grant Richards explained it, we went due south from Paris to Marseilles and then east along the coast of the Mediterranean until we came to the first stopping place he had selected, Agay, where we would spend a few days in peace and quiet, far from the hurry and flare of the café life of Paris, and then journey on the hour or two more which it takes to reach Monte Carlo. Several times on the way south he told me that he had arranged to stop at Agay in order that we might have the journey through France by day, instead of reaching Monte Carlo in the night, as we would have if we had gone straight on. We would rest at Agay for a few days and proceed from there in the morning, which would give us, if we had luck—and such luck usually prevails on the Riviera—a sunlight view of the Mediterranean breaking in rich, blue waves against a coast that is yellow and brown and gold and green by turns.

Coming south from Paris I had the same sensation of wonder that I had traveling from Calais to Paris—a wonder as to where the forty-odd millions of the population of France kept itself. They were not visible from the windows of the flying express. All the way we traveled on through an almost treeless country, past little white towns and vineyards; and I never realized before, although I must have known, that these same vineyards were composed of separate vines, set in rows like cornstalks and standing up for all the world like a gnarled T. Every now and then a simple, straight-running, silvery stream would appear, making its way through the perfectly level land and set on either bank by those tall single lines of feathery poplars. These trees either grow naturally or are made to do so, very tall and without branches, terminating in a small, leafy feather at the top. The French landscape painters have used them over and over, and they demonstrate exactly the character of the country from which the illustrations are drawn. To me, outside of Paris, France had an atmosphere of silence and loneliness, although considering the character of the French people, I cannot understand how that could be.

On the way south there was much badinage between Grant Richards and Sir Hugh as to the character of this adventure. One had brought two hundred pounds, the other sixty, to lose at the gaming table. A certain young friend of Grant Richards's daughter was then resident at Lyon; and it was Grant Richards's hope, according to Lane, that his daughter's friend would bring him a basket of cold chicken, cake, fruit and wine. It seems that he had urged Gioia to write her friend that he was passing through, and I was hourly amused at Lane's biting reference to Grant Richards's "parental ruse," which he trusted would come to nothing. It was as he hoped, for at Lyon the young lady and her parents appeared, but no basket. There was some animated conversation on the platform for the few minutes during which the train paused, and then we were off again at high speed through the same type of land, until we reached a lovely mountain range in the south of France—a region of low huts and heavy ox-wains. It reminded me somewhat of the mountain regions of northern Kentucky. At Marseilles there was a long wait in the dark. A large number of passengers left the train here, and then we rode on for an hour or two more, arriving by moonlight at Agay, or at least the nearest railway station to it. On the way south we had seen two young women journeying together, clad in the smart winter dress of the Parisians, and at Lyon they got off, apparently to send telegrams. They seemed to speak only French, and I paid slight attention to them, except that it seemed to me they were inclined to be flirtatious. After Lyon I lost all sight of them and did not see them again until some time later at Monte Carlo.

The character of the world in which Agay was located was delicious. After the raw and cold of Paris (it had turned wintry there the last few days), this satin atmosphere of moonlight and perfume was wonderful. We stepped out of a train at the little brick station of this summer coast to find grass growing, the trees covered with leaves, and—strangest of all to me—great palms extending their wide fronds into the warm air. There was much chatter in French while the cabbie struggled to get all our numerous bags into one vehicle. When it was all accomplished and the top lowered so that we could see the night, we set forth along a long white road between houses which had anything but a French aspect, being a showy development of things Spanish and Moroccan, and past bright whitewashed walls of stone, over which these magnificent palms leaned. It was wonderful to see the moonlight on the water, the bluish-black waves breaking in white ripples on sandy shores, and feel the wind of the south. I could not believe that a ten-hour ride from Paris would make so great a change, but so it was.

We clattered up finally to the Grand Hôtel d'Agay; and although it possessed so fine a name, it was nothing much more than a country inn—comparatively new and solidly built, with a charming vine-covered balcony overlooking the sea and a garden of palms in which one might walk. There was no elevator here, seeing that it was only three stories high, and neither gas nor electric light. We used candles. But the rooms were large and cool, the windows, I discovered by throwing open mine, commanded a magnificent view of the bay, and the food, so Grant Richards assured us, would be passable. I stood by my window transfixed by the beauty of the night. Not in France, outside this coast, nor in England can you see anything like this in summer. The air was like a caress. Under this white moon you could see the main outlines of the coast and the white strip of sand at the bottom. Below me, anchored near the garden, were some boats and to the right white houses sheltered in trees and commanding the wonder of the water. I went to bed breathing a sigh of relief and feeling as if I should sleep soundly—which I did.

The next morning revealed a world, if anything, more wonderful. Now all the whiteness and the brownness and the sharpness of the coastline was picked out by a brilliant sun. The bay glittered in the light a rich indigo blue, and a fisherman, possibly, putting forth to sea, hoisted a golden sail. I was astonished to find now that the houses, instead of being the drab and white of northern France, were as likely to be blue or yellow or green—and always there was a touch of color somewhere, blue windowsills ornamenting a white house, brown chimneys contrasting with a blue one, the charm of the Moorish arch and the Moorish lattice suggesting itself at different points—and always palms. I dressed and went below out on the balcony and through the garden to the water's edge, sitting in the warm sun and tossing pebbles in the water. Flowers were in bloom here—blue and yellow blossoms—and when Grant Richards came down, we took a delightful morning walk up a green valley which led inland between hills. No northern day in June could have rivaled in perfection the wonder of this day, and we talked of English poetry and the stagey make-believe of Parisian nightlife as contrasted with this and the wonder of spring generally.

"I should think the whole world would want to live here in winter," I said.

"The fact is," replied Grant Richards, "it is becoming a little banal. It has been overdone, and the best people do not come here."

"Where do they go?" I asked.

"Oh, Switzerland is now the thing in winter—the Alps and all that relates to them. The new rich have overdone this, and it is becoming a little dull."

"They cannot alter the wonder of the climate," I replied, "and that should restore it some day to its rightful place."

"Oh, it may come back," he replied. "I think it will if you give it time enough."

There are bits of scenery which, when connected with an idling trip of this kind, stamp themselves indelibly on the memory. I shall never forget the first day on this wonderful coast with the blue sea at the bottom and the tall hills raising their great bulk straight from the water. We had a table put on the balcony at eleven and our morning fish and rolls and salad put there. I can see Lane now, cheerfully trifling with the cat we found there, the morning sun and the scenery having put him in a gay mood, calling, "*Chat, chat, chat!*" and asking, "How do you talk to a cat in French?" There was an open carriage which came for us at one into which we threw our fur coats and blankets, and then we climbed by degrees for mile after mile up an exquisite slope by the side of a valley that gradually became a canyon and at the bottom of which tinkled and gurgled a mountain stream. This road led to a better view of the sea, under great trees at the top of a range, and I came upon it quite unexpectedly, walking some distance ahead of the carriage. I thought at first I was looking into a great valley where a fog prevailed, until suddenly, as I walked a few feet further around a curving road, the wondrous sea below came into view—white sails, vine-covered hills, a distant pavilion protruding like a fluted toy into the water, and here and there a pedestrian far below.

We made our way to a delightful inn some halfway down and back, where under soaring black pine trees we had tea at little green tables—strawberry jam and bread and cakes. I shall never forget the bitter assault I unthinkingly provoked by dipping my spoon into the jelly jar. All the vials of social wrath were poured upon my troubled head. "It serves him right," insisted Grant Richards treacherously. "I saw him do that once before. These people from the Middle West—what can you expect?" And my only refuge was to assault them with sharp comment concerning decadent Europe. It did not help much, for they were rapier-like critics, ready with a critical Roland for every Oliver.

That night a grand row developed at dinner between Lane and Grant Richards as to how long we were to remain in Agay and whether we were to stop in or out of Monte Carlo. Grant Richards's plan was for remaining at least three days here, and then going to a hotel not directly in Monte Carlo but halfway between Monte Carlo and Mentone—the Hôtel Riva-Bella. It appeared that in the Irish knight's mind there was a profound suspicion that Grant Richards, because of previous experiences here, his present sober life, his art and social connections in London, was not anxious to be seen on the Riviera. I had the feeling aroused by this argument that if he were seen here leading a cheerful life and spending money, the creditors of his former failure might pounce on him, or at least make uncomfortable comments. I knew that he had come here at this present time largely to entertain me, and since I would rather have had his presence than the atmosphere of the best hotel in Monte Carlo, it really did not matter so much to me where we went, so long as it was comfortable. Sir Hugh Lane was greatly incensed, or pretended to be, to think I should be brought here to witness the wonders of this world and then be pocketed in some side spot where half the delicious life would escape me.

"Agay!" he kept commenting. "Agay! We came all the way to the south of France to stop at Agay! Candles to light us to bed and French peasants for servants! And then we'll go to Monte Carlo and stop at some third-rate hotel in order to escape our creditors! Well, thank heaven, I haven't any creditors to escape, and I'll not stop at any third-rate hotel anyhow. You can go to the Riva-Bella if you choose. I am going to the Grand Hôtel where I can see something, and at least I will have a decent bed. I am not going to be packed off any ten miles out of Monte Carlo and be compelled to use a streetcar that stops at twelve o'clock or spend thirty francs getting home in a carriage. I prefer to spend some of my time in Monte Carlo, not all of it riding back and forth between the Riva-Bella and the casino."

This insistent bickering kept up until bedtime, with Grant Richards offering solemn explanations of why he had come here, why it would be advisable for us to refresh ourselves at the fountain of simple sunny nature after the fogs of London and the theatric flare of Paris. He had a fine argument for the Riva-Bella as a dwelling site: it was just halfway between Monte Carlo and Mentone, it commanded all the bay of Monte Carlo and was within ten minutes' walk of the bay on which Mentone stood. The high cliffs of the coast range rose sheer behind it. Cap Martin, with the hotel of that name, here thrust its sharp rocky point far out into the sea. A car line passed the door. In a half-hour either way we could be in either Mentone or Monte Carlo. The food he thought was excellent, the price moderate.

"Who wants to be in Mentone?" demanded Lane. "I would rather be an hour away from it instead of a half-hour. If I came to see Monte Carlo, I would not be bothering about Mentone. I, for one, will not go." And then he began to explain to me how foolish I was to allow my travels to be directed by a man whose interests in their arrangement was purely selfish. I kept out of this argument as much as possible, trusting to their united good judgment to bring us around to something satisfactory.

As it turned out, we did go to the Riva-Bella after all. It was not long before I learned that Sir Hugh did much protesting but equally much following. The patient silence of Grant Richards, coupled with direct action at the decisive moment, usually won. Lane's arguments did result in one thing. The next morning, instead of idling in the sun and taking a carriage ride over the adjacent range, we gathered all our belongings and awaited the train at a nearby station. It finally arrived after Grant Richards and I had climbed to the top of an adjacent hill where was an old water pool and had taken our last look at the lovely, high-colored, fluorescent bay of Agay. I can see even now some pearly clouds, tinted a faint peach-blow hue, with opalescent depths of blue and green which hung over the sea. And the white sails! Then the long train with drawing room cars from all parts of Europe rolled in, and we were off again.

One of the horrors which developed as impending at this time was "Old Box." As the train threaded its way in and out of towns, emerging after each dash of darkness upon some thrillingly opalescent bay, the rich, bluish-green water laving the sheer walls of brown and red and gold and with outposts of the Italian hill cities appearing on the land side, Grant Richards revived the personality and presence of old Bax. He resided at Nice. Grant Richards had been compelled to send him a telegram from Paris in order not to be exposed as a conscienceless friend. He was, or rather they were—for there was a Mrs. Bax—relatives of Grant Richards's, either Mr. or Mrs. Bax, I forget which. I think it was Bax. The latter was a famous writer on economics, an authority, and Grant Richards was his publisher. At Nice he expected to encounter him, and Sir Hugh groaned in anguish. "Old Box," he commented in his best and most critical manner. (He could bite like a serpent and sting like an adder. "Baron Wasp," I finally nicknamed him—"Lord Scorpion"—and we called him "Scorp" for short. Sir Hugh is naturally rather cold, and while cherishing the worldly connections of Grant Richards and his associates, he reserves the privilege of groaning and complaining by the way, looking down amusedly from a lofty, artistic standpoint and insisting that all is dull and not worthwhile, but clinging to it nevertheless.)

"Old Box with his stuffy old coat and his cane, and his wife with her moldy ermine and pink feathers!" continued Sir Hugh. "I can see him now, getting on with his hand to his ear." (I learned later from observation that Mr. Bax did not hear very well.) "'Did you come straight from London?' I can hear him ask," Lane complained. "'Are you going to stay long in Monte Carlo? Were you in Paris? Did you stay long there?'—and then running to me behind Richards's back and asking me whether what Richards has just told him is really so. 'Has he any money now? Did he waste any money in Paris? Is he getting on well in the publishing business?'"

It was just possible Bax had invested some money in Grant Richards's business and was consequently interested.

Lane went on to indicate a fussy, nosing, inquisitive old person who was meticulous in his social clatter to the verge of desperation and who, besides being dry and fussy, was a little malicious in his mood. While Lane was absolutely free and bitter in his criticisms of Grant Richards at times, he reserved this privilege for himself, and any information Bax got from him would be after having suffered the jabs of a phalanx of barbed and poisoned critical spears.

Grant Richards sat in the corner of the carriage, dumb as usual under this downpour of critical sarcasm, philosophically inured to all such thrusts. He obviously did not welcome the thought of Bax any more than Lane, but with that subtle understanding of the economic value of social occasions and persons, he was mentally determined to use us to feather his own nest by manipulating our movements so as to give Bax a lunch or two and perhaps a literary and artistic evening at his home. He could thereby assuage the old gentleman's flustered monetary emotions upon seeing him here reveling at Monte Carlo and perhaps build up the dusty author's appreciation of him as a publisher.

He grinned and called my attention to the first of the umbrella trees, of which I was to see so many later in Italy, coming into view in the occasional sheltered valleys which we were passing. Orange groves and lemon trees and the gorgeous orchids of the south were flourishing on either hand. The lovely fronds of palms seemed almost to brush the train, hanging over white enclosures of stone. Green shutters and green lattices, red roofs and bright blue jardinieres, the half-Italianized Frenchman with his swarthy face and burning eyes. Presently the train stopped at Cannes. I struck out to walk in the pretty garden which I saw was connected with the depot, Grant Richards to send a telegram, Lane to show how fussy and cantankerous he could be. It was wonderful to stand in this first resort station of the south and look at palm trees waving over the surrounding walls and at white houses glistening in the sun. Here were long trains that had come from St. Petersburg via Vilna and Vienna, others from Munich, Berlin and Copenhagen with diners labeled *Speisewagen* and sleepers *Schlafwagen*. Those from Paris, Calais, Brussels, Cherbourg were labeled *Compagnie Internationale des Wagons-Lits et des Grands Express Européens*. There was a long black train rumbling in from the south with cars marked Napoli, Roma, Firenze and Milano. You had a sense, from merely looking at this station, that the idleness and the luxury of all the world was pouring in here at will. I bought picture-postcards and wondered whether I should ever see Cannes again.

In ten minutes we were off again—Grant Richards expatiating solemnly on the fact that in England a homely girl was left to her own devices with no one to make anything of her, she being plain and that being the end of it, while here in France something was made out of the poorest specimens.

"Now those two young ladies," he said, waving his hand oratorically in the direction of two departing visitors, "they are not much, but look at them. See how smartly they are gotten up. Somebody will marry them. They have been encouraged to buck up, that there is always hope." And he adjusted his monocle cheerfully, only to find Lane fixing him with beady eyes.

"Now as for Old Box—you may depend on it that I'll have nothing to do with him. I'll not help pay for any social courtesies by my presence."

"Listen to the irreconcilable Lord Scorpion," I said, and Grant Richards sat down, to say nothing.

In a half-hour Bax appeared, shuffling somewhat like a horseshoe crab across the platform at Nice, a large shawl over his arm, a hooked cane in his hand, his pearl-gray felt hat looking much too small for his large head and his general expression being one of puffy comfort, inquisitiveness and intellectual superiority.

"Oh, there is he!" exclaimed Lane solemnly. "There he comes. Well, I'll have nothing to do with it. I am going out to smoke. You can entertain him yourself."

"Now do be reasonable," insisted Grant Richards. "Don't be so cross.

He's not uninteresting, and he'll leave us at Monte Carlo. I'll get rid of him some way."

"Yes, yes! I know how you'll get rid of him. You'll spoil a good lunch by him. You have him on your hands, and you expect us to entertain him."

By now Bax was puffing cheerily and inquisitively up the corridor, and Grant Richards was beaming on him with his seductive eye. Sir Hugh, for all his snarling, was preparing to be civil. There were languid handshakes, easy references to London and Paris. I was introduced as an American author of repute and dismissed at a glance, Bax being an author himself. Then came the fusillade of questions as predicted: "Did you come directly from London? Were you in Paris? Are you going to stay long in Monte Carlo? Did you see the ———s in London? Are they coming to the Riviera? Is your mother still in Rome? I suppose you expect to gamble some at Monte Carlo?"

Sir Hugh fixed me with a suggestive eye, his pale hand over his mouth. "What did I tell you?" he asked enigmatically, while Bax, as voracious as a fish, assailed Grant Richards with new questions and every now and then turned to us for confirmation. Again the Irish knight surveyed me with great wisdom. He did not have to say, "What did I tell you?" I exploded and opened a nearby window for relief. A passing bay, luminous blue against red-brown rocks, quieted my humor, and Lane came out. "Ha! ha! ha! What did I tell you? What did I tell you? Now we'll have him on our hands for the rest of the day. The old leech. But you and I can run away. We'll leave Richards to lunch with him alone. I know a very excellent restaurant. Let's not be put upon." He could be as soothing and persuasive as Grant Richards when he wished to further some cause of his own. I agreed, though I did not see how it was to be done, but I knew that Grant Richards would find a way to trap us both. There was no hope of escaping his oily machinations, so I might as well encourage Lane ad lib, which I did.

Amid the inquiries of Bax we proceeded to Monte Carlo. I had the usual vague idea of a much-talked-of but never-seen place. "I can hear the boys calling '*ascenseur*,'" exclaimed Grant Richards to Lane prophetically when we were still a little way out—all the product of his youthful, enthusiastic fancy. He was as keen for this adventure as a child—much more than I was. I could see how much he set store by the pleasure-providing details of this life, and Sir Hugh, for all his lofty superiority to it all, was equally keen. They indicated to me the great masses of baggage which occupied the platforms, all bright and new and mostly of good leather—such boxes and trunks as Miss Longfellow had coming across on the *Mauretania*. I was interested to see the crowds of people—for there was a train departing in another direction—and to hear the cries of "*ascenseur*" as predicted—the elevators lifting to the terrace in front of the casino. The tracks enter along a shelf of a declivity considerably above the level of the sea and somewhat below the terrace of the casino. The place was all that it should be—gay, rococo houses white and cream with red roofs climbing up the sides of the hard brown hill which rises to La Turbie above. It is a tight little place, all the houses and institutions packed closely together in narrow little streets, the grounds of the casino itself comparatively small and very artificial.

We did not stop but went on to Mentone where we were to lunch, while Grant Richards informed me that Monte Carlo consisted of at least twenty-five thousand people and that the prince of Monaco, who owned most of it, lived at Monaco, an island-like projection of land that looked more like an onyx set in a ring of blue water than anything else. We arrived at Mentone where I fairly swelled with interest; and stepping out from the platform, we walked two by two up the principal thoroughfare: Grant Richards and Bax, Lane and myself—the Irish knight walking with me because he wished to escape a worse fate.

I bought some postal cards, listened to an account of the origin of a double row of palms that graced a portion of the way and admired the new casino and the orange trees with oranges on them, and the profusion of flowers and the delicious summer atmosphere generally. It was so charming to see the striped awnings—pink and white and blue and green—gay sunshades of various colors and ladies in fresh linens and silks and men in white flannels and an atmosphere of outing. I think a sort of summer madness seizes on most people under such circumstances, and dull care is thrown to the winds, and you plan gay adventures and dream dreams and take yourself to be a singularly important person when you are not at all. And to think that this atmosphere should always be here, winter and summer, and that it can always be reached, out of the snows of Russia and the bitter storms of New York and the dreary gray fogs of London and the biting winds of Berlin and Paris!

"Walk fast!" said Lane in the chipperest of moods, "and maybe we'll get rid of Old Box." And when we hurried we heard Bax complaining—which elicited a cacophonous "Ha! ha!" from the Irish knight. "Oh, hear him. He says he has rheumatism. We must hurry and get away. Let's you and I find a place to eat." But the old author was not so lame but what he came clattering up, and then it was that Sir Hugh, out of sheer perversity of spirit, a determination to be appropriately cantankerous, excused himself and hurried away. He had no other engagement, but he did not propose to be put upon; but he agreed to come and find us. His desertion made us rather sad, but we bore up as best we could, and taking Bax by the arm, we bore him off to the Admiralty, one of those *restaurants célèbres* which Grant Richards was always talking about, a place where the *haute cuisine* of France was to be found in its perfection, where balconies of flowers commanded the Côte d'Azur; and the mingled architecture of France and Italy, with its bastard complement of Byzantine and rococo, was delightfully visible, and the brown and red sails which distinguish Capri and Venice were in delightful evidence. It was beautiful.

CHAPTER XLII

Before I go a step further in this narrative, I must really animadvert to the subject of restaurants and the *haute cuisine* of France generally, for on these matters Grant Richards was as keen as the greatest connoisseurs are in the matter of pictures. He loved and remembered the quality of dishes and the method of their preparation and the character of the men who prepared them and the atmosphere in which they were prepared and in fact everything which relates to the culinary and gastronomic arts of the gourmet. I am not prepared to say whether this is or was an affectation or not. Personally I should say it was not, though Sir Hugh Lane maintained that it was. He was never tired of expatiating upon the subject of Grant Richards's affectations and the fact that he was really not a true gourmet at heart, or if he was, that it was a low and unworthy ambition. There were constant exchanges of shrapnel on this score between them, or rather a steady fire on Lane's part with no response on Grant Richards's and no seeming result from the constant pattering of the guns. Grant Richards went his way as unconcerned as though Sir Hugh were the most rapturous and silent of followers.

In Paris and London Grant Richards was constantly talking of the restaurants of importance and contrasting the borrowed French atmosphere of the best English restaurants with the glories of the parent kitchens in France. He literally schooled me in the distinction which was to be drawn between the Café Anglais, Voisin's and Paillard's, and those smart after-supper restaurants of the Montmartre district where the cuisine of France had been degraded by the addition of negroes, tinsel, dancers and music. Nevertheless he was willing to admit that their cuisine was not bad. To breakfast at Henry's, to dine at the Ritz and to sup at Durand's was approved by him as good form; but if I chose to substitute the Café de Paris for the Ritz at dinner I was not going far wrong. He knew that M. Braquesec, the younger, was now in charge of Voisin's and that Paul was *maître d'hôtel* and that during the Commune Voisin's had once served *consommé d'éléphant, le chameau rôti à l'anglaise*, and *le chat planqué de rats*. He thought it must have been quite excellent because M. Braquesec, the elder, supervised it all and because the wines served with it were from twenty to forty years of age.

When it came to the Riviera he was really well aware of all that region had to provide, from Cannes to Mentone, and he could nicely differentiate the advantages of the Café de Paris; the grand dining room of the Hôtel de Paris, which was across the street; the Hermitage, which he insisted had quite the most beautiful dining room in Monte Carlo; the Princess, which one of the great stars of the opera had very regularly patronized some years before; the restaurant of the Grand Hôtel, which he considered very exceptional indeed; and the restaurant at the terminus of the La Turbie mountain railway—which he emphatically approved and which commanded a magnificent view of the coast and the sea.

I was drilled to understand that if I had *mostelle à l'anglaise* at the Hôtel de Paris I was having a very excellent fish of the country, served in the very best manner, which is something to take into consideration. If we went to the Princess, the *maître d'hôtel*, whom he knew from an older day, would serve us midgeon in some marvelous manner which would be something for me to remember. At the Café de Paris we were to have *soupe monégasque* which had a reminiscence, so he insisted, of bouillabaisse and was very excellent. The *supions* were octopi, but delicate little ones—not the kind that would be thrust upon me in Rome. I was lost among reminiscences of Ciro, whose famous restaurant was no longer in existence; the value of the Régence at Nice; the art of M. Fleury, now the manager of the Hôtel de Paris; and what a certain headwaiter could do for one in the way of providing a little local color, as Grant Richards termed it, in the food. To all of this, not being a gourmet, I paid as strict attention as I could, though I fear me much that a large proportion of the exquisite significance of it all was lost on me. I can only say, however, that in spite of Lane's yowlings, which were constant, the only time we had really wonderful luncheons, dinners and suppers was when Grant Richards ordered them.

This first luncheon at the Admiralty was an excellent case in point. Grant Richards, being on the Riviera and being host to several, was in the most stupendous of artistic moods. He made up a menu that was delicious: hors d'oeuvres—which he insisted should never have been allowed to take the place of soup but which, alas, the custom of the time sanctioned—and the caviar of which was gray—a point which he wished me particularly to note; *sole Walewski;* roast lamb; *salade niçoise;* and Genoese asparagus, in order to give our meal the flavor of the land. We had coffee on the balcony afterwards, and I heard much concerning the wonders of this region and of the time when the Winter Palace was the place to lunch. A grand duke was a part of this day's ensemble, and two famous English authors, before whom we paraded with dignity. I was secretly cross-examined at intervals by Bax to find out whether the things Grant Richards was telling him were really true, and also whether I was really an American author of any note or not.

After lunch we dispensed with Bax by putting him safely on a train, and after that, seeing Lane hovering in the offing, we picked him up and made our way to the hotel which Grant Richards, in spite of Lane's complaints, had finally selected. It was the Riva-Bella, standing on a splendid rise between Mentone and Monte Carlo; and here, after some slight bargaining, we halted, having three rooms *en suite* with bath, our breakfasts served in the rooms, and the remainder of the meals optional. Being the guest of honor in this party, I was given the corner room with two balconies and a flood of sunshine and such a view as I have never seen from any window before or since. Straight before me lay the length of Cap Martin, an olive grove of thousands of trees reflecting from its burnished leaves the rays of the sun. To the right lay the bay of Monte Carlo, the heights of La Turbie and all that glittering world which is Monte Carlo proper. To the left lay Mentone and the green and snow-capped mountains of Ventimiglia and San Remo faintly visible in the distance. Never an hour but what the waters of the sea were a lighter or a darker shade of blue, and never an hour but what a lonely sail was crossing in the foreground. High above the inn at La Turbie, faintly visible in the distance, rose the ruined column of Augustus, a broken memory of the time when imperial Rome was dominant here and when the Roman legions passed this way to Spain. At different hours I could hear the bugle of some frontier garrison sounding reveille, guard-mount and the sunset call. Oh, those wonderful mornings when I was waked by the clear notes of a horn flying up the valleys of the mountains and sounding over the sea!

It was immediately settled that once we had changed our linen and made a swift toilet that we would start for Monte Carlo. Grant Richards was anxious to get the preliminaries of admission to the gambling rooms over with and to do a little gambling. He had sixty pounds which he was perfectly willing to lose in the hope of possibly winning, and Sir Hugh had two hundred more. I made a solemn vow that seeing that I was a struggling author, fifteen to twenty pounds should be my utmost. We departed in gay feather, ready to bring back tremendous winnings—I eager to see this showy world, the like of which, Sir Hugh insisted, was not to be found elsewhere.

"Oh yes," he said, "I have been to Biarritz and to Ostend and Aix-les-Bains, but they are not like this. I like to see the adventuresses who have lost their last dollar and the Russians and Spaniards who play here. We really should live at the Grand, where we could walk on the terrace in the morning and see the pigeon-shooting." He told a perfectly wonderful story of how, once having a toothache, he came out of the card rooms of the casino into the grand lobby and attempted to pour a little laudanum out of a thin vial onto his aching tooth. "I stepped behind a column," he explained, "so that I might not be seen, but just as I was pouring it on my tooth, four guards seized me and hurried me out of the place. They thought I was taking poison. I had to make plain my identity to the management before they would let me back."

We arrived at the edge of the corporation which is Monte Carlo and walked in, surveying the character of the place. It was as gaudy and rococoesque as one might well expect this world to be. It reminded me in part of that Parisian world which one finds about the Arc de Triomphe in Paris, rich and comfortable, only there are no carriages in Monte Carlo to speak of. The distances are too slight and the grades too steep. Most of the traveling is done by train. When we reached the square of the casino, it did not strike me as having any especial charm, being small and sloping, and laid off in square beds of reddish flowers with greensward about and gravel paths going down either side. At the foot lay the casino, rococo, cream-white, with a glass and iron canopy over the door and a swarm of people moving to and fro. It did not strike me that it was an idling throng but rather that it had an air of considerable industry about it, quite as one might expect to find in a business world. People were bustling along as we were to get to the casino or to go away from it on some errand and get back. We hurried down the short length of the sward, checking our coats, after waiting a lengthy time for our turn in line, and then entering the chambers where credentials are examined and cards of admission sold. There was quite some formality about this, letters being examined, our personal signature and home address being taken, and then we were ready to enter.

While Grant Richards attended to some additional duty, Sir Hugh and I strolled about in the lobby observing the inpouring and outpouring throng. He showed me the exact pillar where he had attempted to ease his tooth. This was an interesting world of forceful people, whose characteristics I attempted to devour rapidly. The German, the Italian, the American, the Englishman and the Russian were easily recognizable. I expected to see a blazing world of jewels and showy costumes. To a certain extent I was disappointed. It was a smart throng, smartly dressed, the men very often in the rigorous cutaways of the afternoon with all the niceties of the toilet observed, the women perfect in the best their dressmakers could provide. Now and then a woman of amazing smartness or beauty or both would appear—hard, well-groomed, efficient, attended by some servitor in the shape of a husband or admirer and walking with the air of a born ruler.

Sir Hugh was convinced that the faces of the winners and the losers could be distinguished, but I am afraid I was not sufficient of a physiognomist to do this. If there were any who had just lost their last dollar, I did not detect them. On the contrary, it seemed to me that the majority were abnormally cheerful and were having the best time in the world. A large bar at the end of the room opposite the general entrance to the card rooms had a peculiarly American appearance, and the flavor of the whole place was Parisian—or, better yet, American—very active. The one thing that was evident was that all here were healthy, vigorous people with the lust of life in their veins, eager to be entertained and having the means in the large majority of cases to accomplish this end. It struck me here, as it has in so many other places where great pleasure-loving throngs congregate, that the difference between the person who has something and the person who has nothing is one of intense desire and of what, for want of a better phrase, I will call a capacity to live. Some people can live more, better, faster, more enthusiastically in less time than others—can think so—that is the great difference.

The inner chambers of the casino were divided into two groups, one, the outer, being six (I think) in number, somewhat less ornately decorated and housing those who for reasons of economy prefer to be less exclusive; and the other, the inner, being six in number, more ornately decorated, and having of an evening, it is said, a more gorgeously dressed throng. I could not see, after some experience, that there was very much difference. The players seemed to wander rather indiscriminately through both sets of rooms. Certainly we did. An extra charge of five louis was made for the season privilege of entering the inner group or "*cercle privé*," as it was called.

I shall never forget my first sight of the famous gaming tables. Aside from the glamour of the crowd—which was as impressive as that of an opera first night or grand reception—and the decorative quality of the room, which was unduly rich and brilliant, I was taken with the sight of the quantities of real money scattered so freely over the tables, small piles of gold louis, stacks of eight, ten, fifteen and even twenty-five franc pieces, layers of pale, crisp bank notes whose value was anywhere from one hundred to one thousand francs. The mechanism and manipulation of the roulette wheel I did not understand at first, nor the exact duties of the two croupiers seated at each table. Their peculiar cry and the scraping together of all the fascinating wealth with the little rakes and the subsequent throwing back of silver, gold and notes to the lucky winners gripped my attention like a vise. "Great God!" I thought. "Supposing I were to win a thousand pounds with my fifteen! I should stay in Europe an entire year." Visions of easy wealth dawned before my eyes, and I yearned to be able to instinctively pick the lucky numbers which brought such delicious piles of gold to so many.

Like all beginners I watched the process with eager eyes, and then seeing Grant Richards get back five gold louis for one placed on a certain number, I adventured one of my own. Result: three louis. I tried again on another number and won two more. Result: I saw myself (in fancy) the happy possessor of a thousand pounds. My next adventure cost me two louis, whereupon I began to wonder whether I was such a fortunate player after all. Meanwhile Grant Richards, playing first one column and another, had won eighteen and was in high feather.

"Come with me," he said, coming around to where I stood as I adventured my small sums with indescribable excitement and taking my arm genially. "I want to send some money to my mother for luck. I've just won eighteen pounds. I want to telegraph some flowers to Angèle, too."

I wonder if the reader remembers Angèle. We met her in the Rat Mort at two o'clock in the morning and took her home to her very charming apartment.

"Talk about superstition," I replied, coming away from the table. "I didn't think you would."

"I'd better," he smiled philosophically. "Besides, I want to send some sweets to the children."

We strolled out into the bright afternoon sun, finding the terrace comparatively empty, for the casino draws most of the crowd during the middle and late afternoon. It was strange to leave these shaded, artificially lighted rooms with their swarms of well-dressed men and women sitting about or bending over tables, all riveted on the one thrilling thing—the drop of the little white ball in a certain pocket—and come out into this glittering white world with its blazing sun, its visible blue sea, its cream-colored buildings and its waving palms. We went to several shops—one for sweets and one for flowers, *hauts parisiens* in their atmosphere—and duly dispatched our purchases. Then we went to the post office, plastered with instructions in various languages, and saw that the money was sent to Grant Richards's mother. Then we returned to the casino, and Grant Richards went his way, gambling at a distant table, while I wandered from board to board, studying the crowd, risking an occasional louis and finally managing to lose three pounds more—all I had won. In despair I went to see what Lane was doing. He had three or four stacks of gold coins in front of him at a certain table—all of five hundred dollars. He was risking these in small stacks of ten and fifteen louis and made no sign when he won or lost. On several occasions I thought he was certain to win a great sum, so freely were gold louis thrown him by the croupier, but on others I felt equally sure he was to be disposed of quickly, so easily were his gold pieces scraped away from him.

"How are you making out?" I asked.

"I think I've lost eight hundred francs. If I should win this, though, I'll risk a bee-a."

"What's a bee-a?"

"A thousand-franc note."

My poor little three louis seemed indescribably small. A lady sitting next to him, a woman of perhaps fifty with a cool, calculating face, had perhaps as much as two thousand dollars in gold and notes piled up before her. All around the table were these piles of gold, silver and notes. It was a fascinating scene.

"There, that ends me," observed Lane all at once, his stacks of gold on certain numbers disappearing under the rake of the croupier. "Now I'm done. We might walk out in the lobby and watch the crowd." All his good gold so quietly raked in by the croupier was lingering painfully in my memory. I was beginning to see plainly that I would not make a good gambler. Such a loss distressed me.

"How much did you lose?" I inquired eagerly.

"Oh, a thousand francs," he replied with a grand air.

We strolled out and were presently overtaken by Bax, who was here also, shuffling about with his cane.

"Ha! ha! There he comes!" sighed Lane dolefully. "Now he'll want to know how much I've lost. Unquestionably the most inquisitive person I've ever known. And he's so afraid Richards is wasting his money he doesn't know what to do. I've a mind to tell him Richards has lost five hundred pounds."

The old gentleman puffed up, quite eager.

"Enjoying yourself? Ha! Did you lose much? Where is Grant Richards? Has he lost anything?"

Lane put him off with a chilly explanation of his own losses. He said he had not seen Grant Richards. "Nosy old person!" he finally commented when he managed to get rid of him, "Stuffy and inquisitive! And his wife is just like him. It's a wonder she isn't here with him. They're like a pair of leeches when they fasten on you. I told Grant Richards in London not to get in touch with them, but he did it. Now he expects to unload his agony on us. It's good policy for him to keep in touch with them financially, I suppose, but that is no reason why he should inflict them on you and spoil your trip here."

He strolled up and down commenting sarcastically on one type and another and yet with a genial tolerance which was amusing.

I remember a charming-looking cocotte, a radiant type of brunette, with finely chiseled features, slim, delicate fingers, a dainty little foot, who was clad in a fetching costume of black and white silk which fitted her with all the airy grace of a bon-bon ribbon about its box and crowned as to feature by a wonderful confection of a hat; she stood looking uncertainly about, seemingly as if she expected to meet someone.

"Look at her," Lane commented with that biting little "Ha! ha!" of his, which involved the greatest depths of critical sarcasm and indifference imaginable. "There she is. She's lost her last louis and she's looking for someone to pay for her dinner. Ha! ha! ha!"

I had to smile myself at the man's croaking indifference to the lady's beauty. Her obvious charm had not the slightest interest for him.

"See the fat German!" he commented at another time, as a pursy person in light-gray tweeds and gold glasses stalked solemnly by. "I venture to say he's a German official or a banker. It's amazing how the Germans have been pouring in here in the last few years."

Of another lovely creature who went by with her head held high and her lips parted in a fetching, coaxing way he observed, "She practices that in front of her mirror, don't you know! Ha! ha! ha!" and finding nothing else to attack, finally turned on me.

"Oh, I say! It's a wonder you don't take a cocktail. There's your American bar."

"It's the wrong time, Lane," I replied. "You don't understand the art of cocktail drinking."

"I should hope not!" he retorted morosely.

Finally, after much more criticism of the same sort, Grant Richards arrived, having lost ten louis, and we adjourned for tea. After tea there was more gambling by a system which Grant Richards called Labouchere and by which the two of them, after various ups and downs, succeeded in losing twenty more louis. By that time they were both ready for dinner.

Much to my astonishment, an interesting argument arose, now not only as to where we were to dine but how we were to live our very lives in Monte Carlo. As usual—I say as usual, for I am now looking back on my experiences as a whole—Lane was critical of Grant Richards's arrangements and general conduct of affairs.

"Now, I should think it would be nice if we were to dine at the Princess. You can get excellent sole and *canard à la presse* there, and their wines are excellent," said Grant Richards.

"I certainly don't see why we should dine there and spend all the good money it will cost, when we can dine quite as well—sensibly, anyhow—at our own hotel. You might like to dine at the Princess and spend all the money you have, but I don't want to. I shouldn't think Dreiser would either." He fixed me with a saving, ascetic eye.

"I don't see what the value of his coming to the Riviera is," replied Grant Richards, speaking for me, "if he isn't to see the characteristic life of the place. The restaurant life here is quite as much a part of what he should see as anything else. How else is he to write an interesting book?" Grant

Richards turned to me, expecting to find ardent support but was doomed to disappointment. I wanted nothing to do with this managerial bickering. All that came to my mill was grist, even this quarrel. I wanted to travel as inexpensively as possible, of course, consistent with attractive living, but I reasoned that I could trust any compromise which Sir Hugh might compel Grant Richards to accept. Without some such check he was inclined to the wildest extravagance.

"Well, I'll not go," insisted Lane dogmatically. "You two can if you will. I shall go back to the hotel and dress."

This was a very serious defection, and Grant Richards contemplated him with a weary and somewhat disturbed monocled eye. "Well, what would you suggest?" he inquired by way of parley. "We can't dine at the Riva-Bella *every* evening. The cuisine is terrible."

"Not at all! Not at all!" replied Lane. "Besides, a little fasting would not do you any harm. You need not waste all your money on your stomach. Ha! ha! ha! Now what I would suggest would be that we go sanely back to the Riva-Bella, change our clothes, dine simply and inexpensively" (this from the man who had just lost a thousand francs), "come back here, buy our tickets for the *cercle privé* and gamble inside. What is the use of gambling in these outer rooms? You say you want Dreiser to see the typical life of the place, and yet you balk at paying the extra money required to go into the *cercle privé*." (I had not noticed that Grant Richards had balked at this. I merely fancied that he was reserving it for a slightly later impression. We had not got around to it as yet, but Lane would not have it so.) "Here we trifle around all afternoon among a lot of frumps" (Lane, as a matter of fact, had been lost in gambling, not really paying any attention to anyone.) "and now we are not to be allowed to enter the *cercle privé* tonight. First we go to Agay and spend a doleful time among a lot of peasants, and now we hang around the outer rooms of the casino. If I were Dreiser and were employing the services of a guide to show me around Europe, I would get someone who evinced some slight sense of discrimination. I shouldn't assume that my stomach was the only thing that needed consideration in Europe. Ha! ha! ha! We can't live at the Hôtel de Paris or enter the *cercle privé*, but we can dine at the Princess. Ha! ha! That's because he eats the most," he added quite bitingly, turning to me, "and we pay our pro rata share."

Grant Richards merely contemplated the ceiling of the lobby, where we were gathered, while Sir Hugh rattled on snake-wise in this fashion.

"I *expected* to get tickets for the *cercle privé*," he soothed.

"Yes, after you've been driven into it. If I had said nothing you wouldn't."

"It will cost at least twenty francs to drive over to the Riva-Bella."

"Exactly!" replied Lane, "As I predicted. We can't live in Monte Carlo, but we can pay twenty francs to get over to Cap Martin. Thank heaven there are still streetcars. I do not need to spend all my money on shabby carriages, riding out in the cold." (It was a heavenly night.)

"I think we'd better dine at the Princess and go home early," pleaded Grant Richards. "We're all tired. Tomorrow I suggest that we go up to La Turbie for lunch—that will prove a nice diversion—and after that we'll come down and get our tickets for the *cercle privé*. Come now. Do be reasonable. Dreiser must see something of the restaurant life of Monte Carlo."

There was more bitter wrangling, my claims as a sightseer and writer of a book being uppermost, used as a club by both, and as usual Grant Richards won. We *did* go to the Café Princess. We *did* have *sole normande*. We *did* have *canard à la presse*. We *did* have several bottles of excellent wine, and Grant Richards was in his glory. He beamed ruddily. He joked the waiters. He suggested that we telegraph Mme. de Villiers, insisting that I needed feminine companionship on the Riviera.

He wrote his mother a delicious letter at table, telling of the simple life he was leading and the difficult time he was having with his intractable charges, parts of which Lane and I helped compose. "Dear Mother," I suggested as a suitable missive. "Here I am on the Riviera, quite lonesome. It is now nine o'clock, and I have retired for the night. Mr. Dreiser and my friend Sir Hugh Lane, both conservative men, are already in bed. We looked in at the casino a few moments this afternoon, but merely to see it. All of us are opposed to gaming. Tomorrow we are going for a long walk in the mountains to get out of this feverish atmosphere of vice and crime. Only the contract which compels Mr. Dreiser to write a book brings us here at all. But we will lead the simple life and depart soon. Your loving, ascetic son, Grant Richards."

Needless to say this letter did not go.

CHAPTER XLIII

It was while we were at Nice that I firmly gained the impression that Grant Richards was manipulating a world of females for his own entertainment and, to a very minor extent, mine—which interested me greatly. His attitude towards sex was as curious and as interesting as any I have ever encountered.

It is more than probable that he is a sensualist of a very experienced type, but that did not alter the fact that, insofar as I could see, it was interwoven with a very pleasing atmosphere of art and romance. No one could be a greater stickler for the proper adornment of a woman. I invariably noticed that only such women as were charmingly dressed, possessed of natural finesse and a certain amount of awareness and sophistication, were of interest to him. His eye was fixed on youth and beauty charmingly arrayed, but after that, it admitted the maturer woman if she were really attractive. His excuse for the cocotte was that she was primarily poor, artistic and ambitious. The ordinary conventional means of her state gave no room for the exercise of her fancy or her tastes—hence the easy way, vice. He thought that most cases of variation from the social norm sprang from seduction through affection or disappointed love, and after that, vice as a means to social and artistic privilege was obvious. Clever men of means like bright, attractive women, hence the cocotte with her fine dresses, her various trunks and her abnormal appetite for entertainment and pleasure.

In Paris, as I have indicated, he introduced me to Mme. de Villiers and several others in order that I might not be lonely and that I might be socially entertained. It would not be possible, he thought, for a family of ordinary conventional French respectability to show me the things which I ought to see, and what he could not provide himself, he made shift to have provided by others. Here at Monte Carlo he kept indicating that really this world was not what it ought to be without women, that feminine companionship of the smart kind gave that last touch of show and romance which made Monte Carlo so attractive. There was really an innocent, social, romantic phase to his mood on this score, and I am sure that he was more interested in having an attractively gowned maiden of real beauty and mental facility as a companion than he was in anything else. My own attitude could never be quite so remote—although, in a way, it partook of much of the feeling which dominated his own.

My great handicap in all this situation was that I could not speak either French or Italian, and French was dominant here. I had to fall back on Grant Richards as an interpreter, and he was usually busy talking for himself. Sir Hugh Lane had absolutely no interest in women whatsoever. He viewed them all with a chill and pessimistic eye. Oh yes, they were interesting, but they had far too many reprehensible qualities. They were evil, rather glorious and showy spiders spinning nets for none too satisfactory men. When they were too loud in their dress, he refused any comment whatsoever. It was only when they approximated the charm of conservatism that he shot his bitter arrows. Interesting as a spectacle, but worthless; weeds masquerading as true social flowers; creatures really feeding on youth and virtue, and creating spendthrifts and wrecks. I can see his melancholy eye as he followed them, saying, "There they go. Some other poor fool to pay their expenses. If it weren't for them, I suppose some of these shops would not know what to do." Then he lifted his eyebrows in infinite disgust, and no demimondaine ever received an encouraging glance from Lane. Once Grant Richards proposed that I encourage Sir Hugh in an adventure—an experience which he felt sure would broaden his horizon and brighten his life—but of that more anon.

What set me thinking was that Grant Richards was invariably slipping away to send a telegram or industriously writing sudden communications, which caused me to fix him with an inquiring eye. How often I said to him: "I know what you are up to, you stiff. Don't you try to fool me." To which he would reply in his grandest manner, "My dear fellow, what is a stiff? I don't understand you. Some American animal, I presume."

"A stiff is a mutt," I replied, "and a mutt is a dub, and a dub is a bluffer, and a bluffer is a cardsharper who has something up his sleeve, and you are he."

"Really?" The monocle beamed noncommittally, and he refused to confess.

At Nice, however, I thought I saw the younger of the two young women who had met us on our arrival in Paris, and a previous remark of his to the effect that it was just possible we would encounter them here set me thinking. "Oh," I said, "that is where the telegrams have been going, and they are coming down here. No doubt he has them concealed somewhere already, and he is going to leave Lane and me to our own devices. Now he will not come any such game with me." On the other hand, I was not so much interested in these two particular women, for after Mme. de Villiers and the companionship of Miss Rice and the world of clever women I had seen in the cafés, I had decided that they were not so interesting mentally as I had first imagined. Neither were they as smart as many I had seen since—much too gross, in fact—and I was not greatly cheered by the thought that they might be inflicted on me. Besides, the thought which Grant Richards kept constantly uppermost—that they and all women of their type were expensive to entertain and that a liaison easily ran into a thousand francs—was a deterrent. Nevertheless and notwithstanding, the sight of the one that I took to be the younger, radiant in garnet silk and opals, lounging in the waiting room, was a great excitement, and when I smiled and she seemed to recognize me, I hurried off to Grant Richards to reproach him with his treachery. Oh yes, here they were, and he had not said a word. To my astonishment, he denied it vehemently. "You don't tell me! Impossible! I give you my word that I had nothing to do with it. Where did you say she is? Let me see her."

We bounded up the steps from the general garden to the public waiting room three steps at a time, determined to settle this mooted question. Grant Richards was outraged to think I would not accept his word. He was keenly interested, however, to see if his acquaintances had really arrived and no doubt was prepared for the worst or the best. When we confronted her approaching us with an idle air, she gave not the slightest sign of recognition, and I realized that I had made a great mistake. It was not the lady at all. I was nonetheless right in expecting that they were coming, however, for although he denied correspondence, he knew that they were to arrive; and on the night of their appearance, as usual, we were luckily present to receive them. But I am getting ahead of my story.

The next day we spent quietly exploring Cap Martin, that long point of green olive trees which stretches out into the sea between Monte Carlo and Mentone, and hearing Lane expatiate upon the virtues of the simple life. I am amused when I think of the solemn manner in which he viewed our feverish interest in this world and the constant counsel to sobriety which he was giving. "Now you know, Grant Richards, what your failing is. You have no interests beyond the table and these wretched women. You might at least show Dreiser some of the conservative features of the Riviera. It doesn't all consist of the gambling tables and immodest women. Now I should think it would be very nice if we would stay here today and walk out through the olive grove to the Cap Martin Hotel for tea. The Empress Eugénie lives there, and there is that splendid view of Mentone through the umbrella trees. Afterwards we can go to the Soleil if you wish. I should think that would be interesting. Isn't Coppélia dancing there? I understand she is very good."

Grant Richards, who had been drawing a long face over the olive trees and the residence of the Empress Eugénie and tea at the Cap Martin, cheered up the least bit at the mention of Coppélia. At the end of a long, dreary day, Coppélia might help. At least she was in the center of Monte Carlo where all good things were, a part of an excellent restaurant-theater where expensive dinners were served and where he could order wine to his heart's content. So it was agreed, after many bitter remarks on the subject of an alleged love of art which was limited solely to the region of gambling rooms and restaurants, that if we spent a quiet day as described, we were to have the delights of the Soleil at night. We walked with Lane in the green shadows of the thousand-year-old trees and passed the villa of the ex-Empress as scheduled and sat on the rocks under the Cap Martin listening to the sounding sea, and afterwards we had ourselves photographed on the lawn of the Cap Martin watching the carriage of a grand duke, with its attendant moujiks in costume, and later drinking tea on the balcony. The gnarled umbrella trees were duly inspected, giving a wonderful view of Mentone in the setting sun, with its red roofs, its occasional spires, and the brown wall of the mountains all tenderly lighted. We three crossed swords on many delicious points of view and philosophy, arguing fluently every step of the way, and finally it was dusk and we were dressing for the Soleil. Grant Richards now was once more amazingly cheerful, and with more sarcasm as to a love of art that must be constantly well-fed, we were off.

I do not remember much concerning the Soleil except that Coppélia was not present. She was ill. But as we dined splendidly on a balcony overlooking a mediocre vaudeville performance, two acts of which were American—Lockart's elephants, for one—we had the pleasure of contemplating the arrival of a youthful relative of a far-famed English diamond prince who had inherited all the latter's wealth and who was now dining here with women of extraordinary beauty. We had their full history from Grant Richards, part rumor and part fact. And then, very much disappointed at the loss of Coppélia, we adjourned to the gambling casino. It was now that our many good louis were expended to enter that inner sanctum of superior gambling, the *cercle privé*, where Lane was certain that we would see the most striking of women and enjoy the most perfect spectacle of gay license which the Riviera presents.

If I was interested in the gambling chambers at Nice, I was equally interested, and I think more so, in these rooms here. They seemed to me to be built on a surer base of prosperity. The crowd was larger, fairly thick, the costumes of the women quite as striking, and there were more of them. The tables had that rich, feverish atmosphere which is the key to the interest of this region. We gambled at different tables, Lane assuring me from time to time, when I found him, that he was winning, Grant Richards that he had just lost ten pounds or had just won fifteen.

The time passed until near midnight, and then, just as I was gathering up three louis from a table, having lost all track of my companions, I was suddenly conscious of a young girl beside me who was talking rapidly in French as if she knew me. I did not take any notice of her dress and her appearance at first any more than to realize that she was quite young and very beautiful, charmingly so, with none of the sophisticated cynical expression which so many of these young faces wear. She seemed gay and buoyant, and reminded me of the young girl of our hometown with whom I used to go to school.

I could not understand what she said. If I say that I heard "Paris," "Monte Carlo," "Lyon," "*Est-ce que vous n'êtes pas le monsieur que j'ai vu en venant de Paris à Lyon le dernier samedi?*" I would be well within the facts. She said this and much more, as I afterwards learned. She took my arm and led me to a divan, seating herself and indicating that I should, while she still prattled to me in her native tongue. I was so amused and entertained that I laughed out loud. "But I don't speak French," I said, feeling helpless and only for that reason wishing to get rid of her. I was really more interested in a German girl whom I had seen, a maiden of the Marguerite type whose braided coiffure of flaxen hair had attracted me and with whom I had exchanged a few words earlier in the evening. I could talk with her, which was more than I could with any of the others.

"*Non, non, non!*" my delightful companion replied when I indicated that it was "no, no"—hopeless. She beat her knees with very pretty little hands in obvious disappointment at finding that I could not talk to her. For the first time in my life I had a clear demonstration of what the impatience of a pretty Frenchwoman may be. She shook her pretty little shoulders in opposition to circumstances, and I believe would have stamped her foot—to all of which I smiled blandly, very sorry to think that I was to lose the companionship of anyone so charming. She was not through with me, however. She put her hand to her chin in obvious contemplation for a moment, and then suddenly seized me by the arm again. "Come with me," she must have said in French, for she led the way with almost impatient enthusiasm. Only a Sir Hugh Lane could have refused her, and then I think he would have been a little sorry. She was the quintessence of gay, black-haired, rosy-cheeked charms, and her charms were not artificial. She had youth and shapeliness and amazing vigor on her side, and her eyes fairly danced with a smart native intelligence. I shall never forget her "A-h-h, *bien triste*" as she looked at me, realizing that I could not talk to her. To make up for it she squeezed my arm and my hand and smiled at me winningly. You would have imagined that she had known me for years and years.

Her object, as I discovered, was to find her companion with whom she had traveled from Paris, one Mme. Goldschmidt, a young girl as attractive as herself whom, to my astonishment, I found tabled with Grant Richards enjoying a liqueur and chatting gaily. "A-h-h," my friend began—a long, excited speech and explanation, which ended in Grant Richards's explaining to me that these were the two young women who had come down on the train with us from Paris to Monte Carlo whom we had seen getting off at Lyon to telegraph and who had decided on first sight that they wished to know us better. It even transpired, according to this explanation, that they had picked their favorites and divided the spoils of war in advance. The one who had chosen me here—Mlle. Marcelle Itam, no less—was the one who had picked me for her own on the train; and Mme. Goldschmidt had decided on sight that she preferred Grant Richards. They had been greatly grieved on learning that we had left the train before reaching Monte Carlo and had lived in the hope of finding us somewhere in these chambers. Tonight was their first opportunity, and they had immediately taken us in tow. Mlle. Itam was so grieved, I understand now, to find that I did not speak French, but nevertheless, so far as I could judge, she did not intend to relinquish me here.

"I think you will have to do the best you can," Grant Richards said, "whether you speak French or not. The lady seems to like you."

"Leave it to me," I said, looking into Marcelle's shining eyes. "She is very nice. I like her. I can talk to her in some other language than French, and she will understand me quite as well."

We finished our liqueurs, talking of the trip south and explaining why we had not spoken to them. I was fearsome lest Sir Hugh Lane should appear to rebuke us for our levity. We crossed the street to the Café de Paris, but Mlle. Itam and I took a detour, for she could not get her wraps as quickly as her friend, and we were left behind. She wanted to walk around the little formal gardened square. Not a word could we speak, and yet so keen is sentiment and goodwill that we made an excellent shift at exchanging sympathies. When a companion looks cheerfully and enthusiastically in your eyes, you are really not suffering for want of conversation. Mlle. Itam made herself plain enough in a score of ways. I never knew how easy it was to make oneself understood in another tongue without speaking a word of it.

Mlle. Itam, or Marcelle, as she quickly informed me her given name was, had a most pleasing voice, a voice not as wonderful as Mme. de Villiers's, but so very characteristic and soothing. She had a curious rising inflection which she gave to most words and all sentences, and so often the words had a ring to them, a marked emphasis on the last letters. It was delightful to hear her call herself "Marcelle" ("Marsail," she pronounced it) in order to identify herself and get me to tell her my first name. "*Moi*," she explained emphatically, beating her pretty chest with her gloved hand, "Marsail. *Vous—qui?*"

"Theodore," I said.

"*Qui?*"

"Theodore."

"Oh, *oui*," she announced, nodding her head very wisely. "*Oui, oui. Vous êtes* Tayadore. *Moi*—Marsail—*Vous* Tayadore."

"Exactly," I said, laughing.

"*Oui?*"

"Exactly."

"*Oh, oui. Je comprends. Anglais:* exactly. *Français: exactement.*"

"*Oui*," I replied, delighted, "exactly: *exactement.*"

We congratulated each other on how well we were getting on by squeezing hands and laughing foolishly.

I could not tell you how many little things like this transpired in just this one little short walk around the square. I know that all the while Marcelle kept tight hold of my hand, squeezed my arm, and began a short course of French in order to bring me nearer to her intellectually. A smarter little piece never lived. She was fairly bursting with energy and life enthusiasm. "*Rue*," she exclaimed, pointing to the street, and "*trottoir*," to the sidewalk. A flight of steps was indicated to me as *escalier*, an electric light as *lumière*, a window as *fenêtre*, and so on. She touched my lips, exclaiming "*lèvre*," my hand as *main*, my arm as *bras*. I can hear the euphonious ringing sound of her words yet and recall the delightful emphasis she put on them. She was so anxious for me to know that if sheer force and emphasis could have driven French into me instantly, I would have had it. As it was, she reached my naturally eager intellect in the subtlest ways, indicating remarkable mental resourcefulness on her own part.

I cannot wonder now that I took to her so quickly. She was mentally compatible, resourceful, gay, youthful. She had a swinging, self-sufficient, self-reliant little walk which amused and delighted me. Above all she had taste, chic and yet was not unduly forward. I could not help momentarily contrasting her with Mme. de Villiers and at the same time with American girls of their own age. Mme. de Villiers and Marcelle were as radically different as night and day, and yet they held much in common: taste, beauty, good sense, sympathy, appreciative understanding. The vast difference lay in their types of coloring—Mme. de Villiers light and Marcelle dark—and in their respectively fearsome and courageous natures. Marcelle breathed at once defiance and dominance in life, hope, enthusiasm, assurance; Mme. de Villiers reflected a soft, wistful, hopeless philosophy, a be-that-as-it-may attitude which was charming, winsome and yet oppressive. The woman had no real courage. She would breed fear in almost anyone. I found her dangerously depressing at times. Marcelle made me instantly think of success and the worthwhileness of activity and many other things of that sort.

After walking about the block we entered the Café de Paris and there found Grant Richards and Mme. Goldschmidt. Champagne was on the table, of course, and some broiled chicken or the like. It was sup once more, with the spectacle of the café chantant and dancers before us, for no one of these Parisian or Riviera restaurants is complete without them. It was the atmosphere of the Place Pigalle all over again, of the Rat Mort, the Café Américain and of Maxim's. If anything, this particular restaurant outdid Maxim's in the free and pervasive atmosphere of its immorality. Those who were here seemed to take it for granted that all this was intended as a prenuptial entertainment and that you had either brought or were about to select your companion for the night.

Champagne was everywhere, of course. Cocottes were as thick as flies and as beautiful as goldbugs. The dancing was all risqué and, at most times, wildly suggestive. The invariable and frequent passing of the hat, or rather tambourine, for the benefit of the musicians, the tossing of money to admired dancers or singers, and the persuasion toward the consumption of more champagne were common. Money, money, money was the keynote here, and it had to be handed out freely and liberally. Marcelle on several occasions demanded five-franc pieces in order that she might toss them to singers with whom she sympathized, and other pieces of silver had to be provided her in order that she might contribute freely to the tambourine-equipped collectors. I was amused to see how matter-of-factly she took all this, how it never occurred to her but that where attentions and goodwill were directed, there money would flow freely.

I consulted with Grant Richards as to the wisdom of trifling with so expensive a person, but he assured me with his grave eye that she liked me, that it would be hard, once I had gone so far as to be pleasant to her, to evade my responsibilities in this connection. "She expects you to take her home, I am sure," he counseled wisely. "For the life of me, I do not see how you are going to get out of it." "Besides," his manner seemed to say, "you are on the Riviera now, and a little frolic will do you good. You are too much of a stay-at-home as it is." I think he wanted to drive me into sentimental and romantic experiences in order that I might catch the true significance of this world, but as a matter of fact I needed little driving.

Marcelle was attractive and reassuring. There was some frank conversation between her and Grant Richards in which my prudent fears were disposed. He informed her, I believe, that I was an American author and not rich. What else he told her, God only knows, for he is an amiable person with courageous notions about putting the hard facts of life simply, though tactfully, before us all. He may have said that I was sentimental, in need of romance, deeply smitten or something of that sort. At any rate, Marcelle squeezed my hand and told Grant Richards to say that she liked me very much, that she was drawn to me in the train, that I must be nice to her, and that all would be well. After that there was absolutely nothing to do but keep her company, which in due time I did.

Shall I relate what transpired in the boudoir of Marcelle? She was living at the Hôtel de Paris at the time, the place where all the cocottes and adventuresses, to say nothing of the best society in Europe, stop. It is an imposing institution, standing at right angles with the casino and facing the hard green formal little square. It had been indicated to me the first day we arrived as a center of cocotterie in Europe, a place where they received the adventuress with open arms on her arrival—if she had money—and seized her baggage if she failed to prove successful. Her presence in their great restaurant is the thing which gives it the tang or edge which draws smart society. Marcelle had a room on the fourth floor adjoining a room occupied by Mme. Goldschmidt and commanding a view over the city. I can see Marcelle yet marching briskly in at three o'clock in the morning, as much at home and as pleased as though she were in her own apartment. The attitude of servitors and maids to these women is one of utmost politeness, for they expect large fees.

We could not speak a common tongue, and yet we did quite as well as though we could talk. It was no trouble for Marcelle to show me the nice gowns she had, or those possessed by Mme. Goldschmidt, or to show me the charming view over the city, or to indicate that she thought it beautiful, or by a certain movement of the hand or a gesture of contempt indicate that the maid was avaricious, or any one of a hundred other things which she did quickly and easily. It was charming to see her look at me when everything was arranged, standing with her back to her dresser, her pretty back reflected in the mirror, asking me by signs and facial expression if I did not think she looked very charming indeed. The air of the Frenchwoman with her lover is captivating, smart, chic, lively. Marcelle was really as gay as a butterfly, a black one, and as beautiful. She lifted her skirt the least bit to show me her foot, and turned her shoulder the least bit in order to show me the fine line of her arm. "*Très bon?*" she inquired. "*Oui? Très chic?*"

"Marcelle, you little imp," I said in English. "Come here."

And then, because of the spirit of the occasion and the sense the French have of the fitness of things, the desire to make the spirit of any occasion right, she shook her head and pursed her lips and pretended shyness, and said, "Tst, tst, tst—*non, non, non*, Tayadore."

I merely looked at her with pleasure, amused at her cuteness, and then suddenly she ran swiftly, rustling her silks and jumping into my lap. She could see that I really admired her, and she was very pleased. Her face and neck and shoulders had such delicious outlines, and she was charming from every point of view. She began at once smoothing my hair, kissing me, explaining what arms were in French, what a kiss was, what the lips were, and I had a beginner's lesson in the French for all the features of the face, accompanied by appropriate demonstrations. I never saw a prettier figure than Marcelle's, with her short black hair shaken down over her shoulders; and as, after a time, she removed each additional garment, she first pretended shame, and then posed. There was some dance that had just come into vogue, a certain prancing step taken very quickly and within a very small space, and this she illustrated in her silk stockings and slippers.

The rest need not be related, except that once in the early morning I stirred and looked at her in her sleep, her nose tucked charmingly in her pillow, and when I accidentally disturbed her, she woke to say "*Dodo*," which I learned later meant, "Go to sleep." She had all the superior manners of a mother with a spoiled child, so far as I was concerned, and ruled, as I soon learned she would rule with anyone, by coquetry, by subtlety, by quickness of wit, and by hard unbreakable force if necessary.

Marcelle was a real personage, one fitted by nature to take a very interesting position in life if fortune favored her in the least. This trip to Monte Carlo, as I learned later, was a smart adventure, undertaken with little money and with a daring worthy of a better cause. I had not heard then, and I do not know that I believe it now, that she was the daughter of a cabdriver in Paris. If so, she is a fine example of how wonderful flowers of beauty and ability spring up in unexpected places. Unquestionably circumstances would be against the daughter of a cabdriver in Paris. And yet here she was, holding her own with the best in Monte Carlo and not at all imagining that her life was a failure or that she was not educating and bettering herself very carefully and rapidly.

I saw by my conversation with her, such as it was, that night that she took it as an achievement that she and Mme. Goldschmidt had been able to interest two such men as Grant Richards and myself. Her intellect was as sharp as my own, and I could not see that there was any difference in her appreciation of things in general from mine. Certainly her taste in dress and matters of the toilet was excellent, sufficient to win the hearty approval of Grant Richards, who estimates these matters with the eye of a connoisseur. If there had been any notable flaw, he would have indicated it quickly. And in the end, as it transpired, he came to prefer her to Mme. Goldschmidt, whom he admired very much.

She indicated to me in this one night, bantering and coquetting at the same time, perhaps a half hundred very necessary French words, drilling me in them and insisting that she would teach me French quickly. She also said, as plain as words could say, that I should come to Paris, and that if I liked her very much she would come to New York with me. She learned where I had been before coming to Monte Carlo, and where I was going when I left. When I told her that I was going to Rome, Venice, Florence and Milan, she picked the cities which she preferred—Venice and Rome—and said "Tayadore—Marcelle *à Rome*." It was like playing with a child at once very old and very young. She fascinated me by making me see how wonderful she thought this conversation was we were holding without having a common language and how much she valued mind—pure reasoning ability. More than once when we achieved some exceptionally fine results in exchanging thoughts, she clapped her hands in approval, exclaimed, "Bravo!" and on one or two occasions evinced actual astonishment when I caught her meaning with swiftness and accuracy. "Oh," she exclaimed, "*Merveilleux! Extraordinaire!*" and then putting her finger to my forehead exclaimed, "*Très excellent*," and pointing to her own forehead indicated that she also had mind, a very excellent one, and that we would be delightful companions.

I left her at eight o'clock in the morning, coming out to find it raining as it sometimes did early in the day, and wondering what that censor of our perambulating morals, Sir Hugh, would think when he saw me arriving home at this hour. His room was next to mine, and I could already see his beady, reproachful eyes. "Good Lord!" I reflected, "this is tough!" And then I consoled myself with the thought that since Mme. Goldschmidt had not returned to her room, Grant Richards had possibly not arrived home either, and that he would help me share the withering glances of our moral censor. Alas, he had made sharp shrift to get in before dawn, and was ready to deny solemnly, as usual, that he had been out at all. He maintained, with the air of a judge, when I confronted him, hoping to compel a helpful admission, that he had left Mme. Goldschmidt twenty minutes after I had left him, and that thereafter he had gone straight home.

What was I to do? I could not prove that this was not so, and Sir Hugh had probably been sound asleep when he arrived. Anyhow, I can see him tiptoeing over the thick carpets in the hall, endeavoring to make no noise whatsoever and succeeding admirably. It was then that I was compelled to realize that I must face Sir Hugh alone, so I decided to put the best face on it imaginable, to "'fess up" completely and uphold it as a suitable and important adventure. How well I succeeded remains to be related, but I walked past Sir Hugh's door with an uncertain step, and wished sincerely that he might still be asleep.

CHAPTER XLIV

The charms of Monte Carlo are many. The next morning, to the sound of a horn blowing reveille in the distance, I was up betimes enjoying the wonderful spectacle from my balcony. The sun was just peeping up over the surface of an indigo sea, shooting sharp golden glances in every direction. Up on the mountains, which rise sharp and clear like great unornamented cathedrals back of the jeweled villages of this coast, it was picking out shepherds' huts and fallen mementos of the glory that was Rome. A sailboat or two was already making its way out to sea, and below me on that long point of land which is Cap Martin, stretching like a thin green spear into the sea, was the splendid olive orchard which I noted the day before, its burnished leaves showing a different shade of green from what it had then. I did not know it until the subject came up that olive trees live to be a thousand years old and that they do as well here on this little thin strip of coast, protected by the high mountains at their back, as they do anywhere in Italy. In fact, as I think of it, this lovely projection of land, no wider than to permit of a few small villages and cities crowding between the sea and the mountains, is a true projection of Italy itself, its palms, olive trees, cypresses, umbrella trees and the peasants and architecture. I understand that a bastard French—half-French, half-Italian—is spoken here and that only here are the hill cities truly the same as they are in Italy.

While I was gazing at the morning sun and the blue sea and marveling how quickly the comfortable Riviera Express had whirled us out of the cold winds of Paris into this sun-kissed land, Grant Richards must have been up and shaving, for presently he appeared, smug and clean in his brown dressing gown, to sit out on my lovely balcony with me.

"You know," he said, after he had commented on the wonder of the morning and the delicious, soothing quality of the cool air, "Lane is certainly an old fuss-button. There he lies in there now, ready to pounce on us. Of course he isn't very strong physically, and that makes him irritable. He does so love to be contrary."

"I think he's a good running mate for you," I observed. "If he leans to asceticism in the matter of food, you certainly run to the other extreme. Sybaritic is a mild expression for your character."

"You don't mean it!"

"I certainly do."

"In what way have I shown myself sybaritic?"

I charged him with various crimes, the last one that the wine he had consumed the evening before had made him exceedingly gay. Lane had repeatedly insisted (in jest) that he was intoxicated.

"I leave it to you now, in all fairness," he jested, "could you conscientiously say that one bottle of wine would make anyone, let alone me, drunk?"

"I certainly could, and do. Besides, you drank more than one bottle. You drank nearly all of mine and most of Lane's."

"Impossible!"

"But you did."

"I can't believe it. I was as sober as a judge. A little cheerful, but sober."

"You were as full as a tick. You were as drunk as a lord. You were shamelessly drunk. You disgraced us all."

"Oh no!"

"Oh yes! And a man of your age!"

"What about my age?"

"It is too much."

"Oh, dear, no! I feel very youthful."

"You acted like a child."

"I can't believe it. You are jesting. You must be." So we chattered.

Finally it came time to order our rolls and coffee, and we decided to consume them in the company of Lane. We knocked at his door.

"Enter!"

There he was, propped up in bed. His ascetic face, crowned by his brownish-black hair and set with his burning dark eyes, had an almost classic significance for me. He had such pale, thin hands.

"Ha! ha! ha!" he began in his soft critical way. "Here he comes! The gourmet's guide to Europe! Ha! ha! ha!"

"Now do be cheerful this morning, Lane, do be," cooed Grant Richards. "Remember, it is a lovely morning. You are on the Riviera. We are going to have a charming time."

"You are, you mean, ha! ha! ha!" commented Lane. "It doesn't make so very much difference about the rest of us, so long as you are satisfied. Ha! ha! ha!"

"I am the most sacrificial of men, I assure you," said Grant Richards. "I would do anything to make you happy. We will go up to La Turbie today, if you say, and order a charming lunch. After that we will go to Eze, if you say, and on to Nice for dinner, if you think fit. We will go into the casino there for a little while and then return. Isn't that simple and satisfactory?"

"Yes, with Old Box and his wife lurking somewhere around the corner to join us!"

"Haw! haw!" chortled Grant Richards. "I give you my word, no such thing is contemplated or can happen. It will be just us three, with no one to disturb us. Dreiser and I will walk up to La Turbie. You can join us at one for lunch. You think he ought to see Eze, don't you?"

"Yes, if there isn't some Café de Paris hidden away up there somewhere where you can gourmandize again. If we can just manage to get you past the restaurant."

There was more badinage of this character, with Lane looking for flaws, and finally he agreed that this should be done. Grant Richards and I would walk; Lane would follow by train. To make ourselves truly appropriate, seeing that the day was so perfect, all those special articles of adornment purchased in London for this trip were extracted from our luggage and duly put on—new suits, shoes, hats, ties, shirts in all their splendor, and then we set forth. The road lay in easy, swinging S's, up and up past terraced vineyards and garden patches and old stone cottages and ambling muleteers with their patient little donkeys heavily burdened. Automobiles, I noticed, even at this height, came grumbling up or tearing down—and always the cypress tree with its whispering black-green needles and the graceful umbrella tree made artistic architectural frames for the vistas of the sea.

Here and now I should like to pay my tribute to the cypress tree. I saw it later in all its perfection at Pisa, Rome, Florence, Spello, Assisi and elsewhere in Italy, but here at Monte Carlo, or rather outside of it, I saw it first. I never saw it connected with anything tawdry or vile, and wherever it grows, there is dignity and beauty. It is not to be seen anywhere in immediate contact with this feverish casino world of Monte Carlo.

The wonder of this tree is that it is as proud as beauty itself, as haughty as achievement. By old ruins, in sacred burial grounds, by worn gates and forgotten palaces, it sways and sighs. It is as mournful as death, as somber in its mien as great age and experience—a tree of the elders. Where Rome grew, it grew, and to Greek and Roman temples in their prime and pride it added its sacred company.

Plant a cypress tree near my grave when I am dead. If there is such a thing as consciousness after this seeming of life, I should like to think of its charm and beauty joined with the memory of me. To think of its tall, spear-like body towering like a stately monument near my grave would be all that I could artistically ask. Its voice would be that of my own moods and emotions. As it sighs, so have I. If some of this illusory substance which seems to be that which is I, physically, here on this earth, should mingle with its fretted roots and be builded into the noble shaft of its body, I should be glad. It would be a graceful and artistic way to disappear into the unknown.

About halfway up we came to a little inn called the Corniche, which really hangs on the cornice of this great range, commanding the wide, blue sweep of the Mediterranean below; and here, under the shade of umbrella trees and cypresses and with the mimosa in full bloom and with some blossom which Grant Richards called "cherry-pie" blowing everywhere, we sat us down at a little green table to have a pot of tea. It was an American inn, this Corniche, with an American flag fluttering high on a white pole and an American atmosphere not unlike that of a country farmhouse in Indiana. There were some chickens picking and scratching about the door and at least three canaries in separate bright brass cages hung in the branches of the surrounding trees. They sang with tremendous energy.

Once more, anent a passing muleteer whose spotted cotton shirt and earth-colored trousers and dusty skin bespoke the lean, narrow life of the peasant, we discussed wealth and poverty, lavish expenditure and meager subsistence, the locust-like quality of the women of fashion and of pleasure who eat and eat and gorge and glut themselves of the showy things of life without aim or target. For the peasant on this mountainside, there were perhaps no more than ten cents a day on which he must subsist; for the idle company in the casino below, shining like a white temple from where we sat, thousands upon thousands of dollars to be wasted hourly. The tables there, as we knew, were glutted with gold, and the Prince of Monaco, with his surplus earnings, was building useless marine museums which no one visited. For this muleteer—for the lack of an idea—grime and dust and sweat; and for the grand dukes and German officials and English lords, a surfeit of coin to be gambled away for the sake of amusement. It was a fine thought to be indulged in under sighing cypress trees and in so much lovely morning sunlight.

Our climb to La Turbie was in every respect delightful. We stopped often to comment on the cathedral-like character of the peaks, to speculate as to the age of the stone huts, the far-flung reaches of the Roman Empire which was once here. Not far from the top we met a stout German and his wife, sojourners at Monte Carlo, who wanted to know if they could get down this way. We told them the distance and continued our way, arriving a very little later at La Turbie.

I was constantly forgetting in my peregrinations about the neighborhood how small the principality of Monaco is. I am sure it would fit nicely into ten city blocks. A good portion of Monte Carlo is not in it at all—only the casino, the terrace, the heights of Monaco, and that's all. One-half of a well-known restaurant there, I believe, is in Monaco and the other half is in France. La Turbie, on the heights here, the long road we had come, almost everything, in fact, was in France. We went into the French post office here to mail cards, and then on to the French restaurant commanding the heights, which Grant Richards said he recalled as being capital.

It always surprises me that in America and elsewhere so little is made of exceptional views. This is no doubt due in part to the newness of the country. Near New York there are so many exceptional sites for hotels and restaurants, yet it is difficult to think of more than one or two places where the view is more than commonplace. I am thinking of Briarcliff Manor, The Inn at Upper Montchair, El Paradiso on Grimes Hill, Staten Island and some such places as that. Patronage adjusts all these things, but you would think there would be more patronage in general for restaurants and hotels which command a splendid outlook. Here in Monte Carlo most of the hotels and restaurants, the best ones almost, were without any view at all.

This particular restaurant had, as I have indicated, a magnificent view. The circle about which the automobiles turned in front of its door was supported by a stone wall resting on the sharp slope of the mountain below. All the windows of its principal dining room looked out over the sea and that wonderful view of which I was never weary. The room had an Oriental touch, much too Oriental to be novel, and the white tables and black-coated waiters accorded ill with this. Still, it had that atmosphere of exceptional service which only the French restaurants have.

Grant Richards was for waiting for Lane, who had not arrived. I was for eating, as I was hungry. We waited and waited. Finally we ate when we had about given him up, and as we were consuming the sweet, in he came. His brownish-black eyes burned with their usual El Greco, almost proselytizing, fire. I could always easily think of Lane as a modern Peter the Hermit. If he had been born with any religious, reforming spirit, instead of a penchant for art, he would easily have made a St. Francis of Assisi. As it was, without anything to base it on, except Grant Richards's gourmandizing propensities, he had already established moral censorship over our actions.

"Oh, here you are, eating as usual!" he observed with that touch of lofty sarcasm which at once amused and irritated me. "No excursion without a meal as its object. Sightseeing limited, I should say. Ha! ha! ha!"

"Sit down, El Greco," I commented, "and note the beautiful view. This should delight your esthetic soul."

"It might delight mine, but I am not so sure about yours. Grant Richards would certainly see nothing in it if there were not a restaurant here. Ha! ha! ha!"

"I found a waiter here who used to serve me in the Café Royal in London," observed Grant Richards cheerfully and much pleased.

"Now we can die content," sighed Lane. "We have been recognized by a French waiter on the Riviera. Ha! ha! ha! If another waiter should speak to you, it would make a perfect outing. Never happy," he added, turning to me, "unless he is being recognized by waiters somewhere—his one claim to glory."

We jested through two courses for Lane, who sneered but ate heartily, and then we went out to see the ruined monument to Augustus Caesar so very nearby and to continue our journey to Eze.

I shall never forget the wonder of this monument standing crumbling on this high mountain and commanding the great blue sweep of the Mediterranean below. This way came the Roman legions often, no doubt. I was not sufficiently up on my Roman history to recall the conditions under which this great monument, much larger originally than Grant's tomb in New York, was erected here. Whatever they were, though, they were deemed sufficiently important to warrant the erection of something exceedingly significant—quite as notable as the Arc de Triomphe in Paris—and I should say more so. As a matter of fact I saw nothing in Europe which in any way compared with it for size, unless it was the new monument to Victor Emmanuel in Rome, an enormous affair entirely disproportioned to the deed it celebrates.

There were a number of things in connection with this monument which were exceedingly interesting. It illustrated so well the Roman method of construction: a vast core of rubble and brick coated over with marble. Its original form was only in part suggested by what was left, a square marble base surmounted by a marble drum, and above that what? I did not have the historic knowledge, and I have never looked the matter up. Grant Richards informed me that only recently the French government had issued an order preventing the removal of any additional marble, much of which had already been stolen, carted away or cut up here into other forms. Immense marble drums of pure white stone were still lying about, fallen from their place in truly noble columns; and in the surrounding huts of the peasant residents of La Turbie could be seen parts of these noble pillars set into the fabric of their shabby walls or used as cornerstones to support their pathetic little shelters. I recall seeing several of these immense drums of stone set at queer angles to the proper walls of the huts, the native peasants having built on them as a base, quite as a spider might attach its gossamer net to a substantial bush or stone.

So great aims and great dreams fall low and are clambered over by weedlike masses of aimless, dreamless souls who use the best of their earthly days drowsing by a fire or snoring in a corner. The world wags without significance for such, and Caesars come and Caesars go to no effect. That is what terrifies me about life. Great minds build up great dreams, but the sodden masses batter sullenly against them, as the sea against reared dikes, and presently all is as it was before, or nearly so. The process of mass enlightenment is slow.

This village of La Turbie, although in France, gave me my first real taste of the Italian village. High up on this mountain above Monte Carlo, in touch really with the quintessence of showy expenditure—clothes, jewels, architecture, food—here it stood, quite as it must have been standing for the last three or four hundred years. I was amazed to see those narrow streets which had astonished me in the Marais, in Paris, the clambering, up-and-down character of the walks. No roadways and sidewalks separate and distinct in these old towns; they are both one. The houses of gray stone or brick, covered with gray lichens, vegetatious in crannies, and having a cool, damp feel and smell generally, arch over the streets or passages—street is too pretentious a word—and form cool, shadowy tunnels wherein idlers take the shade and where at night perhaps no more than one solitary lamp burns to light the pedestrian on his way. I could not help thinking of Benvenuto Cellini and the streets of the Italian town to which he was accustomed, Rome in particular, where he always turned the corners in as wide a circle as possible in order to save himself from being surreptitiously stabbed and to give himself time to draw his own knife quickly.

Dirt and age and quaintness and romance! It was in these terms that La Turbie spoke to me. Although anxious to proceed to Eze, not so very far away, which they both assured me was so much more picturesque and characteristic, we yet lingered looking up and down narrow passages where stairs clambered gracefully, where arches curved picturesquely over streets and where plants, nurtured no doubt lovingly in this simple world, bloomed bravely in spotted, crumbling windows. Age! Age! And with men, women and children of the usual poverty-stricken Italian type—not French, but Italians. Women with bunchy blue or purple skirts, white or colored kerchiefs, black hair, wrinkled yellow or blackish-brown faces, glittering dark eyes and claw-like hands. I love Italy if for no other fact than that it has produced a vigorous artistic type.

Not far from the center of this moldy scene, flourishing like a great lichen at the foot of Augustus, his magnificent column, was a public fountain, of what date I do not know—the one I was thinking of when I wrote of the public washhouse in London. It was a simple affair, a stone head in a wall pouring a stream of water into a handsome marble basin. In any well-ordered community no public fountain of any such charming character would ever come into such disrepute or neglect as to be used by the housewives of the community. But here they were, as you may see them in other parts of France and Italy, scrubbing their dirty—shall I say linen?—and piling it in soapy masses on the stone ruin. Such a situation has furnished many a French writer a scene for a dramatic action, and they have chosen well.

These women were like a lot of flies around a jar. They were pattering and chattering, their sleeves rolled up to their shoulders, their necks and bosoms well exposed, their skirts bunched heavily about their hips, their heads wound about quite dramatically with cloths of different colors. The French and Italians are all quick in their gestures, no matter how heavily built, and so were they here, chattering, gesticulating quaintly and artistically at the edge of this mossy green fountain. I could not help contrasting this with the washhouse scene I had witnessed in London—the difference of the spirit of the women, the glory of this sky as against the gray of London's dreary heaven. Daudet tells somewhere of some French poet who married a lovely washgirl he observed beating her clothes by a riverbank, and of the tragedy that followed. I can well believe it. After seeing this scene, I could imagine why he married her. She partook of the blue sky, the gold sunlight, the warm, touching, inviting art of the landscape of some such delicious fountain as this. Why, a young girl in short skirts, healthy and buxom, with bare limbs, a purple skirt and white kerchief, standing by one of these old walls or under one of the lovely arches, would be a fit subject for any artist. It would be a thing well worth painting from a poet's point of view.

With many backward glances, we departed, conveyed by one of the boniest horses it has ever been my lot to ride behind. The cheerful driver was as fat as his horse was lean and as dusty as the road itself, as dull and content as any fly driver should be. We were wedged tightly in the single green cloth seat, Lane on one side, I on the other, Grant Richards in the middle, expatiating as usual on the charm of life—explaining, consoling, being properly lambasted, and in other ways accepting and enduring cheerfully all the cares and difficulties of his exalted and self-constituted office of guide, mentor and friend.

CHAPTER XLV

Deep green valleys, dizzy precipices along which the narrow road skirts nervously, tall tops of hills that rise about you craggily or pastorally—so runs the road to Eze, and we followed it jestingly, Lane so dizzy contemplating the depths that we had to hold him in, Grant Richards so gay and ebullient that he had to be incontinently suppressed. I never knew a man who could become so easily intoxicated with life. He is what I would call a wineless drunkard. In the presence of the splendor of nature or of pageant he mounts as an eagle on strong, sure wings.

"There you have it," said Lane, pointing far down a green slope to where a shepherd was watching his sheep, a cape coat over his arm, a crooked staff in his hand. "There is your pastoral, lineally descended from the ancient Greeks. Grant Richards pretends to love nature, but that would not bring him out here. There is no *canard à la presse* to it, no *sole Walewski*."

"And see the goosegirl," I exclaimed, as a maiden in bare feet, her skirt falling halfway below her knees, crossed the road.

"All provided, my dear boy," assured Grant Richards, beaming on me through his monocle. "Everything as it should be for you. You see how I do: goosegirls, shepherds, public fountains, old monuments to Caesar, anything you like. I will show you Eze now. Nothing finer in Europe."

"Nothing nearer a large food supply," suggested Lane bitterly. "His pursuit of art is limited to the short distance his stomach will go between meals."

"I leave it to you, now, Dreiser," protested Grant Richards. "Didn't I insist on coming to Eze? Wasn't I the one to rise this morning and join you at sunrise, while he was lying in bed? Wasn't I the one that proposed that we walk to La Turbie?"

"In a new spring suit and new shoes! Ha! ha!" commented Lane.

"You were," I replied.

"There!" exclaimed Grant Richards triumphantly. "There you have it. I did it. I was the one. I am really the only true friend of art, in spite of criticism."

We were nearing Eze around the green edge of a mountaintop, and there I saw it, my first hill city. Not unlike La Turbie, it was old and gray, but with that spectacular dignity which anything set on a hill possesses. Grant Richards explained that in the older days—some few hundred years before—the inhabitants of the seashore and plain were compelled to take to the hills to protect themselves against marauding pirates. But the idea is older than that. The hill city dates from the earliest times in Italy and was common to the Latins before the dawn of history. Rome was built on seven hills, but originally on only one, the Palatine. How old the idea is in France I do not know. Eze towered up completely surrounded by a wall, the only road leading to it being the one on which we were traveling. We crossed a narrow gully, dividing one mountain height from another, and then, discharging our fat cabman and his bony horse, mounted to the open gate or arched door, now quite unguarded. Some of the village children were about, selling the common flowers of the field, and a native in tight dusty trousers and soft hat was entering.

I think I ate up the strangeness and glamour of Eze as one very hungry would eat a meal. I examined all the peculiarities of this outer entrance and noted how like a hole in a snail shell it was, giving not directly into the old city, or village, but into a path that skirted the outer wall. Above were holes where defenders could look out and shower arrows, shot, stones, hot water, boiling oil, anything. There was a blind passage at one place, leading nowhere at all, or to the rock of the hill, intended as a devilish pocket no doubt in which to pocket men. If one gained this first gate and the second, which gave in to narrow, winding, upward-climbing streets, the fighting would be hand to hand and always upward against the men above you. The citadel, as we found at last, was now a red and gray brick ruin of which only some arches and angles were left; it crowned the topmost point, the extreme summit, from which the streets descended like the whorls of a snail shell. Gray cobblestone and long narrow bricks set on their sides form the streets or passages. The squat houses of brick and gray stone followed closely the convolutions of the street.

It was a silent, sleepy little city. Few people were about. The small shops were guarded by old women or children, and seemed to do only a casual business. Everybody, I am quite sure, knows everybody else in Eze. The men, as I found later, were sheepherders, muleteers, gardeners and farmers on the slopes below. Anything that is sold in this high-placed city is brought up to it on the backs of slow-climbing, recalcitrant donkeys. One blessed thing: the sewage problem of all these older high-placed Italian-French cities takes care of itself—otherwise, God help the cities. Grant Richards insisted that there was leprosy here, which gave me a real chill. My next fright was the sudden, unexpected braying of a donkey behind the doors of what I thought was a stone hut for men. "Wah-hee!" began suddenly and violently, and I leaped about three feet. Lane's face assumed an artistic look of contempt. Why leap at the bray of a donkey? Why, indeed?

Climbing up and around these various streets, peering in at the meager little windows where tobacco, fruit, cheese and modest staples were sold, we reached finally this topmost height, where for the first time in Italy—I count the Riviera Italian—the guide nuisance began. There was one here, an old woman. She did not speak good French, Grant Richards said, but she insisted on telling us all about the ruins. Imagine the garbled nature of this account. Lane kept repeating, "No, no, my good woman. Go away," and I said in English, "Run, tell it to Grant Richards. He is the bellwether of this organization." Grant Richards clambered to safety up a cracked wall of the ruin, and from his dizzy height he eyed her calmly through his monocle. "No, no," he said cheerfully, seeing himself beyond all harm. "Go away." Nevertheless we eventually contributed, as we always did, to get rid of her. Meanwhile we stared at the Mediterranean, at olive groves, distant shepherds, lovely blue vistas and the pale threads of roads, and speculated on life and time and death and human achievement. Alas! Alas!

As we made our way down towards the one gate again we came upon a picture of that poetic poverty which has been sanctified by the American short-story teller—the poor, lean priest whose flock is too small and too meager in its means to support him. There was a little platform of cobblestones in front of his aged church, which commanded a heavenly vista down a green gap to the sea. He must have seen us coming or have been forewarned by some member of his perhaps loving congregation, for when we were still on a street high above him, I looked over the protecting wall and saw him looking upward in a vague anticipatory way. He was very lean and very old and, I fancy, very inefficient. His long black cassock was thin and worn. On sight of me looking down, he fell to his prayers and paced solemnly to and fro. When we eventually reached him by winding paths, his pathetic eye said much louder than any phrase might have, "Won't you look at my little church, and then perhaps you will give me something."

We went in, of course, for Eze is very old, and we were interested in the little church. There was nothing there, as I recall, save a feeble glitter of gilt about the altar and some poor religious art highly colored. The thin father opened the door for us, and I wondered what he lived on. When we came out, he was near the door, his breviary in his hand, a wan, half-fed smile on his face—half-appeal, half-blessing—and I, for one, contributed a franc. I did not watch the others. But all the way down the mountain I thought of the thin old priest wearing out a pathetic life in a place like Eze, his church tinsel and moss, his flock starvelings. I would have given ten francs to have seen him on his way to the dying, up one of these narrow streets, preceded, as I know the priests are in France, by the cross, the censer and the bell. It would be worth more than that seen in Eze.

We were so anxious to get to Nice in time for dinner, and so opposed to making our way by the long, dusty road which lay down the mountain, that we decided to make a short cut of it and go down the rocky side of the hill by a foot-wide path, which was pointed out to us by the priest or some attendant old woman—I forget which. We were a noble company on this narrow mountaineer's track—Grant Richards in his brilliant checked suit, white hat and monocle and Lane in his sanctified, properly tailored black. My best yellow shoes (ninety francs in Paris) were involved in this feat, and you can wager, as I started down, that I decided to choose my steps carefully. As we proceeded, however, and scene after scene unfolded, I grew more and more enthusiastic. I was so pleased to find myself as agile as ever and that these somewhat sharp and narrow angles overlooked small precipices and not dizzy ones. I became more and more sure of myself and went faster and faster, leaving my two friends far above to jeer at my progress and comment on my goat-like antics. Lane spoke of forced agility and theatric calisthenics. I begged him to flap down to the station, some mile or so below, assuring him that he could do it easily in two flights. It would have cheered me greatly to see him sailing through the air clad in His Majesty's best black suiting and looking like a reforming Peter the Hermit coming swiftly to the rescue of a degraded world. Alas, he would not do it.

"No, no," he said in his best sarcastic mood. "You may have a monopoly of circus tricks. I do not pretend to be a performer. Ordinary human motions will be sufficient for me." And they followed at leisure.

We passed shepherds tending sheep on sharp slopes, a donkey driver making his way upward with three donkeys, all heavily laden, an umbrella tree sheltering such a peasant as may have endured from Grecian days, and olive groves whose shadows were as rich as that bronze which time has favored with its patina. It seemed impossible that halfway between Monte Carlo and Nice—those twin worlds of spendthrift fashion and pampered vice—should endure a scene so idyllic. The vale of Arcady is here; all that art could suggest or fancy desire, a world of simple things—poverty, sheep, a shepherd's hut, the crook, the meal of fruit—all those things concerning which poets have sung and artists have painted. I believe, now that I think of it, that Lane indicated that such scenes as this were favored by his great artistic admiration—Daubigny.

We found a railway station somewhere, with passengers such as one sees at Scarborough and Tarrytown, and flashing trains serving this popular coast, and then we came to Nice for dinner. Once more absolutely brilliant coruscating arguments between Grant Richards and Lane. We would take tea at Rumpelmayer's—we would *not* take tea at Rumpelmayer's. We would dine at the Régence—we would *not* dine at the Régence. We would pay I forget how many louis and enter the baccarat chambers of the casino—we would *not* do anything of the sort. It was desired by Grant Richards that I should see the wonders of the seawalk with the waves spraying the protecting wall. It was desired by Lane that I should look in all the jewelry shop windows with him and hear him comment on the prices and the cut of the jewels displayed. How ever these matters were finally adjusted, God only knows. We were progressing and arguing at the same time, creating really a public scene as we went.

We *did* have tea at Rumpelmayer's, however—a very bright but commonplace affair in the Avenue de la Gare (I fancy every town in France has an Avenue de la Gare)—and then we loitered in front of a jewelry shop window where Lane pointed out really astounding jewels offered to the public for fabulous sums. One great diamond he knew to have been in the possession of the Sultan of Turkey, and you may well trust his word and his understanding. A certain necklace here displayed had once been in his possession and was now offered at exactly ten times what he had originally sold it for. A certain cut-steel brooch, very large and very handsome, was designed by himself and was first given as a private gift to a friend. Result—endless imitation by the best shops. He dallied over rubies and emeralds, suggesting splendiferous uses for them.

And then finally we came to the casino, the Casino Municipal, with all the wonders which it contains—its baccarat chambers, its great dining rooms, its public lounging room with such a world of green wicker chairs and tables as I have never seen. I thought the great piers at Atlantic City, with their dancing halls, skating pavilions and the like, were large, but they are not as large, and by no means as fashionable, as this Casino Municipal at Nice. It was filled to overflowing with a brilliant throng—cocottes assorted from all parts of Europe, I should judge: staid Frenchmen, Germans, Italians, Americans, Englishmen and their wives; adventuresses of python-like force and Circe charms; card-loving officials of the most pronounced type; and a showy, pleasure-loving world generally in evening clothes.

Lane ranted as to what we should have for dinner. The mere suggestion that it should be *canard à la presse* and champagne threw him into a dyspeptic chill. "I will not pay for it. I will not spend my money parading in front of a lot of half-baked waiters in the hope that they will speak to me. The little art that I have managed to collect has not been gathered in that way. You can spend your money showing off if you choose, but I will eat a simple meal somewhere else."

"Oh no," protested Grant Richards. "We are here for a pleasant evening. I think it important that Dreiser should see this. It need not be *canard à la presse*. We can have sole and a light Burgundy."

"You can have a light Burgundy if you choose. I will drink water. And please see that it is put on my bill. I do not propose to be overcharged."

So sole it was, and a light Burgundy, and a bottle of water for Lane, and we once more discussed the wonders of this world and what it meant to Europe generally.

Not having as yet been in the *cercle privé* at Monte Carlo—those five or six inner chambers about which Lane fumed—I was perhaps unduly impressed by the splendor of the rooms devoted to gambling in this amazingly large Casino Municipal. I think it is something to see seven or eight hundred or a thousand people perhaps, all in evening clothes, all having paid a heavy admission fee for the mere privilege of being in the chambers, gathered about handsome, green-covered mahogany tables under glittering and ornate electroliers, playing a variety of carefully devised gambling games with a fervor that at times makes martyrs in other causes. I am really not used to the high world of society and fashion. I know very little about it, save as the occasional spectator may. But to see a dozen different nationalities of men and women, their hands manicured to perfection, their toilets all that a distinguished occasion might require, their faces showing in every instance a keen understanding of the world and how it works, was—to say the least—impressive.

The outer fringe of life and circumstance is at best so beggarly. If you walk away from these centers of social perfection, where health and beauty and sophistication and money abound, you come upon the side streets and the outlying regions of the dingy and the narrow and the poor and the unsophisticated. To such, life wears a shabby fringe at the edge. My old priest with his hungry face and his beggarly parish was not over a mile or two away, and in London and Paris I saw hundreds and hundreds who seemed to be begging of life that they should not die. Here in Nice the vast run of the citizens were as poverty-stricken as any, and this collection of nobility and gentry, of millionaires, adventurers, intellectual prostitutes and savage beauties was recruited from all over the world. I hold that is something to see.

There various tables were fairly swarming with a fascinating throng, all interesting as individuals, all very much alike in their attitude and their love of fame, but still individual and interesting. I venture to say that any one of the people I saw in this room, if you saw him in a crowd on the street, would take your attention. A native force and self-sufficiency went with each one. I wondered constantly where they all came from. It takes money to come to the Riviera; it takes money to buy your way into any gambling room. It takes money to gamble, and what is more, it takes a certain amount of self-assurance and individual distinction to come here at all. By your mere presence you are putting yourself in contact and contrast with a notable standard of social achievement. Your intellectuality, your ability to take care of yourself, your breeding and your subtlety are at once challenged—not consciously, but unconsciously. Do you really belong here? the eyes of the attendants ask as you pass. And the glitter and color and life and beauty of the room is a constant challenge.

It did not surprise me in the least that all these men and women in their health and attractiveness carried themselves with cynical, almost sneering hauteur. They might well do so—as the world judges these material things—for they are certainly far removed from the rank and file of the streets; and to see them extracting from their purses and their pockets handfuls of gold, unfolding layers of crisp notes that represented a thousand francs each, and with an almost indifferent air laying them on their favorite numbers or combinations was to me surprising, fascinating and strange.

I know that to the denizens of this world who are fascinated by chance and find their amusement in such playing, this atmosphere is a commonplace. It was not so to me. I watched the women—particularly the beautiful women—who strolled about the chambers with their escorts solely to show off their fine clothes, to win those excited glances which said louder than any words, "How splendid she is!" You could see a certain type of youth here who seemed to be experienced in this gay world and its allied phases in other parts of Europe, for you would hear such phrases as "Oh yes, I saw her at Aix-les-Bains" or "She was at Karlsbad last summer." "Is that the same fellow she was with last year? I thought she was living with ———" (this of a second individual). "My heaven! How well she keeps up!" or "This must be her first season here—I have never seen her before." Two or three of these youngbloods would follow a woman all around the rooms, watching her motions and admiring her beauty, quite as a horseman might examine the fine points of a horse. And all the while you could see that she was keenly aware of the critical fire of those eyes, vain because of it, fairly strutting with a peacock-like strut, as much as to say, "Am I not beautiful indeed? You will have to be very exceptional if I condescend to notice you at all."

At the tables was another type of woman whom I had casually noticed at Monte Carlo but to whom I had paid no particular attention: a stout, not too good-looking, rather practical and perhaps disillusioned type of woman—although, now that I think of it, I have the feeling that neither illusion nor disillusion have ever played much part in their lives. They looked to me like women who, from their youth up, had taken life with a grain of salt and who had never been carried away by anything much, neither love nor fashion nor

"My heaven! How well she keeps up!"

children nor ambition. Perhaps their keenest interest had always been money—the having and holding of it. And here they sat—not good-looking, not apparently magnetic, interested in chance, and very likely winning and losing by turns, their principal purpose being, I fancy, to avoid the dullness and monotony of an existence which they are not anxious to endure. I heard one or two derogatory comments on women of this type while I was abroad, but I cannot say that they did more than appeal to my sympathies. I felt a little sorry for them. Here they sat day after day, putting their gold pieces on numbers—now winning, now losing; now losing, now winning—and waiting for the call of a number or watching with interested eyes the spin of a wheel, the fall of a card. To me it was intensely dull, seeing that no one ever really makes a fortune here—and if they do, they come back to lose it again. I did not see how anyone should want to do that.

But to look at it from another point of view, supposing you were a woman of forty-five or fifty. Men and their silly pretensions and their sex interests were a bore to you, children a thing of the past or nothing at all. You might have had an agonizing husband, or a collection of dreary relatives, or the ennui of a conventional neighborhood with prejudices that were wearisome to your sense of liberty and freedom. If by any chance you have money, here on the Riviera is your resource. You can live in a wonderful climate of sun and blue water; you can see nature clad in her daintiest raiment the year round; you can see fashion and cosmopolitan types and exchange the gossip of all the world; you can go to really excellent restaurants—the best that Europe provides; and for leisure, from ten o'clock in the morning until four or five o'clock the next morning, you can gamble if you choose, gamble silently, indifferently, without let or hindrance as long as your means endure. If you are of a mathematical or calculating turn of mind you can amuse yourself infinitely by attempting to solve the strange puzzle of chance—how numbers fall and why. It leads off at last, I know, into the abstrusities of chemistry and physics. The esoteric realms of the mystical are not more subtle than the strange abnormalities of psychology that are here indulged in. Certain people are supposed to have a chemical and physical attraction for numbers or cards. Dreams are of great importance. It is bad to sit by a losing person, good to sit by a winning one. Every conceivable eccentricity of thought in relation to personality is here indulged in; and when all is said and done, in spite of the wonders of their cobwebby calculations, it comes to about the same old thing—they win and lose, win and lose, win and lose.

Now and then some interesting personality—stranger, youth, celebrity or other—wins heavily or loses heavily, in which case, if he plunges fiercely on, his table will be surrounded by a curious throng, their heads craning over each other's shoulders, while he piles his gold on his combinations. Such a man or woman for the time being becomes an intensely dramatic figure. He is aware of the grandeur of the thing he is doing, and he moves with noble gestures, an air of hauteur, the manner of a grand seigneur. I saw one such later—in the *cercle privé* at Monte Carlo—a red-bearded man of fifty, tall, intense, graceful. It was rumored that he was a prince out of Russia—almost anyone can be a prince out of Russia at Monte Carlo! He had stacks of gold, and he distributed it with a lavish hand. He piled it in little golden towers over a score of numbers; and when his numbers fell wrong, his towers fell with them, and the croupier raked great masses of metal into his basket. There was not the slightest indication on his pale impassive face that the loss or the gain was of the slightest interest to him. He handed crisp bills to the clerk in charge of the bank and received more gold to play his numbers. When he wearied, after a dozen failures—a breathing throng watching him with moist lips and damp, eager eyes—he rose and strolled forth to another chamber, rolling a cigarette as he went. He had lost thousands and thousands, and I would have agonized much more over a five-franc piece, I am sure.

CHAPTER XLVI

Our early homecoming the night before was rather soothing to Sir Hugh's moral nature, and consequently he was in a rather cheerful frame of mind. He was not feeling well, however, and was inclined to lie in bed, while we did what we chose, saw any sights we pleased. There was much talk of an automobile trip up through a mountain pass somewhere—you entered a tunnel on one side, leaving green trees, palms and flowers on one side and emerging into snow on the other—but it never happened. Lane was never in the mood for it. Grant Richards was anxious that I should see Ventimiglia, a little town in Italy only a few miles away, and so after lunch at the hotel we took the train there. It was, as usual, a fine day, with a fresh wind blowing, and as we boarded the train, Grant Richards told me to watch how the character of the population changed once we had crossed the border. "It is surprising," he said, "what a difference a few miles will make. On one side is France—vigorous, up-to-date, good houses, good roads, good engines and cars; on the other Italy, with poor roads, poor houses, poor cars. The climate is better too. They're a lot of robbers in Italy."

I did not ask what provoked this last comment but looked out at the changing scene. The Riviera extends in all its beauty some twenty miles into Italy—to San Remo, and how much farther I do not know. At Genoa, perhaps one hundred and fifty miles farther on in Italy, I understand it is not nearly so pleasant. All the way to Ventimiglia it was lovely except, as Grant Richards predicted, the character of the population changed completely. Instantly as we crossed the border, it was as he said. Life seemed to have gone out of the people to a certain extent—dropped to a lower key. The freight cars that we saw standing on side tracks were not so new or well-built, and the gatemen's houses were not as spruce as those in France. I could scarcely believe that a mile or two of distance, an imaginary line of government, would make so much difference. Yet so it was.

The station at which we arrived is, by agreement between France and Italy, the seat of customs for this district—your baggage going into or coming out of Italy is opened at this point. I saw for the first time the Italian soldier on his native heath, their round flat hats with their burnished rooster feathers and their capes of blue, to say nothing of the uniformed Italian stationmaster in his red cap and blue cape. This was the first time since leaving Paris that I had seen any soldiery to speak of, and they attracted my attention. I noticed at once that the *sorties* of France became *usciti* here, and *le grand bagage* became *bagaglio*. We had a time getting out, let me tell you, for foreigners without baggage, and particularly Englishmen, were an anomaly. We should, according to all the known rights and privileges of the Italian customs officers, have had seven trunks and paid liberally for their inspection. As it was, we merely wanted to get out into the streets to see the town, and this offered no real basis for extortion.

"They're all bandits here in Italy," observed Grant Richards irritably as he peered through some window, endeavoring to explain his mission in French. There was great to-do, which I am sure could have been nicely adjusted for a lira, but finally we were let out into the piazza in front of the station and allowed to proceed unmolested to the heights of Ventimiglia.

I think I may as well make my opening remarks on Italy here, although I am not yet through with France. The character of the landscape here was rugged and picturesque, and during all the time that I was in Italy I never saw it otherwise. We crossed a bridge over a small, almost waterless, river-bed, up the reaches of which I saw lovely snow-capped mountains with the sun shining on them. Although we were not more than ten or twelve miles from Mentone, the city was as different as it could be—gray, solemn, lifeless. Here was the native Italian just as we know him in America in our Italian colonies—his dirt, his leathery countenance, his earrings, his love of color and his wonderful eyes. I think actually the Italians have the most expressive eyes in the world. They are almost always, in the young and old, lusterful, wistful, emotional. Italy should always be wonderful, for it is wonderful in its very texture—its mountains, its valleys, its lakes, its seas.

We climbed up the hill on which was located the old Ventimiglia before the railway came and at the time when it was necessary to occupy a mountain fastness in order to be safe. A little to my disappointment, it was Eze all over again—the narrow streets, the beggarly church, the overhanging arches where passages cut under houses, the interminable ascending and descending steps. I did not know at this time how very common the hill city is in Italy, for I had not traveled south to Rome nor north to Milan, but from what I saw from the trains alone, there must be hundreds of them, crowned almost invariably by a stronghold or a church. Ventimiglia was no different from any other that I saw during my stay—as beautiful, as old, as gray, as dirty.

As I turned quaint corners and emerged out of dark passages where a man could be stabbed so easily, I fairly thrilled to contemplate a coat-of-arms or a shrine set in a wall. Here it was that I first saw those little shrines of the Virgin set in niches cut in the houses—a little blue sky with gold stars painted back of her and a lamp which the faithful may fill with oil. If I had seen nothing else, this alone would have won me to Italy, for faith is so wonderful, even the colorful reminiscence of it. In these doorways, as at Eze, sat old men and women, brown, pathetic, idle. I think all the young work in Italy; I saw no idleness. No corner loafers, so common to our poorer sections. There came to my mind, while I was walking here, the picture of an old Italian I once saw on the East Side of New York chasing his recalcitrant son with an uplifted shovel, and fiercely throwing it after him. When I remonstrated with him for his seeming brutality, he exclaimed, "No worka. No taka de shovel. No damn good—lika de Irish." And I learned then that the Italians love to work. I saw no idling boys in Eze and Ventimiglia or at any time afterwards.

We mounted later to an old fort or stronghold five hundred and sixty-five feet above the sea, of which Grant Richards knew nothing except that it was old and in ruins. Later I learned that it was a Genoese stronghold, used no doubt in those interminable quarrels between the Guelphs and Ghibellines which make up the history of Genoa. We idled all over it for an hour, exploring dark underearth passages, marveling at the thickness of the walls, the immensity of the chambers, and the size of the great stairs that led from the dividing valley that lay between the fortress and Ventimiglia proper. I put my head through a small hole in one wall and peered down into a great empty, dusty room that might have been either a prison chamber or a storehouse, for it was located down among the foundations of the original structure. We speculated concerning the tremendous feuds which had torn Italy from time to time and wondered whether any prisoners had really suffered greatly here. Then we took our last look at the Mediterranean from this height and retraced our steps. I recall an old woman in black picking sticks, like an old crone out of a fable, gathering fagots for her evening fire—and we went off, as usual, into a long discussion of age and death and the unrecordable multiplicity of life and beauty. For once Grant Richards became a little melancholy, noticeably so. He shook his head.

"What's the matter?" I asked.

"Well, I think of it going on in all its splendor, and you and I will not be here to see it."

We went back into Ventimiglia and were assailed by an old woman who gibbered historic information which we could not understand. We were determined to escape without feeing her, but she was so active and enthusiastic in her witch-like way that we were at last compelled to surrender. I never saw an old woman so active. She reminded me, for sharpness, of those peaked-hat witches that used to be astride broomsticks, gamboling in the air. She fairly ran ahead of us in order to be able to turn and gesticulate and explain.

"There you have it," said Grant Richards, thinking of our experience of the night before. "Pounds for harlots, and not a lira for this wrinkled creature." We both contributed at once, while we entered upon a grand philosophic discussion of what it is that life pays for most gladly, and why we gave so freely to irresponsible femininity and to the gaming table and to the restaurant and nothing to age of this type. It finally ended, if I recall rightly, in our deciding that we paid only for the selfish satisfaction of our whims, getting what we valued above all else—diversion. The old lady did not really divert us, so we were stingy and indifferent.

That night we went to Monte Carlo again, and to my surprise, after finding Lane at a gaming table, I won three louis by the simple process of laying a five-franc piece on a number which Lane described as *quatre premier,* and this revived my interest in gambling tremendously. I won two more louis by some other process, and then I thought I was on the road to fortune; but I finally lost the most of it and departed for the Sporting Club for more gambling in great gloom. There must be something in this matter of luck and personality in gambling, for I never win at all at anything. I saw people here who seemed to win steadily—that is, they were obviously having a run of luck whether they subsequently lost it or not. I have never had such a thing as a run of luck, although I have frequently had such a thing as a run of loss—which I think is highly unfair. I fancy that many people are magnetic when it comes to fortune and that they draw wealth to them. There is no question that ability in any line is a gift and that nothing is created by taking thought. Taking thought is the result of ability that has been created beforehand and given without let or hindrance.

I was in for another adventure on this night, although I did not anticipate it at this time. It turned out that Grant Richards was interested in Mme. Goldschmidt and apparently anxious to follow her up. He was constantly manipulating the movements of Lane and myself so as not to lose track of us and yet to give himself the greatest leeway in maneuvering his flirtations to a satisfactory outcome. He evidently did not know what Mme. Goldschmidt was going to do with her time that day, and was anxious to find out whether he could have it for himself. He finally sent a note to the Hôtel de Paris, which he explained might bring Mme. Goldschmidt and Marcelle to supper at the café. It did not turn out that way, however, for about twelve o'clock, gambling having lost its charm and the hour having arrived when they would be due if they were to meet us at all, we entered the Café de Paris to find them, alas! dining with others. It was a great blow.

Grant Richards had a method of entering a dining room which was positively appalling to the uninitiated and the common herd. With his white shirtfront, his fur overcoat and his monocle, he presented a grand air, to say the least, and invariably he threw back his head and tilted his nose upward in a most superior manner, which left me spellbound. The least I could do was to look as dignified as possible, which resulted in a progress that sent waiters and servitors scurrying before us. We saw our favorites of the night before, delightfully arrayed and evidently being carefully looked after by three male friends who were with them. Grant Richards remarked that he thought one of the men was the famous Parisian tenor of whose friendship these two maidens boasted, and it turned out to be so, for months later Marcelle admitted that the said tenor had commented on Grant Richards as a snob. Marcelle learned to mock his walk and manner, which amused him greatly. They paid no attention to us, but it turned out that Grant Richards's ladylove was more faithful to him than I expected, for when he retired to a lounge in the rear and signaled, she followed, and a little later, with true French sagacity, so did the gentleman who was with her. There came near being a scene, but not before an understanding had been reached which resulted an hour or so later in Grant Richards's disappearing for the night.

At his suggestion he and I now adjourned to the Carlton—another famous café nearby—where evidently suitable developments were to be awaited. It was here, after three-quarters of an hour, that Grant Richards disappeared, saying that if he were coming back, he would send me a note in twenty minutes. I waited and, for amusement, started talking to a young girl who looked very much like an American to me, although it turned out that she was French. She spoke English very well, and told me after a few moments that she had lived in England and was, to a certain extent, connected with the entertainment offered by this restaurant—that is, she danced here. I was interested in her from the first because she was a startling type of the pure blonde, very young, very shapely and very beautiful. Later this same night after an argument she showed me her French birth certificate, which fixed her age as twenty-one.

I stop to discuss this particular girl, for in sophistication and world-weariness she was the most depressing creature I had met in years. I could not understand how anyone so youthful, so healthy and so beautiful could be so utterly weary of life. When I first observed her, she was dancing in the central space surrounded by the tables, which is always left for singers, dancers and entertainers generally. She had on a large, soft-brimmed, lemon-colored straw hat trimmed with pale blue ribbons and pink roses. Her shoes were of white canvas and her dress of pale, pink-flowered lawn with a sash of some harmonizing ribbon and dainty bows ornamenting the flounces. I should have said that she was innocence itself, for she had a face like a doll, but to my astonishment she talked to me with the weariness and the sophistication of one who has seen the whole world.

"Perhaps you would like to pay for my wine," she said, after I had first begun to talk to her, "and then we can sit and talk."

"I do not believe that I will do much wine-buying or talking tonight," I replied, "because, if I am not mistaken, I have only five louis all told." Grant

Richards had borrowed some money from me on leaving me, and an examination of my coin purse showed exactly five louis.

"Oh, that is all right," she said good-naturedly. "Buy a half bottle, and then it won't cost so much. It isn't the wine I want."

"You dance very gracefully," I said. "I saw you out on the floor just now. You must be very young."

"I am not very old," she said, with a flickering smile. "Old enough, though. I do not care anything about dancing. I just dance." She looked at me with round blue eyes that were really amusingly innocent-looking and smiled a very weary smile.

"My, what a tired young person!" I said. "This life is palling on you."

"No, I like it," she said, "or I wouldn't be here."

"Well then, it must be that you haven't anyone in whom you are really interested. The Riviera is pretty enough."

"Oh, I get very tired of it at times."

"You're not English," I said. "You talk with such a curious accent."

"I'm French. But I lived in England. I lived in London for over a year."

We fell to discussing the Riviera and the different people in the room, what nationality they were, or what she thought they were. Grant Richards, according to a grand story he had brought me the night before last concerning this same restaurant, had discovered a little innocent English girl here, only sixteen years of age, so unsophisticated that the management had to assist in protecting her against a savage world. She was dancing on this floor, and just before he left, he had brought her over to me and introduced her as a really lovely flower of girlhood flourishing uncertainly in a cesspool of evil. I asked my new acquaintance what she knew of her and whether she was really so innocent, seeing that they were both fairly intimately connected with the same institution.

"What do you mean?" she asked uncertainly. "Do you want to know whether she has ever been with a man?" She seemed puzzled as to what the standard was by which I was trying to estimate her young colleague—conventional virtue being, apparently, of all things, the most remote to her. I had to smile.

"Yes," I replied. "My friend says that she is an entirely innocent young girl who is being looked after by the management."

She smiled her young-old smile, very sad and wan, and, putting up a plump little finger, signaled gracefully to the Spanish *danseur* who, in exceedingly tight black trousers and a red shirt, was dancing violently near us.

"Louis," she said. "You know that little Miss ———. Do you know, has she ever been with a man? Has she a lover?"

I looked on in soul-stirring amusement at this matter-of-fact conversation. The young man looked away as if trying to recall the whole situation in connection with her.

"Oh, I theenk so," he said. "She drinks with the men. I know one or two give her money. I theenk so—yes."

"My friend wanted to know," commented my companion, and the dancer whirled away, rattling a tambourine as he went.

"I don't know myself," she added, "but I think she must be like the rest of us, or she wouldn't be here. They like to lie, you know—these young ones—to get money out of the men." I thought I would tell this to Grant Richards when I saw him again and let him investigate further.

But as for me, this very casual acquaintance interested me as much as anything else on the Riviera. I was wondering whether early vice produced this early ennui and whether it could always be depended on so to do. My friend informed me that her English name was Lily Delsy, and her real French name Antoinette Thérèse Michel.

"My, what a pretty name!" I said. "Were you really named that way, or did you take it?"

"Oh no," she replied with a charming accent. "That is my real name. If you will come over to my room, I will show you my birth certificate. I would not lie about a thing like that—at my age. I do not have to lie."

"No, I shouldn't think you would," I said. "You are certainly young enough and pretty enough to have any nice name and any nice age. Tell me about some of the people here, and about how these restaurants are run. How is it you come to be dancing here?"

Her reply was simple, straightforward and good-natured. She came to Monte Carlo because she was tired of her lover in England—an English bank clerk—and because this was no time to be in Paris, but in Monte Carlo. "Sometimes," she said, with a rather full-sounding voice, and as though she had something in her mouth, "I make much money, and sometimes I don't. It does not make so much difference, so long as I have nice clothes. Now I have it, and now I don't." She shrugged her shoulders very prettily.

"That is a rather uncertain kind of life, isn't it?" I suggested.

"I am young yet," was her answer.

"Do you expect to get married," I asked, "ever?"

"How should I know that?" she shrugged. "If someone will have me. I do not care. If I like someone, maybe."

"Then you don't like anyone now?" I asked.

"No. I get tired of men. They are nice, but I get tired of them."

"How is it you dance here?" I said. "You dance so charmingly. Where did you learn?"

"Oh, I dance. I learned in Paris. The English do not know how to dance.

They are awkward. I came here often. The manager, he see me dance with someone. He ask me if I will not dance with Louis now and then as a favor. They let me have champagne without charge, and then when I have someone rich, they charge it to him. That is the way they do."

"Oh, my poor five louis!" I said to her. "That will not go far here."

"A-h-h," she said reproachfully, "I do not want everybody to buy me champagne. You need not buy me champagne. We can sit here and talk. They will not mind. If you come to my room, I will show you how old I am. We can talk there."

"But after I pay for this champagne," I said, "I shall have only four louis, and then what?"

"Oh, that is all right. You can come with me. I have no one. You can talk to me."

"Very well," I said. "But let's stay here and watch this. It is so interesting."

We had some sandwiches, which took all the loose silver I had. Then we sat, and shall I say enjoyed this scene? It was Saturday night, between two and four. What was left over of the throng that had been in the casino and the Sporting Club and the other restaurants was now here. Even while we talked, Grant Richards having gone, the scene was taking on a sort of wildness. I think there is a certain type of woman that comes from almost the ends of the earth to indulge in license, and I think a fair percentage of them are Americans. I saw two or three who seemed to suggest Sioux Falls and Denver and San Francisco and that their fathers had lots of money and gave it to them to spend. They were, for the most part, showily and, in some cases, suggestively dressed. I think it is not hard to detect the morbidly sexual nature in women, the emotionally overwrought, and there were a few here.

All of these restaurants have a man or two, usually Spanish in get-up, very proficient in the matter of suggestive dancing, with whom anyone can dance—the female guests, if they choose. I saw an American woman—about twenty-eight, very beautiful, but bearing the marks of extreme dissipation, with those moist eyes and red lips which suggest emotional animalism—come out on the floor after three o'clock in the morning and dance wildly, quite in the most sensual Bacchanalian mood, with our Spaniard Louis. She was well along in her cups, a little unsteady on her feet, and once or twice she slipped and fell in a sensuous heap, laughing wildly at the same time. A little later in her peregrinations, she found that her flowing silk skirts impeded her progress, and after one or two futile efforts to seize them, she finally secured them at the bottom and pulled them up high, displaying her shapely legs to above the garters and evoking an enthusiastic burst of applause. My own Thérèse Michel commented that the American lady was feeling good this evening, and I noticed that her slippers and stockings were of black silk and her garters brown. She fell again after a time, quite orgiastically, and was assisted to a table, but the management did not seem to think anything of it. There were others who were dancing less drunkenly but no less sensuously. Thérèse Michel, or Lily Delsy, as she liked to be called, got up after a time, at the request of a girlfriend, and did a final dance which appealed to me as being the extreme of gracefulness and very dainty. She came back after a time, and then, because the crowd was getting a little seedy in its appearance, I decided to leave.

"Will you come over with me to my room?" asked my acquaintance.

"Oh yes," I said. "Remember the four louis."

"Oh, you need not stay," she said. And we strolled out together, her acquaintances nodding to her on one side and the other as we went. She had a blue silk evening cape trimmed with ermine which reached above her ankles and which she put on over her pink-flowered tulle, and we walked up past the formal gardens, charmingly distinguishable in the dark, to her chambers in a nearby apartment house. I was struck again, as I was always at Monte Carlo, by the startling resemblance of everything to the newer quarters in Paris.

We mounted a wide stair which gave into a large hall, and off this, airy and comfortable, were her two rooms and bath. I surveyed them with interest, for a twenty-year-old girl occupying such chambers on the Riviera was a curiosity to me. They were papered in cream-yellow with some faint design in it, set with handsome straw-colored furniture—a tall pier mirror, a dressing table, a chest of drawers, a handsome brass bed, and perhaps six or seven chairs of different designs. I was interested in a handsome lamp with a body of blue china and a shade of pink silk. "Where do you get all the nice furniture?" I asked her, thinking that perhaps she was the mistress of some man, after the fashion of Angèle in Paris.

"Oh, they are furnished this way by the management," she replied indifferently. "I rent them just as they are."

I wondered, for I knew that they must command a good price. My four louis seemed an outrage. One of the things that interested me about her was that she asked absolutely nothing about myself. I do not think that she asked me my name or where I came from or what I was doing in Monte Carlo or how long I was going to stay, or anything. I fancy she knew that I was an American. She did not ask me whether I liked her rooms or her appearance in her blue silk cloak but threw it wearily aside and sat down in a wicker chair under the lamp. I seized on the only rocker and entertained myself by rocking to and fro and looking at the furniture.

"Well," she said after a time, "you think my name is Antoinette Thérèse. I will show you." She went to all the pains of unlocking a trunk, hunting for a small box, and finally produced a certificate issued by the authorities in some small town in Normandy telling all about her.

I was amused at her naive desire that I should see this, for I was very little interested in where she came from and whether she was really telling me the truth about her name. She sat down in her chair, and I said to her, "You know, you are so lovely I can hardly believe my eyes. You are more like a child dressed for a May Day parade than a lady on the Riviera."

She smiled again, her bored little smile, and tilted back her straw hat, which she had not yet removed.

"I'll tell you what you do," I said. "You look so very nice and you dance so very nicely. Dance for me. I should like to see you."

"Oh," she said, "but I have no music. I cannot dance without music."

"Oh yes, you can," I replied. "Imagine you hear music. Come now."

"You think I'm pretty," she said, "don't you?"

"You have no idea," I replied, "how really pretty I think you are—only you are too tired of life."

She got up and took off her hat, throwing it on a settee nearby, and holding out her arms in the position of one who is leaning on a partner began skipping and turning, doing quaint little steps and kicking her heels in an airy-fairy way. This pleased me immensely, and I complimented her, but as I did so, I began to get an inkling of the reason of her interest in me. For all her ennui she was still vain, proud of her looks, and I flattered her in a rather direct way. She paused before her mirror and struck various poses, finally saying, "I do not do very well. My corset is too tight."

"Take off your corset," I said, "and dance without your clothes. You will look nicer."

She pursed her lips moodily and then went behind a pale green screen and undressed, hanging up her clothes very carefully as she did so. She finally appeared in her slippers and stockings and a long strip of pink gauze which she wrapped around her waist. And then she danced after the Turkish fashion but finally ended by posing before her pier mirror, admiring the different positions that she took. I really do not think that she was very conscious of me at all. Exposure of this character is such a commonplace to women of this type and the vagaries of emotion and sex so dreary that my interest in her must have been unimportant. She came over finally to where I was sitting, and said, "Well, what do you think of me?"

"Oh, I think you are a charming little girl," I said. "You have a beautiful figure and a face like a doll." I took her smooth round arms and examined them, and turned her about to look at her hips and her feet. I touched her side at one place, unfortunately, where there was a slight mole, and she became angry in an instant.

"You are like all men," she said, "You think I am diseased, don't you?"

I really had not thought anything about it, for I had no intention of indulging myself sexually with her up to this time, but now that she mentioned it, it occurred to me that it was just possible, though not probable.

"Oh, I don't know," I replied indifferently, "How should I know? I don't suppose you are, although I don't see how you could be sure yourself whether you are or not. A disease need not necessarily show its effects on you for weeks after you have contracted it, and I might contract it from you without your knowing anything about it. That is common."

True to the sensitive French in her, she was hurt by what I said, for I fancy she had been led by my genial admiration to expect complete approval. Her pretty little doll-like face darkened, and her lips parted, a little savagely, I thought.

"Oh, you need not go with me," she said. "I do not need your money. I am all right, just the same." And she walked away from me over to the dresser and began to put some things to rights.

"Now don't be silly," I said. "I did not mean to hurt your feelings. What I say is exactly so. You might be diseased and not know it. Why should that make you so angry?"

"H-oh!" she fumed. "As though I would not know! Don't I go to a doctor every week? Haven't I preventives that keep me all right? Why, I have my card to the *cercle privé*. Do you think I could go in there if I were diseased?"

I did not know until just now how ramified the control of the management of the casino over their women was, but it appeared from this that they exercised a form of physical inspection, which was quite a surprise to me.

"Now don't let us quarrel, Antoinette," I said. "What is the use of your being so angry about that? It is all right. Come here to me. I like you very much."

"No," she said irritably and defiantly. "I won't. You need not go with me. I do not want your money."

"You are going to get my money whether you want it or not," I replied, "—such as it is. And if I meet you again before I go, perhaps we will make this up. But don't be angry. It is late now, and I ought to be going back anyhow. Perhaps I shall see you tomorrow."

I had never removed my coat, and now I stood before her in my evening clothes, while she leaned back over the dresser, quite defiantly and quite nude. She looked like a little sylph out of Arcady.

"Tell me one thing. You must make a good deal of money at times. Is this a bad year?"

"Oh no," she said, slightly mollified. And she told me of one Don James, a pretender to the throne of Spain, who saw her one day in the casino dressed in a very simple little dress and asked her to come to the Hôtel de Paris, where, for three hours of her companionship, he gave her two thousand francs. She told me, with considerable defiance, I think, and with a desire to show me how unimportant I was, of a rich French lace manufacturer of Lyons or Rouen or some place, who found her in Paris and took her on an automobile tour through Holland, Belgium, France and Spain. I think she had traveled with him some six months. Because I had been so foolish as to question her physical integrity, she was determined to punish me now, and although she did not refuse my very unimportant four louis, she let me go—a little to my satisfaction and a little to my sorrow. I was sorry to think that I had hurt her feelings and to think that she should think that I was so indifferent a gallant.

As I stepped out of her door, I heard a perfect uproar of bells which I thought must be some civic alarm over a conflagration. I hurried out into the street, where the first blue haze of dawn was beginning to show itself, and on in the direction of the main thoroughfare, which I knew led toward the Riva-Bella. I had decided to walk home along the sea in order to get the fresh air and to enjoy the morning, but as I came to the main thoroughfare, I was made to realize that my alarm of fire was nothing more than a group of church bells in a nearby church sounding the call to early mass.

An idea struck me. It would be fine to go to mass. So I went up the long flight of yellow steps into the still, dark church, where a group of candles were blazing on the distant altar, and took my seat in a rear pew. I tried to meditate on the distinction between vice and religion, but I could not make it out. I felt no better in my church than I did in Antoinette's room, or the orgiastic precincts of the Carlton. They were nothing but spectacles to me—spectacles grounded on illusion and emotional belief—the orgy as well as the mass. I came out by the sea and walked along, admiring its wonderful color in the increasing light. It was so fair and blue and still. The white houses with their red roofs and surrounding palms were so silent. Over near the Riva-Bella I encountered a company of sisters conducting some inexperienced little schoolgirls of native birth to mass. I think they were members of a private school somewhere in the vicinity.

When I arrived at the hotel, Sir Hugh was waiting watchfully, but I explained quite frankly and fully, and seeing that I had been merely enjoying a spectacle without indulging in the last crime against God and man, he forgave me. When I told him I had been to church, he was quite soothed, and Grant Richards, denying that he had any adventure of any kind and asserting that he had arrived at this hotel within an hour after he had left us, sat down, eager to hear all that I had to relate. I do not wish him the fate of either Ananias or Sapphira, but I fear that he is surely doomed.

CHAPTER XLVII

The more I think of Sir Hugh Lane, the more I wonder at the charm and humor of the ascetic temperament. He had few, if any, vices—no single visible one, so far as I could make out. He gambled here at Monte Carlo, but in a very deliberate way, indeed. He had planned to lose two hundred pounds as a part of the pleasures of this trip at the gaming table, and his daily losses, so far as I could judge, cost him not the slightest qualm. He had lost ten pounds the night before, but when I arrived on the scene the next morning, it was not his losses that were worrying him; he was truly concerned about my character and the damage I was doing my better self. Actually, he was lying in bed, as was his custom, until the noon hour, recuperating his rather enfeebled nerves and speculating on how Grant Richards and I were conducting ourselves, and what a wretched thing it was anyhow to misbehave in regard to women. He had, as I have said, absolutely no use for the adventuress or the cocotte. He looked upon all the women in that showy world which centered around the gaming tables and the cafés as dangerous to social order and the state of things generally.

He resented Grant Richards's "gourmandizing," as he called it, and his penchant for headwaiters, *maîtres d'hôtel* and loose-moraled, smart women generally. He literally resented Grant Richards's leading me into any paths where my inexperience and enthusiasm for life and my love of novelty would aid in seducing me. While he was, as I found, quite ready to reprimand me for what he considered my shameless conduct—and in saying this, I am describing his attitude exactly—he was angry with Grant Richards for being the leader in this escapade, the bellwether marching towards impropriety, the hardened and incorrigible advocate of the devil.

When I came in, after having divested myself of my evening clothes in the dull morning light and having had a bath and a change of linen, he looked at me with a pitying, critical eye. My disturbance on this score amused me—for, after all, I was paying my own way and seeing the Riviera as I wished. I looked upon my adventure with Marcelle as a rather charming idyll in a much too flamboyant atmosphere; for, insofar as I could make out, Marcelle was as far removed from the type of cocotte that had first greeted me on my arrival in Paris as night is from day. She was a clever woman or girl with artistic tastes and emotions that were not yet hardened or coated over by vulgarity or greed. She was intellectually attractive, very, and had I met her in any walk of life, I should have been pleased to know her. She was really as bright intellectually as she was beautiful physically. Grant Richards was quick to tell me on this morning after I had returned that she and her friend Mme. Goldschmidt were the intimate friends of a celebrated Parisian tenor then on the Riviera and that it was Marcelle who was the favored one in that case.

To Sir Hugh Lane, however, an evil woman was an evil woman, and no mental or social connections or accomplishments served to palliate the evil of their condition or their deeds. I think at first his intention was to ignore me entirely, to punish me by having nothing more to do with me whatsoever; but seeing that Grant Richards was to blame and that I was a personage of some note and that there was no reforming either Grant Richards or myself by ignoring us, he fixed me with a reproachful, questioning eye, and after a dry "Ha! ha!" which was the invariable opening and ending of most of his thrusts—a "ha! ha!" so soft that it was almost like a low rasping cough—he said, "I see you are back. No doubt you enjoyed your evening, or I should say your morning. It must be pleasant riding home in evening clothes."

"Oh, I didn't mind," I said defiantly. "I had a very pleasant time indeed."

"No doubt. Ha! ha! ha! I suppose Grant Richards was with you. He thinks I didn't hear him tiptoeing in at six o'clock—ha! ha! ha!—but I did. He is always so careful to cover his tracks that he thinks if he is making little noise he is not making any. He is like the ostrich with his head in the sand. I heard him, though."

"No doubt of that," I said. "You serve as censor on this moral pilgrimage, and a fine one you are. I didn't see Grant Richards after three o'clock, so I don't know when he came in."

"You must be getting rather lively impressions for your book!"

"Very," I said. "Do be cheerful—I had a most interesting evening. It was an intellectual treat for me."

"Quite so. I know the type of interest," Lane said.

Just then Grant Richards came in, and to my intense relief, the shafts of sarcasm and ridicule were turned in his direction. "Oh yes, here he comes—the conservative guide for American authors, the pseudo-gourmet, showing us how to come to Monte Carlo without really coming to it." A perfect storm broke as to his responsibility for my actions and emotions.

"I leave it to you now, Dreiser," he explained defensively at one point. "Did I, or did I not, introduce you to any woman?"

"You did not," I said. "She introduced herself to me, and a charming person she was, too."

"Ha! ha! ha! No doubt. A Western type of beauty, I suppose?"

"She was very nice," I declared. "Highly intelligent. Very attractive. As contrasted with the average dull woman with virtue and nothing more, there is very much to be said for her."

The storm broke. I could not possibly stop to indicate all its ramifications. We got the Lane idea and the Grant Richards idea and my own idea of life properly juxtaposed for once. It appeared from the general details of this that Lane's idea of a suitable existence for man and beast consisted of abstinence—the form of abstinence which relates to the sexual relation outside the bonds of holy wedlock. I never saw a more staunch supporter of society as it is ideally conceived than he. As a matter of fact he applied the term "good woman" only to those women who are morally conservative; who apply their life and energy to the care of a home, the rearing of children; and who seek by precept and example to inculcate the social virtues as they are currently accepted. Such women as we had been having to do with were anathema to him, and I marveled, as I looked at him lying in bed, his black eyes burning, how it ever came about that he came to associate himself or had anything to do with George Moore. The latter's views in regard to sex and morality were certainly at pole extremes from his own. Yet he was friendly with Moore, as I have indicated, and, in his way, admired him greatly. I have often wondered what part wealth, fame and position played in Sir Hugh's estimate of an individual. I think, on the whole, that he was rather lax where talent was concerned, and if a man had genius, he forgave him almost everything, though he deplored and discountenanced the vices and weaknesses which seemed to accompany their greatness.

On the other hand, Grant Richards had the idea—which he never openly advocated, however—that it was necessary to create and maintain a social seeming, insofar as morality was concerned, under cover of which the individual might be free himself, anyhow. He would never admit to personal variations from the current standard of morality, though he countenanced them and apologized for them in others—men and women of talent. I never knew a man who had more reverence for literary and artistic ability—the capable, constructive mind. His sympathy for all life and effort was keen and even tender, but he had a special warm corner in his heart for the artist in any walk, the great artist.

Grant Richards considered all effort at happiness, where it demanded the best to satisfy it and however it manages to satisfy it, an outward and physical sign of an inward and spiritual artisticness which was admirable and laudable, even though it resorted to prostitution to achieve it (as in the case of Marcelle, for instance). All striving of the human heart which related to bettering one's state—socially, mentally, artistically, any way you will—when not coupled with crass brutality of method and savage selfishness of purpose, are laudable or at least forgivable, and I agree with him in that. All methods of self-betterment, when not coupled with utter antagonism to the Golden Rule, are very much worthwhile and are of their very nature artistic. They constitute the body and substance of art. Now if, perchance, as almost invariably happens, the conventional theories of life run counter to these desires, or at least to their ready fulfillment, if the lust for life is great and the ability via conventional methods to fulfill them small, you have these sad infractions which Lane so much deplores. From the social point of view they seem truly sinful, and they do ignore the care of the home, the well-being of children, the conventions and delights of the monogamous state, but unquestionably they create, erect, other things. The exceptional restaurant; the progress of styles; the existence of the exceptional dressmaker, of the ultra equipage, of the gambling resort such as Monte Carlo, of the watering place such as Ostend, of the perfect hotel or palace such as Versailles—all ultimately depend on these infractions. For Versailles was not built for home-loving, conventional women, nor Monte Carlo created nor maintained by either men or women opposed to social infractions—on the contrary. And indeed, every artistic spectacle of life is largely remote from the current understanding of how things should be done. It is only the dull who do not know this.

For myself, my views agree with those of Grant Richards as above expressed, except that instead of attempting an obviously futile concealment in regard to everyone, I would make no mystery of my attitude, particularly insofar as the cognoscenti were concerned. They know how life works as well as the next one. And to my intimate friends I would gladly explain my attitude, as I always have. You can, then, if you are interested, see the peculiar flavor of this early morning conversation, with us three holding the opinions above described—Lane frowning sourly on any infraction of the moral code; Grant Richards pretending a liberal attitude which did not affect his own personal conduct beyond the mere beholding of the eyes; I frankly admitting that I had been with Marcelle, defending the adventure on intellectual and romantic grounds, defending the artistic temperament that fights its way to the top at any cost and over any obstacles.

I declared, and I am satisfied that I am right, that Marcelle in her philanderings with men was merely struggling to reach a better state than she had previously known and that, other things being equal, she was entitled to do so. After all, life is for the individual as much as it is for the state and the nation, if not more so. By temperament I incline to the Greek idea which gives all to the individual and nothing to the state, rather than to the Roman idea which gives all to the state and nothing to the individual. I know that various religionists have told us how we must live, and life presents an open-faced system based on these theories; but, after all, if it were not for the individual, radical and unconquerable, life would be plain hell, a dreary beehive, the wings and bodies of whose denizens would be dusty and torn with labor in their old age—and to what purpose? Nothing under the sun is so dull as the conventional home, and if life were made for that, let me die right now. Monte Carlo is immoral, but it is a spectacle, a glittering variation from the norm of a humdrum existence, and, as such, it is worth almost any price to attain. Certainly the glittering art of the Parisian dressmaker is not based on any mass idea of how man should be garbed, and if it were, God help Parisian dressmaking art. It is not based on any virtuous conception of how life should be lived, or any theories of not robbing the poor, or any notion that virtue must be maintained at any cost. It is more concerned in its triumphant effects with seduction than with moral conservatism, and the veriest tyro knows it.

If this is true, if the art of the *modiste* is art for art's sake without regard to mass theories and conventions, then the radical individual, the seductive contravener of conventions, the unmoral lover of beauty whom the Parisian tailor adores, is the answer. Art at its best is made for them, and not for the religionist and the moral theorist except insofar as he is able to appreciate the value of the art offered. This is equally true of the great hotel and the great restaurant, the palace—any rich thing. It is not made for the mass but for the individual, and for the individual whose theories are not governed by those of the mass. Now I come back to Marcelle and the night before.

My contention was that Marcelle was an individual, seeking some way out to a better life for herself. Being the daughter of a cabdriver, if she was, and being raised in poverty, she would not necessarily have those opportunities and suggestions which would lead to a perfect appreciation of standards of value and social conditions. Desiring to get up—to see more of life, to entertain herself—and having an instinct for the best which the world had to offer, she was busy seeking it. I maintained that it was useless and unfair to say to Marcelle that she must work at some simple, conventional employment until she earned her way, dollar by dollar, to the heights which she could already see. Convention might applaud her, but it would not give her more than three or four dollars a week, and long before she earned enough to purchase the beauty and pleasure which she saw, her capacity for enjoyment would be gone.

"Now, Lane would maintain," I said argumentatively, looking at Grant Richards, "that the thing for Marcelle to do would be to smother her instincts and make her life a sacrifice to the religious and social ideals of the time. My answer is that it is a question whether the religious and social ideals of the time are either unchangeable or important, and that whether they are or not, side by side with the masses there has always stood the individual who has done as he pleased; and unless we accept a soul-destroying socialism, he will remain. From everlasting to everlasting is the individual with ideas and the individual without them—the leader and the led, the strong and the weak—and the leaders do as they please. The only other thing he could say," I added, "would be that I, as a respectable member of society, should not countenance such gross unconventionality; and my answer is that I have never posed as a respectable member of society. I hate to make Lane feel bad," I said, looking him in the eye, "but I think Marcelle an exceptional woman and the experiment very much worthwhile to me. Now I suppose I will be shunned as bad company, but I must say I am having a very good time."

"I confess," said Grant Richards very cautiously, "that I see nothing much in Dreiser's conduct except a love of novelty and romance. It seems all very innocent to me."

"Yes, you!" said Lane severely. "You're the cause of it all. You're always leading the way to some wretched place and then pretending it is for the benefit of someone else. I know if it hadn't been for you that Dreiser would not have met his Marcelle, and you can't tell me anything else. Always pretending."

Grant Richards looked most persuasively and apologetically through his monocle.

"Now, really, I don't see that there's any occasion for any feeling. Dreiser is writing a book, and he must see something of the life here. He could have come home if he had wanted to."

I waived all this discussion. "Let's not fight," I said. "What are we going to do today?"

It transpired that Lane was so dissatisfied that he really cared to have little to do with us. His plan was to go to Monte Carlo and gamble respectably. Grant Richards, by some hocus-pocus, so he said, had let himself into a luncheon engagement with Bax and his wife at Nice, which Lane resented even more violently than he did my immoral conduct. He would not go to Nice, and what was more, he did not propose to be left alone this way to his own devices. He had come along with Grant Richards to the Riviera, he said, anticipating that he would be accompanied and entertained, and if he was to be treated this way, he was going to desert us and move over to a hotel in the heart of the city where he could see something. "I will not live eight miles away in an eighth-rate hotel and pay cab fares only to be left alone." (It was about two miles.) "First Agay and then the Riva-Bella and now a lot of lunches with the Baxes."

Grant Richards apologized profoundly. He insisted that this was the last, that he would never see them again. He begged me to accompany him in order to avoid the agonizing ennui, and out of sheer good nature I did. I did not know until later that there was something else in the wind and that to carry out his prearranged plans, which he nevertheless stoutly denied afterwards, it was necessary that I should be with him. It was no more nor less than the arrival of the sisters Belliard from Paris—the two cocottes whom we had entertained on the night of my first arrival, and with whom Grant Richards had unquestionably been in communication.

We had an amusing lunch with the Baxes at the Régence, during which he lied to them most shamefully and made a jest of their every serious question. After lunch we went to the casino, and I discovered after a while that he was merely restlessly roving about, looking for someone. At about four-thirty, when we were leaving to go to Rumpelmayer's for tea, we encountered them—radiant and healthy. After having discovered Marcelle and getting along so well in that direction, I was not the least interested. My two beauties, who looked so glittering on the night of my arrival, looked anything but as important. I suspected at once that Grant Richards had come over especially to meet them in this casual fashion and that the lunch with the Baxes was a ruse to escape from Lane. I reproached him with it, but he denied it vehemently. It was all the merest chance.

We had tea at Rumpelmayer's, and to my astonishment—largely, I think, because of the discovery of Mme. Goldschmidt, a much more artistic type—he was anxious to get away from them. He explained that he found them a little showy, after Marcelle and Mme. Goldschmidt, a little loud. I think, now that he saw them again, that he was a little fearsome of being seen in their company here in Nice, and he suggested that we take them over to Monte Carlo and accidentally lose them in the Casino. "My God," he said in his most dramatic manner. "I don't believe I can stand this, I shall have to get out of it some way." Since he had arranged to have them come here, it was necessary to take them to dinner, and by some jugglery of excuses, he managed to arrange it so that they went over to Monte Carlo on one train and we on another, or on different parts of the same train. I recall even now with slight distaste my realization that they were of much coarser fiber than I had imagined in Paris—not nearly as refined and imaginative as Marcelle and her friend. We returned by train about seven and met them by arrangement in the Café de Paris, where, to Grant Richards's horror, he found them surrounded by waiters like lumps of sugar surrounded by flies. It is a custom of all these pandering restaurants to use the cocottes as the basis for exorbitant bills, and they are offered everything freely and attentively in order that they may partake and be properly charged.

"Come now," said Grant Richards to the waiters impatiently. "Some of you clear out of here. Get me the manager. This is outrageous!" and to me he said, "My God, this is awful! We'll be disgraced for life!"

The headwaiter arrived, and the waiters were shooed away. We were apologized to for this ambitious attempt. And then we dined. All these meals where only French was spoken were dreary to me except when I was with Marcelle, for she took pains to make her quips and her humors understood and to really entertain me. We taught each other English and French the while. But with the sisters Belliard it was different. To tell you the truth, they were a little dull and very animal, in spite of their charming looks. They exchanged quips principally concerning sex, and Grant Richards informed me that my particular affinity was anxious to establish a temporary relation with me in order to have a good time here. He felt it incumbent on himself, seeing that he alone spoke French, to gain some preliminary understanding as to the financial expenditure involved in order that I might not be robbed out of hand. I never could understand exactly how he managed this sort of thing, and when I made some casual inquiry as to how it was done, he said, "You may well believe that it isn't the easiest thing in the world. I can't just ask them. This thing takes a little management."

I learned after a time, by one expression of disapproval after another, that something in connection with their attitude did not please him. "My God, you had better not have anything to do with these people," he informed me eventually. "They will rob you. They are really not what I took them to be." I never could understand from his attitude whether he was consulting my convenience or his own, or whether I was being artistically left out of something. The young lady who had been so pleasant to me in Paris was particularly eager here, and when he seemed in doubt as to how the evening was to be conveniently concluded, I volunteered to take my particular mademoiselle off his hands. He was sure that it was inadvisable, however, and the more he trifled with them, the more disgusted he became. We started for the Casino eventually with the plan in mind of deserting them, and after securing their entry tickets we did so, but not before the younger had borrowed a hundred or two francs from Grant Richards as a slight token of his interest. He was enraged. "Why, they are regular leeches!" he said to me. "They would bleed us thoroughly."

I went off into a long discourse on the type of creature that eats largely to be eating. I finally likened the mass of these women to a swarm of locusts descending on the Riviera to eat up everything in sight, and he agreed with me heartily. He was so afraid that I would get in with these women a little earlier in the negotiations that once when he heard me suggesting that the young lady was deserting me instead of me deserting her, he came back and said, "Now cut that out. You are spoiling it all. Here I am working to get loose, and you are fixing it so we will have to stay." I assured him not. But at ten we were actually free, and for once, like respectable citizens, we took a fly and returned to the Riva-Bella at, I think, not much later than eleven o'clock—the earliest return yet made. I breathed a sigh of relief, for the pace at which we had been traveling was not exactly conducive to peace of mind, and I remember writing my notes and arranging my belongings with a feeling of great conservatism and respectability. Sir Hugh, on this particular occasion, did not return till about two A.M.—a case in point.

CHAPTER XLVIII

This same Sunday was dull and unimportant, for it rained, and we journeyed to a local *casino municipal* which lies, as I understand it, in that part of Monte Carlo which is in France, not in the principality of Monaco. There was endless bickering between Lane and Grant Richards over the folly of eating interminably at expensive restaurants. As I understood it, this was to be an inexpensive day. It was horribly boring.

I myself was out of sorts, for a letter had come from Marcelle asking for a sum of money which Grant Richards, who translated the communication for me, said I had promised her. This was not true. When I gave her the original eight louis, which I thought was sufficient the morning I left her, she had expressed not opposition but a kind of coaxing reproach which I thought under the circumstances was not well based, seeing that she understood in the first place that I was not rich. When I tried to make her understand that I had very little money with me, and that even if I wanted to I could not now, she seemed satisfied. On this Sunday morning, then, I was very much distressed when this letter arrived asking, or demanding, something, I never learned exactly what, for Grant Richards translated it with his easy, good-natured desire to make everything pleasant. I did not care to contemplate the loss of Marcelle's friendship because of a mere matter of money, or not enough money, and I did not like to think of her as so grasping that she would seek a pretext for exacting more money from me. Grant Richards waived it all lightly aside. There was some misunderstanding. He would see her and make or extract an explanation. He was sure she liked me personally, and there was some unconscious error here on both sides. He wanted to know if by any sign I had promised her more money, but I really had not. The whole matter made me a little angry and depressed.

This day passed in a funk, and at six I deserted my friends and went home to bed. The next morning it was lovely and sunshiny again, and I felt much better. Sitting out on my balcony high over the surrounding land, commanding, as it did, all of Monte Carlo, the bay of Mentone and Cap Martin, I made many solemn resolutions. This gay life here was meretricious and artificial, I decided. Gambling was a vice, in spite of Sir Hugh's lofty predilection for it; it drew to and around it the allied viciousness of the world, gourmandizing, harlotry, wastefulness, vainglory. I resolved here in the cool morning that I would reform. Marcelle had taken it upon herself to introduce an element of discord into this situation. It could now rest. I would see something of the surrounding country and then leave for Italy, where I would forget all this. I started out with Grant Richards about ten to see the Oceanographical Museum and to lunch at the Princess, but the day did not work out exactly as we planned. We visited the Oceanographical Museum, but I found it amazingly dull—the sort of thing a prince making his money out of gambling would endow. It may have vast scientific ramifications, but I doubt it. A meager collection of insects and dried specimens quickly gave me a headache. The only case that really interested me was the one containing a half-dozen octopi of large size. I stood transfixed before their bulbous centers and dull, muddy, bronze-green arms studded with suckers. I can imagine nothing so horrible as to be seized upon by one of these things in the naked, and I fairly shivered as I stood in front of the case. Grant Richards contemplated solemnly the possibility of his being tackled by one of them—monocle and all. He foresaw a swift end to his career as a publisher.

We came out into the sunlight and viewed with relief, by contrast with the dull museum, the very new and commonplace cathedral—oh, exceedingly poorly executed—and the castle or palace or residence of His Highness, the Prince of Monaco. I cannot imagine why Europe tolerates this man with his fine gambling privilege, unless the different governments look with opposition on the thought of any other government having so fine a source of wealth. France should have it by rights, and it would be suitable that the French temperament should conduct such an institution. His palace was as dull as his church and his museum, and the Monacan army drawn up in front of his residence for their morning exercise looked like a company of third-rate French policemen.

I secured as fine an impression of the beauty of Monaco and this whole coast from this height as I received at any time anywhere during my stay, for as I have said somewhere, it is like the jewel of a ring projecting out of the sea. You climb up to the Oceanographical Museum and the palace by a series of stairways and walks that from time to time bring you out to the sheer edge of the cliff overlooking the blue waters below. There is expensive gardening done here everywhere, for you find vines and flowers and benches underneath the shade of palms and umbrella trees where you can sit and look out over the blue sea. Such lovely panoramas confront you in every direction, and below, perhaps as far down as three and four hundred feet, you can see and hear the waves breaking and the foam eddying about the rocks. The visitor to Monte Carlo, I fancy, is not greatly disturbed about scenery, however. Such walks as these are empty and still, while the Casino is packed to the doors. The gaming tables are the great center, and to these we invariably returned.

My days in Monte Carlo after this were only four exactly. In spite of my solemn resolutions of the morning, the spirit of this gem-like world got into my bones by three o'clock; and at four, when we were having tea at the Riviera Palace Hotel high above the Casino, I was satisfied that I should like to stay here for months. Grant Richards, as usual, was full of plans for enjoyment, and he insisted that I had not half exhausted the charms of the place. We should go to some old monastery at Laghet where miracles of healing were performed and to Cannes and Beaulieu in order to see the social life there. We did make a return trip to Nice some two days later, in company with Marcelle and Mme. Goldschmidt, but only after my relations with the former young lady had been readjusted by the tactful maneuvers of Grant Richards. I never could prove how intimate his relations with Mme. Goldschmidt were, and so I could never explain his apparent determination to keep the four of us together, but he was obviously set on it like a grand captain who is constantly maneuvering to bring about a brilliant atmosphere of feminine companionship, and these two were as interesting as any that offered. One thing he understood about me clearly—that personally I craved feminine companionship for the mere mental pleasure it gave me, if nothing else. I have to smile now when I think how industriously he worked to bring about a harmonious understanding between Marcelle and myself, although if I had spoken French I am satisfied that I would not have stood so much in need of his aid.

He bestirred himself this evening to secure the companionship of Mme. Goldschmidt and Marcelle for dinner, but they had a previous engagement. They decided to come at midnight, or at least Marcelle did, to see me; and at half-past twelve when we were finally in the Café de Paris, having escaped the clutches of Sir Hugh Lane, she arrived. As on the previous occasion, she was very winning in her manner and immediately took my hand and beamed on me with the good nature of one who likes you. As usual she was very attractive and surging with a forthright energy that was positively fascinating. I could not help contrasting her with Lily Delsy, so far removed was the latter in color and mood. The one was as fair as the morning and as weary of life as age itself. Marcelle had the spirit of an unfed child—hungry, but tremendously confident. She talked with Grant Richards about what had been going on in her life for the last two or three days, every now and then giving me a glance or a nod or telling Grant Richards something to say to me. It was such a bizarre and naive situation.

"She wants you to stay with her," Grant Richards announced quite calmly after one of his conversations, and I promptly announced that I was charmed. We sat and watched the dancers for an hour and supped, while Grant Richards and Marcelle conversed about life in general. There was one scene in which one of the women singers threw the Spanish dancer about the floor and pulled his hair, making dramatic representations of rage the while she sang, and Marcelle exclaimed, touching my arm, "See—Marcelle, Theodore." And Grant Richards explained that she added, "After a while." We took our wraps about three o'clock in the morning and strolled out into the night, Grant Richards accompanying us to our temporary abode.

I often smile when I think of the matter-of-factness of it all, although in reality it was not in the least matter-of-fact. On this occasion I had plenty of money in my pocket, but I did not know of any hotel, and so Grant Richards came along to adjust matters. He seemed to have a working knowledge of local conditions in this respect. At the Hotel of the Flowers he explained something to the porter, and then lifting his hat grandly departed. Marcelle immediately asked advice of one kind and another, and after throwing open the windows and viewing the showy city in the night closed them again. The moon was very bright in the sky. There was a summer feel to the breeze. In the vicinity somewhere we heard music. I can see her quick moving head as, on hearing it, she turned and said with sparrow-like pertinence—"*Ah—la musique—très belle, très charmante*." Then she began looking after the conveniences of the room quite like a little housewife, and you would have thought we had lived together for years. On mature thought I sometimes think that Marcelle was not cut out to be a cocotte at all, but to be the brilliant wife of a fairly clever man. She would have made the fortune of a middle-class official in France if she had been willing to try, for she had all the graces of those who are truly brilliant.

She made a leisurely toilet, combing her hair with the brushes and combs which the maid provided and polishing her nails and teeth. Then she came to me with the enthusiasm of one who really craves passionate companionship. I wonder sometimes how much acting there is in this and how much desire, particularly in such a case as this. I really think at bottom it is all art, figured out as any other industry is planned. The art of the stage is all I can think of by way of comparison, but after the worst had been said you would have to admit in the case of Marcelle that it was good art. She was far more charming in her dark way, although I may have given a very unsatisfactory picture of her.

The last I saw of Monte Carlo—and Marcelle at Monte Carlo—and of all this Riviera life was three days later on the platform of the railway station when I was waiting for my train for Rome. A part of one of these days Grant Richards, Lane and I spent viewing a performance in Mentone. Another day Grant Richards took Mme. Goldschmidt, Marcelle and myself to Laghet and Nice, beginning with a luncheon at the Riviera Palace and winding up at the Hôtel des Fleurs. The last day we were in the Casino, gambling cheerfully for a little while, and then on the terrace viewing the pigeon shooting, which Grant Richards persistently refused to contemplate. This (to me) brutal sport was evidently fascinating to many, for the popping of guns was constant. They have an automatic method of throwing live pigeons in the air out of traps which are set level with the grass. When the trapdoors are opened, the live pigeons in the baskets beneath are sprung into the air, and as they begin to fly are fired upon, the idea being to see how many of the half-dozen thus tossed upward out of each trap may be killed by one man using a six-chambered rifle. I could barely look at it myself—the live, flying bird dropped so quickly to a foundering, bleeding object on the grass. I saw one trap opened, and then I took a violent dislike to the gunnery and to the system which permitted it, although Sir Hugh Lane seemed to be not in the least disturbed thereby. It is so curious how radically our views differ in this world as to what constitutes evil and good. To Lane this was a legitimate sport. The birds were ultimately destined for pies anyhow; why not kill them here in this manner? To me, the crippling of the perfect winged thing was a crime. I would never be the one to hold a gun in such a sport.

There was a re-encounter over a bottle of wine in the Café de Paris, and then it was that I said to Marcelle, in such way as I could, "Come with me as far as Ventimiglia," never thinking for a moment that she would. "*Oui,*" she replied, "*oui, oui,*" and seemed very cheerful over the prospect.

"Now," I said to Grant Richards, "I'm in for it. Get an extra round-trip ticket for her, will you please?"

"You know, I think she must really like you," he said, "or she would not do that."

The idea had some charm for me, although I really did not see what was to come of it all. We separated to meet at the train, and as I was hunting around the lobby of the hotel to find Sir Hugh, I had my last encounter with Miss Longfellow, who had just this day arrived fresh from Rome in her automobile and was full of raw, showy comments on the life she had seen there.

"Oh, say," she said in her affected voice, "it's magnificent! Say! You want to go see the churches. I never saw anything like it. St. Peter's is a dream—and the sculptures in the Vatican—don't miss 'em." Her lover was close behind her and came up now, rosy and vigorous, to shake hands with me.

He stated in his conservative English way that they had been having a very pleasant trip indeed and were going north into France. They were going to gamble here for a few days, and I could see her in my mind's eye wasting his money at the tables. She presented an exquisite picture of the luxury of her class—very radiant, very bold, and very showy. By a few minutes after four we were all at the depot, Grant Richards looking after his own luggage and mine, for he was leaving for Paris and London one half-hour before I left for Rome. Sir Hugh was there to bid us a fond farewell, for in spite of endless criticism and innate opposition to such a shameless career as mine, to say nothing of Grant Richards's, he had a sort of fondness for me. I kept assuring him that in spite of his wrath, I had a deep regard for him and that he must smile affectionately on me as I left. "Smile sardonically, you mean," he sighed, but he smiled nevertheless.

Marcelle arrived some fifteen minutes before my train was due, but owing to explanations conducted through Grant Richards at the table, she was not to speak to me until we were on the train. It took some maneuvering to avoid the suspicions of Lane, for his shrewd, rook-like eyes would have instantly detected any signaling, and he was with me all the time.

Grant Richards left for the north at four-thirty, swearing a great fondness for me, assuring me that we would meet in Paris in April and ride at Fontainebleau, that we would take a walking tour in England. He had suggested that it would be nice to have Marcelle and Mme. Goldschmidt meet us in Paris and go with us to Fontainebleau. I was a little depressed, for the day before, owing to some maladjustment in his own affairs, he had borrowed for the time being all but one hundred and twenty pounds of my money, assuring me that he would return it. It meant something that I did not like to have introduced into my affairs at this stage, the need of watching my p's and q's financially. However, I took it in as good part as I could and decided that I would come out all right—perhaps it was just as well that I did not have much in hand.

After he was gone, Lane and I walked to and fro, and then it was that Marcelle appeared. I had the feeling that Mme. Goldschmidt had gone to Paris with Grant Richards, but I could not prove it. I had no French wherewith to interrogate Marcelle. If Mme. Goldschmidt had gone, it was managed very carefully. He may have picked her up at Nice or Cannes. Anyhow, the Riviera was over for me, and I was not sorry. I had to smile as I walked with Lane, thinking how wrathful he would have been if he had known that every so often we were passing Marcelle, who was by turns standing still or walking about. The platforms, as usual, were alive with passengers and baggage. My train was a half-hour late, and it was getting dark.

Some other train which was not bound for Rome entered, and Marcelle signaled to know whether she was to get into that. I shook my head and hunted up the Cook's tourist agent, always to be found on these foreign platforms, and explained that he was to go to the young lady in the blue suit and white walking-shoes and tell her that the train was a half-hour late and ask her if she cared to wait. With quite an American *sang froid* he took in the situation at once and wanted to know how far she was going. I told him Ventimiglia, and he advised that she get off at Garaban in order to catch the first train back. He departed and presently returned, cutting me out from the company of Sir Hugh by a very wise look of the eye and informed me that the lady would wait and would go. I promptly gave him a franc for his trouble. My own pocket was bulging with Italian silver lire and paper five- and ten-lire pieces, which I had secured the day before. Finally my train rolled in, and I took one last look at the sea in the fading light and entered. Sir Hugh gave me parting instructions as to simple restaurants that I would find at different places in Italy—not the showy and expensive cafés beloved of Grant Richards. He wanted me to save money on food and have my portrait painted by Mancini, which I could have done, with a letter from him, he assured me, for three hundred dollars. He looked wisely around the platform to see that there was no suspicious lady anywhere in the foreground and said he suspected one might be going with me.

"Oh, Lane," I said, "how could you? Ladies are not to be so easily induced. Besides, I am very poor now."

"The ruling passion—ha! ha! ha!—strong in poverty," he commented, and waved me farewell.

I walked forward through the train looking for my belongings and encountered Marcelle. She was eager to explain by signs that the Cook's man had told her to get off at Garaban.

"*M'sieur Thomas Cook, il m'a dit—il faut que je descende à Garaban—pas Ventimiglia—Garaban.*" She understood well enough that if she wanted to get back to Monte Carlo early in the evening she would have to make this train, as the next was not before ten o'clock.

I led the way to a table in the dining car still vacant, and we talked as only people can talk who have no common language. By the most astonishing efforts, Marcelle made it known that she would not stay at Monte Carlo very long now and that if I wanted her to come to Florence when I got there, she would. Also she kept talking about Fontainebleau and horseback riding in April. She imitated a smart rider holding the reins with one hand and clucking to the horse with her lips. She folded her hands expressively to show how heavenly it would be. Then she put her right hand over her eyes and waved her left hand out to indicate that there were lovely vistas which we could contemplate. Finally she extracted all her bills from the

Hôtel de Paris—and they were astonishing—to show me how expensive her life was at Monte Carlo. But I refused to be impressed. Grant Richards had taken all my money, and I could not have helped her if I had chosen. It did not make the least difference, however, in her attitude or her mood. She was just as cheerful as ever, and repeated "*Avril—Fontainebleau*," as the train stopped and she stepped off. She reached up and gave me an affectionate farewell kiss. The last I saw of her she was standing, her arms akimbo, her head thrown smartly back, looking after the train. The next I saw of her was in London, a few days before I left for home.

We talk boastfully of our railway services at home in America—the fine trains and the long distances they travel—but I do not see that they compare in any way for real comfort with the international trains which ply through different parts of Europe. This through train from Marseilles to Rome was equipped with a diner and many vestibuled, corridored sleeping cars, as comfortable as they could be. I was so pleased to find myself eventually in a separate room, with a little washroom attached, hooks for my clothes, a mirror to shave by and a lamp and table to read by or take tea from if I chose. It was conveniently lighted with a lamp in the ceiling, one over the table and one over the berth so that I could lie and read in comfort. After the abominable American sleeping car which I had once thought so perfect, I realized that this was a vast advance, even if we were in so-called backward Italy. The cars were comfortably finished in green velvet cushions and well-woven carpets and were as clean as any American car ever was. Before I secured my separate compartment, however, I encountered an Italian bandit in the shape of the conductor, who, in spite of the fact that there were six or seven empty compartments in this train, put me in one occupied by another man who eyed me antagonistically. After I had been given a taste of what it would mean to occupy one of these sections with a stranger, he came around and said in stilted English, pausing over each word as though he were very uncertain as to whether it was the right one or not, "I give you room to yourself after Ventimiglia."

I smiled and said "Thank you," knowing, according to my ticket, that I was entitled to it not after Ventimiglia but from Monte Carlo on. But he still continued to look at me as much as to say, "If you do not tip me, you will be doing a great injustice to someone who is doing you a great favor."

I caught the significance of his glance and said, "That will be all right," and he went away, very solemn and very soldier-like. He did not wait until we reached Ventimiglia, however, for the porter came in two or three minutes and removed my belongings and made me comfortable. It was in my comfortable section that I remained until we reached Pisa.

It was due to a railroad wreck about twenty miles beyond Ventimiglia that I owe my acquaintance with one of the most interesting men I have met in years, a man who was very charming to me afterwards in Rome. As I understood it, we were due in Rome the next morning at ten o'clock. I would have dismounted at Pisa at eight and in consequence would have known nothing of this very charming person. Somewhere beyond Ventimiglia the train came to a dead stop in the dark. I had been routed out at that place by a most ferocious-looking inspector with round eyes and toothy mouth encased in black whiskers, who exclaimed much concerning *le grand bagage* and signaled me to come with him. I understood well enough what was wanted and came out into a baggage car, where there appeared to be three or four officers and a railroad employee with a flaming torch. I opened my trunk and was promptly dismissed after the contents had been pulled up on all four sides. Then I went to my section and fell asleep while reading a book concerning Italian art and marveling at the peaceful progress of an Italian train. We were not moving at all!

The next morning we were still stalled where we had stopped the night before. I had risen early under the impression that I was to get out quickly but was waved back by the porter who repeated over and over, "*Beaucoup de retard!*" I understood what that meant well enough, but I did not understand what caused it, or that I would not arrive in Pisa until two in the afternoon. I went into the dining car and there encountered one of the most obstreperous English women that I have ever met. She was obviously of the highly intellectual class but so haughty in her manner and so loud-spoken in her opinion that she was really offensive. She was having her morning fruit and rolls and some chops and was explaining much of the character of Italy as she knew it to a lady who was with her. She was of the type that never accepts an opinion from anyone but invariably gives her own or corrects any that may be volunteered. At one time I think she must have been very attractive, for she was moderately tall and graceful, but her face had become waxy and sallow and a little thin—I will not say hard, although it was anything but ingratiating. My one wish was that she would stop talking and leave the dining car, she talked so loud; but she stayed on until her friend left and her husband arrived. I took him to be her husband by the way she contradicted him.

He was a very pleasing, intellectual person—the type of man, I thought, who would complacently endure such a woman. He was certainly not above medium height, quite well filled out, and decidedly phlegmatic. I should have said from my first glance that he never took any exercise of any kind, and his face had that pleasing pallor which comes from much brooding over the midnight oil. He had large, soft, lustrous black eyes and a mop of black hair which hung low over a very high, white forehead. I must repeat here that I am the poorest judge of people whom I am going to like of any human being. Now and then I take to a person instantly, and my feeling endures for years. On the other hand, I have taken the most groundless oppositions based on nothing at all. Perhaps my groundless opposition in this case was due to the fact that the gentleman was a little old, or a little stuffy, or that he had such a loud-talking wife. Anyhow, I gave him a single glance and dismissed him with contempt. I was far more interested in a stern, official-looking Englishman with white hair who ordered his bottle of Perrier in a low, rusty voice and cut his orange up into small bits with a knife.

After he was gone, I heard a German explaining to his wife what the trouble about the wreck ahead was. We were just starting now, perhaps twenty-five or thirty miles from Ventimiglia, and were dashing in and out of rocky tunnels and momentarily bursting into wonderful views of walled caves and sunlit sweeps of sea. The hill-town, the striped basilica, with its square, many-arched campanile, was coming into view. I was delighted to see open plains bordered in the distance by snow-capped mountains and dotted sparsely with little huts of stone and brick—how old, heaven only knows.

It was true, as Grant Richards said, that Italy was so much poorer than France. The cars and stations seemed shabbier, the dress of the inhabitants much poorer. I saw natives, such as I used to see around the little backwoods towns in Indiana, staring idly at the cars as we flashed past or taking material away from the platforms in rude carts drawn by oxen. So often vehicles appeared to be rattle-trap, dusty, unpainted; and some miles this side of Genoa—our first stop—we ran into a region where it had been snowing and the ground was covered with a wet, slushy snowfall. After Monte Carlo, with its lemon and orange trees and its lovely palms, this was a sad come-down, and I could scarcely realize that we were not so much as a hundred miles away. I often saw, however, distant hills crowned with a stronghold or a campanile in high browns and yellows which made up for the otherwise poor-looking foreground. Often we dashed through a cave protected by high surrounding walls of rock, where the palms came into view again and where one could see how plainly these high walls of stone made for a tropic atmosphere. I heard the loud-voiced Englishwoman saying, "It is such a delight to see the high colors again. England is so dreary. I never feel it so much as when we come down through here."

We were passing through a small Italian town, very splotchy as to its coloring, rich in whites, pinks, browns and blues—a world of wash-lines showing between rows of buildings, and crowds, pure Italian in type, plodding to and fro along the streets. It was nice to see windows open here and the sunshine pouring down and making dark shadows. I saw an Italian woman wearing a pink-dotted dress partly covered by a bright yellow apron and looking out of a window, and then it was that I first got the tang of Italy—the thing that I felt afterwards in Rome and Florence and Perugia—that wonderful love of color that is not rampant but just deliciously selective, giving the eye something to feed on when it least expects it. That is Italy.

When nearly all the diners had left the car, the English lady left also, and her husband remained to smoke. He was not so very far removed from me, but he came a little nearer and said, "The Italians must have their striped churches and wash-lines or they wouldn't be happy."

I am sure I said "yes," but in a gingerly way, and it was some time before he volunteered another suggestion, which was that the Italians along this part of the coast had a poor region to farm. I took that statement about as I took the other, making no particular comment and avoiding the conversation which I felt impending. I got up and left after a little while because I did not want to have anything to do with his wife. I was so afraid that I might have to talk to her, which seemed to me a ghastly prospect.

I sat in my berth and read the history of art as it related to Florence, Genoa and Pisa, interrupting my paragraphs with glances at every interesting scene. The value of the prospect changed first from one side of the train to the other, and I went out into the corridor to open a window and look out. We passed through a valley where it looked as though grapes were flourishing splendidly, and my Englishman came out and told me the name of the place, saying that it was good wine that was made there. He was determined to talk to me whether I would or not, and so I decided to make the best of it and succumb. It just occurred to me that he might be the least bit lonely and, seeing that I was very curious about the country through which we were passing, that he might know something about Italy. The moment that it dawned upon me that he might be helpful to me in this respect I began to ask him questions, and I found his knowledge to be delightfully wide. He knew Italy thoroughly.

As we proceeded he described how the country was divided into three valleys separated by two mountain ranges, and what the lines of its early, almost prehistoric, development had been. He knew where Shelley had come to spend his summers and knew spots that had been preferred by Browning and other famous Englishmen. He talked of the cities that lie in a row down the center of Italy—Perugia, Florence, Bologna, Modena, Piacenza and Milan—and of the fact that Italy had no educational system whatsoever and that the priests were bitterly opposed to it. He was sorry that I was not going to stop at Spezia, because at Spezia the climate was very mild and the gulf very beautiful. He was delighted to think that I was going to stop at Pisa and see the Cathedral and the Baptistery. He commented on the charms of Genoa—commercialized as it had been these later years—

saying that there was a very beautiful Campo Santo and that some of the palaces of the quarreling Guelphs and Ghibellines still remaining were well worth seeing. When we passed the quarries of Carrara, he told me of their age and of how endless the quantity of marble still was. He was going to Rome with his wife, and he wanted to know if I would not look him up, giving me the name of a hotel where he lived by the season.

I caught a note of remarkable erudition, for we fell to discussing religion and priestcraft and the significance of government generally, and he astonished me by the breadth of his knowledge. We passed to the subject of metaphysics from which all religions spring, and then I saw how truly philosophic and esoteric he was. His mind knew no country, his knowledge no school. He led off by easy stages into vague speculations as to the transcendental character of race impulses, and I knew I had gotten hold of a profound scholar as well as a very genial person. I was very sorry now that I had been so rude to him and tried to make it up to him by evincing great interest in all his observations. By the time we reached Pisa we were fast friends, and he told me he had a friend, one Paul Sabatier, who was a resident of Assisi, and that he would give me a letter to him which would bring me charming intellectual companionship for a day or two. I promised to seek him out at his hotel, and as we passed the Leaning Tower and the Baptistery, not so very distant from the railroad track as we entered Pisa, he gave me his card. Fortunately I recognized the name as being connected with some intellectual labors of a distinguished character, and I said so. He accepted the recognition gracefully, and asked me to be sure and come. He would show me around Rome.

I gathered my bags and stepped out onto the platform at Pisa, eager to see what I could see in the three or four hours that I wished to remain. It struck me as incongruous that I should be coming along a double-track railroad in a modern sleeping car to see the Leaning Tower of Pisa and the Campo Santo, but so it was.

CHAPTER XLIX

Baedeker says that Pisa has a population of twenty-seven thousand two hundred people and that it is a quiet town. It is. I caught the spell of a score of places like it as I walked out into the open square facing the depot. The most amazing botch of a monument I ever saw in my life I saw here—a puffing, swelling, strutting representation of Umberto I, legs apart, whis-

tice had made him perfect, for by giving each note sufficient space to swell and redouble and quadruple itself, he finally managed to fill the great chamber with a charming harmony, rich and full, not unlike that of a wind-harp. I know that acoustically this is very difficult, and I should fancy it would be trying work speaking from Pisano's perfect pulpit, but I fancy little speaking has ever been done here, and besides, it is better to have much harmony of sound than many words. An echo as pure and clear as this is a delightful accident and a delicious novelty. I felt a keen desire to stay here a long while, just in this one room, but without were the Leaning Tower and the Cathedral, and I knew I had much to see in Italy, so I left.

If I fell instantly in love with the Baptistery I was equally moved by the Leaning Tower—a perfect thing. As I looked at it over the level grass and standing a little to one side of the apse of the Cathedral, I was amused to think how quickly some American foundation company, some "Rooney Brothers" or "Thompson-Starrett Contraction Company" would quickly right this old tower and think they were making a fine job of it if the Italian government would let them. "Begob!" I can hear some Irish mason-foreman explaining, "we'll have that straight in no time," and he would, too. It would be no trick at all, today, in this era of the skyscraper and the deep excavation.

But if I had to smile I had to sigh too, for a thing of beauty is not only a joy forever but a pain also, when one thinks of the frailness of all perfection. If man is wise and thoughtful from now on, he can keep the wonders of great beauty by renewing them as they wear; but will he remain wise and thoughtful? So little is thought of true beauty. Think of the guns thundering on the Parthenon and of Napoleon carrying away the horses of St. Mark's! I mounted the steps of this tower—one hundred and seventy-nine feet, the same height as the Baptistery—walking out on and around each of its six balustrades and surveying the surrounding landscape, rich in lovely mountains showing across a plain. The tower tilts fourteen feet out of plumb, and as I walked its circular arcades at different heights, I had the feeling that I might topple over and come floundering down to the grass below.

As I rose higher, the view increased in loveliness; and at the top I found an old bellman who explained by signs why the heaviest of the seven bells was placed on the side opposite the overhanging wall of the tower. He also pointed in the different directions which presented lovely views, indicating to the west and southwest the mouth of the Arno, the Mediterranean, Leghorn and the Tuscan Islands, to the north the Alps and Mount Pisani where the Carrara quarries are, and to the south, Rome. Some Italian soldiers from the neighboring barracks came up and made a great to-do over the general effect. I came down and entered the Cathedral, which I consider as perfect as any which I saw abroad. The Italian Gothic is so much more perfectly spaced on the interior than the Northern Gothic, and the great flat roof, coffered in gold, is so much richer and more soothing in its aspect.

The whole church is of pure marble yellowed by age—relieved, however, by black and colored bands. I did my best to unravel the mysteries of tombs and pictures, the art of Andrea del Sarto and Giuliano da Maiano and Cimabue and Sodoma, for I was new to Italy—but I was baffled; I did not have time. With the exception of the altarpieces by del Sarto and the entombment by Sodoma, I had to let them go. The thing that did interest me, although it became a great bore in later churches, was the presence of a large number of priests mumbling their afternoon orisons in the most matter-of-fact way. I saw one with his legs crossed looking wearily over his book as much as if to say, "Good heavens, I wish this were done with!" And others looked as if they could barely pump up sufficient interest to repeat the words. Yet here they were, sitting around like a flock of ducks in this magnificent structure, mumbling aimless prayers. I am not particularly anti-Catholic in my mood, but I should say off-hand that obviously if there is anything the matter with Italy, it is the priesthood. The Catholics of the world are supporting a large number of churches in Italy which had better be shut as churches and opened by the state as museums and objects of art. They are far more significant in that light than as religious edifices.

I came away after a time and entered the Campo Santo—the loveliest thing of its kind that I saw in Europe. I never knew, strange to relate, that graveyards were made, or could be made, into anything so artistically impressive. This particular ground was nothing more than an oblong piece of grass, set with several cypress trees and surrounded with a marble arcade, below the floor and against the walls of which are placed the marbles, tombs and sarcophagi. The outer walls are solid, windowless and decorated on the inside with those naive, light-colored frescoes of the pupils of Giotto. The inner wall is full of arched, pierced windows with many delicate columns through which you look to the green grass and the cypress trees and the perfectly smooth, ornamental dome at one end. I have paid my tribute to the cypress trees, so I will only say that here, as always, whenever I saw them anywhere—one or many—I thrilled with delight. They are as fine as any of the monuments or bronze doors or carved pulpits or perfect baptismal fonts. They belong where the great artistic impulse of Italy has always put them—side by side with perfect things. For me they added the one final, necessary touch to this realm of romantic memory. I see them now and I hear them sigh.

I walked back to my train through highly-colored, winding, side-walkless, quaint-angled streets crowded with houses, the facades of which we in America today attempt to imitate on our Fifth Avenues and Michigan

Avenues and Rittenhouse Squares. The medieval Italians knew so well what to do with the door and the window and the cornice and the wall space. The size of their window is what they choose to make it, and the door is instinctively put where it will give the last touch of elegance. How often have I mentally applauded that marvelous discrimination and reserve which will use one panel of colored stone or one niche or one lamp or one window—and no more. Such space as they have is never artistically destroyed by the uniform repetition of anything. There is space—lots of it—unbroken by any window, until you have had just enough, and then it will be relieved just enough by a marble plaque framed in the walls, a coat-of-arms, a window, a niche. I would like to run on in my enthusiasm and describe that gem of a palace that is now the Palazzo Communale at Perugia, but I will refrain. Only these streets in Pisa were rich with angles and arcades and wonderful doorways and solid, plain fronts which were at once substantial and elegant. Trust the Italian of an earlier day to do well whatever he did at all, and I for one do not think that this instinct is lost. It will burst into flame again in the future or save greatly what it already has.

I was sorry when I took the five o'clock train for Rome that I had not studied that ancient city more diligently in my youth. I was not absolutely without a knowledge of Roman history or of Roman art, for I have read my Gibbon and my Froude, but what I knew at this time was a little vague. As we sped southward through a level plain that was tufted with cypress trees in little darksome companies and humanized every now and then with lone shepherds watching their sheep in the dusk, a confused jumble involving the palaces of the Caesars, the tombs of the Appian Way, the Colosseum, St. Peter's, the Pantheon and the Forum Romanum heaped themselves upward in my mind. Because of what was left over of Gibbon and other writers, I had a notion of a great city, far-flung in its power. The mystery of the Catholic Church, in which I was raised as a child, came back to me. I thought of the stuffy priests who used to boast from the altar of a Sunday that they had been privileged to go to Rome and kiss the foot of the Holy Father. Rome—that used to seem to me the center of the world, where sat the pope, who was infallible. Dear God! Later Caesar and Mark Antony and Galba and Nero became my wonders and my apexes of human terror and achievement. I can remember as a boy sitting in our simple schoolroom in Warsaw and reading of the dramatic progress of Galba from Spain to Rome in his flight to seize the Empire. The Castle of Saint Angelo, the ruined walls, the Pantheon—all the things which made ancient Rome—came back, but so disorganized as to give only the faintest suggestion of a real world. Now I was on the *qui vive* to see it and impatient with wonder as to what the morning would reveal.

I was bound for the Hotel Continental—one of the very good hotels, I understood, close to the great terminal, and the abode, for the winter at least, of Grant Richards's mother, the widow of a departed Oxford don. From all he had told me of her I expected to encounter a severe and conservative lady of great erudition who would eye the foibles of Paris and Monte Carlo with great severity. As a matter of fact, Grant Richards had told me a story of how once when he was at the Normandy in Paris, his mother had sought him there, and finding that he had not been there during the night before and was not expected to return shortly, suspected a liaison of some kind and had wept bitterly afterwards. In her distress she had lost a purse containing five hundred francs. He was constantly writing her suave, cautious and reassuring letters which painted his career in the most sober colors. "My mother, you know," he used to say to me, "is a very conservative person. She is greatly concerned about me and as a rule depresses me greatly. She always speaks of me as 'poor Grawntie'—why, I haven't the slightest idea. But do, for heaven's sake, when you see her, try to cheer her up and give her a good report of me. I don't doubt you will find her very interesting, and it is just possible that she will take a fancy to you. She is subject to violent likes and dislikes."

I fancied Mrs. Richards as a rather large woman with a smooth, placid countenance and a severe intellectual eye that would see through all my shams and make-believes on the instant. I had warned Grant Richards that I would go to the hotel and be nice to her for a few days but that if she bored me I would promptly leave. Lane had constantly assured me that Grant Richards's mother was shallow and very conventional—a recommendation which from him meant much. I could see her as I came in on the train waiting for me, ready to pick flaws in my deportment, and so I decided to be on my guard as much as possible.

It was midnight before the train arrived, however, and as we flashed into the outskirts of Rome I forgot all about her, wondering whether I should see anything which would be of importance historically. It was raining, and as I pressed my nose to the window pane viewing the beginning lamps I saw streets and houses come into view—apartment houses, if you please, and streetcars and electric arc lights and asphalt-paved streets and a general atmosphere of modernity. We might have been entering Detroit or Cleveland or Cincinnati or Pittsburgh for any particular variation it presented. But just when I was commenting to myself on the strangeness of entering ancient Rome in a modern compartment car and of seeing box cars and engines gathered on a score of parallel tracks and seeing coal cars and flat cars loaded with heavy material, a touch of the ancient Rome came into view for an instant and was then gone again in the dark and rain. It was an immense, desolate tomb, its arches flung heavenward in great curves, its great, rounded dome rent and jagged by time. Nothing but ancient Rome could have produced so imposing a ruin, and it came over me in an instant, fresh and clear like an electric shock, like a dash of cold water, that this was truly all that was left of the might and glory of an older day.

I recall now with delight the richness of that sensation. Rome that could build the walls and the baths in far Manchester and London; Rome that could occupy the Ile-St.-Louis in Paris as an outpost; that could erect the immense column to Augustus on the heights above Monte Carlo; Rome that could reach to the uppermost waters of the Nile and the banks of the Tigris and Euphrates and rule. Here it was—the city that St. Paul had been brought to, where St. Peter had sat as the first father of the Church, where the first Latins had set up their shrine to Romulus and Remus and worshiped the she-wolf that had nourished them. Yes, this was Rome, truly enough, in spite of the apartment houses and the streetcars and the electric lights. It was not all gone, and I was eager to step out and see it.

I came into the great station at five minutes after twelve amid a clamor of Italian porters and a crowd of disembarking passengers. I made my way to the baggage room, looking for a Cook's guide to inquire my way to the Continental, when I was seized upon by him.

"Are you Mr. Dreiser?" he said.

I replied that I was.

"Mrs. Richards told me to say that she was waiting for you and that you should come right over and inquire for her."

I hurried over, followed by a laboring porter, and found her waiting for me in the lobby—not the large, severe creature I had imagined, but a small, enthusiastic, gracious little lady, who was as motherly as a woman could well be, and as kindly and obliging. She told me that my room was all ready and that the bath that I had demanded was connected with it, and that she had ordered some coffee sent up, but that I could have anything else that I chose. She began with a flood of questions—how was her "poor dear Grawntie?" And her daughter in London? And had we lost much money at Monte Carlo? And had we been very nice and quiet in Paris? And had I had a pleasant trip? And would I like to go with her here and there for a few days, particularly until I was acclimated and able to find my own way about? I answered her freely and rapidly, for I took a real liking to her and decided at once that I was going to have a very nice time. She was so motherly and friendly. It struck me as so charming that she should wait up for me and see that I was welcomed and comfortably housed, and I can see her now with a loving memory in her charming gray silk dresses and black lace shawl. She was as much of a mother to me during my stay in Rome as any woman could be, and it grieves me sometimes to think that perhaps I was not as consistently kindly in return as I might have been; but we made friends and have stayed friends, and that is something. I still send her letters and cards, and she shortly became, and still remains, "Ma" to me.

CHAPTER L

The first morning I arose in Rome it was raining, and I thought that possibly this meant some such long period of wet weather as we know in America when a rain begins; but I was mistaken, for in an hour or two the sun came out, and I saw a very peculiar city. Rome has about the climate of Monte Carlo, except that it is a little more changeable, and in the mornings and evenings quite chill. Around noon every day it was very warm, almost invariably bright—deliciously bright—but dark and cool where the buildings or the trees cast a shadow. I was awakened by some huzza-ing, which I learned afterwards was for some officer who had lately returned from Morocco.

Like the English, the Italians are not yet vastly accustomed to the bathtub, and this particular hotel reminded me of one in Manchester, with its bath chambers as large as ordinary living rooms, except in this case the builders had sense enough to put the toilet in with the bath and not eight dreary blocks down the hall. My room looked out into an inner court which surmounted the lobby of the hotel and was set with palms and flowers which flourished mightily. I looked out through an opening in this inner court to some brown buildings over the way—brown as only the Italians know how to paint them, and bustling with Italian life. It was interesting to think that I was surrounded by thirty-eight million Italians instead of forty million Frenchmen or forty million Englishmen.

Mrs. Richards had kindly volunteered to show me about this first day, and I was to meet her promptly at ten in the lobby. I had the usual continental breakfast of coffee, rolls, honey and butter in my room and then went down to meet her. She wanted me to take a streetcar to begin with, because there was one that went direct to St. Peter's along the Via Nazionale and because there were so many things she could show me that way. We went out into the public square which adjoined the hotel, and there it was that she pointed out the Museo delle Terme, located in the ancient baths of Diocletian, and assured me that the fragments of wall that I saw jutting out from between buildings in one or two places dated from the Roman Empire.

The fragment of the wall of Servius Tullius which we encountered in the Via Nazionale dates from 578 B.C. and the baths of Diocletian, so close to the hotel, from 303 A.D. The large ruin that I had seen the night before on entering the city was the temple of Minerva Medica, dating from about 250 A.D. I shall never forget my sensation on seeing modern stores—drugstores, tobaccostores, bookstores, all with bright, clean windows—adjoining these very ancient ruins. It was quite something for the first time to see a fresh, well-dressed modern throng going about its morning's business amid these rude suggestions of a very ancient life.

Nearly all the traces of ancient Rome, however, were apparently obliterated, and you saw only busy, up-to-date streets with streetcars, shops, stores and a gay metropolitan life generally. I have to smile when I think that I mistook a section of the old wall of Servius Tullius for the remnants of some very plain warehouse which had recently been removed. All the time in Rome I kept suffering this impression—that I was looking at something which had only recently been torn down, when as a matter of fact I was looking at the earlier or later walls or the remnants of famous temples and baths. This particular streetcar line on which we were riding was a revelation in its way, for it was full of black-frocked priests in shovel hats, monks in brown cowls and sandals, and American and English old maids in spectacles who carried their Baedekers with severe primness and who were, like ourselves, bound for the Vatican. The conductors, it struck me, were a trifle more civil than the American brand—but not much—and the native passengers were a better type of Italian than we usually see in America. I sighted the Italian policeman at different points along the way—not unlike the Parisian gendarme in his high cap and short cape. The most striking characteristic, however, was the great number of priests, who were much more numerous than policemen and taxi drivers in New York. It seemed to me that on this very first morning I saw bands of priests going to and fro, but, for the rest of it, Rome was not unlike Monte Carlo and Paris combined, only that its streets were comparatively narrow and its colors high.

Mrs. Richards was most kindly and industrious in her explanations. She told me that in riding down this Via Nazionale we were passing between those ancient hills, the Quirinale and the Viminale, by the Forum of Trajan, the Gallery of Modern Art, the palaces of the Aldobrandini and Rospigliosi and a score of other things which I have forgotten. When we reached the open square which faces St. Peter's, I expected to be vastly impressed by the huge size of the first Roman church of the world, but in a way I was very much disappointed. To me it was not in the least beautiful as Canterbury was beautiful, as Amiens was beautiful and as Pisa was beautiful. It was large and impressive, but only in a stodgy way. I was not at all enthused by the semi-circular arcade in front with its immense columns. I knew that I ought to think it was wonderful—but I could not. I think in a way that the location and arrangement of the building do not do it justice, and it has neither the somber gray of Amiens nor the delicate creamy hue of the buildings of Pisa. It is brownish and gray by turns. As I drew nearer, however, I realized that it was very large—astonishingly large—and that by some hocus-pocus of perspective and arrangement this was not easily realizable. By comparison with it, the nearby castle of St. Angelo, which is quite large in itself, is small, and there is no other modern building in Rome which rivals it for size. The baths of Caracalla and Diocletian are much larger in extent; the Colosseum, although not so much larger, is vastly more imposing, though its position is even less advantageous. I was eager to see its interior, however, and waived all exterior consideration until later.

What I saw in the way of marbles and sculpture and paintings and jeweled richness generally staggered me, but that I thought it was beautiful I cannot admit. If a vast heap of gold is beautiful, the interior of St. Peter's is beautiful; if a staggering mass of amazingly carved marble of a great warmth of color can be called lovely art, here you have it. Otherwise, not. But that it was amazing and impressive and astounding, I freely admit. If I wanted to steal any quantity of marbles, statues, tapestries, paintings, in order to *make* something truly beautiful and artistic, I would loot St. Peter's first. A truly great artist could do wonders with what is there. It was so interesting to me. As we were first going up the steps of St. Peter's and across the immense stone platform that leads to the door, a small Italian wedding party arrived, without any design of being married there, however—merely to visit the various shrines and altars. The gentleman was so smug in a long black frock coat and high hat, a little, brown, be-mustached, dapper man whose patent leather shoes sparkled in the sun. The lady was a rosy Italian girl, very much belaced and besilked, with a pert, practical air; a little velvet-clad page carried her train. There were a number of friends—the parents on both sides, I took it—and some immediate relatives who fell solemnly in behind, two by two; and together this little ant-like band crossed the immense threshold. Mrs. Richards and I followed eagerly after—or at least I did, for I fancied they were to be married here, and I wanted to see how it was to be done at St. Peter's. I was disappointed, however, for they merely went from altar to altar and shrine to shrine, genuflecting, and finally entered the sacred crypt, below which the bones of St. Peter are supposed to be buried. It was a fine religious beginning to what I trust has proved a happy union.

St. Peter's, if I may be permitted to continue a little on that curious theme, is certainly the most amazing church in the world. It is not beautiful—I am satisfied that no true artist would grant that, but after you have been all over Europe and seen the various edifices of importance, it still sticks in your mind as astounding, perhaps the most astounding of all. While I was in Rome I learned by consulting guidebooks, attending lectures and visiting the place myself, that it is nothing more than a hodgepodge of the vagaries and enthusiasms of a long line of able pontiffs. To me the Catholic Church has such a long and messy history of intrigue and chicanery that I for one cannot contemplate its central religious pretensions with any peace of mind. It always pains me to see the ignorant faithful approaching with such reverence things which are mere shams and hodgepodges of illusion and gigantic memorials of selfish ambition, lust, trickery, murder and all the sins in the decalogue. St. Peter's is just that. I am not going into the history of the papacy nor the internecine and fratricidal struggles of medieval Italy, but what veriest tyro does not grasp the significance of what I mean? Julius II, flanking a Greek cross basilica with a hexastyle portico to replace the Constantinian basilica, which itself had replaced the oratory of St. Anacletus on this spot, and that largely to make room for his famous tomb which was to be the finest thing in it; Urban VIII melting down the copper roof of the Pantheon portico in order to erect the showy baldachino! I do not now recall what ancient temples were looted for marble nor what popes did the looting, but that it was plentifully done I am satisfied, and von Ranke will bear me out. It was Julius II and Leo X who resorted to the sale of indulgences, which aided in bringing about the Reformation, for the purpose of paying the enormous expenses connected with the building of this lavish structure. Think of how the plans of Bramante and Michelangelo and Raphael and Carlo Maderna were tossed about between the Latin cross and the Greek cross and between a portico of one form and a portico of another form! Wars, heartaches, struggles, contentions—these are they of which St. Peter's is a memorial.

As I looked at the amazing length (six hundred and fifteen feet) and the height of the nave (one hundred and fifty-two feet) and the height of the dome from the pavement in the interior to the roof (four hundred and five feet) and saw that the church actually contained forty-six immense altars and read that it contained seven hundred and forty-eight columns of marble, stone or bronze, three hundred and eighty-six statues and two hundred and ninety windows, I began to realize how astounding the whole thing was. It was really so large and so tangled historically and so complicated in the history of its architectural development that it was useless for me to attempt to synchronize its significance in my mind. I merely stared, staggered by the beauty and the cost of the immense windows, the showy and astounding altars. I came back again and again, but I got nothing save an unutterable impression of overwhelming grandeur. It is far too rich in its composition for mortal conception. No one, I am satisfied, really consciously realizes how *grand* it is. It answers to that word exactly. Browning's poem "The Bishop Orders His Tomb at St. Praxed's Church" gives a faint suggestion of what any least bit of it is like. Any single tomb of any single pope—of which it seemed to me there were no end—could have had this poem written about it. Each one appears to have desired a finer tomb than the other; and I can understand the eager enthusiasm of Sixtus V (1588), who kept eight hundred men working night and day on the dome in order to see how it was going to look. And well he might. Murray tells the story of how on one occasion, being in want of another receptacle for water, the masons tossed the body of Urban VI out of his sarcophagus, put aside his bones in a corner and gave the ring on his finger to the architect. The pope's remains were out of their receptacle for fifteen years or more before they were finally restored.

The Vatican sculptural and art museums were equally astonishing. I had always heard of its eleven hundred rooms and its priceless collections; but it was astonishing and delightful to see them face to face—all the long line of Greek and Roman and medieval perfections chiseled or painted, transported from ruins or dug from the earth—such wonders as the porphyry vase and Laocoön, taken from the silent underground rooms of Nero's house where they had stood for centuries, unheeded in all their perfection, and the river god, representative of the Tiber. I was especially interested to see the vast number of Roman personalities—known and unknown—which gave me a face-to-face understanding of that amazing people. They came back now or arose vital before me—Claudius, Nerva, Hadrian, Faustina the elder, wife of Antoninus Pius, Pertinax, whose birthplace was near Monte Carlo, Julius Caesar and Augustus Caesar, Cicero, Antoninus Pius, Tiberius, Mark Antony, Marcus Aemilius Lepidus and a score of others. It was amazing to me to see how like the modern English and Americans they were and how practical and present-day-like they appeared. It swept away the space of two thousand years as having no significance whatever and left you face to face with the far older problem of humanity.

I could not help thinking that the duplicates of these men are on our streets today in New York and Chicago and London—urgent, calculating, thinking figures—and that they were doing today much as these forerunners did two thousand years before them. I cannot see the slightest difference between an emperor like Hadrian and a steel trust president like E. H. Gary or a banker like Lyman J. Gage. P. D. Armour had his forerunner in a personality like Titus or Tiberius, and the head of a man like Lord Salisbury, the famous premier of England, is to be found duplicated in a score of sculptures in various museums throughout the Holy City. I got the feeling that any one of hundreds of these splendid marbles, if separated from their populous surroundings and given to a separate city meager in artistic possessions, would prove a great public attraction. To him that hath shall be given, however, and to those that have not shall be taken away even the little that they have. And so it is that Rome fairly suffocates with its endless variety of artistic perfection—one glory almost dimming the other—while the rest of the world yearns for a crust of artistic beauty and has nothing. It is like the Milky Way for jewels as contrasted with those vast, starless spaces that give no evidence of sidereal life.

I wandered in this region of wonders attended by my motherly friend until it was late in the afternoon, and then we went for lunch. Being new to Rome, I was not satisfied with what I had seen, but struck forth again, coming next into the region of Santa Maria Maggiore and up an old stairway that had formed a part of an old Medici palace now dismantled—only to find myself shortly thereafter and quite by accident in the vicinity of the Colosseum. I really had not known that I was coming to it, for I was not looking for it. I was following idly the lines of an old wall that lay in the vicinity of San Pietro in Vincoli when suddenly it appeared, lying in a hollow at the foot of a hill, which I afterwards learned was the Esquiline. I was rejoicing in having discovered an old wall that I knew must be of very ancient date and a group of cypresses that showed over a very ancient wall, when I looked—and there it was.

I was so surprised that I stopped in astonishment and tried to think whether I was really impressed. It seemed, from this height, not to be so large—and I had fancied, for some reason or other, that it lay far outside the city on the Via Appia. I was not more than ten or fifteen minutes' walk from my hotel. It was exactly as the pictures have represented it—oval, many-arched, a thoroughly ponderous ruin. I really did not gain a suggestion of the astonishing size of it until I came down the hill past tin cans that were lying on the grass—a sign of the modernity that possesses Rome—and entered through one of the many arches. Then it came on me—the amazing thickness of the walls, the imposing size and weight of the fragments, the vast dignity of the uprising flights of seats, and the great space now properly cleared, devoted to the arena. All that I ever knew or heard of it came back: the Christian martyrs fighting with lions (which never occurred here at all but in the Circus Maximus, now completely disappeared); the ancient gladiators—one with a trident, the other with a net and short sword, calling "I have nothing against you. I merely want to catch the fish"—referring to the ornament on the rival's helmet. Byron's pyrotechnic lines on these same ruins and all the artistic representations of scenes presumed to have transpired here flashed before me. I wondered where the animals had been kept and which ones were the particular doors through which they entered.

I sat on the cool stones and looked about me while other travelers, principally from America and England—though there were both French and Germans—walked leisurely about, their Baedekers in their hands. It was a splendid afternoon. The sun was shining down in here, and it was as warm as though it were May in Indiana. Small patches of grass and moss were detectable everywhere, growing on and in between the stones. The five thousand wild beasts slaughtered in the arena at its dedication, which remained as a thought from my high school days, were all with me. I read up as much as I could, watching several workmen lowering themselves by ropes from the top of the walls, all the while they picked out little tufts of grass and weeds beginning to flourish in the earthy niches. Its amazing transformations—from once being a quarry for greedy popes by whom most of its magnificent marbles were removed, to its narrow escape from being a woolen mill operated by Sixtus V—were all brooded over here. It was impossible not to be impressed by the thought of the emperors sitting on this especial balcony; the thousands upon thousands of Romans intent upon some gladiatorial feat; the guards outside the endless doors, the numbers of which can still be seen, giving entrance to separate sections and tiers of seats; and the vast array of civic life which must have surged about. I wondered whether there were vendors of anything who sold sweets or food, and what their cries were in Latin. One could think of the endless vehicles that must have appeared here, bearing the nobility and citizens of means.

Time works melancholy changes. We think our day is so new and so different in the universe, that never has life presented the pictures or held the glamour and thrill which we see and feel. But human emotions and human spectacles are old, old; and I cannot see but what this city of several millions—with its keen intellectual interest and the far-lying reaches of mysterious countries which it ruled, and with its ruins which serve even now to amaze all who come fresh from the colossal wonder of London, Paris and New York—must have been as thrilling and as spectacular as the human consciousness could expect or desire. It must have been so, for the ruins of this Colosseum, like those of the baths of Diocletian and Caracalla, are tremendously impressive.

I left as the sun was going down, reflecting upon the wonder of the old life that was utterly gone. It is something like finding the glistening shell of a departed beetle or the suggestion in rocks of an ancient Jurassic world. As I returned along the thoroughly modern streets with their five- and six-story tenement and apartment buildings and their streetcars and customary vehicles, I tried to restore and keep in my mind a suggestion of the magnificence that Gibbon makes so significant. It was hard, for be one's imagination what it will, it is difficult to live outside of your own day and hour. The lamps already beginning to flourish in the grocery stores and the butcher shops, the cigar stores, apothecary shops, jewelry stores and tailor shops, all smartly arranged, distracted my mood. The old Roman world has been lost almost completely in the drift of centuries and particularly in the development of modern life. Since 1880 even Italy has been made over, with telephones, railroads, and electric lights. The native Roman is but little concerned with the glory that was Rome. He is more anxious to be able to pay his rent and to see the moving pictures than to know the intricacies of an ancient imperial life. Sad, grass-grown, mossy touches of it remain, perking out or obtruding themselves between modern galleries, department stores, theaters, and medieval palaces; but even the latter are *de trop*. A newer life has come, and in the swirl of it Rome is making parks and showplaces of such things as the Capitoline Hill, the Forum and the Colosseum. But they are of a showplace character entirely, of little more significance than the British Museum or the Louvre, if even that. A newer Rome is building apartment houses which it is anxious to rent and running stores and developing industries which it is anxious to make successful. Let the dead past bury its dead.

CHAPTER LI

The second evening I was in Rome I was introduced at the hotel by Mrs. Richards to a certain Mrs. Armstrong, an American woman with two children who, according to Mrs. Richards, was traveling abroad alone and who was very charming. "Oh, I am going to introduce you to such a nice woman," Mrs. Richards told me in the morning in her very enthusiastic way. "She is so charming. I am sure you will like her. She comes from America somewhere—New York, I think. Her husband is an author and playwright, I believe. I heard so." She chattered on in her genial, talk-making way, and I evinced some little interest, for while I did not know the lady's husband or herself I knew at least one friend of theirs, or two, and perhaps others.

"You know, I think it's just possible that there is some trouble between her and her husband. I don't understand these American women. Mrs. Armstrong is very nice, but they go about traveling without their husbands. Now you know in England we would not think of doing anything of that kind," and she pronounced the England with a high-flown, Oxford-like "Eengland," which was somewhat impressive. "Ma," as I finally came to call her, was decidedly conservative in her views and English in manner and speech, but she had the saving proclivity of being intensely interested in life and realized that all is not gold that glitters. She preferred to be among people who know and maintain good form, who are interested in maintaining the social virtues as they stand accepted and who, if they do not actually observe all of the laws and tenets of society as they stood, evoluted or at least maintained a deceiving pretense. She had a little coterie of friends in the hotel, as I found: a Greek traveler and merchant, retired, who spoke English, French, German and Italian, to say nothing of his native tongue, quite as fluently as one might wish; an American banker by the name of Bevan, whom I saw once but did not particularly care for; an Italian countess of great age who spoke English quite as well as I did, and better; an American newspaper woman, secretary to the Japanese ambassador at Rome, who stopped here occasionally; and then friends outside, such as artists, newspaper correspondents and officials connected with the Italian court and the papal court.

I never knew a more industrious social mentor in the shape of a woman, though among men her son outstripped her. She was apparently here, there and everywhere about the hotel, in the breakfast room, in the dining room, in the card room, in the writing room, greeting her friends, planning games, planning engagements, planning sightseeing trips—a most industrious and useful woman. She was pleasant, too; delightful, in spite of Lane's bitter criticism, for she knew what to do and when to do it; and if she was not impelled by a large constructive motive of any kind, nevertheless she had a sincere and discriminating love of the beautiful which caused her to excuse much for the sake of art. I found her well-disposed, kindly, sympathetic and very anxious to make the best of this sometimes dull existence, not only for herself but for everyone else. I liked her very much.

She had, I presume, sometime before I arrived, taken Mrs. Armstrong in tow, made her a member of her numerous card parties, exchanged the civilities of the day with her regularly and invited her on occasional excursions which were very cheerfully accepted. Mrs. Armstrong, I found on introduction, to be a beautiful woman of perhaps thirty-three or -four, with two of the healthiest, prettiest, best-behaved, though eagerly romping, children I have ever seen. She was medium tall and well built, with a little swagger at times in her walk, but in the main presenting a wholly self-reliant, kindly and considerate attitude. In a little less than three minutes' conversation after dinner, when Mrs. Richards brought her over, I found her to be an amazingly intellectual and brilliant woman, combining her Nietzsche-like philosophy with a love of life and society, horseback riding, automobiling, sightseeing and, above all, an overwhelming desire to get the psychology of history and of current human action straight. She was intensely interested in Europe as contrasted with America, the wonder of our nationality, the march of progress or change, and things of that sort. In addition to a mobile, Greek face, light-brown and plentiful hair, shrewd, keen, intelligent brown eyes and shapely, artistic hands, she had a fund of wit and humor quite man-like, which took me quite by storm. Best of all, she displayed excellent, though conservative, taste in dressing, which was a relief after Paris and Monte Carlo and the ultra-smart drawing rooms of London.

"I trust I see an unalienated American?" I observed as Mrs. Richards brought her forward, encouraged by her brisk, quizzical smile.

"You do, you do," she replied smartly, "as yet. Nothing has happened to my Americanism except Italy, and that is only a second love. I just happen to be a bit crazy about Italy by now."

She had a laugh which was a little hoarse and jerky but very pleasant and agreeable nevertheless. I felt the impact of a strong, vital temperament, self-willed, self-controlled, intensely eager and ambitious.

"And where did you come from last?" I inquired, as Mrs. Richards smiled and walked away. "I see a long conversation between you two," she called back.

"Florence," she replied cheerfully and with a buoyant smile, "and before that Munich, and before that Leipzig and Dresden."

"And are you going to be here long?"

"Oh, I don't know. I'm just taking my time, ambling about. I thought I'd stay here a month or so, if I felt like it, and then I thought I'd step along to Naples and maybe from there to Algiers or Gibraltar. I have a kind-of-a-sort-of-a-notion that I'd like Gibraltar," she said with that condescending, patronizing, slangy self-sufficiency of the American, which (to me) is not irritating but merely suggestive of the exuberance and youth of America. She went into an enthusiastic explanation of why she thought she would like Gibraltar—the hot, hard boniness of it all. Sometime, if not on this trip, she was going to Spain to stay a whole year, and on some other occasion, God willing, to Egypt. She made no mention of her husband, whom, as she must have known, I knew of by reputation at least, which was sufficient indication to me that she was not happily mated. I wondered at once, seeing that she was truly such a worthwhile personage, what the trouble could be.

We changed seats to another corner of the room after a while, seeing that we were getting along so swimmingly, and there our mutual social and intellectual proclivities were manifested. Intellectually she suited me to a T. She was intensely interested in history, which is one of my great failings and delights. She liked absolutely vital, unillusioned biography such as that of Jean Jacques Rousseau's *Confessions*, Cellini's *Diary* and the personal reminiscences of various court favorites in different lands. She was interested in some plays but cared little for fiction, which I take to be commendable. Her great passion at the moment, she told me, was the tracing out in all its ramifications of the history and mental attitude of Cesare Borgia, which I look upon as a remarkable passion for a woman. It takes a strong, healthy, clear-thinking temperament to enjoy the mental vagaries of the Borgias—father, son and daughter. She had conceived a sincere admiration for the courage, audacity, passion and directness of action of Cesare, to say nothing of the lymphatic pliability and lure of Lucrezia and the strange, philosophic anarchism and despotic individualism of their father, Alexander VI.

I wonder how much the average reader knows of the secret history of the Borgias. It is as modern as desire, as strange as the strangest ramifications of which the mind is capable. I may as well relate it, for it indicates so well the best of Mrs. Armstrong's intellectuality. She was "up" on the literature of the Borgias, to say nothing of the majority of other distinguished Italian families, the Cenci, Medici, Barbarini, Farnese, Sforzas and the like. She admired their subtlety, craft, artistic insight, political and social wisdom, their governing ability and, as much as anything, their money-getting and money-keeping capacities. The raw practicality of the Italian family thrilled her.

To get the true significance of all this, the history of the Borgia family will have to be outlined accurately. Rodrigo Lanzol, a Spaniard who afterwards assumed the name of Rodrigo Borgia because his maternal uncle of that name was fortunate enough to succeed to the papacy as Calixtus III and could do him many good turns afterwards, succeeded himself to the papacy by bribery and other outrages under the title of Alexander VI. That was August 10, 1492. Before that, however, as nephew to Calixtus III he had been made bishop, cardinal and vice-chancellor of the Church solely because he was a relative and favored by his uncle; and all this before he was thirty-five. He had proceeded to Rome, established himself with many mistresses at his call in a magnificent palace, and at the age of thirty-seven, his uncle Calixtus III having died, was reprimanded by Pius II, the new pope, for his riotous and adulterous life. By 1470, when he was forty-nine, after having had many other mistresses, he took as his favorite Vanozza dei Cattani, the former wife of three different husbands. By the very charming Vanozza he had four children, all of whom he prized highly—Giovanni, afterwards Duke of Gandia, born 1474; Cesare, 1476; Lucrezia, 1480; Geoffreddo or Giuffré, born 1481 or 1482. There were other children—Girolamo, Isabella and Pier Luigi, whose parentage on the mother's side is uncertain; and still another child, Laura, whom he came by via Giulia Farnese, the daughter of a famous family of that name who was his mistress after he had tired of Vanozza some years later. Meanwhile his children had grown up or were fairly well grown when he became pope, which opened the most astonishing chapter of this strange family.

Alexander, as Mrs. Armstrong pointed out to me in all her brilliant talks, was a curious compound of paternal affection, lust, love of gold, love of women, vanity and other things. He certainly was fond of his children, or he would not have torn Italy with dissension in order to advantage them in their fortunes. His career is the most ruthless and the weirdest I have ever heard of.

He was no sooner pope (about April 1493) than he proposed to carve out careers for his family, his favored children by his favorite mistress. In 1492, the same year he was made pope, he made Cesare, his sixteen-year-old son studying at Pisa, a cardinal, showing the state of the papacy in those days. He proposed to marry his daughter Lucrezia well and, having the year before, when she was only eleven, betrothed her to Don Cherubin de Centelles, a Spaniard, he broke it at once and had Lucrezia married by proxy to Don Gasparo de Procida, son of the Count of Aversa, a man of much more importance, who, he thought, could advance her own and his fortunes.

Italy, however, was in a very divided and disorganized state. There was a king of Naples, a duke of Venice, a duke of Milan, a separate state life at Pisa, Genoa, Florence and elsewhere. In order to build himself up and become very powerful, and in order to give great preferment to each of his sons, some of these states had to be conquered and controlled; and so the old gentleman, without conscience and without mercy except as suited his whim, was for playing politics, making war, exercising treachery, murdering, poisoning, persuading, bribing—anything and everything—to obtain his ends. He must have been well thought of as a man of his word, for when he had made a deal with Charles VIII of France to assist him in invading and conquering Naples, the king demanded and obtained Cesare, Alexander's son, aged twenty-one, as a hostage for faithful performance of agreement. He had not taken him very far, however, before the young devil escaped and returned to Rome, where subsequently his father, finding it necessary to turn against the king of France, did so, although without any advantage to himself to any extent.

But to continue. While his father was politicking and trafficking in this way for the benefit of himself and his dear family, young Cesare was beginning to develop a few thoughts and tendencies of his own. Alexander VI was planning to create fiefs or dukedoms out of the papal states and the kingdom of Naples and give them to his eldest son, Giovanni, and his youngest, Giuffré. Cesare would have none of this. He saw himself as a young cardinal being left out in the cold. Besides, there was a cause of friction between him and his brother Giovanni over the affections of their youngest brother Giuffré's wife, Sancha. They were both sharing the latter's favors, and so one day, in order to clear matters up and teach his father (whose favorite he was) where to bestow his favors and so that Cesare might have Sancha all to himself—the mere presence of his brother not mattering—he murdered his brother Giovanni. The latter's body, after a sudden and strange absence, was found in the Tiber, knife-marked, and all was local uproar until the young cardinal was suspected, when matters quieted down and nothing more was thought of it. There was also thought to be some rivalry between Cesare and Giovanni over the affections for their sister, Lucrezia, which is now, however, considered to be doubtful.

After this magnificent evidence of ability, the way was clear for Cesare. He was at once (July 1497) sent as papal legate to Naples to crown Frederick of Aragon king of Naples, and it was there that he met Carlotta, the daughter of the king, and wanted to marry her. She would have none of him. "What, marry that priest, that bastard of a priest!" she is alleged to have said; and that settled the matter. This may have had something to do with Cesare's desire to get out of holy orders and return to civil life, for the next year (1498) he asked leave of the papal consistory not to be a cardinal any longer and was granted this privilege "for the good of his soul." He then undertook the pleasant task as papal legate of carrying to Louis XII of France the pope's bull annulling Louis's marriage with Jeanne of France in order that he might marry Anne of Brittany. He proceeded there in the utmost magnificence, encountering meanwhile Carlotta of Naples, who refused him again. On this journey he met Charlotte d'Albret, sister of the king of Navarre, who accepted him and whom he married. He was given the duchy of Valentinois for his gracious service to Louis XII and, loaded with honors, returned to Rome in order to further his personal fortunes with his father's aid.

In the meanwhile there were a number of small principalities in Romagna, a territory near Milan, which his father, Alexander VI, was viewing with a covetous eye. One of these was controlled by Giovanni Sforza, lord of Pesaro; at a time when Alexander wanted the strength of Milan against the subtle machinations of the king of Naples, he caused Lucrezia, his daughter, then only thirteen years of age, to marry Sforza in 1493, her union with the count Aversa having by this time been severed. Some few years later, when he needed Lucrezia in order to marry her to someone else, he annulled this marriage on the grounds of impotence on the part of her husband, causing the latter to go up and down Italy declaring that it was false and offering to prove to anybody's satisfaction that it was not so if he were given a chance. But to continue. Cesare needing an estate and the king of Naples having become friendly or Alexander VI having won the friendship of the king of Naples, Alexander decided to proceed against the princelings of Romagna and confiscate their property. Cesare was tolled off as general to accomplish this for himself, being provided men and means. Young Sforza, who had married Lucrezia, found himself in a treacherous position—his own brother-in-law, with the assistance of his father-in-law, plotting against his life—and fled with his wife, the fair Lucrezia, aged fifteen, to Pesaro. There he was fought by Cesare who, however, not having sufficient troops, was checked for the time being and returned to Rome. A year or so later, *Papa* Alexander being in a gentle frame of mind—it was Christmas and he desired all his children about him—invited them all home, including Lucrezia and her husband. Then followed a series of magnificent *fêtes* and exhibitions in honor of all this at Rome, and the family, including the uncertain son-in-law, husband of Lucrezia, seemed to be fairly well united in bonds of peace.

Unfortunately, however, a little later (1497) *il Papa*'s mood changed again. He was now, after some intermediate quarrels, once more friendly with the king of Naples and decided that Sforza was no longer a fit husband for Lucrezia. Then came the annulment of this marriage on the ground of impotence and the re-marriage of Lucrezia to Alphonso of Aragon, duke of Bisceglie, aged eighteen, handsome, and a relative and favorite of the king of Naples. All was apparently peace and quiet once more along the Potomac, but alas, no sooner was this fairly begun than new complications arose. The pope thought he saw an opportunity to destroy the power of Naples as a rival with the aid of the king of France, Louis XII. He lent assistance to the latter, who came to invade Naples; and young Bisceglie, now fearing for his life at the hands of his treacherous father-in-law, deserted Rome and Lucrezia and fled. Louis XII proceeded against Naples. Spoleto fell, and eighteen-year-old Lucrezia, Bisceglie's wife, as representative of the pope was sent to receive the homage of Spoleto!

But the plot merely thickens. There comes a nice point in here, on which historians comment variously. Incest was the basis of all this. It was one time assumed, and Mrs. Armstrong from her reading seemed convinced of it, that Alexander, the father, was constantly having sexual relations with his daughter during all of these various shifts and was exceedingly fond of her on this score. Cesare was also a favorite recipient of her favors, adoring her incestuously. Father and son were rivals, then, for the affections and favors of the daughter-sister. To offset the affections of the son, the father had the daughter lure her husband Bisceglie back to Rome. From all accounts he was very much in love with his pawn of a wife, who was beautiful but dangerous because of her charms and the manner in which she was coveted by others. In 1499, when he was twenty and Cesare twenty-three, he was lured back; and the next year, because of Cesare's jealousy of his monopoly of his own wife (Cesare being perhaps denied his usual freedom), Bisceglie was stabbed while going up the steps of the papal palace by Cesare Borgia, his brother-in-law, and that in the presence of his father-in-law, Alexander VI, the pope of Rome. According to one account, Mrs. Armstrong told me, on sight of Cesare jumping out from behind a column, Alphonso sought refuge behind Alexander, the pope, who spread out his purple robe to protect him, through which Cesare drove his knife into the bosom of his brother-in-law. The dear old father and father-in-law was severely shocked. He was depressed and almost prostrated. He shook his head dismally. The wound was not fatal, however. Bisceglie was removed to the house of a cardinal nearby, where he was attended by his wife, Lucrezia, and his sister-in-law, Sancha, wife of Giuffré, both of whom he apparently feared a little, for they were compelled first to partake of all food presented in order to prove that it was not poisoned. In this house—in this sick chamber doorway—suddenly and unexpectedly one day there appeared the figure of Cesare. The ensuing scene (with Lucrezia and Sancha present) was not given. Bisceglie was stabbed in his bed and this time died. Was the crime avenged? Not at all. This was *Papa* Alexander's own dominion. This was a family affair, and father was very fond of Cesare, so the matter was hushed up.

Witness the interesting final chapters. Cesare went off in October 1500 to fight the princes in Romagna once more, among whom are Giovanni Sforza, one of Lucrezia's ex-husbands. In July 1501, Alexander left the papal palace in Rome to fight the Colonna, one of the two powerful families of Rome, with the assistance of the other powerful family, the Orsini. In his absence Lucrezia, his beloved, was acting pope! On January 1 (or thereabouts), 1501, Lucrezia was betrothed to Alphonso, son and heir to Ercole d'Este, whose famous villa near Rome is still to be seen. Neither Alphonso nor his father was anxious for the union, but *Papa* Alexander, pope of Rome, had set his heart on it. By bribes and threats he brought about a proxy marriage, celebrated with great pomp at St. Peter's—Alphonso not being present. In January 1502, Lucrezia arrived in the presence of her new husband, who fell seriously in love with her. Her fate was now to settle down, and no further tragedies befell on account of her except one. A certain Ercole Strozzi, an Italian noble, appeared on the scene and fell violently in love with her. She was only twenty-three or twenty-four. Alphonso d'Este, her new husband, became violently jealous and murdered Ercole. Result: further peace until her thirty-ninth year, during which period she had four children by Alphonso, three boys and one girl. She died in 1519.

As for brother Cesare, he was, unfortunately, leading a more checkered career. On December 21, 1502, when he was only twenty-six, as a general fighting the allied minor princes in Romagna, he caused to be strangled in his headquarters at Senigallia Vitellozzo Viletti and Oliveralto da Fermo, two princelings who with others had conspired against him some time before at Perugia. Seeing him getting stronger, they had been so foolish as to endeavor to placate him by capturing Senigallia for him from their allies and presenting it to him and allowing themselves to be lured to his house by protestations of friendship. Result: strangulation.

On August 18, 1503, father Borgia, Pope Alexander VI, a charming society figure, a polished man, a lover of the chase, a patron of the arts, for whom Raphael, Michelangelo and Bramante worked, died. He and Cesare had fallen desperately sick at the same time of a fever. When Cesare recovered sufficiently to attend to his affairs, things were already in a bad way. The cardinals were plotting to seat a pope unfriendly to the Borgias. The Spanish cardinals on whom he relied did not prove friendly, and he lost his control. The funds which *Papa* Borgia was wont to supply for his campaigns were no longer forthcoming. Pope Julius II, succeeding to the throne, took away the territories assigned him by his father "for the honor of recovering what our predecessors have wrongfully alienated." In May 1504, after he had gone to Naples on a safe conduct from the Spanish governor of that city, he was arrested and sent to Spain, where he was thrown in prison. At the end of two years he managed to escape and fled to the court of his brother-in-law, the king of Navarre, who permitted him to aid in besieging the castle of a refractory subject. Here, on March 12, 1507, while Lucrezia was peacefully residing with her spouse, he was killed.

I have given such a feeble outline of this charming Renaissance idyll that I am ashamed of it. Mixed in with it were constant murders or poisonings of wealthy cardinals and the confiscation of their estates whenever cash for the prosecution of Cesare's wars or the protection of papal properties were needed. The uxorious and child-loving old pope was exceedingly nonchalant about these little matters of human life. When he died, there was a fight over his coffin between priests of different factions and mercenaries belonging to Cesare Borgia. The coffin being too short, his body was jammed down in it, minus his miter, and finally upset. Think of so much ambition coming to such a shameful end. He achieved his desire, however. He wrote his name large, if not in fame, at least in infamy. He lived in astonishing grandeur and splendor. He had the curious affection of his children, and he died immensely rich—and as pope. The fair Lucrezia stands out as a strange chemical magnet of disaster. To love her was fear, disappointment or death. And it was she and her brother Cesare who particularly interested Mrs. Armstrong, although the aged Alexander amused her.

It was of all this that we talked, only vaguely and uncertainly at first until we came to an intellectual understanding, and then delightfully and eagerly as we found that we were mutual students of the vagaries of this strange phantasmagoria called human life, in which to be dull is to be a bond slave and to be wise is to be a mad philosopher, knowing neither right from wrong nor black from white.

CHAPTER LII

The character of this conversation was very liberal, as may be imagined. I did not know it at the time that Mrs. Armstrong was an earnest student of psychology, a reasoner of no mean ability, a woman who before her difficulties with her husband had aided much in the construction and staging of his plays. She was truly a brilliant conversationalist and fascinated me by her endless jesting.

"I have always been interested in *Papa* Alexander's easy, generous attitude toward his children," she observed once, "He grieved a little to think his son should stab his son-in-law in his presence, but was philosophic. Bearing up very well, thank you, after a day or so, dear old soul."

She fixed me with an amused, intelligent eye.

"I know," I replied. "There is no sounding the depths of adaptability, pliability, acceptation in nature. It will do anything." We turned to the fair Lucrezia, and she declared she was fascinated by what must have been the wonder of this woman's personality, the chemic, distracting poison of it. Cesare's bitter ambitions, his mad rivalry both with his sister's husbands and with their own father for her affection were also the basis of strange, moody enthusiasm in Mrs. Armstrong. The Borgia family obviously held her in a tether.

This conversation, with side references to Munich, New York, Dresden, Leipzig and England, where she had been, lasted until nearly midnight. She had been scheduled to take part in a set at whist, but she lost her place. We palavered enthusiastically, finding our moods and points of view in the main identical, and then when Mrs. Richards returned discontinued for the night. I saw at once that in her I had someone who would make my stay here very pleasant indeed, with whom I could go about and discuss many things with which she was already familiar.

It so turned out. Together we visited the Borghese and Barberini palaces, the Villa Doria, the Villa Umberto, the Villa d'Este and the Appian Way. We paid a return visit to the Colosseum and idled together in the gardens of the Pincio, the paths of the Gianicolo, the gardens of the Vatican and along the Tiber. It was a pleasure to step into some old court of a palace with her where the walls were encrusted with fragments of monuments, inscriptions, portions of sarcophagi and the like found on the place, or in excavating, and set in the walls to preserve them—and hear her comment on the way the spirit of life builds shells and casts them off. She was not in the least morbid. The horrors and cruelties of lust and ambition held no terrors for her. She liked life as a spectacle.

The first Sunday I was in Rome I began my local career with a visit to the church of Santa Maria Maggiore, which faces the Via Cavour not far from the Continental Hotel where I was stopping, and afterwards to Santa Prassede close beside it. After Canterbury, Amiens, Pisa and St. Peter's, I confess churches needed to be of great distinction to interest me much; but this church, not so divinely harmonious, exteriorly speaking, left me breathless with its incrustations of marbles, bronzes, carvings and gold and silver inlay. There is a kind of beauty or charm or at least physical excitation in contemplating sheer gorgeousness which I cannot withstand, even when my sense of proportion and my reason are offended, and this church had that. Many of the churches in Rome have just this and nothing more. At least what else they have is not of sufficient distinction to warrant enthusiasm.

This particular church is such an excellent example of the hodgepodge of history, wealth and religious illusion or chicanery that make up so many of them that I like to think of it. In the first place, it is very old, dating from 352 A.D., and the Virgin herself had indicated just where the basilica in her honor was to be built by having a small, private fall of snow which covered or outlined the exact dimensions of which the church was to be. I was interested to learn that they had here five boards of the original manger at Bethlehem enclosed in an urn of silver and crystal which is exposed in the sacristy on Christmas Eve and placed over the high altar on Christmas Day; here were the tombs and chapels of Sixtus V and Paul V and Clement VIII of the Borghese family and, too, a chapel of the Sforza family. Nevertheless, the hodgepodge of history, wealth, illusion and contention, to say nothing of religious and social chicanery which go to make up a church of this kind, is a little wearisome, not to say brain-achy, when contemplated en masse.

The churches of Rome are full of just such religious junk, magnificently encrusted as is displayed here—tombs of forgotten cardinals, families, saints, relics and the like. I was amused by the story of how Gregory VII, seeing Sixtus V—then only a cardinal—beginning the construction of his magnificent chapel here, suspended his allowance on the ground that he must be a rich man to incur such an expense. Some other gentleman by the name of Fontana came forward and placed at the cardinal's disposal all of his savings, which resulted in his receiving fat privileges later when the cardinal became pope. In this same chapel are reliefs commemorating the battle of Lepanto and Pope Pius V's sending assistance to Charles IX for the persecution of the Protestants—glory be. It is such details as this that make up the sacred memories.

I strolled about admiring the marbles, the handwork, the endless artificery of almost endless artists, but not a thrill of delight did I get out of the general design or its proportions or its artistic restraint or fineness of feeling. Rich, yes, but oh, my! It was the same with almost every other church of importance in Rome that I visited, outside of St. Paul Without The Walls. On different days and in different moods I visited St. John Lateran, Santa Pudenziana, Santa Maria in Cosmedin, San Lorenzo fuori le Mura, Santa Croce in Gerusalemme, San Sebastiano, Santa Maria in Trastevere, Santa Maria in Monte Santo and others, and except insofar as they commemorated the growth and early phases of Christianity, they were the veriest trash. It seemed to me toward the end that a good portion of my time had been spent in stepping in and out of churches contemplating gaudy interiors; with the exception of St. Paul's, which I described, and St. Peter's, which is important in its immensity and gorgeousness run mad, I brought away nothing worthwhile. The guidebooks are full of intricate details, hundreds of pages of them, relating to saints, popes, relics, marbles, family histories, battles, miracles and the like, but when all is said and done, what of it? The Roman ideal is much more important to me than the Christian ideal which replaced it, and good art was replaced by bad illusions. One might as well try to recollect all the glens, hollows, trees, flowers and roads of a summer vacation—that would be better, for those in a general way you might remember. But these churches! Unless you are especially interested in a pope or a saint or a miracle or a picture or a monument or an artist, they are nothing save intricate jewel-boxes—nothing more.

St. John Lateran is a gorgeous structure, homely on the outside, with endless Italian beggars at the doors who fight among themselves for the privilege of opening the door or holding back the leather curtain in order to gain the penny which you may give them, but it is not beautiful. Like Santa Maria Maggiore, and even more so, it is an incrustation of great magnificence. It has a long history which any Baedeker will give you: all the details of architectural changes since the time of Constantine; the fact that it was once the site of the residence of the Emperor Marcus Aurelius; that previous to 1870 the popes were crowned here, etc. Its principal charm to me was that it stood on a rise, commanding a lovely view of the Alban hills, that a portion of the old Roman Wall ran outside it and that some cypress trees were in evidence. The present-day Italians of the lower walks have the pleasant habit of making a latrine of every nook and cranny, which spoils your mood before you enter many structures, but beyond that they are well enough. As usual my mouth was agape at the richness of the interior, the astonishing columns, tapestries, paintings, statuary and jeweled altars and chapels, "each one finer than the other." The private burying chapels and tombs of the Corsini, Torlonia and Massimo families are here, to say nothing of a charming cloister, one of the loveliest I have seen.

It seems to be a fashion in Rome for a cardinal who has become rich or been made pope to erect himself a chapel in connection with one of these magnificent churches and encrust it with marbles and rare stones. If you look into any of these chapels of famous families, you are sure to find that one or two of their members at least were popes or cardinals—at the very lowest archbishops, but cardinals and popes as a rule. They are commemorated by magnificent, almost gaudy, effigies of Pontifex Maximus in trailing robes, their miters on, praying at their own tombs or sitting or standing lost in deep thought. It lends great dignity to a family, of course, to have a chapel of this kind and a shrine. I can see the vanity of the younger generations of the Torlonia, Corsini and others, strutting out to take the Roman air, adequately conscious that one of their ancestors was a pope and that they have a magnificent private chapel in St. John Lateran. Dear me! The minor churches such as the Scala Santa, Santa Croce in Gerusalemme, Santa Sabina and the like that have only sacred relics are not so interesting.

I had one interesting half-hour in Santa Croce in Gerusalemme, for here, after giving a lira to as greasy a priest or friar as you would wish to see, I was shown fragments of the true cross, some nails and thorns, a portion of the Title with its trilingual inscription from the same place and some sacred soil from Jerusalem. All these things, with the exception of the sacred soil, were rediscovered in the apse in 1492 enclosed in a leaden box and are now still viewed reverently by the faithful. There were two ladies in the dusky chapel with me when these things were shown, and they crossed themselves solemnly. I felt a little ashamed of my idle curiosity in wishing to look at this trash. But I suppose it is something to see superstition going on in this way, enacting its old roles, which now, interestingly enough, are crumbling to decay. The world will have to give birth to a new set of superstitions if it is to entertain itself in this fashion much longer, for the old ones are losing their force. As I stood looking at this priest holding out his dusty relics and mumbling endless prayers in a bored fashion, I could not help thinking how his job, which once must have been very sacred and important, was now a cheap, discountenanced service. He personally could not respect himself nor his wares nor those who took them seriously, and so there he stood, obtaining money under false pretenses, a self-convicted charlatan with a half-baked, poorly-paying company as an audience. The fact that these relics will be shown to all and sundry, Jew and Protestant alike without let or hindrance, for a lira or whatever you choose to give, is a fair indication of how low the Christian ideal has fallen. We still cling fatuously to a few shreds and patches of what was once an unpunctured theory, but since Locke and Darwin and the advance of modern historical criticism, its decay has been swift. We need no new illusion for the masses, if I judge aright, though I fear me much that in the vagaries of nature we are apt to get them.

For the first five or six days I bestirred myself—sometimes alone, sometimes with Mrs. Richards, sometimes with Mrs. Armstrong—following a certain Signor Tani, who was delivering peripatetic lectures at the principal places of interest in Rome. This is a curious development of the modern city, for so numerous are the travelers and so great their interest in the history of Rome that they gladly pay the three to twelve lire each which is charged by the various lecturers for their discussions and nearby trips. There was a Nashville, Tennessee, chicken-and-egg merchant who, with his wife, was staying at this hotel and who was making the matter of seeing Rome quite as much of a business as that of chickens and eggs in Tennessee. He and his wife were delightfully naive and amusing people, and I think I will describe them.

He was a man of only medium height, dark, pale, neat, and possessed of that innate courtesy, reserve, large-minded fairness and lively appreciation—within set convictions—which is so characteristic of the native, reasonably successful American. We are such innocent, pure-minded Greeks—most of us Americans. In the face of such tawdry vulgarity and vileness as comprises the underworld café life of Paris, or before such a spectacle of accentuated craft, lust, brutality and greed as that presented by the Borgias, a man such as my chicken-merchant friend or any other American of his type, of whom there are millions, would find himself utterly nonplussed. It would be so much beyond his ken or intention that I question whether he would see or understand it at all if it were taking place before his very eyes. There is something so childlike and pure about the attitude of many strong, able Americans that I marvel sometimes that they do as well as they do. Perhaps this very innocence is their salvation. I could not have told this chicken merchant and his wife, for instance, anything of the subtleties of the underworld of Paris and Monte Carlo as I encountered them, and if I had, he would not have believed me; he would have recoiled from it all as a burned child would recoil from fire. We, as a nation, still believe firmly in the home as it is constituted, and in the wisdom and duty of having children and raising them, and in the duty of a man to his neighbors and to God and the government. This man did. He was as simple and interesting and practical as a man could be, and yet so thoroughly efficient that at the age of forty-five he had laid by a competence—perhaps as much as fifty or a hundred thousand dollars—

and was off on a three-year tour of the world. He was going to Naples from Rome, thence to Sicily, Algiers, Egypt, Palestine, India and so on. He had come south through France and Italy from Holland and Belgium, and if I recall right he had been in England—London, anyhow.

Mrs. Chicken Merchant was a large woman—very stout, very fair, very cautious of her thoughts and her conduct, thoroughly sympathetic and well-meaning. Before leaving her native town, she told me, she had inaugurated a small library, the funds for which she had helped collect. Occasionally she was buying engravings of famous historic buildings, such as the Colosseum and the Temple of Vesta, which would eventually grace the walls of the library. They felt that they were educating themselves and that they would return better citizens, more useful to their country, for this exploration of the ancient world. They had been going each day, morning and afternoon, to some lecture or ancient ruin, and after I came there they would seek me out of an evening and tell me what they had seen.

I took great satisfaction in this, because I really liked them for their naive point of view and their thoroughly kindly and whole-hearted interest in life. It flattered me to think that I was so thoroughly acceptable to them and that we should get along so well together. Frequently they invited me to their table to dinner—although it was all the same to me and to them, since the food was included in the day rate of the hotel—but on these occasions my friend would open a bottle of wine, concerning which he had learned something since he had come abroad, and in his innocent way he liked to indicate that he knew it was very exceptional.

"I would have given fifteen cents if you had been with me today over at this here Rag Fair," he said to me one evening very gaily. "Two of these Italians came pretty near having a fight with each other over something my wife was doing. I want to tell you it looked like the real thing to me for a minute."

"Why, what was the trouble, Mr. Brantwood?" I inquired.

"Well, my wife was looking at a jet necklace over here in this Rag Fair somewhere, and the man at the next stand signaled to her that he had a better one, and the first fellow saw him. Well, I want to tell you there was something to pay right then and there. They had to get the police. I thought they were going to stab each other and us, too. I want to tell you we made our way out of there pretty quick, although I told the officer that if he wanted me to come as a witness next morning I'd do it. I expect, you know, that that first fellow will stab the other one sometime if he don't look out. By George! I thought he was going to do it today!"

"Yes indeed," chimed in Mrs. Chicken Merchant cheerily, "I certainly thought we were in for a bad spell there for a minute. I liked that jet necklace, too. I think I'll go back tomorrow or next day and see if I can find it."

"Then you didn't get it?" I sympathized.

"No indeed. I was too frightened. I was glad enough to get out of there with my life."

"You want to look out for these Italians," I said. "They're a dangerous lot. They think all Americans are their just prey, and I don't wonder they stab each other over us."

Well, it was Mr. Brantwood who gave me a full description of the different Roman lecturers, their respective merits, their prices and what they had to show. They had already been to the Forum, the Palatine, the Colosseum and the House of Nero, St. Peter's, the Castle of St. Angelo, the Appian Way, the Catacombs and the Villa Frascati. They were just going to the Villa d'Este and to Ostia, the old seaport at the mouth of the Tiber. They were at great pains to get me to join the companies of Signor Tani who, they were convinced, was the best of them all. "He tells you something. He makes you see it just as it was. By George, when we were in the Colosseum you could just fairly see the lions marching out of these doors; and that House of Nero, as he tells about it, is one of the most wonderful things in the world."

I decided to join Signor Tani's classes at once and to see these sights under his guidance, thus saving myself the trouble of constantly looking them up in my Murray and Baedeker. Besides, the thought of trailing around in the company of a dozen or more sightseers, English and American, was interesting to me. I persuaded Mrs. Richards and Mrs. Armstrong to accompany me at different times, thus being amply provided with suitable companionship.

I must say that in spite of the commonplaceness of the idea, my mornings and afternoons with Signor Tani and his company of sightseers proved as delightful as anything else that befell me in Rome. He was a most interesting person, born and raised, as I learned, at Tivoli near the Villa d'Este, where his father controlled a small inn and livery stable. He was very stocky, very dark, very ruddy and very active. He always reminded me of the Japanese version of the American word industrious—that is, "industorious." Whenever we came to the appointed rendezvous where his lecture was to begin, he invariably arrived swinging his coattails, glancing smartly around with his big black eyes, rubbing and striking his hands in a friendly manner, and giving every evidence of taking a keen interest in his work. He was always polite and courteous without being officious, and never for a moment, so far as I saw, either dull or ponderous. He knew his subject thoroughly of course; but what was much better, he had an eye and a nose for the dramatic and the spectacular, so that every now and then some delicious fact would be brought out which would set his little audience agape and cause them to exclaim in wonder. I shall never forget how in the center of the Forum Romanum he lifted the cap from the ancient manhole that opens into the Cloaca Maxima and allowed us to look in upon the walls of that great sewer that remains as it was built before the dawn of Roman history. Then he exclaimed dramatically: "Now, the water that Caesar and the emperors took their baths in no doubt flowed through here just as the water of the Roman bathtubs might today. It is over 2500 years old today and is built to last as much longer," he explained, and I noticed every face present lighten with interest.

On the Palatine, when we were looking at the site of the palace of Elagabalus, he told how that weird worthy had a certain well, paved at the bottom with beautiful mosaic, in order that he might leap down upon it and thus commit suicide, and how he afterwards changed his mind—which won a humorous smile from some of those present and from others a blank look of astonishment. In the House of Nero, in one of those dark underhill chambers, he told how once Nero had invited some of his friends to dine and when they were well along in their feast and somewhat intoxicated, no doubt, it began to rain rose leaves from the ceiling. Nothing but delighted cries of approval was heard for this artistic thought until the rose leaves became an inch thick on the floor and then two and three, and when they became four or five inches thick the guests tried the doors. They were locked and sealed. Then the shower continued until they were a foot deep, two feet deep, three feet deep and the tables were covered. Later the guests had to climb on tables and chairs to save themselves from their rosy bath, but when they had climbed this high they could climb no higher, for the walls were smooth and the room was thirty feet deep. By the time the leaves were ten feet deep, the guests were completely covered, but the shower continued until the smothering weight of them ended all life.

No one of Signor Tani's little wide-mouthed company seemed to question whether this was plausible or not, and one American standing next to me exclaimed, "Well, I'll be switched!" My doubting mind set to work to figure out how I could have overcome this difficulty if I had been in the room, and in my mind I had all the associated guests busy tramping down rose leaves in order to make the quantity required as large as possible. My idea was that I could tire Nero out on the rose leaf question. The thought of tramping Romans cheered me greatly. In the crypt of St. Peter's, Signor Tani described how Otto the Great and some then reigning pope, meeting each other in the basilica which Otto had unwarrantably invaded, fell to fighting and rolled all around the floor. I was amused to note that this little historic set-to won only grins of amusement from all those present, including several American and English old maids and a most pompous-looking, new-rich American who was present with his three rosy sons.

In the Catacombs Signor Tani chose to tell how some venturous traveler had been lost for days in those labyrinthine paths—which caused all his little flock to gather close around him. And he it was who in the Castle of St. Angelo described how Beatrice Cenci murdered her father and how Benvenuto Cellini effected his very dramatic escape. Signor Tani had a little knack of astonishing his American guests by using current American slang, such as "He was from Missouri and they had to show him," "What do you know about that?" and phrases of that sort. At one time he had lived in New York, being connected with some Commission concern there, and of late years, he told me, he had developed quite a demand for his services in the summertime, when there are few travelers in the city of Rome, as a guide to American families or parties traveling in other parts of Europe—Norway, Holland and elsewhere. It was in Hadrian's Villa that he told the story of the boy who, when asked by the priest who were the four apostles, replied that the four apostles were three, Luke and John.

After my first morning with Signor Tani I decided to take his whole course; and following dutifully along behind him, listening to his interesting and good-natured disquisitions, I think perhaps I gathered more of the wonderful atmosphere than I could have gathered in any other way, unless I had cared to do extensive reading. Oh, those delightful mornings and afternoons in the Forum, on the Palatine, in the Catacombs, on the Appian Way and in the villas at Frascati and Tivoli! Rome is an amazing storehouse—the most wonderful and dramatic in all Europe. There is more here to thrill the intellectual and poetic-minded, I should say, than almost anywhere else. I shall never forget how clearly and succinctly the crude early beginnings and characteristics of Christianity came home to me as I walked in the Catacombs, seeing the wretched little graves hidden away in order that they might not be desecrated and the underground churches where they might worship free from molestation and persecution. I am sure that from all my historic reading about Rome I never got so clear a notion of the congested character of the early political and social life there as I did in hearing a discussion of the narrowness of the streets and the height of the buildings as we walked in the Forum. Most of those noble structures and temples which we see depicted in numerous engravings hung in American homes and libraries were scarcely fifteen or twenty feet apart, facing the winding streets in which they stood. The Sacra Via would not make a good-sized American alley, and the temple of Augustus and the House of the Vestals must have been quite hidden by the structures crowded so closely upon them.

On the Palatine the fact that almost endless palaces were built one on top of the other—the old palace leveled by means of the sledge and the crowbar and the new one erected upon the smoothed-over space—is easily demonstrated. They find the remains of different ruins in different layers as they dig down, coming eventually to the early sanctuaries of the kings and the federated tribes. It is far more interesting to walk through the House of Nero accompanied by someone who loves it, and who is interested in it, and who by fees to the state servitors has smoothed the way, so that the ancient forgotten chambers are properly lighted for you, than it is to go alone. And to hear a friendly human voice expatiating on the probable arrangement of the ancient culinary department and how it was all furnished is worthwhile. I know that the wonder and interest of the series of immense, dark rooms which now underlay a hill covered by trees and grass, but which formerly were exposed to the light of day before the dust and incrustation of centuries had been heaped upon them, came upon me with great force because of these human explanations; and the room in which in loneliness and darkness for centuries stood the magnificent group of Laocoön and the porphyry vase, now in the Vatican, until some adventuring students happened to put a foot through a hole, thrilled me as much as though I had come upon them myself.

Until you go in this way to the site of the Circus Maximus, the Baths of Caracalla, the ruins of Hadrian's Villa, the Castle of St. Angelo, the Forum, the Palatine and the Colosseum, you can have no true conception of that ancient world. When you realize, by standing on the ground and contemplating these ancient ruins and their present fragments, that the rumored immensity of them in their heyday and youth is really true, you enjoy a thrill of wonder; and if you are of a morbid turn, you experience sad speculations as to the drift of life. I cannot tell you how the mosaics from the palace of Germanicus on the Palatine affected me, or how strange I felt when the intricacies of the houses of Caligula and Tiberius were made clear. To walk through the narrow halls which they trod, to know truly that they ruled in terror and with the force of murder, that Caligula waylaid and assaulted and killed, for his personal entertainment, in these narrow alleys which were then the only streets, and where torches borne by hand furnished the only light, is something. A vision of the hugeness and audacity of Hadrian's Villa, which now stretches apparently, one would say, for miles, the vast majority of its rooms still unexcavated and containing what treasures heaven only knows, is one of the strangest of human experiences.

I looked in wonder at this vast series of rooms, envying the power, the subtlety and the genius which could command it. Truly it is unbelievable, one of those things which stagger the imagination even when presented. You can hardly believe that even an emperor of Rome would build so beautifully and so vastly. At the Villa d'Este a conception of the grandeur of medieval Italy returned, and in the Castle of St. Angelo all the deviltry and ambition of time seems to be concentrated. Rome is so vast in its suggestion that it is really useless to apostrophize. At times I felt as though I must shout for joy, and at other times that I must cry to think that things and times so truly wonderful should have completely gone. "Where are the snows of yesteryear?" asked Villon gaily. "Where are the palaces and the magnificences of Rome?" you will ask yourself over and over. That vast empire that stretched from India to the Arctic was surely fittingly represented here. And while we may rival the force and subtlety and genius and imagination of these men in our day, we will not truly outstrip them. Mind was theirs—vast ardent imagination; and if they achieved crudely it was because the world was still young and the implements and materials of life were less understood. Given a Caesar, a Nero, a Galba, a Tiberius today, we should soon see. Perhaps they would do as forcefully and as subtly. If so, the world might see another Rome. If so, the world would once more stand in awe and amazement. They were the great ones—the Romans. We must still learn from them.

CHAPTER LIII

In passing I should pay my respects to the palaces and villas of Rome, for while there remain in many cases only traces of the one hundred and one palaces and sixty-two villas, there are sufficient perfect specimens of at least the villas of the High Renaissance to give one a sense of that exquisite taste and noble superiority of mood which is purely Italian. It does not matter that the founders of these were in their day considered capricious upstarts or that, like the Barberini, the Farnese, the Borgias and others, they robbed their contemporaries, desecrated the ancient Roman ruins to secure marble and statuary or excavated without permission, using what they discovered to ornament their loggias, porticoes, courts and gardens. The essential thing, as one sees it all by sunlight or moonlight in that hard transparency which is the atmosphere of Rome, is that they had an appreciation of beauty as to location and a sense of dignity and more often of grandeur in their theories as to how it was their lives were to be lived.

You look in vain in the rest of Europe for that clear, artistic definiteness of intention, that perfection of form and detail which is here, one might almost say, a commonplace. Whether it is the imposing cornice of a Palazzo Farnese by Michelangelo or a capricious colonnade of Doric columns by Borromini or a terraced array of fountains such as that at the Villa d'Este, surrounded by ilex and cypress and avenued and colonnaded by box and lofty pines, it is one and the same. From the earliest Roman specimens of the villa to that which one encounters in the outlying sections of Rome today—

comparatively recently executed—it is all the same. In the Italian heart must exist an undying love of beauty, a taste in architecture that is almost faultless, a love of grandeur that is princely.

I stood in the grounds of the Villa Wolkonsky near the piazza that faces the Lateran and brooded over the picturesque arches of the Neronian aqueduct which still stand there and which, so my faithful Murray told me, carried the Claudian waters from the Porto Maggiore to the Caelian. The region is all but ruined now by a modern apartment house invasion, but there was enough left when I looked at it in passing to give me a sense of that exquisite Italian taste which has sufficient sense to understand the value of the old and to continue it gracefully with the new. In an older day, before the brown and whitish walls of apartment houses came to disturb it, this must have been a lovely spectacle across the wide greensward where avenues of box and ilex and those lovely arrangements of cypress in clumps and ordered processions lend so much natural grace and beauty.

This is equally true of the Villa Medici and the Villa Doria, where fragments and statues of an older life are deliciously visible and where a sarcophagus or a burial inscription are apt to be presented as a garden monument or set in a wall as a relief. More than once on a sunny afternoon, when the labors of sightseeing—particularly that of the interiors of museums—have palled, I have taken one of those light little vehicles that ply so gaily and cheaply about Rome and been carried out to the gate of some villa in order that I might restore my soul among its avenues and walks or sit upon some moss-tinted stone bench commanding a lovely fountain or an aisle of trees. With the wind stirring faintly in the trees, some far-distant hills or the Tiber over a space of grass in view with a fountain playing, or with effigies in stone casting the glamour of their whiteness upon the walks and the grass, there would come to me at times a sense of the perfection of romance when it is sheltered by greatness, fanned by the winds of fame, and made ornate by the wealth, the taste and the courage of hard and brilliant ability.

With the delicious effect which the gardens and villa interiors present, the cypress and the climate of Rome have much to do, for here they harmonize perfectly. It is so easy for a lover of beauty in gardening to set cypress trees to such perfect advantage here and to place fountains or statues or gateways against their dark background so as to achieve the last touch of artistry in arrangement. The Villa Medici presents as charming a picture of the spirit of the Italian villa as any—located on the site of the celebrated gardens of Lucullus, that wealthiest and most luxurious of the Republican nobles, and afterward the property of Messalina by right of murder, where she celebrated her marriage with Silius. On the same rise that constitutes the Pincian (one hundred and fifty feet), it commands a lovely view of the

Vatican in one direction and picturesque hills in another. The front of it, which looks into the garden, is set with a number of interesting fragments of ancient sculptures, including a curious relief of Horatius at the bridge, the Judgment of Paris, and representations of temples and other edifices of ancient Rome. This is so characteristic of the loggias, the porticoes and the gardens of the palaces and villas of modern construction, and even the cloisters of so many churches are given a villa-like grandeur by the use of these same elements: the ancient fragment, the cypress and the fountain.

I went one day with Mrs. Armstrong to visit the Villa d'Este at Tivoli, that seat of ancient splendor so enthusiastically sung by whores and virgins. The town now has a population of only thirteen thousand or a little over. The river Anio, which flows through it and across the Campagna to join the Tiber, here displays itself in the form of magnificent falls—some eleven in number—dropping perhaps a depth of three hundred and twenty feet, making a number of perfect rainbows which you see as you skirt the high road which encircles them on the ridge like a horseshoe and which are the chief ornament of a splendid landscape in which palaces, temples, the valley of the Campagna and the distant silvery windings of the Anio are a part. From here what is left of Hadrian's ten square miles of villa is faintly visible in the distance, and the lovely cypress-guarded terraces of the Villa d'Este are suggested.

Since first meeting, Mrs. Armstrong and I had become something more than good friends—due, as I have said, to our almost absolute agreement of disposition and our mutual interest in art and the psychology of life. We had been together, as I have said, to a number of the villas, including the Villa Medici and the Villa Doria Pamphili, and had talked over the virtues of the Italians in the respects that I have indicated. By her temperament I think she is peculiarly suited to live among the Italians, for she has some little money and was wildly adoring of their artistic discretion and their ruthless grandiose ability. Seeing that Tivoli was eighteen miles away, we decided to join one of Signor Tani's excursions for the sake of convenience, for he provided a car, conveyances and lunch, and he left you free to follow him or not as you chose. It was a perfect day—warm and crystal clear, as so many of the days of Rome are, but not hot—and as we rode she continued the story of the Borgias as she had begun to outline it to me and also gave me her brilliant but bitter opinion of the Germans.

According to her, fresh from that progressive land, it was the most abominable country in the world from the point of view of temperament, although she freely admitted their material and executive ability. She admired Wagner and the sentiment of Heine, although she had little to say for the rest of their artistic achievements. Most of their philosophers and poets were an abomination to her, and their architecture, to quote her vivid slang, was a scream. She had visited a palace or two constructed by the Mad King of Bavaria, to say nothing of others located about Munich, and to her, their dull, coarse, thick-witted inartisticness was indescribable. She told me of some famous chamber of glass somewhere that was an imitation of the green floral depths of the sea, and the picture she gave of the meticulous care with which each particular leaf and frond had been set forth was positively maddening. She was particularly opposed to the art of René Reinicke and his peers, which she considered to represent nothing save beefy sensuality. And as for the present temperamental attitude of the Germans—no words could fitly characterize the depth of her personal opposition to it. She was a beautiful woman, and the German officers and young philanderers tried constantly to attract her attention, according to her—and I am quite ready to believe it, seeing how attractive she was—but they received short shrift from her. "I could never look into a German art window," she confided to me once, "but what I would encounter before long one of those wretched pictures—a fat German and his mistress crawling out of bed, or a blear-eyed German faun making love to a nude nymph of about the size of a German housewife." While she admitted the splendor of the German officers' uniform, the vileness of the man inside it was indescribable. She was perfectly willing to admit the efficiency, the courage and the endurance, but the mental point of view of the Germans spelled nothing less than explosion if brought in contact with her. I have never met anyone so thoroughly dissatisfied with the Germans before or since.

On the other hand, her love of the Italians knew no bounds. "It doesn't matter to me," she said on this trip, "that their streets are narrow and their houses dirty, and that their clothes look as though they were sewed on for the season. I don't care whether they make a latrine of every palace or not. And if they are as poor as church mice and beggars—that is all right, too. There is something really inherently great in this nation, and it will bloom again. Oh, I tell you I am crazy about them, with their dirty old clothes and moving picture shows and their patched trousers and high-colored shirts. Now, there you have it—that's what I adore," and she nodded her head to a rather bedraggled dooryard scene where a half-dozen Italians and their wives, to say nothing of six or seven frowsy-looking children, were lounging in the shade of trees against a background of brown wall. It was nearing the noon hour, and these men had come in from the fields. They were drinking the cheap red wine of the country and cutting themselves large slices of dark-colored bread, munching and gesticulating the while. A few broken-down wagons stood about, and several dogs lolled in the sun. They were as healthy and gay as children, and somehow the Roman landscape behind them, a bit of ruin in the distance, a group of ilex trees standing low on the Campagna, gave them just that touch of homely perfection which somehow is not to be seen anywhere outside of Italy. You get a suggestion of it in France, particularly on the Riviera, but not elsewhere.

"Now tell me," she said, "where else will you find that? In Germany?"

"In spite of the German temperament which you dislike so much, they have their own type of simplicity, which is delightful also. The peasants would be fat and those would be beer-steins in their hands, and they would wear fat German smiles."

"That's just the point," she replied, "and the flavor would be gone for me."

At the same time she sang the praises of the Americans as something new, as great and imaginative in spirit as the Italians, but untrained. "We are the only ones," she said, "who can renew the splendors of Rome—outside of the Italians, and they will not do it soon again. They are too poor."

We came to Tivoli and rode about the winding road before lunch, looking at the numerous waterfalls making rainbows and the olive groves shining like burnished metal. As I have said, we had reached a sympathetic understanding which was based not so much on romance as on intellectual understanding and appreciation.

"Why don't you come with me to Florence?" I suggested. "I am going to Assisi, Spello and Perugia, and you say you have not seen those places. We can idle about for a week, and then you can come back here. It would be so much more fun with you along. Will you?"

I had risked a rather broad proposition, seeing that we had known each other not much more than two weeks, if so long, but in a way, to my surprise, she took it in good part. She was very much interested in me and had told me the principal details of her marital troubles, which had been produced, she was inclined to believe, by other women. Her husband was unfaithful to her. I saw it from another angle, and that was that she and her husband were mutually incompatible and that she had a stronger leaning to conventional standards than he. Hence she resented his infidelity though she could not have been flattered with the enforced attentions of someone who did not care for her. There was much argument as to his duty to the children, but she herself saw the point after a few moments—had probably seen it a score of times before, ignoring it, however. Now she owned that he would not live with her and that a divorce was the important thing, but she wanted to get it on sufficient grounds to command a suitable alimony. She had some money of her own, but he had considerably more, and she thought it was only fair that if she raised the children, he should provide for them amply. Yet she was not inclined to waste her life in loneliness either, seeing that she was humanly passionate and that he would have nothing to do with her.

I have to smile at the peculiarity of the situation, though I think from some points of view it was commonplace enough. She had been so devoted to her husband that she had seen but little of men except in a *soi-disant* social way, and she was not now inclined to libertinage. She knew all the vagaries of animality, as it were, without sharing in them to any extent or approving of them. Still, on this occasion, because she was so comfortable with me, she was inclined to stay with me, and I saw that my suggestion had weight with her, seeing that I must soon leave Rome.

"It would be lovely," she replied, looking at me curiously out of the corner of her eye for a moment and then looking quickly away again.

"Well, then?"

"I want to think. I wonder whether I had better?"

"Aren't the falls wonderful?" I observed, giving her time to meditate. It was all so beautiful hereabouts that it was like a dream. We returned to Tivoli and at lunchtime found a table at the little restaurant which hangs over the Grotto of Neptune and offers a view, a little way above it, of the Temple of Vesta. Here we sat and talked, looking down occasionally into the whirlpool far below, into which one thin stream of the Anio was pouring and at the mouth of which a lovely rainbow was constantly fading and reappearing. I don't wonder that Horace sang so ardently of the charms of this region.

"Well," I said when we were seated, a bottle of the wine of the country before us and our plates of soup, piping hot.

"I'm still thinking," she said. "I haven't quite made up my mind."

"Think of Assisi," I said, "and the tomb of St. Francis. You will like that." She smiled. "And think of Spello. I understand there are wonderful cypresses there. When we get to Assisi we will find some charming old room there and then drive to Spello. Or Perugia! My guidebook says that is eighteen hundred feet above the sea."

"Oh yes, I know," she replied, smoothing my hands, "but just supposing now that—" she was thinking, as she afterwards admitted, of some possible detective her husband might have on her trail. "The best alibi is never to have been there."

"What are you talking about?" I exclaimed.

She explained.

"Then you won't come?" I said.

"I didn't say that," she replied archly.

She looked so truly charming in a light cream-colored straw hat and striped blue silk that it was a shame on her part to tease me, I thought. We went up to the ancient Temple of Vesta, dating from the time of Augustus, a perfect thing with an entablature festooned with flowers and ox-skulls, the architrave bearing in broken letters "L. Gellio L." Hundreds of feet below spread a lovely view of the valley and the falls.

"This is the ideal place to settle this," I said. "The temple of Vesta. L. Gellio would approve of it, I am sure. Will you come?"

"L. Gellio might, I am sure," she replied. "He was a healthy Roman. But I don't believe Mademoiselle Vesta would applaud very much."

She hung over the stone parapet and looked into the depths below.

We journeyed from there to the palace proper that we had come to see, the wonderful Villa d'Este. I was questioning her as to whether this was not the same Villa d'Este to which Lucrezia Borgia had eventually retired at twenty-four after her amazing youth, having married the d'Este that was Duke of Ferrara—but she was not sure. This gave endless grounds for bantering until we left it, an hour later, for the Villa Hadrian.

I think, of all things that I saw in Italy that related to private living, the Villa d'Este impressed me most. It hangs upon a slope of one of the Sabine Appenines, in the region of the Sabine farm of Horace and the Villa Hadrian, and it commands a magnificent view of the Campagna with its remnants of ancient Rome and the windings of the Anio. I have no doubt that Horace loved this region as he wrote, for it was worthy of a wild poetic affection. I could not learn much about it save that it was built in 1549 for Cardinal Ippolite d'Este, son of Alfonso II, Duke of Ferrara, who was the final husband of Lucrezia Borgia, and that therefore the lovely Lucrezia was his mother. Pirro Ligorio was the architect, and the frescoes, now in poor condition, were by Zucchero, Muziano and others, whoever they were. It was interesting to see that they represented events in the wonderful history of Tivoli.

It is not so much the building proper which is beautiful (though it is large and ornate and exclusive) as its lovely commanded surroundings, which take a poetic, architectural advantage of the slope on which it stands. I scarcely dreamed before that a villa could be so lovely. You come out of a splendid hall, cooled by fountains that are arranged quite as fireplaces are in an ordinary mansion so that the water flows in lovely ripples over the back where the flames would ordinarily be, out onto a balcony and angled staircase which descends in broad flights into the gardens, paths, bowers and grottos of the slope below. The slope on which the estate is located is terraced within its confines, and from every terrace appears the same lovely view of the Campagna and the Anio, upward gleaming vistas of the villa itself and charming bits of stairway, fountains, statues, stone urns and arched aisles of ilex and cypress. It is said that in its early days magnificent entertainments and summer receptions were here given and that open house was kept for the talented and the mighty. It should be so. Only the exquisite in perception should be permitted to grace the halls and walks. I pointed out one spot on a balcony, commanding a wide view of the Anio, to Mrs. Armstrong, suggesting that once we were located here, this was where we would have breakfast served, and she smiled archly. Along a certain aisle of cypresses, exquisitely murmurous in the wind, I told her we would take our moonlight strolls.

"You know," she said at one point as we were strolling about admiring an immense marble box or trough, hundreds of feet long, exquisitely carved in relief, into which perhaps a hundred jets or more, issuing from carved heads, poured the clear waters of the Anio, "I have had so much trouble and bad feeling over the matter of affection in the last two or three years that I sometimes think I am out of love with love. But at other times—" She looked at the wide view and the exquisite trees, and then she smiled.

"Only death is the end of dreams of affection," I replied, "even for the strongest. They never utterly cease—it makes no difference how faint they may become."

We talked of cypresses and silks and satins and how great ladies and rare Italian and French and Spanish beauties would look descending these magnificent stairways to the gardens below for their morning stroll. The fanciful concoctions of a Watteau or a Boucher were not too much to expect under circumstances such as these. We came out finally to take our carriage for Hadrian's Villa, truly rapturous over the charms of the Villa d'Este.

At Hadrian's Villa it was much the same, only here it was the memory of magnificence rather than the presence of any actual grandeur. We sat on the grass in the lengthening shadows of the trees and listened to Signor Tani as he discoursed on what the Emperor Hadrian's original plan had been: that of representing here in miniature all the wonderful things—to him the most wonderful—he had seen in his extended travels, such as the Lyceum, Academy and Poecile at Athens, the Serapeon of Canopus at Alexandria, the Vale of Tempe, a stream called the Euripius and so on. Here he erected or laid out copies of all these and in addition Greek and Latin libraries, Greek and Latin theaters, thermae, a hippodrome, an imperial palace, lodgings for slaves, barracks for the Praetorian guard, a Tartarus, Elysian Fields, Myphaeun and numerous temples. When they were all completed, it covered an area eight to ten miles in circumference, and although a fair portion of this has been owned since 1871 by the Italian government, it is only partially excavated. There are vast series of chambers filled with earth and rubble, above which the grass and trees grow and which may contain—what? Long tiers of excavated rooms are now visible, parts of mosaic floors rich in color and charming in design, a portion of a theater, of baths, of barracks and the like, but one could see little in an afternoon or a day. I tried hard to get a mental picture of it all as it must have been when Hadrian was emperor of the world, but the human mind is weak when it comes to suggesting the intricacies of the past. Power is built on such a far-flung base. The Castle of St. Angelo, which was formerly his tomb, showed that he had exquisite taste; that he had judgment and force, his head, so frequently to be encountered in the Roman museums, makes perfectly plain.

CHAPTER LIV

The question as to whether we were to travel together to Assisi, Perugia and Florence was not settled on this particular outing, though I was fairly satisfied from her uncertainty that she would eventually refuse to go. A love of life was battling strongly with a sense of caution in her. We came back from the Villa Hadrian singing American songs together and glorying in the beauty of the Campagna, now much healthier than it was a few years ago.

The remainder of my days in Rome were only three or four. I had seen so much of it that has been in no way indicated here. True to my promise, I had looked up the able Mr. Conybeare at his hotel (the Pincio) and walked about some of the older sections hearing him translate Greek and Latin inscriptions of ancient date with the ease with which I put my ordinary thoughts into English. Together we visited the Farnese palace, the Mamertine prison, the Temple of Vesta, Santa Maria in Cosmedin and other churches too numerous and too pointless to mention.

It was interesting to me to note the facility of his learning and the depth of his philosophy. In spite of the fact that life, in the light of his truly immense knowledge of history and his examination of human motives, seemed a hodgepodge of contrarieties and of ethical contradictions, nevertheless he believed that through all the false witness and pretense and subtlety of the ages, through the dominating and apparently guiding impulses of lust and appetite and vanity, seemingly untrammeled by mercy, tenderness or any humane consideration, there still runs a constructive, amplifying, art-enlarging, life-developing tendency which is comforting, dignifying and purifying, making for longer and happier days for each and all. It did not matter to him that the spectacle as we read it historically is always one of the strong dominating the weak, of the strong battling with the strong, of lust, pretense and false witness. Even so, the world was moving on—to what he could not say. We were coming to an ethical understanding of things. The masses were becoming more intelligent and were being better treated. Opportunity of all sorts was being more widely diffused, even if grudgingly so. We would never have again a Nero or a Caligula, he thought—not on this planet. He called my attention to that very interesting agreement between leading families of the Achaean League in lower Greece in which it was stipulated that the "ruling class should be honored like gods" and that the subject class should be "held in subservience like beasts." He wanted to know if even a suspicion of such an attitude today would not cause turmoil. I tried out his philosophy by denying it, but he was firm. Life was better to him—not merely different, as some might take it to be.

I gave a dinner to ten at my hotel one evening in order to pay my respects to those who had been so courteous to me and put it in charge of "Ma." She was desirous of nothing better. She was so fond of managing. We had some special dishes prepared, several kinds of wine provided, and the table decorated with bright flowers. Mrs. Armstrong sat at my left and Mrs. Conybeare at my right, and we made a gay hour out of history, philosophy, Rome, current character and travel. The literary executor of Oscar Wilde was present, one Oscar Browning, and my Greek traveler and merchant, Mr. Couris. An American publisher and his wife, then in Rome, had come, and we were as gay as philosophers and historians and antiquarians can be. Mr. Conybeare drew a laugh by announcing that he never read a book under fifteen hundred years of age anymore, and Oscar Browning told the story of Oscar Wilde to the effect that the more he contemplated his own achievements, the more he came to admire himself and the less use he had for other people's writings. One of the most delightful stories I have heard in years was told by Conybeare, who stated that an Italian thief, being accused of stealing three rings from the hands of a statue of the Virgin that was constantly working miracles, had declared that as he was kneeling before her in solemn prayer, the Virgin had suddenly removed the rings from her finger and handed them to him. But the priests who were accusing him (servitors of the Church) and the judge who was trying him, all firm believers, would not accept this latest development of the miraculous tendencies of the image, and he was sent to jail. Alas! Alas! that true wit should be so poorly rewarded!

One of the last things I did in Rome was to see the Pope. When I came there, Lent was approaching or was already in force, and I was told that it would be rather difficult. None of my friends seemed to have the necessary influence, and I had about decided that I would not attempt further to see him, when one day I met the English representative of several London dailies who said that sometimes, under favorable conditions, he introduced his friends but that recently he had overworked his privilege and could not be sure. On the Friday before leaving I had a telephone message from his wife, whom I had met at the studio of an English artist, saying that she was taking her cousin and asking if I would come. Though it was early morning, I raced into my evening clothes and was off to her apartment in the Via Angelo Brunetti, from where we were to start.

Presentation to the Pope is one of those dull formalities made interesting by the enthusiasm of the faithful and the curiosity of the influential who are frequently non-Catholic or anti-Catholic but magnetized by the amazing history of the papacy and the scope and influence of the Church. All the while that I was in Rome I could not help feeling the power and scope of this organization—much as I condemn its intellectual stagnation and pharisaism. Personally I am of the opinion that the world is, by degrees, reaching the place where it will accept vast underlying principles as furnishing rules of conduct and see man as individually (chemically and spiritually) identified with an overruling intelligence; man's true temples and shrines are of understanding and conduct and nothing else, and the Golden Rule is the only safe guide. I do not say there will not be other religions before this is achieved, that possibly there may be once more intellectual dark ages—centuries of superstition. It may be so. But if I read six thousand years of history aright, the tendency is to a larger and larger understanding of life, with greater intellectuality, material prosperity and individual freedom to each human atom. Religion will become identical with moral understanding, and art will be called to embellish the signs and monuments by which humanity chooses to signify its faith and approbation—without, as in most instances in the past, aiding to overawe and enslave the intelligence of the weak. Let us hope so, anyhow.

I was raised in the Catholic Church but outgrew it at an early age. My father died a rapt believer in it, and I often smile when I think how dull he was and how astounded he would have been if the true history of the papacy and the Catholic hierarchy could have been forced upon him. His subjugation to priestly influence was truly a case of the blind leading the blind. To him the Pope was truly infallible. There could be no wrong in any Catholic priest, and so on and so forth. The lives of Alexander VI and Boniface VIII would have taught him nothing.

In a way, blind adherence to principles is justifiable, for we have not as yet solved the riddle of the universe, and one may well agree with St. Augustine that the vileness of the human agent does not invalidate the curative or corrective power of a great principle. An evil doctor cannot destroy the value of medicine; a corrupt lawyer or judge cannot invalidate pure law. Pure religion and undefiled continues whether there are evil priests or not, and the rise and the fall of the Roman Catholic hierarchy has nothing to do with what is true in the teachings of Christ.

It was interesting to me as I walked about Rome to see the indications or suggestions of the widespread influence of the Catholic Church—priests from England, Ireland, Spain and Egypt and monks from Palestine, the Philippines, Arabia and Africa. You met them everywhere—students, priests, monks, nuns. I was standing in the Rag Fair in the Campo de' Fiori, where every morning a vegetable market is held and every Wednesday a fair where antiquities and curiosities of various kinds are for sale, when an English priest, seeing my difficulties in connection with a piece of jewelry, offered to translate for me, and a little later a French priest inquired in French whether I spoke his language. In the Colosseum I fell in with a German priest from Baldwinsville, Kentucky, who invited me to come and see a certain group of Catacombs on a morning when he intended to say mass there, which interested me, but I was prevented by another engagement; at the Continental there were two priests stopping from Buenos Aires; and so it went. The car line which led down the Via Nazionale to St. Peter's and the Vatican was always heavily patronized by priests, monks and nuns, and I never went anywhere that I did not encounter groups of student priests coming to and from their studies.

The morning that we drove to the papal palace at eleven was, as usual, bright and warm. My English correspondent and his wife, both extremely intelligent, had been talking of the steady changes in Rome, its rapid modernization, the influence of the then Jewish mayor in its civic improvement and the waning influence of the Catholics in the matter of local affairs. "All Rome is probably Catholic," he said, "or nearly so, but it isn't the kind of Catholicism that cares for papal influence in political affairs. Why, here not long ago in a public speech, the mayor charged that the papacy was the cause of Rome being delayed at least a hundred years in its progress, and there was lots of applause. The national parliament which meets here is full of Catholics, but they are not interested in papal influence. It's all the other way about. They seem to be willing to let the Pope have his say in spiritual matters, but he can't leave the Vatican, and priests can't mix in political affairs very much."

I thought, what a change from the days of Gregory VII and even the popes of the eighteenth century!

The rooms of the Vatican devoted to the Pope—at least those to which the public is admitted at times of audience—seemed to me merely large and gaudy without being impressive. Versailles is much better, although that is far too showy and extensive to be interesting. One of the greatest follies of architecture, it seems to me, is the persistent thought that mere size without great beauty of form has any charm whatsoever. The Houses of Parliament in England are large, but they are also shapely. As much might be said for the Palais Royal in Paris, though not for the Louvre, and almost not for Versailles. The Vatican is another great splurge of nothing—mere size without a vestige of charm as to detail.

All I remember of my visit is that arriving at the palace entrance we were permitted by papal guards to ascend immense flights of steps and that we went through one large red room after another where great chandeliers swung from the center and occasional decorations or over-elaborate objects of art appeared on tables or pedestals. There were crowds of people in each room, all in evening dress, the ladies with black lace shawls over their heads, the men in conventional evening clothes. Over-elaborate, uniformed guards stood about, and prelates of various degrees of influence moved to and fro. We took our station in a room adjoining the Pope's private chambers, where we waited patiently while various personages of influence and importance were privately presented.

It was dreary business waiting. Loud talking was not to be thought of, and the various whisperings that went on on all sides as the company increased was oppressive. There was a group of ladies from Venice—whence the Pope hailed, my guide informed me—who were obviously friends of the Holy Father's family. There were two brown monks, barefooted and with long gray beards, patriarchal and El Greco–ish types, who stationed themselves by one wall near the door. There were three nuns and a mother superior from somewhere who looked as if they were lost in prayer. This was a great occasion to them. Next to me was a very official person in a uniform of some kind who constantly adjusted his neckband and smoothed his gloved hands. Some American ladies, quite severe and anti-papistical, if I am not mistaken, looked as if they were determined not to believe anything they saw, and two Italian women of charming manners had in tow an obstreperous small boy of, say, five or six years of age in lovely black velvet, who was determined to be as bad and noisy as he could. He beat his foot and asked questions in a loud whisper and decided that he wished to change his place of abode every three seconds, all of which was accompanied by many "shushes" from his elders, whisperings in his ear and severe frowns from the American ladies, and general indications of disapproval, with here and there a sardonic smile of amusement.

Every now and then a thrill of expectation would go over the company. The Pope was coming! Papal guards and prelates would pass through the room with speedy movements, and it looked as though we would shortly be in the presence of the Vicar of Christ. I was told that it was necessary to rest on one knee at least, which I did, waiting patiently the while I surveyed the curious company. The two brown monks were appropriately solemn, their heads bent. The sisters were praying. The Italian ladies were soothing their restive charge. I told my correspondent friend of the suicide of a certain journalist, whom he and his wife knew, on the day that I left New York—a very talented but adventurous man—and he exclaimed "My God!

Don't tell that to my wife! She'll feel terrible." We waited still longer and finally, in sheer weariness, began jesting foolishly; I said that the Pope and Merry del Val, the papal secretary, must be inside playing jackstones with the papal jewels. This drew a convulsive laugh from my newspaper friend Mr. Pooley, who began to choke behind his handkerchief. Mrs. Pooley whispered to me that if we did not behave we would be put out, and I pictured myself and Mr. Pooley being unceremoniously hustled out by the forceful guards, which produced more laughter. The official beside me, who probably did not speak English, frowned solemnly. This produced a lull, and we waited a little while longer in silence.

Finally the sixth or seventh thrill of expectation produced the Holy Father, for guards and several prelates made a sort of aisle of honor before this door, and then he came. All whispering ceased. There was a rustle of garments as each one fixed himself in his final sanctimonious attitude. He came in, a very tired-looking man in white wool cassock and white skull-cap, a great necklace of white beads about his neck and red shoes on his feet. He was a stout man, closely knit, with small, pig-like eyes, a low forehead, a high crown, a small, shapely chin. He had soft, slightly wrinkled hands, the left one graced by the papal ring. As he came in, he uttered something in Italian, and then starting on the far side opposite the door he had entered, he came about to each one, proffering the hand, which some merely kissed and some seized and cried over, as if it were the solution of great woe or the realization of a too-great happiness. The mother superior did this and one of the Italian ladies from Venice. The brown monks laid their foreheads on it, and the official next to me touched it as though it were an object of great value.

I was interested to see how the Supreme Pontiff—the Pontifex Maximus of all the monuments—viewed all this. He looked benignly but rather wearily down on each one, though occasionally he turned his head away or, slightly interested, said something. To the women whose tears fell on his hands he said nothing. With one of the women from Venice he exchanged a few words. Now and then he murmured something. I could not tell whether he was interested or very tired or whether he was slightly bored. Beyond him lay room after room crowded with pilgrims in which this performance had to be repeated. Acquainted with my newspaper correspondent, he gave no sign. At me he scarcely looked at all, realizing no doubt my critical unworthiness. At the prim, severe American women he looked quizzically. Then he stood in the center of the room and having uttered a long, soft prayer, which my friend X. informed me was very beautiful, departed. The crowd arose. We had to wait until all the other chambers were visited by him and until he returned, guarded on all sides by his soldiers, and disappeared. There was much conversation, approval, and smiling satisfaction. I saw him once more, passing quickly between two long lines of inquisitive reverential people, his head up, his glance straight ahead, and then he was gone.

We made our way out, and somehow I was very glad I had come. I had thought all along that it really did not make any difference whether I saw him or not and that I did not care, but after seeing the attitude of the pilgrims and his own peculiar mood I thought it worthwhile. Pontifex Maximus! The Vicar of Christ! What a long way from the catacomb-worshiping Christians who had no Pope at all, who gathered together "to sing responsively a hymn to Christ as to a God" and who bound themselves by a sacramental oath to commit no thefts, nor robberies, nor adulteries, nor break their word, nor deny a deposit when called upon and who for nearly three hundred years had neither priest nor altar nor bishop nor Pope, but just the rumored gospels of Christ.

CHAPTER LV

The strangeness and charm of Rome to me is the mingling of the clerical, the political and the international in the matter of personage on the one hand and of the ancient, the medieval and the modern—historically and intellectually speaking—on the other. I was there some twenty or twenty-five days, endeavoring to read for myself the riddle of its personality, and when I left, instead of getting closer to it, it seemed to me that I was getting farther away. I had some six or seven books—Murray's *Guide to Rome*, Baedeker's volume on the same subject, Grant Allen's two volumes of classical and Christian Rome, Marion Crawford's *Ave Roma Immortalis* and several other volumes literally put upon me by well-meaning friends. I confess they did me little good. I used to look at them regularly mornings and evenings as they stood in an orderly row on my table and wished that I might read them all carefully and so become very wise in all matters Roman—but I never did. To examine Murray's five hundred and sixty pages was an intellectual satisfaction, for it was so amazingly thorough. No least fact escaped it. But I never read that either. I read at it in spots whenever I found some building about which I really wanted to know. For the rest, I pieced together memory, conversations at the hotel with other travelers, lectures by Signor Tani and bits and scraps out of my guidebooks.

The climate of Rome during the February that I was there was delightful. It was so bracingly chill and fresh when you would first get up in the morning—from seven until half-past nine—and then it would become delightfully warm and stay so until four o'clock. Around that hour, or a little later—not always—it would become disturbingly chill, and you would wish for an overcoat, but by half-past five or six you would be used to this new temperature, and then you would not care whether you had an overcoat or not. From then on until morning it was apparently very pleasant if you were out late, but after you had gone to bed and risen again, it was chill.

I marvel constantly at the fact that although Monte Carlo was considerably farther north, it was, in the main, warmer there, or at least more stable than in Rome. It was explained to me that the winds blowing over the snowfields of the Appenines were the cause of the coolness in the sunless hours. I never felt the sirocco or southwest wind which was supposed by those who lived here to bring moisture and great heaviness of feeling with it. All my days in Rome were bright and invigorating, full of brilliant sunshine, but I found that after such a few days it caused a faint irritation or eruption all over my body which was amazing. The crystalline atmosphere revealing trees, houses and mountains as sharp-cut as though they were void of circumambient air seemed to me at times to be too hard and bright to be attractive. I felt as though I were being put out of sorts by something which I could not control, but at other times this very hardness and crystallinity, when revealing distant houses, landscapes, tombs—such as that of Cecilia Metella—and groups of cypress trees was so wonderful that it was positively thrilling.

It was delightful to walk in the gardens of the Pincio, looking across to the dome of St. Peter's or the Pantheon, or to walk or drive along those wonderful paths that ornament the Gianicolo and survey the swelling, undulating undulations of the Campagna or the range of distant snow-capped hills from Soracte to Monte Cavo, or to survey the whole city of Rome lying charmingly congested and compact at your feet. You could pick out so many things—St. John Lateran, Holy Trinity above the Spanish Steps, St. Paul Without The Walls, the amazing monument to Victor Emmanuel, the Colosseum and the Castle of St. Angelo, all standing out in the clear sunlight and seeming to take on especial charm from this wonderful atmosphere. In Rome the sunlight picks out the details of the city with the accuracy of a fine-cut cameo.

I think the first thing I did after visiting a half-dozen churches this first Sunday morning was to seek the Tiber and follow its right and left banks up- and downstream from the Piazza of the Army, where it enters the city, to the region far beyond the Trastevere station downstream towards the sea, which is not so far from St. Paul Without The Walls. I remembered that my histories had told me that once the Tiber had no walls and that it overflowed its banks greatly and that the early Romans, long before the Roman empire came, used to ground their boats on its muddy flats. In its day, it carried vast flotillas of triremes and later the gaudily-panoplied barges of the popes.

It is a muddy, fast-moving little thing, more like the Arno than any other stream that I saw in Europe and quaint but not wonderful. It is given great charm by the fourteen or fifteen bridges, several of which are really beautiful, and by the presence of such structures as the Castle of St. Angelo, St. Peter's, the old monastery gardens on the heights of the Aventine and the Temple of Vesta near the Palatine Bridge. For long sections it is fronted by private dwellings and apartment houses of a very modern aspect indeed. There is a new Jewish synagogue which faces it with considerable distinction at one spot, and then in other places, collections of ancient streets huddled that look as though it would be worth your life to enter them after dark. Muddy and commonplace as its waters are, the Tiber has a great distinction—partly compounded of its wonderful history, which it is impossible to put out of the mind, and partly because of the thrill and dignity of the life along its banks. Now it runs between high walls, with no landings for boats anywhere that I could see. Wide sea walks and drives fully lighted keep it company for almost its entire length. The little open one-horse taximeter cabs which were so common in Paris are even more numerous here. They buzz up and down like flies with jeweled eyes at night. It is strange to see the large modern streetcar crossing the Tiber near the Castle of St. Angelo or near the Temple of Vesta or running parallel with the river for a certain way. Nowhere, however, are there any shops nor any of that bright commercial atmosphere which characterizes so much of the Seine. Neither are there any factories, but a solemn, classical ecclesiastical atmosphere to it all which is pleasing but reserved. I noticed so often those little groups of priests or companies of novitiates making their way to and fro along the banks, and now and then the rather subtle-looking Italian soldier; but, in the main, it is not a much frequented promenade, but only a lounging place for occasional idlers and a source of view for strangers. It is not as rich in atmosphere as the Thames, not as brilliant as the little Seine, but thoroughly characteristic of Rome.

The other central areas of interest, the showplaces to which all go first, after St. Peter's and the Vatican, are the Forum Romanum—that hodgepodge of a former central civic life—the Palatine, where all the palaces of the Caesars were, the Baths of Caracalla below the Avenue Aventino and the Baths of Diocletian. After these there are many things—heaven only knows how many gorgeous churches, perhaps fifty temples or their sites, undoubtedly a hundred ruins or traces of them, to say nothing of museums, villas and views in profusion. I saw but a fraction, and I bestirred myself constantly about my sightseeing labors.

Unquestionably the most impressive thing in Rome to me was the Baths of Caracalla and after that the Baths of Diocletian and the sepulchral House of Nero. The most beautiful thing of all was St. Paul Without The Walls. I saw the Baths of Caracalla the second Sunday I was in Rome—a vast pile of walls so significantly large that the importance of Rome came over me as it had never done before. I did not know until I consulted my faithful guide-book—my illuminating Murray—that they originally covered a space of one hundred and forty thousand square yards, and that on the old Via Nova, the most magnificent street of Rome in its day, they had a frontage of twelve hundred feet. That would be equal to about six short New York blocks up-town. They were commenced by Septimius Severus in A.D. 206, chiefly built by Caracalla, enlarged by Elagabalus and completed by his successor, Severus Alexander, in 222 A.D. or in sixteen years. If such a structure were undertaken today, intended to be arranged and decorated in the same lavish manner, I question whether it would be done as quickly. The New York Public Library, which is perhaps as artistic and lavish a structure as America has yet produced and far more distinguished than any building of the same purpose that I saw in Europe, required ten years; if the archaeologists and historians, to say nothing of the evidence of one's own eyesight, are to be believed, there is no modern building which either in size, design or luxurious equipment can compare with these ancient baths. If you don't believe me, consult your *Encyclopedia Britannica*.

As I stood in these tremendous rooms, about which you may wander as you would a small park, I was trying to think what rooms I had seen in my time that compared with them for size. No doubt the naves of Amiens and St. Peter's compare with some of these rooms in length, breadth, height and dignity, but they are but two interiors. The waiting room of the new Pennsylvania depot in New York bears considerable relationship to some of these chambers—which now, of course, are roofless and open to the sky. There was no interior that I saw in either London, Paris or Berlin that was at all significant by comparison. The Romans always built walls of brick and rubble of tremendous thickness first and then coated them thinly with marble of the richest quality and color. They prepared great niches and colonnades for statuary and arched it all over with amazing domes—domes that, strange as it may seem, sometimes traverse each other at different angles. I looked at these tremendous chambers that have weathered seventeen hundred years, walls thick as an ordinary hall bedroom soaring perhaps one hundred and fifty feet in the air, and realized that in spite of the fact that they had been stripped by greedy conquerors, popes, cardinals, dukes and princes of the medieval period of Italian life, they are nevertheless in themselves possessed of an inalienable grandeur so long as they are not utterly destroyed.

It was a delight to stand here and read of the size of the hot, warm and cold swimming basins, the measurements of which I roughly guessed to be two hundred by one hundred—vast tanks of marble surrounded by amazing chambers of great beauty. If you walk in the galleries of the Vatican or those of the Museo delle Terme or stand in the piazza of the Trinity at Florence, you can see fragments of the columns and marbles which were once a part of this great structure. It is said that Shelley gained his inspiration for *Prometheus Unbound* from gazing at these chambers, and well he might. There were bits of mosaic pavement which remain from the first floor or have fallen from the upper floors and from the columns and capitals which lie scattered about. There was a system of subterranean arches and vaults by which the numerous slaves in service could appear from underground without interfering in any way with the freedom of the persons in the upper halls. You could even see the remains of passages or flues by which hot air and steam and water were distributed to the various chambers, to say nothing of the remains of the aqueduct which brought the vast quantity of water needed from across the Campagna.

There were sixteen hundred baths here, and they were all properly served, and in the outer enclosures were tennis courts, running tracks and sloping tiers of seats for the use of spectators. Here, according to the historians, the patricians and their clients, the senators and their adherents, the literati and their admirers lounged or strolled and discoursed. It was the great political center of Rome. But now that is all gone. It is not even within the confines of the city anymore. The city streets and houses proper cease long before you reach this space. The Italian government, wise in its consideration of the importance of the traveler, is making parks and preserves of these historic areas—the Forum, the Palatine, the Aventine and these baths—which now stand in a fenced enclosure of their own. An admission fee will no doubt eventually be exacted, and that is as it should be, although it has been only since 1870 that the slightest municipal or national interest has been taken in these matters. Old Rome extended far beyond this, in the direction of the Via Appia and the region which is now the desolate Campagna.

As you stand under these immense arches, framing only the blue of the sky and vistas of distant landscape, the significance of it all—of Rome, its imperial power, its luxury and the mad insatiable lust of its body politic—comes back. Three of the emperors involved were murdered, as were the vast majority of that amazing line of power-seekers who sought so eagerly, struggled so ruthlessly, endeavored to build so amazingly to perpetuate their names, and this is what it all has come to—vast staggering masses of dull brick, which the passing traveler associates with a single name of which he knows nothing. My one thought was, in what way has the modern world surpassed this wonder of architecture and convenience? How much more thoroughly, if at all, do we build walls; in what way, if any, has our taste increased in the matter of decoration; how have we improved in sculpture; what is newer in the thought of public convenience? It is a strange thought. Even our furnace-heating is discounted by a similar method two thousand years old. It is presumed we have gained in literary significance, mechanical and electrical convenience and human tenderness or consideration. Be it so. Let those be sure who can.

St. Paul Without The Walls is very different. It is a church the forerunner of which was commenced by the emperors Valentinian II, Theodosius and Arcadius in 388 A.D., completed in 395 and restored by Leo III in the eighth century. It is four hundred and twelve feet long and two hundred and sixteen feet wide except in the transepts, where it is two hundred and seventy-nine feet wide. It was completely destroyed by fire on July 16, 1823, after Christians had worshiped in it uninterruptedly for nearly seventeen centuries. The nave had eighty Corinthian columns in four rows which were completely destroyed, as were all but forty portraits of the popes in lunettes of mosaic above the columns, which formed one of its most distinguishing features. This church, which had always been under the protection of the English kings previous to the Reformation, was rebuilt by the Catholic hierarchy, just as it had been before—Catholic sovereigns, princes and successive popes contributing large sums of money. It was finally dedicated in 1854 by Pius IX in the presence of one hundred and eighty-five cardinals and prelates assembled in Rome for the promulgation of the dogma of the Immaculate Conception. It had cost over fifteen million dollars then, and when I was in Rome they were still working on the west facade, making extensive improvements.

I came upon it one idle afternoon when I was still further exploring the Tiber downstream toward the sea and had reached a sunny meadow, unenclosed, where the grass was soft and green and where some Roman wide-horned cattle were browsing. Rome is odd in that its surroundings are like those of a village consisting of open unfenced fields. So often you can wander at random, coming upon old tombs, well tops and former suggestions of civic life which are now far outside the confines of the present city. I had fancied Rome had a population of at least a million and was surprised to find that it had only five hundred thousand, highly concentrated entirely within the ancient walls.

When I came opposite this particular church, graced in its surroundings by a few cypresses standing up sharp and clear upon the green plain, I thought it was an old monastery of charming design. The ancient basilica is never imposing as to height. It was brown and ornate with the usual campanile at the farther end, a portico with distinguished columns looking over the river to the west and apparently a garden or cloister surrounded by a wall. I signaled to a river man who was plying one of the quaint, snub-nosed Italian punts in the river that I wanted to get on the other side. He drew near. I scrambled down the steep bank, congratulating myself that there was a streetcar line on the other side which I could see would take me back into the city. It was about half-past three in the afternoon with a slanting sun, and as we poled across I had a charming view of its western facade, looking up from the bosom of the Tiber. It is all of a creamy-brown color, very simple, which in this almost permanent spring-like atmosphere was delightful. Before it is a square atrium supported by large columns of pink and gray granite, and the facade is ornamented with modern mosaics of four prophets, the sheep between Bethlehem and Jerusalem, and Christ between Saint Peter and Saint Paul.

I never saw a more individual nor a more beautiful interior in my life. The usual entrance is by a Corinthian portico supported by twelve columns of marble, opening into the north transept, which looks toward Rome. One of the city's car lines comes straight to the door. I had an impression at once of a vast, highly-polished interior, glistening like a mirror. You would have to see it to realize how beautiful it all is—far more beautiful, though much less imposing, than St. Peter's. This interior is only three hundred and ninety feet long as compared with St. Peter's six hundred and fifteen, and only seventy-five feet high as contrasted with the latter's one hundred and fifty-two-and-a-half (the dome is four hundred and five feet), but size is not always important in connection with true distinction. These wonderful proportions, three hundred and ninety feet by one hundred and ninety-five—just twice as long as it is broad, broken only by the ordered rows of glistening gray granite marble with white Corinthian capitals, and its vast floor and walls shining with polished marble—are sufficient to leave you spellbound as to its richness, simplicity and symmetry.

It is the only truly beautiful basilica of the standard form that I saw anywhere abroad. It can only be compared with St. Peter's, which is Romanesque in design, and with the Cathedral at Pisa, which is Italianized Gothic. It is as rich as either, simpler in its lines and more symmetrical, though it could not possibly be more beautiful than the Cathedral at Pisa. Beside the great west door are two columns of Oriental alabaster (yellow streaked with chalky white), polished until they shine like glass and soaring to the roof above. There are four more shafts of the same material which support the canopy or baldachino over the main altar, which stands in the center where the transept crosses the nave. The ceiling is a vast flat expanse of coffered carving and gilding, said not to be as effective as the plain, open wooden roof of the church that was destroyed. This may be true, but you will not miss it. It is supremely beautiful.

Fortune has been kind to this church. It is not stuffed with sarcophagi or monuments. Outside of the central altar and the imposing, glistening columns, of which there are one hundred and thirty-eight all told, there is practically nothing to arrest or disturb the eye—just a vast, beautifully-formed space of polished marble that reflects and shines in the warm light. Above the piers of the transept and over the columns of the nave and aisles (of the latter there are four, two on each side of the nave, divided by granite columns) are the richly-colored medallion portraits of the popes, five feet in diameter, all portraits since Innocent I (401 A.D.), executed in the mosaic workshop at the Vatican. They follow, so my guidebook said, the tradition of the likenesses as they were first produced in the fifth century. I fancy they must concern the painters' idea more than they do the popes'.

Beneath the high altar, which stands under a Gothic canopy, which, in turn, stands under a larger baldachino supported by the four columns of alabaster previously mentioned, lies the body of St. Paul, it is said, but not the head, the latter being in St. John Lateran. The gravestone over his body is a plain marble slab, rudely engraved with the letters *Paulo Apostolo Mort.* A great tribute, this church, to the most significant of all the apostles.

It was not because the church had any religious charm for me that I rejoiced in it. I suppose the faithful get some cheer out of contemplating this testimony to the doctrines of Christ. As a piece of pure, artistic church-building, I think it can safely hold its own against all and sundry. There is nothing finer, though many may rival it in varying perfections. When I think of that glistening expanse of pure creamy marble, broken only by those four rows of gray granite columns, ornamented above their white capitals with the colored mosaic medallions of the popes, words fail me. There are no benches or chairs or stone seats of any kind in this church, just as there are none in most of the show-churches in Europe, which is fortunate. There are no inscriptions to speak of, no paintings, no blemishes or extra ornaments of any kind. Just space—space, beautifully divided, beautifully ceiled, richly colored, glistening. I came out and went around to the cloister, said to be a beautiful example of the monastic architecture of the thirteenth century. I can only say that it is extremely beautiful. A black-cowled priest or monk took me through for a consideration. I was amazed at the variety, slenderness and beauty of the spiraled and twisted and fluted columns which support the cloister roof. In connection with these churches in Italy there is always one of these cloisters which is a dream of simplicity and peace. From the grass within the enclosure, or looking from some central well top, or out from behind the simple arches of the heavenly arcade, you may see the blue sky, the top of the adjacent campanile, perhaps a pigeon or two, and above you relics of a former period of the world's life.

Here on the walls were Roman and early Christian inscriptions and several sepulchral monuments that once stood in the old basilica before it was burned. My guide informed me that a copy of the Vulgate, the Latin version of the Bible, dating from the eleventh century, exists in the monastery, its library, and that here Pope Pius VII lived for many years as the Benedictine monk Gregorio Chiaramonti. He was on his deathbed when the fire which destroyed the old church broke out, but he never knew, for he was never told. On the grass outside the monastery walls, I found some young Italian student candidates for the priesthood in their black cassocks playing football. They spoke only Italian. An old, sober father of the church in a black cassock sat against the wall, reading in his breviary and listening, no doubt, to hear whether the language employed in exciting moments was sufficiently circumspect. On a little balcony of the monastery some distance back and overhead stood a black-robed priest or monk, his arms akimbo, looking west over the winding Tiber to a white, brown, red and blue village and some green cypress-sentineled hills, behind which the sun was setting. Over the river a white, square house with a stone wall, the corners and gates of which were surmounted with lovely, shapely amphorae, had one single tall, black cypress tree standing on solemn guard over its gracefully carved door. This is truly Italy, I thought. This is the lovely world that for centuries has, like a lovely woman, been harried for its art and beauty. This beautiful church, a mile or more without the walls, standing free and clear in a grassy plain, without, no doubt, a single parishioner, preserved in all its exquisite beauty for the sake of that beauty itself. That is Italy. That was the last I saw of St. Paul Without The Walls.

CHAPTER LVI

My last day in Rome was spent in visiting several churches which I had not yet seen: San Pietro in Vincoli, to look at the *Moses* of Michelangelo, that one imposing figure out of the tomb of Julius II that never was; Santa Maria degli Angeli, in the Baths of Diocletian, the great central hall of which Michelangelo converted into a church or designed for those who wished to do so; San Lorenzo, outside the walls, and the cemetery adjoining it; and lastly, one last look at the lovely precinct of the Museo delle Terme, in the Baths of Diocletian, which of almost anything in the city I thought smacked the most of ancient Rome.

I have said scarcely anything of this museum, though I went there four times in all—once with Mrs. Richards, once with Mrs. Armstrong, and twice alone. It was filled with such interesting fragments of ancient Rome, bits of walls and ceilings, portions of mosaic from floors and niches, charming statues of Greek and Roman origin, fragments of columns and pediments from houses and temples, to say nothing of the fact that it is all located within the precincts of the ancient baths themselves—within the very rooms which were once Roman chambers devoted to ablutions.

I cannot fitly indicate what a soothing poetic effect these fragments of ancient walls—very thick, very high, beautifully arched and in some cases still domed in part, but stripped of all their ancient marble facing—have on the collections which are located within them. In most cases the chambers containing important sculptures are covered, but the remainder is open to the blue Italian sky, with the sunlight casting heavy shadows and a hint of moss touching the walls and fragments of ancient marbles in most places. I thought the Musée Carnavalet and the Musée de Cluny in Paris were exquisite. This is much the same thing, only here are no objects of art other than sculptures—no paintings, decorations or craftwork of any kind, unless you wish to think of ancient fragments of wall decorations and floor mosaics as such. You stroll about here for the most part on earthen floors, in the shade of brick walls over sixteen hundred years old, look at the heads of emperors, dream over plans of ancient Rome and of Roman forts in England, Germany, Spain and Asia Minor, see fragments from ancient Roman towns and summer palaces, and get thoroughly into the spirit of a world that is forever gone. I never realized until I loitered in this museum how truly far-flung Rome was, how exquisite were its sculptural and architectural ideals, how freely and richly it borrowed from all the known world. I could stroll about Rome day after day, looking at one great ruin after another, but here I could come into an atmosphere of the utmost historic beauty and sweetness and see the whole thing epitomized.

I was walking one day in one of the rooms with Mrs. Richards, and we were pausing in front of one of the Roman ceilings, a decorated fragment with gay, dancing figures of nymphs and fauns, and I saw her furtively wipe a tear from her eye. I knew what the trouble was, of course. Lane had said that this woman was dull, lacking in an innate artistic feeling, but he was wrong. The magic of this ancient world, its art executed in the most remote, etherialized mood, touched her deeply. Here was no sense of sex nor any thought of religion, but just gay, youthful poetry of motion such as one finds in children. I pressed her arm gently and said, "There, Ma, don't cry. It's exquisite, of course, but you can't help the drift of this sad world."

"I can't help it," she replied. "I'm glad to cry."

Thereafter "Ma" was precious to me for her real artistic feeling.

Another day I stood in the great central court of this museum looking at some ancient fragments of sarcophagi, bits of columns, an ancient carved well top and the like. There was grass here and some climbing, blooming roses, if you please, and finally I found a little column or monolith of marble standing on a base of the same, the four sides of the latter carved with ox-skulls interlaced with roses. By the side of the little column, on top of the base, as if perchance there had been a nymph or dryad standing beside the carved head of a satyr which may once have crowned the top of the column, were a pair of tiny, white-stone feet, very shapely and tinted slightly with age. Then I cried, and I could not say exactly why. Some trick of sunlight and blue sky and red walls and green grass and the atmosphere of ancient Rome did it. I choked down a delicious, sad, joyous emotion, because, I suppose, I was sorry that so much exquisite beauty was not to endure forever for me, that I could not always be young and the like. That was why I went finally to walk quickly and lovingly through the Museo delle Terme.

And another thing I did was to visit a fragment of the ancient Roman wall which surrounds the city between the Porta Pinciana and the Porta Pia, along what is now known as the Corso d'Italia. That is a neighborhood in which new and imposing apartment houses with their elevators and automobiles have crowded close to this ancient wall, with here and there the gardens of some estate (*villa* or *palazzo*), protected by a high wall, over the tops of which stately cypresses may be seen intervening. It was a moonlit night or evening, this last one, with many lamps gleaming in the windows of this modern region and automobiles honking. But I wanted to see again this juxtaposition of the very old and the very new—this wall that contained the city of the best days of the Roman Republic and these very modern, New York-ish and Parisian apartment houses. The cypresses, too, showing their stately, spear-like heads over the walls, the moon silhouetting in a silver haze their shapely blackness. It was a delicious last touch, after San Lorenzo with its jewel-box interior and Santa Maria with its reminders of Michelangelo. I went back to the hotel and in a rather remote mood decided to eat alone in the private restaurant, but I was not long there before Mrs. Richards sought me out to give me last messages and pleasant thoughts, and after she went came Mrs. Armstrong.

Because of her recalcitrance in the matter of my proposed trip with her to Assisi, Spello and Perugia—she was afraid of her nurse or maid who had charge of the children—I decided to write her a pleasant farewell in the morning and escape without further argument, but here she came. She was a little piqued, I fancy, because I had not looked her up either Saturday or this day, but now that the last evening had come, she was in a melting mood.

"I can't go with you," she said as she sat, a silver-spangled lace shawl about her shoulders. "I would if I could, but I'm afraid. Oh, my life is so twisted up!"

Hot, angry tears welled up in her eyes, and she put her arms on the table in a solemn, contemplative way.

"Don't cry," I said, half-sarcastically, half-sympathetically. "You're perfectly safe—you're not going."

"Oh, it isn't that," she replied. "I want to go. It's just that all the things that I have worked for so long have come to nothing. I thought I was settled for life, and here I am at thirty-two, with two children to look after, my life torn up, and I have to lead a celibate life in the bargain. I'll get a divorce, though, soon, I hope, and then I can arrange my life in a different way."

We talked of her husband, the law governing divorce in New York State, the right of alimony for the children's sake, and then we went into the general parlor and talked some more. At midnight we were still talking—America, ways of living one's life, whether she would return soon, what she would do when she returned. She agreed that if she were back in the spring or summer when I arrived, she would look me up.

"I will now," she said. "I promise you that. Only I can't do anything to interfere with my divorce plans. I owe some adjustment to the children."

The peculiarity of this woman's mood, combined with her intellect, interested me greatly. She was so very good-looking, so clear-minded and so forceful. She had an easy, superior grace which was tactful, daring and yet cautious. When there was no one present she fixed herself in such a position that I could see that she had on lavender silk stockings and how shapely her foot and leg were. She took my hand, and when I smoothed her arm she said, "We'd better be careful. Old John Nightclerk over there is dying to see what he can see." I had to smile. She suggested that she might come to the train with me if I were going late, but I was leaving early, and Mrs. Richards had already arranged to come with me. The situation could not be readjusted. She went to her rooms after a time, and I followed to get one last farewell, which resulted in a pretty struggle. Unfortunately the Cerberus of a maid was present, sleeping in an adjoining room with the children, and a bumped chair made too much noise to be ignored. I had to leave, but she promised faithfully to write me, which she did, and finally put her smooth arms around me in a quick, vigorous farewell. That was the end until—but, after all, this isn't the story of my life, merely of this trip abroad.

Never shall I forget the morning of my departure. It was gray, and I was decidedly sorry to leave Rome. As usual, though I did not know it was usual at the time, the ticket man at the gate of the large terminal held up my four parcels of luggage, saying that it was too much to take into my compartment with me. Be it known that under the rules of foreign travel the ticket man at the gate has absolutely nothing to say (in theory) as to whether you take one or ten pieces of luggage with you in your carriage, providing that the remainder of the passengers in your section do not complain. That is a matter for the conductor of the train to adjust. As a matter of fact, if you travel first-class there are as a rule not more than one or two other passengers in the same section with you, the majority of the passenger traffic going second and third. If you are carrying much hand-luggage to avoid excess luggage, it is just as well to travel first-class, for as a rule you still save something on the total cost, you have the advantage of a section almost exclusively to yourself, and you get more attention from porters and servitors generally. It always amused me to see how carefully these fierce Italian, French and Belgian banditti scrutinized the amount of their tips before wreathing their faces in smiles and saying "Thank you" in whatever language they spoke. But to continue.

Although theoretically the man at the ticket gate has nothing to say about whether you take one package of luggage with you or many, he does so just the same. His scheme is simple. If you do not hand him a lira or thereabouts as you pass, he makes some guttural remark to your porter who is carrying your belongings, who immediately puts them all down. Unless you speak the language it will require some time then to find out what the trouble is. After a while it becomes clear. You have forgotten to pay a lira. But if you are green or dull, as I was, it does not come over you on the instant. Mrs. Richards, by the way, had left me in order to secure me some folders. Perhaps, seeing that your baggage has been so unceremoniously put down and your train is about to leave, you resent being held up in this manner and, once angry, refuse to pay at all. Witness, then, an amazing, astonishing process by which the money is finally extracted. You can, if you are really wise, see that a lira is wanted and go back and pay it; or you can go back and gather up all your luggage yourself, find your car and your section somewhere and get in it. That, unless you know the depot, is at once difficult and humiliating. So if you are a dunce, as, for example, the writer, you fume and rage, grow hot under the collar, prepare to fight the whole Italian government, all porters, ticket-takers, trainmen and the like. In vain! In vain!

There your baggage stays. You swear. You start to pick it up. Another underling protests. You seek the baggage master or a Cook's guide or a policeman, or anybody. In vain. They all tell you that it may or may not be against the rules, but somehow the trainmen have you at their mercy. Even the Cook's guide, who knows which side his bread is buttered on, advises you to pay. In my case, before Mrs. Richards had returned, I had found out where my train was, fought my way to it, and amid a storm of protest was about to deposit my luggage in any old section, saying that I would adjust everything with the conductor when I was on the train, when that personage arrived. He was interested, bland, pleasant. Ordinarily he would not charge me anything, he said, never did, but such a row had been made that the baggage master had been compelled to take notice, or had taken notice, and had rated me for a charge of three lire. Why not compromise for the original lira wanted and let it go? The gateman would be satisfied, the baggage master would forego his charge, all would be well. I saw Mrs. Richards arriving in the distance. I wished to appear calm and sensible. That dog of a ticket-taker, mind you, in this great terminal, had left his post (probably in charge of another) and was hovering in the offing to see the end of this great row. I finally produced a lira and, to my chagrin, saw him stalking off showily. His power of extortion had been vindicated. Thereafter in Italy, or anywhere else in Europe, I never argued. Whenever I heard that guttural command to my porter bearing my luggage on entering a depot, I produced a lira and let it go at that. My departing troubles were then over.

On departing from Rome I was really sorry to leave "Ma." She was so intellectual, so high-Oxfordian in her manner, and withal so human, sensible and kindly. She was always talking about "poor, dear Somebody," from the Japanese ambassador, who was a good friend of hers, down to Mrs. Armstrong, her son, her daughter, and, I fancy, myself when she was talking of me to others. I used to tease her, as we went about together, about "poor, dear Caesar" and "poor, dear Nero," "poor, dear Alexander VI," and "poor, dear Cesare Borgia."

"Oh yes, now, you know," she replied, "but everyone has some good traits, hasn't he?" She always spoke with the faintest suggestion of a lisp, which amused me greatly.

"I'll tell you, Ma, how it will be with you," I said to her one day as we were walking in the gardens of the Vatican, those beautiful walks and gardens, with the sunken villa (courteously called a casino) of Pius IV lying before us, "if you should ever reach the home of Satan, which I firmly trust you won't, you will patronize him. 'Poor, dear devil! Poor, dear Satan! He is such a nice devil! It is a question now whether the Lord really did right in throwing him out of heaven.' And you will have all the minor devils standing around you, leaning on their pitchforks, their tails curled over their arms, absolutely neglecting their duties while they listen to you. There you have it. That is just what will happen, I'm afraid."

"Ma" looked at me humorously. "Oh, no," she replied.

"Oh, yes, exactly. You will 'poor-dear' the devil."

On this day I saw her as the train pulled out, bustling back to her *poor, dear Rome* and her *poor, dear ambassador,* while I turned my face to Italy of the north and home.

The trip up the central valley of Italy from Rome to Florence I count the most picturesque of any that I made in Europe. The trip from Paris to the Riviera was charming, suggestive. From Monte Carlo to Rome along the coast it was rich, showy, splendid, but this from Rome to Florence was naive, pastoral, archaeologic and, above all, suggestive of that medieval plotting and counter-plotting, the marchings to and fro of the kings of France and the armies of the popes, the wars of the princely families over Perugia, Foligno, Spoleto and Arezzo, to say nothing of those battles which concerned the dominance of the Romagna.

I do not know what Italy can mean to one who knows nothing of Roman or early Christian history, the rise of the popes, the struggles with the Holy Roman Empire, the revival of art and learning, and particularly the amazing development of art and painting, especially in such cities as those of Perugia, Orvieto, Pisa, Florence, Ravenna, Venice and Genoa. I know little enough, and the guidebooks tell you much, but without a keen intellectual and emotional interest in the development of this amazing country, a love of architecture, of painting, of sculpture and of hot, eager human ambition, what can it mean? True, it has an amazing natural beauty which would be delightful if there were nothing more, but these other things are so gorgeous. They furnish the mind with so much to think on.

Assisi, when I reached it, I found delightful. As we proceeded up the valley toward it I speculated on how often this valley had been traversed by soldiery of almost every description, from that of Rome to that of Napoleon, Garibaldi and the first king of United Italy. On this train were soldiers of the new Italy, officers, several of whom had a small white cypress tree on their caps as an emblem of some region or regiment. Smart, dandified youths they were, sons of good families obviously, with uniforms of good cloth cut to perfection and with swords and other accoutrements of metal polished to a nicety. They laughed and jested, dismounting at Spoleto, whither they were bound.

And that reminds me that I was never weary of looking at the soldiery of Rome. The costumes of the officers at least were exceedingly varied and picturesque. Feathers, buckles, hats bent into the most amazing shapes, long swinging capes, swords, spurs—you would imagine you were in medieval Italy at times. The Corso Umberto, the Via Nazionale and the Corso Vittorio Emanuele, the principal streets in Rome, were alive with them. Perhaps the current *opera buffa* war with Turkey had something to do with it. On several occasions I watched them change the guard at the papal palace, the Quirinale, while the band played in the Palazzo del Quirinale, and the released soldiers ran down the hill afterwards in perfect forward, the bushy feathers on their hats fluttering, their guns carried loosely in one hand swinging lightly, the buglers in front of them, bugling as they ran, and I thought I had never seen a more inspiring scene. It was quite exciting and made Italy seem young, forceful, new. That was the strange thing that I noted about Italy everywhere—the fact that its youth had that peculiarly unsophisticated, child-like enthusiastic look in their eyes, which I have noted always in the boys of our Middle West and South in America.

Assisi, when we reached it after several hours' riding, was not near the station at all at which we dismounted. I could see it in the distance on a high ridge, perhaps fifteen or eighteen hundred feet up. There was no car line, only a few scrubby carriages and buses. I had planned my itinerary with the aid of Grant Richards, several Englishmen and Americans in Rome, and to a certain extent in accordance with my own special wishes. Assisi had been added at the suggestion of Mr. Conybeare, who gave me a letter to his friend and savant, Mr. Sabatier. Spello was Grant Richards's suggestion, because of some magnificent cypresses which I should see there. Perugia was Grant Richards's choice, Venice that of my American publisher friend, who begged me, since I valued my future peace of mind, not to miss it. I wanted to see Milan for a day anyhow, and the Lake of Lucerne, even if all the hotels were closed. I had decided on hunting up my father's birthplace, a little town called Mayen, lying near the juncture of the Rhine and the Moselle, and in reaching it I found that I was compelled to go to Frankfort and thence, via Mayence, bad luck to it, down the Rhine. From there I was going to Berlin, much against Grant Richards's wishes, who told me his impression was that it was dull, and from Berlin I was going to Holland and Belgium for a few days in order that I might return to Paris by easy stages. Amsterdam, Rotterdam, The Hague, Antwerp, Brussels, Waterloo, and at Grant Richards's request Bruges or Ghent, probably Bruges. Then I was to spend a few days with him in Paris, we were to return together to London or parley a bit at Fontainebleau or take a walk in the "Wessex" country of Thomas Hardy. I anticipated a delightful, though speedy, trip and entered upon the labor of seeing Assisi with enthusiasm.

CHAPTER LVII

St. Francis is one of the few pleasant memories of my Catholic school days. We used to study an *Eclectic Reader*, published, I think, by Benziger Brothers of Cincinnati, Ohio—at least that name was identified with most of my Catholic schoolbooks—and in it was the story of how St. Francis preached to the birds. I barely understood in my youth that he was a very poor and good man who, because he was spiritually inclined, had decided to follow Christ; that he had taken literally the words out of Matthew: "Go ye, preach, saying, The Kingdom of Heaven is at hand. . . . provide neither gold nor silver. . . . nor scrip for your journey"; and that he had established a great order of mendicant friars whose business it was to preach to the poor and to assist them. His preaching to the birds had made a particular impression on me, for as I recall it, there was a picture of a thin, pale man of kindly but ascetic countenance in the plain black habit of a friar, a halo about his head, holding up one thin, white hand, while before him upon the ground and ranged upon the thin limbs of a small tree were a number of birds who were listening intently, some with heads reverently bowed, if such a thing could be. He said, as I have since learned by consulting one of the accounts of him: "My sister birds, you should be much bound to God, your Creator, and you should always, in every place, praise Him, for He has given you liberty to fly, and vestments double and triple, and has preserved your seed in the Ark of Noah, and also He keeps you in the air, which He has made for you, and besides this He feeds you and gives you the fountains and rivers to drink from and the valleys for your refuge. And because ye do not know how to spin and sew, God clothes you, therefore keep yourselves, my sisters, from the sin of ingratitude."

I count that a good preachment! It does not matter that it may not accord with this, that or the other theory of life. It is lovely, poetic thought and allied with hope and beauty and faith and joy and gratitude for life itself. This latest account that I have read says that when St. Francis made the sign of the cross, the birds rose up and spread themselves to the four quarters of the world to signify that the preaching of the cross should spread everywhere.

I do not propose to introduce here a history of St. Francis. All of us who know anything about him know that there are a score of interesting 'Lives,' but as I approached Assisi on the train, and even before that, I looked up some facts in connection with him in order to refresh my memory. Then it all came back: the fact that he had been born here of a fairly well-to-do man; had led a gay life in his youth; had seen a vision of duty or experienced a change of heart which caused him to embrace poverty, the care of the poor and needy and to follow Christ exactly in that idealistic dictum which says, "Lay not up for yourselves treasures upon earth . . . where moth and dust doth corrupt and where thieves break through and steal, but lay up for yourselves treasures in Heaven, where neither moth nor rust doth corrupt, and where thieves do not break through and steal, for where your treasure is there will your heart be also." I found in one of the little books I had with me, *Umbrian Towns*, a copy of the prayer that he devised for his order, which reads:

"Poverty was in the crib and like a faithful squire she kept herself armed in the great combat. Thou didst wage for our redemption. During Thy passion she alone did not forsake Thee. Mary, Thy Mother, stopped at the foot of the cross, but poverty mounted it with Thee and clasped Thee in her embrace unto the end; and when Thou wast dying of thirst as a watchful spouse she prepared for Thee the gall. Thou didst expire in the ardor of her embraces, nor did she leave Thee when dead, O Lord Jesus, for she allowed not Thy body to rest elsewhere than in a borrowed grave. O poorest Jesus, the grace I beg of Thee is to bestow on me the treasure of the highest poverty. Grant that the distinctive mark of our Order may be never to possess anything as its own under the sun for the glory of Thy name and to have no other patrimony than begging."

I wonder if there is anyone who can read that without a thrill of response. This world sets such store by wealth and comfort. We all pile on, batten on luxury as far as our means will permit—many of us wallow in it; and to find a man who could write such a prayer as that *and live it* made my hair tingle to the roots. I can understand Pope Innocent III saying that the rule offered by St. Francis and his disciples to ordinary mortals was too severe, but I can also see a poetic enthusiast like St. Francis seeing Christian service only in terms of the greatest poverty. I found myself on the instant in the deepest accord with him, understanding how it was that he wanted his followers not to wear a habit and to work in the fields as day laborers, begging only when they could not earn their way. The fact that he and his disciples had lived in reed huts on the site of Santa Maria degli Angeli, the great church which stands in the valley near the depot, far from the town, and had practiced the utmost austerity came upon me as a bit of imaginative poetry of the highest sort. Before the rumbling bus arrived which conveyed me and several others to the little hotel, I was thrilling with enthusiasm for this religious poet, and anything that concerned him interested me.

In some ways Assisi is a disappointment, if you expect anything more than bare picturesqueness, for it is very old and, I fancy, as modern Italy goes, very poor. The walls of the houses are for the most part built of a cheap gray stone, a commonplace granite, which lends a leaden aspect to the place. If there was manufacturing of any kind, I did not see it—nothing save the small barter and trade that goes with farming. I could see as I entered that the streets climbed up hill and down dale, as at Eze and Ventimiglia: hard, winding, narrow, stony affairs, lined right to the roadways, by those bare, inhospitable-looking houses. No yards, no gardens—at least none visible from the streets—but between walls and down street stairways and between odd angles of buildings the loveliest vistas of the valley below, where were spread great orchards of olive trees, occasional small groups of houses, distant churches and the mountains on the other side of the valley. Quite suited to the bare, self-abnegating spirit of St. Francis, I thought, but probably bearing no resemblance at all to the town as it was in his day—1182!

As I came up in the bus, looking after my very un-St. Francis-like baggage and my fur overcoat, I encountered a spare, ascetic-looking Catholic priest, or abbot, as he finally turned out to be, a Frenchman. *L'Abbé Guillemart, Vicaire Général, Arras (Pas-de-Calais), France*—he wrote out his address for me—and looking at me over his French Baedeker every now and then, he finally asked in French, "Do you speak French?" I shook my head deprecatingly and smiled regretfully. "*Italiano?*" Again I had to shake my head. "*Très triste!*" he said, as if he were sorry, and went on reading. I saw that he wanted to make friends with me, and I was sorry myself, for he had such a very pleasant, interesting and intelligent face. He was clad in a black cassock that reached to his feet, the buttons ranging so nicely down his chest, and carried only a small portmanteau and an umbrella. We reached the hotel, and I found that he was stopping there. Once on the way up he waved his hand out of the window and said something. I think he was indicating that we could see Perugia further up the valley. I smiled. In the dining room, where I found him after being assigned to my room, he offered me his bill of fare and indicated that a certain Italian dish (we had the choice of two meats) was the best. I smiled again.

This hotel to which we had come was such a bare little affair. It was new enough—one of Cook's offerings to which all the tourists traveling under the direction of that agency are sent. The walls were quite colorless, white and clean. The ceilings of the rooms were high, over high, latticed windows and doors. My room, as I found, gave out onto an exquisite balcony which commanded the wonderful sweep of plain below. It reminded me of the veranda of the Catskill Mountain House, in the Catskills, and also of one or two of the high-view hotels in New England.

The dining room, as I found, contained six or seven other travelers, bound either south towards Rome or north towards Perugia and Florence. It was rather a hazy day, not cold and not warm, but cheerless. I can still hear the clink of the knives and forks as these few guests ate in silence or conversed in low tones. Travelers in this world seem almost innately fearsome of each other, particularly when they are few in number and meet in some such out-of-the-way place as this. My Catholic abbé was longing to be sociable with me, I could feel it, but this lack of a common tongue prevented him, or seemed to. As I was leaving I asked the proprietor to say to him that I was so sorry that I did not speak French, that if I did I would be glad to accompany him; and he immediately reported that the abbé asked if I would come along anyhow. "He haav ask," said my proprietor, a small, stout, dark man, "weel you not come halong hanyhow?"

I smiled. "Certainly," I replied. And so the Abbé Guillemart and I, apparently not understanding a word of each other's languages, started out sightseeing together—I had almost said arm-in-arm.

Now there is a fortunate aspect of the Baedekers, covering different countries: and that is that they are arranged much the same in all languages. That is, if on page 478 of the English Baedeker on Central Italy you find a reference to St. Francis of Assisi, somewhere in the French Baedeker on the same subject at about that page, or near it, you will find the equivalent of it. It is not hard to detect. I soon learned that while my French priest did not speak English, he read it after a fashion, and if he took ample time he could form an occasional sentence. It took time, however. He began—quite as Marcelle did, though not in so vivid or enthusiastic a fashion, to be sure—to indicate what the different things were as we went along.

Now the sights of Assisi are not many. If you are in a hurry and do not fall in love with the quaint and picturesque character of it and its wonderful views, you can do them all in a day—an afternoon, if you skimp. There is the church of St. Francis, with its associated monastery (what an anachronism a monastery seems in connection with St. Francis, who thought only of huts of branches or holes in the rocks!) and with its sepulcher of the saint in the lower church and the frescoed scenes from St. Francis's life by Giotto in the upper; the church of St. Clare (Santa Chiara) with its tomb and body of that enthusiastic imitator of St. Francis; the Duomo, or cathedral, begun in 1134—a rather poor specimen of a cathedral after some others—and the church of St. Damiano, the chapel of which was given to St. Francis by the Benedictine monks of Monte Subasio soon after he had begun his work of preaching the penitent life. There is also the Hermitage of the Carceri, where in small holes in the rocks the early Franciscans led a self-depriving life, and the new church raised on the site of a house belonging to Pietro Bernardone, the father of St. Francis, who was in the cloth business.

In spite of my enthusiasm for the principles of St. Francis, I cannot say that I followed with too much enthusiasm the involved architectural, historical, artistic and religious details of these churches and chapels. St. Francis, wonderful "jongleur of God" that he was, was not interested in churches and chapels so much as he was in the self-immolating life of Christ. He did not want his followers to have monasteries at first. "Carry neither gold nor silver nor money in your girdles, nor bag, nor two coats, nor sandals, nor staff, for the workman is worthy of his hire" (Matthew X, 7–10). I liked the church of St. Francis, however, for in spite of the fact that it is rather gray and bare, as befits a Franciscan edifice, it is a double church—one below the other and seemingly running at right angles. They are both large, charming Gothic churches, each complete with sacristy, choir nave, transepts and the like. I was always pleased with it because of the fact that in spite of the un-St. Francis-like idea of it, it has a lovely cloister in the best Italian manner, and through the interstices of the walls wonderful views of the valley below may be secured. In it, as in Rome, are some few fragments of earlier Gothic and Roman architecture, some sepulchers and the like. I cannot see how the Franciscans could have strayed so far from the poetic (not bleak) idea of their founder as to want anything so beautiful and luxurious, and to establish it in his hometown, too—but such is life.

The lower church, gray and varied in its interior, is rich in frescoes by Cimabue and others which deal with the sacred vows of the Franciscans; the upper (the nave) is decorated with frescoes by Giotto, illustrating the life of St. Francis. The latter interested me immensely because I knew by now that these were almost the beginning of Italian and Umbrian religious art, and because Giotto, from the evidences his work affords, must have been such a naive and pleasant old soul. I fairly laughed out loud as I strolled about this great nave of the upper church—the abbé was still below—at some of the good old Italian's attempts at characterization and composition. If you are a founder of a whole line of great artists, called upon to teach them something entirely new in the way of life-expression, it is no easy thing to get all the wonderful things you see and feel into a certain picture or series of pictures, but Giotto tried it and succeeded very well, too. The decorations are not great, but they are quaint and lovely, even if you have to admit at times that an apprentice of today could draw and compose better. He couldn't "intend" better, however, nor convey more human tenderness and feeling in gay, light coloring—and therein lies the whole secret!

There are some twenty-eight of these frescoes ranged along the lower walls on either side: St. Francis stepping on the cloak of the poor man who, recognizing him as a saint, spreads it down before him; St. Francis giving his cloak to the poor nobleman; St. Francis seeing the vision of the palace which was to be reared for him and his followers; St. Francis in the car of fire; St. Francis driving the devils away from Arezzo; St. Francis before the sultan; St. Francis preaching to the birds; and so on. I was delighted to see this last, to see how it coincided with the drawing of my youth, but it was very different. The birds were larger and my single sprig of a tree was not present, but the artist seems to have been moved by the picture of natural beauty that he was set to paint. It was very charming. I could not help thinking what a severe blow has been given to religious legend since those days—how, except in the minds of the very ignorant, saints and devils and angels and stigmata and holy visions have all but disappeared. The grand phantasmagoria of religious notions as they relate to the life of Christ have all but vanished, for the time being anyhow, even in the brains of the masses at the bottom, and we are having an invasion of rationalism or something approximating it, even at the bottom. The laissez-faire opportunism which has characterized the men at the top in all ages is seeping down to the bottom. Via the newspaper and the magazine, even in Italy—in Assisi—something of astronomy, botany, politics and mechanics, scientifically demonstrated, is creeping in. The inflow seems very meager as yet, a mere trickle, but it has begun. Even in Assisi I saw newspapers and a weekly in a local barbershop. The natives—the aged ones, very thin, shabby and pale—run into the churches at all hours of the day to prostrate themselves before useless and helpless saints, but nevertheless the newspapers are in the barbershops. Old Cosimo Medici's truism that governments are not managed by paternosters is slowly seeping down. We have scores of men in the world today as able as old Cosimo Medici and as ruthless. We will have hundreds and thousands after a while, only they will be much more circumspect in their ruthlessness, and they will work hard for the state. Perhaps there won't be so much useless praying before useless images when that time comes. The thought of divinity *in the individual* needs to be more fully developed.

While I was wandering thus and ruminating, I was interested at the same time in the faithful enthusiasm my abbé was manifesting in the details of the art of this great church. He followed me about for a time in my idle wanderings as I studied the architectural details of one of the earliest of Gothic churches and then he went away to himself, returning every so often to find in my guidebook certain passages which he wanted me to read, pointing to certain frescoes and exclaiming, "Giotto!," "Cimabue!," "Andrea da Bologna!" Finally he said in plain English but very slowly, "Did—you—ever—read—a—life—of—St. Francis?"

"Do you speak English?" I asked, rather astonished.

He shook his head and smiled.

I nodded that I had, not being able to explain, however, that my knowledge was vague or at least fragmentary.

We continued our way, and finally we found a Franciscan monk who spoke both English and French. This was a very peculiar-looking man, tall, athletic, who looked as though he might be very experienced in the world indeed. He explained more of the frescoes, the history of the church, the present state of the Franciscans here and so on.

I must confess that my knowledge of the intricacies of Italian art, aside from the lines of its general development, the intellectual state of the time in which it appeared, the personal characteristics of its chief exponents, the charm of their work and the difficulties and influences under which it was done, is slim. I know much of the history of Pisa, Florence, Venice and Genoa, to say nothing of Milan and Rome, and how art in these regions came to be furthered and why, but when it comes to the finer subtleties of influence—one school on another, one country on another, one individual on another, and in particular the influence of one minor individual on another minor individual—I, as they say in poker-playing, pass! If one has an intense love of Italian art and has the business in hand of writing a history of it, well and good. Otherwise I should think a general theory of its development and precise information concerning certain pictures would be sufficient.

Alas, dabbling in Italian art, and in art in general, is like trifling with some soothing drug—the more you know, the more you want to know. At Assisi, as in Pisa, I found myself becoming curious as to exact details, reading with enthusiasm why it was that the upper church of St. Francis was so long in getting its frescoes done. You will have to read a life of St. Francis to get that—to see how the leaders after his death quarreled among themselves as to whether the severe, simple life as he planned it was to be followed or not. It was followed, and it was not—by turns—as one head of the order after another died or was deposed. This problem set by St. Francis was one of the most amazing and significant that has ever been put before the mind of man, and I have never wondered that the good brothers quarreled and that there were zealots, moderates and reactionaries among them. Some of the good brothers, most enthusiastic in their insistence that the work of St. Francis should go on exactly as he originally saw it, were burnt for their pains—the most zealous of them!—but such is life. No great idea makes its way without difficulty, but the gospel according to St. Francis seems to be growing weaker and weaker in its influence just at present, largely because the Catholic Church is so dull in refusing to adjust the inherent sanity of its principles to the psychology of the time.

CHAPTER LVIII

The other places Franciscan, as I have said, did not interest me so much, though I accompanied my friend the abbé wherever he was inclined to go. I could see that he was religiously minded, that he liked me, and we Marcelled our way through considerable information in regard to each other. He had come from Germany into Italy and was going back into France via Spain. He wanted to know—it is almost impossible to make clear the process—how I liked Rome.

"Roma! Oh! Très bon, oui? Très charmant, oui? Magnifique! Oui?"

When he asked after New York, he looked up and waved his hand upward, as indicating great height, great buildings, and I knew he was thinking of our skyscrapers, and then he made me understand that Americans of wealth were very numerous everywhere. "American bar!" he said, twittering to himself like a bird. "American stim-eat" (steam heat). "American 'otel."

I had to smile.

Side by side we proceeded through the church of St. Clare, the Duomo, the new church raised on the site of the house that belonged to Pietro Bernardone, the father of the saint, and finally to the church of San Damiano, where after St. Francis had seen the vision of the new life he went to pray. Thereafter it was given to him by the Benedictines, and he set about the work of repairing it, and when once it was in charge of the Poor Clares, he, after resigning the command of his order, returned to rest and compose the "Canticle of the Law." I never knew until I came to Assisi what a business this thing of religion is in Italy—how valuable the shrines and churches of an earlier day are to its communities. Thousands of travelers must pass this way each year. They support the only good hotels. Travelers from all nations come—English, French, German, American, Russian, Japanese. The attendants at the shrines reap a small livelihood from the tips of visitors, and they are always there, lively and almost obstreperous in their attentions. I saw the oldest and most faded of all the guides and attendants about these churches and shrines of Assisi, so old and faded that they seemed almost epics of poverty.

My good priest was for praying before every shrine. He would get down on his knees and cross himself, praying four or five minutes, while I stood irreligiously in the background, looking at him and wondering how long he would be. He prayed before the tomb of St. Francis in the Franciscan church; before the body of St. Clare (clothed in a black habit and shown behind a glass case) in the church of St. Clare; before the altar in the chapel of Saint Damiano, where St. Francis had first prayed; and so on. Finally, when we were all through and it was getting late evening, he wanted to go down into the valley, near the railroad station, to the church of Santa Maria degli Angeli, where the cell in which St. Francis died is located. He thought I might want to leave him now, but I refused. We started out, inquiring our way of the monks at Saint Damiano, and found that we had to go back through the town. I had to smile as we were doing this, for one of the monks, a fat, barefooted dub of a man, signaled me to put on my hat, which I was carrying because I wanted to enjoy the freshness of the evening wind. It had cleared up now, the sun had come out, and we were enjoying one of those lovely Italian spring evenings which bring a sense of childhood to the heart. The good monk thought I was holding my hat out of reverence to his calling. I put it on.

We went back through the town, and then I realized how lovely the town life of a small Italian town is in spring. Assisi has a population of about five thousand. It was cool and pleasant outside. Many doors were now open, showing evening fires within the shadows of rooms. Some children were in the roadways. Carts and wains were already clattering up from the fields below, and church bells—the sweetest echoes from churches here and there in the valley and from the several churches here in Assisi—exchanged melodies. We walked fast because it was late, and when we reached the station it was already dusk. The moon had come up, however, and lit this great edifice, standing among the ruck of small homes, quite clearly. A number of Italian men and women were philandering with each other around a pump—those same dark, earringed Italians with whom we are now so familiar in America. The church was now locked, but my abbé went about to the cloister gate, which stood at one side of the main entrance, and rang a bell. A brown-cowled monk appeared, and they exchanged a few words. Finally, with many smiles, we were admitted into a moonlit garden, where cypress trees and box and ilex showed their lovely forms, through a long court that had an odor of malt, as if beer were brewed here, and so finally by a circuitous route into the main body of the church and the chapel containing the cell of St. Francis. It was so dark by now that only the heaviest objects appeared distinctly, the moonlight falling faintly through several of the windows. The voices of the monks sounded strange and sonorous, even though they talked low. We walked about looking at the great altars, the windows and the high, flat ceiling while I wondered how all the monks I saw in the garden and elsewhere made a living. We went into the chapel, lined on either side by handsome benches, occupied by kneeling monks and lit by one low, swinging lamp which hung before the cell in which St. Francis had died. There was much whispering of prayers here, and the good abbé was on his knees in a moment, praying solemnly while I too knelt in the background this time, occupying one of the benches and meditating.

St. Francis certainly never contemplated that his beggarly cell would ever be surrounded by the rich marbles and bronze work against which his life was a protest. He never imagined, I am sure, that in spite of his prayer for poverty, his order would become rich and influential and that this, the site of his abstinence, would be occupied by one of the most ornate churches in Italy. It is curious how barnacle-like the spirit of materiality invariably encrusts the ideal! Christ died on the cross for the privilege of worshiping God "in spirit and in truth" after he had preached the Sermon on the Mount; and then you have the gold-encrusted, power-seeking, wealth-loving papacy, with women and villas and wars of aggrandizement and bastardy as the principal concomitants. And following St. Francis, imitating the self-immolation of the Nazarene, you have another great order whose churches and convents in Italy are among the richest and most beautiful. It must be that lust and riches and show and gourmandizing love to seem what they are not, to furnish themselves forth in the livery of their opposites in order that they may satisfy a faint scratching of the spirit that is so thickly coated over that it is almost extinguished. I can scarcely reason it out any other way.

Or it may be that the ideal is always such an excellent device wherewith to trap the unwary and the unsophisticated. "Feed them with a fine semblance, and then put a tax on their humble credulity" seems to be the logic of materialism in regard to the masses. Anything to obtain power and authority! Anything to rule! And so you have an Alexander VI, Vicar of Christ—poisoning cardinals and seizing on estates that did not belong to him, leading a life of almost insane luxury and adultery—and a Medicean pope interested in art and the development of a pagan ideal. Well has this earthly scheme of things been called a riddle! It is a nightmare. It is a wild, disordered dream in which the cap and bells of the jester are far more significant than either the cross or the temple.

We returned at between seven and eight that night. After a bath and with a candle gleaming in my room (the only light furnished), I sat out on the large balcony, or veranda, commanding the valley, and enjoyed the moonlight. Both the burnished surface of the olive trees and brown fields already being plowed with white oxen and wooden shares gave back a soft glow that was somehow like the patina on bronze. There was a faint odor of flowers in the wind, and here and there were lights gleaming. From some street in the town I heard singing and the sound of a mandolin. It was perfect.

At breakfast—coffee, honey, rolls and butter—my abbé gave me his card. He was going to Florence, I to Spello, seven miles away. He asked the hotel man to say to me that he had had a charming time. I replied that I had enjoyed our conversations. He smiled. Would I not come to Pas de Calais (France) and visit him? "When I learn to speak French," I replied. So after breakfast I called a little open carriage, such as they use in Rome, Paris and Monte Carlo, and was off for Spello, and he took an early omnibus and caught his train.

Spello, I shall not linger long there. It dates from Roman days, possibly earlier, and contains the wonderful view of cypresses argued for by Grant Richards, the remains of a large amphitheater outside its walls and a Greek temple of Minerva inside. I thought my contract with my driver fixed it so that I should be driven through the town, wherever I wished to go, but I soon found otherwise. When we reached the gate, an old Roman one, he calmly drove his vehicle into an angle before a tap-house and dismounted. "Here," I said, "this will never do. Up! On!" and I moved my hand to the winding road that obviously led upward.

"*Non! Non!*" he replied and shook his head. Nothing doing.

I groaned. I expostulated. I frowned.

He never budged. Instead he covered his horse with a dirty blanket—to protect him from the heat, I fancy. I went off disgruntled after a time, all my lovely thoughts concerning St. Francis and charity dispelled, but I soon recovered. I climbed up, up, up, for this was another hill-city; you begin to climb upward from a ridge already thirteen hundred feet high. As I walked, I idled before little stores, a small market, several churches, entering the latter to see if there was anything to show in the way of art. There was nothing to speak of. A few frescoes by Pinturicchio in the Duomo, a small collection of silver hearts and tinsel gifts—votive offerings—before a shrine of the Virgin in the church of St. Andrea. For once I was glad to get away from art for a half-day and study railroad-less, streetcar-less, electric-lightless Italian hill-town life.

Spello apparently is not yet spoiled. You do not see any such thing as the newfangled automobile except on the highroad below. I had not encountered one. Instead there were donkeys, carrying large bundles of twigs for firewood on their bags, and odd two-wheeled cars of the vintage of sixteen-something, I fancy. There were, however, modern supplies of tinned oils, shoe polishes, leather goods, hats and caps, but nothing intended apparently for people of means and taste. All the women wore bunchy, high-colored skirts, with occasional bright scarfs; the men thin, earth-colored, tightly-strapped trousers and rakish caps or soft hats. There were no Italian soldiers in either Assisi or Spello—just a low-keyed, simple Italian farming life. Olive orchards, grapevine fields, some flocks of goats and sheep—nothing more.

I looked in many of the low, dark houses and saw not the spinning wheel but the Singer sewing machine, but along with it were women balancing bundles and buckets on their heads and occasionally carrying two buckets of water slung on a yoke laid over their shoulders. Up at the top of Main Street, which climbed and climbed via stairs and slopes until it reached the utmost knoll, I encountered a small chapel and monastery gardens, into the latter of which I ventured without let or hindrance. I do not recall now exactly how I did get in, but I know I entered from a small plaza, which commanded a wide and lovely scene and where stood a tall wooden cross, through a dark, whitewashed hall where some village calciminers were at work. When I had got beyond them, I found myself in a small brick-paved court, one entrance of which gave out onto a path that led under olive trees and between some bushes to a small shrine of the Virgin, perhaps four or five hundred feet farther on. To the right was an orchard of plums and a rose garden, to the left an acre or two enclosed by a stone wall devoted to a more prosaic garden. One could see where a winter crop of potatoes had been protected by straw in order to make them grow advantageously, and in a cow-shed not far from the shrine of the Virgin I found a charming drawing of a little child on its knees done in charcoal.

From every angle of this monastic garden you could, by looking over its gray stone walls, command majestic views of all the country that for centuries has been harried by one power after another. Assisi, with its gray fortress-like monastery frowning like a battlement, lay seven miles to the east. Far down in the valley across a world of olive trees Santa Maria degli Angeli was visible, an imposing feature of the vale of Spoleto. Farther eastward still were the dim outlines of Perugia, that master city, from which such humble cots as Spello occasionally sought protection. The long roads were like white ribbons of dust, the Tiber a dim thread, and below me, not far from the ruins of the ancient Roman amphitheater, was the wonderful mass of cypresses outlining walks and drives in some princely villa, which Grant Richards had admired years before. There were cypresses in this garden, a row of them following the line of a stone wall, and they looked like tall black soldiers or heavenly spears, sighing as usual in the light air.

I wandered about at will without finding a soul, and I thought at first that possibly the place had been deserted in order that the workmen might finish their task of calcimining the rooms; but coming to a little garden full of violets on the other side of the monastery I discovered a series of terraces and below me, in one of them, in the cool shadow of the monastery itself, a brown-cowled Benedictine, a basket on his arm. He was bending over picking here and there a vegetable, probably for his noonday pot. I saw him take up several parsnips, a few beets, some potatoes and turnips, and then, perhaps disturbed by my gaze, he looked up, and a kindly smile spread over his fat features. He nodded genially, pointed to the fine view and then went on gathering his vegetables. On this brilliant morning, in the dewy shade of his monastic walls, he reminded me of that Friar Lawrence in *Romeo and Juliet* whom Romeo encounters filling up his osier cage "with baleful weeds and precious-juiced flowers" for medicinal purposes. Come to think of it, that was a Benedictine also, and the scene was Italy. I thought my friar might come up after a time, but he did not, and finding no one else about, I made my way out into the stairway streets of the town, where little donkeys were still ambling up with vast bundles of faggots, their long ears flicking occasionally, their little feet being placed as mincingly as those of a finicky lady, going as slow as occasional curses, threats and blows would permit. I knew that they were having the most terrible imprecations heaped upon them, but it did not seem to disturb their philosophic souls.

You know, I take it that in this section of Italy the world presents as fine a contrast between the old and the new as is to be found. Imagine Spello—not a streetcar, not an electric light, not an automobile, not a gas tank, not a modern factory, not a railroad, and yet sustaining an ancient population of lineal descent of perhaps three or four thousand. "Spello is unspoiled," someone has said, and it is so true. The modern tide of manufacture, travel and trade that is following in the valley below has not yet spattered to this high top. You can see it—not exactly perhaps, but very much as it was when Pinturicchio painted here, when St. Francis preached in the fields about, when the Baglioni and the guilds were quarreling in Perugia, when Michelangelo fled on horseback past here to Florence in order to escape the machinations of Julius II, when Otto came to conquer Rome. It is so old that the early Umbrians must have yielded sway to Rome here without a murmur, for Perugia and Assisi did. One of these days soon a trolley car will run along these heights from Spello to Perugia, stop in the main square at Assisi and let you off at the tomb of St. Francis, if you ask the conductor. There will be a gasworks and an electric light plant in this vicinity, as there are already at Assisi and Perugia. A trolley car will wind up this long road that leads to the monastery I have described. I am sure that there must have been a moving picture show there already, although I did not find it. It would be almost the only Italian town in which there is not one—indeed, many. I did not see any phonographs in the windows nor any pianos for sale, but if they are not there, poverty alone prevents. A little prosperity, and all these things will be added unto them—and I am in nowise a prophet, either.

I made my way down and found my driver comfortably seated with a group of Italians outside the tap-house door, exchanging the pleasantries of the day. He came and unblanketed his horse, and we trotted cheerily back along the highroad above the valley to the hotel at Assisi. I forgot to say that I tried to present my letter to M. Sabatier, the French savant and authority on St. Francis, but he was off in some other part of Italy, and so I left my card. I gathered up my bags, feed nine underlings who gathered expectantly about the door and hurried off to make the twelve-twenty train in order that I might have my noonday meal in Perugia. I was really anxious to reach Florence and Venice and then jump into Germany, particularly Berlin, in order to contrast this antique life with the ultra-commercial progressiveness which I should find there. I did want to stop once more in the church of Santa Maria degli Angeli in order that I might see how it looked by day, but I had not the time, and by one o'clock I was in Perugia, eating my good meal and drinking my good red wine and wondering what I should see before nightfall.

CHAPTER LIX

Of all the hill-cities I saw in Italy, certainly Perugia was the most remarkable, the most sparkling, the most forward in all things commercial, with as great a sense of up-to-date-ness as Florence or Milan. Although as old in aspect, it is more modern than Florence, much more varied than Pisa or the little I saw of Genoa. It stands high, very high above the plain as you come in at the depot, and a very fine plush-seated, wide-windowed trolley car carries you up to the principal square—the Piazza Vittorio Emanuele—stopping in front of the modern hotels which command the wide sea-like views which the valley presents below. I never before, in all my life, saw a city of sixty thousand so beautifully located. Wonderful ridges of mountains fade into the most amazing lavenders, purples, scarlets and blues, as the evening falls or the dawn brightens. If I were trying to explain where some of the painters of the Umbrian school, particularly Perugino, secured their wonderful sky touches, their dawns and evenings, I should say that they had once lived in Perugia. Perugino did.

It seemed to me, as I wandered about it the two days that I was there, that it was the most human and industrious little city of sixty thousand that I had ever walked into. Every living being seemed to have so much to do. They were trotting here and there with the greatest interest in life, hurrying into the most up-to-date shops of all kinds—dressmaking establishments, drugstores, piano stores, haberdasheries, jewelry shops, bookstores and the like. You could hear as you went up and down the most amazing of streets—streets that ascend and descend in long, winding stairways step by step for blocks—pianos playing, anvils ringing, machinery humming, saws droning and, near one great abattoir where cattle were evidently slaughtered all day long, the piercing squeals of pigs in their death-throes. There was a marketplace that I found held every morning from dawn until noon, crowded with the good citizens of Perugia buying everything from cabbages and dress-goods to picture-postcards and hardware. Long rows of fat, Perugian old ladies sitting with baskets of wares in front of them, all talking genially and dispensing to purchasers at the same time. There was a parade in the public square, running from the Esplanade facing the great hotels back perhaps as much as four or five blocks to the famous fountain of Perugia in the Piazza del Municipio in front of the cathedral, where nightly between seven and ten the whole spirited city seemed to be walking. Boys and girls, young men and young women, middle-aged men and middle-aged women, soldiers, officers, travelers—a whole world of gay, enthusiastic life that would remind you of an American manufacturing town on a Saturday night—only this happens every night in Perugia.

When I arrived there I went directly to the Palace Hotel, which faces the Piazza Vittorio Emanuele, and there I encountered one of those staggering attempts on the part of modern Italy to be up-to-date—a really exceptionally American-like, or at least Parisian-like, hotel. It was excellent, charmingly built, beautifully located, with a wide view of the Umbrian plain which is so wonderful in its array of distant mountains and so rich in orchards, monasteries, convents and churches. I wish you would read the attached description of its charms, just as it was printed in the little booklet which the hotel management furnished, in a staggering attempt on the part of Perugia to catch a part of that all-desired English and American traffic, which now perhaps passes gaily by without stopping. No letter or comma has been touched in any attempt to improve or modify it:

In the most elevated part of Perugia facing the beautiful Piazza Vittorio Emanuele stands a fine building, quiet that in the year 1903 was finished the PALACE HOTEL. If ever a Hotel corresponds to, such a name, it will undoubtely be that in Perugia, for there are a very few within the limits of Italy which can be of such a luxury in all their accomadation. The London Health Resort, in an article devouted to Perugia says: Such a luxurious Hotel is indeed rearely found ouside the great capitals of the world, even the most exacting travellers accustomed to the ever increasing comfort and luxury of the twentieth century hotels could not fait to be satisfied here. It is indeed a constant surpris to newcomers, that anyone should have been enterprising enough to errect this veritable palace not in Rome or Naples, but in comparatively unknown though deeply interesting Perugia.

To the fine and pleasant architecture of the front corresponds every room within the entirely fireproof building, especially the high, bright and airy bedrooms furnished with the latest acquisitions of sanitary furniture—engineering will enjoy full appreciation by visitors. Comunicating suits of rooms including separate bath and toilet correspond in every way to the requirements of modern comfort and compensate especially during a long stay very nearly their own homes.

At any time double and single rooms on any demand.

The public rooms offer in every respect all imaginable comfort either by their dimensions or their happily choosen luxury. The drawing room with delightful ceiling-paintings by Brugnoli exites the admiration of every visitor. Besides this, deserve special mentioning; the large Billiard-and Smoking-room, the Dining-room and the Restaurant both in rococostile and the Wintergarden. This latter, the favourite-room of the visitors is able in virtue of its dimensions to accomodate easily all the visitors of the full house. Beautiful palms and other plants of a carefull selection adorn the eleven metres high, skylighted room and complete the impression of a stay in the open air. News papers of the principle languages are found here and many a day one could imagine to be in Rome or Florence or in any other capital of the continent rather than in quiet Perugia.

The broad and lofty corridors and the majestique staircase still remain to be spoken of; especially the latter with its monumental design and with fragments of etruscan art decorated ceiling-paintings (also by Brugnoli) is quite an attractive curiosity of Perugia.

Rich electric light illuminates every room and steam heating keeps them in a most agreeable temperature. The most secure elevator of latest construction is electric and a special electric saloon-car meets every train at the two miles of the town and 250 metres below its level situated station and brings the traveller up in no more than ten minutes to the hotel. No hotel can have such a delightful station-service, moreover the fare is not exceeding that of a common Omnibus in any other town.

Every improvement for modern comfort has been made here in order to meet the pretensions of modern times. System of separate tables is introduced for the "table d'hote" and in the restaurant, meals are served at fixed prices as "a la carte."

Auto-Garage, Post, Telegraph Office in the hotel.

Whoever stayed at the "Palace" in Perugia and on a fine spring- or autumn-day has contemplated from the terrace on the top of the roof one of the magnificent sunsets over Umbria will ever remember this happy sidestep on his Italian trip.

I count that a worthy attempt, not to be too much sneered at, for the hotel is all that its simple little soul claims and more. The only trouble with the "Palace" and with much else in Perugia is that it hasn't reached the period of pretentiousness and self-esteem which will surely come later. Alas, that it ever should!

The first afternoon that I was in Perugia I spent walking in the various sections of the town that I could reach, looking at the Duomo, glancing at the famous fountain, studying the objects in the Etruscan Museum and giving a passing glance to the interior of the Perugian Gallery of Art, very much discussed in a book on Umbrian towns which I had with me. The next morning I completed my observation of these institutions and idled about the city generally.

I am sorry to state that my preliminary study of Perugian art and architecture did me little good. No one save a historical zealot could extract much pleasure from the complicated political and religious history of this city, which runs through the Carolingian and Teutonic empires, the politics of the French kings and the popes, and winds up in an apparently unbroken dullness which has endured for hundreds of years. Once upon a time there was a guild of money changers and bankers which built a hall called the Hall of the Cambio, which is very charming, and at another time (or nearly the same time) there was a dominant Guelph party which, in conjunction with some wealthy townsmen known as the "Raspanti," built the Palazzo Publico, or Palazzo Comunale, in what is now known as the Piazza del Municipio, which I think is perfect. It is not a fortress like the Bargello at Florence, but it is a perfect architectural thing, the charm of which I have never for a moment forgotten. The guidebook I had spoke of its principal facade as being over-elaborate and wanting in breadth and boldness, but that is mere borrowed architectural tommyrot, I am sure. It is a beautiful structure, one that serves charmingly the uses to which it is put—that of a public center for officials and a picture gallery.

It was in one of these rooms devoted to a collection of Umbrian art that I found a pretentious collection of the work of Perugino, the one really important painter who ever lived or worked in Perugia—and the little city now makes much of him. The work of his which is here is not very remarkable, however, and nothing very good can be said of the cathedral either, which stands nearby and hopes to be taken seriously. Between this palace and the cathedral, the fountain designed by Niccolò Pisano and executed by Giovanni Pisano and Arnolfo di Cambio is really beautiful. It contains an upper and a lower cistern, set upon a small flight of steps and enclosed within a railing that consists of sculptured panels which attempt to set before one a complete philosophy of life and society by means of symbols, personifications, historical personages and scenes, Bible stories and fables, but for that I had no time. They were charming, as were some of the pictures in the public gallery, but after the wonders of Rome and Pisa I drew little satisfaction from the pretentious discussion of their artistic value in the catalogues. Perugino, except in a few pictures, seemed dull. The little pictures of Pinturicchio were unimportant. The Hall of the Merchants I thought was perfect, but outside of that there were few things of which the artistic value was rated high that I found interesting.

If I felt like ignoring the long-winded art discussions of comparatively trivial things, the charm and variety of the town and its present-day life was in no way lost upon me. I think I never saw a place with so much variety of scenery, such curious twists of streets and lanes, such heights and depths of levels, and platforms on which houses, the five- and six-story tenement of the older order of life in Italy, are built. The streets are all narrow, in some places not more than ten or fifteen feet wide, arched over completely for considerable distances and twisting and turning, ascending or descending as they go, but they give into such adorable squares and open places, such magnificent views at every turn, that I do not see how the humblest dweller can avoid seeing something in the way of beauty and view if he has the taste for it.

And the unheralded things, the things which the guidebooks do not talk about, are so charming. I found it so entrancing to descend of a morning by lovely, cool, stone passages from the Piazza of Vittorio Emanuele (everything now in Italy is either Corso or Piazza Umberto or Vittorio Emanuele or Garibaldi, particularly the first two—heaven knows why!) to the Piazza of the Army and watch the soldiers, principally cavalry, drill. Their parade was a space about five acres in extent, as flat as a table, set high above the plain with deep ravines descending on either hand and the quaint houses and public institutions of Perugia looking down from above. To the left, as you looked out over the plain across the intervening ravine, was another spur of the town, also built on a flat ridge, with the delicious church of St. Peter and its charming Italian Gothic tower, and with the white road that swept along the edge of the cliff, making a delightful way for carriages and automobiles. In another section of the town, along the Via dei Priori and the Via dello Conco, I took delight in seeing how wonderfully the deep, green ravines separated one section of the town from another. You could stand, your arms resting upon some old brownish-green wall, and look out over intervening fields to distant ranges of mountains or towns, like Assisi and Spoleto. The variety of the coloring of the plain below was never wearying.

I do not know whether what I am going to say will have the force and significance that I wish to convey, but a city like Perugia, taken as a whole—all its gates, all its towers, all its upward-sweeping details—is like a Gothic cathedral. You would have to think of the ridge on which it stands as providing the nave and the transepts and the apse, and then the quaint little winding streets of the town itself with their climbing houses and towers would suggest the pinnacles, spandrels, flying buttresses, airy statues and crosses of a cathedral like Amiens. I know of no other simile that quite suggests Perugia or that is really so true to it.

The first night I was there I spent walking in the Corso Vannucci, the principal street that runs from the Duomo and the fountain and the Communal Palace—all located in the Piazza del Municipio—to the Piazza Vittorio Emanuele, where the hotel at which I was stopping was located. For a street or parade that must have borne very much of this aspect for the last four or five hundred years, it was exceedingly sprightly and modern indeed. The thing that I noticed first was the peculiar up-to-dateness of the great crowd that was walking here, men and women alike. The women especially were Parisian, or, better yet, American, wearing such costumes as you would see on Upper Broadway of a Sunday afternoon. The tailoring of their costumes was in every respect smart and tasteful, and their hats exhibited all the flare and variety that characterizes good American millinery. Their shoes, too, were good (a window I noticed advertised American shoes), and their general stature and physical proportions corresponded very favorably with those to which we are accustomed on the western side of the Atlantic. The men, in most cases, were smaller than American men, more dapper and less hardy, but they were efficient enough. The soldiery, of whom there were a plentiful supply from the neighboring barracks, were much more rugged, no doubt being drawn from the rural districts. If I had not heard the Italian language everywhere about me, I might have imagined that I was in New Brunswick, New Jersey, or Roanoke, Virginia.

At the same time the windows along this particular parade were so brightly lighted. In one music store I saw a lot of American coon songs and the Indian waltzes displayed in the windows. In another I saw an excellent collection of china and glassware and in a large grocery store those handsome jars of preserved fruit with which we are so familiar on our principal thoroughfares. I have mentioned the phonograph but not the moving picture theater which was here, nor the very metropolitan-looking window full of gloves, neckties, canes and the like. The people walked to and fro here for all of three hours, laughing and chatting, while a great clock somewhere, possibly in the cathedral, chimed the hours and half-hours. I heard four young soldiers whom I took to be Italian and who were sitting on the wall at the end of the parade which commands the great Umbrian valley hundreds of feet below. To my astonishment one of these young men in a uniform of the Italian army with the Bersaglieri hat jumped down and exclaimed in English, "Gee, there goes a pair of beauts! Let's follow 'em!" I could scarcely believe my ears and thought once I would interrogate them, but they were so busy with their thoughts of conquest that it was not possible. I took it that they might have been Americans of Italian parentage who had returned to fight in the war against Turkey.

This Italian valley was so beautiful that I should like to say one more word about the skies and the wonderful landscape effects. North of here in Florence, Venice and Milan they do not occur so persistently and with such delicious warmth at this season of the year. At this height the nights were not cold, but cool, and the mornings burst with such a blaze of color as to defy the art of all save the greatest painters. They were not so much lurid as richly spiritualized, being shot through with a strange, electric radiance that conveyed to me a feeling of spiritual elevation and delight. This did not mean, as it would so often in America, that a cloudy day was to follow. Rather, the radiance slowly gave place to a glittering field of light that brought out every slope and olive orchard and distant cypresses and pines with amazing clearness. The bells of the churches in Perugia and in the valley below were like muezzins calling to each other from their prayer towers. As the day waxed, the features of the landscape seemed to be set in crystal, and the greens and browns and grays seemed at times to have a metallic quality. Outside their walls in the distance were churches, shrines and monasteries, always with a cypress or two, sometimes with many, which stood out with great distinctness, and from distant hillsides you would hear laborers singing in the bright sun. Well might they sing, for I know of no place where life would present to them a fairer aspect.

The people in Perugia proper seemed cheerful and good-natured, pattering up and down their endless stairs with their baskets, walking through the streets with tools of one kind and another in their hands and tinkering industriously at tables drawn close to open windows. There was one place outside the walls where women came to wash, and it seemed to me as if there must have been thousands of white garments here bleaching in the sun. In another place an old Doric temple-shaped building was turned into a sawmill, and in still another part of the town a well-preserved church of attractive proportions had been turned into a weaving and dyeing industry. After the score of churches that I had already seen here, fitted out in some instances with their tinsel trappings, I took it that some of the others might have been spared to the same good purpose. There were a number of others, though, such as St. Peter's and that of San Francesco, which were perfect jewel-boxes of carvings, frescoes, mosaics and the like. The faces of several of these churches were executed in that bizarre, almost arabesque-like pattern of alternate black and white squares. What was left of the Roman ruins, such as the arch of Augustus and the ancient walls and gates, was also really beautiful and impressive in its way.

The country north of Perugia as far as Florence retains much of this brilliant, cypress-pointed atmosphere which I have described. As the train traveled northward from noon until evening, I was never weary of looking at the Italian laborers in the fields, always plowing with white oxen, always accompanied by their wives or perhaps daughters and one or two children, to say nothing of a pig or two that kept close at their heels in order to seize upon any roots or herbs that might perchance be released. The colorings of the buildings—houses, barns, churches, inns and castles—continued to be as they were in the south: gray, brown, cream-white, cream-pink, pink, red and sea-green, with stripings of white and pink or brown and red now and then, and always finished with moss-tinted red and brown roofs. The hill-cities continued also, crowning almost every imposing height with the square campanile and the round-arched monastery. We were entering a place which had but little resemblance to the quaint architectural effects of the older cities. Now and then you would see a round-topped stone well covering that looked not unlike the small observatory domes used in astronomy, but these were not frequent. A newer form seemed to be taking their place. And near the stations occasionally electric light plants were visible, modern freight houses, and those rows of sidetracks with the small Italian freight cars standing on them which makes Europe alike everywhere. At the better stations those rolling stands containing refreshments and periodicals were in evidence, propelled from car to car by hawking vendors, and toward evening the daily newspapers of Rome and Florence were called out. I could see no difference between the American train guards and these Italians running to and fro as the train stopped, calling out the stations and signaling the conductors when all was ready to go on.

Some time before we reached Florence, but as we were coming into striking distance of it, the commercial aspect of Italy seemed to improve. The crossings in a few instances were guarded by gates. For miles we followed a winding stream, possibly the Arno or the Tiber, beautifully set with villas at times, and looked down upon castled heights. As we neared Florence—that city so sacred to medieval grandeur—I was surprised to notice an occasional manufactory, smoke issuing from its chimney and freight cars pushed onto a siding. It was an idyllic, spring-like evening, and with all the treasures of my historic reading in mind from the lives of the Medici and Savonarola to that of Michelangelo and the Florentine school of artists, I was keen to see what it should be like. Mrs. Armstrong had described it as the most individual of all the Italian cities that she had seen. She had raved over its narrow, dark, cornice-shaded streets, its fortress-like palaces, its highly individual churches and cloisters, the way the drivers of the little open vehicles plied everywhere cracking their whips, until, she said, it sounded like a Fourth of July in Janesville. I was keen to see how large the dome of the cathedral would look, whether it would really tower conspicuously over the remaining buildings of the city and whether the Arno would look as picturesque as it did in all the photos I had seen. If we crossed it at all, it was some distance out, so that I had no sight of it whatsoever until I had reached my hotel. The air was so soft and the sun so bright, although sinking low in the west, that I was pleased to accept, instead of the ancient atmosphere which I had anticipated, the wide streets and rows of four- and six-family apartment houses which characterize all the newer sections. They have the rich browns and creams of the earlier portions of Florence, but they are very different in their suggestion of modernity.

The distant hills about the town, as I could see from the car windows, were dotted with houses and villas occupying delightful positions above the town. I remember thinking that it suggested the spirit of the environs of places in the United States like Cincinnati and Louisville. Suddenly I saw the Duomo, and although I knew it only from photographs I recognized it on the instant. It spoke for itself in a large, simple, dignified way. Over the housetops it soared like a great bubble, and some pigeons flying in the air gave it the last touch of beauty that it required. We wound around the city in a circle; I could tell this by the shifting position of the sun, and I remember thinking how strange it was that there should be a railway system in Florence. There were great yards of railway tracks with scores of engines and lines of small boxcars, and then I saw a small stream—nothing like the Arno, of course—a bridge, a canal, and next we were rolling into a long crowded railway station, the guards calling "Firenze" and the porters signaling eagerly that they wanted to take our luggage. I got up, gathered my overcoat and bags into my arms, signaled a *facchino* and gave them to him; and then I sought a vehicle that would convey me to the hotel for which I was bound—the Hôtel de Ville on the Arno. I sat behind a fat driver while he cracked his whip endlessly above the back of a lazy horse, passing the while the showy facade of Santa Maria Novella, striped with strange bands of white and bluish gray or drab—a pleasing effect for a church. I could see at once that the Florence of the Middle Ages was a much more condensed affair than that which now sprawls out in various directions from the Loggia dei Lanzi and the place of the cathedral.

The long, narrow streets were alive with people, and the drivers of vehicles everywhere seemed to drive as if their life depended on it. Suddenly we turned into a piazza, very modern and very different from that of Santa Maria Novella, and then we were at the hotel door. It was a nice-looking square, I thought, not very large, clean and gray. To my astonishment and delight, I found that my room opened directly onto a balcony which overlooked the Arno, and that from it, sitting in a chair, I could command all of that remarkable prospect of high-piled medieval houses hanging over the water's edge. It was beautiful. The angelus bells were ringing, there was a bright glow in the west where the sun was going down, the water of the stream was a light turquoise blue and the walls of all the houses seemingly brown. I stood and gazed, thinking of the peculiarly efficient German manager I had encountered, the German servants who were in charge of this hotel and the fact that Florence had long since radically changed from what it was. A German porter came and brought my bags; a German maid brought hot water; a German clerk took my full name and address for the register and possibly the police; and then I was at liberty to unpack and dress for dinner. Instead I took a stroll out along the stream banks to study the world of jewelry shops which I saw there and the stands for flowers and the idling crowd.

It was so plain that this river again was different from the Tiber in Rome, the Seine in Paris and the Thames in London. Here it is nothing more than a dammed stream, shallow before it reaches the city, shallow after it leaves it, but held in check here by great stone dams which give it a peculiar, still mass and depth. The spirit of the cabmen was not the same as that of those in Rome or other cities; the spirit of the crowd was different. A darker, richer, more phlegmatic populace, I thought. The people were slow, leisurely, short and comfortable. I sated myself on the housefronts or backs below the Ponte Vecchio and on the little jewelry shops of which there seemed to be an endless variety, and then, feeling that I had had a taste of the city, I returned to the hotel. The Duomo, the palaces of the Medici, the Pitti Palace and

I sated myself on the housefronts or backs below the Ponte Vecchio

the dignified goings to and fro of the old Cosimo Pater and his descendants were what I wished to see and realize for myself if I could. I think now, of all the places that I saw in Italy, perhaps Florence really preserves most of the atmosphere of the past, in spite of its changes. But that is surely not for long either, for it is growing and the Germans are arriving. They were in complete charge of this hotel and of many other places, as I shortly saw, and I fancy that the future of northern Italy is to be in the hands of the Germans.

I ate my dinner in one of the best-managed and most methodically-conducted dining rooms that I have ever been in, and I wondered then whether this was a foretaste of what I was to experience in Germany. After dinner I wandered out into the streets of Florence again—dimly lighted and shadowed by great cornices. But of this and much else I shall tell in another chapter.

CHAPTER LX

I dare not imagine what the interest of Florence would be to anyone who did not know her strange and variegated history, but I should think, outside of the surrounding scenic beauty, it would be little or nothing. Unless one had a fondness for mere quaintness and gloom and solidity, it would in a way be repulsive or at best dreary. But lighted by the romance, the tragedy, the lust, the zealotry, the brutality and the artistic idealism that surrounds such figures as Dante, the Medici, Savonarola, Donatello, Michelangelo, Brunelleschi and the whole world of art, politics, trade and war, it takes on a strange luster to me—that of midnight waters lighted by the fitful gleams of distant fires.

I never think of it without seeing in my mind's eye the Piazza della Signoria as it must have looked in 1494 on the morning (or was it an afternoon?) of that famous fiasco in regard to "the test by fire" entered into between Savonarola and the Franciscan monks—those long, ridiculous processions of Dominicans and Franciscans, Savonarola bearing the chalice aloft; or that other day when Charles VIII of France, at the instance of Savonarola, paraded the streets in black velvet and a mantle of gold brocade, his lance leveled before him, his retainers gathered about him, and then he disappointed the people by getting off his horse and showing himself to be the insignificant little man that he was, almost deformed and with an idiotic expression of countenance. Neither can I forget the day that Savonarola was beheaded and burnt for his religious zealotry in this same Piazza della Signoria; nor will I forget all the rivals of the Medici hung from the windows of the Palazzo Vecchio or beheaded in the Bargello! Think of the tonsured friars and grave citizens of this medieval city under Savonarola's fiery incitement, their heads garlanded with flowers, mingling with the overwrought children called to help in purifying the city, dancing like David before the ark and shouting "Long live Christ and the Virgin, our rulers!"; of the days when Alessandro Medici and his boon companion and cousin, Lorenzo, rode about the city on a mule together, defiling the virtue of innocent girls, roistering in houses of ill repute and drinking and stabbing to their hearts' content; of Fra Girolamo preaching to excited crowds in the Duomo, and of his vision of a black cross over Rome and a red one over Jerusalem; of Machiavelli writing his brochure *The Prince* and of Michelangelo defending the city walls as an engineer. If any other city can match this spectacular, artistic, melodramatic progress in so short a space of time, or present the galaxy of artists, the rank company of material masters such as the Medici, the Pazzi, the Strozzi, plotting and counterplotting to the accompaniment of lusts and murders, I should like to know it. Other cities have had their amazing hours, all of them, from Rome to London. But Florence!

It has always seemed to me that the literary possibilities of Florence, in spite of the vast body of literature concerning it, have scarcely been touched. Any one of its astounding figures would be sufficient to grace novels of Dumas-like intricacy and significance. George Eliot's *Romola* is a botch, considering the material ready to her hand, a fitting commentary on the Victorian era in general, and the histories of the Medici and of the city are as a rule too commonplace. The city and its amazing eras remain fresh to the novelist's hand, practically unexploited—only a Gibbon, a Grote, a Froude or a Balzac should ever undertake it!

Personally, I had to refresh my memory to get a grasp on its intricate details. The art section alone is so vast and so brilliant that one of the art merchants told me while I was there that at least forty thousand of the city's one hundred and seventy thousand population is foreign (principally English and American), drawn to it by its art merits, and that the tide of travel from April to October is amazing. I believe it. You will hear German and English freely spoken in the principal thoroughfares. Because of a gray day and chill, following the warmth and color and light of Perugia and Rome, Florence seemed especially dark and somber to me at first, but I recovered. Its charm and beauty grew on me by degrees, so that by the time I had done inspecting Santa Maria Novella, Santa Croce, San Marco, the Cathedral group and the Bargello, I was really desperately in love with the art of it all, and after I had investigated the galleries—the Pitti, Uffizi, Belle Arti—and the cloisters, I was satisfied that I could find it in my heart to live here and write—a feeling I had had in so many other places in Europe.

My European loves! Everywhere in Europe I was finding some place in which I could live and write—at Chelsea and Seven Kings in London; at Canterbury and Oxford outside of it; at Issy and the Montmartre and Luxembourg sections in Paris; on the Riviera; almost anywhere in Rome; in Assisi; in Perugia; even in Spello (I dreamed of taking a cell in the old Franciscan monastery there) and now Florence! After I had seen San Miniato and Fiesole on one and the same lovely day, I was quite ready to believe that I could live indefinitely in Florence. So much for being impressionable.

Truly, however, there is no other city in Europe just like it. It has all the distinction of great individuality. My mood changed about at times as I thought of the different periods of its history, the splendor of its ambitions or the brutality of its methods, but when I was in the presence of some of its perfect works of art, such as Botticelli's *Spring* in the Belle Arti, Michelangelo's tombs of the Medici in San Lorenzo, Titian's *Magdalen* or Raphael's *Leo X* in the Pitti or Benozzo Gozzoli's fresco (the journey of the three kings to Bethlehem) in the old Medici palace, then I was ready to believe that nothing could be finer than Florence. I think now that of all the cities in Europe that I saw Florence was possessed of the most distinguished art atmosphere, something that creeps over your soul in a grim realistic way and causes you to repeat over and over "Amazing men worked here—amazing men!"

It was so strange to find driven home to me, as it was by degrees, here even more than in Rome, that illimitable gulf that divides ideality of thought and illusion from reality. Men painted the illusions of Christianity concerning the saints and the miracles at this time better than ever before or since, and believed something else. A Cosimo Medici, who could patronize the papacy and make a cardinal into a pope with one hand, could murder a rival with the other; an Andrea del Castagno, who was seeking to shine as a painter of religious art—madonnas, transfigurations and the like—could murder a Domenico Veneziano in order to have no rival in what he considered to be a permanent secret of how to paint in oils; the same munificence that could commission Michelangelo to design and execute a magnificent facade for San Lorenzo (it was never done, of course) could suborn the elective franchise of the people and organize a school on the lines of Plato's Academy! In other words, in Florence, as in the court of Alexander VI at Rome, we find life stripped of all sham in action, insofar as an individual and his conscience were concerned, and filled with the utmost subtlety insofar as an individual and the public were concerned! Cosimo and Lorenzo Medici, Andrea del Castagno, Machiavelli, the Pazzi, the Strozzi—in fact the whole "kit and caboodle" of the individuals comprising this illustrious life that foregathered here—were cut off the same piece of cloth.

They were, as we know, one and all (outside of a few artistic figures), shrewd, calculating, relentless and ruthless seekers of power and position; lust, murder, gourmandizing and panoplizing were the order of the day. Religion—it was to be laughed at; weakness—it was to be scorned. Poverty was to be misused. Innocence—it was to be seized upon and converted. Laughing at virtue and satisfying themselves always, they went their way, building their grim, dark, almost windowless palaces, preparing their dungeons and erecting their gibbets for their enemies. No wonder Savonarola saw a black cross over Rome! They struck swiftly and surely and smiled blandly and apparently mercifully. They had the Asiatic notion of morality—charity, virtue and the like, combined with a ruthless indifference to them. Power was the thing they craved—power and magnificence—and these were the things they had. But, oh, Florence! Florence! How you taught the nothingness of life itself! its shams! its falsehoods! its atrocities! its uselessness! It has never been any wonder to me that the saddest, darkest, most pathetic figure in all art, Michelangelo Buonarroti, should have appeared and loved and dreamed and labored and died at this time. His melancholy was a fit commentary on this age, on life and on all art. Oh, Buonarroti, loneliest of figures! I think I understand how it was with you.

Bear with me while I lay a flower on this great grave. I cannot think of another instance in art in which indomitable will and almost superhuman energy was at once so frustrated and so successful. In Rome I saw so many things by him—the statue *Moses* in San Pietro in Vincoli: large, grave, thoughtful, the man who could walk with God; in St. Peter's, in the dome of which he said he would raise the Pantheon into the air; in the Sistine Chapel, the ceiling and *The Last Judgment;* in the Paolina Chapel of the Vatican, the *Conversion of St. Paul* and the *Crucifixion of St. Peter;* in the great central hall of the Baths of Diocletian, his church of Santa Maria degli Angeli; in the heart of Rome the Piazza del Campidoglio; in S. M. Sopra Minerva, the statue of Christ; and so many more. The man was so industrious, and his life was so long. I have stood in profound awe before the wonders he has accomplished.

I am sure I am not mistaken when I say that there is a profound sadness running through all that he ever did. His works are large, gargantuan and profoundly melancholy. This particular *Moses* that I have been talking of, to say nothing of the statues or the tombs of the Medici in San Lorenzo at Florence, fill me with great sadness. I saw them in Berlin, reproduced there in plaster in the Kaiser-Friedrich-Museum, and once more I was filled with the same sense of profound, meditative melancholy. It is present in its most significant form, here in Florence in San Lorenzo, the facade of which he once prepared to make magnificent, but here he was again frustrated. I saw the originals of these tombs—deep, sad figures that impressed me as no other sculptural figures ever have done. *Dawn* and *Dusk; Day* and *Night*! How they dwell with me constantly.

I was never able to look at any of his later work—the Sistine Chapel frescoes, the figures of slaves in the Louvre, the *Moses* in San Pietro in Vincoli or these figures here in Florence—without thinking of how true it was that this great will had rarely had its way and how throughout all his days his energy was so unfortunately compelled to war with circumstance. Life plays this trick on the truly great if they are not ruthless and of material and executive leanings. Art is a pale flower that blooms only in sheltered places, and to drag it forth and force it to contend with the rough usage of the world is to destroy its perfections. It was so in this man's case, who at times, because of unlucky conjunctions, was compelled to fly for his life or sue for the means to complete that which life should have been honored to bestow upon him. I can never look on the frescoes of the Sistine Chapel or on the tombs of the Medici but that their vast, unconquerable melancholy becomes apparent, something so sad that it all but forces tears to the eyes. In the quaint, shapely chamber in which the latter appear—the new chapel of San Lorenzo—there is actually an atmosphere of melancholy so profound and colorful as to fill the whole chamber with a great grief. It is not the petty grief of earthly bereavement, a sense of loss in connection with any given individual, but that greater grief that springs from the mystery and the nothingness of life. How well this man must have known the mood of Shakespeare, who produced that magnificent:

> Who would bear the whips and scorns of time,
> The oppressor's wrong, the proud man's contumely,
> The pangs of despised love, the law's delay,
> The insolence of office, and the spurns
> That patient merit of the unworthy takes. . . .

or the mood of Keats: "Joy, whose hands are ever at his lips, bidding adieu."

Even so. I think, as you look at the figure of Lorenzo de' Medici, lost in profound thought, or at those sad, brooding, half-roused spirits of *Dawn* and *Dusk; Day* and *Night,* typical to me of the Inexplicable, it all comes home. Here you have expressed that profound melancholy that sees in life only mystery, uncertainty, necessity, compulsion. Michelangelo, as well as those comparatively adjacent figures of his own age—Dante, Shakespeare and Villon—saw the aimlessness of things terrestrial and brooded in a great fog of speculative woe. Out of such a mist of sorrow, and only so, have come these figures that now dream here year after year in their gray chapel while travelers come and go, draining their cup of wonder—rising ever and anon to the level of the beauty that they represent. I can see Browning speculating on the spirit of these figures—*Night,* with her heavy lids lost in great weariness and *Day* with his strong eyes. I can see Rodin gathering substance for his *Thinker* and Shelley wondering at the suggestions which Michelangelo gives. There is none so great as this man, for it is he alone who is Phidias plus melancholy, medieval gloom and mysticism plus the art of Greece.

I never think of the great tomb for which the *Moses* in San Pietro in Vincoli and the *Slaves* in the Louvre were intended without being filled with a vast astonishment and grief to think that life should not have permitted this design to come to fulfillment. To think that a pope as powerful as Julius should have planned a tomb so magnificent, with Michelangelo to scheme it out and actually begin it, and then never permit it to come to pass. All the way northward through Italy this idea of a parallelogram with forty figures on it and covered with reliefs and other ornaments haunted me. At Florence, in the Belle Arti, I saw more of the figures (casts)—strange, unfolding thoughts half-hewn out of the rock which suggest the source from which Rodin has drawn his inspiration. Before I was out of Italy, Michelangelo and his genius and the mere dreams of the things he hoped to do enthralled me so that to me he has become the one great art figure of the world. Colossal is the word for Michelangelo—so vast that life was too short for him to suggest even a tithe of what he felt. But even the things that he did—how truly monumental they are!

I could never come into the breakfast room either here or at Rome or Venice or Milan without encountering a large company of that peculiarly American brand of sightseer, not enormously rich, of no great dignity, but comfortable and, above all, contented and enormously pleased with themselves. They belong to what might be called the genus fatwad or fathead, or both! I could never look at any of this tribe, comfortably clothed, staggeringly hungry at times, very pursy and fussy, without thinking what a far cry it is from the temperament which makes for art or great originality to the temperament which makes for normality—the great, so-called sane, conservative mass. God spare me! I'll admit that for general purposes—the value of breeding, trading, rearing of children in comfort, producing the living atmosphere of life in which we find ourselves and from which art, by the grace of great public occasions, may rise—they are very essential. But seen individually, dissociated from great background masses, they are—but let me not go wild. Viewed from the artistic angle, the stress of great occasions, great emotions, great necessities, they fall into such pygmy weaknesses—almost ridiculous. Here abroad they come so regularly, Pa and Ma, Pa not infrequently a little vague-looking from overwork and limited vision of soul, Ma not infrequently a little superior, vain, stuffy, envious, dull and hard. I never see such a woman but that my gorge rises a little. Life should do so much better. The one idea of a pair like this, particularly of the mother, is getting their children (if there be any) properly married, the girls particularly, and in this great phase of family politics Pa has obviously little to say. Their appearance abroad, accompanied by Henry and George, Junior, and Mary and Annabel, is for—I scarcely know what. It is so plain on the face of it that no single one of them has the least inkling of what they are seeing. I sat in a carriage with two of them in Rome, viewing the ruins of the Via Appia, and when we reached the tomb of Cecilia Metella the remarks of both were as follows:

"Oh, yes. There it is. What was she, anyhow?"

"He was a Roman general, I think, and she was his wife. His house was next door, and he built this tomb here so she could be near him. Isn't it wonderful?"

"Beautiful!"

"Such a nice idea!"

What matter which said what?

As far as I could make out from watching this throng, the principal idea was to be able to say that they had been abroad. Poor old Florence! Its beauty and its social significance passed unrecognized. Art, so far as I could judge from the worst examples of sightseers present, was for crazy people. The artist was some weird, spindling, unfortunate fool, a little daft perhaps, but tolerable for a strange furor he seemed to have created. Great men made and used him. He was, after his fashion, a servant. The objectionable feature of a picture like Botticelli's *Spring* would be the nudity of the figures! From a

Rubens or a nude Raphael we lead brash, unctuous, self-conscious Mary away in silence. If we encounter, perchance, quite unexpectedly a *Leda* by Michelangelo or a too-nude *Assumption* by Bronzino, we turn away in disgust. Art must be limited to conventional theories and when so limited is not worth much anyhow.

It was amazing to see them strutting in and out, their good clothes rustling, their shoes almost creaking with newness, an automobile in waiting, noisily puffing the while they gathered aimless "impressions" wherewith to browbeat their neighbors. George and Henry and Mary and Annabel, protesting half the time or in open rebellion, were duly led to see the things which have been the most enthusiastically recommended, be it a palace or a restaurant.

I often wondered what it was—the best—which these people got out of their trip abroad. The heavy Germans I saw I always suspected of having solid Teutonic understanding and appreciation of everything; the English were uniformly polite, reserved, intelligent, apparently discriminating. But these Americans! If you told them the true story of Antonius, whose head I saw them occasionally admiring, or forced upon them the true details of the Borgias, the Sforzas, the Medici or even the historical development of art, they would fly in horror. They have no room in their little crania for anything save their own notions—the standard of the wooden Methodist church at Keokuk. I think, sometimes, perhaps it is because we are all growing to a different standard, trying to make life something different from what it has always been or appeared to be, that all the trouble comes about. Time will remedy that. Life—its heavy, interminable processes—will break any theory. I conceive of life as a blind goddess pouring from separate jars, one of which she holds in each hand, simultaneously, the streams of good and evil, which, mingling, make this curiously troubled existence, flowing ever rapidly onward to the sea.

One last word, and I am done. I strolled out from Santa Croce one evening, a little confused as to the charm of all I had seen and wondering how I could best bestow my time for the remaining hours of light. I tried first to find the house of Michelangelo, which I fancied was somewhere in the vicinity. Not finding it, I decided to go to the Opera della Croce, a sort of a graveyard of medieval scraps, but as I reached there, a monk was just coming out who warned me that it was too late. I then turned idly away and came finally to the Arno, which I followed upstream. The evening was very pleasant, quite a sense of spring in the air and of new-made gardens, and I overcame my disappointment at having failed to accomplish my original plan. I passed new streets, wider than the old ones in the heart of the city, with streetlamps, arc lights, modern awnings and a trolley car running in the distance. Gradually I came to a portion of the Arno lovelier than any I had yet seen, for of course the walls through which it flows in the city had disappeared, and in their place came grass-covered banks with those tall, thin poplars I had so much admired in France. The waters were a Nile green at this hour, and the houses that approached it at times in small groups were brown, yellow, or white, with red or brown roofs and brown or green shutters. The old idea of arches with columns and large projecting roofs still persisted in these newer, outlying houses and made me wonder whether Florence would always keep this characteristic.

As I got further out, the houses grew less frequent, and lovely bluish-black hills appeared. There was a smokestack in the distance, just to show that Florence was not dead to the idea of manufacturing, and beyond, in a somewhat different direction, the dome of the cathedral—that really impressive dome. Some men were fishing in the stream from the bank, catching nothing. In the distance children were playing about at different points, boys and girls, with occasionally their mother or father, or both, the former carrying babies. I noticed the lovely cypresses of the south in the distance, the large villas on the hills and in different places those tall, thin trees of France, not conspicuous elsewhere on my journey. In one place I noticed the largest display of washing I have ever seen, quite the largest—a whole field of linen, no less, hung out to dry—and in another place some slow-moving men cutting wood.

It was very warm, very pleasant, slightly suggestive of rain, with the smoke going up straight from the stacks, and after a while, when the evening church bells were beginning to ring, calling to each other from vale and hill, my sense of springtime and pleasant rural and suburban sweetness was complete. Italy has too much of blind religion perhaps—I am not sure—but none too many beautiful churches. Laughter carried, I noticed, in some peculiar, echoing way. The music of the bells was essentially quieting, and I had no sense of Florence old or new, but just spring, hope, new birth. And as I turned back after a time I knew I had acquired a different and very precious memory of Florence—something which would last me years and years. I should always think of the Arno as it looked this evening—how soft and gracious and still. I should always hear the voices in laughter and the bells; I should always see the children playing on the green banks, quite as I used to play on the Wabash and Tippecanoe, and their voices in Italian were no less sweet than our childish voices and no more. And I had a feeling that somehow the spirit of Italy was like that of America, and that somehow there is close kinship between us and Italy, and that it was not for nothing that an Italian discovered America, or that Americans of all people have apparently loved Italy most and rivaled it most closely in its periods of greatest achievement.

CHAPTER LXI

Whatever the medieval atmosphere of Florence may have been—and when I was there the exterior appearance of the central heart was obviously somewhat akin to its fourteenth- and fifteenth-century predecessors—today its prevailing spirit is thoroughly modern. If you walk in the Piazza della Signoria or the Piazza del Duomo or the Via dei Calzaioli, the principal thoroughfare, you will encounter most of the ancient landmarks, a goodly number of them, but they will look out of place, as in the case of the palaces, with their windowless ground floors, built so for purposes of defense, their corner lanterns, barricaded windows and single great entrances easily guarded. Today these regions have, if not the open spacing of the modern city, at least the commercial sprightliness and matter-of-fact business display and energy which is characteristic of commerce everywhere.

I think we make a mistake when we assume that the manners, customs, details, conversation, interests and excitements of people anywhere were ever very much different from what they are now. Three or four hundred years from now, people in quite similar situations to our own will be wondering how we spent our daily lives. Quite the same as our ancestors, I should say, and no differently from our descendants. We arose, washed our faces and hands, if not our bodies (I am speaking of mass movements), thought of the weather, the duty or engagement in hand, dressed, ate, went to our place of business, met our associates and conducted ourselves much as the Florentines of 1492 or 1512 and much as our descendants will do in 5690 or 6012. Life works about the same in all times. Only exterior aspects change. In the particular period in which Florence (and all Italy for that matter) was so remarkable, Italy was alive with ambitious men—strong, remarkable, capable characters. They made the wonder of the life, not the architecture, and not the routine movements of the people. Florence has much the same architecture today—better, in fact, but not the men. Great men make great times, and only struggling, ambitious, vainglorious men make the existence of the artist possible, however much he may despise them. They are the only ones who in their vainglory and power can truly call upon him to do great things and supply the means. Witness Raphael and Michelangelo in Italy, Rubens in Holland and Velázquez in Spain.

In walking out into the Piazza della Signoria, where Savonarola was burned and so many malcontent princes murdered, and later in the Piazza del Duomo, which remains as it was in the fourteenth and fifteenth centuries, it was interesting to me this first night to find the usual electric lights blazing, restaurants, cigar and saloon stores exhibiting their usual activity, various lines of cars turning about the Duomo and a general sense of current European and American life prevalent everywhere. I came to the Piazza della Signoria quite by accident, following a dark, heavily corniced street from my hotel, and at once I recognized the Palazzo Vecchio with its thin, angular tower; the Loggia dei Lanzi, where in older times public performances were given in the open; and the equestrian statue of Cosimo I. I idled long here, examining the bronze slab which marks the site of the stake at which Savonarola and two other Dominicans were burned in 1498, the fountain designed by Bartolommeo Ammanati, the two lions at the steps of the Loggia and the Benvenuto Cellini statue of *Perseus* with the head of Medusa. A strange genius, that one. This figure is as brilliant and thrilling as it is ghastly.

It was a lovely night. The moon came up after a time, as it had at Perugia and Assisi, and I wandered about these old streets, feeling the rough brown walls, looking in the open shop windows, most of them dark and lighted by streetlamps, and studying always the wide, overhanging cornices. All really interesting cities are so delightfully different. London was so low, gray, foggy, homey, drab and commonplace; Paris was so smart, swift, wide-spaced, rococo, ultra-artistic and fashionable; Monte Carlo was so semi-Parisian and semi-Algerian or Moorish, with sunlight and palms; Rome was so higgledy-piggledy, of various periods, with a strange mingling of modernity and antiquity, and over all blazing sunlight, and throughout all cypresses; and now in Florence I found the compact, dark atmosphere suggestive of what Paris once was, centuries before, but with this distinctive feature that the wide cornice is here an essential characteristic. It is so wide! It protrudes outward from the building line at least three or four feet, and it may be much more—six or seven. One thing is certain, as I found to my utter delight on a rainy afternoon: you can find shelter under its wide reach and keep comparatively dry. Great art has been developed in making it truly ornamental, and it gives the long, narrow streets a most individual and, in my judgment, distinguished appearance.

It was quite by accident, also, on this same evening, that I came upon the Piazza del Duomo where the streetcars are. I did not know where I was going, wandering idly as I was, until suddenly, turning a corner, there I saw it—the Campanile at last and a portion of the Cathedral standing out soft and fair in the clear moonlight! I shall always be glad that I saw it so, for the strange stripe and arabesque of its stonework—slabs of white or cream-colored stone interwoven in lovely designs with slabs of slate-colored granite—had an almost eerie effect in the moonlight. It might have been something borrowed from Morocco or Arabia or the Far East. As I drew nearer, the dome and the Baptistery also soared upwards in a magnificent way, and although afterwards I was sorry that the municipality has never had sense enough to tear out the ruck of buildings surrounding it and leave these three monuments—the Cathedral, the Campanile, and the Baptistery—standing free and clear, as at Pisa, on a great stone platform or square; nevertheless, cramped as I think they are, they are surely beautiful. The Campanile is certainly the most pleasing of any, after St. Mark's at Venice. It is rich in its coloring and so simply balanced in its design. I ascended it afterwards, the day I was leaving, and took one last look at all I had seen, but it never appealed to me so much as on this first night when I saw it in the moonlight.

I was equally touched by the beauty of the Cathedral. Unlike Canterbury, Amiens, Pisa and St. Paul Without The Walls in Rome, the beauty of this cathedral is all on the outside. Within is nothing. After admiring the exterior charm and splendor of Canterbury, Amiens, Pisa, St. Paul's in Rome, you enter to fresh wonders, almost greater delights. Here you pass, as I did the next morning, into a great, bare, creamish-brown interior which leaves you astonished at its reaches—but nothing more. A round choir under the dome, not unlike an immense baptismal font, is one novelty. A homely, seemingly modern pulpit is another—and yet it is the same from which Savonarola thundered! The altars and chapels are pleasing but not splendid. Only in Rome did I see the really amazing chapel and the truly splendid altar.

But although there is little within you can, if you are interested in architecture, walk for hours outside. The different aspects of the Cathedral and its attendant Baptistery and Campanile are all pleasing—grand at times. Every city, I should think, ought to have a truly great cathedral, not so much as a symbol or theory of religion as an object of art, something which would indicate the perfection of the religious ideal. Here you can stand and admire the exquisite double windows with twisted columns, the infinite variety of the inlaid marble work and the quaint architecture of the niches supported by columns. It was after midnight, and the moon was high in the heavens, shining down with a rich spring-like effect, before I finally returned from the Duomo square, following the banks of the Arno, admiring the shadows cast by the cornices, and so finally reached my hotel and my bed.

The next morning I was up and active, visiting first the Cathedral, as I have said, and then later Santa Maria Novella and Santa Croce, but not before I had finally decided to change my plan and visit Venice, for until I had reached Florence I had not yet decided to go there. As I have indicated somewhere, Grant Richards's advice was against it: it would be gray and chilly, he thought; but when I reached Rome I encountered an American publisher fresh from Algiers, and he was fearful lest—or, as he put it, I should make the mistake of my life if I did not see Venice. "You are here now," he said. "It is only a few hours from Florence. For heaven's sake, don't go back without seeing it. It may be cold, but it may not be. I have seen splendid days there at this time of year. You will see the one thing that you will never forget. It is a city without a disappointment." And so here at Florence, on this first morning, I altered my plans, changed my tickets at Thomas Cook's and crowded Venice in between Florence and Milan. I gave myself a stay of four days, deciding to lengthen it if I chose, and then went on about my business of seeing Florence.

I really think that every traveler of today owes a debt of gratitude to Thomas Cook and Sons. I never knew until I went abroad what an accommodation the offices of this concern is. Your mail is always courteously received and cared for; your routes and tickets are changed and altered at your slightest whim; your local bank is their cash desk; and the only advisors you have, if you are alone and without the native tongue at your command, are their clerks and agents at the trains. It does not make any difference to me that this is their business and that they make a profit. In a foreign city when you are quite alone, you would grant them twice the profit for their courtesy. And it was my experience, the little use I made of their services, that their orders and letters of advice were carefully respected and that when you came conducted by Thomas Cook, whether you took the best or the worst, you were politely and assiduously looked after.

One of the most amusing letters that I received while abroad was from this same publisher who wanted me to go to Venice. Not so long before I had left Rome he had arrived there with his wife, daughter and a young girlfriend of his daughter whose first trip abroad they were sponsoring. At a luncheon they had given me, the matter of seeing the pope had come up, and I had mentioned that I had been so fortunate as to find someone who could introduce me, and it was just possible, if they wished it, that my friend would extend his courtesy to them. The young girls in particular were eager, but I was not sure. I left Rome immediately afterward, writing to my British correspondent, bespeaking his interest in their behalf, and at the same time wrote my publisher that I was doing so. As an analysis of girlhood vagaries keen and clever, read this:

"Hotel de Russie,
Rome, Feby. 29.

"My dear Dreiser:

"The young woman who thinks she wants to see the pope goes under the name of Margaret Hamilton—but I wouldn't try very hard to bring it about, because if Margaret went, my daughter Elizabeth would want to go, and if Margaret and my daughter went, Mrs. Ellsworth would feel out in the cold. The old man can stand it.

"Margaret's motives are simply childish curiosity—possibly combined with a slight desire to give pleasure to the Holy Father.

"We miss you. Do not consider the matter of sending back the lire—just go to Venice and spend it in the manner suggested.

"But don't try to get that papal interview for Margaret unless you can get it for all the ladies. You will introduce a serpent into my paradise.

"Sincerely,
"W. W. Ellsworth."

CHAPTER LXII

My days in Florence were few and very active. I walked about the city in the mornings before the museums and churches opened and evenings after they were closed, speculating as to the character of the life here and visiting by turns Santa Maria Novella, Santa Croce, the church and monastery of St. Mark, San Lorenzo, San Miniato and all the museums and other places of interest. The Arno as a stream interested me first off, and I followed it up and down, noting the gardens, villas and small collections of houses outside the city limits and wondering whether Florence was to have a great rebirth and grow someday into a great, modern city. It is a question.

The Arno here is so different from the Tiber at Rome and yet so much like it, for it has in the main the same unprepossessing look, running as it does through the city between solid walls of stone but lacking the spectacles of the Castle of St. Angelo, St. Peter's, the hills and gardens of the Aventine and the Gianicolo. There are no ancient ruins on the Arno—only the suggestive architecture of the Middle Ages, the wonderful Ponte Vecchio and the houses adjacent to it. With many things I was not impressed at first, such as the Pitti Palace and those of the Medici and the Strozzi; but later they grew on me and became wonderful. I spent hours in the Uffizi, the Pitti and the Belle Arti, examining in detail the vast collections of paintings and sharpening my understanding of the growth of Italian art. I never knew until I reached Florence how easy it is to trace the rise of Christian art, to see how one painter influenced another, how one school borrowed from another and how one idea in painting gave rise to another. It is all very plain. If by the least effort you fix the representatives of the different Italian schools in mind, you can judge for yourself.

The Uffizi and Pitti collections of paintings are absolutely the most amazing I saw abroad. There are other wonderful collections—the Louvre being absolutely unbelievable for size—but here the art is so uniformly relative to Italy, so identified with the Renaissance, so suggestive of the influences and the patronage which gave it birth. The influence of religion, the wealth of the Catholic Church, the power of individual families such as the Medici and the dukes of Venice are all clearly indicated. Botticelli's *Adoration of the Magi* in the Uffizi tells the whole story, showing the proud Medici children, the head of Cosimo Pater Patriae, and the company of men of letters and statesmen of the time all worked in as figures about the Christ child. Art was flattering to the nobility of the day. It was dependent for its place and distinction upon religion, the patronage of the Church, and so you have endless "Annunciations," "Adorations," "Flights Into Egypt," "Crucifixions," "Descents From the Cross," "Entombments," "Resurrections" and the like. The sensuous "Magdalena," painted for her form and the beauty of suggestion, you will encounter over and over again. All the saints in the calendar, the proud popes and cardinals of a dozen families, the several members of the Medici family—they are all here. Now and then you will encounter a Rubens, a Van Dyck, a Rembrandt or a Frans Hals from the Netherlands, but they are rare. Florence, Rome, Venice, Pisa and Milan are best represented with small bits from Perugia, Ravenna and elsewhere.

I do not know that any tribute I can lay at the feet of Florentine art and art collections—the wonderful assemblages of the Uffizi, Pitti, Belle Arti and Bargello, to say nothing of its churches—will be of any value, but I cannot refrain from expressing my wonder and astonishment at the things that I saw. Rome for sculpture, frescoes, jewel-box churches, ancient ruins, but Florence for paintings and the best collections of medieval artistic craftsmanship. I returned three times to look at Botticelli's *Spring* in the Belle Arti, that marvelous picture which I think in many respects is the loveliest picture in the world, so delicate, so poetically composed, so utterly suggestive of the art and refinement of the painter and of life at its best. The *Three Graces*, so lightly clad in transparent raiment, are so much the soul of joy and freshness, the utter significance of spring. The nude figures to the left do so portray the cold and blue of March, the warmer April and the flower-clad May. I could never tire of the artistry which could have March blowing on April's mouth, from which flowers fall into the lap of May. Nor could I weary of the spirit that could select green, sprouting things for the hem of April's garment or above Spring's head place a winged and blindfolded baby shooting a fiery arrow at the three graces. To me, Botticelli is the nearest return to the Greek spirit of beauty (grace and lightness of soul) combined with the later delicacy and romance that the modern world has known. It is so beautiful that for me it is sad—full of the sadness that only perfect beauty can inspire.

And the cells and cloister of San Marco—shall I ever forget those? I went there on an Italian spring morning when the bright light outside filled the cloister with a cool brightness, and I studied the frescoes of Fra Angelico and loitered between the columns of the arches in the cloister proper, meditating upon the beauty of things here gathered. Really, Italy is too much. One should be a poet in soul, insatiable for art, and loiter here forever. Each poorest cell here has a small fresco by Fra Angelico, and the refectory, the chapter house, and the foresteria are filled with larger compositions, all rich in that symbolism which is only wonderful because of the art feeling of the master. I lingered in the cells, the small chambers once occupied by Savonarola, and meditated on the great zealot's imaginings. In a way, his dreams of the destruction of the papacy came true. Even as he preached, the great Reformation was at hand—only he did not know it. Martin Luther was coming. The black cross was over Rome! And also true was his thought that the end of the old order in Italy had come. It surely had. Never afterward was it quite the same and never would be again. And equally true was his vision of the red cross over Jerusalem, for never was the simple humanism of Jesus so firmly based in the minds of men as it is today, though all creeds and religious theories totter wearily to their ruin. Savonarola was burned, but not his visions or his pleas. They are as fresh and powerful today, as magnetic and gripping, as are any that have been made in history.

It was the same with the Bargello, the tombs of the Medici, San Miniato and the basilica and monastery at Fiesole. That last stands fixed and clear in my mind, with the wind singing in the cypresses, a faint mist blowing down the valley of the Arno, all Florence lying below and the lights of evening beginning to appear. I saw it for the last time the evening before I left. I sat on a stone bench overlooking a wonderful prospect, rejoicing in the artistic spirit of Italy which has kept fresh and clean these wonders of art, when I was approached by a brown Dominican, his feet and head bare, his body stout and comfortable. He asked for alms. I gave him a lira, not for his sake but for that of Savonarola, who belonged to this order and—simply because of the spirit of Italy which in the midst of a changing, commercializing world still ministers to these shrines of beauty and keeps them intact and altogether lovely.

The climate of Florence is so different from that of Rome. They have fine days here, excellent ones, with a crystalline atmosphere, but on no one of them that I saw did they have that hard, dry sharpness which at times makes Rome astonishing, almost irritating. Instead, there is almost always a touch of moisture which contributes a delicious softness, and on many days there are gray, heavy clouds and damp and rain and cold, which makes the great difference between Florence and Rome.

As I walked about this city—lingering in its doorways, brooding over its pictures, reconstituting for myself the life of the Middle Ages—I could not help thinking how soon it must all go. No doubt the churches, palaces and museums will be retained in their present form for hundreds of years, and they should be, but soon will come wider streets and newer houses, even in this older section, the heart of the city, and then farewell to the medieval atmosphere. In all likelihood, the wide cornice, now such a significant feature of the city, will be abandoned, and then there will be scarcely anything to tell how Florence was. Already the streetcar, as I have said, clang-clangs its way through certain sections. You can get to the Duomo, that large, wonderful church, from anywhere, for almost all cars start from the Duomo, and as for the remaining sights—San Miniato, Fiesole and Vallombrosa—the outlying points, they are almost all available by trolley. The railway trains are convenient and good.

In brooding over the almost endless treasures of the city, I ambled into the Strozzi Palace one afternoon, that perfect example of Florentine palatial architecture, then occupied by an exposition of objects of art, reproductions and originals purporting to be the work of an association of Italian artists—after I had seen, cursorily, about all the other treasures the city had to show. By that time I had been through Santa Maria Novella, Santa Croce, the church and monastery of St. Mark, the cathedral and all the museums. I had wandered up and down the Arno, examining the new life and the old and seeing how the city had been slowly changing from its medieval characteristics to its present, semi-modernized state. I was struck with some of the oldest nooks and crannies, houses in the heart of the city that had been turned into blacksmith's shops, butcher shops, machine shops and the like, and I was wont to linger by the half-hour at various doorways and in various vicinities just looking in. They reminded me of those houses in the Marais in Paris and some of the narrowest and most crowded sections of Rome and London.

In this particular Palazzo Strozzi, after steeping myself in all these wonders of art, I encountered a thing which I had long heard of but never seen—an organization for the reproduction, the re-duplication, of all the wonders of art, and cheaply, too. The place was full of marbles of the loveliest character; replicas of famous statues in the Vatican, the Louvre, the Uffizi and elsewhere; and in many instances also copies of pictures. There was beautiful furniture, imitated even as to age, from many of the Italian palaces—the Riccardi, Albizzi, Pazzi, Pitti, Strozzi and others—and as for garden-fittings, they were all present—fountains, fauns, cupids, benches, metal gateways, pergolas and the like. There were marvelous reproductions from some of the most perfect villas, with all the patina of age upon them, and I thought at first that they were original. I was soon undeceived, for I had not been there long strolling about before an attendant brought and introduced to me a certain Professor Ernesto Jesurum, a small, dark, wiry man with clear, black, crow-like eyes, who made clear the whole situation.

The markets of the world, according to Mr. Jesurum, were being flooded with cheap imitations of truly worthy objects of art from Italian stone benches to landscapes by Corot or portraits by Frans Hals, masquerading as originals. It had been decided by this association of Italian artists that this was unfair, not only to the buyer and the art-loving public generally, but to the honest craftsman who could make an excellent living reproducing, frankly, copies of ancient works of merit at a very nominal price, if only they were permitted to copy them. Most, in fact all of them, could make interesting originals, but in many instances they would lack that one touch of personality which makes all the difference between success and failure, whereas reproducing the masterpieces of another, they did it perfectly. So they had banded themselves together into this very same association of Italian artists that was holding this exposition here and were determined to do better work and sell more cheaply than the fly-by-night rascals who were confounding and degrading all good art. The artists were determined to say frankly, each and all, "Here is a perfect reproduction of a very lovely thing. Do you want it at a very low cost?" or "We will make for you an exact copy of anything that you see and admire and wish to have, and we will make it so cheap that you cannot afford to dicker with doubtful dealers who sell you imitations of the same originals *as originals* and charge you outrageous prices."

I have knocked about sufficiently in my time in the showy chambers of American dealers and elsewhere to know that there is entirely too much truth in what was told me. The rejection of the Hearn collection of pictures by the Metropolitan Museum of Art in New York and the discovery after the death of a certain great builder in New Jersey that his collection, valued at several millions, was largely fraudulent are interesting cases in point. This same Professor Jesurum had not long before been to Kansas City, Missouri, he told me, where he had seen a notably famous collection of six hundred pictures, every one of which was an imitation. "How much better it would be," he said to me, "if they were honestly labeled as such and so exhibited. They are very good. They have been terribly overpriced and the buyer overcharged, but beyond that they are very satisfactory. After all, when you come right down to it, it takes an expert to tell the difference. In the case of most of the pictures I could not have done so myself except for the fact that I knew where the originals were. This uncertainty as to whether the *Mona Lisa* which has disappeared from the Louvre is the original or not is a case in point."

I listened to this gentleman with a great deal of interest. He took me through all the rooms of this very fine Strozzi Palace, and I could not help thinking what a charming place it was in which to exhibit his wares. The rugs, tapestries, Italian period furniture, lamps, bronzes, ironwork, china and statuary showed up to amazing advantage. Several of the heavy, high-ceiled, dark, medieval rooms had been hung with tapestries (imitations of Flemish and French originals) and set with heavy Italian furniture of early thirteenth- and fourteenth-century origin (imitations), and the effect was splendid. He told me how stone, leather, wood and bronze were made to take on this ancient vintage by acid solutions, strong or weak. "I can age a stone bench," he said, "in thirty minutes so that you cannot tell it from an original a thousand years old, and I can take new leather and in three or four weeks give it such a quality of age that no one could tell it from an original piece with hundreds of years of service. Besides, I can sell it to you for about one-twentieth of what the original would cost, and it will be as good as the original—nearly, not quite." I gasped.

He named me the acids, oils and colors, and I had to smile—he was so earnest about it all. He invited me to come out to some garden, wanted to take me, where this work was done, but I declined. I am sure he wanted to sell me a garden set or an interior of ancient vintage, but I informed him quite frankly that I was too poor to buy—I could only admire. His attitude did not change, however. Instead he went on explaining, keeping with me almost entirely the whole afternoon.

The wonder of Florence grew a little under the professor's quiet commercial analysis, for after exhausting this matter of reproducing art cheaply we proceeded to a discussion of the present condition of the city.

"It's very different commercially from anything in America or the north of Europe," he said, "or even the north of Italy, for as yet we have scarcely anything in the way of commerce here. We still build in the fashion they did five hundred years ago—narrow streets and big cornices—in order to keep up the atmosphere of the city, for we are not strong enough commercially yet to go it alone, and besides I don't think the Italians will ever be any different. They are an easygoing race here. They don't need the American 'two dollars a day' to live on. Fifty centimes will do. For one thousand dollars (five thousand lire) you can rent a palace here for a year, and I can show you whole floors overlooking gardens that you can rent for two hundred (seventeen dollars a month). The garden that I have been telling you of, which we use as a workshop here in Florence in the heart of the city, we rent for four hundred a year."

"What about the Italians' idea of progress? Aren't they naturally constructive?" I asked. Mr. Jesurum was a Jew.

"Rarely the Italian. Not at this date. We have many Jews and Germans here who are doing well, and foreign capital is building street-railways. I think the Italians will have to be fused with another nation to experience a new birth. The Germans are mixing with them. If they ever get as far south as Sicily, Italy will be made over; the Germans themselves will be made over. I notice that the Italians and Germans get along well together."

I thought of the age-long wars between the Teutons and the Italians, from the fifth to the twelfth century, but those days are over. They can apparently mingle in peace now, as I saw here and farther north.

CHAPTER LXIII

If I left Florence with a sigh, which I did, I looked forward to Venice with a thrill. Venice—the city I had always wondered about. For how many years had I studied those lovely paintings of William Turner, portraying the Salute, San Giorgio, the Ducal Palace, the bridge of the Rialto, the Bridge of Sighs and the wonders of the Grand Canal. In studying out my itinerary at Florence, I came upon the rather commonplace advice in Baedeker to the effect that "care should be taken in embarking and disembarking, especially when the tide is low, exposing the slimy lower steps." That as much as anything I had ever read conveyed the wonder of Venice to me. But how shall I ever suggest what I really felt—those subtle moods which the city suggests and inspires!

It was lovely afternoon when I left Florence, or rather evening. These Italian cities, not being large, end so quickly that before you can say "Jack Robinson" you are out of them and away, far into the country. For a time after we left Florence, the country was much the same as it had been in the south—hill-towns, medieval bridges and strongholds; the solid whites, browns, pinks, grays and blues that had prevailed in the architecture of the south; the white oxen, pigs and shabby carts; but gradually as we neared Bologna things seemed to improve, or rather take on the very modern air which in a way I was coming to detest—factories, wide streets, thoroughly modern suburbs and the like. It grew dark shortly after that, and the country was only favored by the rich radiance of the moon, which made it more picturesque and romantic but less definite and distinguishable.

Ever since leaving Rome, true to my mood at the time, I was looking forward to new developments in the matter of sex, for I have never been able to go very far in this world without some phase of femininity intruding itself, and not always because of any direct seeking on my part. At Assisi, Perugia, Spello and even Florence I considered my time so short that I had no opportunity to do anything save see the sights, yet I would have welcomed any form of companionship if it had been comfortably available. I am not a gallant of the Grant Richards type, able to forward my feminine interests under the most adverse circumstances. Besides, it has always required the temperamentally exceptional—"my kind," as a friend of mine used to put it—and they, as I have always known, are not conspicuously numerous. There have been enough, but not too many.

This evening, on my train which was traveling swiftly and smoothly, I found myself in company with two women in my compartment, one obviously a wife bound for Bologna, the other a young girl of twenty or twenty-two, rather sensual and phlegmatic, I judged by her appearance, decidedly good-looking and not very well placed in the matter of this world's goods. Her clothing was neat and fairly substantial, but not overmuch so, and the leather bag she carried was old. She had no jewelry of any kind and exhibited at first a restless and inquiring air. Later she settled down and pretended to rest, but I am quite sure she was never in any particular mood for slumber. She reminded me of Mme. de Villiers.

The married Italian lady was small and good-looking and bourgeois. Considerably before dinnertime, as we were nearing Bologna, she opened a small basket which she carried and took from it a sandwich, an apple and a bit of cheese, which she ate. For some reason she occasionally smiled at me good-naturedly, but not speaking Italian, I was without the means of making a single observation. Naturally I grieved over my lack of training in the languages. Nevertheless, at Bologna I assisted her with her parcels and received a smiling backward glance, and then I settled myself in my seat, wondering what the remainder of the evening would bring forth. I was not so very long in discovering.

Once the married lady of Bologna had disappeared, my single companion took on new life. She rose, adjusted her dress at the waistline, smoothed her sleeves and throat at the neck and went to look out the window. Later she returned and propped herself languorously in her seat, her cheek laid close against a velvet-covered flange, and looked at me occasionally out of half-closed eyes. She finally tried to make herself more comfortable by lying down, and to be appropriately friendly, I offered her my fur overcoat as a pillow. She accepted it with a half-smile.

About this time a porter or servant of the dining car came through to take a memorandum of those who wished to reserve places for dinner. We looked at the young lady, but she shook her head negatively. I made a sudden decision. "Reserve two places," I said. The servitor bowed politely and went away. I scarcely knew why I had said this, for I was under the impression that my young lady companion spoke only Italian, but I trust much always to my intuitions.

A little later, when it was drawing near the mealtime and my young companion had favored me by a peculiarly daring position, I said, "Do you speak English?"

"*Non*," she replied, shaking her head.

"*Sprechen Sie Deutsch?*" I added, in the vain hope that the obvious German invasion of this northern half of Italy had brought her some slight knowledge of that.

"*Ein wenig,*" she replied, with an easy, babyish, half-German, half-Italian smile.

"*Sie sind doch Italienisch,*" I suggested.

"*Oh, oui!*" she replied, and put her head down comfortably on my coat.

"*Reisen Sie nach Venedig?*" I inquired.

"*Oui,*" she nodded. She half smiled again.

I had a real thrill of satisfaction out of all this, for although I speak abominable German, just sufficient to make myself understood to a really clever person, yet I knew that by the exercise of a little tact, I should have a companion to dinner and just possibly pleasant companionship in Venice.

"You will take dinner with me, won't you?" I stammered in my best German. "I do not understand German very well, but perhaps we can make ourselves understood. I have two places."

She hesitated and said, "*Ich bin nicht hungrig.*"

"But for company's sake?" I insisted.

"*Oh, oui,*" she replied indifferently, using the French expression.

I then asked her whether she was going to any particular hotel in Venice—I was bound for the Royal Danieli—and she replied that she was going home.

"So you live in Venice?" I inquired.

"*Oui,*" she replied.

I think, all told, that my adventure with Maria Bastida, as her name finally proved to be, was one of the most interesting I have ever enjoyed. She was a large girl, as I have perhaps indicated, pallid, with a full, rounded body and face, semi-drooping eyelids, very light brown hair, almost flaxen, and somewhat too large but not unshapely hands. She seemed, as I came to know her during those few days, strangely world-weary and yet strangely passionate—the kind of mind and body that does and does not care. Obviously she was passionate. I could tell from all her movements that there was a kind of dull, smoldering fire burning within her, and yet she seemed always indifferent in the bargain. I sat on the seat beside her after a time, and she tried to tell me something of Venice in answer to my inquiries, smiling occasionally, and occasionally looking bored. I trustingly let the matter of our future carefully rest, but when she began to ask me an occasional question about New York, I knew that my hopes were not in vain. We dined, and though wine was proffered she drank little and, true to her statement that she was not hungry, ate little. She told me in soft, difficult German that she was trying not to get too stout, that her mother was German and her father Italian and that she had been visiting an uncle in Florence who was in the grocery business. I wondered at times, in spite of her charm, how she came to be traveling first-class.

The time passed. Dinner was over, and in several hours more we would be in Venice. We returned to our compartment, and because the moon was magnificent, we stood in the corridor and watched it shining on clustered cypresses, on villa-crowned hills, on great stretches of flat prairie or marshland, all barren of trees, and occasionally on little towns, all white and brown, glistening in the clear light.

"It will be a fine night to see Venice," I suggested, "for me. I have always wondered how it would look."

"Oh, oui! Herrlich! Prachtvoll!" she replied.

I liked her command of sounding German words.

"When we get there, will you come with me?" I inquired.

She looked out of the window, pretending not to hear.

I dropped the matter for a time, while she told me the names of stations at which we stopped and which the guards were calling. Finally, because the country had become absolutely flat, with occasional streams or small bodies of water in view, all bright in the moonlight, we came in and sat down.

"Well, we are almost there," I said, pressing her arm genially. "Are you coming with me?"

"I should go home," she replied.

"Do you expect anyone to meet you?"

"No."

"Well, then, why not?"

She meditated curiously.

"Never mind," I said, "you will."

She smiled a pale, weary smile.

"I shall have to go tomorrow," she said. "I have no clothes. I have been away two weeks."

"Very good," I replied, "we can talk about that then," and for the first time she gave me her hand. I put my hand to her smooth, cool cheek and pulled her head down. She merely pressed it gently and then after a few moments exclaimed quite gaily, as if at last she was interested in the adventure, "Now we are here! The Lagoon!"

I looked out, and we were speeding over a wide body of water, not unlike Newark Bay at Elizabeth, at which the train crosses on a trestle or stone arcade. It was beautifully silvery, and in the distance I could see something—the outlines of a city, but not very bright. Very shortly we were in a car yard, as at Rome and Florence, and then under a large train shed, and then, convoyed by an enthusiastic Italian porter, we came out on the wide stone platform or sidewalk that faces the Grand Canal and receives and discharges all the passengers in gondolas. I could scarcely believe my eyes—it was so wonderful. The white walls of marble buildings in long, waving lines; a great street of water; the gondolas, black, shapely, numerous, a great company of them nudging each other on the rippling water; green-stained stone steps, sharply illuminated by electric lights, leading down to them; a great crowd of gesticulating porters and passengers. I pressed Maria's arm, for I had learned her name by then, and exclaimed in German, "Wonderful! Wonderful!"

"*Es ist herrlich!*" (It is splendid), she replied.

We stepped into a gondola, our bags being loaded in afterwards, and I said to her enthusiastically, "Are you glad you came with me now?"

"*Oui*," she replied.

Then as I stood up and looked around she took my hand in a friendly way.

"You are like a schoolboy," she observed. "You like it very much, don't you?"

"Oh, do I!" I replied.

I was something like a poet with the fever for expression upon him. Venice had easily won my absolute enthusiasm, as it has that of so many millions before me.

* * *

I think I cannot do more at this place than to incorporate, before going on with the general details of my impressions, a number of those spasmodic, almost involuntary, comments which I jotted into my notebook during the five days I was in the city. They had nothing, or very little, to do with the general trend of my affairs—that is, visiting churches, museums and the principal restaurants of the city. Yet as I think of them, they constitute the best of all I saw, the true spirit of the city. I give them as they came to me. No re-statement of them would have any value as compared with their original mood, so here they are:

"The Grand Canal under a glittering moon. The clocks striking twelve. A horde of black gondolas. Lovely cries. The rest is silence. Moon picking out the ripples in silver and black. Think of these old stone steps, white marble stained green, laved by the waters of the sea these hundreds of years. A long, narrow street of water. A silent boat passing. And this is a city of a hundred and sixty thousand!"

"Wonderful painted arch doorways and windows. Trefoil and quatrefoil decorations. An old iron gate with some statues behind it. A balcony with flowers. The Bridge of Sighs! Nothing could be so perfect as a city of water."

"The Lagoon at midnight under a full moon. Now I think I know what Venice is at its best. Distant lights, distant voices. Someone singing. There are pianos in this sea-isle city, playing at midnight. Just now a man silhouetted blackly under a dark arch. Our gondola takes us into the very hallway of the Royal Danieli."

"Water! Water! The music of all earthly elements. The lap of water! The sigh of water! The flow of water! In Venice you have it everywhere. It sings at the base of doorsteps, it purrs softly under your window, it suggests the eternal rhythm and the eternal flow at every angle. Time is running away, life is running away, and here in Venice, at every angle (under your window) is its symbol. I know of no city which at once suggests the lapse of time hourly, momentarily, and yet soothes the heart because of it. For all its movement, or because of it, it is gay, lighthearted, without being enthusiastic. The peace that passes all understanding is here—soft, rhythmic, artistic. Venice is as gay as a song, as lovely as a jewel (an opal or an emerald), as rich as marble, and as great as verse. There can only be one Venice in all the world!"

There can only be one Venice in all the world!

"I don't know what there is about shadow and moss and gray stones, but they constitute a trilogy which when combined with water and the artistry of masonry make up a combination that is irresistible to me. Venice is so rich, so soft—it is like a cooing dove. It has true mellow temperament, the most soothing temperament, of perhaps any city I have ever seen. No horses, no wagons, no trolley cars. Just the patter of human feet. You listen here, and the very language is musical. The voices are soft. Why should they be loud? They have nothing to contend against. I am wild about this place. There is a sweetness in the hush of things which woos, and yet it is not the hush of silence. All is life here, all movement—a sweet, musical gaiety. I wonder if murder and robbery flourish in any of these sweet streets. The life here is like that of children playing. I swear, in all my life I have never had such ravishing sensations of exquisite art-joy, of pure, delicious enthusiasm for the physical, exterior aspect of a city. It is as mild and sweet as moonlight itself."

"This Hotel Royal Danieli is a delicious old palace, laved on one side by a canal. My room commands the whole of the Lagoon. George Sand and Alfred de Musset occupied a room here somewhere. I must find out. Perhaps I have it."

"Venice is so markedly different from Florence. There all is heavy, somber, defensive, serious. Here all is light, airy, graceful, delicate. There could be no greater variation. Italy is such a wonderful country. It has Florence, Venice, Rome and Naples, to say nothing of Milan and the Riviera, which should really belong to it. No cornices here in Venice. They are all left behind in Florence."

"What shall I say of St. Mark's and the Ducal Palace—dreams, jewel-boxes, mosaics of history, utterly exquisite. The least fragment of St. Mark's I consider of the utmost value. The Ducal Palace should be guarded as one of the great treasures of the world. It is perfect."

"Fortunately I saw St. Mark's in the morning, in clear, refreshing, spring-like sunlight. Neither Venice nor Florence have the hard glitter of the south—only a rich brightness. The five domes are almost gold in effect; the nine frescoes of the facade, gold, red and blue; the walls, cream and gray. Before it is the oblique quadrangle which necessitates your getting far to one side to see the church squarely—a perfect and magnificently individual jewel. All the great churches are that, I noticed. Overhead a sky of blue. Before you a great, smooth pavement, crowded with people, the Campanile (just re-completed) soaring heavenward in perfect lines. What a square! What a treasure for a city to have! Momentarily this space is swept over by great clouds of pigeons, like attendant angels. The swish of their wings is like some sad orchestral opening to a fugue. On the pavement sweeps the shadow of them, like the spirits of rose leaves. The new reproduction of the old Campanile glows with a radiance all its own. I honor Italy for having restored it. Oh, the treasures of Italy! This one soars and sings. Above all, the gilded crosses of the church. To the right the lovely arcaded facade of the library. To the right of the church, facing the square, the fretted beauty of the Doges' Palace—a portion of it. As I was admiring it, a warship in the harbor fired a great gun—twelve o'clock. Up went all my pigeons—thousands, it seemed, sweeping in great restless circles—while church bells began to chime and whistles to blow. Where are the manufactories of Venice?"

"Riding on the Grand Canal I now suspect, for the first time for myself, where the Gothic came from. It may have been imported out of the East, from Morocco, Turkey, Arabia and India. There is a kinship. So-called Venetian Gothic shows nothing but a northern modification of the Orient."

"At first you don't realize it, but suddenly it occurs to you—a city of one hundred and sixty thousand without a wagon, a horse, without a long, wide street anywhere, without trucks, funeral processions, streetcars. All the shops doing a brisk business, citizens at work everywhere, material pouring in and out, but no wagons—only small barges and gondolas. No noise save the welcome clatter of human feet; no sights save those which have a strange, artistic pleasantness. You can hear people talking sociably, their voices echoed by the strange, cool walls. You can hear birds singing high up in pretty windows where flowers trail downward; you can hear the soft lap of waters on old steps at times—the softest, sweetest music of all."

"I am naturally fond of moving water. I can sit by the hour and watch straws and chips float idly by on some slow-moving stream. To hear and see water sipping at doorposts, lintels, over steps and beneath windows is to realize a dream. Imagine my wonder, then, when I found steamboats running as trolley cars do elsewhere and people using the canals as other people use sewers and highways. I found boxes, papers, straw, vegetable waste, all cast indifferently into the water and all borne swiftly out to sea. People open windows and cast out packages as if this were the only way."

"I walked into the Banca di Napoli this afternoon, facing the Grand Canal. It was only a few moments after the regular closing hour. I came upon it from some narrow lane—some 'dry street.' It was quite open, the ground floor. There was a fine, dark, columned hall opening out upon the water. Where were the clerks? I wondered. There were none. Where that ultimate hurry and sense of life that characterizes the average bank at this hour? Nowhere. It was lovely, open, dark, as silent as a ruin. When did the bank do business? I asked myself. No answer. I watched the waters from its steps and then went away."

"One of the little tricks of the architects here is to place a dainty little Gothic balcony above a door, perhaps the only one on the facade, and that hung with vines."

"Venice is mad about campaniles. It has a dozen, I think, some of them leaning, like the tower at Pisa."

"I must not forget the old rose of the clouds in the west, the islands, the sails, the water and the green grass. And just now I heard a bird twittering."

"A gondolier selling vegetables out of a gondola and crying his wares in pure music. At my feet, white steps laved by whitish-blue water. Tall, cool, damp walls, ten feet apart. Cool, wet, red brick pavements. The sun shining above, making you realize how lovely and cool it is here, and birds singing everywhere—canaries in cages."

"Gondolas doing everything—carrying casks, coal, lumber, lime, stone, flour, bricks and boxed supplies generally, and others carrying vegetables, fruit, kindling and flowers. Only now I saw a boat slipping by crowded with red geraniums."

"Lovely pointed doors and windows, houses with colonnades, trefoils, quatrefoils and exquisite fluted cornices to match, making every house that strictly adheres to them a jewel. It is Gothic crossed with Moorish and Byzantine fancy. Some of them take on the black and white of London smoke, though I have no idea why. Others, being colored richly at first, are weathered by time into lovely half-colors or tones. I never saw before such delightful balustrades, such charming recessed windows, such quaint oriels, lunettes, ovals. If Oxford were surrounded by and involved and ribboned with water, England might have something of the kind, not otherwise."

"These little canals are heavenly! They wind like scattered ribbons, flung broadcast, and the wind touches them only in spots, making the faintest ripples. Mostly they are as still as death. They have the most exquisite bridges crossing in delightful arches, and wonderful doors and steps open into them, steps gray or yellow or black with age, steps that have green and brown moss on them and that are alternately revealed or hidden by a high or low tide. Here comes a gondolier now, peddling oranges. The music of his voice!"

"Can you imagine latticework in England or the United States or France? I can't very well, and yet there are examples. Here latticework is everywhere, and it has the authority of, one might almost say, necessity or compulsion—it looks so in the scene. Latticework in the churches, the houses, the public buildings. Venice loves it. It is Oriental and truly beautiful."

"I find myself at a branch station of the water-street-car service. There are gondolas here, too, a score, for hire. This man hails me genially, his brown hands and face and his small, old, soft roll hat a picture in the sun. I feel as if I were dreaming or as if this were some exquisite holiday of my childhood."

"One could talk for years of these passages in which, amidst the shadow and sunlight of cool, gray walls, a gleam of color has shown itself. You look down narrow courts to lovely windows or doors or bridges or niches with the Virgin or a saint in them. Now it is a black-shawled housewife or a fat, phlegmatic man that turns a corner; now a girl in a white skirt and pale green shawl or a red skirt and a black shawl. Unexpected doorways, dark and deep with pleasant industries going on within, greet you at every turn; bakeries with a wealth of new, warm bread; butcheries with red meat and brass scales; small restaurants where appetizing roasts and meat pies are displayed. Unexpected bridges, unexpected squares, unexpected streams of people moving in the sun, unexpected terraces, unexpected boats, unexpected voices, unexpected songs. That is Venice."

"I looked into a small court behind a gray stone portal, shut by an iron gate, in which was a gray, moss-covered well head of antique design; a pair of pretty cupids, brown and green with moss, embracing each other; a Venus triumphant, one foot gone; a head of some solemn, bearded old man; a lovely arcaded fountain; a scrolled and beveled coat-of-arms, yellow with age; a marble eagle, its wings outspread; a wide-basined urn containing flowers; and the fragment of a white arm. They were all standing or lying about in aimless disorder, a carpet of grass beneath, a blue sky overhead, outside the branch of a canal and a bridge with a lovely parapet. What more could one ask?"

"Today I took a boat on the Grand Canal to the Giardino, which is at the eastern extreme of the city. Venice is not, largely, utterly compact. It was evening. I found a lovely island just adjoining the gardens, a Piazza d'Arena. Rich, green grass and a line of small trees along three sides. Silvery water. A second leaning tower and more islands in the distance. Cool and pleasant, with that lovely sense of evening in the air which comes only in spring. They said it would be cold in Venice, but it isn't. Birds twittering, the waters of the bay waveless, the red, white and brown colors of the city showing in rich patches. I think if there is a heaven on earth in which youth and love might find their abode, it is Venice in spring."

"Just now the sun came out, and I witnessed a Turner effect. First, this lovely bay was suffused with a silvery-gold light—its very surface. Then the clouds in the west broke into ragged masses. The sails, the islands, the low buildings in the distance began to stand out brilliantly. Even the Campanile, Santa Maria Maggiore and the Salute took on an added glory. I was witnessing a great sky and water song, a poem, a picture—something to identify Venice with all my life. Three ducks went by high in the air, honking as they went. A long, black flotilla of thin-rowed coal barges passed in the foreground. The engines of a passing steamer beat rhythmically, and I breathed deep and joyously to think I had witnessed all."

"Bells over the water, the lap of waves, the smell of seaweed. How soft and elevated and ethereal voices sound at this time. An Italian sailor, sitting on the grass looking out over it all, has his arms about his girl."

"It would be easy to give an order for ten thousand lovely views of Venice and get them."

CHAPTER LXIV

My adventure with Maria Bastida was as interesting and curious as any that has ever befallen me. Because of the very poor German spoken by both of us, it was very hard for me to extract any really definite information beyond those commonplace facts which almost anyone can gather. She was of a phlegmatic and none-too-communicative type, but passionate and sympathetic. I marvel at times at the variety of character, male and female, that goes to make up this world.

In America the cognoscenti of various strata know the type of woman that can be saluted and engaged in conversation on trains. They are not all adventuresses, by any means, and not all dull. A spirit of romance and youthful adventure is frequently at the bottom of it. Abroad, not always perhaps, it takes a more practical turn. Yet I did not find Maria Bastida either apparently adventurous or practical. She certainly was not greedy for money. She was passionate and a little vague.

One of the strangest of temperaments that I encountered abroad was that of Mme. de Villiers in Paris, but Maria was another. Through my arrangement with Cook & Son, a room and bath had been reserved for me, and this we occupied the first night without comment. The young lady was presentable. The management took good care to see that the difference in price for one extra person was booked, but beyond that no sign was given that a room for two had not been ordered. They have no "John Smith and wife" system of entry abroad—certainly not in France and Italy.

As we rode through the Grand Canal and the narrow water street that runs back of the Doges' Palace into the principal lagoon, I was so curiously divided in my mood for Venice and my interest in the personality of my companion that I scarcely knew how to adjust them. I had found her suggestive and alluring in the dining car without being able to indicate what I felt. She had looked at me occasionally and smiled sedately, a provoking and yet hardly intended smile, which made me abnormally eager. I think, as I look back over life, that there are temperaments unconsciously provocative of passion—loco weeds, poison flowers—against which responsive temperaments must struggle with the aid of principles or else succumb quite brutally. Cantharides acts in a strange way, as does hashish, yet they are no worse than certain temperaments, and we all have certain allied types to which we are strangely responsive. Or it may be that a certain state and fire of youth is the guilty agent. I sometimes think that the provocation to immorality or sex contact under any circumstances is a syllogism, a form, a theorem. Given a certain combination of lines and colors, you produce desire in the male. The thing is no doubt worked out mathematically by the governing intelligence that produces millions upon millions of passions annually and nightly, and all by the same trick or combination.

Anyhow, we journeyed through the Grand Canal and the Lagoon, I with such impressions and feelings as I have indicated—Maria with what, I cannot tell. Venice was an old story to her. Come to think of it now, she suggested in her mood and actions much of the impression I gained from surveying the underworld masses of Venetians whom I met pattering their marvelous dry streets. They were dull, silent, friendly, a little morbid perhaps, and moving with many misty moods within. It was the same with her.

When we came into this hotel room, she took the hotel situation with no particular enthusiasm and no noticeable nervousness. Neither had she the gay effrontery of Marcelle.

"It is nice," she said, looking out of the window onto the Lagoon where San Giorgio and the Salute were in evidence. I gazed myself in wonder, for this moonlit bay was suggestive of the peculiar history of Venice to me—the flight of the early mainlanders to these inhospitable mud islands before the invading Lombards—and its subsequent magnificent development under the doges. I knew just enough about the Council of Ten, the Bridge of Sighs and the development of Venetian art to make it fascinating.

I turned to her immediately afterward and found her before the mirror undoing her collar, which seemed to irritate her smooth neck. She was so matter-of-fact and so strangely phlegmatic that she fascinated me. I offered to unbutton her dress in the back, but she said to me quite sweetly, "I can do it better than you can." She opened her valise and took out a pretty, clean nightgown, which cheered me greatly. I had risked companionship on a rather spruce exterior, but that is not always indicative. When she finally, after some becoming signs of reserve, yielded herself quite nude, she revealed a body not so beautifully modeled as languorous and provocative. She had smooth, rounded arms and legs and a shapely back. She developed a deep though quiescent animality, holding me close and smoothing my hair.

Of all things in this world, passion is the strangest. I think true passion is silent and lust is deadly. For a very large number of people, in youth particularly, the sole reason for existence seems to lie in sex; and for others, such personalities as the Lane type, it has small meaning. I often wonder whether George Moore's faith is true that all men are thinking eagerly of at least one given woman at any given time. Personally I see no significance to the relation beyond a proper ebullition of fancy between two, and I cannot see why any particular condemnation should be attached to it. The aspect in which passion is least attractive is when it is involved with lack of refinement or false expressions of affection, declarations of undying faith, excuses, pretenses, denials and lies (where someone is trying to win a temporary delight and has no real interest in the person beyond the body) or both. That latter aspect is certainly unpleasant and scarcely worth the effort involved. Beyond that, where two have a common mental understanding of the situation or a temperamental inclination toward each other, I can see no harm. No one else is injured. A sense of companionability and satisfaction in life is gained. Pleasant memories for two, as a rule, are created, and life has been prevented from assuming that aspect of dull disappointment it wears for so many. I see much, very much, in sex companionship, though I suppose no one need advocate its value very strongly. It takes care of itself.

The next morning at just about the hour when we were both most anxious for rest, pandemonium broke loose. Let me say right here at the start-off, in spite of all I have said of the peace of Venice, that it is a little mad in the matter of early morning noises. Bells, bells, bells! I never heard such a rattle and clatter as went on this first morning between five-thirty and seven-thirty, and just when I was *so* tired. Bells began ringing at five-thirty, ceased and resumed again at six, ceased and resumed again at six-thirty, and so on until seven and eight, by which time I was nearly wild. There were whistles, too, the weirdest cry from war vessels anchored in the harbor, and some incoming or outgoing steamer, and in addition to all this, reveille sounded from some nearby battleship or public square, and finally bands on several warships visible from my window felt it incumbent upon them to play. There were cries and calls as if bedlam had broken loose. It seemed impossible that anyone could sleep here anymore, ever. But it quieted down after that and I was allowed to resume my repose. I had to laugh at Maria Bastida, who, seeing me jump up to inquire what the trouble was, blinked her eyes sleepily and observed, "*Ach! Es ist immer so!*" (Oh, it is always this way!)

"How can you sleep?" I asked.

"You get used to it," she replied.

It was eight before I really got to sleep again, but by eleven we both had enough and were ready for breakfast. It was very pleasant to me, after the loneliness of Assisi, Spello and Florence, to again be in the company of a woman, even if only so temporarily, because for me they contribute a pleasing working atmosphere or at least a sense of pleasurable companionship that is difficult to obtain in any other way. I do best in their presence—at least I feel best. She got up after a time and went leisurely about her dressing, interrupted to a certain extent by my attentions and smiling, I think, to think she was so welcome. It was interesting to see her do up her hair and bathe, not thinking of me so much, I fancy, and contributing bits of information concerning Venice and her own life. There was an Englishman and his bride in the next room, a none-too-discreet pair who had billed and cooed rather loudly the night before, and once she threw her head in their direction—"They are having a good time, too," she said. She told me that she lived with her mother and father not very far from this hotel in an apartment—"not as nice as this"—I have forgotten the name of the *calle* at the moment, but she said that I could come there. Her father did not come home often. It would be all right. He was engaged in some transfer business—he may have been a gondolier. She and her mother lived much alone, she said. She had been both to Florence, as I saw, and Milan, but never to Rome. "I expect to go someday," she observed. She was interested in Paris, London and New York, but more in New York. Some Italian friends of hers had gone there.

"Do you know a street called Newark?" she asked naively.

"It isn't a street," I informed her. "It's a city."

She was a little doubtful. It must be a street.

"No, it's a city," I said, "very close to New York—twenty minutes."

That explained it for her.

She was faintly interested in Germany, where I was going—her mother's parents came from Bavaria, although her mother was born in Milan.

"Do you ever think you will come to New York?" I asked.

"Maybe. Who can tell? Would you come to see me?"

She pointed out some of the wonders of Venice from the window—the Lido, where there is bathing in summer, on the Adriatic, San Giorgio, where a fine view of the city was to be had, the Salute—"Very nice inside. You should go." She mentioned certain inland streets as very interesting, and when I asked her if she would come with me, she replied, "If you want me to, but I have to go home first."

This going home puzzled me. She had to leave at one o'clock or about then, because a train came from Florence around that time, but she would meet me later in the day and dine with me. "I can meet you in St. Mark's Square," she suggested, "or you can come to the house. It isn't so nice as this."

I saw she was a little ashamed of it.

"Let me come to the house," I said. "I should like to see an apartment in Venice."

She agreed.

Later that afternoon, because of uncertainty of directions, I gave a gondolier the number and was soon there. It was in the Rio di Santa Marina, up three flights, a neighborhood not very excellent, perhaps, but like everything else in Venice—quaint. I could never find a place there, in my newness and enthusiasm, which I could call bad, though some were obviously old, dark, damp and musty. I made my way uncertainly upward and knocked at what was the proper door. Maria herself answered, in a different dress, not so conventional as the one she had worn on the train. She bade me welcome, and I looked curiously about, for this apartment, though not so materially different from any other anywhere else, was different to me because it was in Venice.

"You are curious, aren't you?" she asked in her soft German.

I would have given much to have gathered the actual working arrangement of this Venetian ménage, but I never did. I was in it four times before I left, but it revealed nothing to me but a rather stout, undersized woman of obviously German origin working about several rooms which were beyond the one occupied by Maria. I thought once that she might be lying and that this old woman was her housekeeper, but I could not tell. They talked in Italian. The steps that led up to this ménage were narrow and of stone, with an iron handrail and niches for lamps or candles. There was neither gas nor electricity in this house, but only lamps of rather commonplace glass with silvered reflectors. The floor was of stone or cement, I think cement, and covered in part by strips of carpet. The furniture was old and solid, of walnut or cherry and of a type that has long since been displaced in America and, I fancy, England by lighter designs. Maria's room had a plain, cement-floored alcove with a large, heavy bed in it, a window hung with a red-and-yellow striped stuff of loose weave, and several lithographic reproductions of French beauties. The window, which opened out from this, looked down on one of the one hundred and fifty canals of Venice—a narrow one, but with touches of the architecture that I so much admired. Because of our first night at the hotel I felt thoroughly at home with her, and in spite of the none-too-attractive neighborhood (it was in the vicinity of a church called Santa Maria dei Miracoli), I liked it. I had no letters to any resident in Venice, and I was not particularly anxious for companionship by day, but at night or during the late afternoon it was pleasant to be able to seek Maria out, and after dining at one of the restaurants (*trattorie*), we would ride on the canals or walk in Merceria, Frezzeria, the Salizzada San Moisé or the Piazza of St. Mark's. In the latter there were really interesting stores containing leather goods, jewelry and ornaments of all kinds for women, and here one night I bought her a pretty purse for fifteen lire and another time a set of amber combs for eighteen.

During the days I spent in Venice I saw much of her, but mostly, as I have said, late in the afternoon or evening. She was very practical in her relationship and would agree to meet me in the Piazza of St. Mark at any hour—three, four, five or later—and go wherever I saw fit. One evening after an hour in the gardens at the east end of Venice, some suggestion of which I have given in my notes, we went to the Lido, a distant island over the Lagoon, and had dinner, an indifferent one, at the Grande Hotel Lido. At another time we went to the Restaurant Pilsen, near the northwest corner of the Piazza of St. Mark, and a third time she suggested a cheap, crowded restaurant in the Calle dei Fabbri, because it was like Venice. Not understanding Italian, it was not startling, but Maria was always pleasant and informative in a way when I could make myself understood.

On leaving, and when I saw her last (which was on the station platform at Milan as I was departing for Lucerne), I gave her fifty lire (I had given her fifty the first morning) and her ticket back to Venice. She was to take a later train, and whether she returned or not immediately is a question. She liked Milan and had been there before. I took it, after our first conversation, that she occasionally went with men, that she met foreigners, who are the most prosperous of any here—Germans or Italian-speaking English or Americans—and found it fairly profitable. I am satisfied that she was not a prostitute of the ordinary grade, but of the Marcelle or Mme. de Villiers type with Italian variations. She was very pleasant at all times and on occasion quite gay in a queer semi-Italian, semi-German way. In the main I am satisfied that the Venetians are not as fiery as the remainder of the Italians—the southern Italians anyhow—and more phlegmatic. They seemed a meditative, peaceful people, and Maria was no exception. Altogether, including hotel bills, dinner and railroad fare, she cost me sixty-five dollars, American money, which seemed a trivial sum in comparison with the pleasure I took in her companionship.

CHAPTER LXV

Aside from the Cathedral of St. Mark's, the Doges' Palace and the Academy or Venetian gallery of old masters, I could find little of artistic significance in Venice—little aside from the wonderful art of the city as a whole. As a spectacle, viewed across the open space of water known as the Lagoon, the churches of San Giorgio Maggiore and Santa Maria della Salute, with their domes and campaniles strangely transfigured by light and air, are beautiful. Close at hand, for me, they lost much romance which distance gave them, though the mere space of their interiors was impressive. The art, according to my judgment, was bad, and in the main I noticed that my guidebooks agreed with me—spiritless religious representations which, after the Sistine Chapel in Rome and such pictures as those of Michelangelo's *Holy Family* and Botticelli's *Adoration of the Magi* in the Uffizi at Florence, were without significance. I preferred to speculate on the fear of the plague which had produced the Salute and on the discovery of the body of St. Stephen, the proto-martyr, which had given rise to San Giorgio, for it was interesting to think, with these facts before me, how art and spectacles in life so often take their rise from silly, almost pointless causes; a plain lie is more often the foundation of a great institution than a truth. Santa Maria did not save the citizens of Venice from the plague in 1630, and in 1110 the Doge Ordelafo Faliero did not bring back the true body of St. Stephen from Palestine, although he may have thought he did—at least there are other "true bodies." But the old, silly progress of illusion, vanity, politics and the like has produced these and other institutions throughout the world and will continue to do so, no doubt, until time shall be no more. It was interesting to me to see the once large and really beautiful Dominican monastery surrounding San Giorgio turned into barracks and offices for government officials. I do not see why these churches should not be turned into libraries or galleries. Their religious significance is quite gone.

In Venice it was, I think, that I got a little sick of churches and second- and third-rate art. The city itself is so beautiful, exteriorly speaking, that only the greatest art could be tolerated here, yet aside from the Academy, which is crowded with canvases by Bellini, Tintoretto, Titian, Veronese and others of the Venetian school, and from the Ducal Palace, largely decorated by Tintoretto and Veronese, there is nothing, save of course St. Mark's. Outside of that and the churches of the Salute and San Giorgio—both bad artistically, I think—there are thirty-three or -four other churches, all with bits of something which gets them into the catalogues—a Titian, a Tintoretto, a Giorgione, or a Paolo Veronese—until the soul wearies and you say to yourself, "Well, I've had about enough of this—what is the use?"

There is no use. Unless you are tracing the rise of religious art or trying to visit the tombs of semi-celebrated persons or following out the work of some one man or group of men to the last fragment, you might as well desist. There is nothing in it. I sought church after church, entering often dark, pleasant, but not often imposing interiors, only to find a single religious representation of one kind or another hardly worth the trouble. In the Frari I found Titian's famous *Madonna* of the Pesaro family and a pretentious mausoleum commemorating Canova, and in Santa Maria Formosa a picture by Palma Vecchio—St. Barbara and four other saints, which appealed to me very much—but in the main I was disappointed and made dreary. After St. Peter's, the Vatican, St. Paul Without The Walls, Pisa and the great galleries of Florence, Venice seemed to me artistically dull. I preferred always, in fact I was quite eager, to get into the streets again to see the small shops, to encounter the winding canals, to cross the little bridges and to feel that here was something new and different and more artistic than anything which any church or museum could show.

One of the strangest things about Venice to me was the curious manner in which you could always track a great public square or marketplace of some kind by following some thin trickling of people you would find in some vicinity making their way in a given direction. Suddenly in some quite silent residence section with all its lovely waterways about you, you would encounter a small, thin stream of people going somewhere, perhaps five or six people in a row, over bridges, up narrow alleys, over more bridges, through squares or triangles where churches or small stores were, and constantly swelling in volume, until you found yourself in the midst of a small throng turning now right, now left, until you came out on the great open marketplace or piazza to which they were all tending. They always struck me as a sheep-like company, pattering here and there with vague, almost sad eyes. They were so different, it seemed to me, from the citizens of Paris, Rome, London, even Florence. Europe presents no counterpart to the American, so he is almost negligible—the bright, smart, self-sufficient, upstanding, newspaper-reading American. Here in Venice I saw no newspapers displayed at all, nor ever heard any called or saw any read. There was none of that morning vigor which characterizes an American city. It was always more like a quiet village scene to me than any aspect of a fair-sized city. Yet so it was. Because I was comfortable in Venice, and because all the while I was there it was so radiantly beautiful, I left it with real sorrow. To me it was perfect.

The one remaining city of Italy that I was yet to see, Milan, was of small interest to me because already I had seen so much of Italy and because I was eager to get into Switzerland and Germany. For the sake of companionship—I had to ride from five-forty-five to eleven-ten to get there—I took Maria Bastida with me, and we spent the next day glimpsing what little there was to see. Outside of a half-dozen early Christian basilicas, which we sedulously avoided (I employed a guide), there was only the Cathedral, the now-dismantled palace and fortress of the Sforzas masquerading as a museum, and the local art gallery, a tremendous affair crowded with that same religious artwork of the Renaissance which, one might almost say in the language of the Milwaukee brewer, had made Italy famous. I was, however, about fed up on art. As a cathedral, that of Milan seemed as perfect as any—great and wonderful. I was properly impressed with its immense stained-glass windows, said to be the largest in the world, its fifty-two columns supporting its great roof, its ninety-eight pinnacles and two thousand statues. Of a splendid edifice such as this there is really nothing to say. It is like Amiens, Rouen and Canterbury—simply astounding. It would be useless to attempt to describe the emotions it provoked, as useless as indicating the feelings some of the pictures in the local gallery aroused in me. It would be Amiens all over again, or some of the pictures in the Uffizi. It seemed to me the newest of all the Gothic cathedrals I saw, absolutely perfect in all its details, and as modern as yesterday—yet it was begun in 1386.

To me, the wonder of this, and of every other cathedral like it that I saw, was never their religious but their artistic significance. Someone with a splendid imagination—an individual or a group of men with a sense of grandeur—must always have been behind them, and I can never understand the character or the temper of an age or a people that will let anything happen to them. To me the spirit of a general who would shell a temple like the Parthenon or a pope who would dismantle the Colosseum or the Pantheon, is beneath contempt. Nothing is too dull for such a spirit not to do. Their souls encumber the earth.

Outside of the Cathedral (from the top of which, by the way, I saw for the first time the Alps, Mont Blanc, Mont Cenis, Monte Rosa, covered with snow), there was only really the medieval fortress of the Sforzas—so suggestive of the immense personal ambitions of medieval Italy—and the art in the Palazzo di Brera, some thirty or forty chambers crowded with Mantegnas, Bellinis, Carlo Crivellis, Titians, Tintorettos, Veroneses, Raphaels and selections from Van Dyck, Rembrandt, Jacob Jordaens and others. One would want days and days to attempt even a cursory examination of these, and I did not feel that I had the time. The patient Maria, not new to Milan, kept me company, and now and then she found something she liked. In the main I think she was dreadfully bored.

In the palace of the Sforzas I found considerable to meditate upon concerning the mood and mental attitude which would cause the construction of such an immense fortress. Life was certainly unsettled and insecure. It looks as dull and threatening as any palace-fortress could look, and yet it is impressive and, in a way, beautiful. One can understand how seriously these medieval princelings took themselves when you look at this, but now, like a storm-wrecked bark, it lies stranded on the shore of modern democracy, filled with quaint bits of sculpture from a hundred ancient churches, marbles from the work of the Romans in northern Italy, a collection of costumes and stuffs, a very unimpressive collection of modern pictures, armor, ivories, tapestries and the like. The one thing that really touched me in all this was an effigy of Gaston de Foix from his tomb or sarcophagus, a lovely stone knight lying cap-a-pie in one of these great halls for all to look at. Nearby was a lovely arched window and outside the sunlit green grass—the kind of grass that is described in all medieval tales of knighthood. He was a charming individual, Gaston de Foix—very knightly indeed. You should read of him in the old chronicles.

But if I found little of thrilling artistic significance, after Rome and the south, I was strangely impressed with the modernity of Milan. You read constantly—or we have in America—that Europe is old, run-down at the heels. I wonder how it is that Americans of rank and file get the notion that all Italians are dirty, all Germans fat, all Frenchmen immoral, and all Englishmen poseurs—or, as we used to hear them spoken of in the West, "la-de-das." Europe, to me, is not so old in its texture anywhere. Most European cities of large size are of recent growth, just as American cities are. So many of the great buildings that we think of as timeworn, such as the Ducal Palace at Venice and elsewhere, are in an excellent state of preservation—quite new-looking. Venice has many new buildings in the old style. Rome is largely composed of modern tenements and apartment houses. There are elevators in Perugia, and when you reach Milan you find it newer than St. Louis or Cleveland—much newer.

Except in rather dreary sections of the old city, from which the inhabitants are gradually moving into the bright suburbs, and where you find narrow streets and heavily corniced houses, the rest of Milan is wide, bright, amazingly modernized and as thoroughly equipped with conveniences as any other city. Buffalo is no different, with the exception perhaps that it is not as well-built nor as new-looking. Streetcars (electric, of course) run everywhere. One large union station receives all trains. There are a number of good hotels with elevators, and as you walk the principal streets the shop windows show as many modern book stores, flower stores, music stores, barbershops, leather goods emporiums and anything else that you like, as any other. If there is any medieval spirit anywhere remaining, I could not find it. The shops are bright and attractive. There are large department stores like those in Philadelphia, Boston or Pittsburgh, and the honk-honk of the automobile is quite as common here as anywhere. I could not see, from the crowds and enthusiasm for industry displayed, that it is any different from Kansas City, Chicago or St. Louis. It has a population of only five hundred thousand, but even so, it evidences great commercial force. If you ride out in the suburbs, as we did, you see new houses, new factories, new streets, new everything. Unlike the people of southern Italy, the population looks large physically, and I did not understand this until I learned that they are freely mingled with the Germans. The Germans are in force here—in control of the silk mills, the leather manufactories, the restaurants, the hotels, the book stores and printing establishments. It is a wonder to me that they are not in control of the opera house and the musical activities, and I have no doubt that they influence it greatly. The director of La Scala ought to be a German if he is not. I got my first suggestion of Paris and the north in the tables set before the cafés in the arcade of Vittorio Emanuele. I got my first taste of Germany in the purely German beer halls with their orchestras of men or women, where for a few cents expended for beer you can sit by the hour and listen to the music. In the hotel where I stopped, the German precision of regulation was as marked as anywhere in Germany. It caused me to wonder whether the Germans would eventually sweep down and possess Italy, and if they did, what they would make of it—or what Italy would make of them!

CHAPTER LXVI

If one could fall down and adore wonderful mountain scenery, then Switzerland is the place for perpetual adoration. I entered it at Chiasso, a little way from Lake Como in Italy, and left it at Basle, near the German frontier, and all I saw were mountains, mountains, mountains—some capped with snow and some without, tall, sharp, craggy peaks and rough, sharp declivities with here and there a patch of grass, here and there a deep valley that could easily be walled up and filled with water, here and there a lonely, wide-roofed, slab-built house with immense, projecting eaves of that finicky style of decoration made familiar to us of New York by those shabby adaptations which constitute our L stations.

I cannot say that I enjoyed Switzerland, certainly not as I did Italy, though I was compelled to admire it. I was more overawed, chilled, than impressed. Mountains oppress me at times, almost always—great shut-in valleys surrounded by peaks—and as our train plunged in and out of tunnels as black as night, along dizzy brinks, very high, where snow was, and down into valleys where the grass was pleasantly green and some trees still had foliage or had newly acquired it—my one thought was, "Now, if I were a boy here, born without money, how would I get out of this oppressive land?" Coming north from Milan, I saw my last shade trees and cypresses (though it was cold enough in Milan, in all conscience, as compared with Rome), and when we reached the Swiss border I expected and perceived a great change. The landscape hardens perceptibly a little way out of Milan. High slopes and deep lakes appear.

At Chiasso, the first stop in Switzerland, I handed the guard a half-dozen letters I had written in Milan and stamped with Italian stamps. I did not know until I did this that we were out of Italy, had already changed guards, and that a new, Swiss crew was in charge of the train. "*Monsieur*," he said, tapping the stamps significantly, "*vous êtes en Suisse*." I do not understand French, but I did that, and I perceived also that I was talking to a Swiss. All the people on the platform were *Schweizer*, as the Germans call them—fair, chunky, stolid-looking souls without a touch of that fire or darkness so generally present a few miles south. Why should a distance of ten miles, five miles, two miles, one mile across an imaginary boundary line make such an astounding change? It is one of the strangest experiences of travel to cross an imaginary boundary line and find everything different—people, dress, architecture, landscape, often soil and foliage. It is surely interesting that different regions should produce different people, but so it is.

Now that I was started, really out of Italy, I was ready for any change, the more marked the better, and this was one. I was fully satisfied before I was done. Switzerland is about as much like Italy as a rock is like a bouquet of flowers—a sharp-edged rock and a rich, colorful, odorous bouquet. And yet, in spite of all its chill, bare bleakness, its high ridges and small shut-in villages, it has a kind of beauty—terrible but real. As the train sped on toward Lucerne, I kept my face glued to the windowpane on one side or the other, standing most of the time in the corridor, and was rewarded constantly by a magnificent panorama. Such bleak, sharp crags as stood always above us! such cold, white fields of snow! Sometimes the latter stretched down toward us in long, deep canyons or ravines until they disappeared as thin, white streaks at the bottom. I saw no birds of any kind flying, no gardens or patches of flowers anywhere, only queer brown or gray or white chalets with heavy, log-braced, overhanging eaves and an occasional stocky, pale-skinned citizen in a short jacket, knee trousers, small, round hat and flamboyant vest. I wondered whether I was really seeing the national costume. I was. I saw more of it at Lucerne, that most hotel-y of cities, and in the mountains and valleys of the territory beyond it toward Basle. Somebody once said of God that He might love all the creatures He had made but He certainly could not admire them. I will reverse that for Switzerland. I might always admire its wonders, but I could never love them. England may have *die Schweiz* as a summer playground. Not for me.

And yet after hours and hours of just this twisting and turning up slope and down valley, when I reached Lucerne I thought it was utterly beautiful. Long before we reached Lucerne the lake appeared and we followed its shores, whirling in and out of tunnels and along splendid slopes, commanding delightful views of sharp ridges come square to the water's edge. Nothing is more wonderful than a sheer wall of hard rock rising sharp out of still, cool water, and this is Lucerne.

On the train with me, in my first-class compartment, was one of those very characteristic American couples from, I should have said, Indiana, Ohio, Missouri, Illinois, Wisconsin or anywhere in the Middle West: a short, stout, stocky, dusty little man with a fringe of hair sticking offensively over his coat collar, and his medium-built, sedate, complaisant, commonplace wife. They were obviously graduates from some chicken business, successful farm or very likely successful livery business. From somewhere they had imbibed a keen desire to see the world, and here they were seeing it in a pleasant, good-natured way. "Ma" was a little tired; I could see that. She had traveled much, more to please "Pa," or "Henry," as she called him, than for any great joy she got out of it herself. He was very cocky, superior, self-content and inclined to lord it over her.

"There you are, now, Ma," he said, when Lucerne came into view. "That's Lucerne. There must be eighteen mile o' that, as I calculate it."

She had to watch it to please him. Long traveling and many scenes had wearied her. She was solid and phlegmatic, much too solid to be an enthusiastic traveler.

Before coming to Lucerne we had passed through the St. Gotthard tunnel. There must be a score of tunnels or more between Chiasso and Lucerne. As we entered each new one and remained for a few moments he remarked, "Well, I guess this is the St. Gotthard, all right," but when we flashed out into the sunlight again, he invariably added, "No, I'm wrong." He drew forth a map finally and, following the line of the towns, located himself by the next station. "Here we are," he observed at last. "It's just beyond this place. Now I'll time this run and see how long we take." He pulled out his watch and sat in the half-light as we entered St. Gotthard. "Eight minutes and fourteen seconds," he finally announced as we emerged. "That's pretty good time for this place. I calculated they'd make it in about nine." His wife said nothing, looking indifferently at the window and at him.

It struck me again, the oddity of two people thus running together for years, making finally a dual personality with a single point of view. I wondered what "Ma" really thought of him and his fussy interest in things. He was constantly calling her out to see something, some deep ravine or strange chalet on a slope or chill, bluish-white glacier—she never went of her own accord nor commented on anything.

"Here you are, Ma! Come look at this!" he would call, and as she arose, "Now, mind how you stand. These curves'll throw you over if you don't look out."

"I told you to watch out once," he triumphed when the motion of the train threw her in her seat after she had been up to inspect something. "This ain't no ballroom floor." She seemed to be pleasantly accustomed to him and he to her. They had three or four parcels, a bundle done up in a rug, a large grip and several umbrellas. His clothes and hers looked about like those you would see in any small Midwest town—some town of about fifteen hundred to three thousand inhabitants.

Lucerne, when we reached it, I found to be all that I had ever imagined it, and more. One expects of a renowned summering-place true beauty, and as a rule there is no disappointment, though often the introduction is unsatisfactory. Here, however, at the very door of the station the mountains, lake and city of Lucerne spread out before you in a delicious panorama. The world has long since been familiarized with the curiosities of Swiss, German, Bavarian, Tyrolean and allied types of architecture, which I need not describe; but seeing them actually present is a different matter—in force with all their oddities of gables, their sharpness of conical or hexagonal steeples, their queer little balconies, low, overhanging eaves, oddities of gingerbread towers and ornate, over-elaborate scrollwork between windows and doors or between one floor and another as a border, frieze or belt, and on the underside of eaves, and all that against a towering background of horny, granite mountains with a lovely lake spreading out smooth and silvery at your very feet. When I came out into the piazza which spreads before the station to the very edge of the lake, I was instantly glad that I had included Lucerne in my itinerary. It was evening, and the lamps in the village (it is not a large city) were already sparkling, and the water of the lake not only reflected the glow of the lamps along its shores but some pale, lingering pinks and mauves over the tops of the peaks in the west. There was snow on the upper stretches of the mountains, but down here in this narrow valley filled with quaint houses, hotels, churches and modern apartments, all was balmy and pleasant—not at all cold. My belongings were bundled into the attendant bus, and I was rattled off to one of the best hotels I saw abroad, the National of the Ritz-Carlton system—very quiet, very ornate and with all those conveniences and comforts which the American has learned to expect, plus a European standard of service and politeness, of which we can as yet know nothing in America. We have not even a system of training servants which will produce them.

Here everyone, as I saw at a glance, was expected to dress for dinner. Here a valet offers to unpack your bags and put your belongings away. An unobtrusive and efficient maid is at your service. The rooms themselves, all of them I am sure, are beautifully appointed, decorated in pretty whites, blues, olive greens and browns and kept pleasantly warm. One could see at a glance that Lucerne caters to a large, pleasure-loving, well-to-do summer and, even in a light way, winter patronage. This hotel, which was all of four hundred feet long by perhaps a hundred feet wide, had only one section of it open for winter service, but there were other hotels which were in full operation. The great majority of the rooms had pretty, ornamental balconies, overhanging the lake and commanding a magnificent mountain panorama, to which one could retire from the heat of the rooms and meditate. There are lovely places all over the world where one may idle in peace in summer with every attraction of nature to caress the soul. Lucerne is one.

After I had had time to feed upon Lucerne's exquisite beauty to my heart's content I made a solemn vow, twenty-four hours after I arrived, that never again would I go abroad anywhere unless I had someone with me with whom I might exchange companionable opinions and express something of the ideas and emotions which scenes of beauty and interest naturally evoke. There is no fun whatsoever in knocking about alone. Here I was in Lucerne. The surrounding landscapes were exquisitely beautiful, the town itself was of the most delightful architectural variation from that of Italy. The hotel at which I was stopping was absolutely perfect in every detail—food, attendance, arrangement, decoration, everything—and yet I was very lonely.

I sat on my balcony for a while before and after dinner, looking at the still waters of the lake, some ducks splashing cheerfully about, some little boats rowing picturesquely in the distance, and speculated on how truly unhappy I was. I would have given anything for the company of Grant Richards, Sir Hugh Lane, Mrs. Armstrong, Maria Bastida, Marcelle, Mme. de Villiers—anybody—in order to take off the curse of loneliness. On the Riviera Grant Richards complained that I had no ability to hold over any of my pleasures in conscience, to regurgitate, as it were, and feed on as a cow chews on its cud. He is quite right; I have not. I was very sorry now that I had not persuaded Maria Bastida, strange, meditative soul that she was, to accompany me even this far, though it would have been rather expensive for me. And of all I have mentioned, I would have chosen her last, attractive as she was in her way, for, while fairly intelligent, she was too involved with the mysteries of her own being to be really and truly satisfactory. I should not have cared so much for Marcelle, although I liked her best of all the women I had met, for the reason that she did not speak English. If I could have had Mrs. Armstrong, or any one of a selection from America, all would have been well. But traveling alone is not conducive to the most cheerful or uplifting thoughts in me.

CHAPTER LXVII

That night I spent in rambling about the nearby shores of the lake and adventuring into several cafés, which I located by the sounds emanating therefrom (none too interesting affairs), full of the Bavarian-Tyrolean type of individual whom I always find interesting to look upon, but rarely companionable. Their minds and moods remind me of the rococo decoration on a German-Bavarian-Tyrolean beer stein, and for that type of artistic decoration I do not care. It is quaint, naive, amusing, anything you will, but a little of it goes a long way. Contrast it with the simple, uninvolved purity of anything Greek or Roman, and you see what the trouble is at once. The thoughts and moods which produce this type of art are fuzzy and kinky. Those that lie back of Greek or Roman design are as clear as water and as good as bread. They are noble, chaste, thoughtful, serene. Imagine trying to think of the average Teutonic carving or ornamentation of any kind—Swiss, German, Bavarian, Tyrolean—as chaste, thoughtful, serene! These are exactly the things it is not.

If, however, it has not the splendor and dignity of the Italian-Greek ideals, it has a charm and silly beauty all its own. It is a sort of jester art, all cap and bells, and will serve for an idle hour. I liked to look at the sturdy men and women sitting in these beer halls, big, fat-bottomed, rosy-cheeked creatures, as sturdy as young oxen and in many instances as dull, who were listening with considerable enthusiasm, though stolid miens, to the rather broad quips and comments involved in the comic songs rendered. I wondered, as I looked at the several entertainers who appeared, what chance—if any—they would stand to amuse any American audience, providing they spoke English. None whatsoever, I should say. The American idea of humor is something very different. Here all that I heard were quips relating to marital unfaithfulness, quarrels over the lack of freedom on the part of one half of the married pair or the other, jests about having children or not having them and jests about marital fighting. As I look back over my American vaudeville experience, I am quite satisfied this was not that sort of thing that makes the average American vaudeville audience laugh, ever. We are more concerned with clever imitations of others—Jews, Irish, Germans, French, Italians, English—and with romance, beauty, dancing, beautiful clothes and songs about love in the moonlight. There is much greater variety to our vaudeville bill o' fare, even our café vaudeville bill o' fare. Think it over for yourself.

It was interesting to feel, even though I was quite lonesome, that I was in an entirely different world from that in which I had so recently been rejoicing for weeks. About me for miles and miles were the Swiss Alps covered with snow. I was in the center of one of the best and most modern of Swiss cities, and this was what it had to offer. Some local Frans Hals had done a series of really interesting pictures about the upper half of the dark wooden walls of one of these cafés—street fights between peasants; maidens swinging milk buckets; a judge listening to the details of a brawl; the interior of an inn such as the one in which I was, with drinkers about the tables; and so on and so forth. They were good, very good indeed—full of a clever interpretation of character, of moods and emotions, and with a subtle eye for arrangement, architectural detail and color. I wondered whether some local individual entirely unknown to fame could have done these things and whether time would eventually do him justice. Fra Angelico was entirely unknown to fame in his day, as was Luini, and hearty Frans Hals of Haarlem never knew that any of his pictures would ever sell for five hundred thousand dollars or that automobiles would crowd about the local *Stadhuis* in later years to study the wonders of his color and his line.

I am afraid I have an insatiable appetite for natural beauty. I am entertained by character, thrilled by art, but of all the enlarging spiritual influences, the natural panorama is to me the most significant. This night, after my first day of ramblings and investigations in Lucerne, I sat out on my hotel balcony overlooking the lake and studied the dim, moonlit outlines of the peaks crowding about it, the star-shine reflected in the water, the still distances and the moon sinking over the peaks to the west of the quaint city. Art has no method of including, or suggesting even, these vast sidereal spaces. The wonder of the night and moonlight is scarcely for the painter's brush. It belongs in verse, drama, great literary pageants such as those of Balzac, Turgenev and Flaubert—but not in pictures. The human eye can see so much and the human heart responds so swiftly that it is only by suggestion that anything is achieved in art. Art cannot give you the night in all its fullness save as, by suggestion, it brings back the wonder of the reality which you have already felt and seen.

I think, perhaps, of the two impressions that I retained most distinctly of Lucerne, that of the evening and of the very early morning, the morning was best. I came out on my balcony at dawn or a little before, this first morning after I arrived, when the lake was lying below me in glassy, olive-black stillness. Up the bank to my left were trees, granite slopes, a small chalet built out over the water, its spiles standing in a soothing, restful way. To my right, at the foot of the lake, lay Lucerne, its quaint outlines but vaguely apparent in the shadow. Across the lake only a little space were small boats, a dock, a church, and beyond them, in a circle, gray-black peaks. At their extreme summits along a rough, horny skyline were the suggestions of an electric dawn, a pale, steely-gray brightening from dark into light.

It was not cold at Lucerne, though it was as yet only early March. The air was as soft and balmy as at Venice and in the parks in Milan. As I sat there, the mountain skyline brightened first to a faint pink, the snow on the ridges took on a lavender and bluish hue as at evening, the green of the lower slopes became softly visible, and the water began to reflect the light of the sky, the shadow of the banks, the little boats on its surface and even some wild ducks flying over its surface—ducks coming from what bleak, drear spaces I could only guess. Presently I saw a man come out from the hotel, enter a small canoe and paddle away in the direction of the upper lake. More ducks appeared, their long necks craned, flap-flapping as they came and lighting finally with a soft, splashy rush in the water. Their loose-stringed, vibrant quack-quacks added much to the glamour of the dawn. No other living thing appeared until the sky had changed from pink to blue, the water to a rich, silvery gray, the green to a translucent green and the rays of the sun came finally glistening over the peaks. Then the rough notches and gaps of the mountains—gray where blown clear of snow or white where filled with it—took on a sharp, brilliant roughness. You could see the cold peaks outlined clearly in the water and the little steeples of the churches. My wild ducks were still paddling briskly about. I noticed that a particular pair found great difficulty in finding the exact spot to suit them. With a restless quank-quank-quank they would rise and fly a space only to light with a soft splatter and quack cheerfully. When they saw the lone rower returning they followed him, coming up close to the hotel dock and paddling smartly in his vicinity. I watched him fasten his boat and contemplate the ducks, which eventually, after he had gone, flew away. I wondered then if they were pets of his. Then with the day having clearly come, I went inside.

This being Sunday and wonderfully fair, I decided to take the trip up the lake on one of the two small steamers that I saw anchored at apparently rival docks. They may have served boats plying on different arms of the lake. By ten o'clock all Lucerne seemed to have come out to promenade along the smooth walks that border the shore. Pretty church bells in severe, conical towers began to ring, and students in small, dark, tambourine-like hats, tight jackets, tight trousers, and carrying little canes about the size of batons, began to walk smartly up and down. There were a few travelers present, wintering here no doubt—English and Americans, presenting their usual severe, intellectual, inquiring and self-protective dispositions. They stood out in sharp contrast to the native Swiss—a fair, stolid, quiescent people whose moods I cannot even suggest. Less florid than the Germans, less vivacious than the Danes and Norwegians, I could scarcely suggest their souls. I fancy they would make good scientists, philosophers, religionists and possibly patriots. I cannot conceive of them as being gay, lively human beings of the French-Italian-American brand. And yet they may be.

Lucerne by day I found to be as clean, spruce and orderly as a private pine forest. I never saw a more spick-and-span place, not even in ge-washed and ge-brushed Germany. Everything, I judged, was exactly as it should be. If there are any microbes in Lucerne, they lead a haggard life. A fly, I am sure, would find it hard to make a decent living. All the stores everywhere were smart and polished. The steps, walks and yards of the little gabled houses were so well ge-browned, ge-scrubbed, ge-clipped and otherwise ge-polished and made presentable that there was no opportunity for comment. You cannot quarrel with cleanliness and order. All the little girls and boys I saw were ge-scrubbed and ge-cleaned. Their pale and phlegmatic or bright and rosy cheeks were polished to a nicety and their flaxen hair done in pretty pigtails. You have seen the little girl writing on the wall, one arm up, one foot raised, in Maillard's Cocoa ads. There are many such girls in Lucerne and, I fancy, in Switzerland. *Pa* Swiss and *Ma* Swiss go gravely forth to church at ten-thirty—severe, pious, righteous and altogether suitable. If you should even mention such things as may be seen in Paris or Monte Carlo, they would suffer severe religious twinges, I am sure. Lucerne is exactly the place for them, shut in as it is by high, cold peaks, and kept by long, cold ranges from all the alarums and terrors of an outer world. Their little houses are often like bird-boxes perched on poles, but so much the better. They belong in them. I felt very clean and refined and religious and pure in Lucerne—very.

The trip up the lake was as delightful as any such trip anywhere, I am sure. Such peaks—how they towered above the little boat as it puffed briskly past small chalets, summer hotels, quaint cottages, quainter villages! Now and then a long, thin point of rock or grass-covered land protruded sharply into the cold, deep water, and the cottages everywhere were mirrored clearly in it. The scene changed every moment. New angles and lights on the snowy ridges were achieved. New vistas up inlets opened. Lovely lawns with Swiss chalets on them, birds flying gaily about, and boats anchored in the water appeared and disappeared. An island now and then graced the still waters. It was a perfect day.

On this trip I fell in with a certain "Major Y. Miyata, M.D., Surgeon, Imperial Japanese Army," as his card read, who, I soon learned, was doing Europe much as I was, only entirely alone. I first saw him as he bought his ticket from the purser on board the steamer at Lucerne and later on deck, where he worked industriously at taking pictures and making notes. After each picture he would write in a large notebook which he drew from his pocket. He was a small, quiet, wiry man, very keen and observant, who addressed the purser in English first and later in German. He came on the top deck into the first-class section, a fair-sized camera slung over his shoulder, a notebook sticking out of his pocket, and finding a seat, very carefully dusted his small feet with the extreme corners of his long overcoat and rubbed his thin, horse-hairy mustache with a small, claw-like hand. He looked about in a quiet way while people smiled at his calm and indifference, and he began to take pictures after the boat started. He had small, piercing, bird-like eyes and a strangely unconscious manner, which in reality was anything but unconscious.

I watched him for a time as he worked practically at his sightseeing, and then decided that I should like to talk to him. Noticing a marvelously embroidered waistcoat on a native Swiss standing on the dock of one small village where we stopped, I said, "You do not often see a waistcoat as wonderful as that."

"No," he returned genially, rubbing his small mustache again. "It must be a custom of the country."

"I am sure of it. I have seen others elsewhere."

We fell to talking of Switzerland, Germany and Italy, where he had been, and by degrees I learned the route of his trip, or what he chose to tell me of it, and his opinions concerning Europe and the Far East—as much as he chose to communicate. He was exceedingly interesting.

It appeared that before coming to Europe this time he had made but one other trip out of Japan, namely, to California, where he had spent a year. He had left Japan in October, sailed directly for London and reached it in November; had already been through Holland, Belgium, France, Germany and Italy; and was bound for Munich and Hungary and, not strange to relate, Russia. He was coming to America—New York particularly—and was eager to know of a good hotel. I mentioned twenty. He spoke English, French, Italian and German, although he had never before been anywhere except to California. I knew he spoke German, for I talked to him in that, and after finding that he could speak it better than I could, I took his word for the rest. We lunched together. I mentioned the little I knew of the Japanese in New York. He brightened considerably. We compared travel notes—Italy, France, England. "I do not like the Italians," he observed in one place. "I think they are tricky. They do not tell the truth."

"They probably held up your baggage at the stations?"

"They did more than that to me. I could never depend on them."

"How do you like the Germans?" I asked him.

"A very wonderful people. Very civil, I thought. The Rhine is beautiful."

I had to smile when I learned that he had done the night cafés of Paris, had contrasted English and French farce as represented by the Empire and the Folies-Bergère and knew all about the Post-Impressionists and the Futurists or Cubists. The latter he did not understand. "It is possible," he said in his strange, sing-songy way, "that they represent some motives of constructive subconscious mind with which we are not any of us familiar yet. Electricity came to man in some such way as that. I do not know. I do not pretend to understand it."

At the extreme upper end of Lake Lucerne, where the boat stopped, we decided to get out and take the train back. He was curiously interested to see the shrine or tomb of William Tell, which was listed as being near here, but when he learned that it was two or three miles and that we would miss a fast train, he was willing to give it up. With a strange, old-world wisdom he commented on the political organization of Switzerland, saying that it struck him as strange that these Alpine fastnesses should ever have achieved an identity of their own. "They have always been separate communities until quite recently," he said, "and I think that perhaps only railroads, tunnels, telegraph and telephone have made their complete union satisfactory now."

I marveled at the wisdom of this Oriental, as I do at that of so many of them. They are so intensely matter-of-fact. Their industry is uncanny. This man talked to me of Alpine botany as contrasted with some of the mountain regions of Japan, and then we talked of Lincoln, Grant, Washington, Li Hung-chang and Richard Wagner. He suggested quite simply that it was probable that Germany's only artistic outlet was music, which amused me while it appealed to me as a fact. He thought their peculiar temperament found its best outlet in song and opera. There is much in that, when you think of it.

CHAPTER LXVIII

I was glad to have the company of Major Miyata for dinner that same evening, for nothing could have been duller than this very charming Louis Quinze dining room filled with utterly conventional American and English visitors. The Major had been in two battles of the Russian-Japanese War and had witnessed an attack somewhere one night after midnight in a snowstorm. He made quite an impression as he entered with me—small, soldierly, erect—and afterwards as he proceeded to explain in his quiet way the arrangement of the lines and means of caring for the wounded (without bothering to indicate the extent of the slaughter), I saw the various diners studying him. He was a very forceful-looking person—very. He told me of the manner in which the sanitary and surgical equipment and control of the Japanese army had been completely revolutionized since the date of the Japanese-Russian War and that now all the present equipment was new. "The great things in our army today," he observed very quietly at one point, "are artillery and sanitation." A fine combination! He left me at midnight, after several hours in the same cafés I have described, and then I returned to the hotel and went to bed.

If a preliminary glance at Switzerland suggested to me a high individuality—primarily Teutonic but secondarily national and different—all that I saw afterwards in Germany and Holland, with which I contrasted it, confirmed my first impression. I believe that the Swiss, for all that they speak the German language and have an architecture that certainly has much in common with that of medieval Germany, are yet of markedly diverging character. They struck me, in the main, as colder, more taciturn, more introspective and markedly less flamboyant than the Germans. The rank and file, insofar as I could see, were not ox-like exactly but extremely sparing, saving, reserved. They reminded me more of such Austrians and Tyroleans as I have known than of Germans. They were thinner, livelier in their actions, not so lusty nor yet so aggressive.

The new architecture which I saw between Lucerne and the German frontier reminded me of much that one sees in northern Ohio and Indiana and southern Michigan. There are still traces of the over-elaborate curlicue type of structure and decoration, so interesting as being representative of medieval Teutonic life, but not much. The new manufacturing towns were very clean and spruce, and modern factory buildings of the latest type—almost all glass—and churches and public buildings that were obviously an improvement, or an attempt at improvement, on older Swiss and Teutonic ideals, were everywhere apparent. Lucerne itself is divided into an old section, obviously honored and preserved for its historic and commercial value, as being attractive to travelers, and a new section, crowded with stores, tenements and apartments of the latest German and American type; and a hotel section filled with large Anglicized and Parisianized structures with, in addition, esplanades, caissons, small lounging squares and the like. I never bothered to look at Thorwaldsen's famous lion. One look at a photo years ago alienated me forever.

Once I had seen this much of Switzerland, I shall never forget how interested I was to get into Germany, "The America of Europe," as an American architect once described it to me. He had gone abroad to study the types of domestic architecture to be found in Italy, France, Germany, England and Switzerland, and he had come away most impressed with Germany. "They are more like we are than any other nation in Europe," he told me. "They walk like we do and talk like us. Why, in Germany you see people going downtown in the morning on streetcars reading newspapers just as you do in Chicago. I didn't see that anywhere else." That was in 1900, however, and twelve years no doubt have brought about great changes everywhere in Europe. Nevertheless I was eager to see what Germany had to show.

I had an interesting final talk on the morning of my departure from Lucerne with the resident manager of the hotel, who was only one of many employees of a company that controlled, so he told me, hotels in Berlin, Frankfort, Paris, Rome and London. He had formerly been resident manager of a hotel in Frankfort, the one to which I was going, and stated that he might be transferred anytime to some other one. He was the man, as I learned, whom I had seen rowing on the lake the first morning I sat out on my balcony—the one whom the wild ducks followed.

"I saw you," I said as I paid my bill, "out rowing on the lake the other morning. I should say that was pleasant exercise."

"I always do it," he said very cheerfully. He was a tall, pale, meditative man with a smooth, longish, waxen countenance and very dark hair. He was the last word as to toilet and courtesy. "I am glad I have the chance. I love nature."

"Are those wild ducks I see on the lake flying about?"

"Oh, yes. We have lots of them. They are not allowed to be shot. That's why they come here. We have gulls, too. There is a whole flock of gulls that comes here every winter. I feed them right out here at the dock every day."

"Why, where can they come from?" I asked. "This is a long way from the sea."

"I know it," he replied. "It is strange. They come over the Alps from the Mediterranean, I suppose. You will see them on the Rhine, too, if you go there. I don't know. They come, though. Sometimes they leave for four or five days or a week, but they always come back. The captain of the steamer tells me he thinks they go to some other lake. They know me, though. When they come back in the fall and I go out to feed them, they make a great fuss."

"They are the same gulls, then?"

"The very same."

I had to smile. "You should see the gulls at Blackfriars Bridge in London," I said, and I described them. He was interested.

"Those two ducks are great friends of mine, too," he added, referring to the two I had seen following him. "They always come up to the dock when I come out, and when I come back from my row they come again. Oh, they make a great clatter."

He looked at me and smiled in a pleased way. It was interesting to me to meet a man so fond of nature and animals. He had such mild, dreamy eyes. Because of my interest in nature, I suppose, when I left he came out and helped put my bags in the smart omnibus, shaking my hand and wishing me a pleasant journey. I have often thought of him and his ducks and gulls since.

The moment I entered the train leaving Lucerne for Frankfort, I realized that I was in another world from now on. It was a through express from Milan to Frankfort with special cars for Paris and Berlin. It was crowded with Germans of a ruddy, solid variety, radiating health, warmth, assurance, defiance. I never saw a more marked contrast than existed between these travelers on the train and the local Swiss outside. The latter seemed much paler and less forceful by contrast, though not less intellectual and certainly more refined. It was good again to see those international signs in these cars which show with what freedom they traverse the different countries of Europe. "No smoking" was invariably given in three and sometimes four languages, "not to put your head out" in three or four, "not to expectorate on the floor," the same. One stout German lady with something like eighteen packages had made a veritable express room of her second-class compartment. The average traveler entitled to a seat beside her would take one look at her defenses and pass on. She was barricaded beyond any hope of successful attack.

I watched interestedly to see how the character of the people, soil and climate would change as we crossed the frontier into Germany. Every other country I had entered had presented a great contrast to the last. After passing fifteen or twenty Swiss towns and small cities, perhaps more, we finally reached Basle, and there the crew was changed. I did not know it, being busy thinking of other things, until an immense, rotund, guttural-voiced conductor appeared at the door and wanted to know if I was bound for Frankfort. I looked out. It was just as I expected. Another world and another atmosphere had been substituted for that of Switzerland. Already the cars and depot platforms were different, more pretentious. Heavy German porters were in evidence. The cars, the vast majority of them here, bore the label of Imperial Germany—the wide-winged black eagle with the crown above it painted against a pinkish-white background, with the inscription *Kaiserliche Deutsche Post* above it. A stationmaster—erect as a soldier, very large, with splendiferous parted whiskers, arrayed in a blue uniform and cap—regulated the departure of trains. The *Uscita* and *Entrata* of Italy here became *Eingang* and *Ausgang*, and the *Bagaglia* of every Italian station was here *Gepäck*. The endless German *Verboten* and *Es ist untersagt* also came into evidence. We rolled out into a wide, open, flat, mountainless plain with only the thin poplars of France and no waterways of any kind, and then I knew that Switzerland was truly no more.

If you want to see how the lesser Teutonic countries vary from this greater one, the dominant German Empire, pass this way from Switzerland into Germany or from Germany into Holland. The difference is just that which makes Germany powerful and the others weak. Such thoroughness, such force, such universal superintendence! Truly, it is amazing. Once you are across the border, if you are at all sensitive to national or individual personalities, you can feel it—a vital, glowing life, entirely superior and more ominous than that of Switzerland, and in many ways less pleasant. It is very much like the heat and glow of a furnace. Germany is a great forge or workshop. It resounds with the industry of a busy nation; it has all the daring and assurance of a successful man; it struts, commands, defies, asserts itself at every turn. You would not want to witness greater variety of character than you could by passing from England through France into Germany. After the stolidity and civility of the English and the lightness and spirit of France, the blazing force and defiance of the Germans comes upon you as almost the most amazing of all.

In spite of the fact that my father was German and that I have known more or less of Germans all my life, I cannot say that I admired the personnel of the German empire, the little that I saw of it, half as much as I admired some of the things they had achieved. As various towns flashed by us en route—Freiburg, Kippenheim, Niederschopfheim, Offenburg, Achern, Steinbach, Baden-Oos and Karlsruhe—it was so easy to see what it was in part that the German nation was doing. It was manufacturing, for one thing, and apparently principally. Great, red factories, pleasingly built in a thoroughgoing way, their furnaces consuming apparently only hard coal, their roofs solidly covered with red tiles, stood out sharply in the sun and rain, speaking clearly of successful business. You would pass stations, small towns and cities where this express did not stop, and see in the distance whole sections of small, red-brick dwellings going up, new streets being laid out, new arc light posts being set up and trolley lines in operation, and nearer at hand factories in full operation. All the stations that I saw in Germany were in apple-pie order—new, bright, well-ordered; big, blue-lettered signs indicating just the things you wanted to know. Soldierly officials in smart uniforms were standing almost at attention as you passed. The station platforms were so well built, of red tile and white stone; the tracks looked as though they were laid on solid, hardwood ties; the train ran so smoothly, as if there were not a flaw in it anywhere, and it ran swiftly. I had to smile as occasionally on a platform—the train speeding swiftly—a straight, upstanding German officer or official came into view and disappeared again, his uniform looking like new, his boots polished, his gold epaulets and buckles shining as brightly as gold can shine, his blond whiskers, red cap, glistening glasses or bright monocle, and above all his sharp, clear eyes looking directly at you, making an almost amazing combination of energy, vitality and superiority. It gave you a startling impression of the whole of Germany. "Are they all like that?" I asked myself. "Is the army really so dashing and forceful?"

As I traveled, first to Frankfort, then to Mayence and Coblenz, and again from Coblenz to Frankfort and Berlin and thence out of the country via Holland, the wonder grew. I should say now that if Germany has any number of defects of temperament, and it truly has from almost any American point of view, it has virtues and capacities so noteworthy, admirable and advantageous that the whole world may well sit up and take notice. The one thing that came home to me with great force was that Germany is in no way loose-jointed, lackadaisical, indifferent or idle, but on the contrary strong, red-blooded, avid, imaginative. Germany is a terrific nation—hopeful, courageous, enthusiastic, orderly, self-disciplining—and if it can keep its pace without engaging in some vast, self-destroying conflict, it can become internally so powerful that it will almost stand irresistible. I should say that any nation that today chose to pick a quarrel with Germany on her home ground would be foolish in the extreme. It is the *beau ideal* of the aggressive, militant, orderly spirit, and if it were properly captained and the gods were kind, it would be everywhere invincible.

However. At Basle we left mountains, once and for all. I saw but few frozen peaks after Lucerne. As we approached Basle they seemed to grow less and less, and beyond that we entered a flat plain, as flat as Kansas and as arable as the immediate Mississippi Valley, which stretched from Basle to Frankfort and from Frankfort to Berlin. Judging from what I saw, the major portion of Germany is a vast prairie, as flat as a pancake and as thickly strewn with orderly, new, bright, forceful towns as England is with quaint ones.

What a far cry from Italy to Germany! Gone, once and for all, the wonderful clarity of atmosphere that pervades almost the whole of Italy from the Alps to Rome and, I presume, Sicily. Gone the obvious *dolce far niente*, the lovely cities set on hills, the castles, the fortresses, the strange stone bridges, the white, hot roads winding like snowy ribbons in the distance. No olive trees, no cypresses, no umbrella trees or ilexes, no white, yellow, blue, brown and sea-green houses, no wooden plows, white oxen and ambling, bare-footed friars. In its place, with the Alps and Switzerland between, was this low, rich land, its railroads threading it like steel bands, its citizens standing up as though at command, its houses in the smaller towns almost uniformly red, its architecture a twentieth-century modification of an older order, of many-gabled roofs—the order of Albrecht Dürer, within its fanciful decorations, conical roofs and pinnacles and quaint windows and doors that suggested the bird-boxes of our childhood. Germany appears in a way to have attempted to abandon the medieval architectural ideal that still may be seen in Mayence, Mayen, the heart of Frankfort, Nuremberg, Heidelberg and other places and adapt its mood to the modern theory of how buildings ought to be constructed, but it has not quite done so. The German scroll-loving mind of the Middle Ages is still the German scroll-loving mind of today. Look and you will see it quaintly cropping out everywhere. Not in those wonderful details of intricacy, Teutonic fussiness, naive, jester-like grotesqueness which makes the older sections of so many old German cities so wonderful, but in a slight suggestion of them here and there—a quirk of roof, an over-elaborateness of decoration, a too-protuberant frieze, grapeviny, Bacchus-mooded, sex-ornamented panels—until you say to yourself quite wisely, "Oh, Teutons will be Teutons still." They are making a very different Germany from what the old Germany was—modern Germany dates from 1871—but it is not an entirely different Germany. Its citizens are still stocky, red-blooded, physically excited and excitable, emotional, mercurial, morbid, enthusiastic, women- and life-loving, and no doubt will be, praise God, until German soil loses its inherent essentials and German climate makes for some other variations not yet indicated in the race.

CHAPTER LXIX

Frankfort, when I reached it, was, in spite of my glowing appreciation of the spirit of Germany, a disappointment to me at first. It is a city of over four hundred thousand population—clean, vigorous, effective—but I saw it in a rain, to begin with, and I did not like it, though a certain spacious up-to-dateness and aggressive American directness about it attracted me. To an American traveler like myself, German cities look exceedingly squat and dull, because the high building fever, or the necessity for it, has not reached them, or because the subsoil will not permit of high buildings possibly, or the conservative German temperament has not yet become interested in them. We had such cities as Frankfort in the United States sixty years ago and longer. I am speaking of such German cities as I saw: Frankfort, Mayence, Coblenz, and Berlin; they are low, fairly widespread, squat. In the main they have no modern distinction of architecture. The idea which they represent architecturally is old, very. Berlin is perhaps the only German city which rises to a true modern standard as the American sees it, and it is too low, considering the amazing width of its streets. It is full of fine buildings, really splendid modern apartment houses, comfortably and properly equipped mechanically, but the streets in a way are too wide for the height of the buildings. This is not true perhaps for the outlying sections, but the great central heart, where the crowd comes, where the business is done, where the showplaces are and where government has its seat, is too squat, in Berlin and elsewhere. There ought to be, in my judgment at least, some architectural variation which would stand out and make the city seem to have a true head and center. It was so in all medieval cities. It was so in ancient times. What has come over the spirit of city governments, directing architects and individual enterprises? Is there no one who wants really to do the very exceptional thing? Isn't the Kaiser, insofar as Berlin is concerned, interested in a vast spectacle with which to mark the center of his empire? I should think so. I, for one, should hope so, and yet apparently it is not true. Berlin has nothing at its heart which architecturally is really worthy of the German empire. The Reichstag is nothing; the executive government palaces are nothing; the cathedral of Berlin is a joke.

But I am getting ahead of myself. The one point I want to make is that no German city I saw has a central heart worthy of the name—no Piazza del Campidoglio such as Rome has; no Piazza della Signoria such as Florence has; no Piazza San Marco such as Venice has; not even a cathedral center, lovely thing that it is, such as Milan has. Paris does so much better in this matter than any German city has dreamed of doing, with its Garden of the

Tuileries, its Champs-de-Mars, its Esplanades des Invalides, its Arc de Triomphe and Place de l'Opéra. Even poor old London—after Paris and Venice and Florence I sympathize with London—has its regions about the Houses of Parliament, St. Paul's and the Embankment which are worth something. But German cities! And yet they are worthy cities, every one of them, far more vital than those of Italy, though not Milan, where they themselves rule.

When I entered Germany it was with just two definite things in mind. One was to seek out my father's birthplace, a little hamlet, as I understood it, called Mayen, located somewhere between the Moselle and the Rhine at Coblenz, the region where the Moselle wines come from. The other was to visit Berlin and see what Germany's foremost city was really like and to get a look at the Kaiser if possible. In both of these I was quickly successful, though after I reached Frankfort some other things transpired which were not on the program.

I should like to relate first, however, the story of the vanishing birthplace. Ever since I was three or four years old and dandled on my father's knee in an Indiana homestead, I had heard more or less of Mayen, Coblenz and the region on the Rhine from which my father came. The Germans are a sentimental, home-loving, fatherland-loving race, and my father, honest German Catholic that he was, was no exception. He used to tell me and the rest of the children what a lovely place Mayen was, how the hills rose about it, how grape-growing was its principal industry, how there were castles there and *grafs* and rich burghers and how there was a wall about the city which in his day constituted an armed fortress, and how often, as a little child, he had been taken out through some one of its great gates seated on the saddle of some kindly-minded cavalryman and carried to a neighboring drill ground, only to be brought back later on in the day. He seems to have become, by the early death of his mother and second marriage of his father, a rather unwelcome stepchild, and so early he had secretly decamped to the border with three others and made his way to Paris to escape being drafted for the Prussian army which had seized this town, which only a few years before had belonged for a while to France, though it is German in character. Later he came to America, made his way by degrees to Indiana, established a woolen mill on the banks of the Wabash at Terre Haute and there, after marrying in Ohio, raised his large family. His first love was his hometown, however, and Prussia, which he admired; and to his dying day he never ceased talking about it. On more than one occasion he told me he would like to go back, just to see how things were, but the Prussian regulations concerning deserters or those who avoided service were so drastic and the likelihood of his being recognized so great that he was afraid he would be seized and at least thrown in prison, if not shot, so he never ventured it. I fancy this danger of arrest and his feeling that he could not return cast an additional glamour over the place and the region which he could never revisit. Anyhow, I was curious to see Mayen.

Another fact on which my interest was somewhat based was this: there are few, if any, individuals of the family name of Dreiser in America. Outside of the immediate members of the family, I know of no others at present. There was once a John Dreiser, a policeman, in New York who was shot and killed by his wife, but that was years ago, and no city directory that I have ever seen has listed another. I wanted to discover if by any chance there were any Dreisers still living in Mayen and, without intruding myself in any way, see what their condition and repute were. So much for not having a full-grown and imposing family tree.

When I had reached Rome and began to make further plans for my trip and what I would and would not see, I looked up this matter of Mayen and decided that I would go there. I did not know then that there were both a Mayen and a Mayence, or Mainz, as it is spelled in Germany, and that they were somewhat over a hundred miles apart in the Rhine country. I only knew of Mayen, but when I consulted with the Cook's agent at Rome he promptly announced, "There isn't any such place as Mayen. You're thinking of Mayence, near Frankfort, on the Rhine."

"No," I said, "I'm not. I'm thinking of Mayen. M-a-y-e-n. Now you look and see."

"There isn't any such place, I tell you," he replied courteously. "It's Mayence, not very far from Frankfort."

"Let me see," I argued, looking at his map. "It's near the junction of the Rhine and the Moselle."

"Mayence is the place. See—here it is. Here's the Moselle, and here's Mayence."

I looked, and sure enough they seemed reasonably close together.

"All right," I said, "let me go to Berlin via Mayence."

"I'll book you to Frankfort. That's only thirty minutes away. There's nothing of interest in Mayence—not even a good hotel. At Frankfort you can stop at the Frankfurter Hof—that's some comfort."

"That sounds something like my father's town," I said, thinking of the fact there was not even a good hotel. It was pleasant to think I could stop at the Frankfurter Hof and get out there in thirty minutes. So I had him make out the itinerary in his way and came on to Frankfort.

Having arrived there, I decided not to send my trunks to the hotel as yet but to take one kit bag, leaving the remainder *im Gepäck* and see what I could see at Mayence. I might want to stay all night, wandering about my father's old haunts, and I might want to go down the Rhine a little way—I was not sure. Before leaving, however, I hurried to Cook's office to look after my mail and to secure the key of my trunk, which had been sent forward from Florence via Cook's in order that my trunk, which I was sending straight through to Frankfort from there, might be opened at the several international borders. My going to Cook's opened up a new situation which I was not now contemplating. To get it straight I shall have to go back to my first days in London.

One of the things I narrated was that the Saturday afternoon after my arrival Grant Richards insisted that I should accompany him to Bechstein Hall in the neighborhood of Harley Street in order to hear a certain Madame Culp sing. She was a Dutch girl by birth, he told me, but a German by marriage, residence and acclimatization, a great musical personality in Germany, a singer of songs, and that her concerts in Berlin and elsewhere—Munich, Vienna, Leipzig—practically amounted to sensations. This was her first visit to England. She was being sponsored in a way by Mrs. Stoop and a number of her friends. I should very likely meet her later, and it would be important to say that I had heard her sing. So I went to that particular concert. I believe I indicated that it made a profound impression on me. She had a bewitchingly tender voice—full, colorful, romantic. Counting encores, she sang all of a score of songs and received an ovation from a curious and unfamiliar audience. Being peculiarly susceptible to the moody, temperamental tenderness of German melodies, I was greatly moved, and quite naturally, in the richness of the moment, identified much of the charm of the melodies with the woman herself. We can do that, too, quite safely, if we make allowance for the commonplace weaknesses and necessities of this mortal state that hedges us all.

A few nights later, perhaps three or four, I met her. Grant Richards had been out to see a cousin of his—the same who was to be the Santa Claus at Bigfrith—and returning late, we stopped to pick her up. He had made arrangements to take her to supper at the Carlton. I thought she was charming, singing on the platform of Bechstein Hall, arrayed in pale, smooth, pearl-tinted satin and carrying roses. At this supper she looked quite as well, wearing a lemon-hued silk with black lace over it and carrying white roses. She was of a medium, full-bodied build, fair, almost florid, like the Germans, with very light brown hair and brownish-gray eyes.

My experiences lead me to believe that true temperamental affinity, much or little, has invariably a chemico-physical basis which has very little to do with anything else—ideas, looks and the like—and that the understanding which people of allied emotions and notions reach takes its rise speedily or slowly, instantaneously or otherwise, from this natural physical relationship. Our ideas and emotions reflect our chemical composition and our blood moods. The words "morbid," "choler," "spleen" are good words. They refer to physical states. Physical attraction is a good phrase. It answers for most of our likes and dislikes.

This night, whirling through these heavy-spirited London streets in a taxi, Madame Culp's very even white teeth gleaming, a light of adventure and gaiety in her eye, we reached instantly a sympathetic understanding. Nothing much was said—nothing need be. I complimented her on her voice, the richness of her emotions, the color, as it were, of her soul. She replied with the most effusive compliments in regard to my book. She had just read it—a part of it. The second chapter had touched her keenly. "Oh," she exclaimed warmly and with a rich, furry quality to her voice, "it is beautiful, beautiful! I like that part about the—the—how do you say that?—the red cloud in the sea of silver. Oh-h-h, that iss bu-ty-tiful!"

I had to smile.

"And that other part where the children went for the coal! . . . And so you liked my singing. I'm glad," and she lingered on the phrase with loving emphasis.

Art is such a charming thing. It is sad sometimes, apparently, that it need ever be associated or defiled, as it were, by necessity, and yet we know so well how deep its roots are embedded in the mire of the commonplace. Back of this woman I felt all of the common characteristics of the day, of life—vanity, ambition, compulsion, unsatisfied longings and the wish to be the perfect things of her dreams. That temperament, that understanding, that type of emotion, I love. I really glory in the true artist in any walk, and this woman was one. Her praises soothed me. Her friendly leaning toward me was the best testimony that life could give me. She was still good-looking, though not beautiful—quick, fiery, eager, in her way a little lustful. Her heart and mind, however, were clearly set on her art.

No two artists, if truly ambitious, truly self-centered—as they must be—should ever think of doing anything more than entertaining each other for a period. Art is selfish, self-centered. The refinement, subtlety, gaiety and emotion of one artist naturally attracts another—when they are not rivals for the same honors. These can be made to do service as provocatives of great pleasure if they are not depended upon to provide the practical, stable virtues and conventions of life. The great artist understands, of course, that they must not be so depended upon. But every true artist is not necessarily great. There are rivulets and Niagaras of art. There is the danger that the minor artist will at times depend on the major for those stabilities of convention and order which can have no basis in fact. Hence—

Madame Culp, however, was not quite so dull. She understood how illusive, how will-o'-the-wispy are the facets of beauty in the purely artistic temperament. Strong for life, however, she, the true artist, was still inclined to dream at times that the impossible might happen.

That night at the Carlton, in Grant Richards's presence, we fell into a kind of flirtation. The mental and emotional temperature of the scene rose perceptibly. I am sure we both saw surrounding conditions in a rosier light than they might normally be made to wear. The restaurant took on an especially gay aspect. We laughed a great deal. Grant Richards was at his best in dispensing a form of cynical persiflage, which threw me into gales of laughter. "Oh yes," he said at one place, "the artistic temperament invariably produces a mirage. It is very insubstantial, however."

This for Madame Culp's benefit. She merely smiled.

"Do sing something soft and low to me," I suggested. "Sing '*Es kommt ein Vogel.*'"

"Oh no," she cooed, shrugging her white shoulders and looking at me very alluringly.

"You're quite right," put in Grant Richards sarcastically. "The rules are very strict here against disorder. Besides, this is pure artistic emotion."

"Do sing," I pleaded, jesting and laughing in her eyes.

"If you will write me something pretty on a piece of paper."

"Autographs of authors are not worth much these days," suggested Grant Richards. "They are over-plentiful."

"The voice of jealousy, I assure you," I said to Madame Culp. "He envies me."

"I know it. I understand," she replied. "And what do you think?" (She almost pronounced it "thing.") "When I sang for him once at my home in Zehlendorf, he went fast asleep. Yes, you did," she said, turning to him and putting up one fat, little finger. "Now, when someone else wants to hear me you are jealous." I could see there was some very genial understanding between them.

"Sing if you like," he sighed. "His interest in music is largely pretense anyhow. He has no real ear for it."

I laughed heartily.

She sang. I wrote some silly nonsense on a piece of paper. We drank champagne forgetfully, and when we came out into the taxi at twelve-thirty and spun away toward her apartment she said cozily, "Now I will sing for you," and sang clearly and sweetly. It was pleasant, in the flare of passing electric lamps, to see the elation of her face, the rosy smile. When we finally left her, she invited me to come the next day to hear her sing, but something prevented—I think Grant Richards. He had another plan for me, while he himself disappeared. In the restaurant, however, I forgot to say, it was suggested by Madame Culp that if I came to Germany at all, I must come to Berlin and Zehlendorf and stay a week or two at her house. She was most encouraging as to this. She was to be there in March. If she were not, I could stay there anyhow. Her husband and his friends would entertain me. I must do this. I left her with the idea that in March when I reached Berlin if she were still so inclined, I would do this. Her voice and personality were real attractions, and Grant Richards told me her home was charming. So the matter stood.

CHAPTER LXX

Certain subsequent developments had caused me to imagine that the bond of union between Grant Richards and Madame Culp was stronger than appeared on the surface. Although he spoke of her always only as a friend, yet I could see that there was or had been much more than friendship. Although he cared little for music, he was most active in her musical behalf in London. For two days after we three had been to supper at the Carlton, he disappeared entirely, and I had a very strong impression as to where he was. The following Christmas, only several weeks away, brought large boxes of candied fruit and presents for the children from her, and he had the dates of her European tour well in hand. He seemed quite sure, in an authoritative way, that she would be pleased to have me stay at Zehlendorf near Berlin, which struck me as indicating a very strong bond of friendship, to say the least.

Besides, I had come to guess by now that mere friendly exchange of ideas was never the basis of any feminine interest insofar as Grant Richards was concerned. He was too busy and too attractive. There were too many women, as I could see, from servants up to society women, actresses, authors, singers, ready to be his devoted slave, to cause him to dangle long at the waist of mere intellectuality and friendship. I have previously indicated the unsolicited testimonials from several of his feminine "friends" in London. It was beginning to be amusing.

In Paris, and again at Monte Carlo, he urged me to write Madame Culp at Zehlendorf and say that I was coming to Berlin for certain and ask if she were going to be at home. "You might as well stop there as at a hotel. It will be so much more comfortable for you."

"But I don't know that she really wants me," I replied. "Outside of that one invitation given under the excitement of that silly evening, I never had another formal invitation. You're very close to her. Why don't you have her write me?"

"Well, the truth is I'm not so close to her as you think. But I'm very sure she likes you. She told me so. I think she'll be glad to have you come there. Why don't you write?"

"Well, let me think it over," I replied. "I'm really not anxious to go there unless she wants me very much. I'd rather go to a hotel. Wait a while."

We argued about this until almost the last day at Monte Carlo, when he came into my room one morning and said, "Have you written Madame Culp?"

"No."

"Aren't you going to?"

"I don't think so."

"Well, why not?"

"I don't propose to force myself on her. She knows I'm coming to Berlin. She knows, if she knows anything, that I'm not going to take that one excited invitation seriously. You've talked with her about this. Why are you so anxious that I should go there anyhow? Why hasn't she written me a formal invitation?"

"She's overlooked it, I suppose. I know she likes you. I know that you will be comfortable there. Why not write and say you're coming and that you would like to call on her?"

There was more of this, and finally I took my pen and wrote a short formal note saying I was coming to Berlin sometime in March and that if she happened to be at Zehlendorf it would give me great pleasure to call on her. I gave three available addresses to cover the next month—Rome, Florence and Milan. Not a word in reply. Rome passed and Florence and Venice, but finally this day at Frankfort I received a special delivery letter, care of Cook's, saying that she was singing at Munich and Leipzig and that she was coming to Frankfort about this very time to sing. She was scheduled to sing on Wednesday of this very week, and this was Monday. Would I wait? She was so anxious to see me. She had received my letter but had not had time to reply! There was a long account of Zehlendorf, the house, its management by a capable housekeeper, etc. Would I go there? I could have her room. If I did, would I wait until she could come back at the latter end of the month? It was quite an enthusiastic letter, and I was troubled to know wherefore this sudden burst of interest. I should say that at Milan I had received a short note from Grant Richards saying he had received a note from her requesting details of my itinerary, but that did not explain this.

Wednesday? Well, I debated whether I would answer her or not. The letter practically begged me to wire her at Leipzig whether I would wait. I was a little angry by this time to think she had let a month go by without a word. I decided I wouldn't answer and went out into the city for an hour, just the business heart, in order to buy a Baedeker and to pass the time until my train should leave. She could go to hell, I said, or words to that effect, and I began to study the character of the streets and shops. Frankfort was not sufficiently interesting to warrant my staying any such time just to see her.

At one corner of one of Frankfort's very fine business streets, I came upon a music store in the window of which were displayed a number of photos of musical celebrities. A little to my surprise I noticed that the central place was occupied by a quite large photo of Madame Culp in her most attractive pose. Not tall or startlingly attractive physically, she was still undeniably good-looking. This photo did her ample justice. It stood out quite attractively among the others. I stood and looked at her a while, and much of the charm with which circumstances had invested her in London came back to me. After all, she was a celebrated singer and entitled to moods as well as another. A nearby billboard contained a full announcement of her coming. I meditated somewhat more mellowly after this and finally returned to Cook's to leave a telegram. I would wait, I said, here at Frankfort until Wednesday. That was all. I fancied my Mayence and Frankfort sightseeing would last until then. So having done this and secured my Baedeker, I hurried again to the depot just in time to make my train for Mayence.

The Mayence that I was going to was not the Mayen that I wanted, but I did not know that. You have heard of people weeping over the wrong tombstone. This was a case in point. Fortunately I was going in the direction of the real Mayen, though I did not know that either. I ran through a country which reminded me very much of the region in which Terre Haute is located, and I said to myself quite wisely, "Now I can see why my father and so many other Germans from this region settled in southern Indiana. It is like their old home. The wide, flat fields are the same. That river over there"—it was the Main, which empties into the Rhine at Mayence and within view of the banks of which we were running—"is exactly like the Ohio at Evansville or the Wabash at Terre Haute." It was moving as flatly as glass between low banks and suggested so many similar rivers in America. When we reached Mayence and I had deposited my kit bag for the time being, I strolled out into the principal streets, wondering whether I should get the least impression of the city or town as it was when my father was here as a boy.

It is curious and amusing how we can delude ourselves at times. I really knew, if I had stopped seriously to consider, that this could not be the true Mayen. My father had described it to me as a small, walled town with frowning castles set down in a valley among hills. He had said over and over that it was located at the junction of the Rhine and the Moselle. I recalled afterward that he told me that the city of Coblenz was very near by, but in my brisk effort to find this place quickly, I had forgotten that. Here I was in a region which contained not a vestige of any hills within the city, the Moselle was all of a hundred miles away, and no walls of any medieval stronghold were visible anywhere, and yet I was fairly satisfied that this was the place.

"Dear me," I thought, "how Mayence has grown! My father wouldn't know it." (Baedeker gave its population as one hundred and ten thousand.) "How Germany has grown in the sixty-nine years since he was here! It used to be a town of three or four thousand. Now it is a large city." I read about it assiduously in Baedeker and looked at the rather thriving streets of the business heart—not nearly as up-to-date as Frankfort, however—trying to think how it all might have been in 1843 and while he was a young boy here.

Somehow, however, because of the city's large size and its modernity and the fact that Baedeker's map of southern Germany showed the confluence of the Rhine and Moselle to be some distance away, I had my doubts. It must be, however, with no other Mayen being given, and so finally after plodding the streets a while, I decided to secure my bag and take a room at the best hotel. One night here would not hurt. It would be a pleasure. I took a small, open carriage to the hotel, deposited my belongings in my room, learned the dinner hour and went forth. From then until midnight I was wandering about in the dark and bright streets of Mayence, satisfying myself with the thought that I was really seeing the city in which my father was born.

A dull place. We used to have a word in the Middle West, "Dutchy," which we used to describe all those naive, quaint, un-American phases, notions, details of dress and details of manners which are German, Austrian, Hungarian and Tyrolean, brought from abroad, and which were an abomination, if not in the sight of the Lord, at least in the sight of all youthful Americans. Thick-soled shoes, for one thing, were exceedingly "Dutchy"—terrible. Heavy, unfashionable clothing another. Caps of certain kinds, thick wooly ones, were exceedingly "Dutchy." A red, knitted muffler for the throat, woolen stockings or socks, any round, soft hat, either too large or too small, were "Dutchy." Big ears were "Dutchy," although we occasionally had them ourselves, and white stockings or socks. Big feet likewise, although they in addition were anathema. Long beards, gingerbready houses with conical corners and curlicue or gnomey ornamentations, presented in the form of friezes, square panels or circular plaques, were horribly "Dutchy." In short, there were "Dutchy" men, "Dutchy" women, "Dutchy" children, "Dutchy" streets. I personally, I know, came to have a very definite prejudice against all these things and others because to me they represented an older order of life and a state of civilization which, when introduced into the United States and particularly my hometown, made it out of step with things American and, so far as any "Dutchy" friends came into contact with the family, that also. My father was a typical German. He liked to associate with those who came from Germany, largely because he understood them better. My mother and the children had another point of view. Their intimates were almost exclusively American. There was at times some slight—very slight—feeling on this score, but no friction.

As I grew older, of course, much of this silly prejudice disappeared. I came to admire the sturdy characteristics of the Germans—my father's innate honesty, his love of order and the sobriety, thrift and industry which characterized him and all his friends. German art, especially its wood-carvings as represented by Dürer, had great charm for me. The old, medieval, rococo, flamboyant touches which characterize the architecture of all the older portions of Germany, amused me. I think today the best examples of this old architectural individuality ought surely to be preserved. Old Nuremberg, Heidelberg, parts of Frankfort and Lucerne, if they are ever torn down, will mean a great loss. Still I do not think this sort of thing, except for an occasional helpful architectural suggestion, has any meaning for America at all. It should never be introduced.

Here in Mayence for the second time, I saw this peculiar architecture on its home ground—the first was at Lucerne. People such as I had known in my youth—"Dutchy" Germans—were here in great numbers, too, and unconsciously they aroused a momentary prejudice in me. A little while later I recognized that there is an extreme conflict of temperament between me and all Germans but that I could admire them without wishing to be anything like them. Of all the people I saw I should place the Germans first for sobriety, industry, thoroughness, a hearty intolerance of sham and a desire and a willingness to make the best of a very difficult earthly condition. In many respects they are not artistically appetizing, being gross physically, heartily passionate, vain and cocksure, but those things after all are unimportant. They have, in spite of all their defects, great emotional, intellectual and physical capacities, and these things are very important.

But Mayence was really so "Dutchy." It was in about the condition, exteriorly speaking, that Evansville, Indiana, was about forty years ago. Evansville at that time was practically all German. The cathedral of Mayence is poor. It is full of the gingerbreadiest details, and the various bishops and archbishops and medieval, *hochwürdige* gentlemen are delineated in sculpture with such a gross reality as to destroy all odor of sanctity. Their faces are too blunt and stodgy and scowling, their stomachs too protuberant. You would have thought they never had a light, gay, tender thought in their lives.

The street markets outside—and there were a number, one confined exclusively to crockery and another to chickens, ducks, geese, eggs and the like—were crowded with a heavy-faced mass of old German men and women. The Germans at times—and I think often it is more an exterior seeming than anything else—take life too dolefully. The poorer masses look as though they had never seen a happy day in their lives. Their clothing in the main is too drab, their motions too deliberate and heavy, and they look at you with such low-keyed, moody eyes. I think it is unquestionable that in the main they take life far too seriously. The belief in a hell, for instance, took a tremendous grip on the Teutonic mind, and the Lutheran interpretation of Protestantism, as it finally worked out, was as dreary as anything could be—almost as dreary as Presbyterianism in Scotland. That is the sad, German temperament. A great nationality, business success, public distinction are probably tending to make over, or at least modify, the Teutonic cast of thought, which is gray, but in parts of Germany—here, for instance, at Mayence—you see the older spirit almost in full force.

My stay in Mayence was only until ten the next morning, but by that time I had been there long enough to realize that at least this part of Germany would never appeal to me. The old order depressed me. We have done so much better since these buildings were built and this type of life prevailed. I could see from various examples how charming it might once have been and possibly still was in spots, but it would never do for me. I ate a lonely meal that evening, after which I inspected a local, or rather traveling, Coney Island with tents, sideshow wonders, cane-ringing and Japanese ball-rolling features, after which I went to bed.

Coming into the breakfast room of my hotel the next morning, I encountered a man who looked to me like a German traveling salesman. He had brought his grip down to the desk and was consuming his morning coffee and rolls with great gusto, the while he read his paper, when I said to him, "Do you know of any place in this part of Germany that is called Mayen?—not Mayence." I wanted to make sure of my location.

"Mayen? Mayen?" he replied, "Why, I think there is such a place near Coblenz. It isn't very large."

"Coblenz? That's it," I replied, recalling now what my father had told me of Coblenz. "To be sure. How far is that?"

"Oh, that is all of three hours from here. It's at the juncture of the Moselle."

"Do you know how the trains run?" I asked, getting up, a feeling of disappointment spreading over me.

"I think there is one around half past nine or ten."

"Damn!" I said, realizing what a dunce I had been. I had just forty-five minutes in which to pay my bill and make the train. Three hours more! I could have gone on the night before.

I hurried out, secured my bag, paid my bill and was off. On the way I had myself driven to the old Judengasse, said to be full of picturesque medieval houses, for a look. You know the type. It was. I reached the depot in time to have a two-minute argument with my driver as to whether he was entitled to two marks or one—one being a fair reward—and then hurried into my train. In a half-hour we were at Bingen on the Rhine, and in three-quarters of an hour those lovely hills and ravines which make the Rhine so picturesque had begun, and they continued all the way to Coblenz and below that to Cologne.

CHAPTER LXXI

After Italy and Switzerland the scenery of the Rhine seemed very mild and unpretentious to me, yet it was very beautiful. The Hudson from Albany to New York is far more imposing. A score of American rivers such as the Penobscot, the New in West Virginia, the James above Lynchburg, the Rio Grande and others would make the Rhine seem simple by comparison, yet it has an individuality so distinct that it is unforgettable. I always marvel over this thing—personality. Nothing under the sun explains it. So often you can say, "This is finer," "That is more imposing," "By comparison this is nothing," but when you have said all this, the thing with personality rises up and triumphs. So it was with the Rhine. Like millions before me and millions yet to come, I watched its slopes, its castles, its islands, its pretty little German towns passing in review before the windows of this excellent train and decided that in its way nothing could be finer. It had personality. A snatch of old wall, with peach trees in blossom; a long, thin side-wheel steamer, one smokestack fore and another aft, labeled *William Egan & Co-Gesellschaft;* a dismantled castle tower, with a flock of crows flying about it and hills laid out in ordered squares of vines, gave it all the charm it needed.

I was never weary of looking at the Rhine with its Hudson-like flotilla of towns until Coblenz was reached, when I bustled out, ready to inspect Mayen at once. Another disappointment. Mayen was not at Coblenz but fifteen or eighteen miles away on a small branch road, the trains of which ran just four times a day; but I did not learn this until, as usual, I had done considerable investigating. According to a map I now had, one bought at Mayence, Mayen was very close to the junction of the Rhine and the

Moselle, which was here, but as usual in the hurry of traveling and my eagerness to get there, I forgot to make allowances for map distances. The almost no space on the map was really fifteen or eighteen miles. But be that as it may, I found the Moselle well enough after I asked a small boy dancing along a Coblenz street where the Moselle was. "If you walk fast you will get there in half an hour." It pleased me much to think that I was finally here and that now I should really see the abode of my ancestors. To be talking this way to a small Coblenz boy in his native tongue and not being detected as an American was much. As long as I did not try to talk too much German, I fancied that I was being taken for a German!

When I reached the actual juncture of the Rhine and the Moselle, however, I found I was mistaken. I was entertained at first by a fine view of the two rivers, darkly walled by hills and a very massive and, in a way, impressive equestrian statue of Emperor William I, armed in the most flamboyant and aggressive military manner and looking sternly down on the fast-traveling and uniting waters of the two rivers. Across the Moselle from the tongue of land on which this monument stood, and which, by the way, had been made into a charming little park with this statue as its chief ornament, was vacant land. On the base of the monument, which stood perhaps sixty feet high, was chiseled:

Nimmer mir das Reich zerstöret
(Never will my Empire be destroyed)
Wenn Ihr einig seid und treu.
(If you remain one (in heart) and true.)

I wondered. The ambitions of man run so high. His dreams as a rule are so vain.

Idling about the base of this monument to catch sightseers was a young German picture-postcard seller with a box of views of the Rhine, Coblenz, Cologne and other cities, for sale. He was a very humble-looking youth, a bit doleful, who kept following me about until I bought some.

"Where is Mayen?" I asked as I began to select a few pictures of things I had and had not seen, for future reference.

"Mayence?" he asked doubtfully, "Mayence? Oh, that is a great way from here. Mayence is up the river near Frankfort."

"No, no," I replied irritably (this matter was getting to be a sore point with me). "I have just come from Mayence. I am looking for Mayen. Isn't it over there somewhere?" I pointed to the fields over the river.

He shook his head. "Mayen?" he said. "I don't think there is such a place."

"Good heavens!" I exclaimed. "What are you talking about? Here it is on the map. What is that? Do you live here in Coblenz?"

"*Gewiss!*" he replied. "I live here."

"Very good, then. Where is Mayen?"

"I never heard of it," he replied.

"My God!" I exclaimed to myself. "Perhaps it was destroyed in the Franco-Prussian War. Maybe there *isn't* any Mayen." "You have lived here all your life," I said, turning to my informant, "and you have never heard of Mayen?"

"Mayen, no. Mayence, yes. It is up the river near Frankfort."

"Oh, bosh!" I said and walked off, having paid for what I had taken, however. I hurried back along the river to see if I could find a policeman or some intelligent citizen who would put me right. I was beginning to feel a little uncanny about my father's birthplace. Finally I found a car line which ended at the river and a landing wharf, and I hailed the conductor and motorman who were idling together for a moment.

"Where is Mayen?" I asked.

"Mayence?" they said, looking at me curiously.

"No, no! M-a-y-e-n. Mayen—not Mayence. It's a small town around here somewhere."

"Mayen! Mayen!" they repeated. "Mayen!" and they frowned.

"Oh Lord!" I sighed. "I'm gone. I've come all this way for nothing. I can follow this trail all over Germany and not find it." (I saw my bank account swiftly dwindling in an endless pursuit.) I got out my map. "Mayen—see?" I said.

"Oh yes," one of them replied, putting up a finger. "That is so. There *is* a place called Mayen! It is out that way. You must take a train."

"How many miles?" I asked.

"About fifteen. It will take you about an hour and a half."

"Dear God," I said, "that far off? I thought I was there."

I inquired the train time but he didn't know. So I had to go back to the depot for that and then wait another two hours before my train left. I was getting so that I didn't care whether I ever got to my father's town or not, but having come so far, I hesitated to turn back. No, I decided I would go on, come what may. Perhaps eventually I should find it. The remaining time I used to see Coblenz and to get something to eat and to speculate on what I should find when I really got to Mayen.

The thing that had pleased me with Coblenz on sight was its newness. It was really far newer in its aspect than Mayence, though of course a much smaller place, having only sixty thousand inhabitants. Its streets were so wide and clean and bright in all the newer parts. Its business heart was so brisk. There were several good streetcar lines (electric) traversing its various sections, and the usual details of the brisk American city of the same size. Of course there was an old section, quite quaint—not as quaint as portions of

Mayence, but still possessing a rich old German flavor. The newer portions reminded me for all the world of parts of Rochester, Poughkeepsie and Syracuse, New York. As at Mayence and everywhere else in Germany where there is a river, the bank on the Coblenz side was beautifully treated as a drive with double footpaths, rows of trees, lounging pagodas or shelters and lined for a good portion of its length with attractive residences. Another portion was occupied as a levee with well-made stone piers and solid flights of stone steps leading down to the water.

It was at Coblenz, while waiting for my third train to get me to Mayen, that I secured my first real taste of the German army and the German soldiery generally, as I afterwards saw them, and it induced a vast respect in me for the preparedness of the Germans, whatever the world may think of their military efficiency. Finer-looking soldiers I never saw. While I was talking to the motorman and conductor at the end of the streetcar line, a full regiment of them swung past and crossed a bridge over the Rhine, which was near by. (Coblenz is a military post of considerable importance, as I afterwards discovered, and I myself accidentally ran across the great barracks and parade grounds before I left.) Their helmets were of brass and glittered with a golden sheen. Their trousers were gray and their jackets red, and they marched with a slap-slap-slap of their feet that was positively ominous. Every man's body was as erect as a poker; every man's gun was carried with almost loving grace over his shoulder. They were all big men—stolid, broad-chested, with strong arms and legs. As they filed over the bridge, four abreast, they looked like a fine, scarlet ribbon with a streak of gold in it. They eventually disappeared between the green hills on the other side.

In another part of the city, walking briskly about to see what I could see, I came upon a company of soldiers, perhaps fifty, marching in loose open order, or rather disorder, each man talking to the other—a broken condition which is permitted where parade is not essential. Behind me, coming toward the soldiers, was an officer, one of those bandbox gentlemen in the long, gray military coat of the Germans, the high-crowned, low-visored cap and lacquered boots. I learned before I was out of Germany to listen for the clank of their swords. The moment the lieutenant who was in charge of the men saw this officer in the distance, he gave vent to a low command which brought the men four by four instantly. In the next breath their guns, previously swinging loosely in their hands, were over their shoulders, and as the officer drew alongside a sharp "*Im Gleichschritt marsch!*" brought that wonderful jackknife motion, "the goose-step," each leg brought rigidly to a level with the abdomen, as they went slap-slap-slapping by until the officer was gone. Then at a word, on the instant, they fell into their old, easy, disorderly position and resumed their conversation.

It was surprising to see it. It gave me a sense of extreme, efficient military control. All through Coblenz officers and soldiers were visible, singly or in groups, but never idling anywhere. All the while I was in Germany I never saw a lounging soldier. The officers, all men of fine stature, were so showily tailored as to leave a sharp impression. Their shoulders were always broad and level. Their clothing always looked as though it had just been brought home from the tailor for the first time. Their caps and boots and buckles and spurs and swords all seemed to glow or glisten. They walked briskly, smartly, defiantly, with a tremendous air of assurance but not vainglory. They were so much superior to anything else in Germany that for me they made it, giving it its one note of real distinction and elegance. Everywhere I went the officers and soldiers made Germany for me. But to continue.

At half past two my train departed, and I entered a compartment of the only class they had, which was fourth—hard, wooden-seated little cars, as stiff and heavy as cars could possibly be. My mind was full of my father's ancestral heath and the quaint type of life that must have been lived here a hundred years before. This was a French border country. My father, when he ran away, had escaped into Alsace nearby. He told me once of being whipped for stealing cherries because his father's house adjoined the priest's yard and a cherry tree belonging to that holy man had spread its branches, cherry-laden, over the wall, upon which he had secretly climbed at night. His stepmother, informed by the priest, whipped him. I wondered if I could find that stone wall.

As the train rolled out into this very typical section of old-time Germany, I studied the fields and the towns with great interest. There were plenty of solid, healthy men and buxom women on this train and at the various small but well-built stations. You could feel distinctly a strong note of commercial development here. Some small, new factory buildings were visible at one place and another. An occasional real estate sign, after the American fashion, was in evidence. The fields looked well and fully tilled, sown in season no doubt to potatoes, beets, maize and the standard German crops of vegetables. Hills were always in the distance somewhere. I noticed a strange celebration of some kind going on which, at first, when I saw the first youthful representative of it, made me decide that I was looking at someone escaped from a madhouse, or if not that, one so harmlessly foolish as to be permitted to roam at large. Later I learned it was a very important function and it really occurred all over Germany in exactly the same way. But let me begin right.

As the train pulled into one small station, Metternich by name, I saw a tall, raw-boned yokel, so lackadaisically ambling, yappy, that if by any chance he would have been brought out on a stage as he looked here, he would have evoked a burst of applause as a humorist. He was a mere boy, nineteen or twenty, six feet tall if an inch, broad-shouldered, horny-handed, slightly bow-legged and with as vacuous and inane an expression as it is possible for an individual to possess. A cheap, wide-brimmed, soft hat, offensively new and of a dusty mud color, set low over one ear and around it, to my astonishment, was twined and hung a slim garland of flowers which, interwoven and chained, hung ridiculously down his back. He was all alone on the platform as the train pulled in and left, gazing sheepishly and foolishly about him and yet doing his best to wear his astounding honors with an air of bravado.

"Hello! Here's a village half-wit," I said to myself, "some poor loon too tame to be locked up. What a funny get-up!"

I was looking at his collarless shirt, his big feet and hands and his bow legs, when I heard a German in the next seat, a local businessman obviously, say to another who sat beside him, "He won't look like that long."

"Three months—he'll be fine."

They went on reading their papers and I fell to wondering what they could mean. What was it would make him fine in three months?

At the next station were five more yokels, all similarly crowned, raw, red-faced, horny-handed youths, and around them a bevy of rosy, healthy village girls. These five, constituting a crowd and the center of attention, were somewhat more assured than the lone youth had been, a little loud-mouthed, swaggering and leering foolishly.

"What is that?" I asked the man over the seat. "What are they doing?"

"The drawing for the army," he replied. "All over Germany the young men are being drawn for the army."

"Do they begin to serve at once?"

"Right away."

I paused in amazement at this trick of statecraft which could make of the drawing for so difficult and compulsory a thing as service in the army a gala occasion. With scarcely any compensation—a few cents a day—these yokels and village men are seized upon and made to do almost heroic duty for two years, whether they will or not, and yet they are such silly-billies as to permit themselves to be crowned with flowers and made a show of about the villages, swaggering and drinking and making a noisy spectacle of themselves, the while the remainder of the citizens smile good-naturedly or make such predictions as the one I heard. I did not know then, quite, how intensely proud Germany is of her army, how perfectly willing the vast majority are to serve, how certain the great majority of Germans are that Germany is called of God to rule—*beherrschen* is their vigorous word—the world. Before I was out of Frankfort and Berlin, I could well realize how intensely proud the average boy is to be drawn. He is really a man then; he is permitted to wear a uniform and carry a gun; the citizens from then on, at least as long as he is in service, respect him as a soldier. By good fortune or ability he may become a petty officer. No wonder they crown him with flowers—the girls—and gather around him in admiring groups. What a custom! In a way, what a travesty!

CHAPTER LXXII

The most amusing part of this whole chase after my father's town was that after traveling all this distance and finally reaching Mayen on the railroad, I didn't really reach it after all but only "East Mayen"—a new section of the old town, or rather a new rival of it—and from East Mayen I had to walk to Mayen proper—a distance of over a mile. I first shook my head in disgust and then laughed. For there in the valley below me, after I had walked a little way, I could actually see the town my father had described, a small walled city of now perhaps a population of seven or eight thousand, with an old Gothic church in the center containing a twisted spire, a true castle or *Schloss* of ancient date on the high ground to the right, a towered gate or two of that medieval, conical aspect so beloved of the painters of romance and a cluster or clutter of quaint, many-gabled, sharp-roofed, sharp-pointed houses which speak invariably of days and notions and emotions and tastes now almost entirely superseded. East Mayen was being built in modern style. Some coal mines had been discovered there and manufactories were coming in. At Mayen all was quite as my father left it, I am sure, some seventy years before.

Those who think this world would be best if we could have peace and quiet should visit Mayen. Here is a town that has existed in a more or less peaceful state for all of six hundred years. The single Catholic church, the largest structure outside of the adjacent castle, was begun in the twelfth century. Frankish princes and Teuton lords have by turns occupied its site. But Mayen has remained quite peacefully a small, German, walled city, its inhabitants doing, in part at least, many of the things its ancestors did. Nowhere in Europe, not even in Italy, did I feel more keenly the seeming out-of-placeness of the modern implements of progress. After a pause at the local graveyard in search of ancestral Dreisers, when I wandered down into the town proper, crossed over the ancient stone bridge that gives into an easily-defended, towered gate and saw the presence of such things as the Singer Sewing Machine Company, a thoroughly up-to-date bookstore, an evening newspaper office and a moving-picture show, I shook my head in real despair. "Nothing is really old," I sighed, "anymore. Timbuktu and Lhasa are crowded with automobiles, no doubt. If I ever get to Tomsk or Irkutsk, it will be to see places like Vincennes, Indiana, or Moline, Illinois. Lahore no doubt already has many points in common with New Orleans, and Moscow is like Minneapolis. There is no escape from modernity."

Nevertheless, Mayen I found to be pleasingly old in its atmosphere. Its inhabitants haven't participated to any extent in the rejuvenescence of Germany since 1871. The work of modernizing it has begun, but not so much more than that. Compared to the small manufacturing towns I saw as I came from Basle to Frankfort, it is old. And yet, as I say, even here it is not entirely so. Its streets are narrow, winding, picturesque. Its architecture is of the most delicious, medieval vintage. A little stream called the Nette flows through (and once flowed around) it, and in places its banks skirt massive but now dismantled walls. The only squares of any importance are those at the public market and Catholic church. Beyond those all is confusing, winding streets.

My search for dead or living Dreisers led me first, as I have said, to the local graveyard, the old *Kirchhof*, which I encountered as I came down the hill from East Mayen. "Here we are," I said as I saw it. "Just the place to give me an indication of the presence or absence of Dreisers in these parts for some time back. I'll go in here first," and I hunted vainly around two sides of an old, gray-black wall endeavoring to find an entrance. On the third side I did. It was a pretty graveyard, situated on a slope above Mayen and commanding greenish-gray hills beyond. It was lowering to a rain as I entered, and the clouds hung in rich, black masses over the valley below. It was half after four by my watch. In this graveyard by far the larger portion of the graves were comparatively recent—1800 to 1912—surmounted by lichen-covered slabs ornamented at the top with Gothic crosses. Seriate trees led in two rows from an old stone gate up to a small, old stone chapel which was vacant save for the rudest form of an altar—a shelter, I suppose, in case of rain—when a few last words were to be said. I made up my mind that I would examine the inscriptions of every tombstone as quickly as possible in order to locate all the dead Dreisers and then get down into the town before the night and the rain fell. With that idea in view I began at an upper row near the church and began to work down—a pleasant and peculiar and, in a way, sentimental task.

Time was when the wandering in a graveyard after this fashion would have produced the profoundest melancholy in me. It was so in Paris, after years and years of immunity from feelings of this kind, when in Père-Lachaise I saw that vast company of small stone mausoleums crowded like the small homes of a village and labeled so monotonously, as such things are in France,

"The Family Heurotin," "The Family Arvonet," "The Family Deschot," and so on. There the sounds and the atmosphere of the wonderfully brilliant Paris, which wafted to me like an inciting perfume among those stones from the streets below, speaking of life and love and enthusiasm and desire as contrasted with the vast array of genius, sprinkled like the grains of a sowing between these streets of tombs and on the open hills in simple little rows, depressed me as I have not been depressed in years. It made me morbidly weary and ineffably sad. I saw too many rosebud names of genius—Chopin, Balzac, Daudet, Rachel—withered, alas, to pale, intangible fames, not to be depressed. I hurried out finally, quite agonized and unspeakably lonely, like a shipwrecked man in an open boat at sea, horror-struck in a way by the presence of all-effacing death, the utter forgetfulness of the spirit of life to all that ever was or ever will be.

Here in Mayen it was a simpler feeling that was gradually coming over me—an amused, sentimental interest in the simple lives that too often had had their beginning and their end here. It was a lovely afternoon for such a search. Spring was already here in south Germany, that faint, tentative suggestion of budding life, which suggested the mythical figure of Pan somewhere practicing his stiff fingers upon some simple melody—the first faint tootlings of the flute of spring. All the wind-blown leaves of the preceding fall were on the ground, but in between them new grass was springing, and one might readily suspect windflowers and crocuses, the first faint, green points of lilies and the pulsing tendrils of harebells. It was beginning to sprinkle, the faintest suggestion of a light rain, and in the west, over the roofs and towers of Mayen, a gleam of sunlight broke through the mass of heavy clouds and touched the valley with one last, lingering ray.

"*Hier ruhet in Gott*" (Here rests in God) or "*Hier ruhet sanft*" (Here softly rests) was too often the beginning, but I could easily understand how, often after sickness and pain and perhaps unspeakable sorrow, a narrow bed of soil should suggest soft rest. Yes, yes. Most of the monuments, as I have said, were moderately recent, but for a city or village that dated from twelve hundred and earlier, it seemed to me there were few, if any, really old graves. Graveyards, like human beings, have their day of popularity, their sere and yellow age and their final death and disappearance. Truly there is no death in this universe, only seeming.

I had made my way through the sixth or seventh row from the top, pushing away grass at times from in front of faded inscriptions, rubbing other lichen-covered letters clean with a stick and standing interested before very recent tombstones, all smart with a very recently-developed local idea of setting a black piece of glass into the gray of the marble and on that lettering the names of the departed in gold! It was to me a very thick-witted, truly

Teutonic idea, dull and heavy in its mistakenness, but at worst it was no worse than the Italian idea of putting a photo of the late beloved in the head of the slab behind glass in a stone-cut frame and of further ornamenting the graves with ghastly, iron-shafted lamps with globes of yellow, pink and green glass. That was the worst of all.

As I was meditating how little villages reproduce themselves oyster-like from generation to generation, a few coming and a few going but the majority leading a narrow, simple round of existence, I came suddenly, so it seemed to me, upon one grave which gave me a real shock. It was a comparatively recent slab of gray granite with the modern plate of black glass set in it and a Gothic cross surmounting it all at the top. On the glass plate was lettered:

Here Rests
Theodor Dreiser
Born 16. Feb. 1820
Died 28. Feb. 1882.
R.I.P.

I think as clear a notion of how my grave will look after I am gone, and how utterly unimportant both life and death are anyhow, came to me then. Something about this old graveyard, the suggestion of the new life of spring, a robin trilling its customary evening song on a nearby twig, the smoke curling upward from the chimneys in the old houses below, the spire of the medieval church and the walls of the medieval castle standing out in the softening light—one or all of them served to give me a sense of the long past that is back of every individual in the life of the race and the long future that the race has, regardless of the individual. Religion offers no consolation to me. Psychic research and metaphysics, however meditated upon, are in vain. There is, in my judgment, no death—the universe is compact of life—but nevertheless, I cannot see any continuous life for any individual. And it would be so unimportant if true. Imagine an eternity of life for a leaf, a fishworm, an oyster! The best that can be said is that the ideas of types survive somewhere in the creative consciousness. That is all. The rest is silence.

I found to my great interest in this graveyard various Dreisers: a Theodor who was the son of the above Theodor, who, I failed to state, was my father's brother; a Catharine; a Gertrude and an Elise Dreiser, whose connection I could not trace. In another graveyard which I found later there was a Gottfried and a Johann Dreiser, the latter another brother of my father's, and several additional females, wives and daughters, but no graves dated back beyond eighteen hundred. I wondered whether I should encounter any living Dreisers in the village who could throw any light on the now remote history of the family, and so meditating, I took the road downward again.

Like all the places that were highly individual and different, Mayen made a deep impression on me. To enter this walled town was like entering the shell of some great mollusk that had long since died and finding it occupied by another type of life from that which originally existed there. Because it was raining now and rapidly getting dark, I sauntered into the first shelter I saw, a four-story, rather presentable brick inn, located outside the gate, known as the *Brückentor* (bridge gate), and took a room here for the night. It was a dull affair, run by the dubbiest, most impractical keeper I have ever encountered. He was a little man, sandy-haired, wool-witted, inquisitive, idle, in a silly way drunken, who was so astonished by the onslaught of a total stranger in this unexpected manner that he scarcely knew how to conduct himself.

"*Ich will ein Bettzimmer für die Nacht*," I suggested. (I want a room for the night.)

"A room!" he queried in an astonished way, as if this were the most unheard-of thing imaginable.

"Certainly," I said, "a room. You rent rooms, don't you?"

"Oh, certainly, certainly. To be sure. A room. Certainly. Wait. I will call my wife."

He went into a back chamber, leaving me to face several curious natives—one a hunchback—all of whom went over me from head to toe with their eyes, but not in the smart, alert American fashion. The German race is very different. By this time I had begun to realize that I was not applying at a hotel in the proper sense of the word, but some rooming establishment with a bar and semi-hotel accommodations. There were a few factories in Mayen, and some of the rooms were no doubt rented to laborers. Having applied, however, I decided to chance it.

"Mah-ree-ah!" I heard my landlord calling quite loudly in the rear portion of the house. "There is one here who wants a room. Have we a room ready?"

I heard no reply.

Presently he came back, however, and said in a high-flown, deliberate way, "Be seated. Are you from Frankfort?"

"Yes and no. I come from America."

"O-o-oh! America! What part of America?"

"New York."

"Oh—o-o-oh—New York. That is a great place. I have a brother in America. Since six years now he is out there. I forget the place." He put his hand to his foolish, frizzled head and looked at the floor. "What is that place?" he asked himself.

"Milwaukee?" I suggested.

"No, that's hardly like it. A great city, a very great city," he volunteered.

"Chicago?"

"Yes, I believe that is it. I have a sister living there, too. Wouldn't you like a glass of beer?"

I thanked him, no. I was afraid I was going to have to tell him the story of my life in the presence of these curious idlers. His wife now appeared, a stout, dull woman, one of the hardworking potato specimens of the race. A whispered conference between them followed, after which my host announced my room would soon be ready.

"Let me leave my bag here," I said, anxious to escape, "and then I will come back later. I want to look around for a while."

He accepted this valid excuse, and I departed, glad to get out into the rain and the strange town, anxious to find a better-looking place to eat and to see what I could see.

Mayen was surely not much in the rain at night. For two hours it poured and then ceased, and the stars came out. After buying all the picture-postcards I could find, I followed a street that led to the old Gothic church, a very considerable affair, much larger than I expected it to be. A six o'clock *Via Crucis* service was being held, and all the children of the local schools (Mayen, as I found, was solidly Catholic) were being herded into the church in droves under the direction of male teachers and sisters of some order. I sauntered in and found a place in the back, the atmosphere bringing back my own unfortunate Catholic schooldays. I attended just such a church as this in my time—under compulsion. I can imagine nothing more pathetic than the spectacle of these swarms of children, herded sheep-like under these great arches, compelled to accept as true and significant the doctrines of the Catholic church as laid down by these dull sisters and equally dull priests. I know, from personal experience, what it means to be herded and lectured to upon inane doctrines concerning the Holy Trinity, the infallibility of the pope, the necessity of confession and the sacraments, hell, heaven and all the folderol which goes with maintaining this expensive and showy political-religious hierarchy.

What fools we mortals be and how easily we are led by the nose. Given a strong man or woman, it is nothing for him or her to put a collar on scores, thousands, millions of others and drive them. We have the dominant classes! Why dominant? I have no objection to intellectual leadership that seeks to benefit the individual, but when avarice and craft and dull, malignant ignorance and nepotism sit in the saddle, I object. This church was crowded with poor, dull, blind beginners and weaklings, looking to Jesus Christ and the hosts of calendared saints (reared by priestly subtlety) and the fictitious God the Father, Son and Holy Ghost for escape from terrors heaped on their minds by the same subtlety that created the saints. Dear heaven! And my father, not a bad businessman in his way, accepted this hogwash. It was imposed upon his childish mind in this very church and town. The influences that made a narrow, religious bigot of him were still uninterruptedly at work. Modern Germany, in great part, has still not thrown off the benighting influence of Catholicism and heavy-minded Lutheranism. What a pity it is that dogmatic theology (not religious, of course) cannot be rooted up, root, stock, and branch, and destroyed!

CHAPTER LXXIII

From here, after a time, I went out in the night seeking something to eat, the ancient liturgy of the church ringing in my ears. The Germans label their restaurants and cafés—both almost indiscriminately—*Restauration*; a fit-sounding word, I think, and quite Teutonic. It was quite dark now when I came out of the church, with the sounds of the endless "Our Father-s" and "Hail Mary-s" ringing in my ears, and made my way along the dark little streets. I kept my eye for that mark *Restauration*, although its presence in Germany does not always mean that you can get a meal, any more than the word "café" in America indicates that anything more than liquor is sold. It was easy to drink a glass of beer, though, and so by degrees I got a look into four semi-eating, semi-drinking places, public taprooms, where at this hour the native Mayeners were in part assembled, drinking a friendly glass of beer and discussing whatever news there was to discuss. The atmosphere of these places reminded me of those quaint taprooms that one finds about London and its suburbs, where the native Britisher sits in dour contemplation of his lot. Here the Germans were apparently no more lively, though much more emphatic at times, pounding the tables with their fists or laying down the law in deep, throaty tones.

Nations vary so greatly. They are like fields that have been sown to different kinds of grain or vegetables or flowers. England suggests good, hard wheat, I think; the French, flowering buckwheat or clover; Italy, blossoms only; Switzerland, high mountain corn; and Germany, potatoes. The Germans are a sort of potato in their way—stout, starchy, phlegmatic, seemingly dull but very useful. Here in these small Mayen taprooms they looked the part: heavy, florid potatoes, very simple in their mood, but talking quite big at times—the young ones. "For all the world like animated potatoes," I thought, though I knew there was much more to them than any potato simile would indicate.

I finally came into one *restauration* whose atmosphere suited me exactly, though I could not see that meals were served. It was red and brown in its color scheme. Stamped leather paneling rose to within two feet of the ceiling; on the cornice or molding were ranged the usual pewter plates and tankards and the like. A line of leather-covered seats followed the walls, in front of which were ranged long tables. The center of the room was occupied by a circular wooden post supporting the ceiling, which was low, around the top of which, for amusement's sake and because the founder was probably a wheelwright, was placed a wheel. Tables for cards, writing, dominoes and the like were scattered here and there.

As was the case at my supposed inn outside the bridge gate, my arrival here with a quiet demand for food put a sort of panic in the breast of my small but stout host. He looked not a little like a fat sparrow. He was playing checkers with another middle-aged Mayener when I came in, but when I asked for food, he gave over his pleasure for the time being and bustled out to find his wife. The good neighbor betook himself to an evening (?) paper.

"Why, yes, yes," he remarked briskly on returning, "what will you have?"

"What *can* I have?"

On the instant he put his little, fat hand to his semi-bald pate and rubbed it ruminatively. "A steak, perhaps. Some veal. Some sausage?"

"I will have a steak, if you don't mind, and a cup of black coffee."

He bustled out and upstairs, and in a moment in the distance I heard his voice exclaiming quite nervously, "Katrina, here is one who wants a steak. Can you get that? He is waiting."

I could not catch what she said, but I heard him add, "You must hurry. He is waiting." When he came down, I threw a new bomb into camp. "Can I wash my hands?"

"Certainly, certainly," he replied, "in a minute," and bounded upstairs. "Katrina," I heard him call, "have Anna make the washroom ready. He wishes to wash his hands. Where are the towels? Where is the soap?"

There was much clattering of feet overhead. I heard a door being opened and things being moved. Presently I heard him call, "Katrina, in God's name, where is the soap?" and, when informed, "Run, Anna, and get a towel."

More clattering of feet, and finally he came down, red and puffing. "Now, *mein Herr,* you can go up."

I went, concealing a secret grin, and found that I had dislocated a storeroom, once a bath perhaps; a baby carriage had been removed from a table and on it a pitcher, bowl, towel and soap placed—a small piece of soap and cold water. Finally, after seeing me served properly, he sat down at his table again and sighed. The neighbor returned. Several more citizens dropped in to read and chat. The two youngest boys in the family came downstairs with their books to study. It was quite a typical German family scene.

It was here that I made my first effort to learn something about the Dreiser family.

"Do you know anyone by the name of Dreiser hereabouts?" I asked cautiously, afraid to tell too much for fear of incriminating myself.

"Dreiser—Dreiser—" he said. "Is he in the furniture business?"

"I don't know. That is what I would like to find out. Do you know of anyone by that name?"

"Isn't that the man, Henry," he turned to one of the guests, "who failed here last year for fifty thousand marks?"

"Goodness gracious!" I thought.

"The same," said this other solemnly. (I fancied, by the way he said it, that he had lost some money.)

"There was a John Dreiser here," my host said to me, "who failed for fifty thousand marks. He is gone, though, now, I think. I don't know where he is."

Under the circumstances I thought it might be as well not to identify myself with this Dreiser too closely. They might not look with any goodwill on me. They never asked whether I was a stranger in Germany or not. I finished my meal and went out wondering how, if I was to secure any additional information at all, I was to go about it. The rain had ceased, and the sky was already clearing. After more idle rambling through a world that was quaint as old Canterbury, I came back finally to my hotel. My host was up and waiting for me. All but one guest had gone.

"So you are from America?" he observed. "I would like very much to talk with you some more."

"Let me ask *you* something," I replied. "Do you know anyone here in Mayen by the name of Dreiser?"

"Dreiser? Dreiser? It seems to me there was someone here. He failed for some money. You could find out at the *Mayener Zeitung*. Mr. Schreder ought to know."

I decided that I would appeal to Mr. Schreder and his paper in the morning, and pretending to be very tired in order to escape my host, who by now was a little tipsy, I went to the room assigned me, carrying a candle. That was the way this particular inn was lighted. When I reached it, I found I had been assigned to a very small hall bedroom on the third floor—but what of it? I thought. I was tired, and it was clean. So I put down my candle and began to undress.

I am amused to this day when I think of this room at Mayen. It was so small. Before my arrival it must have been occupied by a small daughter or two of my host. A closet in the corner, which was open, contained some little woolen skirts and petticoats and on a top shelf two of the "dutchiest" little hats, very flat, very pancakey, very wide-brimmed, of cheap, plaited straw, one wheat-colored, the other straw and red. A long, blue ribbon was fastened around the wheat one, a pink ribbon around the straw and red. They were so cheap and so truly German. I could also see, by the presence in one corner of several German flags and emblems of societies and church organizations, that my noble dub of a host was public-spirited. I could see him in my mind's eye leading his packhorse of a wife and his family solemnly off to church on Sundays, their cleanly smocks and yellow-brown pigtails surmounted by these hats! On the wall was a small three-by-four-inch mirror of peeling silver—the only toilet article my poor little German maid or maidens possessed.

That night I slept soundly. The room was cold and over me, in lieu of comforters or a pair of blankets, was an immense, stuffy feather bed, the covering used here. There was no bath in the inn. A small, whitish-yellow bowl and pitcher ornamented a washstand. True to my nature I felt like growling a little, just for growl's sake, but I decided to make the best of it. In the morning I arose early at dawn and, looking out of my one window, saw Mayen, all its medieval towers and housetops spread out before me in the faint morning light. It was beautiful. Below me tumbled the little stream that had served as a moat in earlier days—a good and natural defense. Opposite me was the Brückentor, really strong and impressive-looking. Further on was a heavy, circular sweep of wall and a handsome watchtower. Over the wall, rising up a slope, could be seen the peaked-roof, gabled houses of solid brick and stone with slate and tile roofs. Never before in my life had I looked on a truly medieval city of the castellated, Teutonic order. Nothing that I had seen in either France, England or Italy had the peculiar medieval quality of this. These fat, round towers with conical tops, guarding thick-walled gates, looked so defensive and sure. I could see, in my mind's eye, early Teutonic or Frankish couriers riding up and being halted here. Their showy coats of mail and flaunting feathers would be of no avail against so frowning a wall and solid a gate.

"Who goes there?" some warder might call from that small window above.

A messenger, perhaps, from the Baron This or That.

"Wait, and we will open."

One could almost see the stout, Teutonic soldiers within, their leather jerkins surmounted by breastplates of steel, their heavy helmets and windowed visors ornamented by a feather or two. Swords were really common in those days—pikes and battle-axes—and the iron lanterns of the watchers served to throw a feeble ray on belated visitors. Here, indeed, was precisely such a medieval city, only now these solid gates and towers were dismantled, and the lords who had once flourished here were dead and buried these hundreds of years.

It is hard to evoke a sentimental interest in me for an order of life that is clumsy, gross, contentious and what not, and that has been written to death by the romantic school of fiction; yet face to face with so fine a shell of an older order of existence, I was not unmoved. The conditions here prevailing in Mayen, even the naive architecture, cannot long endure. Who is to pay for the repair of dismantled walls and crumbling towers where crows love to house themselves? Already the hand of modernity is beginning to remove all the pleasing traces of an earlier day. In one of my rambles about the city I noticed where a factory had been permitted to use a segment of the ancient wall as a support. In another region it had been torn down entirely. In still another, a new gate was being cut through quite roughly and inartistically. A second Catholic church was being built, the first one to be constructed since the older edifice, which had been begun in the twelfth century. On the hills back of the town new woolen mills were in operation, and at the noon hour I saw wives, daughters, little children, carrying buckets to their working relatives. A spur of the railroad from Coblenz had been brought over to these, and the modern engine and freight car were to be seen plying to and fro.

No trolley has yet been run out to Mayen, but it will be. Streetcars will enter through the Brückentor, and where once mailed soldiers galloped to and fro, the clang-clang of the trolley bell will be heard. Even here the automobile is no stranger—I saw several—and all the geegaws and mechanical conveniences of modern trade are as readily secured here as elsewhere—the fountain pen, for instance, and collapsible tubes of library paste and mucilage. Nevertheless, in this early morning light, the wedge-like roofs of the old houses rising sharp and clear in the crystalline air, I stood and meditated, dreaming dreams of an older, more picturesque day. Is this not merely the weariness of today talking?

I escaped the importunities of my talkative host by a ruse, putting the two marks charge for the room in an envelope and leaving it on the dresser. I went out and followed the stream in the pleasant morning light, returning via an old Jewish graveyard, very small and very plaintive-looking, and then idling first in one street and then another. I learned from buying a pamphlet on Mayen that there was an old and good museum in the tower over the principal gate and went to that. I bethought myself of my father's house next to the churchyard and went to that to find the exact cherry tree if I could. I visited the Genovevaburg and found the castle half old and half new, the new part forming a horrible excrescence on the old. I mailed postcards at the local post office to all and sundry of my relatives, stating the local condition of the Dreisers insofar as learned, and then sought out Herr Schreder at the office of the *Mayener Zeitung*, but he could tell me nothing of any Dreisers save one. That was the fairly well-respected John Dreiser who had failed in the furniture business. Of other Dreisers he did not know. He advised me to seek the curator of the local museum, a man who had the history of Mayen at his fingertips. He was a cabinetmaker by trade. I could not find him at home. Finally, after looking in the small local directory published by Mr. Schreder and finding no Dreisers listed, I decided to give up and go back to Frankfort, but not without one last look at the private yard attached to the priest's house and the cherry tree which had been the cause of the trouncing.

It is curious how the most innocent and idle of sentiments will lead a person on in this way. Everything in Mayen had been and was of the greatest interest to me. In the little Brückentor museum I had studied with the greatest interest, because it was my father's town, the ancient Celtic, Teutonic, Roman and Merovingian antiquities. It was here that I saw for the first time the much-talked-of wheat discovered in a Celtic funeral urn, which, although thousands of years have elapsed since it was harvested, is still—thanks to dryness, so the local scientist told me—fertile and if planted would grow! Talk of suspended animation! And those who are interested in the abstrusities of metaphysics may meditate on this. What has the inherent life force in the grain of wheat been doing all these years, and how does that affect the theory of personality, individuality, continued existence or non-existence of anything?

Below the town I lingered in the little valley of the Nette, now laid out as a park, and re-examined the gate through which my father had been wont to ride. I think I sentimentalized a little over the long distance that had separated my father from his old home and how he must have longed to see it at times, and then finally, after walking about the church and school where he had been forced to go, I left Mayen with a sorrowful backward glance. In spite of the fact that there was now no one there to whom I could count myself related, still there *had* been. I had found at least the church that my father had attended, the priest's house and garden where possibly the identical cherry tree was still standing—there were several of them. I had seen the gate through which my father had ridden as a boy with the soldiers and from which he had walked finally, never to return anymore. That was enough. I was fond of Mayen for these things, if for nothing else.

CHAPTER LXXIV

My return to Frankfort was swift and straight. I caught a train just about the time I had enough of Mayen, and at Coblenz I had but twenty minutes to wait before I secured a fast express for Frankfort, bringing me there in time for dinner. I was concerned now with the arrival of Madame Culp the next afternoon and the significance of her letter. When I reached Frankfort it was nearly dark and therefore all the more interesting for offering me on the morrow a little companionship such as I might look upon as intimate. That night I can say that I ate one of the very few lone hotel dinners that was truly interesting for one reason—the presence of German officers.

I had never seen such officers. It is possible that Frankfort, being relatively a frontier city as compared to Berlin and others, enjoys more fully the presence of these individuals. Be that as it may, this particular hotel, it seemed to me, was alive with them. Truly, although I had seen army officers in England, Italy, France and the United States, I had never seen anything so fine in my life. The German military cap, as everyone knows, with its high crown and sharply down-turned visor, has become the artistic standard for military caps the world over. The long, broad-skirted, blue-gray military coat, reaching halfway between the knees and the ankles, with its imposing rows of buttons and its interesting sleeve stripes of red or gold, its handsome epaulets and its close-fitting high collar make the most insignificant personage significant, and the German officer is rarely physically small. I never saw uniforms cut out of what I thought was better cloth; I never saw boots so highly lacquered or more appropriately lasted; I never saw spurs so silvery, swords more glistening and clanking, caps so high and distingué, monocles worn with a greater air of superiority, waists drawn in tighter or more shapely by corsets, or such a general air of smartness and physical and social superiority in my life. *Kaiserlich* is the word, and they walk, or rather strut, particularly in a hotel lobby, a drawing room or a theater, as though they thought the Kaiser were then and there looking at them. Asinine? If you will. You feel, as they pass, that to be a mere civilian when one could be an officer is to choose, or be compelled, to be nothing at all. Back, back! Away to the ash heap! There is nothing so fine in all Germany as its military officers. They are truly distinguished.

Here in this Frankfurter Hof on the evening I arrived, there were fully a dozen of them, if not more—young lieutenants with their fathers or mothers, or both; captains and possibly majors with civilian friends or their wives; younger or older officers with their ladyloves or with brother officers of their own age. It was a brilliant spectacle. They strutted like cockatoos and roosters and peafowls. They looked at me and at others, if they chose to look at all, as much as to say, "Who in the world are you? I am a German officer." When they walked with a budding German girl on their arm, as they did very often, you felt as though you must be witnessing a scene in a play and that applause was due somewhere. Scenically speaking, they were just what was needed about a large hotel of this kind to give it a charming touch of color. I was fascinated.

At dinner one young German officer demonstrated a plan of campaign with Metz as a center, laying knives and forks and spoons in various positions as representing trenches, to his father, a very severe, intellectual, professional-looking man with hard, sharp eyes behind brightly-polished, gold-rimmed glasses. I shall never forget the condescending air with which this whippersnapper youth explained to his father nor the latter's fatuous pride (in spite of all his hardness) in the military accomplishments of his son. Obviously they represented the current military thought and spirit in Germany, as well as its better classes socially. They represented the national pride on which the cost of the German army is based. It was wonderful—quite stirring to behold.

The next day while I loafed about Frankfort, judging the city for myself, the hours passed, and finally at three in the afternoon Madame Culp arrived. She was attended, as celebrities usually are, by a maid and a number of satellites, principally women, who were come from Mayence and other places nearby to hear her sing. When I came back from my walk, I found a note from her, artistically cautious, saying that she was here but suffering from a slight cold and that she might not be able to see me for more than a few minutes before the concert, but would I come up at four, when she would send away all her friends? I was in no mood for nonsense. After her failing to answer my letter for so long, it made little difference to me whether she saw me or not, but I was curious as to her sudden impulse to write. Why so eager? I waited until four and then went up to find her very smartly arrayed for the occasion. She was going to serve me tea; I could see that by the little wicker table set with a thin china service, and as for the three or four bouquets of flowers scattered about, I could see that the maid had worked briskly to cause the room to look charming.

"Oh, there you are!" she called when I entered, bustling across the room in a trailing tea gown and surveying me with that warm, bird-like inquisitiveness which had pleased and amused me in London. She was smaller than I had fancied from my London memories but robust, able, not at all bad-looking.

"Yes, here I am," I replied. "And now you're in for a lecture. You shouldn't have written me at all. You've only brought trouble on yourself."

"And why?" she asked, smiling and pouting.

"You know why. Because you didn't answer my letter. Why didn't you?"

I could see she realized that she had a problem on her hands, but, womanlike, she was swift to put a pretty face on it. "Now, you come over here first," she cooed, taking my hand, "and tell me all about yourself. First we are going to have tea, and then you are going to talk to me and tell me where you have been, and then you are coming with me (her "with" was almost "weeth") to the theater, and I am going to sing for you—and then—" She waved a hand gaily and added, "—now, you sit right there, and I will sit here where I can see you."

How silly words are as a rule. They make a little noise, a little fuss, a little rosy dust, sometimes, nothing more. Temperaments talk without words. I could feel a warm enthusiasm here which was based on I could not guess what. Why so friendly? Why all this enthusiasm? She had not written me for a month, and then suddenly she had. The notion, in a way, afterwards, I suppose, that she liked me more than she had at first supposed—the feeling that I was rather close to Grant Richards, of whom perhaps she was unduly fond—what was it? I pondered.

She poured me tea and looked at me. She opened a small jar of preserves, looked, ogled. She put sandwiches on a plate and smiled enthusiastically, looking hard into my eyes. She had a quaint little way of opening her eyes very wide and giving vent to a little, quaint, pig-like grunt which amused and attracted me. It was a bit of artifice left over from or developed by many a flirtation in the past—that was plain. Though not very enthusiastic, I was satisfied to play the role of the pursuer here. She was not unattractive. Germany was not all that it might be without companionship. She was agreeable and she wanted me to flirt with her—that was plain.

"Now you tell me," I said, "you minx. Why didn't you answer me?"

"What is a minx?" she asked. "Iss that something very nice?"

"It is lovely," I replied. "A minx is a muskrat."

"And what is a muskrat?" she queried. Her knowledge of English was not extensive. I could trifle with her as I pleased.

"A muskrat is a semaphore," I replied, and then, amused at my own folderol and the thought that I had accidentally connected her with a danger signal, I burst into a laugh.

"Now you are teasing me," she complained. "Now you are not nice. You mustn't tease me. What is a minx?"

"A minx is a very pretty, fur-bearing animal," I said to her in German.

"Oh!" she exclaimed, not a little unlike Marcelle, "that is very pretty. A little, fur-bearing animal. I like that. You English have such pretty names for women. My *darling, my dearest, my sweetheart*—I like those." (Only she said "swedeheart.")

"My little lump of gold also," I added, quoting the late Alexander Dowie.

She did not get that.

This badinage continued until I asked her again why she had not written.

"I couldn't. I was so busy. I—"

"No, you don't," I commented. "Don't you tell me that. You didn't want to at first and then you did. Why?"

"Don't ask me now—please don't," she pleaded. "Wait until tomorrow. Wait until you come to Berlin, then I will tell you. I will tell you at Zehlendorf."

"But I'm not coming to Berlin."

"Oh, yes! Oh, surely you are! I want you so much there. It is such a nice house. You will have it all to yourself for a few days. Only Minna, my cook, and Fräulein Förster, my housekeeper, are there. They would make you so comfortable. You can have my room."

I smiled at her rapid description.

"Not for me," I replied, "unless you tell me why you didn't write. I'd rather go to the Hotel Adlon. Are you going to tell me?"

"Now you are acting very badly," she complained. "I don't like that. You oughtn't to make me tell you unless I want to."

"Oh, yes, I ought. I'm afraid you don't really want me."

She looked at me quite seriously and then said, "Wait. Until tonight, anyhow. Maybe I will tell you. But you will come to Zehlendorf?"

"Very likely," I said, and we pushed the tea things away.

Now for the big business, as the stage managers say. All during our conversation, much of which has been omitted, she was leaning toward me smiling into my eyes, showing her even teeth, putting her plump little German hand on my arm or my hand and occasionally touching my knee with hers. I suppose in the realms of coquetry this would be considered justifiable homicide. As it was, I felt fairly strongly that incitement towards contact which such things suggest. I had been telling her of my trip to Mayen and the graveyard and the grave of Theodor Dreiser and of a fact which I have not narrated—that all the while I was in the graveyard I was quite unintentionally humming an exquisite little song she had rendered in London, one line of which ran, "*Morgen früh, wenn Gott will, wirst du wieder geweckt.*" (In the morn, if God wills, you will once more be waked.) This pleased her immensely. When I arose she took my hand coaxingly, and suddenly, without notice, I took her in my arms and, forcing her chin up, kissed her mouth. She did not resent it any more than was necessary, but some show of opposition had to be made, of course.

"Oh, you don't understand," she exclaimed, pretending surprise at this sudden onslaught.

"Oh, don't I?" I said. "You tell that to Sweeney." She could not understand the slang, of course.

She was wearing some lilies in her corsage, but they disappeared in the melee, quite crushed. She struggled desperately, telling me that she was really fond of someone else, that she did care for me but that it was not just in this way, at which I merely laughed. She begged me to let her go and, when I refused, cautioned me against the maid. Still I laughed. The upshot was that she finally put her arms around my neck and held me close, kissing me several times.

"Now let me go," she said. "The maid! The maid!"

I let her go.

It was not the end, however. She began a long, confused attempt at a psychologic self-analysis which has interested me to this day but which she never did clear up for herself, principally because she really did not understand herself. I did not get it all then, nor any sufficient part of it, but the subject matter of it was that she had cared very much for Grant Richards and still cared for him in a feverish way, but when I appeared in London, she saw someone who was more in accord with her artistically and whom she could like equally well, if not better. "Oh, if I had only met you first!" she exclaimed in one place. Grant Richards, it appeared, was not what she wanted him to be—to her. He was too distant, too uncertain, too something. He said he was very fond of her, but was he? I foresaw the confessions and woes of another mistress.

"Still, I like you," she suddenly exclaimed, right on top of this, beaming up into my eyes. "Oh, you are so nice. You are so strong and rough and artistic. You love music. Do many Americans love music?" She was planning to tour America the following winter.

I assured her that they did.

She hung about me so close and teasingly, for all her woes over Grant Richards, that I finally picked her up and tossed her on a wide divan that stood in one corner. Words were not necessary; she knew what was coming.

"Oh, not now," she pleaded. "We can't here. Don't you see how it is? The maid is in there. She might come in. She may hear. Wait until tonight. Wait until I come to Zehlendorf. I will be so nice to you. You will be in my room. Please! Please!"

I could not help smiling. The urge was not so great but what it could be repressed even at this late moment. She appeared to be really disturbed about the maid, and so I desisted for the time being, although really in a way it was foolish to have done so. She deserved no respite. I let her go, and then, woman-like, she hung about me again, smoothing my hand, tapping my face with a rose which she took from a vase.

"Stow that!" I said. "I don't think you know what you want. If you tease me any more, you won't escape, that's sure." She sobered a little.

"Are you coming to the concert with me?"

"Yes. At least I shall be there."

"Oh, no. I have my own machine. You are to come with me. Will you?"

"Yes."

"And you will come home with me afterwards?"

"Yes."

"Well, I must rest now. Oh, I am all stirred up!"

She smoothed her hot face.

"I want you to do one thing," I suggested. "Sing for me tonight."

"With pleasure. What shall it be?"

"That little song about 'If God wills we'll awake.'"

"Oh-h-h-h! I weel sing it," she exclaimed with a rising inflection, lifting her eyes, "and you weel sit just below me and look at me. Oh-h-h, that weel be so-o-o nice!"

She fairly gurgled, and I laughed.

Of such is the artistic disposition.

CHAPTER LXXV

The concert that evening, as such things go, was a brilliant success. Madame Culp, insofar as I could judge, had an enthusiastic following in Frankfort, quite as significant, for instance, as a man like Bispham would have in America. An institution known as the Saalbau, containing a large auditorium, was crowded, and there were flowers in plenty for Madame Culp, who opened and closed the program. The latter arrangement resulted in an ovation to her, with men and women crowding about her feet below the platform and suggesting one song and another that she might sing—songs, obviously, that they had heard her sing before. She looked forceful—really brilliant and tender in a lavender silk gown and carrying a portion of an enormous bouquet of lilacs that I had sent her.

This business of dancing attendance upon a national musical favorite was a bit strange for me, although once before in my life it fell to my lot, and tempestuous business it was, too. The artistic temperament! My hair rises! After I left her, I knew Madame Culp was expecting me to do the unexpected—to give edge, as it were, to her presence in Frankfort. So strolling out before dinner (she never ate before singing), I sought a florist's, and espying a whole jardinière full of lilacs—there was enough to pack any large arm—I said to the lady florist (as in France, so many women conduct these small, smart shops), "How much for all those lilacs?"

"You mean all?" she asked.

"All," I said.

"Thirty marks," she replied.

"Isn't that rather high?" I said, assuming that it was wise to bargain a little anywhere.

"But this is very early spring," she said. "These are the very first we've had."

"Very good," I said, "but if I should take them all, would you put a nice ribbon on them?"

"Oh-h-h," she hesitated, almost pouting, "ribbon is very dear, my good sir. Still—if you wish—it will make a wonderful bouquet."

"Here is my card," I said. "Put that in it," and then I gave her the address and the hour. I wrote some little nonsense on the card—about melodies and voices that were akin to spring—and then I went back to the hotel to attend Madame.

A more bustling, aggressive little artist you would not want to find. She had much the irritable, artistic enthusiasm of Marcelle—not quite as much. That little French girl remained positively an astonishing figure to me, virile, hopeful, aggressive. She makes the ordinary dullards of the home look like stuffed mannequins—fish-worms as compared to glittering cobras. Madame Culp was bustling about when I called at eight-thirty—the concert was at nine—being danced attendance upon by three or four musical satellites who could not do enough for her. There was one little girl from Mayence I noticed—a dream of a Jewish girl, with slightly Ethiopian lips, high color in her cheeks and deep, rich, reddish-brown hair and blue eyes—who followed Madame Culp with positively adoring glances. There was something almost uncanny about it—perverted, I should say. There was another woman, or maiden, of thirty, the exact duplicate of a very remarkable woman editor whom I have known for years in New York, who was also caught in the toils of this woman's personality and swept along by her quite as one planet dislocates the orbit of another and makes it into a satellite. She had come all the way from Berlin.

"Oh, Madame Culp," she confided to me upon introduction, "—oh, wonderful! Wonderful! Such a voice! It is always like early spring to me." This woman had an attractive face, sallow and hollow, with burning, black eyes and rich, black hair. Her body was long and thin, supple and graceful. She also followed Madame Culp with those strange, questioning eyes. Life is surely pathetic. I love this atmosphere of intense, artistic enthusiasm.

When the last touches had been added to Madame's coiffure, throat, shoulders and face, a sprig of blossom of some kind inserted in her corsage, a flowing, whitish-gray opera cloak with silver filigree decorations thrown about the shoulders, she was finally ready. So busy was she, suggesting this and that to one and another of her attendants, that she scarcely saw me. Trust the artist to look after her art, to sacrifice everything to it. "Oh, there you are," she beamed finally. "Now, I am *quite* ready. Is the machine here, Marie? Oh, very good. And Herr Steiger! O-h-h!" this last to a well-known violinist who had arrived.

It turned out that there were two machines—one for the satellites and Herr Steiger, who was to play this evening, and one for Madame Culp, her maid and myself. We finally debouched from the hall and elevator and fussy lobby, where officers were still strolling to and fro, got into the machines and were away. Madame Culp was lost in a haze of artistic contemplation, with thoughts no doubt as to her program and her success. Still, she found time to crowd close to me and squeeze my hand. "Now maybe you will like my program better," she suggested. "In London it was not so goot. I haf to feel my audience iss—how you say?—with me. In Berlin and here and Dresden and Leipzig they like me. In England they do not know me." She sighed and looked out of the window. "Are you happy to be with me?" she asked naively.

"Quite," I replied.

When we reached the auditorium, we were ushered by winding passages into a very large greenroom—an artist's salon, as it were—where the various artists awaited their call to appear. It was already occupied by a half-dozen persons or more, the friends of Madame Culp: the local manager, his hair brushed aloft like a cockatoo; several musicians; the violinist, Herr Steiger; Godowsky, the pianist; and one or two others. They all greeted Madame Culp effusively.

"Oh, that was bad weather we had in Munich," I heard her say to someone. "I thought we should have scarcely any audience at all. But it was crowded. And so enthusiastic they were!"

There was some conversation in French here and there, and now and then in English. The room was fairly babbling with temperament.

It is always amusing to hear a group of artists talk. They are so fickle, make-believe, innocently treacherous, jealous, vainglorious, flattering. "Oh, yes, how splendid he was! That aria in C major—perfect! But you know I did not care so much for his rendering of the Pastoral Symphony—very weak in the allegro ma non troppo, very. He should not attempt that. It is not in his vein—not the thing he does best—" fingers lifted very suggestively and warningly in the air.

Some artist and his wife did not agree (very surprising); the gentleman was the weaker instrument in this case.

"Oh!" it was Madame Culp talking, "now that is too-oo ridiculous. She must go places, and he must go along as manager! Herr Spink wrote me from

Hamburg that he would not have him around. She has told him that he affects her playing. Still he goes! It is too-oo much. They will not live together long."

"Where is Herr Schochmann?" (This being incident number three.) "Isn't he leading tonight? But they promised me! No, I will not sing then! It is always the way! I know him well! I know why he does it! It is to annoy me! He doesn't like me, and he disappoints me!"

Great business of soothing the principal singer of the evening, the manager explaining volubly, friends offering soothing comment. More talk about other artists, their wives, flirtations, successes, failures.

In the midst of this, by some miscalculation, in came my flowers (they were to have been delivered over the footlights after the end of the song). They looked like a fair-sized bush being introduced.

"Oh!" exclaimed Madame Culp when the card was examined and they were offered to her, "how heavenly! Great God, it is a whole tree! Oh—wonderful, wonderful! And this be-yutiful sentiment! Oh-h-h!" More ogling and smiling and tender sighs. I could have choked with amusement. It was all such delicious by-play. Quite the thing that artists expect and must have. She threw away the sprig of jasmine she wore and, drawing out a few sprigs of the lilac, carried those instead. "Now I can sing," she exclaimed.

Deep breathings, sighs, ecstatic expressions.

Her turn came, and, as I have said, I heard delicious singing. She had her following. They applauded her to the echo. Her two female satellites sat with me, and little Miss Meyer, as I will call her, of Mayence fairly groaned with happiness at times. Truly Madame Culp was good to look upon—quite queenly, very assured, winding her admirers around her little finger, as it were. At the end of it all came a fifteen or twenty minute ovation, during which she sang the song I liked, looking emotionally down upon me. It was beautiful, truly.

While we were in the greenroom talking between sections of the program and intermediate soloists, I said to her, "You are coming with me to supper, of course?"

"Of course! What else did you expect?"

"Are there any other restaurants besides those of the Frankfurter Hof?"

"I think not."

"How will you get rid of your friends after the performance?"

"Oh, I shall send them away. You take a table anywhere you like and I will come. Make it twelve o'clock."

We were bundled back to the hotel—flowers, wraps, maid, satellites—and I went to see about the supper. In fifteen minutes it was ready, and in twenty minutes more she came, quite rosy, all stirred up temperamentally, inquisitive, defensive, coquettish, eager. We are all greedy animals at best—the finer the greedier. The whole world is looking to see what life will give it to eat—from ideas, emotions, enthusiasms, down to grass and potatoes. We are organized appetites, magnificent, dramatic, pathetic at times, but appetites just the same. The greater the appetite, the more magnificent the spectacle. Satiety is deadly, discouraging. The human stomach is the grand central organ—life in all its amazing, subtle, heavenly, pathetic ramifications has been built up around that. The most pathetic thing in life is a hungry man; the most stirringly disturbing thing a triumphant, greedy one. Madame Culp sat down to our cold chicken, salad, champagne and coffee with beaming, bird-like eyes.

"Oh, it is so good to be with you after all," she declared engagingly. "I was so afraid when I wrote you from Munich that you would not get my letter. That telegram of yours—it was cold. I like that. And I was so glad to get it. I can't tell you how many times I read it going on the train from Munich to Leipzig."

"Yes, but you didn't answer my letter," I suggested.

"You don't understand. It is so hard to tell you. I can't tell you how you appeal to me just now. It is not quite in the way you think. I must talk to you. You are so warm, so sympathetic, so human."

"Quite so," I said, quite wearily, "but how does that help me?"

"How do you mean? Don't you like that? Aren't you pleased?"

"Pleased, to be sure, but—you didn't answer my letter just the same."

"How shall I begin? It is so hard to tell things. Do you know Mr. Grant Richards well?"

"Oh, fairly well. I have known him in a general literary way for ten years or more—all of that, I should say."

"But you don't know anything much about his private life—socially, I mean—the kind of man he is?"

"I have certain things to go by," I replied conservatively. "Yes, I know a little something about him."

"You like him, don't you?"

"I am very fond of him," I corrected. "We can love or admire without always approving everything. I am very fond of the man. I think he is very remarkable, really a great man in his way."

"He is so fond of you," she assured me. "Oh, he admires you so much. What you think must have considerable weight with him. You are like him in so many ways—and so different. He is more—how do you say?—" (she gave the German word for executive) "—you are more the artist."

"A very good definition," I said. "He is executive, quite. But what about it?"

I should say that nearly all of this conversation was a patchwork of German and English, our sentences alternating rapidly in one tongue and the other.

"Where did you first meet him?" she asked.

"In New York."

This holding of the conversation closely to Grant Richards was one of those curious sex developments which interested and at the same time irritated me. It occurred to me for the moment that I was being used in some way, a suspicion which events did and did not really justify but which held for the time being.

"You never knew his wife?"

"No, I only know of her."

"How much do you know?"

"Not so very much. That she is not living with him—that he takes care of the children. What most anyone would know."

"Do you think he is still fond of her?"

"I should judge so—but really, you know I like Grant Richards a lot. I am afraid he would not take it in good part to have his affairs discussed."

"But between us. He is so fond of you. And as for me—I wonder if this will make you angry—he has been the one man in the world I wanted. He is so uncertain, though. He does not satisfy me. I have wanted him to love me, but—"

"Good Lord!" I said to myself wearily, "This settles me! Another full confession of a mistress because I am sympathetic! Farewell to Madame Culp!"

"That was three or four months ago," she went on. "Since I left England, I have been trying to forget him. After all, he is not what I want. His mind is too general, distant. He is fond of me, but that is not enough. I must have affection. And now you have come along. I don't know whether you will understand me, but I am sure if I had just a little time, I could be just as fond of you. I don't know whether I understand myself at times. But oh, I am so glad you waited for me!"

I had to smile. I know so much about the vagaries of human temperament that nothing really surprises me anymore. If the sun were scientifically demonstrated to be a highly-polished brass plate, it would be one and the same thing to me. There is no placing humanity or nature, or even suggestively indicating its vagaries. Nothing but a hypnotizing illusion ever fixes anybody in anything. Life sips and slips and gurgles and murmurs like a moving stream about our feet. It is fluid. It has apparently no verities and no demonstrable stabilities. For a little while—within the memory of man—that is apparently the best that can be said for it.

"You don't really want me," I said. "It's a case of any port in a storm. But tell me one thing anyhow, why didn't you answer my letter? You might have done that, anyhow."

"I'll tell you why. Don't be mad at me. I'll tell you all about it. I have been Grant Richards's mistress. I fell in love with him the first time I saw him. It was at one of my first concerts in London. I knew we should come together the first time I saw him. Then we did. Well, when I left England this last time, I was angry. I wanted to get rid of him—to cure myself, because I do not think we can ever be anything to each other. I think I have—almost—already. When I first saw you in London, we were quarreling. I thought then how fond of you I might have been. Still, you were his friend. I thought once I would get you to come to see me. Then I changed my mind. After I left, I decided not to have anything to do with him anymore and so with you neither. You would remind me of him. Then he wrote me, asking why I didn't invite you, and I didn't even answer the letter for a while. When I did, I gave some excuse. He wrote me that in a way I had rather compromised myself." She laughed.

"Fine!" I commented.

"When I got your note a month ago, I thought I would do nothing. Then I got to thinking about you, and I wrote for your address. It came a few days ago, and, do you know, I was terrified because I thought I was going to miss you! Oh, that nice, cold telegram! Then you answered, and here we are."

"Yes, but you don't want me," I replied, interested, amused, attracted, repelled by this frank confession. To say the least, it was naive, delightful.

"Oh, I don't know. Sometimes I think I am going to go wild about you—then—" She stopped and fixed me with wide, curious eyes. "You appeal to something in me. I get passionate when I get near you. I feel a kind of vibration when I am with you—do you?"

"Yes."

"What is that, do you think?"

"How should I know? I don't understand life," I said. "I know I like you."

"Oh!"—she shook her head and stamped her foot.

"But you will come to Zehlendorf, won't you?"

"What is the use?" I said. "There is really no use."

"Oh, do come. It would be such a pleasure. You will give me that much time. Be nice to me. Wait until I come back. I will be back by the 26th. Can't you wait that long? Berlin is so interesting. Fräulein Förster will be so nice to you. I will write her. You can go in and out of the city every day in twenty minutes. There is a beautiful forest there. I should like you to see my dog Nana. Oh, she is so lovely. There is a beautiful lake there. You can walk. My husband will come home and will show you about. Then I will come."

"Yes, and then—?"

"Oh, then I will be very nice to you. I will sing and play for you, and we will walk and talk, and you can take me to Berlin. I am going to give a big concert there on the 29th. You can hear that. Then you will see what a following I have—oh, a big audience. I will do 'most anything you want me to!"

"Anything?"

"Yes, I think so. Please wait."

"But not here?"

"Oh, I am so excited. Would you want me to? Think of all I have just told you."

"I think not," I said, "but don't sit there and look at me that way. Don't touch my hand."

"How strange you are," she said. "You are not dangerous to me like that—yet. But, oh, I like you!"

"You're mad," I said.

"Why mad?"

"Because you are."

"Oh, no. Many people are like that."

"And your husband?" I said, going back to that peculiar figure. "Doesn't he suspect? What about him? Won't he?"

"Oh, my husband and I," she added lightly, "we have arranged all that long ago. We are good friends. He likes me very much. He helps me. But my artistic life—that is my own."

She began to stare and sigh and tease, and I thought once I should break through all this folderol and settle our relationship preemptorily or go on to Berlin without further ado and without waiting here, but she suggested so many sincere possibilities that I thought finally I would wait. She was going once more to London on the morrow. She would be singing in Leeds, Manchester, Liverpool, Glasgow. When she came back, all would be definitely over with her and Grant Richards, she said. Then—

It was such a curious psychologic and temperamental mix-up that I decided to wait. We finally came upstairs, and I thought of invading her rooms, maid or no maid, but since she seemed sincere in her doubts, I let it go. I am not sure to this day whether she would have preferred it otherwise or not.

CHAPTER LXXVI

The next day in Frankfort was spent—the major portion of it—in sounding out this very peculiar situation, for Madame Culp, who was leaving at two-thirty for England, was anxious that I should drive and lunch with her and in fact see her off, in order, I suppose, that this pleasant beginning might not come to an untimely end. Her house at Zehlendorf had to be secured on the long distance and instructions given Fräulein Förster as to how much attention was to be given me. She also sent a letter off post-haste to her husband. At eleven, after some other details, we set out for a drive in an automobile, ostensibly to see Frankfort. I saw little of it this way. The lady was in a cajoling mood. I could scarcely make her out. For one who was or had been anxious to secure the affection of Grant Richards, she was truly forgetful—flirtatious, coquettish, alluring. When she began petting me, as usual, I said to myself, "I am a fool to listen to this woman's protestations concerning her moods and affections. The next time the opportunity offers I shall make short work of her. It is probably too late here, but if I wait until she comes to Berlin!"

She kept smoothing my cheek and my hands and purring in a kittenish manner near my shoulder.

"You are an imp of satan," I said, and then I had to explain the exact force of that in German.

Frankfort, on the whole, is not a very interesting city—historically, architecturally, artistically. It is true that historically it has a record for various conclaves, and that Johann Wolfgang Goethe lived here, and that in the vicinity of the Römerberg and the old Cathedral there still exists as remarkable a collection of those odd, intricately-carved, exquisitely-paneled and generally be-florated and be-gabled houses which were the last products of medieval Teutonic wood-carving and house-building arts, but beyond that there is nothing. Nothing, I say, unless you agree with me that the social-intellectual aspects of the city, the astonishing force and virility of its modern mood and highly Americanized appearance of its streets, its people and its houses of business are something.

Frankfort is very much like Cleveland, Ohio. It has the same solid, aggressive commercial aspect. It is more virile than either Detroit or Buffalo, much less unique than Pittsburgh. An unimportant sleepy, seepy river, the Main, runs through it or past it—the most uncommercial section of the city is there—but aside from that it is smart, active, quick, thorough-looking and thoroughgoing, well-built and apparently well-managed. The new streets, which constitute the vast majority (the old medieval section being but a mere fragment), are laid out, American fashion, in rectangular lines, mile after mile, so that you get that same sense of order and system which you notice about the great majority of American cities. Its shops and stores are bright and smart. I saw more American-looking men and women; more up-to-date shops and stores; more bustle, go, emphasis, enthusiasm, innate physical force in Frankfort than I saw in any other portion of the continent or even in England, barring Manchester. There was real vigor, self-conviction, intensive thought, determination of purpose, hope, German love of life and love of love in the very air. You could feel it. It set you up, as the English say. It pulled you together. It made you feel that you were once more in a bustling, struggling, enthusiastic, eager, life-hungry world.

I make so much of this fact for the simple reason that nowhere in England outside of Liverpool, Manchester and Leeds (and not so much even in these); nowhere in France outside of Paris; nowhere in Italy or Switzerland that I saw, barring Milan—which is full of Germans, by the way—do you encounter this peculiarly aggressive, progressive, highly commercialized and decidedly American type of life. My American architect was right when he said the Germans are like the Americans. In the matters of commercial astuteness, love of order, love of the latest thing, they are like Americans—only I think in all minor things they do their work more thoroughly than we do. Their streets here in Frankfort, for instance, struck me as better paved, their houses better built. When I say better, I do not mean more artistically. The architectural aspect of a Frankfort street would be likely to strike an American as a little dull. Fifty years ago we built somewhat like they are now building. Then again, the Americans originated the high building, and I think that is very significant when you are considering a race's temperament. Chicago, so far back as 1885 (then a city of a little over 500,000), put up the first ten- and a little later the first thirteen-story building. Why? There was no essential commercial call for such a thing. The city had miles and miles of vacant land within easy reach. Soil conditions were unfavorable to such a structure, the ground below being both sandy and seepy; piles had to be driven. Yet this thing was done! Why?

City temperament, race temperament, a sense of grandeur—now that I am on that theme I should like to descant liberally, for the idea was with me all through Europe and my experiences in Germany, Holland and Belgium merely emphasized my opinions and conclusions.

My idea about life is this: that the most significant thing you can predicate of a man or a nation is his or its ability to do something new, virile, vigorous, forceful, exceptional—above all, artistic. A sense of grandeur in a nation is not necessarily architectural in its final outcome, and yet almost always it has so expressed itself. Greece had a sense of grandeur, and one need only suggest the wonder of the Acropolis to prove it. But aside from that, any perfect Greek temple, any fragment of a pediment, Nike with her outspread wings, the discus thrower, the Venus of Milo would prove it, if the vast welter of Greek fable, sun-lit clouds in a morning sky, did not. Before Greece was Chaldea and Assyria and Egypt, where Babylon and Nineveh and Karnak and Thebes materially justify the claim that a sense of grandeur was there. After Greece came Rome, and no one who has ever stood in the time-gnawed spaces of the Colosseum and the Baths of Caracalla would ever deny that Rome had a sense of grandeur. It reached to the furthermost confines of the Roman empire in camps, walls, memorial shafts and triumphal columns—that desire, because of an innate sense of grandeur, to time and death, "thus did I." In medieval Italy it appeared again, that desire to rear above the dead level of life and say, "Behold, I am not as other men." Alexander VI, his son Cesare Borgia, Julius II, Cosimo Medici (Pater Patriae), Francesco Sforza and Venetian grand dukes—how they fought with the welter of common things to rip from life the ability to do something significant. At Pisa, at Florence, at Venice, at Milan, behold a sense of grandeur in palaces, cathedrals, pictures, sculpture. These men did eagerly, mightily. They would not sink into the mud of time, be numbered with the uncounted thousands.

In Switzerland, outside of nature herself, the divine artificing mother, there is nothing to suggest a sense of grandeur—only a cap and bells, home-making art suitable for a village green. In Germany, aside from the same naive instinct lifted to baronial splendor in the medieval years, nothing. Music? Yes. That is Germany's undeniable claim. An amazing army? Truly. And these things suggest a sense of grandeur in Wagner and von Moltke and Bismarck at least, but when the army is defeated, as time will surely humble it, and Wagner is, mayhap, a superseded memory, what then? Will moldering art and architecture on German soil, by German hands, give man pause and reverence, the loving, pathetic reflection that such things must be? Alas, no, not yet. It has not come. I saw no *new* thing in Germany that might not well be spared, almost joyously spared. It is almost so in Holland and Belgium, architecturally speaking, as I found later. Collections of the old? Oh, yes, there are lovely collections. They represent the sense of grandeur of another day, and are worthy and priceless, but the architecture of the lowlands, unless one excepts the windmill, is unimportant.

When one comes to England, what is there? A native temperament, poetic in many respects, artistic, grand in its sense of government, civic privilege, the sense of Empire, but architecturally only vaguely expressed. Oxford? I have it well in mind. Canterbury? It is adorable, to me England's surest claim to artistic supremacy. St. Paul's? It is a botch, full of the trash of mistaken architectural ideals, however imposing in size. Salisbury? A dream come true—a little dream. Westminster Abbey? A pale reflection of greater efforts elsewhere and choked by memorial trash. England, in spite of a thousand beautiful objects, has not done as Rome did, as Florence did, as Venice did, as Greece did. She has not one cathedral that approaches S. Maria Nascente at Milan, St. Mark's at Venice, St. Paul's or St. Peter's at Rome, for richness of material; not one that suggests the artistic selection of Pisa; the glory of interior design and beauty of St. Paul Without The Walls in Rome; not one that has the architectural sweep and spirit of Amiens. St. Paul's in London, in spite of its enormous dome, is heavy and tasteless. Westminster Abbey is crowded to suffocation with botches of tombs. The Tower of London is a naive fortress. For the rest there is much that is quaint, lovely, poetic, tender—such as the Houses of Parliament, the Royal Palaces, the Inns of Court and the like—but by no stretch of the imagination could these be called grand.

Will we turn to America? Illogical, disreputable, indifferent as we so often are, our streets unpaved or badly paved; our skylines disorganized (to accommodate every householder's whim), our admirations fighting with our pockets, eager, easygoing, elate, we have it—that strange indefinable something, a sense of grandeur. It is a transcontinental railroad that the world wants or needs—vast, staggering enterprises! Certainly, we will build them for you—six or seven, if you wish—and have done so. Cathedrals? You shall have fifty, in as many years, though we may never look inside of them. Bridges? There are none such as span the American rivers. Canals? We can build them too. And on the basic mud of dirty Chicago, dirty and smoky, we have reared such a phantasmagoria of commercial towers as may not elsewhere be seen within the same area, wander where you will.

And as for New York, it is the giant city of a world, a young, fighting cub with a wallop that has already staggered the eyes. They were building the Woolworth Building when I left—it was finished shortly after I returned—and the Singer Building, the Metropolitan Tower and the Pennsylvania Station were accomplished facts. The Capitol at Washington is an old story. But as I left New York, going down the bay, the structures of the city reared up as a cloudy mountain to the west, and never till it reappeared again did I see anything to equal it. Amiens? Rouen? Milan? St. Peter's? Yes, they are wonderful. The suggestion given by the ruins of the Baths of Caracalla is staggering to the initiated. But anyone who has walked the canyons of the financial district or stood in that civic pit known as City Hall Square and looked aloft at the Woolworth Building will forget the wonder of the age that produced it. Say what you will; only a sense of grandeur could father that.

I stood one day, not long since, in the central waiting room of the Pennsylvania Station at 32nd Street in New York and saw through the open lattices of a lunette window high above a flock of pigeons fly in and out, leaving in their flight not so much as a whisper of their wings. They looked like grayish-white petals fluttering about. And the arches and vaulting under which they fluttered sheltered a room as rich in marble, as ornate in design, as spacious as one would wish to see. It identified itself at once, as it always has and does, with my sense of grandeur. It may be new, utilitarian, purely commercial, but it is grand nevertheless. The Americans have that—a sense of grandeur. It is their great distinction. They have learned to do nobly, amazingly, without let or hindrance, that which civically or individually, in a spirit of bravado, vainglory, self-identification or what you will, they see fit to do at all. That is a sense of grandeur.

But to return to Frankfort. This, in spite of American directness and aggressiveness, is just what is lacking. You miss it everywhere in Germany. The local opera house is a trashy repetition of an old idea. The central station for the receipt and dispatch of trains is as commonplace as anything in Europe. The store buildings are good, but like store buildings everywhere. The principal church—the *Dom*—is fit only for an ash-heap. There you have it. Yet I liked Frankfort.

I liked it better than most cities that I saw, for unlike most European cities, it seemed to be fully alive to its opportunities. Life seems all before the people of Frankfort. They walk and look and act as though they had something to strive for. Life is not over for them; it has just begun. If they have no great cathedral, they may have one; if they have no tall buildings, it is just possible they will arrive tomorrow. If they have no truly significant gallery, one may someday be gathered. That is more than you can say for the majority of European cities, and you feel that it is a healthy, invigorating atmosphere in which to be. It made me feel that I could really go on and do a few more things before adding myself to the mortality statistics. Italy, Switzerland, England, even France will not give you precisely that sensation. They weigh a little on the soul. They induce, at times, poetic melancholy.

But to continue. Madame was to be off on the two o'clock train. She grew apparently more feeling as the hour approached. We returned to the hotel and had lunch together, and by two o'clock all was arranged. I was to go directly to Zehlendorf and wait. Her husband was to show me something of Berlin. She would arrive in nine or ten days at the latest. We went to the train together, just we two. The maid and satellites had been dispatched in advance. I commiserated with her on the necessity of departure; she seemed sorry to have to go, just now. She sang me several pretty songs with all the accessories of feeling so easily available to the artist, then the train backed in and finally out, and she blew me a final kiss from the vestibule of one of the coaches. The next morning at eight-thirty I left for Berlin.

CHAPTER LXXVII

Let no one disparage the Germans in my presence. I prefer to do that myself. And I can say as much for as against them. They are a great nation. I think I liked the train ride from Frankfort to Berlin as well as any. It was raining all the way, sometimes pouring, but that did not detract from the distinction of the German cities that we passed—Bebra, Erfurt, Halle and others. What interested me was that it started clear and fair, charmingly spring-like, with soft clouds only flecking a blue sky, and ended with alternate showers and shines; the landscape, for the main, was very flat and sandy, presenting charmingly lowery aspects at times. I think anyone who reconnoiters Germany, even by train rides only, will lose the significance of it if they do not catch the note of rich animal appetites everywhere. It may be that these are involved solidly with conventional nations, though I doubt it. A statistician engaged at the time that I was in Germany in the work of reducing certain German health and birth statistics to order informed me that fifteen out of every one hundred children born in Berlin were born out of wedlock—a slight suggestion as to the German temperament. My own father, thoroughly moral and Christian, highly conservative, had thirteen children in wedlock—another indication.

One need only look at these lusty men and women, ruddy-faced boys and girls who fill the streets, crowd the cars, greet you on trains and elsewhere, to realize that there is a full-blooded animality here, combined with (at times, and in many instances) a sluggishness of mind or body or both, which vents itself in a feverish, unintellectual sex-wallowing which produces much of the atmosphere which one feels. Germany is obviously rich in animality. Its men and women look it. They eat a great deal, drink a great deal and do other things in proportion. If you do not feel this, you are not feeling Germany, and if you do not recognize it, you are a poor observer. They think nothing of it, and I see no harm in such a condition. After the feeble animality of certain classes of Americans—the Sunday-School-Christian-Endeavor religious-so-called educational variety—it is a great relief. We are all animals. What harm in being good ones?

The afternoon before I left Frankfort, after Madame Culp had gone, I accidentally, in rambling about the city in the afternoon sun, chanced upon one of those sights which delighted and in a way suggested Germany to me. I was strolling in the vicinity of a small park when, hearing a sharp rumbling or rather whirring noise nearby, I fancied that a heavy auto-truck was about to turn a corner, although I did not see where it could come from at the moment, there being no immediate corner. Hearing it nearer still and not being able to locate it, I chanced to raise my eyes, and there, high in the heavens, a lovely spectacle, a long, soft, white cocoon floating against a dome of blue, was one of the Zeppelin airships, the seventh to have been experimentally constructed, I think, swinging in a great circle over Frankfort, making a round trip journey from Dresden or Leipzig. The Germans no doubt are as used to that spectacle as we in America are to a mono- or bi-plane floating bird-like in the sky; nevertheless, it created a great deal of excitement. People stopped everywhere the moment they recognized the sound and stood at gaze. Whole families hung out of windows. Vehicles stopped. It was truly impressive. I recalled, as I looked, the number of mishaps that had followed in the train of this inventor's efforts to perfect a passenger-carrying dirigible of sufficient stability to permit a scheduled passenger service and of his repeated and, in many instances, tragic failures. To see it turning thus grandly in the air, a veritable *Mauretania* for size, typified for me that German persistence which has accomplished so much in science, philosophy, religion (I am thinking of Luther) and art (Wagner, Goethe). You would think, after six such failures or mishaps as befell the six preceding Zeppelins, no seventh would have been built, but here it was, sailing in the sky, and German money and German confidence and German hope against hope had put it there. I watched it as it sped feather-like into the eye of the evening sun, and when it had become a mere whitish dot, a dove or a pigeon, I turned. It seemed to me that the spirit of the new Germany was typified there and that a long story of progress and achievement was to follow.

On the train with me was a crusty old German professor who amused me greatly by his innate, though in my case only vaguely indicated, cantankerousness. He got on at Frankfort and, being assigned to my section, stared at me and my several pieces of luggage, rather freely distributed, in a hard, contentious way. I at once put them in better order and gave him ample space. He was a little man, brownish-gray as to hair and beard, very spare of body, very sharp of eye, a fine bracing nose, a good chin and mouth, heavy, bushy, horny-looking eyebrows and well-tonsured, slightly truncated whiskers and mustachios. His large, heavy gold watch chain, most individual, defiant and characteristic; his loose, good shoes, made to fit his feet, do you see; his heavy, gold-rimmed spectacles and collection of papers, manuscripts and solid scientific works carried in a thick, black portfolio of good leather, identified him at once as a rather prosperous professor, savant, philosopher, scientist, anything you like. I had opened the air-vents for a little air, but he promptly closed them without a by-your-leave, if-I-may, sorry or anything. I smiled sweetly, for I know the type—my dear departed father, for one—but he only examined me anew as much as to say "Protest if you dare." Then he stretched himself out on the opposite seat (ordinarily intended for four people) and began reading his papers. There was one redeeming feature which won me to him completely. His nose was the least bit—just the faintest trace—purplish from good *schnapps*. A German savant who loves his *schnapps* is not to be despised.

With him then for a companion, turning ever and anon an inquiring eye on me, I journeyed to Berlin. Dear old soul—I read a thousand hearty German traits behind him. At Fulda I asked him the name of the town. He jerked like an automaton. "Fulda," he said—no more. I fancied him adding, "Upstart American, as usual, no reverence!" At Wartha I asked if some distant castles, visible on a hill, were very old. "Twelfth century," I think he said. Then he sank his short beard into his chest. I was really glad that he was so comfortable and prosperous. I love to see the selfish, individual thinker really well-placed in this world's goods. They are so important to the mental progress of the world.

Weimar, where Goethe lived; Apolda, full of great, new, red factories; Saalfeld, suggestive of older days; Naumburg, crowded with railway crossings and smoking chimneys; all went by in a flash. We were running swiftly, smoothly, in and out of delicious pine forests which came in great black stretches wet with the wind-driven rains, and showing now and then dark, almost black, pools of water. Much of the art of Arnold Böcklin was suggested thereby. The first windmills I had seen in Europe, the windmills that suggest only Holland to me, began to appear. Gone completely was that lovely, subtle, artistic individuality of Italy, now fully six hundred miles away, and in its place this engrossing, entirely different-minded Germany.

As I rode, I fell to figuring out for myself just what the essential differences between the Italian and Teuton are—roughly speaking, of course. It occurred to me at once that the principal optical difference was of course one of size and physical floridity, which of course bespeaks a difference in chemistry and, to a certain extent, soul stuff. The next thought was that the Italians seemed more subtle—not only the Italians of history but the strange, dark Italians of Venice, Florence and Rome of today. They looked to me not so much more mentally incisive as mentally crafty, their minds meditating strange ways and deeds. The Germans, on the whole—all that I had seen of them—seemed to me much more forthright, direct, outspoken, obvious in their intentions. You could tell, in a way, what a German was intending to do; you could count on his love of order, system, theory, government. I could never feel that about the Italians. They reminded me of very uncertain, very undecipherable chemical compounds. They seemed to me to be too highly individual, not really nationally welded. They may love Italy, but do they not love individuality more? And then those dark, glistening, uncertain eyes. Subtlety seemed to me the next great difference, the matter of subtlety that makes all the difference between a crow and a hen, a fox and a bulldog, a snake (I do not use the simile disparagingly) and a snail. The terrible nations and the highly artistic ones have been almost uniformly subtle. The prosperous and constructive ones have been comparatively dull. Both attributes have their great value.

But when one thinks of Italy, with its Cosimo and Lorenzo and Alessandro Medici, its Francesco and Caterina Sforzas, its Alexander VIs, Cesare Borgias, Julius IIs and the like, the Teutonic counterparts are not visible. Bismarck was clever but he was more a mailed fist than a master of chicane; von Moltke was a military battering ram; Frederick the Great had some Italian subtlety, but he does not darkle with the same mystery, subtlety, cruelty, ruthlessness that gives an oily, midnight blackness to the souls of so many of the Italians. Perhaps times are changing. Perhaps the world will never see their like again. Perhaps? Who is to answer for what the universe will or will not produce?

In the dining car I saw one of the most beautiful women I have ever seen, and solidly German. Her body must have been as sound and hard as ivory. She had a Greek face—the straight, delicate, Greek nose, the youthful, moodless, anticipatory Greek mouth—and rich, very rich, reddish-brown hair. A brown-and-gold velvet cap, not unlike the Phrygian, set down about her ears and forehead in peculiarly graceful lines, and her shapely body, clad in brown velvet, was erect and forceful with health, vigor, life-loving determination. Her husband—I took him to be such—was a strong, broad-shouldered, lusty German, who seemed well suited to her physical vigor. They were lost in intimate conversation and enjoyment of their food.

The sight of this woman emphasized the whole women question in Germany for me. The Teutons are so different from the French, the Italians, the English and the Americans that I studied her for my answer. Mrs. Armstrong had told me that all the German women she saw in Munich, Dresden, Leipzig and Vienna were gross—gross! gross!! She could only think of them as Franz von Stuck has shown one of his nude white Venuses, lolling with a satyr in not lascivious but gross animal dalliance. She was ready to grant their possession of all the family virtues, but their lives were spent, the fortunate ones, she thought, in a wallow of animality. Be that as it may, again I see no harm in it. I am a profound admirer of Rubens's beefy women.

After Botticelli's pale perfections I like them best. They are racial, typical, altogether delightful. The souls of them are as good as the souls of any women, with the added charm, for me, that they have a voiceless mistiness of mind that only shadows itself forth in vague emotional mirages, far beyond the realms of expression.

Who gives a damn for the absolutely accurate in art or temperament, anyhow? I despise it. It is not art. The greatest thing in the world is suggestion—the incomplete thing which gives the mind free scope to weave, weave, weave and dream. That is why I go wild over that suggestive reverie of Lorenzo de' Medici, Duke of Urbino, in the new sacristy of San Lorenzo at Florence; over the suggestive, non-interpretable figures of *Day* and *Night, Dawn* and *Dusk;* over the winged Victory, headless and impaired; over the armless Venus, whose ultimate beauty must always be guessed. In the Museo delle Terme at Rome, amid the unguessable splendors of the Baths of Diocletian, facing so often only the fragments of ancient perfections, it was the fragments, the suggestions of possible perfections, that were the perfect things and the only perfect things. Who is to carve beauty? Who to confine for us its ultimate reaches? Has Pegasus been stalled? Ye gods! Farewell to the wondrous thought of him in the free winds of heaven! The dark is not light, and day cannot substantiate its mysterious charm. Beauty is not known: her sanctuary not yet rifled. She is not trailing yet a shining captive beside the triumphal chariot of any artist. Only when her hidden wonders are suggested; only when, in the art of a wild grapevine, perchance in the wind's fingers upon water, the dawn's faint misty palaces, her presence is suggested, the faintest swish of her fancied wings conceived—then—then—

Ah, yes, who is to suggest her lofty realms or to approach save in sandaled simplicity and ashen gray the ultimate sacristy of her mysterious temple?

The charming woman sitting before me was the best of all the Germans (female) I saw in Germany. In Frankfort, Mayence, Coblenz, Mayen, I had seen German women in plenty, but this one was quite as good as Germany need do. More would be inflaming. The women of Frankfort were—a fair percentage of them—reasonably handsome, Amazonian in their build, but far, far from being ungraceful. In my judgment the average English woman has no beauty at all—absolutely none. In the main, they look like hall-racks hung with discarded garments. I am not talking about the perfections which are to be found everywhere. The women of France were, to a high percentage, chic, quick, feminine, alluring. No emancipation of women for them. They seek to rule in another way. The women of Italy, such as I saw at several balls, the carnival in Rome, the afternoon teas at the Excelsior, several receptions and so on, were richly temperamental, occasionally graceful, soft and semi-sensual, but not ravishingly beautiful. The percentage of real physical and mental charm, it seemed to me, was noticeably low. Maria Bastida was as attractive as any that I saw, and she was not fully Italian. In Switzerland I saw few women. Here in Germany another standard impressed itself upon me, a type of beauty that with increasing German power and prosperity is likely to become memorable. Madame Culp, who was Dutch by birth, was not a patch on some of these women. The German woman's temperament, I am sure, is not as yet inclined to force itself into the arena of life. German prosperity, wealth and ambition are demanding of her a greater elegance and subtlety than she has hitherto known, but as yet these delineate themselves upon her in grateful simplicity. She wears them sweetly. The eyes of her—at best or worst—are still soft, moody, uncertain, melancholy. She is trying hard to be proud and vain, but at heart she is a fatalist, and her inmost consciousness bids her be humble. As contrasted with the American women—proud, petted smarties that they are—she would not even seem interesting perhaps, but I am convinced that at heart and artistically she is their equal. Her day has not quite dawned yet. Her hour is still to strike. But when it does, German art, German literature, German drama may well bestir themselves. There are great sex epics coming out of Germany. And what epic is there that has not the love of women as its base?

CHAPTER LXXVIII

Berlin, when I reached it, first manifested itself in a driving rain. If I laugh at it forever and ever as a blunderheaded, vainglorious, self-appreciative city, I shall always love it too, for it is a great city, full of moods, dreams, sorrows, despairs. Paris has had its day and will no doubt have others; New York is having its, with more to come; London is content with an endless, conservative day; Berlin's is to come and come brilliantly. The blood is there and the hope and the moody, lustful, Wagnerian temperament.

I saw it first jogging down Unter den Linden from the Bahnhof (station) Friedrichstrasse to Cook's Berlin agency in Unter den Linden, while seated in a moderately comfortable closed cab behind as fat a horse and driver as one would wish to see. And from there, still farther along Unter den Linden and through the Wilhelmstrasse to Leipziger Strasse and the Potsdamer Bahnhof, I saw more of it. Oh, the rich guttural value of the German *-platz*es and *-strasse*s and *-ufer*s and *-damm*s! They make up a considerable portion of your city atmosphere for you in Berlin. You just have to get used to them, just as you have to accept the *fabriks* and the *restaurations* (isn't that the limit!) and the *weinhandlungs* and all the other *-ichs*, *-ungs*, *-bergs*, *-brückes*, until you sigh for the French *-ries*, Italian *-rias* and the English-American *-rys*. However.

I think that among the first things that impressed me were these: All Berlin streets, seemingly, were wide; five stories was the average height for buildings; everything (literally *everything*) was American new—and newer; and the cabbies were the largest, fattest, most broad-backed, most wide-bottomed and *dutchiest*-looking creatures I have ever beheld. Oh, the marvel of those glazed German cabby hats with the little hard rubber decorations on the side! Somebody should write a wild-eyed panegyric quick. Those heavy, somnolent, red-faced and, I am satisfied, reasonably honest and good-natured creatures were too individual and characterful for words. Nowhere else in Europe is there anything like these cabbies. They do not stand—they sit, heavily and spaciously, alone.

If you imagine for one minute that I did not like Berlin from the very beginning, you are greatly mistaken. The faithful Baedeker, hard-headed, facty, incorruptible, even though his heart may be truly Teutonic, has little to say for Berlin. Art? It is almost all in the Kaiser-Friedrich-Museum in the vicinity of the Kupfergraben, and as for public institutions or spots of great historic interest, they are a dreary and negligible list. But nevertheless and notwithstanding, Berlin appealed to me instantly as one of the most interesting and forceful of all the cities, and that solely because it is new, crude, youthful, human, growing wildly, feverishly, unbelievably, and growing in a distinct and individual way.

None of your smart, light-stepping Parisian atmosphere here—not any, thank you. They want nothing particularly Parisian in Berlin—that is, they do and they don't. They would like to be another Paris, a finer Paris, if you will, in a solid, aggressive, Teutonic way, but nothing more than that. Imagine it—a Paris full of Germans! And they think right now that Berlin is better than Paris, truly. Help! Police! Call out the reserves! The mere thought is too much. Yet they have achieved and are achieving something totally distinct and worthwhile—a new place to go—and after a while, I haven't the slightest doubt, thousands and even hundreds of thousands of travelers will go there. But for many and many a day, the sensitive and artistically inclined will not admire it.

My visit to Cook's brought me a mass of delayed mail, which cheered me greatly. My old German professor, after finding that I was moderately non-obstreperous, condescended to advise me as to how to get to the Potsdamer Bahnhof and Zehlendorf. It was now raining pitchforks, but my bovine driver, who looked somehow like a segment of a wall, managed to bestow my trunk and bags in such a fashion that they were maintained dry, and off we went. I had a preconceived notion that Unter den Linden was a magnificent avenue lined shadily with trees and crowded with palaces. Nothing could have been more erroneous. The trees are few and insignificant, the palaces entirely wanting. It is a very wide business street (the Avenue de l'Opéra of Paris, let us say, or Bond Street of London) lined with four-, five- and six-story buildings—hotels, shops, restaurants, newspaper offices—and filled with a parading throng which I should say is looking principally to see what it can see, but it is not very attractive, not handsome. At one end it gives into an area known as the Lustgarten, crowded with palaces, art galleries, the Berlin Cathedral, the Imperial Opera House, and what not; at the other end (it is only about a mile long) into the famous Berlin Tiergarten, formerly a part of the imperial (Hohenzollern) hunting forest. I am telling you quickly what it took me days to discover. But Unter den Linden, as I saw it this day and afterwards, was principally a disappointment.

The region or suburban area to which I was bound was that which lies between Berlin and Potsdam, the latter being a suburb of Berlin and not more than twenty miles away. Zehlendorf, a handsome and somewhat exclusive suburban section, is on one of those many little lakes or "seas" ("Says," the Germans pronounce them) which surround Berlin in every direction. This whole territory is adjacent to the Baltic Sea. It is flat and sandy, wonderfully sandy, and set with wonderful groves of pines—tall, yellow-shafted specimens which carry a lovely mass of evergreen needles at the top and lend, it seems to me, a peculiar freshness to the atmosphere. After the late March rain in which I arrived, it grew cold and in a few days snowed again, which will give you some slight idea of the climate. Yet the air, though chilly, was not essentially damp but rather dry and bracing. It is just the atmosphere, it seems to me, for a truly great city.

Zehlendorf, when I reached there, made a distinct impression on me, for it was so new, clean, fresh, well-built—much superior to the average English or American suburb. What a charming place it turned out to be! It was not far, as I have said, from a famous public forest or reserve of pines, one of the most pleasing of public preserves and playgrounds I have ever known, and different. It was on a small lake with two or three others in the immediate vicinity. Not far from here, the Havel, a river which connects with the Spree, which in turn intersects Berlin and gives access to boats to and from the Baltic, widens out into the form of a very considerable lake and provides an immense sandy bathing beach and room for all sorts of aquatic sports. Apparently it is a vicinity destined to a wealthy form of suburban life and offering the principal avenue of Berlin's development for years to come.

I was so pleased with the peculiar and individual type of suburban architecture present that I made a note of it. I had always heard that German architects, particularly the architects of Berlin, were achieving something new in the way of apartment and suburban residence architecture, and I was not disappointed in what I saw here. Evidently the men who are building the better grades of German, and particularly Berlin, suburban residences have drawn heavily on the old medieval idea of decoration, but with severe modern variations. The old floridity of design has not been entirely dispensed with, but it has been applied much more sparingly. The conical tower or pinnacle, the outward-mounting wall or bay, the peaked and heavily gabled roof and the rococo, fruity, grapey, cupidy form of relief and decoration are still in force, but not so fulsomely. The moderns are not anxious to be florid. They desire to get a pleasing, compact, moderately ornate effect, and they get it. The houses are plainly as roomy as any other houses of this class anywhere, and of course they have all the modern conveniences, even some that have not come into general use in America as yet. I refer particularly to vacuum cleaning.

The particular suburban residence to which I was bound was a pleasing little thing. It had white-cream walls, a red-and-green roof of tiles and slate, pretty brick-red shutters with ornamental bouquets of flowers painted on them and a brownish-red fence or wall. The effect, because of a plenitude of brownish-shafted, green-topped pines in the vicinity, was exquisite. I had to applaud the discrimination and taste of the architect who built it.

And what a pleasant little ménage it proved to be. The housekeeper-secretary-manager and general official factotum, who had, as she subsequently told me, formerly been connected with a musical agency in Berlin and had known von Bülow, Joachim, Rubinstein and others, was really a delightful and discriminating person—a little old, say fifty, and resigned now, alas, no doubt to a career of usefulness and service, but so polite, courteous, tactful, genial and helpful. She would have to be to hold her position with Madame Culp. When I arrived she was at the gate to greet me—a small, thin, wiry, dark little woman with deliciously intelligent and inquiring eyes, shrewd and canny, and with a sense of humor, who immediately took my fancy.

"Herr Dreiser?" she queried.

"I am he," I replied, "worse luck!"

"Oh, what a bad day to be introduced to our lovely Zehlendorf! How unfortunate! It is usually so lovely. But tomorrow it will be fine. It is sure to be. Then you will see. Now you must come right in. I have telegrams and letters and telephone messages from Madame Culp. She wants me to be sure to make you comfortable. Your room is ready. We will have some tea right away. This is Nana, her pet dog. Down, Nana! Oh, such a cheerful dog she is, so temperamental! And all the young men dogs, they admire her so much. Oh, she is so very popular! They stand outside and admire the walls of the house all day long. But it is a good sign if she likes you. Some people she recoils from dreadfully. A true artist dog."

I had to smile at Fräulein Förster, an old maid, as the "Fräulein" implied.

I entered. A charming little house, warm and cozy and tastefully furnished in part in an old mission, old Flemish manner, with sharp variations and modifications. The music room, for instance, was rather more Sheraton-like than anything else. The dining room likewise. The breakfast room, library, reception room and floral bay were old mission or Flemish, the bathroom snow-white with open plumbing. No English bathroom here. All was warm and cozy with steam heat, gilded radiators, hot and cold water, electric light, telephone and a mail service apparently every hour or less. It was utterly charming.

And Madame Culp's room! A bouquet of early tulips was on the table. There were a few books in evidence, a charmingly recessed nook for the bed, with flowered chintz curtains to shut out the light and a pink silk coverlet. My writing desk was all in order, plentifully supplied with paper, envelopes, even stamps. A three-armed, silver candlestick was present to give me rest if I wearied of incandescent lamps. The bath was at my elbow, the large, deep wardrobe cleared out for my clothes. Fräulein Förster was so solicitous.

"Now, you must tell me what I can do. Aside from wanting to be very nice to you myself, Madame Culp will want to know whether I have been. She will ask me—she will ask you."

"You mustn't trouble," I said. "It is so plain that I am going to spend a happy week or so here. It is charming—those pines over the way."

I paused to look at a rich, dark grove, lowering in the rain.

"Oh, you should see them in the sunlight! In the morning they are—oh, so blue, so brown, so green! It is wonderful! And the thrushes, and the crows! Do crows annoy you?"

"Not at all."

"We have plenty of them here."

Just then I heard one giving vent to a deep, German, guttural caw.

"Plainly those are German crows," I said.

How comfortable I was made I need not say. For the time I was there the house was mine. Herr Merten was not present when I arrived, was not expected for several days, and so I was permitted or compelled to follow my own sweet will; Fräulein Förster and the maid, or cook, or both—she seemed both—were most anxious to see that my every whim was consulted, and so in a way I was quite a lord here.

It is interesting to find, wherever you go in this world, that homes are much the same. I was peculiarly interested in this one because, as I have said, the relations of Grant Richards and Madame Culp interested me, to begin with, and then her uncertain feeling for me and the exceptional position of her husband had strange weight also. I was very curious to see what sort of a man he would prove to be—not much of a one, I fancied, but I awaited his coming with interest just the same. In the meanwhile, I strolled about the neighborhood this same evening and the following day, which was Sunday, and on Monday I went into Berlin quite alone. Monday night Herr Merten arrived, and then I had a new experience.

The character of Zehlendorf and the country around Berlin of which it was fairly typical was, in my opinion, of the best. Sand and pines make a delicious country in which to live, anyhow, and when this is combined with rivers and lakes and a light dry atmosphere, there is little more to be said. Zehlendorf is laid out in wide, rectangular streets ranged with trees; the houses, for the most part, sit in spacious lawns; and tall, yellow-stalked, green-tufted pines form their background. These pines were so beautiful and so refreshing after the variable forestation of south Germany that I became quite enraptured with them. I use the word advisedly.

If you will notice, in much of Arnold Böcklin's and Franz von Stuck's art—two men quite favored in Germany as to their work—the pine is a favorite background, with somewhat of the atmosphere and composition of the cypress of the south, but more of these peculiar and individual pine forests of the north. Again, in the illustrative and romantic pictures of *Jugend, Fliegende Blätter* and *Simplicissimus*, you will find many which reflect quite truly the depth and mystery of these same pine forests. I never knew just where this atmosphere, so distinctive in German illustrative art, came from, nor what true beauty, if any, it really reflected. When I reached Zehlendorf, particularly after the first morning and the first evening, it was quite clear to me. I was a thorough convert to some phases of German illustration, if not painting. These groves of pines which were everywhere hereabout were lovely beyond words to indicate—exquisite.

Imagine, if you can, a great, green forest—its trees although not standing in ordered rows, having a stately regularity, the spaces between each not wide but corridor-like, a clear, limbless shaft reaching upward like a monument in each case, brownish-yellow in tone and crowned at the extreme top by a spreading cone of green. The floor under your feet is smooth and carpeted with brown, dry needles. The air in here is so light and fresh that it seems almost too exhilarating, not sufficiently carbonated for the blood to endure. The wind stirring in the tops of the trees has a far-off sound like the murmur of a distant train. The atmosphere, looking down distant corridors of trees wide and high, is sometimes a pale blue, sometimes a brownish-green. A herd of deer may unexpectedly cross your path!

The first morning that I awoke it was the German equivalent of the American robin that woke me—a brown-bodied, red-breasted thrush. The dawn was only faintly breaking. I got up and dressed quickly, for the pale blue (almost steely) light in the depths of the neighboring groves drew me almost despite my own will. There was a faint, delicious frost on the ground, and the lower trunks of the trees had a thin, white rime. The hollow blue sky back of the trees in the east was streaked with thin, fleecy, golden clouds. In certain directions the aisles of the forest were greenish-black.

I did not know it at the time, but this forest, which extended within a block or two of the house and was visible from it (showing between other houses), was part of a great state forest preserve. It contained lakes, small streams, deer, wild ducks, birds and game of various kinds. As I have said, several of these small lakes were near the house, and reconnoitering the edge of the woods I found one. It was quite lonely now, being early morning and late March, but I could see in various directions little licensed restaurants—summer dining pavilions—now quite still and bare. On the lake, whose waters wore a still, greenish-black look, olive at times, wild ducks were paddling and some busybody crows flying low over the water, wondering no doubt why they were not taught by Allah to swim. As at Lucerne, the ducks lighted every now and then with a soft, low, rushing splash. The tall trees about the bank on every hand were mirrored sharp and clear in the still water.

I adore the dawns and dusks of nature. They are more suggestive of beauty than the days and nights. The other bank, against which the sun struck for a time, had a peculiarly artistic value. Let me quote my notes of the time: "I am looking through silver poplars over water. The water is greenish-black, a dark oil green. The other bank, seen through a spray of silver white poplar, is a rich golden hue as to soil, owing to the morning sun. The trees above are a dark, agate green, but dull of course—a strange rich, almost bluish-green effect. All the tree trunks hereabouts are covered with a faint green moss."

"Just now I met a man. He appeared out of the silent depths of this preserve, his steps unheralded owing to the carpet of needles. A stout, blond, red-cheeked German. How this nation runs to solidity of body!"

"Crows are canny creatures. One of them, possessing a deep, guttural German voice, is eyeing me from a distant limb. They always know whether you have a gun or not. The trees here, under strengthening sunlight, take on a great artistic significance. The trunks, so tall and round and shapely, are now yellowish-gold or brownish-red and flecked with flaring spots of gold where the sun penetrates directly. They are also mottled by the shadows of the green tops of other trees. The lake just now, owing to a breath of air from somewhere, is fluted faintly, like molded glass."

Fräulein Förster—at breakfast, lunch, tea or dinner, whenever it was I happened to be with her—I found to be one of the most interesting of women. It always strikes me as strange, the almost uniform efficiency of the unheralded. We pay so much attention to names and fames, the personality in the spotlight of chance, that we are inclined to forget the man or the woman in the dark. Here was this Fräulein Förster, a thin, pleasant-faced, cheery-eyed soul, very vital, very forceful, refined, delicate, tactful, artistic, whose best days—socially, affectionally and commercially—were over and yet who was all really that a person would need intellectually for entertainment and mental interest. A most companionable and delightful conversationalist and thinker. Do you fancy for one moment that Fräulein Förster did not know what was going on in the world or how the winds of philosophy and doctrine blow—now here, now there? If you do, you are greatly mistaken. I do not know how much in wages she received, but I am satisfied, from her activity, her enthusiasm for her duties, her intense desire to keep all things on an even keel and in good working order, that she was not any too well paid. Her clothes were of the plainest and so well worn, though well looked after. Heaven only knows how much of life such a woman may have seen. It has taught her quite as much about fate and chance as it ever taught Socrates or Plato. Do you fancy she did not know how the world was running—what tricks, subtleties, whims, moods are at large in this mundane state? Oh, thin, little, active Fräulein Förster!

At breakfast, lunch, dinner, tea—not regularly, but occasionally, for I was not there often for more than breakfast—we talked of musical personalities; America, Germany and England in contrast; the imperial German army and how the German public looked upon it; London, Paris, Berlin, Vienna and St. Petersburg in contrast (she had been to all); the Catholic and Lutheran churches in Austria, Hungary, Germany and elsewhere; the wisdom of being kind or of being severe, or both; and such like. Thin little Fräulein Förster! I can see her yet, cutting the breakfast bread, pouring the English breakfast tea, serving the German-made marmalade and German liverwurst or blutwurst. Imagine marmalade, butter, wurst and English breakfast tea, morning after morning for breakfast—the standard in this household. The lovely dog Nana, black and silky, had been carefully trained never to ask for anything and never to take anything from anybody's left hand. She might respond to the right hand, if held before her, containing a tidbit of some kind; the left, not. Nana was so clever. She might *look*—that was the rule—and you might respond if you chose with the right hand, but she must not become too conspicuous or in any way obstreperous.

Clever Nana! How she would talk with those deep, soulful, brownish-black eyes! Talk about a dog with temperament!

"See how she looks," Fräulein Förster observed to me this first day. "She thinks she will ogle you out of something. Offer her something with the left hand."

"Fräulein Zola," as this charming dog was called, heard well enough and understood. Her eyes became coquettishly meek. Do you think *she* would take a bit of bread or a slice of wurst from anybody's left hand? Oh, never! never! I saw her watching Fräulein Förster out of the tail of her eye, to see what effect this fine conduct on her part was having. Nevertheless, when there was no regular member of the family present to reprimand her, I found she would take things out of the left hand, and that right gladly. But if anyone who knew her came in the room—someone who would not connive at her wrongdoing—her manner was instantly one of coy, self-abnegating, conscientious adherence to duty. And still we think our ideas of right and wrong are not built up out of social conditions and necessities but are given out of some far-off Sinai—the voice of an immutable and unchanging God.

But to return to Fräulein Förster. This woman was much keener in her social wisdom than Madame Culp, whom she served. She could outwit a person like myself diplomatically a score of times a day. From all efforts to sound her out intellectually and temperamentally, I could not see but what she was as keen—emotionally, sentimentally, intellectually, artistically—as myself, if not more so. Her knowledge of art and architecture was considerable. Her taste in dress and furnishings was good, only she had no money. She conducted all Madame Culp's affairs with great tact, and Herr Merten told me afterward that she was practically indispensable. Why then a thin, shabby servitor at fifty, earning a few marks a month? Explain me this riddle, gentlemen and ladies of *ability* and fortune. Why isn't Fräulein Förster more than she is? Her keen knowledge of the pettifogging tricks of fate, the scrubby, unfair inequalities of chance did not even (as far as one could see) make her sad. What makes a Napoleon triumphant at Austerlitz, a Diogenes brooding grimly and nakedly in a barrel?

CHAPTER LXXIX

From Zehlendorf as a center of operation, I reconnoitered Berlin and its various outlying regions, beginning Monday and continuing for days afterward with the city proper—its commercial and imperial heart. I think

I get as much satisfaction out of studying the individuality of a city as out of anything else in life. Berlin from the beginning to the end made a distinct and forceful impression on me, establishing itself in my mind as one of the few cities having real individuality—as much individuality as the Germans themselves have. Whether it is due to the one fact merely that it is full of Germans; or that the architecture from end to end has been given a uniformity of expression—forceful, ornate, practical; or that its spirit, commercially and socially, is more modern than that of any other city on the continent; or that it presents phases of thoroughness, responsibility, sincerity of intention and reliability of attitude not suggested elsewhere; but certainly because of its suggestions of character, individuality, innate Teutonic charm or the reverse, as these things strike one, growth, prosperity, promise and the like, Berlin cannot be equaled in Europe. Quite readily I can see how it might irritate and repel the less aggressive denizens of less hopeful and determined realms. The German, when he is oppressed, is terribly depressed; when he is in the saddle, nothing can equal his bump of I-am-ity. It becomes so balloon-like and astounding that the world may only gaze in astonishment or retreat in anger, dismay or uproarious amusement. The present-day Germans do take themselves so seriously, and from many points of view with good reason, too.

I don't know where in Europe outside of Paris, if even there, you will see a better-kept city. It is so clean and spruce and fresh that it is a joy to walk there—anywhere. Mile after mile of straight, imposing streets greet your gaze. Look at a map of the city and see what splendid vistas of streets confront you. The architecture is of a new kind—in a new key as it were. London, outside of a few more prosperous areas, is built like a beggarly hamlet. Paris glows with a great intention to be superior, of an innate conviction of being so. Berlin is superior in its residence districts, and if the national exchequer and the will of the Kaiser and the will of the people and a definitely conceived sense of grandeur would permit, it could quickly be made into one of the wonder cities of the world. Not so much is lacking as it is. A new library, for instance, to cost, say, forty million marks; a new Reichstag, to cost as much more; a cathedral that would not be a bullhead cot like the present one, all cheap rococo facade and no interior, but a splendid Gothic, Byzantine or Italian basilica type would be necessary. It would repay the city a hundred times over. The present Imperial Opera House should be torn down and cast into the scrap heap, and a truly individual structure reared in its place, say for forty million marks more. There should be a new imperial palace, set off entirely by itself, with some distinguishing mark of Empire nearby—an imposing tower a thousand feet high, for instance, or a Washington monument, simple and significant. Berlin needs a great Pantheon, an avenue such as Unter den Linden lined with official palaces (not shops), and unquestionably a magnificent museum of art. Its present public and imperial structures are a joke. They suggest the American-European architecture of 1860–70 or thereabouts, which truly is no architecture at all. The public monuments of Berlin, and particularly their sculptural adornments, are a crime against humanity. Whoever put the gilded, winged Victory in the Königsplatz before the Reichstag? And why was another trashy winged something stuck up in the Belle-Alliance-Platz? Such things as these and the Kaiser Wilhelm monument in the so-called Lustgarten near the Royal Palace and the Cathedral at one end of Unter den Linden are enough to make an ordinary human being weep.

I remember standing and looking one evening at that noble German effort known as the memorial or statue of Wilhelm I in the Lustgarten, unquestionably the finest and most imposing of all Berlin military sculptures. No doubt it is by their beloved Reinhold Begas—I am sure it is—Professor Reinhold Begas. No one really knows how truly noble and fierce the German temperament can become when it tries, or rather when it just does. I am half German myself, and from personal observation of myself I have gathered vague, but only vague, suspicions. They are so lordly, so colossal (*kolo-ssaal*, they love to pronounce it), so "*grossartig*." This statue speaks loudly for all Berlin and for all Germany and for just what the Teutonic disposition would like to be—namely, terrible, colossal, astounding, world-scarifying and the like. It almost shouts "Ho! see what I am!" but the sad part of it is that it does this badly, not with the reserve that somehow invariably indicates tremendous power so much better than mere bluster does. What the Germans seem not to have learned, in their art at least, is that "easy does it." Their art is anything but easy. It is almost invariably showy, truculent, vainglorious. But to continue.

This statue stands in a rather unsatisfactory position on one bank of the Spree, a river or network of interlacing branches of a so-called river (which makes Berlin in part for me)—the helmeted hero of Sedan standing erect and defiant above a perfect storm and welter of furious military sculpture below. Actually you would think there had been a great windstorm or cyclone and that it had blown together, quite as a cyclone will, a small eddy of cannon, guns, swords, helmets, lions, victories—anything and everything which might in any way conceivably have anything to do with war or victory or peace. Four absolutely amazing lions guard the four corners of the base. They crouch on the most uncomfortable-looking heaps of guns, swords and the like, and this last is not written to be witty. There is any amount of good bronze wasted on this helter-skelter, scrap-heap effect. Large figures representing war and peace—classic figures of women, of course—sprawl languorously on the side steps mounting upward. The Emperor himself at the top is led forward by Victory—wreath-bearing or trumpet-blowing, I forget which—and on either side of her are her two sisters, I suppose, each driving a rearing, plunging quadriga. Can you imagine that? The whole thing composes into such a startling mass of military and artistic accoutrements as to be brain-wearying. Art is not multitudinous complexity, in my judgment. Great art is simple. The spirit of bravado and blow-hard in which this is done is not worth considering. Yet it is in the Lustgarten, one of the showplaces and showpieces of the city. This is one of the things that should be immediately torn down and melted up. Another generation of German sculptors will probably do much better.

But the whole neighborhood in which this statue occurs—and the other neighborhood at the other end of Unter den Linden, where stands the Reichstag and the like, all in the center of Berlin, as it were—is conceived, designed and executed (in my judgment) in the same mistaken spirit. Truly, when you look about you before the Cathedral (save the mark!) or the Royal Palace in the Lustgarten or at the winged Victory before the Reichstag itself, and the statue of Bismarck in the Königsplatz (the two great imperial centers), you sigh for the artistic spirit of Italy or the French-Parisian conception of grandeur. The Germans have not done anything as yet in these respects which merits the least consideration, and yet all of these things suggest them in a way. I am told the architecture of the Reichstag is very fine. To me it is beneath contempt. Its lines are neither straight nor reservedly ornate. The eye begs for artistic pauses, level, smooth breathing-places. Your German imperial architect will never supply them. Curlicues, nubs, fluted gulleys, protruding ornaments—until you could throw the whole thing in the river. Why waste good money on such trash?

And this collection of imperial buildings in the Lustgarten! When you pass along Unter den Linden to that region, the Lustgarten, where the Friedrichsbrücke spans the Spree, you instinctively realize that you are in the center of imperial Berlin. Here are foregathered the Kaiserliche Schloss (Royal Palace); the University of Berlin (founded, I believe, by Frederick the Great); the old art gallery; the new National Gallery; the Cathedral, or Dom; the Imperial Opera House; the statue of Emperor Wilhelm I previously mentioned—in fact, it seemed to me, almost everything that had to do with civic and artistic interest, public or imperial. Was it good? I thought, in the main, that it was very bad. I have no quarrel with the arrangement that has been made here, although in my judgment it could be much more spacious and in that way gain speedily in dignity. But if your public buildings have no real distinction, what then?

The National Gallery and the old gallery are attractive—I liked the

National Gallery the best or most of anything that I saw in Berlin. The Royal Palace, over the way on the other side of the atrocious Dom, is inhumanly dull. It could not be worse. Brown wall greets brown wall. Frederick's Bridge, which spans the Spree here, is too flamboyant. No words can do justice to the folly of spending three million dollars to erect such a thing as this Berlin Dom or Cathedral. It is so bad that it hurts. And I am told that the Kaiser himself okayed some of the architectural designs. And it was only completed between 1894 and 1906. What worse could you say? Shades of Bramante and Pisano! When I saw its seemingly imposing dome in the distance, I said to myself, "This must be something important. I must see this." When I reached it I felt like hurrying swiftly away but went inside as a matter of critical duty, as it were. Truly, I could not get out fast enough. Of all the stale, aimless, wearisome places! I have quarreled with the interior of St. Paul's in London and some others, but St. Paul's is a noble achievement compared to this. Nothing worse could happen to any great city than to have such a trashy building thrust upon it. Decorations? There are none! Statuary? None. Charm of proportion? None. No sense of height, space, light, anything. And it cost three million marks in Germany, which would mean that it would cost perhaps six or eight million in America surely. Our magnificent St. Paul the Divine is to cost no more than eight.

But if I seem disgusted with this section of Berlin—its evidence of Empire, as it were—there was much more that truly pleased me. I consider the Siegesallee (Victory Avenue), leading through the Tiergarten (the Central Park of Berlin) from Königsplatz in front of the Reichstag to Kemperplatz, near Leipziger Platz, to the south, a real achievement. I heard much jesting while I was in Berlin concerning the "right leg forward" attitude of the Hohenzollern celebrities commemorated here in stone—monarchs of Prussia and its principalities—but sculpturally and architecturally the effect is good, quite dignified and pleasing. Berlin does not run to the nude in art—in public art, at least—after the fashion of Paris. These are all military figures, practically speaking, all suitably accoutred. They are ranged along either side of this wide avenue at regular intervals of a hundred feet or more, all standing erect on white marble pedestals of modest height, the green of the Tiergarten behind them, a semi-circular stone bench or wall with seat behind each, and each flanked, right and left, with busts of the leading men of their reign. You will hear local stories told of how annually or semi-annually these statues are properly scrubbed with soap and water, after the German fashion, their ears washed, etc., but the public may jest. It is a fine avenue and a fine idea, one you will not soon forget.

The significance of Berlin is not confined to its imperial evidences, however. I found the ground plan of this imposing city as interesting as anything, and the evidence, as I have said, of a somewhat new and effectual architectural spirit in the matter of stores, apartment houses and private dwellings was most engaging. The five- and six-story apartment houses of Berlin—each street limited to a given height and each height corresponding to the spacious stretch of roadway in between—soothed and charmed me greatly. The shabby, broken skylines of so many American cities become abhorrent in the presence of an effect such as this. These streets recede from you in such an impressive way. You pick out individual structures and you see at once that you have something new, quite individual and Teutonic, entirely suited to Berlin and Germany. The exteriors are properly and carefully worked out along a new line of color and decoration. Silver and gray and blue and gold are the commonest forms of apartment-house color and decorative combinations, and they give a peculiar atmosphere to streets—effective, to say the least. Heroes, amazons, griffins, garlands, cupids, lovely full-breasted torsos of women (sometimes exceedingly sensual), rollicking Bacchuses and fauns are all used. They are used, seemingly, to support doors, bay windows, lintels, cornices, and to ornament panels, friezes, balustrades and keystones. It gives a most novel aspect at times. It reminds you—arouses in you, in fact—a keen appreciation of the basic animality of the German mind, full-blooded, ghoulish, healthy and, to me at least, pleasing. I like that sort of thing. No ruling moral cowardice here. Germans take lusty nymphs and amorous fauns as a matter of course, and why not? Imagine an American apartment house decorated exteriorly with naked, lolling nymphs, ruddy cupids and grinning, leering, sensually-minded fauns!

Not only the apartment-house sections, which front mile after mile over seemingly endless areas, but the business sections also give you a sense of something strangely un-European and new. In the matter of commercial and residence areas, Berlin constantly reminded me of Chicago. The soil and climate conditions are curiously much the same, the soil flat as a pancake, the temperature brisk and variable. Such amazingly long streets as Berliner Strasse, Tauentzienstrasse, Frankfurter Strasse, and dozens of others extending mile after mile in a given direction, lined with all the little stores that make up the home supplies of the city, lighted with arc lights, traversed with rumbling cars and brisk with people walking, children playing, storekeepers waiting on customers visible through open doorways, reminded me for all the world of Chicago, only Berlin is so much better built than Chicago in its residence and tenement areas.

But more than that, if you do not conceive of the thoroughgoing German temperament through all this—its moody poverty, its phlegmatic middle-class prosperity, its aggressive commercial, financial, and above all its official and imperial life—you have lost it all. Berlin is shot through like a certain cloth through which a given thread appears and reappears, with the constant suggestion of officialdom and imperialism. The German policeman with his shining brass helmet and brass belt, making him look in his broad-chested, broad-backed solidity like a Roman centurion out of the paintings of the Middle Ages; the Berlin sentry in his long gray overcoat, his musket over his shoulder, his high cap shading his eyes, his black-and-white-striped sentry box behind him, stationed apparently at every really important corner and before every official palace; the German military and imperial automobiles speeding their independent ways, all traffic cleared away before them, the small flag of officialdom or imperialism fluttering defiantly from the foot rails as they flash at express speed past you—these things suggest an individuality which no other European city that I saw quite equaled. It represents what I would call determination, almost vainglorious intention, self-sufficiency, pride and the like. Berlin, all the while, suggests the pride, determination, enthusiasm and condescending superiority of some young hobbledehoy of a giant who is just discovering that he is a giant and wants everyone to know it, without the real tact to conceal the fact that he does. It is new, green, vigorous, astounding—a city that for speed of growth puts Chicago entirely in the shade; that for appearance, cleanliness, order makes London and even Paris in certain sections look cheap and old; that for commerce and traffic suggests only Chicago and other American cities; and that for military precision and thoroughness has no counterpart anywhere. It suggests to you all the time something very much greater to come, which is the most interesting thing that can be said about any city anywhere.

CHAPTER LXXX

One panegyric I should like to write on Berlin concerns not so much its social organization as a city, though that is interesting enough, but specifically its traffic and travel arrangements. To be sure, it is not yet such a city as either New York, London or Paris—the latter having obviously a greater tide of traffic—but at that it has over three million people, a crowded business heart and a heavy, daily, to-and-fro-swinging tide of suburban traffic. In visiting such cities as Paris, Rome, Florence, Milan—in fact any of the European cities, I am sure, outside of London and Berlin—you miss that highly characteristic feature of American urban life, the suburban express or train service and the long distance streetcar service. Even this last is wanting in England. Anyone who has ever lived in any American city of any size (New York, Chicago, Philadelphia, Boston, Pittsburgh, Denver, Seattle or San Francisco) would scarcely know what his daily life was coming to if he did not have to hurry, morning and evening, to catch a local train. Most American cities tend strongly to become shop and office centers, with fairly distant towns or sections of the city as home—or, as someone used to say, "bedroom" areas. This today is equally true of London, Manchester, Liverpool and Berlin. But I caught no suggestion of this suburban residence idea anywhere else, either in Rome or Paris or Milan or Frankfort. It is coming, of course, in all of these cities and others, for European cities are growing quite as fast in many instances as are their American and English contemporaries, but their suburban hour has not struck yet.

In Berlin, as in London, however, I found it in full force. There are a number of railway stations in the great German capital: the Potsdamer Bahnhof, the Bahnhof Friedrichstrasse, the Anhalter Bahnhof and so on, and coming from each in the early hours of the morning, or pouring toward them at evening, are noticeable streams of people, active, hard-working German men and women—their bundles under their arms, their newspapers or publications in their hands, hurrying to their shops or offices or to their homes in the country, just as you will see it in any good-sized city in America or England. You would think, to stand in Friedrichstrasse near the railway station of that name, or on Potsdamer Platz near the railway of that name, or anywhere near any suburban depot, of which there are so many in Berlin, that you were in New York or Chicago or St. Louis or elsewhere in America and that Americans were doing their best to get home or to get to work quickly.

The Germans are amazingly like the Americans. Sometimes I think that we get the better portion of our progressive, constructive characteristics from them. Only the Germans, I am convinced, are so much more thorough. They go us one better in economy, energy, endurance and thoroughness. The American already is beginning to want to play too much. The Germans have not reached that stage.

The Potsdamer Bahnhof, where I arrived and departed so often during the next two weeks, was like any good American railway station—no better and no worse. Excellent railway stations with great switchyards and enormous arched glass and steel sheds where the trains wait are common all over Europe—as much so in Italy as anywhere else. In Berlin I admired the suburban train service as much as I did that of London, if not more. That in Paris was horrible. Rome, Milan, Frankfort and other cities did not appear to have any to speak of. Here the trains offered a choice of first, second and third class, with the vast majority using the second and third. I saw little difference in the crowds occupying either class. The second-class seats or compartments were upholstered in a grayish-brown corduroy, very handsome and kept scrupulously clean. The third-class seats and compartments were of plain wood, nicely colored and polished and also scrupulously clean. There were separate compartments for smokers, non-smokers and travelers with dogs. I tried all three classes and finally fixed on the third as good enough for me, although when I was escorting someone else it was different, of course.

I wish all Americans who at present suffer the indignation of the American street railway and steam railway suburban service could go to Berlin and see what that city has to teach them in this respect. Berlin is much larger than Chicago. It is certain to be a city soon of five or six million people, very soon. The plans for handling this mass of people comfortably and courteously are already in operation. The German public service is obviously not left to supposedly kindly-minded business gentlemen—"Christian gentlemen," as Mr. Baer of the Reading once chose to put it—"in partnership with God." The populace may be underlings to an imperial Kaiser, subject to conscription and eternal inspection, but at least the money-making "Christian gentlemen" with their hearts and souls centered on their private purses and working, as Mr. Croker once said of himself, "for their own pockets all the time," are not allowed to "rub it into" the rank and file.

No doubt the German street railways and steam railways are making a reasonable sum of money and are eager to make more. I have not the least doubt but that heavy, self-opinionated, vainglorious German directors of great wealth gather around mahogany tables in chambers devoted to meetings of directors and listen to ways and means of cutting down expenses and "improving" the service. Beyond the shadow of a doubt there are hard, hired managers, eager to win the confidence and support of their superiors and ready to feather their own nests at the expense of the masses, who would gladly cut down the service, "pack 'em in," introduce the "cutting-out" system of car service and see that the "car ahead" idea was worked to the last maddening extreme, but in Germany, for some strange, amazing reason, they don't get a chance.

What is the matter with Germany, anyhow? I would like to know, really I would. Why isn't the "Christian gentleman" theory of business introduced there? The population of Germany, acre for acre and mile for mile, is much larger than that of America. They have sixty-five million people crowded into an area as big as Texas. Why don't they "pack 'em in"? Why don't they introduce the American "sardine" railway and subway service? You don't find it anywhere in Germany, for some strange reason. Why? They have a subway service in Berlin. It serves vast masses of people, just as the subway does in New York. Its platforms are crowded with people, but you can get a seat just the same. There isn't any yelling of "Step lively!" there. They don't push at your back with their fists in the hope of breaking a rib. Overcrowding isn't a joke over there as it is here—something to be endured with a feeble smile until you are spiritually comparable to a doormat. There must be "Christian gentlemen" of wealth and refinement in Germany and Berlin. Why don't they "get on the job"? Or why don't some of our "Christian gentlemen" go over and "key them up"? The thought arouses strange, uncertain feelings in me. I don't quite see how to solve this problem for myself.

Take, for instance, the simple matter of starting and stopping street railway cars in the Berlin business heart. Insofar as I could see, that area, morning and evening, was as crowded as any similar area in Paris, London or New York. Streetcars have to be run through it, started, stopped, passengers let on and off, a vast tide carried in or out of the city. Now the way this matter is worked in New York is quite ingenious and clever—a splendid illustration of American ability, go, etc., etc. We operate what might be described as a daily guessing contest, intended to develop the wits, muscles, lungs and tempers of the people. The scheme insofar as the street railway companies are concerned is (after running the roads as economically as possible) to see how thoroughly the people can be fooled in their efforts to discover at which side of a crossing or on which corner a car is likely to stop. In New York this matter of fooling the people is wisely left to the discretion of the motorman with the proviso that he is to fool them as often and as exasperatingly as possible. The idea most strenuously enforced is "Make them run for the car, and then when they get there be sure that the car has gone on again." Such a thing as having a fixed stopping place is never to be thought of. That would be robbing the public of what is well known to be a great necessity, a sufficient amount of daily exercise, and would be making of the motorman's life a dull affair. How unhappy he would be if he could not leave a trail of perspiring, swearing, enraged citizens in his wake. No, no, nothing so cruel as that. The public is compelled to guess, to stand on one corner and speculate, calculate, as to just where the car of necessity (the chance crossing of a wagon or something of that sort) will be compelled to stop, then run, and, before it can go on again, clamber on. If an individual makes it, he is applauded by his fellow citizens. If the motorman is able to outwit him, the latter's record for deceiving the public is thereby strengthened. On a motorman's ability to "fool" the largest number of people the most times a day depends his hope of advancement. If his percentage is high enough, he may hope to become a "starter," which is purely an honorary position, as may be seen, and requires no work at all. The American citizen's reputation—for wit, agility, power to "figure out" the secret motives and intentions of another and forestall them—is all based on this system. New York's reputation of being the most congested city in the world at certain hours also rests on this. It is a national institution, so well-grounded now that it would be criminal to attempt to displace it.

In Berlin, however, they have, for some reason, an entirely different idea. There the idea is not to fool the people at all but to get them in and out of the city as quickly as possible. So, as in Paris, London, Rome and elsewhere, a plan of fixed stopping places has been arranged. Signs actually indicate where the cars stop, and there, marvel of marvels, they all stop, even in the so-called rush hours. No traffic policemen, apparently, can order them to go ahead without stopping. They *must* stop. And so the people do not run for the cars, the motorman has no joy in outwitting anybody; and so the Germans are neither so agile, quick-witted or subtle as the Americans. From the New York point of view it is a bad system—one obviously not calculated to develop the utmost capacity of the race.

And then take, in addition, if you will bear with me another moment, this matter of the Berlin suburban service as illustrated by the lines to Potsdam and elsewhere. It is true that the officers and even the emperor, living at Potsdam and serving the imperial German government there, may occasionally use this line, but thousands upon thousands of intermediate and plebeian Germans use it also. You can *always* get a seat. Please notice the word *always*. There are three classes, and you can *always* get a seat in any class—not the first or second classes only, but the third class, and particularly the third class. There are "rush" hours in Berlin, just as there are in New York, dear reader. People swarm into the Berlin railway stations and at Berlin street railway corners and crowd on cars just as they do here. But the rush-hour car service is a great car service—in Berlin. The lines fairly seethe with cars. On the tracks ranged in the Potsdamer Bahnhof, for instance, during the rush hours, you will see trains consisting of eleven, twelve and thirteen cars, mostly third-class accommodation, waiting to receive you. And when one is gone, another equally large train is there on the adjoining track, and it is going to leave in another minute or two also. And when that is gone there will be another, and so it goes.

There is not the slightest desire evident anywhere to "pack" anybody in. There isn't any evidence that anybody wants to make anything (dividends, for instance) out of straps. There *are* no straps, and yet this is an amazingly heavily-patronized line. Swarms of people rush to it in the rush hours. Yet the "Christian gentlemen" operating the suburban services of Berlin here and elsewhere are apparently not "cutting out cars ahead," asking you to "step lively," "reducing the service" just before the traffic falls off and asking managers and employees to see that the cars are packed full before sending them out. Perhaps they haven't any "Christian gentlemen" in Berlin, after all. They don't expect you to pack into the cars apparently, and if they did, I fancy there would be a loud row in downtrodden Germany. These poor, unliberated, Kaiser-ruled people would really kick. They would compel a decent service and there would be no loud cries on the part of "Christian gentlemen" operating large and profitable systems as to the "rights of property," the need of "conserving the constitution," the privilege of appealing to Federal judges and the right of having every legal technicality invoked to the letter—or, if there were, they would get scant attention.

Germany just doesn't see public service in that light. It hasn't fought, bled and died, perhaps, for "liberty." It hasn't had George Washington and Thomas Jefferson and Andrew Jackson and Abraham Lincoln. All it has had is Frederick the Great and Emperor William I and Bismarck and von Moltke. Strange, isn't it? Queer, how imperialism apparently teaches people to be civil while democracy makes tyrants out of upstarts. England teaches you that. So does Italy, apparently; republican France not at all. We ought to get a little "imperialism" into our government, I should say. We ought to make American law and American government supreme, but over it there ought to be a "supremer" people who really know what their rights are, who respect liberties, decencies and courtesies for themselves and others, who demand and see that their government and their law and their servants, public and private, are responsive and responsible to them—not to the eager, indifferent, tyrannical, money-grubbing private-packet-working "Christian gentlemen" who want to "pack 'em in" and to "sweat the dividends out of the straps." It may seem a little strange, but it is true. If you don't believe it, go to Berlin or London—preferably Berlin. It is even more obvious there than in England. But go if you can, and then see if you come home again and believe so cheerfully that this is the land of the *free* and the home of the *brave*. Buncombe! The land of the *dub* and the home of the *doormat*. Nothing more and nothing less.

CHAPTER LXXXI

About the third day, in the evening, Herr Merten arrived, but I did not see him until the next morning at breakfast, a middle-aged, solid-framed, guttural-throated individual whose Teutonic voice echoed without effort throughout the house. An "*echter*" (more real) German you could not hope to see. My, what a Prussian to the core this man proved to be! There was only one country in all the world for him: Germany; and Prussia, his native state, was the only important part of it. The German army! You would have thought he was the Kaiser himself, so proud was he of it, so satisfied as to its ability. The German commercial instinct? Nothing in the world could equal his faith that the German bankers, financiers, merchants and manufacturers are the greatest in the world. England? Poof! America? Nonsense! Germany! Germany! Germany! That is the great country. Never mind the others. Germany does now rule the world in many things and later will in everything. How is that for a fine German-Prussian-Berlinish attitude?

This man interested me so much on sight that I spent all my time at the breakfast-table slyly noticing his facial characteristics. Was he a plain fool or a man of real ability? I asked myself. How was it that his wife could outwit or master him in this matter of what we are accustomed to look on as his marital honor, for outwitted or mastered he was. Madame Culp, I could see from the little I had to do with her in Frankfort, was a woman of great determination and force—soft enough where the matter of her passions or affections were concerned, but as hard as nails otherwise. I wondered all the time that I was there whether this man knew all and had made a rather indifferent commercial bargain with her to keep up appearances because of her artistic and consequently social prestige; or whether he knew little and was only beginning slowly to suspect; or whether, knowing all, he was still fond of her—conquered affectionally, but hoping eventually for a change of heart on her part. I never did get it straightened out exactly to suit me.

Of course at breakfast he was charmingly civil to me in a hard, defiant German way. I must come to lunch with him at noon at a typical German restaurant, he said; I must take coffee afterwards in another; I must take dinner still later at another. Had I been to Potsdam? Did I know where the great army exercise place was? He was helpfully suggestive as to principal things of interest in the city.

"The museums, buildings and streets you can see for yourself," he said at once, with the air of a master regulating my life, "by walking about. I will show you some of the nightlife myself."

"Yes—there he goes," jested Fräulein Förster, who was always at table with us, "he will show you that!"

During the days that followed, this man and I became rather intimate. He had, as I found, in spite of his manner, a real intellect and as unethical (not unmoral) an attitude as you would hope to encounter. Talk about the Darwinian theory of the survival of the fittest—this man accepted it in the coldest, hardest spirit in the world. Yet at the same time he was delightfully human. True to his Teutonic mold and the aggressive time in which he was living, he scarcely believed in luck, and yet I could see that at times he was sour to think that the gods rolled the dice so unfavorably. Some men won, some didn't, even when they fought hard and ably, but fighting hard and ably was the great thing to him.

A fine specimen of a man, this—physically very good-looking. He had nice, shapely, firm hands. His chin was attractive, and his eyes were a fine, hard brownish-black. For all his strength and get-up, he had an emotional pull for me, and I could not explain it. He was like a hard, bony Great Dane. I wondered all the time whether he was truly successful, and yet he appeared to be. By profession he was a sanitary engineer, and obviously a scientific one. He told me at once on the first day at lunch of several important tasks he had executed in Germany—fair-sized cities he had advised as to improvements, and others that he was contemplating advising. There was one particular job or city that held great interest for him. It was in India in a city of five hundred thousand. He was going there, called by the city itself as an expert, to tell it what to do, and he had a most frankly unethical plan in mind. Why he should tell me all this so speedily I do not know, but I think he felt that he had found a brother intellect and that I would look on anything he had to say as mere color, an aspect of the world. He was sailing for India in ten days, and his plan was to examine the physical conditions of the city very carefully, to discover just what was needed and then to tell the city fathers just which European company was best suited to execute this work efficiently and economically. But just here was where the great point came.

"Now," he said to me, with hard Teutonic emphasis, once we had gotten deep into this conversation, "this is a task which will bring some company all of two million marks in business, perhaps more. I mean that much will be expended by this city. My word will be the determining factor. There are two great companies that can do it easily—three, in fact, two here in Germany and one in England. It should be worth a considerable bonus to any one of them to get this task. I want two hundred and fifty thousand marks for my opinion favoring any particular company, and the company that pays me gets the job—not otherwise."

I looked at the man curiously to see whether he was jesting. Why should he tell me this? I asked myself. I should say it was rather bad business to suggest so openly such a buccaneer system of assessing a city without its volition, for of course the city would pay. It was so plain at a glance though that he thought nothing of it. This was the way things were done here. As a matter of fact, he told me—I took good care not to manifest any surprise—that any other sanitary engineer in Germany, saving a fool, would do the same thing. "Why shouldn't they pay me?" he demanded.

I made no reply to this, but I drew definitely from him later the fact that the city in India was paying him a reasonable price for his services as advisor. He could not see but that some one of these big companies should give him at last a really worthwhile tip for his services in favoring them. I should say, in all fairness, that he made it perfectly clear to me that only a worthwhile company, one thoroughly able to execute the work and execute it well, would win his approval, even though he were paid for it.

With Herr Merten noons and evenings during the next ten days I saw considerable of German nightlife—cafés, theaters, music halls, the region of the Tenderloin and two Teutonic houses of prostitution. I cannot say that, after Paris and Monte Carlo, I was greatly impressed, although all that I saw in Berlin had the advantage that it bore sharply the imprint of German nationality. The cafés were not especially noteworthy. I could name a standard list of them—Bauer, Arcadia, Kempinski's, the Fürstenhof, the Hotel Adlon, La Clou, the Linden Cabaret, Piccadilly, the Weinhaus Rheingold, the Weinhaus Trarbach and last, but not by any means least, the Palais de Danse. I do not know what I can say about any of these which will indicate their individuality. Piccadilly was a great evening drinking-place near the Potsdamer Platz which was all glass, gold, marble, glittering with lights and packed with Germans, principally young German men and their girls, husbands and their wives, the latter a little too heavy physically to give the place the necessary spirit. Songs were sung here, the usual cabaret performance

A German dance hall, Berlin

in existence at this time, and smart German, American, French and Austrian music rendered. The American coon song and the Austrian and American musical comedy melodies were in evidence. Beer was the principal liquor consumed.

La Clou was a radically different place, not far from the juncture of Leipziger and Wilhelm Streets in the business heart. In a way it was an amazing place, catering to the moderately prosperous middle class and the medium poor. It seated, I should say, easily fifteen hundred people, if not more, on the ground floor, and every table, in the evening at least, was full. At either end of a great center aisle bisecting it was stationed a stringed orchestra, and when one ceased the other immediately began, so that there was music without interruption. Father and mother and young Lena, little Heinie and the two oldest girls or boys were all here. During the evening, up one aisle and down another, there walked a constant procession of boys and girls and young men and young women making shy, conservative eyes at one another. Both food and drink at reasonable prices were served here.

The Weinhaus Rheingold and the Weinhaus Trarbach were two other interesting places catering to the well-to-do middle classes, providing meals which in New York would average in cost from one dollar and fifty cents to three dollars. Of the two the Weinhaus Rheingold was the more important—an amazing place for size, being a large five-story structure crowded from the ground floor to the roof with dining chambers of different sizes. Many of these rooms were truly imposing, very large, hung with great glass-spangled chandeliers, set with pocket lights, finished in bronze, steel and fine marbles. In no sense could this or its companion restaurants be said to be smart; but Berlin, outside of one or two selected spots, does not run to smartness.

The Cabaret Linden and the Cabaret Arcadia were, once more, of a different character. Those who are familiar with the New York and Chicago attempts at semi-lascivious gaiety can guess their character. In both places—the Cabaret Linden preferred for smartness—you saw a specially selected group of talent sing risqué songs and deliver risqué monologues. I had to laugh at the Berlin variety of this sort of thing, for it was amazingly frank—songs explaining how engaging widows teach young boys to become secret cavaliers, songs of soldiers climbing into the bedrooms of their sweethearts, songs of spring sex madness, the troubles of enceinte girls and the like. There was one woman at the Cabaret Linden who struck me as having real artistic talent of a strongly Teutonic variety—Claire Waldoff, a hard, shock-headed tomboy of a girl who sang in a harsh, guttural voice of soldiers, merchants, janitors and policemen—a really brilliant presentation of local German characteristics.

It is curious how these little touches of character drawn from street boys and girls, chambermaids, policemen, butcher boys, bakers, and the rank and file generally invariably win thunders of applause. How the world loves the homely, the simple, the odd, the silly. There was not a suggestive thing which this woman said or did, coarse and vulgar as it was—and that too where all the other acts were practically suggestive—but she was nevertheless the star feature of the bill. The noisy, champagne-drinking audience could not get enough of her. Through clouds of tobacco smoke she loomed up, a sort of German Albert Chevalier or (drawing an example from America) the once-famous John W. Kelly of Chicago. Her touches were inimitable. She revealed German life at times—those strange twists of character and mood which give each nation individuality like a flash of lightning. I laughed at one little touch after another until I came near disgracing my companion. I fairly choked at times. Yet there would be no way in which to transplant such an artist to either Paris, London or New York. More than likely, her work would seem horribly stale and vulgar—it is so essentially Teutonic. No American Marie Dressler, no English Grossmith, Junior, no French Mistinguett could outrival her. She was as delicious, as naive, as weirdly eccentric and as humorous as any character-singing artist could hope to be.

CHAPTER LXXXII

I have been reserving for the latter portion of this discussion my adventures in connection with two houses of prostitution and the Palais du Danse. I cannot locate the two former very successfully, for my knowledge of Berlin vicinities is not good, but both of them were not far from the corner of Unter den Linden and the Friedrichstrasse, which at night is central for vice, the German cabaret nightlife, the procession of streetwalkers and their pursuers—so common to every city.

Though I have occasionally selected a type for one very distinct reason or another from the streets, almost invariably to extract a certain form of information, I have never been able to see what charm it is that attracts a certain type of man to the average woman of the street. Paucity of female connections and an overmastering, unreasoning, inartistic sex desire must be the one and only answer. In every city, if you study a vicinity of this kind, you find that these women have their patrons—I will not say in plenty, but sufficient to keep a large number of them in the field. It is said of the intellectuals of this world that they are more or less alike everywhere. It is certainly true that the women who make the night street life of the principal cities peculiar, if not mentally elevating, have, exteriorly speaking, much in common. They tend to present a sameness or similarity in flamboyant smartness of garb (shabby-smart) which, however much they may differ temperamentally in New York, Paris, London and Berlin, tends to identify them at once.

This matter of the dressing of these women interests me. When I went abroad, I expected to see some sharp variations in the physical appearance of the street girls of the different countries. To a certain extent there is a difference, but it is more of temperament than of dress. In size, shape, mood, the Parisian streetwalkers in France present often a slenderness and a smartness of garb not otherwise available. They are so remarkable at times that you will frankly admit that not anywhere have you seen the like—naive and almost theatrically strange. In London and New York one sees a more or less American effect, only the London streetwalker looks as a rule light and fair and typically English, for all her American clothes—a little phlegmatic. In Berlin the German streetwalker struck me as doing her best to ape American and French smartness, but you could see that it was a little difficult for the German temperament to get an *air.* They are inclined, I think, by nature to be more mellow and fatalistic than their sisters elsewhere, though not so very much more so. It is hard for them to exercise that cutting candor which first and above all distinguishes the Parisian and secondly suggests the American. The French streetwalker, I am sure, is the only one who thoroughly and practically understands her business and for years deliberately follows it as such. The others in America and elsewhere hope (sometimes I think pathetically) to be lifted out of it all by marriage. The Frenchwoman is perhaps the only one who is not truly hardened by her trade or at least who brings the most philosophy to bear upon the matter.

These women, or girls, rather—they are always girls—in the vicinity of the Friedrichstrasse struck me as having very little to contribute concerning the ultimate details of Berlin life. They were not clever-looking, though they dressed well enough. "I never look at them," observed Herr Merten as we passed through them. They cater to a market (international, I presume) which requires a seeming slenderness and perfection of physique, and so, though the average German girl tended to a sort of rounded solidity (not objectionably so), these were almost invariably slender or corseted to give that effect. The big hat, the high-heeled shoes, the flaring tie were too often in evidence. You would really expect more individuality in this really very individual world. All of them, I suppose, in Paris, New York, London and elsewhere acquire a form of international lingo which they can use, for here in Berlin I was greeted by such calls as "Will you come with me, my darling?" voiced with great difficulty, I could see, and in faraway Milan an

Italian girl near the Cathedral (that great center of Milanese vice) called "'Ello, my sweetheart." Who taught her that?

On the contrary, here in Berlin the women in the bagnios—the two into which I was introduced—were of a purely Teutonic type, a fact which struck me as interesting. These two places, from the point of view of furnishings, were no different from institutions of the same kind in New York and Chicago. I never saw one in Paris or London. They were, as is so often the case, private houses in dark streets. The exteriors gave no suggestion of being even inhabited. I merely wanted to see, and was not disappointed in surveying a type consistently blonde, inclined to physical plumpness, somewhat more gross-looking than the French or Americans, but whether they are temperamentally more so I am inclined to question. In these places, of course, champagne and cigarettes were the necessary mediums.

In introducing me to these realms Herr Merten, it seemed to me, was unnecessarily brusque and frank. "We do not want to have anything to do with any woman," he frankly announced to the madam. "Can my friend be shown some of the rooms?" When one artificially rosy lady approached him and put her hand on his coat, he said quite roughly, "No, no, no! None of that. Talk to him if you wish." The simple-minded denizen, used no doubt to such rude discourtesies, took it all in good part.

Life is truly a hellish, trashy mix-up. Looking at these rather blonde, plump vehicles of lust, decked out in the gaudiest of costumes—red silk evening gowns, low-cut boudoir effects in pink, blue, lavender and even green—their arms and shoulders bare, their hair done in various styles and sometimes very attractively, their legs encased in silk stockings and their feet shod in the gaudiest fashion, silver, gold, blue, pink, yellow—I had to smile as I thought of all the rantings of pulpits, the asinine pamphleteering of vice committees, the silly palaver about reformation (not so much heard these latter years), and the current efforts at medical inspection (the last resource of the defeated). Nothing works like life itself, in my humble judgment. Life ought to concern itself with cure after the fact, and prevention before it, and very little if at all with reformation. Only hard, brutal suffering reforms or destroys—re-forms the person into something very different from what he started out to be. I should like to know, given human nature as we know it to be, what would become of society if we did not have the safety valve of the prostitute and the house of prostitution. The world has not materially changed morally since history began. The average youth, insofar as one can see, is crazy about sex. It is almost more important to him than food. He would consider his life a failure if you cut the crude, meaty female from out of his bill-o'-fare. He loves flesh, responds to the suggestion of female outlines quite as a chemical formula reacts when supplied with the last agent. Who designed all this inter-acting, responding system—chance or God or man? Who gave man a crazy, chemical responsive composition? What is duality for? To reproduce the race? Quite certainly. To lend color to life? Quite as much so. To act as a stimulus to human achievement? Surely, surely, and if you question this, you read life poorly. I always think of a young newspaper manager I knew in New York, a brilliant, pyrotechnic representative of the most important news service in the world. Time and again I have seen his picture in the conservative magazines—those weak-tea purveyors of human life to simple homes (this marvelously ramified illusion called life)—extolling him to the skies as one of those conservative, helpful citizens who are doing "the important work of the world." A young man to be envied, one might say, seeing his picture in the *Independent*—imitated, looked upon as a worthwhile example, interesting because he was brilliantly successful at so early an age.

"My Christ!" he said to me one night as he came bustling in from his work, a boy earning eighteen thousand a year, "I don't know what I'd do if it weren't for women. I need 'em bad. Why, out in 'Frisco I could work harder and fuck more than in any other city I've been in, and I'm always sorry I can't get back there. This New York game is a little slow for me."

I often wondered what his solemn, owlish patrons of the *Outlook*, the *American Magazine*, *Everybody's*, and *McClure's* would have thought of that, particularly the *Christian Outlook*, his chiefest sponsor.

From the last house of "ill repute"—I love that phrase, so deliciously suggestive of only remote understanding—we came away to the Palais de Danse, admittedly Berlin's greatest nightlife achievement. For several days Herr Merten had been saying "Now tomorrow we must go to the Palais de Danse, then you will see something," but every evening when we started out, something else had intervened. I was a little skeptical of his enthusiastic praise of this institution as being better than anything in Paris, London, Monte Carlo—indeed, any other place in Europe. You had to take Herr Merten's vigorous Teutonic estimate of Berlin with a grain of salt, though I did think that a city that had put itself together in this wonderful way in not much more than a half-century had certainly considerable reason to boast.

"But what about the Café de Paris at Monte Carlo?" I suggested, remembering the dish of beauty and lust that had been served there.

"No, no, no!" he exclaimed, with great emphasis; he had a habit of unconsciously making a fist when he was emphatic. "Not in Monte Carlo, not in Paris—not anywhere!"

"Very good," I replied, "this must be very fine. Lead on."

So we went.

Truly, and I say it in all sincerity, after Paris and Monte Carlo I was astonished. Not that I considered what I saw more chic or more lascivious or more rich in that spirit of bravado and devil-may-care which you find in Paris and Monte Carlo, but that any such thing, any approximation of Parisian conditions, should exist in Berlin at all. It was, in its way, amazing, and you would never guess it from its sedate exterior. It did not seem to be very busy, and the front had some such look as a rather commonplace square-shaped opera house might have. The interior was brilliant enough.

"I want to tell you something," said Herr Merten as we climbed out of our taxi—a good, solid, reasonably-priced Berlin taxi. "If you come with your wife, your daughter or your sister, you buy a ticket for yourself—four marks—and walk in. Nothing is charged for your female companions, and no notice is taken of them. If you come here with a cocotte, you pay four marks for yourself and four for her, and you cannot get her past without great trouble. They know. They have men at the door who are experts in this matter. They want you to bring cocottes, but they want you to pay, too. They make their money out of the cocotte, and she makes her money out of them. So she has to pay—or, rather, you do. If she comes alone, she goes in free. How's that?"

Once inside we surveyed a brilliant spectacle, far more ornate than the Café l'Abbaye or the Café Maxim or Américain at Paris, or the Carlton at Monte Carlo. Brilliant is the word. I would not have believed until I saw it that the German temperament or the German sense of thrift would have permitted it, and yet after seeing the marvelous German officer, why not? The main chamber, very large, consisted of a small, central, highly-polished dancing floor, canopied far above by a circular dome of colored glass, glittering white or peach-pink by turns, and surrounded on all sides by an elevated platform or floor, two or three feet above it, crowded with tables ranged in circles on ascending steps so that all might see. Beyond the tables again was a wide, level, semi-circular promenade, flanked by ornate walls and divans and set with palms, marbles and intricate gilt curio cases. The general effect was one of intense light, pale, diaphanous silks of creams and lemons, white and gold walls, white tables, a perfect glitter of glass, mirrors and picturesque paneling. Over the dancing floor was a giant, gold-tinted rococo organ, and within a recess of this, under the tinted pipes, a stringed orchestra.

The place was crowded with women of the half-world, Germans, unusually slender, in the vast majority of cases delicately featured, as the best of these women are, and beautifully dressed. I say beautifully; qualify it any way you want to. Put it dazzlingly, ravishingly, showily, outrageously—any way you choose. No respectable woman might come so garbed, and yet considering the ultra chicness of the European smart world, she might. Many of these women were unbelievably attractive, carried themselves with a grand air, peafowl-like, and lent an atmosphere of color and life of a very showy kind. The place was also crowded, I need not add, with young men in evening clothes. Only champagne was served to drink—champagne at twenty marks the bottle. Champagne at twenty marks the bottle in Berlin is high. You can get a fine suit of clothes for seventy or eighty marks.

The principal diversions here were dining, dancing, drinking. As at Monte Carlo and Paris, you saw here that peculiarly suggestive dancing of the habitués and the more skilled performances of those especially hired for the occasion. As in Paris the Spanish and Russian dancer, the Turkish and Tyrolese specimens, gathered from heaven knows where, are here. There were a number of handsome young officers present who occasionally danced with the women they were escorting. When the dancing began (the music invariably indicated the dance), the lights in the dome turned pink. When it ceased and some purely instrumental composition was rendered, the lights in the dome were a glittering white. The place seemed nothing new to the habitués, quite the blasé atmosphere one encounters in Paris—a rather quick development for Berlin.

It was amusing to me to see the spirit in which Herr Merten took this atmosphere, whether from the point of view of policy—seeing that I knew his wife—or otherwise I could not make out. "Now we are here," he said as we entered. "I want to tell you something. I never associate with these women, I never speak to them. Personally I am through with them—with women. If after a few minutes you think you would like one of them or would like to spend the evening here talking to them, say the word and I will leave. I will sit here as long as you like, but I don't want to talk to them."

I waived the opportunity, of course.

And yet how he did boast of it all! For a man who was interested in this triumph of German vice-life, I thought he was singularly cold. The women looked anything but dull. I fancy the majority may have been essentially vicious. We drank champagne, waved away charmers, discussed London, Paris, St. Petersburg, talked of how Berlin was growing in its patronage of this thing and finally left. But at two or three o'clock, I forget which, before we left, the law apparently compelled the closing of this great central chamber, and after that hour all the patrons were compelled to adjourn to an inner sanctum—quite as large, not so showy, but full of a brilliant, strolling, dining, drinking life, where, I was informed, one could stay till eight in the morning if one chose. There was some drunkenness here, much departing of ladies with their captures for chambers unknown, much coquetting, parading, lascivious dancing. Why, would you say, should Berlin be so proud of this institution? They are proud of it—all the successful cognoscenti. I heard Germans in London speak of it (after I returned there) as being superior to anything in London! What fools and liars, pretenders, we mortals be!

CHAPTER LXXXIII

The most pleasing portions of Berlin to me, the ones most suited to my moods and temperament, are those which relate to the branches of the Spree—its canals and the very large number of lakes about it. It would be very difficult for me to suggest what a romantic value the sight of wild ducks flying over the housetops, over offices and factories of the business heart as well as over buildings of the outlying districts gives to the city—ducks passing from one branch canal to another, or one branch of the Spree to another, their long necks protruding before them, their metallic colors gleaming in the sun.

The rivers of every city have their individuality, and to me the Spree and its canals seem eminently suited to Berlin. The water effects—and to me they are always artistically important and frequent and altogether charming—are plentiful. If you are fond of the Venetian canal idea, it is very easy to find a street in Berlin, the center of which is occupied by one, and if you like the vicinity of a lake, you will have no trouble building or securing a house near one in the suburbs. They are to be found in nearly every direction. I was so interested to see the number of bridges where, much more than in Paris, Rome, Florence or London, one can stand and survey an interesting spectacle of water life—canal boats carrying their apples, coal, potatoes, lumber, all propelled by electricity; or, as in the Tiergarten and some of the better residence streets, with the gulls, ducks and pigeons making idyllic use of the water.

You see quaint things in Berlin, such as you will not see elsewhere—the Spreewald nurses, for instance, in the Tiergarten, with their short, scarlet, balloon skirts emphasized by a white apron, their triangular white linen headdress, very conspicuous, and their very short sleeves and highly colored neck cloths lighting up the landscape like a stage costume. I presume, of course, that it is fashionable for the well-to-do families to employ such nurses and to send them out morning and afternoon in the park with the children. To the zoological gardens people go to see the animals fed, to listen to music in the casino and to watch the children play—a tendency which I could not approve of. It was actually suggested to me as something interesting to do. I went once, but never again. I chanced to come there when they were feeding the owls, giving each one a mouse—live or dead, I could not quite make out. That was enough for me. I despise flesh-eating birds anyhow. They are quite the most horrible of all evoluted specimens. This particular collection—eagles, hawks, condors, owls of every known type and variety, and buzzards—all sat in their cages gorging themselves on raw meat or mice. The owls, to my disgust, fixed me with their relentless, wide-pupiled eyes, the while they tore at the entrails of their victims. As a realist, of course, I ought to accept all these delicate manifestations of the iron constitution of the universe as interesting, but I can't. Now and then—very frequently, in fact—life becomes too much for my hardy stomach. I withdraw, chilled and stupefied by the way strength survives and weakness goes under. And to think that as yet we have no method of discovering why the horrible appears and no reason for saying that it should not. One can actually become surfeited with beauty and art and take refuge in the inartistic and the unlovely! The deformed or so-called ugly in the hands of the artist becomes beautiful.

One of the really interesting things to me was the ice-palace, the which, I take it, has no counterpart anywhere. We have an ice-skating rink in New York, but it is not the same thing. Americans may like to skate and do it as well as the members of any other nation, but the American skating rinks I have seen, roller or ice, do not suggest in any way the charm of this one in Berlin to me. The ice-skating rink in New York is cold, the one in Berlin is warm; the one in New York has two or three rows of hard benches on either side for spectators, this one in Berlin has wide platforms set with tables where food and drink are served. The ice rink in New York has a cheap, third-rate orchestra playing a short melody every fifteen minutes or so because the musical union forbids giving more melody for the money. The one in Berlin has a large excellent orchestra and continuous music. A sort of ice vaudeville performance is given every evening from nine to eleven, and it is an interesting, in many respects beautiful, performance. Never in the rink in New York or elsewhere have I seen such chic skating costumes or as good skaters. I was alternately delighted and terrified by the skill and daring of not a few but a great majority of the skaters.

I hate to inveigh against America so much, but it seems to me that for a nation that is satisfied, because Thomas Jefferson or somebody said so, that it is the chosen of God and that because of its great monetary successes it must have every other merit in proportion, we are as bad off socially as any nation could well be. "Thou shalt not" has been preached from so many fool pulpits and schoolhouses in the United States that the nation as a nation, individual for individual, is terribly ignorant and with little courage for the most ordinary pleasures of life. When I think how once a case of beer landed at our home depot platform was viewed askance—an emissary of hell—I have to smile. If you go to a *respectable* American outing today, beer is barred. So far as I could see, in Berlin everyone drank beer or the lighter wines, the children being present, and no harm seemed to flow from it. I presume drunkenness is not on the increase in Germany. And in Paris the way they sit at tables in front of cafés, men and women, and sip their liqueurs would shock Moline or Cincinnati or St. Louis. Why? It is a very pleasant way to enjoy your life. Outside of trade or the desire to be *president, vice president* or *secretary* of something, we have so often no real diversions. The stage in London, Berlin and Paris is just as good as it is here, if not better. Personally, I think it is better, more human. Their public galleries and places of entertainment (non-theatrical) are infinitely to be preferred. We talk much about our automobiles, but you see just as many automobiles in England, France and Germany as you do here; their railroad service is just as good if not better, and their places to go are much more striking and significant—their seaside resorts, baths and winter mountain pleasures, for instance. Everyone there, insofar as I could make out, takes life so much more matter-of-factly. They are not constantly criticizing their neighbors for this, that and the other variation of the rule. It is the business of each individual to look after himself, and beyond noting the rise or fall of individuals nothing is thought of it. Here our papers and our homes and our pulpits are full of "thou shalt nots." Every little squeak from the village shoemakers up is busy advising. Why, I think the intellectual laissez-faire atmosphere of Europe is positively soothing after New York, Chicago, Philadelphia. We are dull, narrow, inexperienced, idiotically self-opinionated, and we don't know it.

I went one day before Madame Culp returned to Potsdam and saw the Imperial Palace and grounds and the Royal Parade, where one or two of the crack regiments of the empire are drilled. The emperor had just left for Venice. As a seat of royalty, it did not interest me at all. Frederick the Great, insofar as I could learn and see, had laid out and built an imitation of the grounds and palace of Versailles. As an imitation it was fairly satisfactory, without the personality of Versailles, however, and I asked myself over and over why an emperor of Germany should build and accept as satisfactory an imitation of Versailles. What a commentary on German architectural ability and German art! And to this day this defect has not been remedied. You walk through grounds which suggest the French landscape idea and through two palaces, an old one built closely in imitation of the rococo of Versailles, and a new one obviously suggested by the same source. Very dull they are, great rooms containing so-called treasures which are not treasures at all. Depend on it—being an emperor or a member of a royal family has its drawbacks. I tried to be interested in bottle-glass ballrooms, picture galleries, royal auditoriums and the like. Alas, alas! The servitors were just as anxious for tips as any American waiter. Potsdam left a poor impression on me. I returned to Zehlendorf, anxious to stroll in the wonderful forest there, for that was natural, individual, artistic, impressive. I found always that an hour, mornings or evenings, in that great reserve restored my faith in life and its possibilities. Nature, art, beauty seemed once more important and worthwhile.

* * *

It was at the expiration of the ten days originally suggested that Madame Culp returned. Not incuriously, having had time to think over this very complicated situation, I had lost considerable interest in the matter. There had appeared on the scene a cousin of Madame Culp, another Hollander, a very charming young woman who made her living as an accompanist and who had been to America. She had lived in Rochester, New York, for three years and spoke English perfectly. Her husband, a Hollander, was not present and was not expected. They seemed to have some understanding by which they lived apart.

After two or three casual meetings (this young woman came to see Fräulein Förster quite frequently), we became very friendly. She said she liked to play for me because I was sympathetic, and I truly liked to listen to her. She was not a finished artist, but she played with real understanding and regard. We went one evening with Herr Merten to hear Mischa Elman play. And another time I took a walk with her in the great Grunewald forest.

I presume that unless we are fixed by matter of economy, policy, a sense of duty, a religious belief or by some other such binding agent, there is no limit to this matter of sentimental interest between the sexes. A man may crave and delight in ten thousand paintings or objects of art, books, landscapes, specimens of architecture—almost anything you will. With how many poems, pictures, buildings, vistas have I personally been enraptured! It is equally true of women, only the relation could not possibly lead beyond a friendly admiration in most cases. This particular woman, Mrs. Drucker, aged twenty-eight or thereabouts, was of a type quite acceptable to me. She was not, I suppose, good-looking in the ordinary sense. Her face was a little too broad, after the Dutch fashion, and her body too solid, but there was a flower-like charm about her temperament and her point of view that interested and pleased me. Somehow she suggested the waxy pallor and fragrance of the lily or of one of Frans Hals's paintings. She acknowledged frankly and with a phlegmatic acceptance of the inevitable that she had no great talent, let alone genius, for music. She could, she thought, eventually make a fair living as an accompanist. Her husband, she told me, who lived in Amsterdam, had never been able to support her, and besides, they did not any longer feel any particular interest in each other. They were merely good friends. She offered to give me a letter to him. Holland, she thought, was a delightful country, but having only five million people it offered small outlet for the genius of the race. Any talent that appeared in Holland must make its appeal to the world at large. In her opinion, it was not wise therefore for Dutch novelists or playwrights to write in their own language. Better English, German, French. She liked the Germans only fairly well—they were too conceited. The French were too flighty and make-believe for her; the English too cold. "I like the Americans," she said quite simply and exactly, "and I will tell you why. They see things in a larger way, and they are so much more ambitious and hopeful. Their plans are always so liberal."

She certainly had interpreted one phase of the American spirit. Her opinion of the Germans, French and Hollanders was that they were essentially smaller, more conservative, more careful. "Nothing venture, nothing have" appealed to her as something to keep in mind.

Quite outside of any intention, our sympathies united on many points—melodies, landscapes, moods. We talked over the significance of the moods we were in, and then seeing that we were, quite without volition, reaching a sympathetic understanding, she said, "You know, I helped Madame Culp write that letter you received at Frankfort. She isn't very good at English," she smiled quite sweetly, "and she wanted me to help her make it well, you know, nice."

"Did you?" I asked, astonished.

"You like her?"

"Yes. I think she has a beautiful voice."

"Yes indeed! And she has such a following here in Berlin. You should stay and hear her sing. Her concerts are very wonderful."

"I know it," I said.

"I owe her quite a great deal. She can help me in my work here. I wouldn't have you tell her about the letter. She would be furious."

"Do you think I would?"

"I thought not, or I wouldn't have told you."

"What a pity it is that I am not going to be in Berlin longer. She will be returning now in a day or two. You are not coming to Holland?"

"No. There is nothing there for me."

"Nor New York?"

"I'd like to, but I don't think so. It is not wise to move from place to place in this way. I think I shall stay here and in Germany. Altogether it will probably be best, though I like America better."

I sighed. "It is always the way."

"But these moods are not so much," she said very consolingly. "We get over them. It sounds hard, doesn't it, but we do. Madame Culp is very nice."

"Madame Culp—" I growled.

She smiled again. She had a very sweet, philosophic, delicate and refined spirit. "It would not do for me. I could not even be friendly with you. She is very jealous. Sometime, if you come again, perhaps we shall see each other."

"To the devil with sometime!" I said, but just the same I could see her position, and I was scheduled to stay but three or four days more. We met another afternoon quite by accident in one of the streets of Zehlendorf, and I walked with her to the station. She was going into Berlin to some concert.

"Why not come with me to dinner afterward?"

"I would," she sighed, "only there is someone else I have promised, and, as I told you, if anyone saw us—Better not. I may come to New York sometime, or you will come again to Berlin."

She waved me a smiling farewell.

I left her with a real touch of regret.

CHAPTER LXXXIV

Before concluding my account of relations with Madame Culp, I should like to interpolate the incident of Hanscha Jauer, for it occurred the night before her arrival and has cast a significant light over Berlin and Germany for me. Unlike the incident of Lilly Edwards, it was entirely without premeditation—an impulse quickly acted upon. Berlin, like Paris, London and New York, has so many interesting squares or circles. In New York most often they are called squares and in Berlin *platzes*. Like the spirit of all really great individual nations, these *platzes* in Berlin are individual, aglow with a temper all their own. At six o'clock, or anywhere near that time, it was a delight to stand in the Leipziger Platz, the Alexanderplatz or the Spittelmarkt and watch the swirl of metropolitan life, the auto-trucks, automobiles, buses, taxis, streetcars and vehicles of every kind go by in seemingly tangled masses. The big German policeman with his polished brass helmet; the solid German citizen, well-dressed and a little indifferent; the German housewife with her basket or bundle; the well-dressed woman shopper and possibly her daughter, or her daughter alone, progressively smart and attractive; the masses of clerks, laborers, mechanics, small tradesmen, professional men, all hurrying to catch trains or cars, give them a wonderful tone or individuality—the kind of thing you would hope to see in Germany. And then the German signs plastered here, there and everywhere, signs not advertising the same things you see advertised in London, New York or Paris; the German voice, mildly raucous and full of "r's"; the German courage, hope, persistence, and under it all so often the German melancholy—who is it thinks that great melodies are played on human instruments alone? Why, public places sing. Great orchestral compositions are rendered nightly by Trafalgar Square, the Place de l'Opéra, Madison Square and the Alexanderplatz. You can hear almost the ultimate music of this earthly illusion in these central maelstroms of human hope, enthusiasm, effort, desire.

In Berlin I was never tired of seeking out these very individual *platzes*. It was rarely before seven or seven-thirty that I had to keep my appointments in the "down-town" region, and so up to that time I sought almost nightly a new center—Savignyplatz, Arnimplatz, Nikolsburger Platz, Bayerischer Platz, Vinetaplatz and the like. I wanted to find out the localized centers of trade and whether there were immense stores outside of the three or four I heard most frequently mentioned. Berlin has a great trade life, immense. You feel everywhere the throb of true industry. I was constantly assured that it was almost a world-leader in iron-founding, machine-making, wagon, weapon and chemical wares, textiles and the like, and it looked it. In great areas it had the ring of a manufacturing city. I had heard of one hundred thousand individuals so poor that they could only afford to rent a bed in another family's rooms or room, and of thirty-two thousand families living in one-room accommodations. An investigator of real merit gave me the figure of eighty thousand individuals seeking the municipal shelters at night—eighty thousand homeless men and women out of three million or thereabouts.

But be that as it may, these outlying regions—great, smooth, gray streets lined with five-story tenements, all clean and orderly-looking, with other tenements in the rear, all clean and orderly, and still other tenements in the rear of those, all clean and orderly—tenements three-deep—interested me. What kind of solemn German minds filled them? How were they worrying over the morrow, how fighting the battle of today? We grow so smart when we get a little money; we forget the great, shuffling, struggling rank and file. The average man will only look up, not down; forward, not back. It is a part of the cowardly, canting trade-logic of the time.

One evening I went to the Alexanderplatz. I had heard of it as a great center. It was safely removed from all de-Germanizing influences such as prevail about Unter den Linden, the Pariser Platz, the Potsdamer Platz and other places where the German imperial life combines with the European international life to make them less purely German than one might wish.

Not so with the Alexanderplatz. It is purely German. I had heard of a great department store there, the Tietz store, and as those things are always suggestive and illuminating to me, suggestive of the tastes and appetites of a great city, I went there. It was much finer architecturally and materially than any department store I saw either in London or Paris, finer indeed in its marbles, bronzes, decorations and spaces than any store in either New York or Chicago. It suggested somehow the marble glories (brown, cream and yellow) of some of the wonderful churches in Italy.

After I had spent an hour here inspecting what the Berliners buy, seeing all the tricks of presentation, the masses of purely German-made articles—scarcely a single thing imported from abroad—the German floorwalkers, cash-girls, salesgirls and the brisk commercial atmosphere generally, I came out into the evening flare of Alexanderplatz. You know the atmosphere. How twilight seems to blend with sunlight, and electric light with both; how the world seems to be saying, "Now our work is almost done, and we will soon be home." Oh, the promise of the night! I crossed to a central island where streetcars seemed to be stopping in order to get a car to the Potsdamer Platz, when I saw a girl or woman pass me, the type that I think I understand best of all: a vague, wondering soul that does not understand life at all, that wonders with better insight and truer philosophy really what it is all about than those thousands of cocksure, self-protective souls that expatiate by the hour and pay out wise saws and asinine time-maxims like an old-fashioned reel. She was in her way an un-Americanized Jennie Gerhardt, and she looked at me with vague eyes, only to go her way. Not a touch of the coquetry of the Friedrichstrasse, not a suggestion of the international savoir faire of Unter den Linden. You would not have assumed for a moment that she was a street girl—as distinctly she was not at heart. It takes a sort of temperamental capacity to be an efficient streetwalker. There are tricks in all trades, nowhere more so than this. What philosophic raghead was it that called it "the easy way"? There is more innate capacity indicated there than in most of the so-called professions for women.

The sun had just gone down, and the electric lamps were beginning to flare. What an attractive type, I said and paused to watch her. She had on a very light—cream-gray—street suit that fitted her well, principally because nothing could fit her ill. A wide, soft-brimmed, very dark brown hat with no ornament save a pompon of light brown silk went with it. It drooped in graceful lines about a soft, waxy-white face. She had, as I saw afterwards, vague, gray-blue eyes, light brown hair, plump and not too shapely hands and little feet for a woman so solidly built. She was not at all large, but plump after the Teutonic fashion, the type that tends to heaviness and rotundity in later years.

The German street-woman is not allowed to accost any man or to show by sign or motion that her body is for sale. Any man may accost any unaccompanied woman. If she does not want him, she does not speak. He is not promptly arrested for mashing. Yet better than sign or motion is intuition, against the results of which no law can forefend. The average man and woman reach an understanding, law or no law, and the world proceeds about as well as it always has.

I saw this woman go by, and instead of getting on a car, I watched her go down the street. She seemed to me to be coming from some shop and going home. I admired the easy motions of her figure—a frame smoothly and evenly jointed. She disappeared in the great throng of life, and I thought I had lost her, but presently I saw her again taking to the right along a nearby radiating street. I crossed over and watched her draw near along another segment of this great circle. That was evidence enough.

"What a pretty spring dress!" I commented, standing by her near where cars were taking on and discharging passengers.

She looked at me with vaguely questioning eyes, to reassure herself. The faintest effort at a smile lightened her lips. "It is not new," she said.

"Not old, anyhow. Were you going to take a car here?"

"No, I only live a little way. I walk from here."

"You won't mind if I walk with you?"

"No."

"I've just been in that great department store," I observed, by way of conversation. "It's very fine, isn't it?"

"Yes," she said very simply. "I worked there once for a little while."

"Long ago?"

"Two years ago."

"What sort of a neighborhood is this?" I inquired. "Good or bad? It is so busy."

"Oh, very poor. Not bad but poor. This section here is busy, but working people live back through here mostly," and she indicated a long gray cross-street to our right. I thought of the three tenements deep.

"And where you live—is it the same?"

"I have only a room. Yes, it is the same. You had better not go with me all the way. I will go first, and then you can come."

She said it so wearily and matter-of-factly yet so good-naturedly withal that I conceived a real liking for her. Another personage, this, someone to know. Not so much an intellect as a German mood, someone who reflected the more morbid and phlegmatic aspects of the nation, without being heavily despondent. She was really too good-looking to be despondent—yet.

We walked on for blocks through this welter of life. "You are not German," she said.

"No, American."

"I knew you were not German."

We passed a police station.

"The police are very strict?" I suggested.

"Yes, very."

"Do they make the street-women pay here?"

"Not that I know of."

We came to a long street, darkening in the dusk. I decided to have an hour's talk with her and then take her to dinner, perhaps to some typical place she would know. Perhaps, like Lilly Edwards, she could show me something I would not ordinarily see.

"You come in five minutes," she said, with a pretty half-smile. She gave me the number. "Up four flights and the door at the head of the stairs. It will be open."

I waited, reconnoitering a German cigar store, and then went. The door was open, a cleanly tenement. I knocked, and she appeared out of a little closet, her hat off, the blonde Marguerite type of physical charm. Why should a woman as good-looking as this have to be on the streets? I asked myself. Surely some man—a workingman—would marry her. But why should she be compelled to marry a workingman or anybody to escape a social censure that might really not concern her? The price was probably too high.

It was a simple room, quite square, done in brown with a red settee, two red chairs, a center table with a brownish-red cloth on it, and an oil lamp with a large white-and-pink-flowered glass shade. Yellowish-brown shades and white lace curtains were at the two windows—drawn. A quarter-sized bed with a reddish-brown spread on it stood in one corner. In another corner was the closet with some coats and dresses in evidence. It was plain there was no bath here and no steam or furnace heat. Near the window set a patent oil-stove. It was too spring-like tonight to need it.

"My hands are so soiled," I said at a venture. "Have you a washstand?"

"There is a closet in the hall, but I will bring you a bowl. Wait." And she went in a practical way to the hall and returned with a blue-and-white agate ware bowl partly filled with water, a towel and a piece of soap. A little side-table with a drawer, containing possibly tin dishes (I never looked), served as a washstand.

"How do you take a bath?" I asked.

"I have a tin tub."

"In this cold room?"

"It is not so cold. I do not mind."

"There is no heat of any kind?"

"No."

"And what do you pay for this?"

"Eight marks a week."

I tried to figure just what that would mean in American money.

I suppose an equivalent, neighborhood for neighborhood, would be four or five dollars.

When I finished my hands, she waited simply for me to act. Of course I wanted her body, and of course I would act. She stood there, quite clean and fresh-looking. You could see that such smooth, plump flesh as she had, pale but healthy, had never been attacked by any disease. There was not the least suggestion of that morbid blood weariness that shows in the faces of so many—indeed everyone—where disease has entered. This woman was simply healthy.

"Do you go to a doctor?"

"Yes, now and then. I am all right."

She smiled reassuringly.

There is a certain terror that attaches to possible disease springing from promiscuity that is decidedly chilling. It cools my ardor quite thoroughly, while never modifying my interest in a significant type. Instinct has always governed with me and never failed in the few adventures I have made. I have invariably taken all precautions and then thanked heaven that I have escaped scot-free. The best of these women cannot tell what day infection has set in. There is, however, no particular danger in looking at a woman's body, and that is always the lure. So I took her arm and began to unbutton her white shirtwaist.

The thing that pleased me about her was that she was clean, with that honest German cleanliness that begins with the hair and ends with the stockings. She had healthy, light brown hair, plenty of it, and smooth, soft, white arms and hips. There is a rounded plumpness about the average German woman's body which many artists profess to despise. I have listened to their strictures, but I do not share their conclusions. The plump German body reflects the meditative, reflective, melancholy, morbid German temperament. It is not so much dull as emotional and vague. There are different physical responses to the life instinct. The Germans make a very distinguished one, in my humble opinion. When she was fully undressed she made a very pleasing appearance—rounded, not heavy, sensuous, physically disturbing.

"You are nice," I said, looking at her arms and her waist and her neck and chin. "What is your name?"

"Hanscha Jauer."

"And were you born here in Berlin?"

"No, I come from Tilsit."

"Where is that?"

"Oh a long way from here. Near the Prussian frontier."

I thought of long as applied to American distances.

"You said you worked in Tietz's two years ago. Have you been in Berlin long?"

"Nearly five years now."

"Did you come here direct?"

"No, I lived at Stettin" (she pronounced it "Shtetteen") "a little while—two or three years."

"Is that a large city?"

"Oh, three or four hundred thousand."

It was much harder for me to trifle with this woman indifferently than it had been with Lilly Edwards or some others. Her smooth, plump body appealed to me, and what is more, her gray-blue eyes told of a spirit wholly unmercenary. I said to her jokingly, "What is this going to cost me?"

"Oh, anything you like. What you will."

"Well, for instance?"

"Would a gold piece be too much?"

"No," I replied, and smiled.

A gold piece could have been either ten or twenty marks. She did not get that much ordinarily and would have taken less.

I looked at her calmly until she put up one clean, soft hand to my shoulder.

"Don't you like me?" she asked. "I am all right. I am very nice."

"How do you know?"

"I am very clean. See." She went to her closet and produced a bottle containing a scientific German prophylactic with the formula on the label. "I know I am all right," she said.

We went to her couch, where, after teasing her physically, I finally found myself unable to resist. Such a study in suggestive curves as she presented!

CHAPTER LXXXV

The thing that interested me about Hanscha Jauer was her point of view and her mood. Really she was like a still pond, mentally and physically, or one of those dull back eddies where waters pocket themselves without resource to proceed and where straws and sticks go idly about in a ring.

I extracted a portion of her German story. Her father was a carpenter and her mother—well, just her mother. There were not many industries in Tilsit, and she started out to learn to be a weaver but did not like it. The pay was very little. Perhaps that would not have made so much difference, but there was a young blood in the town who fell in love with her, or with whom she fell in love, and who over-persuaded her. I could not get at the romance back of that, but looking at Hanscha, I could imagine it—a youthful fever in the blood. Then he went into the army and left her, and because she was afraid of her father, she ran away to Stettin and the child was eventually sent back to her mother. She tried working in the mills in Stettin, but they made her sick, she said. They were dirty. The work was not nice. She tried working in a store too—"but I am not good at figures. Occasionally I went with a man. I had to."

Somehow, as she said it, I could see the whole picture back of her—mills, stores, streets, men. Tilsit and Stettin, with its factories, stood out as distinct centers of life in my mind.

There was a girl in Stettin who occasionally went with men who became friendly with Hanscha, and the midwife who delivered the child told her what to do. "I did not think so much then," she said, "either. I was still young."

"But you are not old now."

"Next month I will be thirty."

"But that is not old."

"Oh yes, for a woman. I think, always, I will get a man."

"And the child—is it still with your mother?"

"Yes."

"Do you ever see it?"

"No. I send money home, now and then, when I have it."

"Why didn't you stay at Tietz's?"

"I was not quick enough. They don't pay very much either—very little. I would have to go with men just as well if I worked there as I do now, and I would have hardly any time. It is not so easy."

"And well I know it," I said.

"It is not nice, what I do," she went on reflectively, "but I do not see just what else I can do. I am not very clever."

"Don't you ever go into the Friedrichstrasse and Unter den Linden?"

"No. I have not the clothes. One must have fine clothes to go there, and I have not got them."

"But you might get them in time. You are better-looking than most of those women there that I have seen. You are really very pretty."

"Am I?"

"Yes."

She smiled almost sadly.

"You see," she said in explanation, "they are very hard, those women. I do not like them. They are not so much nicer than I am but they are harder. They fight and make men pay them. I cannot do that. I have not the heart. Over here it is not so hard. Someone comes with you, and then maybe he comes again. It is not so expensive here."

"What sort of men do you meet here?"

"Oh, clerks, tradesmen, men who run the stores. They do not expect so much."

"No, but they do not pay you so much either."

"I know," she replied dreamily, "but if one does not go in the quarter where the money is, what is one to do? I cannot dress like that."

What are you to do with such a soul?

"Do you ever go to the Palais de Danse?" I asked.

"The Palais de Danse? What is that?"

"Don't you know what the Palais de Danse is?" I inquired in astonishment.

"No."

"Never heard of it?"

"No."

"Well, bless my soul! Have you ever been to the ice-palace?"

"Once—yes."

"Did you like it?"

"Yes, it was nice."

"Do you skate?"

"I did once. That was a long time ago."

"Let me see now," I went on, curious to see what else of Berlin she had missed. "Have you ever been to the Cabaret Linden or Piccadilly?"

"No," she smiled.

"The Weinhaus Rheingold?"

"I know of it."

"Arcadia?"

"No."

"Come now—you don't mean it?"

"I have never been there."

"Come now," I said, "get on your clothes. It isn't late. I'll show you Berlin." She smiled amusedly. "Have you an evening dress?"

After I mentioned the matter of an evening dress, I was really sorry, for it really did not matter anyhow, and the light dress she wore was sufficiently neat to pass muster.

"I'm afraid I haven't one. But I don't care much to go, anyhow."

"Oh yes. Do come," I insisted. "It isn't late. You'll enjoy it. You haven't had any dinner. We'll go to the Rheingold for something to eat" (I was afraid to venture anything more pretentious), "to Piccadilly for drinks, to Arcadia, to Unter den Linden, and then we'll go to the Palais de Danse and anything else we can find. You ought to see these places. Really, you ought. It will do you good."

"Not the Palais de Danse," she protested simply. "I haven't the clothes. I don't want to go there. The other places I don't mind."

I had unfortunately indicated a little something of the showiness of the Palais de Danse.

She finally agreed and dressed. I noticed that she sought about in her small bureau for a small lace collar, a good one, and put it on. She powdered her face and touched her hair with almost resigned, hopeless touches. She was thinking of her thirty years and her future, I know. I tried to find a taxi, but none careened through this neighborhood. We finally took a car directly to the Weinhaus Rheingold, and after eating walked around to Piccadilly, a very little way. She had never seen it, but it was not exciting to her. We got a taxi there and sped to Arcadia. I think she found it a little dull. Life, after its severe abuses, its ugly, unkindly leers and kicks and blows, can never seem the same—it cannot pretend to be the sweet, smiling thing it seems to some. Hanscha Jauer had seen its ugly face. Melancholy had, I am afraid, marked her for its own. This silly outing merely emphasized her remoteness from it all, her insufficiency, the fact that her day was over.

If you think she was not a pleasing figure hanging on my arm in this Berlin night light, you are greatly mistaken. She did not care to take my arm, would never venture to do so, but I suggested that she should. This same soul, born into a family of means, guarded by self-protective parents and steered aright, would have made one of those pleasing marriages which the world admires. Her pretty face and pleasing disposition would have been an ornament to any home. Life had not soiled her soul even now—it couldn't. It had merely muddied the envelope. Any sensible man of a staid, meditative disposition would have found a charming companion in Hanscha. She was not dull exactly—she was living in vague dreams of her own.

"Supposing," I said to her after we had left the Weinhaus Rheingold—it was in Piccadilly with its flare of silly lights, "that you never get a man. Then what?"

"Oh, I don't know. I shall die, perhaps. I do not want to live very much."

"But your little girl?"

"Boy," she corrected, smiling at my effort to find out.

"What about him?"

"My mother is fond of him now. Oh, I shall work perhaps. I do not know. How can you tell? It is not so easy to get things. I do the best I can."

I could see her in her little room turning in a fog of mystery and misery at times. There was a real pang of suffering in the state of Hanscha Jauer for me.

"Is it so hard to get along in Berlin?"

"There are very many poor people here. They do not pay much."

I thought of the thirty-two thousand families in one room each; the one hundred thousand lodgers able to afford only one bed in the *one room* of another family; the eighty thousand citizens seeking the shelter nightly of the municipal lodging houses. Yes, Berlin is clean, industrious, thrifty, well-built, but it does not escape the pressure of misery either.

"Hanscha," I said, after a time and after we had talked over many other things—or, rather, I had extracted replies to many questions—"what do you think of life, anyhow? What do you think it is?"

"Nobody knows," she replied with a little lift of her hand, deprecating the fact that any such serious question should be addressed to her. "I don't think we live after we die. It doesn't make any difference. I do not want to. It is not very nice."

"You are quite right," I said, "for many it isn't—very many. But if you get a man now, you would live and be happy."

Her brow darkened the least bit. "I'll tell you how it is," she said. "The poor German wants to marry only a woman who will work for him very hard. She must earn him money. If a man has a little store or something, then he can marry a woman who has money, and he will not look at me. If I marry a poor man, I have to be a slave. If one could love, it would be different, but I cannot. So then I must work hard without love, and I would rather die. There are men of course who are nice and who might like me. I don't know."

I wish you could have heard the note of unconscious resignation that ran through this woman's testimony. How dull the world is not to see how life itself, its mere shifting and turning, makes so often for so-called sin and degradation where none is spiritually intended or existent. I can never fathom the block-headed asininity of life. "Ears, and they hear not," said Jesus; "Eyes, and they do not see." Exactly, exactly. And there is neither good nor evil, but thinking makes it so. It is so easy for those born in satisfactory circumstances to moralize. There is but one thing to be said for the best or the worst of them: if they lived long enough, life would surely and rudely rip the scales from their eyes. They would see if they could really live.

We talked of other things. I was curious as to police regulations; as to how, exactly, she divided her hours; whether she had any intimates, women or men, with whom she was truly happy. Of the former obviously none; of the latter I could not learn if there were any. She told me that in many ways she liked Berlin, only she was so much alone—sometimes during the afternoon some of her men friends looked her up, but mostly she was alone. She sewed then or cleaned or dressed or bought anything she needed. At night, unless she had an unusual stroke of good fortune, or some man friend called, which was not infrequent, she appeared in the Alexanderplatz. Insofar as she knew, the police did not know her. She was not regularly there. The janitor in the house did not know. He had too much to do to watch everything and everybody. "If I find a man that I like, I will settle down," she said naively. "I would make a good wife, I think. But I do not want to be a slave."

I do not want to harp too much on this incident, but in its way it seemed quite wonderful to me. I was fascinated by the phlegmatic melancholy of Hanscha Jauer. It fixed Tilsit and Stettin for me. Because of her, the Alexanderplatz and the great gloomy regions behind it took on a strange luster. Mr. Tietz's marble department store was only significant because once she had been discharged from there.

I parted from her at the door two nights later, or perhaps the third, my last in Berlin, and I walked in the swirling life of Leipziger Strasse, aglow with busy shops, crowded with well-dressed people, the windows displaying all those various components which make up homes, dresses, public appearances—the materials of a hopeful life. Somehow, before a great furniture store whose broad plate glass front was set with the details of one of those conventional middle-class dining rooms, "parlors" and bedrooms—all bright, attractive sets—I thought of Hanscha and her possible man. Do you think I could resist the tears? Not me. To me the furniture and all it represented of possible happiness was not worth much—but to her! Why might not life have been kind to Hanscha Jauer?

CHAPTER LXXXVI

The next morning Madame Culp arrived. I had had a letter from her the day before, rather colorfully worded, and a telegram the night before saying she had missed a connection at Ostend, but nevertheless at half after eight the next morning she appeared, brisk, sufficient, authoritative. Depend on it, this household was astir early to receive her. Fräulein Förster was up bright and early. I could hear her in my room stirring around as early as six-thirty. Minna, the combination cook and maid—fair, blonde, of undue growth physically—was "on the job" in the kitchen, putting things to rights. I heard her say of some grocer's boy once—a stocky, red-faced lad—that he was too *frech*, and then I knew where our American slang word "fresh" came from. I never knew before that it was a corruption of the German *frech*.

But Madame Culp when she appeared—bless our souls and bodies, what a manager! Fräulein Förster was nervous, and I could see it. Dear husband was appropriately aggressive, alive, contentious, on the lookout for himself. A gentle, suave, fair, smiling lady this, when all was well, but inclined to rant and thunder when things were not. "Never, never, for my temperament," I said to myself. "She would have to sing a different song for me. What she wants is some peaceful citizen who will dance attendance on her. Grant Richards can have her. I don't wonder she complains that he won't love her enough. He's wise. If he did, he'd dance more attendance than is customarily his wont. The pleasant vales of Holland for me."

However, I was here. I had been for ten days and would be for three or four more. Courtesy demanded that I stay to hear her great concert. She was, in her way, attractive physically, and she could sing. "I'll stick it out," I sighed. "I can make believe in this thing as well as the next one. But if she isn't nice to me, cold weather immediately sets in, and when she comes to New York, I am out of town, that's all. This is entirely too exciting."

When the gate clicked below on her first arrival, all was in a turmoil. Nana, the dog, "friend husband," Fräulein Förster, Minna, the maid—all came in for separate and effusive greetings. I heard the somewhat guttural voice of Herr Merten asking questions. I heard Fräulein Förster explaining volubly many things. "Down, Nana, down!" and then much friendly romping and tumbling with that sentimental animal.

"And where is Herr Dreiser? Good morning, Herr Dreiser! Not up yet? You are lazy this morning."

I put my head out of the door to say I would soon be down to welcome her home. An enthusiastic smile from that direction was my reward. However, now that I was in this so roundly, I was dubious about the whole matter. But such is life.

The most curious thing about this whole household arrangement was the way this dried-up affectional atmosphere was maintained in imitation of its one-time bloom. Herr Merten seemed appropriately solicitous and affectionate. He asked, if not tenderly at least courteously, after her, and she did as much for him. They went off to his boudoir together. Yet of course Fräulein Förster and Minna knew of some of her interests in other directions. They could not have helped it. Fräulein Förster had traveled with Madame in Austria, Russia, Holland and Belgium. Only the day before she handed me my letter and telegram quite matter-of-factly.

Well then, these early greetings being over, I came down to breakfast, to find Madame waiting. Herr Merten had already departed for Berlin. She was engrossed in mail, a large handful. On the table was the customary tea, sausage and marmalade—liver- and blood-sausage and marmalade. I ate both cheerfully, impartially distributed on my rye bread.

Madame was so glad to see me. "And dit you haf a nice time?" I can see her round eyes ogling me. "And wuss Fräulein Förster very nice to you?"

"Indeed! Indeed!"

"Ant were you very happy?"

"Beside myself, all the time."

"I'm so glad." A tender smile.

Very good. So we ate. She was promptly outraged at my eating sausage and marmalade on my bread—after Grant Richards she must have thought me another kind of animal. I laughed at her.

"Oh, but it is terrible. How can you?"

"You will have to endure much worse than that if you run with me," I smiled quite fiendishly—I am sure. "How was Grant Richards?"

Followed an extended description of Grant Richards. She had seen very little of him, of course. He was really not nice enough to her. *Almost all* was over. However, he was sick—some serious chill of the intestines. That worried me. I happened to know that Grant Richards was rather dangerously sensitive in that region. I might wish to disturb him in some of his lady affections, but not in his life. When she saw that I was anxious, she assured me that things were not so bad. He had, she had heard, been getting better.

I could see quite plainly that almost all was not over. She had probably reproached him, using me as a weapon, and had piqued his interest. As a matter of fact, before the breakfast was over, this became quite plain. In Frankfort I had called her "the candy kid," an expression I had used to Marcelle on the Riviera. Marcelle, always repeating like a little parrot everything she heard, had said over and over (I can see the pretty expression of her mouth as she tried to manage the vowels and consonants of the English) "Candy Keed-dah," the nearest she could come to pronouncing it. She had asked Grant Richards for an explanation. He couldn't give it exactly in French, only approximately. This disturbed her. In a store in Monte Carlo one day I made it perfectly clear what candy was, and later found a picture postal card of a pretty mountain kid. That straightened it all out for Marcelle. *"Oh, oui!"* she exclaimed. *"Oui! oui! Très bon! Très charmant! Oh, oui!"* When Madame Culp, coming to London this time, reproached Grant Richards and then asked what the phrase "Candy Kid" meant (she pronounced it "Kanty Kit"), he went off, according to her description, into a gale of Homeric laughter. "Oh yes! Did he call you that? He called every girl he met in Paris and on the Riviera the same thing." Then I laughed heartily at his scoring so neatly.

Nevertheless, in spite of her trip, Madame Culp was not inclined to desert me. After she recovered from the blow of the sausage and marmalade, she squeezed my hand and leaned against my shoulder. As I recall, she had slipped on a loose blue peignoir for comfort, and this gave opportunities. She wanted me to come to the music room—obviously to sing for me—which I did. Before we had been there a half-hour, Herr Merten returned to discuss some business matters with her, and from then on, a number of musical-financial-managerial matters interfered, which irritated me greatly. Nevertheless, just before noon we managed to get away for a stroll in the adjacent forest and around the lake. It was an exquisite day, quite refreshing. She was, unfortunately, in a mood for love-making, not love-doing, which did not interest me so much any more. What actually transpired on this occasion was not so much. It is hard to play the gallant when your interest is slack or elsewhere. A much speedier adjustment of this relationship, if it was to continue at all, was what I wanted. As a matter of fact, I would have been pleased to have gone on at once to Holland, but having stayed so long and seen Berlin with Herr Merten, it was necessary—the slightest courtesy—to remain and hear her sing at her greatest concert. She was most anxious. So I decided to do this. But in trifling about in these woods and along the bank of this lovely lake, I was really bored. So you see how indiscriminate romancing sometimes pays one out.

This greatest concert, by the way, was for Friday night, and this was Wednesday. When I saw how things were running thereafter—accompanists, future concert companions, her Berlin manager and others were interfering, to say nothing of Herr Merten, I was tempted to re-announce that I was going on to Amsterdam, which I did. It evoked a storm. Oh no. This must not be. I must stay and hear her concert. I must be nice to her. Wait a little while. She wanted to walk with me in the woods again. She was going to Amsterdam. I should wait and go with her. Really, I was acting very bad. . . . She appeared at moments to truly crave affection from some source, which made her quite human. At these moments she was not so bossy and commanding.

But nevertheless we got nowhere. If I had been more truly interested, keen, I could have forced this situation and won, but it was not worthwhile. Once, when I was about to compel her—we were in the depths of a forest dingle—she begged most seriously; a plea which would have been worth little if the game had been worth the candle. "Really," she pleaded. "You must not make me go too fast. Remember how strange I feel. I have not made up my mind, even now. You must wait and let me want to very much."

I laughed at this. I upset her lightly on a bank, but she pleaded so hard the danger to herself that I let her go.

It was this way for two days, up to the night of the concert, and I felt that I was being strung along. Meals, friends, letters, business duties interfered. There was, as I found, once she was home, no opportunity for true seclusion in this house; too many people were in it, and too many called. So I spent a day motoring into Berlin for lunch and back with her, during which time, barring an hour, I was with her all the time. On this occasion I thought we had reached a fixed conclusion. Her excuse for the present situation was that unexpectedly there were more musical matters to attend to here in Berlin than she had anticipated. She said when she talked to me in Frankfort, she had presumed that her husband would have gone to India by now—would have been departing this very day in fact. As a matter of fact he was not going now until the following Tuesday, and after that on Wednesday or Thursday, she was going to Amsterdam to give a concert there. Her sister lived in Amsterdam. By the way, she would give me a letter to her. Now if I would wait peacefully until her husband left on Tuesday, all would be well; we would travel together to Amsterdam and perhaps visit Haarlem and The Hague together. If not, wouldn't I go to Amsterdam, after the concert, and wait for her there? I could see Holland. She would join me either at Haarlem or at the best hotel in Amsterdam and go to her sister's afterward. I decided that I would listen to no more promises concerning Berlin. Stay for the concert I would—that was no more than polite. After that I was going to Holland. If she joined me, well and good. If not, I would move on quickly. I indicated as much. She assured me she would come the moment her husband left.

One of the most interesting phases of this whole situation was the matter-of-fact way in which this artist discussed the matter of love, desire, duty, the sex relations generally. How far along the path of life we have come, some of us, how much of the original glamour and illusion has gone out, when we can do this. I should say that the first essential of happiness, that budding wonder which is love, is mystery. Life is only delicious, worthwhile, when it is full of the unexpected, of illusion, of a possibly favorable uncertainty. That is why two young people, ignorant, eager, mutually attracted, find so much of the marvelous, the unreal and yet the delightfully real and gratifying in their state.

But Madame Culp denied that she had much experience in love—said that Grant Richards was really the first, outside of her husband; but I could not accept that at all. It did not appeal to me as probable. There had been some adjustment between her and her husband over somebody—perhaps many—long before Grant Richards appeared. She spoke in too light a way of the passions and attentions of various individuals—which had always been rejected, of course. Her attitude on one point was sound. For physical connection to be worthwhile, there must be a warm, mutual physical response, but over and above that she put the affections—that remote, mutual adoration of personality, which somehow, at times, seems to have little if anything to do with the physical—she understood that.

But her casual discussion of the physical relationship, its stage management and setting, was a little bit too practical for me. She had it all arranged in her mind beforehand just how things were to be. There must be always a nice room with a bath and plenty of light and a view and a good bed. And then there must be flowers and a sort of air of expectancy—a result achieved by making the arrangement some time before. Then as for her, she wanted no clothes at all, just a suggestion of perfume and possibly an ornament—Well, the lusty paramour of this adventure was all that was necessary then. And this was how things were to be in Amsterdam. I have to smile as I think of her matter-of-fact statement of it all, even yet.

The philosophically- and psychologically-minded reach a state in their careers, however, where such description as this is really not significant. The details of life which are intimate to some become commonplace. There is no holy of holies. All the mystery of sex has gone. They have gotten down, as it were, to the naked machinery of it. Not even temperament is significant—or, if it is, it is selected in a practical, matter-of-fact way. A sad state, from one point of view—possibly valuable, philosophically and psychologically, but not otherwise. The only escape from such a condition is via metaphysics, I think. Perhaps sex is leading to a proper understanding of social adjustment, and the quicker it is thrashed out the better. Only I look with a vague regret at times on that period in my life when sex and the world were all mystery, color, illusion, wonder. The flaming mysteries of the morning sky were no more strange or sweet. Sometimes even now, a perfume, a sound, a color, a dream brings it back, a vague suggestion of it. It is then that youth and blood-newness become significant. The potentiality of the tendril is plain. But words fail here—they cannot possibly convey the meaning. Only those who have renewed old emotions in a dream or spell can really understand.

CHAPTER LXXXVII

The concert came and with it quite a revelation of her popularity in Berlin. Like two other musical events in Berlin—the Philharmonic Concert under Nikisch, and the violin recital by Elman—this was held in Philharmonic Hall, one of the most important musical chambers in Berlin. Easily two thousand people could be seated. It was full to overflowing. We had by now reached a mutually sympathetic and expectant attitude which made this affair—its success and effect, at least—a moderately personal matter between us. She wanted to show me how well she could do here. I wanted to have her succeed for its comfort to her. A woman is really only charming when she has done something for which she can be "made over," heartily applauded. Madame Culp was in this position. She was so anxious that I should be properly placed, and so it turned out that along with Herr Merten, the satellites whom I had met in Frankfort, a certain Frau Herzog and others, I was in a box which looked directly down on her and was easily included within the range of her eye. In an adjoining box were Frau von Bülow, the wife of the famous but long since dead pianist, and Godowsky, a popular favorite at this instrument, who had played with her at Frankfort. Other musical personalities of distinction were pointed out to me here and there.

As in London and Frankfort, Madame Culp sang with great charm and magnetism. The finest flavor of her personality was in her music. She seemed to me, as she sang, to take on new qualities of feeling and emotion which it was hard to detect in her daily life. She was not now so gross, not at all so; but rather airy, soulful, gracious and tender. It is almost always so with the artist. It is all in the work. Everything is subordinated to that. Life has little significance to the artist beyond his medium of expression. During her singing, ever and anon she would turn to me, not seeming to in her easy and self-sufficient way, and, throwing back her head, emphasized with the grace of motion the significance of the passage. I caught it all. It was not only good art but good acting. She was charmingly dressed—quite pleasing on the stage, very. Her arms and shoulders were white and round and smooth, and by means of a trailing train, possibly high-heeled shoes, an artistic and pleasing coiffure, she built herself up into a gratifying stature. Roses, lights, applause, recalls made up the brilliant setting which showed her at her best. When it was all over, her private reception room below the stage was crowded to suffocation with admirers. All her friends were there. The place was lined with flowers. In a conspicuous position on her private dressing table I noticed mine.

I made one mistake by not calculating properly as to how many recalls she would be likely to take. In Frankfort she had taken seven or eight, I forget which. The second from the last was a song sung especially for me, my favorite. Tonight, because of a contrary mood, I had not asked her to sing it, but I fancied she would. After the eighth or ninth recall (many people were leaving), I decided that she would not come back any more and had decided not to sing any special song for me because I had not asked. Therefore I decided to go below and compliment her. Others were there already congratulating her. As it was, she expected me to remain in my box, listening in rapt adoration. She really intended to sing a song to me. I had barely left when she was recalled again, and without looking up, as she admitted afterward, she began to sing my song. I should have been there to applaud. Alas, when she did look up, I was gone.

As she came down the stairs into her dressing room, I could see by her face that she was slightly disappointed. "Oh, there you are," she called. "Did you hear your song? Did you hear me sing to you? I sang that for you, and you weren't there!"

"I was listening to it here," I said. "I could tell you more quickly here how lovely I thought it was."

"Yes. See how clever he is," she exclaimed to her friends.

Some of them eyed me oddly.

"Now, I sing for you," she exclaimed pettishly afterward, "and you don't stay!"

"But I thought you weren't coming back. You stayed down so long."

"You should have stayed. I was planning to sing the last one for you. So it is, always."

We finally had done with the congratulations and well wishes, and as Madame changed her dress, the crowd disappeared. Several personalities whom I had not previously met now emerged as part of a theater party—a night-bird party—that was being made up. We were going to supper—where, heaven only knows; an exceptional place. We were going to the Cabaret Linden. We were going to the Palais de Danse, and then we were going home. A Herr Geistler and a Herr Simon, eager admirers both, along with Herr Merten and myself, were now dancing attendance on her. Someone had a machine. This was to be a gala occasion. It was for me, insofar as Madame Culp was concerned. She wanted to be present when I saw certain things. I think she gathered a part of her enthusiasm from the friendly comments of Grant Richards.

Anyhow, after a little while we were off together. A blue and yellow machine, the property of Herr Simon, had been backed into the courtyard of the Philharmonic. At the critical moment Madame Culp took my arm. I did not know until we came out into this court that a crowd of people, men and women, young men and young women, were waiting to have one last look at the star. As we came down together, Madame Culp bowed most genially, the bow of greatness. "This is surely going some," I said to her. We crowded into the machine, the five of us, and amid German hurrahs and prolonged cheers, we were off. I said to her then, "You will have a following sure enough in America if they ever wait at your door thirty or forty minutes after the concert is over to see you off."

"It is the way they do here," she replied, "if they like you."

It probably was, but it surprised me.

The only other thing of this kind that I saw while abroad related to the crown prince of Germany, and I should like to relate that here. As I was walking one evening with Herr Merten outside the Hotel Adlon in Unter den Linden, we saw a large crowd gathering around one of the side entrances of that hotel. A great red touring car was standing there, a very military chauffeur in yellow by the front wheels, and several rotund German policemen contemplating the situation from a respectful distance.

"Aha!" exclaimed Herr Merten, as emphatic as ever. "The crown prince! I knew that too. The Black Hussars are dining here tonight. Now you will see something. He is coming out, otherwise his car would not be here."

The presumption was of course that I would be thoroughly interested, which was true enough, though not inevitably so. We drew near.

I must say that the scene struck me as pleasingly democratic—no soldiers, no policemen other than those who came to gape idly, apparently no detectives—just a growing, friendly crowd of Germans, boys, girls, men and women, and an officer or two of the crown prince's private entourage. Hotel servants there were in plenty, bobbing to and fro bringing intelligence as to whether the various officials were ready to start or not.

"You wouldn't see anything as simple as that in Russia, I tell you," exclaimed Herr Merten as we drew near.

"Nor any more simple in America."

Evidently there were many toasts to be drunk, farewell glasses, for we waited nearly twenty minutes. Finally various imposing-looking officers began to appear, their great capes thrown over their shoulders, their swords and spurs clanking, their impressive caps pulled low over their eyes, going their way.

"Now! Now!" exclaimed someone. There was a great scurrying along an inner hall. A striking company of officers appeared, some in white and blue, others in red and blue, still others in gold and blue uniforms that were as glittering and colorful as any I had seen at Frankfort. The chauffeur was told by somebody to crank up. The auto door was opened. A servitor stood erect at one side, a fur robe over his arm. Then, quite accidentally apparently, bright-colored officers lined the walk from the door to the machine, and immediately there appeared the prince, a well-set-up youth, fairly tall, not too slender, plump, and flushed in his face, smiling a little drunkenly, I thought, and of course foolishly. He climbed in and sank heavily into his corner. After him entered three officers—men slightly older, but not much so—gaily caparisoned. A very callow youth the prince seemed to me, but the German throng obviously followed him with adoring eyes.

Looking straight before him from his corner, seemingly stupefied with liquor, he asked for someone.

"Tell ——— to come," ran along the corridor. Several officers hurried away to see that the message was promptly delivered. Out, finally, hurried another young officer and climbed cheerfully in. The door was slammed. All hats were off. A special imperial horn sounded. The car started. Cheers broke forth. The prince smiled feebly. Then there was a scudding flash around the nearest corner, and the car was off for a record run to Potsdam.

"Auf geht's!" "Hoch!"—such were the cries. My dogmatic friend was as pleased as though someone had given him a new hat. "A fine young man, that," he said. "Nice! Nice! He knows how to conduct himself. He's rich, too, in his own right." Then I heard the details of his fortune by marriage and otherwise, his five automobiles, etc.

We sped, let us say, to Bauer's—anyhow, a first-class midnight restaurant. It was *smart* German. Anyone who has ever read any of Sudermann's or Hauptmann's plays or books, the ones that touch on this sort of thing, will understand. The *smart* German restaurant is so different from the smart Paris, New York or London restaurant. In London, even more than in New York, I felt that *the best* was aping the French. In Berlin, not at all. Whatever other crime may be charged to the Germans, it is not that they ape the French. Do I hear some subtle soul arising to remark that they couldn't? This matter of national temperaments is so elusive, indefinable. You think you have your finger on the exact point, and lo! you haven't at all—it's just one small facet and scarcely indicative.

In this restaurant, though, I noticed that the German men were flushed, spirited, determinate in their national way. No least suggestion of England, France, America. Life is a matter of chemistry and physics, *relatively* understood—beyond that, soundless. Race is equally so. What I felt here particularly, for some reason (perhaps because I was flushed with champagne and delicate; it was the cuisine of this place—German pancakes) was that this effect of guttural, hyperborean lightness was due to the effect of wine, prosperity, German colleges, etc., on the innately stolid, full-blooded, rather matter-of-fact German temperament. Not one of these men could have given any such pyrotechnic, foamy, absolutely baseless display of emotion such as can any Frenchman at any moment, but on the other hand they achieved a sober brilliance such as suggested the flare of a light-struck ruby. Their wit was as good as any, particularly that at our table, but it emanated in a different manner—was surrounded, as it were, with less coruscation. It was smart, coarse, immoral, and yet clever wit.

The Germans are coarse, unquestionably, but they have a value in their coarseness quite as essential as the so-called refinement of another nation. Bird's-eye maple is not mahogany, and teakwood is not withe-willow, but who wants them to be? You can not get the same artistic effects with one that you can get with the other, but you can get different artistic effects, and that is the whole point. I can truly say that the German temperament and its artistic products are truly amazing to me at times, but at others I note that it achieves true distinction. Let it go at that. There must be, unquestionably are, thousands of human temperaments outside of Germany that prefer the Teutonic to either the French or English, and, I may readily add, the American temperament.

But this table situation was so amusing. As I have indicated, I never solved the mystery of Herr Merten's position in his own home, or whether he loved his wife or was jealous of her or what. I *think* he was well aware of what was going on, was jealous, and, by the same token, affectionate but helpless. He had caught a Tartar and had to make the best of it. The pride of having a wife who could win applause from a waiting throng on entering her automobile was truly something—bitter as may have been the remainder.

I have not stated all that I saw or heard at Zehlendorf, by any means. I fancy the young cousin-accompanist I admired so much had been called in to assist before on more than one occasion. In spite of the fact that Herr Merten told me personally that he did not know Grant Richards, and that he persistently refused to talk about him, I saw Madame Culp hand him four neckties—remembrances from Grant Richards on her return, and he take them, seemingly cordially. She had the habit of kissing the heads and cheeks, quite freely, of both her accompanist, a charming dark-eyed musician, and of this same Herr Simon, whom I saw here tonight and whom I saw again the next morning, the owner of the automobile. He was quite wealthy, I learned, not a musician at all, but very devoted to Madame Culp.

Here at the supper table Herr Simon and Herr Geistler vied with each other in doing Madame Culp honors. Insofar as I could see, they were rather rivals for her favor. Herr Merten was obviously no particular friend of theirs, though rather looked after because he was Madame's husband. He was, for one reason and another, a little bulldoggish in his mood, not cheerful, but when Madame cracked the whip of complaint or criticism, he came to with alacrity. For some reason, principally because I was rapidly passing beyond her to other fields of interest, she was especially attentive to me. She put me close to her elbow, clinked all of her wineglasses against mine, served me or saw that I was served momentarily, pressed her white satin slipper on my toe and kept one knee against me all the while. At least three times, perhaps four, she toasted "Amsterdam" sotto voce and assured me "now she knew she was fond of me"—a fine result of a successful concert and champagne.

"This is really getting too wild," suggested Herr Simon to Herr Geistler. "We might as well take a little table in a corner and eat by ourselves."

"I move we all go and leave them together," suggested Herr Merten with a feeble attempt at lightness.

"If you need a minister," jested Herr Geistler to me, "I know a fine one, very good-natured and very poor. He will fix things in a jiffy."

"I hope you name it after me," sighed Herr Simon. "So few have chosen me as godfather."

"It may be possible to name one after each," I whispered to Herr Geistler cheerfully. He retailed it to his friend.

There was loud laughter and more jokes of this kind. Madame Culp took it all in good part. Herr Merten seemed to look on it as usual. We finally escaped between one and two and made straight for the Cabaret Linden, which was nearby.

Unfortunately, insofar as I was concerned, the show was quite the same as I had seen it on two other occasions—with Herr Merten and Hanscha Jauer. Claire Waldoff was really acceptable for a third time. From there we went between two and three to the Palais de Danse, which amused us with its glitter, vulgarities and artistries until dawn. When we came out, after more champagne, a world of immoral women, lascivious dancing, flirtation and the like, the sky was already vaguely gray. Madame crowded next to me on the seat, but she was far too universal in her gay interchanges of wit and affectionate promises to be of any particular interest to me. We sped to Zehlendorf, while Herr Simon made jests to the effect that this tonneau was almost as compact as a lodging-house bed, and the like. In a way I felt a little sorry for Herr Merten, though why I don't know. I should say it would have been the finer part of ethics in his case to leave the lady, although these marital complications are never for outsiders.

"And so this is the lady that is coming to Amsterdam to join me," I thought. "And Herr Geistler and Herr Simon are always at her beck and call here. And the dark accompanist may be a third leading. Grant Richards is a fourth—at present the all-desired. Oh, this dizzy world! Let me get on to Amsterdam and cool off."

So I went to bed, meditating, and the next morning I rose early and packed all my belongings, being quite sure that I was going to be on my way to Amsterdam before midnight—that one thing was sure.

CHAPTER LXXXVIII

Before ending with Berlin and Germany I should like to pay one last tribute to Herr Merten and the German temperament. I think he was fairly successful financially and so typical of a healthy but only moderately contented middle class that he is worth considering, the kind that strives and strives to be something else but does not always succeed. In Leipzig, as I understand it, the word "Prussian" means "angry"; in Thuringia, "exacting"; in Altenburg, "in strained relations"; in Erfurt, "obstinate." Herr Merten was a Prussian. He was so typical of the Berliner, as I observed him at short range, that some thought may be given to the Berliner in general, for he and Herr Merten had much in common.

It would be my opinion that today all Germans incline to a military standard for appearance, deportment, resolution and the like, and that the Berliner is the farthest reach of this inclination. A smooth-shaven chin; a hard, determined glance; an erect, soldierly bearing and an American stride are all the rage. One of the Berliners' most wearying characteristics is a know-it-all atmosphere and attitude. To the few, barring the women, to whom I was introduced, I could scarcely talk. As a matter of fact I was not expected to. *They* would talk to *me*. Argument was, in its way, obviously an insult. Anything that I might have to say or suggest was of small importance; anything they had to say was of the utmost importance—commercially, socially, educationally, spiritually, any way you choose—and they emphasized so much they had to say with a deep voice, a hard, guttural force, a frown or a rap on the table with their fist. Take this series of incidents as typical of the Berlin spirit, and then we will return to Herr Merten.

I had to laugh heartily one day as I walked along Unter den Linden, for I saw a minor officer, who in all likelihood had not been saluted properly, standing in front of a sentry who was not far from his black-and-white-striped sentry box, his body as erect as a ramrod, his gun "presented" stiff before him, not an eyelash moving, not a breath stirring. This endured for possibly fifty seconds or longer. You would not get at the significance of this if you did not realize how strict the German military regulations are. At the sound of an officer's horn or the observed approach of a superior officer there is a noticeable stiffening of the muscles of the various sentries in sight. The possibly drowsy soldier becomes a mechanical automaton, responding to the formula of the occasion like a machine. In this instance, as it appeared afterward—I gathered this from a bystander—the minor officer imagined that he had not been saluted properly, or rather promptly, enough, and that the soldier might have too much beer in him. Hence the rigid test that followed. In my presence he stood before the underling fifty seconds, perhaps three minutes all told, holding him with his eye.

"If he had moved so much as an eyelid," said a citizen to me emphatically and approvingly, insofar as the officer was concerned, "he would have had his gun taken away and been sent to the guardhouse, and rightly. *Schweinehund!* He should 'tend to his duties!"

There you have military regimen in Germany. After the officer was gone, the soldier looked for all the world like a self-conscious house-dog that has just escaped a good beating, sheepishly looking out of the corners of his eyes and wondering, no doubt, if by any chance the officer was coming back.

Coming from Milan to Lucerne, and again from Lucerne to Frankfort, and again from Frankfort to Berlin, I sat in the various dining cars next to Germans who were obviously in trade and successful. Oh, the compact sufficiency of them! "Now, when you are in Italy," said one to another, out of Milan, "you see signs 'French spoken' or 'English spoken'—not 'German spoken.' Fools! They really do not know where their business comes from!"

On the train from Lucerne to Frankfort was another pair (always sanguine and vigorous they were). Said one, "Where I was in Spain, near Barcelona, things were wretched. Poor houses, poor wagons, poor clothes, poor stores. And they carry English and American goods, these dunces! And proud and slow—you can scarcely tell them anything."

"We will change all that in ten years," replied the other. "We are going after that trade. They need up-to-date German methods."

In a café in Charlottenburg, near the Kaiser-Friedrich-Gedächtniskirche, I sat with three others. One was from Leipzig, in the fur business. The others were merchants of Berlin. I was not of their party, merely an accidental spectator.

"In Russia the conditions are terrible. They do not know what life is. Such villages!"

"Do the English buy there much?"

"A great deal. We shall have to settle this trade business with war yet. It will come." (He was referring to war.) "We shall have to fight."

"In eight days," said one of the Berliners, "we will put an army of one hundred and fifty thousand men in England with all supplies sufficient for eight weeks. Then what will they do?"

Do these things suggest the German sense of self-sufficiency and ability? They are the commonest of commonplaces.

During the short time that I was in Berlin, I was a frequent witness of quite human but purely Teutonic bursts of temper—that rapid, fiery, mounting of choler which verges apparently on a physical explosion, the bursting of a blood vessel. There is really only room for one instance. I was going home one night late with Herr Merten from the Potsdamer Bahnhof when we were the witnesses of an absolutely magnificent and spectacular fight between two Germans—so Teutonic and temperamental as to be decidedly worthwhile. It occurred between a German, escorting a lady and carrying a grip at the same time, and another German somewhat more slender and somewhat taller, wearing a high hat and carrying a walking stick. This was on one of the most exclusive suburban lines operating out of Berlin.

It appears that the gentleman with the high hat and cane, in running to catch his train along with many others, severely jostled the gentleman with the lady and the portmanteau. On the instant an absolutely terrific explosion! To my astonishment—and for the moment I can say my horror—I saw these two very fiercely attack each other, the one striking wildly with his large portmanteau, the other replying with lusty blows of his stick, a club-like affair which fell with hard whacks on his rival's head. Hats were knocked off, shirtfronts marked and torn. Blood began to flow where heads and faces were cut severely, and almost pandemonium broke loose in the surrounding crowd.

Fights always produce an atmosphere of intensity in any nationality, but this German company seemed fairly to coruscate with anguish, wrath, rage, bloodthirsty excitement. The crowd surged to and fro as the combatants moved here and there. A large German officer, his brass helmet a welcome shield in such an affair, was brought from somewhere. Such noble German

Teutonic bursts of temper

epithets as "*Schweinehund!*" "*Hundsknochen!*" (dog's bone), "*Schafskopf!*" (sheep's head), "*Schafsgesicht!*" (sheep's face) and even more untranslatable words filled the air. The station platform was fairly boiling with excitement. Husbands drove their wives back, wives pulled their husbands away, or tried to. Men immediately took sides, as men will. "I tell you he is a dog—a cowardly dog! He struck that other fellow first." "I tell you I saw the man strike him with his bag! Why should he? Ha!"

Finally the magnificent representative of law and order, large and impregnable as a beer vat, interposed his great bulk between the two. Comparative order was restored, but men gathered in groups about each, and it looked as though new fights would begin between contentious spectators. It was not so, however. Each contestant was led away in an opposite direction. Some names and addresses were taken by the policeman. Insofar as I could see, no arrests were made, and finally both combatants, cut and bleeding as they were, were allowed to enter separate cars and go their ways. That was Berlin to the life. I was always feeling that such an explosion might occur at any moment almost anywhere. The air of the city, of Germany almost, was rife with contentious elements and emotions.

My last concerns quite another angle of Teutonism, and then I come to Herr Merten. It relates to German sentiment, which is as close to the German surface as German rage and vanity. It occurred in the outskirts of Berlin, one of those interesting regions where solid blocks of gold- and silver-balconied apartment houses march up to the edge of the streetless, sewerless, lightless green fields and stop. Beyond lie endless areas of truck gardens or open commons yet to be developed. Cityward lie miles on miles of electric-lit, vacuum-cleaned, dumbwaitered and elevator-served apartments, and of course streetcars.

I had been investigating a large section of land devoted to free (or practically free) municipal gardens for the poor, one of those socialistic experiments of Germany which, as is always the way, benefit the capable and leave the incapable just where they were before. As I came out of a large area of such land, divided into very small garden plots where the summer farmers had erected small sheds or cottages about the size of small old streetcars (and as valuable), to live or work in or keep their tools in (these things were almost invariably labeled "Villa Schmidt" or "Villa Julius" or "Villa Katrina"—a delightful assortment), I came across a small Berlin graveyard adjoining a small but neat white concrete church about a mile away where a German burial service was in progress. The German graveyard was not significant or pretentious—a poor man's graveyard, that was plain. The little church was too small and too sectarian in its mood, standing out in the wind and rain of an open common, to be of any social significance. Lutheran, I fancied. As I came up, a little group of pallbearers, very black and very solemn, were carrying a white, satin-covered coffin down a bare gravel path leading from the church door, the minister following, bareheaded, and after him the usual company of mourners in solemn high hats or thick black veils, the foremost—a mother and a remaining daughter, I took them to be—sobbing bitterly.

Now the surroundings of the service were generally so flat and unlovely, and the graveyard itself so small, bare and undecorative, that I said to myself, "Here is the worst that dullness and the utterly inartistic can produce," but just then, six choristers in black frock coats and high hats, standing to one side of the gravel path like six blackbirds ranged on a fence, began to sing a German parting song to the melody of "Home, Sweet Home." The little white coffin, containing presumably the body of a girl of sixteen, was put down by the grave, while the song was completed and the minister made a few consolatory remarks.

I have never been able, quite, to straighten out for myself the magic of what followed—its stirring effect on me. Whether it was the size of the graveyard, or the bareness of the ground, or the spectacle of the great city coming up like a wall or a bivouacked army, alive and intense in the distance, or the very poetic and very simple thing that was now done, or all or none, I don't know. Into the hole of very yellow earth, cut through dead, brown grass, the white coffin was lowered, and then the minister stood by and held out first to the father and then to the mother and then to each of the others as they passed a small, white, ribbon-threaded basket containing mixed, small, broken bits of the yellow earth and (tender thought) masses of pink and red rose leaves. As each came forward, crying of course, they took a handful of earth and rose leaves and let them sift through their fingers to the coffin below.

I cried. I could not say why. I cried as pathetically as either the father or mother. The sextet in the background had begun to sing some other song of mellow import, and that hurt me more. I went away crying, over the open fields, toward the city—crying, I suppose, because of all death and all loveliness, for the wonder of songs and white coffins and young hopes and mother-love and foolish father-love and the whole sweet, sad, pathetic illusion of life. Yes, this touch of rose-leaf sentiment, changing the rude necessity of shoveling in earth upon a happy memory, touched me to the quick. I came to the wall of the great city, its new streets and new life, its lights and cars, with wet eyes and a better opinion of the German temperament. It was this that made the raucous sanguinity of the Germans into something finer for me. It glorified Germany and Berlin for me, made the whole Teutonic world more suitable and understandable for having seen it.

And now we come to Herr Merten again. He had not a little of all this—vain, rowing assurance and sentiment involved with and, in the case of sentiment, only concealed under his rugged exterior. A more amusing, typical German I never associated with. So vain he was, so desirous of seeming important, so sensitive to the rights and glories of his nationality. All the while I was there, he was so concerned lest I pay for anything that he made me uncomfortable. I had to force a compromise. So convinced was he of German superiority that it was not only hopeless but impossible to argue with him. So vain was he of the prestige of his wife and her ability that he could not desert her, though she treated him—well, how?

I was sitting with him in the Weinhaus Trarbach one evening when, without let or hindrance, he entered on a grand discussion concerning Germany's superiority. Before he was done, I had the whole history of Germany's army and why it had to be; why Germany would go on building battleships until England was battleship-sick and financially ruined; wherein Germany and particularly Berlin ruled the world—in the matter of certain lines of machinery, textiles, guns, glass, women, dresses and the like. He descanted on the amazing superiority of the German steamship over all others; he told about the German army and its assured sufficiency in war. He, too, repeated the belief that Germany could put an army of one hundred and fifty thousand men in England, with all supplies sufficient for an eight weeks' campaign, in four days. He beat the table firmly, just as so many Germans do, as he assured me that English mechanical engineering—its one great financial asset (allied as it is with England's manufacturing supremacy)—was now second-rate as compared to the thoroughness of the Germans. How are you going to argue with self-conviction and belief of that kind? It is simply colossal.

Leipzig, according to him, is the greatest fur market in the world! Dresden, the greatest china! German supremacy in the matter of South American trade is unquestioned! And so on and so forth. I would have laughed except that I saw that all the other Germans I met or listened to were of the same mind.

But there were one or two little things that happened in connection with him that illustrated not only his own archaic unmoral mind but that of all Germany as well. One Sunday, for instance, while I was there, we went for a walk, and on our way we met a man on a bicycle, riding very swiftly. Herr Merten had Nana with him. "Look at the fool!" he said, why I could not guess, unless it was that the man was riding very fast. But as the man drew near, Nana, who was not leashed as the law provides, ran out and got in his way. It is against the law in Germany (in metropolitan areas) to walk with an unleashed dog.

"Take up your dog, you scum!" called the man on the wheel.

"Go to the devil, you ass!" was Herr Merten's social reply.

"Pig-face!" called the man quite cheerily.

"Sheep-face! Dog's ass!" was Herr Merten's reply. That is Herr Merten, that is Berlin, that is Germany. That is exactly the way they do—rude, hyperborean, direct, contentious. I laughed until I thought I would split my sides.

But there was another thing that happened this day which was even worse. We were on the banks of the Havel, where it skirts the Grunewald and where it widens out into such a fine lake with a sandy beach that from one hundred and fifty to two hundred thousand Berliners come daily in summertime to bathe here.

"Did you ever hear of the free baths?" asked Herr Merten as we came along the heights commanding this beach.

"I never did."

"Well, then, you have missed something the like of which you have never heard of in all your life, I'll venture. There is nothing like it anywhere."

"What is it?"

"Do you see that stretch of beach there?"

"Yes."

"Well, that has been set aside as a free bathing place for the poor of Berlin. They come here every day in summer—every hot day—one hundred and fifty to two hundred thousand strong."

"Yes?"

"Oh, that is something you should see. Such a sight exists nowhere else on earth. You see, there are no bathhouses. Well, they come here, take off their clothes and go into the water together—men, women and children without a stitch of clothing on them."

"Impossible!"

"I tell you it's true. Men, women and children, families, and young men and their girls, I'm telling you, go in here together, just as I say. Young men and young women; old men and old women; fathers and mothers with their children; single individuals. Do you see that place still farther off?"

"Yes."

"Well, there they sit and drink together without any clothes on."

"Are you jesting?"

"Not at all."

"Who watches their clothes?"

"Someone who stays behind. A family will oftentimes bring a big umbrella and put their clothes under that."

"And they wear absolutely nothing—no clothing of any kind?"

"I'm telling you. One and all are naked. And what is more, they cohabit with each other right here on the beach."

"I don't believe it!"

"I'm telling you."

"Impossible!"

"You don't believe me? Wait a little while. We'll ask the first person we meet. If you were here in July, you would see for yourself."

I laughed in wild derision at the thought of it.

"Wait," he exclaimed quite contentiously.

Presently we came in sight of a very pretty young woman of about thirty, out for a morning's stroll. He started toward her. "Now wait," he said quite defiantly, "you shall hear."

"You are not going to ask her?"

"Certainly."

"What sort of a country am I in, anyhow?"

"You Americans—pah! Madame!" he called. "Here is an American who will not believe what I tell him about the free baths. I have said that from one hundred and fifty to two hundred thousand come here in a day in summer, that they wear no clothes and that they do exactly as they please and everything that they please and that no one can interfere. Is that true?"

"Certainly," replied the lady, smiling at me without a trace of embarrassment and twirling her parasol. "It is as he says. They do exactly as they please. The police are not allowed to interfere."

"I stand corrected," I said.

"There you have it," exclaimed Herr Merten, walking on. "You Americans make me sick. You do not know what is going on. You do not know what life is. You're afraid of it. There isn't so much harm in it as you'd think. Those people think nothing of it."

"Nor that young lady," I replied.

"Nor that young lady either. Why should she? It is life. It is true."

Does that give you any indication of Germany or the dogmatic Herr Merten?

CHAPTER LXXXIX

My departure was finally accomplished this day, or the night of it rather, at ten o'clock, but not before I had spent the whole of it practically dancing attendance on Madame Culp. An executive lady, this, always busy with accompanists, future concert associates and the like, and trying to blend romance with business in equal proportions. I did not "see it," as the slang expression has it. These officious souls really need manikins to play with—not men. A strong man of course needs (will only endure) a much softer type of temperament. Nevertheless I visited some lady's Berlin singing school with her, where she paraded as the great I-am, and later went to lunch and to dinner with her. Just before dinner at some Berlin restaurant Herr Merten appeared to say goodbye and, to tell you the truth, I felt sorry for him. He announced that he could not possibly stay, which was of course ridiculous. She did not want him to, and I did not, though if he had, it would not have grieved me much. I wondered just by what process of psychology—compulsion, policy, sense of the inexplicableness of things—he came to do this. He need not have. It was my place to go to him, but Madame Culp saw it in another light and arranged it. I wondered all the while what he thought of me, Grant Richards, her gentlemen (artist and financial) friends. I think a man like Herr Merten has his good points, and anyhow when I contemplate the remainder of humanity, he measures up reasonably well. If there is one human being who by reason of perfection or want of flaws is worth the saving, I should like to meet him. The virtuous are innately dull and narrow-minded, and the so-called evil or able are so cantankerous, treacherous, shifty, hungry, ambitious that they are scarcely worth the killing. It is a mad world we have been born into, my masters, and he knows it best who looks closest.

I came near finding myself in serious straits financially on leaving Berlin; for having stayed so close to Zehlendorf these last few days and having spent my last two days almost uninterruptedly with Madame Culp, I forgot to examine my cash in hand or to draw more against my letter of credit before I left. The result was that I was speeding to the Bahnhof Friedrichstrasse after bidding Madame Culp an affectionate farewell and hearing a last assurance that she would come to Amsterdam a day or two later. She insisted on my taking a letter to her sister, Madame Betsy Rijkens-Culp, which I was to present at once. As I sped to the depot I looked in my purse, to discover that I had just fifteen marks all told. This was Saturday night, and my train was leaving in just thirty minutes. My taxi fare would be two marks. My bags and trunks, deposited earlier in the day in the parcel room of the station, would mean an extra mark in charges. Excess luggage—I saw that looming up swiftly. It could mean anything in Europe—ten, twenty, thirty marks. "Good heavens!" I thought. "I may have to phone to Zehlendorf or go out there—in either case I miss my train. Who is there to cash a letter of credit for me on Saturday night? This is a sweet mix-up!" At the same time I thought of porters, taxis, train-hands at Amsterdam. "If I get there at all," I sighed, "I get there without a cent." However, I hurried on.

At the depot I first had my trunk weighed and found that I should have to pay ten marks excess baggage. That was not so bad. My taxi chauffeur demanded two. My *Gepäckträger* took one more, my parcel-room clerk one mark in fees, leaving me exactly one mark and my letter of credit. "Good God!" I sighed. "I can see the customs officers at the border! Without money I shall have to open every one of my bags. I can see the conductor expecting four or five marks and getting nothing. I can see—Oh, Lord!"

Still I did not propose to turn back. I did not have time. The clerk at the hotel I chose (and I was going to the best one) would have to lend me money on my letter of credit. So I bustled ruminatively into the train. It was one of those long, dusty affairs, coming from St. Petersburg or Moscow, or both, and bound for Holland, Paris and the boats for England. It was crowded with passengers but, thank heaven, all of them safely bestowed in separate compartments or "drawing rooms" after the European fashion. I was so weary of Berlin and art entanglements that I drew my blinds, undressed swiftly and got into bed. Let all conductors rage, I thought. Porters be damned. Frontier inspectors could go to hell. I was going to sleep, my one mark in my coat pocket. I was offering up thanks to think that I had not been compelled to stay one more night in Berlin. And think of all the trouble I would have had over my ticket and reserved berth! So I was preparing to sleep when the conductor called to ask if I did not want to surrender the keys to my baggage in order to avoid being waked in the morning at the frontier. He wanted me to give him a tip for this service, which, of course, I was in no position to do.

"Let me explain to you," I said. "This is the way it is. I got on this train with just one mark." I tried to make it clear how it all happened.

He was a fine, tall, military, solid-chested German. He looked at me with grave, inquisitive eyes. What sort of a yarn was this I was telling him? Only one mark! Tush! Some scheme to avoid a tip! "I will come in a little later," he said. Instead he shook me rudely at five-thirty at some small place in Holland and told me that I would have to go out and open my trunk. The want of four or five marks did that.

Still I was not so downcast. For one thing, we were in Holland, actually and truly, and that was important and interesting to me—quaint little Holland with its five million population, less than New York City, its wooden shoes (in remote sections possibly); its populous cities crowded so close together that you could get from one to the other in a half-hour or a little over; its lovely (to me) memories of Frans Hals and Rembrandt van Rijn, and that whole noble company of Dutch painters who (entirely aside from Rembrandt and Frans Hals) comprise the only school of distinction outside of those that make Italy of the Renaissance and France of its periods so significant.

Dutch art! All my life, I think—all my conscious art life, I am sure—I have been more or less fascinated by those smooth surfaces, spirited atmospheres, radiant simplicities of the kitchens, the dining rooms, the markets, the parlors, the horse ponds, farmhouses, duck ponds, ferries, village fairs, the village inns, windmills, canal scenes, housewives, fishwives, old topers, cattle and nature scenes, which are the basis and substance of Dutch art. I will admit, for argument's sake, that the Dutch costume with its snowy neck and headpiece and cuffs, the Dutch windmill, with its huge wind-bellied sails and nub-like head, the Dutch landscape so flat and grassy and the Dutch temperament, broad-faced and phlegmatic, have had much to do with my art attraction, but over and beyond those there has always been so much more than this—an indefinable something which for want of a better phrase I can only call the wonder of the Dutch soul, the most perfect expression of commonplace beauty that the world has yet seen. So easily life runs off into the mystical, the metaphysical, the emotional, the immoral, the passionate and the suggestive, that for those delicate flaws of perfection in which life is revealed static, quiescent, undisturbed, innocently gay, naively beautiful, how can we be grateful enough! For those lovely, idyllic minds that were content to paint the receipt of a letter, an evening school, dancing peasants, a gust of wind, skaters, wild ducks, milking time, a market, playing at draughts, the fruiterer, a woman darning stockings, a woman scouring, the drunken roisterers, the cow stall, cat and kittens, the grocer shop, the chemist's shop, the blacksmith shop, feeding time, and the like, my heart has only reverence. And it is not (again) this choice of subject alone, nor the favorable atmosphere of Holland in which these were found, so much as it is that delicate refinement of soul, of perception, of feeling—the miracle of temperament—through which these things were seen. *Life seen through a temperament. That is the miracle of art.*

The worst illusion that can be entertained concerning art is that it is apt to appear at any time, in any country, through a given personality or a group of individuals without any deep relation to much deeper mystical and metaphysical things. Some little suggestion of the artistry of life may present itself now and then through a personality, but art in the truest sense is the substance of an age, the significance of a country, a nationality. Even more than that it is a time-spirit (the *Zeitgeist* of the Germans) that appears on occasion to glorify a land, to make great a nation. You would think that somewhere in the sightless substances of things, the chemistry back of the material evidence of life, that there was a lovely, roseate milling of superior principle. "And the spirit of God moved upon the face of the waters." And there was that which we know as art.

I think it was years before those two towering figures—Rembrandt and

Frans Hals (and of the two, Frans Hals is to me the greater)—appeared in my consciousness and emphasized the distinction of Holland for me that the loveliness of Dutch art, the naivety of Wouwerman, the poetic realism of Nicolaes Maes, the ultimate artistry of Vermeer, de Hooch, Ruysdael and all that sweet company of simple painters of simple things, had finally come to mean *to me* all that *I* can really hope for in art—those last final reflections of halcyon days which are the best that life has to show.

Sometimes when I think of the sweet splendors of Dutch art, which in its delicate commonplaceness has nothing to do with the more universal significance of both Hals and Rembrandt, I get a little wild artistically. Those smooth, persuasive surfaces, pure enamel, and symphonies of blue light which is Vermeer; those genial household intimacies and candlelight romances which are Dou; those alleluias of light and water which are van de Velde, Bakhuyzen, van Goyen; those merrymakings, perambulations, doorway chats, pantry intimacies, small trade affections and exchanges which are Terborch and van Ostade! Truly, words fail me. I do not know how to suggest the poetry, the realism, the mood, the artistic craftsmanship that go with these things. They suggest a time, a country, an age, a mood, a spirit which is at once a philosophy, a system, a spirit of life. What more can art be? What more can it suggest? How, in that fortune of chance which combines it with color sense, temperament, craft, can it be exceeded? And all of this is what Dutch art—those seemingly minor phases, after Hals and Rembrandt—means to me.

But I was in Holland now and not concerned so much for the moment with Dutch art as with my trunks. Still, I felt here at the frontier that already I was in an entirely different world. Gone was that fever of the blood which is Germany. Gone the heavy, involute, enduring Teutonic architecture. The upstanding German—*kaiserlich*, self-opinionated, drastic, aggressive—was no longer about me. In his place had come a softer, milder, less aggressive, less military type. The men who were unlocking trunks and bags here were not Germans, and yet they looked not unrelated to them—paler, less florid, not less stout, not so self-conscious, but semi-Teutonic, like Swiss or Swedes.

This mystery of national temperaments—was I never to get done with it? As I looked about me against a pleasant rising Sunday sun, I could see and feel that not only the people but the landscape and the architecture had changed. The architecture was obviously so different—low, modest one-story cottages standing out on a smooth, green level land, so smooth and so green and so level that anything projected against the skyline—it mattered not how modest—thereby became significant. And I saw my first Holland windmill turning its scarecrow arms in the distance. It was like coming out of a

Russian steam-bath into the cool marble precincts of the plunge, to come from Germany into Holland.

Of all the charming water-cities after Venice, commend me to Amsterdam. I suppose there are others. Someone once told me of the naive peculiarities of Bangkok and some of the Chinese water-cities or true "floating populations" of China, but Amsterdam quite satisfies my taste for the picturesque as contributed by water. It is not Venice—far from it. It has not the spacious water significance of New York. But as a water-city, individual and unique, it is not without features of perfection. If the mosquitoes are not a pest in Amsterdam in summer, it must be a haven of delight.

I have shown a preference for so many cities on one score and another that I suppose an additional preference or two will not much matter.

CHAPTER XC

I had no trouble with trunks and bags other than that of opening them and of being compelled to look as though I thought it a crime to tip anybody. I strolled about the station in the early light of a clear, soft day and speculated on this matter of national temperaments. What a pity, I thought, if Holland were ever annexed by Germany or France or any country and made to modify its individuality. Before I was done with it I was inclined to believe that its individuality would never be modified, come any authority that might.

The balance of the trip to Amsterdam was nothing, a matter of two hours, but it partially confirmed all I had fancied concerning Holland. Such a mild little land as it is! I don't wonder that van Ostade and Jan Steen and Ruysdael flourished here. The land could only produce Dutch art. It is so level, so smooth, so green. I began to notice the little stepped roofs, endless variations of which give the individuality to the architecture which it has.

It is always so interesting to me to see what it is that makes up the sum of differences between one country and another and makes us feel that we are far from home and out of our natural element. Aside from the peculiarities of architecture which always force themselves on one's attention in every new land, the language of the signs obtrudes itself on you, and the people look so different. Here one could see signs which seemed such a hodgepodge of German and English badly mixed that I had to laugh. The train passed up the center of a street in one village where cool brick pavements fronted cool brick houses and stores, and on one plate-glass window I noted lettered *haarsnijden*. Would not that as a statement of haircutting make any German-American laugh? Then to see other signs read *telefoon, stoomboot, treinen naar Oostende*, land *te koop* (for sale), and the like brought a mild grin of amusement. In my sleeping car I had already noticed that the Dutch for "no smoking" or *nicht rauchen*, as the Germans put it, was *niet rooken*, another amusing variation.

When we reached Amsterdam, I had scarcely time to get a sense of it before I was whisked away in an electric omnibus to the hotel; and eager to get there, too, in order to replenish my purse, which was now without a single penny. The last mark had gone to the porter at the depot to carry my bags to this bus. I was being deceived as to the character of the city by this ride from the central station to the hotel, for, curiously, its course gave not the slightest indication that the city was full of canals when as a matter of fact its canals are the most charming and distinguishing features of Amsterdam—more so than in any other city in Holland.

And now what struggles for a little ready money! My bags and fur coat had been duly carried into the hotel, and I had signified to the porter in a lordly way that he should pay the busman, but, seeing that I had letters which might result in local invitations this very day, a little ready cash was necessary.

"I tell you what I should like you to do," I observed to the clerk after I had properly entered my name and accepted a room. "Yesterday in Berlin, until it was too late, I forgot to draw any money on my letter of credit. Let me have forty gulden, and I will settle with you in the morning."

"But, my dear sir," he said, very doubtfully indeed and in very polite English, "I do not see how we can do that. We do not know you."

"It is a little unusual," I suggested ingratiatingly, "but you must have done it before. You see my bags and trunk are here. There is my fur overcoat—that is worth a few hundred gulden. Here is my letter of credit. Supposing you speak to the manager and ask him to let me have forty gulden."

The dapper Dutchman looked at my fur overcoat and bags quite critically and disrespectfully, I thought, considering their worth, then retired into an inner office. Presently a polished, connoisseur-like, art-patrony person appeared, dark, immaculate, looking for all the world like a sublimated clothes-brush, and after eyeing me solemnly shook his head.

"It can't be done," he said.

He turned to go.

"But here, here!" I called quite authoritatively. "This won't do! You must be sensible. What sort of a hotel do you keep here, anyhow? I must have forty gulden—thirty, anyhow. My letter of credit is good. Examine it. Good heavens! You have at least eight hundred guldens' worth of luggage there!" He had turned and was surveying me again.

"It can't be done," he said.

"Impossible!" I cried. "I must have it. Why, I haven't a cent! You must trust me until tomorrow morning!"

He smiled wearily. "Give him twenty gulden," he said to the clerk.

"You are an impolite old fossil," I said to him in high dudgeon and very ungratefully. "You do not deserve American patronage. I should think you could see that you could trust me for one hundred gulden."

He merely raised his superior eyebrows and turned away.

"Good heavens!" I said to the clerk. "Give me the twenty gulden before I die of rage," and so he counted them out to me, and I went in to breakfast. I was charmed to find that the room overlooked one of the lovely canals, with a distant view of others, all of them alive with a simple form of canal-boat life, a solid type of placid Hollander poling or steering them about, after the fashion of electric launches, and the spring sunlight giving them a warm, alluring, mildly adventurous aspect. The sense of light on water was so delightful from this breakfast room, great airy place that it was, that I am sure my Sunday morning breakfast eggs and bacon tasted twice as good for being in the proximity of it. I was so pleased with my general surroundings here that I hummed a tune even while I ate.

Amsterdam I should certainly include in my cities of light and charm, a place to live in. Not that it has, in my judgment, any of that capital significance of Paris or Rome or Venice. Though greater by a hundred thousand in population than Frankfort, it has not even the forceful commercial texture of that place. The spirit of the city seemed so much more unbusinesslike, so much slower and easygoing. Before I sent forth a single letter of introduction I spent the entire day idling about its so often semicircular streets, following the canals which thread their centers like made pools, rejoicing in the cool brick walks which line their sides, looking at the reflections of houses and budding but as yet leafless trees in the ever-present water surfaces.

Holland is obviously a land of flower-lovers, but much more than that it is a land of atmosphere. I gained that so strong coming from Venice to Amsterdam, but even more here in this semi-waterside atmosphere. I have often speculated just what it is that the sea does to its children that marks them so definitely for its own, and here in Amsterdam the thought came to me again. It is this: your waterside idler, whether he traverses the wide stretches of the ocean or no, has a seeming vacuity or dreaminess of soul that no storms can shake. I have noted it of every port of the sea that the eager intensity of men melts away at the water's edge. Boats are not loaded with the hard realism that marks the lading of trains. A sense of the idle, devil-may-care waters seems to play about their affairs—the unhasting indifference of the sea. Perhaps the suggestion of the soundless, timeless, heartless deep that is in every channel, inlet, sluice and dock basin is the element that is at the base of their lagging motions. Your sailor and seafaring man will not hurry. His eyes are wide with a strange suspicion of the deep. He knows by contact what the subtlety and the fury of the waters are. The word of the sea is to be indifferent. "Never mind, dearie. As it was in the beginning, so it ever shall be."

I think the peace and sweetness of Amsterdam bear some relationship to this wonderful, soporific spirit of the endless deep. Our own Washington Irving suggested a somnolent spirit as existing in the Dutch—phlegmatic, artistic, realistic—which he did not connect with the sea but which I do, and I think I am right. Our new Amsterdam was not so remote in mood from the old, and New York, for all its seeming haste, has much of the mood of the sea about it. Its thoughts are fixed by the possibilities of far adventure. As I walked along these *grachts* and *kades* and through these *pleins* (seemingly enameled worlds in which water and trees and red brick houses swam in a soft light, exactly the light and atmosphere you find in Dutch art) I felt as though I had come out of a hard modern existence such as one finds in Germany and back into something kindly, rural, intellectual, philosophic. Spinoza was, I believe, Holland's contribution to philosophy, and a worthy Dutch philosopher he was. Both Rembrandt and Frans Hals have indicated in their lives the spirit of this country. I think if you could look into the spirits and homes of thousands of simple Hollanders, you would find that same kindly, cleanly realism which you admire in Dutch art. It is so placid. It is here in Amsterdam. One gathers it from the very air. I had a feeling of peaceful, meditative delight in life and the simplicities of living all the while I was in Holland, which I take to be significant. All the while I was there I was wishing that I might remain throughout the spring and summer and dream. In Germany I was haunted by the necessity of effort.

It was while I was in Amsterdam this first morning that the realization that my travels were fast drawing to a close dawned upon me. I had been having such a good time. That fresh, interested feeling I had had at breakfast every morning for days and days was still enduring—that something to see, to look forward to—but now my splendid world of adventure was drawing to a close. I could now look forward and estimate quite accurately when I would be done with Holland and Belgium, when I would leave for Paris, when I would leave for London, when I would leave for New York. There were interesting things to see yet—Bruges, Brussels, Ghent, the field of Waterloo—but practically it was all over. Coming to Paris a second time could not mean what coming to Paris the first time had—that crystalline bubble of fancy that was all of my own blowing. Coming to London a second time could not mean what coming to London the first time had, though the thought of the Empire City in this swelling spring had more allurement now than the thought of Paris. I had only seen London in damp and raw days. What would it be in warmer weather, with the sun shining yellowly through its pall of smoke! And England—Cookham, Maidenhead, Oxford, Cambridge! I could have idled away all my summer days in England.

But here I was now in Holland, with all the charms of that mellow land under my eyes, and grieving that I could not stay longer in England! The appetites of man!

But as I sat here eating my breakfast, thinking of what I had seen and what I should still see, my mind ran back to the particular wonders, the scenes and objects, that from day to day and month to month had entranced me. First of all, the sea, and then England—rural England—it was such a picture of beauty. Oxford was splendid; then Canterbury; then Amiens; then Paris with all its wonders—the cafés, the Musée de Cluny, Notre-Dame, Madame de Villiers. Back came Monte Carlo, Nice, that very first morning on the Riviera at Agay, with Grant Richards so eager to see that I enjoyed it all and Lane so deliciously cantankerous. Then Marcelle and the casino—what was Marcelle doing? I had not had a picture-card from her in weeks. Smart Marcelle! Then Eze—the first hill-city I ever really saw at close range—then Ventimiglia, then Pisa. What a dream Pisa was, with its Baptistery and its Leaning Tower!

Then came Rome and Mrs. Armstrong and "Ma" and all the company that made my stay there interesting and peculiar. Little "Ma," so solicitous and so truly kind! I think I listed everything I saw in Rome as wonderful, but most of all the Museo delle Terme, the Baths of Caracalla, Tivoli and St. Paul Without The Walls. Then Assisi, gray and sweet, like a sad lichen, and Spello with its cypresses and its brown Franciscan. Then Perugia, high and gay, and Florence, somber, brilliant, sanguine, moody, as rich as the blood of any of its darkest natives.

Then Venice, a jam of water and sweet stone, with Maria Bastida for good measure; then Milan and the Cathedral and the Last Supper only, then Lucerne with its still lake; and after that all Germany. Somehow, now that I was out of it, only the spirit and beauty of the German army officers and the modernity of Germany had any significance to me—those and the mood of Hanscha Jauer. The art of Germany was nothing, and I did not include my visit to my father's town as something really German. That was merely peculiar to me. Here I was now in Holland, as rich a bit of temperament in the matter of land and people as the world holds, and the end of it all was in sight. In about two weeks it would be all over. Naturally I was a little sorrowful, even in my morning joy.

But what a delight, I said to myself, traveling had really been! To get up each day and know that you have something really interesting before you. As a rule life drags so. The endurance of it is in forgetfulness—not to think. For years, just as I did—just as most of us do—we shoot back and forth between home and office, sleep and duty, like a damned shuttle. We think and think, but the scene does not change, and we do not change except imperceptibly. The charm of life, which is the beholding of it with the eyes, is limited to a given scene. Yet the mass of humanity so lives.

To come out this way into the light of the actual, to visit old scenes, walk in the ancient steps of man, is something. It may be true that all is vanity, that what has been will be, that there is nothing new under the sun and nothing really old, but where the moving finger has written—even though it be all but obliterated—is worth seeing. I know that the historical span of man is nothing. Real antiquity and vast catastrophe is written in every rock and on every doorstep, but the business of "going to and fro in the earth" is delightful. Before the Palatine at Rome; the Leaning Tower at Pisa; St. Francis, his cell; or the crumbling walls of so simple a thing as Mayen, it is well to stand. They talk as books cannot; they report as no man can. "Thus was it," "Here stood I," "In the beginning so were the dreams, the hopes, the faiths of man." So say these things, and it is a delight to listen, to walk humbly, to observe patiently, to think reverentially. It was so that my travels and observations had appealed to me.

CHAPTER XCI

The delights of traveling! Never more than at this table, looking out at the canal boats of Holland this fresh spring morning, did I feel more keenly the pleasure and privilege of traveling. Life can be lived, as Thoreau proved, with great intellectual and spiritual distinction in a meager way and in small compass, but oh, the wonder of the world's highways, the going to and fro amid the things of distinction and memory, seeing how, thus far, this worldly house of ours has been furnished by man and by nature.

The days I spent in Holland were exactly five, and for the cursory inspection of Amsterdam, Haarlem, The Hague, Rotterdam and the country between, they were all too short. The city of Antwerp, which I imagined still belonged to Holland, was in Belgium, and I never really consciously knew until I got into Holland that the Rhine, which I oddly enough connected only with Germany, flows through it and empties there into the

North Sea. So much for my earthly geography. Only at Scheveningen near The Hague did I see the protective dikes, or a part of them—a continuous mound of earth which was anything but attractive.

But if Amsterdam was pleasing to me because of its canals—solidly walled in between brick and stone and making for the city its charming local highways—the country round about from Amsterdam to Rotterdam was even more so. I never knew that a windmill—and the Holland windmills have an especial individuality—could be so utterly charming, such perfect works of art. I presume now, since the invention and perfection of the gas-engine and the dynamo, that their days are short. Why windmills which must await a breath of air when you can turn on a current or light a gas-engine? But the utter charm of them! Must all the quaintness pass out of life for want of exceptional utility? The answer is *truly*, but we can sigh without being punished. Obviously, life is utilitarian, and art is an accident, a by-product.

To me, as I sped along the banks of canals in trolleys or trains, witnessing the thirty miles of vari-colored flower-beds in blocks of red, white, blue, purple, pink and yellow that lie between Amsterdam and Rotterdam; standing in the old Grote Kerk of St. Bavo in Haarlem; the Grote Kerk of St. James in The Hague—both as bare of ornament as an anchorite's cell; wandering among the art treasures of the Rijksmuseum in Amsterdam or the Mauritshuis and the Mesdag Museum in The Hague; or wandering in the forests of moss-tinted trees at Haarlem, or again at The Hague, I began to think that Holland had all the charm of a great private estate, beautifully kept, and that (as usual) if God spared me, I should come back here some day to spend a great many happy days.

But the canals of Holland—what an airy impression of romance, of pure poetry, they left in my mind! There are certain visions or memories to which the heart of every individual instinctively responds. The canals of Holland are one such to me. I can see them now, in the early morning, when the sun was just touching them with the faintest pearls, pinks, lavenders, blues—their level surfaces as smooth as glass, their banks rising no whit above the level of the water but lying even with it like a black or emerald frame, their long straight lines broken at one point or another by a low brown or red or drab cottage or windmill! I can see them again at evening, the twilight hour, when in that poetically suffused mood of nature, which obtains then, they lie, liquid masses of silver, a shred of tinted cloud reflected in their surface, the level green grass turning black about them, a homing bird, a mass of trees in the distance or a humble cottage, its windows faintly gold from within lending those last touches of artistry which make the perfection of nature. As in London and Venice, the sails of their boats are brown, and here comes one now, a richly brownish black in the fading light, a healthy Hollander smoking his pipe at the tiller, a cool wind fanning his brow. The world may hold more charming pictures, but I have not encountered them.

Across the level spaces of lush grass that seemingly stretch unbroken for miles, bordered on this side or that with a little patch of filigree trees, ornamented in the foreground by a cow or two perhaps, or a boatman steering his motor-power canal boat, remotely ended by the seeming outlines of a distant city, as delicately penciled as a line by Vierge, ribboned and segmented by straight, silvery threads of water, stand the windmills. I have seen them in the morning, flailing the air with their ambling arms, when it seemed as if they added the last touch of perfection to the scene, the one ultimate, perfect note. I have seen ten, twelve, fifteen, marching serenely across the fields in a row, of an afternoon, like great, heavy, fat Dutchmen of an older day, their sails going in slow, patient motions, their great sides rounding out like solid Dutch ribs—naive, pathetic, delicious things to contemplate. It is just possible that here and there might be one who would consider them commonplace. Not so I. They seemed to breathe of something so naive, simple, solitary, patient, good-natured, that it irked me to think that the passage of time or the change of convenience of method should ever disturb them. There were times when their outlines took on classic significance. They, the utterly level land, the canals and the artistically martialed trees, make the atmosphere of Holland. *That is Holland.* Without them the fleecy, sunny, pearly days which contribute so much more of artistic mood would be nothing.

The second morning of my arrival I sent among others a letter to Madame Culp's sister, Madame Betsy Rijkens-Culp, the wife of an eminent Dutch jurist who had something to do with the International Peace Court. Madame Culp had described her as her "precious sister," the most charming of all the women she had ever known, a "darling." Herr Merten had said of her that she was nice but that she and his wife laughed too much when they were together and that they made sport of everyone and everything. Madame Culp had a picture of her, showing a pretty, mild-eyed woman of obviously Dutch extraction, plump, good-natured and yet meditative. Madame Culp had said that her sister was very happily married and that I would find her husband a charming man. It was not three hours after I sent my letter before I received a telephone call from Madame Rijkens-Culp and heard her very pleasing voice. Would I come to lunch this day? Her husband would be a little late, but I would not mind. Her sister had written her. She would be so glad to see me. I promptly accepted. At one I appeared and was inducted into the house by a maid who looked for all the world like a study by Bols.

The house was near the Rijksmuseum, with a charming view of water from the windows. I can see it now, its very pleasant Holland interior. The rooms into which I was introduced were like a Vermeer interior, designedly so, I presume. The lighting was mild and of a bluish-gray character, the contents spare and in good taste, flowers in abundance, brass and old copper in quaint, suggestive touches. Madame Rijkens-Culp was herself a study in steel blue and silver gray, a very meditative, desirous, reserved and yet temperamental woman.

It always interests me to observe the type of woman who, lacking a strong executive mind or truly ambitious or artistically capable temperament, still tries to make something out of her life. As a rule they are disposed to be meditative, philosophic, fatalistic or merely vague and wondering. She stated with an undecipherable smile that she was so glad to see me, so very glad. Her sister had written her, but better than that she had read my books. A better linguist than Madame Culp, she spoke English perfectly. She had read my book, the latest one, and had liked it, how much she could not say. On sight, after this very airy induction, she folded her hands in her lap, leaned forward and looked at me. "I have been so curious to see what you looked like."

"Well," I replied smilingly, "take a long look. I am not as wild as early rumors would indicate, I hope. You mustn't start with prejudices."

She smiled engagingly. "It isn't that. There are so many things in your book which make me curious. It is such a strange book—self-revealing, I imagine."

"I wouldn't be too sure."

She merely continued to look at me and smile in a placid way, but her inspection was so sympathetic and in a way alluring that it was rather flattering than otherwise. I began to wonder how much I could really like such a woman, whether she represented in any way the summum bonum of earthly merit in femininity.

I think truly that, all other things being equal, the individual fancy being free, affairs and difficulties permitting, every man and every woman if they have not found the engrossing, binding one, male or female, are continually on the search for him or her. Like Shakespeare I would be the last one to admit an impediment to the marriage of true minds. Unquestionably in this world, in spite of endless liaisons, sex diversions, divorces, marital conflicts innumerable, the right people do occasionally find each other. There are true chemical-physical affinities, which remain so until death and dissolution dissolve their mysterious spell. Yet, on the other hand, I should say that this is the rarest of events, and if I should try to formulate the mystery of the marital troubles of this earth, I should devote considerable percentages of actuating motives to (1) ungovernable lust, not willed or able to be controlled by the individual; (2) dull, thick-hided irresponsiveness which sees nothing in the emotional mood of another and knows no guiding impulse save dull self-interest and gluttony; (3) fickleness of that unreasoning, unthinking character which is based on shallowness of soul and emotions (the pains resulting from such a state are negligible); (4) diverging mental conceptions of life due to the hastened or retarded mental growth of one or the other or both of the high contracting parties; (5) mistaken unions, wrong from the beginning, based on mistaken affections—cases where youth, inexperience, early ungovernable desire lead to a union based on sex and end of course in mental incompatibility; (6) a haunting compulsion to seek for a high spiritual and intellectual ideal which almost no individual can realize for another and which yet may be realized in a lightning flash—out of a clear sky as it were. In which case the last two will naturally forsake all others and cleave only the one to the other. Such is sex, affection, mental and spiritual compatibility.

But in marriage, as in no other trade, profession or contract, once a bargain is struck—a mistake made—society suggests that there is no solution save in death. You cannot back out. It is almost the only place where you cannot correct a mistake and start all over. Until death do us part! Think of that being written and accepted of a mistaken marriage! My answer would be that death had better hurry up. If the history of human marriage indicates anything, it is that the conditions which make for the union of two individuals, male and female, are purely fortuitous; that marriages are not made in heaven but in life's conditioning social laboratory; and that the marriage relation as we understand it is quite as much subject to modification and revision as anything else. Radical as it may seem, I predict a complete revision of the home standards as we know them. I would not be in the least surprised if the home as we know it were to disappear entirely. New, modifying conditions are daily manifesting themselves. Aside from easy divorce, which is a mere safety valve and cannot safely (and probably will not) be dispensed with, there are other things which are steadily undermining the old home system as it has been practiced. For instance, endless agencies which tend to influence, inspire and direct the individual or child, entirely apart from the control and suggestion of parents, are now at work. Already, in the rearing of the *average* child the influence of the *average* parent is practically negligible. I should like to ask this one succinct question: Which organization on, say, the East Side of New York, or the South Halsted Street district in Chicago, has most influence on the moods, beliefs, theories and intelligence of the *average* child in those districts—the school or the home? And which individual today really comes nearer suggesting a theory of conduct to a child—the mother or the teacher, or some influential outside stranger? And whose social, political and religious ideals come nearer prevailing in any average workingman's child's mind—the father's or that of the editor of the daily paper? Isn't the cottage plan orphan asylum, as we now know it—twelve children to a cottage—infinitely superior to the *average* home? Can any sane human being avoid the essential implication of these things?

But beyond these things again, look at the ease with which the average home atmosphere is erected or struck like a tent. An apartment such as a king might not have enjoyed four hundred years ago can be thrown together in four days. Man's scope of labor, his ability to change his environment, has increased proportionally. If you cannot live peacefully in New York or Chicago, you can in London, San Francisco, Alaska or Melbourne. The economic and culinary control of a house is even now if not a negligible at least a greatly modified factor. Any average housewife cannot much outshine any other average housewife, and with the ability to attain every household convenience quickly, we are beginning to see, even the dullest, that the home atmosphere and the marriage relation depends on something much more subtle than the material *materials* of which we make it. Mood, soul, suggestion, savoir faire—these are the great things. The rest are necessary but not indispensable. It is easy to get together the materials for a thousand homes. It is often not possible to find one single suitable temperament.

My comment on the whole situation is this. The conditions, in the vast majority of cases, as at present we find them, are execrable. The *average* child instead of being greatly benefited by his home is seriously injured, handicapped, and realizes it clearly in later years. Sometimes he marvels that life was so good as to rescue him from his home atmosphere. Right now the public standards of the school and the newspaper are far in advance of the average home. Intellectual, social, spiritual freedom are constantly being suggested to the individual, but not by the home. People are beginning to see that they have a right to seek and seek until they find that which is best suited to their intellectual, physical, spiritual development, home or no home. It is beginning to be seen that no mistake, however great or disturbing in its consequences, should be irretrievable. The greater the mistake, really, the easier it should be to right it. Society *must* and *is* opening the prison-doors of human misery, and old sorrows are walking out into the sunlight where they are being dispelled and forgotten. As sure as there are such things as mental processes, spiritual affinities, significant individualities, and as sure as these things are increasing in force, volume, numbers, so sure also is it that the marriage state and the sex relations with which these things are so curiously and indissolubly involved will be modified, given greater scope, greater ease of adjustment, greater simplicity of initiation, greater freedom as to duration, greater kindliness as to termination. It cannot possibly be otherwise. And the state will guarantee the rights, the privileges and immunities of the children to the entire satisfaction of the state, the parents and the children. It cannot be otherwise.

CHAPTER XCII

And now that I am on this matter of the sex relationship, or, rather, the duality of sex in life, I should like to advance another theory of mine in regard to it. It is quite probable that in the beginning (biologically speaking) the sexual progenitor of the human race or of evoluted species contained in itself the full chemical content of what has since been evoluted into the so-called male and female. Such being the case, its chemical responsiveness to the movements of the universe—chemical, physical, spiritual, or, let us say, emotional—and to its immediate surroundings was complete in itself. It was not divided into two sexes and therefore not dependent on any alienated portion of itself for its chemical, spiritual, emotional or physical satiation. What happened to it individually and momentarily was all that could happen to it. It needed no complementary organism, no other half or second self, to make its understanding of, its reaction to, life complete.

That is not true today. Man (male or female) appears to be individual and complete, but it is an illusion. The human animal of either sex is not complete without its mate of the other sex. And what mate? The asexual individual of biology has evoluted into the duo-sexual organisms, male and female, and these complement each other and are incomplete the one without the other. They are complete and separate organisms in everything save their chemical responsiveness to the universe which requires their union, not merely physically but spiritually, to be complete. When all is said and done, the greatest mental reaction is between the sexes, and it is by their sex warfares that the race, intellectually as well as physically, has evolved. People—a man or a woman—are individual, and yet they are not. Their union sexually, temperamentally, emotionally, intellectually and so on is required before a full measure of chemical responsiveness to life can be attained in either. It may seem otherwise in individual cases, but it is not so.

Such being the case (and a world of biological data might be here introduced), you have the amazing spectacle of love which confounds all theories of life; which laughs at death and, in its fullest expression, defies all human theory and understanding; acts as a *new*, non-understandable thing, and lets in dreams, emotions, conditions from a deeper world than any of which we know, whereby this shadow called existence is resolved, modified, made over into something else so that it bears no resemblance to its former state. Literally, life is transfigured by it. It is, when love comes, no longer what it was—humdrum and homespun. It becomes, apparently, what it well may be: a dream and an illusion of beauty of pain or delight, or all. Evolutionary progress seems to be based on this non-understandable, mysterious, idealistic reaction and contact which baffles the most searching suggestions and intuitions of the imagination and leaves us awed and dumb before the great classics of desire and passion.

But the great fact, not to be lost sight of, is that love—complete chemical responsiveness to the universe—is only attained in the reunion of the separated chemical constituents of the original asexual individual (that is, the man and the woman), and without love and this union there is no full chemical-spiritual responsiveness to the universe. Man does not soar emotionally into the empyrean except in love, and by "in love" I mean stirred by the sex impulses which make for mate-seeking and union. It does not follow that there need ever be physical satiation to complete this union. Spiritual pollination can spring from the merest accidental contact for a moment with a mate. But the fact remains that the greatest, most complete spiritual and physical responsiveness to the universe (which, after all, is a mere matter of chemical reaction) springs from this responsiveness, which springs from love, and as such our so-called love (desire, passionate chemical response, physical and spiritual) becomes the most significant fact in the universe as we understand it. For what is the universe without intellectual perception on our part, the beholding of it with the eyes, the perception of it with the senses, the responsiveness to it through the emotions?

I have often reflected in this connection on the great sex epics of history—Helen and Pericles and Aspasia; Antony and Cleopatra; Romeo and Juliet; Abélard and Héloïse; Cesare Borgia and his sister Lucrezia; Dante and Beatrice; Rembrandt and his Saskia; Faust and Marguerite; Wagner and his Madame Wesendonck. The great minds of the world have invariably realized that by some strange chemistry of life the one significant, overwhelming, revolutionary thing is love—the great elemental chemico-physical attraction of one for another. Our literature and our art would not be worth their salt except for this. History would be unpalatable sawdust. It is safe to say there would be no history worthy of the name. Life would so quickly be flat, stale and unprofitable. Save for this marvelous instinct to passion, there would be no life.

And how magnificently it flames on occasion! The world really is always looking for evidences of its impending conflagrations. The auroral coruscations of desire—how the world rises early or remains late to see! We pretend a reasonable interest in other things, but by and large this is a makeshift, the stirring in dead ashes after the great original flame is cold. Or there be human ghosts who have never once flamed in the flesh. They are negligible. Of them come nothing. Only the combination of two royal natures in unreasoning chemical attraction is significant. After that neither art nor life have anything much save material accessories to offer.

Having delivered myself of this, I should like to return to Madame Rijkens-Culp and her very Vermeer-like reception room. She was such a physical-chemical possibility, a woman burning with a low fire, smoldering as a haycock smolders, and capable, I should say, of a real conflagration. I wondered at once what personality would be the chemical answer for her. I could see that her life was charming and well-ordered but that it was madly peaceful. She was studying Italian, reading French, practicing temperamentally at her music, wondering what her life would bring her before it was too late for it to bring her anything more at all.

Mijnheer Rijkens was very waxy, very intellectual, very unattached philosophically, apparently, and yet very rigid in his feeling for established principle. The type is very common among intellectuals. Much reading had not made him mad but a little pedantic. He was speculatively interested in international peace, though he did not believe that it could readily be established. Much more, apparently, he was interested in the necessity of building up a code or body of international law which would be flexible and binding on all nations. Imaginatively I could see him at his heavy tomes. He had thin, delicate, rather handsome hands, a thin, dapper, wiry body. He was a little old for Madame Rijkens-Culp—say fifty-five or sixty. She had married him to achieve what—position, name, social connections? He had nice, well-barbered, short gray whiskers, a short, effective mustache, loose, well-trained, rather upstanding hair—some such intellectual Northman as Ibsen intended to give Hedda.

We talked and talked. He wanted to know about America, about England, about Italy, about Germany. He asked me quite frankly whether I liked Madame Culp's husband and whether I liked the Germans. I told the truth. I did and I didn't. Madame Rijkens-Culp sent for her pet dog, an English bull, and demanded to know whether I did not think he was nicer than Nana. I perjured myself like a gentleman. I admired Nana because she was truly temperamental and demure and subtle. This dog was strong and vigorous but plaintively human—a slave to his lady. Every day, she told me, she took him for a walk—as a rule, twice a day. He was such a dear creature. Then we went in to lunch.

I had the impression all the while I was with Madame Rijkens-Culp that she was a somewhat sophisticated Emma Bovary. It must be an interesting thing to be. She was as cool and sweet and intellectually balanced as a heavy, waxy flower—content, apparently, to be charming. I wondered as I talked to her what fancies, unrests, desires her sister's career had put in her mind. She was merely the petted wife of an eminent Dutch jurist, years too old for her. She kept coming back in a sly, provocative way with references to my books—this one book. She was going to get another. Would I write more books like this one? If I wrote fifty they would not be too many for her. The spirit and temperament of Jennie Gerhardt seemed to appeal to her in a very provocative way. I felt all the time that she was talking to me for a purpose—that she was thinking things which she would like to say but never would unless she could establish the conditions which made them feasible. After my rather mistaken experience with Madame Culp I was cautious, and anyhow she was coming here in a day or two. The two of them would be comparing notes. The least evidence of tergiversation or an earlier or continued relation with her sister would prove destructive anyhow. So I was cautiously polite. Mijnheer Rijkens stayed until nearly four o'clock, when I left. Madame begged me to come the next afternoon and walk with her, which I did.

In the meanwhile I visited the Rijksmuseum and ran over to Haarlem, one-half hour away, to look at the Frans Hals in the Town Hall Museum (the quaint but decidedly unimposing Stadhuis).

I think the intensity of my artistic cogitations at Haarlem was even greater than it was at Amsterdam, although the latter has the more important collection, for Haarlem was where Frans Hals lived and where in 1610, when he was thirty years of age, he married, and where six years later he was brought before the burgomaster for ill-treating his wife and ordered to abstain from *dronkenschappe*—a thing which sounds very like good liquor to me. Poor Frans Hals!

The day I was there, there were six automobiles outside the Stadhuis waiting while their owners contemplated the wonders of the ten Regents pictures inside, which are the pride of Haarlem, and when I left London, Sir Hugh Lane was holding his recently discovered portrait by Hals at no less than forty thousand pounds, and probably more. I fancy today any of the numerous portraits by Hals in his best manner would bring two hundred thousand dollars and very likely much more. Yet at seventy-two Hals's goods and chattels—three mattresses, one chair, one table, three bolsters and five pictures—were sold to satisfy a baker's bill, and from then on until he died fourteen years later, his "rent and firing" were paid for by the municipality. "A drunken, roistering, good-for-nothing artist," I hear the conservative saying. Exactly. "He barely saved the character of his second wife, Lysbeth Reyniers, one year after his first wife's death by marrying her," but he had eight children by her all told and he must have loved her. Eight children do not spring from a loveless marriage. I take it that he "got in wrong," as we Americans say, insofar as his first wife was concerned. No wonder he was haled before the burgomaster for drunkenness and abusing his wife. Fate saved an artist by letting his first wife die; probably saved a very great artist from endless misery by letting her die. As it was, he appears to have had his share of misery.

This business of being really great is one of the most pathetic things in the world. When I was in London, Mrs. Grant Allen told me the story of the last days of Herbert Spencer, the Synthetic Philosopher, and how, save for herself, there was scarcely anyone to cheer him in his loneliness. It was not that he lacked living means—he had that—but living as he did aloft in the eternal snows of speculation, there was no one to share his thoughts—no one. This good woman, Mrs. Allen, was perfectly charming as a wife and mother. She was a fitting helpmate to so distinguished a thinker as her husband and would have been a lasting solace to such a man as Spencer if he had chanced to marry her, but alas, it was the fate of that gigantic mind to be lonely. What a pity the pleasures of the bottle might not eventually have allured him. Old Omar knew the proper antidote for these speculative miseries.

And Rembrandt van Rijn—there was another whose pictures I am coming to a little later before I get out of Holland. When I think of his tripartite career I am moved to great spiritual melancholy. It is probably true that from 1606, when he was born, until 1634, when he married at twenty-eight, he was gay enough. He had the delicious pleasure of discovering that he was an artist and that probably the world was going to pay a great deal of attention to him. Then he married Saskia van Uylenburch—the fair Saskia whom he painted sitting so gaily on his knee—and for eight years (until she died) he was probably supremely happy. "Everything," as we say in America, "was coming his way." Saskia had forty thousand gulden to contribute to this ménage. Rembrandt's skill and fame were just attaining their most significant proportions, when she had to die. It does not comfort me in the least that fourteen years later the so-called scandal concerning his Hendrickje Stoffels occurred, or that to all intents and purposes she was a wife to him, a sort of combination housekeeper and mistress. He had lost Saskia, the woman with whom he was getting along splendidly—the woman who could surround him with a pleasant, acceptable, distinguished social atmosphere. He and Saskia probably knew each other's moods to a dot. In the eight years that they were together he had four children by her—a fair test of a connubial bliss. Then, she being dead and he being an artist, his affairs got in a tangle, and you have the spectacle of this other seer, Holland's metaphysician, color genius, life-interpreter tangling himself up with a rather dull housekeeper, losing his money, having all his possessions sold to pay his debts and petering out his last days in absolute loneliness at the Keizerskroon Inn in Amsterdam, quite neglected. The local taste for art had changed. The public was a little sick of Hals and Rembrandt. So there he sat, looking out of heaven only knows what weary old eyes, thinking about it all, no doubt. Pathetic? To me infinitely so. Tragic, surely. That is the way life works. The personality of a Caesar, a Lincoln, a Napoleon is really about as significant in the universe as a last-year's hazelnut—no more and no less. Agassiz said life cares everything for the type, nothing for the individual. He did not put it quite strong enough. Life cares nothing for either type or individual. It will throw even the type away like an old tool when it is through with it. It is only the spirit of man, the superior soul-spirit, that treasures the artistic spectacle—for a time—for a time.

But here in Haarlem, as I sat in the Kroon restaurant, opposite the Grote Kerk, watching some pigeons fly about the belfry, looking at Lieven de Key's meat market, that prototype of Dutch quaintness, and meditating on the pictures I had just seen in the Town Hall Museum, the insignificance of the individual as compared with the business of life came on me with overwhelming force. Frans Hals was the activating cause of this, in a way: the story of his life, and also what I knew of Jan Steen of Leyden, some twenty miles away. Jan Steen of Leyden! The jolly innkeeper, according to some; the low-lived tippler, according to others. What is it, I asked myself, thinking of these two, that makes for earthly preciosity? Why do we value certain things, and who values them, and how? The masses certainly don't care for Jan Steen or Nicolaes Maes or Jacob van Ruysdael or Frans Hals or Rembrandt van Rijn. They don't know who they are, and if they did, they wouldn't care for their pictures. Except for a very occasional soul, here and there, I think there are very few people who either understand or care for pictures anyhow. Color suggests nothing; arrangement pleases in no whit; character is beyond their interpretation; spirit, as shining forth through the movement of life, the paint, its radiating physical presence, is without significance; the wonder of a temperament is beyond them entirely. True readers of life are as scarce as hens' teeth; those with great artistic response practically negligible, and yet we have so much truly great art and such tremendous prices paid for it. No need to wander from Holland to establish this. The Rijksmuseum at Amsterdam, the Mauritshuis at The Hague, and this little Town Hall in Haarlem are sanctuaries of treasure.

But in spite of hundreds of canvases, any one of which today is worth a fortune; in spite of a temperament so rare that you marvel at the restraint that produced the velvet blacks, silver grays, whites that are mellow with a mellowness that suggests magic; a mind so receptive, responsive, that no least shade of the character's emotions, textures of his sitter escaped the deifying subtlety of his brush and palette—yet this man Hals was sold out for want of the price of a baker's bill; and Rembrandt, with even greater canvases to his credit, was forgotten in his own lifetime! Yet any one of eight hundred million middle-class individuals can lay aside enough to pay for fifty thousand bread-bills, if necessary. Such is life.

And Jan Steen! How lightly, for so long, were his family feasts, merrymakings, weddings of ill-assorted couples, quacks and their quackeries, tavern brawls, love-sick maidens and the like, neglected and forgotten. The taste for temperamental realism of that ilk passed. In vain that he was the best colorist of all the school; that he rivaled Hogarth in his suggestion of shabby reality; that he satirized the weaknesses and ridiculed the follies of man with a Molièrian simplicity. A tippler—a Dutch sot—gross. So Jan Steen was all but forgotten.

I suppose it is only the last fifty years that has seen this whole school of Dutch art come into anything like its true perspective. Rembrandt's *Night Watch* has now a room to itself, in the Rijksmuseum. Frans Hals has all of a room in the Town Hall here in Haarlem. In every museum everywhere the Dutch are so placed that you can scarcely escape them. They are pushed down your throat by surrounding bare spaces, magnificent frames, curtains of red or black velvet. But they do not need it. They can stand on their own sturdy legs. The finest attributes of life justify them. But Frans Hals was sold out for a bread-bill, and Rembrandt died quite alone and neglected.

CHAPTER XCIII

In the Rijksmuseum at Amsterdam, whither I went before I saw Madame Rijkens-Culp again, I browsed among three thousand pictures, choosing for myself. Other museums, such as the Louvre, the National Gallery in London, the Pitti and Uffizi at Florence, the Kaiser-Friedrich-Museum at Berlin and Metropolitan in New York, are more catholic in their selection, it seems to me, but the Rijksmuseum is the home of Dutch art, and as such it is inimitable. To begin with, it looks no better than the Hebrew Orphan Asylum in New York—a great, homely, red brick building—and in the next place it always seemed to me that it was highly inflammable—a thought that terrorized me; but otherwise, crowded as it is with Dutch and some Flemish art, it is heavenly. The Rembrandts are in it, for instance—*The Night Watch* and *The Syndics*—and here you may find van der Helst, Vermeer, de Hooch, Hobbema, Maes, Ruysdael and all that long and to me exquisite company, if not at their best at least sufficiently so for all human purposes. The Hals here (*The Buffoon*, *The Artist and His Wife*, *Maria Voogt* and others) are astonishing, but no more so than the Hals everywhere. I never saw anything more virile in my life, more subtly suggestive of the real in mood and texture than this portrait *The Artist and His Wife*. It is not only a wonder of temperament interpretation and reality, but the paint is luminous, vibratory, having the flush and validity of life itself. The Vermeers, Cuyps, Maeses, Ruysdaels and a few others were of especial interest to me but primarily I was anxious to see *The Night Watch* and *The Syndics*, two pictures that are as great drums in art, sounding the rub-a-dub of their merits to the uttermost parts of the earth. Although not a slavish follower of great fames, I hope, still I was interested to see, in common with others, on what transcendent merits so great a fame was based. No engraving or photograph even suggests the spirit or artistry of an original, and so after much pottering by the way I came to it, the first and greatest, *The Night Watch*, set apart in a room hung with velvets and carefully lighted, a veritable prince of a picture enthroned in seclusion and silence.

It was interesting to me, purely as a human spectacle, to see how so great a fame was taken by the average spectator. A number of visitors came in, one or two at a time, and seeing so much space given to a single picture, a whole room ornamented and decorated so as to best set forth its splendors, would tiptoe about and (if two) whisper or stand, curious, often without comprehension, wondering what it was all about. Now and then an individual, interested in a comparative study of Dutch art perhaps, or in related methods of other masters, would examine it in detail. Occasionally a person would glance in, realize it was some vast art mystery beyond his comprehension or interest and pass through. I often wonder why such people go to museums at all, and yet of course I know well enough why they go. We all know why the crowd goes anywhere.

Of the few truly remarkable paintings that I saw abroad—Botticelli's *Spring*, Botticelli's *Worship of the Magi* (in the Uffizi), Michelangelo's *Holy Family* (Uffizi), Titian's *Assumption*, Leonardo's *Last Supper*, Frans Hals's *Officers of the Arquebusiers of St. Andrew* (226 in the Town Hall, I think), Watteau's *Embarcation*, Rembrandt's *The Syndics*—this picture of *The Night Watch* was as significant as any—not more, I should say, than one or two of the others. To me Rembrandt was such a large artistic spirit, and if not sad, a reader of the grim, pathetic face of life. In the Metropolitan in New York are two faces of men that—aside from the wonder of their execution, the spirit of the paint itself, the drawing, the shadowing, the modeling—are instinct with a profound pathos, a profound despair, deeper than any which I know in art. Keats speaks of glutting one's sorrow on a rose. When the profound melancholy fit shall fall, it might well be glutted on these pictures. They speak the heaviness of soul that suggests a Christ and Golgotha; they reflect a true garden of Gethsemane. Why? And whether it was in the subject or Rembrandt, the interpretation is Rembrandt's, and therefore the understanding could only spring from there. What heaviness of soul he must have endured at times—what weltschmerz. One could predicate the largest philosophic comprehension, the deepest, richest, most poetic melancholy from either of these pictures. And the graphic paint mood in which they were done! Deep organ notes of psychology, world echoes of world pathos.

There is such a thing as a soul flare in painting, and *The Night Watch* is one. Never until you dream over a masterpiece at close range—as one reads a great novel, views a great building, catches the spirit of a truly great city (an individual and artistic city) in its very streets—do you come close to the very life spirit of the artist himself or the creative impulse which is back of it all. There is something so eternally wonderful about this matter of temperament, this ability of some souls and bodies to let life come through, not unmodified (for it is that invariably) but modified in such a pleasing way by the color of the soul through which it passes that it is enhanced and in its way glorified thereby. Botticelli's soul! Rembrandt's soul! The soul of Frans Hals! Of Leonardo! There is such a fine sadness in the things of Michelangelo, quite as there is in Keats. There is such a sweetness and poetic delicacy—oh, quite like the budding delicacy of spring—in all that Botticelli ever did, romance and art of the youngest, freshest, most delicate character, and so strangely metaphysical. In Leonardo there is a vast, solemn resignation—so vast and so solemn that in a way it is terrifying, like the vasty deep. In Frans Hals you miss perhaps the sad broodings of a mystic, but—suns and planets!—what realism! The man paints the surface of this life exactly as it was, and you cannot deny it. His people are with you more than your neighbor, your friends. You could almost say of him that he is too great to be great. But with Rembrandt you get a metaphysician who was a Dutch metaphysician, deep, deep, essentially dramatic if you will, sad. Bismarckian, this one—or merely Rembrandtian. Old, courageous, a little weary, but unconquerable, fronting the dark with a contemplative, speculative but not terrified eye.

I like that spirit in the great artist which is forever young. I do not know when *The Night Watch* was painted, but it must have been when Rembrandt had attained to a solid maturity. It speaks of the fullness of things. Yet it is so young in its grasp of life and the love of it, so dramatic where reasonably you cannot expect drama. There is such a thing as a soul flare in paint. This is it. The scene is so commonplace in its way that at first glance it is disappointing. Your catalogue explains that the picture represents Captain Frans Banning Cocq, Lord of Parmerland and Itpendam, whatever they were, and Lieutenant Willem van Ruytenburch, Lord of Vlaardingen, and a small company of the civic guard (each man paid a hundred florins to get in the picture), marching out to go shooting. Among the civic guard is a girl, her fair hair adorned with pearls, a bird hanging from her girdle, "probably the prize for the conqueror in the contest," who probably did not pay one hundred florins, being a guest of the company. There are twenty figures indicated in all and a suggestion of pikes or standards which speaks for still more. The captain is in a dark-brown, almost black, costume. His undersized lieutenant is in a yellow buffalo jerkin, both figures in the full sunlight so that the shadow of the captain's hand is distinctly traceable. The rest recede in a none-too-pleasing order of grouping, a little confused, with deficient rhythm and cross accents—defects which seen in ensemble are not defects at all.

The mystery and charm of this picture is in all likelihood fortuitous, a reflection of a momentary mood. The spirit of adventure and mystery and response to life is so intense and yet so untraceable that it is baffling. There is such a thing as a burst of soul in light and tone—it is here. Color, in the larger sense of the word, is wanting, but color in its farther reaches is so utterly banal anyhow. The chiaroscuro of an imperfectly lighted interior is astonishing. The sense of nervous intensity, perhaps this more than anything else, distinguishes the picture, is inspiring. Why so many alert, nervous Dutchmen? To me the composition, while not bad, is not pleasing, inspiring. Some of the figures seem over- or under-drawn. The dog barking is almost an anachronism. The figure of the stocky dwarf to the left, with the powder horn, is what—a jest? Over all flows Rembrandt's tobacco-juicy atmosphere—a warm, brown, candlelight effect, high lights and deep shadows, but what lighting!

But when all is said and done, what of it? No Botticellian dream of spring, this; no somber psychologic-metaphysical mystery, such as pervades *The Last Supper*. Yet every defect admitted—hands left unpainted, coloring arbitrary, individual figures dull, arrangement poor—this picture sings and sings. It is like Shelley's skylark; it is like Botticelli's *Spring*; it is like the crescendo crash of a symphony. I defy a lover of the charm and mystery of life to stand before it and not find himself coming into a rich, rhythmic harmony with it. Our American Huneker has said somewhere that Rembrandt is a window looking out on eternity. He is. In the great ebb and flow of life, the ratiocination of nature, or the lack of it, in the jetsam and flotsam of blind chance that is weaving endless combinations of matter, endless pictures, Rembrandt van Rijn caught and fixed this one. And the compound of his soul was such—buffs or greens or blues or blacks, phlegmatic Dutchmen or nervous excitable ones; Holland, Belgium, Spain or Italy, he has given us in one fair singing canvas the spirit and flesh and textures and moods of life, its intensity and love of itself. And more than that no man can do. That each guild member paid one hundred florins to have his portrait included is still more a part of the wonder and glory of it all. *The Night Watch* is deservedly famous. I wonder how soon again, if ever, it will be relegated to the limbo of the unimportant, forgotten for a cycle, perhaps only to be resurrected and dreamed over as it is today.

The remainder of the Rijksmuseum was in its various aspects quite wonderful, a true treasure house. I found *The Syndics* illuminating in another way and the various members of the Dutch school true worlds in which to walk. So many, such as Ruysdael, Jan Steen, van Ostade, Vermeer, a score or more, are so brilliantly represented. I have already paid my respects to Dutch art. More I cannot say.

My walk with Madame Rijkens-Culp the same afternoon late was a continuation of the atmosphere of Dutch art for me. She was of its best mood, of a piece with its pearly-silvery Dutch atmosphere. As a matter of fact her temperament suggested Frans Hals coloring. She came into the drawing room of her house clad in a smooth-fitting, dark-blue walking suit and very dull russet shoes. The leaden gray hat she wore, quite smart in design, had a glowing cockatoo's wing and beak on it. Jacco, the bull, was by her side, led by a gunmetal chain.

"Now I will show you the least bit of Amsterdam," she said.

This woman and I, if we had met under other conditions, would probably have been much more than mere social palaverers. She fell into my step quite easily and walked pleasingly, close, her sleeve brushing my arm. We talked first of the water in the canals, its olive green aspect, and how buildings, light and water composed soundless symphonies whereto only the artist might respond. We talked dully of the Germans and her sister and her sister's husband, but dropped them because there was something much more significant in the air. Had I been to Haarlem? Yes. Had I been through the Rijksmuseum? A momentary glance, yes. Was I fond of Dutch art? Yes, I was.

"Oh, it is so lovely today," she said in a soft ecstasy. "Now you must tell me about New York and how you live there and where you come from."

I sketched quickly and roughly a none-too-suggestive biography.

She bit at her lip as she listened to some of the details.

"You are not coming to Holland to live at any time—to write a book?"

"I had not thought of it," I said.

"It is so nice here in the spring. You should come in the spring. Or stay now."

"Would that I could," I said.

We walked a little while longer along a perfect canal in silence. Amsterdam has no vehicles to speak of, no clattering horses and wagons. Streetcars everywhere, yes, unlike Venice. They follow canals and dry streets out to heavenly vistas of lush grass and windmills. Little two-wheeled push-carts seem to do all the business that canal boats cannot. You may have a canal boat at any time laden with hay, straw, potatoes, bricks, lumber, old iron, oil barrels, coal, loitering under your windows. They are so very picturesque, so poetically naive. I showed her how simply the architectural individuality of Amsterdam was achieved by the constant repetition of two or three little Dutch mannerisms. She turned on me a pair of mild, approving eyes.

"Well, now it is your turn," I suggested. "You must tell me all about yourself."

"That is not so easy, but I will. You see, my husband is a very able man, nervously intense, but in a way dependent on me. He is very fond of me, and so I feel I am useful." She smiled. "He needs me. He is working out a history of jurisprudence, and he is connected with international negotiations. It is a great strain. The atmosphere that I make is what he needs. It surrounds him like an envelope without irritation. It is the one buffer between him and life. Under those circumstances I have sometimes thought it ought not to make so much difference to me so long as I can be of so much assistance in this way."

"I understand, exactly," I said.

"But then again," she went on, "since all is so, I dream a little. Music is something. I am studying Italian. An ideal situation may endure, and it may not. I hope of course that it will, for his sake."

Not a word, you see, of her own feeling.

I listened, catching the drift, but I really did not dare speak. It was quite impossible. In the morning I was expecting her sister at the Amstel. We would in all likelihood be going to Haarlem. If I had not trifled with her sister, there would be now no danger of exchanges of confidences.

"I see," I said cautiously.

We walked to her tailor's, who was also by the way an importer of rare laces, Hindu, Chinese and Siamese weaves of silk, some fine tablecloths and Irish laces and linens—a most curious place. We sat and saw a dress tried on a model, then examined rare weaves, some of the most soothing textures, cloths and patterns that were emotional in their quality. Jacco amused himself by growling fiercely under a chair. After perhaps an hour here we came out and followed other canals, to the Koepelkerk, or a view of it and back to the Royal Palace and the Nieuwe Kerk. On the way she took up this matter of the drift of her life. It was too smooth now, she thought. "I am like someone in a boat drifting along a slow-moving stream."

"Perhaps that is just as it should be," I suggested. "You are very happy, or at least you are not unhappy. Why not let well enough alone?"

"When are you leaving?" she asked curiously.

"In a day or two. Just possibly tomorrow. I cannot tell. I am awaiting certain advice."

"You know," she said quite sweetly and with the atmosphere of a fleecy cloud about her, "it is very hard for a woman sometimes to say what she thinks. It really can't be done. She doesn't dare—she can hardly formulate for herself how it is. I say I am happy, yes. But things may change, you know."

"Yes, I know," I said.

"You really ought to come back to Holland some time. The spring is the time."

"I might come here, but if I did, I would be rather lonely. I know no one but you, and I am getting to that time of life where companionship is essential. I cannot endure loneliness. To work hard is really not enough. One has to have a human escape from it. Your husband has found his."

She looked steadily on before her and down.

"I could introduce you to many people," she suggested.

"Yes, I know. I'm sure you could and would."

She walked a little closer and I felt sure that now if I chose, I could say most anything that bore closely on this point of companionship and what she might mean to me. It was inadvisable.

We went into a shop for a pair of gloves—a quaint little Amsterdam shop, very simple, very old-looking and very good. While we were waiting, she said, and it was an effort to say it, "You know I am looking forward to your return in the spring."

I thought at first she said "my sister's return." I really was not thinking.

"Yes, it should be delightful. I know you are very fond of her."

"Not my sister," she corrected, without a smile. "When you come again in the spring."

"Oh, I see," I said. "I wish I could."

"You must."

We went out and back to her door. It was late.

"I have not heard you play or sing."

"You must come another day if you are here. I am expecting my sister in a day or two—three, I think. If you could only stay!"

"I am sure I shall not be able to stay that long. I do not think I shall see you again. You must pay my respects to your husband."

She smiled at me quite dreamily. "It has been so much pleasure. But you will come back. I know you will. I am looking forward to it."

"When I do," I said, "you will see me first."

She rang her bell, and the maid opened to her. She looked out, quite a Vermeerish soul, from the shadow of her hall, nodded and smiled. The door closed. That was all I ever saw of Madame Betsy Rijkens-Culp.

CHAPTER XCIV

When I returned to the hotel this same evening, I was angered to receive a telegram from Madame Culp saying that she could not possibly arrive, that her husband was only leaving Berlin the next morning, but would I wait and see her first at her sister's, where she would arrive just in time for her concert. Later she was going to sing in Rotterdam, and so on. (I had seen a large poster of her well plastered all over Amsterdam.) I would not, I said to myself. Tomorrow I would leave. I would pack my trunk tonight and send it on through to Paris. Tomorrow I would take my bags and visit The Hague and Rotterdam, cities half an hour apart, and possibly Dordrecht, not more than an hour from Rotterdam, and then move on to Antwerp, Brussels, Bruges and Ghent. I vowed that insofar as I was concerned, she and her sister could go to the devil, and with that resolution firm in my mind I packed and later went to bed. It amused me, the psychology of this woman's flirtatious attitude. I could not make it out. It was just possible that her husband was not leaving until the morrow—quite possible—but the thing had such a welcomely fortuitous aspect that I gave up. "No more," I said. "Paris now and London, and then home. I am sick of this loose virtue idea anyhow. It does not really suit my temperament or become me." So I moralized sourly, and the next morning did just as I planned. I packed, stopped at The Hague and Rotterdam, seeking merely a glance of their principal features, and then a little later went on to Antwerp and Brussels. I was so set on this that the next morning as I was leaving, when a porter came running to say that a certain Madame Rijkens-Culp was on the wire, I shook my head. "Say that I have left," I said, and climbed into my taxi. I knew what she wanted to tell me. Her sister was coming; I must wait. But I had enough of the whole troublesome situation and was glad to go on. My one fear was that by some chance I might encounter Madame Culp or her sister at the station.

The ride from Amsterdam to The Hague through Haarlem, and, late that evening, on from there to Rotterdam, where I stayed for the night, was utterly charming. I had seen Haarlem and Amsterdam thoroughly, and now I was to see The Hague and Rotterdam. The land could not possibly have looked fairer. It was bright with a kind of pearly brightness that one finds indicated in the paintings of the Dutchmen, a faint something in the air giving the land an atmosphere as of strong sunlight shining through a rose-leaf thickness of mother-of-pearl. The canals were so still and glossy-black in this light, the grass so green. For all of twenty miles, perhaps thirty, we ran by enormous tulip-bulb farms alight with tulips. I never saw such a spectacle in my life—pinks, whites, yellows, reds, purples, yellowish reds, side by side in great beds. An English-speaking Dutchman (nearly every one speaks a little English in Holland) informed me that these bulbs were shipped in bulk, like potatoes, all over the world, and that fresh tulips, potted and abloom, were sold as far as Berlin, Paris, London and Edinburgh. Every so often great signs told the name of a tulip company, and beside the track at intervals were immense waste piles of pink or red or white or purple blossoms, blooms snipped from the body of the bulb and cast to wither. They make a fertilizing silo of these symphonies of bloom!

Near The Hague I saw a little girl come out to her garden-gate, which opened on the waters of a canal, and dip up a bucketful. She had on, to my almost feverish joy, wooden shoes. I saw so few of these in Holland. Near Rotterdam I saw eleven windmills all in a row, their sails turning, and between The Hague and Rotterdam (the hour was quite six) such glints and gleams of color in the still surfaces of the canals that I was driven to panegyric verse. Useless! Useless! The silver fingers of the twilight left no imprint in them. Only in the elusive, unstable reflection of the sky in the passing surfaces could her unimagined beauty be glinted—unimagined, vaporous radiances such as one sees more gorgeously magnified in the sunset palaces of the west.

The Hague is really naive. It is such an endless amplification of the Vleeshal of Mijnheer Lieven de Key of Haarlem. We moderns know a good thing when we see it. Lieven de Key knew how to step a facade and gable a window, and 's-Gravenhage is the result. It is quaint, but after a while you almost say to yourself, with Hamlet, "something too much of this." I enjoyed the Mauritshuis, with its collection of Dutch and Flemish art, and the Mesdag Museum of modern art. I found my greatest pleasure however, seeing that it was such a perfect day, in wandering idly here and there, meditating on the spirit of the city. Because of the absence of canals such as one finds at Amsterdam, the place lacked that peculiarly vivifying touch which widely-ramified water supplies for me, but otherwise it was charming.

Outside of the approach to it, I did not care for Rotterdam at all. It was too much a port and too little a city. It had a water-city's flavor of international life, but of a seafaring kind—the South Brooklyn–Dover-Vancouver variety. It does not appeal to me. And after looking at its streets and wharves and docks, I was glad to go on. Interiorly, away from the docks and canals, it had much the flavor of Newark, New Jersey, and Paterson—a drabby, matter-of-fact reality which I cannot endure at times. When I came to Antwerp for a day I was more interested. Curiously, that city had much of the full rich atmosphere of France—warm-blooded, sanguine and avid, with just a suggestion, here and there, of the atmosphere of Holland—not much—which I so much liked. Although only an hour or so away from Holland, everything had again changed.

Out from Rotterdam a little way the country through which we were passing seemed swiftly to lose its composed and placid aspect. It was as flat as that of Holland but something had gone. For one thing, the windmills were fewer and different. That strange precision and artistic nubbiness which had characterized them in Holland had gone entirely. For another, the sky-line, instead of showing ranged trees so beautifully put together in groves with canals here and there and windmills and low, precise architecture, was now disordered and to me irritating. The French word *Sortie* replaced the Dutch *Uitgang*. The French *Rue* appeared in place of the Dutch *Straat*. It seemed to me the people were very like the French, dark and energetic, and yet not entirely so. Some buxom solidity was got from somewhere and showed in the women and men. I felt a strange blood change in myself, as I always do when I come in contact with marked, vigorous personalities of another kind.

I cannot say that I liked Belgium all told, and yet I did. Antwerp interested me. In spite of its blazing modernity and trade activity in certain streets and sections, it was charmingly Flemish in others. I remembered, somehow, that Godfrey of Bouillon had been connected with this city, and that Stevenson, somewhere, had descanted charmingly on medieval Flanders. To save time I went first to the Cathedral, where some Easter preliminaries were filling its fine aisles with life, and viewed the *Elevation of the Cross* and *Descent from the Cross* by Rubens, because, I suppose, it was seemingly important so to do. Then I went around a corner nearby and viewed the medieval facade of the Hôtel de Ville, and then I went to the Royal Museum to see more Rubenses and Van Dycks and much other Flemish art.

When I think of Belgium, or rather Antwerp, Brussels and Bruges and Ghent, I scarcely know what stands out most in my mind (they all came so swiftly in a few days)—the pictures of Rubens; the grim, heavy architecture of the Flemish counts (castles, towers and prisons); or the town halls (Hôtel de Ville), *beffrois* and churches and cathedrals, which though serious enough have a lighter character. All Belgium impressed me as a great breeding- and great feeding-ground, purely Flemish, yet with touches of France and Holland thrown in. You have here in this small, narrow, confined Belgian world a strange individuality which is not all French and but little Dutch—dour, thick, dark, and yet in a way Latin and gay. I went so cheerfully about Antwerp first, admiring the Cathedral—one of the most remarkable in Europe, with an amazing tower; the town hall; the old castle called La Steen or het Steen; and all the touches and atmosphere which suggested the Flanders of the thirteenth, fourteenth, fifteenth and sixteenth centuries.

Rubens was so amazingly well represented here in the Cathedral and the Musée Royal (there were over thirty canvases), and Van Dyck and the earlier Flemings were so properly displayed in serried rows for the art lover, that I got sincere satisfaction out of looking at these.

To this day I have never been able to decide whether I artistically thrill with Rubens or merely marvel at him. Such a temperament—such floridity of soul! When I think of all the miles of Rubens's canvases I saw in Paris, Florence, Berlin, London, Brussels and Antwerp, I grow a little weak and even cynical. Tumultuous and overwhelming as he is, there is vast art value here. There is such a thing as having gallons too much of pulsating red blood in your system—even if only a few in the history of the world have ever had it. I always think of Rubens as I think of one of the heavy-footed, vat-bodied Percheron horses bred somewhere in this region. He is so vastly superior in mere physical strength, if nothing more. Think of all his two thousand canvases, even if they were painted by the aid of disciples! His portraits of his first wife, Isabella Brandt, and his second, Helena Fourment, always stagger and yet thrill me. They suit my taste at times. His fat Venuses and the lovely children of his wives, as well as his fleshly bacchic figures generally, have a huge life significance. I learned a good deal about Isabella Brandt and Helena Fourment before I was done with all his pictures. Their white skins, fat-welted bodies and wide, almost animally suggestive eyes came to haunt me after a time. I was persistently contrasting them with Botticelli's slender ladies and (I crave forgiveness) Cabanel and Bouguereau's suggestive nonentities, the latter creatures not to be mentioned in the same breath of course. But in portraying his Venuses, Rubens is the only one, in my judgment, who has a right to be placed alongside of Botticelli, groan as the cognoscenti may. The two men loved women—Botticelli metaphysically perhaps, the poetic idea of them—and knew how to paint them. To me they seem to approach them from related poetic though dissimilar artistic points of view. Strangely, Helena Fourment and Botticelli's central figure in *Spring* at the Belle Arti in Florence are the two nudes that appeal to me most in all the world of art.

But aside from the grossness of his figures and the tumultuous gargantuan bursts of spirit they suggest, there is a fever in the color of Rubens that, to me, transcends translation. Titian is the only other painter who suggests it to me—best in the *Assumption* at Venice. There is color elsewhere, but not of this febrile kind. It is emotional—the very paint has blood flush and fire in it. I imagine all sorts of astonishing things in connection with Rubens, solely because I have not read a history of his life. Although he painted endless religious subjects, I find no religion in them, no faith; merely a Rubensized poetic imagination, or perhaps not even that—a rather florid sense of grandeur.

But outside of a few principal painters—the van Eycks (I admired the realism of their altarpiece in St. Bavon in Ghent), Rogier van der Weyden (there are examples in Antwerp and Brussels), Hans Memling (almost exclusively confined to Bruges), Quentin Massys and the Brueghels, I saw nothing. Fleeting impressions of others remained in my mind for a time and soon disappeared.

But the cathedrals and churches of these cities—Notre Dame at Antwerp; St. Bavon at Ghent; Ste. Gudule at Brussels; and both St. Jacques and Notre Dame at Bruges touched me deeply as being significant architectural examples. The tower of Notre Dame at Antwerp was so obviously out of proportion to the rest of the building and yet so delightful. I think sometimes a supreme artistic effect is secured by what, judging by all the rules of composition and harmony, must be adjudged an error. It is so in life. Genius is quite uniformly abnormal, and nature's most significant effects are so often wildly fortuitous. It is so with so many of the cathedrals which are best for never having been properly completed. St. Bavon at Ghent was so charming, and the interior of Ste. Gudule at Brussels seemed quite like a gorgeous flower to me—perfect in its rhythm and musical harmony.

But of all that I saw in Belgium, Bruges appealed to me most. My guidebook spoke of it as "the Venice of the North." That reference should be dispensed with. Amsterdam has a much better claim. If it were described as thirteenth-century Flanders or purely medieval, it would be so much nearer the truth. It is one of the few European cities (small and dead now it is) that stands out in my mind as having an amazing individuality, something entirely different, disparate from what you may see elsewhere.

I saw it in a rain first, and at night, after having come into Brussels in bright, hot, spring sunshine, the kind that makes you wish you had immediate facilities for changing to tropic clothing. It was hot, and the car was stuffy from Antwerp to Brussels, but before train time I decided to go to Bruges; the weather changed; it grew cloudy and cooler, and finally at eight o'clock at night began to rain. I had a fierce encounter with Brussels transportation bandits, which I will narrate later, and finally got away, only to come upon Bruges in darkness and rain. It seemed, after the crowds, life and dust of Brussels, as though I had come into some dead, silent world from which all suggestion of once-breathing humanity had departed. It was like the lonely precincts of a dream. The buildings of four, five and six stories seemed higher because of the narrow streets, and the tower of Notre Dame climbing upward four hundred feet in the dark and rain gave it even more a suggestion of walled significance. It was not so much so by day, and yet Bruges is literally astonishing, an almost perfect abandoned shell of something rich, old, powerful.

These shells of once-great cities, however they may terrify the life-loving, light-loving metropolitans of the world's great cities, have for the thinker, the critic, the artist, the dreamer almost an unbroken fascination. Much as I prefer the swift, central currents of life for their stimulating effect on my own nerves, nevertheless the moment I enter such an individual world as this, redolent of past efficiency, now quite dead, I feel as though I could reside here indefinitely. Bruges, Canterbury, Venice, Florence, Amsterdam are cities cut off the same piece of cloth, erected in a way on similar intellectual and artistic principles. They somehow reflect quite accurately and emotionally past distinguished periods of human ambition. There are, no doubt, many other cities which I have not seen which suggest at present the same architectural phenomena, but I have not seen them. Bruges is marvelous, beautiful, individual, alluring, in its exterior aspects, and quite dead.

I shall never forget this one morning that I stepped out into it after a peaceful night at the Hôtel de Flandre. I had arrived the night before, trusting to Baedeker to assure me that this was the best hotel. As I came in on my local train from Brussels, a long express from England and Ostend, a boat-train, arrived with passengers bound these early spring days for Vienna, Paris, Rome, Berlin, the Riviera. You could see through cars so marked, and because it was not so late, people peering out to get a single fleeting glance of Bruges. One young woman called to another getting out, "Bye-bye, Bessie. See you in Paris," and then the train pulled out. A great company of the members of some traveling association had debouched and were making for some hotel. My own room was so still that I wondered why the guests who had arrived with me did not make more noise.

But Bruges the next morning, after all my uncertainty as to its importance, repaid my curiosity, for despite its beggarly sixty thousand inhabitants it fairly staggered me with its artistic possessions. What other city of sixty thousand has so much? By turns I brooded over the charms of St. Sauveur, with its magnificent Gothic choirstalls, its wealth of early Flemish art and its relics of Saxon kings; Notre Dame, with its four-hundred-foot tower, its private collection of Flemish art, its tomb of Charles the Bold and its sculptured *Madonna and Child*, assumed to be by Michelangelo; the Hospital Memling, with its devout medallions by Memling; the Musée Communal with more Flemish art; the Béguinage, that strange region of begging lay-sisters; the Halles with its amazing Belfry; the Hôtel de Ville; the Palace of Justice; the Chapelle du Saint-Sang—and it seemed to me a half-dozen other significant institutions and places, including the marketplace. I never saw a city whose architectural facades were, generally speaking, more interesting. One could brood for hours over the solid brown angles, varied arrangements and ornamental faces of its buildings and towers. Its Palace of Justice is a little jewel and is public. The Halles is an impressive suggestion of old-time power. I could readily understand, after seeing Bruges, that once it had a population of two hundred thousand; that seventeen different kingdoms were once represented by factories and trading companies here; and that the worthy burghers, representatives of the Hanseatic League, and the rich bankers of Venice, Florence and the Rhine could readily defy the Louis of France. That was when Bruges was rich and powerful. It is today a brown, sleepy dream, rich, individual, peculiar, like an abandoned casket of rare artistic workmanship.

CHAPTER XCV

After Bruges and Ghent (to which I gave six hours) and before I arrived again in Paris, I gave a day to Brussels. Brussels is a little Paris—the same cafés with chairs outside, the same rococo French architecture, the same tendency to open, charmingly ornamented spaces, the same atmosphere of leisure, wealth, refinement, taste in art, belles lettres, international politics. All the vices and all the charms of Paris, I should say, on a much smaller scale, and with a Parisian-looking company of men and women busy about their varied social affairs. Ste. Gudule was to me all that it should be as a church. Its interior was poetic, dreamy, a song in stone. The new City Hall was suggestive of something new and rather worthwhile in architecture, a modern adaptation of Karnak. The old Hôtel de Ville, with its attendant houses of early date, was as individual and charming as anything to be seen in any of the Flemish cities. What a rich feeling for exterior and interior decoration the architects of those days had. These buildings are really fit and worthy companions of the splendid Gothic cathedrals which they usually attend. In between of course (in Brussels, Ghent, Antwerp, even Bruges) was the ruck of commonplace, or shall we say superior, modern life. Streetcars, tobacco stores, drugstores, saloons, picture-postcard shops, barber shops, moving picture shows, theaters, very, very modern hotels and even automat restaurants—and all this on the soil—in the immediate vicinity of the square—on which the Dukes of Brabant and the Counts of Flanders once held their hearty jousts. The world does move. And the very large population of nearly seven hundred thousand has been brought here almost since 1880!

The modernity of European cities was always impressing me afresh, never more so than in Brussels. When one considers that the telephone, the telegraph, the electric light, the trolley car, the high building and the high-power elevator are comparatively recent American inventions or evolutions, the modernity of the average European city is, to say the least, startling. If I am not mistaken, Brussels had a solid, unbroken wall about it in 1830 with, say, seventy or thereabout striking gates. Formerly there was an inner wall. Not so today. The trolley cars now run swiftly as in any American city to nine or ten outlying suburbs, and the guide who conducted me over the field of Waterloo assured me that there were as many more, still farther out and growing rapidly. The modern ten-story hotel with all conveniences is here, and the Americans and English, to say nothing of other nationalities, are here also in great number, their automobiles honking, their showy evening parties making a great clatter about the halls and foyers of these principal transient palaces. And as for vice, the cocottes and street-women of Brussels seemed as numerous and as striking as those of Paris.

Coming out of Antwerp, Bruges, Ghent, and before that Holland, into this sudden extreme modernity was like being douched with a cold spray or put into a bath of a much higher degree of temperature. Bruges and Ghent were so strangely old in spots. When I looked at the hooded boys and saboted men, the white corduroy trousers of the latter, strangely narrow, and the old women in weirdly flaring black capes and headgear such as I saw at Bruges, and then contrasted all this with the extremely up-to-date and rather sensuous life of Brussels, I felt for some reason as though I had long been out of the world and had just returned. As you begin to draw near Paris, London or New York you feel that way. As I have said, Brussels is a little Paris. At Bruges the night before I had stood and watched a flock of pigeons, peculiarly small-looking, I thought, flying in and out of the tall and beautiful belfry of Notre Dame, at least three hundred and fifty feet in the air. I had a sense of great age. Here in Brussels the next evening I was taking tea and toast along with a score of Americans, English, French and the like, all idling after the best European manner, and all on the *qui vive* with the one dominant thought of the French-Latin life—the satiation of their physical appetites. It was as distinctly sensible here (after Bruges and Ghent and Holland) as if the closest observers were proclaiming it from the housetops. This Palace Hotel, at which I stopped for the night, was alive with cocottes, mistresses, flaring social adventuresses, en route perhaps to Paris and other European centers, and pausing here—I wondered why? Such costumes! Such airs! It was like being back in the Abbaye de Thélème at Paris once more, or Maxim's, looking on at the showy, pleasure-loving companies that frequent those institutions, and seeing the rather tame, conservative non-understanding Americans coming foolishly to pay and look on. Americans do appear to be such yokels at times.

And because I was away from Antwerp, where Van Dyck was born and raised and where he worked for a while and where some very excellent canvases of his may be seen, and, somehow, because Bruges, even more than Antwerp, suggested the atmosphere in which he must have worked, and Brussels the temperament he enjoyed or suffered from, I suddenly developed an interest in his art. Why had I not examined his canvases more carefully at Antwerp? I wondered how many of them were in the Royal Museum here in Brussels and looked them up in my Baedeker. Some twelve were indicated. Good—next day I should see them. I spent an evening gadding the streets of Brussels, conversing with some keepers of shops who talked English, talking with a girl on a corner who also talked English, talking with a cocotte in the writing room who had a charming, silky, black spitz dog who barked at me when I secretly shot paper wads at him, and thus gave me an opportunity to make a remark in English, which was reciprocated genially enough. The lady was stopping here with some individual of material importance or prosperity, who came after a time and took her away. She had a soft, jelly-like, albeit shapely little figure, suggestively clad, and walked with mincing, sensuous steps. What an advertisement such a woman is for the individual who cares for her, I said to myself, and yet how eagerly they are sought. There be those who will pay any price for them. This one had clothes and lingerie and shoes and some few jewels that must have cost a small fortune. My dwindling purse would have permitted no adventurous offers in this direction even if I had been so minded or the lady had been really interested, which she wasn't.

But as to Van Dyck. There is a painter in whom I have always been greatly interested because he satisfies in a certain way a peculiar mood of mine. I think I understand Van Dyck. He was a happy (or shall I say unhappy?) combination of Grant Richards and Sir Hugh Lane. His art—"resemblance with dignity, costume with taste, art with simplicity"—answers for Lane's attitude exactly. His exciting love of the ladies and the incident of the lovely Margaret Lemon, who tried to maim his right hand when he finally married another (and she was only one of many) answers for Grant Richards. His admiration and in a way imitation of the fervor, breadth and sweep of Titian, Rubens, Veronese, to say nothing of their emotional sanguinity, is an indication of his blood temperament. And yet his own work is in a way so cool and polished. Happy Van Dyck!

I found the twelve. They weren't really very good. There are better in Paris and London. Yet the portrait of *An Unknown Gentleman* wearing a huge ruff, and another of a Flemish sculptor, Frans Duquesnoy, gave me a suggestion of his power as a portraitist. Perhaps Rubens was better even at this sort of thing, but his portraits, involved as they usually are in larger canvases, do not show to such advantage. This business of portrait painting had become a science with Van Dyck. Let the heathen, in the shape of the Neo-Impressionists, rage. They cannot sweep this gentlemanly theory of accepting life at its best entirely from the boards. There is something to be said for portraying it fiercely at its worst, but to me both are acceptable. One of Van Dyck's *Crucifixions* is here, but for me he is at his best in the non-religious field.

This Brussels museum, by the way, is a really important affair, one of the world's great galleries. The modern system of setting apart rooms for individuals, schools, periods and types of art is carried out to a nicety. Rubens, the early Dutch and Flemish schools, the late Dutch and Flemish schools, Hals, Rembrandt and the van Eycks, are all represented. The Spanish, French, English and Italian schools dwindle to mere shadows. There was a copy of Rodin's *Thinker*, so immensely popular these days, which I deplore as being a suggestion from Michelangelo's figure of Lorenzo, Duke of Urbino, in the new sacristy of San Lorenzo at Florence—a nude Duke of Urbino it is to me—but that may not irritate many. At the same time I have always felt that Rodin borrowed his idea of semi-revealed archaic figures from Michelangelo's uncompleted (unintentionally uncompleted) figures of slaves for the tomb of Julius II. This may be of no great moment either. I do not decry the validity of Rodin's art. It is life in motion and metaphysics plus emotion and tender humanitarianism, but he has done better than *The Thinker*. However, time cannot impair the significance of Michelangelo any more than it can that of Rodin, strange, rippling metaphysician that he is. There are times when the latter appears to be too much the stormy thunders, but after the pale, pointless nonentities of average sculptural conception he is like God himself. He can create something. Michelangelo was the sad interpreter of life's brooding woes. We cannot spare either.

After a hard day, which included the Brussels Museum and Waterloo, I took the night train for Paris, having given about three hours to the great battlefield. I could see Grant Richards's dull eye in advance as I told him I had been there. Waterloo! Of all dull places to see! So American—such an idea! Nevertheless I went and I was interested, quite excited, over some of the *exact spots* and remaining suggestions. My imagination responds quite readily to war. I remember as a boy that I was always eager to be a general and lead an army of presumably militant Indianaians out from Terre Haute to capture such places as Brazil (Indiana), Vincennes (Indiana), Switz City, Sullivan and Gosport. When I captured them, I scarcely remember what I intended to do with them, but I believe my intention was to declare myself Emperor of Southern Indiana and then war indiscriminately against Kentucky, Illinois, Ohio and Northern Indiana. The vision comes to me yet of my magnificent capitol at Indianapolis and all the natives of my state doing honor to me. Poor Indiana! It lost a great emperor.

However, when we reached Waterloo, it was gray and misting. Hurrying from the Brussels Museum, I had been seized upon by a guide and compelled to listen to his explanations. All the details of Waterloo could be explained in three hours, he told me. Four or five francs was the charge, for here in Belgium we were using French money again, after all the irritating chicken feed of Holland. I have said nothing concerning the money of that country because I am so fond of Holland, but positively it is the worst of all. But who cares about money when you can have Dutch windmills and Rijksmuseums and Mauritshuises? Here in Belgium all was French, and so in this respect at least my troubles were over. I went with this guide, and to my comfort fell in with two Americans doing Europe—two raw West Virginians, living at Wheeling. Italy, Austria, Germany and France had not abashed them in the least. They were going to England for a spring season.

"Gee, get onto the nag," one of them observed as we climbed into the shabby vehicle at Braine l'Alleud (pronounced Braine la Loo) provided for all such poor victims as accept the attentions of guides in seeing such panoramas as Waterloo.

"He looks as though he might have taken part in the battle," suggested the other.

"Nothing weak about that fiery eye, eh? If he came charging down on the enemy there'd be something doing, heh? Yeh, Bo! Go easy there!" We were already ambling down a dirt road to Hougomont and the scene of the attempted turning of Wellington's right.

It was an amusing morning. We had a really interesting Belgian, capable of a fiery description. He looked like an undersized Scotchman—not unlike Harry Lauder—and he confided to me that his grandfather had piloted Victor Hugo over this very field and that he had made a fine job of it.

"Is that where Victor Hugo got his fine description of Waterloo in *Les Misérables?*" I inquired humbly.

"It is," replied my guide.

"What do you know about that!" said one of the Americans, the slimmer, poking the other in the ribs. "Some grandfather, eh?"

Our guide was in no way disturbed.

I am no war-enthusiast, though battles have their charm, but this field of Waterloo drew up interesting memories. I suppose the dullest of us respond when we are on the exact spot. I know that as we went over this ground and found (I presume they were genuine) bullet holes in the farmhouse walls and looked at the well, once choked with dead, and saw the line of the gulley or ditch that Napoleon's field geographers failed to report (there is no gulley there now), the significance of the forceful Corsican's fate came home. I for one have never ceased to regret that he lost. The French would have done as well by the world as the English, and anyhow after his death a natural division of the empire would have followed. Poetically speaking, it is better that he was defeated, for the world needs these great spectacles of grandeur and calamity to make it assume (believe) that life is worthwhile. For without noble tragedy—vast, heroic cataclysms—this human existence would be insufferably dull. Good God, we would have nothing to stir the imagination, to whet it on, and without enlivened imagination life would not be worthwhile. I know a Japanese who maintains that the greatest thing in the world is an illusion, that to create or foster one is the great thing to do. Without illusion, according to him, life is not endurable, and with that I agree. What illusion was it that Napoleon suffered from? What was the one he left in the minds of the many? A sense of grandeur? I think so, and it is the most important contribution he could have made to this humdrum world.

CHAPTER XCVI

When I reached Paris again, it was distinctly *not* like the first time. It was delightful to be coming again, for now it was spring, or nearly so, and the weather was pleasant. People were coming to Paris in droves from all over the world. This through train from Brussels was packed, and three calls were given for dinner in the dining car. The stout Belgians and Hollanders were mingled with smart Parisians, English, Americans and others coming from London or elsewhere via Ostend.

I parted with my two West Virginia friends at Brussels on the way back from Waterloo. They had been charmed with their view of the field.

"I wonder what they did with all the dead," one of them said to me. "There must have been forty thousand dead bodies on this field at one time."

"Quite right," I replied, "but I can't tell you. Perhaps the natives buried them. It couldn't have been very sanitary to have left them lying aboveground."

"Catch anybody burying anybody unless they were paid for it," observed the other American.

"Search me," said the first one, "but it must have been pretty bad if they didn't."

There was talk as to skulls and bones turned up by plows. And muskets and bullets and buckles being found even to this day. I rather doubted that, but it might have been true.

When I reached Paris, it was nearly midnight. My trunk, which I had sent on ahead, was somewhere in the limbo of advance trunks, and I had a hard time getting it. Parisian porters and depot attendants know exactly when to lose all understanding of English and all knowledge of sign language: it is when the search for anything becomes the least bit irksome. The tip they expect to get from you spurs them on a little way, but not very far. Let them see that the task promises to be somewhat wearisome and they disappear entirely. I lost two *facteurs* in this way, when they discovered that the trunk was not ready to their hand, and so I had to turn in and search among endless trunks myself. When I found it, a *facteur* was quickly secured to truck it out to a taxi. And not at all wonderful to relate, the first man I had employed now showed up to obtain his tip.

"Oh, here you are," I exclaimed, as I was getting into my taxi. "Well, you can go to the devil."

He pulled a long face. That much English he knew.

This matter of the European chauffeur or taxi driver, *facteur*, depot attendant, baggage-agent, enraged me as much in Belgium as anywhere, perhaps more so. In England the porter is civil and never unduly greedy. In France he is debonair and indifferent but noticeably greedy. In Italy he works a "stick up and gun" system on you. You give the gateman a lira or you don't get your hand luggage put in the train. In Belgium plain trickery was resorted to.

Instance A: When I came into Brussels the first night, I decided not to bother with it at all but to go on at once to Bruges and return here later. One kit bag was enough. Accordingly I deposited my fur coat, suitcase, blanket, shoebag and other things in the parcel room—the French equivalent for which I now forget. Before doing so, however, I had allowed a *facteur* to carry them out to a waiting taxi.

"Never mind," I said in English. "I will put them in the parcel room."

Great excitement as to my strange, undecipherable intention. Finally, however, it became fairly clear. Do you think my *facteur* led the way back to the parcel room through the door we had just come? Not at all. There was no thieving attendant in charge of that door to profit by my little mistake. Instead he led me around to another door, the regular ticket-taking door where, if I had not had a Cook's tourist ticket to show, I would have been charged a franc or at least thirty centimes to be permitted to carry my bags to the parcel room where I could again pay for storing them. As it was there was a long argument, frothy, tempestuous, before I was made to see that I could not go through here without a ticket (or a tip), not even for so laudable a purpose as bringing some little business to the parcel room. My *facteur* blandly put down all my bags in order to see whether the gateman succeeded in getting a tip or not. He did not—not in this instance. I flashed my tourist ticket on him, and in disgust he wilted. His face took on a sad, contemptuous look. To think that an American, a rich American (we are all rich over there), would resort to any such trashy scheme as this to escape! My *facteur* took up my bags with an air which said as plainly as anything, "This is truly pitiful. This man is the acme of make-believe superiority." He carried them to the parcel room and put them down. I tipped him. Off he went, after he had said a few words to the parcel clerk in French. The latter clattered cheerfully back.

"Fifty centimes," he said.

I paid.

When I was an hour out of Brussels toward Bruges, I looked at my parcels receipts quite indifferently, only to discover that I had paid twenty-five centimes too much, unless I intended to pay for two days in advance, which I didn't. The receipts or stubs called for five centimes per day per parcel. "How did he know that I might leave them two days?" I asked myself. It was a smart mystery.

When I came back from Bruges I went to the parcel room for my bags. How to unravel this strange mystery, said I. The man brought them out.

"Fifty centimes."

"But I paid fifty centimes when I left them here two days ago."

"Fifty centimes."

"But I paid fifty centimes. See here—it says five centimes per day."

"*Non, non, non!* Fifty centimes."

What would you do? Seek justice through a series of railroad officials to whom you couldn't speak French and who very frequently deny that they speak English merely to save bother? I said to one at Monte Carlo, "Do you speak English?" and he replied, "No."

So in helpless rage and to avoid being delayed, I paid fifty centimes more. Then I sought a taxi—to be overcharged as usual.

Instance B: In Ghent on my arrival, I refused a taxi without a meter in order to avoid the arbitrary charge which could be anything when I reached my destination, and instead deposited myself in one with a meter. As I neared St. Bavon, the Cathedral, I noticed that the meter was working overtime. "Here," I said, "this won't do. Look at that thing!"

He stopped the car. The meter still continued to work!

"I'll pay now," I said, "and you can go. In an hour that thing would register thirty francs."

He pocketed three francs for about ten blocks and went his way.

It was even worse at the Gare du Midi at Brussels, where I left my bags for an hour before my departure. The man wanted one franc. The receipt that he gave me called for twenty-five centimes.

When I reached the hotel in Paris, Grant Richards was out somewhere, and instead letters of complaint were awaiting me. Why hadn't I telegraphed the exact hour of my arrival? Why hadn't I written fully? It wasn't pleasant to wait in uncertainty. If I had only been exact, several things could have been arranged for this day or evening. Poor Grant Richards! I realized now that I had been acting rather badly, but I had telegraphed from Brussels. I hadn't given the hour of my arrival because I didn't want him to bother to meet me. While I was meditating on my sins of omission and commission, a *chasseur* bearing a note arrived. Would I dress and come to Gerny's Bar? He would meet me at twelve. This was Saturday night, and it would be good to look over Paris again. I knew what that meant. We would leave the last restaurant in broad daylight or at least the Paris dawn.

It was interesting to see Grant Richards again after two months. A more gracious host one could not wish. Coming down on the train from Brussels, I had fallen into a blue funk, a kind of mental miasma—one of the miseries Grant Richards never indulged in. They almost destroy me. Grant Richards never, insofar as I could see, succumbed to the blues. I, on the other hand, had been meditating that my journey was now practically at an end. A few more days and I would be sailing from Dover or Southampton—I hadn't learned which route had been arranged for. Grant Richards, in managing my finances, had angered me some, for although he had agreed to see that I returned to America with a certain amount, he had never given me a statement of any kind and had manipulated my affairs so that when he was with me, I could never tell whether we were spending much or little—only I knew it was much—or whether our accounting would come out as he predicted or not. At Monte Carlo he had taken charge of the major portion of my cash and left me with what I considered a bare traveling allowance. This had irritated me, but I was not prepared to quarrel about it. As a matter of fact, seeing that his temperament was so interesting and that he had piloted me so effectively, quite affectionately, through all phases of a certain aspect of European life, I did not see that I had any basis for a quarrel or complaint. "Perhaps," I said to myself, "his judgment and discrimination and taste in certain matters, the mere pleasure of being with him, are worth anything I can afford to pay. Only I cannot afford to pay so much. He travels in a much broader realm, socially and sybaritically, than I could ever hope to do."

It always seems strange to me that the human mind and the human body are so arranged as to be compelled or conditionally inclined to seek self-preservation at the expense of almost everything else. Money, as a symbol of self-preservation as well as being a medium of exchange, has come to have undue significance with the masses, though the wise see far beyond it. St. Francis saw something which the average man may never see, and the truly intelligent of all ages have sought only power—money under such circumstances being a mere medium—the thing that it really is. One would think that in such a relationship as this between myself and Grant Richards, money would play only a small part, for after all he had, without any expenditure on his own account and with some advantage in the amusement it afforded him, brought about my present pilgrimage, and that was important to me. Under the circumstances I think he rather looked on my money as his own, to be expended in any general way which would achieve amusing, interesting and possibly artistically developing results for me. He could not look into the depths of my temperament and see the long period I was seeing which related to my life after I returned to America, nor my natural doubts as to the uncertainty of my artistic future. Money (the relatively small amount we had been dealing with) was not the same thing to him that it was to me. All my life I had been dealing in comparatively small sums. His affairs had been laid out on a rather large scale.

So now this matter of the amount I would have with which to return to America was irking me. It was in vain that he had previously pointed out that in his judgment my literary future was reasonably assured. Of a naturally pessimistic turn, I could not see that. Neither was I seeing at the moment the almost inestimable significance, as I have said, of his own personality. I do not know where anyone would turn to find a second Grant Richards as a European guide or mentor. What you got from him really depended on your own capacity and not on his power to give or suggest, which was almost limitless. The man had social, artistic and critical genius.

However, all this had not helped my mood on this particular evening. When, somewhat after twelve, after a most interesting trip through Belgium, I arrived at Gerny's Bar (the restaurant in which I had first seen Madame de Villiers), I was a little doleful. Grant Richards was there. He had just come in. That indescribable Parisian tension, that sense of life at the topmost level of nervous strength and energy, was filling this little bar. The same red-jacketed musicians; the same efficient, inconspicuous, attentive and courteous waiters; Madame Gerny, placid, philosophic, comfy, business-like and yet mother-like, was going to and fro, pleasingly arrayed, looking no doubt after the interests, woes and aspirations of her very, very bad but beautiful "girls." The walls were lined with life-loving patrons of from twenty-five to fifty years of age with their female companions. Grant Richards was at his best. He was once more in Paris, his beloved Paris. Gerny's was central, a kind of headquarters for him. From here, as a vantage point, he could conduct most of his Parisian affairs. He beamed on me in a cheerful, patronizing way.

"So there you are! The Italian bandits didn't waylay you, even if they did rob you, I trust? The German empire didn't sit too heavily on you?

Holland and Switzerland must have been charming as passing pictures. Where did you stop in Amsterdam?"

"At the Amstel."

"Quite right. An excellent hotel. And how did you like Zehlendorf?"

"Very much indeed. A beautiful place."

"I trust Madame Culp did her full duty as a hostess?" (Never a suggestion of undue situations, in that, as you perceive.)

"She was as considerate as she could be."

"Right and fitting. She should have been. The honor was hers, not yours. I saw that you stopped at the National in Lucerne. That is one of the best hotels in Europe. I was glad to see that your taste in hotels was not falling off."

We began with appetizers, some soup and a light wine. I gave a rough summary of some things I had seen, and then, coming to the matter of my sailing date and a proposed walking tour in England, I pulled a long and gloomy face. Retrospective contemplation of my European days told me that in all likelihood, instead of having a considerable balance of cash on which to fall back in America, I should have nothing or less than nothing. I would have to draw against any accumulated royalties, and there were other things which needed adjustment—payments on insurance, land and so on, to the extent of two or three thousand. Delayed work, now that my trip was nearly over, was haunting me, the difficulty of getting a number of things done by so soon as the middle of July—and a walking tour in the south of England would require at least two more weeks. The thought of Fontainebleau, Marcelle and other spring ventures had vanished as I began to look into my affairs after leaving Berlin.

"Now I'll tell you what I think we should do, and then you can use your own judgment," suggested Grant Richards. "By the time we get to London next Wednesday or Tuesday, England will be in prime condition. The country about Dartmoor will be perfect. I suggest that we take a week's walk anyway. You come to Bigfrith—it is beautiful there now—and stay a week or ten days. I should like you to see how charming it is about my place in the spring. Then we will go to Dartmoor. Then you can come back to Bigfrith. Why not stay in England and write this summer?"

I put up a hand in serious opposition. "You know I can't do that. Why, if I had so much time, we might as well stay here and go to Fontainebleau. Besides, money is a matter of prime consideration with me. I am no longer at peace in my mind concerning my future means. I think, in all seriousness, I had best drop the writing end of the literary profession and return to publishing and editing if I can."

Whenever I got on this doleful topic, I noticed that invariably Grant Richards bridled considerably. He had, for reasons of temperament of course, a rather kindly feeling for the type of thing I was trying to do. The geniality and romance that lightened his eye as he thought of the exquisite beauty of England in the spring faded, and his face became unduly severe.

"Really," he said with a grand air, "you discourage me. At times, truly, I am inclined to quit. You are a man, insofar as I can see, with absolutely no faith in yourself—a man without a profession or an appropriate feeling for his craft. You are inclined on the slightest provocation to give up. You neither save anything over from yesterday in the shape of satisfactory reflection nor look into the future with any optimism. Do, I beg of you, have a little faith in the future. Assume that a day is a day, wherever it is, and that so long as it is not in the past, it has possibilities. Here you are, a man of forty, the formative period of your life behind you. Your work is all indicated and before you. Public faith such as my own should have some weight with you, and yet after a tour of Europe such as you would not reasonably have contemplated a year ago, you sink down supinely and talk of quitting. Truly, it is too much. You make me feel very desperate. One cannot go on in this fashion. You must cultivate some intellectual stability around which your emotions can center and anchor."

He stared at me with a hard, monocled eye.

"Fairest Grant Richards," I replied, "how you preach! You have real oratorical ability at times. There is much in what you say. I should have a profession, but we are looking at life from slightly different points of vantage. You have in your way a stable base, financially speaking. At least I assume so. I have not. My outlook, outside of the talent you are inclined to praise, is not very encouraging. It is not at all sure that the public will manifest the slightest interest in me from now on. If I had a large bump of vanity and the dull optimism of the average thick-wit, I might assume anything and go gaily on until I was attacked somewhere for a board bill. Unfortunately, I have not the necessary thickness of hide. And I suffer periods of emotional disturbance such as do not appear to afflict you. If you want to adjust my artistic attitude so nicely, contemplate my financial state first and see if that does not appeal to you as having some elements capable of disturbing my not undue proportion of equanimity." We then went into actual figures from which, to his satisfaction, he deduced that with ordinary faith in myself I had no real grounds for distress, and I from mine figured that my career was quite as dubious as I had fancied. It did not appear, however, that I was to have any money when I left England. Rather, I was to draw against my future and trust that my innate capabilities would see me through.

CHAPTER XCVII

It was definitely settled at this conference that I was not to take the long-planned walking tour in the south of England, lovely as it would be, but instead, after three or four days in Paris, and three or four days in London, I was to take a boat sailing from Dover about the middle of April or a little later which would put me in New York before May. It was, apparently, a little doleful to Grant Richards, who had contemplated a south England outing, and I was sorry, but there were several obstructing elements in my mind, not the least of which, strange as it may seem, was homesickness. It is written of Hugo and Balzac that they always looked upon Paris as the capital of the world. I am afraid I shall have to confess to a similar feeling concerning New York. I know it all so well—its splendid water-spaces, its magnificent avenues, its varying sections, the rugged splendor of its cliff-like structures, the rippling force of its tides of energy and life. Viewing Europe from the vantage point of the seven countries I had seen, I was prepared to admit that in so many ways we are, temperamentally and socially speaking, the rawest of raw material. No one could be more crude, more illusioned than the average American. Contrasted with the savoir faire, the life-understanding, the philosophical acceptance of definite conditions in nature, the Europeans are immeasurably superior. They are harder, better-trained, more settled in the routine of things. The folderols of romance, the shibboleths of politics and religion, the false standards of special and commercial supremacy are not as readily accepted there as here. Ill-founded aspiration is not as rife there as here; every Jack does not consider himself, regardless of qualifications, appointed by God to tell his neighbor how he shall do and live; but granting all this, America, and particularly New York, is to me the most comforting atmosphere of any. London is too remote from any early experiences or emotions. Paris, despite its gripping charm, is, after all, too foreign. Rome, Florence, Venice would do for periods—even Berlin—but for me New York is home. I have lived here too long. The subway is like my library table—it is so much of an intimate. Broadway is the one idling showplace. Neither the Strand nor the Boulevard des Capucines can replace it. Fifth Avenue is all that it should be—the one really perfect show-street of the world. We have no cathedrals as yet, though St. John the Divine begins to suggest its ultimate self; no Garden of the Tuileries, though Central Park is not an unworthy substitute; no Bois de Boulogne, though I think Riverside Drive with its staggering wall of apartments and the surface of the river has a charm not wholly dissimilar. But like or not, deficient or superior, the Atlantic metropolis is the first city in the world to me—first in force, unrivaled in individuality, richer and freer in its spirit than London or Paris, though so often more gauche, more tawdry, more shamblingly inexperienced.

As I sat in Madame Gerny's bar arguing this matter of an English walking trip, the pull of the city over the sea was on me—and that in the spring! I could see upper Broadway, where I love to idle, certain interiors at Sea Gate, the upper Hudson, Staten Island, and the Oranges. *Heimweh* for places and individuals was on me, individuals as unique and forceful as it is possible for individuals to be, and they speak in terms of the American spirit. So I wanted to go *home*.

We talked over the matter of renewing relations with Marcelle and Madame de Villiers, Angèle and Madame Goldschmidt—figures lurking in the background of this brilliant city with whom we could connect yet even this night if we chose, per *chasseur*. It would be expensive. Very likely Marcelle would expect to be taken to Fontainebleau, and Madame de Villiers would be financially distressed. Two thousand francs, say, perhaps more, would be consumed in the ensuing excitement. Did I care to submit to the expense? I did not. I felt that I could not. So for once we decided to be modest and go out and see what we could alone. Our individual companionship was for the time being sufficient.

Grant Richards and I "cut a wide swath" these early spring days. Give him Paris, and life could hold no more. It was complete. Nothing would do but we must revisit all the scenes of our former triumphs—the Bar Fysher, The Rat Mort, Palmyre's Bar, the Abbaye de Thélème, Maxim's, the Café Américain, Paillard and the like. This very night we made the rounds, looking in, palavering to the denizens, ordering champagne, seeing all the things, as we had seen them before. Without a keen sex interest and female companionship, I can imagine nothing duller. It becomes a brilliant but hollow spectacle. There is just one end to this sort of thing, and all intelligent people know what it is. Without that as the ultimate conclusion, the thing lacks significance. That is what it is there for.

The next day was Sunday. Oh, these delicious Paris days in spring! It was warm and sunny as a day could be. The air was charged with a kind of gay expectation. Some English woman with whom Grant Richards had been doing the city had discovered a Neo-Impressionist portraitist of merit—one Hanns Bolz—and both had agreed to have their portraits done by him. This Sunday morning was the first day for a series of three sittings for Grant Richards. He wanted me to come along, first, to see what I thought of the artist's work; second, to see whether I did not want him to paint my portrait. So, to keep him company, I went. But I also planned to look up Miss Rice, the painter, and to see if I could locate a certain Miss Cattell, a writer, whom I had heard was in Paris. I was glad when I finally escaped Grant Richards and was allowed to go my way.

Paris in spring! The several days—from Saturday to Wednesday—were like a dream. With Miss Cattell, who I found as smiling and spirited as ever, I spent an afternoon driving in the Bois, stopping at several of the principal restaurants—the Pavillon de l'Élysée, the Café de Madrid, and the like—idling back to the Pré Catelan and the Café Royal. After that I sought Miss Rice and spent the remainder of the evening with her.

A gay world, full of the subtleties of social ambition, of desire, fashion, lovemaking and all the keenest, shrewdest aspects of life. It was interesting, at the Café de Madrid and the Pavillon de l'Élysée, to sit out under trees and the open sky and see an uninterrupted stream of automobiles and taxis pouring up, depositing smart pairs and groups of people, all looking keenly about, nodding or ignoring each other in a careful, selective social way. Fortunately my companion was not only good-looking but smartly garbed, a condition which brought her many favorable glances. She had produced a new spring hat—one of many, I hope, for she has means—which she wore with chic unconsciousness. Her dotted blue silk walking dress had a gay touch of spring about it, as well as her light gray suede shoes and her cream and lavender parasol. I expected any moment to see Grant Richards stepping out of some one of the endless taxis with his current ladylove—someone whom I had not encountered, of course—but I was disappointed. He did not come. In the evening Miss Rice and myself did the student brasseries and cafés and some of the chairs outside of the restaurants in the Boulevard des Capucines, just to see how Paris did in the spring. A charming woman, this. She talked so entertainingly of art and nationalities and talent and living one's life—I can hear her pleasing voice yet, making the best of things. And Paris was all-in-all to her. Never again would America see her, except on a visit. She adored the Parisians and all things Parisian. When I returned to my room I was fairly hypnotized by Paris—but the night was not done.

On my table was a note from Grant Richards.

"For God's sake, if you get in in time, come at once to the Abbaye de Thélème. I am waiting for you with a Mrs. Murray Bailey who wants to meet you."

So I had to change to evening clothes at one-thirty in the morning. And it was the same old thing when I reached there—waiters tumbling over each other with champagne, fruit, ices, confitures; the air full of colored glucose balls, colored balloons floating aloft, endless mirrors reflecting a giddy panorama, white arms, white necks, faultless faces, snowy shirt-bosoms—the old story. Spanish dancers in glittering scales, American negroes in evening clothes singing coon songs, excited life-lovers, male and female, dancing erotically in each other's arms. Can it be, I asked myself, that this thing goes on night after night and year after year? It was so obvious that it did.

The lady in question was a little remote—not my kind at all; one who would heartily approve of Grant Richards's light elegance, and that only. I expect she said, "This is a dull author," but I have no power of being entertaining without sufficient provocation. We took her home at three or four and continued our rounds—Maxim's and elsewhere—the endless Parisian rounds.

Two things that happened this night interested me greatly. One was the attempt on Grant Richards's part, once he was free of his lady companion, to demonstrate to me that Americans were essentially naive, gauche, unsophisticated and unsuspecting. "They come here to Paris," he observed in his lordly way, "and they haven't the least notion of the significance of the things they are seeing. They have made money in Escanaba or Wheeling or Peoria, and they are reconnoitering this world for the first time. They have happy homes, virtuous wives, children, even religion, some of them, and they certainly don't believe in vice, yet they will bring their wives or daughters here, or both, and literally support and encourage prostitution—unconsciously, of course. Take this man here near the door now" (we were at the Abbaye de Thélème). "In all likelihood he is from your state. Why don't you ask him whether he really understands what he is doing by coming here? You ought to help rectify the moral and social notions of your nation."

"I'll tell you what you do, Grant Richards," I replied. "You reproach him. It is just possible that that noble monocle gleaming on him will hypnotize or terrorize him. It will leave him dumb, helpless, without thought. Reproach him—go ahead."

There was just sufficient champagne in Grant Richards's interior to make him unduly gay and daring. Very much to my astonishment, he leaned over the table of this guest and observed, "My friend, do you realize what it is you do when you come here? Do you understand what sort of an institution it is you are supporting with your money?"

He beamed on him in a solemn, monitory and yet morally helpful way.

"What's that?" asked the American, looking up and, as I suspected, abashed by the distingué countenance bent toward him.

"I say, do you realize what it is that you do by coming to an institution of this kind—supporting it with your money? You wouldn't knowingly support vice in its worst forms, would you?"

"Certainly not," replied the American, curiously disturbed. (He was a mild-looking individual, semi-commercial, semi-professional, tall, slim, slightly gray, a little vacuous, not in the least dynamic and yet fairly intelligent.) "Why, what's the matter with this place? It doesn't seem to be so much worse than any other place. Is it?"

Grant Richards's air was one of sad distress at such density. "Well, look about you. Would you say that what you see here is conducive to morals? Consider the women that you see here. What do they come here for, do you think? That is the quarrel that I have with you Americans. You stand sponsor for morals and ethics in your own country, and then you come over here to Paris and support things of this kind. I am quite sure your ministers and local townspeople wouldn't countenance anything like this. You wouldn't at home."

The man's face was a study. For the time being he was uncertain whether to become angry and resent this intrusion violently or make profound apologies for his presence. His final replies were a faint mixture of both.

"Oh, I don't know that I'm so much worse than anyone else. Why should you select me? You're here. Why do you come here?"

"Ah, that is a very different matter. I'm an Englishman. Our nation is not so militantly engaged on the side of morality. My general experience with Americans has been that they violently espouse the cause of virtue at home. That is why I can never understand their attitude in Paris. They either do not know or they have two opinions—one for America and another for Europe. I thought you might enlighten me."

Grant Richards's manner was by now righteous and sincere.

"Well, I can't answer for other Americans. Personally, I wasn't aware that there was anything so wrong with this place. I am not anxious to support vice any more than anyone else."

"There you have it," exclaimed Grant Richards, taking my arm and pushing me toward the door. "What did I tell you? He comes here and gives his good money to this place—buys champagne and all that—and yet he doesn't know why he does it. You're an American novelist, now. How do you explain that?"

"How should I explain it?" I said. "How do you explain the 'chapel people,' as you call them, in England?" I asked. "How do you explain the East End and West End of London? It looks like a case of sufficient constructive energy to get enough money to come to Paris without much ability to philosophize or see through social conditions. To a certain extent he is probably hypocritical—most people are. Current American notions as opposed to his actual experiences confuse him. He really doesn't know what he ought to think."

"Watch the rest of them. They are all alike. We shall see others. I'll ask some of them. I like to do it, though I can never make them out."

We were entering Maxim's. I had stayed behind to pay the taxi. Grant Richards had gone ahead, and as I received my change, I saw some altercation going on at the door of which he was a part, though what it was I couldn't make out. As I approached, Grant Richards was walking away—

into the restaurant—and I was suddenly confronted by four solid, polished but hard-looking Englishmen in evening clothes, who surrounded me in a trice, their opera hats shoved rakishly back on their foreheads, while one of them—a very sizable person, I took good care to note—leered into my face. They were none the better for liquor and very contentious—bluggy, roistering souls ready for a drunken fight or a frolic.

"Here's the blank-blank-blank-blank—" (about sixteen picturesque though filthy expletives—trust the educated Englishman for that) "——'s partner. Perhaps you'd like to do something for your—" (more magnificent latrine-like characterization) "—friend. For tuppence I'd dec'rate your blank-blank-blank—" endless, variegated expletives of a vile but colorful character "—face. Perhaps you think you might do something to protect your blank-blank friend—you blank-blank-blank (oh, a beautiful, adjectival characterization of me)—!"

"What the devil are you talking about?" I asked of the one who was leering at me so pugnaciously and contemptuously. "What's the row? You certainly don't expect me to fight the four of you without knowing something of what it's all about? What's the trouble?"

"We'll show you what's the trouble, you ————" (more beautiful English characterization). "We'll break your dough-faced head!"

"Land him one in the gut and let him go," suggested another.

"You're a ————————," said another, thrusting an attractive but malicious profile under my nose. "You're afraid to fight, you American ————!"

("Oh joy, oh joy!" I said to myself. "This is really interesting. Here is a fine Parisian street-brawl—the first I've seen!")

"Am I?" I said. "Take your face away, you dope. Do you want me to fight the four of you?"

"You haven't the guts to fight one of us," replied the one nearest me. "Come out in the street, and I'll fight you alone. I'll clean the cobbles with you. You're a ————," etc., etc., etc.

It was really wonderful. Four harder, solider youths I had not met. They fairly creaked strength. Their mood was joyously ugly.

It is astonishing how swiftly and accurately the human mind works under such circumstances. I have never considered myself either brave or cowardly under circumstances, merely a cautious, reasoning animal. Being of a sedentary, contemplative turn, I have only what might be called a sufficient amount of physical strength, neither more nor less than I need. I have been often enough in the face of death or injury to know that neither of those intellectually terrify me—at least my thinking capacity has only been stimulated and strengthened, not deranged thereby. Just now I figured on how I would fare in the event of a struggle with this individual. He looked exceptionally capable, well set up. I started, as a last precaution, to demand the cause of the row, when Grant Richards returned. He saw me entangled.

"What is all this?" I asked.

"I tell you," he said, while now the four antagonists surrounded him, threatening much the same treatment they had threatened me, calling him unspeakable names and begging him to fight, "as I came up from the taxi, these men were coming out. They wanted to know if they could have my machine and I said, yes, if they paid for it. There was nothing more than that said."

"You're a liar!" observed one of them promptly. "You're a—" (this, that and the other). "You know very well what you said." (I never did get straight the enemy's version of what was said. Perhaps there was nothing more than a lofty, contemptuous look on the part of Grant Richards. He was moderately flushed and gay himself.) "You're afraid to fight. I dare you to fight. Come out in the street. Come on, the two of you. I'll beat up you and your—" (this, that and the other) "—friend."

"My dear fellow," retorted Grant Richards in his loftiest manner. "I told you before that I am no fighter. I'm not trained to fight. I don't know how, and I wouldn't if I did. No doubt you are. You like it. I object to fighting. I have told you what was said. My friend here had nothing to do with it. I do not care to argue any more about it." He looked as much as if to say, "Come on," and walked away.

A perfect storm of foul, insulting expletives ensued. I never heard quite so full a British description of a condemned enemy. They wanted to beat us up anyway. Words were all there were to it, however, for Grant Richards walked in, and I followed. Inside was the usual café scene. We gave up our coats and hats and joined the eating, drinking, dancing throng.

"I should like to know what your psychological estimate of that occurrence would be," he observed soberly. "You heard what I said. Would you expect me to fight? I am perfectly sincere in what I said. I have never fought. I object to physical struggles."

"I think you managed it very well," I replied. "Much better than I should have done. If I could see a way to win I might indulge, but your attitude is saner. They are drunk. The result would be bruises, police stations, soiled clothes—most anything. I respect a noncombative attitude if it is sincere."

He smiled. "I mean what I said. I cannot fight."

The last phase of this evening was in this same Maxim's. Three American women and their escorts entered, the latter so new to Paris and Europe that it was a shame to impose on their innocence and credulity; they were so obviously from the Middle or Far West. Unabashed by the occurrence at the door, Grant Richards had selected a table and was looking about to amuse himself. As they entered, he spied them. One of the men, a little one, perhaps thirty-one or -two years of age, was carrying a large crepe-paper bell which he had secured somewhere—a yellow bell such as they sometimes hang up at Christmas time in order to suggest, I suppose, the relation of religion to the occasion. Without warning, Grant Richards signaled him.

"My friend," he said as the man drew near, "you won't mind if I speak to you in a very friendly but frank way, so long as I assure you that it is meant in the best and kindliest spirit?"

"Not in the least," said the young man, very curious. "What is it?"

"I see you are carrying a yellow paper bell there. Do you know the significance of a yellow paper bell in Paris?"

"I don't, no. Is it something so out of the ordinary?" The man's face was a study in wonder, surprise, curiosity, consciousness of possibly grave social error.

"I thought as much," said Grant Richards. "Otherwise, I am sure, you would not be seen with that in your hand. Its significance is such that I cannot very well explain it here. My friend here would not approve of my efforts in that line. I beg of you, however, to put it down at once. You have ladies with you. I know you would not consciously wish to compromise their dignity. I am sorry to be compelled to speak as I do, but I am sure, as I have said, that you will take it in the spirit in which it is offered."

"Why, certainly, certainly," said the young man nervously. "Do you mind if I leave it?" He dropped it in the corner behind my chair. "I did not know there was anything so bad about it. Would you mind giving me an idea of what it is all about? I should like to know so that I could warn anyone else that I might see."

"I would be glad to tell you if it weren't a matter of such subtle depravity. If it were anywhere else—if your lady friends were not waiting—perhaps you would care to call at my hotel? However, other Parisians or your experienced friends will tell you some time. Do not, however, I beg of you, until you have looked into this matter for yourself, ever carry a paper bell again in Paris."

"Thank you, thank you," exclaimed the American effusively. "I certainly won't. I am very much obliged to you, truly. You are very kind. Thank you! Thank you!"

He nodded and walked away, seating himself at his own table and conferring with his nearest male companion in a whisper. They held a long conference.

"There you have it," observed Grant Richards blandly. "Now he will spend a great deal of time unraveling the mystery of the yellow paper bell.

Oh, these Americans! And the French get so much of their money! I must devise some plan for piloting Americans over Europe for a consideration. They really need me."

I looked at my whispering compatriots but gave them up. What can be said about that sort of thing anyhow?

CHAPTER XCVIII

The following day Grant Richards and I returned to London via Calais and Dover. We had been, between whiles, to the races at Longchamps, luncheons at Au Père Boivin, the Pré Catelan and elsewhere. We had finally decided to look up Marcelle, seeing that we had concluded, after due discussion, that I was treating her rather badly in not doing so. Marcelle, since our departure from the Riviera, had sent me an occasional postcard or note, always in French, which I could not read. I had sent her various views en route, penning some weird conglomeration of French words and English thoughts. Now we journeyed to her address in the Rue Marcadet after sending her an invitation the night before to dinner, to which she did not reply. We were curious to see whether she was in town and indifferent or absent. The concierge explained, according to Grant Richards, that she was absent. So the incident of Marcelle was apparently closed. We talked rather dolefully about Madame de Villiers and our duty but finally gave her up, and at the conclusion of his portrait sittings to the Neo-Impressionist, we took the morning train for London. In spite of the utter fascination of Paris I was not at all sorry to go, for I felt that to be happy there, one would want a more definite social life and a more fixed habitation than this hotel and the small circle of people that we had met could provide. I should like to live in Paris with the same social connections that I have in New York. I might even come to prefer it. No city has the indescribable poetic glamour which invests Paris, though it lacks the great force that surges in New York. I took a last, almost yearning look at the Avenue de l'Opéra and the Gare du Nord, and then we were off.

England, when we reached it, was so much more pleasing to me than when we had left it. It was charming then. Now it seemed exquisite. The leaves of the trees between Dover and London were just budding, making that diaphanous tracery which resembles green lace. The endless red chimneys and sagging green roofs and eaves of English cottages peeping out between this vesture of spring were as romantic and poetic as an old English ballad. No doubt at all that England—the south of it anyhow—is in a rut, sixty years behind the times, but what a rut! Must all be new and polished and shiny? As the tower and spires of Canterbury sped past to the right, gray and crumbling in a wine-like air, something rose in my throat. I thought of that old English song that begins:

"When shepherds pipe on oaten straws"—and then—and then—and then—But I can't talk sensibly of rural England. It is too utterly individual, simple, sweet, plainspoken, thoroughgoing. I doubt very much whether the world is through with England. I trust it will never be done with this exquisite rural phase of it, anyhow.

And then London once more and the Hotel Capitol and all the mystery of endless, involute streets and simple, hidden, unexplored regions. I went once to look at the grim, sad, two-story East End in spring. It was even more pathetic for being touched by the caressing hand of nature. I went to look at Hyde Park and Chelsea and Seven Kings. I thought to visit Sir Hugh Lane and Mrs. Stoop and Miss Villars and Miss Longfellow, but I did not have time as things turned out. Grant Richards was insistent that I should spend a day or two at Bigfrith. Owing to a great coal strike, the boat I had planned to take was put out of commission, and I was compelled to sail two days earlier on the boat of another line. Besides, Grant Richards was insisting that somehow I had not treated Marcelle right, that I should have looked her up in Paris earlier or written before arriving or asked him to write, and he kept hinting that it might not be inadvisable to let her come to England for a day or two or three. She could see London or a bit of rural England or both and then go back to Paris as I went to Dover. It would rather even matters up for the way she had been neglected and how nice she had been to me at Monte Carlo. We mutually agreed that Marcelle was a charming, naive, dynamic personality. I still think so.

How this eventually came about is one of those quaint bits of romance that I am not able, even now, to unravel. I know that on the way from Paris to Calais Grant Richards was grieved to think that we had not shown some attention to Madame de Villiers and Marcelle, particularly Marcelle, before I had gone my way. Why Marcelle? Coming up from Dover we went over her charming characteristics and the mystery of personality generally. I am sure now that he personally was very fond of Marcelle but my having somehow (by fortune or misfortune of her personal predilection, poor girl) been originally selected by her, he was content to keep hands off—until I should be out of the way at least. Once at Monte Carlo, when we were arguing one thing and another, I accused him of an undue feeling for Marcelle which was resulting in a secret relationship, and he flared up—almost the only time on the whole trip. "You seem not to be able to understand that there may be some hesitation on my part to follow up speedily in the steps of another. I should think you would credit my personal vanity with something. Promiscuity has its boundaries."

I smiled sardonically, but we got along well enough. In spite of long and sharp claws occasionally exhibited, we shared each other's days in happy fashion.

But on the way up from Dover he kept recurring to Marcelle in such a sympathetic way and with, I think, such a keen desire to lend a last touch of color to London for me—and for him, insofar as this particular visit of mine was concerned—that I felt as though perhaps I had better do something about it. Marcelle had not answered our note in Paris, but, we argued, it was not at all improbable that she was out of the city for a few days, off with her grand opera tenor, Muratore.

"I really think," volunteered Grant Richards, "she likes you, you know."

That soothed me a little. I had often thought of Grant Richards as someone who was painting an impression of Europe for himself, with me as a brush, and this came to me again when he so subtly said this. We were very much akin intellectually and emotionally, so that it was not such an impossible proposition. And then I was such a willing brush and palette, as it were—so very suitable, and Europe such fine paint.

When we reached London, an additional complication was added to the situation. There was, after a day or two, a letter to me from Marcelle in French (which Grant Richards had to translate for me) telling me how sorry she was to have missed me, wishing me bon voyage, hoping I would come to Paris again—and to see her. "I really think she's sorry not to have seen you," suggested Grant Richards. "There's a little feeling here. It would be nice to send for her. She would like it and so would you. You're going to Salisbury Wednesday. She could go along with you. That cathedral would please her. As a matter of fact, if you wanted to invite her, I think you could save your manners and your meat too, for I don't think she'd come. It's doubtful. If she did, ten pounds outside anything you might choose to give her would see you through."

I listened with hesitating but rather willing ears to these Jesuitical suggestions. I could never make the man out—his ultimate reasons. He was as subtle as life. Marcelle was charming enough, in all conscience. None of the women I had met abroad could compare with her for smartness of appearance or seeming sufficiency of soul. A little Trojan that, a fighter, with an eye for art and natural beauty and a taste for wit and dress and smart social life generally. Struggling, too, at the bottom, to get up.

"But I'm not so sure. How much have I left?"

"Oh, perhaps forty pounds outside of your ticket. Not quite so much, I think."

I saw from his manner that I should have to cable to America for funds anyhow, so I succumbed.

"Well, draw up a telegram, and here's hoping she doesn't come. I'd be delighted, but I can't afford it."

His manner brightened immediately. With his usual gusto for such things he drew up the telegram, and here it is. To this day, not knowing French, I do not know exactly what it says but perhaps the reader will.

"London, 4: 10—12

Partant pour Amérique samedi. Venez ce soir par train. Y apportez tailleur et robe pour théâtre. Dreiser. Hotel Capitol, Londres. Rencontrerai ce train à Charing Cross si vous venez."

The telegram sent (along with a cable or two), Grant Richards and I took the train for Cookham, for Marcelle would not start that night, we felt sure. Anyhow we could phone the hotel. And now I was to see Bigfrith once more, in the spring.

After Italy and Holland, perhaps side by side with Holland or before it, England, the southern portion of it, is the most charmingly individual country in Europe. For the sake of the walk, the evening was so fine, we decided to leave the train at Maidenhead and walk the remaining distance to Bigfrith, some five or six miles. It was ideal. The sun was going down and spreading through diaphanous clouds in the west, which it tinted and gilded. The English hedges and copses were delicately tinted with new life. English robins were on the grass, sheep, cows; over one English hamlet and another, smoke was curling, and English crows or rooks were gaily cawing, cheered at the thought of an English spring.

As gay as children Grant Richards and I trudged the yellow English road. Now and then we passed through a stile and cut diagonally across a field where a path was laid for the foot of man. Every so often we met an English laborer, his trousers gripped just below the knee by the customary English strap. Green and red; green and red (such were the houses and fields), with new spring violets, apple trees in blossom and peeping steeples over sloping hillsides thrown in for good measure. I felt—what shall I say I felt?—not the grandeur of Italy, but something so delicate and tender, so reminiscent and aromatic, faintly so, of other field fragrances, that my heart was touched as by music. Near Bigfrith we encountered Spillett going home from his work, a bundle of twigs under his arm, a pruning hook at his belt, his trousers strapped as the fashion of his class demanded.

"Well, Spillett!" I exclaimed.

"W'y, 'ow do you do, sir, Mr. Dreiser? H'I 'm glad to see you again, h'I am." Instead of extending a hand he touched his cap. "H'I 'opes as 'ow you've 'ad a pleasant trip?"

"Very, Spillett, very," I replied grandiosely. Who cannot be grandiose in the presence of the fixed conditions of old England? Money makes you a gentleman to your hirelings. I asked after his work and his health, and then Grant Richards gave him some instructions for tomorrow. We went on in a fading light—an English twilight—talking of how Sir Hugh would snort if he knew that Marcelle was coming to England, if she were coming, and how he would reproach us—Grant Richards most—and how wonderful Italy was and Paris and Holland and this delicious England. "I'm glad you like it," he said quite tenderly. "It always appeals to me as having artistic individuality."

And when we reached the country house it was already aglow in anticipation of this visit. Hearth fires were laid. The dining room, reception hall and living room were alight. I was told that Mrs. Grant Allen, the widow of the deceased novelist, was present and some daughter of an English philosopher. Dora appeared at the door, quite as charming and rosy in her white apron and cap as the day I left, but gave no more sign that I was strange or had been absent than if I had not been. She took my coat and bag, and I went over to look after my room.

The charm of Grant Richards's home! "Now we must make up our minds what particular wines we want for dinner. I have an excellent champagne, of course, but how about a light Burgundy or a Rhine wine? I have an excellent Assmannshäuser."

"I vote for the light Burgundy," I said.

"Done. I will speak to Dora now."

And while he went to instruct Dora, I went to look after all my belongings in order to bring them finally together for my permanent departure. After a delicious dinner and endless, interesting conversation, I called on the phone to see whether a French telegram had arrived. It had. Grant Richards, with the certitude of one who knew the hotel underlings, took charge. He had it read to him. She was making the nine-fifteen train this night and would arrive at Charing Cross at five-thirty in the morning. "That means you will have to catch the eleven o'clock train back," he said to me. "You can change to a larger room. Now I'll tell you just how we'll lay this matter out," and he began to plan the morrow to the last hour as if it were his affair. I was to rise at five and meet the five-thirty. Marcelle was to be allowed to rest. At ten I was to be sure and rouse her so as to be able to make the eleven-fifteen train for Salisbury. He would write instructions in French on a piece of paper which I was to give Marcelle and which would make her understand the necessity of promptness. We were to lunch at the Red Lion in Salisbury. At three-thirty we were to make a train which would get us back at six-thirty. Marcelle was to dress quickly, and we were to go together to see *The Easiest Way*, merely to give Marcelle an idea of an English playhouse. Afterwards we were to come to the Savoy. He would arrange a charming supper. The next day's pleasures we would talk over with Marcelle. He was as pleased apparently as though Marcelle were coming to him.

I smile when I think of Grant Richards even to this day. He was so intensely interested in living. If you would only let him manage, how gladly he would do it and how well. This was quite as much his affair as it was mine, though Marcelle was to confine her physical attentions to me. But he was to be grand master of ceremonies, to be "in on" almost everything; consequently, he was happy.

We called a fly, and I caught the eleven o'clock train to London. Under the spring stars at Cookham I walked up and down the platform wondering how Marcelle would enjoy London—this was her first trip over. I wondered here whether Madame Elaine Goldschmidt, Grant Richards's Monte Carlo inamorata, had been to England and whether his manipulations in favor of the coming of Marcelle was in fulfillment of any promise he had made her on some recent trip to Paris. It looked that way, but I couldn't prove it. Anyhow Marcelle was an interesting companion at all times, a worthy object of contemplation, and so I let it go at that. Her contempt for the fickleness of man I knew must be great, but in spite of her youth and beauty, her toleration, sympathy, good nature and practicality were large.

When I had arranged for a larger room, had a fire laid and some bottled water sent up, I went to sleep and was only roused by the porter beating on my door. It was five o'clock. I dressed quickly and walked out in the dull morning light. London was not astir—the first time I had seen it solemnly quiescent. A solitary pedestrian turned a corner here and there, but of cabs, buses, vehicles of any kind, there were apparently none. And yet in a very little while the morning tide of traffic would be pouring through these streets. I thought of the vastness of London, all the millions slumbering in uniform beds, from the king himself to the wretched hovels of Cunningtown and Southwark. At the Charing Cross station, which was nearby, I saw the empty platforms, manned by a few drowsy porters just coming on duty. The first morning local had not yet arrived, and they were sweeping up the platforms. Out at the end of the train shed were visible the dome of St. Paul's like a large bubble and some winding of the Thames. It was soon five-thirty, but the train was fifteen minutes late.

When it finally did arrive, Marcelle emerged from almost the farthest carriage, as chic and brisk as the day I left her. Because it was chill she had on a long brownish-gray overcoat of thick, soft wool and a thick velvet and wool traveling cap, the shape of a chocolate drop, pulled well over her ears. Her black, curly hair showed beneath it, and her dark eyes glowed with their usual intensity. Those who are opposed to the systematic and calculated use of the power that enthralls and unsteadies men would not like Marcelle. Her principal thought was the beauty of her body and the charm of her temperament as assets in this worldly existence. The uses which are ordinarily calculated as base were merely commonplace and essential to Marcelle. Certain things she had to do to get along and see the world, and she did them with quite an air—with no more irritation or disturbing thought than any other type of woman does anything else. She felt herself to be young, charming and entitled to her fling, and she was in no whit dull—on the contrary.

There was with her when she came out a young Englishman with whom she had come over. He was helping her with her bags until I appeared, a veritable Prince Charming. Marcelle was appropriately superior but interested—I could see that. I called a porter and had a taxi brought. To have heard her chattering, you would have thought we spoke the same language, and at that I gathered about all that she was trying to indicate. The few French expressions she employed, such as "*perfide Tayadore,*" "*sans doute,*" "*mon ami*" (applied to her friend), "*voilà,*" "*tout à fait,*" "*exactement,*" "*à la bonne heure,*" "*pour moi,*" "*pour vous,*" "*je suis,*" "*la nuit,*" "*du jour*" and the like, were perfectly intelligible to me, and on the other hand Marcelle had advanced so far as to be able to gurgle very Frenchily "very well-a," "very nize," "very good-a," "I don't know," "what o'clock is it?" "Where are you going?"—things which I had taught her and a French-English pamphlet had amplified. Though she was tired she looked around curiously at morning London, ready to criticize. The streets were so empty, though, that she felt constrained to suspend judgment.

You would have smiled at the nonchalance of Marcelle. "Oh, my, I had a bad night. The train was crowded." (I got that by signs.) The passage was rough. (Her hand on her stomach indicated that.) The Englishman was very polite, though. "*Très fatiguée,*" she sighed, putting her fingers to her forehead and closing her eyes. I assured her that she could soon sleep. She bundled up close to me and when the hotel appeared so quickly exclaimed, "Oh, very good!" "*Très bon!*"

CHAPTER XCIX

You would have thought to have seen Marcelle settle down in this hotel chamber that we had been married for years. She began immediately to unpack, gesticulating the while. She was not particularly pleased with a nightdress she extracted and complained of it, but a new corset with some lace edging was worth a "*très chic, oui?*" Her skin was particularly fair but

Latin in complexion, and her arms and legs and torso as trim as they were provocative. She had the typical Frenchwoman's body—plump, suggestive hips, short, shapely legs, pretty feet, a full bust, plump arms and nice hands. More than anything else vivacity of soul, health, courage, spirit and a certain electric awareness made Marcelle a temperament to be reckoned with. She had daring and self-sufficiency and, life offering her no solution, she made the best of it she could. She had her bags unpacked in a trice and her clothes put away. In her, to her, unsatisfactory nightgown, she climbed quickly into bed and sighed wearily. "Oh, *très fatiguée! très bon!*" and in not more than five minutes she was sound asleep.

At ten I shook her lightly and made her understand that she must get up. She had a way of bouncing up when awakened, wide-eyed and apparently refreshed, shaking the sleep from her hair and smiling like a pleased child. After teasing her a while I produced Grant Richards's letter of instructions, which made it perfectly clear what we were going to do this day. She was briskly ready for any adventure. "*Oui, oui!*" she exclaimed, "*très charmant!*" and she had me ring for the maid. Her bath was ready, some breakfast served, and while she was dressing, she executed a new dance for me which she had seen in Paris, "La Grizzly Bear." I had to laugh. While she was making her toilet, Grant Richards came in, and then I got (by translation and endless interruption) the full history of her passage. She had been in Paris with Madame Goldschmidt when we wrote and invited her to dinner, but they had just returned from some weekend outing and were tired. Afterwards she was sorry and when my telegram came had decided to come to London. She described how wildly she had flung things together and rushed for the train. She was anything but displeased to come, that was plain, and so at five minutes of eleven we took a taxi for our train to Salisbury.

Every moment of this journey Marcelle evinced the keenest interest in England and London. The little that I knew I had to indicate promptly. She was interested in the London policeman with the strap lying on his chin and in the London mail carrier. At the latter she frowned, as not being smart, but the London police were complimented as "*très bon*" and "*très chic.*" The smoky-golden atmosphere was not bad—she indicated it all with her hand—but Paris was better. The swirl of life gratified her. "*Très intéressant!*" she kept saying, "*très intéressant!*"

On the way out to Salisbury we ran through pleasing English downs, those low, rolling slopes that reveal a distant steeple or nearby chimney to perfection. Marcelle was not very much enraptured. The quaint, type-repeating suburbs of London suited her better. "Sunlight Soap," when the signs attracted her attention, I had to explain was *savon*. A large pottery gave me real trouble. Finally I drew a dish and pitcher on the back of an envelope.

Then she understood. "Oh, *oui, oui!*" I made the great mistake of not securing a seat in the dining car, for these cost nothing and are not available after the train starts. The smaller cars as contrasted with those of the continent interested Marcelle. They were satisfactory but open to question. The English women, too, came in for laughing criticism, for from her point of chicness they were frumps. "*O-a!*" she frowned. "*Terrible! Très* ———, *très* ———. *O-a!*" There was no denying it; they did look dull compared to her, but if they had known Marcelle's point of view, they would have looked worse—threatening.

I was so afraid all the while that Marcelle in her impetuosity or self-willedness would say or do something which would make it perfectly clear that I did not speak French and that this was some wretched liaison which should be publicly suppressed. As it was, seated in this first-class section of an English carriage, surrounded, as we happened to be in this case, by a typical family of the conservative middle class, Marcelle was contrast enough. There was an English girl next to her, about her own age, who was not exactly prim but homely and severe. There was a young man, a brother, two years younger, say, who eyed Marcelle curiously but not with opposition. Mother and father were properly distant, religious perhaps, obviously conservative. Papa had well-trimmed side-whiskers and a long, not too shapely, nose. They looked at Marcelle occasionally while pretending not to, but she was so interested in the English landscape that she did not bother with them. Her trim little body had all the unctuous outlines of Miss Longfellow's, and clad in her brown wool coat and smart cap she stood out quite too youthful, ruddy and attractive. It was almost bad business traveling about the country with her. Still she was so undeniably pretty and reasonably well-behaved that it did not matter.

When we drew near Salisbury, the cathedral came in sight, its single spire rising thin and sharp above all about. Marcelle was so hungry that nothing would do but that we must go at once to the Red Lion, the principal inn, where before we were through, she mortified me greatly. It turned out that she was expecting to find some such inn as one may find near Paris or Monte Carlo where à la carte is the rule and one may have a wide choice of viands. As it eventuated, this was a prix-fixe lunch with no such things as hors d'oeuvres to grace it or any selection of soups, vegetables, wines or cheeses. Marcelle, after surveying the bill-o'-fare and seeing by the arrangement of the various dishes that it was a set lunch, called for the general bill-o'-fare. There was none. What else there was was printed on the back of this one. On having this made plain to her by signs, she frowned.

"Well," (I am merely guessing at her words, which came petulantly), "let's have hors d'oeuvres anyhow."

There were none.

"What, no hors d'oeuvres!" Her eyebrows went up, her pretty forehead knit into lines running at right angles. "No hors d'oeuvres! *Mon Dieu!* What sort of a country is this? In Normandy, Brittany, Picardy—anywhere in France" (I could catch these references), "a country inn is an inn. No hors d'oeuvres! Good heavens! Such are the English, then! And the idea of leaving London to come out to such a place as this, and on my first day in England, too!"

I put my finger on my lips to indicate that she should be more circumspect and suppress her feelings. With a motion of my head I indicated the very conservative and all-too-interested company present. She only shook her shoulders petulantly and defiantly.

"Marcelle!" I said sorrowfully.

"*Non! Non! Non!*" she jerked irritably.

"Marcelle! How you are carrying on now!"

"*Non! Non! Non!*"

"Marcelle!" this pleadingly. "Do behave. *La nuit*—Hotel Savoy. London!"

This soothed her a little. Very well, she would make the best of it, but, oh, these English inns! Shameful! Such wretched inns! In France—anywhere in France—one could get good cooking. How about wine?

I ordered the only wine they had. It was villainous. It tasted like some sort of colored pickling vinegar. Marcelle almost choked. "Oh, the wretched English! The horrible English! Wine! Take it away! It must be poison!"

I asked the waiter to listen to me.

"Now I'll tell you what to do," I said. "The lady is French. She understands no English. She thinks English inns are wretched. You have bottled water, have you?"

"Yes."

"Bring that. And do you make coffee in urns and serve it so?"

"No."

"Could you?"

"I might. I don't know, sir."

"Do you want three shillings for yourself?"

"Yes, sir."

"Well, get the cook to serve me some strong black coffee in a separate percolator. You have cold meats—chicken, ham, tongue and so on?"

"Yes."

"Bring a little of each, some pickles, some lettuce. Have you beets?"

"Yes, sir."

"Some beets."

"Yes, sir."

"Have you any sweets?"

"Suet pudding."

"No, no, no! She'd rise and strike me. Do they sell candies hereabouts?"

"Yes, sir."

"Go out and get me some mint chips, chocolates, ginger and candied oranges or fruit of any kind, and put them in a nice small dish. Now, for heaven's sake, be quick. Bring any other fresh vegetables you have."

He hurried off.

Marcelle looked at me inquisitively. I laid my hand on her arm, put my finger to my lips. "*Très bon! Très charmant!* Everything will be all right now. Wait."

She settled herself peacefully, got out a little mirror from her coat pocket, examined her nose and then began to patter civilly again. It was very bad, these English inns. The women were frumps. The cathedral—was it like Amiens, Rouen?

"*Très bon*," I said. "*Magnifique*."

"Oh, well, then, that would help. I will wait."

So the food came, and we ate. Seeing that she had secured a sample of everything in the place, she was fairly well satisfied. She nibbled at this and that, drank her strong coffee and finally came away smiling and companionable. And to my comfort the cathedral, which was very near at hand, pleased her very much.

It is really an exquisite cathedral, not as large as many another but having such a purely English look. Nowhere except at Pisa (and then not in the same way) will you see a cathedral rising simply and gracefully out of the grass, set in a great space of grass. It rises so perfectly, so ornately. The spire is four hundred and four feet high, with transepts two hundred and thirty feet across and a cloister adjoining which is as perfect in its quatrefoiled and colonnaded elegance as anything in Italy. The interior, because of the absence of stained-glass windows, has a cold, gray aspect, but so fine withal that it suggests carving in jade—pork-fat jade. There was an afternoon service under way, and the arches and aisles were echoing to melody. To me, after Canterbury, it was the one fine, artistic thing I had seen in England, an exquisite national possession. It is so delightful to know that the world really understands now the value of these architectural gems, and by constant restoration seeks to evade the gnawing destructiveness of time. We strolled about the grounds and the interior, viewing the tombs to English knights and earls, and finally came away. Marcelle was really reluctant to leave until suddenly she discovered she had lost a valuable ring—forgotten it, she believed, in the lavatory of the Red Lion.

Oh, such agony! She fairly shriveled with distress. "*Mon Dieu! Mon*

Dieu!" she exclaimed, pointing to her right ring finger. "Oh, *non! Sacrebleu!* We must go right back!"

Sorry as I was for her, I was not nearly so distressed as she was. For one thing, I knew the English better than she did. If the ring had been left in the lavatory, as she fancied, or on the luncheon table, a thousand to one she would find it again. The English are not like the French or Italians—perhaps even better than the Germans when it comes to this matter of mine and thine. The race has evolved a strange fine integrity which rules from coast to coast. Any traveler will tell you that the English are honest. They do not steal. If you lose an umbrella, a cane, a cap, a bag, you will get it again. In any ordinary English inn I would feel safe to forget anything. At the larger hotels, of course, where national gives place to international standards of morality, I would not be so sure, but anywhere else, yes.

On the way back I did my best to make this perfectly plain to Marcelle. "Be easy," I signaled. "Calm yourself. The English are honest. French—no. Italian, no. English, yes." She quieted.

At the inn, sure enough, she found it where she had left it. The maid had not as yet taken it up. Much rejoicing, of course. She bought many postcards of the cathedral, in honor of the occasion, I suppose, and mailed them broadcast. I think the stamps alone cost me two shillings. A more life-greedy little chinch bug I never knew.

The ride back to London, with dinner on the dining car, supper at the Savoy after the theater and a long after-midnight conference in Grant Richards's and later in my room, made up a full day for the young lady. She was so keen to see always more, more. Tomorrow, we decided, she should have a hat—at my expense—tomorrow I would take her to see St. Paul's, Westminster, the Houses of Parliament, the new Catholic Cathedral, Hyde Park, the Embankment and a few things like that. She was a very enchanting person this evening in black silk and minute red velvet ornaments. A red rose gave her clear black hair strong artistic relief. Grant Richards was most interested. I could not help feeling that he was arranging future Paris visits with her after I should be gone. Marcelle was by now, however, a hard, practical soul. It was quite plain she knew how to look after her own interests. And while she admired Grant Richards in a way, she understood him exactly. After he was gone, she would frequently shake her head and smile in a wise way. "*Monsieur Grant Richards! Oh, oui! Très charmant! Très bon! C'est une blague! Madame une, Madame deux, Madame trois, Madame quatre, Madame cinq—*" so she counted naively on her fingers, indicating how many ladies she fancied he had on his list. Grant Richards's comment to me was, "She's a hard little minx, that one." And occasionally, in a moment of unsatisfactory bargaining with her, he would exclaim, "Locust!"—the name I had given the cocotte tribe at Monte Carlo.

CHAPTER C

It was really stacks of fun piloting Marcelle about London. Her joy in the situation, the wonders of the city, rivaled my own. She was so forthright, direct, intellectually honest, I should say. Aimless maunderings of conscience did not trouble Marcelle any. Obviously she had not been raised in an atmosphere where moral theories ran counter to her experiences and the teachings of life. Fortunate Marcelle! To be spared the wearisome pain and labor of having to cut through a world of religious and ethical notions based on dogma—that choking underbrush above which few, so few, really rise. Early the next morning after breakfast we set out, first to buy a hat, then to ride in Hyde Park, then to taxi to this wonder and that. Marcelle was very gay. We were lunching again at the Savoy, dining at the Cheshire Cheese, which Grant Richards believed would amuse her. Afterward we were going to the Empire, to Romano's, to some hotel dance conducted by a literary friend of Grant Richards's and thence to the hotel. Marcelle was to be kept busy—I advocated that myself—so as to avoid the least suggestion of leisure or dullness.

To one who had never possessed a truly imperious mistress, Marcelle was a revelation. She was more than a match for Grant Richards and myself put together. Whatever she wanted she demanded, and as a rule without a "by your leave," "thank you" or anything else. A six-pound hat which I bought her and a pair of gloves got not so much as thanks. The careful prevision of supplying her with a French Baedeker in London did receive a compliment as being sensible. She eschewed open taxis in several instances in favor of the old-style cab, because she said you could see better.

Hyde Park was nice but not as good as the Bois de Boulogne. The Roman Catholic Cathedral was impressive—its strange dusk, which I am afraid will be entirely dispelled when it is lined with marble. Cartloads of marble coating or wall-lining are almost daily being brought to its doors. It was interesting to see this little mistress walking with her superior, almost aggressive air around the great church, looking at the walls, chapels and shrines and exclaiming, "*Magnifique!*" or "*Charmant!*" when the average worshiper therein would have considered her so remote spiritually though perhaps not artistically from the thing she was applauding. Marcelle was really not remote artistically from anything. She had great possibilities, if there had been any way of belting her intellectual flywheel to any intellectual or artistic purpose. But this edifice—devoted, one might say, to penalizing the flesh for its tendencies—being complimented by Marcelle, victim of the toils of the flesh and calculating in all her plans to make its vagaries yield her a living if not a profit, was amusing to me. I could not help thinking if Marcelle had had some artistic gift such as a voice or a talent for acting or even writing—how superior she would have been to a person like Madame Culp. For innate intellectual and artistic comprehension, the latter was not in the same class.

In Westminster, whither we went next, she was doubly amusing. The girl was positively witty and able to transfer her witty suggestions to me by signs, almost voiceless suggestions. Thus all morning she had been trying to teach me a silly French song which ran:

> "*Ah, qu'ils sont bons*
> *Quand ils sont cuits*
> *Les macaronis, les macaronis,*" etc.

Here when we came to the choir, which is peculiarly interruptive in Westminster—disagreeably so, I think—I could only think of the French word "*chantant*" as having any relation to the word "choir."

"*Oui, oui!*" laughed Marcelle quite heartily. "*Ah, qui'ils sont bons.*" How can you have anything but praise for such mental spryness? In one of the chapels we came to a statue of some king—I forget which one—the base of which was surrounded by a series of kneeling angels, devoutly looking upward. "Oh," exclaimed Marcelle on sight, "*Grant Richards et ses maîtresses!*" That got a laugh out of Grant Richards himself later. An English guide, his short chin whiskers protruding defiantly before him, his black gown flaring out in a pompous way, was leading a flock of American sightseers, principally old maids, from one tomb to another. Marcelle gave him a single glance. "*Oh, Chantecler, oui?*" she smiled. The resemblance was perfect. He looked exactly like a smart black Spanish rooster leading a flock of hens.

In the corridors of the Houses of Parliament on Constitution Hill, before the glittering horse guards, Marcelle was bristling with comment. The sight of the latter pleased her immensely. The sight of a small company of Scotch soldiers in their plaids and tarlatans, their rough, bony knees showing, elicited from her a burst of applause. Then we had to go to the hotel for her heavy coat and from there to the restaurant of the Savoy, where she and Grant Richards unraveled, with my assistance, all the mysteries of things she had seen.

For a man who protested that he was merely genially interested in Marcelle as an adjunct to my European impressions, Grant Richards was supremely attentive. He warmed to the labor of entertaining her with far more force and adroitness than I could muster, even had I spoken French. He was cheeringly gay and even brilliant. There was a little hitch (temporary, of course) in this situation, first in my presence and present possession of Marcelle and second in his previous attentions to her friend and companion, Madame Goldschmidt, but of course these might be subsequently removed. I was leaving the next day, and Madame Goldschmidt might easily be cast into the limbo of past experiences. Marcelle's life in Paris was gone into. She admitted living in an apartment maintained for her by someone, who however had recently deserted her. Her unbending superiority was the principal cause. After lunch we went to the Tower, St. Paul's, the Inns of Court, Lincoln's Inn Fields, the Bank of England and then home to dress. Marcelle wanted to see the gloomy East End. I did not blame her, but there was not time left, according to Grant Richards's arrangement. We hurried back, only to find, after we had dressed, that he was patiently awaiting the arrival of some linen which did not come until late. Marcelle was in a rage. To think she could not see the East End, but he could wait an hour for a shirt! Bah! She threw things around her dresser and in the writing room in a tempestuous mood, but at last we were off, and so our last evening in London (Marcelle's and mine) began.

It was such an interesting evening psychologically that I propose to dwell on it at length. Grant Richards was in the gayest of moods, possibly at the thought of getting rid of me the next day once and for all, possibly at the chic presence of Marcelle, who was glowing like an artistic lamp or an orchid, possibly at the full and interesting program for the evening. We were off to the Cheshire Cheese, the naive rudeness of which seized on the French girl's fancy. She was fascinated with it, though the English food did not appeal to her. But the steaming punch bowl and the ale seemed to strike her as worthy. My own was not so pleasant, for just as I had suspected, the financial program Grant Richards had laid out originally had not worked out. Instead of having a number of hundreds of dollars wherewith to begin my work in America, I was not to have any left over, and thus far no answer had come from my American publishers to my cable for additional funds. Fortunately I had my ticket, and after blessing Marcelle with a certain sum—at least a hundred dollars above all expenses to and fro and her entertainment—I should have about twenty or twenty-five dollars left: just enough to take care of all the tips on the steamer. If I did not hear in the morning!

It angered me to hear the pleasant way in which, when I complained, Grant Richards would descant upon my probable future.

"But you forget that I borrowed all of the money on which I came over here in advance."

"Even so. Your books are sure to sell. You have no faith in your own future."

"Own future be damned!" I thought and said, I think, "Prevision is more important. I should return with at least one thousand dollars." Alas, there was no thousand wherewith to return. At the last moment he cheerfully informed me that it had all been dissipated.

But this was not all. I had the pleasing sensation that this occasion was being used to further some future arrangement between Grant Richards and Marcelle. Whatever it was, it would be a purely commercial arrangement, at the start anyhow—that was obvious. Marcelle was in financial straits. She would make a living arrangement with almost any respectable, considerate, socially efficient person. Grant Richards was far from offensive to her, but he would have to make a suitable provision if he proposed to engage her time. I never could quite decipher her attitude toward me, but whatever it was, it was not so practical. On this occasion she would take money from me. She talked about learning English, the absolute necessity of it, and of visiting New York. If I came to Paris to write a book and would take an apartment, she would live with me and keep house. Once when I was gloweringly solemn in the midst of Grant Richards's provocative chatter, she put her slippered toe on mine and pressed it gently—an act of courteous reassurance, to say the least.

But that was not enough. I did not like the way things were working out, and this was my last night in England, and I was fast succumbing to a short period of the blue devils. I get them—the sorried emissaries of gloom. I must say Grant Richards was the soul of courtesy for a long time.

"Do bear up, I beg of you," he urged. "It isn't as bad as you think. Come now, cheer up. You're spoiling the evening. Think of Marcelle!"

"To hell with Marcelle!" or words to that effect, I rejoined.

"Really, you are the worst," he complained. "Do drink a little punch. Have some Burgundy. That will help."

"I'd rather go home," I said.

"Perhaps you'd better, if you are going to go on like this."

"I will," I said, but some interruption of Marcelle to discover what it was all about stayed me.

We went to the Empire. The ballet and the promenade were interesting. They were singing "Alexander's Ragtime Band" and "Everybody's Doin' It," to which Marcelle walked (in the promenade) rhythmically. At Romano's we witnessed the only truly Parisian spectacle which London offers—cocottes, kept women, actresses, a stunning array of feminine beauty in dress and figure; but where in Paris the restaurants of this type open at twelve-thirty and continue until morning, this closes at that hour. From Romano's we went to some very dull hotel dance where Marcelle and I danced once but from which we all escaped within the hour, with apologies. The hotel was all that was left, with wine or liqueurs, or both, and more idle talk. Since I could not speak French, Grant Richards invariably had the best of it. He could monopolize the conversation because there was no way in which to interrupt him.

And yet in spite of it all there was a pleasant understanding between Marcelle and myself. We did not talk, and she knew I was despondent, but she was not without consideration for me, as she afterwards made clear. I did not expect affection of course, merely sympathetic courtesy. Grant Richards talked so long and so gaily and so utterly regardless of my mood in my particular hotel chambers that finally I became angry. He saw what my mood was, I told myself. Why go on flirting with Marcelle—talking over a possible Parisian arrangement, no doubt? Why not postpone it until his next visit to Paris? Courtesy ought to suggest as much. I was out of sorts and consequently out of it.

Besides, by now I had become angry at Marcelle. She was a little too brash in this procedure. Suddenly, in the midst of a very cheerful flow of conversation, I declared myself. "Call it off!" I called angrily from the couch where I was lying. "Cut it out! I've had enough! Postpone your flirtation until another day. Go over to Paris and see her. I'm sick of this. End this thing, for tonight now."

Grant Richards got up. I can see his peculiarly interesting eye now. His brash, artistic acquisition was turning on him, and so rudely—quite like an American.

"I like that," he said. "It's discourteous, to say the least. But let it go. You're certainly rough in your methods!"

"Rough be damned!" I replied. "Enough is enough. I'm through for tonight. Call it off!"

He went out with a light "Goodnight."

Marcelle arose and began to undress. She silently uncoiled her hair, took off her evening dress, unlaced her shoes and finally got into her nightdress. With true French subtlety she crossed and recrossed within the line of my vision, quite nude, her physical outlines being counted on no doubt as worth something. Before getting into bed she stood before me and touched her breast—"*Moi?*" she inquired (because of me?).

"No," I grumbled, but she knew better.

Later in bed she attempted to take my hand, but I removed it definitely from her reach. I wanted none of her just then, and I was perfectly willing to make it quite plain. She took sharp umbrage and removed herself far to the other side, remaining there, quite distant. The next morning I awoke in a slightly better mood, at least ashamed of roughness. I decided to apologize to Grant Richards and, if Marcelle was satisfied, to her. All the points involved were not, I reasoned, sufficient to base an angry quarrel on. Why should I be angry concerning Marcelle? I really did not want her permanently. I really did not expect to see her anymore, ever. As for Grant Richards, he was too interesting and able a man to quarrel with on money or any other grounds. The thing to do was to take matters in my own hands in the future and avoid what I could not cheerfully accept. With that thought in mind I shook Marcelle out of her sleep. Like the white-armed Hera of the Greeks, of whom she always reminded me, she rubbed her eyes and then sat up, smiling and shaking the sleep out of her eyes.

Whatever the French is for "Are you feeling better?"—that she said.

"Very bad last night," I commented, piecing *la nuit* and *mauvais* together in some weird way. "*Très villain. Je pleure.*" She laughed at the "*Je pleure.*" "Do you forgive me?" I added by signs.

"*Oui! Oui!*" she replied. "Was it over me?"

I nodded.

That pleased her fancy, flattered her vanity—Grant Richards and I coming to blows over her. She took my hand. The rest belongs to what might be called the annals of—what?

CHAPTER CI

Later that day we had to leave for our train from Charing Cross and all our belongings were properly weighed and stamped. I saw the last of that pleasant English railway courtesy which is so superior to ours. I was thinking then how different it would be when I reached New York, how coarse and inattentive would be the service offered, and yet I was glad to be going home. Our boasted democracy has resulted in little more than the privilege of every living, breathing American being rude and brutal to every other, but it is not beyond possibility that sometime as a nation we will sober down into something approximating human civility. Our early revolt against sham civility has, insofar as I can see, resulted in nothing save the abolition of all civility, which is sickening. Life, I am sure, will shame us out of it eventually. We will find we do not get anywhere by it. And I blame it all on the lawlessness of the men at the top. They have set the example which has been most freely copied.

The run from London to Folkstone and Dover was pleasant, quite romantic with Marcelle in my keeping. She was not sorry to be going back to France, I think, though she would have been glad to stay longer in England. I could see her retailing to Madame Goldschmidt, with perhaps a touch of superiority, her experiences in London. She was still as keen as ever for impressions, almost more so than myself. Since it was night and dark when she had come up this way before and she was tired, now it was all new. I pointed out the old castle at Rochester and the spires of the cathedral at Canterbury. The English orchards, the slopes of sheep, the nestled chimneys and the occasional quaint, sagging roofs of moss-tinted tiles touched her fancy. I remember at one little vista she shook her head quite moodily, as much as if to say "this is truly beautiful."

On this last run, for some reason, she was not so willful. She came and sat with me on my side of the car and wanted me to teach her an American ragtime song, one called "Hello, My Baby"—only she called it "'Ello, My Babee." It so happened that I remembered it all. All the way to Folkstone, Marcelle practiced that. I had a most difficult time getting her to cease saying "akiss" for "a kiss" and "'oney" for "honey." She would pronounce "rag" "raag" and "heart" "'art." She was like a little parrot mouthing some favored sound. She insisted writing out the words of her song, "*Ah, qu'ils sont bons*" on a sheet of paper and getting me to write out "Hello, My Baby," which she explained in a very pantomimic way that she would be singing in Paris while I would be singing "*Ah, qu'ils sont bons*" in New York. That got her to thinking about the immensity of the sea and how long I should be on the water—eight days on this route—which caused her to shake her head. As we came into Folkstone, she motioned me to kiss her eyes and neck—a bit of French fancy which touched me. Her boat was waiting not thirty feet from the car, ready to get under way, and I no sooner found her a seat and saw her well-placed than the call to go ashore was sounded. She kissed me heartily on the mouth, and as the boat swung out over the chalk-blue water, she held up six fingers to indicate that in six months I would be back in Paris. For the moment I wished I might—she looked so bright, hopeful, alluring.

My own boat was leaving in another hour for Dover, and I had to travel on to Dover—say forty minutes away. The English conductor who had secured me a compartment to myself coming down appeared here, after the Folkstone boat had gone, and I asked him to set me right. He told me not to bother about my luggage, saying that I would surely find it all on the dock when I arrived to take my boat. It was exactly as he said, though having come this way two transfers had to be made. Trust the English to be faithful. It is the one reliable country in which you may travel. At Dover I meditated on how thoroughly all my European days were over and when, if ever, I should come again. Life offers so much to see and the human span is so short that it is a question whether it is advisable ever to go twice to the same place—a serious question. If I had my choice, I decided, as I stood and looked at the blue bay of Dover, I would, if I could, spend six months each year in the United States and then choose Paris as my other center and from there visit any European places that I might choose—England, Italy, Holland, the Riviera. Would I go back to Germany? I wondered. But Paris! That seemed now to have sufficient of what I call world material to make it a fit abiding place for anyone. London is wonderful, but for me let me have Paris first.

And so, after an hour's wait at Dover, while my boat dropped anchor and took on the company of passengers who were going out in a lighter, as at Fishguard, I finally entered the large two-funneled Belgian liner, out of Antwerp, and was under way. The harbor of Dover was lovely in a fading light—chalk-blue waters, tall, whitish cliffs, endless, squeaking, circling gulls and a bugle calling from somewhere, presumably the fort at Dover. And so my trip was over, save for eight days on the water, which would soon pass. This was Saturday night. The following Sunday, or Monday at the outside, I would be in New York. Then would come the humdrum of the old days—days of regular work, evenings and Sundays with familiar people—a world more circumspect and less changeful than I had been viewing for the five months past.

It was with peculiar feelings that I climbed up the gangplank, for now my outing was really over. Eight days of quiet ship rest, and many days of hard work under pressure. It would not be possible to forget this first return (my first, though I hoped not my last), if for no other reason than the sinking of the *Titanic*. This was the week of that disaster. It had sailed only three days before, and Grant Richards had assured me that he had intended booking me on that as a novelty, it being the maiden trip of that ship, only we could not make it in time. He wanted me to stay longer. I found myself in a comfortable stateroom with few differences between this and the ship on which I had gone over save that the passenger list was not so large, nor was it dotted to any extent with significant names. There were, perhaps, no more than a hundred first-class passengers, though the second and third cabins held eighteen hundred. It was a good boat, new—rumored on shipboard, in that self-complimentary spirit which ship companies have, of being one of the easiest sea-riding ships afloat. The service guards which are used to prevent the slipping of dishes and silverware at table were rarely if ever used, it was said. Certainly they were not used on this trip, rough as it was at times.

It was most interesting to me to see on this return trip (I had been too concerned with other things going out to really notice) how the passenger list of a cabin speedily organizes itself into a polity, gets itself divided into working groups, takes sides and does its best to make the best of a series of otherwise dull days. There were various interesting people aboard our boat: a judge or two; a doctor; a Chicago beef company's agent; a priest; a French actress bound for New York; a French daughter of the lower middle classes bound for a sister's home in Lansing, Michigan; a New York commission merchant and his wife, both French-Belgians by birth; a German furrier of New York, back from the great fur markets of Leipzig and London, where he had been buying his next season's goods; a Dutch-Belgian fiancée in the charge of the captain, a charming nineteen-year-old edition of Marguerite, bound for the arms of her betrothed in New York; an English grain agent, bound for Canada (Calgary, if you please); an English-Irish girl of the better class, going to visit a sister at Rochester; and an English tutor and his pupil on a sightseeing tour of America. There were others: several American families—father, mother, daughters and sons of whom we saw little, and a half-dozen silent financial figures who kept reservedly to themselves. The captain, strangely enough, was a sharp, controversial, black-haired, thickset Irishman; the ship's doctor and purser, pure Belgians. The barbers, bath attendants, waiters and so on were Belgians.

For all the ships that man has put on the sea, it is a world which he has not yet invaded. For all the scientific soundings that have been taken, we do not know the deep. The average nature seems to recoil from the monotony of its surface, and it has hours when its vast, flat spaces are too unrelieved. In the main, for me, it was vastly suggestive, grimly poetic. The gray-green swish of water going by in undulating heights and hollows was a never-ending source of delight. The glassy, green walls of water soothed me. The suggestion of unexplored continents of water kept me in a fluid mental mood—vast mountain ranges and plains beneath the floor of the vessel, inhabited by what evolved intelligence?—fin-equipped and scaled. Suppose by any chance this ship should go down; suppose in the night water should begin pouring into my stateroom. That was always a pleasant, poetic thought.

It was a well-finished vessel, with a large drawing room, old English smoking room, writing room, and, for contrast, a colonial dining room. The meals were not bad. After my experience going over, I made a point to begin at once conversation with my right- and left-hand neighbors—on the one hand the ship's physician, on the other the Chicago agent of the dressed beef company. By degrees through these I was introduced to the furrier, the French actress, the Dutch-Belgian fiancée, the English-Canadian grain agent, the judge, the captain, the Irish girl, until by degrees I came to know some twenty or more. In walking the decks or sitting in the writing or drawing rooms after dinner or before lunch, we naturally fell in with each other. I recall that the young Dutch-Belgian girl drew me into a conversation by manipulating the electric light plug which governed the lamp on my writing desk in such a way that I fancied something had happened to the electric equipment of the ship. "Just like a baby, I am," she smiled when I looked up. "I must have something to play with." So I talked about Holland and Belgium to her.

People always, everywhere, are so eager to find out all about each other. I was speedily informed by one person and another as to the personal standing of this and that individual, his honors and emoluments, insofar as known, and with the hope, I took it, that I would have something to communicate in return. I remember the wife of the New York commission merchant smiled at me as she was walking alone in the morning sun the first day (Sunday) and then informed me that the French actress with whom I had seen her talking was going to Chicago and that she was engaged for some production which would shortly appear in New York. "She has very liberal ideas as to life, I can tell you," which led to a full exposition of the moral viewpoint of Madame Farnese, as she chose to call herself. It was not long before I was as thick as thieves with the German-American furrier, the Chicago beef-packers' agent, the ship's doctor, Mlle. Nyssens, the Belgian sweetheart, the French actress, and many others. We made up fours and played shuffleboard. We broke into groups and played "hearts," poker and patience. Before long, solitaire (that phase of it known as Canfield), which is so difficult to work out successfully, began to have a great vogue, and many interested spectators gathered, some betting being done on the number of cards that would be left unturned and drinks being persistently ordered to cheer us on our way. I noticed that for the doctor, the judge, the English grain agent and the Chicago beef agent, the attractive women on board were the main centers of interest, principally the Dutch-Belgian fiancée, the French actress, and a little French middle-class girl whose name was Sylvie Duchesne. Fortunately for me, both the French actress and the Dutch sweetheart spoke English. The French girl, who talked so briskly to others, could only smile at me.

The more carefully I contemplated the life aboard this vessel, the more thoroughly I was convinced that—barring some vast, metaphysical overlordship—life, as I always hold, is, insofar as this earthly spectacle called humanity or animal life is concerned, a mere chemical mixture, subject only to as yet little-understood laws of chemical action and reaction which have very little to do with all the palaver concerning morals, ethics, religion, revelation, or some divine, far-off event. I cannot see either the event or its importance. What *is* is about as important as anything that can be. If I seem to wander, bear with me, for it has some point in connection with this ship. I scarcely believe that there is a soul even temporarily enduring beyond death, and if there is, all its manifestations are probably dependent on physical conditions. Anyhow it would seem so. To me love, hate, pity, gaiety, melancholy, morality and immorality are just chemical processes springing from chemical conditions, and their resultant habits, theories, etc. congealed in the past. Consciousness seems to be nothing but the consequences of physical or chemical changes in the body, and the best answer anyone has for his beliefs, intuitions, faiths and the like is that he has them, that he *feels* them to be true. A majority anywhere for anything is without significance insofar as its relation to the universe is concerned. A majority in Asia or Africa will always think one way, because of climate; a majority in Lapland or North America will think another, because of climate, and the resultant chemical reaction of the average body to it. Cut off the oxygen supply, and in a few seconds all consciousness disappears. Supply it, and you have the phenomenon called thought. If that is exceptional, superior, then the whole universe has it. What phenomena of thought other and larger chemical combinations than those we witness in the human body may generate, I do not know. Perhaps Sirius, which is forty times the size of our sun, or Rigel, which is some thousand times the size of Sirius—a vast, glittering vortex of which we can know nothing—has chemical or "thought" reactions which govern staggeringly in ways we can never suspect. I am ready to believe it. On that basis there may be gods and—I cannot dispute it—an everlasting, omnipotent intelligence. Be it so. Apparently it governs but indifferently in such spindling circumstances as constitute human affairs. Or perhaps in this swirl of the illogical, passionate, self-contradictory and enthusiastic which we call life, we are witnessing the highest wisdom. Be that so also.

CHAPTER CII

But to come back to this interesting ship's company. For ten days, as it eventually worked out, I had a chance to observe this small company closely, rocked on the bosom of the illimitable deep, and all that I saw coincided with the above theory, or lack of one, to a dot. We will begin with the captain. He was a Christian Scientist, believing in the nothingness of matter, the immanence of spirit or a divine idea, yet he was, as events proved, greatly distressed because of the perverse, undismissable presence and hauntings of mortal thought. He had "beliefs" concerning possible wrecks, fires, explosions—the usual terrors of the deep—and one of the ship's company (our deck steward) told me that whenever there was a fog, he was always on the bridge, refusing to leave it, and that he was nervous and "as cross as hell." So you can see how his religious belief squared with his chemical intuitions concerning the facts of life. A nice, healthy, brisk, argumentative, contentious individual he was and very anxious to have the French actress sit by him at dinner when things were going right.

Madame (or Mrs.) Van Dyk, the wife of the French-Belgian commission merchant doing business in New York, was a fair sample of the moderately attractive, self-conserving, reasonably educated, liberal and yet conventional and non-thinking woman. Liberal she surely was in most things, but on the question of the home, morals, the advantage of monogamy she was quite fixed. All this came out anent Mlle. Farnese, because Mlle. Farnese was a moral (or immoral) firebrand. The truth was she had no morals at all. Obviously a fair actress, high-strung, irresponsible, somewhat emotional but above all temperamental, passionate and enthusiastic, she shared no conventional view as to how this earthly life ought to be ordered. She did not know how to share them. Any attractive man was fair prey, though that she did not consider every man or even many men attractive was quite plain. She liked the ship's doctor, who was short, slightly bald, good-natured, witty and essentially an individual for ladies. He had the faculty for entertaining amusingly, which makes friends everywhere, and was very immoral. She liked the commission merchant, which might have had something to do with his wife's strictures concerning her. I am sure it did. Nevertheless Mr. Van Dyk, a tall, lank, ambling person, well-dressed, witty and genial, loved to linger in her vicinity. His favorites were the French actress, the Belgian heiress sweetheart (I forgot the heiress part), and the French family girl. Mlle. Farnese also liked the Chicago beef-packers' agent, who was solid, American, young, cheerful and yet reticent and who loved to sit in the smoking room by himself, play solitaire and drink brandy and soda and liqueurs.

She took me into her confidence also, after the second day, told me her plans, invited me to her hotel in New York, and sought my advice as to certain theatrical agencies and persons. Before we reached New York, I was in and out of her stateroom frequently. She was a little woman, comparatively speaking, slender, graceful, very vigorous, with very dark-brown, almost black, hair, and brown-black eyes. She was the soul of gaiety and humor.

Madame Van Dyk, however, who was mentor to some, put down her foot in private argument against any such attitude as that represented by Mlle. Farnese.

"Very nice, yes; very clever, very attractive" (she pronounced it "aattraactif"), "but it is no way to live, I should say. Perhaps it is all right for the stage—I have nothing to say about that—but in private life, no one could live as she thinks she has a right to live. If she wants to act like that, then she must confine herself to people who are connected with the stage. I know of course there are all sorts of men who will have to do with her if she will let them, but still I maintain it is no way to do. She says she is a typical Frenchwoman. I deny that. The Frenchwomen are not like that—not all of them, certainly. We have our theatrical and art classes there, just as you have them here, but to advocate freedom the way she does for herself and others is no way to do. She is not wise in that. I should say she is very dull."

Madame Van Dyk fixed me with shrewd, inquiring, black eyes which gleamed behind gold-rimmed glasses. She had black hair and a cream-white skin too. I wondered what the ambling Monsieur Van Dyk had to say about all this.

The German furrier, who sat opposite me at table, was as interesting and intelligent a German-American as you would wish to know. He had come to America in 1865, a third son in a family that had been in the fur business in Cologne. There was no way to peacefully divide the local Cologne fur business, so the eldest son was allowed to buy out the others, the second boy went into the wholesale fur business in Leipzig, and the last one (the one here on board with us) came to New York and opened a small store in Maiden Lane. He had prospered mightily. He was now well-to-do. He in turn had three sons whom he was trying to place properly in this world. His wife was dead. I am sure the world would approve of Mr. Weiss as a hard-working, intelligent, shrewd, kindly man. He had all the virtues and all the vices, if we can call them such, of the practical, conservative tradesman. Outside of his business, which he understood very well, he practically knew nothing. History, literature, art, even music—though not entirely music—were almost sealed books. On very short acquaintance—because I was sympathetic, I suppose—he wanted me to come and visit him at his summer home on Lake Mahopac, where his boys appeared to be having a delightful time. I agreed that I might. He was perhaps fifty-eight or sixty years of age, well-preserved, inclined to be a little talkative, vain of his business, vain of his powerful friends, who probably did not know that he looked upon them as friends, grateful for any courtesies extended—a mere chemical force. I noticed that the ladies tolerated him, but that was all. Their interests were elsewhere.

Mlle. Nyssens, the heiress going to be married, was a personage of rare flavor. I have described her exactly when I say that she looked like the average opera Marguerite, except that the lid of her right eye drooped a little, which gave her countenance a strange, outré flavor at times, very delightful. A firm believer in the significance of temperaments—knowing as I do that life holds no fate but that, and that art is life seen through that, as through a glass, richly—I was interested in noting how significant Miss Nyssens's was—one of the kind that I prefer myself. I have said that she was nineteen. She had the wisdom of sixty-five, a sad fatality of thought, which was concealed by her radiant youth and spirits. The most attractive of all the women—and there were a number—she was easily the principal focus of interest for the men and most of the women. The women, particularly the Madame Van Dyk type, were interested in her because she was going (or coming) to America to get married and because she had money. The men of the beef agent (Wallis) and the grain agent (Pemberton) type were interested because she was beautiful, of good family apparently, and being removed thus speedily from the sphere of eligibles. The doctor and Mlle. Farnese looked on her as a human possibility about to be spoiled by marriage. I don't believe Herr Weiss had an opinion one way or the other. As for myself I was curious to learn whether it was true love that was moving her, whether her fate was really sealed, whether she was happy at the prospect, whether she liked the thought of America or not. I found out all I wanted to know. The little Irish girl, the judge and the English tutor, who was unconsciously a bit of a snob and an ass, were more or less retiring, meditative, uncertain whether they should mingle in this ship's life or not. The Irish girl was Catholic with views fixed for her by others through which she had never broken.

But the thing that interested me was the welter of confused notions that prevailed here as everywhere about life. Mlle. Farnese was the base of the general division because she was at once immoral and attractive. She had a following. Miss Nyssens, the heiress, liked her and spent much of her time with her, though Madame Van Dyk did her best (and succeeded) to make everything quite plain. The pretty Irish-Catholic girl took up with her—for the ship's trip only, I suppose. Herr Weiss, the furrier, was a little afraid of, but was socially charming to, her. Monsieur Van Dyk was always near her, or Miss Nyssens, or both, when he was not with his wife. Most always his wife was present, sharing the general tête-à-tête. Being on the treacherous sea, fresh from Europe, all strange to each other, we had so much to talk about. It concerned everything under the sun—morals, ethics, death, trade, politics, everything imaginable. It was all so fluid.

Miss Nyssens confided to me that she had once thrown over the man she was now going to marry and had fallen in love with another, but that she had changed her mind again. She told me that she was sure that it was not marriage that helped to make a life but your own philosophy and endurance. Convent-bred, she had already read Tolstoy, Turgenev, Flaubert, Maupassant and Wells, and above all preferred Maupassant. She had never heard of any American author save Poe, but had never read him. Madame Van Dyk's conservative worries amused her. "She is afraid of Mlle. Farnese," she smiled. "I like Mlle. Farnese. She is bright. Whether she is a good actress or not, I don't know." The ship's doctor was a delight to her, and the American judge someone "to make a fool of," because she could; "because," as she put it, "he must like me because I am pretty. I know that."

The third day we were out, news came by wireless that the *Titanic* had sunk after collision with an iceberg off Labrador or thereabouts. It was Herr Weiss who, busy about everything and everybody, had gleaned it as a sea secret from the wireless man. He had been keeping the latter in cigars. It was a terrible piece of news, grim in its suggestion, and when it finally leaked out, it sent a chill over all on board. I heard it first at nine o'clock at night. A small party of us—Wallis, Monsieur Van Dyk, Pemberton and myself—were seated in the combination card and smoking room, a most comfortable retreat from the terrors of the night and the sea, when Weiss entered, very mysterious-looking and eager to find us. We had been playing shuffleboard all afternoon, but a fog had come up about four-thirty combined with a wet wind, which ended it all. After that we met at dinner, but separated again, drifting one by one back here, for the night was inclement. This drifting back here, one by one, was always significant, I discovered, for when the nights were fair, the stars out, a pleasant wind blowing, the company broke up into pairs or quartets, men and women, and walked or lounged and talked outside. If the sea were gloomy but not ominous, we were apt to gather in the library or drawing room and listen to playing by Madame Van Dyk, who was not a bad pianist, and singing by Mlle. Farnese and Miss Nyssens. The latter, by the way, sang very simply and feelingly, Dutch, German, English and French songs. She was a very fair linguist. When the sea was ominous, as it so often becomes, somehow men and women, the men first, drifted back into the card room and ensconced themselves in comfortable leather-upholstered corners, sometimes, I thought, because the card room looked less like the sea than any place else on the ship.

This matter of the sea looking ominous was a curious thing. You could not escape its dread suggestion. As a rule, when this happened, a fog would have settled unexpectedly down, the decks would be wet, the wind damp. Instead of the ship plunging doggedly ahead as it did in fair weather, it slowed down now, at times seemed to stop entirely and drift, the great foghorn began mooing like some Brobdingnagian sea cow wandering on endless, watery pastures. The spirits of the passengers invariably sank until they could be gotten together in groups in the card room, where, played upon by scores of lights, served with drinks and reacted upon one by the moods of the others, a temperamental combination took place which served to dispel their gloom. At that it was not possible to escape entirely, for the starting and stopping of the ship, the grim moo of the horn and the sound of long, swishing breakers outside spoke of the immensity of the sea, its dark depths and terrors. Every now and then, I noticed, someone would rise and go outside to contemplate, no doubt, the hopelessness of it all. If there is anything more unpromising to this little lamp, the body, it is the dark, foggy waters of a midnight sea.

This particular evening when Weiss came seeking us was such a one.

"I got sumpin to tell you gentlemen," he said very secretly, bending over us. "You better come outside where the ladies can't hear." There were several in the room. "I just been talkin' to the wireless man upstairs."

We arose and followed very nonchalantly, as he advised, and one by one, wondering what it was all about.

"What do you suppose old Weiss has got up his sleeve?" Mr. Wallis asked me.

"Not the slightest idea. Perhaps Taft has been killed, or the Standard Oil Company has failed."

He laughed, but we were interested.

When we reached an open space which fronted the first cabin baths, we found Weiss. He was very concerned.

"What do you think I just heard from the wireless man? You know I've been friendly with him. I keep him in cigars, and all that. The captain's given orders to keep it a secret until we reach New York. The *Titanic* went down last night with nearly all on board. Only eight hundred saved and two thousand drowned. She struck an iceberg off Newfoundland."

"Good God!" exclaimed Wallis, his whole healthy, debonair manner changing. "What do you think of that! Two thousand!"

"You don't say!" exclaimed Pemberton, such a mild, quiet little man he was too. "Most dreadful! The president of the White Star Company was on that boat—was he drowned?"

"John Jacob Astor was on it," returned Weiss, "but they don't know yet if they were drowned. That looks kind of bad to me—only eight hundred out of twenty-eight hundred people saved. You gentlemen must promise me faithfully not to tell the ladies, otherwise I shuttn't have told you. I promised the man upstairs. It might get him in trouble."

We promised faithfully.

All the while we were discussing this, though, the swish of the sea could be heard and the regular moo of the horn—the great sea cow roaming the endless meadows of the deep.

"And this is only Tuesday," suggested Monsieur Van Dyk in his amusing, practical way. His face showed a true concern. "We got a week yet on the sea, the way they will run now. And we have to go through that region."

He took off his cap and scratched his hair in a foolish, thoughtful way.

There now began a low but animated discussion. The terror of the sea had come swiftly and directly home to all. I am satisfied that there was not a man of all the company who heard but felt a strange sinking sensation as he thought of the endless wastes of the sea outside—its depths, the horror of drowning in the dark and cold. I for one thought of all the strange fish I had ever seen—*Gastrostomus bairdii*, with its cavernous mouth; *Halimochirurgus centriscoides*, with its amazing eye and snout; *Aphyonus gelatinosus*, blind and colorless; *Diaphus lucidus*, with its incandescent lamps. To think of a ship as immense as the *Titanic*, the largest that ever had been built—new, shining, finished in expensive woods, fabrics and metals, sinking in endless fathoms of water! And the two thousand passengers routed like rats from their berths only to float helplessly in miles of water, praying and crying.

I confess I felt the chill of terror, and yet I am not afraid to die. To me fear is an idea which can be firmly repressed, made to slink away like a whipped dog. I went to my berth in due season, thinking of the pains and terrors of the two thousand, a great rage in my heart against the fortuity of life, the dullness or greed of man that prevents him from coping with it. For an hour or more I listened to the swish of the water, the vibrations of the ship, trembling at times like a spent animal as a greater or lesser wave struck at it with smashing force. The thought of icebergs was in my mind—vast cakes of submerged ice and the weariness of drifting until cold and numbness made clinging to wreckage no more possible or even desirable. Then I slept, the souls of the victims of the *Titanic* keening in the endless spaces that are not water or air or earth but—what?

CHAPTER CIII

I found by careful observation of those with me that I was not the only one subject to disquieting thoughts. Wallis, the Chicago beef man, pleased me most, for he was so frank in admitting his inmost emotions. A lover of strong drink, this vigorous young buck, but never more than rosily warm with liquor at any time and usually quite free of it, he was always frank and straightforward. He came down to breakfast the next morning looking a little dull. The sun was out, and it was a fine day. "You know," he confided genially, "I dreamed of those poor devils all night. Say—out in the cold there! And then those big waves kept hitting the ship and waking me up. Did you hear that smash in the night? I thought we had struck something. I got up once and looked out, but that didn't cheer me any. I could only see the top of a roller now and then going by."

"I know well enough how they look," I replied.

Another evening, sitting in the deepest recesses of the card room, he explained that he believed in good and bad spirits, and the good spirits could help you "if they wanted to."

Monsieur Van Dyk was nervous, in a subdued, quiet way, despite his continued interest in the ladies. He never ceased commenting on the wretchedness of the catastrophe, nor did he fail daily to consult the chart of miles made and course traveled. He predicted that we would turn south before we neared the Grand Banks because he did not believe the captain would "take a chance" running into the icefields that held the iceberg which sank the *Titanic*. He would blurt out harrowing suggestions at times when three or four of us were together, showing that his mind was on the subject. I am sure he told his wife and that she told every other woman, for the next day Miss Nyssens confided to me that she knew and that she had been "stiff with fear" all the night before.

The Englishman, Pemberton, gave no sign one way or the other. Weiss was like a man with a mania. He talked of it all the time. The American judge talked solemnly with all who would listen, a hard crab of a man whose emotions found their vent in the business of extracting information. The women talked to each other but pretended not to know.

It took three days of more or less pleasant sailing to relax the tension and nervous excitation which pervaded the whole vessel. The captain did not appear again at table for four days. On Wednesday, following the Monday of the wreck, there was a fire drill—that ominous clanging of the fire-bell on the forward deck which brought many troubled spectators out of their staterooms and developed the fact that every piece of hose employed was rotten, for every piece put under pressure burst—a cheering thought! The bucket-passing drill showed that as a rule it must have been neglected, for it was a farce, only quarter-filled buckets being passed along when the passing was forced. I thought we should see a boat-drill with rusted davits developing as a result, but none was had. This made the passengers even more cheerful, but as the days passed and we did not sink, we began to take heart again. The philosophers of the company were unanimously agreed that as the *Titanic* had suffered this great disaster through carelessness on the part of the officers, no doubt our own chances of safely reaching shore were thereby enhanced.

"It stands to reason," said Weiss, who spoke a deliciously flavored English, "dey ain't goin' to take any more chances now dan dey can help. Why should dey? Ain't dis de same company? Dey don't want a second disaster. What?"

"You're right," coincided Wallis cheerfully.

We fell to gambling again, to flirting, to shuffleboarding, just as we had always done. By Saturday, when we were passing in the vicinity of where the *Titanic* went down, only much farther to the south, our fears had been practically dispelled. Only we were all eager to see the newspapers or to get additional intelligence by wireless, none of which was forthcoming. Insofar as any evidence of the calamity came from the ship's officers, no wreck had ever occurred.

It was not until we reached Sandy Hook the following Tuesday—a hard, bright, clear, blowy day—that we really learned. The customary pilot was taken on there, out of a thrashing sea, his overcoat pockets bulging with papers—a *Herald*, a *World*, a *Times*, an *American*—all flaring with headlines describing the awful disaster, and all giving the full first- and second-cabin passenger list as well as painfully vivid word pictures by eyewitnesses, survivors.

I shall never forget the scene in the smoking room when the papers were brought in. Weiss, as usual, first and foremost, had secured them. He had warned us (some of us) that he would, and true to his word, no sooner had the pilot got on board than he appeared with them. A fair-sized company of men gathered, those who most frequented the smoking room, and we took turns reading—Weiss, Wallis, Judge Andrews and myself. The softhearted German, encountering details as to the struggles of women and children in the water in the dark, broke down and cried. He did not try to read any more. Young Wallis, somewhat better fortified by alcohol, read a while but gave up, his voice clouding badly with emotion. Judge Andrews did better reading the passenger list, and I found no difficulty doing so, though the chance bitterness of it all was not lost on me. There was a great rage engendered in all present at the parsimony and neglect of the company in not furnishing a sufficient number of lifeboats, in allowing so large a number of the crew to escape, leaving the passengers to sink, in not warning everyone on board that the vessel was certain to go down. I never listened to a greater palaver of rage nor one involved with more emotion born of the terror of it all. There were sneers for the president of the corporation controlling the ship, who had managed to escape, and applause for the individuals who, knowing their lot to be hopeless, faced it with that stoicism which we all adore. Weiss, who had gone away to dry his eyes, presently returned and was intensely interested in the fact that the very young woman who had married the American multimillionaire who had gone down on the vessel after bowing her into a boat would now be very rich in her own right and able to marry again soon if she chose. For a German furrier of some sixty, he was about as human and pleasing a piece of humanity as you would want to meet.

Thus discussing the great disaster and looking after our luggage and preparing our declarations for the customs inspectors and making our farewells, one to the other, we came finally to quarantine, where American doctors came aboard, and a statement as to our individual physical condition was demanded. It amused me to see how in these last hours the rather vigorous ardors of ship-friendship that had been engendered by the days spent together began to cool—how all those present began to think of themselves no longer as members of a coordinated ship's company, bound together for weal or woe on the bosom of the great deep, but rather as individuals of widely separated communities and interests, to which they were now returning and which of necessity would sever their relationship perpetually. I saw, for instance, the American judge—who had unbent sufficiently after we had been three days out, to play cards with so humble a person as Van Dyk the commission merchant and Weiss—begin to congeal again into his native judicial dignity. Madame Van Dyk, who had apparently been rather intimate with Miss Nyssens, was now rather cut by her, or as it were gently eliminated. And this was not a conscious process on the part of Miss Nyssens half so much as it was preoccupation with her coming affairs. It could not be expected that she and Madame Van Dyk would be apt to move in the same sphere. Weiss himself, who by degrees had become the gayest of the gay, dissolving under the genial influence of ship companionship into probably native boyishness, now began to take on much of the executive dignity of his successful fur business. He was thinking of his store and his awed employees. He had on, as might be imagined, a handsome fur coat, his field glasses slung over his shoulder and his derby hat pulled low over his eyes. He looked quite smart, cool, anything but emotional, and I secured a sharper impression of him as a successful, quick-minded merchant than I had yet been able previously. He was very interesting. With many of those with whom he had been most friendly, he was now less so—with others he craved future relationship.

The Englishman, the English tutor, the little Irish girl and the French actress, while still very friendly, were quite remote—other worlds were calling them. Mlle. Farnese reminded me of my promise with a day and hour, but I was a little wary of her; I sensed—I scarcely know what. Little Sylvie Duchesne, seeking guidance until her friends from Lansing, Michigan, should meet her, was most amusing in her kitten-like hoverings. She craved care and got it. Monsieur Van Dyk ambled about in a gay way, glad to get back. Although born in Belgium (Lille), he was no longer interested in Europe. He made the remark I had often heard made by Americanized foreigners, that the Europeans were too concerned with little things; they did not see life in the broad, easy, tolerant way Americans did. I wondered.

And now all of this goodly company were so concerned as to whether they could make a very conservative estimate of the things they were bringing into America and yet not be disturbed by the customs inspectors that they were a little amusing. What is honesty, anyhow? Foreign purchases to the value of one hundred dollars were allowed, yet I venture to say that of all this charming company, most of whom prided themselves on some form of virtue—from chastity and commercial honesty on and up—not one made an honest declaration. They were all as honest as they had to be, as dishonest as they dared be—no more so. Yet what a storm if anyone had said this to them. Monsieur Van Dyk frankly confessed to me that he never declared more than two hundred. Mlle. Farnese was carefully figuring out the lowest estimate which would cover her importations. The American judge, as I saw later, knew some of the inspectors at the pier. Mr. Weiss admitted that he declared some things at what he considered a fair value. Miss Nyssens considered customs duties more or less outrageous and a farce anyhow. Wallis and Pemberton, the Englishman, kept their own council, but I judged they were arranging their lists with discretion. I saw Wallis fee an inspector later in order not to be bothered. Poor, pretending humanity! We all lie so. We all believe such untrue things about ourselves and about others. Life is literally compact of make-believe, illusion, temperamental bias, false witness, affinity. The so-called standards of right, truth, justice, law are no more than the wire netting of a sieve through which the water of life rushes almost uninterrupted. It seems to be regulated, but is it? Look close. See for yourself. Christ said, "Eyes, and they see not; ears, and they hear not." Is this not literally true? Begin with number one. How about *you* and the so-called universal standards?

The last two hours of this clear April day were spent in coming up from quarantine and berthing the boat. It had been so cold and raw down the bay that I could scarcely believe, as we neared Manhattan Island, that it was going to be so warm and spring-like on land as it proved. When we first sighted Long Island and later Long Beach, it was over a thrashing sea, the heads of waves of which were being cut off by the wind and sent flying into white spindrift or parti-colored rainbows. Even above Sandy Hook the wind made rainbows out of wave-tops, and the bay had a tumbled surface. I was pleased to see the stately towers of the lower city as we drew near, that mountain of steel and stone cut with its narrow canyons. They were just finishing the upper framework of the Woolworth Building—that first cathedral of the American religion of business—and now it reared its stately head high above everything else. Mlle. Farnese, Sylvie Duchesne, Miss Nyssens and the English tutor and his pupil watched it all with untiring eyes. "Oh, it is fine," observed Miss Nyssens and Mlle. Farnese; and Sylvie Duchesne, who could speak English, agreed that it was *magnifique*. I think all three were a little frightened by the spectacle of the giant metropolis ahead. "A stranger in a strange land," I thought. I recalled how New York frightened me coming from the West years before.

There was a great crowd at the dockside to receive us. Owing to the sink-

New York harbor

ing of the *Titanic*, relatives were especially anxious, and all incoming ships were greeted with enlarged companies of grateful relatives. There were reporters on hand to ask questions as to the voyage—had we encountered any dead bodies? had we struck any ice?—and lovers, relatives, friends. I was first allowed to inspect Miss Nyssens's intended through her binoculars from the middle of the Hudson, and later was introduced to him—a tall, grave, sentimental-looking man who was obviously feverish because of her. By Wallis I was invited to dinner at the Knickerbocker, whither he was bound; by Weiss, to come to his summer place at Mahopac. As an act of charity, I personally took charge of little Sylvie Duchesne's customs difficulties and promised Mlle. Farnese certain introductions. Madame Van Dyk and I had some last sharp words as to life, religion, morals. She was a little resentful of her unfortunate conditional mediocrity, I think, and yet contentiously defensive in consequence. Pemberton was leaving this same night for Montreal and Calgary—that utterly new town in the far west of Canada. The judge and others not of "our crowd" were solemnly making their way to parts unknown.

When I finally stepped on the dock, released my baggage and Miss Duchesne's, called a few final farewells and took a taxi to Upper Broadway, I felt really once more that I was at home. New York was so suggestively rich to me this spring evening. It was so refreshing to look out and see the commonplace life of Eighth Avenue, up which I sped, and the long cross streets, and later Upper Broadway, with its rush of cars, taxis, pedestrians. On Eighth Avenue negroes were idling at curbs and corners, the Eighth Avenue type of shopkeeper lolling in his doorway, boys and girls, men and women of a none-too-comforting type making the best of a humdrum and shabby existence. In one's own land, born and raised among the conditions you are observing, responsive to the subtlest of modifications of speech, gesture, expression, life takes on a fresh and intimate aspect which only your own land can give after a trip abroad. I never quite realized until later this same evening, strolling out along Broadway to pay a call, how much it is one loses abroad for want of blood affinity and years and years of residence. All the finer details, such as through the magnifying glass of familiarity one gains at home, one loses abroad. Only the main outlines, the very roughest details stand revealed as in a distant view of mountains. That is why generalizations on so short an acquaintance as a traveler must have are so dangerous. Here, each sight and sound was significant.

"And he says to me," said one little girl strolling with her picturesque companion on Upper Broadway, "if you don't do that, I'm through."

"And what did you say?"

"Good night!!!"

If the foreigner traveling in America were as deficient in English as I was in Italian, French, Dutch, even rural and cockney English, how would he "get that," do you think?

THE END

Historical Commentary

THE COMPOSITION AND PUBLICATION OF A TRAVELER AT FORTY

Theodore Dreiser began writing *A Traveler at Forty* in November 1911, one month after the formal publication of his second novel, *Jennie Gerhardt*, on 19 October.[1] Unlike his previous work, *A Traveler* does not deal with subject matter he had been contemplating for years; rather, the book was inspired by a fortunate moment that offered not only a trip to Europe but also a new career as a travel writer. In July, right after he had sent all chapters of the *Jennie* manuscript to the press, and continuing through August, while the first galleys were arriving, Dreiser returned to the novels he had already begun, *The "Genius"* and *The Financier*, both of which he now offered to Harper's. The firm favored the latter, and Dreiser energetically fell to work, telling his friends that he was to become a one-book-a-year writer. He wrote rapidly, and that October he sent a letter to William C. Lengel reporting that he had finished twenty-six chapters.[2] The book, conceived in the manner of Zola, was to be the true story of a representative captain of industry whose life was familiar to Dreiser and who was still remembered by the American public. Interlacing the search for wealth and power with a quest for beauty, the life of Charles Tyson Yerkes seemed ideally suited to Dreiser's purposes. Although not exactly a regular rags-to-riches tale, it nevertheless contained similar swings of fortune, the high and the low life, a pattern of economic as well as moral rises and falls, the public working world and private sexual interest, the sphere of money and the realm of art. The various stages of Yerkes' career, from his youthful beginnings to his 1905 death in New York, were tied to different settings: the banking years in Philadelphia; the years of building the transit system in Chicago; and his final big venture in London, where he converted the city's subways from steam to electricity and thereby tried to gain control of the Underground system. As Dreiser was following his hero from locale to locale, he had been aware for some time of the impending crux; after having completed the Philadelphia and Chicago sections, he would have to take the narrative to Europe, where the tale, at this point still planned as one big novel, would end.

The wish to travel abroad seems to have first crossed Dreiser's mind in 1908. At the end of a 6 March 1908 letter, Grant Richards, a London publisher who had started a correspondence with Dreiser in 1905 and who showed a vivid interest in the forthcoming novel *Jennie Gerhardt*, reminded the author of his "vague idea of coming to England" that summer.[3] Dreiser postponed his visit year after year, however, while Richards repeated his invitation and even offered to serve as the writer's personal guide.[4] Dreiser, then the editor of the *Delineator,* one of the Butterick publications, may have been tied up at his desk; he may have hesitated to accept an invitation that he felt was motivated by Richards's desire to become his English publisher; or he may still have too much resented the fact that Richards, a good friend of Mr. and Mrs. Doubleday, had likewise refused his first novel, *Sister Carrie,* despite the praises of Frank Norris. But by early November 1911 the situation had changed considerably. Richards's interest in the American writer had been rekindled, and Dreiser, with a recently published book in his hands and a new novel whose completion required European travel, decided to respond to the publisher's note and consult Richards, who from 1906 to 1913 made annual November visits to New York, where he regularly stayed at the Hotel Knickerbocker. Although the two men's descriptions of the events differ somewhat in detail and emphasis,[5] the initial few meetings between them, the first of which occurred on 5 November, resulted in a plan by Richards to win over this seemingly promising author and his next novel for the Century Company and his own firm. To force this transfer, Dreiser was to confront Harper's with a demand for a steep advance on *The Financier,* which the managers were not expected to meet. In addition, the Century Company was to help finance the European trip Dreiser needed to complete *The Financier* by paying for three articles to appear in *Century* magazine. Richards's plan worked, but not in the manner he and his friends at Century had wished and imagined, for Harper's—to Dreiser's delight—did not part with the author of *Jennie* but instead paid the advance on *The Financier* on the basis of the thirty-nine chapters already received for storage. The Century Company, equally impressed with Dreiser's critical success, held up its promise of an advance for three articles "embodying [his] personal impressions of Europe" and also provided an option for a book "containing not only these articles but other material about Europe" that was to grow out of his "coming journey."[6]

On 18 November, a Saturday, the Century Company's president, Frank H. Scott, sent the letter acknowledging the agreement. He added a personal note, written the day before, expressing his pleasure at the prospect of having Dreiser and his wife for a private dinner on the following Monday. For Dreiser, this invitation was the culmination of an extraordinary development that not only freed him from financial worries for the next few months but also guaranteed him a publisher for *The Financier* and two publishers for his future travel book. Citing Arnold Bennett's praises, Richards had already added to his high spirits by suggesting that 1912 might see the author of *Sister Carrie* and *Jennie Gerhardt* become the first American to receive the Nobel Prize in literature. This secret hope, which Dreiser confided to his friend H. L. Mencken, further fueled his motivation to travel to England, where, he thought, he might personally contribute to raising a favorable sentiment that might also improve critical opinion in America.[7]

Fate, as he liked to call it, having thus arranged his affairs to his best advantage, Dreiser and Richards left for England on the *Mauretania* on 22 November 1911. Before the departure, when Dreiser and the officers of the Century Company were at a luncheon in the writer's honor at the Aldine Club, the editor Robert Underwood Johnson had told him that he was expected to furnish "a type of social essay article."[8] The traveling writer thus immediately began to keep notes on his experiences, setting down some of his impressions while still on board the ship, as the dates in the early chapters suggest. In fact, a diary fragment that Thomas P. Riggio discovered in 1987 in the Dreiser Collection of the Alderman Library at the University of Virginia is the earliest version of the first chapter's initial passage, representing a stage midway between a diary note and the *Traveler* text.[9] It contains a short note of 4 November recording Richards's message from the Hotel Knickerbocker and a longer entry about the same day written on 25 November. It is not clear how much of the early text was first set down as notes—Dreiser cites from his diary in chapter 6—and how much was composed straight for publication.

After he reached England, Dreiser apparently followed Richards's advice that he continue to set down his observations while they were still fresh in his mind. On 19 December he wrote in his journal, "I finished the chapter on Mrs. Stoop—her reception." He even gave these descriptions to Richards to read.[10] This practice can be inferred from several passages in *A Traveler at Forty*,[11] as well as from a letter of 24 January 1912 in which Richards objects to specific points in the portrayal of Dreiser's visit to the publisher's country home at Bigfrith, Cookham Dean, in Berkshire.[12] Since the holograph manuscript has not been recovered, it is impossible to assess how much of the later text was drafted in this initial stage. It can be shown, though, that Dreiser not only kept a scrupulous daily record in his diary[13] but also actively prepared for the book in more than one way. In his characteristic manner he engaged friends and acquaintances to furnish him with material he thought might interest his prospective readers. In Italy he asked Rella Abell Armstrong to set down the history of the famous Borgia family, which he then integrated into his text.[14] He left a blank space in the manuscript where he intended to insert an anecdote he had heard from Richards—a blank, by the way, that was never filled in any of the surviving typescripts.[15] He sent a second inquiry to his English friend and travel companion in France to ask for the transcript of a typical dialogue with a Paris guide that he had been unable to follow, because he did not know French.[16] To support his memory, he collected maps, train schedules, concert programs, tickets, menus, and hotel and laundry bills, all of which he carefully filed with his copious diary notes in chronological order.[17] He also bought numerous picture postcards to refresh his visual memory.[18] From Richards he received not only a diary book for 1912 but also a number of books providing much-needed information. Thus he received a copy of Baedeker's *England* and a book on the postimpressionists, as well as other unspecified books he had requested.[19] In April 1913 Richards exhorted the American author to return a guide to northern France on which Dreiser had apparently been relying for specific details.[20] In his travelogue Dreiser explicitly quotes Baedeker on Pisa, Venice, and Berlin, but there are more instances in which he uses Baedeker to refresh his memory or to verify his notes, as a direct comparison with the tour books will reveal. In chapter 49 he even writes a long laudatory passage on this most renowned of travel guides.[21]

Despite these promising beginnings, the writing of his travel book was delayed. After Dreiser returned to America aboard the *Kroonland* on 23 April 1912, his contract with Harper's forced him to work first on *The Financier*. On 26 May he tells Richards that Harper's would issue the Cowperwood tale as a trilogy, a volume to appear every six months, which might allow him to stop work on *The Financier* for a while. He reports a talk with Johnson of the Century Company about the travel essays to appear in the magazine, expressing his intention to write the travel book before going on with the second volume for Harper's. He concludes, "I do not want my European experiences to grow cold."[22] The following day Douglas Z. Doty, an editor and secretary for the Century Company, sent him the contract for *A Traveler at Forty*. It appears that the title was also determined at this time. Dreiser finished the first volume of his *Trilogy of Desire* in July, but the revision of the bulky manuscript kept him occupied until the beginning of October 1912.[23] It is not clear when he returned to the account of his travels; presumably he did so by late July. In the original agreement with the Century Company, the firm's president had suggested 1 July 1912 as the deadline for the delivery of the three magazine articles. Dreiser was duly reminded of his obligations by Johnson in a letter of 11 July 1912 but seems to have been able to negotiate for more time.[24] In late September he reported that the book was progressing nicely.[25] On 13 November 1912 Doty informed Dreiser that he had begun to read "the new travel stuff."[26] Although he approved of including more material about Dreiser's actress acquaintances, he recommended discussing these episodes "rather briefly."[27] This advice, though gentle, foreshadows the differing attitudes of writer and publisher that would eventually lead to a seriously truncated text. When Richards arrived for his annual November visit to New York that year, disagreement on the subject matter of the travel articles and the book increased vehemently. Richards, sorely disappointed by having failed to obtain the English publishing rights for *The Financier*[28] and by what he considered Dreiser's double-dealing, was further enraged when he was given the manuscript to read. Highly displeased with the description of friends into whose homes he had introduced Dreiser, he chafed: "No confidence was sacred, no actual, or imagined, secret respected. Luckily Doty allowed me, encouraged me even, to cut and cut. I did."[29] Eager to protect his personal interests, he even threatened a lawsuit in case of Dreiser's noncompliance.[30]

Opposition was also brewing on the American side, and despite Dreiser's efforts, the publishing procedure halted. At the end of 1912 Dreiser had completed the holograph manuscript of the book. A 30 December 1912 letter to H. L. Mencken shows him already in Chicago doing research for the second volume of the Cowperwood trilogy.[31] A few days later Doty formally confirmed the receipt of the original diary notes and the full original text of the book.[32] A typing bill lists the first amount due as of 31 December 1912.[33] Although initially set for the spring of 1913,[34] the publication date was postponed until September by mutual consent. It appears that after having read the first few chapters, Johnson had serious doubts as to whether the book or any of the articles were publishable.[35] The *Century Magazine*, a continuation of *Scribner's Monthly*, had been established as the leading literary periodical of its time under the lifelong editorship of Richard Watson Gilder. It had published such famous writers as William Dean Howells, Mark Twain, and Henry James. Johnson, himself a poet of the genteel tradition and—like Dreiser—educated in Indiana, had only recently become editor-in-chief, having taken the reins following Gilder's death in 1909. Holding firmly to his nineteenth-century views and heeding the antivice legislation of the Comstock era, he had not only opposed the publication of Edith Wharton on moral grounds—she had written about divorce—at the turn of the twentieth century but continued his rigid stance far into it, ignoring what Cynthia Ozick calls "a volcanic alteration of taste and expression."[36] Dreiser's candid description of European society as well as his frank relation of his own sexual affairs and discussions of marriage and free love must have deeply offended Johnson's sense of propriety and decency, an attitude that was confirmed and strengthened by the English publisher's objections.

Dreiser was thus in a situation that strikingly resembled his troubles at the beginning of his writer's career. He had found a respected publisher, but one who was unwilling to take any risks with an established readership and did not think it wise to publish the travelogue as it was. Doty, belonging to a younger generation, appears to have secretly sympathized with the author, but caught between two fires, he shifted the responsibility to Richards and continued to send chapters to England, asking for Richards's consent. Apparently nothing much happened between January and April, when typing was finally resumed and Doty firmly promised Dreiser that he would return to editing the manuscript.[37] The appearance of the "Lilly Edwards" chapter in the June issue of *The Smart Set,* which had come out in the middle of the preceding month, may have helped Dreiser to secure a contract for the book, which he was offered on 27 May.[38] This new development may also reflect the corrective course of the trustees of the Century Company, which resulted in Johnson's resignation in June. Johnson's successor was W. W. Ellsworth, who had met Dreiser during his travels in Rome in 1912 and had shown his enthusiasm for the travel book as soon as he had read the first chapters in December 1912. When Ellsworth became president of the Century Company, things began to move. Dreiser received the first batch of proofs,[39] and the three articles were allowed to go into print for the *Century Magazine*. "The First Voyage Over" came out in August 1913; "An Uncommercial Traveler in London," in September; and "Paris," in October. Dreiser even prepared a fourth essay entitled "Berlin," which survives as setting copy.[40] Evidently too late to be included in the November issue of the magazine, it had to be sacrificed, since *A Traveler at Forty* was published on 25 November. Meanwhile Richards, coaxed by Ellsworth, had signaled his approval of the revised text's first seven chapters at the end of September. While Century pressed on toward publication, Richards continued to be difficult, and Ellsworth had to negotiate more compromises on the text. By this time Doty had cut literally half the original text. He had reduced the 103 chapters of the "First Typescript" to a mere 53. The number of pages decreased from 1,165 to 525 in the "Revised Typescript." The new numbering, in red, still totaled 562 pages, but the text as finally published in 1913 is only 526 pages long. The countless changes reflect the ongoing battle over what would eventually go into print. Dreiser unflinchingly continued to work on the text until the very end. He smoothed over the marred transitions, made minor stylistic changes, and, with the tacit support of Doty and Ellsworth, reinserted text whenever possible. The chapter titles were added during the last stage of corrections.[41] The many alterations resulted in costs that were almost three times as high as those of the first typing, $150.00 versus $58.35.[42] The illustrations, the last batch of which arrived in the middle of October, were greeted with unanimous approval. Doty, signing his letter "Yours, much more cheerfully," reported, "[W]e all think they are immense."[43] The drawings were the work of William J. Glackens (1870–1938), a realist painter of the Ashcan school who was strongly influenced by the French impressionist Pierre-Auguste Renoir. Taking the key lines directly from Dreiser's text, he shed a humorous light on the human figures and sketched the European scenes with a true sense of place.

The extensive revisions severely affected the travelogue's overall cast. An astute critic such as Mencken could not fail to notice the unbalancing effect. The cuts altered not only the pace of the narrative, which became curiously uneven ("The whole Italian section is dragging in tempo," he complained),[44] but also the internal and thematic structure. The removal of many chapters in which Dreiser had described his experiences with women[45] led to a number of blind motifs, dark passages, and a striking lack of coherence. The narrative centering on the famous Dutch singer Julia Culp, which provides a continuous sentimental plotline, is largely reduced to her appearances on stage, since the private encounters in Frankfurt and Berlin were radically cut. The same holds true for the Parisian chapters, on which a bewildered Mencken commented, "But in the latter I note an effect of reticence. You start up affairs which come to nothing."[46] The drastic surgery diminished the autobiographical and, at times, highly confidential quality of the narrative. In the first half of the book, the large-scale cuts inadvertently increased the emphasis on the character of Richards, who was disguised as "Barfleur," while simultaneously reducing the importance of the author's own personality. Whereas many pages on Dreiser himself were dropped, practically none of the passages on Richards were removed. The result was a considerable shift in focus and a lack of sufficient background information, both of which inevitably led readers to misconstrue facts. The first passage that strikingly shows the effect of these cuts is the story of Richards's ingenious arrangement of Dreiser's grand tour, which appears to be accomplished by a deus ex machina in the opening chapter of the 1913 edition.[47]

Equally hampered were the underlying metaphor of life as a journey and the theme of death, which Dreiser had carefully elaborated, starting with the suicide of a friend on the day of his departure, climaxing in the visit to the ancestral graveyard at Mayen, and ending with the disastrous news of the sinking of the *Titanic*.[48] Many of the smaller incidents and observations by which he had supported this motif were edited out. Further, to make the work fit the conventional conception of a travel book as a record of places, the longer chapters and passages in which the traveler pauses and investigates his own personality and the meaning of life were either extensively or completely excised.[49] *A Traveler at Forty* contains an important early statement of Dreiser's philosophy, but by removing the reflective passages, the editors at Century made the few remaining statements sound random and incoherent. Also gone were passages that underline Dreiser's belief in intuition and fate.[50] Other cuts endangered what is typically Dreiserian, such as detailed descriptions of the financial arrangements for the trip or the physical appearance of the ship's interior.[51] As a further measure, personal names were disguised to meet the objections of Richards, who feared possible libel suits and had demanded still more extensive cuts. This precautionary editorial decision deeply affected the nature of the narrative, which thus acquired the quality of a roman à clef. Many vivid Balzacian portrayals of types and characters were discarded, which impaired the unsparing picture of European society, both high and low, that Dreiser intended to draw. Examples include the vignette of the German baron in the second chapter and the Hanscha Jauer chapters.[52] In the original text Dreiser gives a much more candid account of the particulars of his journey, one meant to amuse and instruct the American reader at home. What may have seemed like trifling remarks, and were therefore deleted, often help to spice up solemn and dry material, as in the case of his comment on the statue of Umberto I.[53] Since the editor's pencil eliminated a number of dialogues as well, the colloquial quality of the narrative suffered accordingly.

After having had to compromise to this extreme extent, Dreiser suffered intensely. He began to cast around for a new publisher who would grant him "freedom," and he solicited Mencken, whom a year before he had asked to become his literary executor: "After I am dead please take up my mss of The Financier, Titan & Travel book & restore some of the woman stuff—or suggest that it be done."[54] Despite Dreiser's misgivings, the critical reception of the book was mainly favorable; *A Traveler at Forty* received nationwide attention when it appeared on 25 November.[55] In an 18 December 1913 letter, Doty expressed the Century Company's general satisfaction: "Good notices continue to come in, and the book has had a very nice start in point of sales."[56] Critics recognized Dreiser's special achievement in having produced not a run-of-the-mill record of travels but a narrative sifted through his own philosophy. E. F. Edgett of the *Boston Evening Transcript* defined the novelty of the book to "be sought in the adventurer's own mind, not in the scenes he sees and describes," and called the author "no ordinary tourist."[57] Similar praise came from the West Coast. The *San Francisco Bulletin* wrote: "[H]is ability to portray character is recognized by all critical readers"; "[H]e . . . boldly disregards the conventions that he may give an accurate report of things as they are and not as they seem to the average tourist."[58] Most critics agreed that as a travel book the volume was "uncommon," "unusual," and "unprecedented" and that there was "no other travel book just like this one."[59] A few also noticed inexplicable flaws, however, with one reviewer calling it "deadly dull in places" and wondering about such abortive descriptions as the one of the lady with a small white donkey: "[A]nd when we finally encounter the lady she only smiles, and assures us that she doesn't like the idea of her children's toys being made in America."[60] The reviewer blamed Dreiser, but in fact responsibility lay with the editor, who had excluded most of the text on Richards's neighbor. Other readers seem to have been equally puzzled at times. Answering a letter from a female admirer in 1914, Dreiser assured her that "[t]he ms. of A Traveler & all matter relating to it is locked up in a trunk in the Manhattan Storage House, New York," and promised that he would be "glad to dig out the missing material" for her.[61]

The first printing sold out quickly, and the second printing followed immediately in January 1914; the third, in September of the same year.[62] In 1914, too, Richards issued the British edition. Century shipped 250 unbound copies of *A Traveler at Forty* to England in February, but as Richards later admitted in his memoirs, he was less than enthusiastic in marketing it: "I did not exactly repeat the Doubleday–*Sister Carrie* trick, but I certainly was not very zealous in pushing the book."[63] *A Traveler at Forty* continued to sell in a small but steady way. After World War I Century prepared the fourth printing, which was ready for the market by the end of February 1920.[64] The book was printed from the same plates, but the cover title and page edges now lacked gilt stamping. Dreiser apparently disliked its cheaper appearance, and the publisher apologized: "The use of gilt on covers or edges is at present prohibitive."[65] The fifth printing was done in October 1923. Century restored the original binding and appearance in this printing after Boni and Liveright had begun to negotiate for a transfer of rights on 8 March. Given what he called the book's "very steady sale," Century's treasurer was not very willing to give up the rights and offered the plates for a fairly steep price.[66] Horace Liveright declined but continued the negotiations. He told Dreiser: "We'll jockey a bit with The Century Company on A Traveler at Forty."[67] The copyright for *A Traveler at Forty* was finally transferred to the author on 25 July 1926.[68] In April 1929 Dreiser contracted with Liveright for the publication of all his works. As a result, Liveright finally acquired the publishing rights to *A Traveler at Forty* and issued the sixth printing, which became available by August 1930. Except for its saffron binding, this printing, too, is an exact copy of the 1913 edition.

By 1917 Dreiser seems to have lost hope of a complete edition of the manuscript while he was still alive. An entry in his diary on 31 May, however, records his firm will to save the text for posterity. On that day he handed the first portions of the holograph to his friend Estelle Bloom Kubitz, who in 1912 had traveled to Germany to visit with relatives there.[69] Dreiser asked her to type the manuscript "in order that it may be left intact when I die."[70] Kubitz seems to have got past the Lilly Edwards chapters by 1 June: "During dinner we have long discussion of prostitution—Lilly of London (see *A Traveler at Forty*)."[71] On the following day he took the last half to her to copy.[72] On 2 August she was still "bringing several chapters" she had finished.[73] After Dreiser's death Robert H. Elias arranged to have this typescript, along with other papers, sent to the University of Pennsylvania, where it is filed as "The 1st Typescript." A handwritten note in the old file lists states: "Ms. In 1922 loaned to someone who wants to retain it. Can be recovered. TD to W. W. Lange 12.12.22." The holograph manuscript, however, has not been recovered.[74]

Notes

1. Donald Pizer, Richard W. Dowell, and Frederic E. Rusch, *Theodore Dreiser: A Primary Bibliography and Reference Guide*, 2d ed. (Boston: G. K. Hall, 1991), 5.

2. Theodore Dreiser to William C. Lengel, 15 October 1911, in Robert H. Elias, ed., *Letters of Theodore Dreiser: A Selection*, 3 vols. (Philadelphia: University of Pennsylvania Press, 1959), 1:122.

3. Grant Richards to Theodore Dreiser, 6 March 1908, Theodore Dreiser Papers, Annenberg Rare Book and Manuscript Library, University of Pennsylvania, Philadelphia.

4. Richards to Dreiser, 9 June 1909 and 13 June 1910, Archives of Grant Richards, reel 15, letter 509, and reel 17, letter 296, Rare Book and Special Collections Library of the University of Illinois, Urbana; Richards to Dreiser, 22 November 1910, Theodore Dreiser Papers. See also Lucia A. Kinsaul, "The Letters of Grant Richards to Theodore Dreiser: 1905–1914" (M.A. thesis, Florida State University, 1990).

5. For example, in his memoirs Richards dates their encounter 13 November, whereas Dreiser, having called and left a note on 4 November, has them meet the following day for breakfast. See Grant Richards, *Author Hunting: Memories of Years Spent Mainly in Publishing* (1934; London: Unicorn, 1948), chaps. 15–16; Dreiser to Richards, 4 November 1911, *Letters of Theodore Dreiser*, ed. Elias, 1:125; Thomas P. Riggio, ed., "Dreiser: Autobiographical Fragment, 1911," *Dreiser Studies* 18, no. 1 (Spring 1987): 15; and Dreiser's narrative in this edition of *A Traveler at Forty*, 8–9.

6. Frank H. Scott, president of the Century Company, to Dreiser, 18 November 1911, Dreiser Papers.

7. Dreiser to H. L. Mencken, 11 November 1911, in Thomas P. Riggio, ed., *Dreiser-Mencken Letters: The Correspondence of Theodore Dreiser and H. L. Mencken, 1907–1945*, 2 vols. (Philadelphia: University of Pennsylvania Press, 1986), 1:82–83. Dreiser took a big case of clippings on his travels through Europe. Richards describes how on 30 December, near the end of Dreiser's stay in England, the adverse criticism in the *London Nation*—due to anti-German and anti-American sentiment—spoiled these hopes; see *Author Hunting*, 157. Dreiser notes in his diary on 6 January that he decided against having an interview, citing "[n]o London interest" (Dreiser Papers).

8. See p. 12 of this volume.

9. See Riggio, ed., "Dreiser: Autobiographical Fragment," 12–21.

10. For a more detailed discussion of Dreiser's method of working, see Renate von Bardeleben, "Dreiser's Diaristic Mode," *Dreiser Studies* 31, no. 1 (Spring 2000): 26–42; von Bardeleben, "Dreiser's English Virgil," in *Literatur im Kontext—Literature in Context: Festschrift für Horst W. Drescher zum 60. Geburtstag*, ed. Joachim Schwend, Susanne Hagemann, and Hermann Völkel, Scottish Studies 14 (Frankfurt: Peter Lang, 1992), 362–64.

11. See pp. 78, 96, 108–9, and 236 of this volume.

12. Richards to Dreiser, 24 January 1912, Dreiser Papers.

13. The diary notes in the Dreiser Papers cover the period from 4 December 1911 to 25 April 1912.

14. *A Traveler at Forty* (New York: Century, 1913), 329–35. The narrator, called Mrs. Q. in the 1913 edition, is Rella Abell Armstrong; see Dreiser's diary notes of 16, 17, and 23 February 1912.

15. See "1st Typescript," 223, Dreiser Papers, and appendix. The preceding sentences, by which Dreiser introduced the anecdote, were omitted in the 1913 edition.

16. Richards to Dreiser, 27 March 1912, Dreiser Papers.

17. See the file boxes of the diary notes, Dreiser Papers.

18. See boxes with postcards, Dreiser Papers.

19. Grant Richards and Pauline Hemmerde to Dreiser, 29 December 1911, Dreiser Papers.

20. Richards to Dreiser, 30 April 1913, Dreiser Papers. Richards had published various travel guides written by his uncle Grant Allen, including *Florence* (1897), *Paris* (1897), and *Venice* (1898), and a guide to Paris (1908) written by Leonard Williams. Richards himself later wrote and published a travel guide to the French Riviera under the title *The Coast of Pleasure* (London, 1928).

21. "1st Typescript," 638–40.

22. Dreiser to Richards, 26 May 1912, *Letters of Theodore Dreiser*, 1:144.

23. Richard Lingeman, *Theodore Dreiser*, vol. 2: *An American Journey 1908–1945* (New York: Putnam, 1990), 68.

24. Robert Underwood Johnson to Dreiser, 11 July 1912, Dreiser Papers.

25. Douglas Z. Doty to Dreiser, 28 September 1912, Dreiser Papers.

26. Doty to Dreiser, 13 November 1912, Dreiser Papers.

27. Ibid.

28. See Richards to Dreiser, 27 July and 8 August 1912, Dreiser Papers.

29. See Richards's account in *Author Hunting*, 154.

30. Richards to Doty, 12 December 1912, qtd. in Lingeman, *Theodore Dreiser*, 70.

31. Dreiser to Mencken, 30 December 1912, in *Dreiser-Mencken Letters*, ed. Riggio, 1:113.

32. Doty to Dreiser, 6 January 1913, Dreiser Papers.

33. A survey of the typing expenses from 31 December 1912 to November 1913 was provided in the monthly statement of Dreiser's then current account with the Century Company on 31 March 1914; see Dreiser Papers.

34. Dreiser to Mencken, 26 May 1912, in *Dreiser-Mencken Letters*, ed. Riggio, 1:94.

35. Doty to Dreiser, 27 January 1913, Dreiser Papers.

36. Cynthia Ozick, "Annals of the Temple: 1918–1927," *Portrait of the Artist as a Bad Character and Other Essays on Writing* (Chatham, Kent: PIMLICO, 1996), 265; see also 265–79.

37. Doty to Dreiser, 26 April 1913, Dreiser Papers.

38. Doty to Dreiser, 27 May 1913, Dreiser Papers.

39. James Abbott to Dreiser, 6 June 1913, Dreiser Papers.

40. Archived at University of Pennsylvania's Dreiser Papers collection. The arrangement of this text differs considerably from the book's.

41. Dreiser to Mencken, 10 November 1913, in *Dreiser-Mencken Letters*, ed. Riggio, 1:124. Both the First Typescript and the Revised Typescript have only a few chapter titles.

42. For typewriting costs from 31 December 1912 through 27 March 1913, see the

statement of Dreiser's account with the Century Company, 31 March 1914, Dreiser Papers.

43. Doty to Dreiser, 18 October 1913, Dreiser Papers.

44. Mencken to Dreiser, 16 November 1913, in *Dreiser-Mencken Letters*, ed. Riggio, 1:125.

45. See also Thomas P. Riggio, "Europe without Baedeker: The Omitted Hanscha Jower Story—from *A Traveler at Forty*," *Modern Fiction Studies* 23 (1977): 423–40.

46. Mencken to Dreiser, 16 November 1913, in *Dreiser-Mencken Letters*, ed. Riggio, 1:125.

47. See von Bardeleben, "Dreiser's English Virgil," 366–67.

48. For a more detailed discussion of the major themes in *A Traveler at Forty*, see Renate von Bardeleben, "Central Europe in Travelogues by Theodore Dreiser: Images of Berlin and Vienna," in *Images of Central Europe in Travelogues and Fiction by North American Writers*, ed. Waldemar Zacharasiewicz, 144–58 (Tübingen: Stauffenburg, 1995); idem, "Theodore Dreiser's European Encounters: The Case of Oxford," in *Transatlantic Encounters: Studies in European-American Relations; Presented to Winfried Herget*, ed. Udo J. Hebel and Karl Ortseifen, 232–44 (Trier: Wissenschaftlicher Verlag Trier, 1995); and idem, "The Shock of the Ancestral Quest: Theodore Dreiser's *A Traveler at Forty* and Cynthia Ozick's *The Messiah of Stockholm*," in *The Self at Risk in English Literatures and Other Landscapes: Honoring Brigitte Scheer-Schäzler on the Occasion of her 60th Birthday*, ed. Gudrun M. Grabher and Sonja Bahn-Coblans, 95–108 (Innsbruck: Institut für Sprachwissenschaft der Universität Innsbruck, 1999).

49. E.g., "1st Typescript," chaps. 2 and 3.

50. E.g., "Revised Typescript," 10, Dreiser Papers.

51. "1st Typescript," pp. 15, 43, 46, and 49–52.

52. Chapters 84, 85, and 87; they were first published by Thomas P. Riggio in "Europe without Baedeker," 423–40.

53. See chapter 49.

54. Dreiser to Mencken, 18 November 1913, in *Dreiser-Mencken Letters*, ed. Riggio, 1:127.

55. See the scrapbook on *A Traveler at Forty*, Dreiser Papers; Jack Salzman, ed., *Theodore Dreiser: The Critical Reception* (New York: David Lewis, 1972), 141–68.

56. Doty to Dreiser, 18 December 1913, Dreiser Papers.

57. E. F. Edgett, *Boston Evening Transcript*, 3 December 1913; repr. in Salzman, *Theodore Dreiser*, 141–42, quotation at 141.

58. *San Francisco Bulletin*, 6 December 1913; repr. in Salzman, *Theodore Dreiser*, 145.

59. Israel Solon, "A Novelist in Europe," *Chicago Evening Post*, 5 December 1913; W. J. C., *Detroit Tribune*, 21 December 1913; H. L. Mencken, "Anything But Novels," *Smart Set* 42 (Feb. 1914): 153–54; *Washington Evening Star*, 20 December 1913; all repr. in Salzman, *Theodore Dreiser*, 142–43, 150, 152, 159–60, quotations at 142, 150, 152, 159.

60. *Life*, 22 January 1914; "Mr. Dreiser," *New York Times Review of Books*, 763; both repr. in Salzman, *Theodore Dreiser*, 152–54, 156, quotations at 154, 156.

61. Dreiser to Mabel Cheyney, 6 April 1914, Swarthmore Library, Swarthmore, Pennsylvania. Dreiser describes an encounter with the correspondent, Mabel Cheyney, in a diary fragment from April 1914; see Theodore Dreiser, *American Diaries 1902–1926*, ed. Thomas P. Riggio (Philadelphia: University of Pennsylvania Press, 1982), 447–48.

62. The dull red used for the first two printings' cloth covers became much more lively in the third printing.

63. Richards, *Author Hunting*, 154.

64. The title page says "1920," but Horace Liveright lists "December 1919" for the fourth printing. For the exact date, see George L. Wheelock to Dreiser, 28 February 1920, Dreiser Papers.

65. Wheelock to Dreiser, 17 March 1920, Dreiser Papers.

66. Wheelock to Dreiser, 12 March 1923, Dreiser Papers. The Century Company demanded $1,000, "stock to be taken over in addition at cost price."

67. Horace Liveright to Dreiser, 16 March 1923, Dreiser Papers.

68. W. B. Jones to Dreiser, 20 November 1926, Dreiser Papers.

69. See the diary notes of her trip, archived in the Dreiser Papers. Kubitz stayed in Germany from 24 July to 1 September 1912.

70. Dreiser, *American Diaries*, 160.

71. Ibid., 161.

72. Ibid., 162.

73. Ibid., 169.

74. In a passage on the collector W. W. Lange, Vrest Orton claims that the holograph was destroyed; see Orton, *Dreiserana: A Book about His Books* (New York: Haskell House, 1973), 75.

Theodore Dreiser

(Annenberg Rare Book and Manuscript Library, University of Pennsylvania)

The *Mauretania*

Julia Culp

(Friese Pers Boekerij/Uitgeverij Noordboek)

Theodore Dreiser, Grant Richards, and Sir Hugh Lane at Cap Martin

(Annenberg Rare Book and Manuscript Library, University of Pennsylvania)

Charles Tyson Yerkes

(National Portrait Gallery, Smithsonian Institution)

HISTORICAL NOTES

Notes are supplied for persons, places, historical background, literary quotations or allusions, abbreviations, colloquialisms, and foreign words or phrases. The editor has tried to identify all significant persons and places mentioned in the text and to provide all relevant information whenever available. In a few cases it has not been possible to trace persons, because either too much time has elapsed or no additional records exist.

Each note is preceded by a page and line reference that indicates the subject's location in this edition. Running heads, chapter titles, and blank lines were not counted in assigning these numerical references. The keywords or -phrases are set in boldface type.

In addition to standard dictionaries, encyclopedias, guidebooks, and biographical works, the following sources have been consulted:

Abrams, M. H., gen. ed. *The Norton Anthology of English Literature*. 5th ed. New York: Norton, 1986.

Alighieri, Dante. *The Divine Comedy*. Trans. Carlyle-Wicksteed. New York: Random House, 1944.

The Association of Research Libraries. *A Catalog of Books Represented by Library of Congress Printed Cards*. New York: Pageant, 1959.

Baedeker Belgium and Holland including the Grand-Duchy of Luxembourg. Leipzig: Karl Baedeker, 1910.

Baedeker Berlin and Environs: Handbook for Travellers. Leipzig: Karl Baedeker, 1912.

Baedeker Central Italy and Rome: Handbook for Travellers. Leipzig: Karl Baedeker, 1909.

Baedeker Großbritannien: England (außer London), Wales, Schottland, und Irland; Handbuch für Reisende. Leipzig: Karl Baedeker, 1899.

Baedeker Italien: Handbuch für Reisende; Erster Teil Ober-Italien, Ligurien, das [sic] *nördliche Toskana*. Leipzig: Karl Baedeker, 1891.

Baedeker Italien von den Alpen bis Neapel: Kurzes Reisehandbuch. Leipzig: Karl Baedeker, 1926.

Baedeker London und Umgebung: Handbuch für Reisende. Leipzig: Karl Baedeker, 1909.

Baedeker Mittelitalien und Rom: Handbuch für Reisende. Leipzig: Karl Baedeker, 1908.

Baedeker's Northern France from Belgium and the English Channel to the Loire Excluding Paris and Its Environs: Handbook for Travellers. Leipsic [*sic*]: Karl Baedeker, 1894.

Baedeker's Northern Italy. Leipsic [*sic*]: Karl Baedeker, 1895.

Baedeker's Paris and Its Environs with Routes from London to Paris. Leipsic [*sic*]: Karl Baedeker, 1900.

Baedeker's the Rhine including the Black Forest and the Vosges. Leipzig: Karl Baedeker, 1911.

Baedeker Die Riviera; Das südöstliche Frankreich; Korsika. Leipzig: Karl Baedeker, 1906.

Baedeker's Southern France from the Loire to the Spanish and Italian Frontiers including Corsica: Handbook for Travellers. Leipsic [*sic*]: Karl Baedeker, 1891.

Baedeker Die Schweiz nebst den angrenzenden Teilen von Oberitalien, Savoyen, und Tirol. Leipzig: Karl Baedeker, 1909.

Balzac, Honoré de. *La Comédie humaine*. Dijon: Imprimerie Bibliothèque de la Pléiade, 1952.

Bartlett, John. *Familiar Quotations: A Collection of Passages, Phrases, and Proverbs Traced to Their Sources in Ancient and Modern Literature*. 15th ed. Boston: Little, Brown, 1980.

Blackbeard, Bill, ed. *100 Jahre Comic-Strips*. 2 vols. Hamburg: Carlsen, 1995.

Boyer, Paul S., Clifford E. Clark Jr., Joseph F. Kett, Neal Salisbury, Harvard Sitkoff, and Nancy Woloch, eds. *The Enduring Vision: A History of the American People*. 3d ed. Lexington, Mass.: Heath, 1996.

Brown, Joanna Cullen. *Figures in a Wessex Landscape: Thomas Hardy's Picture of English Country Life*. London: W. H. Allen, 1987.

Browning, Robert. *The Poetical Works of Robert Browning*. Oxford: Oxford University Press, 1905.

Brüllmann, Richard. *Lexikon der Martin Luther–Zitate*. Wiesbaden: VMA Verlag, 1983.

Butt, John, ed. *Wordsworth: Selected Poetry and Prose*. Oxford: Oxford University Press, 1964.

Castle, Charles. *La Belle Otéro: The Last Great Courtesan*. London: M. Joseph, 1981.

Chalon, Jean. *Liane de Pougy: courtisane, princesse, et sainte*. Paris: Flammarion, 1994.

Cook, Jean M., ed. *Great Marlow: Parish and People in the Nineteenth Century*. 1991. Marlow: Marten, 1992.

Cruickshank, J. W., and A. M. Cruickshank. *The Umbrian Towns*. Grant Allen's Historical Guides Series. [London: Grant Richards, 1901.] New York: Wessels, 1902.

Darby, Stephen. *Place and Field Names, Cookham Parish, Berkshire*. N.p.: n.p. ["for private circulation"], 1899.

de Sabincourt, Ernest, ed. *The Poetical Works of Wordsworth*. Rev. ed. Ed. Thomas Hutchinson. London: Oxford University Press, 1936.

Dickens, Charles. *The Personal History of David Copperfield*. London: Cassell, 1867.

Dictionary of National Biography. Ed. Sir Leslie Stephen and Sir Sidney Lee. Oxford: Oxford University Press, 1993.

Drabble, Margaret, ed. *The Oxford Companion to English Literature*. Rev. ed. Oxford: Oxford University Press, 1998.

Dreiser, Theodore. *American Diaries 1902–1926*. Ed. Thomas P. Riggio. Philadelphia: University of Pennsylvania Press, 1982.

———. "Dreiser: Autobiographical Fragment, 1911." Ed. Thomas P. Riggio. *Dreiser Studies* 18, no. 1 (Spring 1987): 12–21.

———. *Dawn: An Autobiography of Early Youth*. 1931. Ed. T. D. Nostwich. Santa Rosa, Calif.: Black Sparrow, 1998.

———. *The Financier*. 1912. New York: New American Library, 1967.

———. "The First Voyage Over." *Century Magazine* 86 (Aug. 1913): 586–95.

———. *Jennie Gerhardt*. 1911. Ed. James L. W. West III. Philadelphia: University of Pennsylvania Press, 1992.

———. "Lilly Edwards: An Episode." *Smart Set* 40 (June 1913): 81–86.

———. *Newspaper Days*. 1922. Ed. T. D. Nostwich. Philadelphia: University of Pennsylvania Press, 1991.

———. "Paris." *Century Magazine* 86 (Oct. 1913): 904–15.

———. *A Traveler at Forty*. New York: Century, 1913.

———. "An Uncommercial Traveler in London." *Century Magazine* 86 (Sept. 1913): 736–49.

Eagle, Dorothy, and Meic Stephens, eds. *The Oxford Illustrated Literary Guide to Great Britain and Ireland*. 1981. 2d ed. Oxford: Oxford University Press, 1992.

Elias, Robert H., ed. *Letters of Theodore Dreiser: A Selection*. Philadelphia: University of Pennsylvania Press, 1959.

Ellsworth, William Webster. *A Golden Age of Authors: A Publisher's Recollection*. Boston: Houghton, [1919].

Enciclopedia italiana di scienze, lettere, ed arti. Rome: Istituto della Enciclopedia Italiana, 1949–2001.

Enciclopedia universal ilustrada europeo-americana. Madrid: Espasa-Calpe, 1958.

Encyclopédie des citations. Comp. P. Dupré. Paris: Éditions de Trévise, 1959.

Foner, Eric, and John A. Garraty, eds. *The Reader's Companion to American History*. Boston: Houghton Mifflin, 1991.

Frauenholz, Eugen von. *Das Heerwesen des XIX. Jahrhunderts*. Munich: Beck, 1941.

Gill, Stephen, ed. *William Wordsworth*. Oxford: Oxford University Press, 1984.

Die Gothaischen Genealogischen Taschenbücher des Adels. Freiherrliche Häuser B. Gotha: Justus Perthes, 1937.

Grand Larousse encyclopédique. Paris: Librairie Larousse, 1964.

Grant [Blairfindie] Allen, Charles. *Florence*. Grant Allen's Historical Guides. London: Grant Richards, 1897.

———. *Paris*. Grant Allen's Historical Guides. London: Grant Richards, 1897.

———. *Venice*. Grant Allen's Historical Guides. London: Grant Richards, 1898.

Green, V. H. H. *A History of Oxford University*. London: B. T. Batsford, 1974.

Grillandi, Massimo. *La bella Otéro*. 2d ed. Milan: Rusconi, 1980.

Grote Winkler Prins Encyclopedie. 25 vols. Amsterdam: Elsevier, 1980.

Guide through Mayence and Environs. Mainz: Verkehrsverein Mainz, 1911.

Hardy, Thomas. *Tess of the d'Urbervilles: A Pure Woman*. 1891. Intro. P. N. Furbank. The New Wessex Edition. London: Macmillan, 1975.

Hart, James D. *The Oxford Companion to American Literature*. 4th ed. New York: Oxford University Press, 1968.

Hartnoll, Phyllis, ed. *The Oxford Companion to the Theatre*. 4th ed. Oxford: Oxford University Press, 1983.

Historische Kommission bei der bayerischen Akademie der Wissenschaften, ed. *Neue deutsche Biographie*. Berlin: Duncker und Humblot, 1964.

The Holy Bible and International Bible Encyclopedia . . . Authorized or King James Version. New York: Garden City, 1940.

Horn, Maurice, ed. *The World Encyclopedia of Cartoons*. 2d ed. Philadelphia: Chelsea House, 1999.

———, ed. *The World Encyclopedia of Comics*. Rev. ed. Philadelphia: Chelsea House, 1999.

Hugo, Victor. *Les Misérables*. London: Penguin, 1982.

Der illustrierte Ploetz: Weltgeschichte in Daten und Bildern von den Anfängen bis zur Gegenwart. Würzburg: Ploetz, 1973.

Information Leaflet, Holy Trinity Church, Penn. Penn, U.K.: n.p., n.d.

Irving, Washington. *The Sketch Book of Geoffrey Crayon, Gent*. 1819–20. Ed. Haskell Springer. Complete Works of Washington Irving, vol. 8. Boston: Twayne, 1978.

James, Henry. *The Wings of the Dove*. 1902. Harmondsworth: Penguin, 1965.

Jeffares, A. Norman. *George Moore*. London: F. Fildner, 1965.

Jeffrey, David Lyle, gen. ed. *A Dictionary of Biblical Tradition in English Literature*. Grand Rapids, Mich.: Eerdmans, 1992.

Jens, Walter, ed. *Kindlers Neues Literatur Lexikon*. Munich: Kindler, 1992.

Johnson, Robert Underwood. *Remembered Yesterdays*. Boston: Little, Brown, 1923.

Kershner, R. Brandon. *Joyce, Bakhtin, and Popular Literature: Chronicles of Disorder*. Chapel Hill: University of North Carolina Press, 1989.

Kipling, Rudyard. *Plain Tales from the Hills*. New York: Manhattan, n.d.

Kleber, John E., ed. *The Kentucky Encyclopedia*. Lexington: University Press of Kentucky, 1992.

Leitermann, Heinz. *Zweitausend Jahre Mainz: Bilder aus der Mainzer Geschichte*. Mainz: Verlag Dr. Hanns Krach, 1962.

Letters of Grant Richards to Theodore Dreiser, 1905–14. Archives of Grant Richards. British Publishers Archives on Microfilm. Cambridge: Chadwyck-Healey, 1981.

Lewis, Arthur H. *La Belle Otéro*. New York: Trident, 1967.

Lingeman, Richard. *Sinclair Lewis: Rebel from Main Street*. New York: Random House, 2002.

———. *Theodore Dreiser*. Vol. 1: *At the Gates of the City 1871–1907*. New York: Putnam's, 1986.

———. *Theodore Dreiser*. Vol. 2: *An American Journey 1908–1945*. New York: Putnam's, 1990.

Lord, Walter. *A Night to Remember*. New York: Holt, 1955.

Magnusson, Magnus, gen. ed. *Chambers Biographical Dictionary*. Edinburgh: W. and R. Chambers, 1990.

Martini de Chateauneuf, Charles. *M'En Avisou: Menton à la Belle Epoque*. Breil-sur-Roya: Editions du Cabri, 1990.

McCart, Neil. *Atlantic Liners of the Cunard Line from 1884 to the Present Day*. Wellingborough: Patrick Stephens, 1990.

McCormick, David, ed. *Scottish Literature: An Anthology*. Vol. 1. New York: Lang, 1996.

Mencken, H. L. My *Life as Author and Editor*. Ed. Jonathan Yardley. New York: Knopf, 1993.

Mills, A. D. *A Dictionary of English Place Names*. 1991. Oxford: Oxford University Press, 1994.

Moore, George. *Memoirs of My Dead Life*. London: Heinemann, 1928.

Morton, Peter, comp. *Grant Allen (1848–1899): A Bibliography*. Queensland: University of Queensland Press, 2002.

Mott, Frank Luther. *A History of American Magazines*. Vol. 4: 1885–1905. Cambridge, Mass.: Belknap, 1957.

———. *A History of American Magazines*. Vol. 5: *Sketches of 21 Magazines, 1905–1930*. Cambridge, Mass.: Belknap, 1968.

Mumby, Frank Arthur. *Publishing and Bookselling: A History from the Earliest Times to the Present Day*. London: Jonathan Cape, 1954.

Das Neue Lexikon der Musik. Stuttgart: Metzler, 1996.

New Dictionary of American Slang. Ed. Robert L. Chapman. New York: Harper, 1986.

Nicholson, Harold. *King George the Fifth: His Life and Reign*. London: Constable, 1953.

Noyes, Russell. *William Wordsworth*. Rev. ed. Boston: Twayne, 1991.

Ochaim, Brygida, and Claudia Balk, eds. *Varieté-Tänzerinnen um 1900: Vom Sinnenrausch zur Tanzmoderne*. Frankfurt: Stroemfeld, 1998.

Osborne, Harold, ed. *The Oxford Companion to Art*. Oxford: Clarendon, 1970.
Otéro, Caroline. *Les Souvenirs et la vie intime de la belle Otéro*. Ed. Claude Valmont. Paris: Editions Le Calame, 1926.
Ousby, Ian. *The Englishman's England: Taste, Travel, and the Rise of Tourism*. Cambridge: Cambridge University Press, 1990.
Partridge, Eric. *A Dictionary of Slang and Unconventional English*. London: Routledge and Kegan Paul, 1984.
Perkin, Harold James. *The Rise of Professional Society: England since 1880*. London: Routledge, 1989.
Pizer, Donald, Richard W. Dowell, and Frederic E. Rusch. *Theodore Dreiser: A Primary Bibliography and Reference Guide*. 2d ed. Boston: Hall, 1991.
Poe, Edgar Allan. *Collected Works of Edgar Allan Poe*. Vol. 1: *Poems*. Ed. Thomas Ollive Mabbott. Cambridge: Belknap, 1969.
———. *Essays and Reviews*. 2d printing. Library of America 20. New York: Literary Classics of the United States, 1984.
Pougy, Liane de. *My Blue Notebooks* [*Mes cahiers bleus*]. Trans. Diana Athill. New York: Harper and Row; London: A. Deutsch, 1979.
Priestley, J. B. *The Edwardians*. London: Heinemann, 1970.
Rey, Alain, ed. *Le Petit Robert: Dictionnaire universel des noms propres*. Paris: Dictionnaires Le Robert, 1994.
Richards, Grant. *Author Hunting: Memories of Years Spent Mainly in Publishing*. 1934. London: Unicorn, 1948.
———. *The Coast of Pleasure*. London: Grant Richards, 1928.
———. *Memories of a Misspent Youth, 1872–1896*. London: Heinemann, 1932.
Riehle, Wolfgang. *Geoffrey Chaucer*. Reinbek bei Hamburg: Rowohlt, 1994.
Rosenthal, Harold, and John Warrack. *Concise Oxford Dictionary of Opera*. London: Oxford University Press, 1972.
———. *Dizionario enciclopedico dell'opera lirica*. Oxford: Oxford University Press, 1991.
Rowse, A. L. *Oxford in the History of the Nation*. London: Weidenfeld and Nicolson, 1975.
Schneider, Robert, ed. *Berlin aus der Luft: Zerstörungen einer Stadt 1903–1993*. Berlin: Nicolaische Verlagsbuchhandlung, 1994.
Scholes, Percy A. *The Oxford Companion to Music*. 8th ed. London: Geoffrey Cumberlege/Oxford University Press, 1951.
Schüller, Hans, and Franz-Josef Heyen, eds. *Geschichte von Mayen*. Mayen: Geschichts- und Altertumsverein Mayen, 1991.
Shakespeare, William. *The Complete Works of William Shakespeare*. Ed. John Dover Wilson. London: Guild/Cambridge University Press, 1984.
———. *Henry IV: Part I*. Ed. A. R. Humphreys. The Arden Shakespeare. London: Methuen, 1960.
———. *Macbeth*. Ed. Kenneth Muir. The Arden Shakespeare. London: Methuen, 1951.
Silver, Nathan. *Lost New York*. New York: Weathervane, 1967.
Spevack, Marvin. *The Harvard Concordance to Shakespeare*. Hildesheim: Georg Olms, 1973.
Strong, James. *The Exhaustive Concordance of the Bible*. Nashville, Tenn.: Broadman and Holman, 1994.
Swanberg, W. A. *Dreiser*. New York: Scribner's, 1965.
Twain, Mark. *Mark Twain Speaking*. Ed. Paul Fatout. Iowa City: University of Iowa Press, 1976.

Warren, Mark D., ed. *The Cunard Turbine-Driven Quadruple-Screw Atlantic Liner "Mauretania."* Wellingborough: Patrick Stephens, 1987.

Webster's International Dictionary. Ed. W. T. Harris. London: G. and C. Merriam, 1903.

Wendland, Folkwin. *Der große Tiergarten in Berlin: Seine Geschichte und Entwicklung in fünf Jahrhunderten*. Berlin: Mann, 1993.

Wier, Albert E., ed. *The Book of a Thousand Songs: The World's Largest Collection of the Songs of the People, Containing More than a Thousand Old and New Favorites*. New York: Carl Fischer, 1918.

Williams, Leonard. *Grant Richards's Waistcoat-Pocket Guides: Paris*. London: Grant Richards, [1908].

Wilmeth, Don B., and Tice L. Miller, eds. *Cambridge Guide to American Theatre*. Cambridge: Cambridge University Press, 1993.

Woolley, A. R. *The Clarendon Guide to Oxford*. 5th ed. 1983. Oxford: Oxford University Press, 1990.

Wordsworth, William. *The Prelude; or, Growth of a Poet's Mind*. 1805. Ed. Stephen Gill. London: Oxford University Press, 1970.

CHAPTER I

3.19 ***Jennie Gerhardt*** Published in 1911 after extensive cuts (the original manuscript was reduced from 723 to 425 pages), *Jennie Gerhardt* was Dreiser's second novel and first literary success.

3.22 **"The Financier"** Dreiser's third novel, *The Financier*, is based on the life of the financial tycoon and railway magnate Charles T. Yerkes. With its publication in 1912 by Harper and Brothers, Dreiser was able to give up freelancing and devote himself more fully to his own writing.

3.27 ***Sister Carrie*** Published in 1900 by Doubleday Page and Co., *Sister Carrie* did not initially achieve great commercial success, leading to the author's fears that his publisher was actively suppressing the book.

3.30 **Zola's *Fecundity*** This novel (*Fécondité* [1899]) by Émile Zola (1840–1902) was the first in a series of four novels (*Les Quatre Evangiles*), the last never completed, in which he optimistically depicts social ideals.

3.31 ***An Englishwoman's Love-Letters*** Dreiser refers to a collection of letters by Laurence Housman (1865–1959), originally published anonymously in 1900, which enjoyed some notoriety and was widely parodied at the time.

5.12 **my mother was first a Mennonite and later a convert** Dreiser's mother grew up as the daughter of prosperous Mennonites near Dayton, Ohio. She was disowned by her family, who were militant anti-Catholics, when she ran off and married John Dreiser, a devout Catholic, in 1851.

5.16 **the State University of Indiana** Indiana University at Bloomington (founded 1820). Dreiser was enrolled there for the 1889–90 academic year.

6.15 **"Boy and the Owls"** Dreiser alludes to Wordsworth's "There Was a Boy," which was included in *Lyrical Ballads* (1798). Dreiser probably remembers the poem as "Boy and the Owls" because of its contents and its appearance without a title in *The Prelude* (1799/1850 ed.).

6.41 **Nathan Hale** An American Revolutionary officer, Hale (1755–76) was hanged without trial for spying on the British.

7.4 **owing $175.00 on a piece of land** In a manuscript discovered by Thomas P. Riggio ("Autobiographical Fragment"), Dreiser is more specific: "There is $175 due on a note which completes the payment of two lots at Grand View on the Hudson, N.Y." (17).

7.33 **an old publisher friend of mine in England** Franklin Thomas Grant Richards (1872–1948) founded the World's Classics (now issued by Oxford University Press) and was perhaps best known for having published nearly all of George Bernard Shaw's works.

7.42 ***à la* Joseph Chamberlain** Chamberlain (1836–1914) was a British businessman, social reformer, radical politician, and ardent imperialist having a slight frame, incisive features, and a ribboned monocle.

8.6 **Butterick Publications** Dreiser worked for this publisher of dress patterns and ladies' magazines from 1907 until 1910, when he was fired as a result of a scandal revolving around his extramarital platonic involvement with the eighteen-year-old Thelma Cudlipp, daughter of Annie Ericsson Cudlipp, a widow from Virginia who was an assistant editor and in charge of the company's stenographic pool.

8.9 **Mrs. Dreiser** Dreiser refers to his first wife, Sara Dreiser (1869–1942), née Sara Osborne White, who was called "Jug."

8.37 **the *Bookman*** A respected literary magazine, *The Bookman* was founded by Frank Howard Dodd of Dodd, Mead and Company and ran from 1895 to 1933, publishing such authors as Edith Wharton, Aldous Huxley, and Theodore Dreiser.

9.22 **my friend Mr. Scott tomorrow at the Century** Frank H. Scott was president of the Century Company, the publishing house of the *Century Magazine*, which, like *Harper's*, was a leading illustrated monthly between 1885 and 1913.

9.41 **at the Knickerbocker** Dreiser refers to the Hotel Knickerbocker, located on Forty-second Street at Broadway.

10.21 **family heirloom** The manuscript of *The Financier* has been deposited at the University of Pennsylvania in Philadelphia. Grant Richards's hopes of acquiring the new novel for his publishing house failed.

CHAPTER II

11.2 **my story** Dreiser refers to his novel then in progress, *The Financier*.

11.33 **Mr. Doty** Douglas Z. Doty (1874–1935) served as secretary and editor for the Century Company until 1917 and for the Cosmopolitan Company thereafter. He was responsible for the publication of *A Traveler at Forty* (1913) and also published some of Dreiser's short stories.

12.4 **the Aldine Club** The clubhouse of the Aldine Association, located at Eighteenth Street and Fifth Avenue, formally opened on 12 February 1890. One of the highlights of the Aldine Association's numerous activities was a dinner it gave to Mark Twain on 4 December 1900; see *New York Times*, 5 December 1900.

12.7 **Mr. Johnson** Robert Underwood Johnson (1853–1937) was editor-in-chief (1909–13) for the *Century Magazine*.

12.11 **the Hoffman House** The Hoffman House was located at Broadway and Twenty-fifth Street. In *Newspaper Days* Dreiser describes the hotel as a center for "more smart political and social life."

12.29 **I have obligations to them** Dreiser had already agreed in writing to deliver *The Financier* to Harper and Brothers.

13.13 **"Honor . . . catechism"** From *Henry IV, Part I*, act 5, scene 1: "What is that honour? . . . Who hath it? He that died a-Wednesday. Doth he feel it? No. Doth he hear it? No. 'Tis insensible, then? Yea, to the dead. But will it not live with the living? No. Why? Detraction will not suffer it. Therefore I'll none of it. Honour is a mere scutcheon—and so ends my catechism."

13.22 **Mr. Ellsworth** William Webster Ellsworth (1855–1936) was a vice president at the Century Company in 1911. He became its president in 1912.

14.2 **the late Joe Cannon** This may be a reference to Joseph "Joe" Gurney Cannon (1836–1926), a staunchly conservative Republican and long-term member of the House of Representatives. He left the office of speaker of the House in 1911, which may be the reason for Dreiser's "late" reference.

14.26 **"Of the Shining Slave Makers"** This story appeared as "The Shining Slave Makers" in the June 1901 edition of *Ainslee's* (issue 7, pp. 445–50); when it was revised for *Free and Other Stories* (1918), it was retitled "McEwen of the Shining Slave Makers."

17.6 **Baron R.** Dreiser mentions a letter from a Baron Rodech in a 21 December 1911 diary note. He seems to refer to Freiherr (Baron) Anton Gabriel Cyrill von Rodich, born on 17 September 1872, a retired lieutenant colonel. Rodich had a daughter born to him on 18 May 1910 at Monte Carlo and may have been a gambling acquaintance of Grant Richards, a regular traveler to this pleasure resort. His brother Georg, who died in 1910, had been a consul, and one of his sisters, Helene Marie, was a lady at the court of Prince Leopold Maximilian of Bavaria (1846–1930) of the Wittelsbach dynasty, dating back to the twelfth century. Some members of the Wittelsbach family were kings of Germany and, from 1806 to 1918, kings of Bavaria.

17.7 **the Ritz** The Ritz Company was founded by César Ritz (1850–1918), a Swiss hotel owner who built the first Ritz hotel in Paris in 1898 and then quickly expanded by opening hotels in other major European cities. The New York hotel (the Ritz-Carlton) was located at Madison Avenue and Forty-sixth Street; it was demolished in 1951.

17.8 **Mrs. Havemeyer** Louisine Waldron Elder Havemeyer (1855–1929), known as Mrs. H. O. Havemeyer, was an American philanthropist, advocate for women's suffrage, art collector, and museum patron.

17.10 **Harpers** Harper and Brothers was Dreiser's publisher at the time of his trip to Europe.

22.16 **Miss Burke** Sarah Burke (?–?).

22.25 ***The Easiest Way . . . Sister Carrie*** Eugene Walter's (1874–1941) *The Easiest Way* was performed on Broadway in 1908. The play's main character is a young woman whose talent lies not so much in acting as in her abilities as a mistress.

22.35 ***The Little Millionaire*** Written by George M. Cohan (1878–1942), *The Little Millionaire* was first performed in 1911.

25.12 **the Merry Widow dance** From the highly popular operetta *Die lustige Witwe* (*The Merry Widow*), by the Hungarian composer Franz Lehár (1870–1948).

25.13 **Anna Held** Held (1873–1918) was a French actress who became famous in 1896 via promotions by Florenz Ziegfeld, whom she married in 1897.

26.24 **amiably** Dreiser may be alluding to *Caviare* (London: Grant Richards, 1912), in which Grant Richards disguises himself with the name "Amiable Charles."

27.26 **Corot** Jean-Baptiste-Camille Corot (1796–1875) was a highly influential French landscape artist.

27.26 **Detaille** Édouard Detaille (1848–1912), known for his historical paintings and paintings of soldiers, was one of the nineteenth century's most popular painters, providing accurate, if perhaps chauvinistic, portrayals of the Franco-Prussian War (1870–71).

27.37 **Gainsborough** Thomas Gainsborough (1727–88) was an influential English portrait and landscape artist.

27.39 **"thou . . . eyes"** *Macbeth,* act 3, scene 4: "Thou hast no speculation in those eyes / Which thou dost glare with."

CHAPTER III

30.15 **Mr. Hitchcock** Ripley Hitchcock (1857–1918) was an editor at Harper and Brothers.

30.19 **at the condition of the sales of** *Jennie Gerhardt* Although sales of *Jennie Gerhardt* were expected to rise to 10,000 copies by the end of 1911, Dreiser had been hoping for higher returns and was discouraged.

32.27 **ship** Dreiser was traveling on the *Mauretania* (entry into service: 1907; gross tonnage: 31,938; overall length: 790 feet; breadth: 87 feet, 6 inches), the *Lusitania's* sister ship. For more than two decades the *Mauretania,* built by Swan, Hunter, and Co. in Wallsend-on-Tyne, was known as the "Queen of the Atlantic." It was first launched on 20 September 1906 and made its initial voyage on 16 November 1907 from Liverpool to New York. The ship held the Blue Riband for twenty years and set many new records for crossing the Atlantic. For example, in December 1910 it completed a voyage from Liverpool to New York and back in a little over twelve days. By May 1911 the *Mauretania* averaged 27.04 knots (31.12 mph), and although it was surpassed in size by the *Olympic* (White Star Line), it continued to be the fastest ship for another eighteen years. During World War II it served as a troop transport and a hospital ship. Its last passenger sailing was from Southampton to New York on 30 June 1934. The *Mauretania's* final fate was to be bought for £80,000 by Metal Industries Ltd., of Glasgow, for scrap.

CHAPTER IV

35.34 **Miss Longfellow** Malvina Longfellow (?–?) was an American actress.

35.35 **Mr. Kahn** Otto H(ermann) Kahn (1867–1934) was a Jewish American financier of German descent (he was the youngest son of a Mannheim banking family) and one of the most generous patrons of the arts in U.S. history (for many years he was chairman of the Metropolitan Opera). Despite his many achievements, Kahn was disliked by Dreiser's friend of this period, the journalist and critic H. L. Mencken (1880–1956). In his autobiography *My Life as Editor and Author* (first published in 1993), Mencken describes him as "an extremely offensive Jew who had a great deal of money and was one of the leading figures of New York in his day. He was little more than five feet in height, but he was a very vain fellow and fancied himself as a lady's man" (84). Mencken's attitude may have negatively affected Dreiser's view.

37.11 ***Heimweh*** Dreiser paradoxically uses this German word for "homesickness" at the beginning and the end of *Traveler* to express his sense of America as his true home.

37.40 **George W. Smalley** Smalley had been a London correspondent for the *New York Herald;* see chapter 6, pp. 56, 59, and 62.

39.5 **David Garrick** Garrick (1717–79) was an English actor, producer, dramatist, and poet.

39.5 **Edwin Booth** Booth (1833–93), an American actor, was renowned in his day and best remembered for his portrayal of Hamlet.

42.8 **"the kingdom of heaven . . . cometh not by observation"** Luke 17:20.

43.30 **Karl Kitchen** Karl Kingsley Kitchen (1855–1935) was a New York journalist who wrote for the *New York World, Photoplay Magazine, New York Sun,* and other papers, as well as the author of *The Night Side of Europe as Seen by a Broadwayite Abroad* (Cleveland: David Gibson, 1914) and *Pleasure—If Possible, a Passport to the Gay Life Abroad* (New York: Rae D. Henkle, 1928).

CHAPTER V

49.31 **Shade of Addison** Dreiser refers to Joseph Addison (1672–1719), an English essayist, poet, and dramatist considered a master of English prose and known for his informal style and ability to popularize the ideas of various philosophers.

CHAPTER VI

53.20 **The wreck of the *Bourgogne*** *La Bourgogne,* of the French Compagnie Générale Transatlantique, collided with the British ship *Cromartyshire* on 4 July 1898 and sank, killing 549 people.

53.31 ***The Vista of English Verse*** A collection of English poetry compiled by Henry Spackman Pancoast (1858–1928) and published by Henry Holt, New York, in 1911.

54.30 ***Sands of Pleasure* . . . meeting its author** Dreiser met the author of this book, (Alexander Bell) Filson Young (1876–1938), on 7 December 1911. This encounter is described in chapter 16.

56.22 **Captain Turner** William T. Turner, a Liverpool man who had previously been captain of the *Lusitania,* assumed command of the *Mauretania* in late December 1909 and remained captain until he resumed command of the *Lusitania* shortly before it was torpedoed by a German submarine on 7 May 1915.

56.30 **tuft-hunter** One who meanly or obsequiously courts the acquaintance of persons of rank and title.

58.41 **Velázquez . . . Rembrandt** The Spaniard Diego Rodríguez de Silva y Velázquez (1599–1660) and the Dutchman Rembrandt Harmensz van Rijn (1606–69) were painters known for realism in their portraits.

59.29 **the *Baltic* and the *St. Louis*** Both ships (of the White Star and American Lines, respectively) ran between New York and Liverpool around the turn of the century.

61.36 **the Shuberts** Lee (1875–1953), Samuel S. (1876–1905), and Jacob J. Shubert (1880–1964), successful theatrical managers and producers of the time, founded a chain of theaters bearing their name.

62.9 **the Wallace Collection** The art collection of the earls and marquesses of Hertford, known for its seventeenth- and eighteenth-century French and English paintings and sculptures.

63.7 **Madame de Sévigné** Marie de Rabutin-Chantal, marquise de Sévigné (1626–96), became well known for her long correspondence with her daughter, in which she provides a perceptive account of Paris under Louis XIV.

63.17 **Bernhardt . . . Moore** Sarah Bernhardt (Rosine Bernard [1844–1923]) was an internationally renowned French actress. Coquelin (Constant Coquelin [1841–1909]), also known as Coquelin Aîné, was a French actor; his younger brother Ernst (1848–1909), known as Coquelin Cadet, was a comic actor. Réjane (Gabrielle Réju [1856–1920]) was a Parisian-born French actress who owed her success to her interpretation of a modern repertoire. Edmond Huot de Goncourt (1822–96), born in Nancy, and his brother Jules (1830–70) were French naturalist writers known especially for their *Journal*. Charles-Augustin Sainte-Beuve (1804–69) was a French writer, critic, and literary historian born in Boulogne-sur-Mer. Jules Michelet (1798–1874) was a Parisian-born French historian known for his liberal ideas and his *Histoire de France* and *Histoire de la Révolution*. Guy de Maupassant (1850–93) was a French realist writer. George Augustus Moore (1852–1933) was an Irish novelist who was influenced by Flaubert and Zola and who championed impressionist painters.

64.31 **"Pilate asked what is truth?"** John 18:38.

65.17 **Sir William White** Sir William White, K.C.B. (1845–1913), was a British maritime engineer and renowned ship architect who designed more than 250 warships for the British Admiralty.

65.22 **"Alice, Where Art Thou?"** The lyrics of this popular British song by J. Ascher describe a melancholy man's yearning for his lost ladylove.

66.23 **"I Love a Lassie"** This song was popularized by Sir Harry Lauder (1870–1950), a Scottish music-hall comedian who became famous throughout the English-speaking world as a singer and composer of homely Scottish songs.

66.33 **"true religion and undefiled"** Dreiser alludes to James 1:27: "Pure religion and undefiled before God and the Father is this, To visit the fatherless and widows in their affliction, and to keep himself unspotted from the world."

68.21 **St. Paul writes, "And we being exceedingly tossed with a tempest"** Dreiser quotes Acts 27:18, a reference to the storm Paul encountered during his voyage to Rome.

CHAPTER VII

68.30 **it might be eight-thirty or seven** During the journey the onboard clocks were repeatedly moved forward to match local time, which explains Dreiser's confusion.

68.32 **Kipling's "White Horses"** Rudyard Kipling's (1865–1936) poem "White Horses" was published in 1897. The passage that Dreiser seems to have had in mind is the poem's second stanza, which reads, "*Who holds the rein upon you?* / The latest gale let free. / *What meat is in your mangers?* / The glut of all the sea. / 'Twixt tide and tide's returning / Great store of newly dead,— / The bones of those that faced us, / And the hearts of those that fled."

69.13 **Fishguard** This Welsh port in Pembrokeshire was developed by the Great Western Railway Company as a port of call for the Atlantic liners. Disembarking at Fishguard saved passengers of the first and second classes five hours on the sea journey to London or the Channel ports. Third-class passengers got off at Liverpool. On 30 August 1909 the *Mauretania* became the first ship of the Cunard line to use Fishguard.

69.37 **Watt . . . engine** James Watt (1736–1819), Robert Fulton (1765–1815), and George Stephenson (1781–1848) played important roles in the development of steam power. Watt developed the first economical engine (his "tea kettle"); Fulton applied this engine for use on ships; and Stephenson did the same for use in locomotives.

71.33 **Whistler** James Abbott McNeill Whistler (1834–1903) was an American painter known for his realistic portraits.

72.6 **Offenbach's "Barcarole"** Jacques (né Jacob) Offenbach (1819–80) was a composer whose famous barcarole originally appeared in *Die Rheinnixen* (1864) and was introduced into *Les Contes d'Hoffmann* when this opera was orchestrated posthumously in 1881.

73.3 **Du Maurieresque** George (Louis Palmella Busson) Du Maurier (1834–96) was a British novelist and caricaturist whose illustrations for *Punch* commented on Victorianism.

74.3 **Mrs. Wharton's Jew in *The House of Mirth*** In her novel *The House of Mirth* (1905), Edith Wharton (1862–1937) included the character of Mr. Rosedale, a Jewish financier who wishes to marry the main character, Lily Bart, but only as long as she maintains her position in society.

74.4 **Sam Bernard** Sam Bernard, né Barnett (1863–1927), was an English-born comedian who as a boy made a career for himself in American variety shows (1876–84).

CHAPTER VIII

78.7 **Cookham** A town twenty-seven miles northwest of London where Dreiser was to stay at Grant Richards's country home.

79.20 **coon songs** A then-current slang term for songs sung by American blacks or popular songs meant to resemble these.

80.33 **"dead . . . doornail"** Shakespeare, *Henry VI, Part II*, act 4, scene 10.

81.28 **"The Oceana Roll"** "The Oceana Roll" (1911; music by Lucien Denni, lyrics by Roger Lewis) was a popular ragtime song of the period.

82.8 **family resemblance** Dreiser is describing some of the smaller steamers of the Cunard line, such as the *Campania*, the *Lucania*, the *Ivernia*, the *Saxonia*, the *Pannonia*, the *Slavonia*, the *Carpathia*, the *Caronia*, or the *Carmania*.

82.12 **Oxo. . . . Liebig's** Liebig's Extract of Meat Company was founded in London in 1856. While conducting scientific studies, Justus Freiherr (Baron) von Liebig (1803–73), a German chemist, had invented a meat extract that could be used to flavor soups and drinks.

82.20 **In a collection of essays . . . "The Flight of Pigeons"** Dreiser refers to *The Color of a Great City* (New York: Boni and Liveright, 1923), which includes "The Flight of Pigeons." The essay was first published under his pseudonym "Edward Al" in the *Bohemian*, Oct. 1909.

87.32 **Barrie** The British dramatist and novelist Sir James (Matthew) Barrie (1860–1937) created Peter Pan.

87.33 **Jerome K. Jerome** Jerome K(lapka) Jerome (1859–1927) is best known for his story of a rowing holiday on the Thames, *Three Men in a Boat (to Say Nothing of the Dog)*, published in 1889.

CHAPTER IX

90.22 **George Moore's "Doris" in "The Lovers of Orelay"** This character appears in chapter 8 ("The Lovers of Orelay") of the Irish author George Moore's 1906 novel *Memoirs of My Dead Life*. Moore (1852–1933) describes her in much the same terms as Dreiser does Miss Burke, that is, small, delicate, like a Dresden china figure, and so on.

92.5 **the dead Lucy** Dreiser refers to several poems by William Wordsworth (1770–1850), "Strange Fits of Passion Have I Known," "She Dwelt among the Untrodden Ways," "Three Years She Grew," "A Slumber Did My Spirit Seal," and "I Travelled among Unknown Men," which editors typically group as "The Lucy Poems." In all these poems the poetic persona mourns the death of a girl named Lucy.

92.7 **"The Solitary Reaper"** Written by William Wordsworth in 1805 and published in 1807, the poem tells of a young woman in the Scottish Highlands. It is filled with loneliness and melancholy as it details a "solitary Highland Lass! / Reaping and singing by herself."

92.22 **"Saw you the weird sisters?"** *Macbeth*, act 4, scene 1.

92.23 **"All hail to thee. . . . hereafter!"** *Macbeth*, act 1, scene 3.

92.39 **Thomas Leaf. . . . Tess D'Urberville** Representative of English country life in the nineteenth century, these characters appear in Thomas Hardy's (1840–1928) works: Thomas Leaf, in *Under the Greenwood Tree* (1872); Joseph Poorgrass, in *Far from the Madding Crowd* (1874). The name of the protagonist of Hardy's *Tess of the D'Urbervilles* (1891) is Tess Durbeyfield, not Tess D'Urberville, but her family is said to have descended from the "ancient and knightly family of the d'Urbervilles, who derive their descent from Sir Pagan d'Urberville, that renowned knight who came from Normandy with William the Conqueror."

93.12 **George Inness** Inness (1825–94) was an American landscape painter who sought the mystical in nature, representing it through a wide range of light effects.

93.13 **Turner** Joseph Mallord William Turner (1775–1851) was the foremost English romantic painter and landscape artist, best known for his increasingly abstract portrayals of light, space, and the elemental forces of nature.

94.23 **Mr. T.** Mr. T. is unidentified.

95.38 **One eats his hard-earned crust in the sweat of his face** Genesis 3:19.

96.11 ***Les Misérables*** *Les Misérables* (1862), a portrayal of the life of the poor in the faubourgs of Paris, is perhaps the best-known novel by Victor Hugo (1802–85).

96.39 **Millet. . . . *The Man with the Hoe*** Jean-François Millet (1814–75) was a French painter known for his peasant subjects. His success began with *The Man with the Hoe*, which was exhibited in 1863.

97.37 **Otéro . . . Liane de Pougy at Monte Carlo** Both women were prominent figures in the Parisian demimonde who rivaled for elegance and beauty. Caroline Otéro (1868–1965) was a Spanish-born courtesan and dancer known as "la belle Otéro"; her memoirs were published in 1926 under the title *Les Souvenirs et la vie intime de la belle Otéro*. Liane de Pougy (1869–1950) was a French princess, courtesan, dancer, and writer; her notebooks, *Mes cahiers bleus*, were translated into English and published under the title *My Blue Notebooks* in 1979.

98.39 **Sir Edward Grey. . . . some Moroccan difficulties** Dreiser alludes to one of two Moroccan crises (the first was in 1905–6) in which Germany made a show of aggression in response to France's handling of Moroccan affairs. Although an international treaty gave France policing rights in the country, Germany sent a gunboat to Agadir in July 1911, presumably to protect its economic interests during a local uprising but in reality to test the strength of the British-French alliance. Sir Edward Grey (1862–1933) responded to this provocation in the fall of 1911, indicating that Britain was prepared to defend France against Germany.

101.8 ***Punch*** *Punch; or, The London Charivari* was an English illustrated periodical founded in 1841 and well known for its satiric humor, caricatures, and cartoons. The name originates from Punchinello, the main figure in the Punch and Judy show.

101.8 ***Pick Me Up*** An English illustrated periodical published from 1889 to 1909 by the Pick-Me-Up-Office, in London.

101.11 **W. W. Jacobs** William Wymark Jacobs (1863–1943) was an English author known for his tales of the macabre (e.g., "The Monkey's Paw" [1902]).

101.27 **Miss Hemmerde** Pauline Hemmerde.

102.14 **Omar** Dreiser refers to *The Rubáiyát of Omar Khayyám*, Edward Fitzgerald's (1809–83) translation of the quatrains (or *rubais*) of the eponymous twelfth-century Persian mathematician, astronomer, teacher, and poet. The poem's pessimistic and at times cynical mood, as well as its mocking attitude toward the transience of human grandeur, links *The Rubáiyát* with the motif of *vanitas* in Ecclesiastes (1:2: "Vanity of vanities . . . all is vanity"). Dreiser was deeply impressed by Fitzgerald's rendering of the Persian poet, as can be seen not only in his additional reference to "old Omar" in chapter 92 of *A Traveler at Forty* but also in the concrete intertextual relations between Fitzgerald's translation and Dreiser's later works *The Hand of the Potter* and "The Road I Came" (from *Moods, Philosophical and Emotional* [1935]); the latter work was read by Charlie Chaplin at Dreiser's funeral.

102.15 **"There is a grievous evil I have seen under the sun."** Ecclesiastes 5:13: "There is a sore evil which I have seen under the sun"; Eccl. 6:1 and 10:5: "There is an evil which I have seen under the sun." See also Eccl. 1:9 ("[A]nd there is no new thing under the sun") and the following passages in Ecclesiastes, which might have inspired Dreiser to engage in the preceding meditations and to think of *The Rubáiyát:* "So I returned, and considered all the oppressions that are done under the sun: and behold the tears of such as were oppressed, and they had no comforter; and on the side of their oppressors there was power; but they had no comforter" (4:1); "Then I beheld all the work of God, that a man cannot find out the work that is done under the sun: because though a man labour to seek it out, yet he shall not find it: yea farther; though a wise man think to know it, yet shall he not be able to find it" (8:17).

CHAPTER X

102.23 **Bigfrith** Grant Richards lived in this section of Cookham Dean. In 1609 it was described as an "open wood and common; by estimation 200 acres, well set with young beech."

104.25 **Hamlet's father, his ghost . . . in that tragedy** This quotation, one of the text's many references to death, comes from the first act of *Hamlet,* in which the ghost of Hamlet's father makes its first appearance. The crowing cock heralds the dawn ("cockcrow") and compels the ghost to depart. See act 1, scenes 1 and 2.

105.29 **Burne-Jones-y** Sir Edward Coley Burne-Jones (1833–98) was an English painter whose works exhibited an otherworldly, dreamlike quality corresponding to the qualities Dreiser attributes to Grant Richards's daughter ("spiritual," "delicate," "remote," etc.).

CHAPTER XI

108.22 **Marlow** This parish (town), which contained about 6,000 inhabitants at the beginning of the twentieth century, is located in the Wycombe district, Buckinghamshire, on the River Thames. Dreiser's consistent misspelling of Marlow as "Marlowe" in his manuscript (not corrected in the 1913 edition of *A Traveler at Forty*) illustrates Dreiser's confusion and association of its name with the poet and playwright Christopher Marlowe (1564–93).

111.12 **The Compleat Angler** The inn is named after the eponymous discourse on fishing, first published in 1653, by Izaak Walton (1593–1683), also mentioned in Washington Irving's story "The Angler," in *The Sketch Book of Geoffrey Crayon, Gent.* (1819–20), with which Dreiser was familiar.

111.13 **the church** Dreiser refers to the Great Marlow Parish Church of All Saints (known as the All Saints Church). The church was rebuilt between 1832 and 1835 after damming of the river made the earlier church subject to flooding.

111.14 **The Lion and Elk** Possibly the George and Dragon, an alehouse located behind the church.

111.16 ***Sketch*** A popular English periodical issued by the International News Company in the United States.

111.30 **a list of the resident vicars . . . some long-since-forgotten soul** A plaque inside the All Saints Church records the names in two lists: "Rectors of Marlow: A.D. 1204–1473" and "Vicars of Marlow: 1495–1902."

111.33 **This bridge . . . seventy years before** The structure that Dreiser saw in Great Marlow was a suspension bridge completed in 1831. This bridge succeeded the wooden bridge built in 1789, which had failed after only about forty years because it had been built from wood used in the previous bridge.

115.37 **"Annie Laurie"** This Scottish ballad was based on a poem (presumably written in 1685) by William Douglas (ca. 1672–1748). It is a love song to Annie Laurie, the daughter of Sir Robert Laurie, baronet of Maxwellton.

115.37 **"Auld Lang Syne"** A recasting by Robert Burns (1759–96) of a popular song (probably originally a folk song), published in its final form in 1794.

115.37 **"Sally in Our Alley"** A ballad and love song by Henry Carey (ca. 1687–1743), an English poet, playwright, and musician.

119.9 **"fly"** A light one-horse covered carriage—a hansom or other cab—for hire.

CHAPTER XII

121.26 **the Savile Club** Founded in 1868, this establishment was originally known as the Eclectic Club. In 1869 it was renamed the New Club, and in 1871 it became known as the Savile Club. In 1927 it moved to its present location, 69 Brook Street. The club boasts a strong literary tradition; members have included R. L. Stevenson, Hardy, Yeats, L. Strachey, H. James, and S. Potter.

121.28 **a noble pile** When King Edward VII died in 1910, his consort, Queen Alexandra, moved into Marlborough House.

121.29 **dark-looking building** Although the duke of Portland (William John Arthur Charles James Cavendish-Bentinck [1857–1943]) owned or resided at several locations in the area (Cavendish Square, Grosvenor Square, and Arlington Street), it seems likely that Grant Richards was pointing out the duke's Arlington Street home, for it is closest to Piccadilly.

122.26 **Rittenhouse Square** Named in 1825 to honor David Rittenhouse (1732–96), an astronomer, clock maker, and the first director of the U.S. Mint, Rittenhouse Square (located at Eighteenth and Walnut Streets) was a residential area filled with elegant mansions in Dreiser's time.

123.34 **a certain German singer** Julia B(ertha) Culp (1880–1970), Grant Richards's Dutch singer friend, was then a resident of Berlin and married to Erich Gustav Wilhelm Merten (1869–1933), an engineer. See also historical notes 597.11 and 651.37.

123.39 **Beau Brummell** George Bryan Brummell (1778–1840) was an English dandy and fashion authority at the beginning of the nineteenth century.

125.24 **$2.50 gold piece** Dreiser refers to the gold quarter eagle, which Congress authorized in 1792. The first of these gold coins were delivered to the Philadelphia Mint in 1795.

127.23 **the Plaza** The Plaza Hotel, located at Fifty-ninth Street and Fifth Avenue, was to be a favorite haunt of such literary figures as Sherwood Anderson, John Dos Passos, and F. Scott Fitzgerald.

127.24 **the Manhattan** The Manhattan Beach Hotel, on Long Island, was patronized by millionaires, actors, and important politicians.

127.24 **the Belmont** The Belmont Hotel was located on Park Avenue between Forty-first and Forty-second Streets, across from the Grand Central Terminal; it was demolished in 1939.

127.25 **the Lafayette** The Lafayette Hotel, located at University Place and East Ninth Street, was demolished in 1953.

127.25 **the Brevoort** The Brevoort Hotel, which stood just north of Washington Square, attracted literary figures including Mark Twain and H. L. Mencken. It began to decline just before the turn of the century and was eventually demolished.

128.9 **Mrs. Stoop** Mrs. Stoop is unidentified.

128.19 **Lady O.** Lady O. is unidentified.

128.20 **Miss Villars** Meg Villars (?–?) was an English dancer and later a news correspondent in Paris.

128.31 **Bechstein** Bechstein Hall, located at 36 Wigmore Street, in London, opened in 1901 and was renamed Wigmore Hall in 1918.

128.36 **near Berlin** Julia Culp's house stood in Zehlendorf, which is now a part of Berlin but at that time lay at the outskirts of the city.

129.36 **London subways** This material was developed in *The Stoic*, the third volume of *The Trilogy of Desire*, written between 1928 and 1945 after a second visit to London.

CHAPTER XIII

131.2 **Reynolds** Sir Joshua Reynolds (1723–92), an English portrait painter and aesthetician, dominated English artistic life in the middle and late eighteenth century.

131.2 **Greuze** Jean-Baptiste Greuze (1725–1805) was a French painter and pioneer of anecdotal genre subjects.

131.2 **Cabanel** Alexandre Cabanel (1823–89) was a French painter known for historical paintings.

131.7 **Epstein** Sir Jacob Epstein (1880–1959) was an American portrait sculptor.

131.35 **Réjane** Gabrielle Réju, known as Réjane (1856–1920), was a famous French actress who, after divorcing the theater director Porel in 1905, bought the Nouveau-Théâtre in Paris, later renamed Théâtre Réjane.

131.35 **Mrs. Leslie Carter** Née Caroline Louise Dudley (1862–1937), this American actress was known for her highly dramatic style and was therefore often called the "American Sarah Bernhardt."

132.3 **Joanne** Dreiser refers to Joanne Adolphe Laurent (1813–81), who published travel guides, maps, and geographical dictionaries, mainly on France.

132.5 **warlike goddesses** These are figures in Richard Wagner's (1813–83) opera cycle *The Ring of the Nibelung* (produced 1870–76).

132.34 **Threadneedle Street** The Bank of England stands on this London street; the name is used metonymically for the bank or its directors.

133.25 **Mr. K., a dwarf** Mr. K. is unidentified.

136.6 **Lucrezia Borgia** Lucrezia (1480–1519) was a central figure in the Borgia family; her three marriages served both to establish and to sever the family's political alliances. Dreiser writes about her at length during his trip to Rome; see chapter 51.

136.32 **Henry Lamb** (1883–1960) was an English artist whose work was deemed worthy of major exhibitions in his time.

140.26 **Strathnairn** Hugh Henry Rose, Baron Strathnairn of Strathnairn and Jhansi (1801–85), was an English field marshal and war hero (in India and elsewhere) born and educated in Berlin. The equestrian bronze statue of Strathnairn by E. Onslow Ford is located at the junction of Knightsbridge and Brompton Road and was unveiled in June 1895.

140.33 **the Oratory** Brompton Oratory, also known as the London Oratory of St. Philip Neri, is located on Brompton Road, south of Kensington Gardens, next to the Victoria and Albert Museum.

141.16 **How often . . . signifying nothing!** Dreiser alludes to *Macbeth*, act 5, scene 5: "Out, out, brief candle! / Life's but a walking shadow, a poor player / That struts and frets his hour upon the stage, / And then is heard no more: it is a tale / Told by an idiot, full of sound and fury, / signifying nothing."

142.2 **"I am the vine, ye are the branches"** John 15:4

CHAPTER XIV

143.18 **a typical London chophouse** A restaurant specializing in mutton chops, beefsteaks, and so on.

143.21 **looked like King Edward VII** King Edward was a big man with an impressive beard and a warm personality. He dressed well and had a great appetite, eating five large meals a day. By middle age, he had a forty-eight-inch waist.

143.28 **John Sargent** The American painter John Singer Sargent (1856–1925), born in Boston and educated in Europe, was especially known for his fashionable society portraits, such as *The Sitwell Family*, and his landscapes.

143.28 **Percy Grainger** Percy (Aldridge) Grainger (1882–1961) was an Australian-born American composer, pianist, and conductor.

145.15 **Gill** Dreiser possibly refers to (Arthur) Eric (Rowton) Gill (1882–1940), a British sculptor, engraver, typographer, and writer.

147.7 **Paderewski. . . . Byronic head** Dreiser refers to the Polish composer, pianist, and statesman Ignacy (Jan) Paderewski (1860–1941), who reminds him of Lord Byron (1788–1824).

147.23 **a certain Archibald Russell** Archibald George Blomefield Russell (1879–1955) was an English critic of art and literature known for his work on William Blake (1757–1827).

CHAPTER XV

148.3 **Mr. Eric MacLagan** Eric Robert Dalrymple MacLagan (1879–1951) was an art critic, a translator, and an assistant keeper at the Department of Architecture and Sculpture at the Victoria and Albert Museum, South Kensington.

150.13 **Johnnie** A nickname given to Englishmen in Mediterranean countries.

151.5 **Let him who is without sin cast the first stone** John 8:7

151.14 **Soho** This neighborhood in the city of Westminster, Greater London—bounded by Oxford Street (to the north), Charing Cross Road (to the east), Coventry Street (to the south), Regent Street (to the west), and Piccadilly Circus—was home to famous residents including William Blake, William Hazlitt, and Karl Marx. An animated, multiethnic quarter famous for its restaurants, food shops, and street markets, Soho was and still is one of London's prostitution districts.

151.15 **Cheshire Cheese** An ancient Fleet Street eating-house where the Rhymers Club (including Yeats) met in the 1890s.

153.27 **Lawrence . . . Rubens** Sir Thomas Lawrence (1769–1830) was an English romantic painter; Jean-Antoine Watteau (1684–1721) was, as was Chardin, an eighteenth-century French painter important before the Revolution; Sir Anthony Van Dyck (1599–1641) was a seventeenth-century Flemish painter second only to Rubens in prominence; Peter Paul Rubens (1577–1640) was a Flemish baroque painter and one of the greatest artists of his age.

153.31 **De Quincey** Thomas De Quincey (1785–1859), an English essayist, journalist, and critic, wrote, among other things, *Confessions of an English Opium Eater* (1822/56).

153.31 **Lamb** Charles Lamb (1775–1834) was an English critic, essayist, and poet.

154.40 **a celebrated English novelist and naturalist** Dreiser refers to (Charles) Grant (Blairfindie) Allen (1848–99); see historical note 236.8.

155.29 **Jerrard Grant Allen** A son of Grant Allen, Jerrard (1878–?) was a theatrical agent; he was married to the comedienne Violet Englefield at the time of Dreiser's visit. In 1916 he moved to the United States.

155.34 **where Doctor Johnson lived** Samuel Johnson (1709–84) lived at no. 2 Staple Inn in Holborn from 1759 to 1760.

156.30 **Mrs. Bicknell** Ethel E. Bicknell (?–?) was a British author of travel guides, such as *A Guide to South-West Cornwall* (1902), *The Channel Islands* (1910), and *Paris and Her Treasures* (1913), and of two children's books, *A Dog Book* (1902) and *Praise of the Dog: An Anthology* (1902). Some of these titles were published with Grant Richards, London.

156.33 **an American who came to London to make a fortune** Dreiser refers to Charles Tyson Yerkes (1837–1905), the American railway magnate who built the Chicago transit system and then, in 1900, went to London, where he was responsible for the expansion and electrification of the London Underground. Yerkes inspired Dreiser to write his *Trilogy of Desire: The Financier* (1912), *The Titan* (1914), and *The Stoic* (1947).

157.2 **department store . . . American idea** Although the first department store was the Bon Marché in Paris (founded as a small shop in the early nineteenth century), Dreiser seems here to invoke Chicago's Marshall Field and Company. Founded by Marshall Field (1834–1906) and Levi Zeigler Leiter (1834–1904) in 1868 and located on State Street, for a time it was the largest department store in the world and served as a prototype for all later stores of its kind.

158.1 **John Bull** This conventional personification of England or the English character was invented by the Scottish author John Arbuthnot (1667–1735) for his *History of John Bull* (1712) and popularized in the middle to late nineteenth century by the cartoons published in *Punch*.

158.3 **George Grossmith, Junior** Grossmith (1874–1935) was a British actor-manager, playwright, and well-known figure in musical comedies. The son of the entertainer and light-opera singer George Grossmith, he first appeared on the stage at the Criterion Theatre in 1892.

158.4 **Sir Thomas Lipton** Sir Thomas Johnstone Lipton (1850–1931) was a British merchant and the founder of the Lipton tea empire.

158.33 **Wish Wynne** This music-hall singer is applauded in a 1911 review in the *Pall Mall Gazette* as "a new variety of singer" and "a performer whose every word is of value." The 1913 August edition of *Nash's* includes an article entitled "Wish Wynne: The Hit of the London Season."

159.11 **Hogarth's pictures . . . Joseph Andrews** Dreiser refers to William Hogarth (1697–1764), an English painter and engraver famous for his satirical representations of vanity, hypocrisy, and vice, and Henry Fielding (1707–54), an English novelist and playwright. Dreiser's mention of Joseph Andrews is a reference to Fielding's novel *The History of the Adventures of Joseph Andrews* *and His Friend Mr. Abraham Adams* (1742), in which the main character encounters all manner of thieves and ruffians on the road between London and Somersetshire.

159.35 **"Over the Hill to the Poor House"** This sentimental poem appears in *Farm Ballads* (1873), a collection by Will Carleton (1845–1912). Carleton's other collections include *Farm Legends* (1875) and *City Ballads* (1885). In *Dawn: An Autobiography of Early Youth* (1931) Dreiser writes that the poem always reminded him of his "brother Paul's attitude toward his mother" and that it moved the Dreiser children to tears when it was recited by one of the family's boarders (105–6).

CHAPTER XVI

162.24 **Harlem Casino** A cabaret located at the corner of 124th Street and 7th Avenue.

163.18 **Mr. T.** Mr. T. is unidentified.

164.34 **a Mr. Filson Young** (Alexander Bell) Filson Young (1876–1938) had published *Sands of Pleasure* (1905), the "novel that made a considerable stir," a fictionalization of Young's love affair with a European prostitute. His "subsequent volumes" were *The Wagner Stories* (1907), *Mastersingers*, and *More Mastersingers* (1911). While editor of the *Delineator* (1907–10), Dreiser had published several of Young's short stories at the suggestion of Grant Richards.

165.13 ***English Review*** A journal published in London from 1908 to 1937.

167.2 **the Roman Catholic Cathedral** Dreiser refers to Westminster Cathedral, the principal Roman Catholic church in England, which was built in neo-Byzantine style in the late nineteenth century and was opened in 1903.

167.16 **Grub Street** This term—originally a street in Moorfields in London (renamed Milton Street in 1830) home to many writers working for hire or purely for the money—has become synonymous with literary hackwork; see, for example, George Gissing's novel *New Grub Street* (1891).

CHAPTER XVIII

180.1 **a Welsbach burner** A trademark used for a lamp consisting of a gas burner and a gauze mantle impregnated with cerium and thorium compounds that becomes incandescent when heated by the burner.

180.16 **a certain one somewhere** Dreiser refers to Thelma Cudlipp; see historical note 8.6.

CHAPTER XX

195.18 **Whistler . . . Chelsea** While living in London, Whistler (1834–1903) painted a number of "nocturnes," night scenes of London, particularly of Chelsea.

195.29 **the tall chimneys of Lambeth** At the time of Dreiser's visit, clusters of chimney pots rising from virtually every roof were a characteristic feature of Lambeth and other boroughs of inner London.

197.37 **Lupus Street** Dreiser alludes to the medical meaning of the term *lupus* (Latin for "wolf"), "an ulcerous disease of the skin" (Lat.: *lupus vulgaris*) reminiscent of a wolf's face.

197.39 **coster** Short for "costermonger," a London vendor who sells fruits and vegetables from an open cart.

198.42 **a stranger in a strange land** Exodus 2:22: "And she [Zipporah] bare him [Moses] a son, and he called his name Gershom [from the Hebrew *gur:* "to be a sojourner"]: for he said, I have been a stranger in a strange land." In American literature this phrase or similar phrases and images have been used for scenes of arrival in the New World. In the final chapter of his travelogue, Dreiser gives the motif of the "stranger in a strange land" an ironic twist when he uses it to describe his mixed feelings on returning to the United States; see chapter 103.

CHAPTER XXI

199.13 **John Masefield** John Edward Masefield (1878–1967) was a British author. Dreiser is probably referring to the stir generated by Masefield's narrative poem *The Everlasting Mercy* (1911), which shocked literary orthodoxy with its coarse language.

199.30 **the Whitechapel murders** Jack the Ripper committed his murders in or near the Whitechapel district in 1888.

200.17 **the Great Eastern Railway Goods Station** Presumably Dreiser means the Bishopsgate Goods Depot, which is located just off of Great Eastern Street.

203.39 **costers with buttons all over their clothes** By the mid-1800s the costers had begun mimicking the fashions of the rich by sewing mother-of-pearl buttons onto their clothes. This earned them the nickname "Pearlies."

CHAPTER XXII

204.32 **Baedeker . . . threw it down in disgust** Although elsewhere in *A Traveler at Forty* Dreiser praises Baedeker travel guides for their thoroughness and reliability, here the guidebook's prosaic enumeration of facts blatantly conflicts with his momentary poetic mood.

205.4 **Cleopatra's Needle** Dreiser refers to the Egyptian obelisk that stands in New York's Central Park. In the late nineteenth century the government of Egypt divided a pair of obelisks, giving one to the United States and the other to Great Britain. The second obelisk stands on the Thames embankment in London. They are known as Cleopatra's Needles, although they have no historical connection to the Egyptian queen.

206.21 **London Stone** This small block of limestone is kept behind an iron grill within the exterior wall of the Overseas Chinese Banking Corporation.

206.22 **the site of a house of Chaucer** Chaucer lived above the Aldgate (one of London's city gates) for twelve years beginning in 1373.

206.25 **Billingsgate Market** Principally a fish market, Billingsgate was the oldest market in London until its closure in 1982, when the operation was moved to a large warehouse in the Isle of Dogs area. The original market was situated at the north end of London Bridge, under the monument that commemorates the outbreak of the Great Fire of September 1666.

206.37 **Peck Slip** Together with Ferry, Spruce, Chatham, Catharine, and South Streets, this is one of the areas marking the boundary of Manhattan's Lower East Side.

207.4 **Frans Hals** Hals (1581/85–1666) was a Dutch portraitist famous for his originality and technical ability and best known for his group portraits. Since the nineteenth century, Hals has been considered second only to Rembrandt among seventeenth-century Dutch painters.

209.14 **Sir Thomas More** The humanist and statesman Sir (or Saint) Thomas More (1477–1535) served as chancellor of England (1529–32). He was beheaded for refusing to accept Henry VIII as head of the Church of England. He was canonized on 19 May 1935 by Pius XI and is now recognized as a saint by the Roman Catholic Church.

CHAPTER XXIII

209.33 **Sir Hugh Lane** Sir Hugh Percy Lane (1875–1915) was an Irish art dealer known for his collections of impressionist paintings. Lane set up his own art gallery in London in 1898, established a gallery of modern art in Dublin, and also acted as an adviser to South African art galleries in Johannesburg and Cape Town. He was knighted in 1909 and appointed director of the National Gallery of Ireland in 1914. He died in the sinking of the *Lusitania* on 7 May 1915. The origin of the nickname "Sir Scorp" is explained on p. 378.

210.11 **He had an uncle. . . . Grant Richards's father . . . and there was still another uncle** In his autobiography, *Memories of a Misspent Youth* (1932), Grant Richards details the academic careers of his father, Franklin Richards, and his two uncles, Herbert and John Richards, at Oxford. Franklin Richards received a scholarship at Queen's College, and Herbert Richards and John Richards did the same at Balliol. Richards's father taught Latin and Roman history, first at the University of Glasgow and later as a don in Oxford, where Grant Richards spent most of his childhood and youth.

210.22 **a place called Penn . . . whence William Penn had come originally** Penn is the ancestral village of William Penn (1644–1718), the English Quaker leader and founder of the Commonwealth of Pennsylvania. For over six centuries members of the Penn family have been buried in vaults below the chancel of Penn's Holy Trinity Church.

211.35 **C. H. Shannon** Charles Hazelwood Shannon (1863–1937) was a British lithographer and painter.

211.35 **John Lavery** Sir John Lavery (1856–1941) was a British painter and portrait artist.

211.35 **William Orpen** Sir William Orpen (1878–1931) was a British painter and portrait artist.

211.36 **John Sargent** See historical note 143.28.

212.1 **Christopher Wren . . . Inigo Jones** Sir Christopher Wren (1632–1723) and Inigo Jones (1573–1652) were both English architects.

212.32 **Marlow** See historical note 108.22.

212.35 **High Wycombe, Lane End and Hazlemere** The first is a town and the other two are parishes, all in the county of Buckinghamshire. Their names evoke the quaint and poetic atmosphere Dreiser has in mind.

213.5 **Goldsmith's "Traveller" and "Deserted Village"** Oliver Goldsmith (1730–74) was a British writer. In both these poems, "The Deserted Village" (1770) and "The Traveller" (1764), Goldsmith laments the decline of rural life.

213.5 **Gray's "Elegy"** Thomas Gray (1716–71) was an English poet whose "Elegy Written in a Country Church-Yard" (1751) probably refers to the cemetery at Stoke Poges in Buckinghamshire and expresses the poet's thoughts on "the forefathers of the hamlet."

214.36 **the flight and return of Charles II** Charles II (1630–85), also called the Merry Monarch, reigned as king of England and Ireland from 1660 to 1685, a period in English history known as the Restoration. He was defeated at Worcester by Cromwell in 1651 and became a fugitive. Hunted through England for forty days, he eventually escaped to France in October 1651. He was finally restored to power in 1660 with the help of George Monck, one of his leading generals.

214.36 **"Songs of the North"** This is a reference to a collection of Scottish ballads edited by A. C. Macleod, Harold Boulton, and Malcolm Lawson and published by Leadenhall Press, London, in 1869. The three songs mentioned in the text were rearranged by Percy Grainger (see historical note 143.28).

215.6 **Roman Catholic Cathedral of Westminster** Westminster Cathedral is an archiepiscopal see; it and Liverpool Cathedral are the two most important Catholic churches in England. Located west of Westminster Abbey, it was built in Romanesque-Byzantine style between 1895 and 1903 on the foundations of a previous basilica. Its crypt contains Thomas Becket's miter and what are alleged to be fragments of the Holy Cross.

215.20 **Adam** Robert Adam (1728–92) was a widely imitated Scottish architect.

216.17 **Burns** Robert Burns (1759–96) was a Scottish poet and songwriter. In his highly successful collection *Poems, Chiefly in the Scottish Dialect* (1786) and in *Tam o'Shanter* (1791), Burns both celebrates and satirizes Scottish rural life.

217.4 **Lorenzo the Magnificent** Lorenzo de' Medici (1449–92), who ruled Florence from 1469 until his death, was an immoral and tyrannical ruler but contributed greatly to making Florence prosperous and participated actively in its intellectual achievements.

217.22 **Oscar Hammerstein** Originally from Germany, the inventor, composer, and theatrical manager Hammerstein (1847–1919) immigrated to New York in 1863, where, through a series of inventions, he amassed a large fortune. On 3 December 1906 he opened the Manhattan Opera House, which rivaled the Metropolitan for several years. In 1910 the Metropolitan bought his interests and stipulated that he not produce opera for ten years. After his New York defeat, he went to England, and his London Opera House opened on 13 November 1911. After only one season, however, he returned to New York, where he hoped to once again produce opera, but his legal obligations to the Metropolitan restrained his plans.

217.29 **Koster and Bial's** Koster and Bial's Music Hall was a famous house of light entertainment; it closed on 26 August 1893 when John Koster and Albert Bial moved to their New Music Hall. Their old theater was operating at this time under the name of Bon Ton.

218.36 ***Pelléas et Mélisande . . . Thaïs . . . Louise . . . Salome*** These works are operas by (Achille-) Claude Debussy (1862–1918), Jules Massenet (1842–

1912), Gustave Charpentier (1860–1956), and Richard Strauss (1864–1949), respectively.

218.39 **Gounod** Charles-François Gounod (1818–93) was a French composer, famous for his opera *Faust* (1859).

218.40 **Tetrazzini, Cavalieri, Mary Garden** Luisa Tetrazzini (1871–1940) was an Italian opera singer, as was Lina Cavalieri (1874–1944) who was also married (1913–27) to the tenor Lucien Muratore, whom Dreiser mentions in chapter 98. Mary Garden (1874–1967) was a Scottish opera singer whose portrayal of the title character in Strauss's *Salome* was one of her most celebrated roles; her performance of the "dance of the seven veils" caused a scandal in Chicago.

219.7 **Puccini** Giacomo (Antonio Domenico Michele Secondo Maria) Puccini (1858–1924) was an Italian composer who introduced realism into Italian opera. His operas include *La Bohème* (1896), *Tosca* (1900), and *Madame Butterfly* (1904).

219.37 ***Oxford and Its Colleges* by one J. Wells** Dreiser refers to an illustrated scholarly pocket guide written by J(oseph) Wells (1855–1929) and published by Methuen (London, 1889).

223.7 **Shelley's essay . . . monument** The "Necessity of Atheism" was published anonymously at Oxford in 1811; Shelley's monument is located across from All Souls College.

223.8 **where some English bishops . . . religious beliefs** Dreiser refers to Thomas Cramner (1489–1556), archbishop of Canterbury; Nicholas Ridley (1503–55), bishop of Rochester; and Hugh Latimer (1485–1555), bishop of Worcester. All were Protestant martyrs who were burned at the stake in Oxford's Broad Street during the reign of Queen Mary I.

CHAPTER XXIV

225.28 **Nippur or Nineveh** These were ancient Mesopotamian cities. Nippur, in Sumer, lay south-southeast of Babylon, in what is now Iraq's Muhafazat Ad Qadisiyah. Nineveh, the capital of Assyria, lay to the north along the east bank of the Tigris, opposite modern-day Mosul, in Iraq.

226.6 **he gave Dublin a really fine gallery** See historical note 209.33.

226.18 **Philip Wilson Steer** The Englishman Steer (1860–1942) is considered the greatest British landscape painter of his generation.

226.40 **Van Dycks, van der Neers, de Heems** All three men were painters. Sir Anthony Van Dyck (1599–1641) was Flemish; Aert van der Neer (1603–77) and Jan Davidsz de Heem (1606–83/84) were Dutch.

226.42 **Mancini** Antonio Mancini (1852–1930) was an Italian painter whose work, introduced by John S. Sargent, was celebrated and exhibited in London during the 1870s.

227.3 **Van Dyck . . . John Oxenstierna** Van Dyck's *Johan Oxenstierna* (n.d.) is a portrait of Johan Axelsson Oxenstierna (1611–57), son of Axel Oxenstierna (1583–1654), who was chancellor of Sweden from 1612 until his death.

227.4 **Gustavus Adolphus at the Peace of Münster** These are references to Gustavus Adolphus (1594–1632), king of Sweden (1611–32), and the Peace of Westphalia (1648), ratified in the city of Münster, which concluded the Thirty Years' War (1618–48).

228.24 **Demidoff Rembrandt** The painting by Rembrandt seems to have been owned by Sir Hugh Lane. Demidoff probably refers to the Demidoff family as the former owners. Their villa in San Donato, near Florence, was famous for the artworks it contained.

228.28 **Elizabeth Bas** The portrait of Elizabeth Bas, now exhibited in Amsterdam's Rijksmuseum, was acknowledged as a Rembrandt until 1911, when it was attributed to a pupil of Rembrandt, Ferdinand Bol (1616–80). Although this opinion is still generally accepted, there has been renewed support for Rembrandt as the author.

229.6 **Botticelli** Sandro Botticelli (1445–1510) was an Italian Renaissance painter.

229.19 **Ruysdael's *The Hill of Bentheim*** Jacob (Isaakszoon) van Ruysdael—also spelled Ruisdael (1628/29–82)—painted *Bentheim Castle* (1653), which is likely the object of Dreiser's reference.

229.19 **Snyders's** Frans Snyders (1579–1657) was a Flemish baroque painter.

229.20 **Metsu** Gabriel Metsu (1629–67) was a Dutch painter from Leiden who died in Amsterdam. Metsu is best known for his intimate scenes of middle-class life, for example, *Mother and Sick Child* (Rijksmuseum, ca. 1660).

230.1 **Mrs. Y.** Mrs. Y. is unidentified.

230.31 **We do not live by bread alone** Matthew 4:4.

231.6 **young Jewish architect, Solomon** See textual note 231.6

231.17 **Kaffir's kraal** *Kaffir* or *Kafir* (Arabic: "infidel") is a formerly used (and frequently pejorative) name for the Xhosa, a cluster of related Bantu-speaking tribes living primarily in the Transkei (South Africa); *kraal* refers to an enclosure or a group of houses surrounding an enclosure for livestock, common among some African and particularly South African peoples.

231.33 **"We are all living in terror . . ."** Sir Hugh Lane refers to the third part of George Augustus Moore's autobiography, *Hail and Farewell* (3 vols.), which was published in 1911–14.

232.11 **Spencer** Herbert Spencer (1820–1903) was an English (largely self-taught) philosopher and sociologist whose evolutionary philosophy influenced naturalist writers on both sides of the Atlantic. His magnum opus, *The Synthetic Philosophy* (1896), contains volumes on the principles of biology, psychology, ethics, and sociology.

233.25 **The portrait of Père Tanguy** One of Vincent Willem van Gogh's (1853–90) masterpieces, the work was painted in 1887–88.

233.41 **Fortuny** Mariano José Bernardo Fortuny y Carbo (1838–74) was a Spanish painter known for the brilliant color used in some of his paintings.

233.41 **The *Wayside Christ*** Dreiser refers to (Eugène-Henri-) Paul Gauguin's (1848–1903) *Le Christ jaune* (1889).

234.2 ***Primavera*** Botticelli's *Primavera* was painted in 1477–78 for the Medici family.

CHAPTER XXV

235.14 **"Christmas in England" . . . Washington Irving** Dreiser alludes to Washington Irving's essay "The Christmas Dinner" in *The Sketch Book*.

236.4 **Housman's *A Shropshire Lad*** A(lfred) E(dward) Housman (1859–1936) wrote *A Shropshire Lad* (1896), a series of sixty-three nostalgic poems set in a fictitious area called Shropshire.

236.8 **a famous litterateur** Dreiser refers to Grant Richards's uncle (Charles) Grant (Blairfindie) Allen (1848–99), one of the most prolific authors of the Victorian age. He is best known for the novel *The Woman Who Did* (1895), the story of a woman who refuses to marry her lover because she feels that the marriage laws are unfair to women. The book caused a scandal when it was published.

237.18 **a nearby abbey church** Bisham Church.

238.20 **"This is something like!"** This now-antiquated phrase expresses approval; here it means that the image of the woman was just what Dreiser needed.

242.39 **the protest against state support. . . . "chapel people"** The protest to which Dreiser refers revolved around the Church of England, which all English subjects, including non-Anglicans, had to support. Those who dissented were pushing for the disestablishment of the state church, and because these dissenters generally belonged to Protestant sects that met in their own chapels, they were dubbed "chapel people" by the public at large. Dreiser provides more insight into what was meant by "chapel people" in chapter 28.

243.41 **Sir Robert Hart** Hart (1835–1911) was a British statesman who directed the Chinese customs bureau and satisfied Western demands for an equitable Chinese tariff. He was knighted in 1882 and awarded a baronetcy in 1893.

244.29 **"if my bark sinks, 'tis to another sea"** The line comes from William Ellery Channing's (1780–1842) poem "A Poet's Hope" (1817).

244.37 **ultimate significance** Dreiser here refers to Herbert Spencer's categories of the knowable and the unknowable.

245.4 **"A mighty fortress is our God," sang Luther** From "Ein' feste Burg ist unser Gott" (1529): "A mighty fortress is our God, / A bulwark never failing. / Our helper He amid the flood / Of mortal ills prevailing." See Psalm 46.

250.33 **Pepys** Samuel Pepys (1633–1703) was a naval administrator most famous for his *Diary*, which he kept from 1 January 1660 to 31 May 1669. The work remained in cipher (a system of shorthand) until 1825, when it was deciphered by John Smith. Newly transcribed by R. Latham and W. Matthews (1970–83), it is considered one of the most important diaristic texts in English literature.

CHAPTER XXVI

251.19 **laboring and living conditions . . . agitators** At the time of Dreiser's visit, employee lockouts, squalid living conditions, and the lack of a minimum wage had led to Britain's worst labor difficulties to date. These difficulties included over 870 strikes in the milling, mining, railway, and shipping industries in 1911 alone, as well as periodic violence and street fighting in cities such as Manchester and Birmingham.

251.24 **Mrs. Stubbs . . . K. Kabura** Dreiser's hosts in Manchester were Mr. and Mrs. Stubbs; Mr. Stubbs sold machinery to textile mills around England and in the United States. Dreiser was also introduced to a Mrs. Mitchell, who, he notes, was married to a "Damascus Jew."

252.21 **Earl of Crewe** Dreiser probably means Robert Offley Ashburton Crewe-Milnes (1858–1945), the second baron Houghton (since 1885) and first marquess of Crewe (since 1911). Crewe-Milnes was an influential politician and diplomat, both in Great Britain (e.g., he was the leader of the Liberals in the House of Lords, 1936–44) and in its colonies (e.g., he was Minister for India, 1910–15). The town of Crewe in Cheshire was created when the Grand Junction Railway Company opened its Liverpool-to-Birmingham line in 1837. The company's railway works were transferred to Crewe in 1843. Crewe has continued as a railway center.

252.22 **I was reminded of Pittsburgh** As he relates in *Newspaper Days*, first published in 1922 under the title *A Book about Myself*, Pittsburgh was the location where Dreiser saw the poor living conditions of the steel workers in Carnegie's mills. See chapters 68–77 in the 1991 University of Pennsylvania Press edition of *Newspaper Days*.

254.10 **the Midland** This hotel, located on Peter Street, was subsequently named Holiday Inn Crowne Plaza Midland Manchester.

254.26 **Galt House of Louisville, Kentucky** This sixty-room hotel opened in 1835 and soon earned a national reputation for its excellent food and lodging. It burned down in 1865, but the second Galt House opened in 1869 at First and Main and quickly became the center of Louisville's social scene. The declining hotel was razed in 1921. The latest Galt House was built in 1972 in the grand tradition of its name.

CHAPTER XXVII

257.25 **mill strike. . . . recognition of the unions** As Dreiser's diary notes and as historical studies indicate, the trouble first revolved around a mine workers' strike and then spread to the textile and other industries.

259.21 **"A good name is rather to be chosen than great riches, and loving favour rather than silver and gold."** Proverbs 22:1.

260.38 **football** Dreiser means rugby.

CHAPTER XXVIII

265.41 **blue laws** These laws, regulating the practice of businesses on Sunday, are said to be so named because they were originally printed on blue paper.

266.36 **Pullman** The Pullman Palace Car Company was organized in 1867 by George M. Pullman (1831–97).

267.15 **God save the King . . . we mean the government** Mr. Stubbs is emphasizing the fact that England is a constitutional monarchy and that the British elite view the national anthem's glorification of the king or queen as metaphoric.

267.25 **establish a republic in China** This movement to overthrow the Manchu (Ch'ing) Dynasty (1644–1912) was led by Sun Yat-sen (1866–1925) and culminated at the time of Dreiser's visit to Europe (the Chinese emperor abdicated on 12 February 1912).

CHAPTER XXIX

271.31 **"The Cotter's Saturday Night"** The poem "The Cotter's Saturday Night," written by Robert Burns (1759–96) and published in 1786, describes—among other things—the typical home of a Scottish peasant.

272.3 **the song of the clogs** Dreiser here alludes to the poem "The Song of the Shirt" (1843), by Thomas Hood (1799–1845), which, from the perspective of an underpaid seamstress, deplores the harsh life of the poor working woman. Contemporary artists, including John Leech (1817–64), used the poem's theme for illustrations and caricatures in periodicals such as *Punch*.

273.41 **John Bright** Bright (1811–89) was a British reform politician from Rochdale, Lancashire.

274.1 **Society of Equitable Pioneers** The Rochdale Society of Equitable Pioneers was a cooperative business founded in 1844 as a means for various types of tradespeople to pool their resources and sell their wares.

CHAPTER XXXI

281.9 **the Hon. T. P. O'Connor** Thomas Power O'Connor (1848–1929) was an Irish journalist and politician who was elected as member of Parliament for Galway in 1880 and for Liverpool in 1885. An Irish nationalist, he founded several radical newspapers, including *TP's Weekly* (1902).

281.24 **Mr. M.** Mr. M. is unidentified.

281.31 **Westminster Hall** This was the only portion of the original eleventh-century Westminster Palace to survive the fire of 1834 (its medieval wooden roof was destroyed in 1941). Having been the assembly place for the House of Lords for centuries, it now serves as the entrance to the building.

281.32 **the deposition of Edward II** Hoping to settle the dispute with Charles IV of France over his territories in France, Edward II sent Queen Isabella—his wife and Charles's sister—to mediate. Isabella sided with her brother, however, and together with her lover, Roger de Mortimer, landed in England in 1326, taking Edward captive and forcing him to abdicate.

281.33 **the condemnation of Charles I** Charles's reign (1600–1649) was marked by years of struggle for power between the king and Parliament that eventually led to civil war. Forced by the army, the "Rump Parliament" of only seventy-five members prepared a charge of treason against Charles I. The king was beheaded on 30 January 1649.

281.33 **the trial of Warren Hastings** Warren Hastings (1732–1818), a governor-general of India, was charged with misgovernment and personal corruption. The trial opened in Westminster Hall on 13 February 1788 and lasted more than seven years.

281.34 **the poling of the exhumed head of Cromwell** As a posthumous punishment for the regicide of Charles I, Cromwell's body and those of others were exhumed and hung on the gallows in 1661, twelve years after the king's execution. Cromwell's head was then set on a pole atop Westminster Hall, and his trunk was buried under the gallows.

282.41 **Lloyd George** David Lloyd George (1863–1945), the first earl of Dwyfor, was a Welsh Liberal statesman and social reformer who was elected a member of Parliament for Caernarvon Boroughs in 1890. From 1908 to 1915 he served as chancellor of the Exchequer. His budget for 1909–10, which provided money for social purposes, was rejected by the House of Lords, bringing about a constitutional crisis and leading Parliament to pass an act that renounced the lords' power of veto in 1911.

283.26 **Mr. Bonar Law** Andrew Bonar Law (1848–1923) was a Canadian-born Scottish statesman and Unionist member of Parliament from 1900. In 1911 he succeeded Arthur Balfour as the Unionist leader in the House of Commons.

283.27 **Mr. Winston Churchill** The English statesman Sir Winston Leonard Spencer Churchill (1874–1965), although having been elected a Conservative member of Parliament for Oldham in 1900, joined the Liberal Party in 1906. In 1911 he was appointed First Lord of the British Admiralty.

285.4 **Wellington and Marlborough** Sir Arthur Wellesley (1769–1852), the first duke of Wellington, was the British army commander during the Napoleonic Wars and prime minister of Great Britain (1828–30). John Churchill (1650–1722), the first duke of Marlborough, was a British general.

286.4 **Paul Potter** Potter (1625–54) was a Dutch painter who primarily used animals as subjects.

287.22 **the Fleur de Lys** The Fleur de Lys Inn stood at 34a High Street. First mentioned in 1376, the inn was demolished in 1958 and replaced by a shop.

288.9 **St. Augustine and King Ethelbert** St. Augustine of Canterbury (?–604/605) was the first archbishop of Canterbury; with the support of King Aethelberht (or Ethelbert) I of Kent (560–616), he founded the Christian church in southern England.

288.9 **Thomas à Becket** St. Thomas Becket (1118–70), the archbishop of Canterbury from 1162 to 1170, was murdered in Canterbury Cathedral following a dispute with King Henry II.

288.10 **Laud** William Laud (1573–1645) was an archbishop of Canterbury who was executed by the House of Commons for his persecution of the Puritans.

291.1 **Mrs. Wilkins Freeman** Mary Eleanor Wilkins Freeman (1852–1930) was known for her realistic stories of New England life, the best of which are contained in the collection *A New England Nun* (1891).

291.27 **the Black Prince** Edward the Black Prince (1330–76) was the son and heir apparent to Edward III of England and an important commander in the Hundred Years' War.

292.32 **the monastery of St. Augustine** St. Augustine's Abbey, founded by St. Augustine in 598, following the success of his evangelical mission from Rome to King Ethelbert of Kent, is one of the oldest monastic sites in England.

CHAPTER XXXII

294.22 **Lord Warden Hotel** In 1856 Charles Dickens (1812–70) stayed at the Lord Warden Hotel, then called the Ship, a fictionalized version of which features in *A Tale of Two Cities* (1859). Located on Lord Warden Square close to Snargate Street, the building is now called Southern House and serves as the local headquarters of the Southern Railway company.

295.16 **Bolton** An industrial town near Manchester.

295.21 **coronation of the king and queen at Simla in India** Although King George V was crowned in London on 22 June 1911, he had been planning the unprecedented further step of traveling to India and crowning himself emperor at Delhi. Various complications, however, made this event (on 12 December 1911) not a second coronation but rather a royal audience aimed at calming the growing Indian nationalist movement. While in India the king and queen also visited Simla, a district of Calcutta.

299.16 ***Figaro*** Published in Paris and named for the title character from *The Barber of Seville*, *Le Figaro* was founded in 1826 as a sardonic and witty gossip sheet on the arts.

299.16 ***Gil Blas*** The paper takes its name from Alain-René Lesage's (1668–1747) *Histoire de Gil Blas de Santillane* (1715–35). The novel is generally considered to rank with Cervantes's *Don Quixote* and the works of Rabelais among the greatest foreign influences on eighteenth-century English comic fiction.

300.22 **Amiens** The capital of the Somme district and ancient Picardie and an episcopal see.

301.6 **cathedral** The cathedral at Amiens is the largest in France, famous for its thirteenth-century Gothic style.

301.14 **Villon** François Villon (1431–after 1463), although often associated with brawls, disreputable society, and crime, is considered the finest poet of medieval France.

301.17 **Ruskin** John Ruskin (1819–1900) was an English writer and critic who later became a social reformer. He expressed his philosophy of art in numerous volumes, including the series *Modern Painters* (1843–60), *The Seven Lamps of Architecture* (1849), *The Stones of Venice* (1851–53), and *The Bible of Amiens* (1880–85). He brought about the revival of interest in Gothic architecture and advocated a basically religious aesthetic.

301.17 **Morris** The English artist, architect, designer, novelist, poet, and social reformer William Morris (1834–96) cultivated a passion for medieval art and architecture. He is best known for his utopian socialist fantasy *News from Nowhere* (1890/91), a critical response to Edward Bellamy's (1850–98) *Looking Backward* (1888). Morris's private home, Red House at Bexley, was a significant landmark in English domestic architecture, adopting late Gothic methods to nineteenth-century needs.

302.18 **a treaty between France and Spain** Dreiser refers to the Treaty of Amiens, between France and Spain on the one side and Great Britain on the other, which was signed in 1802 and stipulated, *inter alia*, cessions and restitutions of Continental and overseas possessions.

CHAPTER XXXIII

303.40 **Café de Paris** This establishment, located at 41 Avenue de l'Opéra, was ranked by Baedeker (1900) as a "restaurant of the highest class."

303.41 **Folies-Bergère** Located at Rue Richer, this music hall was built in 1867 on the site of the Colonnes d'Hercule stores, which sold bedsprings ("sommiers"). Designed to entertain its audience with a variety of genres and attractions such as operetta, fantasia, and pantomime, as well as chansons, "gymnastics," and dancing, the establishment opened under the risqué name of Café du Sommier élastique (The Bobbing Bedsprings Cafe) on 2 May 1869. In November 1871 the quick-change artist Sari added a promenade gallery and renamed the music hall "Folies-Bergère."

303.41 **Abbaye de Thélème** This cabaret, located on the Place Pigalle and named after the eponymous utopian abbey in François Rabelais's (1494–1553) *Gargantua et Pantagruel* (1532–64), was known for its liberty and epicureanism ensuing from the fictitious abbey's motto, "Fay ce que vouldras" (Do what you like).

305.24 **E. V. Lucas** Edward Verrall Lucas (1868–1938) was a British journalist and essayist.

306.4 **Hôtel Normandy** Although Baedeker (1900) lists this hotel, located at 7 Rue de l'Echelle and 256 Rue St-Honoré near the Opéra, the guide omits it from the category "Hotels of the Highest Class" and instead describes it as being "of almost equal rank."

307.25 **Greuze . . . soft, buxom, ruddy womanhood** Jean-Baptiste Greuze is valued not only for his genre paintings but also for his unmoralized portraits of girls and women, for which his wife usually served as model (e.g., *Girl with Doves*, Wallace Collection); see the historical note for Greuze at 131.2.

309.5 **the newest sensation of Paris, Mistinguett** Jeanne-Marie Bourgeois, known as Mistinguett (1875–1956), was a French comedienne noted for her stage personality and beautiful legs but not necessarily for her talent as a dancer or singer.

310.21 **Maxim's** The famous Parisian cabaret on the Rue Royale was founded in 1893 by a former waiter, Maxime Gaillard, after whom the new establishment was named. From modest beginnings Maxim's soon became a famed meeting place for the rich and beautiful, including celebrities such as the son of Queen Victoria and king of England, Edward VII; the king of Belgium, Leopold II; the Vanderbilts; and Liane de Pougy.

CHAPTER XXXIV

313.7 **Rue St-Honoré . . . Balzac** The Rue St-Honoré, one of the oldest streets in Paris, is the extension of the Rue Faubourg du St-Honoré. Rue Balzac is a small side street that, at its intersection with the Avenue de Friedland, has a statue of Honoré de Balzac (1799–1850). The house at no. 25 bears a plaque commemorating Balzac, who bought this house and died there at the age of fifty-one.

313.15 **Rue de l'Echelle . . . the Swiss Guards** Rue de l'Echelle intersects with the Rue St-Honoré near the Palais Royal, which was built by Cardinal Richelieu between 1619 and 1636. The Swiss Guards housed in this neighborhood served in many European countries before the establishment of national armies.

313.32 **Foyot's** Situated at 22 Rue de Vaugirard and 33 Rue de Tournon on the Left Bank, this is a first-class restaurant in the vicinity of the Théâtre de l'Odéon.

313.34 **Anne Estelle Rice** Rice (1877–1959) was a Philadelphia-trained American modernist painter and illustrator who lived in Paris from 1907 to 1913. Dreiser portrayed her as "Ellen Adams Wrynn" in *A Gallery of Women* (1929).

313.34 **J. D. Fergusson** John Duncan Fergusson (1874–1961) was a Scottish painter; he met Anne Estelle Rice in 1907.

313.35 **Mme. Wanita de Villiers** "Mme. de Villiers" is not Meg Villars, whom Dreiser had also Frenchified and introduced as "Miss Villiers" in the typescript version of *Traveler*. In a letter dated 17 January 1912 and inserted in Dreiser's travel diary, Grant Richards ironically comments on the possible confusion arising from the similarity of the aforementioned names: "[W]e met Madame de Vill[i]ers (when you have been to see Meg Villars whose address you now have, you will have quite a collection of different sorts of Villiers on your list)."

315.39 **Issy** Issy-les-Moulineaux lies to the southwest on the surrounding hills, about ten miles from the center of Paris. The area near the Seine is the site of various industries.

316.11 **"green hour"** L'heure verte, the hour when Parisians had a drink of absinthe, a green liqueur made from wormwood and anise.

317.33 **secessionists** The term describes movements against and within impressionism, neoimpressionism, symbolism, and expressionism. The term derives from the various *Sezession* movements in Munich, Berlin, and Vienna. Progressive artists seceded from the previously mentioned schools, founded separate associations, and organized their own exhibitions when their work was not accepted by the traditional art institutions.

319.12 **Halle aux Vins** The building was formerly located to the north of the Jardin des Plantes.

319.24 **Sainte Geneviève** Geneviève (ca. 422–512) is the patron saint of Paris.

319.24 **Saint Denis** Saint Denis (?–258?) was the first bishop of Paris and is the patron saint not only of the original Christian church built on the site now occupied by Notre-Dame but also of France as a whole. Legend has it that after being decapitated for religious reasons, he picked up his head and, led by an angel, walked from Montmartre to the abbey church of St. Denis.

319.27 **Panthéon** Designed in the classical style by the architect Jacques-Germain Soufflot (1713–80) and built from 1764 to 1790 on the site of Saint Geneviève's tomb, the building served as a church until 1791, when the Revolutionary Convention resolved to convert it into a national memorial temple named the "Panthéon." Repeatedly reconsecrated, the cruciform building was secularized again in 1885 for the obsequies of Victor Hugo and has since been used as a mausoleum for notable French men and women.

320.4 **Gothic chapter house** The place where a chapter (i.e., the general assembly of the canons of a cathedral church) meets to read a chapter of its rule and to allow the members to consult one another or transact affairs of the order.

320.35 ***Great Man from the Provinces . . . Wild Ass's Skin*** *Un Grand Homme de province à Paris* (1839; publ. as the second part of *Illusions perdues*) and *La Peau de chagrin* (1831) are both part of Balzac's (1799–1850) great series of interconnected novels and stories known collectively as *La Comédie humaine* (written 1827–47).

321.16 **Musée Galliera** Built by the duchesse de Galliéra (d. 1888), it is a municipal museum of art and industry.

321.21 **the new city hall in Brussels** Dreiser may be referring to the almost complete reconstruction (1873–95) of the Maison du Roi, which is located directly opposite the Brussels town hall.

323.21 **Café d'Harcourt** This famous café, located at the corner of the Place de la Sorbonne and Boulevard St-Michel, was a favorite haunt for artists.

323.21 **Bullier's** This Parisian dance hall dates back to the French Revolution. Located at 31 Avenue de l'Observatoire and known variously as the Prado, La Closerie des Lilas, La Chartreuse, Garden Bullier, the Bal Bullier, and finally the Bullier, it was frequented by glamorous grisettes and famous for erotic dancing.

CHAPTER XXXV

324.23 **great department store** In 1909 Rice was given a mural commission for the Wanamaker Store in Philadelphia.

325.13 **Restaurant Prunier** Located at 9 Rue Duphot, to the south of the Madeleine, this restaurant, which Baedeker (1900) rated as being in "the highest class," was most famous for its fish and oysters.

325.15 **Théâtre des Capucines** A theater situated at 39 Boulevard des Capucines.

325.16 **Gerny's Bar** A bar and restaurant located at 8 Rue de Port-Mahon.

328.7 **Mr. R. and Mr. N.** Mr. R. and Mr. N. are unidentified.

333.10 **Monico** A famous cabaret located in Montmartre.

CHAPTER XXXVI

337.3 **no more Marais** Saved from complete deterioration by extensive restoration, this former center of seventeenth-century feudal life has once more become a lively quarter of Paris and a major tourist attraction on account of its numerous famous palaces, called "hôtels."

337.34 **Chauchard** Alfred Chauchard (1821–1909) was a French art lover who bequeathed the Louvre an important collection of bronzes and paintings, including works by Corot, Daubigny, Decamps, Delacroix, Meissonier, and Millet.

337.36 **the Winged Victory of Samothrace** Discovered in 1863 and also called Nike of Samothrace, this statue is considered to be the finest Hellenistic Greek sculpture in existence and is on display at the Louvre.

337.40 **Watteaus . . . Paters** Jean-Antoine Watteau (1684–1721), Jean Honoré Fragonard (1732–1806), François Boucher (1703–70), Nicolas Lancret (1690–1743), and Jean-Baptiste-Joseph Pater (1695–1736) were all French painters.

338.2 **Meissonier . . . Daubigny** Juste Aurèle Meissonier (1695–1750) was a goldsmith and decorator. Charles-François Daubigny (1817–79) was a French landscape painter of the Barbizon school, which propagated the love of landscape for its own sake, and one of the earliest exponents of plein-air painting in France.

338.10 **van Ostade and Metsu and de Hooch** Adriaen van Ostade (1610–84), Gabriel Metsu (1629–67), and Pieter de Hooch (1629–83) were Dutch painters known for their depictions of landscapes and everyday scenes.

338.19 **church of the White Mantle** Notre-Dame-des-Blancs-Manteaux, located at 12 Rue des Blancs-Manteaux in Paris, is a seventeenth-century monastery of the Servites de Marie, a mendicant order wearing white mantles.

338.34 **Gambetta** Léon Gambetta (1838–82) was a French statesman who helped direct the defense of France during the Franco-Prussian war and founded the Third Republic.

338.34 **M. de Yiesville** M. de Yiesville is unidentified.

339.7 **George W. Cable** George Washington Cable (1844–1925) was an American author who generally wrote about Louisiana Creole society. *The Grandissimes* was published in 1880, and *Old Creole Days*, in 1879.

339.35 **the time of Francis I** François (Francis) I (1494–1547) was the king of France from 1515 to 1547.

339.37 **St. Martin at Pontoise** This abbey is located in the town of Pontoise, which is picturesquely situated on the west bank of the Oise.

339.40 **the Visigoth King Recceswinth** Recceswinth was known for having promulgated the *Liber judiciorum*, the kingdom's legal code, in 654.

340.2 **Château Villette** A picturesque country estate outside Paris.

340.4 **the gold rose of Basle, presented by Pope Clement V to the Prince Bishop of Basle** The golden rose is an ornament of wrought gold set with gems that is blessed by the pope on the fourth Sunday in Lent and bestowed on a distinguished individual, group, or community. Pope Clement V (1260–1314; ruled 1305–14) bestowed the golden rose on the prince bishop of Basel.

340.21 **Hale, a Boston publisher whom I had met in London** Dreiser refers to Ralph Tracy Hale (1880–?), of the Boston publishing house Small, Maynard and Company.

342.31 **Knights of Pythias** A secret order founded in Washington, D.C., in 1864 for social and charitable purposes.

344.2 **a Merovingian tower known as the tower of Clovis** This clock tower, located in the Henri IV Lycée at the side of St. Étienne-du-Mont, is the last surviving part of the Abbaye Sainte-Geneviève.

344.4 **John Calvin** Calvin (1509–64) studied in Paris from 1523 to 1528 and again from 1531 to 1534.

CHAPTER XXXVII

349.39 **Marguery's** A first-class restaurant located on the Boulevard Bonne-Nouvelle, adjoining the Théâtre du Gymnase.

351.1 **Boulevard des Halles** Rue des Halles.

351.17 **Sacré-Coeur** Designed in Romano-Byzantine style by Paul Abadie (1812–84), the Basilica of the Sacred Heart was built from 1876 to 1914 on the butte of Montmartre and consecrated in 1919.

CHAPTER XXXVIII

353.1 **my new friend** Dreiser means Ralph Tracy Hale; see historical note 340.21.

353.17 **Mr. Dawson** George Geoffrey Dawson (1874–1944) was an English journalist and editor of the *Johannesburg Star* (1905–10) and the *London Times* (1912–19; 1923–41).

354.34 **the election of Fallières** (Clément-)Armand Fallières (1841–1931) was the president of France (1906–13) at the time of Dreiser's visit.

354.38 **Edward Garfield Wriothesley Russell** Dreiser may be referring to George William Russell (1867–1935), an Irish nationalist poet, dramatist, editor and political essayist. Russell's pseudonym was "Æon," more widely known under its clipped variants "Æ," "AE," or "A.E." By replacing Russell's pen name and his initials G and W with the names *Edward*, *Garfield*, and *Wriothesley*, Dreiser may have attempted to disguise the poet's identity.

357.7 **Père-Lachaise** The "Père-Lachaise," or "Cimetière de l'Est" (eastern cemetery), is the largest and most important of the Parisian burial grounds. It is named after Père François de La Chaise (1624–1709), the Jesuit confessor of King Louis XIV, whose country seat occupied the site of the present chapel. Inhabitants of the northeastern part of Paris are interred there, as are persons of distinction from all parts of the city. The monuments in this vast necropolis number around 20,000, many of them noteworthy for their artistic excellence.

357.12 **Rachel** Elisabeth-Rachel Felix (1821–58), known as "Rachel," was a street singer who, despite an incomplete education at the Conservatoire, became a celebrated actress at the Comédie-Française (1838–55). Her interpretation of the protagonist in Racine's (1639–99) *Phèdre* (1677) received international critical acclaim.

357.12 **Abélard and Héloïse** Pierre Abélard (1079–1142) was a prominent and controversial theologian who secretly married his student, Héloïse (ca. 1098–1164), after she gave birth to their illegitimate son—a situation that prompted Héloïse's family to have Abélard castrated, after which he entered a monastery and she entered a convent.

357.12 **Daudet** Alphonse Daudet (1840–97) was a French short-story writer and novelist most famous for his *Lettres de mon moulin* (1869).

357.13 **de Musset** (Louis-Charles-) Alfred de Musset (1810–57) was a poet and playwright of the French romantic movement best known for the melancholy and anxiety (known as the *mal du siècle*) expressed in his work and for his notorious liaison with George Sand (1804–76).

358.20 **the "Turkey Trot"** This American ballroom dance to ragtime music, whereby dancers bob up and down, rising on the ball of the foot and then dropping to the heel, originated in the 1910s and was considered an exotic step on the order of the bunny hug.

359.10 **Baudelaire** Charles Baudelaire (1821–67) was a French poet; his *Fleurs du mal* (1857), a series of 101 lyrics in a variety of meters, including many sonnets, is one of the great collections of French verse.

CHAPTER XXXIX

362.37 **a certain American poet and novelist** Dreiser recounts this episode in his diary notes. He writes that Mme. de Villiers told him of a Roberts and "his crazy dancing." This Roberts may have been Kenneth Lewis Roberts (1885–1957), an American journalist, poet, and novelist.

362.41 **American short story writer . . . friend of the poet's** Mme. de Villiers mentioned a Roy Norton in the same breath as she does Roberts (see previous note), and this may have been the friend to whom Dreiser refers in this passage.

364.19 **Mistinguett** See historical note 309.5.

CHAPTER XL

365.20 **Mr. Flexner** Abraham Flexner (1866–1959) was an American social investigator and innovator in the field of education. Flexner made Dreiser's acquaintance while performing a study of European prostitution for the Rockefeller Bureau of Social Hygiene. This meeting was brought about by the American publisher W. W. Ellsworth, who had introduced Flexner to Grant Richards. The latter was to further the interests of science by acting as a guide to the seamier side of Paris.

365.25 **a fifth person** This person was William Webster Ellsworth (1855–1936), then a vice president at the Century Company.

366.28 **Mlle. Freyl** Mlle. Freyl is unidentified.

368.35 **Revolution or the Commune** Dreiser refers to the French Revolution (1789–99) and the revolutionary government in Paris (Commune de Paris) from 1789 to 1795. Between 1793 and 1794—a period known as the Reign of Terror—the Committee of Public Safety, led by Maximilien de Robespierre (1758–94), carried out most of the revolutionary measures, in which women were actively engaged. Another insurrectionary government, the Commune of 1871, took possession of Paris in the spring of 1871 after Prussian troops had withdrawn.

CHAPTER XLI

372.28 **Mentone** This is the Italian name of Menton, a town numbering 10,000 inhabitants at the beginning of the twentieth century. It had been part of Monaco until 1848, when it became a free city; it was bought by France in 1861. Menton then developed into a winter resort for English, German, and Russian tourists.

372.33 **Agay** A small town with a train station at the Cap Esterel, it lies twenty miles from Cannes and forty miles from Nice.

376.13 **a critical Roland for every Oliver** Dreiser alludes to the Battle of Roncevaux (778) as greatly fictionalized in several accounts, including the medieval French poem *Chanson de Roland*. Oliver is recorded as having prudently urged Roland to call for assistance, which he refused to do until it was too late.

377.34 **"Old Box"** Ernest Belfort Bax (1854–1926) was a social historian who had published numerous books with various publishers, six of them with Grant Richards (in 1900, 1901, 1906, 1911, 1912, and 1913).

379.6 **Cannes** Located at the Bay of Napoule, this town was home to 30,000 inhabitants in the first decade of the twentieth century and a preferred resort for the English, German, Russian, and French aristocracy.

381.4 **La Turbie** A village of 2,400 inhabitants at the time of Dreiser's visit.

381.16 **origin of a double row of palms** The Promenade du Midi was built across a former torrent and lined by palm trees; it extended from the railway bridge to the sea, linking two former gardens and thus creating the Jardin Public, which was partly destroyed when the new casino was built in 1934.

381.40 **the Admiralty** The former Restaurant de l'Amirauté located at 3 Porte de France, overlooking the Baie de Garavan.

CHAPTER XLII

382.26 **Café Anglais** The most illustrious of all nineteenth-century Paris restaurants, the Café Anglais stood at 13 Boulevard des Italiens, on the corner of the Rue de Marivaux, and was the social and culinary center of Parisian high society until it closed in 1913.

382.26 **Voisin's** Standing at 261 Rue St-Honoré and 16 Rue Cambon, it is described in Baedeker (1900) as "a long-established house."

382.26 **Paillard's** Located at 2 Rue de la Chaussée d'Antin and 38 Boulevard des Italiens.

382.30 **Durand's** Restaurant Durand was located at 2 Place de la Madeleine and Rue Royale and in the nineteenth century was a favorite gathering place for politicians, artists, and writers, including Émile Zola.

382.31 **Café de Paris** The Restaurant de Paris, located in the Grand Hôtel.

383.5 **Hôtel de Paris** This hotel was situated on the Place du Casino in Monte Carlo; Baedeker (1891) described it as providing services "on a grand scale."

383.6 **the Hermitage** Located on the Rue de la Scala, Monte Carlo.

383.7 **the Princess** A restaurant on the Boulevard des Moulins in Monte Carlo.

383.9 **the Grand Hôtel** According to Baedeker (1891), the Grand Hôtel Continental, located on the Rue de la Scala in Monte Carlo, was "palatial and expensive, especially during the season (15th Dec. to end of April)."

383.10 **the restaurant at the terminus of the La Turbie mountain railway** Hôtel-Restaurant du Righi d'Hiver, a first-class restaurant.

383.13 ***mostelle*** A Mediterranean fish similar to cod or rockling.

383.20 ***supions*** Little squids.

383.21 **Ciro** Ciro's Restaurant, located in the Galerie Charles III in Monte Carlo.

383.22 **the Régence at Nice** The Hôtel-Restaurant Régence is situated on 9 Avenue de la Gare, now called Avenue Jean Médecin.

383.37 ***sole Walewski*** The dish is named for Alexandre, compte de Walewski (1810–68). A French politician born in Walewica, Poland, he was the illegitimate son of Napoléon I and the Countess Walewska and served as a minister under Napoléon III.

383.40 **Winter Palace** A noble restaurant in Menton, situated on a hill north of the station, now classified as a historical monument.

383.40 **A grand duke** The duke is unidentified.

383.41 **two famous English authors** The authors are unidentified.

384.7 **the Riva-Bella** Located on Cap Martin about three miles to the west of Menton, the building is now in private use. Baedeker (1906) notes its "splendid view."

384.21 **column of Augustus** The tower of Augustus is a trophy erected in memory of the subjection of the Ligurians in A.D. 13.

386.28 **louis** Equivalent to twenty francs.

388.1 **"What's a bee-a?"** In familiar usage the French *billet* indicated 1,000 old francs.

389.22 **Labouchere** This roulette system is also known as "split martingale," "cross-out," or "cancellation."

389.31 ***canard à la presse*** This roast-duck dish is served with a sauce made from juices pressed from the duck and cooked with cognac and butter.

CHAPTER XLIII

394.18 **Cap Martin Hotel** The Grand-Hôtel du Cap-Martin.

394.18 **The Empress Eugénie lives there** Eugénia Maria de Montijo de Guzmán (1826–1920), known as Eugénie, was the wife of Napoléon III (1853–70) and empress of France; she lived in the Villa Cyrnos at Cap Martin.

394.20 **Soleil** Casino Palais du Soleil in Beausoleil, Monte Carlo.

394.21 **Coppélia** Charles Nuitter's and Arthur Saint-Léon's ballet-pantomime *Coppélia ou la Fille aux yeux d'émail* (Coppélia; or, The girl with the enameled eyes) was first performed in Paris at the Théâtre Impérial de l'Opéra, 25 May 1870 (music by Léo Delibes). At the Casino Palais du Soleil the ballet was staged as a matinée performance on 2–5 February 1912.

395.7 **Lockart's elephants** This was a popular number by the American comedian G. Lockart (?–?). The second American sketch was performed by the duo Mallya-Bart, who were announced as "Extraordinaires Comiques Américains."

395.35 ***"Est-ce que vous . . . le dernier samedi?"*** Are you not the gentleman I saw [on the train] coming from Paris to Lyon last Saturday?

396.1 **Marguerite type** Dreiser alludes to Marguerite in *Faust* (1859), a very successful opera by the French composer Charles Gounod (1818–93). The plot is based on Johann Wolfgang von Goethe's drama *Faust*, part 1 (1808). Marguerite corresponds to Goethe's Margarete/Gretchen. According to the penultimate line of part 2 (1832), she symbolizes the "eternal feminine."

398.32 **Café Américain** A restaurant at 4 Boulevard des Capucines in Paris.

CHAPTER XLIV

406.1 **marine museums** The Oceanographic Museum, or Musée océanographique, was founded in 1899 by Prince Albert of Monaco to house his important private collections; the Anthropological Museum was built at the beginning of the twentieth century.

407.3 **El Greco** Domenikos Theotocopoulos (1541–1614) was a Greek painter, sculptor, and architect who did most of his work in Spain. Interest in his oeuvre, particularly his religious paintings and portraits, was revived at the end of the nineteenth century.

407.4 **Peter the Hermit** Pierre L'Ermite (ca. 1050–1115) was a French ascetic instrumental in launching the first crusade.

407.17 **Café Royal in London** The Grand Café Royal, located at 68 Regent Street.

407.25 **ruined monument** Built in 6 B.C., the Trophée d'Auguste, a Roman tower, commemorated the subjugation of the alpine population. It formed the basis of a fortress, built around 1550, that was destroyed by the French in 1706.

407.36 **monument to Victor Emmanuel** Built from 1885 to 1911 and made of white Brescian limestone, this immense monument had been criticized for its pompousness and dubbed "the Birthday Cake." After World War I the tomb of the Unknown Soldier was placed in front of the statue, and the monument is now known as "Altare della Patria."

408.34 **Benvenuto Cellini** Cellini (1500–1571) was a Florentine goldsmith, metalworker, and sculptor whose work gained a wide reputation when his autobiography, *La vita* (1728), was translated by Goethe in the eighteenth century. In 1537 he was imprisoned in Rome for embezzlement.

409.11 **a public fountain** The drinking fountain built in 1824 near the Trophy of Augustus at La Turbie.

CHAPTER XLV

410.24 **Caesar** Gaius Octavius (63 B.C.–A.D. 14) was the first emperor of Rome. After being adopted by his granduncle Julius Caesar, he called himself Gaius Julius Caesar Octavianus. In 28 B.C. he was made *princeps senatus*, and in 27 B.C. he received the honorary title Augustus, by which he is known.

413.33 **vale of Arcady** Dreiser refers to the mythic and idealized pastoral world described in the eclogues of Theocritus (ca. 308–ca. 240 B.C.) and Virgil (70–19 B.C.) and immortalized in English literature by Spenser's *Shepheardes Calender* (1579) and Sidney's *Arcadia* (1590).

413.38 **Daubigny** Charles-François Daubigny (1817–78) was a French landscape painter who links romanticism and pre-impressionism.

414.2 **Rumpelmayer** A high-class café located at 26 Boulevard Victor-Hugo.

414.13 **Avenue de la Gare** French for "Station Road."

416.25 **Aix-les-Bains** A spa in Savoy, France.

416.25 **Karlsbad** The German name of Karlovy Vary, a spa in Bohemia, Czech Republic.

CHAPTER XLVI

421.11 **the Guelphs and Ghibellines** These were two opposing factions in medieval Italian politics; *Guelph* and *Ghibelline* are derived from the German names *Welf* and *Waiblingen* and designate propapal or proimperial leanings, respectively.

429.41 **one Don James, a pretender to the throne of Spain** Don Jaime (1870–1931) was the prince of Madrid and only son of Don Carlos (or Charles de Bourbon [1848–1909]).

430.41 **Ananias or Sapphira** Dreiser uses this biblical allusion to suggest that Grant Richards is lying about the way he spent the night. The reference is to Acts 5: 1–14, which recounts the discovery that Ananias and his wife, Sapphira, failed to give the community all their earnings from the sale of a piece of land and lied to God. As a result, both fall dead at the Apostle Peter's feet.

CHAPTER XLVII

432.2 **celebrated Parisian tenor then on the Riviera** Dreiser probably refers to Lucien Muratore (1878–1954), who began his career as an actor—appearing on stage opposite Réjane and Sarah Bernhardt—and then studied voice at the Paris Conservatoire, making his debut as a tenor at the Paris Opéra-Comique in 1902. In 1943 Muratore settled in Paris and became the manager of the Opéra-Comique. At his death he was well known as an actor, a vocalist, and a teacher.

CHAPTER XLVIII

441.13 **Laghet . . . miracles of healing** Dreiser refers to the pilgrimage to the *Madone de Laghet*, for which Laghet is known. Laghet is part of the community of Eze (Alpes-Maritimes *département*, Nice *arrondissement*) and is situated northwest of La Turbie.

442.17 **Hotel of the Flowers** Hôtel des Fleurs.

450.17 **Paul Sabatier** Sabatier (1858–1928) was a French Protestant theologian and historian whose *Vie de Saint-François d'Assise* (1894) is considered a standard work on the subject. Louise Seymour Houghton's English-language translation, *Life of St. Francis of Assisi*, was published by C. Scribner's Sons (New York) in the same year.

CHAPTER XLIX

450.35 **Umberto I** Umberto (1844–1900) was the duke of Savoy and king of Italy from 1878 until 1900, when he was assassinated.

451.18 **I wanted to see the Arno because of Florence and Dante** Dante was from Florence, and his works contain numerous references to both the city and the Arno (which flows through it).

451.30 **Niccolò Pisano** Nicola (or Niccolò) Pisano (ca. 1220–78/84) was an Italian sculptor. By combining the antiquing techniques in his art with Byzantine and Gothic elements, he established a new relief style and created a new type of pulpit architecture in Tuscany, where he lived and worked after 1250. His pulpit in the Cathedral of Pisa was completed in 1259/60.

453.1 **steel railroad bridge** The Ponte di Ferro.

453.3 **fortress** The Antica Fortezza.

453.4 **fortified palace** The Cittadella d'Artiglieria.

454.3 **Bonannus of Pisa** Bonnano Pisano (?–?) was a twelfth-century engineer in charge of building the bell tower now known as the Leaning Tower of Pisa.

454.3 **William of Innsbruck** Guglielmo di Innsbruck (?–?) was a twelfth-century architect who, beginning in 1173, worked with Bonnano Pisano on the construction of the bell tower at Pisa.

454.4 **Diotisalvi** This twelfth-century Italian architect (?–?) was responsible for the initial phase of construction of the baptistery in Pisa, as an inscription at the base of a pillar inside the building attests.

455.21 **thing of beauty . . . joy forever** Dreiser refers to the first line of John Keats's *Endymion: A Poetic Romance* (1818), which reads, "A thing of beauty is a joy for ever."

455.26 **Napoleon carrying away the horses of St. Mark's** At the end of 1797 the four gilded horses of St. Mark's were shipped off to Paris, where Napoleon had them set atop the Arc de Triomphe du Carrousel. The 1815 Congress of Vienna sent most of Napoleon's loot back to Venice, and the horses were reinstalled on the loggia of St. Mark's. Believed to have been cast in the fourth century, this is the only quadriga to have survived from classical antiquity.

456.6 **Andrea del Sarto** The Italian painter del Sarto (1486–1531) was a contemporary of Michelangelo and Raphael, which has often led his work to be overshadowed and neglected.

456.6 **Giuliano da Maiano** Da Maiano (1432–90) was a Florentine woodworker and architect and a brother of the sculptor Benedetto da Maiano (1442–97).

456.7 **Cimabue** Cenni (Bencivieni) di Pepo (ca. 1240–1302) was an Italian painter and mosaicist. Dante Alighieri refers to him in *The Divine Comedy*. See also historical note 520.6.

456.7 **Sodoma** Giovanni Antonio Bazzi Sodoma (1477–1549) was an Italian painter and leading Sienese artist of his time.

457.21 **Gibbon** The British historian Edward Gibbon (1737–94) is most famous for his *History of the Decline and Fall of the Roman Empire* (1776–88).

457.21 **Froude** James Anthony Froude (1818–94) was a British historian and biographer known mainly for his twelve-volume *History of England* (1856–70) and his four-volume biography of Thomas Carlyle (1795–1881). Here Dreiser seems to refer to Froude's *Caesar: A Sketch* (1893).

457.34 **Galba** Servius Galba Caesar Augustus (3 B.C.–A.D. 69; original name Servius Sulpicius Galba) was the emperor of Rome from 68 to 69.

CHAPTER L

460.33 **Museo delle Terme . . . baths of Diocletian** The museum in question is the Museo Nazionale Romano delle Terme Diocleziane. The Thermae of Diocletian were Rome's most extensive thermae, or hot baths, completed by Diocletian (245/48–313/16) and his coregent Maximian in 305–6.

461.1 **Servius Tullius** Tullius (578–34 B.C.) is traditionally considered the sixth king of Rome.

461.4 **temple of Minerva Medica** This ruin of an ancient ten-sided nymphaeum (a shrine to a nymph or nymphs) lies on the Viale Principessa Margherita, to the southeast of Rome's principal train station, the Stazione di Termini.

461.35 **Gallery of Modern Art** The Galleria Nazionale d'Arte Moderna was built in 1880–83 by the Italian architect Pio Piacentini (1846–1928).

461.35 **Aldobrandini and Rospigliosi** Ippolito Aldobrandini (1536–1605) and Giulio Rospigliosi (1600–1669) became Popes Clement VIII and Clement IX, respectively.

462.10 **Caracalla** The Thermae (hot baths) of Caracalla, or Thermae Antoninianae, were begun in A.D. 212 by Caracalla (188–217), extended by Heliogabalus (204–22), and completed by Alexander Severus (208–35).

463.13 **Julius II** Born Giuliano della Rovere, Julius (1443–1513) served as pope from 1503 to 1513. He was the greatest art patron of the papal line and one of the most powerful rulers of his age. He commissioned Michelangelo's *Moses* and paintings in the Sistine Chapel, as well as Raphael's frescoes in the Vatican.

463.15 **St. Anacletus** The second pope (76–88 or 79–91), he was the immediate successor to St. Peter.

463.17 **Urban VIII** Born Maffeo Barberini (1568–1644), he served as pope from 1623 to 1644.

463.20 **von Ranke** Leopold von Ranke (1795–1886) was a German historian noted for his innovative presentation of sixteenth- and seventeenth-century history.

463.21 **Leo X** Born Giovanni de' Medici (1475–1521), he served as pope from 1513 to 1521. Among the most extravagant of the Renaissance popes, Leo X made Rome a center of European culture and raised the papacy to significant political power in Europe. He excommunicated Martin Luther in 1521.

463.24 **Bramante** Donato di Angelo Bramante (1444–1514) was an outstanding Italian architect of the high Renaissance.

463.25 **Carlo Maderna** (1556–1629) was a leading Italian architect of the baroque period.

464.2 **Browning's poem, "The Bishop Orders His Tomb at St. Praxed's Church"** In this poem Robert Browning (1812–89) describes the final hours of a bishop who details, among other things, the marvels meant to adorn his tomb.

464.7 **Sixtus V** Born Felice Peretti, Sixtus (1520–90) served as pope from 1585 to 1590. He reformed the Curia.

464.24 **Nerva** Nerva Caesar Augustus (30–98), born Marcus Cocceius Nerva, was the Roman emperor from 18 September 96 to January 98. He was the first of the so-called "five good emperors."

464.24 **Faustina the elder, wife of Antoninus Pius** Antoninus Pius was an emperor of Rome (138–61) whose reign was a time of great peace and prosperity for the empire. When Faustina, his beloved wife, died in 141, he had her declared a goddess ("Diva Faustina") and had millions of coins made bearing her portrait.

464.25 **Pertinax** Publius Helvius Pertinax (126–93) was a Roman emperor from January to March 193, at which time he was murdered because of his attempt to enforce unpopular economies in both civilian and military expenditures.

464.27 **Marcus Aemilius Lepidus** Lepidus was a Roman patrician (died 13 B.C.) who, together with Antony and Octavian, formed the Second Triumvirate.

464.36 **steel trust president like E. H. Gary** Elbert Henry Gary (1846–1927) was a U.S. jurist and the first president of the Federal Steel Company, which merged with the United States Steel Corporation in 1901.

464.37 **Lyman J. Gage** Lyman Judson Gage (1836–1927) served as secretary of the U.S. Treasury (1897–1902) in the McKinley and T. Roosevelt administrations.

464.37 **P. D. Armour** P(hillip) D(anforth) Armour (1832–1901) was an American entrepreneur and innovator and the head of Armour and Company from 1875 until his death.

464.38 **Lord Salisbury** Robert Arthur Talbot Gascoyne-Cecil (1830–1903), third marquis of Salisbury, was the British prime minister from 1885 to 1892 and from 1895 to 1902.

465.17 **San Pietro in Vincoli** This structure is also named the Basilica Eudoxiana, after Eudoxia, the wife of Valentinian III (419–55), who erected the church around 442 to hold what was reported to be the chains of St. Peter, which Eudoxia had presented to Pope Leo I.

467.7 **the glory that was Rome** Dreiser alludes to the second stanza of Edgar Allan Poe's poem "To Helen" (1831), the fourth and fifth lines of which read, "To the glory that was Greece, / And the grandeur that was Rome." Poe was inspired by John Augustus Shea's (1802–45) lyric "The Ocean" (1830), which includes the lines "The glory of Athens, / The splendor of Rome," and by William Wordsworth's (1770–1850) "Stanzas: Composed in the Simplon Pass" (1822), in which the poet celebrates "The beauty of Florence, and the grandeur of Rome."

467.17 **Let the dead past bury its dead** This is the second line to the sixth stanza of Henry Wadsworth Longfellow's (1807–82) poem "A Psalm of Life" (1838).

CHAPTER LI

467.20 **Mrs. Armstrong** While in Rome Dreiser made the acquaintance of Mrs. Rella Abell Armstrong, with whom he had an affair that continued after they had returned to the United States. "The surviving correspondence . . . indicates that they collaborated on 'The Financier,' a dramatization of *The Financier* and *The Titan*. Although completed in 1926, 'The Financier' was never produced, probably because it was too long. In a letter to Mencken, dated 21 December 1916, Dreiser suggests that he had for years relied on Mrs. Armstrong's critical judgment of his writing" (Thomas P. Riggio, in Theodore Dreiser, *American Diaries*, ed. Riggio, 151n; see also Robert H. Elias, ed., *Letters of Theodore Dreiser*, 1:244). Armstrong's husband, Paul, was a noted playwright. In *My Life as Editor and Author* Mencken refers to Armstrong as an "insatiable nymphomaniac" (218) and speaks of the couple's "violent" and "delirious" affair (134, 141).

469.40 **Jean Jacques Rousseau's *Confessions*** Rousseau's (1712–78) *Confessions* (1781–88) were written as exercises in self-justification and self-analysis. Rousseau's narrativization of the complexity and individuality of a personality and a sensibility, which in his day was unprecedented for its candor, detail, and subtlety, remains a landmark in the history of autobiography.

470.3 **Cesare Borgia** A famous scion of the Borgia family, Cesare (1475/76–1507) played a role in numerous political assassinations, which earned him a rather unsavory reputation for ruthlessness.

470.9 **Alexander VI** A corrupt, worldly, and ambitious pope, Alexander VI (1431–1503) is known for his neglect of the spiritual inheritance of the church, which contributed to the development of the Protestant Reformation.

473.19 **quiet . . . along the Potomac** Dreiser refers to the poem "All Quiet along the Potomac," about a soldier on sentry duty who is hit by a sniper's bullet. The poem, by Ethel(inda) (L.) (Eliot) Beers (1827–79), was published in the 3 November 1861 edition of *Harper's Weekly* and originally titled "The Picket Guard." Set to music by John Hill Hewitt (1801–90) and others, it enjoyed tremendous popularity on both the Union and Confederate sides during the Civil War.

CHAPTER LII

476.34 **Pincio** The *collis hortorum*, or "hill of gardens," of the ancients was named Mons Pincius after the Pincii, an influential family of the later period of the empire. Here were the gardens of Lucullus, in which Messalina, wife of Claudius, celebrated her orgies.

476.34 **the paths of the Gianicolo** Dreiser refers to the Passeggiata Margherita, which leads up to the Ianiculum, now called Monte Gianicolo in Trastevere (Ital.: *tras* [beyond] and *Tevere* [Tiber]), a hill named after the Roman god Janus and situated on the west bank of the Tiber.

477.9 **Continental Hotel** This first-class hotel located at 5 Via Cavour, opposite the central train station, served an English and American clientele.

477.28 **Paul V** Camillo Borghese (1552–1621), Italian pope from 1605 to 1621.

477.35 **Gregory VII** Presumably Dreiser means Gregory XIII (Ugo Buoncompagni [1502–85]), who was a contemporary and the immediate predecessor of Sixtus V (1521–90).

477.39 **Fontana** Domenico Fontana (1543–1607) was a renowned baroque architect whose fame rests largely on his having been commissioned as architect to the papacy by Sixtus V, for whom Fontana had worked when the former was still a cardinal.

478.1 **battle of Lepanto** A naval battle on 7 October 1571 between Christian forces and the Ottoman Turks over the control of Cyprus.

478.1 **sending . . . Protestants** Pius V (1504–72) was pope from 1566 to his death, during which time he is known for having encouraged European rulers to ruthlessly suppress Protestantism. This included sending troops to France to help Caterina de' Medici (mother of reigning teenaged king Charles IX) put down the Huguenots.

478.8 **St. Paul Without The Walls** San Paolo fuori le Mura was founded as an early Christian basilica in 386 by Valentinian II. Destroyed by fires in 1840 and 1891, it was each time gorgeously restored.

478.9 **St. John Lateran** San Giovanni in Laterano was founded by Constantine the Great in a palace of the Laterani family that he had presented to Pope Sylvester I. The basilica, which suffered from earthquakes and fires, has been frequently altered and was finally modernized in the baroque style by Francesco Borromini; see historical note 486.32.

479.12 **Pontifex Maximus** Chief priest of ancient Rome.

480.8 **a certain Signor Tani** Aristide D. Tani (?–?) was an Italian scholar and author of guidebooks and popular histories, such as *Sketches of Ancient Roman Life* (1914) and *Guide of Rome Illustrated with a Map and 25 Views* (1920). In 1912 he was giving promenade lectures on the sights and historical places of Rome, his native city.

482.10 **House of Nero** The "Golden House," a lavish palace erected after the burning of Rome in A.D. 64, fell to decay soon after Nero's death in 68.

482.10 **Castle of St. Angelo** Castel Sant' Angelo, originally a tomb Hadrian erected in A.D. 136 for himself and his successors, was later converted into a fortress and, after 923, used as a stronghold. Destroyed in 1379, it was restored and enlarged by the popes. A thorough reconstruction began in 1901.

483.8 **Elagabalus** A Roman emperor who was also known as Heliogabalus, Elagabalus (218–22) is famous mostly for his eccentric behavior.

483.34 **Otto the Great** Otto I (912–73), king of Germany and Holy Roman emperor (962–73), was called "the Great" for having subdued revolts of nobles and defeated the Magyars in the great battle on the Lechfeld (955). In 963 he deposed Pope John XII.

484.2 **Beatrice Cenci** An Italian noblewoman executed by Pope Clement VIII in 1599 for taking part in the murder of her father.

484.20 **the villas at Frascati and Tivoli** The villas Falceneri, Torlonia, Lancelotti, Aldobrandini, and Mondragone are located in Frascati; Hadrian's Villa and Villa d'Este, in Tivoli.

484.26 **underground churches** These date from the fourth century and served only for the celebration of ecclesiastical festivals in honor of the martyrs; ordinary services were held in the private homes in the city, not in the Catacombs.

484.35 **House of the Vestals** The Atrium Vestae, or Palace of the Vestal Virgins, which dates from the first and second centuries, is located on the Sacra Via.

486.1 **"Where are the snows of yesteryear?"** Reference to the line "Mais où sont les neiges d'antan?" in François Villon's (ca. 1431–after 1463) best-known poem "Ballade des dames du temps jadis," first printed in *Le Grant* [sic] *Testament* (1489).

486.6 **Mind . . . vast ardent imagination** Dreiser here seems to have adopted the romantic concept of spiritual geography from Edgar Allan Poe, who in his May 1842 review of Hawthorne's *Twice-Told Tales* writes, "Thus the field of this species of composition, if not in so elevated a region on the mountain of Mind, is a table-land of far vaster extent" (Poe, *Essays and Reviews*, Library of America 20 [New York: Literary Classics of the United States, 1984], 573).

CHAPTER LIII

486.32 **Borromini** Francesco Borromini (1599–1667) was an Italian architect and the chief formulator of baroque architectural style.

487.4 **Villa Wolkonsky** Now called the Villa Campanari.

487.4 **the piazza that faces the Lateran** The Piazza di Porta San Giovanni in Laterano.

487.39 **Messalina . . . Silius** Messalina Valeria (22–48) was the third wife of the Roman emperor Claudius (10 B.C.–54 A.D.), whom she convinced to execute numerous senators. Her affair with Gaius Silius and presumed marriage to him resulted in her own execution.

489.8 **René Reinicke** Reinicke (1860–1926) was a German painter.

491.40 **Temple of Vesta** The Temple of the Sybil (Tempio di Sibilla), also called temple of Hercules Saxanus, stands on a rock above the waterfalls.

492.22 **Pirro Ligorio** An Italian architect, painter, and antiquarian, Ligorio (1500–1583) designed the Villa d'Este at Tivoli.

493.20 **Hadrian's Villa** The Villa Adriana at Tivoli, although depleted of its art treasures, continues to be noted for its magnificent 160–acre grounds. Hadrian assigned the names of celebrated buildings and localities of antiquity to the various parts of this architectural marvel.

CHAPTER LIV

494.13 **Mr. Conybeare** The reference is to Fred C. Conybeare. Dreiser had met this person (whom he calls "my Englishman" in chap. 48) on the train to Pisa.

494.16 **the Mamertine prison** Carcer Mamertinus, which was the Roman state prison, is now part of the church of San Pietro in Carcere.

495.2 **the Achaean League** Twelve cities in ancient Greece formed this confederation to fight piracy. The league was dissolved in 146 B.C. following quarrels with expansionist Rome. A smaller league, however, continued into the Roman imperial age.

495.15 **Oscar Browning** A celebrated history lecturer at King's College, Cambridge, Browning (1837–1923) was the author of a biography of George Eliot (1890).

495.16 **An American publisher** William Webster Ellsworth of *The Century Magazine*; see historical note 13.22.

495.36 **English representative** J. A. Sinclair Pooley represented the *Daily Express*, *Roman Herald*, *Evening Times*, and *London Telegraph*.

495.40 **an English artist** In his diary notes Dreiser identifies the artist as "Mr. Prentice."

496.31 **Boniface VIII** Boniface VIII (ca. 1235–1303) was pope from 1294 to 1303. Dreiser may have confused him with Boniface VII (?–985), who was known for murder, unjust imprisonment, and theft from the church treasury.

496.37 **Pure religion and undefiled** James 1:27; see historical note 66.33.

497.20 **the then Jewish mayor** Ernesto Nathan (1845–1921) was the first nonaristocratic mayor of Rome (1907–13) and the head of the "blocco popolare," which united radical, socialist, and republican forces. He fought for the municipalization of the city's public services.

497.30 **Gregory VII** Saint Gregory (Hildebrand [1020–85]) served as pope from 1073 to 1085. He was one of the great reform popes of the Middle Ages and attacked various abuses in the church.

500.9 **"to sing . . . God"** Dreiser quotes from the tenth book of Plinius Caecilius Secundus (Pliny the Younger), epistle 96.

CHAPTER LV

500.22 **Grant Allen's two volumes of classical and Christian Rome** Dreiser refers to Henry Stuart Jones's *Classical Rome* (New York: H. Holt; London: Grant Richards, 1910) and J. W. Cruickshank's *Christian Rome* (New York: A. Wessels, 1906), both published in Grant Allen's Historical Guides series.

500.23 **Marion Crawford's *Ave Roma Immortalis*** F(rancis) Marion Crawford, *Ave Roma Immortalis: Studies from the Chronicles of Rome* (New York and London: Macmillan, 1898).

501.22 **Cecilia Metella** The daughter of the patrician consul Quintus Metellus Creticus, Cecilia Metella married Crassus, the eldest son of Caesar's general in the Gallic War. Her tomb was built in 30 B.C. and later incorporated into a medieval fortress and monastery.

501.39 **Trastevere** Regio Transtiberina was annexed by Augustus as the fourteenth quarter of the city. The quarter always retained the character of a suburb; at the time of Dreiser's visit, it was inhabited almost exclusively by the working classes.

502.3 **triremes** Ancient galleys used primarily as ships of war in Greek and Roman times.

503.11 **Septimius Severus** Severus (146–211) was a Roman emperor (193–211).

503.12 **Severus Alexander** Alexander (208–35) was a Roman emperor (222–35).

503.27 **Pennsylvania depot** Pennsylvania Station, bordered by Thirty-first and Thirty-third Streets and Seventh and Eighth Avenues, opened in 1910 and in its day was the largest building for rail travel. Its 277-foot-long waiting room was designed to resemble the Roman baths of Caracalla and the Basilica of Constantine. It was torn down in 1964.

505.10 **Valentinian . . . Leo III** Valentinian II (371–92) was emperor from 375 to 392; Theodosius I (347–95) was the eastern Roman emperor from 379 to 392 and sole emperor from 392 to 395; Arcadius (377–408), the son of Theodosius I, ruled conjointly from 383 to 395 and alone from 395 to 402; Leo III (?–816) was pope from 795 to 816.

505.23 **Pius IX** Giovanni Maria Mastai-Ferretti (1792–1878) served as pope from 1846 to 1878.

508.7 **Pius VII** Born Barnaba Gregorio Chiaramonti (1742–1823), he served as pope from 1800 to 1823.

CHAPTER LVI

511.29 **Cerberus** In Greek mythology Cerberus is a three-headed dog who guards the entrance to the infernal regions.

513.25 **Pius IV** Born Giovanni Angelo de' Medici (1499–1565), he served as pope from 1559 to 1565.

513.37 **home** Seeing his funds dwindle, Dreiser had firmly announced to Richards in a 20 February 1912 letter that, because he was "handicapped financially," he wished to complete his journey after seeing Berlin and sail home.

514.17 **Assisi** This episcopal see, which had a population of 5,000 inhabitants at the time of Dreiser's visit, is the birthplace of St. Francis. The town lies on a hill two and a half miles from the station.

514.20 **United Italy** In 1861 the Sardinian king Victor Emmanuel II was proclaimed king of Italy, uniting all the various territories except Venice and the States of the Church, which were integrated in 1870. A centralized government like France's was established.

514.25 **Spoleto** An industrial town and archiepiscopal see with about 10,000 inhabitants in 1912.

514.33 **war with Turkey** Italy's war against Turkey (1911–12) for the possessions in northern Africa, especially Libya.

515.10 **Spello** A small town of about 5,000 inhabitants at the time, situated on a mountain slope.

515.18 **Mayence, bad luck** The German city Mainz on the Rhine is called "Mayence" in French, a fact that will contribute to a later confusion of Mayen, the birthplace of Dreiser's father, with Mainz (see chapter 71).

515.25 **"Wessex" country** Dorsetshire, the region that the naturalist writer Thomas Hardy (1840–1928) portrayed in his fiction and poetry, for example, in the *Wessex Poems* (1898).

CHAPTER LVII

515.34 **"Go ye . . . journey"** Matthew 10:7–10.

516.10 **"My sister birds . . . ingratitude"** A free rendering of St. Francis of Assisi's (1182–1226) "Sermon to the Birds" (ca. 1220).

516.33 **"Lay not up . . . be also."** A reference to Matthew 6:19–21; in verses 19 and 20, however, the biblical text refers to "moth and rust," not "moth and dust."

516.37 ***Umbrian Towns*** A travel guide by J. W. and A. M. Cruickshank, first published in Grant Allen's Historical Guides series by Grant Richards (London, 1901; first American edition, New York: A. Wessels, 1902).

517.14 **Pope Innocent III** Born Lotario de' Conti di Segni (1160/61–1216), Innocent III served as pope from 1198 to 1216. His approbation of St. Francis's rule of life marked the official founding of the Franciscan order.

517.21 **Santa Maria degli Angeli** The church was built on the site of the original oratory of St. Francis; its construction was begun in 1569 and completed in 1640.

518.3 ***L'Abbé Guillemart*** Charles Guillemart (?–?), "vicaire général d'Arras," is the author of a three-volume biography of Bishop Pierre-Louis Parisis, *L'Evêque de Langres* (1916), *Le Champion de l'église* (1917), and *L'Evêque d'Arras* (1925), all published by Librairie Lecoffre, Paris.

519.17 **Giotto** Giotto di Bondone (ca. 1267–1337) was an Italian painter and a principal player in the revival of naturalism, which is regarded as one of the most important features of the Italian Renaissance.

520.6 **Cimabue** Cenni di Peppi (1240–1302) was an Italian painter. In actuality his frescoes are located in the upper church of San Francesco in Assisi.

520.26 **St. Francis in the car of fire** The *Vision of the Flaming Chariot* is one picture in a cycle of frescoes by Giotto di Bondone in the upper church of San Francesco in Assisi; the work depicts the life of St. Francis.

521.7 **Cosimo Medici** Cosimo de' Medici (1389–1464), founder of one of the main lines of the Medici family, is also known as Cosimo the Elder or Cosimo Pater Patriae.

521.20 **Andrea da Bologna** Dreiser probably refers to Andrea dei Bruni (c. 1355–77), an Italian fresco artist.

CHAPTER LVIII

523.7 **the Poor Clares** A Franciscan order for women begun by St. Francis and St. Clare in 1212.

523.9 **"Canticle of the Law"** Dreiser possibly refers to St. Francis's "Canticle of the Creatures."

526.7 **Pinturicchio** Bernardino di Betto (ca. 1454–1513), known as Pinturicchio, was an Italian painter of the Umbrian school known for his frescoes in the Collegiate Church at Spello.

526.32 **calciminers** Workers who whitewash walls with calcimine.

527.27 **"with baleful weeds and precious-juiced flowers"** *Romeo and Juliet*, act 2, scene 3.

528.5 **Baglioni and the guilds** In the thirteenth century representatives of the seven major guilds formed a government whose oligarchy was subsequently challenged by revolts of the mostly powerless workers and peasants. These revolts were squashed by militias, and the guild government was gradually replaced by ruling families such as the Baglioni. The Baglioni were Umbrian nobles who dominated Perugia between 1488 and 1534.

528.6 **Michelangelo . . . machinations of Julius II** Michelangelo and Pope Julius II's friendship suffered recurrent strains as a result of their overly similar personalities. In 1505 Michelangelo began work on the pope's tomb, but the two soon quarreled, and in 1506 Michelangelo secretly fled to Florence to escape Julius.

528.7 **Otto came to conquer Rome** Dreiser is probably referring to Otto III (980–1002), a German king and Holy Roman emperor who planned to re-create the glory and power of the ancient Roman Empire in a universal Christian state governed from Rome.

CHAPTER LIX

529.13 **Perugino** Pietro Vannucci (1445/50–1523) was a prolific Italian painter from Umbria whose works include the decoration of the Audience Chamber of the Collegio del Cambio at Perugia (completed with Raphael).

529.33 **Piazza del Municipio** This plaza has since been renamed the Piazza Quattro Novembre.

530.34 **Brugnoli** Annibale Brugnoli (1843–1915) was an Italian fresco painter who contributed to the interior decoration of the Palazzo Cesaroni, built in 1898, which served as the main building of the Palace Hotel until 1925.

531.37 **the Hall of the Cambio** The Collegio del Cambio, which Dreiser later calls the "Hall of Merchants."

531.42 **the Bargello** The national museum in Florence.

532.14 **Giovanni Pisano** Giovanni (fl. 1265–1314) was the son of Niccolò Pisano (fl. 1258–78); both were sculptors.

532.14 **Arnolfo di Cambio** Di Cambio (fl. 1265–1302) was an Italian architect and sculptor.

534.17 **Bersaglieri hat** The Bersaglieri (Ital.: "sharpshooters" or "daredevils") are light, fast-moving infantry troops formed by the House of Savoy in 1836 as an elite corps. Their distinctive leather-and-felt hats featured symbols of their bravery and fighting ability: a copper or brass insignia over a tricolored cockade on the front and a showy plume of rooster feathers on the side.

536.6 **possibly the Arno or the Tiber** The Arno.

536.12 **Savonarola** Girolamo Savonarola (1452–98) was an Italian preacher, reformer, and martyr who established a republic in Florence in 1494 when the Medici were overthrown.

537.5 **Hôtel de Ville** The Excelsior Hôtel de la Ville is located on the north bank of the Arno at 3 Piazza Manin.

537.41 **Pitti Palace** Situated on an eminence at the Piazza Pitti, the Palazzo Pitti was designed and begun by Brunelleschi about 1440. Since the sixteenth century the palazzo had been the residence of the reigning sovereign. The upper floor of the left wing houses the famous Pitti Gallery, which contains numerous masterpieces, including works by Perugino, Andrea del Sarto, Raphael, Titian, Tintoretto, Bronzino, Rubens, Van Dyck, Rembrandt, and Dürer.

538.1 **Cosimo Pater** See historical note 521.7.

CHAPTER LX

539.1 **Donatello** Donato di Niccolò di Betto Bardi (1386–1466) was an Italian sculptor and the leading artistic figure in Florence of the early fifteenth century.

539.2 **Brunelleschi** Filippo di Ser Brunellesco (1377–1446) was the best-known Florentine architect of the fifteenth century.

539.5 **Piazza della Signoria** This square had been the center of urban life in medieval Florence. The events to which Dreiser refers occurred when, because of the constant warfare between the Guelphs and the Ghibellines, the leaders of the major guilds united and took over the city's administration.

539.26 **Fra Girolamo . . . his vision** Savonarola impressed the masses by his sermons and visions. Although he stated, "I have never absolutely declared myself a prophet," he did report seeing a black cross of divine wrath rising from Rome, followed by the red cross of mercy and compassion over Jerusalem. See also historical note 536.12.

539.28 ***The Prince*** *Il Principe* (1513), by Niccolò Machiavelli (1469–1527), is a treatise on statecraft advocating the use of power and political cunning.

539.32 **the Pazzi** A family rivaling the Medici.

539.32 **the Strozzi** A family of Florentine merchants.

539.38 **George Eliot's *Romola*** *Romola* (1863), a historical novel by the English writer George Eliot (Mary Ann Evans [1819–80]), is set in fifteenth-century Florence during a crucial period of transition between feudal and modern society. Based on extensive research on Renaissance Italian culture, the novel deals with moral failure and moral aspirations, the historical figure of Savonarola serving as one of Romola's two mentors. Criticism centered on the book's "shadowy life" and museumlike reconstruction of the period.

540.1 **Grote** George Grote (1794–1871) was a British historian noted for his works on ancient Greece.

540.32 **Benozzo Gozzoli** Benozzo di Lese (ca. 1421–97) was an Italian painter of the Florentine school.

541.4 **Andrea del Castagno** Andrea di Bartolo di Bargilla (ca. 1423–57) was a Florentine painter.

541.6 **Domenico Veneziano** Domenico (?–1461) was an Italian painter.

543.1 **Who would bear . . . unworthy takes** *Hamlet*, act 3, scene 1.

543.6 **Keats: "Joy, whose hands are ever at his lips, bidding adieu."** Dreiser quotes John Keats's (1795–1821) "Ode on Melancholy" (1819/20), the poet's best-known statement of his recurrent theme of life's mutability and contrarieties. The third and last stanza of Keats's poem begins with the famous lines "She [i.e., melancholy personified as a goddess] dwells with Beauty—Beauty that must die; / And Joy, whose hand is ever at his lips / Bidding adieu."

543.21 **Phidias** An Athenian sculptor, Phidias (or Pheidias [ca. 500–ca. 432 B.C.]) was the artistic director of the construction of the Parthenon.

545.3 **Bronzino** Agnolo (or Anigolo) di Cosimo (1503–72), called il Bronzino, was a Florentine painter and poet.

545.17 **Antonius** Mark Antony (i.e., Marcus Antonius [ca. 82–30 B.C.]) was a Roman orator, ruler (in the so-called Second Triumvirate), and general.

545.22 **Keokuk** This town in southeast Iowa had about 12,500 inhabitants at the time. Dreiser cites it as an example of the small-town America depicted later in Sinclair Lewis's novels *Main Street* (1920) and *Babbitt* (1922).

546.35 **the Wabash and Tippecanoe** The larger Wabash River runs through Terre Haute and the smaller Tippecanoe River runs through Warsaw, Indiana, towns in which Dreiser spent his childhood.

CHAPTER LXI

547.5 **Via dei Calzaioli** This street, whose name means "hosier street," is located north of the Piazza della Signoria.

548.4 **Palazzo Vecchio** Erected in 1298 by Arnolfo di Cambio and situated between the Piazza della Signoria and the Uffizi, this castlelike building originally served as the seat of the Signoria, the government of the republic, and subsequently as the residence of Cosimo I. At the time of Dreiser's visit it was used as a town hall.

548.5 **Loggia dei Lanzi** Located south of the Piazza della Signoria and originally called "Loggia dei Signori," the Loggia dei Lanzi is an open-vaulted hall that was erected in 1376 for public ceremonies. Its present name dates from the time of Cosimo I, when the latter's German spearmen, or "lancers," were posted there as guards.

548.6 **Cosimo I** Cosimo de' Medici (1519–74), also called Cosimo the Great, was the second duke of Florence.

548.9 **Bartolommeo Ammanati** Ammanati (1511–92) was an Italian architect and sculptor.

548.11 **A strange genius, that one** Dreiser here refers to Cellini.

CHAPTER LXII

552.2 **the dukes of Venice** The *doge* (duke) was generally an elected office whose power varied in scope throughout the history of Venice.

552.41 **Fra Angelico** Fra Giovanni da Fiesole (1387–1455), also called Guido di Pietro Angelico or Beato Angelico, was an Italian painter, many of whose works are displayed at St. Mark's.

554.35 **Riccardi** The Palazzo Riccardi, located at 1 Via Cavour, was built from 1444 to 1460 by Michelozzo (1396–1472) for the Medici family and sold to the Marchesi-Riccardi family in the seventeenth century.

554.35 **Albizzi** A leading Florentine family of the fourteenth and fifteenth centuries that fell from power in 1434.

554.41 **Professor Ernesto Jesurum** Jesurum (?–?) was the acting president of the Association of Italian Artists (Associazione degli Artisti Italiani) at the time of Dreiser's visit.

555.23 **Hearn collection** Dreiser refers to the collection of paintings by George A. Hearn (1835–1913), a trustee of the Metropolitan Museum of Art. In 1906 Hearn established an eponymously named fund to buy art by living American painters. Hearn was also reported to have been a victim of the leading New York art dealer T. J. Blakeslee, who committed suicide in 1913 after the discovery of his dishonesty.

CHAPTER LXIII

559.21 **Royal Danieli** Located east of the Doges' Palace on the Riva degli Schiavoni, it was the home of Alfred de Musset and George Sand in 1833.

561.7 **Maria** The diary entries confirm neither the dinner invitation on the train to Venice nor the gondola ride to the hotel. Rather, Dreiser expresses regrets at having lost the train acquaintance as a companion.

561.35 **Trefoil and quatrefoil** These are architectural ornaments resembling three- and four-lobed leaves, respectively.

563.17 **George Sand** The French author Amandine-Aurore-Lucile (Lucie) Dudevant, née Dupin (1804–76), wrote under the pseudonym of George Sand. Her lovers included de Musset, Liszt, Chopin, Berlioz, Delacroix, and Balzac. Sand's literary fame is based on a series of romantic tales (e.g., *Lélia* [1833]) and artfully told idylls of rustic life (e.g., *La Mare au diable* [1846]) that portray the struggle of women against social constraints and celebrate the natural moral integrity of peasants and laborers, respectively. Her autobiography, *Histoire de ma vie*, was published in 1854–55.

CHAPTER LXIV

568.26 **Cantharides** A preparation made from the dried bodies of beetles (typically *Lytta vesicatoria*, or Spanish fly), cantharides was formerly thought to be an aphrodisiac.

569.7 **before the invading Lombards** The event occurred in A.D. 568.

569.9 **the Council of Ten** A policing agency established in 1310 to protect the established government of Venice and (ruthlessly) suppress opposition.

572.15 **Santa Maria dei Miracoli** Located at Calle delle Erbe, south of the Campo Santa Maria Nova.

CHAPTER LXV

573.11 **Academy** Accademia di Belle Arti, located in the Scuola di Santa Maria della Carità on the Canale Grande.

573.25 **St. Stephen** Stephen (?–A.D. 36) was the first Christian martyr; he was stoned to death after defending his views before the Sanhedrin.

573.30 **the Doge Ordelafo Faliero** Ordelafo Faliero was the thirty-fifth doge of Venice (1102–18).

574.7 **Bellini** This could be any of three members of the Bellini family of painters: Jacopo (father) or sons Gentile (1429–1507) and Giovanni (1430/40–1516).

574.7 **Tintoretto . . . Veronese** Dreiser refers to the painters Jacobo Robusti Tintoretto (1518–94), Tiziano Vecellio (ca. 1487–1576), and Paolo Caliari Veronese (ca. 1528–88).

574.13 **Giorgione** Giorgio Barbarelli Giorgione (1475–1510), also known as Giorgio del Castelfranco, was a historically controversial Venetian painter because most of his works were not signed and dated. After his death, many unfinished canvases were completed by his students.

574.20 **the Frari** The church of Santa Maria Gloriosa dei Frari, located on Campo San Rocco.

574.21 ***Madonna* of the Pesaro family** An altarpiece by Titian (1519–26).

574.22 **Canova** Antonio Canova (1757–1822) was an Italian neoclassical sculptor.

574.22 **Santa Maria Formosa** Located on the eponymous Campo.

574.23 **Palma Vecchio** Jacomo Negretti Palma Vecchio (1480–1528) was an Italian painter who worked in Venice.

574.23 **St. Barbara** A virgin martyr of the early church and the patron saint of artillerymen.

575.11 **Milan** The capital of Lombardy and an archiepiscopal see, it had 520,000 inhabitants in 1912.

576.5 **Palazzo di Brera** The "Brera," or Palazzo di Scienze, Lettere ed Arti, located at the corner of Via di Brera and Via Fiori Oscuri, contains a famous picture gallery, the Pinacoteca, which includes works by Raphael, Mantegna, Crivelli, Palma Vecchio, Rubens, Van Dyck, and Rembrandt.

576.6 **Mantegna** Andrea Mantegna (1431–1506) was an Italian painter who worked in Padua.

576.6 **Carlo Crivelli** Crivelli (ca. 1430–95) was an Italian painter of the Venetian school.

576.7 **Jacob Jordaens** Jordaens (1593–1678) was a Flemish painter of Antwerp.

576.23 **Gaston de Foix** Gaston Phoebus (1331–91), count of Foix from 1343, was a soldier and passionate hunter who, when he suspected his son of trying to poison him, had him imprisoned for life.

577.29 **the arcade of Vittorio Emanuele** The Galleria Vittorio Emanuele.

CHAPTER LXVI

578.2 **Chiasso** A village of 5,000 inhabitants in 1912.

578.3 **Lake Como** Named for Como, a town of 31,500 inhabitants in 1912 that sits on the southwestern edge of the lake.

578.3 **Basle** Basel, which straddles the Rhine, is a manufacturing city that had around 130,000 inhabitants in 1912.

580.4 **St. Gotthard tunnel** Built in 1872–80, this tunnel measures 14,998 meters in length.

581.6 **Lucerne. . . . village** This town, the capital of the canton of Lucerne in central Switzerland, numbered about 37,000 inhabitants in 1912.

581.14 **the National** Grand Hôtel National, located at the Quai National, bordering the lake.

582.9 **hold over any of my pleasures** Dreiser alludes to the quick changes of mood from which he suffered occasionally.

CHAPTER LXVII

583.28 **one of these cafés** The Restaurant Stadthof, located at Stadthofstraße 4, existed from 1872 to 1968, when it was demolished to make room for an office building.

583.36 **Luini** Bernardino Luini (ca. 1482–1532) was an Italian painter who achieved great popularity during the Victorian era.

584.8 **Turgenev** Ivan (Sergeyevich) Turgenev (1818–83) was a Russian realist novelist, short-story writer, and playwright and the first major Russian author to be successful in the rest of Europe. His best work includes the novel *Fathers and Sons* (1862) and the play *A Month in the Country* (1850).

585.10 **two small steamers** Steamship service on Lake Lucerne was begun in 1835, and the sole company that runs all navigation was formed in 1869. The steamboats *Uri* (1901), *Unterwalden* (1902), and *Schiller* (1906) are still in service.

585.37 **Maillard's Cocoa ads** Victorian trade cards depicting idyllic scenes of little girls drinking cocoa.

587.22 **Empire** The Empire Theatre of Varieties, located at Leicester Square in London.

587.29 **boat stopped . . . train back** Dreiser here refers to Flüelen, the boat and train station twenty-four miles from Lucerne.

587.31 **shrine or tomb of William Tell** Built at the beginning of the sixteenth century, William Tell's Chapel is located on Tellsplatte, the spot where, according to legend, the Swiss national hero Tell leaped ashore to liberty in 1307. A statue of him was erected in nearby Altdorf in 1895.

587.33 **a fast train** The Gotthard Railway, inaugurated in 1882.

588.2 **Li Hung-chang** Li (1823–1901) was the leading Chinese statesman of the nineteenth century.

588.2 **Richard Wagner** Wagner (1813–83) spent 1866 to 1872 in Lucerne, where he composed *Die Meistersinger* and the *Götterdämmerung*.

CHAPTER LXVIII

588.9 **Louis Quinze** An eighteenth-century style of decoration popular during the reign of Louis XV of France.

589.15 **Thorwaldsen's famous lion** Dreiser refers to the *Lion of Luzern* monument, a sculpture after a model by the Danish neoclassical sculptor Bertel Thorwaldsen (1768–1884). Begun in 1819 and completed in 1821, it was dedicated to the Swiss guards slain while defending the Tuileries in Paris in 1792.

589.30 **company that controlled** The Ritz-Carlton hotel company; see historical note 17.7.

590.26 **Frankfort** Frankfurt am Main, a city in Hessia numbering about 440,000 inhabitants in 1912.

591.20 **poplars of France** Napoléon I ordered poplars to be planted along the Rhine; the tree thus became a characteristic feature of the upper Rhine Valley.

592.1 **Freiburg . . . Karlsruhe** Cities and towns in the upper Rhine Valley in Baden.

592.26 **Coblenz** On 26 May 1926 the spelling of this town was officially changed from *Coblenz* to *Koblenz*.

593.19 **Albrecht Dürer** Although also a painter, Dürer (1471–1528), a German from Nuremberg, is best known for his woodcuts and engravings, especially the large series of the *Apocalypse* (1498), the *Great Passion* (1510), and the *Life of the Virgin* (1510).

593.23 **Nuremberg** Known in German as Nürnberg, this city in Franconia had about 330,000 inhabitants in 1912. Germany's secret capital during the Middle Ages, the town is towered over by the Kaiserburg.

593.23 **Heidelberg** A town on the Neckar, counting about 45,000 inhabitants in 1912, which is famous for its medieval castle and the oldest German university.

593.35 **1871** Following the Franco-Prussian War (1870–71), the German Empire (Kaiserreich) was founded in 1871. This marked the beginning of an era of industrialism and capitalism as well as new nationalism.

CHAPTER LXIX

595.24 ***grafs*** *Graf* (pl. *Grafen*) is German for "count." By referring to grafs and rich burghers, Dreiser characterizes the leading section of late medieval society. Mayen was ruled not by the nobility but by the Roman Catholic Church, and the castle as a symbol of power was built by the archbishop of Trier. Grafs lived in the surrounding countryside, as did, for example, the Grafen von Virneburg, who owned property in Mayen as well.

595.31 **with three others** Dreiser's father went to Paris together with a brother and two sisters.

595.31 **the Prussian army . . . to France** The area west of the Rhine and in particular the Moselle region, where Mayen is located, were placed under French control in 1793 and recaptured in 1814 by a coalition consisting of Prussia, Russia, and Austria.

595.33 **Later he came to America . . . large family** Dreiser's father, John Paul Dreiser, left for the United States in 1844 and worked in woolen mills in New York, Connecticut, and Dayton (Ohio). After marrying Sarah Maria Schänäb in Piqua, Ohio, on 1 January 1851, he took on a job at a woolen mill in Fort Wayne, Indiana, moving to Terre Haute in 1858. The couple had thirteen children, of which the first three died in infancy.

595.37 **dying day** John Paul Dreiser died on 25 December 1900, at the age of seventy-nine.

595.39 **Prussian regulations concerning deserters** According to the 1808 and 1844 Articles of War for the Prussian Army, peacetime deserters were to be confined to barracks when not performing military duties, which they were to carry out under constant surveillance. The duration of this sentence ranged from six months to life, depending on the circumstances and the number of offences; in 1844, however, the mandatory life sentence for third-time offenders, as stipulated in the 1808 articles, was modified to ten to fifteen years of hard labor in a chain gang. Punishments for wartime deserters included beatings or death.

597.11 **Madame Culp** Julia B(ertha) Culp (1880–1970) was a Dutch concert singer who is considered her generation's most important mezzosoprano singer of lieder and oratorios. Refusing to perform on the opera stage, she was best known for her interpretations of lieder by Brahms, Richard Strauss, and Hugo Wolf. After her premiere in Magdeburg in 1901, she gave celebrated concerts all over Europe and, from 1913 on, in the United States as well. She withdrew from the public eye at the height of her career when she married her second husband, Wilhelm Ginzkey (1856–1934), a Czechoslovakian millionaire industrialist, in 1919. See also historical note 123.34.

597.29 **a cousin of his** Jerrard Grant Allen; see historical note 155.29.

599.27 **Zehlendorf** In 1912 Zehlendorf, a village of 18,000 inhabitants whose first known textual mention comes from 1241, was rapidly developing into a colony of suburban villas. In 1920 it became a part of Groß-Berlin (Greater Berlin).

CHAPTER LXX

603.18 **the best hotel** During his visit to Mainz, Dreiser stayed at the Hotel Hof von Holland, located at Rhein-Straße 77.

604.38 ***hochwürdige* gentlemen** "Hochwürdige Herren" (reverend gentlemen) or "Hochwürden" (reverends) are used as forms of address for priests and bishops.

605.24 **cane-ringing and Japanese ball-rolling** Dreiser refers to traditional Japanese juggling performances, which include acts with an umbrella and objects such as canes, balls, and rings. The Japanese influence on European circus and vaudeville culture has been considerable.

606.4 **Judengasse** The Jewish community in Mainz dates back to early Roman times; it flourished in the tenth and eleventh centuries, when it attained leadership in the Rhineland. Pogroms in the wake of the Crusades, especially in 1056, threatened to extinguish the Jewish population, but it revived and continued to live in the very heart of the old town. In 1912 the community numbered 3,400 Jews.

606.8 **Bingen** A town of then 10,000 inhabitants at the confluence of the Nahe and the Rhine.

CHAPTER LXXI

607.14 **statue of Emperor William I** Erected in 1897 at the confluence of the Rhine and the Moselle—a point of land called the "Deutsches Eck" (German corner), after a former Teutonic Knights lodge—the monument of William I (1797–1888), German emperor from 1871, comprises a forty-six-foot-high copper equestrian figure of the emperor accompanied by a thirty-foot-high attendant bearing the imperial crown. The statue was destroyed at the end of World War II; a replica was set up in 1993.

610.21 **stepmother** Catharina Schink was the second wife of Johannes Dreiser, who remarried in August 1824, a year after his first wife's death.

CHAPTER LXXII

612.7 **"East Mayen"** Mayen-Ost is the main station, where trains coming from Koblenz stop. It is located one mile from the town center, the marketplace; the station Mayen-West (West Mayen) is only a half-mile from the center and serves the towns of Daun and Gerolstein. The account in both the First Typescript and the 1913 edition confuses the two stations. The preceding facts and the description of his walk into town indicate that Dreiser arrived at the East Mayen station.

612.12 **a population** In 1912 Mayen had 13,500 inhabitants.

612.13 **an old Gothic church** Dating back to the twelfth century, this building, the St. Clemens Catholic Church, is predominantly Gothic and known for its grotesquely twisted steeple, the result of a fourteenth-century structural flaw. After its destruction in World War II, the steeple was carefully restored to duplicate the unique original.

612.13 **a true castle or *Schloss*** The ancient castle Genovevaburg, built in 1280.

612.14 **a towered gate or two** One enters Mayen through the Brückentor, the gate bridging the Nette River. The other gates are the Neutor (New Gate) and the Obertor (Upper Gate). The Wittbendertor (Wittbender Gate) was destroyed during World War II.

612.19 **coal mines** In *Dawn* (1931, p. 9) Dreiser proudly mentions that "one cousin owned stone and coal yards." This was Johann Dreiser (1851–1937). The family was dealing in coal.

612.24 **single Catholic church** The parish church of St. Clemens.

612.30 **the local graveyard** The old cemetery, located outside the city walls at the Chapel of St. Veit, was used as a burial ground from 1784 to 1904; in the 1920s it was converted into a park.

612.34 **Singer Sewing Machine Company** Before World War I the Singer Sewing Machine Company had a store at the Markt-Platz (upper market square) near the former Reichsbank.

612.34 **bookstore** Louis Schreder owned a modern bookstore located at Brückenstraße 1.

612.35 **moving-picture show** The first movie theater was situated in a restaurant on Neustraße.

614.40 **black piece of glass** A piece of polished black marble that gives the impression of glass.

615.14 **Theodor Dreiser** An older brother of Theodore Dreiser's father.

615.35 **son of the above Theodor** Born on 20 September 1858, Theodor's son died on 3 February 1898.

615.36 **Catharine** Katharina Dreiser (1823–1907), one of the twins born after Dreiser's father, Paul.

615.36 **Gertrude** Gertrud Dreiser (1889–91), the daughter of Johann Dreiser (1851–1937), is mentioned in his diary notes.

615.36 **Elise** Elisabeth Dreiser (1891–93), the daughter of Johann Dreiser (1851–1937), is mentioned in his diary notes.

615.37 **another graveyard** After the old cemetery was expanded several times, a new cemetery on the eastern side of Mayen was established at the beginning of the twentieth century.

615.38 **Gottfried** Gottfried Dreiser (1886–1909) was a son of Albert Dreiser (1860–1945), who was a son of Theodor Dreiser (1820–82).

615.38 **Johann** Dreiser misidentifies this person, listing in his diary notes a Johann Dreiser (1815–1905) who is not directly related to his father's family. Johannes Dreiser (1817–78), Dreiser's uncle, was the second oldest brother of Paul Dreiser.

616.8 **brick inn** The Felsenkeller was located at Bachstraße, opposite the Brückentor.

616.15 ***Bettzimmer*** Dreiser uses a literal translation of *bedroom*, a word not available in the German language; this no doubt explains the host's perplexity.

617.21 **solidly Catholic** For 1910 Mayen records 13,689 Catholics, 421 Protestants, and 307 Jews.

617.22 **of some order** The order of Saint Charles Borromeo (1538–84).

CHAPTER LXXIII

619.1 **one *restauration*** The restaurant, Im Römer, is located at Marktstraße 46.

620.28 ***Mayener Zeitung*** The local newspaper was edited by Louis Schreder, who also published the local directory (mentioned later).

622.12 **A second Catholic church** The Herz-Jesu-Kirche (Heart of Christ Church), in neo-Roman style, was built in 1911/12 and consecrated in July 1912.

622.32 **an old Jewish graveyard** The Jewish cemetery was located near the railroad tracks adjacent to the shooting club. After destruction from bombing in World War II, the graveyard was moved to the Waldstraße. See also historical note 617.21.

622.35 **my father's house** The house of Dreiser's paternal grandparents was located in the Feilsgraben, near St. Clemens. It has since been replaced by a home for senior citizens.

622.37 **Genovevaburg . . . half old and half new** Genovevaburg was originally built as a fortress in the thirteenth and fourteenth centuries and was expanded into a residence in the eighteenth century.

623.2 **failed in the furniture business** Dreiser's relatives and the town of Mayen have not confirmed this account. Dreiser's cousin Johann Dreiser (1851–1937), a moderately prosperous son of Theodor Dreiser (1820–82), moved his family to a new house in Mayen in 1905. There is a second Johann Dreiser (1885–1934), the son of Dreiser's cousin Georg Dreiser (1854–1920), and a third Johann Dreiser (1887–1971), the son of his cousin Theodor Dreiser (1858–98).

623.2 **other Dreisers** In 1912 there were six Dreiser families living in Mayen.

623.3 **the curator** The master cabinetmaker Peter Hörter.

623.15 **much-talked-of wheat** These carbonized wheat kernels are catalogued as Nummer 666 in the museum.

623.17 **the local scientist** Dr. Josef Knörtzer.

623.33 **my father . . . with the soldiers** These were Thuringian cuirassiers of the Prussian army stationed in Mayen. In 1830 the Eighth Prussian Army Corps was in a training camp near Urmitz when the news of the July Revolution in Paris arrived. The Prussian army was mobilized immediately, and border guards were posted. These soldiers remained in Mayen for some time.

CHAPTER LXXIV

624.12 **this particular hotel** Grand Hotel Frankfurter Hof, located on the Kaiserplatz.

624.27 ***Kaiserlich*** This word, which means "imperial," came to denote the military power, pomp, and arrogance associated with the reign of the last German emperor, Friedrich Wilhelm II, who abdicated in 1918.

625.9 **Metz** This fortified city in Lorraine became a part of Germany in 1871 and returned to France in 1919. The description of defense strategies against France reflects the latent atmosphere of war.

627.1 **Alexander Dowie** John Alexander Dowie (1847–1907) was a U.S. evangelist and faith healer who founded the Christian Catholic Church and the City of Zion (Illinois).

627.16 **Hotel Adlon** This first-class hotel, opened in 1907 and located at Unter den Linden 1, stands in the center of Berlin.

627.33 ***Morgen früh, wenn Gott will . . .*** Lines from the lullaby "Guten Abend, gut Nacht" (1868/69) by Johannes Brahms (1833–97). The text of the first stanza, which includes these lines, was taken from Achim von Arnim's (1781–1831) and Clemens von Brentano's (1778–1842) anthology of German folk poetry *Des Knaben Wunderhorn* (1808).

627.41 **You tell that to Sweeney** This threatening colloquial expression of disbelief derived from Sweeney Todd, a barber who murdered his customers and was later portrayed in a play by George Dibdin-Pitt (1799–1855).

CHAPTER LXXV

629.18 **Bispham** David Bispham (1857–1921) was an early twentieth-century American recitalist.

629.19 **Saalbau** Opened in 1861 and renowned throughout Europe for its excellent acoustics, the Saalbau was designed as a site for concerts, theatrical performances, and other cultural and social events in Frankfurt. The original building was destroyed in 1944.

630.16 **Marcelle** Dreiser refers to Marcelle Itam from Paris. See chapter 100 for a further comparison of Julia Culp and Marcelle Itam.

631.24 **Godowsky** Leopold Godowsky (1870–1938) was a Lithuanian-born pianist and composer and, at the time of Dreiser's visit, one of the highest-paid and most sought-after artists.

631.34 **Pastoral Symphony** The speaker refers to Beethoven's (1770–1827) Symphony No. 6, Op. 68 (*Die Pastorale*), composed in 1808.

CHAPTER LXXVI

637.23 **Johann Wolfgang Goethe** Johann Wolfgang von Goethe (1749–1832), the renowned German poet, playwright, and novelist, as well as a minister at the ducal court in Weimar and a researcher in science, was born and spent his youth in Frankfurt.

637.24 **Römerberg** The marketplace in front of the Römer, the municipal offices, a group of twelve separate old houses and the new Rathaus (city hall).

639.26 **von Moltke** The Prussian field marshal Helmuth (Karl Bernhard), Graf von Moltke (1800–1891), was the leading general in the Franco-Prussian War (1870–71), chief of the German General Staff (1858–88), and a member of the Reichstag (1867–91). His military theories and strategies led to German victories in Denmark, Austria, and France and ultimately to German unification in 1871.

640.5 **S. Maria Nascente at Milan** The Milan Cathedral, the city's religious heart and symbol, was built from 1386 to 1682 and dedicated to the birth of the Virgin Mary.

CHAPTER LXXVII

643.8 **Zeppelin airships** Ferdinand (Adolf August Heinrich), Graf von Zeppelin (1838–1917), invented these rigid dirigible airships. When, after ten years of experimenting with his "lighter-than-air craft," Count Zeppelin completed a twenty-four-hour flight in 1906, he received commissions for an entire fleet from the German government.

644.13 **Fulda . . . Wartha . . . Weimar . . . Apolda . . . Saalfeld . . . Naumburg** Towns in Hesse, Thuringia, and Saxony-Anhalt, ranging between 20,000 and 50,000 inhabitants.

644.26 **Arnold Böcklin** Böcklin (1827–1901) was a Swiss painter particularly known for his mythical landscapes.

645.26 **cap, not unlike the Phrygian** A soft felt or wool cone-shaped cap, the tip of which generally curls forward.

645.37 **Franz von Stuck** A German art nouveau (*Jugendstil*) painter known for his allegorical pictures, von Stuck (1863–1928) helped to found the Munich Academy and taught both Wassily Kandinsky (1866–1944) and Paul Klee (1879–1940).

646.9 **Lorenzo . . . *Dusk*** In Michelangelo's New Sacristy (Medici Chapel) of San Lorenzo, the Medici are depicted above figures representing day and night (meant to symbolize the active life), and dawn and dusk (symbolizing the contemplative life).

646.40 **the Excelsior** The Grand-Hôtel Excelsior, located at the corner of Via Boncompagni and Via Veneto in Rome.

CHAPTER LXXVIII

647.32 **Potsdamer Bahnhof** Situated to the south of Potsdamer Platz, this train station was destroyed in World War II and subsequently razed.

648.19 **Kaiser-Friedrich-Museum** Located on the Museum Island, this museum was renamed the Bode-Museum in 1958 after its founder, Wilhelm von Bode (1845–1929).

649.11 **Berlin Cathedral** This domed structure, built in 1894–1905 in the style of the Italian Renaissance, rests on the site of another cathedral, built in 1747–50.

649.11 **Imperial Opera House** Königliches Opernhaus, built in 1741–43, is located on Unter den Linden.

649.18 **Potsdam . . . suburb** Located in the Greater Berlin area, the town, which numbered 62,000 inhabitants in 1912, was the seat of government for the province of Brandenburg, a position it regained after reunification. It boasts numerous splendid palaces erected by the Prussian kings.

649.38 **considerable lake** Wannsee.

650.27 **von Bülow . . . Rubinstein** All are references to musical celebrities of the late nineteenth and early twentieth centuries: Hans (Guido) Freiherr von Bülow (1830–94), German pianist and conductor; Joseph Joachim (1831–1907), Hungarian violinist; and Anton Grigoryevich Rubinstein (1829–94), Russian composer and pianist. See also historical note 699.16.

651.1 **Nana** The dog's name was Fräulein Nana Zola.

651.6 **Fräulein Förster** Julia Culp's housekeeper.

651.9 **Sheraton** This furniture style, developed by Thomas Sheraton (1751–1806), became typical of the late eighteenth century.

651.37 **Herr Merten** Erich Gustav Wilhelm Merten (1869–1933) was a German engineer and Madame Culp's first husband. Culp was the famous singer's Dutch maiden name, which she used professionally.

652.24 ***Jugend . . . Simplicissimus*** These were avant-garde German publications around the turn of the century. *Jugend,* an illustrated magazine published from 1896 to 1940, was the namesake for German art nouveau—that is, *Jugendstil; Fliegende Blätter* and *Simplicissimus* were satirical magazines published from 1844 to 1944 and 1896 to 1944, respectively. (Franz von Stuck contributed to the former.)

655.31 **Napoleon . . . Austerlitz** In the Battle of Austerlitz (a town in Moravia), the army of Napoléon I of France (1769–1821) engaged those of Franz (Francis) II of Austria (1768–1835) and Alexander I of Russia (1777–1825) on 2 December 1805, with Napoléon winning a decisive victory.

655.31 **Diogenes . . . barrel** Diogenes of Sinope (ca. 400–ca. 323) was a Greek Cynic philosopher who, by leading an ascetic life, criticized conspicuous consumption, illustrated by the anecdote of his taking up temporary residence in a barrel.

CHAPTER LXXIX

656.33 **cathedral . . . bullhead cot** Dreiser here joins the numerous critics of the architectural blunders of the Berlin Cathedral, built to please the exceedingly pompous notions of Emperor Friedrich Wilhelm II.

656.36 **present Imperial Opera House . . . in its place** The Opera House was completely destroyed during the bombing raids of World War II. It was rebuilt according to historical designs and reopened in 1955.

656.38 **There should be a new imperial palace . . .** Destroyed by World War II bombing, the Imperial Palace (referred to in the text as the "Royal Palace" and the "Kaiserliche Schloss") was razed in 1951 by the East German government. In its place was erected the Palast der Republik, a building now scheduled to be torn down. The rebuilding of the imperial palace is a favored plan for the future.

657.6 **winged Victory . . . Königsplatz** The Siegessäule, a massive column unveiled in 1873, was moved from the Königsplatz to the Tiergarten.

657.8 **Belle-Alliance-Platz** Although the Belle-Alliance-Platz was renamed Mehringplatz after the German writer Walter Mehring (1896–1981) in 1945, the "trashy winged something" (the Friedenssäule) has remained.

657.13 **statue of Wilhelm I** This pompous equestrian statue by Reinhold Begas, unveiled in 1897, did not survive World War II, but its pedestal still exists. It is located near the Königliche Schloss, the Royal Palace.

657.15 **Reinhold Begas** Begas (1831–1911), a leading figure in Prussian sculpture, was the most famous German sculptor of his time.

657.31 **hero of Sedan** Dreiser refers to Emperor Wilhelm I. On 2 September 1870 Emperor Napoléon III was taken prisoner after his defeat at Sedan, near the Franco-Belgian border, which ended the French Empire. In January 1871 King Wilhelm I was proclaimed German emperor at Versailles. The "Sedanstag" became a national holiday.

658.18 **statue of Bismarck** This monument memorializing the famous German chancellor Otto von Bismarck (1815–98) was erected by Reinhold Begas in 1901 and relocated to the Tiergarten in 1938. Its somewhat unintelligible allegorical details have been criticized.

658.22 **Reichstag** The Reichstagsgebäude (Hall of the Imperial Diet) was built in 1884–94 from designs by the German architect Paul Wallot (1841–1912).

658.32 **University of Berlin** The Friedrich-Wilhelm-Universität was donated by King Friedrich Wilhelm III in 1810. Implementing Wilhelm von Humboldt's (1767–1835) new university concept—the unity of research and teaching—it became the model for all German universities. In 1949 it was renamed Humboldt University after its founder.

658.33 **old art gallery** Located on the Museum Island and built in a Greek style, the Altes Museum (Old Museum) contains antique and applied art.

658.33 **National Gallery** Built in 1866–76 in the form of a Corinthian temple, it houses a collection of German painting and sculpture from the eighteenth to the twentieth centuries.

659.5 **spending three million dollars** Building the new cathedral cost 11.5 million marks.

659.19 **St. Paul the Divine** Dreiser may mean the Cathedral Church of St. John the Divine (Episcopal), the world's largest cathedral, built in 1892 at the corner 112th Street and Amsterdam Avenue in Manhattan.

659.23 **Siegesallee . . . Kemperplatz** Neither the statues, which were deemed too militaristic by the Allied occupational forces after World War II, nor the Siegesallee survived the war and the relandscaping of the Tiergarten.

CHAPTER LXXX

663.14 **"Christian gentlemen" . . . Mr. Baer** George Frederick Baer (1842–1914) was an American lawyer and industrialist. While president of the Philadelphia and Reading Coal and Iron Company, he responded to a coal miners' strike by saying, "The rights and interests of the laboring man will be protected and cared for—not by the labor agitators, but by the Christian men to whom God in his infinite wisdom has given the control of the property interests of the country" (qtd. in *The Encyclopedia Americana—International Edition* [Danbury, Conn.: Grolier, 1998], vol. 3, p. 46).

663.19 **Mr. Croker . . . "all the time"** Richard Croker (1841–1922) was a controversial political boss in New York City toward the end of the nineteenth century. During a judicial examination, he once described his interest in the city's government as follows: "I am working for my pocket every time."

666.12 **von Moltke** See historical note 639.26.

CHAPTER LXXXI

667.27 **great army exercise place** The Exerzierplatz was located to the north of the Tiergarten.

669.11 **Bauer** Located at Unter den Linden 26.

669.11 **Kempinski's** Located at Leipziger Straße 25.

669.11 **Fürstenhof** Located at the Potsdamer Platz.

669.12 **Linden Cabaret** Located at Unter den Linden 22.

669.12 **Weinhaus Rheingold** Located at Bellevuestraße 19–20, just off the Potsdamer Platz. See historical note 647.32.

669.13 **Weinhaus Trarbach** This large establishment stood at Behren-Straße 47 (near Friedrichstraße).

669.13 **Palais de Danse** The Metropol-Palast (Metropolitan Palace), which contained a large ballroom ("Palais de Danse"), was located to the west of Friedrichstraße 53–54.

670.37 **Claire Waldoff** Clara Wortmann (1884–1957), a Berlin actress and popular singer who worked in various cabarets from 1910 to 1933, went by the stage name Claire Waldoff.

671.8 **Albert Chevalier** A popular British actor and music-hall entertainer, Chevalier (1861–1923) was known as the "costers' laureate" because of his Cockney-dialect songs on common London life.

671.16 **Marie Dressler** A Canadian-born actress and vaudeville comedienne, Dressler (1869–1934) made her screen debut as Charlie Chaplin's partner in the 1914 film *Tillie's Punctured Romance*. In 1930 she starred in two motion pictures, *Anna Christie* and *Min and Bill*, the latter winning her an Academy Award.

671.16 **Grossmith, Junior** See historical note 158.3.

CHAPTER LXXXII

677.3 **What fools . . . mortals be!** Dreiser paraphrases Puck in Shakespeare's *Midsummer Night's Dream*, act 3, scene 2: "Lord, what fools these mortals be!"

CHAPTER LXXXIII

678.18 **ice-palace** The Berliner Eispalast, located at Luther-Straße 22–24, boasted a rink of 7,000 square feet.

680.12 **a cousin of Madame Culp** Julia Culp's cousin Frau Drucker.

680.22 **Mischa Elman** Previously a child prodigy, Elman (1891–1967) was one of Europe's leading violinists at the time of Dreiser's visit.

CHAPTER LXXXIV

683.14 **Savignyplatz . . . Vinetaplatz** All these squares are located in the center or to the west of Berlin.

684.2 **Tietz store** Tietz's warehouse, located at Leipziger Straße 46–50 and extended to Dönhoff-Platz in 1912, opened in 1905. It was founded by Hermann Tietz (1837–1907), who built several department stores, such as the KADEWE (Kaufhaus des Westens) in Berlin. The Hertie (short for Hermann Tietz) department stores still bear their founder's name. The Tietz store Dreiser mentions was destroyed in World War II and replaced by the Centrum-Warenhaus, called the Galeria Kaufhof since the 1990s.

684.23 **Jennie Gerhardt** Dreiser refers to Jennie Gerhardt, the heroine of his second novel. She is a patient, intelligent young woman who has an illegitimate child and suffers from the lower-class situation of her immigrant family.

688.1 **Tilsit** This middle-sized town lies near Königsberg (now Kaliningrad), in east Prussia. Tilsit was renamed "Sovetsk" in 1945, when it was acquired by the Soviet Union; it is now part of Russia.

688.9 **Stettin** Dating back to the early Middle Ages, the town belonged to Pomerania and in 1815 became a part of Prussia. After World War II it became Polish and was named "Szczecin."

CHAPTER LXXXV

689.2 **not many industries in Tilsit** Tilsit's economic activity centered principally on agrarian production (e.g., of cereals, cheese, wood), as well as textile and shipbuilding industries.

689.10 **mills in Stettin** This may refer to any facility in the town's shipbuilding, electrical, machine-construction, textile, or food industries.

692.34 **"Ears, and they hear not . . . Eyes, and they do not see** Dreiser refers to either Matthew 13:13 ("Therefore speak I to them in parables: because they seeing see not; and hearing they hear not, neither do they understand") or Mark 8:18 ("Having eyes, see ye not? and having ears, hear ye not?").

692.35 **And there is neither good** Dreiser paraphrases *Hamlet*, act 2, scene 2: "There is nothing either good or bad, but thinking makes it so," a line quoted at the beginning of *Science and Health with Key to the Scriptures* (1875), by Mary Baker Eddy (1821–1910), a textbook in Christian Science to which Dreiser occasionally refers in his writing.

CHAPTER LXXXVI

694.3 **fresh** The *Oxford English Dictionary* mentions the possible semantic influence of the German *frech* ("saucy" or "impudent") on the American *fresh*.

CHAPTER LXXXVII

699.3 **Nikisch** Professor Arthur Nikisch (1855–1922) was a renowned conductor who led the Berlin Philharmonic Orchestra from 1897.

699.3 **Elman** See historical note 680.22.

699.4 **Philharmonic Hall** The Philharmonie was located at Bernburger Straße 22.

699.14 **Frau Herzog** Mrs. Herzog is unidentified.

699.16 **Frau von Bülow** The actress Marie von Bülow, née Schanzer (1857–1941), became the second wife of Hans Guido Freiherr von Bülow (1830–94), a German pianist, conductor, and composer. Von Bülow had married her in 1882 after divorcing Liszt's daughter Cosima (who then married Richard Wagner in 1870).

699.17 **Godowsky** See historical note 631.24.

701.12 **crown prince of Germany** Friedrich Wilhelm Victor August Ernst (1882–1951) was the crown prince of Germany from 1888 to 1918.

701.19 **The Black Hussars** This famous Prussian regiment, which existed from 1740 to 1892, was named "Die Schwarzen Husaren" because of their extravagant uniform (a black dolman with white braids and a cap featuring the skull and crossbones as a sign of bravery). Renamed the Leib-Husaren-Regiment in 1806, its aristocratic members included the crown prince of Germany.

702.22 **Bauer's** See historical note 669.11.

702.23 **Sudermann's** Hermann Sudermann (1857–1928) was a leading writer of the German naturalist movement.

702.24 **Hauptmann's** Gerhart Hauptmann (1862–1946) was a German naturalist playwright and author who received the Nobel Prize in Literature in 1912. His most important plays are *Vor Sonnenaufgang* (*Before Sunrise* [1889]) and *Die Weber* (*The Weavers* [1892]).

703.21 **He had caught a Tartar** The term *Tartar* as used here refers to "a person of a violent, intractable, or irritable temper . . . too strong for his assailant" (*Webster's New International Dictionary of the English Language*, unabridged, 2d ed., s.v. *tartar*).

703.32 **accompanist** Julia Culp's accompanist that evening was Erich J. Wolff (1874–1913).

704.24 **Claire Waldoff** See historical note 670.37.

CHAPTER LXXXVIII

705.8 **"Prussian"** The German word *preußisch* ("Prussian") connotes certain qualities (as in "Prussian virtues") that formerly were expected to characterize a Prussian soldier or official and later were extended to all Prussian subjects: a certain rigid observance of law and order, dutifulness, personal rectitude, parsimony, and self-discipline. The "meanings" Dreiser lists for the different locations reflect the political relations between the state of Prussia and its neighbors.

705.9 **Altenburg** A middle-sized town near Leipzig, Saxony.

706.29 **café . . . near the Kaiser-Friedrich-Gedächtniskirche** The popular Charlottenhof Restaurant near the Charlottenburger Chaussee and the Emperor Frederick Memorial Church.

708.29 **municipal gardens** Named after the physician and pedagogue Daniel Gottlieb Moritz Schreber (1808–61), who created them, the Schrebergärten, or Laubenkolonie, were playgrounds for children and gardens for adults that developed into small garden plots, usually equipped with a small cabin, called a "Laube."

709.34 **foolish father-love** Connecting it with the memory of his German father, Dreiser here borrows the German expression "närrische Elternliebe" (foolish parental love).

710.11 **Weinhaus Trarbach** See historical note 669.13.

711.13 **"Did you ever hear of the free baths?"** Seeking to escape the stifling atmosphere of Berlin's slums, people went out to enjoy nature and fresh air after work or on weekends. Since Berliners mostly ignored the ban on free bathing, a 400-meter stretch of the Havel beach was set aside for them in 1907; it later became the Strandbad Wannsee.

711.28 **without a stitch of clothing** According to the "Lebensreform" (life reform) movement at the turn of the century—which also propagated vegetarianism, abstinence, and moderation in general—being nude meant being in harmony with nature. The first clubs in Berlin date from 1910. Dreiser here reports the first outraged reactions of bourgeois society.

CHAPTER LXXXIX

713.21 **It is a mad world** Dreiser alludes to Charles Dickens's (1812–70) novel *David Copperfield* (1849–50), in which Mr. Dick, a lunatic himself, tells David: "I shouldn't wish it to be mentioned, but it's a— . . . it's a mad world. Mad as Bedlam, boy!"

715.27 ***Life seen through a temperament*** Dreiser quotes Émile Zola's definition of art as formulated repeatedly in *Mes haines: Causeries littéraires et artistiques* (*My Hatreds* [1866]), *Le Roman expérimental* (*The Experimental Novel* [1880]), and "Le Naturalisme au théâtre" ("Naturalism in the Theatre" [1881]): "Une oeuvre d'art est un coin de la création vu à travers un tempérament [A work of art is a corner of creation viewed through a temperament]."

715.39 **"And the spirit of God moved upon the face of the waters"** Genesis 1:2.

716.3 **Wouwerman . . . Terborch** Dreiser mentions several Dutch painters: Philips Wouwerman (1619–68), Nicolaes Maes (1634–93), Jan (Johannes) Vermeer (1632–75), Salomon van Ruysdael (ca. 1600–1670), Gerard (Gerrit) Dou (1613–75), Ludolf Bakhuyzen (1631–1708), Jan van Goyen (1596–1656), and Gerard Terborch (1617–81). See also the historical note on Ruysdael at 229.19.

716.13 **van de Velde** Dreiser could be referring to any of several seventeenth-century Dutch painters with this surname. The six generally regarded as important (and the most likely to be the referent of Dreiser's invocation) are Esaias (1590/91–1630), Jan the Younger (1593–1641), Jan Jansz (1619/20–after

1662), Willem the Elder (1611–93), Willem the Younger (1633–1707), and Adriaen (1636–72).

716.16 **van Ostade** See historical note 338.10.

CHAPTER XC

717.23 **Jan Steen** Steen (1626–79) was a Dutch painter best known for his animated scenes of taverns and popular feasts.

720.9 **Our own Washington Irving . . . phlegmatic, artistic, realistic** Using the pen name Diedrich Knickerbocker, the American writer Washington Irving (1783–1859) depicted the stereotypic Dutch burgher in his burlesque *A History of New York from the Beginnings of the World to the End of the Dutch Dynasty* (1809).

720.20 **Spinoza** Benedict de Spinoza (1632–77) was a Dutch Jewish philosopher and one of the foremost exponents of seventeenth-century rationalism.

722.15 **"going to and fro in the earth"** Dreiser quotes Job 2:2, where Satan, when asked by God where he has been, replies: "going to and fro in the earth."

CHAPTER XCI

723.18 **Grote Kerk of St. Bavo** A late-Gothic church erected in the fifteenth century and restored in the last decade of the nineteenth century.

723.18 **Grote Kerk of St. James** A Gothic church of the fifteenth and sixteenth centuries.

723.21 **Mauritshuis** This building was erected in 1633–44 for Count John Maurice of Nassau, the Dutch West India Company's governor of Brazil; since 1821 it has housed the Royal Picture Gallery, a collection surpassed only by that of the Rijksmuseum.

723.21 **Mesdag Museum** Opened in 1903, the museum contains the art collections (especially works from the nineteenth century) of the painter Hendrik Willem Mesdag (1831–1915), which he donated to the Dutch government.

724.7 **Vierge** Daniel Vierge (1851–1904) was a Spanish-born artist often referred to as the "father of modern illustration." He is best known for his illustrations for nineteenth-century editions of classic Spanish picaresque novels, such as Cervantes's (1547–1616) *Don Quixote* (1605) and Quevedo's (1580–1645) *La vida del Buscón* (1626).

724.25 **an eminent Dutch jurist** Dreiser here disguises the profession of R. Rijkens, whose business card, contained in Dreiser's diary notes, shows him to have been a physician.

724.39 **Bols** Hans Bols (1534–93) was a Dutch painter best known for his portraits and idealized landscapes.

725.13 **my book, the latest one** Dreiser refers to his second novel, *Jennie Gerhardt* (1911).

725.32 **marriage of true minds** Dreiser quotes Shakespeare's Sonnet 116, "Let me not to the marriage of true minds" (1609).

727.1 **cottage plan orphan asylum** Dreiser refers to a movement that went back to the early decades of the nineteenth century and spread after the American Civil War. Orphan children lived as "families" in "cottages" and "villages" instead of institutions. Dreiser had a lifelong interest in orphaned children. As an editor of the *Delineator* he organized a child-rescue campaign that continued for three years, and in his will he bequeathed part of his estate to an orphanage for black children.

CHAPTER XCII

729.30 **Madame Wesendonck** Mathilde Wesendonck (1828–1902) was a a poetess with whom Wagner was romantically involved and some of whose works he set to music as the *Wesendonck Lieder* (composed 1858).

730.28 **Ibsen . . . Hedda** Hedda, the main character of the play *Hedda Gabler* (1890), by Henrik (Johan) Ibsen (1828–1906), is unenthusiastic about her marriage to George Tessman, a sincere, methodical intellectual devoted to his work.

730.40 **a somewhat sophisticated Emma Bovary** Dreiser refers to the heroine of the novel *Madame Bovary* (1857), by the French writer Gustave Flaubert (1821–80), which deals with the dissatisfied life, adulteries, and suicide of a doctor's wife in provincial Normandy.

731.19 **the Town Hall Museum** The Stadhuis contained the artwork of Frans Hals, which has been displayed in the Frans-Hals-Museum since its opening in 1913.

731.23 **Frans Hals . . . ill-treating his wife** Here Dreiser reports Hals's biography as narrated in Baedeker's *Belgium and Holland* (1910; p. lxvii). According to the *Oxford Companion to Art* (1970), the story that Hals was a drunkard and wife beater "is based upon a mistaken identity" (523).

731.26 ***dronkenschappe*** The Dutch word *dronkenschap* means "drunkenness."

731.40 **Lysbeth Reyniers . . . must have loved her** Hals married Reyniers in 1617, two years after the death of his first wife, Annetje Harmensdochter Abeel, whom he had married in 1610 and with whom he had two of his ten children.

732.9 **Herbert Spencer** See historical note 232.11.

732.17 **Old Omar** See historical note 102.14.

732.25 **Saskia van Uylenburch** The daughter of a Friesland lawyer, she married Rembrandt in 1634 and died in 1642.

732.31 **Hendrickje Stoffels** Rembrandt's common-law wife, Stoffels (?–1663) was some twenty years younger than the artist and bore him two illegitimate children.

733.7 **Agassiz** (Jean) Louis (Rodolphe) Agassiz (1807–73) was a Swiss-born American naturalist, geologist, and teacher.

733.14 **Lieven de Key's meat market** The Vleeshal, famous for its rich ornamentation, was erected in the Renaissance style by Lieven de Key (ca. 1560–1627) at the Grote Markt in 1602–3. Shortly before Dreiser's visit it had been restored for use by the Dutch National Archives.

CHAPTER XCIII

734.29 **Hebrew Orphan Asylum in New York** This institution, located on New York's Amsterdam Avenue, was founded in 1822 as the Hebrew Benevolent Society and underwent several name changes until 1906.

734.34 ***The Night Watch*** Rembrandt's perhaps most celebrated work, painted in 1642 and long held to be a nocturnal scene, represents a company of arquebusiers emerging from their guild house. For his description Dreiser has partly adopted the text of Baedeker's *Belgium and Holland*, which he had purchased in Berlin.

734.34 ***The Syndics*** *De Staalmeesters* ("Stampmasters"), painted in 1662, presents the syndics of the clothmakers' guild.

734.34 **van der Helst** Bartholomeus van der Helst (1613–70) was a Dutch portrait painter.

734.35 **Hobbema** Meindert Hobbema (1638–1709) was a Dutch landscapist.

735.2 ***The Artist and His Wife*** This painting (ca. 1624) has since been referred to as *Married Couple in a Garden*.

735.8 **Cuyps** Aelbert Cuyp (1620–91) of Dordrecht was a Dutch painter of portraits and animals.

735.33 ***Officers of the Arquebusiers of St. Andrew*** Begun by Frans Hals in 1633 and completed by Pieter Codde in 1637, this painting, also known as *The Meagre Company*, depicts Captain Reynier Reael's Company of Arquebusiers.

735.41 **Keats speaks of glutting one's sorrow on a rose** Dreiser refers to Keats's 1819 "Ode on Melancholy": "But when the melancholy fit shall fall . . . Then glut thy sorrow on a morning rose."

737.31 **Shelley's skylark** Dreiser refers to Shelley's poem "To a Sky-Lark" (1820), which uses the (European) skylark, a bird that sings only in flight, to embody a nonmaterial spirit of pure joy beyond the possibility of human experience.

737.34 **Huneker** James Gibbons Huneker (1860–1921) was an American music, art, and literary critic.

739.35 **Koepelkerk** The Ronde Lutherse Kerk (also called Koepelkerk) was erected in 1668–71 and is located at 11 Singel. With its circular floor plan, this classicist-style Lutheran church is unique in the Netherlands and of special architectural value.

CHAPTER XCIV

742.24 **'s-Gravenhage** Official Dutch name for The Hague.

742.25 **"something too much of this"** *Hamlet*, act 3, scene 2, l. 76.

743.20 **Godfrey of Bouillon** Godfrey IV of Bouillon (?–1100) was the duke of the lower Lorraine in 1087 and leader of the first crusade. Henry IV bestowed Antwerp on him in 1076.

743.21 **Stevenson . . . Flanders** Dreiser refers to the Scottish author Robert Louis Stevenson's (1850–94) book *An Inland Voyage* (1878), which describes a canoe tour in Belgium and France.

743.23 ***Elevation of the Cross*** **and** ***Descent from the Cross*** Rubens painted these two altarpieces in Antwerp's Our Lady cathedral in 1610 and 1612–14, respectively.

743.39 **the old castle called La Steen** Originally a part of the Castle of Antwerp, this building dates from the tenth century. It was given to the burghers of Antwerp in 1549 and later turned into a museum.

744.2 **Musée Royal** Erected in 1879–90, the museum houses important Rubens and Van Dyck collections, as well as a collection of old masters and a gallery of modern paintings.

744.13 **Percheron horses** These draft horses were originally bred and raised in Perche, a district in northeastern France.

744.15 **His portraits of . . . Helena Fourment** Dreiser refers to Rubens's *Portrait of Helena Fourment* (ca. 1630; Musées Royaux des Beaux-Arts, Brussels). Helena (Hélène) Fourment appears frequently in his later paintings.

744.23 **Cabanel and Bouguereau's suggestive nonentities** Both Alexandre Cabanel (1823–89) and William-Adolphe Bouguereau (1825–1905) were French painters. Dreiser saw Bouguereau's *Study for Nymphs and Satyr* (1873) in New York's Hoffmann House Café when his brother, the songwriter Paul Dresser, introduced him to the city in 1894.

745.1 **the van Eycks** Jan (ca. 1390–1441) and Hubert van Eyck (ca. 1370–1426) were two early fifteenth-century Flemish painters. The altarpiece in Ghent was begun by both but completed by Jan when his brother died.

745.2 **St. Bavon** The Cathedral of Ghent, a massive building of plain exterior, was founded in the tenth century and mainly built from the eleventh to the fifteenth centuries.

745.2 **Rogier van der Weyden . . . Massys** Rogier van der Weyden (1400–1464), Hans Memling (1430–94), and Quentin Massys (1465/66–1530) were Flemish painters.

745.4 **the Brueghels** This family of Flemish painters (also spelled Breughel and Bruegel) included Pieter Bruegel (1525–69) and his two sons Jan Brueghel (1568–1625) and Pieter Brueghel the Younger (1564–1638).

745.37 **Notre Dame** An early Gothic building dating from the twelfth century, with a late Gothic addition in the fifteenth century, it was restored in 1907.

746.16 **Hôtel de Flandre** A first-class hotel, located at 38 Rue Nord-du-Sablon.

746.30 **St. Sauveur** Built between 1183 and 1527 and named a cathedral in 1834, the church combines early and late Gothic styles.

746.33 **Charles the Bold** The last of the great dukes of Burgundy (1467–77), Charles (1433–77) led the Burgundian state to its most extensive power.

746.35 **Hospital Memling** The Hospital of St. John, which dates from the twelfth century, houses some of the finest paintings by Hans Memling (1430–94), a representative of the early Flemish school, among them the altarpiece of St. John and the reliquary of St. Ursula.

746.36 **Béguinage** Dating from the thirteenth century, the low, whitewashed houses formed the abode of the religious sisterhood of the Beguines and later of the sisters of St. Benedict.

746.37 **the Halles** This storage building, which forms a large rectangle, was erected in the thirteenth and fourteenth centuries.

746.37 **amazing Belfry** The tower, 353 feet tall, offers a splendid view. It is described in Longfellow's poem "The Belfry of Bruges" (1846), which is cited in the Baedeker guide that Dreiser used for his travel book.

746.37 **Hôtel de Ville** A Gothic building of the fourteenth and fifteenth centuries.

746.38 **Chapelle du Saint-Sang** The name of the church derives from what are claimed to be drops of Christ's blood that Theodoric brought from the Holy Land in 1150.

747.6 **Hanseatic League** Beginning in the eleventh century and formally established in 1356, the Hanseatic League, or Hansa (Ger.: *Hanse*), was founded by north German towns and German commercial groups abroad to defend their mutual trading interests. Bruges became the leading city of the "Flemish Hansa in London" by practically monopolizing the wool and cloth trade with England.

747.7 **defy the Louis of France** The treaty of Verdun (843) made Flanders a part of France, which resulted in its long-lasting struggle against France. After the assassination of Charles the Good (1127), the prosperous burghers opposed the French King Louis VI (1081?–1137) by electing Count Theodoric of Alsace as their sovereign and the count of Flanders.

CHAPTER XCV

747.18 **Ste. Gudule** Begun in 1220, this imposing Gothic church is built on the site of St. Michael and dedicated to St. Gudule, the patron saint of Brussels.

747.21 **Karnak** Dreiser refers to the temple ruins of Karnak, in Egypt.

747.21 **Hôtel de Ville** The Brussels city hall (Stadhuis) is one of the most beautiful buildings of its kind in the Low Countries. Construction on the building began in 1402; its Gothic-style façade, which faces the marketplace, is richly decorated with statues of the dukes of Brabant and other celebrities.

747.29 **automat restaurants** The first restaurant with food-vending machines—an American innovation—the Automat Restaurant was opened in Philadelphia in 1902.

747.31 **Dukes of Brabant and the Counts of Flanders** Former rulers of the region in which Antwerp is located.

749.7 **Royal Museum** The Palais des Beaux-Arts, built in 1875–81 in the classical style, houses the royal collections of sculpture and paintings.

749.28 **"resemblance with dignity, costume with taste, art with simplicity"** Dreiser here quotes from *Lectures on Painting, Delivered at the Royal Academy of Arts* (1809), by John Opie (1761–1807), a British historical and portrait painter.

749.31 **Margaret Lemon** An English courtesan who was Van Dyck's lover until 1639, when he married Mary Ruthven.

749.39 **Frans Duquesnoy** Frans (or Francis) Duquesnoy (1594–1643) was a Flemish sculptor who spent most of his life in Italy.

750.14 **Rodin's *Thinker*** During the last twenty years of his life, François-Auguste-René Rodin (1840–1917) worked on *The Gates of Hell*, inspired by Dante's *Divine Comedy*, Ghiberti's *Paradise Gate*, and the art of Blake. Comprising 186 figures and never completed, it provided the basis for many of his most famous sculptures, among them *The Thinker*.

750.19 **Michelangelo's . . . the tomb of Julius II** Work on the tomb of Julius II was interrupted because of a quarrel between Michelangelo and the pope. *Moses* and two *Slaves* were all that were actually carried out of the project.

751.28 **Harry Lauder** Sir Harry (MacLennan) Lauder (1870–1950) was a Scottish music-hall performer and songwriter.

751.30 **Victor Hugo . . . *Les Misérables*** Dreiser refers to part 2, book 1, of *Les Misérables*.

CHAPTER XCVI

757.3 **the Amstel** The Amstel Hotel, located on the Buiten-Amstel at 1 Tulp-Plein, is a first-class hotel.

CHAPTER XCVII

759.34 **Garden of the Tuileries** The Jardin des Tuileries was built next to the Louvre in 1563 by Caterina de' Medici and in 1664 extended to contain the park designed by André Le Nôtre. The castle (deriving its name from the tile kilns that originally occupied this site) was destroyed during the regime of the Communards in 1871.

759.35 **Bois de Boulogne** Bordering the Seine, the park derives its name from Notre-Dame-de-Boulogne-le-Petit, erected by pilgrims on their return from Boulogne-sur-Mer. Originally a royal hunting ground, but also a hiding place for thieves and robbers, it was turned over to the municipality in 1852 and became a favorite promenade for Parisians.

760.6 ***Heimweh*** See historical note 37.11.

760.10 **Marcelle** Marcelle Itam.

760.11 **Madame Goldschmidt** Elaine Goldschmidt.

760.23 **Café Américain** See historical note 398.32.

760.35 **Hanns Bolz** After studies at the Kunstakademie (academy of art) in Düsseldorf, the German painter Bolz (1885–1918) went to Paris, where he worked from 1908 to 1910 at Montmartre and Montparnasse, followed by a year in Munich. In the spring of 1912 he returned to Paris and became a member of the Dome group of artists. During World War I he was exposed to poison gas, which led to his death in 1918.

760.39 **Miss Rice** See the historical note on Rice at 313.34.

761.4 **Pavillon de l'Élysée** The restaurant of the Hôtel de l'Élysée, which is located at 12 Rue des Saussaies, close to the Palais de l'Élysée and the Champs-Élysées.

761.4 **Café de Madrid** This first-class restaurant is located at the Porte de Madrid. The name *Madrid* (for a section of Neuilly) derives from a castle that once stood near the racecourses of Longchamp in the Bois de Boulogne.

761.5 **Pré Catelan** A gourmet restaurant situated on the Route de Suresnes, Bois de Boulogne.

761.5 **Café Royal** Pavillon Royal, a first-class restaurant located on the Route de Suresnes in the Bois de Boulogne.

763.28 **chapel people** See historical note 242.39.

764.5 **bluggy** A euphemistic English pronunciation of *bloody* that Dreiser uses here to characterize the stylish Englishmen who are lusting for a fight.

CHAPTER XCVIII

767.8 **Au Père Boivin** A restaurant located at 6 Avenue de Clichy.

767.9 **Marcelle. . . . Rue Marcadet** Marcelle's address in Paris was 220 Rue Marcadet.

768.6 **"When shepherds pipe on oaten straws"** *Love's Labour's Lost*, act 5, scene 2.

769.13 **Muratore** See historical note 432.2.

770.9 ***Partant pour Amérique. . . . vous venez*** The French passage translates: "Leaving for America Saturday. Do come tonight by train. Bring suit and [a] dress for theater. Dreiser. Hotel Capitol, London. Will meet the train at Charing Cross if you come."

771.41 ***The Easiest Way*** See historical note 22.25.

773.14 ***"perfide Tayadore," . . . "du jour"*** French words and phrases meaning "fickle Theodore," "no doubt," "my friend," "that's it," "quite," "exactly," "that's fine," "for me," "for you," "I am," "the night," and "of the day."

CHAPTER XCIX

774.36 **Salisbury** Located in southwestern England, about eighty-three miles from London in Wiltshire County, the town had 16,000 inhabitants in 1912. The cathedral, built in 1220–60, is one of the finest examples of early Gothic style.

CHAPTER C

779.13 **the Empire** The Empire Theatre of Varieties, located on Leicester Square.

779.13 **Romano's** A high-class restaurant in the West End, at 399 Strand.

780.24 ***Chantecler*** The rooster in *Le Roman de Renart* (written between 1174 and 1250).

782.32 **"Alexander's Ragtime Band" and "Everybody's Doin' It"** These two hit songs, published in 1911, were written by the composer Irving Berlin (1888–1989). "Alexander's Ragtime Band" was Berlin's first major success.

784.6 **Hera** A daughter of Cronos and Rhea, this Greek goddess was both sister and wife of Zeus. Greek mythology portrays her as an impetuous, jealous wife who persecutes her husband's many mistresses.

CHAPTER CI

785.10 **"Hello, My Baby"** Song written by Joseph Howard (1867–1961) and Ida Emerson (?–?) in 1899.

786.7 **Belgian liner** The *Kroonland* was built in 1902 by W. Cramp Sons at Philadelphia for the International Mercantile Marine Company's Red Star line (entry into service: 1902; gross tonnage: 12,760; overall length: 560 feet; breadth: 60.2 feet). It set out on its initial voyage, from New York to Antwerp, on 28 June 1902. In 1908 it was put under the Belgian flag (Société Anonyme de Navigation Belgo-Américaine, or SANBA) and sailed between Antwerp and New York until 13 January 1912, when it reverted to the U.S. flag.

789.12 **Sirius** Appearing in the constellation Canis Major and also called the Dog Star, it is the brightest star in the heavens.

789.12 **Rigel** A first-magnitude star in the left foot of the constellation Orion.

CHAPTER CII

791.32 **opera Marguerite** See historical note 396.1.

791.36 **through a glass, richly** The biblical phrase that Dreiser intertextualizes is "through a glass, darkly" (1 Corinthians 13:12).

793.30 **Brobdingnagian sea cow** Dreiser refers to the giant inhabitants and animals of the fictional country of Brobdingnag in *Gulliver's Travels* (1726), by Jonathan Swift (1667–1745).

794.9 **Taft** The Republican William Howard Taft (1857–1930) was the twenty-seventh U.S. president (1909–13).

794.22 **The president . . . John Jacob Astor** Dreiser refers to J. Bruce Ismay (1862–1937), president and managing director of the White Star Line. Unlike John Jacob Astor (1864–1912), who died in the sinking, Ismay was saved from the *Titanic*.

CHAPTER CIII

796.39 **passing in the vicinity of where the *Titanic* went down** The *Titanic* sank about 360 nautical miles southeast of Newfoundland.

799.19 **"Eyes, and they see not; ears, and they hear not"** See historical note 692.34.

799.32 **Woolworth Building** A sixty-story neo-Gothic skyscraper designed by the American architect Cass Gilbert (1859–1934), it was under construction from 1910 to 1913.

799.38 **"A stranger in a strange land"** See historical note 198.42.

Textual Commentary

EDITORIAL PRINCIPLES

The copy-text for the present edition of *A Traveler at Forty* is the "First Typescript," as completed in 1918 from Dreiser's original holograph manuscript by his friend and experienced secretary Estelle Bloom Kubitz. The designation of this manuscript is misleading from a chronological point of view, for the first typed copy had been prepared for the Century Press in 1913. This copy was then radically cut and altered by house editors. Real events were fictionalized by changing the names of living persons and places, and new passages were introduced to bridge textual gaps ensuing from the cuts. The result—the first edited typescript of 1913—is no longer extant. The numerous alterations then required a second typed copy to serve as setting copy. This "Revised Typescript" of the same year, containing still further cuts, changes, and corrections, has survived together with the First Typescript of 1918. Also preserved in the archives of the University of Pennsylvania's Annenberg Rare Book and Manuscript Library are the corresponding diary notes, Dreiser's daily record of his travels in Europe, and his collection of picture postcards.

This new edition presents the fullest known text of *A Traveler at Forty*. The version of the travel book published by Century in 1913 is a different book, a historical document that reflects the specific circumstances and pressures of its time of production. It is and will remain of interest for this particular reason. Dreiser himself considered the published book to be a mere selection from his work. He took care to distinguish it clearly from the uncut version. In his own hand, he labeled the Revised Typescript as follows: "A Traveler at Forty. Typewritten selected portions which were published in the volume of that name." The Kubitz, or First, Typescript, however, carries the note: "A Traveler at Forty. Typewritten copy of the original uncut and unedited pen copy. It contains much material not in the published book."

The revisions on which the Revised Typescript and the published book are based gave a different direction to the work, especially by removing the more private passages and reflections on social mores that both the American and the English publishers considered inappropriate or too daring for the reading public of their time. For the present edition, the authorial revisions in these texts were considered carefully. They have been categorized as those that were required by the editorial policy—the overruling adjustment to outside pressures—and those that aimed at improving the original text. A number of these revisions have been chosen to emend the text of the First Typescript. In the case of *A Traveler at Forty*, Dreiser apparently benefited from the reading and advice of the Century editor Douglas Z. Doty, who, being on friendly terms with Dreiser, seems to have tried to serve him in the double capacity of personal and professional editor. Doty, although sharing Dreiser's views to a certain extent, had to put the considerations of his publishing house first, and so he found himself more than once in an unpleasant dilemma. Moreover, a business friendship of longer standing with the English publisher Grant Richards and the threat of legal pressure further complicated an already difficult situation. Thus, despite Doty's genuinely good-natured approach, his alterations needed to be reviewed critically. It should be noted that H. L. Mencken was not involved in the editing of the travel book. Despite Dreiser's promises in a 9 August letter to send proofs "shortly," none were mailed until 10 November.[1]

The First Typescript, although a fair copy for the most part, requires editing in various respects. Since the holograph is missing, it is impossible to tell, except by inference from other manuscripts prepared by Kubitz, which changes and corrections were introduced during the process of typing. Although typing mistakes or misreadings can be easily detected and corrected, intentional changes may remain hidden. Whenever corresponding passages were available, it was necessary to collate the First Typescript and all extant variant forms to create a working ground for redaction.

The most obvious problems in the First Typescript, although small in number, are the blank spaces, representing sometimes a word or words the typist could not read, sometimes a word or name the author meant to insert later, and sometimes pages missing from the holograph version;[2] spelling errors (outright typing mistakes or errors in personal names, place names, and foreign words); and inconsistent spellings. The more subtle problems occur on grammatical and stylistic planes. The strategy throughout has been to form the appropriate decisions on the basis of the work itself and its intended meaning. There are several cruxes in the text of the First Typescript. The first crux is the generic change in the beginning, where Dreiser gradually abandons the form of the travel journal in favor of the travel narrative.[3] The second crux concerns the abrupt narrative break in chapter 1. A third crux is the occasionally mixed use of real and disguised names. The fourth crux is the logical sequence of the London chapters and the integration of a supernumerary chapter (chap. 30a). The fifth crux is the missing description of Dreiser's visit to the Houses of Parliament in the company of the Honorable Thomas P. O'Connor. The sixth substantive crux is the problem of the chapter titles.

Crux one. Dreiser, following instructions from his English publisher, Grant Richards, starts his book in diary fashion. Following the chapter numbers he lists the day of the week and the date before beginning the narrative proper. He continues this method, with intermittent lapses, until 20 December, when he reports on the events of 4 December 1911, the day he begins chronicling his experiences in a separate diary, to be elaborated on his return. Although he cites from his journal from time to time, he gives up the diaristic mode as impracticable in chapter 15 and replaces it with a less time-bound and time-conscious narrative. While keeping all references to specific days and dates in the chapters, the editor has removed the dates placed before the opening sentences in chapters 1, 7, and 8. Since the dates are repeated within the text, however, they remain accessible to the reader.

Crux two. Chapter 1 furnishes an interesting case of early rewriting. Preserved as a fragment and variously titled as "Autobiographical Attack on Grant Richards" and "Dreiser: Autobiographical Fragment," this piece, which contains two diary entries for 4 and 25 November and is housed at the University of Virginia,[4] is the first version of the beginning of the book. It stops abruptly in the middle of a sentence, "Here I was writing, owing $300 on an insurance policy which." The fragment itself, however, precisely fills the lacuna in the corresponding passage of the First Typescript, "was just about to fall due . . ." The preceding paragraph starting "In some respects" has also been incorporated in order to fill the logical gap in the narrative.[5]

Crux three. With few exceptions, Dreiser used real names in the First Typescript, but for reasons of discretion the American and the English publishers decided to disguise names of both persons and places. Occasionally these substitutes, such as "Bridgely Level" for Bigfrith and Cookham Dean or "Wilhelmsruhe" for Zehlendorf, occur along with the real names in the same chapter and even on the same page. Dreiser generally preferred to use the real names and obviously disliked the disguise.[6] Dreiser's dominant practice in the First Typescript has therefore been adopted for the present edition, and whenever needed, the real names have been restored.[7]

Crux four. The sequence of the narrative events, especially in the London chapters, was subjected to considerable rearrangement in the 1913 edition. Chapters were cut up and portions reassembled according to the editor's seeming preference. Although cutting complete chapters presented no problems in the process of recopying, the London chapters, which apparently had also been renumbered, caused some confusion, as is reflected in the First Typescript. To restore the narrative's chronological order, the following changes were made to the presentation of the First Typescript. First, chapters 14 and 15 appear in reverse order, and chapter 11 (Dreiser's visit to Penn and Oxford on 16 and 17 December 1911) has been placed just before chapter 24. The short chapters 24 and 25, which relate a day's visit to Sir Hugh Lane's home, have been brought together as one chapter. Chapter 30a, which describes the Christmas celebrations at Richards's country house, is now chapter 25. The present chapters 26 to 30, which describe the trip to Manchester and its environs, are numbered in brackets as chapters 26a to 26e respectively in the First Typescript. One can only speculate that these portions were later inserted by Dreiser and that, starting with chapter 27, Kubitz had to renumber all following chapters in the book. A further case of a disordered text and a mention of missing pages occurs toward the end of chapter 94. Kubitz's note on the gap is followed by a passage identical to one in chapter 95.[8] The duplicate text has therefore been removed from chapter 94.

Crux five. Another irritating case of pages missing from the First Typescript is the vignette of Dreiser's walk with the Honorable Thomas Power O'Connor in chapter 31, alternatively numbered 26f and probably also inserted at a later point. Here, right at the beginning of this chapter, the typist has stated in brackets: "The first part of this chapter has apparently been torn off and taken to England by Richards—Dreiser."[9] The chapter proceeds with the continuation of a walk to the new Roman Catholic cathedral. The corresponding diary entry reveals that, earlier that day, Dreiser and O'Connor had visited the Houses of Parliament. Curiously, this is the only case of an episode that appears in the 1913 edition but not in the original version or the Revised Typescript. The note suggests that, after noticing the gap at the start of the chapter, Kubitz asked Dreiser, who blamed Richards for the missing text. Nevertheless, as in the case of Dreiser's description of the Carlton Hotel in London, to which Richards had vehemently objected, the text was later restored by Doty. In the case of the O'Connor passage, however, it cannot be known whether the visit to the Houses of Parliament represents the entire missing text.

Crux six. Titles were provided for the fifty-three chapters of the 1913 edition. They seem to have been selected at the last minute. There is no record documenting who chose them and why they were added. Of the First Typescript's 103 chapters, only chapters 11, 12, 19, 23, 26, 32, 33, 34, and 45 have titles. In the Revised Typescript only three chapters bear a title. The reason for adding titles may have been the publisher's wish, first, to identify the book more clearly as a discussion of persons and places in Europe and, second, to suggest a firm, coherent structure in a book whose narrative had been seriously impaired by enormous cuts and substantial alterations to the remaining portions. Dreiser does not seem to have planned to introduce titles, an opinion supported by the fact that in 1912 he had expressed his wish to have the chapter titles removed from the plates of *Sister Carrie*.[10] Since the Dreiser Edition seeks to avoid any unwarranted emendations, the chapters are identified only by the original roman numerals. As a part of the textual history, however, the 1913 edition's chapter titles appear in the apparatus.

In the matter of accidentals such as spelling, punctuation, and word division, the various Traveler texts present certain problems. The punctuation of the "Lilly Edwards" chapter as published in *The Smart Set*, for example, differs strikingly from that in the same passage as printed in the 1913 edition.[11] The house-styling of the latter is marked by some conspicuous features, such as abundant hyphenation (e.g., *to-night*), a characteristic absent from the First Typescript. The present edition follows the Kubitz typescript version throughout in the matter of accidentals. Although Dreiser tended to delegate decisions on accidentals to others, both literary friends and professional editors, it does not follow that their way of handling these textual specifics should be adopted. While he may have followed his house's guidelines perfectly, the copy editor did not take into account the work's specific nature as a personal record. In an autobiographical narrative it is imperative to stay as close as possible to the author's version. Because Dreiser preferred a light manner of pointing, an increase in punctuation beyond the basic requirements of clarity would have affected his easy-flowing style and deeply altered the general impression of his narrative.

For questions that cannot be cleared up by referring to the extant edited forms of the travel book, the diary notes—the immediate source of composition—offer guidance. These notes, which Dreiser carefully stored along with the Kubitz typescript, provide reliable information as to names of persons and places, as well as to the sequence of the events described. Usually the spelling of proper names in the diary is more dependable than in any of the later versions, and several substantive problems have been resolved on the basis of these precise details. Since these entries occasionally project the wording of a particular passage, they have also been consulted in cases of dubious words and phrases. Moreover, all doubtful realia have been traced, checked, and verified with the help of extratextual sources.

The collation based on the text of the First Typescript assembles the corresponding portions of the Revised Typescript, the four magazine articles, the autobiographical fragment, and the first impression of *Traveler* (1913). After all later changes had been entered into this diplomatic text, the editing of the copy-text was performed. A precise color-coded record of all emendations has been kept, and responsibility, whenever it can be assigned, has been indicated. Emendations that had to be made throughout the text for the sake of consistency have been noted in a master list. The complete record of emendations has been deposited at the Annenberg Rare Book and Manuscript Library for the use of interested readers. For this publication, a selective list of emendations has been added, strictly limited to substantive and significant accidental emendations. A list of the block cuts that created the 1913 edition, the Revised Typescript, and the magazine articles has also been appended.

Notes

1. Thomas P. Riggio, ed., *Dreiser-Mencken Letters: The Correspondence of Theodore Dreiser and H. L. Mencken, 1907–1945*, 2 vols. (Philadelphia: University of Pennsylvania Press, 1986), 1:123–24.

2. The text missing from chapter 1 I have since been able to identify as a portion of a holograph manuscript preserved in the Dreiser Collection of the Alderman Library at the University of Virginia, where it is listed as "Autobiographical Attack on Grant Richards." This fragment was originally discovered by Thomas P. Riggio. See Riggio, ed., "Dreiser: Autobiographical Fragment, 1911," *Dreiser Studies* 18, no. 1 (Spring 1987): 12–21. See textual notes 3.1, 5.10, and 6.29.

3. See Renate von Bardeleben, "From Travel Guide to Autobiography: Recovering the Original of *A Traveler at Forty*," in *Theodore Dreiser and American Culture: New Readings*, ed. Yoshinobu Hakutani (Newark: University of Delaware Press, 2000), 177–86.

4. See the historical commentary, p. 807.

5. See Riggio, ed., "Dreiser: Autobiographical Fragment," p. 19, ll. 10–28; First Typescript, p. 5, l. 20, to p. 6, l. 1; and this volume, p. 6, l. 31, to p. 7, l. 4.

6. The Revised Typescript shows the various stages of the ongoing battle over Grant Richards's name. See textual note 8.15.

7. In his memoirs, published in 1934, Grant Richards revealed some of the names that had been disguised in the 1913 edition; see Richards, *Author Hunting: Memories of Years Spent Mainly in Publishing* (London: Unicorn, 1948 [1934]).

8. See First Typescript, 1077–80.

9. First Typescript, 387.

10. See James L. W. West III, "Editorial Principles," *Sister Carrie* (Philadelphia: University of Pennsylvania Press, 1981), 583.

11. On the first page alone punctuation varies in thirteen cases.

November 18, 1911

My dear Mr. Dreiser:

I have pleasure in sending you inclosed our check for $1000, and in this connection make a record of the arrangement between us, as follows:

This payment is for three articles embodying your personal impressions of Europe, to be prepared for The Century Magazine after further consultation with the editors. If you should decide to write a book, containing not only these articles but other material about Europe - growing out of your coming journey - we are to have an option of publishing the book upon a payment to you of a royalty of 15% of the retail price. If you should for any reason be unable to deliver the three magazine articles satisfactory to our editors by say July 1, 1912, this payment is to apply as an advance on account of royalties on the book; or if the book should not be published by us it is to be considered as a loan, to be repaid without interest.

Sincerely

Frank H. Scott

Theodore Dreiser, Esq.
3609 Broadway,
New York.

Letter by Frank H. Scott

(Annenberg Rare Book and Manuscript Library, University of Pennsylvania)

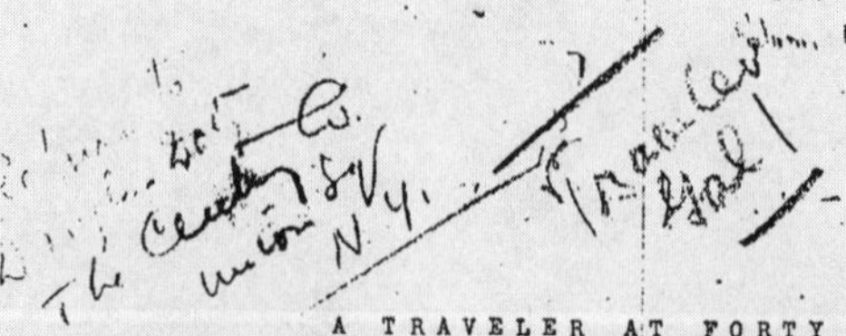

A TRAVELER AT FORTY

To begin this record right I should say that on this date, Saturday November 4th, 1911, I am living in an apartment on upper Broadway, New York. I enjoy those things which go to make up the best type of apartment life in New York City - the first city in America. I have just turned forty. I have seen a very, very great deal of life. I have been a newspaper man, editor, magazine contributor, author and before these things several odd kinds of clerk before I found out what I could do.

This past winter I have been engaged in writing a novel which is just now on the market and, thank Heaven, much to my astonishment, doing fairly well. This fall I have been at work on another novel which I hope to complete by the spring of 1912. About one third of it is done. I am not very well fixed financially at this moment but because of the unexpected success of this book, critically at least, I begin to see my way clear. A distinct unequivocal literary reputation is worth something financially in the United States. Eleven years ago I wrote a novel, which was issued by a New York publisher and suppressed by them. Heaven knows why.

Edited page from the Revised Typescript

(Annenberg Rare Book and Manuscript Library, University of Pennsylvania)

Estelle Bloom Kubitz

(Annenberg Rare Book and Manuscript Library, University of Pennsylvania)

TEXTUAL NOTES

In the following list, the leftmost page-line references indicate the starting point of the passage in question; bracketed page-line references following the boldface key phrases indicate the endpoints. In addition, the First Typescript is abbreviated as FTS throughout; the Revised Typescript, as RTS.

CHAPTER I

3.1 **To begin this record right** The date at the beginning of the text has been removed, for Dreiser repeats it in the following sentence. The diary mode of narrating was practiced systematically only from 4 to 25 November. Exceptions are chapters 38, 63, and 78, in which Dreiser quotes from his diary notes. The beginning of the first sentence of *A Traveler at Forty* is identical to the beginning of the first sentence of Riggio, ed., "Dreiser: Autobiographical Fragment," 14.

3.22 **"The Financier"** Although titles of published books are italicized, "The Financier" has been left roman in this case, because it was an incomplete manuscript at the time and is used here by Dreiser as a working title for the later trilogy.

3.24 **my second book** To clarify the chronology of Dreiser's writings, the word *second* has been added to parallel the next paragraph's use of the word *first*, which had already been introduced in the revised and the printed versions. Without the change from "this book" to "my second book," "the unexpected success of this book" could be misinterpreted as referring to *The Financier* instead of *Jennie*.

4.5 **too much . . . actively dangerous** [4.22] In the RTS Dreiser added several words that, because they further explain his meaning, have been entered into the copy-text: "generally not to talk about that too much" and "Most of us believed that to understand life was not only to become evil, passively so, by reading but to be by the very act of so reading actively dangerous."

5.10 **1844** The incorrect date 1849 in the FTS, which seems to be a misreading by the typist, has been emended. The correct date, 1844, is given in Riggio, ed., "Dreiser: Autobiographical Fragment," 15.

6.13 **"Ode on a Grecian Urn"** The title of the poem Dreiser calls "Ode to a Grecian Urn" has been corrected to its true title, "Ode on a Grecian Urn."

6.29 **I am not a simple-minded man** The incomplete sentence on page 7 of the FTS continues Riggio, ed., "Dreiser: Autobiographical Fragment," 19. As can be seen in chapter 1 of the FTS, Dreiser did not change the diary form, and he hardly changed the first sentence: "To begin this record right . . . " A further indication that Dreiser used the text of the fragment is the sentence "Life was not only to become but to be very bad" (Riggio, ed., "Dreiser: Autobiographical Fragment," p. 17, para. 2, l. 10), which reappears unchanged except for a comma in the FTS (p. 3). The sentence "But perhaps instead of telling you about my book" (which seems to refer to *Sister Carrie*) does not make much sense without the passage on *Sister Carrie* from "Dreiser: Autobiographical

Fragment, 1911," for otherwise Dreiser will not have told the reader about that book.

7.33 **old publisher friend . . . I shall publish them** [9.13] In the RTS Dreiser changed "publisher friend" to "literary friend." Changes of this kind have not been adopted because they reflect the pervasive spirit of discretion as reflected in the 1913 edition. This is also true for Dreiser's changing Grant Richards's promise "I shall publish them" to "I will see that they are published."

8.15 **Grant Richards** *G. R.* and *G——— R———* have been rendered consistently as "Grant Richards." In his correspondence Richards always signed with his full name. The name was variously disguised, as "G." and "X." in the magazine articles and as "Barfleur" in the published version of 1913. In the RTS "G. R." was blue-penciled into "Barfleur," and this correction was then reversed back to "G. R." In the final stage of production, the American publisher suggested to Richards that he not hide behind a fictitious name.

10.19 **an American publisher** Dreiser's handwritten change of "with an American publisher" to "with both an American and an English publisher" in the RTS has not been adopted, for it was motivated solely by discretion.

CHAPTER II

25.2 **The young couple** The antecedent of "These two" is grammatically unclear; since the phrase logically refers to the young couple mentioned earlier, "These two" has been emended to read "The young couple."

27.39 **"thou hast no introspection** The *Macbeth* quotation reads "Thou hast no speculation in those eyes / Which thou dost glare with." Dreiser changed the key word to *introspection* and omitted the ensuing relative clause. The misquotation has been left unaltered because it reflects Dreiser's intention better than the accurate quotation would.

CHAPTER III

32.39 **I acknowledge the Furies** The final sentences in this chapter are among the few Dreiser remarks to have made their way into Bartlett's *Familiar Quotations* (15th ed. [1980], 732): "'I acknowledge the Furies, I believe in them, I have heard the disastrous beating of their wings' (*To Grant Richards [1911]*)."

CHAPTER IV

33.18 **B deck** The ship's decks are designated in an inconsistent manner. The present edition thus uses the form "B deck" rather than "B. deck," "B-deck," or "(B) deck," all of which appear in the FTS.

CHAPTER V

47.32 **Miss Burke . . . Miss Longfellow** Grant Richards's reference to "Miss Brook" has been changed back to "Miss Burke." Two lines later (47.34), "Miss Brook" has been emended to read "Miss Longfellow," since the story line and the logic of the narrative clearly suggest that it is Miss Longfellow, rather than Miss Burke, with whom Dreiser is "at swords."

51.35 **Mr. Vulgar Kahn** Dreiser's descriptive use of a pejorative adjective as a first name has been maintained rather than change "The Mr. vulgar Kahn" of the FTS to "The vulgar Mr. Kahn" or "vulgar Mr. Kahn"; the preceding definite article has been removed. To emphasize its intended function as a first name, the adjective has been capitalized.

52.5 **cu-aw-rious** At first glance the word *cuawrious* looks more like a typing error than imitated speech. Therefore hyphens have been introduced so that it reads more easily as a reproduction of Grant Richards's pronunciation.

CHAPTER VI

62.10 **an American citizen** The word *American* has been inserted into the sentence "He has a brother who has become an [blank] citizen and resides in New York."

63.24 **values. How does he** A redundant FTS passage—"Bernhardt was entirely satisfactory to him. . . . I asked myself"—has been cut; it appears in the appendix.

68.21 **"And we being exceedingly tossed** In the RTS Dreiser corrected the phrase "and when we were come by Patmos after much trouble," a rather free rendering of Revelation 1:9 ("I John, who also am your brother and companion in tribulation, and in the kingdom and patience of Jesus Christ, was in the isle that is called Patmos") and a reference to the fact that John wrote the Book of Revelation on this island. Instead Dreiser selected Acts 27:18 ("and we being exceedingly tossed with a tempest"), which is a reference to the storm Paul encountered during his voyage to Rome. Since the corrected phrase is more suggestive of Dreiser's mood at the end of this chapter, the author's correction has been adopted.

CHAPTER VII

68.31 **The sea is** Dreiser's change of tense in the RTS can be attributed to his adaptation of diary text to a more narrative style. Since Dreiser's diary style has been left exactly as it appears in the FTS, this change of tense has not been adopted.

CHAPTER VIII

78.35 **I am a silly person** Dreiser's revision of his frank statement in the FTS "I am a silly person from many points of view" to "I think most of us are a little silly at times, only we are cautious enough to conceal it" in the RTS seems to have stemmed from his effort to comply with the publisher's general policy of "genteel" presentation of living persons. Therefore, the revised version has not been adopted.

81.27 **"Swanee River"** Dreiser seems to refer to Stephen Foster's song "Old Folks at Home," which mentions the "Swanee River." Dreiser's spelling in the FTS has been preserved and not emended to "Suwannee," as was done in the 1913 edition.

CHAPTER IX

92.8 **"The Boy and the Owls"** The title of the Wordsworth poem that Dreiser calls "'The Boy' and 'The Owls'" in this chapter of the FTS has been emended to read "The Boy and the Owls," to harmonize it with the form of the title he uses in the first chapter of *A Traveler at Forty*. See also historical note 6.15.

CHAPTER XI

108.19 **After I had been at Cookham . . .** To restore the chronological order of the narrative, the original chapter 11, Dreiser's visit to Penn and Oxford, has been placed just before chapter 24.

112.1 **Sacred to the Memory** The text from the church wall to which Dreiser is obviously referring but that is missing from the FTS has been inserted as it appears on the memorial plaque inside the All Saints Church in Marlow.

CHAPTER XII

122.20 **again. At first I thought** The following sentences from the FTS were cut to avoid redundancy: "These white spots were quite like scars. The truth is, it was quite the other way about. They had been snow-white and had been sooted by the smoke until they were now nearly coal-black. And only here and there had the wind and rain whipped bare white places which looked like scars or the drippings of time."

128.8 **present. While we were sipping** The FTS contains an incomplete episode—"While we were dining G—— R—— told me the following story. . . . (Missing)"—that has been deleted; it is reproduced in the appendix.

129.8 **take the train to Cookham** The change to "until train time" in the RTS has not been adopted, for it seems to have been motivated by the pressure to obscure the precise destination of Cookham, Grant Richards's address. The FTS's more explicit phrase "until time to take the train for Cookham" has been emended to read "until it was time to take the train to Cookham."

129.36 **concerned my next novel, "The Financier"** Dreiser changed "Since the London subways concerned my next novel, The Financier," in the FTS to "concerned a future novel" in the RTS. This change has been omitted to preserve a uniform temporal perspective, although given that the *The Financier* had just come out when he made the revision, Dreiser may have felt he had to adjust this information—his original plan—to correspond with the recent decision to handle the material in a trilogy and to postpone the London subway material for later use.

CHAPTER XIII

131.21 **I was ushered upstairs** Since the book provides information about Dreiser's movements in Mrs. Stoop's home earlier than the copy-text does, this passage has been inserted into the copy-text here, where it fits the chronological sequence of events. The FTS sentence "I had been ushered into a drawing room one flight up" has been removed from line 29 of the copy-text.

CHAPTER XIV

143.1 **London is lost in a fog . . . I would not stop** [148.1] The FTS chapters 14 and 15 appear in reverse order to correspond with the progression of the story.

CHAPTER XV

148.25 **action. Of course** The FTS version is marred by a lacuna here: ". . . of great ease in action, which is really not ease nor insouciance but [blank] of what he is thinking and saying, and what you are thinking and saying." The copy-text ends after the first full prepositional phrase, with the word *action*.

150.36 **so confined** In the FTS this chapter suffers from several textual gaps, all of which have been emended. For example, in the sentence reading "The circumstances from which they spring are obviously so [blank] and confined," the word *and* has been deleted and the blank ignored.

CHAPTER XVI

160.10 **was delicious . . . as I have indicated in a way** [166.2] Dreiser's handwritten additions to the RTS, most of which appear in the 1913 edition, have been integrated into the copy-text.

164.34 **a Mr. Filson Young** In the FTS Dreiser uses the pseudonym "Mr. Tyne" for this "other" critic, but he identifies him as Filson Young in the diary notes (see historical notes 54.30 and 164.34). Accordingly, we have substituted the true name for "Mr. Tyne" and have cut the following lines from the FTS: "I do not care to give the name of the writer, for his affairs are too intimately connected with those of G—— R—— to permit of it. At that time I did not know this."

CHAPTER XX

196.34 **not new, like those in New York or Rome or Berlin or Paris or Milan** In the course of his travelogue, Dreiser gradually moves from a diaristic to a novelistic mode. Here the author anticipates his second visit to London at the end of *A Traveler at Forty*. He retrospectively compares it to the cities he saw on the Continent, thus summing up his European travel experiences.

197.4 **Tower—there are no fine buildings** Since Windsor is not situated in London, it has been removed from the FTS sentence "Outside of some of the old palaces and castles in London—St. James, Buckingham, the Tower, Windsor—there are no fine buildings."

CHAPTER XXIII

212.35 **Hazlemere** A blank in the enumeration of place names has been filled in to read "Hazlemere." Either the typist could not read the word or Dreiser did not remember the name and meant to add it later. The context makes it fairly certain that the town in question is Hazlemere (Buckinghamshire County). Having passed Lane End and High Wycombe, the party had to pass through Hazlemere to reach Penn. Dreiser insists on the poetic quality of the place names, which may have been suggested to him by the suffix *-mere*. He may have associated the name with those of the Lake District spots cherished by the romantics, such as Windermere and Grasmere, and made famous by poets such as Wordsworth. Dreiser often links place names with literature, as can be seen from the fact that he unfailingly misspells *Marlow* as *Marlowe*, thus making it match the English playwright's name. The other option—to omit the name—would have required a substantial alteration of the text, which reads "but they are only three . . ." To change this phrase to "only two" would have impaired Dreiser's style, since the tradition of citing three examples is an imperative one observed by Dreiser in many other instances.

CHAPTER XXIV

225.18 **Among the most interesting . . . I am sure** [230.23] The short chapters 24 and 25 have been merged because they form a narrative unit. Chapter 13 (renumbered 30a in the FTS by Estelle Kubitz, the secretary) has been numbered 25 in keeping with the chronology of the narrative.

231.6 **Solomon** In an 18 January 1912 typewritten letter from Grant Richards to Dreiser, the name of the South African architect appears as "Solomon." Accordingly, the FTS spelling "Salaman" has been changed to "Solomon."

CHAPTER XXVIII

265.38 **One of the amusing things** The syntax of the following FTS sentence has been extensively emended: "One of the amusing things was that this being Sunday, no liquor of any kind was supposed to be served but in spite of the blue laws without, the 'chapel people,' as the religious-minded are dubbed in England, who are strong enough to prevent it, nevertheless champagne was being consumed here in large quantities." It now reads "One of the amusing things was that this being Sunday, no liquor of any kind was supposed to be served—the 'chapel people,' as the religious-minded are dubbed in England, are strong enough to prevent this—but, in spite of the blue laws without, champagne was being consumed here in large quantities."

CHAPTER XXXI

281.1 **One evening** In the FTS this chapter starts with the following parenthetical comment: "(The first part of this chapter has apparently been torn off and taken to England by Richards—Dreiser.)" Given that part of this chapter corresponds to chapter 10, pages 81–83, in the 1913 edition and that Dreiser's visit to the Houses of Parliament (pp. 83–88 in the 1913 edition) is the only instance in which the 1913 edition contains an episode missing from the FTS, it can be assumed that this episode constitutes at least part of that missing text.

CHAPTER XXXII

293.4 **One of the things** The first four sentences of this chapter are ambiguous in the FTS: "One of the things which dawned upon me in hearing about England,

and particularly as I was leaving it, was the reason for the inestimable charm of Dickens. I do not know that anywhere in London or England I encountered any character which spoke very forcefully of those he described. It is probable that they were all exaggerated—somewhat. But of the charm of his setting there can be no doubt." They have been rearranged as follows: "One of the things which dawned upon me in moving about England, and particularly as I was leaving it, was the reason for the inestimable charm of Dickens. I do not know that anywhere in London or England I encountered any types which forcefully manifested the characters he described. It is probable that they were all exaggerated—somewhat. But of the charm of Dickens's settings there can be no doubt." The second, redundant instance of the phrase *no doubt* has been eliminated.

298.37 **secure** Forms of the verb *to secure* appear in conspicuous abundance and have therefore been emended: one instance of the verb has been kept, and the other two have been replaced with *had* and *attract*.

300.20 **sickening Pullman. Grant Richards** In the FTS Dreiser notes that pages are missing. This gap has been smoothed over as follows: "I can no longer take pleasure in the stuffy Pullman, with its sickening [paragraph break] (pages gone here) [paragraph break] he slept until we neared Amiens . . ." has been emended to ". . . in the stuffy, sickening Pullman. [paragraph break] Grant Richards slept until . . ."

CHAPTER XXXIII

302.25 **As we came . . . The run from Amiens to Paris** [303.26] Since the first sentence of this chapter ("The run from Amiens to Paris requires several hours") is out of the place in the FTS, it has been deleted here and inserted where it logically belongs, namely, at the end of the third paragraph on page 303.

CHAPTER XXXIV

321.17 **the Petit Palais** Given that the Petit Trianon (to which Dreiser refers in the FTS) is located in Versailles and that Dreiser is referring to "all these great institutions in Paris," Dreiser is probably referring to the Petit Palais in Paris. Therefore, the latter has been used in the copy-text.

CHAPTER XXXVII

348.38 **The Paris subway** The following sentences have been linked: "The Paris subway does not go outside the walls. It turns in circles and cross-sections within it. Neither do many of the Paris electric lines or bus lines. They run from one important point in the city to another." The passage in the copy-text now reads this way: "The Paris subway, which turns in circles and cross sections, does not go outside the walls. Neither do many of the Paris electric lines or bus lines, which run from one important point in the city to another."

350.23 ***Figaro* as a guide** The FTS reads "if you will accept Figaro, [blank], as a guide to what is Parisian in this matter"; it has been rendered "if you will accept *Figaro* as a guide to what is Parisian in this matter."

CHAPTER XXXVIII

353.1 **The next day** To restore the chronological order of the narrative, the puzzling phrase "The rest of the day" has been changed to "The next day."

CHAPTER XXXIX

361.36 **Her gay girlfriend** To make the antecedent clearer, "friend" has been changed to "girlfriend" and "She" [361.40] to "Mme. de Villiers."

CHAPTER XL

371.35 **adjourned to another place** An omission in the FTS has been bridged: "Thereafter the four of us adjourned to the [blank]" now reads "Thereafter the four of us adjourned to another place."

CHAPTER XLI

377.34 **"Old Box" . . . Bax** [377.39] "Old Box" is clearly indicated to be the nickname of Ernest Belfort Bax (see historical note 377.34). Although Dreiser consistently uses the nickname in his narrative, it can be assumed that he does so solely to respect Grant Richards's wish to protect his friend's privacy. In addition, the discussion on the same page reveals the origin of Sir Hugh Lane's nickname—which, however, is used rather inconsistently. The use of "Bax" in the sober narrative and of "Old Box" in the dialogues underlines the joking nature of the conversation.

CHAPTER XLII

384.19 **lonely sail** Since the word *lovely* has been changed to *lonely* in both the RTS and the 1913 edition, and since it fits the mood of the passage, this emendation of a possible misreading of the word in the holograph has been incorporated into the copy-text.

386.23 **"cercle privé"** Although Dreiser writes "Cirque Privé," the casino's official description uses "cercle privé"; as a result, the latter has been substituted. Dreiser's version seems to have resulted from the fact that when pronounced rapidly, the French word *cercle* sounds like "cerc," which Dreiser may have confused with the French word *cirque*, which means "circus."

CHAPTER XLIII

393.9 **a stiff** Dreiser seems to use less common meanings of the word—"migrant," "vagabond," or "someone who is cheating"—to tease Richards, as his later explanation confirms.

CHAPTER XLIV

404.4 **His ascetic face, crowned** Since it is impossible to determine the end to Dreiser's passage "his ascetic face looking like a figure out of [blank]," the reference has been removed.

407.29 **doubt. I was not** Since it is impossible to determine whom Dreiser meant when he wrote, "Near here, as our Badaeker [*sic*] told us, [blank] was born," the sentence has been omitted.

408.14 **stone. So great aims** The last sentence of the first paragraph has been removed. The second paragraph fully develops the comparison that has been introduced in the first paragraph—thus, the FTS's phrase "The parallel is quite apt" has been deleted.

CHAPTER XLV

413.18 **antics. Lane spoke** Given that Dreiser's omission in Grant Richards's "comment which involved the [blank] as an illustration" cannot be resolved, this part of the sentence has been removed.

415.19 **spectator** Since the word *speculator* in the FTS does not make sense in this context, it has been emended to *spectator*. The RTS and the 1913 edition confirm this correction: although they phrase the passage differently, they use the word *spectacle*.

CHAPTER XLVII

437.4 **Belliard** "Baillard" has been emended to read "Belliard," based on the spelling of the name of the sisters in a 2 February 1912 diary entry.

437.7 **lunch with the Baxes at the Régence** As indicated in a 2 February 1912 diary entry, Dreiser's lunch with the Baxes took place at the Régence, not the Regis (which is not listed anywhere in the guides of the period and appears to be a misreading by the typist).

CHAPTER XLIX

456.7 **Cimabue** The spelling of the Italian painter "Cimabue" as "Cimolene" in the FTS seems to have stemmed from a misreading of Dreiser's handwriting.

CHAPTER LI

470.37 **Giuffré** Dreiser here uses one of five possible variants of the name, including "Giuffré," "Giuffrè," "Gioffre," "Joffré," and "Jofré."

472.41 **Cesare was tolled off** The tenses of the Borgia narration have been changed in entire paragraphs for consistency's sake.

CHAPTER LII

482.36 **knew his subject** Here and on the following pages Dreiser's handwritten corrections to the RTS have been adopted.

CHAPTER LIII

487.18 **apt to be presented** To avoid a too frequent use of *as*, two instances of it have been removed in the phrase "where a sarcophagus or a burial inscription are as apt to be presented as a garden monument or set in a wall as a relief as not." It now reads "where a sarcophagus or a burial inscription are apt to be presented as a garden monument or set in a wall as a relief."

488.22 **Since first meeting, Mrs. Armstrong and I** To make Dreiser's meaning perfectly clear, the FTS's clause "Since first meeting Mrs. Vallon we had become" has been changed to "Since first meeting, Mrs. Armstrong and I had become."

CHAPTER LV

505.14 **1823** The correct year is 1823; "1873" reflects either a misreading or a typing error. See *Baedeker Central Italy and Rome* (1909, p. 445).

CHAPTER LVI

509.32 **a decorated fragment** An omission from the FTS has been edited out: "a fragment of decorated . . . with gay, dancing figures" now reads "a decorated fragment with gay, dancing figures."

CHAPTER LVII

515.28 **St. Francis** The FTS fragment "(Page missing) [blank] until it reaches the town" has been deleted.

CHAPTER LVIII

522.26 **Marcelled** Dreiser here coins a neologism to characterize an improvised foreign-language communication he had previously practiced with Marcelle.

527.8 **cots** Humble places of shelter.

528.26 **feed** Gave a fee to, paid.

CHAPTER LIX

535.31 **entering a place** The omission in the phrase "We were entering a [blank] which had but little resemblance . . ." has been filled with the word *place*.

537.41 **The Duomo . . . were what I wished to see** The omission in the FTS passage "The Duomo, the palaces of the Medici, the Pitti Palace, and that world which concerned the [blank] of Florence, and the dignified goings to and fro of the old Cosimo Pater and his descendants, was the thing that I wished to see" has been resolved as follows: "The Duomo, the palaces of the Medici, the Pitti Palace and the dignified goings to and fro of the old Cosimo Pater and his descendants were what I wished to see."

CHAPTER LX

543.20 **Michelangelo gives . . . Michelangelo and his genius** [543.33] Dreiser mentions several other artists in the middle of his discourse on Michelangelo, rendering the referent of the FTS's "this man" ambiguous. Therefore "this man" has been changed twice to "Michelangelo."

CHAPTER LXII

555.1 **Mr. Jesurum . . . was a Jew** [556.36] To avoid redundancy and an undue emphasis on ethnicity, the apposition "a Jew" has been removed from the first of these two sentences. The attribution "Mr. Jesurum was a Jew" remains on page 556.

CHAPTER LXIII

557.6 **of William Turner** "of [blank] and Turner" has been corrected to "of William Turner."

559.36 **I trustingly . . . watched it shining** [560.6] To avoid repetition and redundancy, the FTS passages "I let the matter of our future carefully rest, trusting to the future" and "because the moon was shining magnificently we stood in the corridor and watched it shining" have been rearranged to read "I trustingly let the matter of our future carefully rest" and "because the moon was magnificent, we stood in the corridor and watched it shining."

CHAPTER LXV

576.2 **Mont Cenis** The missing geographical name, *Cenis*, which had been added in the RTS, has been inserted here.

576.34 **"la-de-das"** The plural form of *la-de-da* (also *la-di-da*), a derisive term for one who affects gentility, a "swell."

CHAPTER LXVI

578.37 **different regions should produce different people** The text that appears here in the 1913 edition, "It proves that countries are not merely soil and climatic conditions. . . . Races like animals . . . judge for yourself," reads like lines written by Dreiser and inserted at the last minute, an impression reinforced by the fact that it does not occur in the RTS. Dreiser apparently expanded the text to clarify his meaning. Since there is no definite proof of this, however, and the same argument can be found elsewhere in *Traveler*, the FTS text has been chosen for the copy-text.

CHAPTER LXVII

583.39 **his line. I am afraid** A redundant paragraph from the unedited portion of the FTS ("The next day being Sunday . . . I had come out on my balcony") has been cut. Although it anticipates the later narrative, it disrupts the reflections on the subject of beauty, which start with art and proceed to natural beauty.

585.26 **ge-washed and ge-brushed** Dreiser adds the prefix *ge-* to words in these chapters to give the text a German-language feeling. This prefix is found in most German past participles.

CHAPTER LXVIII

592.11 **factories in full operation** An omission in the FTS has been edited out: "and nearer at hand factories labeled [blank] in full operation" now reads "and nearer at hand factories in full operation."

CHAPTER LXXII

613.1 **Timbuktu** "Tombouctou," the most modern spelling of Dreiser's "Timbuctoo," has been rejected in favor of the more commonly known variant "Timbuktu," in keeping with the general tendency of Dreiser's spelling.

616.15 ***Ich will ein Bettzimmer*** Dreiser's misspellings in German have been corrected, but any incorrect usage has been preserved. See also historical note 616.15.

CHAPTER LXXIII

621.30 **"Who goes there?"** The call that Dreiser imagines hearing from the tower, "Who comes here," has been changed to "Who goes there," following English usage, for Dreiser does not attempt a literal translation of the corresponding German phrase *Wer da,* as the reader might assume him to have done.

CHAPTER LXXV

630.17 **virile** Dreiser uses *virile* in the now obsolete sense of "nubile."

CHAPTER LXXVII

647.7 **not a patch on** Colloquial for "in no way comparable to."

CHAPTER LXXXIII

680.14 **Rochester, New York . . . Mrs. Drucker** [680.31] The FTS furnishes no name for Madame Culp's cousin and disguises her by using a different place of residence in America. Following the information in the diary notes, "Mrs. . . ." has been replaced by "Mrs. Drucker" and "Cleveland, Ohio," by "Rochester, New York."

CHAPTER LXXXIV

682.19 **Hanscha Jauer** Based on the spelling in the diary, Hanscha's last name has been corrected to "Jauer," a name frequently occurring in eastern Germany.

CHAPTER XC

719.32 **Venice to Amsterdam** The FTS passage "I gained that so strong coming from [blank] to Amsterdam" has been changed to "I gained that so strong coming from Venice to Amsterdam." The missing place name was derived from the corresponding 31 March 1912 diary note.

CHAPTER XCII

731.26 ***dronkenschappe*** "from 'dronkenschappe'" is a quotation from the chapter on Frans Hals in *Baedeker Belgium and Holland* (Leipzig: Karl Baedeker, 1910) lxvii, which Dreiser has used for his description. Although *dronkenschap* is the Dutch word meaning "drunkenness," *dronkenschappe* is an inflected form used in the seventeenth-century source.

CHAPTER XCIII

739.36 **Nieuwe Kerk** There is no Grote Kerk in Amsterdam—although both The Hague and Haarlem have one—so that Dreiser must be referring to the Nieuwe Kerk, which is located near the Royal Palace.

CHAPTER XCIV

741.12 **go to the devil** The omission from the FTS—"I vowed that in so far as I was concerned she and her sister could go to [blank]"—has been resolved by inserting "the devil."

747.10 **workmanship** Page 1077 of the FTS bears the note "(pages missing)," followed by a lengthy excerpt of duplicated text from chapter 95 (pp. 750–52 in the present edition). Accordingly, that passage ("and Italian schools dwindle to mere shadows . . . he could have made to this humdrum world.") has been cut from chapter 94.

CHAPTER XCV

747.11 **After Bruges and Ghent** To clarify the chronology, the FTS's sentence "After Bruges and Ghent (to which I gave six hours), and Brussels (to which I gave a day), I arrived again in Paris" has been emended to read "After Bruges and Ghent (to which I gave six hours) and before I arrived again in Paris, I gave a day to Brussels."

749.26 **in a certain way** The first instance of the word *peculiar* has been replaced by *certain* to avoid repeating it in a single sentence.

CHAPTER XCVII

766.1 **Grant Richards had selected** To avoid repetition of the word *secured* in consecutive sentences, the first sentence has been changed to "Grant Richards had selected a table."

CHAPTER CI

784.17 **Later that day** Pages missing from the FTS required the creation of an acceptable transition at the beginning of the chapter. The incomplete sentence has thus been emended as follows based on the diary notes: "Later that day we had to leave for our train from Charing Cross."

788.11 **Farnese** All forms of the name *Farnasinia* (e.g., *Farnesinia* in chapters 102 and 103) have been changed to *Farnese* in the copy-text; in a diary entry for 20 April 1912 Dreiser writes, "Miss Farnese (She's borrowed that name from Italy)."

CHAPTER CII

795.3 ***Diaphus lucidus*** The omission in "[blank], with its incandescent lamps" has been filled with "*Diaphus lucidus*," a typical representative of the family Myctophidae (lantern fish); those in the genus *Diaphus* have specially developed luminous "headlight" organs.

Textual Apparatus

SELECTED EMENDATIONS

The following table lists selected substantive emendations made in preparing this edition of *A Traveler at Forty*. The complete textual record, including a list of all relevant emendations, is on deposit in the archives of the University of Pennsylvania's Annenberg Rare Book and Manuscript Library. Emendations to the deposited version of the copy-text are color coded. Editorial emendations appear in light blue; emendations adopted from the 1913 Century edition, in green; those from the Revised Typescript, in red; and those from Dreiser's articles "The First Voyage Over," "An Uncommercial Traveler in London," "Lilly Edwards: An Episode," and "Paris," in dark blue. When adopted, Dreiser's additions and corrections to the Revised Typescript have been marked in brown.

The page-line citations in the following table refer to the present edition. Chapter titles, running heads, and blank lines were not counted in determining these numbers. The initial text in each entry is the emended reading; it is followed by a righthand bracket that should be read as "emended from" and then by the text from the First Typescript.

3.24	my second] this
3.25	I am beginning] I begin
5.10	1844] 1849
5.13	Terre Haute, and when] Terre Haute, Indiana. When
6.11	poetry books] poet books
6.13	"Ode on a Grecian Urn"] "Ode to a Grecian Urn"
12.3	*Century Magazine*] Century
12.15	"The Financier"] "The Financier" (in England we call it Fee-nance-yer)
16.3	$1,500] one thousand, five hundred dollars
22.16	Miss Burke] Miss B
25.2	The young couple] These two
25.31	sex feelings could grow] sex feelings could loose themselves and grow
25.41	loose itself] loose itself and talk more freely
28.4	gay-sounding waltz] gay sound waltz
28.19	principle] principal
30.15	Mr. Hitchcock] Mr. H.
32.25	Mr. Scott] MR. S
32.31	times] lines
35.10	flower beds] beds
35.34	Miss Longfellow] Miss L
36.6	these women] them
38.30	has even occurred] always occurs
38.31	these temperamental race differences] it
40.1	complementary] complimentary
40.34	pleasant] great

41.38 lovely] pretty
43.18 as sweet a pair of lips] a pair of as sweet lips
47.32 Miss Burke] Miss Brook
47.34 Miss Longfellow] Miss Brook
48.37 race] force
48.41 Grant Richards] He
52.5 cu-aw-rious] cuawrious
53.31 *The Vista*] a Vista
54.18 That thing never works, quite] That things never work, quite
55.15 The second class occupy] The second occupy
61.30 ever] never
66.40 Kadato] Kadata
67.24 There was sixty-four pounds] I . . . the ship for sixty-four pounds
68.12 Switzerland, Germany] Spain
68.29 November 26] Sunday, November 26
68.36 washstands, and closets] washstands, closets and the like
70.7 whirling] whistling
71.39 Malvina] M
74.1 Mr. Kahn] Mr. K
74.17 touches of white and silver] touches and white and silver
74.25 Miss Longfellow] Miss B
75.17 masses] mass
76.25 forty] twenty-five
77.4 said] thought
79.41 lowering] lowery
81.40 Welsh] English
82.39 enameled] jewel
84.5 English] first-class
86.32 the low be] law
88.16 mere] were
91.18 really] actually
91.18 It was not at all strange to me, for in books and pictures I had seen it all my life, but here were the actual hills and valleys] It was not at all strange to me in books and pictures. I had seen it in those all my life, but here were the actual hills and valleys
92.8 "The Boy and the Owls"] "The Boy" and "The Owls"
92.41 Tess D'Urberville is present] Tess D'Urbeville and . . . are present
93.10 dark] dank
93.13 the English] your own
93.15 the charming] those lovely
95.27 between the tall hills where our train was following a stream bed] between the tall hills where we were following a stream bed—our train
95.41 except] expect
96.16 gaunt] grim
96.39 I have always had it] and I can't tell you why
97.28 She seemed to think poorly of gentlemen who hunt and shoot] She seemed to think poorly of hunting and shooting gentlemen
98.34 others have] some

101.27 Miss Hemmerde] Miss S
101.39 trams] trains
104.3 blacked] blocked
105.10 own native] early
105.20 eleven] seven
106.1 ten] twelve
107.9 how he managed to] whether he could
107.13 h'ighteen] 'ighteen
107.14 hawfter] aafter
107.40 about London at this distance] about London at this distance, or in England
108.23 small country town] village
109.34 border] line
110.19 quiet's] quit's
111.34 Cromwell] Cornwall
113.3 peered] peeked
113.33 filled] fulled
114.40 inquired] asked
116.12 a sandy-haired] a small, dapper, sandy-haired
117.25 in his every gesture] sticking out all over him
121.4 After a few days] Yesterday
122.10 generally] universally
123.13 from an American house] to American concerns
123.21 Georgian] colonial
123.25 business] publishing
125.6 this I followed] I have been following this also
126.29 In London] Here
126.37 problematic] probable
126.37 looks as though he were to be] looks to be
127.1 shall be able] am
127.11 imposing] distinguished
127.15 showy, ornate] glittering
127.16 hardwood heavily mirrored] woodwork
127.18 constitute a blazing curio case—a glittering museum] are things of beauty
127.29 those of the Brevoort] the Lafayette
127.30 repainted] painted
127.36 Jewish] Jew
128.6 hotel . . . But] real first-class hotel—but
128.20 Miss Villars] Miss V
130.29 wholly geometric, metaphysical and symbolic] wholly symbolic
132.13 shouted] insisted upon for her
132.40 continued] said
133.33 called my attention to Picasso's] produced his
133.37 lustrous] lustreful
133.39 morbid] marked
134.1 this conception] the idea if [*sic*] this work
134.3 has rather haunted me] I am hourly thinking
135.22 Use better English] use better
135.25 clear] good

136.1 Mr. K.] Mr.——
136.32 Henry Lamb] H L
137.3 Mr. Lamb] Mr. L
137.23 that he . . . at it] and Mr. H—— L—— . . . solemnly
138.35 unable . . . any] to . . . no
141.15 found] thought
145.14 wonder whether] wonder
145.18 was swathed] swathed
147.6 Mr. Percy Grainger] Mr. P G
147.27 Mr. Archibald Russell] Mr. A R
148.3 Mr. Eric MacLagan] Mr. Ian MacLaghan
149.12 Henry Lamb, who] Henry Lamb, an artist who
151.23 navigator] vanigatos
152.31 seemed to be] were seemingly
153.1 worst] worth
153.21 moot] mooted
154.25 settees] settles
155.18 Jerrard] Gerald
155.35 I also saw] Also
162.29 eyebrows] eyes
164.10 well-guarded] [blank]-guarded
164.34 the other of whom—a Mr. Filson Young—] the other of whom
164.38 Mr. Young] Mr. Tyne
164.41 thirty-three] -three
165.13 *English Review*] English Reviews
165.21 us] me, and G—— R—— who came along
165.25 dressed] arrayed
165.30 of course] I am quite sure that
167.8 an excellent] a splendid
168.2 Mr. Russell] Mr. R
176.9 join me] come
176.13 looked over her shoulder at me and smiled] looked at me quite interestedly
176.19 where they paused] somewhere pausing
177.31 Titchfield] Litchfield
180.24 Lilly] Lily
182.5 sullenly] suddenly
183.28 a dreadful] an awful
183.32 decided] got the idea
187.31 profitable] significant
188.17 to that Cheapside place] there
190.12 arranged] ranged
191.8 Miss Edwards] Miss E
191.14 about reclaiming] about it to reclaim
196.6 the tiny fish] them
196.6 the gulls] them
196.9 thrilled] delighted
196.13 minnows] ones
197.4 Tower—] Tower, Windsor—

197.37 Churton Street] Churleton Street
199.8 drab] drabby
199.22 whippet] whiffet
202.19 pictures of life] things
202.26 find] see
205.23 admired] saw
207.4 Frans] Franz
207.16 Most of them] They
207.22 amusingly novel] comic
208.23 according to how] according as
209.32 Cookham] Bridgeley Level
209.33 Sir Hugh Lane] Sir Scorp
209.34 some of the finest Manets] the finest collection of Manets
210.23 whence] from whence
211.35 C. H. Shannon] J. J. Shannon
212.35 and Hazlemere, but] and . . . , but
213.1 once prevailing but now obsolete] which once prevailed but which now obviously is obsolete
214.16 carefully gone over annually] gone over carefully annually
214.31 Ireland also. That evening] Ireland also. I would go on with this . . . experiences [*sic*]. That evening
217.1 their great impulses] the great impulses of princes
218.36 *Pelléas et Mélisande* by Debussy, *Thaïs* by Massenet, *Louise* by Charpentier, *Salome* by Strauss] "Pelleas and Melisande," "Thais," "Louise," "Herodiade" [*sic*] by Strauss
219.22 the children and I] myself and the children
219.38 twenty-two] twenty-one
220.21 Gioia] Berenice (Gioia)
221.5 Cookham] Bridgeley
221.30 which is perfection] which is the perfection
222.14 twenty-two] twenty one
222.15 colleges and halls] colleges
223.21 Christ Church] Christ College
225.21 Cookham Dean] Bridgeley Level
225.29 delve into] in
225.34 near] by way of
225.35 by hook or by crook] by hook and by crook
226.18 Philip Wilson Steer] [blank] Steer
227.3 John Oxenstierna, Count of Södermöre] John Oxensteirn, Count of Sadremare
227.4 Münster] Minster
230.37 invest] put
231.6 young Jewish architect, Solomon] young Jew architect
232.6 bent on] bent after
234.16 paintings] painted
235.30 There was] The personality
235.32 Jerrard Grant Allen] Gerard Grant Allen
237.13 Miss Hemmerde] Miss M

238.29 make him prick] cause him to prick

239.31 Eric Saunders] George Shepherd

242.9 Mrs. Grant Allen] Mrs. G A

243.41 late] last

245.1 an infinite] a finite

245.17 occurred] recurred

246.35 chattering] clattering

249.5 their father] G R himself

249.21 his funny] a high, falsetto

250.7 Nana] Mrs. A

250.32 adjourned] adjoined

251.24 Mrs. Stubbs] Mrs. Carton

253.28 Peterborough] Petersborough

254.13 had not been] had been

254.20 That was the end] There was an end

254.26 Galt House] Gault House

258.21 socialized] enobled

263.1 Mr. Stubbs] Mr. C

269.2 *haut*] haute

270.9 virtually] practically

270.22 through] past

270.22 partly] partially

270.24 relative to] near

271.6 rain] dark

271.41 poured] trickled

273.12 relatively minute] so small

274.8 flaring] flary

275.40 The one that I encountered this afternoon] This same restaurant

276.5 substituted] very cheap

277.16 a city of a population of one hundred thousand] a city of a hundred thousand population

284.22 Another afternoon we went] We went from this club

285.4 dusky] dusk

286.29 forgotten] overlooked

286.34 stertorously] industriously

287.15 moldy] mouldering

287.21 the Dover express] my through Dover express

288.31 hominess] home-ness

289.28 overhung with broken arches that had fallen] overhanging arches broken and fallen

290.5 tinny-voiced] tiny-voiced

291.11 a guide] one

292.36 stationery] stationary

293.4 moving] hearing

293.7 types] character

293.7 which forcefully manifested the characters he described] which spoke very forcefully of those he described

293.9 Dickens's settings] his setting

293.14	Landport] London
295.26	regions] country
296.39	faithfully] truly
297.8	Conservatism] Conversation
297.23	brighter] lighter
297.33	bleak in appearance] bleak-looking
298.37	had] secured
298.40	attract] secure
299.24	Gallic] Gaelic
299.28	rigorously] vigorously
301.9	towers, arches] spandrels
303.10	dreary-looking] dreamy-looking
303.16	chattering] clattering
303.30	bustling] hustling
304.32	remembrance and flavor] rumor
305.19	Louvre] Louis's
307.16	most common] commonest
310.39	wild] perfect
312.9	satisfaction or weariness, or both] satiation
312.12	from Russia] from the Russian
312.19	considered himself insulted] considered that he had been insulted
313.10	French men and women] Frenchmen and women
313.34	J. D. Fergusson] F. F. Ferguson
314.37	dashing] clashing
315.1	thence] from here again
317.38	seceded] receded
318.1	Boulevard] Boule
319.25	the latter] this particular
321.17	Petit Palais] Petit Trianon
321.37	with a little Gothic] with Gothic in little
322.18	Mr. Fergusson] Mr. F
322.19	Miss Rice] Miss R
322.29	astonishing] delightful
323.10	artist] art trio
323.19	down] dawn
324.1	exceedingly high] exceeding high
324.4	calling here] entering
325.7	one of his charcoal sketches] a charcoal sketch
325.14	reserve] secure
327.30	dog or child] dog
328.21	blend] type
328.31	festive] festival
332.14	did not know] did know
332.26	much as if to say] as much as to say
333.23	expensive] expansive
333.32	was plain] is seen
335.11	rouge] red madder
335.16	demimondaines] demi-mondes

339.30 collections] connections . . .
340.21 Hale] Dibblefield
343.7 Hart] R
343.26 Hart] H
344.27 was drawn] was to be seen
345.3 all the spirit] any spirit
346.23 told me] explained
347.4 still] yet
347.17 establishment] one
347.19 as long as they consent] unless they would consent
347.27 Port de la Conférence] Quai de la Conference
348.15 Then] When Monday comes
350.4 since this was] this being
350.15 dull, green-painted] painted a dull green
351.31 range from . . . in rent] rent for from
353.1 The next day] The rest of the day
353.17 Mr. Dawson] Mr. W
355.20 Mr. Dawson] Mr. Watson
358.41 affectionate] affectional
361.36 girlfriend] friend
361.40 Mme. de Villiers] She
362.30 the fact of his impending marriage] the fact
364.22 Jiv me akeess] Jive me akiss
365.20 Mr. Flexner] Mr. Simon
366.31 Mistinguett] Mees Tinquette
368.40 extended an indifferent hand] shook hands
369.18 though] through
370.26 we wound up being invited] it wound up by our being invited
371.35 another place] the [blank]
373.27 One had brought] They had brought, the one
375.3 as likely to] as like to
375.12 perfection] perfectness
376.1 suddenly, as I walked] suddenly walking
376.2 vine-covered] wine-colored
376.19 Riva-Bella] Bella Riva
377.8 bay of Monte Carlo] bay on which Monte Carlo stood
378.2 Bax] Old Box
378.19 is really so] is so
379.6 I struck out to walk] I to walk
382.15 expatiating upon] animadverting on
383.11 emphatically approved] considered very fine
384.19 lonely] lovely
385.30 This was] It was full of
386.12 for want of a better phrase] for a better phrase
386.37 Visions] Visitors
387.7 I stood as I adventured] I stood adventuring
394.16 gambling] gaming
395.36 *le dernier*] dernier

396.34 Itam] Itain
397.29 *oui*] qui
401.39 *excellent*] excellente
405.10 pride] ruin
405.17 illusory] pointless
405.33 skin] brogans
405.38 no more than] so much as
406.8 to speculate as to the age] the problematic date
407.41 construction] building anything
408.35 accustomed] used
408.37 and to give himself time] in order to give him time
409.8 claw-like] clawy
410.17 the ancient Greeks] Greece
410.19 *canard à la presse*] *canape a la presse* [*sic*]
411.1 mountaintop] mountain, its top
411.28 arches and angles were left; it crowned] arches and angles of which were left, crowned
411.41 real chill. My next fright] real chill, and my next fright
415.19 spectator] speculator
415.38 people] individuals
416.23 this gay world] this world
416.29 woman] given beauty
423.8 lounge] loungingroom
426.21 ends of the earth] earth-ends
426.29 female] women
426.33 Spaniard Louis] Spanish Louis
427.3 no less] not the less
431.28 My disturbance on this score amused me] It amused me—my disturbance on this score
432.40 woman with virtue and nothing more] woman of virtue with nothing more
437.4 Belliard] Baillard
437.7 Régence] Regis
442.23 turned and said with sparrow-like] turned and with sparrow-like
444.32 Mme. Goldschmidt] she
445.28 *descende*] descends
447.13 fell asleep while reading a book] fell asleep reading
447.31 one] own
447.36 above medium height] above the medium in height
448.10 what the trouble about the wreck ahead was] what the trouble was
448.22 carts] ox-carts
448.23 some] this, added to the fact that many
448.30 Often we] So often we
448.38 crowds, pure Italian in type] companies of the pure Italian type
448.40 wearing] in
450.28 incongruous] so strange
451.13 I had not learned] I had learned
451.41 knowledge] erudition
452.5 Karl Baedeker's books] Karl Baedeker—his books

453.9 Niccolò Pisano] Pisano
453.21 *campi santi*] Campo Santos
453.30 beautiful] lovely
453.40 studded] jeweled
457.15 earlier] elder
460.23 Italian] this foreign
462.32 band] bank
463.17 finest] first
464.27 Marcus Aemilius Lepidus] Aurelius Lepidus
466.34 reflecting upon] tremendously impressed with
467.15 if even that] if so much
467.20 Mrs. Armstrong] Mrs. Vallon
468.33 best-behaved] well-behaved
468.38 Nietzsche-like] intellectuality and Nietzsche-like
470.12 relate] indicate
470.13 Mrs. Armstrong's] her own
470.34 By the very charming Vanozza] By her, who was very charming
470.39 still another] a still other
471.10 made] created
471.16 advance] advantage
471.31 necessary] to his advantage
472.2 so that Cesare might] to
472.8 Cesare and Giovanni] them
472.22 On this journey he met] He did meet
472.27 principalities] princes
472.30 Alexander] he
473.13 *il Papa's*] papa's
473.25 eighteen-year-old] (aged eighteen)
473.33 a favorite recipient] a favorite, or rather a recipient
474.37 1519] 1511
476.34 Pincio] Pincian
477.5 horrors] terror
477.12 exteriorly speaking] exteriorly
478.1 Pope Pius V's sending assistance] the sending by Pope Pius V of assistance
478.24 that would be better] better
479.22 after giving a lira to as greasy a priest] for a lira, by as greasy a priest
480.8 following] accompanying
480.9 who was delivering peripatetic lectures] whom I have mentioned as lecturing
482.36 knew his subject thoroughly of course] had the history . . . at his fingertips
482.40 lifted . . . from] took . . . off
483.28 doubting] resourceful
483.29 could have] would set about to
483.32 thought] spectacle
484.26 desecrated] decorated
484.37 the fact that almost endless palaces were] the almost endless palaces that were
485.7 interest] force
485.29 A vision of the] The
486.1 snows of yesteryear] roses of yesterdays

486.12 learn] live and learn
487.23 sit] seated
487.32 they] the cypress and the climate
487.35 so as] to such advantage as
488.22 Mrs. Armstrong and I] Mrs. Vallon we
490.22 idle about for a week] idle a week about it
491.16 offers a view . . . of] commands
494.25 seemingly] apparently
494.31 Even so] still it was so
495.2 Greece] Italy
495.16 Mr. Couris] Mr. Bouris
495.41 asking if I would come] would I come
496.12 man's true] its
496.13 nothing] nowhere
496.28 subjugation to] leadership by
499.4 convulsive] foolish convulsive
499.4 from my newspaper friend Mr. Pooley] from—I will call him X
499.5 Mrs. Pooley] Mrs. X.
500.1 and smiling satisfaction] smiles of satisfaction
500.26 as they stood] standing
500.33 Signor Tani] a most delightful lecturer whom I discovered
502.1 Roman empire] Empire
502.5 It is given great charm] that gives it its great charm
502.14 the Tiber has] it has
503.3 I saw the Baths of Caracalla] The first I saw
503.15 I question] it is a question
504.9 There were] Aside from the
504.14 You could even see] and see
504.36 involved] had to do with this
504.37 power-seekers who sought] seekers after power. They sought
505.14 1823] 1873
505.29 meadow] mead
509.32 a decorated fragment with] a fragment of decorated . . . with
510.7 dryad] homodryad
512.16 some time] some little time
512.24 wise, see . . . pay it; or you can go back] wise (1), see . . . pay it; (2), go back
513.2 lira] one
518.4 *Guillemart*] Guillmont
518.37 the abbé asked if I] the Abbé said, would I
518.38 haav] have
520.6 which deal with] dealing with
522.25 minded] inclined
524.5 dusk] dust
524.32 barnacle-like] barnacle-wise
525.4 fine semblance] fine-seeming
525.25 Pas de Calais (France)] France (Pas de Calais)
525.30 possibly earlier] and earlier possibly
525.33 inside] within

529.2 commercial, with as great a sense of up-to-date-ness as Florence] commercial, and really with as great a sense of up-to-date-ness, although it is fifteen hundred feet above the plain, as Florence
529.4 varied] vicarious
529.9 sea-like] sea, like
529.33 Piazza del Municipio] Piazzo Municipio
532.25 artistic] art
533.17 like a Gothic cathedral] like a cathedral in itself, a Gothic cathedral
534.13 I heard] To my astonishment I heard
534.14 whom] what
534.16 To my astonishment one of these young men] young men . . . one of them
537.7 bands] stripes
538.2 what] the thing that
538.17 solidity] solidarity
539.17 nor will I forget] nor
539.27 Rome and a red] Rome, a red
542.28 force] cause
543.6 the mood] that other
543.16 ever and anon] ever and ever
543.20 Michelangelo] this man
543.34 genius and the mere] genius, the mere
544.19 getting their children] the getting her children
544.37 examples of sightseers present] examples present
545.34 vicinity. Not finding it] vicinity, but not finding it
546.12 manufacturing] manufacture
547.17 spent] took
551.7 city in the mornings] city, mornings
552.40 on an Italian spring morning] on a spring morning (spring in Italy)
555.15 The artists were] and were
556.41 Italy will be made over; the Germans themselves will be made over] Italy will be made over
557.6 of William Turner] of [blank] and Turner
557.11 slimy] shiny
557.12 anything I had ever read conveyed] anything conveyed
557.36 the temperamentally exceptional] the exceptional temperamentally
558.5 bound for Bologna] traveling from Florence to Bologna
559.12 I knew that by] I knew, by
559.21 that she was going home] "No, her home."
560.5 was magnificent] was shining magnificently
561.2 it was so wonderful] so wonderful was it
561.20 I think I cannot do more] I cannot do more, I think
563.32 five] four (?)
565.18 realize] know
565.28 though I have no idea why] though why I have no idea
568.19 suggestive and alluring] suggestive . . . , alluring
569.24 such personalities as the Lane type] such as personalities of the Lane type
569.29 be attached] attach
570.13 as if] until it seemed as if

571.11 where there is bathing] where the bathing is
572.4 glass] glass type
575.26 Rouen and Canterbury] Rouen, Canterbury and Cologne
578.17 acquired it] acquired, foliage
579.37 much, more to please] much to please
580.30 Midwest] middle west
581.14 the National . . . system] a Frenchified version . . . in New York
581.35 after I arrived] after I was
582.7 Mrs. Armstrong] Mrs. A
582.9 hold over any of my pleasures] hold any of my pleasures over
584.1 after my first day of ramblings] after my rambling
584.14 of the very early morning] of the morning (the very early morning)
584.18 over the water, its spiles standing in a soothing, restful way] over the water
584.21 dock] clock
585.37 such girls] such
586.16 Miyata] Myata
586.30 which in reality was] which was
587.29 Lake Lucerne] Lucerne
588.26 in Germany] in Switzerland, Germany
589.11 travelers, and a new section] travelers. A new section
589.28 I had an interesting final talk] It was so interesting, my final talk
590.38 veritable] regular
591.37 amazing] significant
592.20 boots] shoes
592.26 then to Mayence and Coblenz, and again from Coblenz to Frankfort] then to Mayence, Coblenz and Cologne, and again from Cologne to Frankfort
593.19 fanciful] forceful
593.37 women- and life-loving] women-loving and wine-loving
595.6 those of Italy] Rome or Florence or Venice
595.29 and second marriage of his father] and a second marriage on the part of his father
596.3 revisit] overcome
596.17 as it is spelled in Germany] as it is sometimes spelled, in Germany
596.41 I could see at Mayence] I could see
597.7 back to my first days in London] back to London, my first days
597.17 should very likely meet her later] should meet her very likely later
597.30 Bigfrith] Bridgeley Level
599.2 she, the true artist] (the true artist), she
603.9 sixty-nine] sixty-five
603.15 map of southern Germany] south-Germany map
605.5 The poorer masses look] They look, the poorer masses
605.10 Teutonic] Teuton
606.7 fair reward—and then hurried into my train] fair reward
606.26 aft] after
608.2 Mayen] that
610.12 I entered a compartment of the only class] I entered the only class
612.7 East Mayen] West Mayen
613.13 and once flowed around] once around

614.15 too often had] had, too often
615.25 the life of the race] the race life
617.22 male teachers] men-teachers
618.8 root, stock, and branch] stock and branch
619.4 were ranged] of which were ranged
619.22 bustled] brustled
620.13 my host] he
620.16 any goodwill] any too good will
621.2 wheat] white
621.30 Who goes there] Who comes here
622.12 the first one to be constructed] the first . . . had been constructed
622.37 Genovevaburg and found the castle] Genoveforburg Castle and found it
622.41 Schreder] Scheder
625.2 Who in the world] Who is in the world
625.20 Madame Culp] Madame G.
627.8 Zehlendorf] Wilhelmsruhe
627.12 Förster] Stolz
629.11 weel] will
631.3 Is] Iss
632.24 Miss Meyer, as I will call her] Miss Meyer (I will call her)
635.27 feel] fell
637.23 that Johann Wolfgang Goethe lived here] that Martin Luther, Johann Wolfgang Goethe and [blank] lived here
643.25 feather-like] feather-wise
648.3 French *-ries*] French
648.3 *-rias*] rics
648.20 Kupfergraben] Kupferdamm
651.37 Herr Merten] Herr C
652.26 I never knew] I never knew, until I reached
653.4 woke me] did it
655.6 Zola] Nana
655.21 sound out] sound
658.3 each driving a rearing, plunging quadriga] driving, each, rearing, plunging quadriga
659.5 dollars] marks
659.24 Kemperplatz] Kemp [blank] Platz
661.11 speed] rate
661.25 One panegyric] The one panegyric
665.24 dear reader] dear, darling reader
666.33 more real] right
667.10 slyly] slying
669.3 work] world
669.8 greatly] unduly
669.10 especially noteworthy] so much
673.13 mediums] mediums of introduction
673.29 efforts at] effects at
675.21 Américain] American
678.37 monetary] money

679.28 Royal Parade] Royal Parade grounds
680.14 Rochester, New York] Cleveland, Ohio
680.31 Mrs. Drucker] Mrs.——
682.19 Jauer] Jower
683.24 one-room accommodations] one room
688.9 "Shtetteen"] "Stetteen"
689.19 what] how
693.33 Förster] ——
693.34 up] astir
700.33 Geistler] Schmock
700.33 Simon] Pfleister
702.17 *Auf geht's*] So gehts
703.24 was truly something] was something
708.26 dumbwaitered] dumbwaiter
710.38 drew near] drew
713.30 Betsy Rijkens-Culp] Helena Stoveren Verhack
715.38 milling] willing
716.25 Dutch] Dutch or Italian
717.12 matter] matter. Amsterdam, I should . . . (No more)
719.32 coming from Venice] coming from [blank]
719.38 port] part
719.39 melts away] fritters itself away
719.39 the water's] their
723.21 the Mesdag Museum] the [blank] Museum
724.35 Madame Rijkens-Culp] Madame S
725.37 formulate] solve
729.39 auroral] aurora
730.15 Mijnheer Rijkens] Mynheer S
731.31 no less than] at least
731.41 eight] ten
732.17 bottle] battle
732.17 might not eventually have allured him] might not have eventually allured him
732.30 proportions, when she] proportions. Then she
732.31 Stoffels] Jaghers
734.4 million] billion
734.26 Kaiser-Friedrich-Museum] Kaiser Friedrich
735.2 *The Artist and His Wife*] the "Portrait of a Man and His Wife"
735.8 Maeses] Maes
738.9 van Ostade] Ostade
738.24 olive] alive
739.36 Nieuwe Kerk] Groote Kerk
743.23 *Elevation of the Cross*] Ascent
743.24 *Descent from the Cross*] Descent of the cross
743.27 Rubenses] Rubens'
745.40 shell] shall
747.2 The Halles] Halles
747.11 After Bruges and Ghent (to which I gave six hours) and before I arrived again

in Paris, I gave a day to Brussels] After Bruges and Ghent (to which I gave six hours), and Brussels (to which I gave a day), I arrived again in Paris

749.26 certain] peculiar

750.29 After a hard day, which included the Brussels Museum and Waterloo, I took the night train for Paris] Brussels, after a hard day, which included the Museum and Waterloo, and I took the night train for Paris

758.28 attacked] attached

758.28 somewhere] sometime

760.37 first . . . second] (1) . . . (2)

761.9 Pavillon de l'Élysée] Elysee

761.32 Mrs. Murray Bailey] Mrs.——

764.10 dec'rate] decrate

766.1 selected] secured

767.24 people that we had met could provide] people we had met had provided

768.6 straws] strains

768.15 Hugh] High

768.16 Mrs. Stoop] Mrs. S

770.9 Y] le

771.21 Assmannshäuser] [blank]

773.14 *Tayadore*] Theador

777.17 I will] She would

780.15 *Oui*] Qui

780.15 *bons*] bon

780.19 *et ses maîtresses*] et maitresse

782.32 Ragtime] Big Brass

782.32 Doin'] Doing

784.17 Later that day we had to leave for our train from Charing Cross] Cross

788.13 Nyssens] Oatzang

790.1 Van Dyk] Goyen

790.29 brown-black] blown-black

791.16 Weiss] Salz

792.3 Wallis] Wiggins

792.3 Pemberton] Coventry

792.34 Maupassant] de Maupassant

793.31 sank] sank (were subdued)

794.27 shuttn't] shuttint

795.3 *Diaphus lucidus*] [blank]

795.15 smashing] titanic

796.31 safely reaching] safety in reaching

797.16 Andrews] Maple

799.28 spindrift] [blank]

799.41 crowd] company

BLOCK CUTS

The following table records substantial First Typescript passages that were cut from the 1913 Century edition; the Revised Typescript; and Dreiser's articles "The First Voyage Over," "An Uncommercial Traveler in London," "Lilly Edwards: An Episode," and "Paris." Each opening page-line citation refers to the beginning of the passage in the present edition; the closing one, to the end. Brackets indicate language that the editors have removed from the copy-text.

CHAPTER I

Omitted from the 1913 edition (ch. 1, pp. 3–6)

3.1 [Saturday, November 4th:] To begin this record right . . . the first city in America. [3.15]
4.20 Most of us believed . . . nothing of its mysteries. [6.22]
6.26 I was raised . . . and complete my book. [7.30]
8.4 He had been over . . . Sunday morning, which he did. [November 15:] [8.21]
9.14 "Why? Why?" . . . for the English market. [10.16]

Omitted from the RTS (ch. 1, pp. 1–6)

3.1 [Saturday, November 4th:] To begin this record right . . . the first city in America. [3.15]
5.7 But perhaps . . . nothing of its mysteries. [6.22]
8.4 He had been over . . . Sunday morning, which he did. [November 15:] [8.21]
9.14 "Why? Why?" . . . for the English market. [10.16]

Omitted from "The First Voyage Over" (pp. 586–87)

3.1 [Saturday, November 4th:] To begin this record right . . . the first city in America. [3.15]
4.2 No doubt all of these . . . was to keep us so. [4.18]
4.20 Most of us believed . . . nothing of its mysteries. [6.22]
6.26 I was raised . . . and complete my book. [7.30]
8.4 He had been over . . . Sunday morning, which he did. [November 15:] [8.21]
9.14 "Why? Why?" . . . for the English market. [10.16]

CHAPTER III

Omitted from the 1913 edition (ch. 1, p. 6)

29.1 The Monday following . . . at eight o' clock, and there I was. [32.29]

Omitted from the RTS (ch. 1, p. 6)

29.1 The Monday following . . . at eight o' clock, and there I was. [32.29]

Omitted from "The First Voyage Over" (p. 587)

29.1 The Monday following . . . at eight o' clock, and there I was. [32.29]

CHAPTER IV

Omitted from the 1913 edition (ch. 1, pp. 6–13; ch. 2, pp. 16–17)

33.18 B deck, at least, the main lobby . . . cut flowers overcame all that. [35.15]
37.27 his adventure and in me . . . contrary notwithstanding. [38.9]
41.3 In the confusion of observations . . . highest form of earthly bliss [42.14]
42.37 So I looked at Miss Longfellow . . . even better than the first. [43.32]
44.4 I am not one such . . . an almost enduring quarrel. [47.11]

Omitted from the RTS (ch. 1, pp. 6–17)

33.18 B deck, at least, the main lobby . . . cut flowers overcame all that. [35.15]
37.35 "You have a spare copy . . . contrary notwithstanding. [38.9]
41.3 In the confusion of observations . . . highest form of earthly bliss [42.14]
42.37 So I looked at Miss Longfellow . . . even better than the first. [43.32]
44.4 I am not one such . . . an almost enduring quarrel. [47.11]

Omitted from "The First Voyage Over" (pp. 587–88)

33.18 B deck, at least, the main lobby . . . cut flowers overcame all that. [35.15]
37.27 his adventure and in me . . . contrary notwithstanding. [38.9]
39.9 On the contrary, the women of the stage . . . managerial skill of Grant Richards, for [40.15]
40.37 I like to see what he thinks . . . highest form of earthly bliss [42.14]
42.37 So I looked at Miss Longfellow . . . an almost enduring quarrel. [47.11]

CHAPTER V

Omitted from the 1913 edition (ch. 1, pp. 13–14)

47.32 He made an agreement with me . . . a line on things generally. [48.24]
48.40 [if you are at all inclined] . . . at the time I wrote these lines. [53.11]

Omitted from the RTS (ch. 1, pp. 17–21)

47.32 He made an agreement with me . . . a line on things generally. [48.24]
48.40 [if you are at all inclined] . . . at the time I wrote these lines. [53.11]

Omitted from "The First Voyage Over" (pp. 588–89)

47.12 This interesting ship life proceeded . . . a line on things generally. [48.24]
48.28 This day had been a little stormy . . . at the time I wrote these lines. [53.11]

CHAPTER VI

Omitted from the 1913 edition (ch. 1, pp. 14–15)

53.12 Let me take out of my notebook . . . I knew nothing of it before. [65.10]
65.20 from one point of view . . . and so went to bed. Oh, no. [68.4]

Omitted from the RTS (ch. 1, pp. 21–23)

53.12 Let me take out of my notebook . . . I knew nothing of it before. [65.10]
65.20 from one point of view . . . and so went to bed. Oh, no. [68.4]

Omitted from "The First Voyage Over" (p. 589)

53.12 Let me take out of my notebook . . . I knew nothing of it before. [65.10]
65.20 from one point of view . . . and so went to bed. Oh, no. [68.4]

CHAPTER VII

Omitted from the 1913 edition (ch. 2, pp. 16–23)

69.10 Mr. Owen, Mr. McGee, Miss Longfellow . . . After lunch [69.28]
70.23 Mr. Gillingham, the chief engineer . . . [Sunday, November 26th, 1911] [73.39]
73.40 I stopped in the writing room . . . He returned after a moment [74.24]

Omitted from the RTS (ch. 1, pp. 23–32)

69.10 Mr. Owen, Mr. McGee, Miss Longfellow . . . After lunch [69.28]
70.23 Mr. Gillingham, the chief engineer . . . [Sunday, November 26th, 1911] [73.39]
73.40 I stopped in the writing room . . . He returned after a moment [74.24]

Omitted from "The First Voyage Over" (pp. 589–90)

68.29 Sunday, November 26 . . . [Sunday, November 26th, 1911] [73.39]
73.40 I stopped in the writing room . . . He returned after a moment [74.24]
75.20 fully enough, but I shall add . . . if you do the same things. [76.29]
77.18 He loves power, authority . . . we all went to bed. [77.38]

CHAPTER VIII

Omitted from the 1913 edition (ch. 3, pp. 24–31; ch. 4, pp. 32–36; ch. 6, p. 47)

82.11 On the face of one part of the . . . through the abyss of space. [82.37]
84.10 I knew of course that that was . . . American scheme of things. [85.12]

Omitted from the RTS (ch. 2, pp. 33–50)

82.16 to me. But when I came up on deck . . . through the abyss of space. [82.37]
84.10 I knew of course that that was . . . American scheme of things. [85.12]

Omitted from "The First Voyage Over" (pp. 590–93)

82.11 On the face of one part of the . . . through the abyss of space. [82.37]
83.11 Miss Burke was looking for . . . should see them no more. [83.21]
84.6 a semi-octagonal-looking . . . delighted me. [87.38]

CHAPTER IX

Omitted from the 1913 edition (ch. 5, pp. 37–46)

88.27 They clicked along as gaily . . . be left safely in her hands. [91.14]
94.21 So Grant Richards did not object . . . As we traveled, and [95.6]
96.18 The threshing machines . . . and dull minds and so on. [96.31]
98.35 Well, then, presently it was too dark . . . boil for that heat. [101.4]
101.11 but I did not see anything . . . capable-appearing young woman. [101.29]
102.3 Joy is the same here as elsewhere . . . to speak for any other man. [102.20]

Omitted from the RTS (ch. 3, pp. 51–67)

88.27 They clicked along as gaily . . . be left safely in her hands. [91.14]
94.21 So Grant Richards did not object . . . As we traveled, and [95.6]
96.18 The threshing machines . . . and dull minds and so on. [96.31]
98.35 Well, then, presently it was too dark . . . boil for that heat. [101.4]
101.11 but I did not see anything . . . capable-appearing young woman. [101.29]
102.3 Joy is the same here as elsewhere . . . to speak for any other man. [102.20]

Omitted from "The First Voyage Over" (pp. 593–95)

88.27 They clicked along as gaily . . . from the boat to the train. [91.38]
93.30 Miss Longfellow and her charming . . . As we traveled, and [95.6]
96.8 But these queer, weird, hard, sad, . . . to speak for any other man. [102.20]

CHAPTER XII

Omitted from the 1913 edition (ch. 7, pp. 57–65)

124.12 to be measured for waistcoats . . . consulted in moments of doubt. [124.40]
126.40 All my life—certainly all my literary . . . things had gone long ago. [127.21]
129.6 After the concert . . . Grant Richards brisk and smiling. [130.9]

Omitted from the RTS (ch. 3, pp. 88–100)

121.4 After a few days I went to London . . . and quite like life. [122.14]
124.12 to be measured for waistcoats . . . consulted in moments of doubt. [124.40]
129.15 (the older portions) . . . merely an index of precedent. [129.31]

Omitted from "An Uncommercial Traveler in London" (pp. 736–38)

122.39 "Here is a famous bachelor . . . was new and interesting. [126.25]
127.35 As for the crowd . . . [The art is his, not mine.] [128.8]
128.28 being rich . . . and thence to bed. [130.17]

CHAPTER XIII

Omitted from the 1913 edition (ch. 8, pp. 66–71)

130.30 —a phase of art . . . and I admitted that. [131.18]
135.8 However, I agreed with her . . . live in glass houses, etc. [135.23]
135.35 I worked this out later . . . "I hope so. It would be a pleasure." [136.18]
136.27 There was a fine line from the forehead . . . She moved to my side. [137.13]
138.8 Lady Macbeth in the sleepwalking scene . . . And so it is. [142.37]

Omitted from the RTS (ch. 3, pp. 101–10)

130.30 —a phase of art . . . and I admitted that. [131.18]
135.8 However, I agreed with her . . . live in glass houses, etc. [135.23]
136.27 There was a fine line from the forehead . . . She moved to my side. [137.13]
138.8 Lady Macbeth in the sleepwalking scene . . . And so it is. [142.37]

Omitted from "An Uncommercial Traveler in London" (pp. 738–42)

130.20 and some personalities that interested . . . and I admitted that. [131.18]
135.8 However, I agreed with her . . . live in glass houses, etc. [135.23]
135.35 I worked this out later . . . "I hope so. It would be a pleasure." [136.18]

136.27 There was a fine line from the forehead . . . She moved to my side. [137.13]
138.8 Lady Macbeth in the sleepwalking scene . . . And so it is. [142.37]

CHAPTER XVI

Omitted from the 1913 edition (ch. 10, pp. 77–81; ch. 9, pp. 72–76)

164.26 But her French count . . . did prove very interesting. [164.38]
165.5 It always interests me . . . was my crescent reputation. [165.29]
166.40 Mr. Russell invited me . . . modeled objects of art. [167.11]

Omitted from "An Uncommercial Traveler in London" (pp. 742–45)

162.6 I recall venturing . . . kind to let them. [164.32]
165.5 It always interests me . . . was my crescent reputation. [165.29]
166.40 Mr. Russell invited me . . . modeled objects of art. [167.11]

CHAPTER XVIII

Omitted from the 1913 edition (ch. 13, pp. 113–21)

174.3 I went this same . . . her car sped away. [174.33]
175.14 Shall I phone . . . went out into the rain [176.11]
179.1 "Yes. They're soft and pleasant . . . attempt to build out of that. [179.28]
180.14 I took off my hat . . . "I'm not." [181.23]
182.6 "More likely . . . than her state. [182.26]
184.33 I pitied her weak, sweet eyes . . . grew sorry watching her. [185.10]
185.35 You won't do it . . . wasn't as bad as I thought her. [186.15]

Omitted from the RTS (ch. 6, pp. 135–45)

174.3 I went this same . . . her car sped away. [174.33]
175.14 Shall I phone . . . was not pretty enough. [176.8]
179.1 "Yes. They're soft and pleasant . . . attempt to build out of that. [179.28]
180.14 I took off my hat . . . "I'm not." [181.23]
182.6 "More likely . . . than her state. [182.26]
184.33 I pitied her weak, sweet eyes . . . grew sorry watching her. [185.10]
185.35 You won't do it . . . wasn't as bad as I thought her. [186.15]

Omitted from "Lilly Edwards: An Episode" (pp. 81–84)

174.3 I went this same . . . her car sped away. [174.33]
175.14 Shall I phone . . . was not pretty enough. [176.8]
179.1 "Yes. They're soft and pleasant . . . attempt to build out of that. [179.28]
180.14 I took off my hat . . . "I'm not." [181.23]
182.6 "More likely . . . than her state. [182.26]
184.33 I pitied her weak, sweet eyes . . . grew sorry watching her. [185.10]
185.35 You won't do it . . . wasn't as bad as I thought her. [186.15]

CHAPTER XIX

Omitted from the 1913 edition (ch. 13, pp. 121–27)

187.38 , where the society women go." . . . but we talked on. [188.9]
189.22 and even exceptional . . . the Dewey, Sharkey's and the like. [189.41]
191.2 although in the matter of size . . . Broadway and 42nd Street! [193.33]

Omitted from the RTS (ch. 6, pp. 145–53)

187.38 , where the society women go." . . . but we talked on. [188.9]
189.22 and even exceptional . . . the Dewey, Sharkey's and the like. [189.41]
191.2 although in the matter of size . . . Broadway and 42nd Street! [193.33]

Omitted from "Lilly Edwards: An Episode" (pp. 84–86)

187.38 , where the society women go." . . . they were always full of girls. [188.16]
189.17 If a few silly phrases would aid . . . Piccadilly from everywhere. [190.28]
191.1 From this first place we went . . . cheap gauds and desires. [194.4]

CHAPTER XX

Omitted from "An Uncommercial Traveler in London" (pp. 745–46)

197.5 Even the new Christian Science . . . a stranger in a strange land. [198.42]

CHAPTER XXII

Omitted from the RTS (ch. 7, pp. 163–71)

206.35 In spite of all this . . . I could talk [207.11]
208.5 including such things . . . proper at Battersea Bridge. [208.31]

Omitted from "An Uncommercial Traveler in London" (p. 749)

204.9 [One of the things that interested me] . . . wet wind and rain. [205.11]
206.9 I smelled printing plants . . . what it must be like. [206.27]
206.35 In spite of all this . . . I could talk [207.11]
207.20 I remember going to some barber . . . [I could fancy such a man as Turner or Whistler or Carlyle or Rosetti [*sic*] finding it comfortable here.] [209.21]

CHAPTER XXIII

Omitted from the 1913 edition (ch. 15, pp. 136–47)

211.14 seemed opposed to taking . . . general caught my fancy. He [211.30]
211.35 generally. He seemed to know . . . according to Wren and Jones. [212.10]
213.6 The sweetest of these little homes . . . [I would go on with this and with the interesting discussion that followed our return to Big Frith afterwards if it were not for the journey to Oxford the following morning, which, for all that it rained a drizzling rain all day long, was one of the most delightful I have ever experiences [*sic*].] [214.31]
215.16 I rejoice in the Roman modification . . . I think [216.12]
217.18 We could not get anywhere . . . to aid it by his good word. [218.2]
218.20 They are coming over here . . . I had to cease. [219.18]
219.32 Tea, perhaps, was to be had . . . the thought that we would not go. [220.22]
223.26 Sir Hugh had missed out . . . we started on the return trip. [224.22]
224.24 a knit glove, of great comfort . . . make a wonderful combination. [224.37]

CHAPTER XXVII

Omitted from the 1913 edition (ch. 17, pp. 171–74)

259.10 An old thing in any of these . . . average soul to contend with. [259.24]
259.37 What resources thoughts of infinity . . . anything to do with this. [260.27]
260.38 One of the things I did see . . . its vicinage are one sort. [262.14]

Omitted from the RTS (ch. 7, pp. 172–75)

259.10 An old thing in any of these . . . average soul to contend with. [259.24]
259.37 What resources thoughts of infinity . . . anything to do with this. [260.27]
260.38 One of the things I did see . . . its vicinage are one sort. [262.14]

CHAPTER XXIX

Omitted from the 1913 edition (ch. 17, pp. 174–79; ch. 18, pp. 180–81)

269.1 After my dinner . . . I was well repaid. [269.12]
269.30 I was delighted that anything . . . St. Louis, what you will. [270.4]

Omitted from the RTS (ch. 7, pp. 176–83)

269.1 After my dinner . . . I was well repaid. [269.12]

CHAPTER XXX

Omitted from the 1913 edition (ch. 18, pp. 181–87)

274.27 It was misting or about to rain . . . In several places I found [275.35]
277.11 This matter of a city's restaurants . . . It is always so. [278.2]

Omitted from the RTS (ch. 7, pp. 184–91)

274.27 It was misting or about to rain . . . In several places I found [275.35]
277.11 This matter of a city's restaurants . . . It is always so. [278.2]

CHAPTER XXXI

Omitted from the 1913 edition (ch. 10, pp. 81–83; ch. 19, pp. 188–97)

284.25 It was interesting to come out . . . innocent of any marble. [284.35]
292.30 examining the shops of High Street . . . as artistically deficient. [293.3]

Omitted from the RTS (ch. 7, pp. 200–213)

284.25 It was interesting to come out . . . innocent of any marble. [284.35]
292.30 examining the shops of High Street . . . as artistically deficient. [293.3]

CHAPTER XXXII

Omitted from the 1913 edition (ch. 7, pp. 198–209)

295.17 The two should have been side . . . still came from somewhere. [295.39]
296.16 I spent the last half-hour . . . home-loving citizen. [296.26]
300.4 church with white walls . . . (pages gone here) . . . the national air at once. In [300.31]

Omitted from the RTS (ch. 7, pp. 214–27)

295.17 The two should have been side . . . still came from somewhere. [295.39]
296.16 I spent the last half-hour . . . home-loving citizen [296.26]
300.4 church with white walls . . . (pages gone here) . . . the national air at once. In [300.31]

CHAPTER XXXIII

Omitted from the 1913 edition (ch. 20, pp. 209–10; ch. 21, pp. 211–24)

304.1 and after that, if the ladies . . . we reached Paris. [304.14]
312.22 Between the amount . . . When we were in the taxi [312.32]

Omitted from the RTS (ch. 7, pp. 228–43; ch. 8, pp. 244–48)

304.1 and after that, if the ladies . . . we reached Paris. [304.14]
312.22 Between the amount . . . When we were in the taxi [312.32]

Omitted from "Paris" (pp. 904–8)

302.25 [The run from Amiens to Paris requires several hours.] . . . others must do that. [305.38]
308.12 It is as good a place . . . any particular difference. [308.24]
312.22 Between the amount . . . When we were in the taxi [312.32]

CHAPTER XXXIV

Omitted from the 1913 edition (ch. 22, pp. 225–34)

314.27 Look as you will . . . and ornamented in every notable way. [314.39]
318.16 There may be as many as thirty . . . which is purely Parisian. [318.31]
319.15 The striped black-and-white . . . chapter house for a score of it. [320.4]
320.16 It is too hard and bare . . . still so many things to see. [322.7]
322.10 He had, as I have said . . . for the cooking is perfection itself. [322.26]

Omitted from the RTS (ch. 8, pp. 248–59)

319.15 The striped black-and-white . . . chapter house for a score of it. [320.4]
320.16 It is too hard and bare . . . have the past come back is hard. [322.4]
322.10 He had, as I have said . . . similar reputation in America. [322.24]

Omitted from "Paris" (pp. 908–10)

314.14 Only the fancy of a monarch . . . in the conduct of his business. [315.2]
317.16 and I studied some of them . . . which is purely Parisian. [318.31]
319.9 The church of St. Étienne-du-Mont . . . still so many things to see. [322.7]
322.10 He had, as I have said . . . similar reputation in America. [322.24]
322.38 A lunch which had been ordered . . . enthusiasm for life. [323.32]

CHAPTER XXXV

Omitted from the 1913 edition (ch. 22, pp. 234–37; ch. 23, pp. 238–46; ch. 24, pp. 253–54)

328.34 It was a peculiar and an amusing . . . keep their appointment. [329.5]
329.8 Like Foyot's it was decidedly . . . between Paris and New York. [330.2]

Omitted from the RTS (ch. 8, pp. 260–64; ch. 9, pp. 265–75; ch. 10, pp. 278–79)

328.34 It was a peculiar and an amusing . . . keep their appointment. [329.5]
329.26 In Germany . . . the difference between Paris and New York. [330.2]

Omitted from "Paris" (pp. 910–15)

323.33 Since the two studios . . . and appropriately cheerful. [325.12]
326.18 A charmingly proportioned girl . . . lived in Paris for years. [327.22]
328.32 It was high time . . . our meal in comfort. [329.18]
329.26 In Germany . . . between Paris and New York. [330.2]
330.5 before he should leave . . . into a silvery dawn. [333.12]

CHAPTER XL

Omitted from the 1913 edition (ch. 24, pp. 248–52)

365.36 I really groaned within my soul . . . miss his interesting wares. [366.22]
369.21 The only one who compared with her . . . and mine to Rome. [372.25]

Omitted from the RTS (ch. 10, pp. 276–85)

365.36 I really groaned within my soul . . . miss his interesting wares. [366.22]
369.21 The only one who compared with her . . . and mine to Rome. [372.25]

Omitted from "Paris" (pp. 912–15)

365.13 I did not see him when he first . . . miss his interesting wares. [366.22]
369.21 The only one who compared with her . . . and mine to Rome. [372.25]

CHAPTER XLI

Omitted from the 1913 edition (ch. 25, pp. 255–63)

377.34 One of the horrors which . . . appreciation of him as a publisher. [378.39]
379.28 only to find Lane fixing him . . . Lane ad lib, which I did. [380.28]

Omitted from the RTS (ch. 34, pp. 384–97)

377.34 One of the horrors which . . . appreciation of him as a publisher. [378.39]
379.28 only to find Lane fixing him . . . Lane ad lib, which I did. [380.28]

CHAPTER XLII

Omitted from the 1913 edition (ch. 26, pp. 264–74)

388.16 We strolled out and were . . . and spoil your trip here." [388.33]
389.33 "I certainly don't see why . . . that we go sanely [390.16]
391.13 He beamed ruddily . . . Needless to say this letter did not go. [391.28]

Omitted from the RTS (ch. 37, pp. 398–415)

388.16 We strolled out and were . . . and spoil your trip here." [388.33]
389.33 "I certainly don't see why . . . The cuisine is terrible." [390.13]

CHAPTER XLIV

Omitted from the 1913 edition (ch. 27, pp. 275–83)

403.22 the last one that the wine he had consumed the evening before had made him exceedingly gay . . . So we chattered. [403.41]

405.41 with his surplus earnings . . . a very little later at La Turbie. [406.13]

409.24 The French and Italians are all quick in their gestures . . . from a poet's point of view. [409.38]

Omitted from the RTS (ch. 11, pp. 286–95)

403.22 the last one that the wine he had consumed the evening before had made him exceedingly gay . . . So we chattered. [403.41]

409.24 The French and Italians are all quick in their gestures . . . from a poet's point of view. [409.38]

CHAPTER XLV

Omitted from the 1913 edition (ch. 27, pp. 283–87; ch. 28, pp. 288–92)

410.26 "Nothing nearer a large food supply . . . in spite of criticism." [410.36]

412.19 As we made our way down . . . worth more than that seen in Eze. [413.3]

413.11 were involved in this feat . . . And they followed at leisure. [413.26]

Omitted from the RTS (ch. 11, pp. 296–307)

412.19 As we made our way down . . . worth more than that seen in Eze. [413.3]

413.11 were involved in this feat . . . And they followed at leisure. [413.26]

CHAPTER XLVIII

Omitted from the 1913 edition (ch. 28, pp. 292–94; ch. 29, pp. 295–305)

439.7 This same Sunday was dull . . . my friends and went home to bed. [439.34]

441.15 We did make a return trip . . . waiting for my train for Rome. [443.2]

443.29 "Now," I said to Grant Richards . . . but he smiled nevertheless. [444.13]

446.8 The next I saw of her was in London . . . until we reached Pisa. [446.40]

447.2 As I understood it . . . not moving at all! [447.15]

Omitted from the RTS (ch. 11, pp. 308–23)

439.7 This same Sunday was dull . . . my friends and went home to bed. [439.34]

441.15 in company with Marcelle . . . waiting for my train for Rome. [443.2]

446.18 It was conveniently lighted . . . until we reached Pisa. [446.40]

CHAPTER XLIX

Omitted from the 1913 edition (ch. 30, pp. 306–14; ch. 31, pp. 315–17)

456.5 I did my best to unravel . . . that light than as religious edifices. [456.21]

457.18 I was sorry when I took . . . the faintest suggestion of a real world. [457.39]

Omitted from the RTS (ch. 11, pp. 324–34; ch. 11[2], pp. 369a–c)

456.5 I did my best to unravel . . . that light than as religious edifices. [456.21]

457.21 As we sped southward . . . the faintest suggestion of a real world. [457.39]

CHAPTER L

Omitted from the 1913 edition (ch. 31, pp. 317–26)

467.3 The old Roman world has been lost . . . dead past bury its dead. [467.18]

Omitted from the RTS (ch. 11, pp. 335–45)

467.3 The old Roman world has been lost . . . dead past bury its dead. [467.18]

CHAPTER LI

Omitted from the 1913 edition (ch. 32, pp. 327–36)

469.16 "And where did you come from last?" . . . she suited me to a T. [469.37]

Omitted from the RTS (ch. 11, pp. 346–59)

469.16 "And where did you come from last?" . . . she suited me to a T. [469.37]

CHAPTER LII

Omitted from the 1913 edition (ch. 32, p. 336; ch. 33, pp. 337–44)

476.4 The character of this conversation was . . . It so turned out. [476.31]
477.33 The churches of Rome are full . . . you might remember. But [478.25]
478.28 St. John Lateran is a gorgeous structure . . . are apt to get them. [480.6]
481.25 "I would have given . . . stab each other over us." Well [482.7]
483.33 In the crypt of St. Peter's . . . apostles were three, Luke and John. [484.13]

Omitted from the RTS (ch. 11, pp. 360–69)

476.4 The character of this conversation was . . . It so turned out. [476.31]
477.33 The churches of Rome are full . . . you might remember. But [478.25]
478.28 St. John Lateran is a gorgeous structure . . . are apt to get them. [480.6]
481.25 "I would have given . . . stab each other over us." Well [482.7]
483.33 In the crypt of St. Peter's . . . apostles were three, Luke and John. [484.13]

CHAPTER LIV

Omitted from the 1913 edition (ch. 34, pp. 345–53)

496.9 Personally I am of the opinion . . . Let us hope so, anyhow. [496.23]

CHAPTER LVII

Omitted from the 1913 edition (ch. 35, pp. 354–61)

515.28 (Page missing) until it reaches . . . to refresh my memory. [516.28]
522.5 At Assisi, as in Pisa . . . to the psychology of the time. [522.22]

CHAPTER LVIII

Omitted from the 1913 edition (ch. 35, pp. 361–64; ch. 36, p. 365)

525.30 Spello: I shall not linger long there . . . I should see before nightfall. [528.35]

CHAPTER LIX

Omitted from the 1913 edition (ch. 36, pp. 366–70; ch. 37, pp. 371–73)

530.7 I wish you would read . . . and architecture did me little good. [531.32]
532.10 The work of his . . . that I found interesting. [532.25]
533.24 The first night I was there . . . to fight in the war against Turkey. [534.22]
535.1 The people in Perugia . . . an idyllic, spring-like evening, and [536.10]
537.31 It was so plain that this river . . . I shall tell in another chapter. [538.13]

CHAPTER LX

Omitted from the 1913 edition (ch. 37, pp. 373–79; ch. 39, pp. 390–97)

542.32 I can never look . . . in a great fog of speculative woe. [543.14]

CHAPTER LXI

Omitted from the 1913 edition (ch. 38, pp. 380–82; ch. 39, pp. 392–94)

547.13 I think we make a mistake . . . life prevalent everywhere. [548.2]
549.8 I was leaving . . . are all pleasing—grand at times. [549.23]

CHAPTER LXII

Omitted from the 1913 edition (ch. 38, pp. 383–85; ch. 39, pp. 387–95)

555.23 The rejection of the Hearn . . . entirely the whole afternoon. [556.18]

CHAPTER LXIII

Omitted from the 1913 edition (ch. 40, pp. 398–408)

557.27 Ever since leaving Rome . . . of Mme. de Villiers. [558.12]
560.14 "When we get there . . . interested in the adventure [560.35]
561.10 and I said . . . so here they are: [561.28]

Omitted from the RTS (ch. 37, pp. 416–30)

557.27 Ever since leaving Rome . . . of Mme. de Villiers. [558.12]
560.14 "When we get there . . . interested in the adventure [560.35]

CHAPTER LXV

Omitted from the 1913 edition (ch. 41, pp. 409–14)

575.38 To me the spirit of a general . . . in the old chronicles. [576.28]
577.3 Except in rather dreary sections . . . that you like, as any other. [577.13]

Omitted from the RTS (ch. 37, pp. 431–37)

576.9 The patient Maria, not new to Milan . . . in the old chronicles. [576.28]
577.3 Except in rather dreary sections . . . that you like, as any other. [577.13]

CHAPTER LXVI

Omitted from the 1913 edition (ch. 42, pp. 415–17)

578.11 I cannot say that I enjoyed . . . perceived a great change. [578.21]
579.24 commanding delightful views . . . at your very feet. [581.5]
581.18 We haven't even a system . . . uplifting thoughts in me. [582.21]

Omitted from the RTS (ch. 37, pp. 438–40)

578.11 I cannot say that I enjoyed . . . perceived a great change. [578.21]
579.24 commanding delightful views . . . at your very feet. [581.5]
581.18 We haven't even a system . . . Lucerne is one. [581.33]
581.39 Here I was in Lucerne . . . uplifting thoughts in me. [582.21]

CHAPTER LXVII

Omitted from the 1913 edition (ch. 42, pp. 417–22)

582.22 That night I spent . . . I had come out on my balcony. [copy-text omits the last paragraph] [583.39]
585.27 Everything, I judged, was exactly . . . It was a perfect day. [586.15]

Omitted from the RTS (ch. 37, pp. 441–46)

582.22 That night I spent . . . I had come out on my balcony. [copy-text omits the last paragraph] [583.39]
585.27 Everything, I judged, was exactly . . . It was a perfect day. [586.15]

CHAPTER LXVIII

Omitted from the 1913 edition (ch. 42, pp. 422–23; ch. 43, pp. 424–30)

589.17 I shall never forget . . . what Germany had to show. [the copy-text begins "Once I had seen this much"] [589.27]
593.8 What a far cry . . . not yet indicated in the race. [593.39]

CHAPTER LXIX

Omitted from the 1913 edition (ch. 43, pp. 430–32)

594.7 and dull . . . It was so in ancient times. [594.25]
596.5 Another fact . . . I only knew of Mayen, but [596.19]
597.2 Before leaving, however . . . So the matter stood. [600.8]

Omitted from the RTS (ch. 37, pp. 457–60)

594.7 and dull . . . It was so in ancient times. [594.25]
596.5 Another fact . . . I only knew of Mayen, but [596.19]
597.3 and to secure the key . . . So the matter stood. [600.8]

CHAPTER LXX

Omitted from the 1913 edition (ch. 43, pp. 433–36; ch. 46, p. 454)

600.9 Certain subsequent developments . . . but finally this day at [601.28]
603.25 A dull place . . . after which I went to bed. [605.25]

Omitted from the RTS (ch. 37, pp. 460–65)
600.9 Certain subsequent developments . . . care of Cook's, saying [601.29]
603.25 A dull place . . . a momentary prejudice in me. [604.24]
604.34 But Mayence was really so "Dutchy." . . . low-keyed, moody eyes. [605.8]

CHAPTER LXXI

Omitted from the 1913 edition (ch. 44, pp. 437–43)
608.32 but having come so far . . . stone steps leading down to the water. [609.8]

Omitted from the RTS, "The Quest for My Ancestral Home" (pp. 466–73)
608.32 but having come so far . . . stone steps leading down to the water. [609.8]

CHAPTER LXXII

Omitted from the 1913 edition (ch. 44, pp. 443–48)
613.1 Timbuktu and Lhasa . . . those all is confusing, winding streets. [613.16]
613.38 after years and years of immunity . . . depressed in years. [614.7]
617.16 Mayen was surely not much . . . root, stock, and branch, and destroyed! [618.8]

Omitted from the RTS, "The Quest for My Ancestral Home" (pp. 474–80)
613.1 Timbuktu and Lhasa . . . those all is confusing, winding streets. [613.16]
613.38 after years and years of immunity . . . depressed in years. [614.7]
617.17 After buying all the picture . . . root, stock, and branch, and destroyed! [618.8]

CHAPTER LXXIII

Omitted from the 1913 edition (ch. 45, pp. 449–53)
618.9 From here, after a time . . . any potato simile would indicate. [618.36]
620.32 That was the way this . . . German maid or maidens possessed. [621.9]
621.25 These fat, round towers . . . the weariness of today talking? [622.28]

Omitted from the RTS, "The Quest for My Ancestral Home" (pp. 481–86)
618.9 From here, after a time, . . . seemingly dull but very useful. [618.32]
620.32 That was the way this . . . German maid or maidens possessed. [621.9]
621.25 These fat, round towers . . . the weariness of today talking? [622.28]

CHAPTER LXXIV

Omitted from the RTS, "The Quest for My Ancestral Home" (p. 487)
624.1 I caught a train just about . . . Of such is the artistic disposition. [629.15]

CHAPTER LXXV

Omitted from the RTS, "The Quest for My Ancestral Home" (pp. 487–95)
634.6 This holding of the conversation . . . to have his affairs discussed." [634.18]
634.23 "This settles me! Another full . . . Wait until I come back. [635.36]
636.1 and then—?" "Oh, then I will be very nice . . . . otherwise or not. [636.35]

CHAPTER LXXVIII

Omitted from the 1913 edition (ch. 47, pp. 462–66)

649.17 The region or suburban area . . . grimly and nakedly in a barrel? [655.32]

Omitted from the RTS, "The Quest for My Ancestral Home" (pp. 496–98)

649.17 The region or suburban area . . . grimly and nakedly in a barrel? [655.32]

CHAPTER LXXIX

Omitted from the 1913 edition (ch. 47, pp. 466–68)

655.33 From Zehlendorf as a center . . . hopeful and determined realms. [656.15]
656.24 Look at a map of the city . . . monument, simple and significant. [656.41]
657.29 This statue stands in a rather . . . probably do much better. But [658.12]
658.19 or the French-Parisian conception . . . here is too flamboyant. [659.4]
659.9 When I saw its seemingly imposing . . . cost no more than eight. [659.20]
659.22 I consider the Siegesallee . . . in its residence and tenement areas. [660.37]

Omitted from the RTS, "The Quest for My Ancestral Home" (pp. 498–501)

655.33 From Zehlendorf as a center . . . hopeful and determined realms. [656.15]
656.24 Look at a map of the city . . . monument, simple and significant. [656.41]
657.29 This statue stands in a rather . . . probably do much better. But [658.12]
658.19 or the French-Parisian conception . . . here is too flamboyant. [659.4]
659.9 When I saw its seemingly imposing . . . cost no more than eight. [659.20]
659.22 I consider the Siegesallee . . . in its residence and tenement areas. [660.37]

CHAPTER LXXX

Omitted from the 1913 edition (ch. 47, pp. 468–73)

661.31 In visiting such cities as Paris . . . I found it in full force. [662.12]
664.20 In New York this matter of fooling . . . attempt to displace it. [665.3]

Omitted from the RTS, "The Berlin Public Service" (pp. 502–7)

661.31 In visiting such cities as Paris . . . I found it in full force. [662.12]
664.20 In New York this matter of fooling . . . attempt to displace it. [665.3]

CHAPTER LXXXI

Omitted from the 1913 edition (ch. 48, pp. 474–75)

666.30 About the third day, in the . . . even though he were paid for it. [669.4]
671.7 Through clouds of tobacco . . . artist could ever hope to be. [671.18]

Omitted from the RTS, "Night-Life In Berlin" (pp. 508–9)

666.30 About the third day, in the . . . even though he were paid for it. [669.4]
671.7 Through clouds of tobacco . . . artist could ever hope to be. [671.18]

CHAPTER LXXXII

Omitted from the 1913 edition (ch. 48, pp. 475–78)

671.19 I have been reserving for . . . . of only remote understanding [674.24]
676.20 It was amusing to me to see . . . may have been essentially vicious. [676.32]

Omitted from the RTS, "Night-Life In Berlin" (pp. 510–13)

671.19 I have been reserving for . . . . of only remote understanding [674.24]
676.20 It was amusing to me to see . . . may have been essentially vicious. [676.32]

CHAPTER LXXXIII

Omitted from the 1913 edition (ch. 48, pp. 478–80)

678.16 The deformed or so-called ugly . . . and we don't know it. [679.26]
680.9 It was at the expiration of the . . . with a real touch of regret. [682.17]

Omitted from the RTS, "Night-Life In Berlin" (pp. 514–16)

678.16 The deformed or so-called ugly . . . So far as I could see, [679.4]
679.10 The stage in London . . . and we don't know it. [679.26]
680.9 It was at the expiration of the . . . with a real touch of regret. [682.17]

CHAPTER LXXXVIII

Omitted from the 1913 edition (ch. 48, pp. 480–85)

705.3 Before ending with Berlin . . . American stride are all the rage. [705.17]
709.29 I cried. I could not say why . . . or the dogmatic Herr Merten? [712.32]

Omitted from the RTS, "Night-Life In Berlin" (pp. 517–22)

705.3 Before ending with Berlin . . . American stride are all the rage. [705.17]
709.29 I cried. I could not say why . . . or the dogmatic Herr Merten? [712.32]

CHAPTER LXXXIX

Omitted from the 1913 edition (ch. 49, pp. 486–91)

712.33 My departure was finally accomplished . . . best who looks closest. [713.22]
717.3 Of all the charming water-cities . . . will not much matter. [717.12]

Omitted from the RTS, ". . . (continued)" (pp. 523–28)

712.33 My departure was finally accomplished . . . best who looks closest. [713.22]
717.3 Of all the charming water-cities . . . will not much matter. [717.12]

CHAPTER XC

Omitted from the 1913 edition (ch. 49, pp. 491–93; ch. 50, pp. 494–96)

720.35 I could now look forward . . . observations had appealed to me. [722.22]

Omitted from the RTS, ". . . (continued)" (pp. 529–34)

720.35 I could now look forward . . . it would be all over. Naturally [721.40]
722.1 But what a delight, I said . . . observations had appealed to me. [722.22]

CHAPTER XCI

Omitted from the 1913 edition (ch. 50, pp. 496–500; ch. 51, pp. 501–3)
722.30 The days I spent in Holland . . . accident, a by-product. To me, as [723.15]
726.34 I should like to ask this . . . far in advance of the average home. [727.26]

Omitted from the RTS, ". . . (continued)" (pp. 535–41)
726.34 I should like to ask this . . . far in advance of the average home. [727.26]

CHAPTER XCII

Omitted from the 1913 edition (ch. 50, p. 500; ch. 51, pp. 501, 503–5)
728.3 And now that I am on this . . . to bring her anything more at all. [730.14]
730.29 We talked and talked . . . and walk with her, which I did. [731.17]
733.18 Frans Hals was the activating . . . died quite alone and neglected. [734.22]

Omitted from the RTS, ". . . (continued)" (pp. 541–43)
728.3 And now that I am on this . . . to bring her anything more at all. [730.14]
730.29 We talked and talked . . . and walk with her, which I did. [731.17]
733.18 Frans Hals was the activating . . . died quite alone and neglected. [734.22]

CHAPTER XCIV

Omitted from the 1913 edition (ch. 51, pp. 503, 505)
741.1 When I returned to the hotel . . . The ride from Amsterdam [741.29]
741.30 where I stayed for the night . . . Near The Hague [742.10]
742.11 bucketful. She had on, to my almost . . . a lighter character. All [743.33]
743.35 thrown in. You have here in this . . . [to this humdrum world.] [747.10]

CHAPTER XCV

Omitted from the 1913 edition (ch. 51, p. 506)
747.12 the same cafés with chairs outside . . . to this humdrum world. [752.15]

Omitted from the RTS, ". . . (continued)" (p. 544)
747.12 the same cafés with chairs outside . . . to this humdrum world. [752.15]

CHAPTER XCVI

Omitted from the 1913 edition (ch. 52, pp. 507–11)
752.19 This through train from Brussels was . . . When I reached Paris [753.1]
753.16 This matter of the European . . . called for twenty-five centimes. [754.40]
755.18 from Dover or Southampton . . . on this particular evening. [756.24]
757.14 I pulled a long and gloomy face . . . my affairs after leaving Berlin. [757.25]

Omitted from the RTS, ". . . (continued)" (pp. 544–52)
752.19 This through train from Brussels was . . . When I reached Paris [753.1]
755.18 from Dover or Southampton . . . quarrel or complaint. "Perhaps," [755.31]

755.35 It always seems strange to me . . . on this particular evening. [756.24]
757.14 I pulled a long and gloomy face . . . my affairs after leaving Berlin. [757.25]

CHAPTER XCVII

Omitted from the 1913 edition (ch. 52, pp. 511–14)

761.13 Fortunately my companion was not only . . . night was not done. [761.29]
762.7 Two things that happened . . . that sort of thing anyhow? [767.5]

Omitted from the RTS, ". . . (continued)" (pp. 509–12)

761.13 Fortunately my companion was not only . . . night was not done. [761.29]
762.7 Two things that happened . . . that sort of thing anyhow? [767.5]

CHAPTER XCVIII

Omitted from the 1913 edition (ch. 53, pp. 515–17)

767.9 seeing that we had concluded . . . the morning train for London. [767.21]
768.20 Besides, Grant Richards was insisting . . . could phone the hotel. [770.14]
771.26 endless, interesting conversation, . . . "Oh, very good!" "*Très bon!*" [773.30]

Omitted from the RTS, ". . . (continued)" (pp. 512–15)

767.9 seeing that we had concluded . . . the morning train for London. [767.21]
768.20 Besides, Grant Richards was insisting . . . could phone the hotel. [770.14]
771.26 endless, interesting conversation, . . . "Oh, very good!" "*Très bon!*" [773.30]

CHAPTER CI

Omitted from the 1913 edition (ch. 53, pp. 518–19)

785.5 touched her fancy. I remember . . . say forty minutes away. [785.29]
786.10 And so my trip was over . . . the highest wisdom. Be that so also. [789.20]

Omitted from the RTS, ". . . (continued)" (pp. 553–54)

785.5 touched her fancy. I remember . . . say forty minutes away. [785.29]
786.12 This was Saturday night . . . the highest wisdom. Be that so also. [789.20]

CHAPTER CII

Omitted from the 1913 edition (ch. 53, pp. 519–21)

790.1 Madame (or Mrs.) Van Dyk, . . . I am pretty. I know that." [792.40]
793.8 when Weiss entered, very . . . leather-upholstered corners, [793.23]

Omitted from the RTS, ". . . (continued)" (pp. 554–57)

790.1 Madame (or Mrs.) Van Dyk, . . . I am pretty. I know that." [792.40]
793.8 when Weiss entered, very . . . leather-upholstered corners, [793.23]

CHAPTER CIII

Omitted from the 1913 edition (ch. 53, pp. 521–26)

797.18 He did not try to read any more . . . our farewells, one to the other, [797.39]
798.10 Madame Van Dyk, who had . . . Americans did. I wondered. [798.36]
800.4 —and lovers, relatives, friends . . . their way to parts unknown. [800.17]

Omitted from the RTS, ". . . (continued)" (pp. 557–62)

797.18 He did not try to read any more . . . our farewells, one to the other, [797.39]
798.10 Madame Van Dyk, who had . . . Americans did. I wondered. [798.36]
800.4 —and lovers, relatives, friends . . . their way to parts unknown. [800.17]

CHAPTER TITLES

The following list records the chapter titles printed in the 1913 Century edition of A *Traveler at Forty*. In each entry the numeral and the title to the right of the slash refer to the Century text. The numerals to the left of the slash refer to the corresponding, untitled chapters in the present edition.

I / I	BARFLEUR TAKES ME IN HAND
II / —	[not in Century edition]
III / I	BARFLEUR TAKES ME IN HAND
IV / I–II	BARFLEUR TAKES ME IN HAND + MISS X.
V / I	BARFLEUR TAKES ME IN HAND
VI / I	BARFLEUR TAKES ME IN HAND
VII / II	MISS X.
VIII / III + VI	AT FISHGUARD + THE BARFLEUR FAMILY
IX / V	THE RIDE TO LONDON
X / VI	THE BARFLEUR FAMILY
XI / XII	MARLOWE
XII / VII	A GLIMPSE OF LONDON
XIII / VIII	A LONDON DRAWING ROOM
XIV / —	[not in Century edition]
XV / —	[not in Century edition]
XVI / X + IX	SOME MORE ABOUT LONDON + CALLS
XVII / —	[not in Century edition]
XVIII / XIII	LILLY: A GIRL OF THE STREETS
XIX / XIII	LILLY: A GIRL OF THE STREETS
XX / —	[not in Century edition]
XXI / XIV	LONDON; THE EAST END
XXII / —	[not in Century edition]
XXIII / XV	ENTER SIR SCORP
XXIV / —	[not in Century edition]
XXV / XVI	A CHRISTMAS CALL
XXVI / —	[not in Century edition]
XXVII / XVII	SMOKY ENGLAND
XXVIII / —	[not in Century edition]
XXIX / XVII–XVIII	SMOKY ENGLAND + SMOKY ENGLAND (CONTINUED)
XXX / XVIII	SMOKY ENGLAND (CONTINUED)
XXXI / X + XIX	SOME MORE ABOUT LONDON + CANTERBURY
XXXII / VII	A GLIMPSE OF LONDON
XXXIII / XX–XXI	EN ROUTE TO PARIS + PARIS!
XXXIV / XXII	A MORNING IN PARIS
XXXV / XXII–XXIII + XXIV	A MORNING IN PARIS + THREE GUIDES + "THE POISON FLOWER"
XXXVI / —	[not in Century edition]
XXXVII / —	[not in Century edition]
XXXVIII / —	[not in Century edition]

XXXIX / —	[not in Century edition]
XL / XXIV	"THE POISON FLOWER"
XLI / XXV	MONTE CARLO
XLII / XXVI	THE LURE OF GOLD!
XLIII / —	[not in Century edition]
XLIV / XXVII	WE GO TO EZE
XLV / XXVII–XXVIII	WE GO TO EZE + NICE
XLVI / —	[not in Century edition]
XLVII / —	[not in Century edition]
XLVIII / XXVIII–XXIX	NICE + A FIRST GLIMPSE OF ITALY
XLIX / XXX + XXXI	A STOP AT PISA + FIRST IMPRESSIONS OF ROME
L / XXXI	FIRST IMPRESSIONS OF ROME
LI / XXXII	MRS. Q. AND THE BORGIA FAMILY
LII / XXXII–XXXIII	MRS. Q. AND THE BORGIA FAMILY + THE ART OF SIGNOR TANNI
LIII / —	[not in Century edition]
LIV / XXXIV	AN AUDIENCE AT THE VATICAN
LV / —	[not in Century edition]
LVI / —	[not in Century edition]
LVII / XXXV	THE CITY OF ST. FRANCIS
LVIII / XXXV–XXXVI	THE CITY OF ST. FRANCIS + PERUGIA
LIX / XXXVI–XXXVII	PERUGIA + THE MAKERS OF FLORENCE
LX / XXXVII + XXXIX	THE MAKERS OF FLORENCE + FLORENCE OF TO-DAY
LXI / XXXVIII + XXXIX	A NIGHT RAMBLE IN FLORENCE + FLORENCE OF TO-DAY
LXII / XXXVIII + XXXIX	A NIGHT RAMBLE IN FLORENCE + FLORENCE OF TO-DAY
LXIII / XL	MARIA BASTIDA
LXIV / —	[not in Century edition]
LXV / XLI	VENICE
LXVI / XLII	LUCERNE
LXVII / XLII	LUCERNE
LXVIII / XLII–XLIII	LUCERNE + ENTERING GERMANY
LXIX / XLIII	ENTERING GERMANY
LXX / XLIII + XLVI	ENTERING GERMANY + THE ARTISTIC TEMPERAMENT
LXXI / XLIV	A MEDIEVAL TOWN
LXXII / XLIV	A MEDIEVAL TOWN
LXXIII / XLV	MY FATHER'S BIRTHPLACE
LXXIV / —	[not in Century edition]
LXXV / —	[not in Century edition]
LXXVI / —	[not in Century edition]
LXXVII / —	[not in Century edition]
LXXVIII / XLVII	BERLIN
LXXIX / XLVII	BERLIN
LXXX / XLVII	BERLIN
LXXXI / XLVIII	THE NIGHT-LIFE OF BERLIN
LXXXII / XLVIII	THE NIGHT-LIFE OF BERLIN
LXXXIII / XLVIII	THE NIGHT-LIFE OF BERLIN
LXXXIV / —	[not in Century edition]
LXXXV / —	[not in Century edition]

LXXXVI / —	[not in Century edition]
LXXXVII / —	[not in Century edition]
LXXXVIII / XLVIII	THE NIGHT-LIFE OF BERLIN
LXXXIX / XLIX	ON THE WAY TO HOLLAND
XC / XLIX–L	ON THE WAY TO HOLLAND + AMSTERDAM
XCI / L–LI	AMSTERDAM + "SPOTLESS TOWN"
XCII / L–LI	AMSTERDAM + "SPOTLESS TOWN"
XCIII / —	[not in Century edition]
XCIV / LI	"SPOTLESS TOWN"
XCV / LI	"SPOTLESS TOWN"
XCVI / LII	PARIS AGAIN
XCVII / LII	PARIS AGAIN
XCVIII / LIII	THE VOYAGE HOME
IC / —	[not in Century edition]
C / —	[not in Century edition]
CI / LIII	THE VOYAGE HOME
CII / LIII	THE VOYAGE HOME
CIII / LIII	THE VOYAGE HOME

PEDIGREE OF EDITIONS

The following printings of *A Traveler at Forty* have been published in the English language. All were printed from the plates for the 1913 edition.

New York: The Century Company, (November) 1913.
Second printing, (January) 1914.
Third printing, (September) 1914.
Fourth printing, 1920 (December 1919).
Fifth printing, (October) 1923.

London: Grant Richards, (May) 1914. The sheets for this edition were printed in the United States and shipped to England.

New York: Liveright, (August) 1930. Unlike previous editions, this one ran the illustrations broadside, with their tops toward the book's spine.

Appendix

APPENDIX

The following text includes two redundant FTS passages that were cut from the Illinois edition of A *Traveler at Forty* and an originally handwritten page from the FTS that constitutes a short note for an essay Dreiser intended to write on English civility and American incivility.

The following First Typescript passage, from the middle of chapter 6, has been removed from page 63, line 24, of the present edition.

Bernhardt was entirely satisfactory to him—her life, her art, the plays she interpreted, which, as we all know, have been various and peculiar; Rejane and the Goncourts, those enthusiastic lovers of all art forms, were without trouble to him, but when it came to Flaubert, Balzac, de Maupassant, he was silent. Where is the difference? I asked myself.

The following passage from the middle of chapter 12 has been cut from page 128, line 8, of the copy-text. It is an introductory passage to a story Dreiser had asked Richards to send him.

While we were dining G—— R—— told me the following story concerning a certain publisher who came in and sat down near us and whom I know slightly, and since it is so very remarkable here, I tell it. It is worthy of de Maupassant and as such made up for any lack of grandeur which my earlier reports of London had led me to expect. I give it exactly as he told it. The art is his, not mine. [paragraph break] (Missing).

The following passage has been preserved as a loose leaf at the end of the First Typescript. Dreiser also announces his burgeoning plan at the end of a 16 January 1912 letter to his literary agent, Miss Holly: "I should like to write a paper on English civility."

American Incivility

"Our boasted democracy has resulted in little more than the privilege every living, breathing American has of being rude and brutal to every other, but it is not beyond possibility that sometime as a nation we will sober down into something approximating human civility. Our early revolt against sham civility has, in so far as I can see, resulted in nothing save the abolition of all civility, which is sickening."

INDEX

RENATE VON BARDELEBEN is a professor of American literature and culture at the University of Mainz in Germany. She is the author or editor of nine books and has published one book and numerous articles on Theodore Dreiser.

The University of Illinois Press
is a founding member of the
Association of American University Presses.

Composed in 10.5/13 Goudy
with Goudy display
by Jim Proefrock
at the University of Illinois Press
Manufactured by Thomson-Shore, Inc.

University of Illinois Press
1325 South Oak Street Champaign, IL 61820-6903
www.press.uillinois.edu